JOHN R. MOTT

1865-1955

*A sense of mission that could not be mistaken was
written on his face.*

JOHN R. MOTT
1865-1955

A Biography

By
C. Howard Hopkins

WILLIAM B. EERDMANS PUBLISHING COMPANY
GRAND RAPIDS

Copyright © 1979 by the National Board of the Young
Men's Christian Associations
291 Broadway, New York 10007
Published by arrangement with William B. Eerdmans
Publishing Company,
255 Jefferson, S.E., Grand Rapids, Michigan. 49503

Library of Congress Cataloging in Publication Data

Hopkins, Charles Howard, 1905–
  John R. Mott, 1865–1955.

  Bibliography: p. 779.
  Includes index.
  1. Mott, John R., 1865–1955. 2. Young
Men's Christian Associations—Biography.
BV1085.M75H66   267'.392'4 [B]   79-15069
ISBN 0-8028-3525-2

To John Livingstone Mott, Irene Mott Bose, Frederick Dodge Mott, and Eleanor Mott Ross, the children of John R. and Leila White Mott, who carried on in our generation the spirit of their parents, and who were of indispensable help to the author; and also to a great teacher who opened to me the world of scholarship: William H. Roberts of the University of Redlands.

Preface

*T*HIS IS an account of how a provincial midwesterner grew into what Karl Barth once called a universal, if American, personality. John Mott was unique. The biographer or historian may look in vain for his counterpart. He was early possessed by a sense of destiny and of mission, yet unlike most builders and prophets, lived to see the fruition of his dream. As the embodiment of that hope, he was a hero to thousands.

From the day when, as a boy of eleven, Mott added the initial "R." to his name and thus proclaimed his individuality, to his last public utterance eighty years later, he was committed to one purpose. The tortures of adolescence were resolved in his sophomore year through prayer and wrestling that led to one irrevocable vocation enforced by "decision of character." He largely created the organization that would be the vehicle for his career, then extended it and its progeny to the ends of the earth.

His capacity for friendship and his inborn charisma led not only to the cementing of private friendships and working partnerships with professional colleagues, but resulted in a worldwide network of women and men who contributed not only money and time but things of the spirit. Thus, as Paul B. Anderson has said, he became a channel for the expression of the best in those who were committed to the building of Christian society; they needed a person of integrity, wisdom, power, and personality to vicariously carry out their own ambitions. His management of the far-flung enterprises they made possible was of a quality such as Vannevar Bush once characterized as a braid of technique and art. But pervasive throughout all of Mott's multitudinous and varied actions was an inner mystical apprehension of the spirit of God in

Jesus Christ. This was not simply the "practice" of the presence of God; it was a part of Mott. Persons of every estate felt with Bishop Hans Lilje that "he cared for and respected" them as individuals; when Mott spoke to one, that person felt honored for the rest of his life.

Mott was not a prophet in the usual sense. His was a prophetic stance toward persons and situations, much akin to what John C. Bennett has recently called "transforming social justice." His attitude toward mission was to discover and nurture indigenous leadership for rising nations, to lay spiritual foundations. The race problem, whether in America, the Congo, Australia, or South Africa, could be met only by understanding each human situation and bringing the "missionary and inclusive" Christian spirit to bear upon it, thus breaking down barriers between man and man. He took the World's Student Christian Federation to Tokyo in 1907, an international "first" in the Orient, and to Constantinople in 1911, to open doors between western and Orthodox Christians.

To thousands, Mott was a hero. In an era suspicious of heroes and sure that the dead ones were frauds, we need to remind ourselves, as Reynolds Price has written, that lasting and useful heroes are objects of love. They are public men, Paul Zweig contends, made not only "of muscle and courage" but of values. No old saw is more worn than the pretense that no man is a hero to his valet, yet Mott held the full esteem and affection of the men and women who worked most closely with him.

André Maurois declared a half-century ago that the cult of the hero is as old as mankind, setting before men "examples which are lofty but not inaccessible, astonishing but not incredible." In this narrative biography of John Mott, I have tried to describe his life as he lived it, and in the perspective of his times. I have included the humdrum and the heroic, trivia as well as greatness. Maurois also commented that no writer would ever have the luck to find "a life perfectly grouped round a single passion." On that score, my luck was good, but Mott's single-mindedness is incomprehensible to our age. Paul Murray Kendall once wondered who would be willing or able to spend the requisite dozen years necessary to write a biography of a person for whom he had no feeling. The biographer of a great American novelist commented that after nine years of captivity with his subject, he was not a better man but a wiser. I once heard Mott speak, and later spent several hours with him. I believe I am a better, and a wiser, man for having spent fifteen years with his intimate and public papers, his family and hosts of friends, and visiting and contemplating the world scene of his activities.

C. HOWARD HOPKINS

Claremont, California

Contents

CHAPTER 3: **Students of the World United:
Europe, the Near East, Ceylon, and India**

CHAPTER 8: **"Then Came the Test"**

CHAPTER 9: **Mission to Russia**

CHAPTER 12: **Retrospect and Reward**

1

Young Man
from Iowa

*It has been my ever present ambition to do something
for the world.*

O N A FALL DAY in 1865 the McGregor Western Railway train
wheezed to a well-earned stop at the high prairie settlement of
Postville, Iowa, after a stiff climb through forested coulees from the ferry
terminal on the Mississippi. Some of its passengers had traveled from the
East through Chicago over the new Chicago and Northwestern Railroad
and the Milwaukee and Prairie du Chien Railway to the latter's river
terminus in southwestern Wisconsin. Crossing the Father of Waters to
McGregor, Iowa, by ferry, they realized that they had truly reached the
"New Northwest."

John Stitt Mott, his wife Elmira, and his mother Lydia had come
from Sullivan County, New York, with two small daughters and a husky,
brown-eyed boy of four months called Johnnie. In all probability they
had stopped overnight in McGregor with "Diamond Jo" Reynolds, a
distant relative who had once owned a grist mill and a tannic acid plant
in Sullivan, and was now a grain merchant and steamboat entrepreneur.
After a night's rest the seemingly interminable ride over bumpy new
roadbeds and half-wild prairies ended with the short twenty-six mile pull
through the scenic northeastern corner of Iowa.

Several miles before they reached Postville the Motts could see
ahead the town's one conspicuous landmark—a grain elevator. Built by
Reynolds the year before, it symbolized the hope of ambitious farmers to
reap from virgin soil bumper wheat crops to be sold at inflated prices
created by the war just ended. But even as they descended from the train
Elmira's heart must have sunk as she involuntarily contrasted the dusty
and almost treeless barrenness of this raw "town by the tracks" with the
luxurious flower garden she had left a week earlier on the bank of an
ever-flowing stream.

1

Postville, named for the first settler to build a log house on the site less than a generation earlier when the region was an unbroken wilderness inhabited by Indians, was laid out on the gridiron pattern fixed on the American West by the examples of Philadelphia and the Northwest Ordinance but imposed as a blueprint upon a thousand towns by the expanding railroads. After a short stay on a farm, the Motts would move into Postville to become its first family, and through sixteen golden years the subject of this biography would grow to adolescence in its friendly warmth. Whether Johnnie was born with the wanderlust or was hypnotized by the rhythms of the 1,200-mile journey from the East, he would be fascinated by trains, and the narrow iron bands that brought the Motts to Postville would open the world to him as a youth and later take him to college and a life of travel to the ends of the earth.

PART 1: The Motts of Rockland, Sullivan County, New York

The Motts traced their ancestry to seventeenth-century English and Dutch immigrants, although they were vague about the forbears of the Revolutionary patriot Thomas Mott of Peekskill, New York, who had wintered with Washington at Valley Forge and risen to the rank of lieutenant in the Westchester Militia. About 1791 he claimed his soldier's land warrant and with his large family, goods, and farm animals pushed westward "over the mountain"—the Shawangunk—through primeval forests abounding with game, hostile Indians, and predators. He settled on the Willowemoc River, a tributary of the Beaverkill, which in turn emptied into the Delaware River, at a strategic location for log-rafting. Within the larger township of Rockland, this settlement was long known as Purvis, but was later named Livingston Manor. In 1813, the year of his death, Thomas Mott conveyed to his son John a four-acre tract on the river bank for a home.[1] There John farmed in summer and in winter cut logs to float to the Philadelphia market; several children were born to him and Lydia Wright Mott, among them John Stitt, the father of the subject of this biography, in 1823.

The burgeoning growth of American cities created an insatiable demand for lumber. As the primeval forests of the coastal areas were cut over, loggers pushed up the tributaries of the Delaware. Pine and hemlock were felled in winter when the ground was frozen; the logs were accumulated in or near creeks where spring floods carried them downstream in rafts of varying size guided by men who rode them. Log-rafting to Philadelphia became important in the late eighteenth century and reached its height in the mid-nineteenth. This epic endeavor was a feature of the conquest of the North American continent. Three generations of Motts pursued it, poling their way from the Willowemoc to tidewater, then staying in Philadelphia until the timber was sold.

John S. Mott's apprenticeship began when he was a teen-ager. During the run of 1839, while John Mott was at the bow and the son, not quite sixteen, was steersman, their raft struck a submerged rock and the father was thrown into the water. Although a good swimmer, he struck his head under the raft and was drowned. The boy completed the mission, returning home with the proceeds of the sale. He now shouldered the responsibility for the family, farming in summer, and for twenty-five years continued his father's lumber business, including the operation of a sawmill.

For his own or his steersman's guidance, he printed directions in a pocket notebook, including reliable stopping points and hazards along 200 miles of the Delaware to the "head of steam navigation and tide water" near Trenton. Several beaches afforded "safe flood landing" but one place was "a smoky old whiskey hole," doubtless not a place to stay overnight. Directions were "run Penn" or "run Jersey." Bridge piers required careful maneuvering. Not far below the "giant romantic scenery" of the Delaware Water Gap the channel was "40 feet from Jersey shore": he must "look out for big rock in middle of river and reaf below." If this was where his father was drowned he did not note the fact. Exact directions were given for sighting by landmarks the safe channel through the white water of Wells Falls just below present-day New Hope/Lambertville. A few miles further Washington had crossed "in times of the Revolution" as his grandfather must have known only too well. The last peril was Trenton Falls, which required expert navigation between rocks plainly visible to the twentieth-century Metroliner passenger, and two sets of bridge piers. Then "you can land as soon as you choose." The Philadelphia market was a school in salesmanship; the homely pocket guide to navigation bespoke traits later imparted to a son who would never ride a log raft to market but would sail the seven seas.

In 1853, when John Stitt Mott was twenty-nine, he married Elmira Dodge, who was six years his junior.[2] A vigorous, attractive, self-educated woman with an insatiable interest in history and the broader world, she was an omnivorous reader, a strong Methodist, and a professional seamstress to Rockland; her ledger listed the town's leading inhabitants and served as a roster of the local emigration to Iowa in the 1850's.

Several Dodges and Motts went, including John's brother James and Elmira's brothers Joel and Israel. They never stopped urging John and Elmira to join them.

PART 2: **From Purvis to Postville**

The physical demands of J. S. Mott's work were too great for his limited strength. Occasionally he took a naturopathic course of mineral baths and treatment at a spa such as Clifton Springs, New York, or Battle Creek, Michigan. He struck up many acquaintances among his fellow-patients, learning much about other parts of the country from them and keeping addresses and directions to their homes by rail—all of which suggests that he long considered a move. Yet his health, uncertainty as to the best place to settle, the distraught state of the nation, and prosperity in the lumber business—all contributed to persistent postponement of a decision. Mary Alice, their first child, arrived in 1859, a year in which Mott was supervisor of Rockland. Then the Civil War came: lumber and farm products sold well. A second daughter, Clara Myrtle, was born ten days before the first battle of Bull Run.

The Iowa fever would not down. Elmira's younger brother Joel, a volunteer in the Tenth Iowa Regiment, bombarded the home folks from various army camps with arguments and pleas to join their relatives and friends in the Hawkeye State. "I hope that John will make up his mind to emigrate to Iowa before many more years roll around," he wrote from Corinth, Mississippi. "You live in the wilderness of the earth in old sullivan county," declared her other brother Israel in the last letter that came to her, just before his death on the march to Shiloh. In 1862–63 John Mott was again a Rockland supervisor. Wounded and mustered out, Joel described a wheat harvest he had helped reap; it averaged sixteen bushels an acre: "Corn and wheat are the two staple products. Land that will raise them will raise anything."

Word came back not only about Reynolds' grain elevator but there was also glowing praise of northeastern Iowa from that entrepreneur. The guidebook *Iowa As It Is* emphasized the need for lumber and the availability of immense supplies of it for the "large farms, and lots of them" that were being broken out of the prairie in Allamakee County, a "well-watered, well timbered, fertile and productive" region adapted to "all kinds of grain, fruit, and grazing." The War was approaching its end, the country would return to normal, and a torrent of migration be released. John S. Mott was not the man to take his family to the raw frontier. Doubtless he read the *Prairie Farmer* and the *Iowa Homestead* and about this time went to Iowa and bought an improved farm near Postville, which was becoming a farming center and was already the head of a Methodist circuit. Then Elmira became pregnant again.

John Mott (the "R." came later), the third child and only son of John Stitt and Elmira Dodge Mott, whom this book is about, was born in the family home near Purvis (Livingston Manor), Sullivan County, New York, May 25, 1865, six weeks after the assassination of Abraham Lincoln. That September the family joined the thousands bound for the trans-Mississippi West. As their train clattered across New York State it passed near a new campus being laid out above one of the Finger Lakes, on which a sophomore from Iowa would find himself and the direction of his life twenty years later.

From the Postville depot it was a two-mile drive behind a new team along "Makee Ridge" via the old military route toward Fort Atkinson— one of Hamlin Garland's *Main Traveled Roads*—to the Motts' new home, doubtless a white frame house erected by one of those Yankee pioneers who had so stamped the culture of Maine upon the area that settlers from Indiana and Illinois had dubbed the high prairie "Penobscot!" The McGregor Western tracks now extended twenty-five miles toward St. Paul from Postville, noisily close to the Mott farmhouse. Passing trains would make an indelible impression on young Johnnie.

PART 3: A Civilized Town on the Prairie

The Motts came to Iowa as "civilized farmers," in Frederick Jackson Turner's descriptive term for the last phase of western settlement before the advent of cities. John S. Mott, however, was not rugged enough to manage 160 acres of wheat and the technology had not quite reached the point at which machinery made it possible to farm sitting down. But the demand for lumber was growing in a new area rapidly filling with new families not only from just across the Mississippi or even from Ohio. The second largest immigrant group in Iowa in 1870 was, like the Motts, from New York State. Northeast Iowa had a large Norwegian population and there were substantial numbers from Germany, Great Britain, Canada, and Sweden.

Although this was the great era of log rafting on the Mississippi, with colossal export from adjacent Wisconsin both by rail and by water,

J. S. Mott did not return to that business. Instead, he soon bought a partnership in a retail lumber yard in Postville, absorbing his partners' interests before long, then buying out his competitors until for a time he enjoyed a monopoly. A line of hardware for the growing farms was added. When the town was incorporated he became its first mayor; a subdivision was named for him. His business prospered as population and wealth increased. Corn gradually replaced wheat as the staple crop and the foundations were being laid for the region to become the heart of the nation's dairy industry. There were years when the Mott enterprises netted more than $5,000. The depressions that shook industrial and urban America through the seventies were hardly felt in this corner of Iowa. Mott held on to the farm and invested in town lots, timber acreage, and small industries related to dairying. By 1885 he could cal- culate his net worth at $55,000.

On this economic base, the Motts, as Postville's first family, helped to build, if Turner's phrase may be stretched, a "civilized town" in the midst of "one of the most prosperous agricultural economies the world has ever seen," in a region where each year the rains, the summer heat, and the rich soils "produced the broad-leafed fields" of dark green corn. This was where John R. Mott grew up.

Richard Hofstadter opened *The Age of Reform* with the comment that the United States had been born in the country but had moved to the city; he was referring chiefly to the migration of thousands from the exaggerated grubbiness of Hamlin Garland's farms to the alleged advan- tages of the raw new cities. Postville never became a city, but in its controlled environment its children were surrounded by the conservative values of Victorian and American life. The family of the future Cornell professor Carl Becker enjoyed in Waterloo, Iowa, "a synthesis of physical and spiritual well-being" that started Becker in the direction he chose. Xenia, Ohio, was formative for Arthur M. Schlesinger, who at age four- teen had read 598 books from his family's and the town library's shelves. A comparable social microcosm in China, Maine, shaped the life and career of Rufus M. Jones, a contemporary of Mott.[3]

John S. Mott soon built a large pleasant house on West Williams Street. With spacious rooms and many windows, it became the unifying center for its six residents—a third daughter, Harriett Belle having com- pleted the family circle in July, 1867 (Grandmother Lydia Mott died in 1869)—a focus for affection, "culture," charity, Christian faith, practical learning, and community leadership. Within the warmth of that circle young Mott acquired from his mother, a person of even temperament, broad understanding, and a fine sense of humor, an insatiable desire for knowledge, to be obtained chiefly through reading. It was said that in her childhood an unsympathetic stepmother had papered the cabin walls with newsprint; when she found Elmira reading it she put it on upside-down, but the girl mastered it and retained the skill. Her interests ranged through history and public affairs, both of which became Johnnie's absorbing youthful concerns. *Harper's Weekly, The Youth's Companion,* a *Methodist Advocate,* and the *Guide to Holiness* were received and read. There was an early purchase of the *Encyclopedia Britannica* in return for the boy's pledge to neither smoke nor drink before age twenty-one. Many years afterward John recalled his mother's wide interests: her love of flowers, her passion for reading, her interest in foreign countries and in great rulers and other eminent leaders.

Sister Clara showed a musical talent, so a piano was obtained in addition to the family organ; Johnnie practiced on it and sang a bit. Elmira improved the large corner lot with a diversity of unusual flowers, generously supplying everyone. And as the years passed the trees grew until Postville's bare silhouette on the prairie height disappeared beneath a green or grey-brown umbrella, like the older civilized towns back East.

Johnnie Mott was a vigorous, fun-loving boy given to practical jokes and much good-humored banter and play with his three sisters and the town's children. Of course he cared for the chickens, milked the cow, rode or drove the family horses; there were no organized sports, the adults assuming that work and chores provided exercise enough. This was Black Hawk country and there were Indian rock carvings and mysterious mounds in Allamakee County, but the boys did not play at Indians. Cattle abounded in the region but no one played cowboy: the realities were too near, and Buffalo Bill was not yet. But Johnnie and his friends did play at the greatest game of the time: railroading, the biggest business of America and the wave of the future. They laid out and operated extensive rail lines in back yards and on the wooden sidewalks until a night wheelbarrow express "ran into a leading citizen and shattered him and his basket of eggs," whereupon Mayor Mott dealt with son John "conclusively—and shut down our whole system." For a time John surreptitiously helped the train crew care for their locomotive when Postville became the terminus of a second railroad.

At the age of eight, while visiting the relatives in Newton who had first gone to Iowa, he wrote back that he wasn't especially homesick, had practiced the piano some, and that the children had gone "out on the prary and got all the strawberrays we could eat." Then there was a steamboat trip to St. Paul, probably via the "Diamond Jo" Line on passes from its owner Reynolds. When he was eleven, Johnnie went to Newton again, this time reporting back the details of the train schedules and signing himself "John R. Mott": the added "R." was an initial only, to distinguish himself from his father; such was a custom of the time.[4] That same year, 1876, the entire family visited the Centennial Exposition in Philadelphia, where all stood in awe before the great Corliss engine that symbolized the age of steam power.

When he was fifteen, young Mott drove the family horse and buggy 125 miles across the prairie to Newton and back, accompanied by his sister Harriet. They followed a map he had made, passing through many cross-roads settlements like West Branch, off their route to the south, where a small boy named Herbert Hoover, with whom John would become intimate, was growing up. The youthful Motts stopped at farmhouses overnight. This excursion under the June sky bore in upon John the sublimity of the prairie. Unique in the North American landscape, the undulating vastness of the Iowa prairie, in contrast to the flat plains, was an unforgettable sight. It was, Herbert Quick would write in *Vandemark's Folly*, "like a great green sea" with some of the hillsides "as blue as the sky," the wind sweeping a flock of white clouds before it while under them "went their shadows, walking the lovely hills like dark ships over an emerald sea . . . the newest, strangest, most delightful, sternest, most wonderful thing in the world."[5] Mott never forgot those "far views" and "retreating horizons."

It was early understood that the family business would be John's when he was ready for it. He began working in it as a boy, learning the need for bookkeeping and a meticulous inventory, together with criteria for judgment of materials. When his father initiated the grading of lumber it became the husky youth's duty to help sort and stack the various sizes, grades, and woods, as each freight car was set out on the Mott siding, a job that taxed both brain and brawn. John also served a multi-lingual clientele and observed the idiosyncrasies of customers with names such as Adams, Goerthoffner, Negel, Olson, Roberts, Swenson, or Vanhooser. He was paid for his services, and like his father kept careful account of his money and spent it judiciously.

It was once remarked that Mott learned the essentials of the gospel at "a Methodist family altar." Evangelical Christian faith was presupposed in the household on West Williams Street, but it was not overemphasized. The son of that home once reminisced about his mother:

> The truly Christlike life she lived created in me, even in the tender years of childhood, the longing and inclination and purpose to go Christ's way. Her

religion was not simply thought out, it was not talked out, it was lived out. In the deepest sense it was contagious.

She inculcated also a genuine loyalty to the Church and such of its institutions and activities as the Sunday School, the midweek prayer meeting, the camp meetings in the pioneer days, and above all a reverential regard for the Christian minister. Through all the years in our home town the presiding elder, or the bishop, or other church officials were entertained in our home.[6]

When the great Methodist Bishop William Taylor, an advocate of Wesleyan Holiness, was a guest, young Johnnie, then five, was heard to ask in an audible whisper: "Is that God?"

The Protestant ethos assumed that adolescent boys and girls would undergo conversion and join the church at an impressionable moment. A turning point came in February, 1879, when Johnnie was thirteen. The Iowa State YMCA pursued an active program of rural evangelism. Its agent, J. W. Dean, "a Quaker evangelist and a remarkable Bible teacher or expositor," conducted an interdenominational revival in Postville, during which, as Mott once put it, "he led my father, two of my sisters, and me to Christ." More significantly, there came shortly to Postville, in the endless succession of Methodist circuit-riding pastors, an exceptionally able young graduate of Cornell College, Iowa, and of Drew Theological Seminary, the Reverend Horace E. Warner, who was only ten years Johnnie's senior. Long afterward Mott recalled:

He would let nothing crowd him out of his study for the better part of two days and a half every week. He preached sermons of distinction in our little village. . . . This rarely equipped pastor identified himself with me. Again and again he visited me while I was at my work in the lumber yard. He interested himself in my reading. He generated in me the desire and purpose to get a college education and convinced my parents so that they made this possible.[7]

In 1910 Mott wrote the introduction to Warner's *Psychology of the Christian Life,* acknowledging its author's influence. Few small-town boys were fortunate enough to come under such tutelage and still fewer were able to gain so much from it.

PART 4: Upper Iowa University

By the summer of 1881, that unending summer through which the nation agonized while President James A. Garfield lay at the point of death from an assassin's bullet, young Mott had exhausted the resources of the Postville schools. Under the urging of Warner and the president of a nearby coeducational Methodist college, Upper Iowa University, he entered the preparatory department of that school at the age of sixteen, though not until Elmira had been convinced that it did not turn out atheists. In Fayette, about thirty miles from home, Upper Iowa had opened in 1857 with a hundred students who had paid $46 for each of three fourteen-week terms per year. When Mott entered, the cost had risen to $50. In the main line of the nineteenth-century church-related college tradition, which included its ambitious name, UIU contributed its share of leaders to various walks of life as well as to the clergy, including a Speaker of the House of Representatives. At the time of Mott's arrival by train and stagecoach on a cold September day it was housed in a conspicuous, buff-colored, three-story stone building on a bare hill. That fall he lived on the third floor and joined an eating club that cost $1.80 a week.

He promptly reported these arrangements to the folks at home, thus establishing a weekly letter-writing pattern to which he would adhere as long as either of his parents lived. His mother kept most of his letters, written, as the years went by, on trains and ships and from all corners of the globe, but none of hers has survived. From the beginning he would first describe things of interest to them before recounting his own affairs. He invariably signed himself "John R." or "John R. Mott."[8]

Fayette was "not such a place as I supposed," he complained in his first letter. Compared to Postville it was "terribly dull": one couldn't see "three teams on Main Street at one time." First courses would be algebra, grammar, Latin, bass voice lessons; he could see that "a person has got to study." He opened at once a ledger more detailed than his father's, recording every expense of five cents or more, which also became a life-long habit. He also kept an exact transcript of his courses, teachers, grades, and class rank. After a flurry of letters home, acquaintances grew into friendships and some homesickness vanished. Yet for three years his letters would betray adolescent dissatisfaction with himself and the college, doubtless exacerbated by his father's poor health and consequently his own duty to the family, uncertainty about his vocation, but above all his inability to win debates and oratorical contests.

The principal agency in resolving most of his problems was the Philomathean Literary Society, which he joined early in his first term. It was a fraternity of sorts that helped to banish alienation, a laboratory for every form of public speaking—debate, oratory, mock trials, elaborate lawsuits, and, as Basil Mathews, his biographer of 1934, says, a focus for "a vast amount of hilarious nonsense" in which Mott was normally involved. Yet there were two notable achievements of this long training period: mastery of Robert's *Rules of Order,* the manual of Western parliamentary procedure, and learning to speak without notes.

In his first term Mott defended the labor side of the old question of capital versus labor. He was first in two of his classes. He mourned the death of Garfield. During winter term he lived off campus, took algebra, Latin, and "natural philosophy," claimed to have studied harder, and again stood at the head of two classes and second in a third, which became a pattern. There were no athletics or group sports at UIU, but John kept a boat on the Volga River that flowed through the town. He walked a great deal and rose to first sergeant of the college military drill unit. He was the first business manager of the student paper, the *Fayette Collegian.* John's acting in several Shakespearean plays surprised both Professor Chauncy Colegrove who coached and his fellow-students by his insights into the characters of Shylock and Macbeth.

In the spring of 1882 he wrote home that he was reading a chapter a day in the New Testament. Colegrove told Mathews that during a religious meeting in the fall of 1883 Mott had arisen "and in manly, simple, eloquent language" described his religious experiences at home. He had kept them a secret at college but was now "determined to live an open, active, religious life." When a college YMCA was organized not long afterward, he was a charter member "and one of the most efficient and faithful workers."[9]

Yet the success he yearned for in debate and declamation eluded him. John stayed out of school during the spring terms of 1883 and 1884 and it was not until the beginning of what was to be his final year at Upper Iowa that rewards did come and that he began to enjoy his classes, now in economics, history, and the natural sciences, with preferences for botany and English literature. That Mott did not become a college drop-out was due to the personal help given by friends and professors. Colegrove, who taught English, proved to be a wise counselor. The Philomathean Society served as fraternity, safety-valve, and forum. An alumnus who lived nearby, the Reverend Mr. Paine, coached John until he won a first debate. William Larrabee, the region's most prominent politician and successful candidate for governor in 1885, encouraged him.

In the summer of 1884, during which Mott worked in the lumber yard, he prepared for a debate on the relative importance of the defeat of the English at Orleans versus the surrender of Burgoyne at Saratoga. The event came early in the term: "I proved too quick for them on the answering argument and won," he exulted to his father; "it did me $5 worth of good. I *do* want to be a good debater and speaker and shall do all in my power to become such." A political speech delivered that same night would be published in the *Collegian*. This letter concluded with a virtual directive to his father to take time off for the sake of his health. If necessary John would leave college to help if brother-in-law James McAdam could not handle the business.

The next letter recounted John's taking the unpopular protectionist position against his entire economics class and the professor; when the issue was debated before a crowded Philomathean Society, two of three judges voted in his favor. In recognition of these triumphs he shared the honor of writing his name with other winners on the wall of the room in which the Society met. Six decades later Mott astonished President Eugene E. Garbee by locating the spot on the then renovated wall and declaring that "right here in this room" he had had "the inspiration to take the gospel to the world."[10]

The college year 1884–85 was one of the most formative times of Mott's life. It brought out the firstfruits of maturing abilities and interests. John now possessed his own techniques of public speaking and found that they worked. Success followed success. The *Collegian* published his pieces on "An Anchored Life" and "The Causes of the Reformation." He won two more debates and gave several orations. He portrayed "Spartacus to the Gladiators" so effectively that Professor Colegrove judged that he had "plenty of fight in him to make a lawyer."

That same winter Mott adopted a set of physical, "mental," social, and religious "Regulations" based on Benjamin Franklin's that bade him become acquainted with both the Methodist Church and *the Universal Church*. He attended Methodist class meetings regularly, kept abreast of Methodist affairs, and rejoiced when his roommate and debating partner John W. Dickman, who would be professor, dean, and president of UIU, was converted in a February revival. The climax of Mott's four years at Fayette came with victory in the prestigious Alumni Prize oratorical contest. His subject was "What the Nineteenth Century owes to the Twentieth." It was inspired by an address by Andrew Dickson White, the founding president of Cornell University.

During 1884–85 Mott weighed the merits of transferring to "some more advanced college" such as Yale, Harvard, Johns Hopkins, Wisconsin, Michigan, or Cornell. The UIU authorities vacillated over his class rank, and the caliber of the student competition he would have during two more years there was not impressive. He wrote home his settled belief that if he were to enter a profession he could not obtain the preparation needed at UIU. If necessary, because of Pa's health the business should be sold, but hopefully "the money that goes into my mind will come out some day." Then he added:

> I am so thankful that you have been so situated that you have been able to give me such opportunities to improve and I assure you I am improving them as far as time and strength will allow. I am more thankful that you brought me up with an interest in lasting things rather than in cigars, profanity, loafing, etc.

After careful canvassing of the materials that came from the universities named above, Mott decided, with the advice of Colegrove and others, to enter Cornell, with Michigan as second choice. As he much later looked back on this decision, he claimed to have been getting "somewhat uncomfortable" in the overly religious atmosphere of UIU where there were pressures to go into a religious profession rather than the law.

Among the items he had received from Cornell was a speech of White's given at Yale that set forth the Cornell founder's philosophy of education. White pleaded for creative leadership to raise American standards in the arts, politics, religion, philosophy, science, and literature as a bulwark against the increasingly materialistic and "mercantile" spirit that was engulfing the nation. Many years afterward Mott wrote on this yellowed sheet (possibly for the benefit of a biographer) that it had led him to Cornell. In 1885 he marked this passage:

> We must do all that we can to rear greater fabrics of philosophic thought, literary thought, scientific, artistic, political thought; to summon young men more and more into these fields... as a patriotic duty; to hold before them, not the incentive of mere gain or of mere pleasure or of mere reputation, but the ideal of a new and better civilization....[11]

White's appeal not only fired Mott's oratory; it fed his own growing sense of mission.

John opened the oration on the debts of the centuries with a picture of the "glorious drama of progressive civilization" and his generation's duty to hand on the best. He saw the mercantile spirit as the chief enemy of mental progress and the root of the conflict between capital and labor, symbolized by "the red flag of communism" which he himself may have seen "flaunted" in the streets of Chicago. Hand in hand with education must go the quickened conscience! Why do nations rise and fall, "like billows on the ocean?"

> Because those nations were not bedded on the eternal rock—Moral Princi-
> ple. Upon the great truths of Christianity our forefathers established this
> nation. The conscience of our fathers kept it from disunion. Christianity
> has given birth to the greatest triumphs of progress.

> When the portals of the twentieth century swing open ... let it be the
> opening of time's most brilliant vista, revealing a land whose only citadels
> are temples of worship; whose protecting wall is the trained mind and
> unstained conscience; whose people are moving in harmony and expand-
> ing in culture ... bearing the banner inscribed as by the hand of God with
> that watch-cry which alone can lead the nation on to victory, "Righteous-
> ness exalteth a nation, but sin is a reproach to any people."[12]

Andrew Dickson White had won another recruit for Cornell.

Mott worked hard in the lumber yard that summer. He reconsidered
the possibility of enrolling at the University of Michigan where he might
major in history under Charles Kendall Adams, for he had not heard that
White had retired from Cornell and Adams had taken his place. Early in
September the Philomathean Society held a farewell party for this "old
and respected member who was about to leave for Cornell University,
Ithica [sic], New York." In response to the many "extemporary speeches"
and replies, Mott urged members "to be prompt in attendance, energetic
and determined in their work, systematic and faithful" in all their under-
takings. "'Aim high in life,'" he counseled, and do not live "'for self
alone, but for God and humanity.'"[13] He would return to Fayette many
times. In 1943 he expanded the above theme: "ever stand proudly on this
hill—a watch tower—a light to the world—to ... purify politics, to
elevate the professions, to quicken the industries, to consecrate wealth,
to sanctify the home, to inspire patriotism, to evangelize the world, to
glorify God." Thus was a part of the debt of the twentieth century repaid
to the nineteenth.

PART 5: Cornell Sophomore

Early in the morning of September 12, 1885, a Michigan Central express
train stopped on the great cantilever bridge over the Niagara River for its
passengers to enjoy the view of the Falls. John Mott, now twenty and on
his first great venture away from home and the West, looked out the
window in awe. His first impulse was to share his emotions with his
parents. A hastily scribbled note described the several scenic stops for
viewing the Falls; later in the day he wrote his mother brief impressions

of gardens and estates in Rochester. This route was not the most direct from Chicago to Ithaca. He had taken it to verify the situation at the University of Michigan.[14] Cornell had been the right choice.

Upon arrival in Ithaca that Saturday night Mott was met by representatives of the university Christian Association (CUCA); he "put up" at a hotel until he would find a boarding house the next Tuesday.[15] Sunday morning he attended the Aurora Street Methodist Church, a warm-hearted Holiness congregation, and in the evening the State Street Methodist Church, finding "a wide difference" between them. He joined the former and the CUCA the next Sunday, both momentous decisions. This first Sunday afternoon, armed with the student handbook and a map, he oriented himself to Ithaca and the University. First impressions were of a "simply grand" natural landscape of lake, hills, and forest; the view across Lake Cayuga was the most beautiful he had ever seen. "It is going to be a new world for me," he wrote home, realizing that he had "a hard fight" ahead, yet he declared that if "the intellectual merit" of the school were even one-fifth as great as its financial power and natural advantages, he could not complain. The streets were "spotted with dudes" but he was confident that he would meet young men of "sterling worth and genius" in classroom, debating society, and church—the last being the first place "that seemed natural."

On the advice of his new pastor and the student YMCA, he took rooms with "a Methodist lady" at 91 East Buffalo Street. The other boarders were from Long Island, Ohio, and Illinois. Costs were much higher than in Fayette, but he expected this. The ledger was reopened and kept with precision down to expenses of two and three cents. The daily mile-long ascent of the campus-crowned hill would be good exercise. Sunday, September 10, he began weekly letters home to parents now alone: Alice was married, Hattie had gone to Cornell College, Iowa, and Clara to Germany to study music. Before the week was out he had obtained a good roommate, George W. Ames, an engineering freshman from Vermont, a Methodist, Mott's own age, a "quiet, industrious" fellow who had no bad habits "unless it be that he is a little careless about keeping things picked up in the room."

Mott had been admitted to Cornell as a sophomore with a few deficiencies. During his first year he took the classical courses required—Latin, French, German, Ancient and English History—but enjoyed geology the most (there were field trips on the lake); it was making him "more observing" just as botany did at Fayette, and it was enlarging his views "of the greatness of creation and of the truth of

Genesis." He confessed that he would have to learn how to use the library of 55,000 books and "some little experience" would be required to decide "what lectures to attend and what to skip." Although Charles E. Courtney was beginning his phenomenal career as crew coach, Mott did not go out for this or any organized sport, preferring long rambles in the country, usually with others, and obtaining a good deal of physical exercise from military drill, being promoted to artillery because of his Fayette experience. And there was always the Buffalo Street hill!

His September 20 letter declared that Cornell was already disgusting him with "the common legal profession" and giving him more respect for labor and "enlightened citizenship." For a man intent on escaping from religious influences while dedicated to the law, Mott's first week was a disaster, or his alleged pursuit of a career in law and politics was a much later rationalization. Men with those goals, for whom he expressed some contempt, shunned church and Christian Association, went out for athletics, joined fraternities, and found friends among "dudes."

The early part of the term was marked by hard study, a few carefully selected social events, regular church and CUCA attendance, with careful analyses of the sermons in Sage Chapel reported in dutiful letters home that revealed some homesickness; he was especially impressed by Lyman Abbott, Edward Everett Hale, and Washington Gladden. Two geology trips down the lake were "very instructive and we also had some fun." At a CUCA reception for President Adams he met and became acquainted with "several good boys." Finding that little stress was laid on oratory at Cornell he postponed joining a debating society. He had agreed with Hattie to write regularly to Clara, who would be "the most lonesome of us all." He believed she would return "changed for the better if she is true to herself" in fulfilling their agreement of daily Bible reading and meditation. This concern for his sisters would not only continue as long as they lived but would expand to professional colleagues and associates as Mott's web of friendships widened.

John also wrote occasionally to his older sister Alice and her husband James, varying the content to their interests. It was to "Dear Brother James"—the only brother he had, several years older than himself—that he described his "first public speech" right after joining the Cornell Mock Congress as a Republican from Iowa:

> I did not intend to participate in the work last night but when the High Liscence bill was brought up a big headed dude who never saw beyond the Mississippi made a speech in which he cast slurs on Iowa Prohibition—this fired me up and I got up and pitched into him and forced him to amend his bill.

Next day he led a CUCA meeting at which President Adams was present, carrying it off "quite successfully," he confided to James, adding that he had been elected a delegate to the state college "Y" convention, an organization it would pay him "to know more about." In conclusion he hoped "you men of Iowa" would elect his friend William Larrabee next Tuesday: "the eyes of the East are closely watching you." Larrabee was elected Governor.

That Sunday letter of November 1, 1885, chronicled the upturn of Mott's affairs at Cornell. To his mother he wrote that a sermon by the Reverend C. N. Simms, President of Syracuse Methodist University, had so inspired him that if he could get to be as powerful a preacher "and do as much good" as Simms he would fit himself for the ministry "directly." He confided to her that his life work "must reveal itself" soon; he had long felt that he "was meant for something more than a business life; it has been my ever present ambition to do something for the world." He had also conquered his homesickness. The campus Association had brought him into contact with "the best young men of the school," and by the end of November he could express delight that the Cornell elective system would allow the choice of "just what studies" he wanted during his junior and senior years.

At this juncture he had to defend himself against Pa's regret that he had not sent him to a commercial school, a parental myopia not infrequent in families whose children are the first generation to seek higher education. John could not see that he had been "changed one iota for the worse" in college, he had acquired no pernicious habits, his health had been good, his religious life had been deepened; his mind had not been "turned into dudism" (his word for frivolous living) and had in fact been "greatly broadened," enabling him to reason out problems "in one half of the time and with trible [sic] the strength" he formerly could. He had also "in a measure aquired the habit and power" of expressing his thoughts and learning to others.[16]

John Mott was nearing the top rung of the ladder of independence. On December first the annual business meeting of the CUCA surprised him by electing him vice-president and to the executive committee—"something that very rarely takes place in a student's first year." It is "our determination to make our Association the best of all the college YMCA's in the United States and we will do it," he continued to his parents, adding that he would be the business manager of a new venture, *The Association Bulletin*. Fulfillment of the Association's goal would be the means of his own self-realization, though he could not have known its significance at that time. Then: he would need a new suit next term.

"I have dressed as poorly as any student in the University and just as I did at Fayette, but it will be necessary to dress better than I have done in order to avoid humiliation as I get farther along in my course." Being well-dressed would become a rule of life. He completed the fall term with five honors grades and two C's, but after that only honors.

The Christmas vacation of 1885 was given to visiting family friends and relatives in Sullivan County, New York, where John was born; he was warmly welcomed. The hardships of his father's early life were made real at the sawmill "where you worked so hard day and night," and the stream where 150,000 feet of lumber was lost in a spring flood. Family history "from the time of the Revolution" was carefully taken down in a long-lost notebook, but an indelible impression remained that his ancestors had been Dutch. He liked the "earnest, common sense, honest people" and reported to Postville on the health and situations of a score of relatives and former neighbors. The incidence of tuberculosis was much higher than in Iowa. John expressed genuine concern for the distressed, the senile, and his distant cousins caught in unproductive jobs. Rather than disappoint an ignorant uncle who believed that he had valuable coal deposits on his hard-scrabble farm (some practical jokers had planted pieces of it), John took specimens to show his geology professor although he was certain that they were not indigenous.

PART 6: "Your Prayers Have Been Answered"

During the autumn Mott had read Methodist Bishop Matthew Simpson's Yale *Lectures on Preaching,* which were full of common-sense advice but emphasized the necessity for conviction and compassion; Mott needed the former. Through an expanding friendship with a new roommate, Arthur H. Grant, now president of CUCA, John formed a kinship in dilemma, for Grant was involved in a comparable inner struggle. The two had often discussed the claims of the ministry, but on a Tuesday afternoon, January 12, 1886, they put their books away to concentrate "right down to the bottom of things," talking over "the whole matter candidly and coolly" and "closely examining" one another, as Mott wrote his parents the next Sunday. On their knees God told both that they must work "in His vineyard." They verified the vision by opening their Bibles at random, fixing upon relevant verses. Mott came upon Daniel 12:3—"They that be wise shall shine as the brightness of the firmament; and *they that turn many to righteousness* (Mott's underlining) as the stars forever and ever." Grant found the Great Commission: "Go ye into all the world and preach the gospel to every creature." Mott then recalled God's assurance to Joshua to "be strong and of a good courage" for the Lord would be with him.

John wrote home next Sunday that he was now "free from a great load" though deeply aware of "weakness and imperfection," Holiness terms his mother would understand. He was seeking to be "wholly consecrated"—perhaps the best clue we have to his life's dedication. And would she send him copies of the *Guide to Holiness* "as fast as you are through with them." A bundle came at once.

On Friday of the same week there arrived on the Cornell campus as a guest of the CUCA, the famous English cricketer, J. E. K. Studd, who had captained the Cambridge eleven, chaired D. L. Moody's evangelistic meetings at Cambridge in 1882, and was now first honorable secretary of the London Polytechnic Institute. The national student YMCA staff had arranged an American tour in the hope that, as one of the world's best-known athletes, Studd would attract students to hear his missionary message and description of the "Cambridge Seven" who had rejected status and wealth to volunteer for foreign missions. He also brought a message from the students of Britain. Grant and Mott, as the ranking officers of the host organization, must have had a hand in the arrangements.

For some unaccountable reason Mott was late to Studd's first meeting that Friday night, dropping into a back seat just as Studd was declaring his text: "Seekest thou great things for thyself; seek them not. Seek ye first the Kingdom of God." These words were meant for him, Mott recalled on several occasions later, and sent him out to a sleepless night of wrestling with his conscience, some of which took place in the solitude of the Cascadilla Gorge. Studd invited students with serious questions to call on him. "With great wisdom," Mott said long afterward, Studd led him to "a reasonable and vital faith" in the course of several interviews in which he advised the youth to "look Christ-ward" into the Biblical sources. When Mott himself began early in his professional career to advise students, he followed the same prescription: study the New Testament and cultivate a personal relationship with Christ. This was Mott's "second conversion," according to Clarence P. Shedd, historian of the Student Christian Movement; it was "the decisive hour of Mott's life," in the judgment of Basil Mathews, who interviewed both Mott and Studd in the early 1930's.[17]

In the light of Mott's experience with Grant a few days before, it appears more probable that Studd simply reinforced John's own resolution by giving him practical suggestions. In his home letter that next Sunday, he did not mention Studd but described his and Grant's studies and decisions in some detail, nor did he ever name Studd to his parents, preferring, it appears, to give them the impression of a steady and unemotional development, building on his experiences at UIU. In a rare autobiographical sketch of 1944 he did not speak of Studd nor was the incident included in a life-list of his "most creative experiences" compiled in old age. The importance of the encounter with Studd would therefore appear to have been the further resolution of the tension built up earlier in the week. Forty or more years afterward, Mathews may have been influenced by the fact that Studd was then Lord Mayor of London—which could also have influenced Mott's later interpretation of the incident. Before returning home Studd reported to his hosts in New York that Mott had the greatest potential "as a leader in your work" of any student he had met on his tour. The national staff began to lay plans to snare Mott for that work.

PART 7: What I Am to Do in Life

Whether or not this was Mott's "second conversion," or a step toward his "second blessing," it was revolutionary, for it plunged him into almost frantic, immediate preparation for the ministry—the most obvious route to full-time Christian service. He began a rigorous program of Bible study for an hour before breakfast every morning. He and Grant held a Bible class in their room each Sunday at 9:30, requiring the six men who came to study at least thirty minutes a day. With William O. Moody, another CUCA officer, he started Sunday religious services at the local jail, with gratifying results, although his mother never understood why he did it. He became more active in his church and consulted with his sympathetic pastor, the Reverend John F. Clymer. Before long he was writing to brother James that he was planning on the ministry and craved the home folks' prayers that he might be "built up in holiness."

In following Studd's suggestions, John directed his early morning Bible study to the Gospels, seeking to verify the credibility of the resurrection of Christ. At the climax of this pursuit he achieved "entire sanctification," the "second blessing," or the "higher life" as the Holiness perfectionists put it. His own term was often "this higher ground." The goal, available to any devout believer who would consecrate himself wholly, meant supplanting one's "bent toward sin" with "perfect love" as his sole motivation until a spiritual plateau was reached. John's experiences with Arthur Grant and Studd, not to mention his home training and the motherly influence of his class leader in the warm fellowship of the Ithaca Church to which he belonged, provided the stairway for his upward climb.

Sherwood Eddy once commented that it was almost impossible for a later generation to understand the intensity of the religious experiences of the youth of the late nineteenth century. Mott never forgot the morning when, with his notes scattered over the desk and on the faded rag rug on the floor, as he recalled it, he was able "with St. Thomas to say to Christ with intellectual honesty, 'My Lord and my God.'"[18] This was his "second blessing." It signified the total commitment of his Herculean energies to the bringing in of the Kingdom. D. L. Moody had often remarked that it had yet to be demonstrated what a person fully consecrated could accomplish; Mott, perhaps unconsciously, set out to be that person, certain that achievement depended upon dedication and love and the guidance of the Holy Spirit. Thus he also reached complete independence and would henceforth make his own decisions. Maturity was not far away.

"I have glad news for you for your prayers have been answered," he had written his mother on January 17, the Sunday after Studd's visit. Her reply must have stunned him. It has not survived, but it hastened his growth toward adulthood. In what appears to have been a tear-stained yet respectful and affectionate reply he tried to set at rest her fears that his new direction would leave her and Pa in neglect in their old age. "Far from it," he promised, but the call to serve his Master, "who has done even more for me," must come first. He reviewed the careers open to him: a "leading phrenologist" had recently assured him that he could achieve a "marked success in scientific husbandry," and there were also law, politics, and business. But in his roommate's verse, the still, small voice said, "Go ye...."

Other aspects of Mott's new-found purpose included the beginning of what became a life-long preoccupation with biography; that winter he read Wesley, Whitefield, and Moody. He strove to improve his image with his classmates of '88 and recruited some twenty delegates to the state YMCA convention. The first issue of The Association Bulletin appeared, carrying a description of Studd's visit. John drew up for himself a new daily discipline that emphasized "spiritual development" through prayer, Bible reading, devotional literature, meditation, and "work for others" through a prayer band, the Association, the church, "conversa-tion," and "visitation." In all this he was more indebted to Charles G. Finney than he knew.

Throughout the spring his letters home repeated the need for thoroughgoing preparation for the ministry; he planned to study Greek next fall. When James M. Buckley, the well-known editor of the New York *Christian Advocate*, spoke at Sage Chapel, Mott sought a confer-ence. By mid-April John was wishing there could be forty-eight hours of Sunday, "there is so much Christian work to do in this place." But before and above all learning there must be an unshakable faith in God and a knowledge of the Bible. He found new meanings in old words and phrases in the *Guide to Holiness*, that advocate of the "second blessing," absorbed the magazine's advocacy of evangelical unity, and perhaps noted that in England a "Morning Watch" society had been formed to encourage "early rising and early communion with God."

Mott had hardly satisfied his parents' anxieties when a new crisis arose. In April the Cornell Association selected him to represent it at the evangelist Dwight L. Moody's first "College Students' Summer School" to be held at Mount Hermon, Massachusetts, in July, on the campus of Moody's new school for boys. This was something new even to those who were promoting it—Luther D. Wishard and Charles K. Ober of the national student YMCA;[19] it was to be the successful pioneer of that great American invention, the summer student conference. Pastor Clymer was convinced that John should go "by all means," for he would derive more from Moody in a month than from a theological school in a year. Needing parental approval, John relayed Clymer's comment that the opportunity was "a direct provision of Providence" to Postville: "Dear Parents," he announced, "I have made the first decision of any importance, which I have ever made without your advice." He will go: a declaration of independence one month before his twenty-first birthday.

But he still needed their assent and in a five-page brief anticipated all possible objections including his previous promise to work at home all summer. He was not going to Mount Hermon for his own pleasure; it was God's will that he do his utmost to improve his ability to win souls. Therefore Mount Hermon must take precedence over Postville. They might sell the *Britannica* or draw interest from his own savings if they felt they couldn't give him the money. And then: "God had some other purpose in sending me to Cornell besides fitting up my mind." On May 5 he burst out to Pa in Holiness phraseology:

You and Mother do not recognize the change that has gone over me since I was with you. You look at me as the same impulsive, hot-headed boy, jumping at conclusions or reasoning everything out, and you also think of me as the same *selfish* creature. Thank God I am above this and "that I live *yet not* I but Christ liveth in me." . . . When I gave up to God in this way I settled forever the question what I am to do in life. It is to be *soul saving*.

"Forever" would be at least sixty-eight years. "While life lasts I am an evangelist," he declared at his final public appearance, in 1954. Pastor Clymer wrote the Motts "with joy" on John's behalf, testifying that their son was showing "clear and unmistakable proof of having received a wonderful baptism of the Holy Spirit." He and his congregation regarded John as "a chosen vessel of God." The Mount Hermon invitation was the privilege of a lifetime. Approval finally came. John promised that the folks would never have occasion to regret it.

Secretary Charles K. Ober came to Cornell with the good news that the Association might have more delegates to Mount Hermon and helped Mott recruit ten men. John urged his old friends at UIU to send a delegation. At the instigation of his Methodist class leader, Mrs. Purdy, who was without doubt a major influence upon him during his years in Ithaca, he joined the youth missionary society of the church and got it to support "two heathens in Japan" instead of one. The study of German broadened his comprehension of the impact of European culture upon sister Clara; he sent her a copy of the immensely popular Holiness tract, *The Christian's Secret of a Happy Life,* a copy of which he would also take home. He joined and would push the program of the White Cross Army, a CUCA program in sex education and purity, one of the first such in the country.[20]

As his new commitment developed momentum John no longer yearned for forensic achievement: he now possessed the reality of speaking and working with persons and groups rather than the shadowboxing of oratory or debate, yet he would always construct his speeches like legal briefs. At UIU he had learned to speak effectively and to move judges; now he had a vital message to move men's hearts and minds. Ambition was satisfied through the CUCA, the life changes he helped bring about in the prisoners he met each week (who were, he inadvertently wrote home, not unlike the plain people he'd met in Sullivan County), and through self-expression in his Methodist class which he was endeavoring to lead "up to the high and *safe* ground" of "perfect trust in Christ." He wrote home that he was also working on both Clara and Hattie "in this same line." This was the language of Methodist preaching, of his class leader, his mother, and the *Guide to Holiness*.

In reviewing the year to his parents he could say that even at "old infidel" Cornell, men were beginning to follow the lead he and Grant had initiated and he intended that the trend should continue. "I feel," he concluded, that God "has placed me here to do a work akin to that of the Wesleys at old Oxford."

PART 8: Mr. Moody's Summer School

When he was about eighty-five, Mott drew up a list of a dozen of "the most creative experiences" of his life; the first one was his month at Mount Hermon, Massachusetts, in July, 1886. He made the trip there from Ithaca a leisurely combination of travel by train, hiking, and rowing. Needing rest as well as change, he stayed with friends, at country inns, and with college mates. He fell among Spiritualists at Homer, New York, reserving judgment about their beliefs but noting that such could only be held by "ignorant, superstitious, and highly imaginative minds." A friend joined him at Schenectady; they hiked to Saratoga Springs and took a narrow-gauge railway up Mount McGregor, from which the view was the "broadest" young Mott had yet seen. The superlatives invoked in describing it to the home folks were a foretaste of his accounts of the inspiration that mountain-top views would afford throughout his life.

That night the boys found it necessary to stay with Irish immigrants in the desolate country north of the mountain; the following day they rowed the length of Lake George, most of the work falling to Mott because his companion had drunk too freely of the mineral water at Saratoga. Both the geology and the scenery were fascinating, as were the "sacred ruins" of Fort Ticonderoga. They spent the Sabbath with George Ames in Vermont and reached Mount Hermon Monday evening; two friends from UIU arrived shortly.

Although Mott had not been among the students who shared in the planning of the conference, his leadership emerged early. He assembled the Cornell delegation daily; before the conference ended, they had the following year's campus program in order, a fact not overlooked by Wishard and Ober, who were following Studd's advice about Mott. Years afterward Ober remembered that the Cornell men had regarded Mott as their chief. He had handled them without friction, making no display of his leadership; "they loved and respected him."

Mott's ecumenical friendships that would ultimately encircle the world started with Moody. From Wishard he absorbed the concept of a worldwide fellowship of Christian students. From Wishard and from Robert P. Wilder, the son of a missionary to India, just graduated from Princeton, he caught an enthusiasm for foreign missions. The "School" refined his methods of Bible study and sharpened his resolve to study daily; the speakers at Mount Hermon shamed him into confessing that although he was working at it, there was really no book "so misused, so neglected" as his Bible. By the end of the first week he was writing home that the conference had confirmed God's call to him.

"Mount Hermon 1886" is best seen through the eyes of Mott and his fellows. John's first impression of Moody, the central figure, was of "a very fleshy, short man—not very good-looking" but possessing "a strong personal magnetism which draws"—an indefinable characteristic the twentieth century would call "charisma." The evangelist's enthusiasms, his infectious religious convictions, his *joie de vivre*, immediately endeared him to the students, especially as he shared in their games, outings, and stunts. Although each guest speaker contributed uniquely, Mott declared that Moody not only presided over the conference but "pervaded it."[21]

Moody announced the "key-note" of the sessions to be "He that winneth souls is wise," from Proverbs 11:30 (King James Version), a striking parallel to Mott's verse of the past January 12. John wrote home the first Sunday that in spite of Moody's insistence there was no program, everything was moving "right along that line—to fit us for that work"—evangelism. The opening address on the inerrancy of the Bible was by the Reverend James K. Brookes of St. Louis, a leader of the Niagara Bible Conferences and editor of the militantly conservative *Truth,* the mouthpiece of those forms of adventism known as millennialism and dispensationalism. It aroused "a buzz of discussion among the students by reason of its extreme position." The student editors of the conference *Souvenir* credited Brookes with stimulating them to "personal investigation of the Word itself." Another aggressive conservative was the Reverend William G. Moorehead, of Xenia (Ohio) Theological Seminary, whom the student writers thought "a remarkably pleasant speaker." Although several of the conference preachers were ardent evangelicals whose anticipation of the second coming of Christ lent urgency to what became the main theme of the conference, they did not, as some have supposed, dominate the gathering or the Student Volunteer Movement that grew out of it: Moody dominated Mount Hermon 1886 and every subsequent student conference at nearby Northfield where they were held henceforth.

Mott described the atmosphere in his second letter to Postville:

> Here are 225 young men all of whom are solid Christians and more-over who are all imbued, with the Y.M.C.A. characteristic—*work for souls.* I know of no other such meeting in this country at least. They are all impressed with the feeling of responsibility also—I doubt very much if there is a fellow here but what will enter some active religious work such as the Y.M.C.A., Foreign Missions or Ministry.
>
> It seems good to be in a place where you see not a puff of cigar-smoke, hear not a single oath—where the very countenances speak of the higher life—where you can enjoy sympathetic Christian fellowship or wander in the pine woods and be alone with your God.

By the end of another week the attention of the conference was being focused on foreign missions.

Three years before, a small group at Princeton led by Wilder had covenanted, "God permitting, to become foreign missionaries." Wilder's sister Grace had been identified with a similar group at Mount Holyoke College. Both had prayed for a thousand volunteers for the foreign mission field. Wilder, who had been consulted by Wishard on the planning for Mount Hermon, had set off for the conference with his sister's prayers ringing in his ears.

The Mount Hermon missionary "gusher"—Ober's phrase; this was early in the drilling of oil wells—was the result of Wilder's and Wishard's manipulation of Moody's scheme of "no program." A handful of students quietly promoted the cause. Mott told a later Northfield conference how Wilder caught him:

> The first time I heard about missions down there half-way to the river a fellow began to talk to me on German philosophy in which he had heard I was interested. Before long he wove in the subject of missions. I evaded it. He tactfully held me to it. That was Robert Wilder. To Wilder I trace the great interest in missions in the colleges more than to any other man; to his sister, more than to him, the spirituality and higher success of the Movement. Early in the conference he began to find out about the men who were interested in missions. Soon he handed in a notice, the reading of which surprised us, for all interested in missions to meet. Fourteen met. Soon there were twenty-one.
>
> They had the spirit of propagation. Probably Wilder himself did not secure more than eight or ten. They got one another. They multiplied. I suppose the most sacred ground here is that grove back of this hall. There probably is not a foot of ground that has not been prayed over. I never went into that grove but that there were men praying there in groups or alone. Men talked missions everywhere—running, tramping, eating. [22]

The Reverend Arthur T. Pierson of Philadelphia, another millennialist, whom the student reporters of the conference described as wonderfully versatile, brought the missionary interest into the open with the challenge, "All shall go, and shall go to all." As enthusiasm and concern grew, the China missionary veteran and promoter, the Reverend William Ashmore, who arrived late and virtually uninvited, fanned the fire and asked his hearers to "show cause why you should not obey the command of Christ, 'Go ye forth.'" Mott talked with Ashmore, who thought John "a grand fellow." Wilder secured Moody's permission for a testimonial service at which students representing ten nations each urged their fellows in "pithy, burning, three-minute speeches" to volunteer as missionaries to those countries. By this time, July 23, there were fifty volunteers. On July 30 Mott wrote home that

> The Holy Spirit is working with mighty power here. He has brought about the greatest missionary revival the world has ever known. Up to this noon over 80 of the students have consecrated themselves to the foreign missionary work and ere Sunday night I know they will number 100. It thrills me through and through to record the fact. I have received a far richer anointing of the Spirit than I had dared to ask for before I came here.

His prophecy was fulfilled. At a final prayer meeting ninety-nine men on their knees were joined by one more.

These were the "Mount Hermon Hundred." Wilder printed their names that fall in a tiny *Catalogue of Y.M.C.A. Students of Summer School for Bible Study who have decided to enter the Foreign Missionary Work.* They were listed in the order in which they had signed the Princeton pledge. Mott was number 23. About half indicated the mission fields they anticipated. Wilder named Southwest India, to which he later went. Mott left that column blank, though he also was interested in India.[23] This was the beginning of what was organized two years later as the Student Volunteer Movement for Foreign Missions, of which Mott would be chairman for thirty-two years.

The final meeting of the Hundred resolved to spread "the missionary spirit, which had manifested itself with such power" to those "thousands of students in the colleges and seminaries who had not been privileged to come in contact with it at its source." Two days before this, Mott had suggested

> to a few of the volunteers and leaders of the Conference, while on a tramp over the hills near the Vermont border, that a deputation, something like the Cambridge Band, be sent among the colleges. This famous band was

composed of seven Cambridge students noted for their scholarship, their prominence in athletics, and above all, their consecration and spirituality. Before going out to China they made a memorable tour among the British universities, creating a great missionary revival among the students—felt also more or less by the entire Church. When this plan was mentioned to the volunteers it was heartily and prayerfully adopted; and a deputation of four students were selected to represent the Mount Hermon Conference and to visit during the year as many institutions as possible. [24]

The members of the Band made up a gospel quartet; the reporter for the *Springfield Daily Republican* thought they sang well. Mott was the bass.

On Monday morning, August 2, almost 200 students straggled along the road from the campus to the little Mount Hermon station, where they would take the train. Moody, who had responded to the boys quite as happily as they to him, appeared in his buggy and turned the singing and cheering procession into a roadside farewell meeting, enhanced by a few remarks from his popular choir leader, Ira Sankey. "The boys had a hearty send-off at the depot, and 'God-bless-yous' were heard on every hand," a reporter wrote. The members of the Band stayed another day to plan the year's work with Ober and Wishard.

Thus did John Mott learn his first lessons at the feet of Dwight Moody. In the September Cornell *Association Bulletin* he described "One Month on Mount Hermon":

> Great had been the expectations concerning Mr. Moody, but none too great. He is unquestionably the mightiest man of this day in Christian faith and practice. He knows his Bible; he knows his God; he knows human nature. He has infinite tact and consecrated common sense. He keeps his hand on the pulse of the meetings and does not let them go to sleep. In spite of all this he does not make himself prominent, for he holds up Christ so clearly that you forget all about Moody. His humility is marvelous, but the secret of his power is fervency of spirit. This shows itself in everything—in the earnestness of his prayers, in his unremitting activity in which he finds time to do nothing but his Father's business. His influence on those young men will never die. [25]

Mott found Brookes' exhortations to "stand by every word of the Bible" and to "be separate from the world" congenial, but did not mention the particular viewpoints of any of the speakers except Pierson's "suggestive and convincing" lectures on "prophecy and the scientific accuracy of the Bible." John's article emphasized missions, Bible study, consecration, and the working of the Holy Spirit.

Another lesson learned at Mr. Moody's School was the subordination of abstract doctrines to the compelling central Christian thrust toward action. In his biography of Moody, James F. Findlay, Jr. points out that the foreign missionary emphasis at Mount Hermon was contrary to the evangelist's previous interests in urban and rural home missions. Yet Moody went along with it at least in part because of its interdenominational YMCA connections, long a mutually supportive relationship. This ecumenical example may well have been the most important lesson Mott learned at Hermon. He must also have attended the several conference sessions on the YMCA secretaryship as well as model Bible study classes.

What Mott and the Volunteer Movement derived from the conservative pulpit orators who helped Wilder and his cohorts build up the missionary enthusiasm was the Biblical sense of crisis that was to characterize the Student Volunteer Movement—"the evangelization of the world in this generation"—which was likewise compatible with Mott's own mood of urgency. John must have been excited to learn of the international aspects of the student missionary movement, already organized in Britain and Scandinavia. Doubtless he heard about Moody's connections in Great Britain and why J. E. K. Studd had visited the American colleges and universities the previous winter. Yet one may wonder with Findlay whether the thousands of youthful and often ill-prepared Volunteers to be recruited later might have accomplished more for the Kingdom had the emotions that seized them been directed toward the Christianization of that growing American "mercantilism" that Mott had decried in his prize-winning oration at Fayette, rather than toward the almost hopeless odds they were to face in the Orient and elsewhere. Findlay rightly assesses Moody's greatest impact upon the generations of students who first came under his tutelage in 1886 and who were to provide in large degree the leadership of American Protestantism up to the First World War, as that of his person:

> Mott and the others inherited the best of Moody's outlook. The warmhearted spirit and enthusiasm of evangelical Christianity shaped their deepest personal predilections; at the same time they possessed an ecumenical viewpoint that would have pleased their mentor in Northfield.[26]

As he took a fast train home to Iowa, little might Mott have imagined that he would himself become Moody's heir as evangelist to students as well as chairman of succeeding Northfield student conferences. In 1944 he recalled that at Hermon "All of us delegates were brought into intimate touch with him, not only in listening to his powerful sermons and pungent Bible expositions, but also out under the elms plying him by the hour with our questions." To him, Moody was still, decades afterward, "the greatest evangelist of the last century."

In the very different atmosphere of Postville in August, 1886, John decided that rather than travel with the Band, his primary duty during the coming year was to the Cornell Christian Association, of which he would become president due to Arthur Grant's inability to return to college. In writing to another member of the Band, he magnified his parents' objections to his going on tour, but there were also the compulsion to get on with his education and the still unsettled question of the specific form his Christian service would take. He in no way repudiated his missionary dedication; the demand of the moment was to obtain the very best preparation.

Mott's defection created consternation. Wishard thought John's reasons pointless but refused to argue; in terms of the Mount Hermon challenge, no one ought to go to any field if he could possibly rationalize an alternative. Then two more withdrew, leaving only Wilder, who was, after all, the best qualified; he found another Princeton graduate, John N. Forman, to visit 162 institutions with him that winter. They recruited 2100 Volunteers, to the astonishment of the Protestant world. Mott, a "hindered" Volunteer, would be the chief agent in channeling that gusher into the Student Volunteer Movement.

PART 9: President of the Cornell University Christian Association

Mott returned to Cornell as a junior early in the fall of 1886 to insure a head start on the Association program; he soon found himself "swallowed up" in work. The sheer excitement of learning permeated his home letters from then until graduation two years hence. Now that he had fulfilled his requirements, the Cornell elective system, less radical than Eliot's plan at Harvard but destined to be more widely followed in America, gave him almost unlimited choice of courses during his junior and senior years. The new courses were exhilarating.

Eager to begin concentrating in history, he enrolled in a three-term course on Prussia taught by President Charles K. Adams, with whom he had considered studying at Michigan. "General History" or what is now known as Western civilization, was an eye-opening survey for an eager young man from Iowa, but Mott's delight was his work in American history with Moses Coit Tyler, who, in 1881, had begun a distinguished

career at Cornell as the first professor of American history in an American university. At that time the history curriculum had been reorganized
and a combined major with political and social science set up. This was
Mott's major; it led to the bachelor of philosophy degree. Tyler introduced his students essentially to what in the twentieth century is called
American studies; he had been an influence upon the young Washington
Gladden. Mott likewise received a new understanding and appreciation
of his native land and its culture. Instruction in education—"pedagogy"
at the time—was introduced at Cornell that fall and Mott found a course
in it absorbing. "Education," he wrote his sister Alice, "is finding out
what you don't know and where you are weak—it is not simply cramming
the head full of facts but sharpening and strengthening the mind for the
more subtle and actual conquests of real life," an idea also congenial to a
young instructor at Bryn Mawr who was a visiting lecturer at Cornell that
year—Woodrow Wilson, who thought the Cornell student body
thoroughly Philistine.[27] John did not enroll then, or ever, for Greek, a
requirement at most theological seminaries. It was a decision by default
against the pastoral ministry.

Although Mott claimed that he had accepted the presidency of the
Christian Association with reluctance, the work received all the attention and energy that he could bring to bear upon it; this was the first
demonstration of his almost infinite capacity for hard work and care for
details. When his father chided him for overworking, he replied that he
had the affairs of the Association so organized that they did not interfere
with his studies. The secret was the delegation of responsibility so that
his chief duty was supervision. That he was responsible for the religious
program of the university weighed heavily but he wrote home that he
faced the job humbly, courageously, and "with perfect trust for I know it
is God's work and He will give me grace and strength to perform it." The
office

> is not only enabling me to do much good but I can see that it is doing me a
> wonderful amount of good. I have to overlook the religious interests of the
> whole student body of 800 and lay out work for and keep at work 200 of the
> members of the Association. I have to be acquainted with every de-
> partment . . . in order to see that everything is done properly. Moreover I
> have to be posted on the work better than any other man in order to be in
> advance so that I may be a leader.
>
> It is a fine discipline in studying human nature for as you know it
> requires tact to assign men to proper committees, to keep them at work and
> to make everything move harmoniously. It trains one to be prompt, to
> think for himself, to be methodical, and gives one tact. I do not know of

> any position that I could ever occupy that would be any better mental
> drill. . . . I have systematized all my work so thoroughly that it does not
> interfere with my University work or my health.

He had never felt better, which he laid to going to bed at ten, regular
exercise (not to mention the Buffalo Street hill which wore out four pairs
of rubbers that winter), a daily cold bath, an hour outdoors, and an hour
in prayer and meditation every day. In addition, he was learning not to
fret about anything, "because as Wesley used to say, 'to fret is just as bad
as to curse and swear.'" Again he asked that the *Guide to Holiness* be sent
on after the family had read each issue.

Not only were there a dozen committees to supervise in the standard
student YMCA program of that period, but the membership drive among
new students was so successful that attendance at the regular Sunday
afternoon meetings grew to 160 and had to be moved to the largest
lecture hall. By January, membership had climbed to 290. Therefore, like
Yale, the Cornell Association must have a building of its own, Mott
challenged the University community in the *Association Bulletin.* Hardly
an issue passed without an article depicting "Y" programs on other
campuses—Michigan, Yale, Toronto. John reported progress on the
building fund to the home folks regularly; he raised $2,000 of the first
$4,100. The building would cost $50,000, "but it is going to come": the
Association "is doing God's work and He will not be cramped." By
February the fund reached $7,000 of which $5,700 was in $100 pledges
including his own. At the end of May it stood at $9,000.

To facilitate his personal Bible study, John bought a copy of Young's
Concordance, on the recommendation of Horace Warner. Early in the fall
he ordered a year's subscription to *Divine Life and International Expositor,*
the leading periodical of the Keswick movement (which Mott would
experience later) in Britain. Its editor was Asa Mahan, former president
of Oberlin College (Ohio), and "the grandest link" between Charles G.
Finney, Holiness, Moody, and British and American revivalism. Mahan's co-editor was Asbury Lowrey, prolific author of books on "the
higher Christian life." Among the international contributors to *Divine
Life* were several men whom Mott would ultimately meet and work with.
Both *Divine Life* and the *Guide to Holiness* emphasized Christian perfection as the central thrust of Christianity.

Divine Life welcomed "with great joy" every evidence that the sectarian spirit was "passing away from amongst the children of God." The
Guide's editors emphasized their "Catholicity" of outlook, believing in
"the one universal Church of Christ—a body with many members."

There is in nature and in grace, they contended, *"unity in diversity."* [28] In greeting new members at the Association reception that fall Mott welcomed "all sects" and stressed that the organization emphasized "no denominational lines." We aim, he declared, "to avoid all weakening criticism that comes from clashing sects." And as if his hearers had not heard him the first time, he added: "We want to forget church denomination lines, class lines, society lines and come together as co-workers in the cause of kindness and love." Soon the society would return to its earlier coeducational inclusiveness. Later that autumn Mott closed a talk to the Methodist Alliance with an exhortation "to avoid sectarianism— to guard against thinking our own denomination is the only one of any note, but to have honor and reverence for all branches of the Holy Catholic Church."

As the fall term drew to a close, Mott was re-elected to the presidency of the CUCA by a unanimous vote. He was invited to a Christmas party at the women's college—a delightful evening when he "became young again," quoting his sister Clara. In planning a holiday trip to New York City he explained to Postville that he could include only a few days in Sullivan County because "this life is too short and too important to spend much time in idle visiting. I must make vacations as well as terms count in fitting me for greater usefulness in my Master's work-field." To his sister Alice he revealed the struggle he was having between his innate shyness and reserve and the demands of his position to be outgoing, activistic, and friendly:

> This hermit life is a good thing in the wilds of the Far West where one cannot help it but in the land of humanity it is better for a man to be able to walk across the drawing room floor without tripping himself up—and be able to talk about something else beside the last snow storm.

John's description of New York City was written from Sullivan County where among the "quiet white hills of the Willowemoc" he could draw "a deep honest breath of pure air" after the dirt, crowds, and noise of the metropolis. A full day had been devoted to YMCA business, during the course of which he had outlined the program at Cornell and had the pleasure of meeting several leaders of the movement including the great city secretary Robert McBurney. He spent most of a day at the new Metropolitan Museum of Art, and in the company of his former Cornell roommate Arthur Grant, walked the Brooklyn Bridge, visited several YMCA's, and climbed a 225-foot building for the view. Other adventures included a 100-foot descent to the main tunnel of the new

Croton water system, an evening with two other Cornell men slumming in "the lowest part of the city" where they saw how the devil "has got his foot pretty well planted." The boys visited two missions where the gospel was being preached "in the purest and most simple words." The singing was the "most stirring and tender I ever heard"—a night that did John "more good than all else" he saw in the city combined.

Christmas Eve was at Grant's home and Christmas Day at Temple Emmanuel, it being Saturday, and at St. Patrick's cathedral; dinner was with "the Purvis girls"—friends from Sullivan County. Thence to the Five Points Mission, and then "to the docks where I went aboard two large ocean steamers and sized them up from hold to upper deck." That evening he went to a YMCA reception for "young men away from home," and on Sunday heard the Brooklyn pulpit orator T. DeWitt Talmage's Christmas sermon. On the return trip to Ithaca Mott celebrated New Year's Day in the home of a girl he had met at college.

PART 10: "Decision of Character"

Back at Cornell "to fight ignorance for another three months," John went to an orientation lecture by Cornell founding president Andrew D. White, probably his first opportunity to hear White. The ex-president addressed himself to students perplexed by the choice of courses that the elective system opened to them, and for which the majority were poorly prepared. He emphasized the importance of intelligent choices made in the light of the high purposes for which the University had been established, and urged the cultivation of the habit of "decision of character," an idea that took hold of Mott with extraordinary force. During his presidency White had provided students at his own expense with copies of an essay that had once been helpful to him, "Decision of Character," by John Foster (1770–1843), a once popular but virtually forgotten English man of letters. Mott hurried to the library, where, given the freedom of the stacks by his friend George L. Burr, the Librarian and a staunch supporter of the Association, he found the Foster essay and devoured it then and there. Later he testified that it "exerted a greater influence" on his mental habits than anything else he ever read or heard.

John found here a scheme for the ordering of the forces of his own person. Foster's words were suggestive of the man Mott would become:

> A man without decision can never be said to belong to himself, but to whomever can capture him; he is subservient to events. With the man of

decision, you would feel an assurance that something would absolutely be done; he will not re-examine his conclusions with endless repetition. He cannot bear to sit still among unexecuted decisions and unattempted projects. When a firm decision spirit is recognized, the space clears around a man, and leaves him room and freedom; he will obtain also by degrees the concurrence of those in whose company he is to transact the business of life.[29]

Much depends upon the physical constitution: the action of strong character seems to demand something firm in its material basis, as massive engines require. Physical nature is a proud ally of the moral one.

The first prominent mental characteristic of the person whom I describe, wrote Foster, is a complete confidence in his own judgment, based upon clear perception and perspective, rather than servility to the moods of his feelings.

> A strenuous will must accompany conclusions of thought, and constantly incite the utmost efforts to give them a practical result. The intellect must be invested with a glowing atmosphere of passion, under the influence of which the cold dictates of reason take fire and spring into active powers. Such a person's systematic energy will be displayed in its most commanding aspects in those grand schemes of action that have no necessary point of conclusion but extend even beyond the individual's life span. A capital feature of the decisive character is a ruling passion that sweeps away all trivial objections and little opposing motives and seems almost to open a way through impossibilities.
>
> Courage is an essential part of the decisive character. The decisive energy of rational courage, if it confides in the Supreme Power, is sublime: that man will retain his purpose unshaken amidst the ruins of the world, as in the cases of Luther and John Huss. The decisive mind must have the discipline of Plato's charioteer: unless the chief forces act concurrently, there can be no inflexible vigor, either of will or execution.[30]

Foster cautioned against tyranny or inhumanity, admitting that men of decision had not in general possessed "a large share of tenderness." An effect of strong character would be recognized through the peculiar charm imparted by it to "the gentle moods and seasons." Opposition may "continually strengthen the principle of re-action," putting the mind in the habit of defense and self-assertion. In conclusion, Foster declared that the process of thinking should be subjected to "strong and patient discipline," a process "in which all the parts at once depend upon and support one another"; but this sequence must be followed on to "a full conclusion." Any question must be disposed of before it is dropped. And whatever decisions may be reached should be "of a dignified order, so as to give the passions an ample scope and a noble object."

Mott read and reread Foster's advice until it became part of him. Although it may seem to have been antithetical to his avowed dependence on the leading of the Holy Spirit, it was not; there was wide room in Holiness thought for administrative judgment and methodical decision-making, and it should be remembered that Wesley was a Method-ist! Perhaps Elmira Mott was such a person as Foster described. Like President White, Mott shared Foster with later generations by bringing out an abridged version of the essay twenty years later; it was widely distributed throughout the student Christian movements of the English-speaking world.

PART 11: Cornell Junior

During the Christmas vacation Mott had found time to work out "quite an elaborate committee system," assigning seventy-five members to fourteen working groups. "The secret of the whole business," he wrote home, "is to get men to work. It is better to set ten men to work than to do the work of ten men even if one is able to do so"; he could have been quoting Foster or Moody. Some of the workers were women, but Mott did not mention them in his letters to his parents.

In addition to history courses which were now dealing with the Reformation and with colonial America, he took psychology and audited the history of education and chemistry lectures during winter term. In mid-February, 1887, he attended the State YMCA convention at Utica; a few weeks later he gave a banquet at his rooming house for the Mount Hermon delegation of the past summer, waiting on the tables with his roommate. The toasts and songs continued until midnight; one of the speeches was entitled "Christ for the students of the world, and the students of the world for Christ."

For a time during the winter John considered leaving Cornell for a theological school the next year, but decided against it—a pivotal vocational decision. He wrote to his grandfather Dodge that in addition to the pastoral ministry, the claims of home missions, the YMCA secretaryship, evangelism, "Christian lectureships in colleges," and religious editing were also possibilities. He conferred with Pastor Clymer, wrote to Methodist leaders with whom he had had some contact, and told his father that he was confident that if God wanted him to go elsewhere He would "develop events in my life and communications" that would make it clear.

The most significant event in the life of the Cornell Christian Association that winter was the visit of the Wilder-Forman team, the Princeton pair who carried out Mott's Mount Hermon proposal of a missions deputation. Armed with maps and charts of heathen lands and projecting an emotionally charged appeal, they found at Cornell an Association that had already organized a missionary group. Thirty-five Cornell students signed the pledge, Mott commenting that some of them might be used in this country. He subscribed to the *Missionary Review of the World,* of which Robert Wilder's father was editor. The lead article in the January issue for 1887 was by A. T. Pierson and could well have been a résumé of Pierson's remarks at Mount Hermon the previous summer. Mott also subscribed to *The Watchman,* the national organ of the YMCA.

As problems arose concerning the new Association building, and there were many of them, Mott took them to Director Robert H. Thurston of the Sibley College of Mechanical and Mechanic Arts of Cornell. This acquaintance resulted in an invitation to join the engineering students' annual "inspection tour" of "some of the leading manufacturing establishments of the country" in western Pennsylvania over the spring recess. John made the trip in the company of his friend George Ames. They went to Harrisburg, Altoona, Pittsburgh, and Buffalo. Mott was thrilled by the Bessemer process, the great machines that made or lifted heavy equipment, the Horse Shoe Curve on the Pennsylvania Railroad west of Altoona, a luncheon with George Westinghouse and his top brass, "a glorious ride" up the Allegheny Valley in a private car with a "darkey porter" lent by a railroad president, and the fact that the 1100-mile tour cost a mere $22! He reported to his father that

> Besides giving me an opportunity to study mechanics and mining it also enabled me to study social problems to some extent. . . . I saw a great deal of new country. . . .
>
> I feel ready for study. My mind is rested, for in all that time I did not think of my school work. I gained five pounds, and, in spite of complex fare, varying all the way from that millionaire dinner down to an alms house rail road lunch of dusted sandwiches and eggs boiled a year ago last fall, I have an appetite that will not bring disgrace on my past record.
>
> My conviction is deeper than ever that the secret of the triumphs of genius in business and invention that God has permitted me to look upon during the last few days lies in the one fact that these men worked, worked, worked, and thought, thought, thought and the fires of my ambition to go and do likewise in my preparation burn brighter than ever.
>
> N.B.—I am out of money.

John made good use of his observations of wages and living conditions in the industrial cities in a new and stimulating course that spring.
Frank B. Sanborn, secretary of the Massachusetts Board of Charities, a
non-resident lecturer, gave a course in "Modern Philanthropy," in which
he dealt with "Prisons, Reformatories, Pauperism, Insanity, Crime and
Vice." To illustrate his lectures he took the class on Saturdays to institutions such as the reformatory at Elmira, which Mott explained to the
home folks was "the best in the new world." The value of this to John
was that because of the alarming increase of insanity, crime, and other
social problems "in this fast age" he must "get intelligent ideas on them."
In political science his class was concerned with "the Rail Road problem
and more especially the Inter State Commerce Bill recently passed."

Basil Mathews recounts an incident of the spring of 1887, told to
him by Ransford S. Miller, Cornell '88, who would be Mott's senior
roommate. Mott had been nominated for senior class president on a
reform ticket and was well on the way to victory when he suddenly
withdrew for the sake of class harmony.[31] In spite of his earlier professed
interest in law and politics, Mott had no real stomach for political conflict. He dropped out of the race to protect the neutrality and ecumenicity of the Christian Association, whose leader could not assume a political stance. Only once in the future would he forget that lesson.

Toward the end of the year 1886–1887 the CUCA was host to an
extraordinary young Hindu, the Pandita Ramabai, who was in the
United States to raise funds for a non-sectarian school; a "Ramabai
Circle" was organized out of the admiration and confidence aroused,
according to the *Association Bulletin.* It was about this time that Mott and
his friends founded another society called the "Religious Union," into
the common fellowship of which were drawn "not only Christians, but
also Jews, Buddhists, Moslems, and Mormons." Ober visited the campus
in May, "not only to observe the developments of the Association work
in Cornell under Mott's leadership," but "to have fellowship with Mott
in his personal problem" of a specific vocational choice. They talked
shop but also "of the things of the spirit," the intimacy of their personal
friendship deepening.[32]

John anticipated getting home to Postville for the summer by sending ahead a copy of the new *Freshman Handbook* the production of which
he had supervised and could therefore "take some pride in." Among the
last items entered in his ledger that spring were "boat hire," a "sociable,"
and an "excursion down lake." His departure from Ithaca was hastened
by the death of Mary B. Hill, an active CUCA member, in Jamestown,

New York; John attended the funeral and laid a flower cross from the Association on the grave. He did not go to Moody's second conference that summer, but en route home stopped next at Ann Arbor to persuade the University of Michigan Association to organize a Ramabai Circle. In Iowa he visited Cornell College, his sister Harriet's school, for the same purpose.

PART 12: Cornell Senior

The summer of 1887 was John's last extended stay at home. The lumber yard had been sold so he was free to devote the entire vacation to rest, recreation, extensive and intensive reading and study, correspondence, and long conversations with his parents, Harriet, and Alice and James who lived nearby. He must have planned it this way to fulfill those frequent written promises to share his experiences and insights. In the big house on West Williams Street there was leisure for all these things— time to meditate on the pros and cons of the various forms of ministry that were opening before him, and freedom to luxuriate in the affection- ate circle of his family, so much missed at college. In order to have a head start on his courses for fall, he devoted three hours a day to directed study of the antecedents of the Reformation, prescribed by his mentor George L. Burr; he read and outlined Ullman's *Reformers Before the Reformation,* an example of the influence of German scholarship on the Cornell fac- ulty.

One night after he had gone to bed a messenger brought a telegram from Burr bearing the astonishing news that Alfred S. Barnes, a New York publisher, philanthropist, and Cornell trustee, had given $40,000 to complete the Association building fund! Both presidents White and Adams had been friendly to the CUCA, attended its meetings, spoke before it, and supported its program. They were sensitive to the wide- spread criticism of Cornell as a godless institution. Burr, who served as White's private secretary as well as Librarian, was himself an effective fund-raiser and may well have proposed the building fund to Barnes at the 1887 commencement. However this may have been, and whether or not Mott was the unwitting agent of White and Adams to change the godless image of Cornell, a role he would have been glad to play, there could be little else as important to plan for that summer unless it was his own final vocational decision. In mid-summer he wrote Burr, who as White's protégé had access to the University's decision-makers, that he had sent the authorities his ideas on "the character and arrangement of the rooms" in the new building but he respected Burr's judgment and would trust him to represent the Association on the ground.

Such was the pace of the summer of 1887, notable also for unhurried saturation in the Iowa milieu that John loved so well, until July 28 when Postville was devastated by a fire that wiped out a large part of the wooden town in a few hours. There could have been no more fortunate circumstance for the Mott family than that John was there to steady them through the traumatic experience. The next day he wrote to Burr that his father had lost property valued at $10,000: "It may prevent my returning in the fall but I hardly think so." The hardware store was adequately insured and was rebuilt; the home was not involved.

Returning to Ithaca early, John directed the freshman activities of the Association and supervised the multitudinous details of the year's program, which grew to such proportions that he soon began to yearn for the end of his term as president. During the summer the university authorities had selected the site for what would be named Barnes Hall, whose donor had increased his gift to $50,000; construction was begun in October. Mott was much involved with details of the plans; the students wanted a lunch room but Barnes vetoed it. The project encountered so many problems that the historian of Cornell intimated that they must have been caused by "the hostility of the foul fiend." Barnes died during the winter. So did his daughter, the superintending architect, the contractor, and an important sub-contractor, each under totally unrelated circumstances. The sculptor of the stone ornamentation was stricken with tuberculosis so that the carvings had to be omitted. [33]

Mott's courses that fall were "by far more beneficial than ever before"; he expected the year to be "characterized by more development" than any he had yet spent in college. In the philosophy seminar with Professor Jacob Gould Schurman, one of Cornell's greatest teachers, a Christian layman, first incumbent of the Sage chair of philosophy, and Adams' successor as president, Mott ran into what he called "the most difficult thing I have yet grappled": Kant's *Critique of Pure Reason.* One had to "abstract himself from everything in the world and give himself up to pure thought . . . a great mental stimulus." This was welcome, he wrote home, because "one gets very little time to think in college." Work under Tyler continued, with plans for the senior thesis.

Hardly had Mott settled into something resembling a routine, when Burr devastated him with an offer to accompany him to Europe as research assistant during the latter part of the year already begun. The project was both for Burr's own advancement as an historian and to obtain materials for Andrew D. White's writing. John outlined the pros and cons of the proposal to the home folks in a six-page brief which was followed soon by a letter indicating that he had about decided not to accept. Clara wrote "a withering rebuke" in reply to his description and refusal of the plan.

Visitors to the Association that fall widened the range of Mott's ecumenical friendships. The Pandita Ramabai returned. James B. Reynolds, who had studied in Europe while promoting the student movement there and was now YMCA secretary at Yale, came to describe Bible study methods and organization. Luther Wishard brought the famous Glasgow professor Henry Drummond, widely known as the recent author of *Natural Law in the Spiritual World*, who had been featured at Northfield the previous July. This was the beginning of Mott's meaningful relationship with Drummond. Wishard described his own plans for a world journey to organize student Associations in the Orient.

Mott's tour of duty as president of the CUCA ended with the annual meeting on December 5, 1887. In October he had entertained thirty committee chairmen to dinner for an evening of planning. His annual report, covering every phase of the Association's activities, filled twenty printed pages in the *Bulletin*: unwittingly he had prepared his own job analysis for the next several years, for the document described the organization he had built into the largest and most effective student Christian Association anywhere. The report, he told his parents,

> shows the world that Cornell is no longer an infidel hot bed; but on the contrary that its Christianity is more on the alert and more active than in many of the largest religious colleges in the East. I am thankful that God has used me in raising the religious tone of this University and in putting the Association on such a solid and enduring basis. I am often led to think that this is the main reason that I was ever brought here.

In conclusion Mott wrote his first universal or ecumenical challenge, in the implementation of which he would himself be the chief agent:

> The energies of the C.U.C.A. have been confined to its own development. In a great measure this has been necessary; but it must be no longer self-centered. Now that it has done a good work for Cornell it must begin to reach out and touch the outside world. God grant that Cornell may give birth to some religious movement that will influence the world—just as the Intercollegiate Y.M.C.A. movement, originated by our Princeton brothers, is the most potent religious factor in American colleges to-day, or

as the American Foreign Mission movement, which took its rise among a few young men by that old haystack at Williams College, is lifting every fallen nation on the globe.[34]

A couple of weeks later, in the relaxed atmosphere of winter recess, he let himself go in a mood of high humor to the home folks: "Another term, examinations over, a third of the Senior year gone and 1887 almost on file."

> Now time enough to take breath, have some extra fun, and do a little close thinking. Which of the three shall I specialize on during the vacation? Judgment says "breath." But human nature adds "take a little fun as well."

He went to Livingston Manor (formerly Purvis), Sullivan County, for Christmas. As it happened, Burr was on the train, en route to Europe. "I had a delightful visit with him," John wrote home, "he has done more for me—led me out more and been kinder to me perhaps than any person whom I have met in the East, and that is saying much."[35] This trip produced the worst Christmas Eve of Mott's life: he spent from 2:00 P.M. till 6:00 Christmas morning at isolated railway junctions waiting for late trains. Enjoying the holiday with distant relatives, he next day inspected the newest wood-working plants, which were turning out vast numbers of baseball bats, Indian clubs, and dumbbells. But Rockland needed "a genuine stirring revival"; it pained him to see how many of his relatives were "deaf to the claims of religion—all wrapped up in the humdrum cares of the present—leading good moral lives but entirely empty of the Spirit of God." Yet the mood of humor continued:

> No man ought to undertake to visit even the people that I have visited during these four days, in less than two weeks. It is ruinous. I have been received as well as President Cleveland was on his Western tour and have had a good time but it wears on me more than college work . . . they shed tears unless you founder yourself at every meal. Good-bye Sullivan County at meal times. . . . let all students who want to have a clear head for thinking dodge taking their meals among the Dodge's, etc.

John H. Vincent, presiding bishop of the Methodist Church (North), came to Cornell shortly after the winter term opened; John visited with him, writing home his own ambition to "stand high in our church." Vincent advised obtaining the most thorough preparation including some foreign travel. A few days later Professor Schurman proposed that John apply for a fellowship in philosophy at Cornell for the coming year. Then the CUCA asked him to be its first paid secretary for that year; the two offers could be combined. Further, he had been invited to attend the

New York State YMCA conference in Harlem in February, at which time there should be ample opportunity to obtain advice from several men whose judgment he trusted.

Mott now found himself in an agonizing dilemma. In spite of Foster's advice, decision was impossible. Waiting seemed almost intolerable. "Keep praying for me," he asked his mother in mid-January, "that the Holy Spirit may direct in all my planning as He has done during the last two years. He never makes a mistake." Then he described the course of study he was following with his classmate Ransford S. Miller on the topic of the Holy Spirit, which was making him "a Holy Ghost Christian through and through." Then to his mother he said:

> I have been thinking to-day how much I owe to you. I very seldom speak of this subject but think of it very, very often. A boy never forgets his mother. How many times the thought has enabled me to throttle temptation—I do not know. Your living example of Christian strength, of purity, of *patience*, of silence—even when misunderstood or wronged—will never fade from my memory but has molded and will mold me more than any force from earth. That I may prove worthy of such a mother is one of my purest and most living ambitions.

PART 13: A Job for One Year Only

The February trip to Harlem, then a comfortable Manhattan suburb, was a turning point in Mott's vocational dilemma. He was assigned a topic on which to address the convention briefly. The subject was absurd—"The opportunity our members have for personally benefitting one another." John worked hard to prepare a creditable speech, which he gave before an audience of 1500, following the well-known philanthropist and YMCA leader William E. Dodge.

A whirl of sightseeing, partly in the company of his former roommate W. O. Moody, now Association secretary at Corning, New York, included a climb to the torch of the Statue of Liberty, the new Fulton Fish Market, and two hours aboard the *Etruria*, "one of the largest ocean steamers of the Cunard line," little dreaming that in 1895 he would cross the Atlantic on it with his wife on the first leg of his first trip around the world. He spent an afternoon at Drew Theological Seminary in Madison, New Jersey, conferring with President Buttz, one of Horace Warner's teachers. Another excursion was to New Haven, to see the new Association building, confer on program, and obtain personal advice, doubtless from Reynolds.

The College Committee of the national YMCA asked him to stay over in New York a day in order that they might offer him a position as traveling secretary to fill the vacancy created by Wishard's going on a world tour. He would receive $1,500 a year and all expenses, with the expectation of raises to $2,500 within five years. "So you see," he reported to his family, "I am in demand on all sides." Reminding them of his rejection of an offer by Ira Sankey the past year to become secretary of a city YMCA supported by the singer, he still felt that preparation was more important than any present job opportunity, and at the moment inclined toward the fellowship in philosophy.

Writing home in March just after the "great blizzard of '88"—"I do not consider the storm anything wonderful as compared with some I have seen in Iowa"—he was still on the fence, but leaning toward the Cornell proposition. Several prominent Methodists had advised him not to enter a seminary until after a year of graduate work. Analyzing each situation in agonizing detail even to daily schedules of the proposed jobs, he filled most of twelve large pages. During this exercise he realized that he was already prepared for the YMCA position. At best, the Cornell proposals were temporary. Now in a twenty-page letter home he convinced himself that the intercollegiate secretaryship was in potential influence "as great as that of any minister." What of his Volunteer pledge? Well, Ober and Wishard had been instrumental in leading great numbers to become missionaries.

At this point, Ober, who had not been at Harlem, made a special trip to Ithaca to urge Mott to accept the YMCA offer on a one-year trial basis. John went to the station with him, and, Ober recalled long afterward,

> while waiting for the train we stepped under a shed near the platform, out of the rain. The casual observer would not have noted any change in posture or overheard our muttered words, but we were mindful of the injunction: "Commit thy way unto the Lord; trust also in Him; and He shall bring it to pass."[36]

Mott promised to decide within a month. Writing to Harriet he declared that he had "ceased to worry about the matter by trying to settle the question of life. God only asks me to take a *step* at a time—not the whole of life's journey." The impression was growing upon him that he had better try the traveling secretaryship for "one year at least."

He kept his word to Ober, giving him a tentative affirmative on April 16, with full acceptance about ten days later. On the twenty-eighth he wrote his father that although almost everyone at Cornell had been set on holding him there he had reached the decision by himself and with "the guidance of the Holy Spirit," who leads "in harmony with the *Word, reason, conscience* and *providential events,* —never in harmony with *feeling* alone." He was undertaking the work with "a deep distrust" of his own abilities—which had been his chief reservation all along. He expected to meet "all sorts of disappointments, trials, hardships, cold blankets. . . ." Could he stand the rigors of travel?

In August he related the steps toward his decision to Burr: he had concluded that the intercollegiate secretaryship had a claim upon him as a life work "*equally* as strong as that of any other branch of religious work—if not a stronger claim," provided he was adapted to it. The only way to answer that question would be "to give it a fair trial." The best time to make that trial would be the coming college year.[37] He had written out his argument and read it, seemingly without embarrassment, to Professors Tyler and Schurman, his pastor, four students including Ames and Miller, and had sent it to his family. "They could not escape my conclusions." All agreed that even if he were to spend only one year in it, the experience might be "the best possible preparation for any calling in this country." A year devoted to "practical work—dealing with all kinds of men, problems and things" would be "a most helpful change after six years spent largely in book-work."

That last phrase was an unwitting clue to the decision: Mott was not an intellectual for whom a teaching career might beckon, although Schurman's fellowship proposal indicated that he had the capacity. Doubtless John's growing friendship with Charles Ober was a factor; he had been Ober's first choice of several candidates. The fellowship of the YMCA's religious activism was attractive, and the "Y" wanted him. Ober reminisced forty years afterward that John had been "strong, clearheaded, well-poised and dependable" if not scintillating; "I saw that he had leadership." Mott had been conscious of his ability, "but he was not an egotist." The ecumenical stance of the YMCA was congenial. Mott admired power and prestige; the men he had met in New York ranked high in the business world and this job would bring him into immediate contact with them. Whether he recognized it or not, Mott loved travel. Strangely, too, in spite of the warm relations between him and his pastor and congregation, he was apparently never asked to fill the pulpit, nor taken under care as a ministerial candidate.

The remaining weeks of the spring term were almost an anticlimax after the momentous decision was made. It was far more momentous than Mott could have imagined. First he had to reassure his mother that he had made the right choice: he regretted that she was disappointed by it but reminded her that she had really not answered his basic premises. To meet the Association's needs at Cornell, he had selected Ransford Miller, whom he knew intimately, for the secretaryship. A large delegation was going to Northfield that summer so there would be a "strong, reliable band of workers" in the CUCA next year. He would himself return for the opening of the term "to help start the work off."

His senior thesis on the Reformation accepted and examinations passed, Mott received honors in history and was named one of nine student commencement speakers. He hastily recast the thesis into an oration on "The Influence of the Reformation upon America." Election to Phi Beta Kappa came as "the greatest honor which can fall to a man at Cornell." The requirements, he wrote his parents, were high scholarship and high moral character; eleven had been tapped from his class of 120. It was unusual for a student who had not been at Cornell four years to be chosen. Membership in this "republic of letters" would be "worth something," even though he was obliged to buy a gold key for $7.00. He would never be seen without it.

Commencement came and went. Although his parents were visiting in Sullivan, they did not attend, an enigma never explained. The CUCA *Bulletin* bade him godspeed: "With our knowledge of Mr. Mott's valuable past services to the Association we can forsee nothing but success." He returned to Cornell during the next college year as planned, and throughout his life at least once a year. "When I come," he told a group of professional colleagues meeting there in 1931, "I speak in the University Chapel, but by night I walk beneath the stars and think of what God did for me when I was a student on this campus."[38]

2

"My First Love"

This work among students, first in one's own country and then across the many years throughout the world, was my first love.

JOHN MOTT was an immediate success as the intercollegiate secretary for the North American Student YMCA. Ober's first estimation of him as sane but not spectacular was soon improved upon by the students of a hundred colleges for whom Mott early became "the chief." There were, however, greater resources within him, of which the senior secretary had not been aware that spring evening at the Ithaca station when he had urged Mott to try the job for a year. These would drive Mott not merely to success but to world recognition as he expanded the student enterprise to five continents.

PART 1: The Preparation of an Intercollegiate Secretary

Mott once confessed that he had been born with an "instinct" for travel, the *Wanderlust*, as the Germans say. Before he could talk he would clamor to be taken out in front of the Postville farmhouse to see the Milwaukee trains. As an adolescent he collected the routes and timetables of most American railroads; like the old Indian fighter General Hugh Scott who once told him that he could find his way in the night on horseback from Canada to Mexico, Mott believed that as a boy he could have found his own way by train "all over this country." Travel, he said, became "almost a second nature" to him.[1] Extensive travel was still somewhat of an ordeal in 1888, but Mott reveled in it in spite of train sickness at first; dedication overruled minor complaints. An astute observer of men and customs, he delighted in the constant unfolding of new scenes and ex-

47

periences. For more than half a century he would average thirty to forty thousand miles a year by rail and ship.

Ober must have been aware of the prestige that Cornell would lend to Mott's name: it was the best-known·of the newer American universities and all well-informed student Association leaders knew that its campus "Y"—surrounded by a secular environment—was the world's largest and most effective. Had Mott come from the University of Michigan, which he once considered, he would not have radiated the aura of educational progress associated with Cornell. Had he graduated from Yale or Harvard he would have been backed by tradition and his achievement taken for granted.

Nor had Ober recognized the effectiveness of Mott's unique combination of intellectual, social, and spiritual training at Fayette and Ithaca. Few young Americans of Mott's generation finished college as well trained for their careers as did he. His Cornell degree represented his entire formal education; it furnished him with a critical mind, skills in research and information retrieval, an acuteness that was almost uncanny in judging the character and qualifications of men, and the ability to express himself clearly and forcefully in both speech and writing. He had gained understanding and appreciation of the latest trends in science and philosophy from some of the best teachers of his day but had kept his evangelical convictions intact. Some have wondered whether the decision against graduate study was the right one, but as he visited the universities of America and then of the world, his real education continued, far more effectively than if confined to specialization.

Thus prepared, John R. Mott at the age of twenty-three, a large six feet tall with handsome features and impressive bearing (in spite of a stubborn crop of reddish-brown hair that stood straight up) set out in September, 1888, to visit the colleges and universities of the United States and Canada. His remarkable facility to recognize and remember persons and their names—a later colleague called it a sixth sense—and to engage them at once in serious conversation, would be assets as he moved among the 173 college Associations and their 15,000 members. People might notice his open, earnest, and vigorous face, but they would be moved by his joyous Christian faith and message of unity, and his fellow-students would adopt his secrets of organization and program. Although he possessed a "normal though hidden" sense of humor, he was, as a colleague once said, "terribly in earnest," even in the early days.

Almost from the moment of acceptance of Ober's offer, Mott's main thrust had been preparation for the job. He did not linger at Cornell in June but as in 1886 made a vacation of the trip to Northfield, where the summer conference would provide important training for the new work. His mother couldn't understand why he wanted to go there again, but he looked toward "a rich experience." That it was, and he replied that the conference was affording him "a splendid opportunity" to fit himself for his new job; the acquaintances he was forming would prove "of great value" as he would move from college to college. In addition, he was meeting men of "wide experience in the Y.M.C.A. work" from whom he was "extracting many valuable suggestions," but the most significant contacts were interdenominational.

Among them were J. Hudson Taylor, founder of the China Inland Mission, and the Reverend Henry Clay Trumbull of Philadelphia who would influence Mott in such a way that his portrait would join those of four other, better-remembered personalities in Mott's study during his own later years.[2] Alexander McKenzie of Cambridge spoke on the book of Genesis and Professor John A. Broadus of Louisville, a leading Southern Baptist Bible scholar, on evangelical themes. Amos Alonzo Stagg of Yale directed the sports program. Mott met Edward I. Bosworth who would in a few years provide the Movement with its most successful Bible lessons; William Rainey Harper illustrated his method of Bible study in a lecture on the prophet Amos; Wilder talked on the evangelization of the world. Among the delegates destined to missions was Max Wood Moorhead of Amherst. Charles Foster Kent of Yale would found the National Council on Religion in Higher Education in 1923. A student was drowned in the "treacherous" Connecticut River; "the sad responsibility for taking the body home to the boy's mother was laid on Mott."

Wishard and Ober brought to Northfield a delegation of ten men from three Oxford colleges, and from Cambridge, Edinburgh, and Utrecht. They were "from some of the best families of Britain, fine scholars and above all very consecrated men," Mott wrote home. During a session addressed by student speakers, Mott's words made the deepest impression. Moody turned to Richard Morse, seated next to him, and remarked: "You ought to keep your eye on that young man!" to which the national secretary replied, "it is because already we are doing so that he is speaking here today." Later in the conference a student asked Moody to identify the new intercollegiate secretary. Mott stood up and was recognized. "Without knowing it," Morse recalled, "Moody was really introducing to us the man who was to succeed him for many years as president of the

Northfield Student Conference." At the closing session Mott declared that God had "brought us up here to form a link in a great chain of circumstances."[3]

When the conference closed Mott was, to his delight, put in charge of the European delegation, guiding them to Niagara, the Thousand Islands, Toronto, Montreal, and the Hudson River Valley. This, his first international responsibility, ended in New York City, where he waited impatiently for his sister Clara to arrive from Germany. Finally he preceded her to Jamestown, New York, to visit Mary Hill's parents. Clara joined him and together they enjoyed the trip to Postville, where John filled a month with preparation, belated Cornell business, and much correspondence.

PART 2: John Mott and the Age of Energy

When in 1970 Howard Mumford Jones described the American experience between 1865 and 1915 as *The Age of Energy*, he was not acquainted with John Mott's career, though he did mention Dwight L. Moody. It was an age, said Jones, that was fascinated by energy, whether produced by steam, war, or personality. It was expressed in American mobility, in the Corliss engine, the extravagance of hyperbole in literature from Ella Wheeler Wilcox to Mark Twain, in the steam locomotive, and in much of American Victorianism. It was epitomized in the "robber barons" such as Vanderbilt, Rockefeller, Carnegie, Stanford, or in George A. Custer, the Hearsts, Roscoe Conkling, Theodore Roosevelt, or Henry Ward Beecher.[4] None of these personified the age of energy more fully than John R. Mott, who set out in 1888 to weld the Christian students of North America into a unity and then to apply the pattern to the world.

The age of energy produced the mushrooming cities that dominated the nation before the turn of the century. Mott's career opened at the very apogee of *The Rise of the City*, as Arthur M. Schlesinger described the growth of urban America.[5] The Minneapolis to which Mott made his very first professional visit grew from a small town to a city of 200,000 in less than twenty years. The growth of Chicago, where he would set up an office for the Student Volunteer Movement, was "meteoric," in the word of another authority on *The Urbanization of America*.[6] Every section of the nation shared in this development of which Seattle's almost sixfold growth in two decades may have been extreme, but the phenomenon was universal. In every one of these cities there was a thriving YMCA, a center for the constructive channeling of male energy.[7]

This was also the golden age of the railroad. The imperial schemes that projected the roads from coast to coast with branches everywhere bound cities, towns, and even villages together. Mott soon became an urban man whose "life of travel" was made possible by the rail network that opened hamlet and metropolis alike to the traveling salesman. His specialized ministry to students—at the beginning of his career; it was expanded to the urban YMCA's later—early acquired an aura of prestige marked by the glamor of arrival and departure at one of the social centers of every community—the railway station. The wonder of train travel still surrounded the visiting promoter with a sort of halo, and as time passed a protocol of welcome developed.

Within a few years of entering this race, Mott was in full cooperation and competition with an astonishing number of the business leaders of his time, meeting if not surpassing their expenditure of energy. Some who had inherited millions from parental "malefactors of great wealth" early trusted him to spend, or invest, a part of their surplus in instrumentalities dedicated to human betterment through religious agencies. It was also the golden age of invention: he merely needed to ask for funds to support almost any project; he was rarely refused. One cannot avoid the conclusion that in these pre-income tax days the rich really did not know what to do with their wealth and so welcomed the opportunities he proposed that could be balanced over against their diminishing capital of social responsibility.

As executives these business leaders would admire his judgment and power of decision, his inventiveness, his business efficiency, his singleness of purpose. His powers of concentration enabled him to consult with colleagues or dictate in train or taxi; his sponsors paid his deluxe rail and steamship fares so he could carry on more business. A rapid reader who schooled himself to take notes to everything, he could digest or write a complex report in a minimum of time and with extraordinary clarity. And before long, there would be a talented wife to edit, revise, or rewrite.

The Mott enterprises that captured the imaginations of his supporters befitted the age of energy. The college youth with whom he worked were full of it. The Student Volunteer Movement was bent on evangelizing the world in this generation. It was, as Jones points out, an era of exuberance in language, attitudes, ambition, altruism. Challenge, dedication, commitment, were still sources of power; they had not yet been adulterated by the caustic acids of modernity. The age of the crusade was not over; Mott's career was to coincide with, even aid and abet it to reach its high-water mark.

Mott stood squarely in the middle stream of religious tradition that assumed an energetic attitude toward its goals. Immediacy had been a favorite term of Charles G. Finney, and no later evangelist could afford to let his converts' ardor cool before bringing them into the fold. To pursue this is beyond our present interest, but the Holiness that motivated Mott was an energetic quest. George Williams, the founder of the YMCA, wanted young men to be "strong to serve." No soul could rest in quietism, even after a second blessing; there was a "divine impera- tive of practicalness" about it. Throughout his career, Mott's activism would be an enigma to his German friends, but was not American Protes- tantism itself a "lively experiment"?[8]

PART 3: First Assignment: New England and the Maritimes

Mott's first official duty as assistant secretary of the College Department of the International Committee of the Young Men's Christian Associa- tion was a quick trip to Minnesota in mid-September, 1888. Taking the train from Postville, right past the old Mott farm, he had a "very success- ful" visit at Carleton College where he arrived for the Association's opening reception. At the University of Minnesota, "a different atmo- sphere" from Carleton, he held three conferences on Association work, then visited Minneapolis Academy. After a short stay at the teachers' college at St. Cloud, and a stop at Macalester College, he returned to Postville for the week-end, prior to "breaking camp" for the year, as he put it.

On September 10, at Minneapolis, he began a diary in a small pocket notebook, a custom he would follow with variations throughout his life. A few pages have survived covering the first five weeks of his secretaryship; they reveal that methods and concerns that would charac- terize his life work were present at its inception. He noted points of special interest about his travels, and to remind himself of the persons he met, listed those with whom he talked and why they impressed him. Perhaps it was the Puritan in him who entered comments on the effec- tiveness of what he had done, recorded the subjects of speeches, confer- ences, and interviews, and gave himself advice. He found at once that friends from Cornell and Northfield could "open doors," and that the

Cornell Association example was impressive. Ecumenism was implicit: at St. Cloud he spoke on the importance of the Christian Association to the individual, to the campus, to the colleges of America, and "as a world-wide movement." This, he reflected, was "the best talk" he had given as yet, but, he added, "I must improve much more. In fact, the magnitude of the work is just dawning upon me." After the last meeting at Macalester, a number of students asked for personal interviews, as he himself had when Studd came to Cornell; this refinement of Moody's "inquiry room" or Finney's "anxious seat" would characterize Mott's college evangelism.

When he accepted the secretaryship it was agreed that Mott would return to Cornell for several days to help the new team he had picked to get under way. This he now did, but under the sad necessity of electing a new president, for George Ames, his first roommate and partner on the engineering tour, the president-elect, lay at home dying of "brain fever." Mott had a dozen conferences with Ransford Miller, who was to serve as secretary that year, and others, and gave at least half-a-dozen talks on aspects of the program, before going on to Rensselaer Polytechnic Institute at Troy, New York.

Five days were given to conferences in New York with Richard C. Morse, the statesmanlike general secretary of the American YMCA's and hence Mott's superior, with whom he would develop a remarkable rapport, and with Charles K. Ober, his immediate superior and partner in the student work, with whom he enjoyed an intimate spiritual comradeship.[9] Robert Wilder, whom Mott knew from Mount Hermon 1886, who would travel for the Student Volunteer Movement again this year, was there.[10] During the few interludes in these crowded days Mott found time to hear James G. Blaine speak before such a crowd at the Polo Grounds that he was "nearly squeezed to death" but thought Blaine's sketch of the history of the tariff was to the point, it being received with great applause; on Sunday he went with Ober to Brooklyn to hear the famous pulpit orator T. DeWitt Talmage give a sensational gospel message, "steeped in Scripture." On the way back they ran into Robert Weidensall, father of the American student YMCA movement, who, Mott noted in his diary, had "worn himself out" in the service of the "Y."[11]

The climax of Mott's orientation was the planning session of the College Committee, held at Clark's Restaurant following "a banquet of no mean character," for which Cleveland H. Dodge, the chairman, was host.[12] This pleasant affair was attended also by Wishard, Frank Sanders (the Yale secretary who would edit the Intercollegian that year), Henry

Webster (a "prominent New York businessman"), and by the indispens-able Erskine Uhl, office secretary, without whom the Movement could move but little. Ober's and Mott's plans for the year, agreed upon in conference and correspondence since spring, were approved. When the meeting broke up, Mott headed for a sleeper to Boston, a foretaste of a thousand and one nights in his "life of travel."

The morning after the Committee session, he visited the State House and the Boston Common while crossing the city to his train for Maine and the Maritimes. By eight that evening he was at the Maine State College at Orono, having stopped off in Bangor, "a typical New England sea port," for a supper of broiled fresh mackerel and fresh cod steak, which he thought the home folks "would have eaten with genuine relish." All through Maine he had been impressed by "the tidy appear-ance of everything," and although the countryside seemed rough and poor in comparison to Iowa, there was an air of thrift and prosperity "which we do not see everywhere around our Western towns and country places." The countless glimpses of the sea and shore were novel sights for the young secretary from Iowa making his first journey along the Atlantic seaboard.

At Orono he conducted a morning devotional service, at noon held a conference with the "almost lifeless" Association, and at 6:00 gave an address to the student body, following it with a brief evangelistic service. At 8:00 he took a sleeper and awoke in St. John, New Brunswick, finding himself "beyond the limits of my native land," little imagining what a habit that would become. During the long day trip to Halifax he observed the strange landscape, now rocky and forested, now open and fertile, "as level as any Western prairie," and the clear streams everywhere. He was surprised to find much of the country thickly settled and that the grazing land reclaimed from the salt marshes was worth $150 an acre. The fall foliage was "simply gorgeous."

Upon arrival at 7:30 P.M. he was driven to Dalhousie College where he was warmly received by a student audience that was awaiting him. He followed a short speech with an informal conference from which he hoped to derive an approach for his later meetings. The fellows "were very earnest and willing, but their organization was weak." He convinced them that they should begin Bible study, carry on deputation work among the other colleges of Nova Scotia, and open a drive to obtain and furnish a meeting room. He was entertained at the best hotel and in the home of the president of the college, and met with the city Association; a

British naval officer who attended that meeting gave him next day an escorted tour of a man-of-war.

The next stand was at Mount Allison College, a "whole-souled" Methodist school, at Sackville, New Brunswick, where he met with the YWCA as well as with the men. He stayed in a dormitory, and ate in a cheap college club which reminded him of his Fayette days: breakfast of oatmeal, bread, and milk; supper of sauce, two kinds of bread, and tea. He reported to Ober that the organization here was weak also but that he had led the group to organize Bible study classes and adopt a missionary society as an Association department. There was a day's break in his schedule that he devoted to the Amherst, Nova Scotia, city YMCA where he was welcomed "very cordially" and his suggestions accepted "eagerly."

Three days of the second week-end in October were devoted to Acadia College, at Wolfville, Nova Scotia, a "close communion" Baptist school, to which access had been obtained only after considerable negotiation by John S. Maclean, a Halifax businessman who had presided over the International YMCA Convention of 1870. Mott found "everybody braced and prejudiced against the Y.M.C.A.—students, faculty, town church." He wrote. Ober that he had "put in three of the hardest days work" of his life, speaking three times to students and faculty and following each address with "informal discussion of from one to two hours." He had succeeded in converting the president and all six members of the faculty, a majority of the students, and had earned "the respect of all, for our work." He had also spoken at the town church where he secured the "unqualified approval of the pastor and people." The stumbling block was the desire of a determined group of students to call a campus pastor, and the organization of an Association was postponed until that matter could be settled. "I have," he concluded to Ober, "opened their eyes about the Association work so that it has created a wonderful stir throughout the college." There would be "good results" even if no Association were organized: "If ever I have worked in the prayerful spirit and with the consciousness of being led by God, it has been during these three days." He confided to his diary that he "stood a running fire of questions for 2 hrs without getting cornered once." To Hattie he wrote that it was "agreeable" to "feel that you are in the right, and all the crowd against you, and then remove the scales, one by one, from their eyes."

Proof of his effectiveness came next morning: a "large crowd of fellows cut recitations and saw me off at the train," he noted in his diary for October 16. This was the first enthusiastic send-off, to be repeated scores of times, usually outside of the United States. Charisma was beginning to emerge. Later in the year a revival broke out at Acadia in which almost "every unconverted man in the college" was converted. [13]

There was a free morning while Mott was in Wolfville which he improved by walking to the village of Grand Pré, made famous by Longfellow's narrative poem *Evangeline* on which every American school child was brought up. John was entranced by the place, the rich farm land surrounding it, the wealth of the apple harvest, the great meadow "as level as a floor" dotted with thousands of cattle and horses. Weaving Longfellow's phrases into his narrative to Hattie, he named a dozen varieties of apples, and described the harvest and processing of shiploads of fruit to be sent to Europe. The return journey to the States began with a mercifully smooth passage across the Bay of Fundy to St. John. Mott noted the great tides, the fishermen's huts on the headlands, the lighthouses, the fishing boats.

The next stop was the University of New Brunswick at Fredericton, where he was the guest of the president, whose daughter was a remarkably fine vocalist; some of her religious songs were "especially inspiring." Why, Mott asked his mother, "can't our American girls do this sort of thing?" Mott also owed his host a debt of gratitude for initiating him into the "fascinating science" of astronomy and giving him a book on the subject. There were several "helpful" meetings of the University Association, and Mott moved on to Bucksport Seminary, of his own church, in Maine. His work there was gratifying: the Association was scattering and needed organization, yet the students had taken hold of his ideas and suggestions "eagerly and with good spirit." A young teacher at Bucksport suggested a call on two "lady teachers": it was "a good lively call," Mott told his mother, but averred that in his work he was "obliged to put on a bold front and run a never-ending gauntlet of young women as well as young men; but I guess that I shall stand fast," he concluded, perhaps ruefully.

Shortly after returning to New England, Mott described to his parents the differences he had observed between the Provinces and the States. In Canada, "everybody moved deliberately. There was no hurry or worry. I had time to attend to all my business and to write also." But in the States it was a "pell-mell, insane, selfish rush, rush, rattle, rattle, get gain, get gain." If one could look down from above on the various parts of the world our country would present the appearance of "a vast, unending conflict." Still, he liked "the way Americans put push and snap into things." After his experience of the rocky coast line he couldn't help but repeat a story he had heard of a sailor who declared that he had been all over the world but here for the first time he was out of sight of both land and sea. "Rocks, rocks, rocks, are all you can see in some places."

The itinerary now took Mott to Colby College and then to Bowdoin, which he recalled had been Longfellow's alma mater, where he was in charge of the college sessions of the annual state YMCA convention, and to which the college "Y" was host. Here Mott met President William DeWitt Hyde and shared experiences and an evening seminar with Wilder. As was the custom, members of the Convention spoke in the churches on Sunday; Mott gave his addresses to Methodist, Freewill Baptist, and Congregational audiences, and to a "union mass meeting." From Bowdoin Mott and Wilder went to Bates College where in spite of serious handicaps they organized both a YMCA and a YWCA. A man was converted in a business session: Mott promptly turned it into a consecration meeting; he expected a revival to break out in the college.

Summaries of his activities and speeches show that young Mott had already appropriated as his own the basic principles of YMCA student work and that he was looking beyond some of them: the program must concentrate on students; it should be so thoroughly organized that every man has a definite task; each Association should emphasize its intercollegiate relationships; it is part of a *worldwide* movement; it should exalt the Word of God. The Maine State Convention report later that year declared that the parish of the YMCA "is the world."

In Boston—it was now the beginning of November—Mott could devote only a few hours to the city-wide Intercollegiate YMCA serving the 2500 students of the major colleges and universities. He made the acquaintance of Walter C. Douglas, the general secretary of the Boston "Y," known as "the best man in the country for Association work."[14] En route to New York Mott stopped in Springfield to "inspect" the "YMCA Training School" later to become Springfield College. In New Haven he "spent two hours with the Yale boys," arriving in New York late at night.

This first New England tour had been an eye-opener to the young man from Iowa. He wrote Hattie that we "may well be proud of the genuine New Englanders." They have put their stamp upon the whole country, especially in moral reforms, in giving us Thanksgiving Day, and remember, he joked, people eat baked beans "even in the Rocky

Mountains." The only trouble with these New Englanders was that they knew that "their record has been a good one in the past and they are leaning on that. And they are dreadfully conservative."

> It beats all how they love beans in New England. They are omnipresent. Why I was at one college in Maine and they had beans six meals in succession—and not as a side dish either but as the center platter.

PART 4: Learning the Ropes from Luther Wishard

A day was given to reporting to chairman Dodge and preparing for the next circuit, which would be in the Midwest. New York was "fairly boiling" with political excitement on the eve of the presidential election; so was Chicago. It was a great disappointment to John that he could not get home to vote for the first time on November 6, 1888, for the Republican candidate for the presidency, Benjamin Harrison. On Thursday after election day he wrote his father that he had never felt "quite so much like cutting loose and shouting as I do now to know that we are rid of that great national disgrace—Grover Cleveland." A little later he wrote to his sister that he had learned that "during all the rush and excitement" of his campaign, "Mr. Harrison never missed preaching service or prayer meeting. It seems good, don't it, to know that we are to have a man and a family at the head of this nation which will have family prayers in the White House and no wines on the tables."

Mott devoted election week to Albion, Hillsdale, and Adrian Colleges in Michigan, where in spite of the political excitement he was able to straighten out several groups that were pursuing programs tangential to the main lines of Association student work. He then went in to Chicago for a day of rest and conference with Wishard; he selected some samples of suiting to send for his mother's approval, noting that Wishard's tailor offered a ten percent discount. The next stand was in Wisconsin. A week later he noted that he had traveled 2500 miles and spent five out of seven nights in Pullman cars.

Part of the reason for this was to attend the annual conference and dinner of the International secretaries in New York with the Committee:

> I would not have missed it for $100. It gave me an idea of the vast scope, the strong backing and dignity of the movement which reading and conventions cannot give.... We met at Clark's Restaurant in an elegant private parlor.... I presume there were at least a dozen millionaires present. We first sat down to a meal the like of which I never saw. I do not

know how many courses there were. . . . The Secretaries each made an eight minute speech on their special work. Then the members of the International Committee and the visitors followed with vigorous practical addresses. I tell you this movement has gotten hold of the hearts and pockets of the Christian business men of this country as no other religious movement has.

These laymen had gotten hold of John Mott also!

To obtain an extended visit with Wishard before the older man left for Europe, Mott traveled with him to Iowa, leaving after the banquet. "I cannot afford to lose this opportunity of drawing from his rich experience in the work during nearly twelve years." Luther D. Wishard was the world's first full-time student secretary.[15] Upon the foundations laid by Robert Weidensall, he had built the North American intercollegiate YMCA movement; his plans for a world missionary tour had opened the position Mott was now filling. Although in later years the two men would drift apart—Wishard subsequently left the YMCA—he now shared with Mott not only his own life story that paralleled the development of the student movement and its relation to the parent body, but reviewed the major problems and issues facing it. For Mott's benefit, Wishard went over every conceivable phase of the student work, not only in colleges and universities but in prep schools, medical and law schools, commercial schools, theological seminaries, and "normal" or teacher-training institutions. Following this the two canvassed the colleges of the country, state by state, Wishard giving Mott a résumé of the conditions in every one together with names of key persons. Then they reviewed the attitudes of the various denominations and societies such as Christian Endeavor to the college work. Wishard listed his closest friends and supporters over the country, authorizing the use of his name in approaching most of them.

Wishard explained the inner workings and the personalities of the International Committee, its divisions and subdivisions, gave Mott a long list of "pointers," some suggestions for reading, and considerable fatherly advice about regularity in meals, sleep, and a rest day every week. "Every college should be visited at least two days each year," "don't allow the YMCA chairman to force you to decisions," "keep lots of college schemes on foot," "be originating and creating new ideas," "get good men for the secretaryship." "You want a life work," he declared, "this is the greatest field in the world." The college Associations have "the greatest possibilities of any organization which is designed for the evangelization of the world." Wishard drew a parallel to the Corliss engine both men had seen at the 1876 Fair, comparing the religious executive to the engineer who directed the power of his machine. Mott took thirty-six pages of notes; they were well-worn before he retired them to his files.

PART 5: Taming the Missionary Gusher

After several hard days in Iowa City and a brief visit to Postville, Mott returned to New York for what proved to be one of the most important consultations of his career, the meeting at which the Student Volunteer Movement was organized. Ober was now convinced that his apprentice had won his spurs in the general college work and that the time had come for him "to take something that would be all his own and see what he could do with it."[16]

Ever since the eruption of the "missionary gusher" at Mount Hermon in 1886 and the surprising enlistment of two thousand volunteers by Wilder and Forman during the following college year, the leaders of both the student YMCA and YWCA had been in a quandary as to how best to channel this growing student enthusiasm. "To be of value to mankind," Ober wrote, a gusher must be controlled, "and the best time to begin to control it is before it begins to flow." He feared that uncontrolled, the movement would "de-missionaryize" the Associations; for the Volunteer Movement to succeed the college Associations must be made responsible for it. So these administrators decided to channel what was obviously a movement into an organization.

No one had traveled among the colleges on behalf of missions in 1887–1888, though hundreds of students had continued to volunteer and the centrifugal forces that were generated threatened to dissipate the movement. Some groups named themselves for Robert Wilder. The leaders had discussed the problem seriously since 1886 but especially at Northfield in the summer of 1888; a committee of which Ober and Mott were members proposed that a full-time man be put in the field and another in an executive relationship to the Movement. Ober, Mott, and Wilder were agreed and during the fall the proposal was submitted to the several constituent organizations and approved by each. Ober provided the organizational key.

The Student Volunteer Movement for Foreign Missions was brought into being on December 6, 1888, after three prayer meetings, by Ober, Morse, Wilder, Mott, and Nettie Dunn, the first traveling secretary of the intercollegiate Young Women's Christian Association.[17] The resulting "wise organization," as Mott characterized it, consisted of an executive committee (which began to function the next month) composed of officers of each of the four bodies involved: Miss Dunn for the student YWCA, Mott for the YMCA, and Wilder for both the American InterSeminary Missionary Alliance and the Canadian Intercollegiate Missionary Alliance. The "SVM," as it was usually called, would be the missionary department of these. It seemed logical that Ober should serve as chairman, but to Mott's surprise and over Morse's objections, Ober insisted upon Mott's taking the position, and carried the point with the International Committee. Thus began, only four months after starting his new job, a major responsibility that Mott would shoulder until 1920, and for which he would carry heavy solicitation all his life. Ober, who later referred to himself as the connecting link between Wishard and Mott in their YMCA service, recalled that in insisting upon Mott's representing the YMCA, he had been

> prompted not solely by solicitude for the future of the Student Volunteer Movement, but also and perhaps chiefly, for the future of Mott as a coming leader in Christian work. I felt that the time had come for him to take some definite responsibility, for his development and for his deeper commitment to what I hoped would become his life work.[18]

Ober was thus the agent who brought Mott into the intercollegiate work and also focused his attention on what would become the next great motivating power of his life—the missionary enterprise. As an ecumenical historian put it: "From that time forward, Mott's bond with the Christian world mission was sealed."[19]

During the discussions in New York Mott defended the proposed organization by pointing to the need to conserve, stimulate, develop, enlarge, and extend its influence to the churches and other bodies. What considerations are essential to the best possible direction of the Movement? he asked: executive oversight, a traveling secretary in the field, an office secretary, and a corresponding secretary to deal with publicity. To combat the male chauvinism of the New York YMCA leadership, he then turned to the duties and qualifications of a YWCA representative.[20] She would improve the missionary department of the YWCA and help to preserve right relations between the missionary bands in the colleges and the Associations. With the YWCA an integral factor in the organization, the SVM traveling secretary would visit both men's and women's campus Associations, thus (though Mott did not say so) fostering a coeducational enterprise. The YW representative would also maintain an acquaintance with women Volunteers in the various denominations, being aware of their progress in preparation and when they would be ready to sail. She would keep in touch with the women's mission boards and the demands for women by the various boards; further, she would direct the women Volunteers. Such a person must be affiliated with the YWCA, be herself a Volunteer, have the time and ability needed for the task, and be located near the national center of collegiate activity. Thus, before the organization had been effected, Mott forecast its ramifications and anticipated its need for competent administration.

PART 6: Bible Lessons for College Students

Mott and Ober now retreated to the latter's home in Beverly, Massachusetts for a week's concentration on plans for the organization's Bible study program. Materials for this had first been prepared in the summer of 1885 when Moody invited the student staff to Northfield to prepare a syllabus, which was used during the following year; a byproduct of that summer collaboration had been the Mount Hermon Conference of 1886. Mott's qualifications for participation in this venture were largely personal. Since Fayette he had met his own needs and been convinced of the value of regular Bible study as basic to the student YMCA program. In addition, he and Ober were both socially and spiritually congenial. Their outlines were in actuality adaptations of William Rainey Harper's topical approaches to the Bible. The purpose was to provide a methodology for student groups dedicated to winning their fellows to Christianity. "I believe that the Spirit is going to use this course" to the great good of hundreds of persons during the coming year, Mott wrote Ober on December 30, suggesting that they should put aside any false modesty and "give God all the glory." Robert E. Speer, a Princeton senior, to whom Mott had shown the plan, endorsed it "highly." Students across the country agreed: the pamphlets reached circulations of 25,000.[21]

The lesson outlines for classes were published with an introduction by Mott in the *Intercollegian* beginning in January, 1889, and in pamphlets. Addressed to lay teachers, the object was "To fit men for leading their fellows to make a personal surrender to Christ." Leaders were urged to use personal cases as examples, to "insist upon members doing actual personal work," and to drill their classes in the Bible passages relevant to the types of problems encountered. Elementary pedagogical suggestions were included, such as a plan for every minute of each class hour. There were answers to most excuses such as "some members say they do not have time to prepare," or they do not attend regularly. One almost sees the Fayette drill sergeant! It was proposed that the leader meet privately with men who claim not to be interested to show them that "since they are soldiers of Christ, they should learn to use the Sword of the Spirit." Above all, prayer was to be the keynote: "conduct the class in the prayerful spirit"—*because you are building for eternity* (italics theirs). But the heart of every lesson and the underlying theme of each course was the person of Christ: for Mott it could not have been otherwise. Also during this time Mott came upon the idea of programming daily Bible study as the "Morning Watch," which proved helpful to his professional colleagues and was subsequently utilized as an evangelistic technique.

The week at Beverly gave Mott his first real exposure to a fishing community and the seacoast. He found it "a keen delight" to walk along the beaches "and watch and listen to the waves and surf as they dash and rush upon the shore and rocks." The coast was literally rock-bound. One morning he "looked into the fishing industry," going on board numerous boats and observing "the drying and salting and smoking processes," the barrels of herring, and cod stacked like cordwood. He delighted in the fish dishes he was served. He also tramped into the woods along the shore, returning with a basket of "beautiful moss and trailing arbutus."

PART 7: A Mandate: Pray for Colleges

Mott arrived home on Christmas Day exhausted. In writing to Ober on December 31 after devoting a full week to correspondence, he complained that neither of them was getting much vacation. Wearied by his first four months' activities, he was wondering whether he should remain in the work when his trial year expired. But while in Postville on that brief winter holiday, he underwent a transforming experience through reading one of the books that Wishard had recommended during their extended conference in November. This was *Prayer for Colleges,* by the Amherst College classics professor William S. Tyler. The book had been a prize essay thirty years earlier, when it was written to arouse support for the work of the "Society for the Promotion of Collegiate and Theological Education at the West." It had now gone through several revisions, and although outdated at the time Mott came upon it was not only a cogent argument for prayer but a virtual handbook of the church-related colleges of the country.

The Amherst professor did not need to convince Mott of the importance of prayer; the special reasons for praying for colleges are the fact of the Great Commission and the needs—next to rulers of the state and nation—of faculty and administrators. Students not only need prayers but deserve them. The colleges were founded by the church and can only be sustained by prayer. Further, we owe the colleges a debt of gratitude; we are dependent on them for leadership, and in praying for them we pray for "the rising hope of our country, the church and the world."

Tyler then described the growth of colleges and the rise in standards of admission in recent years, not only in the West but throughout the country. He believed that religious revival and moral reform had improved the quality of life on many a campus. Mott learned a great deal from this overview about the funding of the colleges and the problems they faced during and after the Civil War (which it must be remembered was then only twenty-three years deep in the national memory). Tyler was conservative in his attitude toward the new secular universities, but took comfort in the religious developments in the older schools, and pointed to the marked effects of the day of prayer for colleges, the chapel services, student societies, and religious activities in some thirty colleges he had surveyed. Although Tyler's statistics were old when Mott read the book, and the latest revision did not include the dramatic growth of the student YMCA's since 1877,[22] Mott not only grasped Tyler's conclusions but saw beyond them:

> The increasing value and necessity of Christian colleges as the only adequate means of sustaining and advancing Christian civilization and Christianity itself. . . .
> The great importance of frequent and powerful revivals of religion in these institutions. . . .
> The sacred duty of the guardians and teachers of institutions that were founded for the express purpose of advancing the cause and kingdom of Christ, not only to keep this object in perpetual remembrance . . . but to devise and contrive ways and means for the conversion of the students, and their advancement in Christian character, not less than for their progress in literature and science. . . .[23]

When Mott first visited Amherst the next year, he called upon Tyler to thank him for a statement that can be described in retrospect as a mandate for his career. Four decades later Mott was incisive concerning the impact of *Prayer for Colleges:* "nothing in all the intervening years has been able to deflect me from this my first love and what I am constrained to believe will be my last love."[24] The question of continuing in the secretaryship after the first year never came up. There would be many tempting offers to move into other fields in the future, but they would all be refused.

PART 8: Discovering the American South

The first six weeks of the new year, 1889, were given to the colleges of the South, which Mott tackled well-briefed by International regional secretary H. E. Brown who oriented him as thoroughly as had Wishard.[25] From Vanderbilt Mott went to a conference at Lebanon, Tennessee, then to Tuscaloosa, Centenary, Tusculum, Emory and Henry colleges, and the University of Virginia. He returned to New York for a meeting of the College Committee February 13–15, and spoke at the New England College conference that week-end, conferred with Ober and Wilder at Beverly right afterward, and then visited Bowdoin, Boston, Watertown, New York, Hamilton College, and Cornell by the twenty-eighth. That day he and Wilder with fear and trembling raised $1,000 for the SVM at a "parlor conference" of rich women in New York; years after they could remember "how cheered we were at the response." This became a favorite technique with Mott.

Then back to the South: Baltimore, St. John's College, Annapolis, President Harrison's inauguration on March 4, Winchester College, Johns Hopkins, Oak Ridge Institute, Guilford College (where he formed both a YM and a YWCA), Trinity (later Duke), Davidson, University of North Carolina, and Wake Forest. By March 24 when he wrote his first annual report for the YMCA *Yearbook* he had visited forty-three colleges in fourteen states and two provinces.[26] A few days later he was begging Ober to let him off from the Bible study preparation due to the pressures of the road, promises made to Sanders for two articles for the *Intercollegian* (one on the day of prayer for colleges had appeared in the January issue) and upcoming speeches at a secretarial conference and the annual Convention of the International YMCA.

There was a break from the road at a state YMCA convention at Wilmington, North Carolina and another for Georgia at Savannah, at both of which, as had been the case at Bowdoin in the fall, he spoke on the college work and thus became known to the wider YMCA fellowship.

Here it was also possible to present the sectional aspects of the student movement to the professors and students who were always present, since the intercollegiate movement had not yet developed its own regional and national gatherings. For these sessions Mott used an effective blackboard technique.

Between these conventions he visited Mercer University. In South Carolina there were five college visits and a state convention; at Claflin College the entire student body came to hear him three times. "It was difficult to turn them off," he wrote home. "I entered right into sympathy with them just as if they were whites." From Atlanta he wrote Ober that he was giving "considerable spare thought" to perfecting the organization of the missionary work but it kept him "on the jump" to "head off separate movements," adding with conviction that "this movement has vitality in it." Toward the end of April he visited in Tennessee again and attended the Alabama State Convention at Huntsville. Thence he returned to New York via Chicago to confer there with Ober and Miss Dunn on the SVM, then stopped at Ann Arbor and Cornell to help recruit large delegations for Northfield. During this visit to Cornell, Mott conducted an evangelistic meeting "of deep power," according to the CUCA *Bulletin,* which also commented that Mott's "splendid equipment for his present work grows more and more apparent." There followed a couple of days with Ober on the Bible study project and plans for Northfield.

Throughout his life Mott would recall with gratitude the warmth of the hospitality he enjoyed on these first travels in the South. One of his important goals was the recruitment of students of both sexes for foreign missions. For a time he and Wilder traveled together; at a small conference they held at Cumberland University in Tennessee they "discovered" a Vanderbilt sophomore, Fletcher Simms Brockman, who would soon join the ranks of Mott's lifetime intimate colleagues. [27] At the University of Tennessee, classes were cancelled for a conference; forty men were converted and a revival started that was carried back to their home colleges by students from Tusculum, Washington, and Maryville, whence eighty-five conversions were subsequently reported.

About this time Wishard wrote from Japan to congratulate his colleagues for their "successful work" on the Bible study program, asking their prayers, and challenging them to find YMCA missionaries for South America, China, and Africa. "I am convinced that this student movement can be carried around the world, if we can only get the right men. . . ." He then asked to be remembered to Mrs. Ober, and to "the future Mrs. Mott if she has materialized." Another letter written at the end of March begged his colleagues to keep him informed because nothing could take the place of their letters since the college work in America was his "first and last love." He rejoiced to hear of Mott's successes and was thoroughly convinced of "the wisdom of our judgment in his selection."

PART 9: A Speaker of Calm Dignity

Mott gave the first half of May to a conference of 450 YMCA secretaries at Orange, New Jersey, and to the International Convention in Philadelphia. A month before, he had reminded Ober that he had never attended a secretaries' conference and asked his superior to "jot down some points when you are on the train and send them to me" with a method of treatment also. We do not know how Ober replied, but at the secretarial assemblage Mott was also asked to deliver a memorial address for the workers who had died since the previous meeting, an odd commission in view of the speaker's youth and the fact that he had yet to serve the Movement a full year. A Swedish visitor remembered long afterward how Mott had carried out the assignment "in a way which met with universal approval":

> He stood erect near the wall and spoke with scarcely any gestures. That dignified bearing and that way of letting the effectiveness of his address depend entirely upon its content has characterized his public speaking throughout his life. He also raises his voice at the end of sentences which he wishes to emphasize particularly, and sometimes uses both head and hands to reinforce something that he regards as particularly important, but in all this one must still say that in his manner of speaking he is characterized primarily by calm dignity, but not at all by stiffness or affectation. [28]

The observer was Karl Fries, who had just begun work as Association secretary in Stockholm and was in the States as a guest of the International Committee. He and Mott became life-long intimates; partly as a result of this American visit Fries, who also met Moody, "started fires" that resulted in the Scandinavian student conference of 1895 at which he and Mott would be two of the half-dozen founders of the World's Student Christian Federation. [29]

At the Philadelphia Convention an event took place that profoundly influenced both men: David McConaughy, general secretary of that city's YMCA, was selected and in a solemn lay ordination ceremony commissioned the first American secretary to India.[30] The quality of McConaughy's spiritual life and dedication became the standard that Mott would uphold in the future choice of missionary personnel in whose selection he would have an increasing share. McConaughy was later one of the founders of the "Quiet Day" prayer group to which Mott was invited soon after its formation.

Returning to the Midwest, Mott enjoyed a brief respite at home, then visited his old college, Upper Iowa, where the daughters of his early mentor Governor Larrabee were enrolled. Mott now found college girls peculiarly immature; they thought him stiff and overly serious.[31] The rest of May went to a round of midwestern Methodist colleges—Cornell, Iowa, Northwestern, DePauw, and Ohio Wesleyan (whose presidency he would some day be offered). Early June saw a whirlwind tour to Toronto, Syracuse, Wesleyan (Connecticut), and Cornell, where he shared in the dedication of Barnes Hall.

The principal address at the dedication was by President Charles K. Adams. He traced the origin of the Association's new home to the history of the society and gave credit to the student initiative and sacrificial giving that had marked the canvass for it. Although Mott was seated on the platform and all Cornell knew that the building was his brainchild, Adams did not acknowledge the fact or mention his name. When Mott rose to speak, one of his first points was to remind his audience of the instrumentality of President Adams in the founding of the first student Association in America at the University of Michigan in 1857–1858; he went on to give a short sketch of the growth of the Movement since then, but emphasized the present and future of the Cornell Association, pointing out its strengths and weaknesses and challenging it to "reach out and stamp its almost perfect organization upon the other associations."

He then confronted his hearers with the SVM watchword—"the evangelization of the world in this generation." He concluded with what was almost a rebuke to President Adams, who had eulogized the chief donor A. S. Barnes:

> This building is a result of prayer. For weeks before any steps were taken in the canvass, individuals were praying for it. The canvass was preceded by a week of special prayer. . . . All seemed to realize that the building must come from God. At the same time each member realized that he must do all he could. This called forth the spirit of sacrifice.[32]

But he would do violence to his "highest feelings" if he failed to recall the exceptional efforts of three fellow-students who were absent: Mary Hill, who inspired greater sacrifice among the women students than had been shown among the men (one cannot but wonder whether Mott's feelings may have been deeply personal as well); George W. Ames, who, "by his faith and personal example," had been "largely instrumental in setting the standard of giving so high"; Boardman Oviatt, who had probably given more time to the canvass than anyone. All three had died since the project began.

PART 10: "Make Jesus King": Northfield 1889

For the secretarial staff, the climax of every college year was the North-field summer conference. While riding on "one of the roughest railroads in the South," in mid-April, Mott had written to Wilder:

> You and I have been praying for the next Northfield meeting for a long time. The time has come when we must begin to lay special plans for it, if we want to make it what it should be. I enclose an outline. . . . We want all who come to Northfield next summer to get *zeal and knowledge*. Let us leave no stone unturned to bring about this result in the Missionary Department. . . . It is one of the greatest delights of my life to pray for you during these days. Rom. 16:20. [33]

Throughout his travels he had recruited delegates, often being forced to recommend Northfield rather than the International Convention, because the student conference would meet "the great need of a few trained men all through the Southern colleges." "We must depend on getting large delegations from the colleges of the Middle States and from the richer colleges of New England and the Central States," he had written Ober from Atlanta. In conference and by correspondence plans were perfected, but a week in mid-June and the Harvard-Yale boat race June 28 must be fixed dates; he would go to Northfield June 29.

Marking a steady upsurge in numbers, the Conference enrolled 431 delegates and thirty-six student guests of whom twenty-two were Japanese studying in this country; one of them had been a member of the Kumamoto Band of 1876, a group of Japanese volunteers that reminded these mission-conscious leaders of the Haystack Band at Williams College who had initiated the American foreign missionary movement in the first decade of the nineteenth century. The remaining dozen represented Oxford, Cambridge, Aberdeen, Edinburgh, Glasgow, Dublin, and Trinity universities. Ober wrote somewhat immodestly in the official report, *A College of Colleges*, that the gathering was "better planned, organized and manned than ever before." Moody was, as always, the presiding officer. He, Mott, and Sanders were the executive committee; Amos Alonzo Stagg of Yale again chaired the athletic committee; Robert E. Speer, just graduated from Princeton, headed the missionary committee. Ober and Mott held seminars each morning on Association methods, and on several evenings presented the claims of the secretaryship as a career. The Student Volunteers met with Speer at a spot that later came to be called "Little Round Top."

Moody, "with his inimitable leadership, tact and naturalness, gave life and power to every session." Novel viewpoints and a few liberal speakers whose presence proved Moody's irenic stance, were there in addition to some of the warhorses of the millennium: Yale professor William Rainey Harper, soon to be the founding president of the University of Chicago, whose fresh "Inductive Bible Studies" reflected the new and possibly feared higher criticism; these "threw a new light on the Old Testament prophecies." Harper's "wide research and eminent scholarship" suggested the values of his "thorough and critical approach" to Bible study which the movement was then adding to its own home-made lessons. Arthur T. Pierson, who had electrified the Mount Hermon Summer School in 1886, spoke powerfully on the SVM watchword, "the evangelization of the world in this generation," for the coining of which he was later to be credited by Mott.[34] The Reverend I. D. Driver defended Genesis with an arsenal of scientific information. Charles H. Spurgeon, Jr., of London, gave an example of his pulpit oratory. Frank Sanders, who had just earned his Ph.D. at Yale under Harper, demonstrated the inductive method of Bible study.

The sensation of the Northfield Conference of 1889 was the development of enthusiasm for YMCA missionary work in Japan. The evening of the Fourth of July was given to a joyous celebration. Unique features of the program were speeches by some of the Japanese delegates, a "song and sword dance in Japanese costume," and a Japanese cheer followed by a "war-song, march and charge up the hill by moonlight." John T. Swift, the YMCA's first secretary to a foreign country, was home from Japan and described his Volunteer decision "in this same room" two years previously. A letter from Wishard was read, but a fever pitch of excitement was reached with the reading of a telegram from Kyoto: "Make Jesus King. Five hundred students. Wishard."[35] This message was another of the links in that chain of circumstances to which Mott had referred at Northfield the previous year, and which would lead ultimately to the formation of the World's Student Christian Federation.

Men came to Northfield from most of the colleges Mott had visited during the past year. Here he had the opportunity to cement friendships that would ripen in many cases into lifelong partnerships in the common enterprise. From Wesleyan (Connecticut) there was Archie C. Harte who would invest his life in India and the Near East, from Yale George Sherwood Eddy who would evangelize in the Orient with Mott in 1912-13, [36] and Horace Pitkin who would travel for the SVM in 1895-96 and be martyred in the Boxer Rebellion. From Michigan Agricultural College came Kenyon L. Butterfield who would work in agricultural missions, from the University of Minnesota Theodore G. Soares, from Princeton the future Presbyterian missionary statesman Robert E. Speer who would travel for the SVM in Wilder's place that fall and whose name linked with Mott's and Eddy's would become one of a household trilogy known throughout Protestant America during the first four decades of the twentieth century. [37] From Cornell there were Mott's friends Ransford Miller and C. H. Lee, from Union Theological Seminary Lawrence L. Doggett, future president of Springfield College, from the College of Wooster David Willard Lyon whose life would be invested in China.

For several years beginning with 1887 the Northfield summer conferences were described in detail in 300-page hard-cover books titled *A College of Colleges*. These comprehensive surveys not only reported the major addresses but provided historical sketches of the Student Movement and the SVM. They listed the names, colleges, and vocational preferences of the delegates. Unlike the student-written and edited report of the Mount Hermon Conference of 1886, these souvenir publications were prepared by professionals. Mott's first task after the conference of 1889 closed was to provide the New York office with copy for what became the first chapter of that year's publication. In it he reviewed the intercollegiate religious scene and described the recent phenomenal growth of student YMCA's. The Northfield "Summer School" has been well called "the World's Convention of the College Associations," he declared, citing examples of students returning to their home colleges to establish new Associations, stimulate Bible study, and carry on revivals. The British delegation of 1888 had called the first intercollegiate religious gathering in Great Britain, and its influence had spread to Japan.

The College Young Men's Christian Association is the largest student organization in the world. It numbers over 300 Associations, having nearly 20,000 members. Associations are to be found in the colleges of the United States, Canada, Japan, India, China, Ceylon, Syria and Turkey. In America alone there are 284 Associations. The most important additions

of the last year have been Acadia College, Emory College, Guilford College and Johns Hopkins University.

Mott could have added that he had organized the last four.

Mott also provided the second chapter of *College of Colleges* for
1889. Titled "The Student Missionary Uprising," it was a history and
description of the Student Volunteer Movement since 1886. He outlined
the plans for the coming college year: Wilder would return to seminary,
Speer—a "thoroughly consecrated man" who was "the leading scholar
and debater" of his Princeton class of '89 and who had been "one of the
most active volunteers in the country"—would travel in his place. Because Speer could not visit more than a fifth of the colleges it had been
decided to appoint a corresponding member in every state and province
"to conserve and extend the movement in that state." Making it clear
that the SVM was "simply the missionary department of the Young
Men's Christian Association," he explained that in some sixty colleges
during the past year local campus missionary societies had merged into
the Association. As of August, 1889, it was believed that there were
3,947 Volunteers ready or preparing. Mott did not mention it here, but
he had arranged for Fletcher Brockman to travel week-ends to the colleges of Tennessee during the next two years.

A revision of this essay became Mott's first printed pamphlet, if his
earlier co-authorship with Ober of the Bible study lessons may be ex-
cepted. Issued in August, 1889, as No. 1 in the "Student Volunteer
Series," it was a tract of twenty pages and along with No. 2, *Shall I Go?*
by Wilder's sister Grace, sold for three cents a copy or $1.50 per hundred.
As such, it received enormous distribution throughout the Protestant
world, which was accustomed to reading tracts on every religious subject.
If the twentieth-century reader finds this fact incomprehensible, he may
be reminded that when Martin Luther utilized the newly successful printing press to spread his views, he initiated a technique that would reach its
apogee in the nineteenth century when tracts of every kind and description poured from the presses by the millions. The American Tract Society, organized in 1825, had distributed millions of them before Mott was
born. The SVM was utilizing the best means available to it for dis-
seminating its challenge and program. Mott would write numerous pamphlets. The content of this one, revised in 1891, comprises the most
authoritative description of the early days of the SVM; in 1946 Mott used
it for the opening essay of the volume on the SVM in his *Addresses and
Papers.* [38]

PART 11: A Job for One Year Only: The Second Year

The second year of Mott's associate secretaryship, 1889–90, began dramatically. It produced new program emphases, visits to prestigious campuses that he had not entered during his first year, the receipt of a substantial unsolicited gift to the work for the first time, a confrontation with the faith missions movement, and a substantial increase in salary. It ended with sudden and unexpected promotion to the senior secretaryship of the student department, a pivotal event in the life of the intercollegiate movement. All of these attested to the rapid unfolding of his capacities of leadership.

Realizing that they were confronted by a growing movement far greater than their ability to guide and administer it, the miniscule staff began the year with a retreat on Baker's Island off the Beverly, Massachusetts, harbor. The team comprised Ober, Mott, C. H. Lee (a Mount Hermon Volunteer fresh from the presidency of the Cornell "Y"), and S. M. Sayford, the Association evangelist; they planned to give themselves unhurriedly to an appraisal of their resources in God "and to think through with Him" their strategies for the year's "campaign." They surveyed the entire intercollegiate program and developed a plan to increase the efficiency of individual college Associations by coaching campus Christian leaders in methods at regional conferences, on the assumption that these men would improve their own organizations and spread the methodology to other colleges. Mott and Ober worked three months that fall and winter selecting seventy men who came to three meetings in the spring; the scheme was effective and became the most important program advance of the year. It was known as the deputation plan.

For quite different reasons the Baker's Island stay was an unforgettable experience for Mott. The four men had hardly settled themselves in their simple quarters when a northeaster blew up, churning the ocean into a raging fury and isolating the party for several days. Mrs. Ober could not reach the Island so each man took his turn cooking, Mott thus being able to satisfy his appetite for fish and lobster. Also, this was his first but far from last real encounter with an oceanic storm. He was fascinated:

> I do not tire of standing on the rocky shore and watching the waves roll in. I have spent hours of every day in walking up and down the shore . . . and roll up the curtain before I rise so I can see the white caps in the distance. Every night I have been out until ten o'clock. There is a grandeur in the ocean at night that baffles description.

From Beverly Mott started a swing through New England. This year he experimented with a card file entry for each college. At Amherst the "Y" existed "simply in name" when he arrived; he left "an Association" after "much personal work with students, faculty and pastor." He took a different tack across town at Massachusetts Agricultural College where he was "very cordially received by the young scientific farmers," and a dozen men agreed to enter training classes. While in Amherst he wrote his father that he had called on Professor Tyler to thank him for the inspiration he had derived from *Prayer for Colleges*: "the tears came to his eyes and he said: 'If anybody helps you always tell him. It makes him feel good'." Mott formed a resolution to carry this out and began in that very letter home: "I should have to tell you and Ma a great deal,—it could never be told." While on the Amherst hill he climbed the Greek revival chapel tower to see the view described in alumnus Henry Ward Beecher's novel *Norwood* which he had recently read.

Between trains at Amherst Junction he climbed Mount Tom (Nonotuck). The overview of the Connecticut River Valley from the Oxbow at his feet to the distant towns of his imagination caused him to "thank God for the Puritans—for Jonathan Edwards, for David Brainerd—for New England with its open Bible—its Christian homes and colleges—its countless spires pointing to God!" In a letter home he expressed deeply-rooted feelings that never crossed his lips in public: Here had been schooled "the conscience and the will which saved the country" in the late Civil War; the scene was in strong contrast to the panorama he had seen the year before from Lookout Mountain over the slums of Chattanooga and the Tennessee Valley where "for well-nigh a century" there had been tolerated "an institution which was directly against the will of God," one that deadened the feelings, "destroyed conscience, stunted the spiritual life—and mocked God." It was but twenty-five years since Appomattox; John's uncle Joel Dodge had lost his life near Shiloh in that Tennessee valley.

At Wesleyan University in Middletown, Connecticut, Mott "met many of the Profs" including Woodrow Wilson, and found "probably the best" Association in New England. [39] He laid foundations to raise it to one of the best in the country; it would provide a "big field" for Speer to canvass on behalf of the SVM. On October fifth and sixth he made his first professional visitation to the Yale Association, where he met with the deacons and conferred with Professor Harper and with A. A. Stagg, the secretary that year; there were no Bible study or other classes "but radical change is now being made." This group possessed stronger individuality than any other college Association he had visited. "It must be handled with great tact," he noted.

His October schedule next took Mott to Chicago for the convention of the Inter-Seminary Missionary Alliance, a constituent body of the SVM. He returned to New England for the Massachusetts State YMCA Convention, then shuttled back to Iowa State to aid in a difficult building fund campaign. Starting east again he found at Michigan Agricultural "the best college Association" in a large public institution with the possible exception of Cornell. At Fredonia, New York, he paid a bedside call to a Cornell friend who was dying of "quick consumption." Back in New England he visited Williams College, the birthplace of American foreign missions, for the first time. Like Wishard before him, he doubtless reaffirmed his missionary commitment at the Haystack Monument. [40] Thence a call at Middlebury College followed by a full day at Rutland with George Ames' parents, for whom he had written a memorial of their son, his first Cornell roommate. Bowdoin, Bates, and Colby rounded out this circuit in November.

Part of the Thanksgiving break was spent in Sullivan County, reported in a sixteen-page letter home, the day itself and dinner with Ober in New York, then witnessing the spectacle of Princeton beating Yale in "the greatest foot ball game in America." That night the two men took a Pullman to Lexington, Virginia, where they conducted a college conference. On his return trip Mott visited the Natural Bridge, which he thought worth a thousand-mile journey to see. We find him next in Boston listening to some "wonderful addresses" on National Needs and Remedies as set forth by social gospel and church cooperation leaders before the Evangelical Alliance of the United States in a gathering representative of sixteen denominations in twenty-three states. This conference had been promoted largely by Josiah Strong, whose pioneering social gospel study Our Country, Mott had read as an undergraduate.

After presenting the student program to the Vermont State Convention he joined Ober for ten days' work on a new course of Bible study lessons. In mid-December he addressed "thirty of the richest business men" of Brooklyn in what his friends told him was "the best speech" of his life. En route to Postville for Christmas he chaired an intensive session of the SVM executive committee in Cleveland, at which the Movement's "work and tendencies" were "carefully examined" in order to conserve its current gains, extend it, and enable it to act as "a helper to the churches and regular missionary boards in leading these now 4,500 volunteers into the field." The "best" student conference of that winter was the New England meeting at Wesleyan, at which Mott furthered his acquaintance with Professor Woodrow Wilson.[41]

Early in 1890 he reported to his parents that his salary had been raised to $2,000, a "marked increase" from the $1,500 at which he had begun, and which he hoped would make it possible to support a missionary, since he could not yet go to the foreign field himself. He also invested in some building lots in Denver which were rapidly appreciating in value. February was notable for the unexpected receipt of a check for $250 from J. Livingstone Taylor of Cleveland, a wealthy department store proprietor and lay YMCA leader whom Mott had never met but would visit shortly. The gift was to be used "for that part of the Lord's work in which you are interested." Although Taylor died prematurely, this was the beginning of a supportive friendship of more than forty years, continued with his widow.[42]

At the end of February Mott made his first official call at Harvard. He reported to Ober that it was "glorious"—one of the most thorough inspections of his life. The chief thrust of his two-day stay at the "oldest and most famous University of America" appears to have been to stimulate the Association to move toward a full-time secretary as a preliminary to a building. A week later Mott was at Johns Hopkins where he was tendered a reception; entertained in the home of a Quaker professor, he attended a Friends worship service which caused him to declare to his mother that this was Holy Ghost religion: "never have I been more conscious of His presence than in that meeting." In the course of a happy letter to Hattie—there was an especially fine rapport between the two at this time—John recommended the devotional classic *With Christ in the School of Prayer* by Andrew Murray of South Africa, a Holiness writer and leader, whose house guest he would be in 1906.

In April the first deputation conference, which had been planned at Baker's Island, met at Asheville, North Carolina. All of the sixteen men who had been invited arrived promptly. Mott wrote home that the gathering was "not only of great practical value but also of rare spiritual power." Mott's friendship with Fletcher Brockman grew, and the younger man was given an especial invitation to Northfield that summer. The two secretaries liked Asheville, "a grand place to go to for recuperation, rest, or study." Before and after the conference they three times rode horseback into the mountains, their final excursion taking them to "the very summit of Gouch's Peak," an inspiring experience. They were lame for days afterward.

The remaining deputation conferences were equally successful, and the two secretaries calculated that their protégés had contributed the equivalent of twenty months' service to the Movement as a result of their training![43] En route to the next one, in Chicago, they stopped at Mammoth Cave where Mott was enthralled by the "beautiful and sublime" sights. On May first he witnessed "the greatest labor demonstration ever held in Chicago," noting that the placards—chiefly supporting the eight-hour day—were "uncommonly fair and elevated in their temper and tone."

The following week-end Mott attended, at Indianapolis, a "secret and select" meeting of some twenty faith missions promoters, convened by the dynamic Kansas state YMCA secretary, George P. Fisher, ostensibly to find "the will of God concerning the evangelization of the world in this generation," as Mott wrote to Wishard. Although he was already familiar with this midwestern YMCA heresy, this was Mott's first active contact with what became known as the Kansas-Sudan Missionary Movement, a simplistic scheme to send untrained missionaries to foreign lands on faith.[44] Ostensibly only those were invited who "had no preconceived notions as to how mission work should be done." Robert E. Speer was there but Mott believed that he had succeeded in keeping him from committing himself "too deeply to the Kansas idea."

When given the opportunity to present a topic of his own choice Mott spoke for four hours on the "Better Use of Existing Agencies," outlining YMCA expansion policies clearly and providing a broad base for future debate on the Kansas errors. He went prepared "to take in everything" including extended kneeling prayer sessions that lasted into the small hours of the night, lest he be thought to be unspiritual. In perspective he told Wishard that he did "receive a big spiritual uplift from waiting so long before the Lord," but at the time he wrote his mother that he was praying and thinking over the possibility of going on faith rather than salary, an alternative that did not remain in his mind for any length of time. It would have run diametrically counter to his current loyalties and his inherent organizational sense, which was as deeply ingrained as was his Holiness profession. He resolved the matter by holding to the best in both positions, and became a mainstay in the YMCA's effort to divest itself of the Kansas embarrassment, which also presented a potential threat to the Student Volunteer Movement. There would be another "Kansas" conference in September; Mott avoided membership on the planning committee, shifting that responsibility to Speer. Wilder had been besieged by Fisher, but Mott had gotten him "solid." Some Volunteers had "yielded." In the meantime Mott began laying plans for a national Student Volunteer convention in the winter of 1890–1891, and by mid-summer of 1890 had obtained approval for it from Morse and all of his colleagues.

From Indianapolis Mott went to Nashville where he presented an address on the metropolitan student work to the annual meeting of some 300 YMCA secretaries. Later he wrote Hattie that while in that city he had addressed his "largest audience"—"a sea of 4000 or more faces," gathered in a tent to generate support for the local YMCA. Going next to Virginia, he was given a conducted tour of Monticello, where he was deeply moved by the humility of Jefferson's epitaph. At the end of May he wrote Hattie that he had traveled 4,000 miles in nineteen states since April. The high point of that hectic month—"one of the busiest of my life" (although he had told her in late March that he was through with his hardest work for that spring and year!)—had been an address to the General Assembly of the Presbyterian Church at Saratoga Springs, New York, on behalf of the SVM. "The Lord used me greatly," he wrote Ober. Unabashed by the presence of ninety-four doctors of divinity in an audience made up of the leaders of "the best-educated church in America"—a little different from facing "a corporal's guard of Sophomores, or even Theologs!"—he broke away from his notes, feeling borne up by the prayers of Volunteers all over the world, for he was speaking at the noon hour when they stopped wherever they were to pray. The speech was received with "more than ordinary favor and brought about several very important interviews" that were in addition to those with denominational mission board officials whom he had been cultivating between other business engagements in New York and elsewhere all year. As had been the case with the YMCA itself two decades earlier, it was imperative that the SVM be tied closely to the churches.

After a ten-day rest at Postville, Mott attended the commencement and alumni functions at Upper Iowa University, made four speeches himself, and met many old friends of both sexes. From there he went to Mount Vernon, Iowa; in reporting to their parents on a full and happy day with Hattie he hoped that her health would be "so guarded" that she could continue her education, because "she has more ability than any of the rest of us children."

Following some business in Chicago he went to Wooster, Ohio, his first but far from last visit to that college town. Invited by a graduating senior of the University of Wooster, John Campbell White, who had attended the recent deputation conference in Chicago, Mott shared in the commencement exercises in which the campus "Y" participated.

Mott gave the "annual address" to a packed house; introduced by White, he "held the attention of the audience through a long, impassioned and masterly presentation" of the college YMCA's potential and how it would be enhanced by a building at Wooster, a hope unfortunately unfulfilled. Mott renewed his acquaintance with Willard Lyon, who had been at Northfield the previous summer; Lyon would join the Mott team upon graduation.

Mott then went to a national YWCA meeting at Oak Park, a suburb of Chicago, where he spoke five times. The next assignment was the Northfield Summer School, "a glorious one," at least in part because among the European delegates Mott met and formed an affectionate regard for Nathan Söderblom, future Archbishop of Sweden, ecumenist, and winner of the Nobel Peace Prize. The vigorous, buoyant Christianity lacking in "unctuosity and Sundayface" that he experienced at Northfield marked "a new chapter" in his life, Söderblom wrote later; this was the beginning of his ecumenical career. "I'll tell you, Mr. Söderblom, I have learned to love you," Mott burst out at the end of the conference; Mott himself made the deepest impression on the young Swede, who felt himself drawn to those who represented "the strong spirit of the unity of the church." Another was Wilfred Monod of France; the three became life-long partners in the ecumenical venture.[45] Also at this eventful conference, Fletcher Brockman was "consecrated" to the student work among the Southern colleges in a dramatic service in which Moody, Mott, and the other leaders laid their hands upon his head.[46]

PART 12: Senior Student Secretary

Following Northfield, Mott and Wilder took a vacation trip together to the White Mountains—at the International Committee's expense—where, after a good rest, they climbed Mount Washington without a guide in spite of a storm, several episodes of fog, losing their way, and following an unnecessarily steep route. They were rewarded by a "glorious sunrise" next morning. Mott admired the deep mosses as well as the grand overviews, and enclosed to his mother a pressed bloom of the Alpine sandwort, "the most prevalent and beautiful of the mountain flowers we saw."[47] Dr. Buckley of the *Christian Advocate,* he added to a letter written at the summit, "has called mountain climbing the best exercise in the world. I am prepared to agree with him."

This respite from the imperious demands of Northfield prepared

Mott for what he and Ober had set up as a second student summer conference at Lake Chautauqua in western New York. To their disappointment few students came and their own program was overshadowed by the adult features of this popular Christian summer resort, watering place, and center of "culture." They admitted defeat by closing early. In the resultant unexpected leisure each man opened his vocational perplexities to the other. Both were "detained volunteers," and were reading Stanley's In Darkest Africa, which reinforced their sense of world need. Ober had a new idea about "a type of missionary work" that he would like to do. Mott, daily becoming more and more involved in the intercollegiate field, was being pulled toward student work in India while the Religious Education movement was urging him to become its general secretary. Ober was increasingly concerned for the city and state YMCA program, which was to his mind "on the rocks in many states." He told Mott that if he wanted "a man-sized job, he need not look any further than his present work," and then proposed that Mott "stay by" the student secretaryship while he (Ober) would return to the general YMCA field work. Unable to resolve matters, they wired Richard C. Morse, their superior, "the wise man, counsellor, coordinator and unifier of the American Association movement," to meet them at Niagara Falls. There in two days of conversation by the river, the three decided to recommend that Ober return to the general supervisory staff of the International Committee, and that Mott, aged 25, be made senior student secretary. From Niagara John wrote his father that he would have "several important matters to present as soon as I reach home."

There must have been excitement in the big house on West Williams Street when the news was broken, but it is not hard to imagine Elmira Mott retiring to her room for prayers and tears; only last spring, when John was in Asheville, she had begged him to rearrange his life so as to live at home again. His answer to that letter, which he had read with feeling, was a pattern for all subsequent replies to persuasion or offers leading to other fields: "Duty and Providence seem to point unmistakably in the direction of my holding to this work—at least for now," he had written. If I had ten lives I should put them all into it. "I also believe that I was called of God . . . certainly I did not seek it." The decision at Niagara was inevitable. The Committee ratified it.

His acceptance would be for a twenty-five year term. Ober could now leave the intercollegiate promotion, gratified that Mott, through his instrumentality, was identified with it "for something more than an

experiment," that the Volunteer gusher was, as Morse put it, "domesticated" into the student YMCA's and YWCA's with Mott at its head, and
that the deputation plan had taken a firm hold as a prophetic program
advance. Mott's debt to Ober was immense, and was fully acknowledged.
Ober recalled in 1926 that his own method of dealing with his protégé
had helped Mott to find himself and to "deal with men." "I treated him
not as an assistant but as an associate, sharing everything with him," the
older man reminisced. "Before I worked out a plan I would get his
thought and cooperation, and I do not think he knows to this day
whether he or I thought of these things first. We worked them out
together." On the archival copy of this interview Mott placed his customary strong emphasis marks—in his own old age.[48]

Mott's assumption of the senior responsibility for the intercollegiate
movement signified the end of the pioneering era begun by Weidensall,
built by Wishard, and brought to fruition by Ober and Wishard with
Mott's recent aid. The year 1890 marked the beginning of an advance so
expansive that the new era thus begun required a separate chapter in the
1951 centennial history of the American YMCA's. Mott was the chief
instrument in that advance.[49]

His apprenticeship behind him, Mott moved aggressively and decisively to promote his "first love." The YMCA was an ideal vehicle
through which to exert leadership. Here were men of decision, who,
although they had not read John Foster, thought and acted "resolutely,"
as the International Committee's doughty chairman and Mott's "boss,"
Cephas Brainerd, had once declared. Mott found himself at home and at
ease in this lay organization, comparatively free as it was from the dog-
mas, tight discipline, and hierarchical handicaps he might have encountered in a denomination such as his own Methodist Church, then
wrenched by the growing tensions between Holiness leaders and its
ecclesiastical authorities. Here in the "Y" he was already near the top
echelon, with direct access to its big business lay leadership and the
comradeship of the secretarial fraternity.[50] He already enjoyed status that
might have had to wait until middle age in an ecclesiastical vocation. In
late June of 1890 the College Committee held a special meeting "at
Cleve Dodge's home at Riverdale." Mott described the occasion to
Wishard:

> After taking a delightful row across the Hudson and along beneath the
> shade of the Palisades—Dodge and Morse at the oars (Princeton [Dodge]
> coming out ahead)—and partaking of a dinner the mere suggestion of

which must cause you to wish for speedy termination of your tour, we took our seats on the piazza and held our heads down to this problem until 10:30 P.M. Dodge, Webster, Morse, Sanders, Ober and myself were there.[51]

Little wonder that consideration of theological training and ordination retreated into the background of John's mind, to surface rarely.

Mott would soon become the chief engineer of a new era in the American YMCA Student Movement. He would also put his mark upon other phases of the Associations' programs as he became responsible for their foreign expansion, and subsequently when, as general secretary, he influenced every aspect of the Movement. He was entering it at a time when the "modern" post-Civil War organization was only slightly over twenty years of age, and just before the pioneers began to turn their responsibilities over to younger men. They, in fact, had chosen him; many of them became his models. William E. Dodge, Jr., president of the influential New York City Association from 1865 to 1876 during its period of most significant national leadership, was "the ideal layman" whose name was linked with almost every aggressive Protestant enterprise; Dodge had supported Wishard's foundation-laying for the student movement.[52]

Throughout his quarter-century chairmanship of the International Committee, Cephas Brainerd had steadily insisted upon the Associations clarifying and adhering strictly to their basic purposes of a four-fold ministry to young men only; in his adroit but firm handling of the Kansas crisis he demonstrated again that decisiveness so admired by Mott, who many years later would characterize Brainerd as "the outstanding layman" of the YMCA's of North America in his day.[53] Robert R. McBurney, "the ideal secretary" of the New York City Association for almost forty years and probably the most creative YMCA leader of the nineteenth century, profoundly influenced Mott, who would work intimately with him.[54] As Mott traveled the country, he sought out others, some of whom have been mentioned; more will appear, but his greatest debt was to Dwight L. Moody, the lay embodiment of American and British evangelical Protestantism.[55] Thus it was that as Mott worked with every Protestant denomination from an interdenominational base, his contribution to the growing ecumenical movement would be universal and lay-centered rather than ecclesiastically oriented.

From the perspective of the last quarter of the twentieth century when the student Christian movement for which Mott labored has all but disappeared, it is difficult to realize that in the final decades of the nineteenth century and the first four of the twentieth, it made one of the most important contributions of American Protestantism to world Christianity.[56] A major source of the ecumenical movement, this youth movement was on the threshold of its greatest development when, in 1890, Mott became the most dynamic force within it. A direct line runs from the Mount Hermon Summer School of 1886 to the World Council of Churches of 1948, by way of the American-Canadian student YMCA, the SVM, their parent Associations, and the World's Student Christian Federation. These were the chief vehicles of Mott's drive which had developed considerable momentum by the fall of 1890, "to weave together all nations." In the early days of electric power, someone compared Chairman Brainerd's leadership of the YMCA's to a "great and invisible dynamo to which all the wires run." As Mott became the central figure of the American YMCA's the wires and the inspirational power would run from the central dynamo through a web of connections that became a world network.

PART 13: The Woman I Am Going to Marry

Although Mott's hectic schedule, now set by himself, appeared to belie his endorsement of one of Moody's aphorisms, "it is better to get ten men to work than to do ten men's work," his first task following the departure of Ober was to find an associate. Speer, who had visited 110 colleges and recruited 1100 Volunteers in 1889–90, had joined the Presbyterian foreign missions board and could not continue; another Volunteer, W. H. Cossum from Colgate, took to the road with part-time assistance by Robert Wilder from a base as a student at Union Theological Seminary in New York City. In the course of the year Cossum touched almost 100 campuses. Brockman, now a senior at Vanderbilt, worked in the colleges of the upper South. Mott supervised and Ober was available to help at strategic points when needed, particularly in projects he and Mott had planned together.

The search for an associate suddenly and unexpectedly resolved another quest that was becoming urgent: John Mott found the young woman who would become his wife and partner. When Mott had spoken at the Wooster commencement the previous June, he had had the opportunity to observe John Campbell White in action and to become better acquainted with him.[57] White had made a favorable impression at the spring deputation conference and he now emerged as the best qualified of several candidates to be Mott's assistant. Like this entire breed of able and enthusiastic young men Mott was beginning to attract, White was a Volunteer and a born promoter; he was a fluent evangelical of United (Covenanter) Presbyterian affiliation in spite of which he often displayed an exuberant sense of humor. Mott would find him lacking at times in judgment and tact, but at this juncture he was impressed by White's fine appearance and rugged constitution which would hold up against the rigors of intercollegiate travel.

Mott could well have been already acquainted with White's older brother Wilbert Webster, a protégé of William Rainey Harper at Yale, with whom he was currently working on a doctorate while starting a teaching assignment at Xenia Theological Seminary. W. W. White's life would be devoted to teaching the Bible and making it central in the education of ministers, enthusiasms that could immediately endear him to Mott; his great work was to be the founding and lifetime presidency of the Biblical Seminary in New York.[58] The brothers would both have tours of duty in India before the end of the decade. "Cam" White was subsequently secretary of the Layman's Missionary Movement and president of Wooster. Further evidence of the spiritual kinship Mott enjoyed with these men lay in the ideas and inspiration they all found in Andrew Murray's devotional classic *With Christ in the School of Prayer,* which John had only recently commended to Hattie, and which would soon precipitate a virtual second conversion in Wilbert White.

When Cam White invited Mott to the "White House"—a delightful example of American folk and White family humor[59]—on the outskirts of Wooster, ostensibly to be briefed on the new job, he added that he had "a mighty fine sister" he wanted Mott to meet. Actually there were three sisters. When Mott met Leila Ada White it was love at first sight: according to YMCA folklore he destroyed his check list of "desirable qualities in a wife," and announced to an intimate, probably Ober, that "this is the woman I am going to marry." But, characteristically, he did not rush into an early marriage, writing his mother only that this was "a genuine Ohio farmer's home" and that he had liked all the members of White's family; they possessed "unusual ability and common sense." He anticipated working well with White, who subsequently traveled for several years for the SVM. Mott treated him, as Ober had done with himself, as an associate; no distinctions or rank were indicated on the official stationary of the Movement.

Leila White was teaching that fall at Monticello Seminary (later Monticello College), a girls' preparatory school in Godfrey, Illinois, "a little town across the river" from St. Louis. It is astonishing how many fund drives, campus visitations, and state YMCA conventions required Mott's presence in St. Louis and the central Midwest that fall, winter, and spring! It was, of course, the year of the International Committee's all-out drive against the Kansas heresy, and Mott had become their most persuasive apologist. He must have regarded these opportunities as providential.

The couple became engaged when Mott spent several days at the "White House" that winter recess. Mott reported to his family that he had been kept too busy to write, though he had accomplished "a great deal of important planning and other work," besides having "a spendid time socially." The sleighing had been good. The Whites were "country people," but made up "a bright, social and intellectual family." Not until spring did John break the news to his family, and then only to his mother, deferring details until he could relate them in person, which was done during a trip to Colorado to visit Alice and James in May.

But just before that he wrote Clara that she had been correct in suspecting that he had "a very strong attraction" in another state: "she is *the one* for me—beyond any possible question." Lest he be thought hasty, he had deliberated "nearly a year." She is, he said,

> a graduate of Wooster University—a prominent Presbyterian institution—standing at the head of her class... she has an unusually good education and a remarkable mind—according to the testimony of all who know her; you would call her good looking—so do I.

He might have added that Leila was a medium brunette of average height, vivacious, slender but not fragile, essentially shy, and quite capable of keeping up with him on almost any ramble. "I know four of the six children," he continued:

> They are all strong in every way; five of the six are graduates of the University; she is a true Christian in every sense of the word—and a member of the United Presbyterian Church; she is in hearty sympathy with my work and with all my tastes and plans and purposes in life. If she has faults I have not discovered them. What more do I want? How much less I deserve!... You need never fear that the love of a woman like this will detract from the strength of my home ties. On the contrary it has, and will continue to strengthen them.

This would also concern Elmira Mott, who naturally dreaded "losing" her only son. As he had done during his vocational crises while at Cornell, he now summoned the resources that strengthened them both to assure her that she would never lose "one iota" of his "affection or loyalty," nor could he ever think "a bit less" of his dear home. The new relationship, he continued to Clara, has "broadened, deepened, enriched, and refined me in every way." This was already apparent in his letters, which became less reportorial, more sensitive to persons and values, and phrased with greater tenderness. He would tell Clara "much more" when they next met.

Hopes for a summer wedding and European bridal trip were frustrated by a long-standing agreement with Wilder to canvass abroad for the SVM prior to the latter's sailing for a missionary assignment in India. Mott went alone. There would be a Thanksgiving Day wedding at the "White House" in 1891.

PART 14: Faith Missions and the First SVM Quadrennial

The first summer conference held at Lake Geneva, Wisconsin, took place in early September, 1890. Mott wrote home with boyish enthusiasm that it had been "the most delightful camping party" he had ever experienced. There were 108 students from sixty-three colleges; the quality of the Bible classes and addresses had been "fully equal" to anything at Northfield. The main thrusts of his travel that year were the student movement and combatting the Kansas heresy. On the assumption that each college in the United States and Canada should be visited at least every two years, he set out at the end of September to canvass the schools of the Maritime Provinces again, this time adding Prince Edward Island to his itinerary and concluding with a conference at Acadia College. He was accompanied by Ransford Miller, his Cornell roommate, now under contract with the International Committee for service in Japan; they thought it would help with his preparation if he could observe Mott's methods.[60] At Fredericton Mott experienced his first Church of England worship service in the cathedral, commenting that he had been "very much interested in the formal ritual." The hard beds in a boarding house at Charlottetown produced a bad pun; the contrasts drawn between Canadians and Americans were similar to those of the previous trip. There was more and rougher ocean travel this year; John learned that he might combat seasickness by remaining in the open air in spite of cold wind and heavy seas.

October was given to a furious round of state conventions eventuating in two days of rest at St. Louis, followed by visits to colleges in "upper Canada"—Guelph, Toronto, Cobourg, Belleville, Kingston, Montreal.

November brought a change of pace while preparing several new pamphlets at New York headquarters and at the Bowne Historical Library at Springfield College. There was time out for the Yale-Harvard football game and hearing Phillips Brooks, the pulpit orator of Trinity Church, Boston, and for inspirational reading of the biography of Ion Keith-Falconer, a brilliant young Cambridge graduate who had recently achieved missionary martyrdom at Aden where he had gone as a lone volunteer, a tale almost as bizarre to twentieth-century readers as were the brash decisions of the Kansas martyrs to Mott.[61]

Returning to the West in mid-winter, Mott revealed his joy in rail travel when he spoke of "sweeping through the grand old York state" on a fast express. In January and February there were college visits and days at Godfrey, Illinois, but he found rail, dining, and hotel accommodations west of Chicago barbaric. The first Student Volunteer Convention at Cleveland at the end of February he believed was the largest Christian student gathering in history. Then more college visits in Missouri; while in St. Louis "Mr. White's sister" came over. White accompanied him to the second deputation conference at Asheville; the next one was in Springfield, Massachusetts, during which Mott stayed with the Merriam family of Webster dictionary fame.

In early May John accompanied Morse and McBurney to Missouri to address the national secretaries' and the International conventions, both held in the Kansas-infected area, for which he had prepared with very great care. En route back East for the Northfield summer conference, he stopped for several days at Wooster. During the last month of the college year 1890–1891 he confessed to his sister Clara that he was "trying to do too much, and should call a halt—making provision to devote more time to my family, relatives and friends." On July 7, right after Northfield, he took a slow ship to Europe, a device he would use many times when needing a complete rest.

From the moment of his assumption of the primary responsibility for the student work, Mott involved himself personally in every aspect of the program. His workbook for that year is an eight- by ten-inch ledger of which 110 pages are devoted to comprehensive outlines, in his handwriting, of all aspects of the program, his addresses and reviews of its history, policies, and organization, plus rosters of the men who attended the deputation conferences the first two years these were held. The prime program emphasis continued to be Bible study: "inductive" or "intellectual," devotional, and for "personal work." It was pushed in all campus visits, deputation conferences, and at Northfield and the new summer conferences at Lake Geneva, Knoxville, and on the Pacific Coast. Mott was continuously on the lookout for new teachers and approaches, bringing his prospective brother-in-law Wilbert White and Robert E. Speer into the picture in the fall of 1891; he kept a tight rein on these projects, not hesitating to make suggestions to White and to "overhaul" Speer's outline. At the same time he was gradually phasing himself out of the actual preparation of the studies, though remaining an avid Bible student; the quality of the lessons was steadily improved as professionals prepared them, and their popularity increased by leaps and bounds.

The next greatest emphasis was on foreign missions through the Student Volunteer Movement. The numbers of Volunteers continued to grow. When the Kansas fever appeared as a threat, Mott called and planned, with real help from Wilder, the first of what would become a sequence of large conventions popularly known as Quadrennials because they were held once in each student generation; they would become the biggest events in the student world. The first one met in Cleveland from February 26 to March 1, 1891. Mott was astonished by it. He had written Wishard the previous summer that he didn't want an attendance of more than 200 or 300, but was amazed when 558 student delegates from 151 institutions, thirty-one missionaries, and thirty-two officers of mission boards came. J. Livingstone Taylor welcomed the convention to the city and to the handsome new hall in the YMCA of which he was president.[62] As the presiding officer, Mott told his enthusiastic audience that there were then, 6,200 Volunteers in the United States and Canada, and that 321 had "sailed" since the Movement began. He revealed that he had received requests from students in Great Britain and Scandinavia "to send a representative to introduce and organize the Movement among their universities." He hoped that this would soon be possible; actually, he would go himself the next summer, and Wilder would bring a British organization into being in the early months of 1892. The report concluded with the hope that "if the students of the Protestant world are linked together by the power of the Spirit in this Movement it will greatly hasten the establishment of Christ's Kingdom throughout the world."

Mott wrote home a week afterward that the conference had been "a wonderful success," having gone "far beyond the expectation of the most sanguine." God had answered their prayers "in a greater measure" than they had dared to ask or even think. "It was indeed the most representative student convention ever held in the world." He had counted many

more missionaries and board members than were officially registered—
125 in fact. "The enthusiasm was absolutely unbounded" and the spirituality "even more marked." He had been kept busier than at any time in
his life; it had been "an immense responsibility for one so young." It was
at this Quadrennial that the watchword, "the evangelization of the world
in this generation," received its first great popular acclaim; as Mott
declared, it constituted at once the SVM's "ultimate purpose and its
inspiration," although he was aware of its motivational roots in evangelicalism half a century earlier.[63]

Although he traveled 31,000 miles in 1890–1891, Mott allocated
only fourteen weeks to thirty-eight campuses, restricting his calls to
"special emergencies, or to inaugurate a more comprehensive policy."
White went to many more schools, mostly in the South. The largest part
of Mott's time, five months, and, one might add, of his energy, was given
to twenty-three conventions, conferences, and summer schools—more
than twice the time devoted to such in any previous year; he met with a
thousand students of 168 colleges during these rounds. In October there
were seven conferences in a row.

Because of Wishard's absence from the country, Mott, at state
YMCA conventions in Kansas, Illinois, Missouri, Indiana, Ohio, and
Iowa, and at the national secretaries' meeting and the International
Convention, was delegated to defend orthodox Association "foreign
work" methods. This comprehensive 5,000-word brief, widely distributed
in pamphlet form, and in the Association house organ, now answered in
the affirmative the question, "Is it incumbent upon the American Young
Men's Christian Associations to promote foreign missions?" Its reasoning
displayed Mott's growing ability to present an almost irrefutable argument, buttressed by facts, logic, and religious compulsion; it not only
helped to quash the Kansas movement but made a persuasive case for
American YMCA expansion to foreign-mission fields.[64] Mott was thus
inadvertently cast in the role of advocate of church-related missionary
vocations for students, and he became the YMCA's most persuasive
advocate, after Wishard, for Association expansion to meet the "needs
of young men in foreign-mission lands." In a few short years he would
be given the "foreign work" portfolio in addition to his duties as student
secretary.

During that eventful year 1890–1891, Mott "helped in the inauguration or promotion" of canvasses for buildings at a number of universities, supervised the movements of the evangelist S. M. Sayford among
the colleges, prepared for and led four deputation conferences, gave

significant leadership at Northfield, and raised funds for both the student work and the SVM. His annual report conveyed a new authority, and the pronoun "I" became prominent.

PART 15: Europe 1891: Dreams of a World Student Union

Mott's trip to Europe in the summer of 1891 was his first. In June he wrote home that he had at least three reasons for going: to measure the prospects for carrying on student work in the American style in European universities; he and Wilder would study this. The World's Alliance of YMCA's would hold its Twelfth World's Conference in Amsterdam in August. Morse and McBurney were going. Mott did not express it in that June letter, but he must have intended to explore the possibilities of a world student Christian organization. He insisted that it be a family secret that he would go alone and not married.

On board the *City of New York* he wrote that this was the "safest ship on the ocean" because of its air-tight compartments, which, he believed, made it "humanly" safer than a train, but from the divine point of view "we are as safe in one place as in another—if we do His will." The eastbound passage was relatively smooth though Mott had a few brief spells of seasickness "but not as much" as he used to suffer on trains; no one should boast on the Atlantic: "it will humble the proudest and strongest." He had an incomparable rest—ten hours sleep and twelve hours in the open air daily.

From the few records that have survived, it appears that Mott, Morse, and Wilder met at Oxford, where they had a season of prayer and shared the knowledge gained from the British delegates to the recent Northfield conference and from James B. Reynolds, Yale '84, who had been traveling on the Continent, as Wilder later put it, "to prepare the way for a world-wide Student Christian Movement." Wilder remained in Britain for the year, beginning in Edinburgh (with Drummond in the chair) a winter tour to enlist students for the Volunteer pledge. As he went from university to university he met men who had been at Northfield or who had been touched by the currents begun by Moody's earlier visits; many were keeping the morning watch. In April he was instrumental in organizing the "Student Volunteer Missionary Union of Great Britain and Ireland," the impetus of which brought the "British College Christian Union" into being the following summer. [65]

There being little that Mott could accomplish among students in mid-summer, he left his friends to tour, on his own, the Lake region of England and the literary and historical spots of Scotland, stopping overnight at the "great Keswick Convention for Deepening Religious Life," the "most noted summer religious gathering of Britain," to attend an evening session of "2,000 or 3,000 in that tent" with "profit" to himself. He would return there in 1894. Going on to Glasgow and thence to Edinburgh, Mott, full of the history of the city, was enthralled. He walked up and down Princes Street as many times as he could; he was stirred to the depths to stand in John Knox's house where "those great Reformation thunder-bolts" had been prepared. He visited the University and "the university settlements among the poor people," and finally just walked about the city to allow its "impressions to deepen." He took tea one evening with the family of a student who had been at Northfield in 1888 and who had gone on the tour that Mott led to Canada that summer. "I am in love with Scotland—but love America more," were the closing words of an eleven-page home letter recounting his experiences and reactions to the historical and literary associations that came alive in a memorable tour. His affection for Scotland would never dim.

En route to London he stopped at Durham and York "to study and admire and stand in reverence before their grand cathedrals." He felt dwarfed and insignificant in London where he spent six days taking in most of the usual sights of this "*metropolis* of the world," little imagining that in less than two decades his own arrivals there would be noted by the *Times*. A three-day stay at Oxford, upon the invitation of a friend, provided a break in the round of sightseeing and "an opportunity to see the greatest University and also meet a number of prominent men." His guide was an undergraduate named Joseph H. Oldham.

Contemporary observers and historians considered the program of the World's Conference of YMCA's at Amsterdam that summer a "dull and indifferent" one. But for Mott the presence of 500 delegates from seventeen nations, the simultaneous translations into four languages, the singing in varied tongues, the forming of "splendid acquaintances among the prominent delegates from different nations," the renewal of friendships such as those with Nathan Söderblom and Karl Fries, and the securing of "a world-wide view of our great work" were exciting.

One of the acquaintances Mott made was with the handsome and youthful Parisian Professor Raoul Allier, who challenged the conference to stimulate young men to assert themselves for justice and fraternity, an advanced position regarding social issues that the Alliance could not embrace for another generation. Thirty years later, Allier remembered an informal occasion at which Mott was present:

> One evening in a little hotel room he and some friends talked together of
> concerns which were common to us. Each of us recounted the things that
> had been happening in the university centres of his own country. It seemed
> to us clear as day that a common work was appearing in every country, that
> this work ought to be undertaken by the Student Christian Association
> and that these Associations ought, in spite of all the ecclesiastical dif-
> ferences and above all the confessional preoccupations, to unite their
> efforts to glorify Christ. We separated with our hearts fixed on this pur-
> pose. [66]

To Mott's surprise, Wishard and his wife were there. The story of
Wishard's world journey, printed in four languages, made a deep impression on the delegates and on Mott, who wrote Ober that it had been
worth the entire trip to have had the week with Wishard, [67] adding that
"the Conference has been an event in my life," and "G.O.M. [Morse]
and wife are in splendid condition." Mott and the Wishards went to
Leyden where they saw the home of John Robinson and the Pilgrims'
church; they also visited the universities of Leyden and Utrecht. From
Holland they went to Berlin and then fulfilled Mott's dream when in
college to see the Luther country—Wittenberg, where John stood at
Luther's desk in the aula, thence to Eisleben where Mott met his "long
looked-for fate" of sleeping between feather beds and visited the houses
in which Luther was born and where he died, and to Eisenach and the
Wartburg. The party made Sunday at the castle a day of devotion more
than of sightseeing, "beginning on the summit" with a review of Luther's
life. They lingered in "the room where Luther translated the New Testament and Psalms," and gave the rest of the day to the castle and the
forest.

On the westbound voyage Mott's ship encountered two severe
storms, one the equivalent of a typhoon, the captain had declared. Some
of the passengers prayed for the first time in their lives, Mott wrote
home, but he had not been "really alarmed," feeling that "we were safe in
the hand of the God of sea and land." He returned saturated in meaningful history, full of dreams of a world student fellowship, and "thoroughly
invigorated and ready" for the eventful year that lay ahead.

PART 16: A Thanksgiving Day Wedding

Although John Mott's mind must have dwelt increasingly on his forthcoming marriage, he pushed himself at the accustomed pace through the

fall of 1891. Already there were the problems of where he and Leila would live; when in Chicago he received advice from "Y" friends concerning living in that city, which then seemed to be the logical site for his headquarters, and as it eventuated, he purchased a lot in suburban Oak Park. October required attendance at several state conventions in the Midwest. The officers of one of them asked for his picture; somehow the request to his mother to forward a photograph was delayed and he replied to her that there was "much temptation to pride in living before the public as I am doing. There are also other perils which can only be withstood by constant communion with Jesus Christ." Nevertheless his photo appeared more and more frequently; YMCA publicity required it, and it was an asset. Following these meetings, Mott went to Winnipeg, which now could be reached from Minneapolis by rail in nineteen hours in contrast to a three weeks' journey only a short time earlier. The University provided an example of the British cluster college plan, which had intrigued Mott the past summer; on Sunday he filled the pulpits of the two largest churches of the city. The visit closed with the first intercollegiate conference ever held in the "Canadian Northwest," a "vast land" destined "to become one of the most civilized and most influential portions of the Anglo-Saxon domain." From Winnipeg a circuitous route via Virginia and the annual International Committee dinner in New York took him to Wooster for Thanksgiving. Thus began one of the most memorable years of Mott's long lifetime.

The "White House" on the outskirts of Wooster was the gathering place for a small clan of brothers and sisters, their wives and husbands, children, and grandchildren. Three of Mott's four children would be born in the plain, square, two-story frame country home which was surrounded by eighteen acres of rolling farmland, garden, orchard, and pasture, watered by two streams with swimming holes; they would remember it with affection. Education for the six White children had begun at the hands of a mother whose consuming ambition was a college education for each of them. It continued at the one-room school across the road, on a diet of McGuffey and the three R's. The goal of these ambitious boys and girls was to enter the preparatory department of the new college on the tree-crowned hill within walking distance—for the boys—of the family home. In fact, the college was not only always in view but was the reason why the Whites came to be at Wooster.

When, soon after the end of the Civil War, the wife of John May White heard that a Presbyterian college was to be established in Wooster, she prevailed upon her husband to move near it. This he did, giving up the trades of carpenter and millwright for farming; known for his feats of strength, White was also of an inventive frame of mind, with interests in the schools, politics, and temperance. Martha Ann Campbell White contributed in a small way to the foundation of the "University"—most midwestern small colleges began as such; she carried her second son Cam as a babe in arms to the inauguration of its first president in 1870, little dreaming that in 1916 she would see him inducted into that office. Wilbert was graduated in 1881, Leila in 1886 after staying out a year to earn money teaching a grade school, Elizabeth the same year, Anna May in 1888, and Cam in 1890.

This was a conservative "Covenanter" Presbyterian family that never omitted morning devotions even during the threshing season; John White read a full chapter from the Bible, the entire family joined in singing a Psalm, and knelt at their chairs while father prayed. Church attendance was as regular as the occurrence of the Sabbath, as Leila would call Sunday in her diaries. The children memorized the Westminster Shorter Catechism, but the family maintained a liberal attitude toward some of their co-religionists' interpretations. Mother White once walked out of a church service and sat in the buggy because of "the too high 'fencing' of the Communion table." Leila would be more conservative than her husband, though she later joined the Methodist Church.

She was salutatorian of her college class, an achievement in view of the outside work and skimping necessary to make ends meet when for a time all three White girls and Cam were in college or the preparatory department at once; Leila tutored other students including Harry K. Thaw, whose mother was a benefactor of the college. Immediately upon graduation she began teaching at the Geneseo Collegiate Institute in Geneseo, Illinois. In 1889 she moved to Monticello Seminary (later College) at Godfrey, Illinois. She pursued no further formal education, the M.A. she received from Wooster being automatically conferred on its graduates by the college two years after graduation. When a Phi Beta Kappa chapter was installed in 1926, she, Wilbert, Cam, and their brother-in-law, Charles R. Compton, were elected to it.[68]

It was apparent to at least one wedding guest that Leila White and John R. Mott would establish a creative partnership. The anonymous YMCA observer who wrote our only description of the event commented that in the choice of his bride, Mott had given "another evidence of the discrimination and good judgment that seems to characterize everything he does."[69] In accepting his offer of marriage, now to be consummated after a year of acquaintance, many dates, and much correspondence, Leila must have realized that his was a unique genius to which many of the usual expectations of a Victorian woman would have to be subordinated. She would choose to go with him rather than to stay with their growing family on the occasions of his extended world tours. She would accept and adapt to his total preoccupation with "my work," as he called his commitment to a day-and-night promotion of the cause he held dear, beginning with organizing student YMCA's on their wedding trip. More than that, she would share his career as editor, confidante, mentor, and "courageous, downright honest critic," as he once put it. Already she must have realized his tendency to overwork, and would when possible slow him down, but never "call a halt" to a "forward-looking proposal" or program. These two created one of the unique husband-and-wife teams of their times.

The "White House" wedding was a "very simple and impressive" ceremony according to Presbyterian order. The bride, "the accomplished daughter of Mr. and Mrs. John M. White" (commented that anonymous Association reporter), who possessed "the characteristics of person and mind and heart that give the sweet charm to womanhood," stood by the side of "that tall manly form with its thoughtful face and keen, pleasing, kindly eye" which "revealed the presence of John R. Mott," whose "rare combination of platform and executive abilities has made him a leading factor in the Christian activities of the colleges of two nations." Cam White was best man. Wilbert White performed the ceremony, assisted by YMCA evangelist S. M. Sayford. Clara and Harriet Mott were there, but John's parents were not. President Sylvester F. Scovel and Professor Elias Compton, father of the three famous Compton scientist brothers who would grow up in Wooster, completed the small party.[70] "When the reception was over and due justice dealt to the appetizing viands the bridal pair took a train headed westward"—to Mansfield, Ohio, then next day to Chicago for overnight, followed by a pleasant week at Postville, Leila with an embarrassing cold.

A week later John wrote his parents from Denver, where he and Leila had enjoyed "a splendid visit" as guests of Alice and James, that he had received railroad passes for most of their trip and had organized "a good YMCA" at Boulder. At Colorado Springs the couple were the guests of the Reverend and Mrs. Horace E. Warner, Mott's Postville pastor, for "a delightful visit" that Leila remembered for the "deep dark eyes and beautiful face of Mrs. W. . . . the presiding angel of that home."[71] In Pueblo they were entertained by the family of one of Leila's pupils at Geneseo. En route again, they gazed from the observation platform of their Pullman "with ever increasing wonder and awe" at the Royal Gorge until they were, as Leila wrote in her diary, "sated with sublimity." The next segment of the trip was over the spectacular Marshall Pass of the Denver and Rio Grande Railroad. During a long wait between trains at Grand Junction the couple dropped in on a prayer meeting in "a rather primitive Baptist church" only to be greeted by name by the pastor: "thenceforth we were one with them." A "blessed meeting" followed, opening to all of them a new sense "of what Christian fellowship may mean." Such encounters would mark their future travels.

After brief stopovers at Salt Lake City and Sacramento they reached Santa Barbara on December 22. Here, in a subtropical paradise the like of which neither of these midwesterners had experienced, John and Leila Mott luxuriated between the "Grand Old Pacific" beaches and rocks, and the Spanish mission which was to Leila "the attraction of the place." John wrote home that "our new life is smooth and happy" and that until after New Year's they would be resting and sightseeing in Southern California; he devoted several large pages to an exuberant description of the roses and other flowers and the exotic plants, wishing that his family could also be transported to "this almost tropical clime."

They next went to Riverside, which John thought "one of the finest little cities in this country"; they stayed at the Glenwood, later the Mission Inn, and walked and drove among the "orange trees everywhere." They attended some sessions of a teachers' convention there, which afforded John "the opportunity of meeting men connected with the different colleges" he would be visiting; Leila was quite as interested in it as was her husband. They lunched with one of the speakers, John's fellow-Cornellian David Starr Jordan, the new president of the new Stanford University just opened that year. Leila noted that Jordan (another devotee of John Foster) was "very tall and strongly-built" with "small piercing eyes, good forehead, a little uneasy and awkward in his bearing, with no hint of the orator—but the personality and the theme command perfect attention." Jordan spoke on "the evolution of a college curriculum."[72]

Then there was a side-trip to San Diego, visiting the ruins of missions San Juan Capistrano and San Diego, walking on Coronado beach, thrilling to "the glorious surf," touring the cruiser *San Francisco,* and having breakfast on the beach. After a brief return to Riverside, where John twice addressed "large audiences" at the local "Y" and thus "came to know some of the finest men of the section," they settled in for two weeks in Los Angeles.

PART 17: Organizing a Score of New Campus "Y's"

On January sixth John's business began in earnest with a trip to Chaffee, Lordsburg (now LaVerne), and Pomona colleges, accompanied by Harry Hilliard, Princeton '86, the college secretary of California, who had prepared the ground and would follow up after Mott's tour. Mrs. Hilliard and Leila were on their own during the absences of the men, but there was no lack of friends and socializing. The Hilliards guided the Motts throughout California and Oregon. In this manner Mott organized a score of new campus Associations on the Coast. He found all the colleges small, but because no one had canvassed them for five years, regarded his work as "largely that of a pioneer." Often classes were dismissed for his meetings, even at the state institutions; everywhere "the faculty received us most cordially." The real clue to his success was that, as he wrote his parents, "we succeed in finding out and making friends wherever we go." In each major center he climaxed his visits with an intercollegiate conference, the first of which, held at the University of Southern California, January 15 to 17, attracted six college presidents, professors from all eight institutions in the area, and 110 students. No such meeting had ever been held in Southern California. [73]

The Motts and Hilliards then transferred their center of activities to San Francisco, which Mott characterized as "preeminently the Association center of the Far West," and where, under the "generalship" of Henry J. McCoy, there had been developed a city Association that ranked "among the very best of the land"—a lengthened shadow of Moody's visit of 1880. Although Mott was depressed by the "wrecks of colleges which were found strewn along the coast from San Diego to Puget Sound," he had more than he and Hilliard could do to visit the survivors. [74] They went to at least thirteen colleges and prep schools within a 100-mile radius of San Francisco.

Drawn to Stanford by his fresh acquaintance with Jordan, and the stir the new university was creating in educational circles, Mott considered the YMCA that he organized there his most significant single professional achievement of the year, devoting a detailed article to it in the *Intercollegian*. He was profoundly impressed by the magnificence of the new campus and buildings, the endowment, and the faculty "of forty carefully selected specialists, all of whom, including President Jordan," were "young men, aggressive, and progressive." Both he and Leila sat in on some classes. Although the students had already organized a liberal coeducational and interconfessional "Christian Association," Mott convinced about sixty men that they needed a student YMCA. This became at once the largest such body on the Coast, and a real rival to that at the University of California. The student Mott would remember for the longest time was a freshman named Herbert Clark Hoover. President Jordan made Mott a flattering offer to join his faculty, which it hardly needs saying was politely refused. After these strenuous activities, they enjoyed a "rest day" at Monterey, the Seventeen-mile Drive, and Point Lobos. Mott's activities in central California were concluded with a conference on the Berkeley campus February 5 to 7 that enrolled 183 students and at least one professor from each institution of the area.

After travel through spectacular winter scenery dominated by Mount Shasta, the Motts and Hilliards set up a base in Portland, from which they visited eleven schools and colleges in Oregon and five in Washington. Leila and Mrs. Hilliard, unhappy with hotel rooms "saturated with tobacco," stayed in a boarding house while the men "radiated" through the colleges. Everywhere there were YMCA's to address, pulpits to fill, city Associations to advise, Cornell friends to look up, receptions for the two couples, until John was "used up" and Leila packed him off to a newly-found friend's home for a full day of rest. The concluding intercollegiate conference at Salem attracted numbers and registered enthusiasm comparable to those in Los Angeles and Berkeley.

The Motts began their return journey East on the last day of February, Leila going ahead to visit her youngest brother in Montana while John went to Whitman College at Walla Walla; his final report of the tour was written in a snowbound train on the prairie "in a typical North Dakota blizzard" that had "just blown some cars from the track—an experience in striking contrast with picking oranges from the trees in northern and southern California in January and seeing flowers all the way from Santa Barbara to Victoria." He had visited thirty institutions and there were now twenty-nine regular Associations where there had been six; in only one-third of the schools had adequate Bible study programs been initiated, but at least forty students had become missionary Volunteers. Five hundred nine college men, including fifty-nine professors, had attended the series of conferences. "When we remember that these colleges are cut off 2,000 miles from the body of the Intercollegiate Movement, the significance of this great student awakening cannot be overestimated."[75] To his parents he wrote that much had surpassed what he had seen on his European trip and in"climate, country, scenery" the Coast had seemed like a foreign country. It had rained only seven days out of seventy-one; the hospitality had been warm, and the railroads had granted full passes for the entire 5,000 miles, for the most part including Leila's passage.

After a stop in Postville the couple checked on urgent business in Chicago including their future home in Oak Park. John spent a day at Wooster, leaving Leila with her family while he planned his spring itinerary from the New York office. The two had a few days together at Postville in May. As summer wore on, John spent increasing periods of time with Leila at Wooster; their first child, a bouncing boy, the image of his father, arrived on October tenth.

PART 18: Driving Moody's Team

Doubtless the most pressing item on Mott's crowded agenda when he returned a week late to his desk at 40 East 23rd Street in New York in mid-March, 1892, was the sobering fact that he would be in sole charge of the Northfield Student Conference that summer. Moody had been seized with the desire to return to Great Britain the previous November and would take a vacation trip to the Holy Land in late spring, returning to England for the summer. In addition, Mott would be responsible for the first regional conferences at Knoxville and at Lake Geneva, Wisconsin. There were also to be the first "Presidents' Conferences" that summer, gatherings of next year's officers of college "Y's," a distinctive leadership training program that Mott developed out of the deputation conferences which also continued. That spring there were important visits to strategic campuses—Brown, Wesleyan, Yale—with time out for a ramble up East Rock and for sailing. In New York he met the Wishards at the pier upon their return from their world journey; he then canvassed the colleges of the "Dutch" region of Pennsylvania, America's "finest farming country," and went on to the national quadrennial Methodist Conference at Omaha and college visitation elsewhere in Nebraska. He wrote home at the end of April, "it is a busy time and I must keep a strong hand on things."

Knowing that Mott would hold the reins with a firm hand, to borrow a phrase from Moody's favorite pastime of driving spirited horses, the evangelist had no apprehension about leaving the Northfield student gathering to him. Attendance was larger than ever before:

As I had to preside at the sessions because of Mr. Moody's absence in England I was kept extremely busy. The Lord gave me necessary wisdom and strength. It was a convention of very great power. Those who had been at preceding meetings regard it as having been fully as strong as any since the days of Mt. Hermon in 1886.[76]

Mott's handling of the program was adroit: he committed it chiefly to his contemporaries and intimates—Speer, John Forman, back on furlough from India, and Wishard, exuberant from his world tour. Warren H. Wilson, Oberlin 1890, a student at Union Theological Seminary, destined to be a pioneer in rural sociology, and for whom a college in North Carolina would be named, edited the *Intercollegian* that year. He reported that this was "a young men's conference," with some of the leaders "no more than four years away from their courses of study." Speer, who gave a Bible study course, a missions talk on Round Top, and addressed the farewell meeting, was the outstanding speaker: "To report Mr. Robert E. Speer is to report the conference, so truly did he voice its spirit," declared Wilson. President Merrill E. Gates of Amherst, Arthur T. Pierson, Anthony Comstock, and Methodist missionary Bishop James M. Thoburn each spoke once or twice. Mott concentrated on Association methods and a missionary institute; the former exerted "the greatest influence on this year's conference," wrote Wilson, emphasizing that the entire session had borne down "more strongly on organization and put more spirit into it" than other aspects of the Northfield programs, a testimony to "Mr. Mott's growing spiritual power." Wilson thought that this, the Seventh (since Mount Hermon, 1886) "World's Student Conference" had proved that the deepest Christian commitment could be successfully channeled into organizational forms. There was a subtle tribute to Mott and his young colleagues in Wilson's conclusion:

> The power of this conference is a mystery. It is not explained by the man-force present. Everyone knew a different presence in the sessions. The open heart needs no other Christian evidence than this untraceable power.[77]

On the way home to Wooster and Postville Mott stopped off at Chautauqua where Bishop J. H. Vincent pressured him again to "enter the ministry" and Thoburn urged him to go to India; of these alternatives Mott preferred the latter to taking "some fashionable church" in one of our large cities, he added to a letter home. But he made no move in either direction.

That summer and fall it was also necessary for Mott to keep a firm hand on the construction of his new home in suburban Oak Park, seven miles west of downtown Chicago and a quick trip by commuter train. He was not unduly surprised that it cost more than he had anticipated. His father helped with the plans; he had earlier given financial assistance by purchasing John's lots in Denver to reduce the indebtedness concerning which the younger Mott was apprehensive. For $2200 Mott had bought two 40-foot lots on Kenilworth Avenue "north of Iowa," there being no house numbers as yet in an unfinished development.[78] The house was built to the Motts' specifications; it cost $4,500. Roomy and comfortable, it resembled a thousand undistinguished midwestern frame houses of the period and would have seemed equally indigenous to Postville or Wooster. His worst problem, John confided in exasperation to his father, was with the plumbers. A new feature was hot water heat.

Delays and minor illnesses postponed moving until spring; the three Motts would occupy their first home in early March, 1893, an exciting time to be living in Chicago, with the opening of the great Columbian Exposition and all the excitement and guests it would bring. Some miles away, in an utterly different part of the city, the pioneer social settlement "Chicago Commons" was being occupied by Graham Taylor and his family of children and graduate students; Taylor may already have contributed a bibliography on the social gospel to one of Mott's program outlines.[79] After a week of settling and daily trips into the city to buy furniture, a kitchen stove, and all the details needed to equip a fully functioning home, all purchases being obtained at discount through friends or connections, John confessed to his mother that in that period he had "learned more about a house and its furnishings" than "in all the rest of my life." The only "drawback" about the house was that there was water in the basement—like every house on the block, until drains were installed. Yet in a rare letter to Clara he expressed "splendid satisfaction" with it. Unknown to Mott, Frank Lloyd Wright, whose designs were beginning to dot Oak Park and its neighboring suburbs, lived only a few blocks away. The two never met.

Mott had postponed his 1892 vacation, normally taken in midsummer, to be with Leila in the fall as the birth of their first child approached. After the round of summer conferences mentioned above he spent a week with Ober in the Berkshires revamping several pamphlets and the Bible study outlines. A staff meeting at West Point opened the year; there were now six men in addition to Mott. Two of them would become his most trusted lieutenants and intimate friends over the years: Fletcher Brockman and Gilbert Beaver, son of the governor of Pennsylvania, who would direct the student movement while Mott traveled around the world in 1895–97.[80]

At Wooster he and Leila devoted themselves that autumn to an intensive study of the life of Christ, having procured eight of the newest biographies, including those by Edersheim, Farrar, Stalker, and Broadus, "a tremendous gold mine," John wrote to Hattie, who had asked him to recommend titles for a missionary library, but "nothing however when compared with the plain Gospel accounts."[81] The books he and Leila were studying ran the gamut of current scholarship from German higher criticism to Southern Baptist evangelicalism; that they could derive both knowledge and spiritual sustenance from them not only evidenced her husband's irenic spirit that Leila was happy to embrace, but showed the influence of Mott's travel among the colleges. Loyalty to Jesus Christ was the guiding principle of his life, but he could not rely upon the impetus of the past to meet either his own needs or those of the increasing numbers of college youth who were looking to him for guidance and inspiration. Unlike Moody and other contemporary evangelists, Mott possessed a compulsion to read and to weave the best scholarship of his time into his message—a partial explanation of his growing popularity as an evangelist to students.

On October 10, 1892, John Mott wrote to his mother: "You shall be the first to know that this afternoon a son was born in this household, and that he and Leila are doing well. It is an event to cause joy, and I am sure that you will all rejoice with us." American Protestants whose churches did not espouse infant baptism or christening often waited until well after a baby's birth to name it. Sometimes delays of several years occurred. Relatives on both sides of this young family expressed their ideas and held to them vigorously; even John Mott's smooth temper was stretched. He and Leila were definite that the boy's middle name was to be Livingstone, an understandable choice by the chairman of the Student Volunteer Movement and his wife. But the selection of a first name was not so simple. They inclined toward Robert, Hugh, Arthur, or John; Mott thought a boy would have greater individuality if his name were different from his father's, but made the mistake of asking his parents' and sisters' advice. Whatever that may have been (it must be remembered that no letters to Mott from his family have survived), the young couple took matters into their own hands in mid-November and announced that they had named him "Dwight Livingstone"—both names John's choice, "although they seem to give universal satisfaction," he wrote home, without having heard from his mother, who was outraged. Elmira, aware of her New England history and obviously not an admirer of Dwight L. Moody, as many were not, wrote to the baby's Aunt Clara that John Mott was odd enough but "Dwight Mott is horrid." If he names him that, she went on, "I'm resolved I shall call him Timothy." John R. paid a quick visit home about that time; on December 30 he confessed to Hattie that they would "have to compromise and call our baby John Livingstone after his grandfather." He is going to make "a lively boy, I assure you," he added. "He keeps things moving all day." All remarked on the child's resemblance to his father, except for his blue eyes.

After leaving Wooster as soon as he could be certain of Leila's well-being, Mott, too, kept moving. This was a season of extended travel, 7,000 miles from mid-October until November 20, surviving "in good trim," during which he covered most of the United States except the Far West, plus Ontario and the Maritime Provinces. He concentrated on the "most prominent" campuses. If the Association at Stanford had been his best single achievement of the past year, that at the new University of Chicago, just opened this fall, was the high point of this year.[82] Travel made it impossible to vote in November; Mott had prognosticated that Harrison would win re-election, but upon Cleveland's victory he observed somewhat glumly to his father that he was glad that the Democrats had made "such a clean sweep if they had to win" so as to put the "whole responsibility upon them." He thought the Republicans would have done better to have nominated Blaine, "the longest-headed statesman in this country." When Blaine died the following January, Mott mourned the passing of "the greatest American of modern times."

On January 12, 1893, Mott, together with Morse, Wishard, Campbell White, and William D. Murray, a member of the International Committee, represented the YMCA at a conference in New York City of officers and representatives of twenty-one foreign mission boards and societies of the United States and Canada. The purpose was to discuss "practical questions of missionary policy" and to lay foundations for cooperation. Only Wishard spoke, assuring the seventy-five delegates that the Associations would follow the lead of the churches in policy matters. Morse led in prayer; Mott did not enter the discussions, but he would be a strong force in the organization that eventuated out of this informal gathering. Fifty years later when he addressed the jubilee meeting of what became the Foreign Missions Conference of North America, he recalled the names of a score of those who had attended in 1893; in 1943 only Speer, White, and himself were living.[83]

PART 19: The Mantle of Moody

In January, 1893, when Mott was in Canada, he obtained an unusual permission to speak to a hastily gathered group of students at Laval University, his first talk needing an interpreter. He made an unannounced call on Cardinal Taschereau and was received by the prelate in person. The Cardinal "listened attentively and respectfully to all that we told him about the Y.M.C.A." While in Montreal Mott met the Reverend Reuben A. Torrey, the evangelist who had been "superintendent" of Moody's Bible Institute in Chicago since 1889. Rather to Mott's surprise, Torrey "extended a call" to him, on behalf of Moody, to become "his colleague in the management of the Institute." Torrey explained that Moody would present the details in person the first time they met. Mott commented to his parents: "I am hardly the man for such a position and work, I fancy. In the midst of all the conflicting calls which come to me it is hard to tell what to do." That spring he had established the offices of the Student Volunteer Movement in one of the Institute buildings. Here it remained for a time. In May, Moody offered him $3,000 a year "to become the Director or Superintendent of his Training School in Chicago." The importance Mott attached to the proposal was indicated by the fact that he made it a brief entry near the end of an eight-page letter home. This summer, 1893, he would share the administration and leadership of the Northfield student conference with Moody, a more difficult task than directing it alone with Moody on the other side of the Atlantic. This time the evangelist would decide to carry on a campaign in Chicago during the fair.

Had the once-eager Cornell sophomore, ambitious to learn Moody's "secret," penetrated that mystery? From a sometimes trying apprenticeship with an often obtuse master, Mott had learned from Moody that commitment was primary; he became fond of repeating an aphorism that Moody had picked up in Great Britain: "The world has yet to see what God will do with a man who is wholly consecrated to him." Mott came to believe that Moody incarnated this truth; he would himself approximate its high goal. The prime requisite to its accomplishment was unswerving devotion to Christ. This, too, was Mott's overriding motivation. Although Moody never explicitly adopted the Holiness doctrine of the "higher Christian life," its spirit was congenial to his outlook and unquestionably served as a bond between himself and the young secretary who would become his successor as evangelist to students. [84] Moody was never ordained, a fact that Mott could not have overlooked. Both men had inexhaustible resources of energy.

Mott also saw the ecumenical ideal at work through Moody: denominations meant little, the unity of Christian effort everything. Both men, as Findlay says of Moody, were drawn "irresistibly and irrevocably" into the mainstream of American evangelical Protestantism through local church and YMCA home missionary projects—Sunday School for street urchins with Moody, prisoners in the town jail for Mott. But again, as Findlay points out in regard to Moody's Chicago school, "care for the soul could not be neatly compartmentalized and set apart from concern for the body." This led Moody to rescue work and home missions. It motivated Mott and his generation toward foreign missions and the social gospel. Furthermore, the YMCA early served as the interdenominational agency for staging Moody's urban campaigns.[85] Likewise, in fund-raising there were no sectarian barriers. Mott's favorite definition of philanthropy as making "the releasing and use of money a pronouncedly spiritual process" was derived from Moody.

When the student staff urged Moody to invite a few liberals to the Northfield platforms, they happily discovered an unsuspected breadth of spirit. Moody's great respect for learning, his own lack of which he never ceased to regret, gave the student secretaries effective leverage with him. Constantly in touch with the university world which could hardly have been other than an enigma to Moody, they found him eager to contribute what he could to what they regarded as its welfare. Thus it came about that the unlettered worker for souls could both sponsor the summer conferences and bring to them men of diverse viewpoints, including some who were essentially hostile—in ideas but not in spirit—to his own stance. So it was that Moody had been instrumental in bringing J. E. K. Studd and Henry Drummond to America and Northfield. In later years, both liberals and conservatives would claim Moody as their own, the former taking their cues from the broader interests represented by the Northfield Schools and the latter centering around the Bible Institute.[86] Mott was not forced to choose sides, though his interests naturally drew him toward the Schools.

Many observers quickly became aware that Moody not only presided over meetings but pervaded them. Mott, who noticed this that first summer at Mount Hermon, came to achieve a comparable ability to guide and dominate almost any gathering he chaired. His more diverse experience and his diametrically opposite manner of speaking and intensive platform training gave him a far more sophisticated control of his audiences than did Moody's guileless but sedate, relatively unemotional manner. Moody injected realism into his preaching by projecting his own feelings into the Bible stories he read or the illustrations he used. His voice had no music in it but he injected humor or pathos into his sermons by his own genuine emotional involvement. Mott's voice was mellow, low-keyed, and inherently persuasive. His talks carried conviction by sheer weight of logic, facts, and forceful delivery; they were never "sermons," but always "addresses" or "speeches." In this regard Mott was more indebted to Charles G. Finney than to Moody; the seriousness with which he spoke and the effect of his mien when he had grown heavy eyebrows on occasion almost frightened some hearers. Moody could be fantastically misunderstood by foreign observers, one of whom was to describe him as a "simple Pietistic peasant."[87] This would never happen to the urbane and polished Mott, who nevertheless admired Moody's straightforward decisiveness; both were secure persons and their platform presence declared the fact.

Although in his early career Moody had been somewhat brash and displayed a tendency toward officiousness and disputativeness, Findlay notes that he toned this down as he matured, refusing to enter into public controversy. Mott, schooled in the techniques of debate that could have produced an argumentative and contentious attitude, was, both temperamentally and by training in the YMCA school of non-involvement in public controversy, inclined to a similar stance. He was, however, neither able to enter fully into the fun and pranks of college youth, nor, as was Moody, capable of being, as another biographer of Moody expressed it, "the biggest and jolliest boy of them all."[88] The story is told that at one of the conferences from which Moody was absent, Speer, who had been a football player at Princeton, donned a comic hat and clowned at the Fourth of July "fun night" but Mott had to be frisked about the platform by some of the boys to break his reserve.

The summer of 1893 brought Moody and Mott together on the Northfield platform, Moody having taken time off from his Exposition campaign in Chicago. Young men were again in charge—Speer, Brockman, Beaver, James McConaughy, James B. Reynolds, and Campbell White who was commissioned to carry the greetings of the conference to the students of India whom he would soon begin to serve. Drummond was there again, as were the Reverend W. H. P. Faunce, later president of Brown University and already a social gospel leader, and Professor George T. Purves of Princeton. Funds were raised for the

SVM and for the intercollegiate "Y." After his talk on Friday morning Moody explained his view of the situation in Chicago and frankly asked the students whether he should go or stay: to a man they voted that he should go. The editor of the *Intercollegian,* presumably Wilson, wrote later that the Spirit of God had both gone with Moody and remained at Northfield, guiding Mott "in presiding over all the remaining sessions up to the farewell meeting," which high point had been described by conference veterans as having never been equalled "in thought and spirit." Mott would owe additional debts to Moody, such as the preparation for his own campaigns in the universities of Great Britain, as will be seen later; throughout his long life he would willingly acknowledge them.

PART 20: The World's Parliament of Religions and the Second SVM Quadrennial

As the World's Columbian Exposition unveiled its "city of palaces set in spaces of emerald," unprecedented throngs came to Chicago in the summer of 1893 to see it. John wrote his family in May that it was "by big odds the most stupendous exhibition the world has ever seen," and that nothing should be allowed to interfere with their visiting it. Both the Postville and Wooster families were invited to stay at the new home on Kenilworth Avenue, Oak Park. Although John, Leila, and young John L. spent a month's vacation at Postville, most of the relatives did come, beginning with the newlywed Campbell Whites. Horace Warner and family came from Colorado Springs with their children; Alice and James brought their brood from Denver.

The cosmopolitan nature of the Exposition with its international exhibits naturally focused the attention on the world beyond America. In July a congress of college and university students heard Mott, Wishard, and James B. Reynolds, now secretary of the thriving new Association at the University of Chicago, describe recent religious movements in the universities of Europe, Asia, and America. One of the sensations of the fair was the World's Parliament of Religions, which met in three sessions daily through seventeen summer days in the largest halls on the grounds. Faiths from Armenian Orthodox to Zen Buddhism were represented, often by colorfully-garbed devotees from exotic places. The sessions were attended by capacity and overflow crowds.

John Mott made his first speech to an international audience at one of these sessions. It was a description, in his best oratorical style, of the

North American Intercollegiate Association Movement, an unashamed proclamation of its evangelical motivation and its ethical, social, and ecumenical aims. Pointing first to the fact that it was a more widespread union of students than any athletic, fraternal, forensic, or other intercollegiate affiliation, he described briefly its remarkable growth, and cited Drummond's recent comment that "there is nothing like it among the students of the world." Its primary purpose is "to lead college men to become followers of Jesus Christ." But that is only a beginning. The Movement seeks to guard students "against the many bodily temptations which beset the college man as fiercely as any other young man; and, moreover, against the more subtle and insidious temptations in the realm of the intellect which assail college men as no other class of men." To undergird this aim the Associations "lay great emphasis upon the development of the spiritual life," chiefly through Bible study.

The Movement also trains men for Christian service as lay leaders, and for the ministry and home and foreign missionary work, the last of which had produced the remarkable phenomenon called the Student Volunteer Movement, which by then had despatched over 600 men and women to various fields under the auspices of church societies. Here Mott repeated the oft-quoted question of President James McCosh of Princeton, asked when the SVM was only a year old: "Has any such outpouring of living young men and women been presented in our age, in our country, in any age, or in any country, since the day of Pentecost?" But the "fundamental purpose" of the Association Movement, he concluded, is "to unite the Christian students of the world," it having already established "a student brotherhood in Jesus Christ"—a forecast of the World's Student Christian Federation. More than this, it is, as no other agency, "uniting in spirit the various denominations of the Church of Christ," since it is organized in the colleges of some forty such bodies.[89]

Three dozen special purpose religious and church-related congresses met during the Exposition, including the YMCA and an interdenominational conference on missions. Mott attended as many of these as possible and met many of their leaders. When added to the Parliament itself the whole became a horizon-widening experience for the chairman of the Student Volunteer Movement.

During the interval since the Cleveland Convention of 1891, the Student Volunteer Movement had occupied a vastly greater share of Mott's time and energy than the preceding pages have suggested. In the spring of 1893, *The Student Volunteer*, a twenty-page monthly, had been started. It contained a variety of short articles, one of which Mott usually supplied, a potpourri of advice and suggestions, brief book reviews, and news of the Movement. D. Willard Lyon, who traveled for the SVM that year from his base at McCormick Theological Seminary, began a series of studies on China, where he would invest his life, in the first issue; Cam and W. W. White contributed, as did Harlan Page Beach later to be a Yale professor, Wishard, Speer, Elizabeth Wilson of the YWCA, W. H. Cossum then in China, and other Volunteers as they reached their fields.

The November, 1893, issue announced a second international convention to be held February 28 to March 4, 1894, in Detroit. The buildup in the *Student Volunteer* forecast that this would be a much larger conference than Cleveland 1891. It was: 1,082 students of thirty-eight denominations in thirty-two states and five Canadian provinces came from 294 institutions of higher education; in addition, sixty-three missionaries and fifty-four mission board representatives, thirty-seven professors and teachers, three dozen YMCA and YWCA secretaries made up the total of 1325 persons attending. Donald Fraser, secretary of the Student Volunteer Union of Great Britain, brought the news that there were then over 700 Volunteers there; his presence suggested the growing international and ecumenical significance of the Movement. He cautioned the Americans against overly emotional taking of the pledge, and invited them to the 1894 British summer conference. Doubtless he and Mott discussed the prospects for a world student organization.[90]

J. Hudson Taylor made a "most impressive appeal" for adequate spiritual preparation by the would-be missionary. Robert E. Speer gave a "masterly analysis" of the Apostle Paul as "the great missionary example." Miss Geraldine Guinness, author of *In the Far East,* presented the needs of China. Arthur T. Pierson, the inventor of the watchword, "the evangelization of the world in this generation," spoke as he had at Cleveland in 1891. Such were some of the highlights selected by the editor of *The Student Volunteer* for his April issue. He would draw upon conference addresses and discussions for months. The official cloth-bound report of the conference, edited by Max Wood Moorhead, who would serve in India, was a 375-page book replete with conference statistics, verbatim transcripts of the speeches, devotions, messages from Volunteers in various fields, and Mott's twenty-page triennial report—"the strongest and most complete presentation of the Movement that has ever been made."[91]

The chairman named two dozen men and women who had supplemented his own propagation of the Movement since 1891—among them Horace Pitkin, Henry Luce, and Sherwood Eddy, Yale 1891, whose pragmatic appeal to the delegates to commit themselves forecast his later prophetic role. The infinitely detailed organization of this immense gathering that taxed the hospitality of the city betrayed behind the scenes a master hand that had devoted months of preparation to it, as is plain from the seventy-page notebook in which Mott worked over every aspect of the meeting under some thirty headings. In spite of the importance of Bible study, no other intercollegiate department received such detailed and loving attention as did missions, for the Volunteer Movement was the throbbing heart of Mott's "first love" and supplied the entire Movement's most potent motivation. After the convention closed, Mott assembled a group of leaders and took careful notes to their criticisms of both the mechanics and the content of the program.

The program had featured orators who would appeal to idealistic youth; it included vivid presentations not only of all the major mission fields but also the need for adequate preparation. Mott himself dealt with the rationale of the organization, and there were section meetings on methods. In May, 1893, there had appeared in the *Missionary Review of the World* the first serious criticism of the Movement, an extended but tolerant delineation of its weaknesses by the veteran Presbyterian missionary John L. Nevius of Cheefoo. Instead of rushing into print with a denunciation of Nevius, Mott wrote his comments on the margins of the article, conceding the justice of some, and focused indirectly on others at Detroit. Nevius' prime targets were the pledge, which did annoy many (it was later changed), and the very small numbers of Volunteers to reach the fields in spite of the missionary gusher.[92]

The Drummonds and the Harpers were not at Detroit. Instead there were orators like Pierson, A. J. Gordon, and returned missionaries who, for the most part, emphasized the evangelistic side of missions. However, James S. Dennis, whose epochal *Christian Missions and Social Progress* would later help to correct an overemphasis on missionary preaching, pointed out the values of educational work. Even in Pierson's address, however, there was less millennialism than there had been at Mount Hermon in 1886 or in his own speech at Cleveland in 1891, evidence that Mott was utilizing the emotional thrust of the conservative or millennial wing of American Protestantism and the appeal of faith missions such as Taylor's China Inland, to enthuse his Volunteers.[93] At the same time, the weighty voices at Cleveland and Detroit were those of the mission boards, of which Establishment Speer was doubtless the most persuasive. Among Mott's primary aims in calling these conventions was the need to tie the Movement to the churches and their mission boards. He thus applied the brakes to the millennial aspect; his own defense of the watchword was pragmatic and logical rather than fundamentalist, prophetic, or utopian. To an earlier generation the slogan "immediate emancipation" had a comparable meaning; to a later one, "with all deliberate speed" conveyed a similar thrust.

PART 21: Britain and the Continent 1894: Toward a Worldwide Union

Early in 1894 Mott became convinced that "the time had at last arrived when a world-wide union of Christian students might be achieved."[94] Stimulated to pursue this goal by his conversations with Donald Fraser at Detroit, he planned a trip to Great Britain and the Continent that summer. Renting the house in Oak Park to the Wilbert Whites and leaving young John L. with Mother White in Wooster, he and Leila took a slow ship from New York on May 11, their expenses underwritten by Mrs. J. L. Taylor. It was a rough voyage and John was ill, but he arrived at Londonderry well rested.

At Dublin University he held "successful" meetings. Fraser met the Motts at Glasgow, his home. In Edinburgh they were the guests of Professor Simpson of the University, "one of the leading medical men of Great Britain," the son of the discoverer of ether. Mott spoke twice at meetings of the Free Church of Scotland, whose Assembly was in session. They were invited to "some of the best homes in the city," meeting "Lord Overton, Professor Drummond, Professor Lindsay, &c." After a return stopover in Glasgow where John shared in a farewell reception for five Volunteers, they arrived in London for the principal event of their trip—the Golden Jubilee of the London (the original) Young Men's Christian Association and the Thirteenth International Conference of the World's Alliance of YMCA's.

The Motts were thrilled to attend the opening exercises in Westminster Abbey and other events at St. Paul's Cathedral, the Guildhall, and the Royal Albert Hall, and to worship at Wesley's City Road Chapel, "the Mecca of Methodism." Morse, Wishard, and David McConaughy were there. Mott made a short, extravagant, but to Morse "very impressive" speech on the student YMCA's of North America, his first to this world body, in which he claimed that the spirit of Christ was capturing both the students and the faculties of the universities and colleges of the world. Prince Oscar Bernadotte of Sweden sought Mott out to urge him to repeat his message across Scandinavia; similar requests came from delegates from Denmark, France, and Switzerland. Karl Fries was so busy with a hundred Swedish delegates and his own address that he had little opportunity to talk with Mott, except to make the most tentative plans for a Scandinavian student conference the next summer, to which Mott would hope to bring representatives from Great Britain and Germany. "The idea of the World's Student Christian Federation was hovering before his inner vision," declared Fries in retrospect.[95] Actually, it had been there for some time.

It seems unlikely that Mott spoke with George Williams, founder of the London YMCA, on the occasion of the Jubilee, shortly before which Williams had been knighted. Mott later claimed to have had a score of conversations with Williams. All of his reports of these interviews indicate that Mott asked, "What was in the minds and hearts of yourself and your associates, Sir George, when you formed the first Association?" Williams replied, "The chief burden on our hearts and minds was to associate ourselves that we might better win our fellow young men to Christ."[96] Mott would tell this story effectively many times.

From London the Motts went to Oxford for three days, where Leila was "carried away" with all she saw. There, as elsewhere, Mott met with students, professors, or chaplains to discuss the religious situation, to learn the strong and weak points of the work among students, to tactfully do anything he could "to promote their organized Christian work," and to pave the way for a forthcoming summer student conference at Keswick. Everywhere he was received warmly—at Cambridge, Trevecca, Aberystwyth, and the universities mentioned earlier. In reporting confidentially to Morse after his return, he summarized the findings of these visits by contrasting the achievements of the British with the American student YMCA program. The British students were "in advance" in their work for boys in the preparatory schools, and in social settlement and off-campus mission activities. But there were fifteen areas in which he had found British students to be "behind the Americans," most notably in organization, membership, strategic programs such as the fall campaign for new students, "personal work," revivals, Bible study, missionary activities, buildings, leadership training programs, and paid secretaries. They were doing "comparatively nothing in the way of promoting the study of Christian sociology"; although we are not doing much either, he admitted, "we have taken some steps in advance of our British friends."[97]

Mott was "greatly impressed" by the Paris Association and its building, but found the work among the students of the Latin Quarter sadly inadequate. It was during the Motts' short stay in Paris that the assassination of the fourth president of the French Republic, Sadi Carnot, took place. Mott was asked to speak at a memorial service; he recalled the grief of the American people on the occasion of Garfield's death, but this minor address was unique in being his second to be interpreted into a foreign language.

The Motts went on to Geneva, "a most thrifty and interesting city," where John met several members of the World's YMCA and laid foundations for a possible student conference the next summer. He and Leila were able to accept two of four social invitations, thus gaining "a most interesting contact with the home life of the best people in Switzerland," further evidence of the "wonderful brotherhood" of the Association, which was giving them an elitist circle of friends "among the choice people of every denomination and of every nation that we have come in contact with." In Geneva, Roman history came alive; the most interesting monument was the cathedral in which Calvin had preached.

Taking the lake steamer to Lausanne they spent a night in the room once occupied by Lord Byron in the Hotel d'Angleterre, where they read "The Prisoner of Chillon" before retiring; early the following morning they visited the Castle before taking a train for the all-day trip to Zermatt. Next morning at 5:30 they were up for an early start on the five-hour tramp to the Görnergrat, which was reached through snow up to their knees; for the last mile "we had to drag ourselves up over rough stones—a little at a time." The scenery was "indescribably grand" on a cloudless day—"the sun burned us pretty badly although the air was cool." The trip down consumed three and one-half hours; they were told they had traversed twenty miles. Twelve hours sleep left "comparatively little lameness." This, John declared in a graphic letter home, is "the best exercise in the world."

There followed "another week of solid enjoyment and upbuilding" with the post-wagon trip from Brig over the Furka Pass to Goeschenen, on the finest roads. John wrote home from the Rigi that the need for better roads in the United States was one thing on which he could agree with Jacob Coxey, whose "army" was drawing attention to the weaknesses in the American economy that were at that very moment causing infinite suffering because of the depression. The Motts' tour continued via the St. Gothard Railway to Flüelen on Lake Uri. Four days were given to "the beautiful lakes of the Forest Cantons," "the region immortalized by Schiller in *William Tell,*" which both had read in German in college and were now reviewing as they journeyed. Then they "walked up the Rigi," an ascent of "nearly 5000 feet above the lake level," spending "a little over three hours" rather than parts of three days as had Mark Twain.

John next wrote home from the Falls of the Rhine that they had been at Interlaken, the high point of which stay was the "inspiring excursion" to Lauterbrunnen and Mürren opposite the Jüngfrau. The "beauty and grandeur of the range" called from Mott a paean of praise such as one may not infrequently encounter on a plaque along an Alpine path. "The mountains," he wrote home,

> deepen, lift and refine. They send you away better—physically, intellec-
> tually, spiritually. They breathe freedom. They call forth reverence. They
> show you the relative proportions of things, and deeper meanings in life.
> They remind you of God—of His eternity, of His greatness, His sublimity,
> of His purity, of His unchangeableness, of His protecting care. "Before
> the mountains were brought forth, or ever Thou hadst formed the earth
> and the world; even from everlasting to everlasting Thou art God."

Then to Berne, Zurich, Cologne where the cathedral inspired John to write to his parents that he was "in full sympathy with the plan and purpose of the Episcopal Church to erect a great cathedral in New York"; Heidelberg, Mayence, and back to London and the student conference at Keswick.

In reporting to Morse, Mott noted that at Keswick one could, without much difficulty, "imagine himself at Northfield." The student conference, he made it clear, was not to be confused with the "Convention for the Deepening of the Spiritual Life" for which this site in the English Lake region was famous. This was, in a sense, a distinction without a difference, because both movements shared largely in the evangelical currents that had swirled back and forth across the Atlantic as such Americans as Charles G. Finney, D. L. Moody, Asa Mahan, and R. Pearsall Smith had visited Great Britain. Moody's "most distinctive" work there had been among students: it was he who aroused the University of Edinburgh and enlisted the youthful Henry Drummond who became "the most powerful student evangelist yet seen." When Moody visited Cambridge in 1882 several leading athletes, the "Cambridge seven," were profoundly touched and declared themselves volunteers for missions.[98] One of them, J. E. K. Studd, had visited Cornell in 1885–1886. Mott was discovering his own roots.

Keswick, which had come into being in the 1870's, was dedicated to "the promotion of practical holiness." It had intimate connections with the British YMCA; Mott had heard two of its spokesmen at the recent Jubilee. These men, F. B. Meyer and Prebendary Webb-Peploe, whose names occur frequently in Holiness literature, also addressed the student conference.[99] Most of the 250 student delegates to *their* Keswick convention came at the end of July in time to sit in on the closing sessions of the larger body; John and Leila Mott were entirely at home in this setting. The student meeting followed a schedule similar to Northfield. Mott explained how to carry on Association work in the American manner. Speer gave Bible study lectures and two influential addresses, on the SVM watchword, and "Christ, our Life." Following each of these there were conversions or missionary volunteering on the part of talented men whose futures would be inextricably linked with the ecumenical movement, most notably Joseph H. Oldham, who with Mott would be the joint architect and engineer of the Edinburgh missionary conference of 1910 and of the International Missionary Council a decade afterward.[100]

Mott spoke six times at Keswick and was "kept busy day and night meeting committees and individual workers," centering his efforts on transforming this Volunteer body into a more inclusive Association-type organization that would employ a traveling secretary; at his instigation sufficient funds were raised to hire one, who he hoped would be Donald Fraser. He had encouraged a German leader, Fritz Mockert, to attend; Mockert brought Johannes Siemsen, a student whom Mott thought a possible secretary for Germany. Together with Jean Monnier of France they discussed the possibilities of a world student Christian union, which was also broached to the British leaders, one of whom was Ruth Rouse who would later become women's secretary of the new world union. In concluding his description of the summer to Morse, Mott noted that since "definite and pressing calls" had come from "at least seven or eight different European countries for us to come over and help them," it would seem that the American Movement faced a "special responsibility."[101] How those calls would be answered will be described in Chapters Three and Four.

PART 22: **A Seven-Year Review**

The Motts returned to Wooster in late August "in splendid trim" to find their boy thriving. John's program that fall was somewhat less hectic than usual, being given to staff and other conferences and to fund-raising. He began to take in earnest Wishard's advice to "go after big men" who could provide large gifts. In spite of "hard times" (his own salary was not always paid on schedule during this period) he obtained several gifts of $500 and $1,000, the latter sum from D. W. McWilliams, who had financed the original Wilder-Forman Volunteer tour of 1886–1887. Mrs. J. Livingstone Taylor, whose husband had died prematurely, could usually be counted on for $1,000. New Associations were formed that winter at the Massachusetts Institute of Technology and at Boston University. At Harvard he held "the best religious meetings the association has ever had there," attendance increasing to the end; they were remarkable because "for the first time in all my visits at the University men sought me to talk about their soul's salvation." This winter he began to bear down heavily on the issue of sexual morality. He wrote home from Brown University that "we had a big revival break out," and that he had been entertained part of the time by John D. Rockefeller, Jr., "the only son of the great business man who is worth probably $200,000,000. He is an industrious, levelheaded fellow—with good habits."[102] This acquaintance ripened into a mutually supportive, intimate friendship and collaboration that lasted as long as Mott lived.

In September John had told his folks that he might have to return to Europe the following August. That prospect was probably never out of his mind during 1894–95. Many of his activities that year can best be understood in the perspective of a possible world journey. Great attention was given to building his staff, beginning with a meeting at Gilbert Beaver's home at Bellefont, Pennsylvania, during which Beaver and Mott raced to the top of a nearby mountain and the Governor regaled his guests with "stirring stories about his experiences" in the Civil War. Mott assembled the SVM staff at "Dr. Strong's Sanitarium" in Saratoga Springs, not only because they would have "plenty of mineral water to drink, and good healthy food," but also because Saratoga was a good place to solicit wealthy visitors. The entire International staff of twenty-five met in New York for a week. Mott then wrote several pamphlets; if the pattern that prevailed later began this early, Leila was joint editor. In the list of challenges that Mott left to the Movement in his absence he included the question, "has not the time come for more of our Associations to interest their members in the burning present-day problems in the realm of Christian sociology, and to lead them to find and take their true place in the Kingdom of God?"[103]

As Mott prepared for his world journey he was increasingly aware of calls for secretaries to establish indigenous Associations in foreign cities, a familiar YMCA story for almost a decade.[104] He had become involved in this specialized missionary expansion almost by the accident of being called upon to protect the SVM and the fledgling YMCA expansion movement from the Kansas-Sudan schism. An added purpose of his forthcoming trip around the world would therefore be to inform himself on the needs for American secretaries in Asian cities. He had spoken on this concern at numerous state conventions and a variety of Association gatherings; his argument had been published throughout the Movement and he had come to be regarded as the leading advocate, after Wishard, of the world outreach of the North American YMCA.

In constructing that argument four years earlier he had dealt not only with broad principles but with specific needs in named cities, most of which he would visit. "We have the men, we have the money, we have the methods," he had said in 1891. He could have added, "We have the evangelical fervor," but that was not necessary in 1891; it was taken for granted. Since then the Volunteer Movement had produced another generation of highly motivated personnel; the YMCA would be accused of skimming the cream of the Volunteer crop. This "one department of our work" is recruiting "the future missionaries of the church," he declared, so our relationship to the Church of Christ demands that we promote it, "the greatest work which today confronts the Church." We are agreed in standing for the unity of the work. In addition, "the life of our Associations depends upon being true to the missionary spirit," which demands that foreign peoples not be referred to as "natives" or "heathen": they should be treated as equals. The greatest need is for "far more definite, intelligent, effectual fervent prayer on the part of our Associations."[105]

Knowing that he would be out of the country for more than a year, Mott gave special attention to his annual report for 1894–95, summarizing the quantitative changes that had taken place since 1888, the year in which he had joined the staff, though that was not mentioned. The figures suggested "many reasons for deep gratitude to God":

1888		1895
299 .	Number of Associations	513
19,000 .	Membership	33,000+
4 .	Associations owning buildings	23
2 .	Associations having general secretaries	20
350 .	Delegates at summer conferences	1,000+
None .	Number Association presidents trained	200+

3	. Publications on college work	35
1,200	. Professed conversions	3,400
2,280	. Men in Association Bible classes	8,000+
None	. Number in missionary study classes	800
1	. Secretaries of Volunteer Movement	7
None	. College secretaries of state committees	6
2	. International college secretaries	5[106]

Mott's superior, Richard C. Morse, whose respect for and admiration of Mott had grown by leaps and bounds since 1888, was probably the best judge of his achievement and potential. After the Northfield Conference of 1895, Morse proposed to Mott that he assume the general secretaryship of the parent body of the North American YMCA's after his world journey. Morse was over fifty years of age and the prospect of continuing in office without a junior associate seemed "very hazardous," but he was willing to serve as a fellow secretary in a supervisory relationship. The interview ended without a favorable reply, but Morse hoped that Mott would accept the offer in some form upon his return. It would be twenty years before that hope would be realized. Morse later wrote that "Mott could not respond favorably to this appeal, because his obligations as a Student Volunteer seemed to him to forbid his acceptance of such a position," which reminded Morse of John's hesitancy to undertake the SVM chairmanship in 1888. Morse did not share Mott's viewpoint but respected it; he placed Mott and others such as Ober or Speer in a special class of "hindered volunteers" who "by serving officially at the home base, accomplish far more for the work on the foreign field than they could possibly accomplish by spending their own lives in foreign lands."[107] One is reminded of the first "hindered volunteer," Samuel J. Mills, Jr., of the original Williams College "Haystack Band" of 1806 that was such an inspiration to Wishard, Mott, and thousands of latter-day Volunteers.

From the day John Mott had written home from Cornell that God must have some reason for sending him there besides "fitting up" his mind, he had been possessed by an increasing sense of destiny—a drive intensified by Foster's *Decision of Character* and Tyler's *Prayer for Colleges*. The seven years chronicled in this chapter brought the rounding out of his personality through a series of straight-line choices all moving in one direction. In love with God in Christ, students, and the world mission, his life shared and fulfilled through his marriage to Leila White, he was now ready to cross the threshold of world citizenship.

3

Students of the World United: Europe, the Near East, Ceylon, and India

The Federation will ... inevitably unite in spirit as never before the students of the world. And in doing this it will be achieving a yet more significant result—the hastening of the answer of the prayer of our Lord "that they may all be one."

The Federation is the work of God.

W HEN JOHN and Leila Mott sailed for Liverpool from New York aboard the "splendid" Cunarder *Etruria* on July 20, 1895, it was their expectation that the world journey on which they were embarking would require fifteen months. Student conferences in Great Britain, Germany, and Scandinavia were to be "the first steps toward the world's federation of all student Christian organizations throughout all lands—which, "with the help of God," Mott hoped "to effect on this tour." It took twenty months. The formation of the World's Student Christian Federation followed by his first globe-circling tour to extend and consolidate it was the most creative achievement of Mott's life.

PART 1: Preparation for a World Journey

Kept on "the ragged edge" of seasickness most of the voyage because of choppy seas, the Motts met few of their fellow-passengers in spite of being accompanied by the gregarious Luther Wishard and his wife. One of them, Frederick Schenck, a New York banker who was then treasurer of the YMCA International Committee, wondered whether this "callow youth" was qualified to start out on a world-encompassing mission to the students of all lands.[1] Neither Schenck nor even Mott's intimates knew that he was already under pressure to take over gradually the general

119

secretaryship of the North American YMCA's, a move on which the decision had been postponed until his return. Callow Mott was not in 1895: his youthful demeanor, although he had just turned thirty, was a real asset for the assignment ahead; it would still be remarked upon at the Edinburgh missionary conference of 1910.

Less than a week prior to sailing, when in Boston to speak before the fourteenth convention of Christian Endeavor, Mott had learned that one of his financial guarantors had suffered brain damage and could not contribute as promised. Mott wrote his parents that he had made the crisis a matter of prayer and decided to approach Cornelius Vanderbilt II, whom he learned was at Newport. He presented his card unannounced at *The Breakers,* Vanderbilt's new seaside Renaissance palace. The railroad magnate "came down and received me very cordially," he wrote home. "I had met him once in New York. After explaining matters to him he told me that he would be good for the $2000. needed." It was agreed that if the original pledge were to be paid, Vanderbilt would receive a refund. He did. All other contributors had paid up "in good shape," so Mott considered himself "well supplied" at the time of departure.

This near-disaster was totally unrepresentative of the care with which Mott had prepared. During the summer of 1894 calls to visit numerous countries in Europe and Asia had come to him, unrelated and unsolicited. Soon after his return home in the fall of that year he had arranged in characteristic memos to himself as many reasons as he could muster for and against the tour at this time: its effects on the intercollegiate and Volunteer Movements, the disruption of his family life, the possible disposition of most of the property he had acquired, the physical wear and tear of such a journey, and the cost. With Wishard's help on every detail of travel, a budget of some $10,000 was set up. Mott considered investing his own savings in the tour, but Morse, who handled the accounts, would never have approved. On the "pro" side of his balance sheet Mott put the benefits to his career if he went now rather than later; the program he was projecting for Europe in the summer of 1895 would be an ideal springboard from which to approach the students of the Orient; the situations as reported to him in India and in Japan were ideal.

To sound out selected members of his constituency, Mott prepared a five-page syllabus setting forth the purpose of the trip, together with a schedule. He spoke of the calls that had come from Great Britain, Germany, Norway, Sweden, Denmark, Switzerland, Asia Minor, Egypt, India, Japan, and China: "This would make a complete chain of visitation and conventions around the world." The purpose would be four-fold: to introduce and promote the American Christian Student Movement's goals and methods among the universities of Europe, to carry out an aggressive evangelistic campaign among the students of the Orient, to unite the 750 American Student Volunteers already on the field in order to "bring their pressure to bear on the students of America," and most important of all, to build "a union of the Christian student organizations in America, Great Britain, the Continent and the Orient—thus effecting a world-wide student federation." The unique word, and it was Mott's word, was *federation*. [2]

He planned on five weeks in Great Britain, Germany, Scandinavia, and Switzerland, almost three months in southern Europe, Egypt, and the Near East, four months in India, ten weeks in China, and at least four and one-half months in Japan and "Corea," returning to America by December, 1896. The itinerary did not include Australia although that possibility was not ruled out; presumably he was awaiting British initiative and financing, both of which were to come while he was in India. All these plans were perfected at numerous consultations, some around Richard Morse's dining table. Wishard shared intimately in them, was made the representative of student movements in mission lands, and was commissioned to go to South Africa. Thus there would be two Americans at the organization of the Federation.

In the course of his travels in the fall and winter of 1894–95, Mott obtained overwhelming approval of the tour as well as pledges of financial support. The pivotal event at which his heart and mind were made up and the principal financial means assured was a small private prayer meeting in late winter. In that list of "some of the most creative conferences of my life" of which Mount Hermon 1886 was first, a second cryptic item recalled the gathering of a few friends: "McWilliams + 2: Dr. Gregg = Mrs. Coburn = WSCF." Daniel McWilliams, the New York transit executive who had paid for the SVM deputations of 1886–87 and 1888–89, gave $1,000. Dr. David Gregg was the scholarly pastor of the Lafayette Avenue Presbyterian Church of Brooklyn, a popular lecturer and author of numerous books, one of the latest of which was based on his own journey to the Holy Land. It was he who opened an avenue to the wealthy Mrs. George Coburn of Boston, who subscribed $3,000. Some ten others, including Cyrus McCormick, Jr., made up the remainder. The project had a strong appeal to the supporters of the SVM. [3]

Mott had spent a morning with Joseph Cook, the famous "Boston

Monday Lecturer," and had conferred with Francis E. ("Father Endeavor") Clark, both of whom had recently made round-the-world journeys. "We shall be much better prepared than they were," John wrote
home, adding that Prince Bernadotte was greatly pleased that he was
coming to Sweden. Mott interviewed many returned missionaries and
mission board secretaries, all of whom he said were "deeply interested in
the tour and will help in different ways." By mid-April the trip was
"practically an assured thing," more calls having come from various
countries "in such a way that we cannot but regard them as providential."

He had been granted a leave by the International Committee with
part salary; having trained Beaver and Brockman he could leave them in
charge with full confidence. The home in Oak Park would be rented and
Leila would accompany him, leaving young John Livingstone, now talking and filling the house with "life and spirits," with Mother White in
Wooster. Matters appeared to be sufficiently well in hand that he supposed he would not have "such a whirl" of work again for two years!
Little did he anticipate the demands that would mushroom at every stop
until near the end of the tour he would become ill from fatigue. He was
yet to learn that God did not expect him to bring in the Kingdom by
himself.

In early May it was agreed that Mrs. J. Livingstone Taylor, the
Motts' friend and benefactor, would accompany them with her secretary
much of the way, an arrangement Mott saw as "a big help" with his
business letters. He and Leila visited her in Cleveland where she out-
fitted them at her department store at wholesale prices, and gave John a
second check for $1,000 for the SVM that would enable him to "leave
the country with all the bills of our Movement paid." He managed a visit
to Postville before the student summer conferences at Knoxville, Lake
Geneva, and Northfield engulfed him. Each of these endorsed the tour
and sent their greetings to the college men of Europe, Asia, and Africa.
The message from Lake Geneva, framed by Robert E. Speer, greeted the
students of other lands in Christ " 'who came not to condemn but to *save
the world* '" and bespoke through Mott their "earnest desire to be linked
with them in a united, definite and believing effort . . . to do God's will
and hasten the coming of Jesus Christ and His Kingdom." On the eve of
departure Mott was presented with a gold watch, the appropriate gift of
affection and good will, by his friends, colleagues, and staff at Northfield
and the New York headquarters.

PART 2: Laying Foundations in Britain

Docking in Liverpool was delayed by an adverse tide, but by "about nine Sabbath morning" the party was through customs and in a "plain but comfortable" hotel. The day, as was the custom, was spent quietly but in the evening they walked three miles to hear Dr. John Watson whose *Beside the Bonnie Briar Bush* they had read on shipboard. By two next day they were established in "a kind of home boarding house" at Keswick, where friends from the previous summer introduced the ladies to a round of religious and social activities while Mott and Wishard plunged into the business for which they had come: to secure the formal endorsement of the world federation idea by the British College Christian Union (BCCU) here assembled. The Union—which adopted this name at this meeting—was only two years old but its recent growth, stimulated by the "zeal, courage and vision" of Donald Fraser, now its traveling secretary and "inspiring first great leader," had been phenomenal. [4]

Mott was delighted that this conference proved to be the largest and most representative gathering of students thus far held in the British Isles, there being 51 colleges and universities, including all the "prominent" ones, represented by over 200 delegates. Building on the foundations laid at Keswick the summer before he could now press his plan with the added impact of official North American Movement authorization. He and Wishard met over lunch with four of the British leaders, all of whom were fully committed to the federation idea and had been in communication since their first cautious exploration of the scheme in 1894. The previous January Mott had written one of them that it was imperative for the Britons and the Americans to "see eye to eye and act as one mind," and suggested that they "go all over the subject together" at Keswick and "arrive at the right plan" before disclosing the proposal to the Conference.

The six agreed so completely that the "main lines" of their findings were to constitute the essence of the Federation organization as it would be adopted later. The Keswick Conference responded with great interest, ratified the proposal, and appointed J. Rutter Williamson, just returned from Northfield as fraternal delegate, to accompany the Americans to the German student conference that would meet shortly near Kassel. Williamson was also authorized to represent the BCCU at the subsequent Scandinavian conference where it was hoped the Federation would be effectuated. [5] Mott's mind usually ranged several steps ahead; at this point he suggested that the president of the new body be a citizen of one of the smaller neutral nations and proposed Karl Fries of Sweden. He could now write home exultantly that this had been "the first step toward the world federation . . . the most important work I have ever undertaken."

Mott was also in constant demand for advice on organizational problems of the fledgling BCCU. Perhaps the most important of these was the adoption of an evangelical basis, a matter on which he held a strong position in view of "our experience in America."[6] In the course of the Conference he gave seven addresses, some on spiritual themes but several intentionally descriptive of American methods of administering the student work, hoping to share the techniques he had developed at home. One of these, for which his notes have survived, outlined the "Intercollegiate Relations of the American College Associations" and sketched the historical development of the Movement, but brought all points to bear upon breaking down the isolation of student groups from one another which he had found in Great Britain: in America, he said, the number of student Christian organizations had increased, the scope of their programs had broadened, Christian life and work had been intensified, spiritual life and Bible study had been revived, other student movements stimulated, and invaluable international ties cemented.

He also counseled with newly elected members and secretaries, helped with plans for the Volunteer Union's convention the following January (which would enact significant legislation affecting his tour), assisted in raising funds for the coming year's budget, and of great importance in his own mind, emphasized the spiritual side of the work.[7] Leila thought that his talk on Bible study laid out enough work "to last them until we come back to Britain." At a fun session he and Wishard sang the Cornell *alma mater* "Far above Cayuga's Waters." On the final Sunday afternoon the leaders and many students met for special prayers for the Motts' and Wishards' tours. Each spoke briefly, outlining his plans on a map of the world. Leila recalled that the assembly then turned to

> very definite prayer that we might be given the physical strength to endure the strain, that the way might be opened and prepared, that we might meet Jesus by the way, that in the days of loneliness we might have the joy of his presence, that great blessings should follow our visit.[8]

It was "a most helpful, blessed meeting," she commented, "surely these prayers and those that will follow us from the Keswick friends shall be heard and answered." Mott's closing word at the evening farewell session challenged his hearers to be obedient to the heavenly visions gained and to translate them into action in terms of "The Ten New Commandments." A few days later he wrote home that the spirit of God had been with them in power: "never have I been so used in a Conference. Scores of students testified as to the help I had been to their lives."

PART 3: Convincing the Germans

From Keswick the two couples traveled to the nearest railroad via horse-drawn coach from the top of which they had delightful views of the Lake District, with stops at the graves of Wordsworth and of Hartley Coleridge. Late arrival in London was followed by supper and a walk to Westminster Abbey. The next day was given to museums and shopping for such items as "pith hats, steamer chairs," and last-minute needs. They took the Channel steamer for a rough crossing that evening, but at Calais no sleepers were to be had, so all five—Williamson had joined the party—"took one compartment and slept five in a bed, heads and feet alternating." Plans to reach Kassel the next day failed so they spent a comfortable night at Düsseldorf, reaching their destination at the village of Gross Almerode near Kassel by evening of August 8. Their hosts expected them to stay in private homes, but the party, wishing privacy and ignorant of local customs and conditions, insisted upon a hotel which proved to have only minimal accommodations: feather beds above and below with bedbugs—"it was a horrible night. Sweat or chill—take your choice." Next day while the men were involved in the conference, the women walked in the hills and picked blueberries, going far enough "to see the picturesqueness of the horribly filthy village"; by evening they had decided to return to Kassel and the YMCA hospitz. The men did better. The second night Mott piled the feather beds on the floor and used his steamer rugs and overcoat for covers. "It takes all kinds of customs to make up the life of the world," he philosophized.

Two more Americans came to Gross Almerode: L. L. Doggett,[9] later president of Springfield College, and J. Ross Stevenson, subsequently president of Princeton Theological Seminary. They and the Mott party found almost one hundred German students whom Leila thought "a fine, mature looking body of men." They represented two-thirds of the universities of the country together with fraternal delegates from Norway, Sweden, Finland, Holland, and Switzerland. This was the sixth German Student Conference. The fate of the federation plan lay in its hands. The students were almost unanimously and enthusiastically in favor both of tightening their own organization and endorsing the federation, but their somewhat dictatorial leader Edvard Graf von Pückler was suspicious of anything Anglo-Saxon. [10]

Mott spoke five times, through an interpreter. He apparently adopted there the unique practice he was to follow throughout his life, different from that of most speakers, of requiring the interpreter to translate sentence by sentence—even with Mott's gestures held—instead of allowing the interpreter to render the sense of a paragraph. This is a clue to Mott's unusual effectiveness with non-English speaking audiences. "Of course," he wrote his parents, "this makes slower work and destroys one's eloquence(!) but it enables you to talk points." He was somewhat surprised to understand much of the German at the sessions (it had been seven years since he studied it at Cornell) but kept an interpreter by his side.

Again Mott brought his American experience to bear upon the organizational aspects of another movement. He urged the Germans to adopt a more comprehensive purpose than the admirable Bible study and social fellowship that had held them together hitherto. He brought their leaders to see the need and feasibility of adding special efforts to help new students, to carry on personal work to win students to Christ, and to promote missionary activity. Above all he was burdened by the "temptations of the students of Germany—particularly impurity, intemperance, rationalism, and ruffianism." Believing that "next to nothing" was being done "to shield them and attach them to Christ," Mott gathered the most spiritual men of the conference and went into the forest one afternoon "where we had most earnest conference and prayer together on preparation for and promotion of a spiritual awakening among the students of Germany."

> O, that there might be raised up some man of commanding intellectual ability, with the heroism and enthusiasm of Peter the Hermit or Luther, and filled with the spirit of God, to help meet the awful spiritual need which is now presented by the universities of Germany![11]

Mott also saw to it that measures were adopted "ensuring a larger participation of the students in the management of the movement," a step that demanded "extended and intense discussion." The adult leadership disparaged student interest in or ability to raise funds but a financial session elicited a splendid response of 6,000 marks or $1500, ensuring traveling secretaries the following year for both the universities and the gymnasia. His American friends had aided in these activities which climaxed in the formation of the German Student Christian Alliance

(Deutsche Christliche Studenten Vereinigung—DCSV) in spite of Graf
Pückler's opposition, finally overcome by lengthy discussion with Mott,
whose "value and significance he always recognised," and by an all-night
prayer-vigil. The new body appointed Johannes Siemson, a recent law
graduate of Berlin who had been at Keswick in 1894, to represent it at
the Scandinavian conference and commit it to the new federation if such
should be formed. At the farewell session the students "with determined
faces and triumphant voices" sped the emissaries on their way with *Ein
feste Burg ist unser Gott*—Mott observing for the home folks "how those
German young men did sound it out. It will sing in my ears for months,
and will never lose its influence on me. It takes the Germans and Welsh
to inspire you with congregational singing."

PART 4: The Founding of the Federation

To Mott, impatient to reach the Scandinavian student conference, Sweden seemed "comparatively plain," reminding him of parts of Maine or
Wisconsin, with many small lakes and much pine land. The language
was almost unintelligible but the people in their varied costumes intrigued him. He liked the smorgasbords at the station restaurants and
thought the red raspberries the finest produced in any land. He was
impressed by the democratic spirit, honesty, hospitality, industry, cheer-
fulness, intelligence, and patriotism of the people. After vicissitudes
comparable to those encountered en route to Gross Almerode, the
Mott-Wishard party, augmented by Siemson and Williamson, finally
reached the conference site at Vadstena, some 150 miles northeast of
Göteborg, on the morning of August 14 to find the third Scandinavian
"Students' Meeting with Christian Programme" of 250 representatives
from the universities of Norway, Sweden, Denmark, and Finland already
in session. Leila thought the students "most friendly" as they almost
overwhelmed the Americans by "pouring in their visiting cards upon us,
expecting ours in return."

Previous Scandinavian conferences had been held in such unusual
settings as an old warship lent by the Norwegian government, so the
Swedish hosts headed by Karl Fries sought a unique location for this one,
perhaps aware that epoch-making events would take place. Let the historian of the WSCF summarize the quest:

> When searching for a suitable conference site for 250 students, Karl
> Fries was staying with the local doctor on a visit to the Y.M.C.A. of the

ancient town of Vadstena, on the shores of Lake Vettern. From his window he spied the beautiful old sixteenth-century royal castle built by Gustavus Vasa, reflected in the moat with its lofty tower and the cupolas of its bulky turrets. Fries saw in a trice it was made for a conference! There was a vaulted hall, big enough for the 250 to eat in; a large Council Room, where sixteenth century Diets had been held; plenty of rooms and corridors for beds. Ideal; but there were a few drawbacks! It was 200 years since the castle had been inhabited: it had not a stick of furniture, nor a window to its name! Such obstacles were as nothing to Fries. His doctor host was building a hospital, and offered beds and other furniture for first use by the students, while the hospital contractor obliged with its future windows. Special permission was necessary to use the castle. Authority after authority refused, until at length the Government itself gave the permit, but with one proviso: no lights whatever were to be used inside the castle. Even this did not daunt Fries. He discovered an electrical engineer in the local Y.M.C.A.; between them, they rigged up a system of lights outside each window to dispel the darkness within; they conjured up a donkey engine to supply power. Just in time the castle was ready. On August 13, 250 Scandinavian students trooped in, plus a tiny band of foreign delegates, two Americans, one Englishman, and one German, there for epoch-making business.[12]

Doubtless this fantastic setting helped to make indelible impressions on those who participated in the stirring events of August, 1895. Mott noted that there was room enough left over to have housed all the students attending conferences anywhere in the world that summer.

The Scandinavian student Christian movement owed its origins to Wishard's cable from Kyoto to Northfield 1889 relaying the message from 500 students in the first such conference ever held in Japan, "Make Jesus King." Richard C. Morse had shared this moving word with Fries, then secretary of the Stockholm YMCA, who received it in Christiania (Oslo), where he read it to some student leaders who were there for a missionary conference. The immediate reaction was to organize Christian students "here in the north." The first Scandinavian meeting was held the next summer. Now in 1895 the Movement was ready to take its place among the charter members of the nascent world body, in the presence of Luther Wishard.[13]

Ruth Rouse, historian of the Federation, detects the desire to "strengthen the spiritual power of the Christian students of the Far East" as a major factor in the crystallization of the Scandinavian Movement. A second factor was "the awakening of love for and confidence in Mott himself." During the Conference Mott devoted two addresses and many interviews to instructing the delegates in basic American principles of student work, urging them to broaden their scope, to engage in evangelism, and to emphasize missions and the spiritual life. He gave the key leaders copies of his pamphlets. Much as he had done in Germany, Mott pushed for "a better [more centralized] organization of the work," seeing to it that a permanent committee was created for Scandinavia and a national committee in each country to supervise the local societies.[14] The result was the "Scandinavian Student Christian Movement" with a permanent international committee, the authorization of Fries and Martin Eckhoff of Norway to represent it in the federation-organizing conference, and to join the new body, which Mott had described to the full Conference.

A Danish leader, later a missionary to India, recalled how Mott nourished the federation idea; on an outing he and the six founders were lying on a grass-clad slope, discussing the plan:

> The kingly thought was John R. Mott's: rather it was indeed the King's own thought, but it was Mott who grasped it, and prepared the way for its realization.... The young American was unpretending and quiet as always, questioning, listening, appreciative of every remark, however irrelevant, the unquestioned centre and leader.... We saw the great possibilities, but some of us knew that our national movements were hardly able to shoulder responsibilities. With his usual sympathetic understanding, Mott assured us 'that the object would be to strengthen not to force the weak movements, to advise and never to control them.' The following day, the Federation was officially founded.[15]

That was August 17, 1895—Saturday. It marked the high point of Mott's career thus far, a goal for which he had worked "ever since I was in England a year ago." The half-dozen sessions in which the World's Student Christian Federation (WSCF) was forged ranged through three days and nine and one-half hours. Mott was chairman, Williamson secretary.[16] Three took notes that have survived; their corrections, clarifications, and doodles bear out Fries' later comment that "though Mott had undoubtedly been clear from the beginning as to the fundamental principles, he made no attempt to force his conclusions upon the rest of us." Differing views were given "scrupulous consideration," continued Fries, and numerous changes were necessary "before we could achieve the simple, but as I believe suitable statutes" that served the Federation as a "leading string" for many years.[17] The prophetically ecumenical character of the group and the organization they set up reflected youth and dedicated cosmopolitanism: only one was ordained and only one was over forty while two were in their early twenties; in experience they represented ten countries and the disciplines of law, medicine, history and philosophy, Semitic languages, and theology.[18] No Orientals were present, but the Federation would outdo itself to correct that imbalance. Fifty years later Mott would list the "little band in the attic of Vadstena Castle" among the most creative experiences of his life.

Appointed "Honorary" (a euphemism for temporary) General Secretary "while on my tour," Mott now had his commission: "I shall seek to induce the students of Asia to join the Federation. This is the first time that the student movements of all Christendom have been united," he wrote home, adding his conviction that this fact "has large promise for the future of the Church and the world." Mott was authorized to invite national movements in the countries he would visit to join if they were college or university oriented, gave evidence of stability based on a permanent committee, and embraced goals "in harmony with the Federation." If they could not meet these standards they might still affiliate through a corresponding member. A simple constitution designed to serve until the first general conference to be held in 1897 set forth the objectives:

1. To unite student Christian movements or organizations throughout the world.
2. To collect information regarding the religious conditions of the students of all lands.
3. To promote the following lines of activity:
   (a) To lead students to become disciples of Jesus Christ as only Saviour and as God.
   (b) To deepen the spiritual life of students.
   (c) To enlist students in the work of extending the Kingdom of Christ throughout the whole world.[19]

These proposals were quite as audacious as had been the watchword of the SVM, of which the Federation was a direct descendant. In addition, they were flexible enough to bring students of Orthodox, Roman Catholic, and non-Christian countries into an ecumenical fellowship. The similarity of the basis of membership to the "Paris Basis" of the YMCA's—the pioneer ecumenical formula of modern times—hardly needs to be pointed out.[20] Long before he had planned this world journey, Mott had become conscious of the uniqueness of every nation and had sought a plan of union that would "encourage the Christian students in each country to develop national . . . movements of their own, adapted in name, organization, and activities to their particular genius

and character, and then to link these together in some simple yet effective federation." This would be in contrast to Wishard's concept of a
worldwide organization of student YMCA's. As Robert Mackie points
out in his introduction to Ruth Rouse's *History* of the Federation, it was
"something new in the university world . . . an experiment in Christian
fellowship which worked."

That it worked was Mott's achievement of the next twenty months,
an assignment that lengthened into a lifetime. The appointment of Fries,
who was three years Mott's senior, as Chairman not only assured a gifted
co-worker but grew into a half-century of "association in service" with
never an instance in which "we failed to see eye to eye and act as one
mind."[21] Siemson was vice-president, a post which after the first conference of 1897 was always held by an Oriental. Williamson was made
corresponding secretary and Wishard treasurer, in which capacity he
received from Eckhoff as the first contribution to the Federation the
surplus from an earlier Scandinavian conference—one guinea!

PART 5: Assignment: The World

Following a day each in Stockholm and Uppsala the Motts and Wishards
took a brief vacation trip in Norway. A student who had been at Northfield accosted John on the street in Christiania (Oslo), causing him to
write Hattie, "the world is very small; it is impossible to lose yourself."
He might have thought of later returning to these university towns, but he
could not have dreamed in 1895 that a half-century later he would
receive one of the world's greatest honors, the Nobel Peace Prize, in this
very place. The route to Bergen via Fagernes, Borgund, and Laerdalsoren
was exhilarating for the transparent mountain air, blue sky, and clearest
mountain sunshine, reminding the party of California. Walking "enough
each day to keep us in good trim," and riding in two carriages drawn by
"tough and eager" fjord ponies, they enjoyed scenery always beautiful and
sometimes grand. Mott marvelled at the berries and cherries so far north
and in characteristic superlatives described the Sögnefjord as "the most
magnificent waterway I have ever seen." The party rested almost a week
before pushing on to Bergen and thence through heavy seas to Newcas-
tle, England.

The two couples now separated, the Wishards going to Edinburgh
prior to starting for South Africa. Since the summer of 1886 at Mount
Hermon the two men had been virtual partners in the promotion of the

world missionary enterprise. On scores of occasions the Motts would find their way prepared by the Wishards' earlier world journey. Each now set forth as an officer of the new World's Student Christian Federation, of which both were architects and were now to be builders. Wishard, with the aid of Donald Fraser, en route to missionary assignment, would bring the South African Students' Christian Association into the fold while the Motts labored in Australia and the Orient.[22]

The next weeks were filled to overflowing with sightseeing, final preparations for the Orient, writing letters and reports, and carrying out assignments agreed upon at Vadstena. Paris was "full of show and frivolity, and yet I suppose it is the finest city in Europe," John wrote to his sister Clara, "you would like it. Everybody does." After laying plans for student work in France, and two lovely days in Geneva climaxed by the alpenglow on Mt. Blanc, he and Leila moved on to Rome where the historian in Mott exulted in "the three greatest days I have ever spent in a foreign land." Rome was "certainly the most impressive, most absorbingly interesting city in all the world," though he might change his mind upon reaching Constantinople and Jerusalem, "but I do not think that I shall." St. Peter's was "simply overwhelming," but what moved them most was going along "the same road and under the same arch" as St. Paul. Mott met Protestant missionaries and addressed the students of a small Methodist college.

Leaving Leila to go to Constantinople with Mrs. Taylor, he went to Florence to meet a young Waldensian pastor to whom he could "commit the student interest of Italy," as had been authorized at Vadstena. There followed "one of the most interesting days of all my life," he wrote his father—on the new World's Student Christian Federation stationery—at Torre Pellice in the Piedmont, the home of the Waldensians, "famous in Church History as the most persecuted Christians in all Europe." There he laid the foundations for "the first Christian Association of students in Italy."

He then returned to Switzerland for a meeting at St. Croix that proved to be "the best conference held on the Continent this year." He had shared the previous summer in the planning of this, the first student conference to be held in Switzerland. At Vadstena a Swiss movement had been regarded as of strategic importance to the building of the Federation because of the location of Switzerland and the international composition of its student population, half of which was foreign. Students and some professors came to St. Croix from most of the French-speaking universities of the country. Six members of the executive committee of the new Federation were there, with the Chairman, Karl Fries, presiding. As at Keswick, Gross Almerode, and Vadstena, Mott's addresses were descriptive of the Christian movements in North America and the other European countries. He outlined program and organizational steps plus a "simple national organization," and appointed a Swiss corresponding member of the Federation. This was "the beginning of a student movement in the mountain republic." He also obtained informal endorsement of the world tour from officers of the World's Alliance of YMCA's, under the auspices of which the conference was held. [23]

His face now "well set toward the Far East," Mott worked his way "by easy stages" to Constantinople. In Vienna he discussed religious conditions with "an able minister" whom he commissioned on behalf of the Federation to investigate the religious status of the students of the country in the hope that a way would open for an approach to "the five thousand students in the university of this wicked city." He found Hungary a "more hopeful" student field; in Budapest he was gratified to come upon a new YMCA with a student program and there appointed a "very capable" young pastor as the Federation's representative in the newly-formed Balkan States. For Athens he discovered "a very rare young man," a Greek, a graduate of Harvard and a Ph.D. of Berlin, to represent the Federation. "Surely it is God's will that a real spiritual work be started among the students of this city, who today worship not so much 'an unknown God' as no God." [24]

Arriving in Constantinople by train, Mott spent six never-to-be-forgotten days there during a reign of terror against Armenians who were being subjected to every atrocity and "shot down like dogs" by the hundreds. He was so outraged that he devoted most of a long report letter to a recital of facts he had personally verified from eyewitnesses, concluding that there could be no real peace "for the Christian peoples scattered throughout Asia Minor and along the beautiful Bosporus until this barbarous Ottoman Government is swept from the face of the earth." Most of his activity was at the American Congregational Robert College, which Mott appraised as "the only institution of higher learning worthy of the name in European Turkey." Its setting was "more beautiful and richer in historic associations than that of any other institution in the world," set as it was in view of the "Towers of Europe" and the "Towers of Asia" fortifications built by Mohammed II the year before he conquered Constantinople, and at the narrowest point of the Bosporus where Darius had crossed into Europe and the Crusaders into Asia.

Reunited with Leila, fresh from her voyage from Rome, this interlude was "a beautiful dream" under a full moon. Only a few meetings were risked, but Mott was impressed by the student YMCA that carried on in four departments according to the languages spoken. Back in the city they witnessed by special permit the Sultan's attendance on Friday prayers and saw dancing dervishes in the streets, "a bit of inane nonsense" to Leila, who was happy to leave this "cruel, sin-cursed place." John cautioned his sister Hattie not to be "scared" by his description of the atrocities since "we are safely out of that wicked city."[25]

Before leaving Europe, Mott reflected on the evidences that were in his mind already establishing the Federation as *"the work of God."* In a report letter from Constantinople he wrote over-optimistically that although the new organization had been in existence only a few weeks it had facilitated his efforts to introduce "organized Christian work" into some of the most difficult "unoccupied student fields," namely France, Italy, Hungary, and Switzerland.[26] He was confident that it would "prove even more helpful in certain fields in the East." It would make possible for the first time "a thorough and comprehensive study of the religious state of the students of the whole world" and enable us "to grapple successfully with the problem of the spiritual welfare of the large numbers of foreign students in different countries." The stronger members were strategically placed where they could be most helpful to the weaker. It would be a clearing house for "the best ideas wrought out in the experience of Christian student organizations in all lands," and would expedite the projection of new plans and policies throughout the whole student world. But most significantly it would stimulate Christian union.[27]

The cruise from Constantinople to Beirut was "a big vacation." Mott envisioned history on both sides—the Hellespont, Troas, Lesbos, Smyrna (Ismir), where a shore visit included ancient ruins and Mott met and spoke to the first of scores of groups of missionaries he would meet on this trip. Some of them he had known in Canada, Vermont, or England, "so you see I am still unable to get where I am not known," he complained to Postville. Then on to Chios, followed by Athens for a four-hour stop and a mad dash to the Acropolis—"the most magnificent ruin in the world"—and what was regarded as Mars Hill where Paul's proclamation of the "God of heaven who 'dwelleth not in temples made with hands' took on new meaning" under the shoulder of the Acropolis crowned with "heathen temples." Back on ship by ten A. M., Leila opened her diary entry for that breathless morning with a flashback to Wooster: "John's birthday—three years old today." "The most enjoyable voyage I have ever taken" continued to Rhodes, where Leila refused to leave the ship, confiding to her diary that "distance lends enchantment to all these Eastern cities"; Cyprus, then Beirut.

Six days at the Syrian Protestant College (The American University) included a trip to Damascus on the new French-built railroad. This, the oldest city in the world with its "continuous existence of over 4,000 years" fascinated them because of its connection with the life of St. Paul. Their missionary hosts showed the Motts the road on which the Apostle had probably come into the city; they went through the gate he must have entered and saw "the wall down which he was let in the basket" to escape his persecutors. They walked along "the street called straight"— "now very crooked"—where Paul had lodged and "where he had received his sight, and the baptism of the Holy Ghost." Because of Moslem unrest it was deemed unwise to hold a meeting for young men.

The return trip to Beirut included a visit to the ruins at Baalbek; next day Mott called at the Jesuit university in Beirut. Back at the Syrian Protestant College he spoke five times, chiefly on "subjects bearing on the practical promotion of the spiritual life," and held two evangelistic meetings, all to audiences of 250 students, large numbers of whom came to his room afterward for counseling. Profoundly impressed by such a cosmopolitan student body, Mott came to respect the College as one of three "most important institutions in all Asia".

> It has practically created the medical profession in the Levant. It has been the most influential factor in promoting popular education in Syria and in other parts of the East. It has been and is the center for real Christian and scientific literature and learning in all that region.

It and the other mission schools and colleges of the Levant

> are laying a great mine underneath the system of Mohammedanism. If that most formidable structure is ever completely shattered—and it will be—it will be as a direct result of Christ's truth and power working through the channel of these educational institutions. [28]

So complete was Mott's rapport with students, faculty, and missionaries that President Daniel Bliss wished that he could stay for forty years!

PART 6: Two Bible Students' Horseback Tour of the Holy Land

The next three weeks unfold one of the most revealing episodes of Mott's life. On this journey we have seen him so far as promoter, organizer, evangelist, administrator, and formal spiritual leader; only exceptionally has he emerged as historian or relaxed involved tourist. He had arranged for a deluxe safari from Sidon, a three-hour sail from Beirut, through Galilee to Jerusalem. This would be a rigorous exercise to which he would give himself with a degree of abandon perhaps unequalled in any other sequence of events of which there is a comparably intimate record. The Holy Land was to evoke his and Leila's deepest religious emotions. To Mott's wide knowledge and lively sense of history he had added, since his sophomore year at Cornell, a comprehension of the Bible that was both factual and in depth.

The attraction of the Holy Land for Americans in the late nineteenth century was an aspect of evangelicalism. Pious individuals and small groups of like-minded Germans and Swedes found its magnetism irresistible.[29] The seventy-odd persons who migrated to Jerusalem from Chicago in 1881 to become the American Colony were not atypical.[30] There was the tragic expedition from Jonesport, Maine, in 1866, one of whose survivors would be the Motts' travel agent.[31] There were only a few Jewish colonies in Palestine in 1895 and Jews comprised less than 8 percent of the population; the Motts' only observations of them were to be at the Wailing Wall and in the Jewish Quarter of Jerusalem where they approached a majority.

Numerous American, British, and Continental mission societies directed their efforts toward Arabs and the adherents of the several Eastern Orthodox and Armenian Christian bodies which Mott was to characterize on this trip as "corrupt" churches. But beyond all such considerations there lay the eternal lure, as a twentieth-century Orthodox writer eloquently expressed it, of the historic place itself:

> Jesus Christ, the Son of God, was born, lived, taught, talked to the woman of Samaria at Jacob's well, suffered, and was glorified *here*—not in Poland or Peru, not in the Cameroons or Korea, not in Florida or France. Therefore Protestant missionaries *had* to come to the Middle East, and a thousand million years from now, Christians from China, or from Mars or some Betelgeuse system, will come here too. . . . Let [nothing] beguile any man into believing that the Near East will ever cease to be a cosmic magnet for all those who know and love Jesus Christ. This is its unalterable destiny . . . it was all determined by Jesus Christ himself.[32]

With the increasing emphasis upon the earthly life of Christ that developed in the late nineteenth century, and as improved means of transportation and the opening of the Suez Canal made such journeys possible, a tour of the Holy Land became a logical extension of the grand

tour of Europe or of a visit to Egypt for tourists from America or western
Europe. Likewise, there were beginning to be large numbers of pilgrims
from the Orthodox countries of eastern Europe, especially Russia. Travel
books satisfied the appetites of those who could not go, and whetted and
directed the enthusiasms of those who could. Bibles with "engravings and
coloured pictures from drawings" made in the Holy Land, the forerunners
of photographs, with coordinated Scripture texts were read by millions. [33]
The serious beginnings of modern archaeology were being published. The
Motts had studied some of this literature and had developed critical
attitudes toward tradition and folklore. They may well have met George
Adam Smith, the biographer of Henry Drummond, for they were reading
Smith's new *Historical Geography of the Holy Land,* and John had consulted Joseph Cook, whose Boston Monday Lectures on the *Orient* described many places he and Leila would visit. [34]

John explained to Postville that because roads were almost non-
existent and no other means of travel were available, they had hired "a
regular Oriental caravan":

> We have a native Syrian dragoman. He knows the whole country as well as
> a farmer knows his farm. He speaks several languages. We have also a
> cook, a waiter, and seven muleteers—making ten men in all. Most of these
> men receive but a few cents a day. To carry us and our outfit and stores we
> have seven horses, two donkeys and twelve mules. We have three sleeping
> tents, one dining tent, and one kitchen tent. The beds are as comfortable
> and the meals as good as you would find in the best hotels. A dinner of
> seven courses is served at 6 P.M. We have a plain breakfast very early in
> the morning in order to get started on our journey before it becomes warm.
> We stop for lunch wherever we find a good place toward the middle of the
> day. [35]

Such outfits, supplied by Thomas Cook, "were magnificent, the equipment sumptuous, and the service excellent," the tents being "lined with
indigo blue, every inch of which was covered with bright patchwork in
arabesque patterns," wrote Bertha Spafford Vester of the American Colony, who would much later entertain the Motts on several occasions. [36]
Mott denigrated the expense "when everything is taken into consideration." The chief consideration was that Mrs. Taylor made it possible.
Another was safety. Palestine in 1895 was grossly misgoverned by the
declining Ottoman Empire, the "sick man of Europe," whose symptoms
the Motts had witnessed in its capital city. It was a backward and desolate
place, well described by Abba Eban's word "stagnant." The land had no
political or administrative identity, subject as it was to the Turkish pro-

vincial system. "There were scarcely any roads, no industry, little profitable commerce and none but the most primitive agriculture, constantly ravished by malaria and pestilence."[37]

As aware of all this as possible prior to first-hand experience, the Motts together with Mrs. Taylor and her secretary, accompanied by a local missionary, mounted their horses in the narrow street of Sidon the morning of October 22 "with considerable inward agitation," as Leila confided to her diary at Tyre that night.[38] The route of the first two days lay along the shore of the Mediterranean. Almost at once biblical sites came into view: this was ancient Phoenicia whose influence spread from Britain to India. Here Elijah had replenished the widow's oil and meal. Tyre, port for stone and timber for Solomon's temple, lay in the destruction prophesied by Isaiah, Ezekiel, and Amos; Christ and Paul had both been here. The canter over miles of hard sand was "most bracing," their mounts so ambitious that the party was asked to slow their pace lest the horses be injured. On Mount Carmel Mott recalled Elijah's calling down the rains after three years' drought; the magnificent view of sea, harbor, hill, and plain included the place of sacrifice where the prophet slew the priests of Baal.

After crossing the plain of Esdraelon and winding through the hills of lower Galilee they rode into Nazareth at sunset "over the road which Christ must have trod hundreds of times," and camped on a hill overlooking the town. The literature had prepared them to adopt a sceptical attitude toward the traditional sites but Mott found two authentic places: "The boy Jesus without doubt often went to the spring with His mother just as I have seen other children doing"; He must also have gone frequently to the hill on the north side of the town. From that vantage point Mott obtained "the most impressive view I have ever had anywhere in the world," not excepting the American West, the Wartburg, or the Görnergrat, "none of which approached it in combination of natural and historical features." He had read of this view in various lives of Christ but it surpassed all that he had seen or heard about it. In words reminiscent of his description of the Connecticut Valley from Mount Tom and quite as eloquent as Joseph Cook's, he wrote home a lengthy and stirring paragraph depicting not merely the topography in full circle but the meaning of the map, seeing "stirring Scripture events in every direction": Carmel and Elijah, Esdraelon—Barak, Sisera, and Gideon, Saul's defeat by the Philistines, Josiah's rout by the Egyptians, Mount Hermon and Christ's transfiguration, the great caravan routes north-south and east-west—how "the peoples and nations have fought for this land" from the earliest tribes, the Phoenicians, the tribes of Israel, the Crusaders, the Turks, to the modern French! "Where in the whole world can one have a view which calls up so much?"

But the "most impressive thought" that came to both Motts in hours of meditation here was that Christ must have climbed this hill many times "not only to take this view, but also (I believe) to have communion with His Father." Leila was reminded of the command to Abraham— "Look eastward and westward, and northward, and southward. It is a wonderful picture." The Sabbath provided a full day of rest at Nazareth: "We had a good day with our Bibles, which became new to us in the land," she wrote. In the evening John spoke to the youth of a new YMCA made up of both Protestants and Orthodox. He brought greetings from North America and from Europe and thought it most appropriate that "there should be such an organization in the city where the Young Man of Nazareth grew up and prepared for his wonderful mission."

The morning they left for Tiberias Mott arose at four to visit the Nazareth hilltop for the third time, watching the sun come up over Mount Tabor, drinking in a sight "even more impressive than on the night before." Part of the day's itinerary lay along the ancient caravan road between Acco (Acre) and Damascus. This one day Leila took a palanquin. The village spring at Cana reminded them of two of Christ's miracles; the homes of the prophets Jonah and Nathanael were noted. In early afternoon the Lake of Galilee, whose "beauty has not been exaggerated," burst upon them. As they descended to it the Motts were reminded of numerous hymns on the theme; John thought "Blue Galilee" most appropriate. They pitched their tents "right on the lake shore outside the walls of the old city of Tiberias," and immediately took a boat, rowing for two hours in spite of the heat. Mott noted that the locations of most of the ruined ancient cities around it were discernible. After supper they went out again, this time by moonlight, finding the water a bit rough, which helped them to appreciate the stilling of the tempest by Christ. John wrote home:

> My heart was deeply moved as I thought of what Christ did and taught around this little lake. . . . A majority of [His] miracles were performed on the lake, or on its shore or in sight of its waters. We recall the healing of the paralytic, the restoring the sight of the blind man, the healing of Peter's mother-in-law. . . the driving of the devils out of the two demoniacs at Gadara (you can see the steep hill where the swine ran into the sea . . .), the walking on the lake, the miraculous draught of fishes . . . the feeding of the five thousand. . . . He also gave some of his greatest teachings . . . in this vicinity. . . . He taught in synagogues, in fields, in boats, along streets

all about this region. Here he called Peter and Andrew and James and John. . . . Next to Jerusalem I think this is the greatest center of interest in the Holy Land. Gladly would we linger here for days. [39]

The next morning Mott took "an exhilarating bath" in the lake before sunrise. Reluctantly mounting their horses early, the members of the little caravan wound their way up out of the deep valley, feasting their eyes on the lake below them until it finally disappeared, never to be forgotten. Now Safed, supposed to be "the city set on a hill which cannot be hid," Lebanon and Mount Hermon, the Horns of Hattin, and Mount Tabor came successively into view before they again reached Nazareth after a brief stop on the now familiar hilltop. That evening Mott spoke to a "very attentive audience" in "the only Protestant church" of the town and was interpreted by the Syrian pastor.

The route toward Jerusalem lay across the plains of Esdraelon and Jezreel and through the rocky hills of Samaria; it was the hottest and most difficult part of the entire journey. Stopping for lunch and siesta and camping overnight in orange, lemon, pomegranate, or olive groves, the sweet odors were welcome relief from the parched roads. This was the olive harvest season and everywhere the fruit was being gathered as from time immemorial. The area brought to mind the Old Testament narratives about Elisha, Saul and Jonathan, Ahab, Naboth. Extensive ruins such as those at Samaria (Sebastia), though at times seen through shimmering heat, made vivid the lives of Omri, Jehu, and Jezebel, and dramatized the Assyrian conquest. Arriving in ancient Shechem (Nablus) John set out at once with a guard to climb Mount Ebal, from whose summit there was another panorama "over almost the entire Holy Land," even to Mount Nebo whence Moses had overlooked the Promised Land. As the party left next morning ten lepers begging at the city gate presented "a most pitiable" sight. At Jacob's well Mott read from the Gospel of John what he called the "interview of Christ with the Samaritan woman." Never, he added, did He "give deeper teaching."

The roads now became like the beds of rocky dry mountain streams, worse than anything back home in Sullivan County! Up and down hill were at times steeper than a stairway, but Leila remarked that they had "somehow learned to trust these sure-footed, well shod horses," riding over "places we would not lead a horse at home." Although they had been somewhat stiff after the first days, they had become hardened to riding and were enjoying it:

This overland trip has been a good thing for us physically as well as in every other way. We have great appetites. We are brown as gypsies. We sleep

soundly at night, and also lie down on the ground under some tree each
noon and take a nap. It has braced our constitutions for our tour in the
tropics.

In an unspeakably filthy town the children crowding in for baksheesh
seemed more like animals than humans so dirty they were, and only partly
covered in rags. Bethel brought to mind Jacob's dream, and Deborah,
Samuel, Elisha, and Elijah, as the party sat Turkish fashion on the porch
of a mosque for their lunch.

It was "an impressive moment" when, rounding the shoulder of
Mount Scopus as had the Romans under Titus in A.D. 70, according to
historian Mott, writing home, "suddenly and strikingly" the domes
and towers of Jerusalem burst into view. Instead of going to a hotel Mott
decided to camp through the week-end among the olive trees of Galilea,
the traditional pilgrims' area on the Mount of Olives, directly opposite
the Golden Gate and above Gethsemane—"the best point from which to
view the city." The moon was full "and such moonlight. We could read
the finest handwriting even. That Passover night so long ago must have
been something the same." But even Jerusalem took second place to
reading the mail from home. The next day, their Sabbath, was devoted
to "reading all in the Bible that took place right near Jerusalem"—"a
great deal"—"and feasting our eyes on it." Mott wrote home:

> My heart burned within me as I remembered that it was Christ's custom to
> come to this mount for communion with His Father. . . . Here He taught
> His disciples some of their deepest lessons. Just below is Gethsemane where
> He had the great struggle and won the victory which makes us free.

At sunset they climbed the minaret near their camp for "a surprising
view" of the wilderness of Judea, the Dead Sea, and the mountains of
Moab. In the future Mott would return to the Mount of Olives, most
notably in 1928 when he arranged for the delegates to the International
Missionary Council meeting to camp on the same spot, where it was
hoped they would be similarly inspired.

The descent from the Mount was according to Psalm 48—"walk
about Zion . . . tell the towers thereof . . . "—except, as Mott noted, they
rode horseback, marking the valleys, the towers, and the walls that had
seen 30 sieges. Some of the ancient olive trees at Gethsemane could have
been there in the time of our Lord. Prepared by their reading and by
other pilgrims, the Motts exercised critical judgment concerning the
authenticity of what they saw, agreeing with D. L. Moody's scepticism on
most of the sites: "but the hills you cannot change or move."[40] Doubtless

they had discussed these matters with him. They remained in "the wonderful city" a week, staying at Floyd's Hotel ten minutes northwest of the Jaffa Gate. Leila wrote twenty-four pages of description while John's letters to Postville filled fourteen closely handwritten pages, on which this account is largely based.

Excavations fascinated them, for "the spade of the archaeologist is constantly confirming the truthfulness of the Scripture records." Permission was obtained to visit Mount Moriah, which was explored at great length under the guidance of Professor Ellis of Bishop Gobat's School. They examined an archaeologist's models of the several temples. These, Mott noted, make "many things in the Bible much clearer." The Roman pavement in the crypt of the Chapel of the Flagellation seemed authentic: "in all probability Christ Himself once walked over this ancient road." The activity at the Wailing Wall was to the Motts a "pathetic sight." Two visits to the Church of the Holy Sepulchre failed to move them or to convince them of the authenticity of the site. The relics, images, and "superstitions" associated with it saddened them: Mott preferred to forget rather than describe these in a home letter, believing the place of the skull the more likely site of the crucifixion. But at any rate, he concluded,

> it fills one with indescribable emotion to reflect that somewhere here where we have been looking and walking took place the most stupendous event of history—the death and resurrection of Jesus Christ. One feels not so much like speaking as being silent.

Pilgrimages were made to Bethany, Jericho, and the Dead Sea. Bethlehem was "undoubtedly the cradle of Christianity." The excursion to Jericho and the Dead Sea—in which they bathed—was by carriage rather than horseback, with an armed escort which Leila described as "one lone armed outrider on a poor specimen of a horse," and was the "hottest, dustiest ride" ever. The sun beat down "with unmitigated ardor." The Jordan proved to be a narrow, crooked, dirty stream, yet probably "the most famous river in all the world." In the course of the "toilsome ascent" back to Jerusalem, which gave new meaning to the biblical phrase "up to Jerusalem," Mott asked a shepherd to call his sheep. Each one had its name and would come no matter where it was in the flock. "How vivid it makes the meaning of Christ's words 'my sheep know my voice and a stranger they will not follow.'" Mott also carried on "considerable work" in Jerusalem, giving seven addresses before two YMCA's and at Bishop Gobat's School. The party met a dozen missionaries, most of them of the Church of England, "some good Lutheran workers and one Friend or Quaker."

In leaving for Egypt the party took the new railroad from Jerusalem to Jaffa. "It seemed strange enough to be rushing behind an American locomotive down the valleys of Judea, among the hills of the Philistines, and across the Plain of Sharon." Mott hoped that better roads would be built for horses all over Palestine, but was not in favor of more railroads. Jaffa, their port of embarkation, reminded them of St. Peter's great vision there, but the reality of the place was "hardly inviting" to Leila, who felt "like stepping high and quickly too."[41] The dangerous reef that caused all shipping to anchor well off shore was safely negotiated, and as their Austrian Lloyd ship lifted anchor at sunset they looked back reverently upon the shores of the Holy Land which they had come "to love very much." Although Mott would rarely if ever mention this experience specifically, it had been "the most instructive and helpful that we have ever spent in any land." More than a year later as they recalled the high and low points of the tour, they would remember the hilltop visions at Nazareth and the Mount of Olives, and the "misgovernment, rottenness, decay, and cruelty" of the Turkish Empire, with its "ruined land and poverty-stricken, wretched people," which they had encountered in Constantinople, Damascus, and Palestine.

Ten days in Egypt were devoted largely to Mott's work, but between engagements they were able to see "the principal sights." The oldest streets of Cairo revealed "a hundred new and strange things in as many steps." They met missionaries, visited several mosques, and thought the mummy of Rameses II looked the part of the oppressor of the Hebrew people. Mott bought a finely illuminated copy of the Koran. They were quietly hissed at the University of El Azhar. They climbed the Great Pyramid where Mott marvelled at the panorama of the "trackless desert," the Nile Valley, Cairo, and the other pyramids. After seeing the Coptic cathedral he commented that American missionaries had been "very successful in their efforts to reach the Copts."

The work to which Mott referred took them to the United Presbyterian mission college at Asyut, some 200 miles up the Nile. From the train he marvelled at the productivity and the semi-tropical fruits of the region under the unique irrigation of the river. The college, with its 400 students, was doing a work comparable to that he had admired at Robert College and the Syrian Protestant College. He brought greetings and news of student Christian movements at home and in Europe to students, faculty, and missionaries; a score of young men dedicated themselves to

Christian work as ministers or teachers in response to his appeal, and steps were taken toward organizing a YMCA. One of the most moving testimonials that came to him on this entire tour was composed by these students and sent on after he had left Egypt. Four meetings in Cairo were well attended, but there were not enough Protestant young men to form an Association. The missionaries urged him to stay on, as they would do everywhere, but steamship tickets had been bought and the schedule in Ceylon and India could not be postponed.

PART 7: Ceylon: A Point of Strategic Importance

November 21 saw the Mott party aboard the Peninsular and Orient ("P. & O.") *Paramatta* bound for Colombo, Ceylon (Sri Lanka). The first passenger they recognized was to their joy the great Methodist India missionary bishop James Mills Thoburn, who had thrilled the Northfield Conference of 1890. Leila was reminded that this was Fletcher Brockman's wedding day. A hurried note to Postville before sailing assured the home folks that they were "in splendid health—in fact never were in better health." John's catarrh seemed to have left. They had avoided the cholera-infested areas of Cairo and were glad to be "under the British flag again." Repeating the mail arrangements, John sought to allay his mother's anxieties by giving her his philosophy of travel: a lady in Edinburgh had given him a pocketbook inscribed in gilt letters: "With God over the sea; without God not over the threshold." Mrs. Taylor planned to send cables home regularly and would include news from the Motts if there were need. There was none.

The voyage was warm, smooth, uneventful, productive. John conducted ship's prayers once, talked with missionaries, and wrote voluminously to New York. At the first port of call he despatched Number Eight of what would be a series of twenty-one Report Letters that had begun with Keswick. These were sent to 125 friends, supporters, and the leaders of the new Federation, the list increasing as the tour progressed; they would also be published in the American YMCA, church, and missions press. To Gilbert Beaver he sent detailed directives for the guidance of the staff and the governance of the Movement; because of the risk of misunderstanding the written word, let us be much in prayer, he concluded to Beaver on another occasion, so that "we may not on the one hand hinder God's work and on the other hand that we may be '*wise master builders.*' " John and Leila observed their wedding anniversary on

Thanksgiving when Mrs. Taylor's American flag was displayed in the dining saloon and the Americans at the captain's table were served extra desserts. The Motts deepened their acquaintance with the Anglican Bishop George Evans Moule who was en route to China. Leila played deck quoits with a Mrs. Goode of Adelaide.

Robett Wilder, now on assignment in India, met them at Colombo early on the morning of December 3, 1895. He and the Motts moved as quickly as possible to the northern peninsula of the island. At Jaffna College, a Congregational school at Batticotta, the first American missionary college, Mott found the oldest and "the best" college Association in the mission field, it having been founded by F. K. Sanders in 1884. In 1889 it had been the site of Wishard's first Asian student conference. Now it was the nucleus for a union of some dozen Associations in the schools, colleges, and villages of the area.[42] Mott and Wilder devoted several days to visiting the surrounding schools and colleges "to secure suitable delegations" and to become acquainted "with the workers and the needs of the field." This travel, some by bullock cart, exposed the Motts for the first time to Oriental religion and to the tropics. To Mott the climate seemed no hotter than at home in August, but pith hats and white umbrellas lined with green were indispensable. Staying in the homes of missionaries made them apprehensive about tarantulas, centipedes, and snakes; of the last "it is said there are 104 kinds of which over 40 kinds are poisonous," he wrote home. Although no missionary had ever been bitten and the Motts did not see even one snake, the stories they heard were enough "to keep one awake nights." Leila observed that the difficulties facing missionaries were very great and that persons "weak mentally or spiritually" should not attempt the work.

The meetings at Jaffna College December 11 to 13 were the first of the many series of student conferences for which Mott had come to the East. Of the 400 delegates, 300 were from the eight Christian colleges and schools of the peninsula, most of which had "suspended their exercises" so that students, masters, and principals could attend, as well as some 30 missionaries, 20 native pastors, the leaders of neighboring village Associations, and the headmaster of a Hindu college who brought 40 students. Sessions were conducted in English and Tamil. They covered a range of topics "that would remind one of the college conferences of the West." Mott drew inspiration from the "attentive faces of this body of young men" who listened to his eight talks, and from their "fervent prayers and hearty singing especially of the Tamil lyrics." The results of this prototype conference revealed that "the spirit of God was wonderfully present," there being a number of conversions and rededications, with 148 delegates pledging to keep "the morning watch—that is, to spend at least the first half hour of every day in Bible study and secret prayer," a fresh emphasis to which Mott directed one of his most effective addresses. Careful plans were laid to conserve the gains of the conference through visitation, the preparation of a prayer cycle, and Bible training classes.[43]

It was necessary to return to Colombo to take ship for India. When unanticipated delay forced them to stay over several days, Mott and Wilder held a "quite well attended" two-day conference of missionaries, students, and teachers. Mott recognized Colombo as a strategically important location for a city YMCA because it was "more nearly at the crossroads of the nations than any other port in the world," being "the half-way station between the West and the far East." It was gratifying to him to announce "to the workers throughout the island" that Louis Hieb, whose experience had been in metropolitan student work in Chicago, had been appointed to the Colombo Association and would soon be on the field. Mott concluded his report letter on Ceylon with the comment that the Roman Catholics had recently opened "the best equipped college in Ceylon" at Colombo with the intention, as he had learned from two Jesuits he had met on shipboard, of making it "the first real university in the island." Why, he then asked his constituency, should not Protestants also recognize what the Jesuits have always acted upon: "that the points of most strategic importance in any country are the institutions of higher learning?"

PART 8: A "Hindered Volunteer" in India

Mott and Wilder set out for Madras via Tuticorin, leaving Leila and Mrs. Taylor to sail directly to Calcutta, the former to spend Christmas with her brother J. Campbell White. In lightering to their ship the women's rowboat was struck by a coal barge, with a major accident narrowly averted. For Mott this was the beginning of 7,000 miles travel that during the next eleven weeks (he later commented that he could have used eleven months) would take him to 30 schools and colleges and five student conferences in Bombay, Lahore, Lucknow, Calcutta, and Madras. The groundwork for these had been well laid in advance by "prominent members of the American and British Volunteer Movements" already on the field.

While in Madura Mott made his first visit to a Hindu temple, finding it "disgusting, saddening, deadening to witness the people worshipping and serving the creature rather than the Creator." He confessed to his parents that two years before at the Parliament of Religions in Chicago "it had sounded very well" to hear these heathen religions exalted and praised, but it was "an entirely different thing to see their practical working out and influence right here on the ground." Beginning in Madras Mott checked over the plans for the forthcoming conference. In every situation he was met, entertained, guided, and advised by YMCA men or missionaries, most of whom he had known at home or in Great Britain; these prepared his way. Their admiration and enthusiasm would help to build his early fame. Forty missionaries attended a reception for him and Wilder in Madras. He spent Christmas with the Wilders at Poona where Robert was working among educated Hindus and Brahmins and on several occasions invited Mott to speak to what had not infrequently been hostile audiences. Mott wrote home:

> It is a great joy to present Christ to men, many of whom have never heard of Him as a personal Saviour. If my work did not call me on, I could find enough to do right here to make a life-work of great influence for Christ.

He also attended some sessions of the Indian National Congress then in its annual meeting, where he marvelled at the diversity of races and creeds represented in "the most picturesque audience I ever saw," wishing he could have a color photograph that would reveal the turbans of 21 different colors. "We cannot, in the West, imagine anything like it." India is more than a country, he wrote his sister Hattie, "it is a vast continent. It is a most bewildering country." It is a mission field of "simply marvellous extent, importance, difficulties, and possibilities. The Church should send an army of her best equipped workers here, to turn the impending crisis for Christ." To further this end Wilder would devote two years to travel among the North American theological schools under the SVM.

Mott was not referring to a political crisis, for the 1890's were one of the most tranquil periods of that century; it was, in fact, a time of unprecedented calm in India's internal affairs. The National Congress he had attended generated "not the slightest trace of anti-British feeling in its deliberations or activities," nor did Mott observe such. The first political assassination was not to take place until 1897, and it was almost another decade before any missionary would espouse the Nationalist cause. [44] This sense of political calm was reflected in missionary reports of the period though some workers worried about the tendency among educated Hindus toward an uncritical emulation of the West that led them to disparage their own culture and neglect their native languages. London Missionary Society representatives on the field believed that " 'a great door, and effectual, is opened to Christian effort in India, though there are many adversaries.' " Throughout the country there were encouraging signs of inquiry about Christianity with a "new spirit of unrest and expectancy" evident among both caste and non-caste populations. Yet there could be no illusions among missionaries when the total Christian population amounted to less than one percent of the whole, nor was there evidence that an indigenous church, the real test of progress, could be anticipated in the foreseeable future.

Mott's first conference was held in Bombay, a "magnificent city," which only two years earlier had been the site of a conference that had discussed seriously cooperation among missionaries and their sponsors. He would become aware that moves toward comity were further advanced in India than elsewhere in the mission field and on his next visit would be much impressed by them.[45] Leila rejoined her husband at Bombay, after a 1400-mile train trip, alone, second class from Calcutta, which had consumed three nights and two days and cost twelve dollars. The conference attracted fifty representatives of missionary societies and 75 Indian students and teachers—nearly all of the Christian students and teachers of the region. There were a handful of decisions for Christ and 30 covenanted to keep the morning watch. "The missionaries all bore testimony to the spiritual and practical help which they had received." Perhaps slightly disappointed by the small attendance, Mott anticipated that his conferences would "get better and better as we advance." They afforded an opportunity to meet many workers and "also to do much more good. It is sort of bringing the mountain to Mohammed," he wrote home.

While in Bombay a cable came from Liverpool that the Student Volunteer Convention that Mott had helped to plan at Keswick in August, had met every expectation, with attendance of more than 700 including good delegations from the Continent. Representatives of "practically all" of the missionary societies of Great Britain had been there. In addition, two hundred pounds toward extending the tour to Australia had been subscribed and was available at a bank in Bombay. Plans and rescheduling for the tour "down under" could now go forward. He and Wilder had earlier cabled, "Asia's crisis demands thousands mountain-removing Volunteers" to the Liverpool gathering.

Mott as tourist marvelled at the Taj—it "cost about $10,000,000—a perfect structure," the tomb being "the finest piece of architecture I ever saw or expect to see." Superlatives failed him; it was quite impossible to describe it to the folks at home. He and Leila bought a small alabaster model and photographs. These monuments far surpassed "in real elegance any European royal palaces we have seen." Yet in India there were fifty million people in a perpetual state of hunger: "in the villages and cities we have ourselves seen multitudes of this class." The gospel was making more rapid strides than the rise in population, and doing so among both lower and educated classes: "my work among the students of the country has enabled me to see this." At St. John's College in Agra he addressed about 200 students, half of whom were Hindus or Muslims. If there had been time and energy he could have had a constant stream of persons coming to him to talk about Christ and Christianity: "in no other country have I seen such eagerness to converse about religious themes."

The second Mott conference was held at Lahore (then in India) where the host was a professor at the American Presbyterian College. Cam White came from Calcutta to assist. Attendance rose to 100 Indian students and teachers, 60 foreign missionaries, and over 50 Indian workers; there were 16 conversions and 20 decisions for Christian work among their own peoples. Mott repeated with suitable adaptations the address he had given at Keswick and at Jaffna on "Bible Study for Spiritual Growth," one of a half-dozen talks utilized throughout this tour that were repeated with various adaptations. If the real test of our discipleship is the quality of our life, he challenged, it cannot be met "apart from devotional Bible study." Replete with biblical citations and biographical examples, the argument moved with relentless logic, beginning with the relevance of his subject to his hearers "as Christians," as Christian teachers, as Christian workers, and as Christian leaders. Hindrances to such a program, especially "lack of time," were ridiculed because everywhere he went men and women claimed to be busier than elsewhere: if it is the will of God that I am to grow spirtually, then "there is time to study the Bible"— the Bible itself, not books about it. Some are afraid to study it, afraid of the light! "How unscientific and cowardly!" As to approaches, there are many. Moody had suggested study of the great doctrines; Mott and his Cornell roommate worked on the idea of the Holy Spirit for a year and found it almost inexhaustible. Prayer, the Kingdom of God, or—a life-long pursuit of Mott's—the reading of biography has "always proved stimulating to the spiritual life." But the most important course is the study of Jesus Christ:

One day in Edinburgh I asked Professor Drummond to name three courses of study which might be recommended to Christians for spiritual profit. After a few moments of thought he replied: 'I would recommend they study, first, the Life of Jesus Christ; secondly, the Life of Jesus Christ; and, thirdly, the Life of Jesus Christ.' He is right. It takes us to the very heart of the subject. Pre-eminent and essential for the spiritual life is the constant and devout study of Christ Himself. [46]

The autobiographical character of this testimony must have fallen on his hearers as if Drummond himself had uttered it, for Mott would more than once be called the "lineal descendant" of Drummond.

For effective study a biblical subject should be broken into suitable daily subdivisions. One ought to study and meditate alone, keeping his spiritual need uppermost, concentrating to avoid sidetracks, being thorough, meditating on the meaning of the words, and finally writing down his findings. Study and meditation must be in "an earnest or intense spirit," dependent upon the Holy Spirit, in a prayerful, childlike, obedient, and practical mood: "All that the Lord hath spoken we will do." Study should be daily, regular, unhurried, at "the very choicest time in the day." Several years earlier Mott had learned of the Morning Watch Movement at Cambridge and had adopted this plan "of spending the first half hour or first hour of the day alone with God."

... I firmly believe that it is the best time in the day. The mind is less occupied. The mind is, as a rule, clearer, and the memory more retentive. But forget these reasons if you choose. The whole case may be staked on this argument: it equips a man for the day's fight with self and sin and Satan. He does not wait until noon before he buckles on his armor. [47]

Citing eight great men who, like John Quincy Adams, found early morning Bible study "the most suitable manner of beginning the day," Mott, doubtless inwardly reliving his recent hilltop experiences in the Holy Land, reminded his hearers that Christ "rose a great while before it was day to hold communion with God." What He found necessary or even desirable can we do without? "Spirituality costs. Shall we pay what it costs?" At the Lahore meetings 157 took up the challenge.

En route to the third conference Mott stopped at Saharanpur to address the students at the Presbyterian Theological Seminary and at Bareilly to speak before the Methodist Seminary, "probably the largest to be found on the foreign field." Two hundred delegates came to the American Methodist center at Lucknow. The obvious success of the several enterprises there—these Methodists were second only to the Anglicans among Protestants in India at this time—seemed to Mott to challenge the churches at home to greater efforts. It was from such first-hand contacts that he built his vast knowledge of the missionary enterprise and constructed the arguments in support of it that would equip him increasingly as a missionary statesman.

In the interval between the Lucknow conference and the fourth one at Calcutta, the Motts visited Benares, "the Jerusalem of India," and Darjeeling where they saw "the most magnificent mountain scenery of this world." Mott described it to his sister Hattie:

> The great Kinchinjanga peak rises to an altitude of 28156 feet above twice as high as the highest mountains we have seen in Switzerland or America. Although this giant peak and its neighboring peaks were 45 miles distant they did not seem a mile off. . . . The upper 17000 feet were snow covered. We obtained our best views at and just before sunrise. After sunrise the clouds often at this season of the year rise and obscure the peaks. The last morning we were there I took a horse and rode about 6 miles to Senchal, 2400 feet higher than Darjeeling, from which place I had a view of Mount Everest, the highest mountain in all the world, 29,002 feet high. Think of a mountain over five miles high. It was 115 miles distant—further off than Cedar Rapids is from Postville—and yet it loomed up as distinctly as if it were five miles away. It is vain to attempt a description of this marvellous mountain scenery. It is equally impossible to describe the emotions which it awakens.

The mountain air braced them for the last few weeks in India. Mott, fascinated by the Tibetan, almost Chinese features of the people, visited a Buddhist temple where he succeeded in buying an ancient book from a priest and later a prayer wheel from Tibet: "The more I see of the religions of the East the more disgusted I become with them, and the more firmly do I become convinced that Christianity is the only true and sufficient religion."

Back in Calcutta the thermometer was "up to white heat." Mott gave the address at brother Cam White's new YMCA's second birthday party, a celebration presided over by Sir Alexander MacKenzie, Lieutenant Governor of Bengal, "who rules over more people than the president of the United States." The Association needed a building desperately: Mott gave White references in Britain which the latter pursued with signal success. The more than 240 delegates who came to the Calcutta conference represented 25 colleges and 27 missionary societies; 101 decided to keep the morning watch. They listened to an opening address by J. Hudson Taylor, founder of the China Inland Mission, and to Mott on Bible study, the secret prayer life, and personal purity. After a whirl of sightseeing, convention business, receptions and teas ("we work so hard at visiting," wrote Leila), the Motts took ship—"the most restful place in the world"—for a quiet four-day voyage to Madras, where the final conference and follow-up national organizational meetings were to be held.

The fifth conference was opened by Wilder with an address on "The Perils of a Conference," followed by Mott's description of the Federation; his usual introductory remarks, everywhere on the tour, were the greetings from the American, British, and Continental student conferences:

> As I bring you this message from the students of the West, I wish I could convey to your minds all that it means. Among other things, I trust it impresses you with the fact that you are not alone. You are bound up in the interest and sympathy and prayers of the students of many lands. The students of the East and West have a community of thought life, of temptations and perils, of spiritual aspirations and purposes. We have one Bible and one Saviour. The spiritual solidarity of the student Christian world is indeed a fact. . . . The most signal fact of recent years in the Christian college world is the formation of the World's Student Christian Federation. It unites the five great intercollegiate Christian movements of the world.[48]

Mott then sketched the history and current activities of each of the national movements and the founding conference at Vadstena. Some separate sessions were held for men and women, Leila speaking at one on the history, achievements, and program of the YWCA. John developed an infected tooth which was pulled in time for him to preside at an important evening session, but shortly afterward he was taken with the "Indian fever." Fortunately the next day was Sunday and he could rest until an afternoon men's meeting, at which against the advice of friends he gave the final address—"the old talk on Personal Purity," he called it in a letter to Beaver, adding that it was "needed on every street corner (I had almost written in every home) in India." The Spirit had worked in spite of his weakness, thirty-two students accepting Christ. As anticipated, this proved to be the largest of the five conferences in India, with 300 students present, although the entire planning group including Leila had beaten the bushes in the neighboring schools for several days to obtain them. Four hundred persons came; there were 170 morning watch decisions. Mott's temperature rose to 103 degrees and the doctor ordered him to "get on the ocean as soon as possible."

PART 9: The Intercollegiate YMCA of India and Ceylon Joins the Federation

The five conferences in India, attended by 759 students from 120 schools—more than at all of the European meetings of the past summer—and by representatives of "nearly all" of the sixty missionary organizations at work in India, were really but preliminary steps toward a national student Christian union, the establishment of which Mott considered to be "of more far-reaching importance." Duly appointed delegates met through parts of three days around the sick beds of Mott and Max Wood Moorhead, one of the Mount Hermon Volunteers, whose fevers continued. An Intercollegiate Young Men's Christian Association was proposed, to be under the auspices of the Indian National Council of the YMCA with strong committee supervision by prominent Indians and several westerners including Campbell White. Mott proposed that India and Ceylon form a unified body on the pattern of the American-Canadian relationship. Delegates had come from Ceylon empowered to authorize such a move, and the Intercollegiate YMCA of India and Ceylon came into being.[49]

The first act of the new organization was to request membership in the World's Student Christian Federation. After "carefully inspecting" the dozen local Associations—this activity had consumed large blocks of his time throughout the eleven weeks in India—and following "thorough consultation with the Council" (apparently from his sick-bed), and after observing the vitality of the Indian Movement as manifested in the five conferences, Mott was "fully convinced that all the conditions laid down by the Federation for the admission of a movement had been fully met." Two Indian leaders, Kali Churn Banurji of Calcutta and S. Satthianadhan of Madras, were appointed to represent the new body on the General Committee of the Federation, where they were to exert significant leadership. Thus the sixth constituent member of the Federation was added, placing the Christian students of India and Ceylon "on an equal footing with those of Britain, Germany, Scandinavia, and America."

The interest in home mission service at all of the conferences had been so great that the leadership planned to organize it at these meetings, to which some delegates had traveled more than 2,000 miles. The result was the Student Volunteer Movement of India and Ceylon, organized like the American SVM. It planned another series of conferences for the next winter, projected a prayer cycle, composed a declaration, authorized local bands to affiliate as departments of college Associations where possible, and set up a program of publications beginning with a 150-page verbatim report of the 28 addresses given at the six conferences starting with Jaffna.[50] Mott and his colleagues believed that this move would have a salutary effect upon the evangelization of the whole world in their generation.

From Madras Leila Mott took her sick husband to Tuticorin, a 30-hour trip by train, March 5–6, in a first-class compartment that was protected against the glare of the sun by tinted glass. He could lie down but they both suffered from the intense heat, though the night became tolerable. They were met and taken to a hotel while awaiting the steamer to Colombo. Upon arrival there they went at once to a resort on the shore where they rested until sailing for Australia on March 8.

Four months later Mott summarized his "dominant impressions." He had come to India "somewhat disposed to look upon educational mission work as less important than directly evangelistic work" but now attached "the greatest possible importance" to education. Nothing in India had impressed him more than the four leading colleges he had seen: Duff, Forman, Lucknow Christian College for Women, and the Madras Christian College. More and more, he concluded, India will be governed and its thought life molded by the student class: the burning question is whether this will be heathen, agnostic, or Christian. For it to be Christian there must be "a great increase in the number of Christian workers among students" and of educational missionaries. The religions of India are a colossal failure; study of the social changes there during the past century will show that every great reform is traceable to the influence of Christianity. "The strongest testimonies to the civilizing and transforming power of Christianity I have ever heard were certain references made by Hindus at the Indian Social Congress." As a mission field India is accessible, dead ripe, and critical: "a forward movement all along the line should be planned and executed." But he warned prospective Volunteers that "the most thorough preparation is essential for a life-work in India." With David McConaughy in mind he cautioned that it must be undertaken only by men who know from personal experience the meaning of being "filled up to their present capacity with the Holy Spirit." Others "had far better not come to India to work."[51]

Thirty-two years afterward, one of Mott's converts on this tour, S. K. Datta, who had been convinced "by the irresistible logic and reasonableness of the thing as he presented it," evaluated the visit:

He came to us... as a new discoverer of the East—of its needs, yes, but more—he made the discovery that there might be those in the East who could themselves make a contribution to the cause of Christ. There were those who insisted that the East would never change, never respond to the Christian appeal. He knew better, and insisted that the opportunity must be given to the East.[52]

4

Students of the World United: Australasia, China, and Japan

A sense of mission that could not be mistaken was written on his face.

T HE 7,000-TON P. & O. *Himalaya* gave the Motts a "perfect voyage" over unusually smooth seas to Adelaide, South Australia. Mrs. Taylor and companion had gone on to China and home. Luxuriating in "absolute rest" after the strain of India, the Motts enjoyed food "always just as good as the day the boat left London," because of a new refrigeration system at which John marvelled; he and Leila read novels and books on Australia from the ship's library and visited with fellow-passengers among whom some gold-seekers fascinated them. They took little part in the deck games and remained aloof from the "dancing, gambling, drinking, smoking and card-playing" that went on "constantly."

John's fever, which rose every afternoon and left him "utterly weak and worthless," finally disappeared soon after the ship crossed the equator, almost as if in response to the gradual temperature drop from 85 degrees at Ceylon to 60 off the south coast of Australia. Leila noted that the passengers were very kind "in consideration of John's pallor." She wrote the home letters to Postville for him, not mentioning his illness, but describing it to her own family with the caution that Mother Mott would worry if she heard. Then, as if she had been challenged for neglecting John Livingstone by leaving him home, she added that she had "never been surer" that she ought to be with her husband. "I don't know what would have happened if he had been alone when he had the fever," she added, but the patient himself wrote Gilbert Beaver that the pressures in India had been "simply terriffic as you will judge when you receive the report letters. I suppose I never had a heavier 2 months schedule even at home"; correspondence had to wait two months and he had been taken with the "treacherous Indian fever." Asking Beaver not to mention the illness lest relatives and others worry, Mott requested

155

prayers that "we may care better for the temple of the Holy Spirit, and also that we may be specially shielded in the terrible climate and exposure" through the East Indies and in China, since that would be "by all odds the most perilous of our tour." Had the Indian experience cooled his ardor for a missionary career in that country?

PART 1: **Australia in 1896**

The Australasian endeavor was to be unique in Mott's career. In India he had been met, guided, and briefed by American or British Volunteers, YMCA men, and older missionaries who arranged his itineraries, entertained him and Leila, and often accompanied them in travel. That prototype tour would be repeated again and again, ten times in Japan for example, throughout his "life of travel" as he would refer to his career forty years and two million miles later.

When John and Leila Mott landed at Adelaide on March 21, 1896, no one met them, although they had received favorable replies while in India from "prominent men in Australia and New Zealand" to whom letters of inquiry had been sent from Norway. A Mrs. Goode and a Baptist pastor with whom they had become acquainted on the *Paramatta* were the only persons they knew. It had not been possible to write ahead to make the usual contacts. They got through customs, though not without a struggle, and to a hotel recommended by a fellow passenger, to be shocked by what seemed exorbitant charges compared with those in India or at home. Yet within a week they were being entertained in the highest social and religious circles of the colony and welcomed at the colleges and university. John's first letter to Postville told how *unexpectedly* busy they were. Mott's person and credentials were so persuasively harmonious with this transplanted Victorian evangelical culture, in spite of some feeling against Americans, that they might almost as well have been at Keswick, Liverpool, London, or Edinburgh.

The key that opened Australia to them was the YMCA. Forty years before the Motts arrived in Adelaide, young men of the type the original YMCA and its founder George Williams had aimed at were finding emigration "down under" to be attractive; many of them came of missionary families, and as Clyde Binfield points out in his biography of Williams, the YMCA was "international and not merely British, European, or American." As the concept of empire began to stir the British people, those who migrated included some of the first families of the London YMCA.[1] When, after a week at the hotel where they worked hard on correspondence and reports, the Motts accepted the hospitality of Mr. and Mrs. Charles H. Goode, they learned that Goode had been a member of the original London Association and was the first president of the Adelaide body, the first one outside of London, in 1880.[2] To their surprise and delight they found that he had also attended the great 1894 Jubilee; the exchange of impressions of Sir George Williams may be imagined. Previous guests in this decidedly Victorian home of a successful wholesale merchant, Baptist deacon, Sunday School teacher, and patron of all good causes (the pun was intentional) had been J. Hudson Taylor, General Booth, and George Mueller—proof that Australia was now on the world evangelistic circuit, and that part of Mott's acceptance was in that role; he was also there at the request of the British Student Christian Movement. When the Motts left Adelaide after two weeks, the farewell party at the railway station included some of the most prominent citizens of the colony.

The Motts visited Australia in a post-depression era. By 1896 the economy was beginning to recover from the "three catastrophes" that had brought a "sudden and painful end" to the post-gold-rush "land boom"—"the great strike, the great depression, and the great drought." Between 1891 and 1894 unemployment had risen to unheard-of heights and most banks had failed, suspended, or reconstructed: the drought lasted until 1902. These conditions rendered Mott's modest fund-raising efforts somewhat remarkable, small as they may appear in retrospect. He found university budgets and student bodies smaller than usual, with few scholarships available and many forced to study in evening schools.[3]

By the 1890's the idea of a single Australian nation was beginning to become popular, although it would not be accomplished until 1901. An increasing majority of the people had by then been born and raised there, Western imperialism was bringing international rivalries perilously close, and the cultural upsurge of the nineties, especially in literature, gave Australians their first recognizable image of themselves as a unique people rather than as mere colonials. Mott's familiarity with Canada prepared him to endorse the federation idea, and doubtless the youth who responded enthusiastically to his call for an intercolonial student union affiliated with the WSCF were motivated by nationalistic and universalistic ideals. The Australasian Student Christian Union was to lead a long and vigorous life during which it would contribute significantly to the world movement.

Australia had not had a distinctive religious history. By the mid-1890's the Salvation Army and the Seventh-Day Adventists had reached there, but no Great Awakening had ever aroused the colonies; nor was there a "burned-over district." Yet Mott would receive a far greater response to his own evangelistic overtures than he expected, suggesting that the churches were still well within the evangelical stream. About one-fourth of the population was Irish Roman Catholic, with about sixty percent "census Anglican." The principal remaining denominations were the Presbyterian, the wealthiest, and the Methodist, which probably had the best church attendance. In both Australia and New Zealand it had been necessary to separate church and state and to base the public schools and universities on secular assumptions, decisions that rankled the churches for generations and forced the development of inexpensive Catholic parochial schools and costly Protestant "colleges," clustered around some of the public universities. These "colleges," in which the Motts labored prodigiously, were, in effect, somewhere between the great public schools of Britain and American private preparatory schools; they served chiefly as feeders to the universities or as "finishing schools." Mott saw them as strategic to his mission; when he returned in 1903 and in 1926 he recognized many in positions of leadership who had come up through the Unions in these "colleges." Both he and Leila noted that the colonial young people did more thinking for themselves and were more independent than those with whom they had previously worked; Mott therefore did not hesitate to organize Unions that enrolled boys and girls of fourteen and fifteen years. Toward the end of his life he frequently expressed the wish that he had devoted more attention to this age group.

In none of the colonies had the denominations possessed the means to furnish the equivalent of the American church-related college that had been such a prominent feature of the nineteenth-century Western landscape. The Australian situation was much more comparable to that of central California—with which Mott was familiar—where the gold-rush philosophy obtained and only one church college survived. Also, unlike their counterparts in the United States, the public universities did not reflect the dominant Protestant climate, which brought out Mott's remark that he was forced to feel his way at every place visited: "rationalist" would probably describe the prevalent attitude. In Australia the denominations did establish some elementary schools, the high schools or "colleges" just noted, and theological colleges.

PART 2: Adelaide, "City of Churches"

Throughout their stay in Australia the Motts were constantly reminded of the States—California, San Francisco, Denver, perhaps Canada.

"There was a push and stir about things which seemed very American—and the voices seemed more American than English" in Adelaide, the "city of churches," a "bright, attractive city." It was also hot, and on the Sabbath, wonderfully quiet—"so good after no Sabbath in India." The marvelous berries and fruits, all of which had been avoided in India, were a tonic to John. Hotel meals, albeit expensive, were excellent in contrast even to the fine ship fare they had enjoyed; when apple pie and cream came on, he burst out with "Praise the Lord!" Above all, "the proverbial hospitality of this great southern land" was the most remarkable feature of their stay "down under." Noted in every letter home, in each report, in almost every diary entry, and repeated in *Strategic Points in the World's Conquest,* John's book-length description of the tour—, it grew until the final send-off from Sydney, 11,000 miles after Adelaide, was almost a public ceremony—a foretaste of the future.

At the first opportunity Mott presented himself to the Reverend David Paton, pastor of the Chalmers Street Presbyterian Church of Adelaide, who promptly took him to call on the Chief Justice of South Australia, doubtless the Colony's leading Protestant layman, the Honorable Samuel James Way, a prominent member of the Adelaide YMCA, who invited the Motts to dinner at his home the next evening. At this very enjoyable affair the conversation centered for some time on "the merits of W. T. Stead"; the event caused Leila to write home that "all along the way we have introductions to people at the top of the heap." She hoped they would not become "highminded," as a Wooster professor had once warned. "John appreciates all these things for what they mean to the work." She liked them for the opportunity "to see the inside life and how to do things." The necessity of formal dress at many affairs might amuse her Ohio relatives but "the English people care more than the Americans for the customs of their ancestors" and the Australians "haven't been away from the customs of their mother country as long as we have." In any case, John looked "stunning" in dress suit and silk hat, which "one must wear in the evening or be considered not a gentleman perhaps." His health was now normal but he tired easily.

The Adelaide University Christian Union had been in existence since 1890. Mott revived and reorganized it, beginning at a meeting chaired by the Chief Justice; the Governor could not attend and sent his regrets. In accordance with Australian custom, Mott was applauded "fifty times if he was once." The Anglican bishop proposed a vote of thanks—another Australian custom—and was followed by several speeches supporting the motion, one of which was by the famous missionary doctor John D. Paton of the New Hebrides. Mott reported to Postville that his meetings in Adelaide were "very successful"; he had founded new Unions in three other colleges. The Chief Justice arranged a breakfast at his home to which he invited "twelve prominent men" to meet Mott, presided at another public gathering (at which Mott gave his address "Is Christianity losing its hold on the students of the world?"), entertained the Motts twice more, and became the chairman of the Advisory Committee of the new Australasian Student Christian Union, to be organized in early June. Further addresses and tutelage with student groups demanded much of Mott, while Leila spoke at several girls' schools and on her thirtieth birthday, April first, meditated on Luke 3:23. On the final day of their stay, J. J. Virgo, secretary of the YMCA, took them on an exhilarating fifteen-mile drive into the country behind a lively team of black horses; at a pause in the conversation he asked if they were acquainted with a Professor White, of Chicago, whom he would like to bring to Australia![4] At the railway station some fourteen persons saw them off to Melbourne. "It hardly seems possible," Leila wrote in her diary, "that two weeks ago we came to Adelaide as absolute strangers. These people seemed like old friends."

PART 3: Ten Days in Melbourne

The overnight trip to Melbourne via Ballarat was enjoyed in the seclusion of an American Pullman compartment. Customs were a farce, Leila wondering if it were because they appeared travel-stained. Taking a carriage to the Grand Hotel (later the Windsor), modern with electric lights and elevator, and situated opposite Parliament House in the heart of this "Chicago of Australia," the Motts were prepared to protect themselves from too much hospitality, a rule to be adhered to increasingly whenever possible. Melbourne, they thought, with its cable cars, attractive shops, its "push and go," could have been set down "any place in America without being recognized as an exotic."

They were hardly in their room when a student called and after tea took John to meet a committee at the university, where there had been an "Alliance" a few years earlier. It was Mott's good fortune to appear when a movement was on foot to revive it. He brought his messages from the students of the West, of India and Ceylon, and of Adelaide. Before the end of this brief ten-day stay—the Motts would return for an inter-colonial conference in Melbourne after their tour of Tasmania, New Zealand, and New South Wales—a new Christian Union would be fully organized at the University of Melbourne. Doubtless it was here that the secular spirit which Mott characterized as the strongest he had ever encountered, not excepting the state universities of the American West, set up a barrier that fell only after "a bitter fight"—words normally absent from the Mott vocabulary:

> In one university the chancellor was opposed even to my speaking in the university buildings. He finally consented on the following conditions: "(1) That no matters of dogma or religious controversy shall be touched upon; (2) that the lecture shall not be given under the auspices of any organization; (3) that there shall be no prayers or singing of hymns before, during, or after the lecture." He also added that he wished me "to do nothing which would in any way interfere with the secular character of the university." Despite his restrictions one of the most powerful organizations in the colonies has been effected in this university. The Christian students petitioned the authorities for the privilege of holding religious meetings in university buildings. The secularist and Roman Catholic parties combined to prevent the granting of the request. After a bitter fight, prolonged through three meetings of the board of governors, the Christian forces won by a vote of eleven to seven.[5]

A union was also formed at Ormond Theological College, and women's groups at the University of Melbourne and the Presbyterian Ladies College.

From the moment of their arrival in India the Motts had slipped further and further behind in their correspondence, report writing, and editing of John's addresses. Three full days were devoted to it in Melbourne, with "some help" from a stenographer enabling them to post eighty-three letters just prior to leaving for Tasmania. Somehow they sandwiched in a few social engagements, one to a suburban vicarage whose resemblance to an English home prompted Leila to confide to her diary that "these cold damp drawing rooms with dark carpets and dark paper on the walls chill my very heart," though this one had been made remarkably attractive with large showy flowers and an open fire. English church people usually said grace before being seated at table; she rather liked the custom. Next day, while John worked with students at the University, Leila received an uncle of J. Livingstone Taylor and "a fine little woman of the Keswick type" who came to ask John to speak at the Wesleyan mission church.

On April 13, 1896, after final preparations for the intercolonial student conference that John hoped and prayed would eventuate from his work and at the end of "a day in a whirl," the Motts took ship for Tasmania. Leila reported to Wooster that

We knew what was coming and got into bed about six. It was none too soon. The little boat began to creak and heave. I intended to read aloud awhile but soon gave that up. I didn't dare to get up to put out the light. The trunk came out from under the bunk and everything began to move. Tin pans were suggestively stuck on each bed. John was sick all night. I held myself together by being very quiet. We hardly slept any.

By morning the ship had emerged from "the boiling cauldron" to cruise quietly up the Tamar River to Launceston. Peaceful, green, fresh meadows and hills on both sides were reminiscent of Ireland. There would be several more such ordeals before they could return to the mainland, but there was no suggestion of complaint or thought of staying home. In fact, they were very happy. John wrote Hattie that he had been "as sick as I ever was," but added that "you are over it the moment you run into still water, or the moment you get on land." Even these episodes would pale into insignificance in contrast to crossing the South Atlantic in 1906. The afternoon train trip to Hobart was a pleasant run through country Mott thought much more beautiful than the mainland he had seen, because it was more wooded; he rejoiced in the fine pears and world-famous apples (he had "enjoyed the apple pies in Australia and Tasmania more than any other of their many good things"), and now that it was autumn the blackberries were also abundant.

He had no apparent success whatever at the university in Hobart, though two representatives were to come to the Melbourne Conference, there being too few students and insufficient interest to consider a Union. The Motts learned that there were only twenty students in the University and that disbandment was being considered. "The sons are taken up with business and gold fever." But it chanced that the Anglican Synod of Tasmania was in session and the bishop asked Mott to speak informally on the SVM at a "conversazione," at which "they hurled questions fast." The outcome was a letter of introduction to the bishops of New Zealand.

PART 4: Dunedin and Christchurch, New Zealand

From Thursday night to Monday morning en route to New Zealand John and Leila Mott endured separate miseries, there being no double cabin available. It was "a cold trip and not stormy but rough enough to keep us humble and in our bunks," and to be compared to the North Sea at its worst. The motion was "something between a pitch and a roll," Saturday was "a horrid seasick day," and no meals were taken after the first dinner when the ship was still in port. John wrote to Hattie, from on land, that if with her fragile health she were ever tempted to wish herself along, she would hardly want to face the sea after a thorough shaking up, and should therefore rejoice in her present lot. "We are having great opportunities and privileges but as in everything else we have to pay the price. Still our God is so good that we should never complain whether abroad or at home." But, he added, "the spiritual state of the Australasian colonies is certainly low. There is need of a great spiritual awakening here."

Although the tone of New Zealand society was essentially Protestant, it was also, as Mott came to realize, "a simple materialism."[6] Colonized originally by Scots Presbyterians at Dunedin and Anglicans at Christchurch, these bodies, together with the Methodists, had impressed their value-systems on the new country; their puritanical and evangelical values were still significantly dominant in 1896. "How good it is to be among them [the Scotch] again," wrote Leila. The New Zealand form of secularism was explained to the Motts by a Dunedin pastor:

> The first settlers were Scotch who came out soon after the Disruption, with all the bitterness of the fierce controversy in them. They were domineering and narrow. Then came the rush of gold seekers made up of all sorts. Inevitably there was friction. They had to live together. So there came about both by the reaction from extreme rigidity and the new element— this fear of religious influence which has come to be a kind of vaunting secularism.[7]

The controversy, which continued through many years, had been especially pointed over the issue of religious instruction in the public schools,[8] and at the time of the Motts' visit was being freshly fueled by the mounting attacks on orthodoxy by the new theories of evolution, biblical criticism, and the nature of revelation—the British debates on which were read avidly in the colonies. Mott tended to avoid controversial issues, but at one university which he did not identify,

> I was respectfully challenged by certain science students to answer publicly questions bearing on the Christian faith. I accepted. All the students of that science faculty were present. It afforded one of the best opportunities of my life for setting forth informally the grounds and claims of Christianity. The meeting resulted in much earnest conversation and, we trust, in settling the conviction of some who were drifting.[9]

The New Zealand churches had sufficient vitality to carry on a vigorous missionary program, especially toward the Pacific Islands and to some extent in Asia; in the 1890's a few clergymen were active in humanitarrian crusades chiefly against sweated labor.[10] That the Protestant population was still strongly motivated by evangelicalism was evidenced by the large turnouts to Mott's popular meetings and the instant response he elicited from students.

Upon arrival in the South Island Monday morning, April 20, a good hotel breakfast (for two shillings) at Invercargil provided "as square a meal as our weak stomachs would stand" and strengthened them for the expensive (five cents a mile) all-day train trip through productive country in full harvest which they compared to Scotland "with the advantage to New Zealand." As always Mott was sensitive to where he was: the sun rose in the northeast and progressed across the northern sky, setting in the northwest; on the southern island of New Zealand they were the farthest south they had ever been or probably would ever be, he wrote home. Moments after arrival in Dunedin he called on two educators and next morning enlisted students to get out invitations to his first meeting, which would be the following night. One of them, A. T. Thompson,[11] later to share in the founding of two colleges, met Mott at the edge of the campus:

> Well does the present writer as a freshman of Otago University, Dunedin, remember an autumn afternoon in 1896. He was on his way to a Mathematics Lecture, and had just reached the Campus Gate when, at its entrance, there descended from a hansom cab, a tall young man, of strong frame, and commanding presence. A sense of mission that could not be mistaken, was written on his face. He came straight towards me. It was his mission, as I soon learned, to capture young students. "Are you a student at this place? Well perhaps you could kindly show me the way to the Registrar's Office." Thus, quite by accident, the honour of being the first New Zealand Student to meet the now world-famed John R. Mott, fell to my lot. The following Sunday was spent in his company—a rare privilege, never to be forgotten.[12]

The twentieth-century ecumenical movement was built in part by just such seemingly casual contacts, multiplied scores and hundreds of times throughout Mott's career. At the first session in Dunedin the vice-chancellor presided over an audience of some one hundred students; the meeting took initial steps toward the formation of a Union. Next day the New Zealand Presbyterian *Outlook* asked for a written interview; in addition to preparing it Leila wrote to the tenth reunion of her Wooster College class. Recapitulating the trip, she emphasized the deep impression "the intense, courageous, beautiful faces of the little bands of missionaries in India" had made upon her, and the beauty of New Zealand which she had been told was less than sixty years removed from cannibalism. In writing home the same day she regretted being unable to reune with her classmates, but preferred "to be here with my husband":

> We were just saying last night how happy we are. This is not that we do not care for home and long to see you all, but we have *no doubt* this is where the Lord wants us just now and we are being led every step of the way so surely and so kindly. We came here as strangers—nobody we had ever seen before—but we are already among friends.

She added that as they were leaving Hobart a parcel had come from "a dear old lady in Melbourne whom I had seen only once. It was a blue serge, flannel lined wrapper to wear at sea. What do you think of being treated like that in a strange land?"

The process of forming Unions in the preparatory schools began with a lengthy evening meeting with students of Otago Boys' High School who "adopted the Adelaide constitution bodily and elected officers." Next was an organization at St. John's (Theological) College. On Sunday afternoon Mott spoke to seven or eight hundred men at the Dunedin City Hall on "Impurity," while Leila took a class at the YMCA mission Sunday School where she told of their visit to Jacob's well and of other experiences in Palestine. In the evening John spoke to a crowded house in St. Andrew's Presbyterian Church on "Personal Work." Next morning, when the Motts departed for Christchurch, all eight theological students "were at the train enmasse" together with other students and perhaps a dozen newly made friends. Mott wrote his father that they had been "most heartily welcomed everywhere in New Zealand although we did not know a living soul anywhere" upon arrival.

While in Dunedin, Mott had received an invitation from three students of Canterbury College, Christchurch, asking him to visit; they met the Motts. One of them, a Maori named Kohere, recognized Mott at the station from a description he had read two years earlier in the English *Our Boys Magazine*. He and another student had initiated a petition signed by seventy students requesting the "Liverpool delegation"—of which they had read in the *Gleaners* magazine—to come to New Zealand, hoping that Mott might be sent. The letter he received was a proposal that the Otago University students also circulate a petition. Mott replied that he would be in Christchurch shortly. Kohere had opened a luncheon conversation with Leila by asking whether Robert E. Speer had played football, and all this information had followed. Mott later cited the incident as a remarkable example of the power of prayer, especially since it had occurred during a period of diplomatic stress be-

tween Great Britain and the United States over the Venezuela boundary
when there was considerable anti-American sentiment in New Zealand.[13]

The Canterbury students had obtained the college hall for Mott's
opening meeting, a precedent-breaking move: the chairman of the board
of governors presided over what proved to be the largest first meeting yet
in Australasia. The motion of thanks was made by the Anglican bishop
and steps toward a Union begun. Leila went to bed with a cold, which
yielded to treatment with eucalyptus oil so that she could attend a dinner
with the bishop next evening. At the Lincoln Agricultural College a
Union was "organized in four hours." The three petitioners accompanied
the Motts on the train to Lyttleton as they left for Wellington; a delayed
sailing provided an evening of fellowship. Leila commented in her diary
that "for a descendant of cannibals" Kohere was "a fine specimen of
Christian manhood." She was impressed by his desire to teach in the
Maori Divinity School and to be "an evangelist among the Maoris."

PART 5: Three Days in Auckland

En route to Auckland, a one-night stop-over in Wellington (where the
best hotel afforded only a single narrow bed) gave Mott the opportunity
to speak on the Federation to "a fine audience" of more than a thousand
in St. John's Presbyterian Church where the singing was "hearty and
good." The next day's long train trip was through forests of trees "completely covered with creepers and parasitic plants," the nearest Leila had
come to a jungle but thought a "tropical and temperate zone forest
united" a better description. Reading for the day was the story of the
Fiske Jubilee Singers. At Wanganui they put up at what had been recommended as the best hotel, but "living and dead flies were too numerous about the table and even in the bread"—the worst in New Zealand so
far. A walk over the hills, with views of mountains and sea, was bracing.
They met an Irishman from Belfast who took John for a Dublin man:

> When we told him we were from America he said he had heard that was as
> dangerous a place as one could come from, that there were places in New
> York where one could not go after night for they would think nothing of
> knocking you over. John told him he was right and that very few people got
> out of America alive.

The journey to Auckland was completed by ship, overnight in separate
cabins, "rocky" until the harbor was entered in a pouring rain.

Met by the Presbyterian pastor, T. F. Robertson, and the YMCA secretary, William Brakenrig, they picked up thirty letters and many papers and settled in at the Bella Vista Hotel, "a good boarding house," for three hours of solid enjoyment of home and other news which after "all these weary weeks of waiting... fairly made us dizzy." John did not feel well enough to speak to the Diocesan Church Congress but next morning began a week that rushed at what was becoming normal Mott pace. His first meeting at Auckland University College was at 11:00, with the Primate of New Zealand, the Right Reverend William Gordon Cowie, presiding. Student attendance was disappointing, but a reporter called Mott's talk "fluent and decidedly interesting and instructive." Lunch was taken with the bishop.

> John spent the afternoon investigating Auckland College and the Wesleyan Prince Albert College. He found only fifty regular undergraduate students in Auckland college and not enough Christian timber on which to found an Association. No sympathy from the Faculty.

In the evening he met some students at the YMCA and at the request of the Primate spoke briefly at the final session of the Church Congress. Next morning he went early to St. John's Theological College and organized its eight students into a Union; later that day he did the same at the Wesleyan Theological College. In the afternoon Leila went horseback riding eleven miles to and around Lake Tahapuna with a "little earnest Christian girl who hopes to go to China" as a missionary. Next day her back "and some other places too" were a bit sore. The following day the Motts visited the Maori exhibits at the museum, marvelling at the "very elaborately carved war canoe 84 feet long" which had been fashioned with stone axes and fire, and the houses and other artifacts that remain the pride of that unique collection. That evening John spoke on "The Great Missionary Uprising among Young Men and Women" in the YMCA hall. Sunday he gave "a powerful and eloquent address" on "Purity" to 700 men at City Hall; they listened "with the utmost attention." Leila spoke to about 150 women at the YWCA on their experiences in Constantinople and Palestine. At night he gave an "impressive" discourse again in City Hall, an evangelistic appeal developed on the theme "I am not ashamed of the gospel of Christ." In aftermeetings that day some twenty "accepted Christ. It was a great day."

Monday there was a trip to the summit of Mt. Eden: "We have seen no other city which commands such a view." At a tea both Motts were accorded speeches of welcome and thanks. John spent the evening "trying to get some ideas and convictions on organization" into the heads of some Auckland College students; he must have succeeded because delegates came to the Melbourne Conference, their expenses met by funds he raised in Auckland. The next day there was a joint meeting of the Unions of the two theological schools to which he gave his address on Bible study, which was really an outline of that movement program. Sandwiched in between these scheduled activities there were conferences with individual students, luncheons, teas, and seemingly endless visits to church or Association-sponsored institutions, fund-raising, or letter writing.

John told his Iowa family that New Zealand compared very favorably with "the best parts of the British Empire," and that they had been "splendidly received." This section of the tour had been "all and much more than we had expected," there having been five student Unions planted where previously there had been none. He had witnessed an ecumenical advance in the uniting of Wesleyans, Bible Christians, and Free Methodists, which might well set an example elsewhere such as in the United States. Educational and religious matters were "far advanced" in the colony. He hoped the threat of war between America and Spain would be settled amicably.

He wrote Gilbert Beaver pointed directions to insure that the American origins of the WSCF be clearly stated in all releases, for he had heard intimations that claimed Keswick as its birthplace. He was finding the Federation "irresistible to students." Cautioning Beaver to "avoid entangling alliances" with the popular youth movements such as Christian Endeavor while working closely with its founder, he also gave confidential charges concerning delicate problems related to the Inter-Seminary Missionary Alliance, and promised to follow the American summer conferences in prayer.

PART 6: **Triumph in Sydney**

From noon Wednesday, May 13, to midnight Sunday, May 17, the travelers experienced another bout with rough seas in a small boat. Two "faithful friends," Miss Grant, with whom Leila had gone riding, and "Y" secretary Brackenrig saw them off in a driving rain storm, remaining on the pier as long as the ship could be seen. Few meals were taken; Leila's berth was in the women's cabin. "All afternoon and night the boat tossed and the screw was out of the water almost as much as in." By Friday both Motts were on deck part of the day. Leila had long thoughts "on the subject of the duties and privileges of motherhood" (though she did not write them down) while observing a German nurse handling three children.

Saturday was calm. The Motts took tea with the captain, "a most earnest Christian," whose cabin was decorated with Bible texts the most prominent of which was "Kept by the power of God." Sunday was "a perfect day at sea." After the evening service, at which the captain spoke, the beam of Sydney's South Head lighthouse was picked up. Within the seemingly narrow heads, festoons of street lights up and down the hills afforded seven miles of scintillating beauty until their ship, the *Waihora*, docked at midnight—a startling contrast to the drab approach to the city in the jet age. "Our good captain piloted us till we were ready to drive to Hotel Metropole," where a good bed and bread and milk awaited—vital preparation for the heavy week ahead.

Mott was exhilarated by Sydney. He believed that it was destined to win the population race against Melbourne, but again, both cities were more American than British. The weather was like a brisk October day in Iowa. The second day after his arrival was one of the high points of the entire world tour: an evening meeting in the Great Hall of the University, then the aesthetic pride of the Colony (long antedating the 1973 Opera House!), a cultural center and the largest building in Australasia. Similar to Westminster Hall in London but slightly smaller, its stained glass, heraldic borrowings from the arms of Cambridge and Oxford, its carvings and open timbered roof whose beams carry symbols of the arts and sciences—all this, together with the large and distinguished audience he faced, inspired Mott to one of the memorable orations of his life.

Neither outline nor text has survived, but it may be assumed that he opened with greetings from the students of North America, Europe, India-Ceylon, Adelaide, Melbourne, and New Zealand, and moved on to the explication of the Federation which is familiar to the reader. The Vice-Chancellor of the University, Dr. P. Sydney Jones, said to be the Colony's most distinguished physician, who presided, characterized the speech as "a remarkable revelation." The principal of another school, who had shared the dais, declared it to be the first lecture he had ever listened to of which he could say it was entirely new. A professor praised Mott as the best platform speaker he had ever heard. A sympathetic commentator wrote after the Motts had left for China:

> Mr. Mott's chief inspiration has been the message of fact which he has delivered... underlying Mr. Mott's calm logical eloquence, and his wonderful memory for figures and facts, which he knows so well how to mar-

shall in imposing array, there has been the overwhelming answer to those who would have us believe—because a few scientists and men of letters are the exception—that the world's mighty company of students and thinkers are turning their backs on the great truths of the Bible, and writing down as impracticable the Christianity of Jesus Christ. . . .[14]

Of the 300 persons present, sixty students remained for an after-meeting which took steps to organize a Union that, Mott wrote his father shortly afterward, had already enlisted "about 80 of the best students in the University." It was destined to exert powerful leadership in the Australasian Movement, beginning with a delegation of twenty-five to the organizing conference in Melbourne two weeks later.

The remaining days in Sydney moved relentlessly, smoothed by a new friendship with a Cornell colleague, Henry Barraclough, an influential member of the Sydney YMCA. There were news conferences, periods of fund-raising to send delegates to Melbourne, talks to various bodies such as the missionary committee of the Anglican diocese of New South Wales, and a midnight session to organize a Union at Hawkesbury Agricultural College at Richmond, forty miles west, where Mott saw a great need because the rural location of the College cut students off from "church influences and privileges"; Catholic students and a Catholic teacher joined. Word came that $20,000 had been obtained for the Calcutta YMCA building, a notable move in the Australian equivalent of "foreign," later "world work." May 25 was Queen's Birthday, a public holiday; John found time to write his parents:

This is my birthday. As I reflect on the years that have past my heart is filled with sincere and deep and affectionate gratitude to both of you for all that you have done for me and all that you are to me, and also to God for His great goodness to all of us. I desire that the coming years shall be better spent in His service than the past.

A group of friends saw the Motts off to Melbourne that afternoon.

PART 7: The Australasian Student Christian Union

Mott plunged at once into Union affairs. These took him first to Ballarat where he organized Unions in the School of Mines, Clarendon College, and Grenville College, and visited the gold mines. Settling in again in Melbourne at the Grand Hotel, the couple were besieged by callers, students, and Movement business until Leila was forced to stay in mornings, "keeping people away from John so he should have time to breathe and think." His primary concern was preparation for the forth-coming conference, but time was found to visit the local colleges so that by June second, seventeen Unions had been organized in the colonies, the same number as in Britain when a national movement was organized.

The founding conference of the Australasian Student Christian Union met in the small and somewhat intimate Wyselaskie Hall of Ormond College whose neo-Gothic dining hall was "the finest in all the colonies," June fifth through seventh. Although the proposal of such a gathering had been met with some scepticism, there was surprise and gratification when 258 delegates came from thirty-four institutions in-cluding three in New Zealand whose representatives were forced to travel 2,000 miles. Two came from Hobart; the largest delegation was from the University of Sydney and included five women. Leila thought them "a fine looking lot of men and maidens." Mott noted that this was a larger convention than "the similar initial gatherings in America, Great Brit-ain, Germany, Scandinavia, or Switzerland." It was the "first student Christian convention ever held in these colonies, or, in fact, in the Southern Hemisphere." He presided and opened each topic, conducting the convention like his presidential conferences at home, as a working body, low-keyed, with frequent interludes of prayer and hymn-singing; he thought the business sessions "remarkably interesting." "Addresses of power were made by prominent clergymen and professors," Mott himself giving eight.

On June 6, a constitution, incorporating the evangelical basis, "doubtless the best thus far adopted by any student movement"—earnestly debated by delegations seated together, as Mott's well-scratched notes reveal—was adopted by a body that indulged at times in "a tremen-dous amount of clapping" and became "very excited and enthusiastic." One of the members of the new General Committee commented on the "eminently practical discussions," the "tone of deep spirituality and ear-nestness," and the "marked absence of any unsound emotionalism what-ever." Much credit for the success of the Movement was given to the special concerts of prayer that had been devoted to it by students in the other Federation countries.[15] Although the technicalities of admission into the Federation remained to be met, this was the eighth national constituent body, Wishard having organized South Africa a few weeks earlier.

The Convention authorized Mott and the new executive to raise funds and hire a traveling secretary for two years, the students themselves subscribing £300 toward a proposed budget of £1400 for the biennium.

Because of his indispensable expertise, Mott was asked to chair the meetings of the executive as long as he was in the country. The first, in his hotel on June 8, decided on Sydney as headquarters and the site of the next conference to be held in February, 1898. Mott was authorized, after lengthy evaluation of possible candidates, to secure a secretary if funds became available. The Day of Prayer for Universities and Colleges was set, a committee for publications was appointed and six pamphlets authorized including a prayer cycle which Mott helped to prepare before leaving for China.

Although the great business of the tour was now accomplished, the Motts remained in the country almost another month, due chiefly to the delay of their ship, but there would be no cessation of activity until they were on board. The second day after the intercollegiate conference John spoke on "Purity" to a packed house in the Independent Church on Collins Street, an event in the schedule of the Intercolonial YMCA then convened in Melbourne. He advised a representative from Hobart on forming a Union, conferred with a select group of clergy and laymen described as a "Council of Churches," addressed a missionary committee in the Church of England cathedral, and gave one of the addresses to an audience of "at least 3,000" in Town Hall at the twenty-fifth anniversary observance of the Melbourne YMCA, a meeting chaired by the Governor, Lord Brassey, who invited him to Government House. During this week Leila formed a Union of the girls at Merton Hall, her third, and doctored their mutual friend J. J. Virgo, secretary at Adelaide, who would later move to Sydney and then to London, England, with eucalyptus steam while he and John planned a fund-raising parlor conference. John spoke at Trinity Church on right relations between the Brotherhood of St. Andrew and the student Unions.

While John was gone to Adelaide, Leila was a guest in the vicarage at Caulfield, attended several fashionable teas, spoke to groups of college girls, and gave some missionary talks but confided to her diary that people tended to regard such speeches "in the light of an entertainment." There was a quiet rainy Sabbath spent by the fire. The day John returned with pledges of £400, she organized her fourth girls' Union, at Tintern College. He turned to the preparations for the Melbourne parlor conference which was to be held by invitation of the Governor at Government House, talked with medical students about medical missions, got to a football match, and witnessed the opening of Parliament. Both Motts were involved in serious discussions of faith missions on several occasions. The day after the parlor conference John, in company with a member of Parliament, canvassed the business district, obtaining the £100 expected but in small sums because the depression had everywhere inflicted terrible reverses, "and many who were rich are now poor. Disaster seemed to fall on innocent and guilty alike for hardly a bank stood." When the Motts left Melbourne a dozen well-wishers gave them three "very lusty cheers."

Met at Sydney by most of the new executive group of the Intercolonial Union, Mott plunged into a concentrated session before an open fire in his hotel room. In the evening he conferred with the University Union cabinet until midnight and the next day organized a women's Union there, to which Leila also spoke. A third parlor conference was held by invitation of the Primate of Australia and Tasmania at his residence but took an odd turn when one of the thirty guests proposed taking up a collection which yielded only £60. Mott recouped the loss by subsequent individual solicitation which produced one contribution of £50 per year for three years. He had started out with a goal of £800, but God had given more than £1400; thus his work would "go on after I leave the colonies," he wrote to his father.

This put the Movement budget into operation and cleared the way to employ a secretary, the selection of whom occupied most of the attention of two more sessions with the executive committee. Mott's choice was William H. Sallmon, a young Canadian then serving as Association secretary at Yale while completing his doctorate. Mott shared with the executive a 5,000-word letter he had composed to Sallmon outlining the position in great detail and urging him to accept: they endorsed the nomination unanimously. It took Leila an entire evening to transcribe the letter. Sallmon, who later went on to a position of leadership in Canada, accepted and enjoyed remarkable success in Australia and New Zealand. The executive voted funds to send one of its members to Northfield to the WSCF conference in 1897, obtained from Mott every bit of advice they could anticipate needing, and urged him to return to America via Australia after his visits to China and Japan.[16]

Sunday evening, June 28, was planned as a "farewell meeting" at the Pitt Street Congregational Church; Mott spoke "powerfully" on the Student Volunteer Movement to a capacity congregation that included many students, a hundred of whom stayed for the after-meeting, deeply concerned about missions. The final week before a much-delayed sailing seemed to accelerate rather than diminish the Motts' obligations, working them until midnight daily. John met with engineering students and again with medical students at the University. Long hours went into the preparation and proofing of the Bible study courses and other pamphlets. Leila gave some more talks but "never allowed John to go near" one. He "rejoiced to hear that the Republicans [had] nominated McKinley" but could not learn who the vice-presidential candidate was; that little-known politician would later play a helpful role in Mott's own career.

On the Fourth of July the Motts were tendered an excursion around "the most magnificent harbor in the world" by the Sydney University students. The government provided a fine steamer; the Minister of Education of New South Wales accompanied the happy crowd of some 200. The Stars and Stripes "hung gloriously" at the bow with the Union Jack at the stern. Gifts and flowers were showered upon Leila. Pictures were taken, tea served, speeches given. John spoke of the common Anglo-American heritage and expressed his and Leila's deep and very real appreciation of the great kindness they had received everywhere. Firecrackers were exploded—"a very notable and glad Fourth." After tea Mott met with the executive until midnight. Next day provided a fabulously interesting introduction to star photography at the observatory; John was fascinated by the southern constellations. That day he spoke at the YMCA.

Monday, July 6, they finally sailed for Hong Kong on the 2450-ton *Taiyuan* of the Chinese Navigation Company at 4:00 P.M. Thirty-five persons gathered at the quay. Flowers and gifts were presented in abundance. "There were the warmest goodbyes." As the steamer moved off, "there were three cheers for us, then one for John Livingstone" back home in Ohio. Henry Barraclough broke out the Cornell colors. The crowd stood waving until the ship was out of sight. Leila wrote in her diary: "It was with real regret and relief too that we were finally on our way. We stayed on deck to see the last of this matchless harbor and beautiful Sydney." Mott told Hattie that they would never "be able to express to God our gratitude for being sent" to the colonies.

The voyage to Hong Kong would last until July 29, due in part to the hazardous navigation through the Great Barrier Reef and the East Indies; the ship was often forced to drop anchor at night. But without such periods of rest and renewal neither of the Motts could have endured the stresses to which they were subjected while on land. Later in life Mott would not infrequently acknowledge this and comment that the sea had become a great source of inspiration. Rest, reading, and deck games alternated with periods of writing, reporting, and accounting. The first letter was a virtual pastoral epistle sent back to the new Unions he had just created. He reminded them of the strengths and weaknesses of a new movement, of the importance of Bible study and daily prayer, of *doing* as well as talking and being, of drawing new students into their fellowship, and other program suggestions. Relaying Leila's as well as his own appreciation of the warm reception they had enjoyed, he concluded that it had not been easy to leave such friends, "but far needier fields summon us."[17] Report letters then had to be brought up to date. At the Australasian executive's request he prepared an itinerary for the new secretary's first tour—beginning in New Zealand at Auckland rather than as he had—the letter crammed with detailed advice. He wrote all the constituent members of the Federation concerning the admission of the new Union, and put its officers on the mailing list for his own reports. To his father he wrote that "if ever God led us to any part of the world He led us here."

Thirty years later, the occasion of Mott's third visit, a participant in the Australasian Movement since 1896 summarized the Motts' 11,000-mile detour of that year:

> It was a short and sharp campaign, but the peculiar genius of Dr. Mott was exhibited in his powers of organization. All the existing, and occasionally moribund, groups of students throughout the Commonwealth were galvanized into new life, new organizations were formed, new avenues of work for students opened up, and the whole student body of Australia and New Zealand was helped into one united whole. When the first convention was held in Wyselaski Hall, in 1896, there was intense enthusiasm, the foundations of future work were securely laid, and a constitution drawn up.
>
> Nor must we forget the changed attitude of the Universities. The intensely secular ideas that had been too long current began to give way. What had previously been ignored or tolerated, and even proscribed, now became recognized as an integral and worthy part of University and college life. It is hard to conceive that in one University library no Bible could be found, and the only copies of sacred writ were presentation copies of Westcott and Hort's Greek Text. Pagan classics could be found in abundance. All that has now been changed, and vastly for the better.[18]

PART 8: Prelude to China

The Motts disembarked at Hong Kong the morning of July 29, 1896, thoroughly rested and ready for what they feared would be the most hazardous segment of their tour. The voyage from Sydney had been the longest, "most interesting and enjoyable" ever, bringing them from the "youngest" continent to the "oldest." For two hours every morning John had read "heavy books chiefly on China" as part of an almost inflexible shipboard routine that began with a seawater bath at seven and ended at ten after an evening of writing or reading. Finally caught up with their correspondence and reports, they mailed eighty letters, but this gained them little enough—fifty-seven were awaiting them at this "decidedly occidental" gateway to China which was "really an English colony."

Putting up at the Hong Kong Hotel, they were barely settled when a typhoon struck. Leila feared the building "would surely go" as window after window blew in and was boarded up. Donning oilskins they joined other guests on the leeward side of the hotel to watch the storm; there was little sleep that night.

Next day was calm: they took the tram up the Peak, Leila being reminded of the funicular from Lauterbrünnen to Mürren in the Bernese Oberland by the steep ascent, but how different the view! No Alps were to be seen here, but only the low brown "nine dragon" hills of Kowloon to the north, and everywhere else the arms of the sea and the steep small islands.

They took the river steamer to Canton the following day, a short and pleasant journey—while on shipboard. Then they were plunged into the revolutionary heart of the China that was on the threshold of a half-century of upheaval that would culminate in Mao's People's Republic.

The China to which Mott came in 1896 seemed to the 5,000 Protestant missionaries then at work to be opening to Western influences, with the traditional indifference if not opposition to all things foreign slowly giving way. China's defeat in the Sino-Japanese War of 1894–95 had eroded Chinese official contempt for modern technological power and was encouraging curiosity about Western thought. The missionary enterprise was feeling the effects. A number of missionary educators were finding audiences among modern businessmen and the young, though not yet among the literati. The interest was in science and education more than in the religious message, yet in 1894 the Empress Dowager had actually accepted a presentation copy of the New Testament in Chinese. Missionaries debated hotly whether their main effort should lie in pure evangelism or in education and social services, yet behind their debate lay some optimism that the impenetrable barrier of Chinese society could be breached by the West. Mott, whose sympathies inevitably lay with the educators, could not help but share in this optimism.

Yet sensitive observers realized that anti-foreign feeling was quiescent rather than extinct. The past five years had seen a number of anti-foreign riots, among them a massacre of missionaries at Huashan,

near Kucheng in the province of Fukien. The latest incident had occurred in Shantung province only a few weeks before the Motts' visit
there, foreshadowing the eruption of the Boxer Rebellion in the North
four years later. There was a deep cleavage between Western Christian
culture and Chinese society that was bound to result in abrasive encounters. China's unique and deeply entrenched culture had produced a
humanistic, secular civilization unlike that of the West. Chinese resistance appears to have been based less on actual hostility to the gospel
than upon the prior contempt for the foreigner and barbarian. Yet
neither Mott nor his contemporaries seemed to realize that evangelism
and dogma, even with concessions to Chinese taste, could not resolve
the differences. They might well have asked: Could China ever be lured
into responding affirmatively to the best the Occident had to offer?
Could her humanistic morality be challenged successfully by a dogmatic
and ecclesiastical religion with its accent upon transcendence? But at the
moment of Mott's visit, in the interlude before the Boxer storm, they
discussed instead the less fundamental questions of technique. To the
challenge of "the evangelization of the world in this generation" Mott
and his colleagues had unique answers: secure the students, develop the
four-fold program of the YMCA into an indigenous institutionalized
force, and later unite missions and denominations in ecumenical endeavor.[19]

The Motts' short visit to Canton began with missionary-guided tours
of the mission stations and hospitals—especially the largest mission hospital in China, whose director, Dr. John G. Kerr, was said to have
treated a million patients—in a city "still strongly anti-foreign" in spite,
or perhaps because, of its having been the first Chinese city opened to
foreigners and the place where missionaries began their work. Unlike
India, China had not been occupied: she had been forced to make concessions. Traffic crossed the canal between the old city and the foreign
settlement, but the cultures did not mix.

Seeing the Chinese city mostly from sedan chairs, the Motts were
fascinated by "the examination halls of Chinese scholars, the Viceroy's
college, the prison, the temple of horrors, the view from the five story
pagoda, the shops, the silk weaving establishments, the constant streams
of people on every street, the countless strange customs, costumes and
noises." To Leila it was an "inexpressible relief" to return to the hotel
from the "pandemonium of sounds" and the mysterious labyrinth of
streets; but months later when John listed "the great days of the tour" he
included this foray into old Canton. Among the thirty-three missionaries

they met were two of Mother White's preparatory-school classmates and others who had children in college at Wooster. Back in Hong Kong for a few hours, John devoted most of the time to an interview with a veteran missionary.

A steamer trip then took the Motts to Shanghai, where they stayed at the Astor House after picking up thirty-five letters and an armful of papers which brought word that Mott's colleagues Beaver, Brockman, and Michener had all married, and John Livingstone was thriving. John made some calls by ricksha in the oppressive heat; this form of transportation made about as good time as the family horse and buggy back home, he noted. Although they remained in Shanghai only one night, a handful of missionaries saw them off to Chefoo in Shantung, where they would escape the heat, rest for two weeks, study, and plan for conferences.

PART 9: Two Conferences in North China

At Chefoo the Motts were guests of Mrs. John L. Nevius, widow and biographer of the outstanding Presbyterian missionary educator who had criticized the SVM in 1893, and who had since died. This quiet period provided many opportunities to visit mission schools, to observe the infinitely strange—"queerest in the world"—Chinese, to hear (and for Leila to write down) much missionary gossip, and to attend an open house aboard an American gunboat.[20] John had time to plan his conferences with his intimate friend and colleague D. Willard Lyon, by whom the Motts' entire tour was being arranged, its purpose, of course, being the same as in India and Australasia—to organize local Associations of college students and unite them in a national body that would affiliate with the Federation.

Lyon, who had come on to Chefoo from Tientsin, had lived with the Motts at Oak Park in 1894–95 and had married and sailed for China to be the American YMCA's first secretary in that country about the same time they had started their world journey. The son of missionaries, Lyon had been born on a Ningpo canal boat and grew up in Soochow. Educated at the College of Wooster and McCormick Theological Seminary, he had traveled for the student movement in the South and Midwest and had been the first educational secretary of the SVM. He had selected Tientsin for his base of operations because of the five government colleges there.[21] Supported in part by Mrs. Taylor, his dream of a building was realized through her gift of $10,000 when she came to China after leaving the Motts in India the previous spring.

The Chefoo conference opened on August 23 and extended through parts of five days. Mott gave the several basic addresses he had developed on the tour, adapted, as always, to each audience, plus a new talk on "Four Saviors." The conference was similar to those held in India and Australia. Some sessions were in Chinese. Leila spoke to several women's groups, where she was surprised by the interest in young John L.; they thought it remarkable that she would leave her only son at home. The conference was attended by more missionaries than students, but Mott felt encouraged and expected that the gatherings would improve as they went along.

From Chefoo the party went by overnight steamer, with considerable discomfort, to Teng Chow, where they were entertained by the redoubtable Calvin Mateer, president of Teng Chow College, one of the best missionary schools; he was a staunch advocate of education in mathematics and the natural sciences for the Chinese.[22] Generally considered among the greatest of all Presbyterian missionaries, Mateer had pioneered with a text *Mandarin Lessons* and had long contended for a curriculum in liberal arts including social studies and the Chinese classics, with a minimum of instruction in English. Among the first sights to be seen was Mateer's science museum which specialized in optics and electricity, most of the equipment for which Mateer had himself constructed. There were plans for a large exhibition hall with a miniature electric railroad running around the walls. "The idea," Leila wrote, "is to catch these students on modern science lines and thus interest them in Christianity." In the evening they were shown a nebula in the constellation Hercules through Mateer's ten-inch telescope.

The Motts had heard that Mateer was not convinced of the values of the Federation and the SVM watchword, so when John spoke on these it was with the specific intent of persuading him and some others. Leila noted that "this speech was heavy firing in both these lines and seems to have 'fetched' them all." Next day Mateer interpreted Mott's Bible study address. Instead of opposing his host by organizing an Association, Mott held a two-hour open discussion period, the upshot of which was that the boys themselves decided to organize.

On the return trip to Chefoo Mott's coolies "took him off into some new wretched quarter of the city and lost themselves and him completely in the darkness. He couldn't speak a word. Mr. Cornwell and Mr. Lyon happened to come along and rescued him." Before going to Tientsin the

Motts made a 173-mile side-trip to the Great Wall, going first class on China's only railroad "in wooden seats arranged like an American train with the aisle in the middle." Mott was fascinated by the Wall. He included his walk along the top of it in his later summary of the "most enjoyable" side-trips of the tour, writing to Iowa that "it was longer than from Postville to New York City." In conversation with a group of Taoist monks he presented himself as a man with a literary degree who, like their viceroy Li Hung-chang, traveled all over the world; for their deference he had to pay extra, Leila commented wryly to her diary, perhaps reflecting her own fatigue after a wrenching ride in a Chinese cart. To that home letter he added a final note: "I hope that McKinley will be elected. It will not do to let the free silver party win."

During the first of two brief stays in Tientsin a mini-conference was held, chiefly for the benefit of the fledgling YMCA Lyon had organized the previous December. At the new government university Leila found the same textbooks that she had known in her own teaching at Monticello School back in Illinois.

En route to Peking, where the next conference would be held, the party took a houseboat which they arranged to have propelled by a double crew using sails, beaver-tail oars, and poles as well as tow to get them non-stop to T'ungchow, a few miles east of the capital, where they were guests of President D. Z. Sheffield of North China College, another prominent educator. [23] The final leg of the journey to Peking was made by donkey back; each man was thrown at least once and Mott's mount ran into the front door of a Chinese cottage, "scaring the children fearfully." Accompanied on part of this trip by the Methodist Bishop Isaac W. Joyce, they stayed at the Methodist compound.

The Mott conference at Peking was attended by 600 delegates, including just under one hundred missionaries. John's address on the Federation—one of five given—was interpreted by Dr. Sheffield. Sightseeing included the major temples, the hall of Confucian classics, and a cloisonné factory; but foreigners were allowed only a distant view of the "wonderful" Altar of Heaven. Mott shopped for ancient coins. Associations were organized in the Presbyterian and Methodist colleges.

Back in Tientsin, Mott laid the cornerstone of the "Livingstone Taylor Memorial" building (which the Boxers would soon wreck) "for the glory of God and the salvation of young men," following an outline he had earlier dictated to Leila. During an informal lunch at the London Mission, the SVM watchword came up for heated discussion. Leila's summation suggests that most of the missionaries present were convinced that China could not be evangelized in their generation because the doors to the upper classes were "practically closed." Their attitude seems to have been precisely contrary to the assumption on which they had come out: "that men of spiritual power could do this work quickly." China had been reported to be "all open to the Gospel" by enthusiasts such as Miss Geraldine Guinness of the China Inland Mission, whose *In the Far East: Letters from China,* they said, had painted an unrealistic picture.

On the return voyage to Shanghai Mott and Lyon turned the ship's small saloon into an office and spent an entire day writing. Mott's letter home was a sad one: word had come to Tientsin of the death of his nephew, Earle McAdam, the first break in the Iowa family circle:

> Our hearts go out in deep sympathy for Alice, James and the children, and we shall not cease to remember them in special prayer that the God of all comfort may be very near and sustain them during these lonely and dark days. Much as we all feel this loss we must not forget that it is Earle's infinite gain, and that the good Lord has far better plans than we can possibly have.

The trip home would be revised to visit the bereaved family in Denver the following spring.

PART 10: Twenty-seven Associations Where There Were Five

Back at the Astor House in Shanghai—the traffic was "as bad as Chicago"—there was again the inevitable round of church meetings, conference preparation, and speeches, interrupted by a restful sail to Ningpo where the Motts were guests at the Church Missionary Society compound, which was inside the city but separated from it by a high wall:

> A clean gateway, a walk bordered with brilliant coxcombs, beyond a rose-bordered path, a tennis court, the vine covered house, the chapel, the boys' school, and the women's hospital—all looked clean and sweet and imposing too.

Both Motts spoke to the students of mission schools, John addressing the boys of the Baptist, Presbyterian, and CMS institutions in the afternoon and again at night; a YMCA was organized.

In Shanghai again, there was a visit to St. John's College with its 150 students and "the finest buildings and equipment we have seen in China," plus an evening address. Leila wrote the home letters because

John was so involved he couldn't do so without taking time from his sleep, though on the ship returning from the north he had sent Beaver five pages of instructions including plans for the first world meeting of the Federation, to be held at Northfield the next summer.

The Shanghai Conference began the morning of September 30 with sessions in both the China Inland Mission Hall and the Union Chapel. It attracted more than 700 delegates. Mott spoke seven times, filled the Union Church pulpit, and gave an evangelistic address to 300 non-Chinese businessmen at the Lyceum Theatre. "There has never been such a meeting in Shanghai," some missionaries commented concerning Mott's unique revivalistic methods. He wrote to Hattie that this demonstrated the desirability of an Association to meet the needs of these men; by 1898 the American YMCA's would have a vigorous secretary on duty and the first formal city Association in China would be organized in Shanghai early in 1900.[24] Leila visited two upper class homes and spoke to several groups. James Stokes, the eccentric New York philanthropist, appeared and talked to the conference. At the end of the gathering Mott was presented with an elegantly bound facsimile copy of the same New Testament translation that had been accepted by the Empress Dowager.

Partly for relaxation after the strain of the conference the Motts and Willard Lyon went to Soochow by houseboat—"the most restful form of traveling" they had yet found, and far more comfortable than "any Pullman car." Meetings with students of three schools resulted in the organization of an Association, Mott's eighth in China.

At a Chinese Christian wedding a band played "the most weird, woe-begone, plaintive, soul-harrowing music that it has ever been my lot to hear," he wrote to Hattie. They sat through some twenty courses of a much longer banquet, but Mott confided that he had "gone light" on delicacies such as bird nest soup, sharks' fins, or boiled aged duck eggs, most of which had gone on the floor as he diverted the attention of the other diners. Dishes like roast duck were splendid, though he found chopsticks awkward. "This is a good country to live in," he enthused, an attitude he would translate into expanded Association programs. His health was excellent, and so was Leila's, and he was constantly astonished to meet missionaries who had worked in China for thirty to fifty years. Concluding a long letter home, he supposed that the political pot was "boiling vigorously," with each party predicting the absolute ruin of the country if the other won, "but America cannot be ruined that easily."

The return to Shanghai was in the luxury of a mandarin's houseboat towed by a steam tug. Plans were readied for the next conference, visits made to various missions including the Catholic center, addresses given. October tenth was "our baby's fourth birthday." Leila set down one of several accounts of the Chinese custom of exposing unwanted infants, describing the missions' efforts to find, sometimes to buy, and by various methods to succor these children in their many orphanages.

A steamer trip now took the party to Foochow for what would be Mott's largest conference, attended by 1277 persons, of whom 570 were students from sixteen institutions. The hopeful outlook for the mission cause had been expressed to Leila by an American Board worker:

> It's glorious to be in China now. What we have seen this year alone is worth all the years we have spent here. I'm sorry for the people at home and those who had to go before this time came.

Leila continued:

> Whether it's the blood of the martyrs of Kuncheng (Huashan) or the prayers of God's people thereby directed here, or the patient sowing of fifty years,—there is now in all the missions a great ingathering and the churches are using the utmost caution to keep out the unworthy. Self-supporting churches are springing up, villages are begging for preachers, the homes of many of the high classes are open to the Gospel, every Chinese who could possibly help has been pressed into service. [25]

In this optimistic atmosphere the three-day conference was held under a large tent in the Methodist compound. John gave the first of eleven addresses to an audience of 930 Chinese.

Leila talked with Mabel Hartford, the only American in the Huashan massacre of the previous summer, who had escaped "almost by a miracle":

> A man rushed at her with a trident but she caught it and warded off the blow. He then knocked her down and beat her with the spear. Her Chinese servant got hold of the spear and threw it as far as he could and then helped her to get into the bushes. She heard the house burning down but supposed all had escaped as she had.

Several Associations were formed in Foochow, one "large and enthusiastic." Miss Hartford gave Leila a tour of her work.

The return voyage to Shanghai afforded two days of rest but the next, devoted to visiting, speaking, and organizing, ended with embarkation for Hankow. The ship's captain was a Maine man devoted to free silver and Bryan's candidacy; his and John's conversations may be imagined. When the steamer touched at Nanking the Motts remained on board for John to dictate a report, while the boat swarmed at one end with Methodists en route to conference and "at the other end" with hundreds of Chinese. The Motts then joined the Methodist gathering for two days where they renewed their relationship with the presiding officer, Bishop Joyce, an earlier guide and traveling companion. Back on shipboard Leila rewrote a paper for John's China report, the exercise giving her "a new conviction of the sinfulness of poor writing," while he devoted the day to correspondence. At Hankow they were entertained at the China Inland Mission, held a small conference, and organized five Associations. Three days in Nanking, "an attractive city," provided John with the opportunity to visit the government examination halls with their 30,000 stalls for scholars, and for Leila to go to the Ming Tombs on a Chinese pony. Both spoke to student groups and three Associations were organized.

They had now visited "practically all" of the schools and colleges of the country. Twenty-seven Associations—"one in every important institution in the empire"—could be counted, whereas there had been but five when they arrived in China thirteen weeks earlier. All had adopted the model constitution with its evangelical basis, and Mott had made a beginning on what would become a widely-recognized method of obtaining information by questionnaire—this one for his first report to the Federation next summer. Over 1200 Chinese had attended his five regional conferences; 800 delegates had pledged to keep the morning watch, and seventy-seven had volunteered—the vanguard of the SVM of China.

PART 11: The College YMCA of China

The climax of the China tour was the national conference that met in Shanghai November third through sixth. It was a small delegated body of eight Chinese and twenty-four foreign representatives from twenty-two of the new Associations, plus guests and advisors. Calling itself the College Young Men's Christian Association of China, the new organization set up "a strong national committee" of seven Chinese and seven foreigners. Plans were laid for a news organ, pamphlets in Chinese and in English, a prayer cycle, and a national convention; a national secretary, Willard Lyon, was called. The real significance of the movement, wrote Mott in *Strategic Points*, "is seen in the fact that old China is passing away; new China is coming on."[26] The national body "fully complied" with the requirements (though not without some quibbling over the evangelical test) and was "at once admitted" to the Federation, and a Chinese was appointed to represent it at Northfield the next summer.

In addition, a Student Volunteer Movement was organized as the missionary department of the national Association.[27] Working once until midnight under Mott's chairmanship, it too laid extensive plans, in part to elicit and focus the interest of the two hundred North American Volunteers in China; the India-Ceylon pledge of "direct work for Christ" in one's own country was adopted and steps were taken toward a similar committee of women Volunteers. The diversity of denominations present was unusual, Leila noting in her diary that "the unity of the Spirit in a body composed of such divergent elements was marked by all." The seventeen college presidents who attended at a cost of from five days to three weeks of their time "seemed to feel abundantly repaid for coming and to have the greatest hope for the future." One of them called the new movement "the greatest event in the line of missionary effort in China." After an unusually moving farewell Leila returned to the hotel wondering "how we shall ever pay the debt of love we owe to friends all round the world." November seventh they sailed for Japan on the *Kobe Maru*, waved out of sight by Lyon and others.

Both Motts were sorry to leave China. The anxieties they had felt concerning safety and diet had proved groundless. Extensive travel had been restful. They were both in excellent condition. Not an hour had been lost "on account of any physical discomfort." Their reception by "a host of as fine Christian men and women as are to be found in any land" had been royal. Mott's work had been "richly blessed," beyond his expectations, he wrote home. Their regard for China was undiminished by the "endless dirt, filth, and no sanitation," the execrable wagon roads, the lack of railroads and postal service:

> It has impressed us more strongly than any other field, I think. Although it may surprise you, I believe that the cause of Christ is advancing more rapidly and securely in China than in Japan.

As he reflected on his experiences two months later Mott's dominant impressions were of China as "the greatest mission field in the world" because of the vast population, the combination of the greatest difficulties, and the largest potential. "The students of the Chinese Government competitive examination system constitute the Gibraltar of the student world." Therefore educational missions are of "the greatest strategic importance." He believed that the new national Association "so ably led" by Lyon was destined to play a large part in the solution of this colossal problem; three or four men should be sent to strengthen his hands. Mott was convinced of the reality of a rising spiritual tide in China, "an awakened desire to know something of the outside world." There would be convulsions in that awakening.

PART 12: **Japan in 1896**

None of the generalizations usually made about the Christian churches in Asia or about the past experience of overseas mission agencies applies to Japan; Japan as a nation and people defies generalization. The primitive, ancient, medieval, modern, and contemporary all exist in Japan in a marvelous *modus vivendi* with one another that is matched nowhere else.[28]

This mid-twentieth-century characterization of Japan by R. Pierce Beaver could almost have been written by Mott following his 1896–97 visit. The country, Mott declared in his second report letter, "is in the midst of the greatest national transition ever witnessed," though at that time it was not at all clear that a *modus vivendi* would be achieved. Less than thirty years had then elapsed since the beginning of the Meiji era, that is, the restoration to the Emperor of central governmental power, the founding of modern Japan. In contrast to China, Japan had intentionally embraced much of Western civilization, chiefly its material culture, within the short period since Commodore O. H. Perry's "visit" in 1853, but it was still ambivalent as to the compatibility of Christianity with Japanese conservatism and nationalism.

The propagation of Christianity was allowed, but the official attitude was largely negative; the Ministry of Education was filled with anti-Christian officials, and the first visit of a member of the royal family to a Christian school would not take place until 1928.[29] As had been the case centuries earlier, with the importation of Chinese and Korean cultures, the Japanese chose those items they would assimilate from the West rather than to imitate it in toto. The conscious adoption of Western technology was a protective measure based on the assumption that modernization was not only the best defense but also the quickest route to the abrogation of the unequal treaties Japan suffered along with China.[30] Her early adoption of military conscription and her consequent imperialistic ventures—the annexation of the Kuriles, Bonins, and Ryukus, and later Taiwan and the Pescadores—were the beginnings of the territorial aggrandizement that would ultimately lead to Pearl Harbor. The Motts' visit came "as Japan moved away from its Western moorings into the open sea, as a mature nation-state."

How Japan shopped the Western world for compatible institutions is a familiar story. Her emissaries found congenial ideas on government, politics, and military science (especially the chief of staff system) in Prussia, naval science in Great Britain, and education at first in France and the United States, but the comprehensive system of schools she finally adopted was based on Prussian concepts and was dedicated to the perpetuation of the state and the subservience of the individual to it, rather than to his liberation or enrichment. This "powerful weapon of control," as Hugh Borton has described it, was

> a conscious and effective way of steering the people away from the exotic Western stream of civilization toward an amplified, intensified, national stream of culture which was to sweep all before it for the next half century.[31]

Unlike the American Bill of Rights, the Japanese constitution subjected the various freedoms to "the limits of law," but within this restriction, Christian groups could be formed in the student bodies of the new government colleges and universities, as we shall see.

Despite the ban against Christianity, the Meiji government had been very lenient from its own inauguration in 1868. In 1873 the edict against Christians, which had been in effect for both Protestants and Catholics since the early seventeenth century, was abolished; following the 1854 treaty with the United States, the Tokugawa government realized that it would be difficult to keep missionaries out, but the latter were very careful not to be overzealous, the first Protestant agent having entered the country in 1859.[32] Rapid growth of Roman Catholics, Protestants, and Orthodox had followed the abolition of the edict against them, resulting in some optimistic claims that the nation could be converted.

At the time of the Motts' visit, there were said to be some 40,000 Protestants in the country, but the annual gain had dropped from well over 5,000 in 1889 to fewer than 1200 throughout the nineties.[33]

Contrary to the situation in China, Christianity had made a visible impression upon the Japanese intellectual classes, marking it, as Mott's activities would delineate, as an elitist movement. The several colleges such as Doshisha that had been established under missionary or other Western religious impulses were now severely hampered by a strong anti-Christian surge. Thus, "the persistent issue in the history of Christianity in Japan" had emerged—

the confrontation of the transcendental perspectives of Christian faith, particularly the Christian obligation to obey God rather than man, with the traditional tendency of Japanese political leadership to make loyalty to the political and social structures of the land a religious obligation surpassing all others. [34]

A unique manifestation of Protestant Christianity had been the several "bands" of young samurai who were converted in the 1870's by able American teachers chiefly at Yokohama, Kumamoto, and Sapporo. When the school that created the Kumamoto band was closed in 1876, the group of about thirty migrated almost to a man to the new Doshisha in Kyoto—a move reminiscent of the migration of the followers of Theodore Weld from Lane Seminary in Cincinnati to the struggling new Oberlin College in 1834—and comprised the entire first class graduated in 1879. Together with members of other bands, these men initiated "the first great wave of evangelization by Japanese." Others rose to positions of leadership in government as well as across the social and economic panorama of the country. They carried the gospel to the interior at a time when missionaries were restricted to the port cities, and gave the Japanese church indigenous leadership of a very high order. Jerome D. Davis, co-founder of the Doshisha, believed that their work changed the history of Japan. [35] Mott would meet many of them and would have one of the high spiritual adventures of his life with the extant band at Kumamoto.

Although there had been YMCA's in Japan as early as 1880, the North American International Committee had sent its first "foreign" secretary there in 1888, on the crest of the wave of Christian success. At the "request" of missionaries, John T. Swift went out as a teacher of English in a government school, but he soon turned his entire attention to furthering the YMCA, especially among students, even diverting a legacy from himself to the construction fund of the first YMCA building in Tokyo. [36] He welcomed and guided Luther Wishard during the latter's nine-month stay in 1888–89. Strongly in favor of Japanese leadership, he brought outstanding men into the secretaryship and insisted upon Japanese boards of directors. From 1891 to 1895 Swift had had the assistance of Ransford S. Miller, Mott's Cornell roommate. When the Motts arrived there were eight Associations in the country. With the reputation of having done "one of the grandest pieces of missionary work thus far accomplished in Japan," Swift had already planned the Motts' itinerary when his card was presented at their cabin door in the harbor at Nagasaki before John was up, early in the morning of November 9, 1896.

PART 13: **A Different Strategy**

The Motts' tour of Japan was to be almost as different from their routines in India, Australia, and China as were those countries. There were no local or regional conferences held, save for a one-day meeting at Kumamoto, emphasis being placed instead on a national gathering in Tokyo after Mott had visited practically every institution of higher learning in the country and formed or strengthened Associations in most. There was more personal evangelism—with more conversions than in any country on the tour, more interviewing to understand the problems of the field, and more concern to undergird the case for increased missionary endeavor, as Mott saw it. Their itinerary provided three weeks in the south, the same in the central part of the country, two weeks during the holidays at Miyanoshita in the Hakone mountains and at Nikko, with a final three-week concentration in Tokyo interrupted by a short trip to Sendai.

A week in Nagasaki was essentially an orientation to the country. "Japan is a new world," Leila wrote home. This hillside city had been a port of entry, Catholic center, and site of persecutions—Swift pointed out the hill that was said to have been covered with crosses—since the sixteenth-century plantings of Francis Xavier. The Motts noted the cleaner and wider streets than in Chinese cities, the custom of bowing, the beauty of trees, parks, gardens, and flowers. Both Motts spoke to students of several schools and interviewed missionaries.

John worked hard organizing Associations. At once he encountered the independence of Japanese students: at a mission school the men had stayed away from classes recently to caucus on the improvement of the institution, presenting the principal with definite proposals charging the incompetence of certain teachers whom they demanded should be dismissed, declaring that there should be a Japanese principal of a Japanese school, that the textbooks were antiquated and should be replaced, that the lecture system should supplant the recitation method, and that young men should not be under such minute rules as were in effect. In treating the petition with amusement as evidence of the perversity of the Japanese mind, the missionaries revealed their lack of understanding of the old custom of petition by those below when conditions were bad. On another occasion there was heated discussion of coeducational attendance at certain of Mott's meetings at which several schools were represented. In another place the missionaries were astonished by a large turnout of 300 men in an area previously marked by indifference.

At Shimonoseki the Mott party, which included Swift and their interpreter Keinosuke Yabuuchi, visited the Buddhist temple where Li Hung-chang, the chief Chinese negotiator, had stayed during the talks that ended the war with China a few months before; they lunched there, Japanese style. A short but beautiful trip on the Inland Sea on a perfect autumn day was followed by an evening journey along a good road to Yamaguchi—"we have hardly seen a prettier spot in all our travels," Leila wrote Clara; the autumn foliage of the Japanese maples was glorious. The missionary home where they stayed was "modern and perfect," finished and furnished in native woods unvarnished but very handsome. An Association was formed. In Fukuoka the party was carried along "as part of the fun" of a local festival as they made their way through the town. It was a unique experience to stay with missionaries living in Japanese style—"very lovely people of the Keswick school looking for the second coming of Christ in the near future." Sabbath was spent in part reading George Adam Smith on *Isaiah*. John refused to speak on purity to a co-educational group.

PART 14: The Kumamoto Band

The Motts' fifth wedding anniversary fell on a rainy day consumed largely by the train ride to Kumamoto, which gave them opportunity to think about their years together. Leila wrote to Alice that people still took them to be on their wedding journey until they learned about young John L., but her husband insisted that they still were on it, and they were agreed that the most recent year had been happier than their first year. At Kumamoto they were met by a deputation of Japanese student descendants of the famous band known throughout the missionary world.

These young men had written to Mott in Australia to inquire how many were required to organize an Association. He had replied that he planned to visit Kumamoto and that a good Association could be formed "by even three Christians, if they were in earnest and united." He found that the three had started an Association and "led eleven of their fellow students to Christ." At a meeting that went on until nearly midnight he was welcomed by a hymn written for the occasion and an address of welcome to which he responded. Next afternoon he was asked to speak without an interpreter. Under his adroit leadership the new Association became an orthodox YMCA on the evangelical basis. A few students had been invited from other schools of the region so that the Kumamoto meetings turned into a mini-conference, with 300 local students thronging to Mott's address on temptation. An evening affair in the Methodist church was also crowded:

> The doors had to be closed and the gates of the yard too. People sat on the floor, in the windows, everywhere. The number of listeners was estimated to be 500. John spoke on the Student Movements and was most respectfully heard by an audience most of whom could not have been in sympathy.

Their host said he had never expected to see such a meeting in Kumamoto.

The pressures created by Mott's schedule worried Leila. "I have been rather anxious about John," she wrote to Wooster, "simply because flesh and blood can't stand it to work as hard as he has been doing in Japan. Here's what he did last Sabbath":

> Got up at five to attend a sunrise prayer meeting at six on a high hill an hour's journey away. This lasted an hour and a half. Home to breakfast. A meeting from 9–12:30 with some twenty picked students from seven institutions of southern Japan—speaking more or less all the time. At 2:30 a public meeting in which he spoke through an interpreter about an hour and a half. Immediately after another meeting with the delegates for two hours and a half—speaking twice—and leading. Home to supper. Another meeting from 8:30 to ten with the Japanese pastors, to explain the student movement and to encourage them in their work. Japan is the most trying country we have been in so far as work goes. You have to handle the people so carefully and they are so difficult to lead that John says it's twice the strain and takes twice as long to do anything as in China. . . .

Yet for John the sunrise prayer meeting was one of the memorable experiences of his life, often mentioned, and fifty years later included in an inventory of great moments in his career. The tradition of the Kumamoto band was very much alive, and now freshly revitalized by their organization into a YMCA, the fourteen members and their nine visitors had honored Mott by inviting him to climb Hanaoka ["Flowery Hill"] in the dark to greet the sunrise with prayer and the singing of "The morning light is breaking." "This morning the sun seemed to be different from what it used to be," wrote one of the young men. At the close of the day's impressive events the Kumamoto men and their guests testified that this had been "the greatest day they had ever seen, and the first time they had ever seen manifested the power of the Spirit of God"; one commented that there hadn't been such an event "since the Doshisha days at Kyoto," a reference to the enthusiasms of the early 1880's.[37] Mott wrote home that

Over 20 years ago about 30 Japanese students went to the same place before daylight for a prayer meeting. They had decided to become Christians and had this meeting to nerve themselves to confess Christ publicly. They wrote a covenant with blood drawn from their own arms promising to remain loyal to Christ and to extend His Kingdom in Japan. . . . It is a most impressive spot. . . . At your feet stretches the Kumamoto plain with the river winding through it. To your left in the distance you catch a glimpse of the sea. In front of you miles away stretches a mountain range the highest peak being a great volcano from which you can see the steam and smoke ascending.

From his own small conference the Japanese delegates were going forth "on fire with the love of Christ to work among their own fellow students and relatives." John concluded his letter by asking if it were true that McKinley's election had resulted in "improved times."

PART 15: Kyoto, Kobe, Osaka, Nara

Moving on to the central part of Honshu via the Inland Sea the Motts immediately identified themselves with the missionary community in Kyoto. John paid a protocol call on the new president of Doshisha, but he found the students cold at first and spent much time conferring with Swift and others. Leila visited the famous crafts shops and met the widow of Joseph Hardy Neesima (Niijima Jo), founder of the Doshisha, an unusual institution governed entirely by a Japanese board but substantially supported by American Congregationalists as well as the Japanese.[38] Both Motts gave addresses, and John was gratified by student conversions and the formation of an Association. A Japanese commented:

> While he [Mott] was working with a single purpose he never overlooked the real worth of learning and industry thus gaining fully the sympathy of other thoughtful people. He knew quite well forms of temptation to which students are generally exposed and taught us the way how to conquer such and lead a Christian life of victory. His speeches were generally practical and always struck the keynotes of religious needs and his presentation was so admirable that he never separated the ideal of religious life from that of the equally important ethical and social life of mankind. I suppose he is one of the best evangelists who know the deep spiritual interests of youthful life.[39]

In Kobe activities centered at Kobe College, unique as a school for women; while there John somehow found time to write his father a description of the construction of Japanese houses, using as examples the homes of the missionaries with whom they had stayed:

> They are more like toy houses than anything else. They are very lightly built. The frame is of light wood. The partitions are mostly sliding panels covered with paper. You can hear the least noise all over the house. You walk in the house without shoes.

He usually spoke standing in his stocking feet, but was getting moccasins which were "allowable."

> In some places where I speak the people sit on the floor. Whenever I speak I have to bow when I begin and when I close my address. As soon as I bow the entire audience bows in return. It is not a simple nod of the head either, but bowing the whole body nearly double.

At Osaka John addressed 700 students, and a conference of missionaries; Leila talked on Palestine. A "day off" was spent at Nara, the eighth-century capital, where they admired the Deer Park, the stone lanterns, and the marvelous plantings of trees, but reacted negatively to the shrines and temples. He and Swift went to Okayama for Mott to address 400 students in the evening; next morning they visited the lovely Koraku-en garden, which Mott pronounced the finest he had ever seen anywhere. He spoke on Bible study in the afternoon and to 500 in the evening on temptation. Back in Kyoto, Nijo Castle was visited. At Nagoya a college Association was formed at the Methodist boys' school.

PART 16: Christmas at the Fujiya Hotel

It was now December 21, Mott was exhausted, and the winter vacation rendered further work impossible until January. It was decided to devote the next two weeks to rest, sightseeing, and planning for the all-important Tokyo conference. From Nagoya the party went by train—the trains, wrote Leila, "are more like the English than the American and are very well managed" but slow, going only about twenty miles an hour—to Shizuoka on the Tokaido Road. Overnight accommodations were doubtless comparable to those offered at the celegrated Minaguchi-ya a few miles further at Okitsu.[40] John had his first experience with massage, being put to sleep in a few minutes. Rising early they took a train through the Hakone mountains:

> We had magnificent views of Fuji. We could see at one point from the snowy summit to the sea—a long line and one of the most beautiful in nature.

At Gotemba, in full view of Fuji and later to be the site of the national
Japanese YMCA's conference center Tozanso, to be visited many times
by Mott, their trunks were "loaded on the backs of some poor old horses"
while the Motts rode in rickshas for the first couple of miles, the Swifts
walking the entire thirteen miles over the ridges to Miyanoshita. After a
steep climb against a cold wind, a summit was reached in about two and a
half hours. Here the party ate their lunch in a shelter warmed by a
roaring fire. The downhill route "was so steep we ran most of the way":

> Then across the valley shut in by the beautiful hills. Bamboos and pines,
> rice and wheat—extremes seem to meet amicably in Japan. Some of the
> hills are quite covered with trees, others are bare and brown. We could see
> the steam from "Great Hell" and "Little Hell"—as they are called, these
> natural hot jets on the mountain side. We reached the hotel about six. For
> an hour before it was quite dark we seemed always in sound of waterfalls.
> We turned a sharp corner and came suddenly on the hotel. Almost the
> whole front is of glass and it is lighted with electricity. It did look beautiful.

This was the Fujiya, then and since the queen of Japanese resort
hotels, set on a cliffside among oriental gardens, pools, streams, and
forests.[41] The Swifts went on home to Tokyo for Christmas, hoping to
return, but he became ill. For eight days the Motts gave themselves to a
leisurely routine of long daily walks and climbs, down into the gorge—
anywhere "you may meet a torii and a wayside shrine"—or up to ever-
changing views of Fuji, to much letter-writing, daily hot mineral baths,
all pervaded by discussion of their future occupation. Three attractive
calls to other positions had precipitated decisions that would need to be
made soon after getting home, now only two months away and for which
both yearned. The pros and cons of each position—nowhere were they
named—were gone over separately and then weighed "impartially from
the standpoint of qualifications and life convictions." The solution
would come dramatically and unexpectedly in Chicago, the day after
arrival.

On Christmas Day they reminisced over the six Christmases since
they had become engaged at the "White House" in 1890: Santa Barbara,
Wooster, Louisville, Postville, and last year separated by the breadth of
India. Christmas dinner at the Fujiya featured twenty-four Western dishes, many with French descriptions; Mott sent a copy of the menu home
for the folks at Postville to judge "whether we are suffering in this Far
Eastern land," and remarking that he had never enjoyed better food "in
the hotels at home." Then he added that the recent election in the
States was "glorious." The hotel was festive, but the Motts kept to

themselves, leaving the dance floor to the "Yokohama crowd"—"we knew nobody in the hotel and didn't care to." Working over their finances, they found they were ahead. John dictated twenty letters to Leila, and wrote to Beaver at great length:

> Without doubt Japan is the most difficult field we have ever visited, and the problems here have taxed my resources more than any I have ever grappled with. I anticipated difficulties... but they have proved to be greater than I had expected to find. It is the first field where I have ever been in which I was put through such a nervous strain as to make sleep almost impossible. This is not explained by my condition when I reached Japan, because I reached here in splendid condition. Nor was it due to worry, or to friction with colleagues; for Swift and I have worked together as an absolute unit, and God has graciously kept us from anxious thought.
>
> I trace it to the awful moral condition of the young men which has drawn on my sympathy in a degree that I have never known, to the crisis in Japan which is terrible in its solemnity, to the necessity of moving the Japanese by indirection on account of their ultra-independent spirit—thus requiring three-fold the time and tact necessary in China, India or America. Notwithstanding all this God is leading us in triumph *in Christ*, largely, I believe, as a result of the prayers of faithful friends. . . .
>
> How I long to see you to talk of the future! The questions that call for settlement within the first few months after my return are very complex and vital. I cannot but feel that it is the will of God that we are to continue to be very closely related to each other in the work of His Kingdom. I rejoice in such a prospect.
>
> I would much prefer that you keep secret what I have written about losing sleep. We are getting a few days rest here before the final pull. Swift is badly used up and has had to go to bed. He has the hardest work of any man in the field in all our force, although I never realized it. May God forgive me for not praying more for him! I have felt all along that the work in India and China needed prayer more than that in Japan.

Then Mott twitted Beaver in a rare display of banter; wishing Beaver and his bride could be there to climb with them,

> We would not rush you up the way you did me on a memorable occasion. Still I would not object to having you run me up Mount Lofty if I could transport myself to Center County [Pennsylvania] (which I understand gave a majority for McKinley) tonight.

A few days later he advised Beaver against rejecting "a good thing" because of his own uncertainty as to the future, but hoped it could wait until their return.

John also found time to write his mother a description of Japan; how you would enjoy "its beautiful hills, its stretches of rice fields, its wonderful landscape gardening," he began:

its finely cultivated shrubs and trees and flowers; its strange and interesting temples and shrines in every grove and on every hill; its houses which remind one of children's houses or cupboards; its perfect roads and paths; its bright, polite, cheerful, active people; its unselfish and godly missionaries; its railways, telegraphs, electric light, postal service, well graded schools, manufactures and other features of modern civilization. It is a wonderful country.

But sin still abounds, and superstition. There are over 30,000,000 of people who know nothing about Christ. Infidelity is gaining ground. The forces of evil are active. More strong consecrated missionaries are needed if the nation is to be saved for our Lord. It is a time of crisis and Japan needs the prayers of the Church as never before.

"We have not been in a hotel we enjoyed more in many a day," wrote Leila after leaving the Fujiya, "we paid six and a half yen a day for the two of us—a little more than $3.25 gold." Some eight servants came to thank them at their departure "and all made profound bows." The route down from Miyanoshita revealed gorgeous views of Fuji plus Oshima, "an active volcano on an island."

PART 17: Nikko, Sendai, and Bishop Nicolai

A hotel in Yokohama seemed "dingy and dirty after our last home," but one night there and one in Tokyo were necessary for business, sitting for photographs, and ordering a new overcoat, before going on to Nikko where they were honored as the first guests of the New Year at the Hotel Arai. Before dark they walked the great avenue of cryptomerias, "probably the finest in the world," and the temple buildings, "not only picturesque but fascinating." Truly, wrote Leila, "the groves were God's first temples," and one cannot but delight in such beauty as this. The mausoleum of Iemitsu she thought "simplicity itself"; the trees "had most to do with the deep impressiveness of this temple, for it is a most wonderful combination of Nature and Art. . . ." On a visit to Japan, General Grant had won the "everlasting love of the Japanese people" by refusing the privilege of crossing the sacred bridge reserved for rulers and representatives of divinity, saying that what was good enough for the common people was good enough for him.

Mott became restive after three days at Nikko, one of which featured the zig-zag ascent to Lake Chuzenji by ricksha, and returned to Tokyo to find that the colleges had not yet reopened. He quickly arranged for a trip to Sendai, utilizing the intervening time for interviews, chiefly those with Seijiro Niwa,[42] the first Japanese YMCA secretary, and C. M. Bradbury, one of the earliest American teachers of English, who had been recruited by the Wilder-Forman team in 1888.[43]

Arrival at Sendai took on some of the features of later Mott travel: the veteran American Board missionary Dr. J. H. DeForest, who was arranging the details, astonished the Motts by appearing on the train with a delegation of students at a stop an hour out; there was also a large welcoming group of students and missionaries at the Sendai station.[44] During a brief stay at what proved to be an inopportune time John nevertheless interviewed the leading missionaries and Japanese Christians, gave several addresses, and laid the foundations for an Association. At a "floor party" reception given by the boys' Christian Club of the Koto Gakko Leila's feet went to sleep and she squirmed so that they brought her a chair. Dr. DeForest accompanied the Motts back to Tokyo; there were some thirty students and half-a-dozen missionaries at the station to see them off in the dark at 6:00 A.M.

The Motts alternated staying at the Imperial Hotel and with the Swifts during the seventeen days in Tokyo before they would sail for Hawaii on January 28, being treated to a heavy snow, and a sharp earthquake that roused John out of bed. Several weeks later he wrote his parents from Honolulu:

> It came in the middle of the night. We were living in Mr. Swift's large brick house. It rocked like a ship on a rough sea. The beams of the house creaked terribly. It was for all the world like an experience on the ocean. It seems mighty strange to have the solid earth sway and heave like the waves of the sea. The whole thing lasted about two minutes. We were sound asleep but it waked us up in a hurry. We did not know what it was at first but it did not take us long to find out. They have one every few weeks in Tokyo. The best houses, like the one we were in, are built scientifically to withstand the earthquake shocks, and they do it admirably. We were glad to have one experience of the kind, but one is enough. You are as safe on sea as on land—I really believe, safer.

Thirty years later, after earthquake and holocaust had devastated Tokyo, Mott would recall this when raising relief funds.

A three-day local conference had been planned in Tokyo prior to the national gathering, posters had been printed and all preparations made, but mourning for the Empress Dowager proscribed all public meetings. Instead, small groups of students met for discussions and Mott visited six area schools, though the most significant use of his time for the ecumenical movement was an extended conversation with the Russian

Orthodox missionary Bishop Nicolai—"Père Nicole" to many Japanese.[45]

This was the beginning of Mott's lifelong love affair with Orthodoxy. Leila wrote that the Bishop impressed him as a great man in body, mind, and spirit, who made him think of Phillips Brooks. John "put him through" the list of questions, which he answered "most frankly and kindly." Mott took copious notes. The Bishop did not believe more Protestant missionaries were needed in Japan. Next day the Motts visited the Orthodox cathedral, which came to be known popularly as the Nicolai-do; a chapel would be consecrated to the Bishop's memory.

> We all fetched up a little after six to hear the famous music. The cathedral stands on one of the finest sites in Tokyo, higher than the palace itself. It is an immense affair and has grouped all about it the Greek schools, Bishop's house, etc. A choir of about 100, both male and female voices, without instrumental accompaniment, sing most of the time for two hours. They keep perfect time and harmony. Strange and almost weird some of it is—but it is also fascinating to a strange degree. . . .

John became so involved that the only time Leila could be sure of him was between midnight and six in the morning.

PART 18: A National Student YMCA Is Formed

A small delegated body representing seventeen Associations, "the final convention to form a national movement," opened at the Tokyo YMCA on January 18, a "dark and rainy day." The group took meals together nearby "to prevent caucusing and to expedite matters." In addition to Mott and Swift there were seven foreigners present, but the majority of the delegates were Japanese. Mott was uneasy lest the rationalistic and nationalistic viewpoints which had been quite vocal in some of his meetings would become dominant.[46] A few delegates became "very excited," fearing that a creed was to be foisted on them, and there was "some sparring" over the evangelical basis.

Mott and Swift got home late the first night and were "very much tired out," but were hopeful that the standard constitution would be adopted next day. This was accomplished, largely, wrote DeForest, through Mott's "frank and tactful" strategies, though the final wording varied from that adopted by all other members of the Federation, the Japanese preferring to state their purpose as:

To bring students to become disciples of Jesus Christ as only Savior—*true God and true man.*

In concluding remarks addressed to Mott as the two-day Convention closed, the new chairman, President Kajinosuke Ibuka of the Meiji Gakuin, fittingly summarized the appropriateness of Mott's visit:

> You have come at a most favorable time, just when our nation is growing out of the narrow national spirit. This is not a national meeting, but an international. Our work does not end with these sessions, it is only begun. [47]

Mott and Swift returned to their wives at midnight "with the joy of victory in their faces and voices."

> It was a great day and so different from the preceding. The opposition had largely swung round and the Spirit of God ruled. A national Student Movement true to Christ was formed. It is the first successful attempt to define evangelical Christianity in Japan. Nobody but John dared to believe that what was really accomplished was possible. Men like Dr. Davis who have had to endure the Doshisha martyrdom rejoiced greatly and were much encouraged. [48]

In the remaining week Mott gave most of his time, as had been the case in the countries previously visited, to the administrative details of establishing the new organization—outlining Swift's duties as national student secretary, aiding in the writing of a prayer cycle, planning a series of pamphlets and a students' magazine, and coaching the new national committee of five foreigners and ten Japanese.

Throughout the visit to Japan Mott stressed the interviewing of Japanese and foreign religious leaders. Using the questions which he had developed, which had now expanded to twenty-five, he carefully took notes, seeking, as Swift explained later, "to form an opinion of the needs and opportunities of the country as a whole,"

> —of its progress and the true state of its new social life, which should be based not upon the impressions of his busy tour, but rather upon the mature judgments of a large number of the more experienced Japanese Christian workers and missionaries. As chairman of the American Student Volunteer Movement for Foreign Missions, he felt it his duty thus to become advised of the truth concerning this, the most misunderstood mission field in the world. [49]

As Swift summarized it, Mott gave time "which others would naturally have devoted to sightseeing" to these conversations concerning student life and the views of the leadership concerning the religious problems of the nation. Catholic, Orthodox, and Church of England people generally believed that there were enough missionaries in Japan but agreed with the Protestants whom he queried that workers needed to be better qualified and trained. Some gave eloquent testimony for ecumenism. Protestants are too much divided, which is "bad for the whole earth," declared Nicolai. DeForest decried the numbers of sects and the sectarian attitude. From fifty interviewees, more than a third of whom were Japanese, Mott accumulated a body of opinion that he would distill in his report letters.

The several thousand words of notes jotted in a fine but legible hand establish that it was about this time that Mott fixed the habit of taking notes on standard size typewriter paper—his letterheads were most often used—folded three times to produce four columns on each side, a device he would often refer to as his "pocket office." Thousands of these sheets, including two score from Japan at this time, have survived, many of them well worn; they comprise one of the most intimate aspects of the surviving record of his life.

Other activities of the last week in Tokyo included several evangelistic meetings, the largest of which attracted a thousand students and extended through three and one-half hours. There was an all-Japanese farewell stag dinner tendered by the directors of the Tokyo YMCA at which Swift commended Mott on his skill with chopsticks, and the speaker of the evening, a member of the original Kumamoto band, spoke on the significance of the words "world" and "Christian" in the name of the Federation. "The men came home in high spirits," wrote Leila, "each one bringing the remains of his feast neatly done up in a wooden box." Next evening the Swifts gave the Motts a farewell Japanese dinner, authentically served, but Leila's diary records that "one meal" had been quite enough of the native cuisine. The next to the last day John spent with Swift, Niwa, and Yabuuchi, their interpreter, in writing, while the ladies visited the Daibutsu at Kamakura. Leila liked it much better than the great images at Kyoto and Nara, quite possibly because the surroundings were fragrant, "quiet and sunny and peaceful," suggesting "Nirvana or at least a good deal of day dreaming." But that night John required a massage to get to sleep.

Finally, January 28, the long-awaited day of departure for Hawaii and home, arrived. A deputation of theological students called before breakfast to announce their decision to organize an Association. Niwa and Yabuuchi presented Leila with a book for John Livingstone, whose picture she had shown them the day before. Accounts were settled with the Swifts and affectionate farewells expressed for their helpfulness and hospitality from the moment of arrival in Nagasaki. The *Doric* of the P. & O. line sailed about noon for Honolulu, on what was an epoch-making voyage for John: for the first time in his life he was not seasick although the vessel rolled and pitched all the way.

Half of the ten-day trip was given to rest and relaxation; John read almost a book a day before feeling up to writing letters and reports. The time spent in Japan had about equalled that devoted to India or China, and in spite of the difficulties anticipated, had been remarkably effective. From the first the tour had taken on a more evangelistic character than elsewhere. He had addressed more than 7,000 in mass meetings, had spoken to students in forty-two educational institutions, converted 225 young men, increased the number of college Associations from eleven to twenty-eight—half of them in public schools—and added another national organization to the Federation. He had won the universal approval and support of the missionaries, more than fulfilling the hopes of the three who had first invited him to come to Japan in the spring of 1894. Swift wrote in retrospect that those who had watched Mott at work had more than once observed the collapse and disappearance of obstacles that had seemed insurmountable; "difficulties of a very delicate nature" were resolved through "brotherly harmony and loving obedience to God's will," pushed forward as it were by "the irresistible momentum of the great body of prayer following it." However, it had not seemed wise to press for a Japanese Volunteer Movement, as had been done so successfully in India.[50]

Mott's own impressions, summarized in his report letters and in *Strategic Points,* were that Japan was on the threshold of advance, that missionary support should be increased rather than diminished, that missionaries going there should be persons of "unusual strength," that the "greatest peril" to Japan was "the secular character of her institutions of higher learning," that Buddhism was "doomed in the land where it has greatest vigor," and that "the cause of Christ in Japan is entering upon a new and remarkable era." One of Mott's most impressive interviews had been with Guido Verbeck, who had baptized two of the first three Protestant Christians in Japan thirty years before. "Now there are over 40,000: God has always been in the life of this wonderful nation, but never so manifestly as to-day."[51]

PART 19: **Hawaii, Portland, Denver, Postville**

Eighteen days in the Sandwich (Hawaiian) Islands convinced Mott of the power of the religion of Christ to transform a country from barbarism to civilization.

> Every practical and fruitful effort being put forth to-day for the promotion of temperance, purity, and other virtues which have so much to do with the well-being of communities, is traceable to the religion of Jesus Christ.

The problems observable in the Islands were "the direct result of the evil forces of civilization" and in no sense whatever caused by Christianity. Several student Associations were formed and a corresponding representative to the Federation appointed for the Hawaiian Republic; such was Mott's success in fund-raising that Leila declared that he had "financial interviewing on the brain."

The diversity of Protestant missionary operations among Chinese, Japanese, Hawaiian, and European communities that they were shown seemed like a recapitulation of the tour. Although annexation was in the wind, neither Mott mentioned it. The names of their hosts, co-workers, and friends made up a roster of pioneer missionary families and second generation aristocrats: Dole, Gulick, Atherton, Damon, Waterhouse, Richards, Rice, Hyde, Bingham. Leila wrote that they had come away from a visit with the last named "feeling that these people were cast in heroic mould." John made a primary objective of their extended stay, caused by the disabling of the *Belgic* off the China coast, the rebuilding of his own health and vigor, taking a series of treatments at the Seventh-Day Adventist sanitarium under Dr. Kellogg of Battle Creek, for which he was able to obtain a forty percent discount.

A large group of missionaries, together with a band, saw them off for Tacoma via Victoria. As John reviewed his impressions of the Islands, he compared them to Ceylon: "God has not worked here in vain," having caused to be planted a Christian nation that is "a great lighthouse and a base of operations for the enterprise of universal evangelization." Hawaii is a veritable cross-roads of the nations:

> This fact has added meaning in our generation in which the Pacific is becoming increasingly the theatre of some of the largest activities of the world. [52]

The voyage home was rough and the food repulsive; few trips were made to the dining salon, but there was time to summarize the tour. Sixty thousand miles had been traversed (actually only a little more than Mott might have covered in the States) and work carried on in 144 schools, colleges, and universities in twenty-two countries, resulting in the organization of seventy new Associations and five national movements affiliated with the Federation, three of which were obtaining secretaries.

They had met 1300 missionaries representing eighty agencies, hundreds of whom John had interviewed. There had been twenty-one conferences attended by 3300 students and teachers from 308 institutions, plus 2200 other delegates. Five hundred young men had been converted, 2200 pledged to keep the morning watch, and about 300 volunteered for Christian work. These results were due to the generous men and women who had made the tour possible, to the years of seed-sowing by missionaries on the fields, to careful planning by colleagues in each country, but above all by "the work of the Spirit of God as a result of the prayers of friends and workers all over the world." Later as he concluded his description in *Strategic Points in the World's Conquest*, Mott testified that the results of the tour were in no sense

> the work of one or two during twenty short months, but rather [were the product] of a world-wide circle of "laborers together with God" reaching through the long years. Some men have planted; others have watered; *God Himself has given all the increase.* [53]

More than half a century later, Willem A. Visser 't Hooft, one of Mott's successors as general secretary of the Federation, himself early caught in the Mott web, held that this tour remained "without the slightest doubt the most fruitful ecumenical journey that anyone has ever undertaken perhaps since the days of St. Paul." [54]

Landing in Tacoma rather than San Francisco gave the Motts relative seclusion, an increasingly elusive possibility. Secretary Henry J. McCoy of San Francisco had planned to have a tender meet their ship in the Golden Gate to bring them to "a royal genuine heartfelt welcome to your homeland" featuring a banquet at the Palace Hotel! It seemed good to be on an American train from Tacoma to Portland, where a hectic week-end awaited. Mott chanced to arrive there at the strategic moment of an Association building campaign, which he aided by an eloquent address on "Why we believe in the YMCA" to an immense audience in the Opera House; the same evening he spoke to a congregation of over 1800 in the Taylor Methodist Church. That such numbers would crowd the largest halls of the city on short notice was an indication of his growing fame. Before leaving for Denver next evening he called on prominent men in the interest of the canvass.

It might be said that the world tour ended at Denver in reunion with John's sister Alice McAdam, whose oldest son had died while the Motts were in India. In spite of the pressure to reach Chicago and New York John had planned on four days of fellowship with a minimum of public distraction. Two extended visits with the Warners, Mott's childhood pastor and family, and a few other intimate friends, filled the time, except for reading a shoebox of sixty letters—"the last big heap of mail"—that came on from San Francisco.

The McAdamses accompanied the Motts to Postville. In Iowa the abundance of corn in storage caused Leila to recall the starvation she had seen in India. John planned four days in Postville, where for the first time in eight years the entire Mott family gathered around a festive table. Bothered by the recurrence of a stiff neck with rheumatic twinges, John spoke only once or twice in the little red brick Methodist church of his youth. Leila addressed a women's meeting where many of her hearers who had known John from infancy embraced her. It was inevitable that some business be transacted: one of John's colleagues came from Minneapolis for a full day of conference; all three of his staff members had suffered breakdowns from overwork during his absence, and all had been married. A happy family saw John and Leila, now only two days away from their son at Wooster, off to Chicago in joyous contrast to the fears they had choked down twenty months earlier when they hardly expected ever to see the travelers again—an explanation of John's repeated assurances of their good health and safety in every letter home.

PART 20: "A Lady in Chicago"

Upon arrival in Chicago—it was now March 23—John met Gilbert Beaver and plunged into business affairs, spending the night with Cyrus McCormick, Jr., who had contributed to the budget for the tour. Leila checked on the Oak Park home, to which they would not return, and took the night train to Wooster, John to follow. No one met her, but when she reached the "White House" young John L., now four and a half, was awakened from a nap:

He didn't know who was there. He looked at me just a moment, then threw himself into my arms. . . . [He] has grown broad and tall too. Says he weighs forty-seven. Hasn't changed so much in looks as in his thot and expression. Has a craze for spelling everything he sees.

But her mother was seriously ill. Leila was immediately engulfed in the exhausting care of a household, even forgetting her birthday on April first in the anxiety about her mother. There was a happy day when she took John and a cousin on a "delightful ramble down by the creek and in the woods as of yore." Her diary of seven books, kept daily throughout the tour and a principal source of our knowledge of the journey, ended on a household note April 8 in Wooster, which would be home until a house could be found in a New York suburb: Mott's burgeoning duties mandated living in the "national metropolis," headquarters for all YMCA activities.

Mott reviewed the tour with the younger McCormick, who raised questions concerning John's vocational and financial future. Promptly next morning the two men called on Cyrus' mother, Nettie Fowler McCormick, who asked similar questions. Both McCormicks had been fascinated by Mott's report letters. Then, as he later recounted it to Leila, John was "unexpectedly to himself" constrained to propose that the McCormick family undertake his support.[55]

There ensued the most strategically important conversation of Mott's life. At Vadstena he had been made general secretary of the Federation for the duration of the world journey. What would he do next? The question had preoccupied him and Leila at least since Christmas in the "Japan Alps." In the box of letters that had been forwarded to Denver there were offers and reminders of offers of at least two important positions. One was the general secretaryship of the North American YMCA, discussed with Morse at the outset of the tour. What the others were, we do not know, but a decision had to be made. At the same time, the leaders of eight of the ten constituent members of the Federation, each without the knowledge of the others, were urging him to become its permanent secretary. This was a clear call.

The discussion in the ornate McCormick mansion on North Rush Street that eventful morning doubtless canvassed all possibilities. Mrs. McCormick asked whether the forces initiated by the Federation and the momentum generated by the tour should be allowed "to pass away like water in a sieve?" Or ought they to be conserved and extended as "the beginning of a world-wide work—the alignment of the forces for a great forward movement among the nations?" To accomplish this there would need to be "one man who will throw himself into it and make it his specialty." Who could be better qualified than Mott with his nine years of experience in student work? There was remarkable agreement among the three. Mott went away to consider this breathtaking offer from the first woman to exert a major influence in the American business world.[56]

Following a day of staff conferences, Mott and Beaver took a night train to Indianapolis hoping to obtain the consent of former president Harrison to speak at Northfield in July. Previous engagements made this impossible for Harrison, but the conversation laid the groundwork for a development more significant for Mott's career. When Mott arrived in Wooster, John L. recognized him at once. The proud father described this moment in a letter to his parents:

> He looked at me a moment and then rushed up and threw his arms around me. He has hung right on to both of us ever since we arrived. Before this he would not leave his Aunt Anna to go with anyone. It is wonderful that he should remember us so well. They have done all they could to keep us in his memory and they have succeeded well. I am glad to say that he is looking very well. He is the picture of health. He is full of vigor and is on the move all day long. We are indeed thankful to God for caring for him so well and bringing us back to him in safety. We hope never to have to leave him for such a long time.

Then he spelled out detailed instructions for sending his sister Hattie to Battle Creek for a series of treatments. The important thing was to have Dr. Kellogg himself examine and prescribe for her; John thought he could obtain a discount, but they need not be concerned about finances. He, too, had returned to home and family responsibilities.

A few weeks later, after lengthy and prayerful consideration and conferences with Richard Morse and a few intimates, Mott drafted an eight-page statement of what would be involved in his acceptance of the McCormick offer.[57] The family approved it and a formal contract was drawn up, in terms of which Mott would receive a beginning annual stipend for salary and expenses of $4200 for one year, renewable annually at the donors' option. This would enable him to feel free to raise additional funds for the Federation which he estimated could run from $10,000 to $30,000 a year under special circumstances. To provide "unembarrassed leadership of the work" he hoped the contract would be renewed through a period of years.[58] His four-page outline of his proposed services to the Federation was essentially a job analysis of what he had been doing.

Thus began a friendship with Nettie Fowler McCormick that was to continue until her death thirty years later, and with other members of the family as long as Mott would live. It grew into a filial relationship bound by common concerns, unmatched ever in Mott's large circle of friends and supporters. He was free to approach her at intervals for special projects, which he did with adroit consideration, never abusing her confidence. Although Mott kept matters on a strictly professional basis, there came to be genuine affection displayed on both sides. For the Motts as for the Henry W. Luces, Mrs. McCormick became "an inestimable source of strength and encouragement." Luce once recalled "her unequalled presence—her face, lighted by an inner glow; the fine eyes, all fire and spirit and keen intelligence; above all, the kindly look. . . ."[59] Mott wrote at once:

> I cannot tell you what an inspiration it would be to work in this way as the representative of the members of your family. You have all shown such an intelligent and sympathetic interest in this work. In sustaining the Federation it is possible to influence all denominations, all nations, and all races; to purify the very fountain of the life of the nations, for as President Cleveland pointed out at Princeton—the universities and colleges furnish the real leadership of the nation. In a day of wars and rumors of war such a work would help unite the nations with a stronger and more enduring bond than arbitration treaties, for it is nothing less than fusing together with the omnipotent spirit of Christ the future leaders of the nations—the students. And in a time when much is being said and written about "Christian unity" the Federation, if in reality it unites the Christian young men of all denominations and races, will present the most remarkable concrete object lesson the world has yet seen—that "there is one body and one Spirit."[60]

The McCormicks and others urged Mott to publish the reports of his tour in book form. Perhaps the most eloquent of these suggestions was a well-reasoned brief from James A. Beaver, Gilbert's father, former Governor and now Chief Justice of the Supreme Court of Pennsylvania, to whom the letters on Australasia seemed to have "something of the flavor of the 16th Chapter of Acts." Judge Beaver proposed that the description of the journey be issued "in such form as to beauty of paper, typography, binding, etc., as to commend it to people of refinement and culture."[61] The book, Mott's first, not devoid of that hyperbole of expression that characterized the age, was published in June, 1897, as *Strategic Points in the World's Conquest: The Universities and Colleges as Related to the Progress of Christianity.*[62] A small volume complete with itinerary and a map of the tour, its worldwide distribution proclaimed the birth and remarkable early growth of the Federation, and established Mott as Protestantism's leading missionary statesman.

PART 21: **Students of the World United: The First Federation Conference**

The first convention of the Federation met as planned at Northfield in July, in connection with the North American student conference, with all ten national movements and others in process represented by men Mott had met on his tour. Leila brought John L. Let Mott describe it, since it was his creation:

> In addition to the 600 students from 136 universities and colleges of the United States and Canada, there were present students and Christian workers representing twenty-five other nations or races. They represented Orient and Occident, Northern Hemisphere and Southern Hemisphere, all six continents of the globe, as well as the islands of the Pacific and Southern Seas. Delegates were registered from not fewer than thirty-six denominations or branches of the all-embracing Church of Christ and from all the five great races of mankind. All classes of institutions of higher learning were represented—state, Christian, and independent—as well as the different faculties or departments of learning—arts, medicine, theology, science, philosophy, engineering.
>
> Round Top is the little hill just back of Mr. D. L. Moody's house, and is famous as being the place where more students have dedicated their lives to the extension of Christ's Kingdom than anywhere else in the wide world. Day after day at sunset the hundreds of delegates from the ends of the earth assembled on this sacred mount to lift up their eyes and look far beyond the beautiful Connecticut Valley and the distant Green Mountains upon the great harvest fields of the world, and to listen to burning messages from their fellow students telling of the triumphs of Christ among their own people and the need for more men to preach the Gospel in regions beyond.

Moody led some of the inspiring sessions. One day the delegates visited "holy ground" at Mount Hermon where the Student Volunteer Movement had been born in 1886; prayers were offered in twenty-one languages to consecrate the site of a new chapel.

After the Northfield meetings, the delegates from abroad and a few others moved to Williamstown for the business sessions of what Mott called the "real convention" of the Federation. Karl Fries, the chairman, was absent on account of illness, but was reelected. T'ing Ming Uong of China nominated President Ibuka to the vice-presidency; he chaired the meetings "with grace, impartiality, dignity, and ability." Mott declared in his report that this was "probably the first world's Christian gathering at which an Oriental has presided, but it will not be the last." Mott was made permanent general secretary; he told the delegates that "a lady in

Chicago" had underwritten his support. There were reports from around the world, general policy set, the constitution amended. Then,

> The high tide of the Federation convention, if not of all student conventions, was marked by a meeting held at twilight one day near the close of the convention at the Williams Haystack Monument.... The battle hymns of the Church were sung with fervor and deep feeling. Praise and prayer were offered in many tongues. The delegates unitedly rang out the words of the haystack band, "We can do it if we will," adding that watchword which during these days is taking such strong hold on the lives of students of all races: "Make Jesus King!" They then joined hands around the monument for closing prayer, but it was not until the meeting had been thrice prolonged and the Doxology sung as many times that this world-embracing circle reluctantly broke up. [63]

Thus were the students of the world united.

5

Apostle of Unity

*There is no other man . . . who could be spread over
the entire globe.*

MOTT rose to the apex of leadership of his "first love" in the years immediately following his return from the first round-the-world journey. Under his direction the North American Student YMCA's enrolled unprecedented numbers whose multitude of activities ranged from Bible study to social service; to these thousands of college youth he was the great evangelist and spiritual leader of the day. The Student Volunteer Movement enlisted ever-growing numbers of missionary candidates, while the hosts attending its quadrennial conventions expanded in both numbers and enthusiasm.

The World's Student Christian Federation, fostered by a second world tour, another trip to Australia, and months in Europe every year, was laying solid foundations for the later ecumenical movement. Secretaries of the "foreign work" of the YMCA could be found promoting the American program in more and more cities of the non-European world. Mott's leadership of these four interrelated organizations and increasing recognition as Protestantism's chief missionary statesman now demanded that his office be in New York City.

As early as 1894, he had written his parents that he might need to move east from Chicago. Upon their return in 1897, he and Leila set up a temporary base for her and John L. at the Wooster "White House" until a suitable suburban home could be found within convenient commuting distance of the "national metropolis," where John would be not only at YMCA headquarters but near "the center of the foreign missionary interests of the country," as the editor of *The Student Volunteer* put it in the first issue published from the new location.[1]

The move was a wrench for both the Mott and White families. John S. Mott's health was deteriorating and Harriett was undergoing periods of depression. Leila's parents were aging and needed care and relief from the Wooster farmstead; the burden of domestic arrangements for them fell heavily upon Leila, who took young Johnny to the White home for long periods when his father was abroad. She returned there for the birth of Irene, their second child, in 1899;[2] John administered his far-flung enterprises from Wooster that summer.

The search for a permanent New York home extended through three long years; after unhappy experiments in renting, and many months spent in Europe, a house at 75 Midland Avenue in Montclair, New Jersey, was purchased. Four children grew to maturity there. From this convenient location, John could readily walk to his New York train each morning, meeting his secretary at the station and when under unusual pressure dictating all the way to his office even in a cab in Manhattan.[3] He would return each evening with a loaded briefcase, and after a family dinner Leila—in later years stretched out on a sofa—would advise, edit, and critique his current writing and the affairs of the day; intimates doubted that he ever made a major decision counter to her advice.[4]

At 75 Midland Avenue, Leila managed the home and family, with domestic help, and when John was away on extended trips, brought the Fennell P. Turners, neighbors and spiritual kin (he was General Secretary of the SVM), who became virtual foster parents to the children, to live with her. When she accompanied John, both felt complete security with the Turners in charge; the children later recalled that at times during adolescence they felt less restraint under the Turners than when subject to their mother's Scotch Presbyterian discipline, which, in turn, was more severe than their father's.

The move to New York brought Leila for a time into a modest whirl of student Young Women's Christian Association activities. She spoke frequently at women's colleges and at student conferences. She had an extended term of service on the national YWCA board. In the winter of 1898-99 she was caught in a blizzard during a tour of women's colleges and became ill from exposure. She did not usually accompany John in domestic travel, but when he adjudged that she was overworking, her schedule was reduced. During the short period covered in this chapter two of her brothers came to live and work in New York, which happily enlarged the family circle and provided not only gay holidays for a bevy of children but also gave John R. Mott joyous moments to recall when alone on the other side of the globe.

John was probably able to visit Postville as frequently as when his

base was Chicago. Each year the responsibility for his parents and unmar-
ried sisters increased. As long as they lived, he tried to write home
weekly, but when that was impossible, Leila took over. His letters might
give spiritual advice to Clara or Hattie, assure his parents on the re-
investment of idle funds through his attorneys Merrill and Rogers, help
them decide on furnishings or improvements to the house on West
Williams Street, or instruct Clara, whom he had introduced to Mrs.
McCormick, on the strictly professional nature of her relationship as
piano teacher to a daughter. The Postville family was never far from his
mind: he not only sent souvenirs and gifts from strange places, but from
India shared their satisfaction over a new bathroom, from Australia advised them to use a local paperhanger and to pay a housemaid adequately,
from a ship nearing Ireland expressed anxiety about Harriett's need for an
operation. In 1900 he enjoyed voting for president the first time, returning to Postville to cast his ballot for McKinley.

For Mott the greatest joy of each year was an extended family
vacation at Lac des Iles, Quebec, in summer. Invited by Canadian
YMCA friends to a wilderness area some sixty miles north of Montreal,
the Motts first found their ideal camp in 1897. John enthusiastically
wrote Hattie a greeting on birchbark, which has survived with superior
legibility. Property was purchased for a song and by 1900 a log cottage
had been built. When forced to work during the summer, Mott would
install Leila and the children at the Lac, coming to them readily by
sleeper from New York as frequently as possible. Usually there were
family or friends also in residence, and the simple cabin was added to and
more land obtained and additional accommodations built. For Mott, this
was another life. Until telephones came, it was as remote as his sea
voyages before wireless.

For at least a decade the fishing was rewarding. Mott would try other
lakes with his neighbors, the Budges, Rosses, and Calhouns. He persisted
in trying to learn to swim, but John L. soon outdistanced him. If the fish
were unresponsive to his lures, he might cuss them in mock solemnity as
if addressing an SVM Quadrennial. He often read aloud and neighbor
children came to listen. On one occasion a ten-year-old boy stopped by
to visit; neither thought it unusual that the talk went on for two hours.
On Sunday mornings an informal Protestant service was held at one of
the larger cottages; Mott usually hammered out, partly through discussion afterward, an important address to be used during the coming year.

Over the years, select friends came as guests. Some were surprised,
but not all, to discover Mott as *pater familias*, doing "much work" with

"his own hands" on the house and its furnishings, as Karl Fries put it. Some thought they had come upon another source of his spiritual power. They at least observed him building up resources with which to combat the solitariness of travel: constant awareness of the intimate ties to wife, children, relatives, and friends augmented the eternal entities by which Mott lived, whether in their immediate presence at the Lac or in their spiritual presence while crossing a tempestuous sea from Australia to New Zealand. Throughout his entire life, the "Lac" would be a retreat, a haven of renewal, a place of joy.[5]

PART 1: The Home Base

The first decade of the twentieth century was "a uniquely creative period" in the development of denominational cooperation in the United States. This movement took at least three directions.[6] Mott, involved in all of them and courted by one, maintained his neutrality among Protestant bodies including his own (Northern) Methodist Church, but built his base in the pioneer interdenominational agency, the Young Men's Christian Association. Tempted, though never seriously, by flattering offers elsewhere, he commited himself ever more closely to the YMCA not only because it was an effective vehicle through which he could accomplish his personal aims but also because of the attractiveness of its fraternal spirit, its lay character, and its rapidly broadening purposes that he was himself increasingly molding.

From his epochal report to the International Convention of 1897 on the WSCF and his world journey to promote it, Mott was held in the highest regard by the YMCA. He was a regular dinner guest at Chairman Cleveland E. Dodge's New York mansion for top-level policy-making. He sat on the planning committee for the Golden Jubilee at Boston in 1901, and "was kept very busy in helping to direct its affairs" during the sessions, as he wrote his parents. In his climactic closing address he proclaimed to an expectant audience that the home base must become "a base of aggressive, world-wide operations on behalf of the Kingdom founded by our Lord and Saviour, Jesus Christ." The "larger significance" of the YMCA lies in its becoming "a mighty force to be wielded on behalf of the evangelization of the multitudinous inhabitants of the earth." The prospect drew an enthusiastic response from all quarters, including the press. No one dissented. As Owen E. Pence says in his incisive appraisal of the Movement, "In the years immediately following 1900, the word was 'Forward'."[7] Mott's name became synonymous with that slogan. A week earlier he had spoken twice at the Jubilee of the Montreal Association, the first in North America, concluding that there was no apparent reason why the next half century should not be "far richer and more fruitful than the past fifty years."

Mott was not only an effective advocate of world outreach but in the eyes of his colleagues embodied the evangelical ideals of enthusiasm, dedication, Bible study, the life of prayer, and full commitment to Christ. When S. Wirt Wiley, to be a national YMCA executive and confidant of Mott, heard him in the late 1890's at Lake Geneva, Mott was eloquent, serious, impressive—then, and always.[8] Whether he was speaking to the railroad "Y," observing the twenty-fifth anniversary of the Rochester City Association, or projecting a hastily-outlined oration such as that for the Portland building campaign right off the ship from the Orient in 1897, Mott's message was that the greatest need of the YMCA is "the power of Jesus Christ."

This appeal brought men such as Wiley into the fraternity in increasing numbers, as secretaries, lay workers, or missionaries, dedicated to the parent YMCA, the student work, the Volunteer Movement, or the burgeoning "foreign work."[9] Mott came almost to embody the Association, as had its revered founder, George Williams, whom Mott knew and liked to quote on the evangelical ideal of confronting men with Jesus Christ. In Richard C. Morse's words, Mott was "the lineal successor of Henry Drummond."[10]

As Mott's popularity grew, he found it increasingly difficult to meet the demands placed upon him and at the same time devote his best efforts to his own portfolios. This brought him in 1900 to the realization that he must "narrow down or be swamped," as Professor H. B. Adams of Johns Hopkins put it to him. It was from about this time that he began to make annual allocations of the number of days to be devoted to each of his responsibilities. It must have been, too, near this juncture that he came to the realization, when reading the Bible with Leila, that God did not expect him to bring in the Kingdom either alone or immediately. From that moment the weight of his schedule was lifted. To keep his complex financial affairs in order, he designed a pocket ledger in which he noted not only his expenses but pledges, promises made or received, loans, bank accounts, funds held for his Postville family, and expenses at Lac des Iles.

In 1902, David McConaughy, the first American YMCA secretary to India, who accompanied Mott home on his second world journey, together with his brother James, Mott, Speer, and "a few other intimate friends," organized a prayer circle that would meet once a year for a "Quiet Day." A monthly circular kept the members in touch; it bore "just a few requests for prayer and for praise for answered prayer." McConaughy later described Mott's participation:

> It has been his habit, along with the rest of us, to speak to one another with utter unreserve of the experiences of the year past, including the books read, and forecasting our plans for the ensuing year. In the intimacy of that circle, I have come to realize the secrets of power in the closeness of his daily walk with Christ, steadying him in the midst of tremendous pressure and exacting demands.[11]

On occasion, old friends such as Luther Wishard and Robert Wilder were invited. Conducted much like a Quaker meeting, the day was given to review of the year's high and low points both in individual and larger perspectives, to Bible reading, prayer, and discussion. At lunch the men shared impressions from books they had read. Some sessions were deeply personal, others absorbed in world problems; each man spoke out of his own thought and experience. There were no speeches. Mott was there unless out of the country; for him, this inner circle nourished a life-long fellowship broken only by death and Fundamentalism. New friends of new generations filled the rare vacancies.

PART 2: The Intercollegiate YMCA

His first love continued as the heart of Mott's activities for eighteen years after his return in 1897; his leadership of the North American Student Christian Movement more than justified Princeton President Patton's 1899 remark that few things had encouraged and inspired him more. Patton's successor, Woodrow Wilson, said in Mott's presence in 1902 that this phenomenon that had taken hold of the colleges had also "taken hold of the nation and in taking hold of the nation [was] taking hold of the nations of the world."[12]

The steady growth of the Movement was clear evidence of the confidence of Americans in the religious and educational institutions of their country during the last years of pre-World War I innocence. Higher education was on the threshold of tremendous expansion, and the Protestant churches were growing faster than the immigration-swollen population. The Student Christian Movement was the central drive of this young man who had taken the world as his parish en route to becoming "the most widely-known figure in the academic life of five continents."[13]

Wilson's remark had followed an address by Mott in which he had described the North American Movement in broad strokes: there were then 648 student Associations, distributed among colleges and universities, theological, law, medical, dental, normal, technological, military, and naval colleges, metropolitan intercollegiate bodies, academies and preparatory schools.[14] In all of these the student YMCA's enjoyed a virtual monopoly of the field. Their primary purpose, Mott always made clear, was to bring students into the Christian life; all activities and programs served this end.

The most productive agent in the promotion of the student work, according to Mott, was the secretary. By 1902 he had built his staff up to ten men—Gilbert Beaver in the New York office and the others deployed across the continent. Mott's genius for selecting young men of unique abilities has already been seen in his choice for special assignments of Robert E. Speer, Robert Wilder, W. W. and J. Campbell White, Fletcher Brockman, D. Willard Lyon, and Galen Fisher. Ethan T. Colton, a Dakotan interested in politics and education until he read an article by Mott in the *Northwestern Christian Advocate,* was invited to the International Convention at Grand Rapids in 1899, quite as Mott had been called to Harlem in 1888, ostensibly to speak at a student session, but actually to be "sized up as a secretarial prospect, much as an animal gets exhibited at a stock sale." Mott sat on the front row, "looking as severely intent as he could then," Colton remembered. The resulting tenure as traveling secretary for fourteen Midwest and Coast states brought Colton into intimate working relations with "The Chief," an acquaintance with Mott that began "with his gentler traits and moods and relaxations from the inner pressures that drove him." In recalling his apprenticeship sixty years later, Colton compared Mott to Gladstone, who had "toiled terribly":

> So did this man. He was misunderstood for disappearing from public sessions without a handshake and a chat with waiting persons down in front. To do it would consume time and strength from the next high-tension responsibility. The exterior he presented was never just a "front." It expressed the sense of mission that claimed the use of all his powers and time. Humor bubbled when appropriate, frequently over events of the day in bedtime postlude with intimate associates. Ginger ale flowed freely—the imported Cantrell and Cochrane brand preferred.[15]

Colton's forte, after four years in student work, would be in fund-raising

for the Foreign Department and from 1917 to 1924 in administration of
the Russian relief program.[16]

Before Mott had ever heard of a vigorous young Texan named Willis
D. Weatherford, Brockman's keen scent had marked him for YMCA
leadership. Just as Weatherford was taking his Ph.D. at Vanderbilt in
1902, a telegram came from Mott, the result of which was a life-long
commitment to Southern youth, race relations, and education, beginning with a three-year tour of duty "up and down and across fourteen
Southern states" to visit some seventy-five colleges every year—as had
Brockman and Mott before him.[17] Each year there were more fresh
recruits, some to travel for a time and move on; "Mott's men" came to be
legion. On each he lavished what one called "wonderful care" for professional development, family crises, or needed holidays.[18]

The administration of his far-flung operation was Mott's exercise
and glory. Since the Baker's Island retreat of 1889 he had found that type
of small staff meeting to be well suited to building morale and fostering
the sense of fraternity. It was the ideal method of coaching his men in the
methodology he had developed; its intimacy and their receptivity to the
higher spiritual life that he possessed produced a high degree of loyalty.
The extent to which the members of the team emulated him is the most
apparent evidence of his success. The results were similar whether it was
a small retreat or, later on, the larger meeting of all International staff
men and key lay leaders. His induction, wrote Colton, took place in
1900 at an Atlantic resort:

> Each man covered the year's progress, his current problems, outlook and
> plans ahead. Committeemen and colleagues bored in, cross-examined,
> challenged and recommended. It was vital give and take all around, in and
> out of sessions. Withal for the newcomer it was exposure both in sweep and
> detail to the far flung operations of that outstanding lay body of the time. It
> served Christian ends consecutively for a half century. We were solemnized
> and instructed about our physical health and intellectual habits and
> growth. The spiritual element pervaded and dominated objectives at all
> angles. I came away sensitive to being more than a cog in wheels of
> organization. Proud to be sharing in so rich a fellowship, I came away to
> put my best and utmost into it.[19]

At the turn of the century, Mott was already concerned with "Perils
in the life of the Secretary," and was being called upon by professional
groups such as the conference just described for advice on "The Spiritual
Life of the Secretary," "Traits the Traveling Secretary should seek to
Exemplify," or "Habits which we as Christian Workers should fasten

upon us as with cords of Steel." Perils were superficiality, narrowness, failure to keep the spiritual work to the front, selfish ambition, starving the spiritual life, working in the energy of the flesh, "failure to win the victory in one's own life," lack of Christian frankness in dealing with one another. On the positive side, Mott counseled the worker to give himself an annual personal inventory and then to do so with a fellowship group, to begin each day with the morning watch, to pray regularly, to observe an occasional quiet day, to be aware of the effect of body states upon the mind, and to cultivate right mental habits, especially of constructive thinking. When Mott compiled his *Addresses and Papers* in 1946–1947, he included three pieces dealing with the physical, intellectual, and spiritual life of the religious worker; their content had changed little from his texts of 1902, 1904, or 1905.[20]

Mott's prescriptions, which were among his more popular talks, inspired generations of YMCA secretaries, Student Volunteers, and religious workers. Thousands of college men and women who listened to Mott the evangelist were helped to clarify their goals and discipline themselves. The similarity of these recipes to comparable exhortations by Henry Drummond is apparent, as are the parallels to more popular "positive thinking," the perils of which Mott avoided by cautioning against pride and constantly referring to the lordship of Christ, even as he had done as a prep school boy at Upper Iowa and as a junior at Cornell. No longer labeled "Holiness," this discipline nevertheless led to a "higher life." It became the new *Guide to Holiness* for Christian youth and their leaders.

The extensive program of the intercollegiate Movement is familiar to the reader. Bible study was being promoted by three secretaries in 1906. Mott saw to it that both liberal and conservative approaches were available to study groups; his brother-in-law, W. W. White, who represented the latter position, taught large classes at the summer conferences at Northfield and Lake Geneva, and Speer's texts continued to be popular. Oberlin professor Edward I. Bosworth's books appealed to the more liberal; in 1899 Mott brought H. B. Sharman, author of *Studies in the Life of Christ*, to the department.[21] The morning watch was significant in the Bible study context; Mott promoted it at every opportunity. The annual Day of Prayer for Students was a worldwide observance of rededication and financial support. Mott emphasized the construction of buildings to house the worship services, discussion groups, classes, and varied activities of the larger campus Associations. (The missionary department, organized as the Student Volunteer Movement, will be treated separately below.) A strong effort, with some success, was made to develop an affiliated movement in the theological schools under the leadership of Robert Wilder, J. Ross Stevenson, and Thornton B. Penfield.[22]

Mott accorded high priority to the student presidents' conferences, which he had begun in 1892. In spite of his growing worldwide responsibilities, he gave them his personal attention, for they were prime sources of lay and staff leadership. Here, again, the final emphasis was upon the qualities of leadership to be nourished by Bible study, the morning watch, and prayer. The members of one such conference in 1904 recognized in a resolution that they were in themselves "wholly inadequate" to meet the duties that confronted them "without a living personal relation" with their Lord and Master, and after promising to work for sixty percent more students in Bible study, pledged themselves to "loving, persistent, personal work" in behalf of their fellows who were not Christians. At the presidents' meetings Mott also helped his protégés with a hundred suggestions on business management, publicity, record keeping, literature, and the whole gamut of program.

By the turn of the century attendance at Northfield had reached 600; in 1903, 1571 delegates came there, to Lake Geneva, Pacific Grove (later Asilomar), and the peripatetic Southern center then at Asheville. Mott assumed full control of Northfield upon the death of Moody, which event had no apparent effect upon the numbers of students who came to the summer conferences. He usually presided at both the men's and women's conferences; the only one missed in these years was 1898, when he was in Europe for World's Alliance and WSCF meetings. Although persistent efforts were made to bring celebrities to these popular events, the evidence is that Mott and his gifted and attractive colleagues such as Colton, Weatherford, Beaver, and others were the principal magnets. Charles K. Ober, whose heart was ever warm toward the student work, described the real purpose of a conference as "the opportunity for spiritual illumination and uplift, 'the stimulation of a few great messages concerning Jesus Christ, some quiet talks together on the secrets of His life and service, conference on the gospel and its present power to transform men's lives. . . ." These, together with "the glory of the vision and the music of the invitation," were "the forces that in the past had wrought changes in men's lives and given them the dynamic of the gospel." Paul Super, post-World War I builder of the YMCA in Poland, was first confronted by Mott at a deputation conference in 1901. He remembered the "world-conquering determination ringing in his voice, authority in his words, compulsion in his ideas, his concentrated gaze penetrating one's inmost soul," one might add, like the earlier evangelist Charles G. Finney. [23]

Financing the growing enterprise was an ever-present spectre that occupied an inordinate share of Mott's time and energy. Because his salary and expenses were met from other sources, he could ask the students at the summer conferences to help support the work; Northfield was raising about $2,000 a year at this time. In a strong lieutenant such as Colton he had an invaluable ally; finances occupied a primary place in the surviving letters between the two for the four years Colton traveled for the student department. At one juncture, Morse and Mott proposed to Mrs. McCormick and the Rockefellers that they endow Mott's office, but the Rockefellers rejected the plan. Mrs. McCormick countered with an unsolicited offer to provide Mott with an assistant. [24]

In spite of such rare windfalls, financing the intercollegiate Movement was a continuous uphill struggle of individual solicitation that became intolerably burdensome during the all too frequent recessions of the period. In later years, Mott acknowledged an immense debt to Richard Morse for coaching him in this technique. [25] Mott's enthusiasm for student Association buildings, grounded naturally in his Cornell experience, ran its course by about 1910, when there were fewer than thirty of the hundred he had once projected; many, if not most, of these lived on into the secularized fourth quarter of the twentieth century, sadly diverted from their original purposes. [26]

In accordance with his resolve to "narrow down," Mott began to restrict his campus visitations to the Ivy League, the larger state and private universities, and other prestige or strategic institutions. After he met Leila he rarely found time to visit Upper Iowa, but beginning in 1898 he started going to the eastern women's colleges. Yet he kept in vital contact with the Movement at large through intimate participation in student conferences, soon to include new ones in Canada, Oregon, and Louisiana, and his tours were scheduled to include stops on the main lines of travel. When he shared the Pacific Grove conference with Colton in January of 1901, there were visits to the University of California at Berkeley and at Stanford, which he called the "most irreligious" university in the country; he thought it "shaken to the center" by his evangelism, though the student newspaper was less impressed. [27] He spoke regularly at Cornell, and as his reputation as an evangelist grew, held student revivals at Toronto, Columbia, Wisconsin, Penn State, Virginia, and Brown at the instigation of alumnus John D. Rockefeller, Jr. [28]

But his favorite American campuses were Princeton, Harvard, and

Yale. Princeton was a shrine to YMCA men because of the beginnings of the intercollegiate Movement there two decades earlier.[29] In January, 1899, Mott wrote Mrs. McCormick from the Princeton Inn the morning after he had observed the Day of Prayer for students on the campus of Old Nassau at the invitation of President Patton. Classes had been dismissed and large numbers of men had assembled in the chapel in spite of pending examinations. His talk on "Temptations of Students in All Lands" had received excellent attention; later he had spoken to the Association on "Points to Emphasize in Our Work," and in the evening there had been an overflow audience in "the old church" for his address on "The Student Movement throughout the World and Princeton's part in it," a forecast of Princeton-in-China, followed by private conferences with students "about matters pertaining to life and service."

Mott's visit to Harvard in 1901, he reported, was in some ways "one of the most remarkable experiences" he had had up to that time. Due to effective planning doubtless stimulated by the resourceful campus "Y" secretary, Edward C. Carter, well-advertised meetings brought out the largest numbers ever, possibly excepting those for Drummond, in spite of Mott's well-known stance on morals. Colton recalled an incident concerning the advance publicity:

> Once in Detroit he gave me a telegram to send to the "broad gauge" Christian Association at Harvard, where a series of evangelistic meetings was being set up on the campus. As the topic for publicizing the opening address, he had given, "Universal Sins in Student Life." He would deal with intemperance, impurity, betting and cheating. The promoters had misgivings about this frontal attack. They proposed a title that sounded academic yet utterly bromidic. The reply, handed me with a grin, read: "No objection to change if it does not involve change in subject matter." And he chuckled: "I can soon dispose of the headline."[30]

When the meetings began, Mott was gratified to notice diverse student interests represented and to be given "intense attention." No public professions were asked for, but there were ten- to fifteen-minute personal interviews day and night: "Nearly forty conversations were held on questions fundamental to Christian faith and Christian life. A large majority of the men dealt with were led to take at least the first step necessary to entering the Christian life." Mott attributed these phenomenal results to the prayers of "a faithful band of Harvard men" and similar groups elsewhere: "No one who was present in the public meetings or in the Preachers Room at Wadsworth House, where the inquirers came, could doubt for a moment that an irresistible, unseen power was at work on the hearts and consciences and wills of men." After the first night, the *Crimson* commented that men rarely had the good fortune to hear such an address as Mott had given: "He spoke on a difficult subject with a frankness and earnestness which impressed everyone who heard him."[31]

But Mott's favorite university was Yale. In early July, 1898, when he was putting the finishing touches on his preparation for the WSCF conference in Germany later that month, word came to him at Lucerne that Yale had conferred an honorary M.A. on him. "I suppose this is about the greatest honor I have yet had," he wrote promptly to his parents, "except that of being counted worthy to serve this great student movement. Whatever honors come to me like this remind me that I owe all to what you have done in bringing me up and affording me facilities for obtaining an education. These honors therefore are yours as truly as they are mine."

Yale was the first university Mott had visited while an undergraduate at Cornell. It had been a close competitor to Cornell in his choice of an eastern college. It was the alma mater of James B. Reynolds, who had laid the European foundations for the WSCF, of Sherwood Eddy, who would be one of his closest collaborators, of Henry W. Luce and Horace T. Pitkin, Student Volunteers whose successors formed Yale-in-China, and of Amos Alonzo Stagg, the legendary athlete and coach who had directed the sports program at Northfield in the early days, and had served a term as Association secretary at Yale. The student "Y," "Dwight Hall," and its winsome secretary, Henry B. Wright, epitomized Mott's ideal of a campus Christian organization.[32] At the turn of the century, Yale men were playing a large role in the Northfield conferences every summer. Mott was probably Yale's most frequent ecumenical visitor during the next third of a century after his return from the world journey of 1895–1897; he was forced to keep a record of his visits and the subjects of his discourses, which, after 1908, had to be held in the new Woolsey Hall, Battell Chapel being too small. He also spoke at Dwight Hall, and his evangelistic campaigns stormed that citadel of infidelity, the Sheffield Scientific School. "His influence," wrote Ralph H. Gabriel in *Religion and Learning at Yale*, "was a powerful force in determining the character of Dwight Hall religion in his day." When Mott came to Yale, "his words extended the horizons of young men in college at a time when the United States was emerging from a century of isolation and, with some awkwardness and confusion, was beginning to assume the responsibilities of a major power."[33]

Mott's emphases in his turn-of-the-century campus evangelism may be seen in the titles of his addresses: "What manner of man we should be," "Spiritual Atrophy," "Why an increasing number of young men believe in Jesus Christ as Lord," "Four kinds of students," "Be sure your sins will find you out," "The power of sin," "Religion primarily a matter of the will."[34] After Mott's visit to Yale early in 1900, Henry Wright wrote of how salutary for the Church it could be that 500 men would graduate from Yale that year "who not only have heard, but who know by experience that a religious awakening among educated men is not only possible, but more than that, necessary." Nearly 100 men had taken a stand or "made things right with the folks at home." Four agnostics who had talked with Mott, Wright continued, were now "meeting twice a week and studying the resurrection and the life of Christ." Late at night, as Wright finished his letter, "another entirely new man" stopped by to tell him that he had "smashed up a picture after your meeting Sunday, began a systematic study in the Bible and feels the power of Christ."

It was true, as Sherwood Eddy saw it in retrospect, that Mott "addressed himself to the reason, the conscience, and the will—not to the emotions. He could not touch the heart of the man in the street, as Moody could. But Mott's method appealed to critical students." A few years after the above events, Eddy continued, "to the amazement of academic circles," the universities of Oxford, Cambridge, and conservative Edinburgh would fall to Mott "like the walls of Jericho."[35]

Eddy's contrast of Mott with Moody was already apparent when in December, 1899, word came that Moody had died. One may imagine the kaleidoscope of memories that thronged Mott's mind as he journeyed with Richard Morse to Northfield for a deeply moving funeral and interment on "Little Round Top," the most sacred spot in the Student Volunteer world. Several times in later life, when called upon to speak about Moody, Mott recalled the high points of the thirteen years of his association with the great evangelist:

Beginning with Mount Hermon 1886, I literally sat at his feet for four weeks. . . . All of us delegates were brought into intimate touch with him, not only in listening to his powerful sermons and pungent Bible expositions, but also out under the elms plying him by the hour with our questions. After that I had face-to-face contacts with him at least once every year. . . . I was permitted to see him in action in some of the most notable and fruitful evangelistic campaigns of his wonderful career. Moreover, as he was the presiding officer of the annual student conference at Northfield, to which I sustained an executive relation, I was brought into close relation with him every day of the conference sessions and as a rule at other times during each year in connection with the selection of speakers and the perfecting of all plans for this chain of creative gatherings. In addition to seeing and talking with him so many times, often in his home, I have been privileged to be well acquainted with the members of his family. Moreover, I had rare opportunities of meeting with nearly all of his leading colleagues in his evangelistic work on both sides of the Atlantic. . . . [36]

This was how Mott learned "Mr. Moody's secret," which he had set out to discover at Mount Hermon in 1886. Richard Morse viewed that thirteen-year period as the time during which the Associations found the successor to Moody whom "God provided for us in the person of John R. Mott."[37]

Early in January, 1900, a memorial service for Moody was held in the new and prestigious Carnegie Hall in New York. Sandwiched in between pulpit orators of national renown, Mott, introduced as "one of the leading Christian Association workers in the world," spoke briefly and pointedly about Moody's influence on students. Beginning with the Princeton revivals of 1876 and 1877 from which the intercollegiate Movement had sprung, he told how the summer conference had spread from Northfield around the world, attracting and training leadership for the Christian enterprise. The SVM "had its origin in these meetings, and under the leadership of Mr. Moody"; the increase in student Bible class attendance from 2,000 to 12,000 was traceable "directly to this source." Moody's evangelism was at its greatest in the revivals at Oxford and Cambridge.

The secret of Moody's influence among thinking young men and women, Mott believed, lay in "his matchless knowledge of the human heart" and his "wonderful honesty": "if he didn't know a thing he said, 'I don't know.'" That gave him the intelligent confidence of the students. His freedom from cant or professionalism appealed to them, as did his challenge to "the heroic or self-sacrificing in young men." Over all this and through it all there was "his abounding fidelity and spiritual life, due to the fact that he was a God-possessed man." His going leaves a great gap, Mott concluded, declaring in Henry Drummond's words, "We must close up the ranks and work hard."[38] If Moody had lived only to be the tool in God's hand to point a few like Studd, Grenfel, Söderblom, and Mott to their callings, declared a Dutch writer of a later generation, we could conclude that his life was of "the utmost importance not only for the expansion and confirmation of the Kingdom of God but also for the Church of Christ in the world of the twentieth century."[39]

PART 3: **Missions and the Student Volunteer Movement at the Turn of the Century**

"You and I today stand at the opening of a new century, with the finest equipment of appliances for great work men have ever had in this world's history, and the finest opportunity for great work men have ever had in this world's history, and the most solemn responsibility resting upon us," cried a British missionary executive to the great "Ecumenical Missionary Conference" at Carnegie Hall in New York in 1900. This ten-day series of meetings, which added the word ecumenical to the twentieth-century Protestant vocabulary, epitomized the expansionist sentiment, the growing missionary fervor, and the thrust toward interdenominational cooperation that characterized the last decades before World War I. As Robert T. Handy has phrased it, the missionary drive of the eighteenth and nineteenth centuries sought to turn the Protestant hope for world civilization into reality, and as the nineteenth century came to a close the belief that Christian civilization would soon dominate the world through Anglo-Saxon agency seemed "very near to fulfillment for great numbers of American Protestants."[40]

By 1900, the North American SVM was a dozen years old, and under Mott's direction was furnishing the primary dynamic of the intercollegiate student Christian movement, from which it was almost indistinguishable. This was also true for the WSCF, both at home and abroad, since Volunteer organizations had been set up in virtually all the countries he had visited on his recent tour. In his address to the Ecumenical Conference, Mott concentrated on the obligation of his generation to evangelize the world. He also chaired three sessions and the committee on "students and young people," but left the description of the SVM to his associates, J. Ross Stevenson, later to become president of Princeton Theological Seminary, H. C. Duncan, chairman of the Student Volunteer Missionary Union of Great Britain, Miss E. K. Price of the Chicago YWCA, and two students—one from Yale and one from Auburn Seminary. Other speakers acknowledged the "large part" the SVM had played in lifting "the whole missionary cause on to a higher level."[41]

At no point was Mott's talent as a judge of men—and women— better displayed than in his selection of the traveling staff for the SVM. During his absence in 1895-1897, Henry W. Luce, Horace T. Pitkin, and G. Sherwood Eddy, all Yale men, went on the road for short assignments before "sailing" to their mission posts.[42] Others to make names for themselves were Harlan P. Beach, Fletcher S. Brockman, Robert R.

Gailey, Robert E. Lewis, J. Ross Stevenson, Fennell P. Turner, S. Earl Taylor, Fred Field Goodsell, and Ruth Rouse, whose major contribution would be to the WSCF.[43] Miss Rouse divided her time between the American SVM and the intercollegiate YWCA for two years. Robert Wilder, who could not endure the climate of India, worked among the theological seminaries for a time. Brockman, Gailey, Lewis, Luce, Pitkin, and Taylor went to China, Eddy and Miss Rouse to India; Turner became general secretary of the Movement. Mott brought Dr. J. Rutter Williamson and Dr. S. Howard Taylor, son of the founder of the China Inland Mission, from Britain for short terms among medical students, and John N. Forman, who had toured the colleges with Wilder in 1886–1887, came from India to canvass the theological schools during his furlough of 1901–1902.

Adequate missionary literature was as basic to the SVM as was Bible study to the general movement. From the first issue of *The Student Volunteer* in 1893, mission study, based on solid information, was a regular feature. In 1893 the veteran China missionary, Dr. John Nevius, had criticized the SVM for superficiality; Moody was uneasy about pledging immature youth to service in countries of which they were ignorant. No program feature could better illustrate Mott's concern for information, or the popular belief of the time that knowledge of facts would produce action. To aid students to volunteer out of knowledge as well as enthusiasm, Mott early designated an educational secretary; Willard Lyon was succeeded in this post by Harlan P. Beach, who moved from it to the first professorship of missions at Yale. Mott made the use of basic literature a major agenda item at all leaders' conferences, and often presided at them himself. The provision of a "comprehensive and progressive system of missionary education for students" was one of thirteen "settled principles" of the Movement promulgated by its executive committee in 1897.[44]

In the winter of 1899–1900, Mott decided to write a mission study book on the theme of the watchword. As had been the case in meeting the publisher's deadline for *Strategic Points*, he nearly became ill under the pressures of compiling information and writing. "It is the hardest work on my health that I ever have to do," he confided to Gilbert Beaver, reminding him of his "trouble about sleeping" during the earlier ordeal: "I have reached the same stage now. . . ." The reception of the book more than made up for the effort that went into it. Issued simultaneously in New York and London in the fall of 1900, it was a 210-page manual of the missionary movement, entitled *The Evangelization of the*

World in this Generation. Translated into half-a-dozen languages and studied in as distant places as South Africa and Calcutta, it initiated Mott's
policy of writing a book on a key theme to appeal to each college generation.

Mott reviewed the history of the watchword, emphasized its biblical
basis, and cited famous missionaries who endorsed it. He surveyed the
world with current facts, figures, and forecasts recently obtained from
leading missionaries. The prospect, he declared, is different from any
time in the history of the world, because today "practically the whole
world is open" and the Church has unprecedented resources. If she will
"improve her opportunities, facilities, and resources," it seems "entirely
possible to fill the earth with the knowledge of Christ before the present
generation passes away." From this premise Mott went on to call for
Volunteers with the highest qualifications, for maximum utilization of
the "native" church, for comity among agencies, for greater support by
the home churches and more awareness of the missionary cause by the
theological seminaries, and the promotion and extension of the SVM as
the churches' most effective agency.

Reviewers agreed that Mott had "made out his case," that he displayed "years of thoughtful reading, innumerable conferences with missionary experts, long-continued and fruitful study of the Bible, and a
practical acquaintance with evangelistic methods and results." The work
contained "an array of missionary information such as can be found in no
other book of its size." All Volunteers know "how much the cause of the
Evangelization of the World owes, under God, to Mr. Mott," declared
one sympathizer. The New York *Homiletic Review* discussed it in a parallel column to Josiah Strong's *Expansion under New-World Conditions.*
Some of the comments and quotations were almost interchangeable.
Noting that Mott was in a sense the embodiment of the SVM, the editor,
who claimed to have waited thirty years for the book, saw it as "an aid in
the new forward movement upward and onward that is agitating all
Protestant Christendom on the threshold of a new century." He found
nothing fanatical or partisan about the work: It is simply "the clear logic
of incontrovertible fact and Scripture." Its theme—the watchword—
"simply translates Christ's last command into terms of obligation concerning our own lifetime." From Strong he endorsed a similar theme: "It
is time to dismiss 'the craven fear of being great,' to recognize the place in
the world which God has given us, and to accept the responsibilities
which it devolves upon us in behalf of Christian civilization."[45]

The summit of each college generation's exposure to missions propaganda was the Quadrennial Convention, from which hundreds of Volunteers dated their decisions, or, as Mott put it, "the men and women kindled at these gatherings became the leaders of various denominational and interdenominational societies and guilds." The first Quadrennial had been held at Cleveland in 1891, with 558 in attendance, and the second at Detroit in 1894 with 1088. In Britain, SVM history was reckoned from an enthusiastic conference at Liverpool in 1896, which, among other things, had raised the funds to enable Mott to visit Australasia. The largest student assemblages of their times, these meetings gave Mott an international platform, since they not only included Canada but always featured foreign guests who carried the message home.

In announcing the "Third International Convention" to meet again in Cleveland at the end of February, 1898, Mott invited 1,500 delegates (entertainment could not be provided for more); 2,214 came from 458 institutions—just a week after the sinking of the battleship *Maine* in Havana harbor. Again sponsored by the Cleveland YMCA as it had been in 1891, the convention had to meet in an armory, yet many local friends, supporters, and hosts to the delegates (the majority of whom were entertained in homes) could not get in. The call showed Mott's concern for details: Cleveland was strategically located for travel (no Quadrennial was ever held in New York, San Francisco, or even Chicago) and there would be reduced train fares. Campus machinery for selecting and sending delegates was suggested: delegations ought to be made up of both Volunteers and non-Volunteers "who are in a position to do much to promote the missionary interests of the institution." If the Convention is to be "a mighty factor and force in the missionary enterprise," he concluded, it must be supported by "faithful, united prayer."[46]

In his 6,000-word report, Mott covered the mission field. He stressed the "ultra-conservative" policy of the Movement in recruiting Volunteers and decried a popular tendency to exaggerate the number of them; nevertheless, during the lifetime of the Movement the number of college students expecting to become missionaries had multiplied five times. Current figures showed that 1,173 had sailed, under forty-six societies, and were "distributed through fifty-three countries in all parts of the world." He had met 1,300 missionaries representing seventy sending agencies in the course of his world tour and they had made "one unbroken appeal" for additional personnel. During the Cleveland Convention, Mott also spoke on the morning watch, shared a panel with Speer, conducted a training session, and gave the closing words—to which we shall return—after a farewell service for those expecting to sail within the year.

Pulpit orators and missions executives were heard at Cleveland, but the emphases were upon "how to" presentations and panels, upon rational choice rather than emotion; none of the millennialist speakers of the past were scheduled. The delegates listened to the first appeal from a southerner asking the Movement to expand into the black colleges. A fraternal delegate from Cambridge University later called the convention "preeminently a reunion of leaders of the Volunteer Movement" past and present. "Have not Messrs Mott, Speer, Wilder, Wishard, and Miss Rouse alone spread the spirit of the Movement into more than twenty countries?" he asked. Every effort had been made, he wrote, to bring Volunteers and missions executives together, and the literature exhibit was the most comprehensive yet displayed. In comparison to other conventions he had attended, this British correspondent found the Cleveland meeting the largest in world history. Its success demonstrated the spiritual solidarity of the WSCF (of which the SVM was a department), and the results of persons praying in thirty-five to forty different countries. The last great meeting of its kind to be held in the nineteenth century, it "would seem to mark the coming of still brighter days," he concluded.[47]

Mott's closing words were entitled "What of the War?" In language replete with Biblical terminology and metaphors of the battlefield, he reminded his hearers that at the opening session the conference had been described as a council of war. But "Where is the war?" With his own version of James S. Dennis' identification of social progress with the missionary thrust, Mott enthralled an audience that was expecting a war in Cuba shortly:

> To-morrow morning we shall fling out the battle line through all the length and breadth of the United States and Canada, and within a few months . . . it will be extended to the very ends of the earth. It is in the Turkish Empire—a war against violence and bigotry and sensuality. It is in the vast continent of Africa—a war against cruelty, slavery and the densest superstition. It is in Japan—a conflict against impurity, materialism and skepticism. It is in China, with her multitudinous inhabitants—a war against avarice, pride and dishonesty, against misrule, against the enslavement and debasement of nearly two hundred millions of women. It is in South America—a strife against ignorance, against blinding and blighting superstition, against gambling and gross immorality. It is in India, that great continent in itself—a war against caste, against conditions enforcing grinding poverty, against false religious faiths, against child widowhood and the degradation of woman. Yes, it is an awful conflict, involving the temporal and spiritual welfare of two-thirds of the human race. . . .

Yet there is another battleground:

That field is our own hearts, and the war is against pride, against hypocrisy, against selfishness, against slothfulness and irresolution, against prayerlessness, against disobedience to heavenly visions and voices. . . . If we can win the battle in our own hearts we shall have victory on all other fields.

Mott never left a challenge hanging in mid-air:

The secret of triumph here consists in taking one day at a time. Let us adopt as a practical thing the words which Wesley placed on the flyleaf of his Bible, "Live to-day." If we would live and fight to-day, triumphantly we must, at the very beginning of the day, put on the whole armor of God. . . . If we keep the morning watch to-morrow as we turn our faces from Cleveland, it will be much easier to observe it the next morning. Thus, morning by morning let us go forth to the day's conflict in vital union with the Lord Jesus Christ. The inevitable result will be that His mighty Spirit will continue to surge into and through these hearts of ours, the colleges of this continent will be shaken, the ends of the earth shall see the salvation of our God. [48]

Eight weeks after the delegates left for home, Spain declared war on the United States.

When the Volunteers next met, 2,957 strong, from 465 colleges and universities, at Toronto in 1902, they were truly an international gathering of English-speaking enthusiasts with numerous representatives from Britain. Mott was fresh off the boat from his second trip around the world and since Cleveland had published *The Evangelization of the World in This Generation;* the Spanish-American War had been won by the United States which was thereby committed to imperialism, the British had reduced the Boers to guerillas, President McKinley had been assassinated, and there was a new boldness in the White House in the person of Theodore Roosevelt.

Mott's role at Toronto was somewhat different from his part at Cleveland. He responded to the official welcome, read the executive committee's twenty-page report which fascinated his audience like the description of a military campaign, spoke on "The Need of a Forward Evangelistic Movement," and brought news and messages from the countries he had just visited. A cable from China challenged the Convention to "fill up the gap" left by the Boxer martyrs, including Pitkin who had been at Cleveland. The telegraph operator had read the message "fill up the map," and the audience chuckled when Mott suggested that either conveyed the same meaning. Richard Morse noted that the most frequently overheard phrase was, "I am going to China to fill up the gap."

Speer, the matchless "teacher of missionary principles," gave the opening and closing addresses. Both Dr. and Mrs. F. Howard Taylor appeared several times, as did other Keswick representatives. There were familiar voices—Wishard, Thoburn, Forman, Sanders, Beaver. David McConaughy had come from India with Mott. Colton was there; William A. Hunton repeated the plea made at Cleveland for the SVM to enter the black colleges of the American South and for mission boards to send blacks as missionaries to Africa.[49] It was reported that 100,000 copies of SVM literature had been sold since 1898; 1,953 Volunteers had now sailed, among the more recent being Samuel Zwemer who later testified that Mott's *Evangelization of the World* had "widened the horizons for many who have gone into foreign fields."[50] Nettie Fowler McCormick, who was underwriting a substantial share of the SVM's expenses, attended some of the week-long sessions; Leila Mott escorted her, expressing afterward the Motts' real affection.[51] The Conference was reported in a 700-page volume that gave all addresses verbatim, indexed and outlined for use by study groups. The Quadrennials of 1906, 1910, and 1914 would each eclipse its predecessors in numbers, enthusiasm, and statistics, due chiefly to the growing hope for global Christian triumph.

The central theme of all SVM rhetoric was the watchword, "the evangelization of the world in this generation." Robert Wilder, who played the largest part in the beginnings of the Movement, wrote in retrospect that it "did not so much produce the watchword, as the watchword—or rather the thought behind it—helped to bring into being the Student Volunteer Movement."[52] Explained and defended, a major theme for apologetics, discussed in the Movement magazine, in pamphlets, in literally hundreds of speeches, it was the beating heart of the Movement. It became the Protestant world's most widely recognized and effective slogan; it was a challenge to the churches and a potential point of controversy at every missionary meeting, including the Carnegie Hall series of 1900. Whatever part the millennialists may have played in its origins—Royal G. Wilder, Robert's father, and A. T. Pierson both used it or an equivalent—Mott was chairman of the Movement when it was adopted in 1889 and now in 1900 had not only tied his wagon to it with *The Evangelization of the World in This Generation,* but had domesticated it into his own balanced Christianity.[53] It was compounded at least of nineteenth-century optimism, Old Testament prophetic thrust, and Mott's driving sense of crisis, duty, and sensitivity to the awful needs of the non-Christian world.

No Volunteer meeting was without discussion of the watchword.

Mott defined it as succinctly as was ever possible, to the Cleveland Quadrennial of 1898:

> It means to bring Christ within the reach of every person in the world that he may have the opportunity of intelligently accepting Him as a personal Savior. It does not mean the conversion of the world because the acceptance of Christ rests with the hearer, and not with the speaker. . . . The Movement stands pre-eminently for the emphasis of the belief that by a great enlargement of all agencies employed by the missionary societies, the gospel can and should be brought within the reach of every creature within this generation. Nor should the watchword be interpreted as a sure word of prophecy. It calls attention to what may and ought to be done, not necessarily to what is actually going to occur. . . . The Christians of today are the only ones to whom the heathen of this generation can look for the gospel. It is our duty to evangelize the world, because Christ has commanded it. His command to us applies to this, the one generation in all eternity for which we are responsible. . . .[54]

Four years later he could report to the Toronto Convention that the North American Movement had stepped up its emphasis on the watchword—"until recently more earnestly advocated and pressed by the British Movement"—partly through the wide circulation of *The Evangelization of the World in This Generation,* its reprint in India and translation into German, Norwegian, Swedish, Japanese, and French. The "advantages" of the watchword were continuing to be "more and more apparent":

> It has exerted a great unifying influence among volunteers and other Christian students throughout the world. It has helped to hold volunteers true to their life purpose. It has arrested the attention and stimulated the thought of a multitude of Christians on the subject of missions. It has presented a powerful appeal to some men to become missionaries, and to others to make their lives in Christian lands tell for the world's evangelization. It has placed a much-needed emphasis on the urgency or immediacy of our missionary obligation. In the case of a large and increasing number of Christians who have taken it as their personal watchword, it has enlarged vision, strengthened purpose, augmented faith, inspired hopefulness, intensified zeal, driven to God in prayer, and developed the spirit of heroism and self-sacrifice.[55]

Yet controversy continued. Lutheran missionary bodies experienced the greatest difficulties with this "modern Anglo-American view of missions." Mott carried the war into the enemy's homeland, calling on Professor Gustav Warneck at Halle and speaking to the theme both on the continent and in Britain. For a time in the middle of the first decade of the new century the British themselves experienced doubts, phrased pointedly by J. H. Oldham. Yet the difficulties of coining a substitute and gaining its acceptance, and the appeal of the old motto prevented a change. In a conversation with Tissington Tatlow, British SVM secretary, Mott noted that the criticism and discussion had "kept the fire of interest burning." They should not be dismayed by criticism: "The day [the watchword] stirs no comment is the day to fear."[56]

The ecumenical significance of the SVM was already apparent. It had played "a creative and central role" in the founding and extension of the WSCF. By the turn of the century it had made substantial progress toward the ideal of "looking steadily at the world as a whole," if we may anticipate Mott's words of 1911. It was "the most important" of all agencies to the missionary cause. If we may appropriate another Mott phrase, its greatest days lay ahead.[57]

PART 4: The Beginnings of the "Mott Era" of YMCA "Foreign Work"

The Student Volunteer Movement and the overseas expansion of the North American YMCA's were twins born of Luther Wishard's pioneering. Less than a year after Moody's summer school for college students in 1886, for which Wishard was responsible, the Wilder-Forman team had convinced two prominent city Associations that they should underwrite foreign projects. At Northfield in 1887, veteran missionaries from India and from Brazil asked for well-trained general secretaries for the major cities in their adopted countries. The YMCA responded favorably, but not until it had received formal requests from the missionaries in each place. The first secretary to Japan went ostensibly to teach English in a government school, but actually at the request of a group of missionaries to work among young men. A decade of "cautious expansion" later, at the time Mott returned from his first world tour, there were thirteen men serving the International Committee in six countries, on a budget of $28,000.[58]

At this point, Wishard left the YMCA. Mott, who had been inextricably involved with the foreign venture since his assignment to combat the Kansas heresy a decade earlier, now assumed an increasing responsibility for the overseas expansion, aided on a part-time basis by his former colleague Charles K. Ober. This was the first move toward Mott's undertaking "a substantial part" of the duties of the general secretaryship that

Morse had urged upon him in 1895; in 1901, Mott officially became associate general secretary for the foreign department, a post he held until 1915. During the 1898–1902 interval, he and Ober increased the foreign staff to thirty and the budget to $80,000.[59] This was the beginning of the "Mott era" of world service, aptly summarized many years later by Sherwood Eddy:

> As foreign and then general secretary, Mott with his fellow-workers sent out nearly six hundred men to foreign fields, for long or short periods; he organized hundreds of local associations, and helped to plant the association movement with its modern developments in thirty-two countries. He quietly helped to raise a fund of some twelve million dollars for over a hundred of the finest modern association buildings in the teeming cities of the Orient, Latin America, and Europe—cities which were rife with temptation for young men—and saw the membership of the associations throughout the world rise to some two million.[60]

This was based on a few fixed policies: Associations established abroad must be self-reliant, indigenous bodies—"self-supporting, self-governing, self-propagating"—according to a slogan borrowed from the Protestant missionary movement. Financial aid would be provided only in support of secretaries from North America, contributions toward buildings, or assistance to national bodies. Invited by resident missionaries, the Associations that were thus founded or strengthened, served as specialized ministries to men and boys as did their counterparts at home and as such supplemented church missions. There were often creative approaches by individual secretaries whose directive was always "to work themselves out of a job" in favor of "nationals."[61]

It was entirely natural for Mott to add the foreign enterprise to his three other portfolios. On his world tour of 1895–97, he had surveyed the general YMCA situation in every city, and therefore was the North American Associations' most knowledgeable authority concerning every outpost, whether occupied or potential. He was intimately acquainted with and had conferred at length with every man on the field and brought back their reports and recommendations. The essentials of the task at the home base were therefore to select the ablest men and obtain funds to support them and, later, provide the buildings to house their programs. We have observed his uncanny ability to choose highly successful personnel for the intercollegiate YMCA and the SVM. Similar but even more exacting criteria were applied to candidates for foreign Associations, with the added requirement of city YMCA exposure. In addition, Mott had come to the conclusion, with David McConaughy of

India, in 1895, that no man should attempt work on "the frontier of darkness" unless he had undergone a profound religious experience not unlike Mott's own or akin to that which, as McConaughy described it, had startled him "out of the sleep of years."[62]

It was during the comparatively short period with which we are dealing in this section that Mott laid the administrative foundations for the procedures that would undergird the vast expansion of the foreign work during the next quarter-century, although the Kansas controversy a decade earlier had clarified most of the issues and confirmed the broad principles. Primary among his tasks were the appointment and delineation of the responsibilities of men going out. Recruitment, allocation of time between agencies, and relations with both mission boards at home and missionaries in the receiving country often called for skilled diplomacy. All of its life the YMCA had been sensitive to "church relations." It was not a denomination, but the servant of the churches for a specialized ministry to young men. Mott had cultivated denominational executives and mission boards from the very beginning of his student secretaryship and was a founder of the Foreign Missions Council of North America, of which the International Committee of the YMCA was a constituent member.

Because most of the men co-opted for foreign service were of above average ability, and the YMCA paid more than most mission boards could afford, the Associations ran the risk of criticism not only from church boards but also from their own city and state organizations for raiding the hinterlands of their own movement. Mott also had to deal with personality and other conflicts on the field, with tensions between British and Americans in India, with the unique issues of membership policies in Roman Catholic countries, with some apprehension on the part of the World's YMCA because American expansion was not fully channeled through or actually administered by that body.

As the number of men serving abroad grew, policies had to be established concerning outfit allowances, housing, salaries, furloughs, physical examinations and health care, assistance toward the education of children, life insurance—most of which were at first handled by Mott on an individual basis but gradually by necessity became institutionalized. As soon as there were several men on duty in a given country, it became necessary to name one as senior secretary. Because Mott was away from headquarters a great deal, he managed his empire to a large extent by letter or cable, not infrequently from remote parts of it, writing often at great length in his own hand.

Mott's ability, "little short of genius," to discover and attract "young men of outstanding promise," wrote the historian of world service, Kenneth Scott Latourette, resulted in his obtaining "some of the ablest of the men who served the Associations abroad." Morse turned the coin over in pointing out that it was this trait that "made possible the steady increase in the number of offices he [Mott] excellently administered." Among those recruited and assigned around the turn of the century were Robert E. Lewis and Robert R. Gailey, who went to China with Brockman in 1898; Benjamin R. Barber and Edward C. Carter to India; Galen M. Fisher, V. W. Helm, George Gleason, C. V. Hibbard, and G. S. Phelps to Japan; Philip L. Gillett to Korea; B. A. Shuman and Charles J. Ewald to Brazil. These became still another fraternity of "Mott's men."[63]

There was no specific training program for these recruits. Virtually all had served the Associations in some capacity. On one occasion Mott conducted a group of five to Montreal to study that city's Association before they left for foreign posts. During his Scandinavian trip of 1899 he had L. P. Larsen, a Danish missionary to India then on furlough, as traveling companion and interpreter, partly to ascertain Larsen's fitness for a YMCA-related post back in India; Larsen then came to America to study Association methods for a time. It was the universal testimony of Mott's protégés that he dealt with them in a straightforward manner and exhibited concern for their personal problems.

In the early days it was almost necessary for a secretary going abroad to find his own patron, individual, Association, or even a church or school group. Mott worked strenuously to institutionalize a budget and administer it through the International Committee. It was not enough that local YMCA's should adopt a man on the field. "We felt that it was vital that the Associations themselves should become missionary and then their missionary enterprise would become the natural expression of the life of the Associations, the missionary fruit of a missionary tree," wrote Ober concerning his work with Mott at the turn of the century. This, of course, was exactly what the SVM was doing in the colleges and the denominations were striving for in their local churches, and it was another effect of the watchword.

Mott and Ober began a campaign of missionary education and enlistment throughout the YMCA, attempting to make the cause an integral part of permanent Movement policy. They issued tracts and booklets, made up an Association missions library, started a prayer cycle and a quarterly called *Foreign Mail*, gave addresses and wrote articles, and conducted leaders' workshops comparable to those they had initiated for students a decade earlier. Since a great deal of the original effort in foreign cities was directed toward students, several hundred copies of *Strategic Points* were distributed throughout the brotherhood. Foreign expansion was the dominant theme of Mott's major speeches to the International Conventions of the period, including the Boston Jubilee of 1901. His fighting words at Grand Rapids in 1899 have probably been the most misinterpreted by latter-day historians: "The foreign enterprise of the YMCAs is a war of conquest, not a wrecking expedition."[64] It produced funds to send seven new secretaries abroad.

Yet through the period under discussion and especially in times of recession, funding the foreign enterprise was discouraging. Mott once confessed his "feeling of loneliness" in promoting it; Colton, then on a trial field tour, replied that he could assure Mott of "at least one sympathizer" after four days in a New England state in which each general secretary he approached regarded the foreign work as "the least of his responsibilities." Mott was not born with an instinctive skill in fundraising, but learned it from his colleagues. It was YMCA folklore, told by Colton, that Hans P. Andersen, the capable headquarters secretary, had, as Colton put it, "taught Mott all he ever knew about financing, and he was a good teacher." Brockman joked that he had to raise money twice—once for China, and again to get it from Andersen. Mott became extraordinarily successful because of personal qualities that elicited the confidence of men and women of wealth, beginning with the J. Livingstone Taylors and the McCormicks, and moving through ever-extending circles of YMCA-minded benefactors such as the millionaire eccentric James Stokes.[65]

Upon his return in 1897 from the first world journey, Mott had begun to cultivate the acquaintance he had made with John D. Rockefeller, Jr., at Brown University just before leaving on that trip. The two men had been drawn to one another from their first meeting; undoubtedly Mott included young Rockefeller on the mailing list for his report letters. No correspondence or other evidence of their growing friendship has survived for the first three years after the tour, but John D., Jr.'s admiration and respect for Mott was evidenced in his asking Mott to teach his men's Bible class at Fifth Avenue Baptist Church in New York in November, 1900.[66] The next spring the Rockefellers not only renewed their annual gift toward his salary but contributed to the budget for Mott's second world tour, at the end of which he secured their pledge of $100,000 toward foreign Association buildings and other facilities to cost $225,000. Paid over a four and one-half year period, this fund was instrumental in attracting other capital gifts to the YMCA foreign work in Nagasaki, Sendai, and Tokyo, Japan, Hong Kong, Hankow, Foochow, Nanking, Tientsin, China, Calcutta, Seoul, Colombo, Rangoon, and Mexico City. In 1902 the Rockefellers began supporting the annual foreign work budget to the extent of $10,000, but they rejected a proposal to endow it. These sums would be increased many times over as both Mott and young Rockefeller raised their sights and their budgets in the next three decades. "I believe in this work and in your special fitness to carry it on," Rockefeller wrote Mott in 1901. A lifetime of cooperation was well under way.[67]

Nevertheless, the years at the turn of the century were lean. Ethan T. Colton came from the student work as Mott's associate in the foreign department after Ober moved out of it. The supervising committee became convinced that Mott was "unduly occupied with securing financial support," and, noting Colton's broad shoulders—he had been a youth of prodigious strength—gave him the primary responsibility for meeting the budget. This load "for thirteen years did not lift for a day and annually grew heavier." The cost of the foreign enterprise increased steadily because the evangelization of the world in that generation required the manning of more and more strategic outposts and the provision of great buildings to house programs like those at home. By 1910 these would cost millions.

PART 5: The WSCF and the World's Alliance of YMCA's

By the time that John Mott came into dynamic relation to the World's Alliance, that body was on its way toward outgrowing its Anglo-Saxon and European limitations; he became a decisive influence in making it truly a world alliance. We know that he attended the Amsterdam conference of 1891 and that he made his maiden speech at the London Jubilee in 1894. It was also at London that he rejoiced to hear his colleague David McConaughy, on furlough from India, declare prophetically that "If we will take our stand at the foot of the Cross of Jesus Christ," we will see from that perspective—the "only point on all the earth high enough"—that "there is no such thing as a foreign field and a home field."[68]

At the Fourteenth World's Conference in Basle in 1898, both Mott and Fries spoke on student work, Mott reviewing the formation and growth of the WSCF. Four years ago, he began, "I was asked to speak on the students' branches of the YMCA in America; today I am asked to say something of the work among students all over the world."[69] Also at Basle, he chaired the "Committee of Delegates," a crucial assignment. Karl Fries, together with "a German and a Scot who both possessed an unusual degree of stubbornness in asserting their views, which were often dictated by a pronounced distrust of Geneva and America," were among the members, as Fries recalled:

> It was no light or easy task to guide the discussions, particularly because we had also among the participants an American who was helping certain Associations in Europe with overwhelming liberality, but on that ground thought he had the right to say how things should be done, and that with about as little tact and delicacy as were revealed by the two other gentlemen. . . . Mott succeeded in getting the most explosive questions referred to a sub-committee consisting principally of Mott and me; in any case it was we who moulded and pounded the not too easily malleable material until it became somewhat presentable. Then, if not before, I came to know Mott as the unrelenting worker who puts everything else in the background in favor of the matter in hand.[70]

Fries went on to say that it was at Basle that the World's Alliance, in no slight measure due to "Mott's broad vision," took action to recognize both the autonomy and the fraternal relationship of the WSCF.

Mott was a member of the Committee of Delegates again in 1902, 1905, and 1909; also during this period he became one of the American members of the executive, replacing Brainerd. At the Versailles Plenary of 1900, he presented a vivid picture of the work of the YMCA's in China and of the sufferings of both Christian Chinese and missionaries in the Boxer uprising; the resulting resolution called for support of the Association movement in China "*not by works and words of retaliation but by Christ's method of overcoming evil with good.*"[71]

Mott reported to the Christiania Plenary of 1902 on his two journeys around the world, informing the assembly that there were now national councils of YMCA's in Japan, China, India, and Ceylon; he stressed his policy of relating them to the World's Committee. He then turned to a problem that had arisen through the failure of some North American secretaries in foreign countries to send their reports to Geneva as well as to New York, an oversight that had given rise to fears that the North American International Committee was a competing operation. In the absence of a policy of dual appointment, this was almost inevitable; it contributed to tensions for a decade in spite of new rules.[72]

When the executive next met at Geneva in 1903, Mott challenged it to a ten-year program of expansion "to build up, or to have built up, at principal centers, Associations of such strength and vitality that they will determine the character of the Association work throughout the region or land in which they are located"—Madrid, Lisbon, Athens, Budapest, Sofia, Belgrade, and Bucharest. "God has not revealed all of his mind regarding the Young Men's Christian Association to any one nation. . . . A World's Committee should reflect faithfully and impartially this wonderfully varied and rich manifestation of the mind of God as seen throughout the world field."[73]

This statement, which could be seen as a criticism of the conservatism of Geneva, was presumably designed to placate both sides to a controversy that had developed over proposed constitutional changes and the future stance of the Alliance. Because the issues had been opened by a paper written but not read by his own superior, Richard C. Morse, who appeared to have advocated two world bodies (differences between Anglo-Saxon and German views producing much disagreement), Mott was placed in a position of the utmost embarrassment, yet by proposing that the executive study the matter during the interval until the next plenary, he brought "order out of disorder," at least for the time. He appears to have had no part in the furious negotiations, chiefly between the British and Germans, of the next three years concerning the nature of the Alliance and of the Paris Basis, which was reaffirmed in its simplicity and ecumenical power at the Paris Jubilee in 1905.[74] On that occasion Mott gave a strong address tracing the achievements of the half century and showing how the YMCA's had done more than any other agency "to realize true Christian unity"—more than any other influence "in hastening the answer of the prayer of our Lord, 'that they all may be one.'"[75]

PART 6: The WSCF: Occupation of the Strategic Points

When the World's Student Christian Federation met in its first conference at Northfield and Williamstown, Massachusetts, in July, 1897, the five founding movements had grown to ten; two more would be admitted during the brief period at the turn of the century which is being surveyed in this chapter.[76] This was, therefore, largely a time of consolidation and extension within the territories to which the Federation laid claim. The vast correspondence in its archives testifies to the infinite care with which Mott advised, cultivated, and nourished each of the national movements he had created, and to his phenomenal memory of persons and situations around the world.

The last note of the doxology sung around the Haystack Monument at Williamstown had hardly died into the Berkshire twilight when Mott was off to account to the British Student Christian Movement for his Australasian campaign. A smooth voyage provided an excellent opportunity not only for much-needed rest but to review with his cabin-mate, J. Rutter Williamson, corresponding secretary of the Federation, the accumulation of materials received from the membership, which would become the nucleus of the Federation archives.[77] There were early reviews of *Strategic Points* to read, and he wrote to Postville that he awaited eagerly the reactions from Iowa friends such as Governor Larrabee and Horace Warner, to whom copies had been sent; later responses from missionaries around the world would be favorable. But this was strictly a "business trip"; he spent only two weeks in England, returning over a very rough sea. To keep his mind off seasickness, he read Stanley's *How I Found Livingstone, Tom Brown's School Days,* and some Kipling and Victor Hugo. Upon arrival he immediately took his family to Canada for their first vacation at Lac des Iles.

The British conference to which he had gone had moved that year from its birthplace at Keswick, and was held at Curbar "among the beautiful hills of Derbyshire." It was the largest yet in Britain, the 333 students representing twenty-four denominations and seventy-three institutions—almost twice the number Mott had met with in 1895; one-third of them were Volunteers for foreign missions. His participation included "public addresses, conferences with groups of men interested in special problems, and extended interviews with leaders of the national movement and of the organizations in different institutions." In a report letter he continued:

> While I do not underrate the value of platform work, I am coming year by year to attach increasing importance to hand to hand work with pivotal men. At Curbar more of this individual work was done than at any preceding conference. By economizing my time I was able to interview every key man in the conference. The aim in all such work was not only to learn all I could regarding the moral and religious life in the British universities, and to come into sympathetic personal relation to the leaders in the various Christian organizations, but also to throw light on their present day problems and to suggest plans for meeting unusual opportunities.[78]

After the conference, he spent a day with the officers of the BCCU and another with those of the SVMU, "discussing national problems and policy." On previous visits it had been necessary to stress matters of organization, but this time he could emphasize "the internal development of the movement." A decade earlier the Americans had begun to cultivate the British by inviting them to Northfield; the progress of the British Movement was now obvious, and it was "beginning to influence our American organizations, and a kindly rivalry exists which is doing much to intensify and to develop work on both sides of the Atlantic."[79] The Federation was being consolidated.

The ecumenical thrust of the Federation was not only its activism: the centrality of Christological affirmation with its consequent emphasis on evangelism, Bible study, and the deepening of the spiritual life of students, exerted a universal appeal that brought diverse groups of college youth into a fraternity that included Wesleyan Methodists, high-church Anglicans, and Orthodox, as well as Anglo-Saxons, Chinese, and Indians. In her history of the Federation, Ruth Rouse, its first woman secretary, shows how it was an organization as well as a movement, citing Mott's investment of days and days on each of his tours—as was very apparent in Australia in 1896—instructing new national officers. "Pioneer visitors," she said reminiscently, "were never satisfied with an enthusiastic welcome and send-off; they must leave behind an organized group of some sort, if no more than a Bible circle with three members." Mott's correspondence, with which she was familiar, testified to his "adaptable wisdom in shepherding and advising Movements at all stages of their growth, and to his genius for personal friendship which played so richly human a part in building both men and movements."[80]

But the organization must be a vehicle of spiritual power; the "Universal Day of Prayer for Students" was adopted at Vadstena and the first call issued for February, 1898, and annually thereafter, always related to a pivotal event in the student world. However diverse the secrets of Federation advance may have been, "its most signal service to the Church" was in introducing the Student Volunteer Movement into countries around the world.[81] These, then, were some of the drives that sent Mott around the globe again, to Europe five times, and to Australasia a second time in the brief period of this chapter, for a total of some twenty-six months.

The conference, still a novelty, was "the warp and woof" of Federation growth, wrote Miss Rouse.[82] Here the diverse threads of nationality, faith and practice, race and language, were woven into the ecumenical pattern. Each gathering was held, doubtless largely because of Mott's sense of history and timing, at a strategic point, beginning with Northfield, site of SVM origins, and Williamstown, birthplace of American foreign missions. The next conference, in July 1898, was at Eisenach, Germany, birthplace of Protestantism. Unlike the immense American

SVM Quadrennials, WSCF meetings were relatively small delegated bodies of some one hundred chosen representatives, preceded by executive meetings; they were considerably subsidized by Mott's wealthy supporters. He prepared for them, as for all conferences, with infinite care for every detail—ventilation, the arrangement of the literature exhibit, seating both in sessions and at meals, recreation, interpreters; as Ruth Rouse wrote out of long experience, "the man of vision is rarely the man of detail. Dr. Mott is both, and taught the Federation not only to think in continents, but to despise no detail which may carry the vision out." This was why there could be "time to deal with matters of justice and the love of God" when a Federation conference met.

At least a chapter, and in some cases a book, could be written about Mott's preparation, journey to, and conduct of a Federation conference. Eisenach, 1898, was the climax of a journey that criss-crossed western Europe from April to July. In January, Mott delegated the administration of the American college work to Beaver. When he sailed at the end of March, war with Spain seemed imminent. "The American flag floating over us is an inspiration," he wrote home as his ship neared Southampton. After sharing a very short vacation with Williamson at Harrogate, which included a visit to Fountains Abbey, he plunged into the British theological students' conference at Birmingham, where he gave four addresses. At the end of April he wrote home from Delft that except for those in England, continental newspapers seemed "to show most sympathy with Spain," due, he thought, largely to "ignorance of the facts."

After a short planning period in Holland, Mott returned to England for a three-week evangelistic campaign at Cambridge and Oxford, just prior to which he spoke to an audience of 3,000 ("thousands were unable to get in") at Exeter Hall, London, at the centenary of the Church Missionary Society—"the largest missionary society of the world." "I was very cordially received and God helped me to deliver my message with power," he wrote to his mother. He spoke on the student movements of the world, a favorite theme since his tour, emphasizing the SVM but reaching an oratorical climax in describing the Federation—"one of the most remarkable developments in the recent history of the Church."[83]

Mott's visits to Cambridge and Oxford were his first specifically evangelistic "campaigns" to students in Great Britain. No such outburst greeted him as had confronted Moody sixteen years before when Cambridge students tapped on the floor with canes and umbrellas and cried "Hear, hear!" to Sankey's solemn music.[84] The *Cambridge Review* editorialized in advance of Mott's coming that he was the author of *Strategic Points* and secretary of the WSCF with "an immense experience of University life in other lands" and anticipated his account of it. [85] His meetings were held in Henry Martyn Hall; interest deepened and attendance increased day by day. He spoke on personal purity, missions, and the Federation. Small gatherings were held in students' quarters, at breakfast, in afternoon groups, and at teas, but he thought especially significant a well-attended breakfast for dons that resulted in the formation of a Christian Union "composed of dons only." [86] Mott was provided with a private parlor where he could meet individuals, of whom there were "over twenty" who came on the final day to talk about personal religion. The last two days at Cambridge were given to an annual interuniversity conference with seventy Oxford men in attendance; Mott was asked to speak twice.

One may imagine some of the thoughts that came to Mott as he moved to Oxford. Perhaps he recalled that he had once written home from Cornell that God must have sent him there as He had sent Wesley to Oxford. He must have visited spots related to Wesley and the "Holy Club." Sherwood Eddy once said that in many ways Mott was "the Wesley of the nineteenth century." [87] He must have been told how Moody's first attempt to read a Scripture had been frustrated by stamping and shouting, and how the students had subsequently apologized. And he must have been aware that the mantle of Moody now rested on his shoulders. The *Oxford Magazine* anticipated that no one could be better qualified to speak about students in different lands, since Mott was "one of the leaders of the great religious movements in the universities and colleges of America." [88]

A final Sunday-night mass meeting packed Balliol Hall, men coming through a pouring rain, which reminded Mott of his meetings in Japan. "Someone said that there had been nothing like [it] since the visit of Moody and the Cambridge Band. There were many evidences of the mighty working of the spirit of God." The *Oxford Review* approved of Mott's "weighty and common-sense remarks," which it said were heartily received, and summarized his address on personal purity, noting that he had pointed out that "temptations in the body were more intense perhaps because of [students'] sedentary habits." Mott had then spoken plainly with regard to certain temptations, and concluded by saying that there was "one rock to which all men who found temptation overcoming them could cling: That rock was Jesus Christ." The last two days at Oxford brought so many inquirers that he was forced to limit the interviews to less than fifteen minutes each. At both Cambridge and Oxford, Mott gave a great deal of time to the student officers of the campus Christian organizations. No criticism appeared in the student newspapers of either university.[89]

From these triumphs he moved, exhausted, to a small conference in Holland, where the slower pace was welcome, and thence to Paris for a week's "work among French students" and the forging of significant ecumenical links.[90] James Stokes, "a rich man of New York, who for 30 years has been a member of the International Committee," insisted upon Mott's being his hotel guest, which proved to be "pleasant" notwithstanding some of Stokes' "objectionable peculiarities," Mott confessed to his parents. He was surprised to find a large colony of British and American students in Paris; "over 300" came to an evening service in the Latin Quarter. Here, also, he met and conferred with Nathan Söderblom, and probably with Wilfred Monod, the coming French Protestant leader, who also had been at Northfield in 1890. Raoul Allier, whom he had known since the Amsterdam Conference of the World's Alliance of 1891, arranged for him to attend and speak to the second summer conference of French students, five of whom followed him to Eisenach, thus building for French admission to the WSCF.[91]

From Paris Mott wrote privately to his parents that he was finding people everywhere on the continent favoring Spain in the war then reaching its climax. He felt that this was due to "jealousy of the Anglo-Saxon race which has been uniting in such a remarkable way recently," to "ignorance of the cruel treatment of the people of Cuba by Spain," and partly to "Roman Catholic prejudice, because among Protestants I find much less of this feeling."[92]

Student conferences had been held in Switzerland each year since 1895, presaging "the beginning of a student movement in the mountain republic." Campus Associations were being fostered at Geneva, Lausanne, and Neuchâtel; Mott spent ten days among them to determine whether the Swiss Movement was ready for membership in the Federation. After a few days in Germany, he went to Norway for a brief stay under the midnight sun with the Wilders at their home at Veldre, not far from Christiania, where there was a student conference to which he spoke four times. There was also "a great Sunday-School convention" which he addressed twice. En route, he had been met at Copenhagen by a delegation of students and Count Joachim von Moltke, who had been begging him since 1894 to come to Scandinavia.[93]

Returning to Switzerland to rest prior to the World's Alliance Conference at Basle and the WSCF at Eisenach, Mott gave himself several days of leisure at Lucerne. Reflecting upon his work on the continent, it seemed almost as badly needed as in Japan. "Intemperance, impurity and rationalism are ruining thousands of students in all these lands," he wrote his parents. We know nothing like it in America. "It is a great thing to find a little band of six or eight earnest Christian students in a university." Surprised at the large number of American students, many of whom lost their faith, he thought sister Clara had done "mighty well to run the gauntlet so successfully for three years." Expecting momentarily to read of "a very bad battle at Santiago," Cuba, which would "help matters greatly," he complained again that the Spanish "and some American papers lie so much that people do not know what to believe." He had followed the New York *Outlook* and the *Christian Advocate* for reliable news and views.

From the Basle Conference of the World's Alliance, during which the battle of Santiago took place, Mott went to the WSCF meeting at Eisenach, Germany, for "the real climax" of his "European campaign." Twenty-four countries were represented by the 102 delegates. Mott had devoted more time to the preparation for this gathering than to any other activity that year unless it had been the Cleveland SVM Quadrennial. The specific purposes of Eisenach were to bring national student leaders together and to focus on the universities of the continent. Fries presided. An organization composed of the movements in the Netherlands, France, and Switzerland was admitted. A worship service was held in the Luther Chapel of the Wartburg. Mott's report of twenty-seven pages recounted the growth of student Associations around the world during the past year, described his own activities, reemphasized basic Federation principles, and outlined immediate as well as long-range goals. His address, "A Spiritual Awakening in a University," which was both an inspirational and a practical challenge, was reprinted and widely circulated.[94] To Gilbert Beaver and the prayer circle that received his report letters, he wrote afterward from London that the conference had been "a fresh and complete confirmation of the value of the Federation idea, methods, and spirit," and that the experiences of Cleveland and Eisenach had convinced him of "the value of special calls to prayer."

Interspersed in this lengthy schedule, parts of which have been lost, Mott spent several of "the most difficult and exhausting" weeks of his experience up to that time among the universities of Göttingen, Breslau, Leipzig, Halle, and Berlin. One wonders whether his bafflement would have been so serious if he had accepted one of the Cornell fellowships and had studied in Germany, which he now concluded was "the greatest student field in the world" not only because of the immense number of students and professors but also on account of the liberal if not agnostic attitudes of the faculties. His usual list of temptations, augmented by dueling, "Ritschlianism, rationalism, and materialism," had at first depressed him, but before the visit terminated this had given way to "confident hope."[95] It had been "an immense help and satisfaction" to be accompanied by Heinrich Witt, the German student secretary who would lay foundations in Russia the next year, and with whom it may be assumed Mott took a walking tour through the Hártz Mountains after his German campaign.

After a day at a British conference at Ripon, Mott sailed for home on August sixth. Santiago and Puerto Rico had fallen and peace with Spain was agreed upon while he was on the high seas. "It is remarkable how few have been killed or wounded," he had written a few days earlier, but "the fever bids fair to do more harm than the bullets and shells."

In 1899 Mott's primary service to the Federation was a first tour of the universities of Scandinavia and a secretive visit to Russia. As the date for his departure, January 28, began to threaten his work schedule, it chanced that his associate Gilbert Beaver inadvertently suggested that John take on a chore that Beaver did not feel competent to handle. Mott's reaction was almost a peevish outburst. Had Beaver realized the "heavy burden" he had "already assumed" he would have tried "to devise some means" of relieving him of some of it rather than adding more, Mott wrote at home the day after Christmas, 1898, in his own hand. He then outlined a score of responsibilities he must handle in a month. The letter provides a rare glimpse into Mott's workaday world:

> The covering of the SVM and Foreign Association finances (involving the salaries and expenses of so many workers) for the probable period of my absence; the meetings of both Executive and Advisory Committees of SVM . . .; the sizing up and calling of seven new secretaries for the two movements before they are tied up with other work . . . the meeting in N.Y. with the summer campaign workers of all denominations to try to prevent serious complications in this rapidly growing work which so much concerns the SVM; the conference of Board secretaries which experience shows I cannot wisely omit as Chairman of the Executive Committee; as chairman of the committee on student and other young people's work for the 1900 Ecumenical Missionary Convention . . . the set-to with the W.S.I. in Chicago along with Morse and Michener on Jan. 6 and 8 involving the Geneva Conference plans for more than one year I fear; the fixing of home matters affecting my parents in Iowa, my sister in Springfield, and my own family so that things will be all right when I am

away . . . ; etc. (In this case etc. includes many definite things which I can indicate)—all these things make it necessary that I count the hours of night and day before I sail as golden.[96]

There followed a thousand words of instructions regarding immediate problems.

He did sail as planned. The day before, he wrote Mrs. McCormick a request for funds to bring several Europeans to America for training experiences, and sent her his itinerary. During a brief stay in London, "the most bewildering and interesting city in the world," he observed his brother-in-law, Wilbert W. White, lecturing on the Bible at nine different centers to 12,000 auditors a week. Mrs. McCormick had arranged for "a professor" to come from Paris to advise him on his Russian trip, for which he also sought advice in London. Tissington Tatlow, newly appointed British Student Movement secretary, took him to the Bishop of London, Mandel Creighton, who had attended the Czar's coronation in 1894. The Bishop, who was well-versed in Orthodoxy, gave him an orientation together with a letter to the Over-Procurator of the Russian Church, K. P. Pobedonostsev, and lent him his own copies of three specially prepared volumes in English interpreting Russia for the Czarina at the time of her marriage.[97]

In the history of the British Student Christian Movement, the "one notable event" of the winter of 1898–1899 was Mott's evangelistic mission the second week of February in Edinburgh University, which, with its 4,500 students, Mott understood to be "not only the leading student center in Scotland but also one of the greatest in the British Empire."[98] A week of daily meetings reached a climax the final Sunday night; with Sir William Muir, principal of the university in the chair, 2,000 young men listened closely to "The Temptations of Students in all Lands." To discourage emotional decisions, Mott invited 350 inquirers to a distant hall, but there were so many that they were forced to return to the large meeting-place where he spoke again for twenty minutes, when "the meeting was taken out of my hands by one man who stood up and said that he wanted to know Christ as Savior. He had been one of the worst men in the university. Another man, a prominent athlete, stood and indicated a similar desire. I then felt I must follow this lead, but counseled men to think calmly and yet conclusively." Seventy-nine stood after further quiet counsel.

Interviews were held in a neighboring hotel, limited to ten or fifteen minutes each. They continued late into the night and all day Monday, delaying Mott's departure by a day. "I was made fairly dizzy by these interviews. My experience was that of Henry Drummond, who said after one such experience that he was ill from the sins of the men with whom he had been talking." Mott's advice to sin-sick youth was similar to Drummond's. The latter advised himself and others to pray, think, "talk to wise people," beware of "the bias of your own will," then "do the next thing (for doing God's will in small things is the best preparation for knowing it in great things)." When decision and action are necessary, go ahead. "Never reconsider the decision when it is finally acted upon." Drummond's mantle fitted Mott. [99]

The subsequent circuit of the Scandinavian universities produced no such responses as at Edinburgh. Mott was "looked upon with some distrust, even by those who professed to be Christians, while those opposed to Christianity largely kept aloof," although he had Fries and Lars P. Larsen, a "keen evangelist" and future principal of United Theological College in India, as interpreters and advance agents. Larsen's diary indicates that Mott was received politely but not enthusiastically, although he did make a deep impression on some, and to a certain extent this critical attitude changed to approval if not acceptance. [100]

There was the least interest at Lund, the most at Copenhagen, where there appears to have been some aura of social respectability attached to meetings sponsored by Count Joachim von Moltke, a Danish court official, in whose mansion Mott was entertained. He was summoned to the royal palace for an interview with the crown princess; they discussed his work "in Kopenhagen and other parts of Scandinavia, also in Japan and India; the work of the Holy Spirit, the importance of prayer, the religious attitude of her three sons, the increased interest in religious matters in court life since her conversion about twenty years ago. She is an earnest Christian woman," he wrote to Postville describing his first interview with royalty.

At Christiania (Oslo), a last-minute surge of interest brought "a large company of students" to see him off at midnight:

> As the train pulled out, they sang, as only Scandinavian students can sing, two verses of that triumphant battle hymn of the Student Movement, "All Hail the Power of Jesus' Name." I can still hear the closing strain: "Og kryn han Allheims Drott! And Crown Him Lord of All!" [101]

In Stockholm, Mott was the guest of Prince Oscar Bernadotte, whom he had met at the London Jubilee of 1894. "After dinner we had a nice visit and at the close knelt in prayer together. Both the Prince and Princess prayed earnestly for me and my work. The Princess also prayed for Leila and John. They are deeply interested in my work among students and keep remembering it in prayer." Although the results at Uppsala appeared to be meagre, Nathan Söderblom later recalled that when he returned there to teach in 1901, Mott's influence could still be felt among young men and women destined for distinguished careers. One was Johannes Sandegren, future missionary bishop in India.[102]

From Stockholm during the first week of April, 1899, Mott, with Fries as his interpreter and companion, voyaged to Finland on an icebreaker. Mott watched spellbound near the prow as the ship broke its way through the floes with "a crushing, cracking, crunching and thundering sound." When the two arrived in Helsingfors (Helsinki), very late, Mott could not sleep until Fries had connived to stop a loud-ticking clock in an adjoining room. Mott was greatly attracted to Finland: "Its thousand lakes, its rugged granite rocks, its forests of pine, its island-fringed coasts, exerted a real fascination over me. It is a wonderful land."

His arrival was opportune, in that there was great unrest because of recent steps toward Russification by the Czar's government. Mott extended his stay at the University of Helsingfors from six to nine days, with two meetings each day. "The political troubles... had led the students to think seriously and helped to open their minds to the earnest consideration of eternal things." Altogether there were "more inquirers in meetings and personal interviews than in any other university or student center I have ever visited, not excepting Edinburgh." Because of the need for translation, interviews consumed up to forty minutes each, "and were necessarily exhausting." At the close of the visit, Mott and Fries were tendered a banquet and two hundred students came to the station when they left, bringing the university glee club. "It was difficult to reach Finland; it was still more difficult to leave."[103]

The Federation kept a "ceaseless watch" for openings into difficult fields, with "a steady barrage" directed toward Russia.[104] While in Helsingfors, Mott and Fries were joined by Baron Paul Nicolay, a Finnish nobleman and pietistic Lutheran who had been deeply touched by the Keswick spirit and was devoting himself to various forms of religiously-motivated social work, some of it in Russia. They had invited Nicolay to share in a conference to discuss the formation of a Finnish Student Christian Movement, and at the same time had asked his advice on Mott's going to Russia in the interests of students. Nicolay had replied that due to the suppression of students because of a national strike he could "promise no meetings," but because Russia was "a land of possibilities," Mott should come and see for himself what could be done.

Nicolay was deeply impressed by Mott's "genuine, unaffected, calm" faith, entertained him in his home in St. Petersburg, and served as his guide and interpreter throughout his stay in Russia. Nicolay's biographer could hardly appraise fully the bond that from then until Nicolay's death held the two men in fellowship. During the three weeks they were together in Russia, they prayed frequently for "open doors." Few did open, then, but an occasion when prayer took on unusual reality caused Mott to enter in that short list of memorable moments of his life which included Vadstena and Flowery Hill at Kumamoto: "Prayer of two of us in hotel room in Moscow."

No public meetings were possible, but a few friends could meet in homes or a group gather under the guise of a German Lutheran society. Mott abandoned his plan to begin with government officials, which would have alienated students, and apparently did not use Bishop Creighton's letter to Pobedonostsev. Instead he sought advice and information from Russians to whom Nicolay introduced him, including the Baron's sisters, several professors, and American and British students. He also had "extended conversations with [Russian] students from ten leading universities and colleges . . . students representing all faculties, both sexes, and all shades of belief and unbelief." He was deeply moved by what he heard.

During an evening at the home of Princess Lieven, while Mott was describing the Federation to a small group, it was borne in upon Nicolay that he was the person to organize a Christian movement among the students of Russia.[105] The two men's prayers were answered during the next fourteen years as Nicolay cautiously but effectively built up a heroic Movement that entered the Federation in 1913, and himself became one of its best-loved leaders. On his return trip from Russia, Mott shared his experiences with the German leaders. Heinrich Witt, his companion of the previous summer, visited Russian universities that fall before going to China, and Dr. Karl Heim cultivated Witt's plantings in 1901; Ruth Rouse went in 1903 and Robert Wilder in 1904. But it was Nicolay who went on opening doors, keeping at it in periods of ill health and depression "for Mott's sake," maintaining constant contact with the general secretary through correspondence, the *Mayak* or YMCA at St. Petersburg, and attendance at Federation conferences until his death in 1919. Mott came home in 1899 convinced that Russia, rather than Germany, constituted "the most needy and difficult student field of all the world," because of the inaccessibility of its students.[106]

Returning through Germany, Mott stopped at Halle to call upon

Professor Gustav Warneck, editor of the leading German missionary periodical and probably the most distinguished figure in German missions, who had been critical of the Student Volunteer Movement's "presumption" in setting "a timetable for God" in its watchword. Robert Wilder joined Mott in a two-hour visit with the Professor in his home, Mott taking copious notes and forming a solid friendship. Wilder remembered pointing out to Warneck that the Shanghai missions conference of 1877 had resolved that China should be "emancipated from the thralldom of sin in *this* generation." Taking the report of that meeting from his shelf, Warneck confessed, "I have never noticed that before."[107] In 1888, Warneck had proposed to the International Missionary Conference in London a plan for missionary unity that was almost a blueprint for the International Missionary Council, of which Mott would be the chief engineer in 1921. In 1901, the German SVM held "the most remarkable student missionary conference ever held on the continent" at Halle; Mott told the North American Quadrennial at Toronto in 1902 that Professor Warneck, "the eminent missionary scholar and authority," had spoken "most appreciatively of this Movement." When Warneck reviewed the German edition of Mott's *Evangelization of the World in This Generation,* his tone was warm and friendly; his reservations concerned the lack of exactness in and the false hopes engendered by the watchword.[108] In 1947 Mott dedicated the volume on missions of his *Addresses and Papers* to Warneck and three others.

To strengthen the French-speaking movements the Federation was nourishing in western Europe, it met at Versailles in 1900, the guest of a devout French banker who lent his estate "Les Ombrages." Fries, the chairman through these years, recalled how Mott "prepared for everything" with "extraordinary foresight" and then with "unswerving punctuality carried everything through." Mott reported that there were then "fully 1,400" local Christian Associations affiliated with the Federation. Raoul Allier, now chairman of the French Movement, had the pleasure of seeing his organization, born of his and Mott's contact a decade before, admitted into membership. The Chinese, Indian, and Japanese delegates came in Oriental garb, which may have stimulated the Federation's first thought of meeting in the Orient. The all-male conference gave some attention to the admission of women to the organization.

The Boer War had created serious tensions between the Dutch and English, the former threatening to boycott any conference attended by the latter. In January, Fries had been to Utrecht to urge the Dutch leaders to send a delegation to Versailles. They did so and Mott succeeded "in uniting the two groups in such a way that since then scarcely two other national organizations in the World's Federation have remained in such close accord," wrote Fries. Mott addressed the conference on prayer and on evangelistic methods.[109] Mrs. McCormick was there for a time and Mott breakfasted with her twice.

Before and after the Versailles Conference Mott saw the Paris Exposition which he thought on the whole inferior to Chicago 1893, attended a concert by the Royal Welsh Choir, and heard a Russian choir "second in rank only to the one in the private chapel of the Czar. The singing was wonderful," he wrote home, "one does not need to understand the language to be deeply moved by it spiritually." He also went to the Passion Play at Oberammergau. On the return voyage Mott shared with a small group in the planning with his brother-in-law Wilbert W. White for what became the Biblical Seminary of New York, the embodiment of White's concept of Bible study as the basis of ministerial training, and of which White would be life president.[110]

PART 7: Around the World in 1901–1902

As early as March, 1900, Mott had sounded out colleagues such as Galen Fisher of Japan on the desirability of another world tour. Now that he was shouldering the major responsibility for the North American foreign work, he felt the need for fresh study of the national movements and face to face conferences with their leaders. There were, he wrote his parents, administrative problems, "and I am the only one who can handle the situation." In the same letter he expressed annoyance that the *Christian Advocate* had published his plans prematurely. He would hold short student conferences in each nation and conduct brief evangelistic campaigns at strategic centers. He also suggested to Fisher that the Japanese delegate to Versailles be instructed to "press the matter with the Federation." Needless to say, the tour was approved and took place between August 17, 1901 and February 11, 1902. Mrs. McCormick provided a secretary, Burton St. John, who, Mott reported to her upon his return, increased his efficiency "fully 50 per cent and saved me from breaking." John D. Rockefeller, Jr., whose wedding the Motts would have to miss, also contributed to the travel fund.[111]

From Vancouver Mott sent YMCA Chairman William D. Murray an eight-page letter explaining the major problems he would confront, concluding that it had not been easy to go on this tour:

What you wrote me about remembering in prayer those whom I leave behind touched my heart deeply and I thank you. Never was it so hard to leave my wife, little children, and aged and feeble parents. Continue to pray for them and that I may come back to them. Pray also that I may be given *wisdom, strength,* and *much of the Spirit of Christ* to meet the many difficulties in the way. [112]

One matter was deliberately omitted from Mott's overly careful review of the pros and cons of this tour:[113] the besetting problem of her aging parents that was distracting Leila; his ingenious and generous solution was held out to surprise her when it became a *fait accompli.*

The day after John left Leila and the children at Postville for a departure from Vancouver, she received his first letter which conveyed the news that he had shared in the purchase of a new home on the eastern edge of Wooster for her family, to which they could move at once and thus be relieved of the burden of the farm before the "White House" could be sold. Her reply is a rare survival from the thousands of letters that were exchanged between the couple whenever they were separated throughout the sixty-two years of their marriage:

My own Beloved Husband:

Your first letter reached us Wednesday afternoon about two. Your thoughtfulness for us so blinded my eyes that I could not for awhile devour the contents. Surely the tie between us was never so strong or so disdainful of distance and barriers. I thank God that I can love you so and do no violence to my best self.

She was discovering in young John L. "a new manliness" since his father had had "the courage and the grace to talk with him." Baby Irene would look up and say every time a train passed, "Papa coming!" Hastily added as the letter was posted was news of the assassination attempt on President McKinley. [114]

During the voyage Mott as usual read both seriously and for recreation, but devoted a great deal of time to the perfecting of his current questionnaire and tried it out in numerous interviews with the many missionaries on board.[115] Doubtless he also thought frequently of that morning the previous spring when he had spoken on the world student movement at Foundry Methodist Church in Washington and President McKinley had been in the congregation. The next day he had called at the White House; the President was cordial and said that he had been impressed by Mott's address, which he thought "a very effective presentation." The President, Mott had written to Postville, "is a very pleasant man and a noble Christian." The first news upon landing was of McKinley's death.

Mott was met at Yokohama by a launch filled with missionaries and "Japanese workers." He at once plunged into a planning session with Fisher and Helm. Next day he met with those whose names are synonymous with YMCA and ecumenical beginnings in Japan: Messrs Fisher, Helm, Gleason, Motoda, Miller, Ibuka, Honda, Ebara, Takai, and student representatives from the leading colleges of Tokyo. There would be others as the tour developed.[116] That afternoon he went with the Gleasons, recently arrived, to Nikko for a three-day conference of the foreign secretaries; its crowded schedule did not prevent Mott from enjoying "the wonderful beauty of the place."

Accompanied by Fisher, his next stand was at Sendai where he was the guest of Dr. J. H. DeForest, who came on the train two stations out as he had in 1897; a delegation of "Christian teachers, pastors, male missionaries, and leading laymen" were at the station, as were more than a hundred Christian students. Next day Mott spoke to a large meeting on "Student Temptations" after a lengthy coaching session with his interpreter, R. Ishikawa. "Four Kinds of Students" was the evening subject. The following morning 600 crowded the main hall of the Koto Gakko, and that evening 580 heard "Be Sure Your Sins Will Find You Out." These addresses were far more powerful and explicit than the versions subsequently published in English. Mott was at his persuasive and logical best as he moved relentlessly (usually in a conversational style) from sowing to reaping, from bodily to mental to spiritual sins, from temptation to victory.[117] Seventy-five gave in their names; Mott considered such results "most fruitful" and clear evidence of "satisfactory preparation" for his coming.

There followed a four-day joint conference of the city and student Associations of Japan in Tokyo, preceded by a reception featuring a song composed for the occasion. Except for Mott and the American ambassador all chairmen and speakers at the conference were Japanese. During the intervals Mott interviewed Japanese business leaders and officials including the Minister of Education and Baron Shibuzawa, the "merchant prince of Japan." After the conference he spoke to several mass evangelistic rallies for students, with gratifying results; most filled halls to their "uttermost capacity" and crowds stood outdoors. He interviewed missionaries of various agencies and talked at length with Orthodox Bishop Nicolai, who remembered his earlier visit, received him "most kindly," provided "many valuable facts" in response to the questionnaire, expressed "hearty appreciation" of his "movement and work" and gave him a photograph of himself, which for years was the only portrait to hang in Mott's office.[118] The climax of Mott's stay in Tokyo was an evening meeting to which 1,300 non-Christian students and professors came an hour early. There were 170 student professions after his address, "Be Sure Your Sins Will Find You Out." Dismissing the non-Christians he then spoke a second time challenging the Christian students to evangelize their country.

At Kyoto, Mott's activities centered at the Koto Gakko and the Doshisha. There were crowded evangelistic services, meetings with pastors, Christian teachers, missionaries, and officers of student Associations. The YMCA staff withdrew to Nara to continue the conference begun at Nikko; they completed a five-year plan for the work in Japan and found time to stroll through the avenues of lanterns and the temple enclosures. At Osaka, 850 heard "Temptations of Young Men." Virtually the entire missionary contingent of Osaka turned out to hear Mott's address on the fundamental principles of the YMCA, which was interpreted by S. Niwa, the national secretary.[119] Three evangelistic rallies attended by some 2,200 resulted in 278 decisions for Christ of which 119 were students. Japanese officers of the Kobe Association came to the train as Mott left to urge a building for their organization. In a few hours at Okayama Mott interviewed the Reverend T. Miyagawa, "the most influential pastor in Japan," and spoke on "Student Temptations":

> The church was packed from the foot of the platform to the remotest corners, and beyond each of the ten open windows and the open door stood crowds of students for nearly one hour and a half consumed by my address on "Student Temptations." Fully 900 students came within the range of the message and not less than 500 stayed to the after meeting, where 206 indicated their desire to become disciples of Jesus Christ as their Savior.[120]

At Kumamoto some 700 succeeded in getting into a church, with 200 more listening outdoors while 500 were turned away; 600 stayed for the after-meeting and "an even 100 decided to become Christians," of whom 73 were students. Sunday morning, seventy climbed "the famous Flowery Hill" for a sunrise prayer meeting "of great spiritual blessing and power." A final evangelistic service attracted 900 "students and other young men" to a second in the series of lectures on temptation; there were 111 decisions, forty-nine of which were students. Afterward Mott coached some forty workers on how to follow up his meetings; members of that audience had come from every part of Kyushu. After a brief stay in

Nagasaki, which included an evangelistic talk to a packed house of 400, Mott sailed for Shanghai, seen off by Fisher, his interpreter Ishikawa, and his old college mate Ransford Miller, who "went out in the sampan to the steamer."

The contrasts to Mott's visit of four years earlier are obvious, beginning with the enthusiastic welcomes he was given everywhere. Work at the grass-roots level no longer required his attention; it was being carried on by a well-organized staff that was increasingly composed of Japanese—evidence of the aggressive spirit that he had once described as "holding in a fast and strong-bitted horse." After a lull, the Christian enterprise was again moving forward in Japan and this was "the time of times," he wrote his parents. He had been instrumental in 1,500 conversions of which 1,000 were students—an "unprecedented work of God." There were also fresh evidences of cooperation among denominations and with the YMCA, which he had emphasized in his address to the workers at Osaka, where he had pointed out that the reasons for the current spiritual upswing were the power of prayer, of self-denial, and of Christian unity.[121] At his instigation, reinforcements had recently been sent and more would follow soon: V. W. Helm, George Gleason, C. V. Hibbard, and G. S. Phelps. The very next year the Tokyo Association would achieve full financial independence, and in 1903 a national union of city and student "Y's" would be effected.[122]

Mott arrived in China in the aftermath of the Boxer uprising, that drastic unmasking of Western imperialism at its worst. Yet this anti-foreign and anti-Christian outburst was proving to be a blessing in disguise to the fledgling YMCA and its miniscule staff, among whom there were no casualties, though Gailey and Lyon lost all of their household furnishings and personal belongings, and the new Livingstone Taylor building in Tientsin, the cornerstone of which Mott had laid in 1896, was destroyed.[123]

The "hundred days of reform" were being swallowed in reaction, but the suppression of the official examinations in many places not only gave the missionary-educated Chinese the opportunity to enter civil service but put a premium on Western-style education, one of the YMCA's primary entering wedges. Somewhat to the surprise of both the Chinese and the American secretaries, the Association began to play a "far larger role in China's modernization than it had expected." As Brockman began to "discover the Orient," his own and his colleagues' horizons broadened to include the urban elite as well as businessmen and students. Brockman, who soon became national secretary, began to work with the elder missionary statesman Timothy Richard on approaches to the literati, Lyon moved into student work, Gailey took over at Tientsin where he reported "a new and friendly air," and Robert E. Lewis, who would set the pattern for city Associations in China, was being welcomed into "the wealthiest homes in Shanghai." They were soon joined by C. H. Robertson, who developed a popular presentation of Western science. [124]

Mott had not intended to visit North China, but so strong was the plea from both secretaries and missionaries, "because of the demoralized condition of all Christian work," that he changed his itinerary and went at once with Brockman to Peking. The improvements in transportation since his visit of 1896 were demonstrated by the four-hour rail trip from Tientsin to Peking which by-passed a four-day trip by houseboat and donkey-back. Although he spent fifteen of his thirty days in China on the water, the time was well utilized in conference and interviews related to the "scientific study" of Chinese young men and students.

Of the 350 persons attending the two-day conference in the capital, Mott was told that "practically every delegate either had been through persecution himself or had relatives terribly persecuted or killed in the massacres."

> Time after time, as I mingled with them, I was reminded of the words of Revelation, "These are they which came out of the great tribulation," and of the words of Hebrews that by faith some "escaped the edge of the sword" and through faith "others were tortured, not accepting deliverance." It was one of the most thrilling experiences of my life to come into such intimate touch with the martyr churches. My faith in the stability and the genuineness of the Chinese Christians was greatly strengthened. A still larger number have been in the fires of persecution, but I could learn of none who had renounced their faith. [125]

The main burden of his messages was "our opportunity as leaders" and the "responsibility to enter upon the heritage of the martyrdoms and self-sacrifices of their own people and of prayers in their behalf by Christians throughout the world." In the intervals between sessions he interviewed some members of the diplomatic corps but chiefly pursued missionaries with his questionnaire.

Back at Shanghai, the Association staff conferred, with their discussions continuing on shipboard en route to Nanking for a national convention, "the principal event" of Mott's Chinese tour. The meetings were held in a "most beautifully decorated" bamboo pavilion on the campus of Nanking University; there were Scripture verses in Chinese characters "beautifully prepared," the flags of many nations, Christian Association emblems, specially ornamented Chinese lanterns, together with a literature exhibit and pictures of Association workers and leaders. There were 170 delegates, 131 of them Chinese, the remainder foreign; they represented thirty-three colleges, fifteen missionary societies, and eight provinces. Fourteen college presidents attended although doing so involved absences from their duties of from one to three weeks. Secretary Niwa came from Japan, Phillip L. Gillett, under appointment to Korea, and Walter J. Southam of Hong Kong gave the conference an international flavor. T'ing Ming Uong, who had been at the Northfield-Williamstown WSCF conference of 1897, was a vice-president.

This was "the most representative and influential gathering of Chinese Christian workers ever held," Mott wrote in his diary, "it united the Christian forces of China as no other occasion could possibly have done," although it was made up almost exclusively of students and professors. After exhaustive discussion it adopted a three-year "advanced policy" expected to introduce "a new epoch in Association work in China." Major goals were evangelistic work among young men, the increase of Christian literature including Bible study courses, a request to North America for thirteen additional secretaries, and plans "to lay siege to the literati."[126] Mott sent press releases to a score of American, Canadian, and British periodicals.

Following the conference, he held evangelistic meetings in Nanking, Shanghai, Canton, and Hong Kong, with 196 conversions, a number he thought remarkable because of the "inevitable social ostracism, political opposition and severe persecution involved. The awful memories also of the recent massacres lead a man to count the cost most seriously. The harvest, however, is ripe." In 1896, the Chinese student situation had been "the Gibraltar of the student world." In November, 1901, as Mott left China for Ceylon, he changed the metaphor to "the Jericho of the student world" because he could see signs that "the walls will some day fall."[127] That day came sooner than expected: in 1905 the traditional examination system was abolished. The YMCA would be ready.

Mott left copies of the addresses he had given in China—they were quite different from his Japan subjects—with the National Committee for publication; they were printed as *Christians of Reality*, a 134-page booklet with a Shanghai dateline of 1902, his third.[128]

En route to Colombo, in the *Paramatta* again—which must have aroused memories of the voyage to Ceylon with Leila in 1895—he improved an overnight stop at Singapore to speak in several schools and advise with missionaries "about the young men" of that city. The Ceylon Associations, most of which were student groups, held a conference at Kandy ("without doubt the most beautiful place which I have ever visited in all the world") to which twice the expected number of delegates came. They adopted a program of advance under Louis Hieb, a Volunteer who had come to Colombo in 1896, partly as a result of Mott's promotional activities during his visit in 1895. Hieb's experience had been in the student department of the Chicago Association, an assignment for which Mott had once coached him; he was soon supported almost entirely by that YMCA. Before his health forced him home in 1905, he campaigned for a building at Colombo and saw it occupied without debt.[129] He now accompanied Mott on the first leg of the India tour, participating in the secretarial conference at Allahabad.

Mott faced India the second time with apprehensions partly comparable to his and Leila's anxieties of 1895–96. This time he was concerned both for his physical well-being and the risk of blundering across some of the fragile boundaries of British sensibilities. His experience there would be, as he had written to the members of his prayer list, "on different lines" from that in either Japan or China. If he still held, even subconsciously, the hope of serving as a missionary there, it was important not merely to make the best possible impression but to contribute significantly. And there were serious personnel problems among the secretaries, some of whom were his best friends of long standing.

On shipboard he had meditated on "How to make the visit to India most profitable":

> More time *alone* in spiritual preparation.
> Live over and readapt addresses.
> Before each address and conference to remind myself of the need of the Holy Spirit and to claim His help for the work at hand.
> Bear in mind the points in my address on the use of tongue.
> Guard health day by day: sleep, siesta, exercise, sun, chill, food, drink, bowels.
> Attempt no more work than can be done well, and in harmony with the above.
> Work for and expect large results. . . . Do not forget prayers of others; the long preparation; the results in Japan, China; God.
> Your *life* in India will count for more than your words and plans.
> Patiently seek interviews and group meetings and keep record.
> Go to bottom of work of each secretary.
> Plan to spend time regularly and freely with the Indians.[130]

When Mott arrived in India in December, 1901, the situation of missions had not changed essentially from what he had observed in 1895, though there were perceptible signs of a renaissance of Hinduism. No missionary had as yet endorsed the growing cause of nationalism, but Mott was more aware than most foreigners that if Christianity were to take root, Indian leadership must be developed. The YMCA was a pace-setter in this regard and was already among the "very few organizations where prominent lay people could use their gifts in a direct Christian service which was relevant to the needs of their country." As Hans-Ruedi Weber points out in *Asia and the Ecumenical Movement, 1895–1961*, it was one through which Asian Christians could express "their urgent desire for Christian unity reaching out beyond denominational, racial, and national barriers." As early as 1893 a veteran missionary in India had declared that the YMCA partially fulfilled "the cry for union" and the "strong desire that there should be one united Indian Church."[131]

By 1901 the YMCA had passed the pioneering stage in India, now having three strong Associations, at Madras, Calcutta, and Bombay. Mott could therefore concentrate chiefly at these centers, dealing with administrative problems, holding conferences, conducting student revivals, addressing "the educated men of India," and recruiting Student Volunteers. There was no hectic beating the bushes for delegates to local or regional conferences that had consumed so much time and energy six years before. The records of this journey indicate that he talked as much, if not more, with Indians than with westerners, and that the concerns of three of his portfolios were intermingled in almost every activity.

Mott had written William D. Murray, his chairman in New York, that a major object in visiting India was to "go to the bottom" of those questions concerning the "relations and rights of the International Committee and the Indian National Council," which were occasioned in part by honest differences between British and Americans. "All experience shows," he said, that such disagreements can be cleared up much better "face to face than by letter. In this case the three parties most concerned—McConaughy [whose colleagues found him difficult], Wilder, and Mott—will be face to face." So it proved to be: in a letter home he noted that "among our secretaries out here I find many difficulties and problems calling for my attention. Every day I see more clearly why God had me make this trip this year," and to his sister Harriett he confided that he was forced to reduce his evangelistic activities in order "to devote most of my energies and attention to the problems of our Association work," which was, he rationalized, a good investment for greater productiveness in the future.

Eddy joined Mott and Hieb on the train from Tuticorin to Madras for discussion of the SVM. A South India Conference was held in Madras from December fourteenth through the seventeenth; Mott spoke on "Men of Reality," "Be Sure Your Sins Will Find You Out," "Why I Believe in the Intercollegiate YMCA of India and Ceylon," and in an after-meeting on the last day appealed to the Indian delegates for Volunteers for their country. He also talked with Indian leaders and with the Volunteers from the West; during "spare hours" there were "long conversations" with Larsen, Smith, and Azariah regarding their work. He took tiffin with the Anglican bishop of Madras and with several others whom he quizzed at length on his questionnaire, which had undergone considerable change by this time.

En route to Allahabad, Mott was joined in the train by Dr. J. Rutter Williamson (a Vadstena founder of the WSCF, now a medical missionary) and by Wilder, for consideration of Association policy. The first meeting at Allahabad, December 22 to 24, was the "regular" secretaries' conference, with "McConaughy, Wilder, Eddy, Barber, Steinthal, Sarvis, Smith, Anderson, McCowen, Grace, Hieb, and Mott of the foreign staff; Azariah, Sircar, George, Cumaraswamy." He spoke to them on "Christian Unity," of which no record exists, unfortunately, and on the physical, intellectual, and spiritual life of the secretary.[132]

Immediately after Christmas "the most representative National YMCA Convention ever held in India" met in the same city. Attended by 142 official delegates, its program featured several distinguished Indians: Professors S. Satthianadhan and N. G. Welinkar, and S. Nath Mukerji and S. V. Karmarkar, two of whom dealt with "how the tie between the Churches and the Association may be made closer." Mott's addresses were on diverse subjects. The National Council was reorganized and an advance program laid out under nineteen headings. The new national committee of twenty-two named seven Indians.[133] At the close of the conference Mott and Eddy held a gospel meeting at which fifty-five Indian students "indicated their desire to know Christ as a personal Saviour." A number of these young men later told Sam Higginbottom, who became a leader in agricultural missions, that they had been persuaded in the mission high schools and colleges that they ought to become Christians but that they had lacked the courage to come out openly until John Mott had presented Christ to them in an irresistible light.[134]

Between conference sessions Mott carried on "prolonged conversations" with Wilder and McConaughy to reconcile the personal differences that had virtually required him to come to India. He also talked privately with every secretary "concerning difficulties and problems in his own work"—the personal touch that characterized Mott's administration—and mediated between the Oxford-Cambridge Mission and the Allahabad Association "on questions in controversy between them." He sat with Wilder, McConaughy, and Eddy to delineate the respective spheres of the YMCA and the Society of Christian Endeavor with the India secretary of the latter movement, a relationship that he handled with great care at home.[135] For a brief rest before a hectic schedule in Calcutta, Mott and Wilder spent a quiet week-end at Agra, visiting the Taj Mahal at noon and again at sunset.

At Calcutta, Mott was the guest of his brother-in-law J. Campbell White, the general secretary of the Calcutta Association, and of student secretary Benjamin Barber, who would years later become his private secretary. Preparation for an evangelistic campaign caused Mott to note in his diary that there was not "a single day that we left our knees without the clear assurance that our prayers for the succeeding public meeting had been answered." One morning he had "a long conversation on work among young men" with Kali Charan Banurji, recently elected chairman of the Indian National Council of the YMCA's, whom Mott believed was "without doubt the most distinguished Indian Christian."[136] A few days later, Banurji invited "about twenty leading Indian non-Christians" to hear Mott "set forth the attitude of educated men toward Christianity and to press the claims of Christ upon the educated men of India, including those present," among whom were Justice G. D. Banurji, Professor Gokhale, P. C. Mozoomdar, P. K. Rav, H. P. Sastri, and R. C. Mitra.

> Although it was not easy to do so, I presented Christ to these men clearly and personally and faithfully. [They] constituted one of the most influential groups of Indian non-Christians who could have been gathered in any place. After my address, fully an hour was spent in discussion. Taking it all in all it was one of the most intense and most interesting experiences of my life.[137]

One must conclude, for he never mentioned it, from the satisfaction thus expressed and his similar reaction six years earlier, that it was this kind of witness that Mott had dreamed of carrying out, had he fulfilled his goal of missionary to India.

The climax of the week in Calcutta was reached in several large evangelistic meetings shared with Wilder, at one of which John

Wanamaker of Philadelphia "gave a short address of encourgement to those who had decided to accept Christ"; at the close, even the non-Christian Indian young men rose for the hymn, an unusual thing. The second night, after a comparable experience, Wanamaker asked Mott what he could do for the young men of India. Mott replied that the "most important thing" would be "to erect a boy's department building for the Calcutta Association," for which Wanamaker gave 50,000 rupees (U.S. $15,600) after further cultivation by White.

Mott conferred again with Banurji and Professor Mukerji on how to reach Indian students, but his conversations and fellowship producing the most far-reaching results were with Larsen and Professor J. V. Farquhar of the London Missionary Society's Bhowanipore college. Farquhar, who had been in India since 1891, was, in Mott's judgment, "one of the foremost missionaries at work among educated men." To Mott's delight, he accepted an offer to become educational or literature secretary for India, "a great accession to our force." His book, *The Crown of Hinduism,* would be a major contribution to the dialogue with Hindus and a force in the changing attitude of Christians toward other religions. [138]

McConaughy joined Mott on the train to Bombay; they would travel together to New York, Mrs. McConaughy having suffered a serious accident that necessitated their leaving the field. Mott confronted his first serious demonstrations during the evangelistic meetings in Bombay. A Hindu group held a counter-meeting in the square opposite the hall, though this had little effect. As the audience entered, each man had been handed a printed message: "Victory to Hind! Resist every kind of temptation. Let every Indian say, 'I will not give up my religion.'" A group of Parsee priests "twice tried their best to break up the meeting, but we succeeded in quieting them." In fact, the disturbance seemed to enhance the message. That evening, although Mott's voice was "about used up," he spoke again; there were more decisions for Christ in Bombay than in Calcutta, thanks to "the prayers of [Max Wood] Moorhead and others." After a morning session with "about seventy-five Indian Christian students and missionaries," and a final coaching period attended by several distinguished Indian Christians on how best to conserve the revival's gains, Mott sailed for home on January 18. [139]

With the fourth SVM Quadrennial due to open in Toronto in a month, he changed ships at Aden and Port Said to catch a fast train from Brindisi. After a speedy run along the Adriatic and through olive and peach and orange groves, the train was snowed in during the night, making the party twelve hours late at Boulogne; such was the storm on the Channel that they did not arrive in London until Sunday morning, February 2. Nevertheless, Mott went to hear the pulpit orator Joseph Parker, and lunched with J. H. Oldham. On Monday he conferred on the SVM watchword with "a dozen or more leaders" of the British Movement. Karl Fries and Count Moltke had come to plan the WSCF conference to be held in Denmark the next summer; Mott was Henry Hodgkin's dinner guest. On Tuesday McConaughy and Mott both spoke at a breakfast given by Lord Overtoun on behalf of the foreign work of the English National YMCA; in the afternoon Mott happened on the Church Missionary Society's regular monthly meeting and was asked to speak; then there was further conference with the English National Council, and the day stretched until after midnight in talk with Fries and Moltke "about Federation interests."

Mott and McConaughy sailed at noon February 5 aboard the *Kaiser Wilhelm der Grosse*—"the most comfortable boat on which I have ever traveled"; it landed them in New York February 11 after a passage of "comparative comfort," and fourteen days before Toronto.

Although this world tour had not been spectacular, there were real grounds for gratitude to God. This unique declaration not only summarized Mott's journey but revealed the man:

OCCASIONS FOR THANKSGIVING SUGGESTED BY
REFLECTION WHILE ON THE HOMEWARD VOYAGE
AT THE END OF THE ASIATIC TOUR OF 1901–02

Convincing evidence in each land visited that the visit there was made at the providential time.

Enabled to meet every appointment.

Shielded from accident and disease and break-down throughout the entire tour of 32,000 miles, although exposed to perils of travel by land and by sea, to deadly pestilence and to extremes of climate, and subjected to unusual pressure of work. Psalm 121.

The entire foreign secretarial force united in policy and in spirit and brought to see eye to eye with the home Committee.

Nearly 2000 young men led in various evangelistic meetings to become disciples of Jesus Christ as their personal Savior and Lord. Large numbers of these are reported as having already gone or as now going forward to baptism.

Nearly if not fully 100 students and teachers led to dedicate their lives to direct Christian work as a life work.

The inestimable privilege of coming into close and mutually helpful relation to the martyr church of North China.

The opportunity of meeting personally so many of the missionaries and native leaders of the Christian forces and of profiting from their experience, knowledge, and counsel in all that pertains to the evangelization and upbuilding of young men.

In at least thirty-two lands the tour was being definitely remembered in prayer.

The works wrought by the Holy Spirit in connection with the visits in difficult fields like Japan and China have stimulated the faith and zeal of workers in all parts of the world.

In the face of the greatest opposition and difficulties I have been enabled to increase and to abound in faith and hope as at no other time in my life.

My work in the home land has not suffered during my absence, but, on the contrary, has been carried on with marked success.

The members of my family have been kept in health and have been preserved from all harm.

More time to meditate and to take my bearings and to see my work in true perspective.

A new, more constant, and more vivid realization of the truth that "the Lord is at my right hand."[140]

Mott wrote a summary of his findings for The Congregationalist and Christian World: The journey had reenforced his judgment of six years previous that "the non-Christian religions are losing their hold, especially on educated men." Christianity "is making greater progress proportionately among students than among other classes." The movement "in the direction of unity and cooperation among the Christian forces is making marked headway." Year by year "the policy of comity as regards the division of the field" is being more generally adopted and observed. The YMCA, although a late-comer, has already become "one of the principal factors making for Christian unity," by uniting young men of different churches in common efforts through its city Associations and by fusing together the future leaders of all Christian bodies in its student groups. Christian Endeavor, the Sunday School Union, and the Bible and literature societies are similar influences.

Mott then cited specific denominational moves toward comity in Japan, China, and India. That "the religion of Jesus Christ has become firmly rooted in the nations of Asia" is attested by the leadership being exerted by "such workers as Honda, Kozaki, Miyagawa, Ibuka, Motoda, and Uemura in Japan; Meng of Paotingfu and Shen of the London Mission in China; Dr. Chatterji of the Punjab, Banurji of Calcutta, the Satthiandhans of Madras and Pundita Ramabai of western India." Mott did not say so, but he had met and talked at length with most, if not all, of these "leaders of genuine Christian experience and of large ability."

The native churches are developing the missionary spirit and are standing firm in spite of "awful massacres and persecutions" such as in North China. The hundreds of missionaries he met made "one unbroken appeal for more men and women of consecration and ability to come speedily to their relief," for "on nearly every mission field there is a real crisis impending."[141]

There was now fresh evidence to support Governor Beaver's remark at the end of the first world tour that no other man "could be spread over the entire globe." Or, as one caught in Mott's web many years later would say, Mott had *acted* on his belief in universality.[142]

PART 8: From Söro to Sydney

In August, 1902, the WSCF met at Söro, in southern Denmark, doubtless to stimulate the development of the Scandinavian Movement. It was not one of the Federation's great conferences but it had significance beyond its immediate actions. Mott's reports reviewed the biennium since Versailles, 1900. In a major address, he reversed the usual West-East relationship by presenting "Lessons for the student movements of the Occident from experiences in evangelistic work among the students of the Orient," from his recent tour. In every place where he had obtained "large spiritual results," he said, there had been at least a few Christians—in some cases fewer than ten—who threw themselves into the campaign earnestly and with self-denial; Christian forces were united; the work was "thoroughly organized"; it was well advertised; the meetings were kept as free as possible from "everything mechanical, sensational, emotional, or anything which might savor of cant"; the most effective messages were those that led men "to recognize their need of Christ, those setting forth the mission of Christ to men, and those designed to influence men to decide to take Christ as their Savior and Lord." Yet more important were the laws of "sowing and reaping," of prayer, of self-sacrifice, and of conservation of results.

Mott wrote home that it was a great pleasure to meet again and work with men he had come to know on his travels in many lands; twenty-nine nations were represented. He also addressed them on "our oneness in Jesus Christ," a theme that was coming to mean to the Federation what the watchword was to the Student Volunteer Movement. "From the beginning," he declared, "unity has been the crowning glory of the Christian student movement," which is "one of the most impressive object lessons" to the various churches. Unity does not mean the sacrifice of independence, the weakening of individuality, or the lessening of freedom of expression of the "national, social, and religious peculiarities" of each constituent movement. Those who are really united in Christ are one in the foundation of their faith, which indicates the indispensable importance of the personal basis of membership in all our movements. Mutual understanding, the headship of Christ, the cultivation of peacemaking, fellowship, and prayer—all these should make for unity within diversity. As St. Paul makes clear in I Corinthians, chapter twelve, "the recognition of our oneness in Christ and the promotion of real Christian unity is the most reasonable course for all Christians"; but Paul well knew that something more was needed than merely to convince the mind, so he threw himself into his marvelous description of the character and power of Christian love as the force that binds Christians together. This love is the gift of God. "And it is shed abroad in the heart by the Holy Spirit."[143] These addresses conveyed an unmistakably pietistic flavor that must have been designed to commend them to the Scandinavian mind.

Also at Söro, the Korean Movement (which Mott had not yet visited) was admitted to the Federation. The growing inclusion of women students in many of the constituent movements brought Mott to declare that the time had come for the Federation to employ a woman secretary, the result of which was that before the next conference Ruth Rouse began her long term of distinguished service, supported by Miss Grace Dodge of New York in response to Mott's request.[144] Also at Söro, Mott took a strong social gospel stand: "our movements," he said in his report, "should be ambitious to become a larger factor in helping to solve the social, moral, and religious problems of our day," and cited the advanced position of the Dutch Movement in this area.[145]

Söro decided to hold the next Federation conference in Tokyo. When first proposed, this seemed fantastic. The delegates from Australasia invited the meeting there, but the great distances and cost appeared insurmountable. The Japanese delegate, with invincible logic, showed that in world perspective his country was as central as Europe. Most of the delegates considered the proposal "more or less of a joke," but Fries, the chairman, remembered that Mott "took the whole thing with unruffled seriousness" and moved that if the Federation's supporters agreed (since they were paying the bills!), the next meeting should be held in Tokyo—evidence to Fries of Mott's bold faith and of his farsightedness.[146] The Russo-Japanese War intervened and the Federation did not get to Tokyo until 1907, but the disappointed Australasian delegates added pressure to previous urgent requests that the general secretary revisit "down under," since they could not anticipate a Federation meeting. Mott acceded, for the next year, 1903. From Söro, he moved north to the World's Alliance conference at Christiania (Oslo). He made the summer's tour a delight for Leila, who stayed in London to witness the coronation of Edward VII—"gorgeous, wonderful, splendid, magnificent"—and then joined her husband, the Morses, and other American YMCA colleagues in a tour of Scandinavia that was enhanced by the hospitality of Mott's royal friends.

Mott's second trip to the southern hemisphere differed markedly from the first, as had the recent tour of Asia. The grass roots had been explored. He told a reporter who met him at Sydney that he had come, in response to three years' requests, to "re-study the moral and religious life of the Universities," to give "a series of addresses at each student centre on topics of vital and absorbing interest to students especially, on moral and religious lines," to "confer at great length with leaders of the organization concerning special problems and difficulties," and to hold a convention to launch a forward movement. The reporter noted that Mott was "in the best of health and spirit," having not missed a single meal on the twenty-one day voyage. He also thought Mott an unusual man:

> A very remarkable man. A man of whom you at once take notice and wish to know more. A man of commanding presence and of frank address—one inspiring confidence. A man of energy and enthusiasm. In manner quiet, earnest, and impressive. A man courteous, gracious, manly. Above all, a man of intellect, power, and purpose—and that to help students. A man who believes that our Universities are to be won for Christ.[147]

To support his mission, Mott brought four large trunks containing two hundred copies of *Christians of Reality* and multiple copies of virtually all student YMCA, SVM, and WSCF reports, pamphlets, and general literature, plus a small library—more than fifty volumes—for his own information and relaxation during six weeks on shipboard.

Upon arrival in this "most distant and isolated but most homelike" land, where he was welcomed by many friends of seven years earlier, Mott went shortly to Adelaide, where he was tendered a public reception by the Governor of South Australia, and was joined by the Richard Morses and Lucien Warners (the latter being chairman of the North American International Committee), who were journeying around the world eastward. Mott would be with them through several segments of his stay. At a meeting in Sydney, all three men spoke. An observer thought they presented a "kind of ascending scale" in oratory:

> Mr. Morse, amongst his many gifts, cannot claim that of popular speech; and (but for the excellence of his matter) would be a somewhat painful person to listen to. Dr. Warner is an improvement on Mr. Morse; and Mr. Mott an improvement on Dr. Warner. Mr. Mott, though hardly a "popular" speaker in the ordinary use of that term, is likely to be popular with cultivated men, and commends himself, therefore, to the audiences of university people.[148]

Morse and Warner cultivated the city and the national YMCA's, which they found "in danger of an arrested development through isolation from one another."[149] Mott was therefore relatively free to work with students and their Union, but he occasionally spoke before a city Association, in one case telling an audience that theirs was the only city of comparable size in the English-speaking world without a YMCA building.

Nowhere did Mott need to "struggle for a hearing" by students, as had been the case in 1896. The five societies with which he had begun on the first trip were now forty-five, and the 70 members he had found in 1896 were now 1,370. His first meetings at Sydney and at Melbourne were each larger than all of his opening audiences put together seven years earlier. The quality of leadership had improved on every campus and the professional leadership of W. H. Sallmon, who had spent three productive years as traveling secretary, was being continued by E. J. Withycombe, who accompanied Mott throughout his tour.[150] Mott now saw at once that a second man was needed, and convinced the national student executive committee, which authorized the move at an informal meeting held "on the cliffs at South Head" overlooking the dramatic entrance to Sydney Harbour.[151] Mott plunged into fund-raising and, in spite of the poor economic situation, obtained £5,000 for a two-year budget. The new position was offered to H. R. Holmes, who had "a splendid record as a scholar, athlete, speaker, and organizer." Mott coached him with care and devoted large blocks of time to advising the leadership on the most detailed problems. For relaxation, John spent a day at the station of the Honorable James Balfour, who had introduced him to leading businessmen in Melbourne from whom he solicited the funds for the second secretary. He wrote home that the station was "something like a ranch in our Western states," it being fourteen miles long and two to four miles wide, but suffering, as was the entire continent, from drought, having only half its normal complement of sheep and these needing to be fed.

The students at the University of Sydney had been preparing and praying for Mott's visit for months. His first meeting was held in the ornate Great Hall, with the vice-chancellor in the chair and an impressive faculty group on the dais; five hundred students listened carefully to "The attitude of students throughout the world to Christianity." As the week unfolded there were three meetings for men and one for women, as well as several that were coeducational. The subjects were "Temptations of students," "Four kinds of students," and "The battleground of student life." The pace and plan differed markedly from Mott's campaigns elsewhere, the meetings being a day apart and the final ones devoted to addresses on the "chief evidences for the truth of Christianity," and to coaching sessions for the members of the Union only. No pressures were exerted on students for decisions; Mott advised them to "study thoroughly for themselves the original document," according to the *Australasian Intercollegian*. The visit not only stimulated the Sydney Union to fresh activity but elicited broader support from its university constituency. A student reporter wrote:

> But the deepest results lie hidden in the hearts of those who felt the power of the Spirit by the agency of His minister, whose lives will henceforth be a strife with evil and temptation, till, by the power of Christ, they win the victory over self and develop into the full perfection of manhood in Christ Jesus our Lord.[152]

A comparable schedule was followed at Melbourne and at five centers in New Zealand. Mott was somewhat surprised that "the great awakening which swept through Australasia last year had not extended to the universities," and that his was therefore "the first special effort of the kind ever made in this part of the student world," except for that of Henry Drummond "at three centers years ago."[153] It was estimated that one-half of the students of Australasia heard one or more of Mott's messages. The preparation had been the most thorough he had experienced. Although he had "deemed it unwise" to ask students for public confessions, in other ways there was "abundant evidence that a deep and genuine work of Christ was wrought in the lives of large numbers." Not even at Kumamoto the year before had he been "more conscious of the presence and actual working of the spirit of God" than at Melbourne, Sydney, Dunedin, and Christchurch. At University College, Auckland, the visit was "the event of the year." A student at Canterbury College pointed out that one could not "set down in cold print the effect of such meetings." At Otago Mott "created a profound impression."

"The most distinctive feature" of the visit was the launching of a "forward movement" for home and foreign missions by holding two conferences, one in the handsome Gothic dining hall of Ormond College at Melbourne, the other in Canterbury College Hall at Christchurch. Mott calculated that the 664 delegates from sixty-one institutions made these events "proportionately the largest student conferences ever held in the world." They were in marked contrast to the secularism and materialism of a decade earlier. Addresses were given by "the most distinguished missionary speakers in Australia and New Zealand," including men with degrees from Oxford, Cambridge, Edinburgh, Glasgow, and Belfast. Mott did "a great deal of committee work" and gave six addresses. At Melbourne, he phrased the Volunteer challenge in both home and foreign mission terms: "the world was treated as a unit," he said later of the meetings, but to his youthful audience he declared:

> Students are needed to throw themselves into the troubled heart of the cities of Australasia in order to make them strongholds and propagating centers for pure and aggressive Christianity. Students are needed to extend the ministry of Christ to the back-block regions and all the rural communities, without which we cannot permanently hold the cities of the nation. Students are needed to evangelize the aboriginal and foreign populations in different parts of the countries who otherwise must be a menace to the nation. Above all, many students of ability are needed for the work of foreign missions. [154]

Mott noted that every Protestant church in that part of the world was represented at the conferences, "as well as every phase of thought in those Churches." The conferences showed "the essential unity of the Churches which is never so impressive or so apparent as when Christians confront the heathen world and are intent on how best to help men and how most to exalt Christ." They also revealed that "large numbers of the choicest spirits in the Australasian universities are ready to throw themselves into missionary service at home and abroad. An adequate outlet for their consecration and energy must be provided." Mott was further impressed by the fact that "the students of Australia and New Zealand are among the strongest and most resourceful in the world. Their educational standards will compare in thoroughness favorably with those of Scandinavia." He discouraged immediate Volunteer decisions, but they came later in rewarding numbers. [155]

Mott sailed home from Auckland. Leila awaited him at San Francisco, at the end of a voyage made pleasant by congenial passengers. It was May 25, 1903, his thirty-eighth birthday. The couple went to Yosemite for a week's vacation.

Such were most of the activities of a "detained Volunteer" during six years at the turn of the century. In the mass of Mott's papers there is no intimation of disappointment or regret that he had become caught up in a "life of travel" rather than a mission to the educated classes of India. He had, in fact, hired two of the most scholarly men he could find, L. P. Larsen and J. V. Farquhar, to carry on that ministry. The "occasions for thanksgiving" at the end of the journey of 1901–02, during which he had seen these men at work, was a full acceptance of his own vocation.

In 1898 Mott had been offered the presidency of Oberlin College, which he had politely refused. [156] Not long afterward, Mrs. McCormick had proposed to endow the senior secretaryship of the Student YMCA, Mott's primary portfolio and the base for all of his far-flung activities. In acknowledging this further evidence of his benefactor's "statesman-like and divinely inspired foresight," he revealed his own commitment:

> When I . . . think of the work itself, and see what a marvellous opportunity a man holding the senior college secretaryship . . . (and therefore the chairmanship of the Student Volunteer Movement) has to influence the one thousand and more institutions of higher learning in North America, and through them the life of the nation and the Church in all its branches, and through the World's Federation, to influence the student movements of all lands—I am convinced that there is no university or seminary professorship the endowment of which is more important than the endowment of this post.

> In the providence of God you have sustained an absolutely unique relation to this world-wide student movement. If we may trust the united testimonies of college presidents, eminent Church leaders, missionaries and statesmen, there has been no development in the life of the Church in many years which has in it larger promise for the extension of Christ's Kingdom than the formation and extension of this world-wide student movement. You had the prophetic eye to see this and acted upon your vision. . . . [157]

The vision had not been solely Mrs. McCormick's.

6

Ecumenical Architect

When we look back on ecumenical history we see a host of men, often of great energy, who sought to give the churches and the missionary bodies a vision of their common world-wide task; but we also see that nearly all of them failed to achieve their objective. When the young Mott appears, however, vision becomes reality and ideas take concrete shape. [1]

IN THE FIRST DECADE of the new century, the winds of change that became known as Progressivism and the social gospel began to penetrate the movements of which John Mott was the leader. [2] His heritage of evangelicalism had sensitized him to poverty and human degradation from the time of his work among prisoners in the Ithaca jail and his tour of industrial Pennsylvania with the Cornell engineers. His political preferences were Republican and conservative, but Holiness, Moody's moral revivalism, acquaintance with Theodore Roosevelt and William Howard Taft, and friendship with Woodrow Wilson, together with wide reading, constant visitation of the great intellectual centers of the world, and awareness of contemporary issues brought him to the evangelical side of the social gospel—a possible "blend of piety and progress" as Robert T. Handy has described it—which he infused into the movements over which he presided during this time of optimism, unprecedented organizational growth, and numerical and financial expansion.

Many years later, Sherwood Eddy said that Mott had not been a prophet, and some lesser authorities agreed. [3] But such a judgment is misleading. In his rightly conceived role of himself as executive and leader, even crusader as his secretary William R. Stewart put it, he was called to build. It was contrary to his character and vocation to criticize, engage in destructive polemics, or attack friends or acquaintances whom muckrakers might smear as "malefactors of great wealth." If Mott did not

274

prophesy, he nonetheless gave strong testimony, some of which was as forthright as that of the prominent social gospel leaders of the day.

PART 1: Winds of Change

In 1893 Mott began an address at Postville that was reminiscent of W. T. Stead's speech at the World's Fair, "If Christ Came to Chicago." If Christ were to travel in our country today, he would be concerned about the poor and [in Andrew Carnegie's phrase] could teach the rich the true "gospel of wealth."[4] But since Jesus does not walk among us, we may go "back to Christ," which in this day means finding him in philosophy, or ethics, or sociology, through which he provides real solutions of the problems of capital and labor, socialism, and anarchism.[5] We recall Mott's closing words at the SVM Quadrennial of 1898 declaring spiritual war on social evils around the world, a theme obviously based on James S. Dennis' *Christian Missions and Social Progress*, from which the SVM reprinted a booklet entitled *Social Evils in the Non-Christian World.*[6] Mott chided the Söro WSCF Conference of 1902 because "probably" no movement was "doing as much as it should to fight and counteract the evil forces and influences which are injuring or ruining the lives of students"; he was aware of the growing social concern in the British Movement.

The American student Associations were introduced to the social gospel through shifts in Bible study emphases, and by a new stress on social service activities, though the influence of speakers such as Rauschenbusch upon college groups should not be overlooked. In 1899 Mott added H. B. Sharman, author of the liberal *Studies in the Life of Christ,* to the Bible study department to prepare outlines that would appeal to those who were becoming restive under the traditional approaches. Probably the most popular course in the decade before 1910 was *The Political and Social Significance of the Life and Teachings of Jesus,* by Professor Jeremiah K. Jenks of Cornell, studied by more than 10,000 students. Such was the impact of the Northfield conferences at this time that one Volunteer thought them, in retrospect, more influential on his career than his own Harvard education. Mott's was the primary impress, greater than Speer's or Eddy's. In 1908 a young Baptist pastor named Fosdick captured his Northfield audience with a vigorous talk on "The Second Mile." Mott urged and aided in its publication, and later wrote an introduction to *The Meaning of Prayer,* thus stimulating the beginning of Fosdick's literary career.[7]

One of Mott's major emphases in college evangelism in this era—there were large campaigns at Penn, Michigan, McGill, Virginia, Texas, Toronto, Princeton, Wisconsin—was to urge students to express their Christian commitment through social service, at a time when agencies such as the Yale Hope Mission were widening their revivalistic purposes to include welfare. Serving mankind during undergraduate days was required by "the best standards of higher education" as well as "the highest and purest patriotism," he told a Dwight Hall audience at Yale in 1905. [8] In these years also, he brought a new generation of student secretaries into the Movement—some for short terms, others for life—many of whom were imbued with the new social viewpoint which he in turn absorbed from them: Richard H. Edwards, D. A. Davis, Arthur Jorgensen, Thornton B. Penfield, Charles D. Hurrey, Charles W. Gilkey, Frank V. Slack, Charles L. Boynton, David R. Porter, E. C. Carter, A. J. Elliott, Gale Seaman—one of whom testified to what was true of many, that Mott "dominated every turning point" in his career.

In 1908 Mott challenged the Association movement to social service as "one of the most distinctive calls of our generation," secondary only to leading men to Christ:

> Jesus Christ is Lord and therefore must reign. He only has authority to rule social practices. He must dominate His followers and all society in all their relationships: domestic, industrial, commercial, civic, national, and international. . . . There are not two gospels, one social and one individual. There is but one Christ who lived, died, and rose again, and relates Himself to the lives of men. He is the Savior of the individual and the one sufficient Power to transform his environment and relationships. The Association is summoned imperatively to give itself more fully than heretofore to discharge its social responsibility. It is summoned by the program and two great commandments of Jesus Christ. [9]

If evidence were needed of the influence of evangelical Holiness upon the social gospel or upon John Mott's awareness of it, the search could end here. It was natural for him to phrase such an appeal in terms of the Lordship of Christ at a time when well-known social gospelers were asserting the authority of "the Christian law" or the "Kingdom of God." The student movements heard and acted, under Mott's and others' goading; the parent YMCA held back.

An interracial program began in 1908 when Willis D. Weatherford, college secretary for the South, asked four blacks and three whites to examine this "thorniest of the nation's dilemmas." They resolved that Weatherford should write a study text. *Negro Life in the South,* based on

solid research and trial runs in student groups, came from the press in
1910. It was a landmark. Fifty thousand students studied it within a few
years.[10] Needless to say, advances such as this met with Mott's
wholehearted approval. Equally needless to say, the main thrusts and
program features of the intercollegiate movement continued on the upswing through these years. Except in 1906, Mott chaired the annual Northfield conferences each year and attended as many of the regional ones as
he could, usually getting to Lake Geneva and Asheville. In the fall of
1908, a thousand delegates—200 of them college presidents, professors,
editors, and college pastors—came to a Bible Conference over which
Mott presided in Columbus, Ohio.[11]

There was, however, one important development in the student
field that Mott appears to have underestimated. This was the beginning
of denominational ministries at state universities. The first Presbyterian
university pastor was appointed at the University of Michigan in 1905.
James C. Baker began at Illinois in 1907 what became the Wesley Foundation. By 1910 several meetings of university pastors had been held; in
that year Mott was invited to speak to an augmented gathering at Madison, Wisconsin, under the chairmanship of Richard H. Edwards, secretary of the University of Wisconsin Association, who would soon join
the national intercollegiate staff. Mott's addresses produced "thorough
and frank discussions" of the place of the Associations in the totality of
campus religious influences and agencies. He held that the YM and
YWCA's were the best agencies to handle "everything that can best be
done interdenominationally" and that denominational work ought to be
"related to the church in its organized local expression." Mott met with
the group again in 1910, but Baker, who became a Methodist bishop and
in the 1940's was Mott's hand-picked successor as chairman of the International Missionary Council, later felt that Mott had "missed the boat"
in failing to tie these two movements together.[12] In any case, the theme
of denominational loyalty was notably absent from Mott's college addresses of this period.

PART 2: The Missionary Enterprise

In October, 1906, the centennial of the Haystack Band—the Williams
College group who inaugurated foreign missions in American Protestantism—was observed at Williamstown, Massachusetts. Mott used
the occasion to urge "coordination and a closer unification of the mis-

sionary forces of the Church."[13] A few days afterward, the New York *Evening Post* editorialized at length on the occasion. Mott clipped the article, noting on it, "Pretty strong for the Grumbler." The present-day missionary enterprise, the newspaper commented, is less concerned with the future life than it is with "extending the civilization of Christian nations"; there is today a struggle of "enlightened progress" against "dark stagnation." The popular image of the missionary is changing from that of preacher to physician or reformer "opposing the vices of civilization on the one hand and those of barbarism on the other." Mott underscored the conclusion, part of which might have described his own activities:

> The missionary sermon of the present resembles the address of a returned ambassador, rather than the exhortation of an evangelist; and the organization of a missionary board is the miniature of a foreign office. . . . Even those whose faith is not ardent must read with admiration the story of missionary enthusiasm and heroism. They cannot fail to recognize in it a force in that wide evolutionary process which goes painfully onward towards the regeneration and federation of the world.[14]

Such winds of change began to be felt in the Student Volunteer Movement.

The British SVM had suffered somewhat of a decline at the turn of the century and in an effort to recoup it scheduled a Quadrennial at Edinburgh in January, 1904. Mott made a special crossing to give what was described as the "most direct and searching address" of the conference on "The Watchword as a spiritual force" to eight hundred British students and one hundred foreigners under the chairmanship of Henry T. Hodgkin. Taking his text from the Haystack Monument inscription, "The field is the world," to which he added that "Christ is Lord of all," he developed the theme that the Kingdom is to be co-extensive with the earth.[15] One who heard the challenge recalled half a century later that it "deeply moved the youthful assembly" and many volunteered. Such appeals were equally effective on this side of the Atlantic; they illustrated what the *Post* had described—the transition from concern for "Niagaras of souls" hurtling to perdition, to loyalty to the command of Christ.[16]

But some of the leaders of the British Movement were wondering whether the watchword should be abandoned. J. H. Oldham, who heard Mott, wrote a few weeks later to thank him for a "quite new conception of the demands and glory of the Kingdom of God," but he was concerned lest the definition of evangelization might be compromised by practical considerations similar to the problems created by those who held that "Christian holiness is attainable and in so doing reduce the standard of what Christian holiness is."[17] The meaning of the watchword would continue to worry student movement leaders, missionaries, and theologians, but its power to recruit eager youth and to undergird the missionary movement remained unabated until after the Great War. Yet in that same letter, Oldham acknowledged that Mott's earlier book, *The Evangelization of the World in This Generation,* had provided the classic statement of the theme and had answered most of the criticisms. It continued to exert a wide influence.[18]

During the winter of 1903–1904, the energies of both John and Leila Mott were focused on a new approach to the mission theme. In mid-April, 1904, Mott gave the Merrick Lectures at Ohio Wesleyan University (for a fee of $600). That summer he was approached for the presidency of Ohio Wesleyan.[19] Later that spring he repeated the course at Yale Divinity School (but "of course for no such price," he wrote his mother). A call to Yale would come later. In the fall of 1904 the lectures were expanded at McCormick and Princeton theological seminaries and published by the Student Volunteer Movement as *The Pastor and Modern Missions, a plea for leadership in world evangelization;* it was a book of 200 pages with a carefully selected "pastor's missionary library" appended.

As several reviewers noted, Mott summarized his argument in the preface:

> The primary work of the Church is to make Jesus Christ known and obeyed and loved throughout the world. By far the larger part of this undertaking is among the non-Christian nations. The world's principal events in recent years have combined to make possible a more rapid and more effective prosecution of the campaign of evangelization. The conditions which obtain at the beginning of the present century favor a great onward movement.
>
> The secret of enabling the home Church to press her advantage in the non-Christian world is one of leadership. The people do not go beyond their leaders in knowledge or zeal, nor surpass them in consecration and sacrifice. The Christian pastor, minister, rector . . . holds the divinely appointed office for inspiring the thought and activities of the Church. By virtue of his position he can be a mighty force in the world's evangelization.
>
> This book seeks to set forth the situation in the churches of Christendom at the beginning of the new century, to show the vital and potent relation that the Christian ministry sustains to the missionary enterprise, and to indicate the means which may be employed by pastors in order to realize the missionary possibilities of the Church. . . .

The work not only revealed Mott's own wide reading and travel but presented a body of data assembled by letter and interview from scores of clergymen and mission leaders—from the French Protestant Pastor M. A. Boegner to Samuel Zwemer or Luther Wishard—based on an 18-item questionnaire.

Mott had submitted his manuscript to about sixty clergymen for their criticisms and suggestions; Leila compiled data on forty-four famous missionaries to try to find their original motivation, and the motives of 1,700 Volunteers had been investigated. Painstaking research showing the sources and amounts of all gifts of more than $100,000 to religious, educational, and charitable objectives in the United States was summarized. Yet, prayer was "the greatest force that we can wield." The most shocking finding was the almost negligible influence of parish ministers on the recruitment of missionaries.

Reviewed around the English-speaking world, the book was generously received. A writer in *World-Wide Missions* declared that it was

> Written in the direct, straightforward style which distinguishes Mr. Mott, whether on the platform or in the printed page, filled to the brim with facts more eloquent than oratorical appeals, arranged in a logical fashion, as compact as a traveling bag, it will make engrossing reading matter for the busiest man in the world.[20]

And he added that Mott was "a young prophet through whom God is speaking directly to this age." The *Baptist Missionary Magazine's* review suggested the esteem in which Mott was held in many denominations:

> Mr. Mott is so sane and terse, so balanced and enthusiastic; his principles are so scriptural, his plans so reasonable, his logic so clear and strong, that he produces deep conviction, sturdy resolution, inspiration to heroic sacrifice and personal help in methods of glad service.[21]

The Manchester *Guardian* thought the book "characterised throughout by practical common sense, and an absence of fanaticism," agreeing with Mott that "The real problem of foreign Missions is in the home Church" and "apart from the ministry it cannot be solved."[22] By the end of 1905 the work had sold almost 30,000 copies and earned $800 for its author. There was no need in this book for endorsements or an introduction by an ex-president or former prime minister; Mott wrote his own preface.

The greatest SVM event in this period was the fifth Quadrennial, to which 4,235 delegates came from 716 institutions to Nashville at the end of February, 1906. William R. Stewart, Mott's private secretary from 1905 to 1910, wrote that his chief had handled the gargantuan preparation for Nashville while also planning his forthcoming tour of South Africa and South America "without any show of being burdened." He had gone into the conference "tired of body, but after four unusually strenuous days" came out "fresher than when he went into the open meeting."[23] Stewart did not mention that Mott had left daughter Irene with scarlet fever, a bedridden mother-in-law, and his wife in the hospital back in Montclair.

Mott and Speer shared the opening session; one who was there could feel their impact more than sixty years later. Eugene E. Barnett, who would be general secretary of the American YMCA's, was among the Volunteers.[24] In his report Mott reminded the convention that 1906 was both the twentieth anniversary of the Mount Hermon "summer school" at which the SVM had originated, and the centennial of the Haystack Prayer-Meeting at Williams College; 2,953 Volunteers had now sailed. They constituted two-thirds of the missionaries being sent out.[25] Winds of change were apparent in the concentration of the speakers on "vital, practical issues," a "breadth in the discussions, not usual in such gatherings, that was at once refreshing and prophetic," and acknowledgments such as Speer's that "of course there is good and truth in the non-Christian religions." Karl Fries recalled Mott on the platform "as a general surrounded by his loyal troops." There was an occasion when, contrary to conference rules, the vast audience broke into applause: Mott rose, stretched out his hands, and said, "It is forbidden," and silence reigned instantly.

As had been apparent at Toronto in 1902, large place was given to speakers from the mission boards, to both recent and older missionaries on furlough from many fields—twenty-six countries were represented—fraternal delegates from abroad, a few ultra-conservatives, and this year an unusual number of distinguished laymen, some of whom had been invited to confer with the student leaders on ways and means to relieve "the financial stringency" that was preventing numbers of Volunteers from sailing. One of these was John B. Sleman, who was "profoundly moved" by "the spirit of the thousands of studying youth with their manifest burning desire to press to the front." Why not mobilize the laymen of the churches to raise such funds? thought Sleman, later seeking Mott's advice. He did not receive "much encouragement" because Mott believed American church life to be already over-organized; Sleman persisted and in the fall of 1906 the Laymen's Missionary Movement came into being. Mott later characterized it as "the most significant development in world missions during the first decade of the present century," and himself supported it with many addresses at its mass rallies in the United States and Canada; he introduced it to Great Britain.[26] He continued to play an increasingly important role in the affairs of what came to be known as the Foreign Missions Conference of North America (FMCNA), especially through its committee on a "Third Ecumenical Missionary Conference" scheduled for 1910.[27]

PART 3: The Home Front (1904–1909)

Mott's apparent preoccupation with the student, missionary, and YMCA foreign work programs did not preclude his continuing to render a variety of services to the general YMCA, to Methodism, and to the growing cause of ecumenism in these years. He had been a Fellow of the Royal Geographic Society for some time, and it was during the period covered in this chapter that he was first listed in *Who's Who*. Leila Mott was a member of the National Board of the Young Women's Christian Association; she had his advice on more than one knotty administrative problem, and he occasionally spoke before YWCA audiences. Because of his own rural background and telling testimony he was often asked to address state YMCA conventions in the Midwest on rural work, a specialization that would later be added to his own foreign mission concern.

It was, however, as an advocate of the higher spiritual life that Mott spoke most frequently to secretarial conferences on themes such as "The Advantages of Difficulties," "Traits of Character the Secretary Should Possess," "The Place of Prayer in Our Movement," or "How to Preserve the Vitality of the Movement." It was this characteristic, as well as Mott's administrative capacity, that moved Richard Morse in 1905 to urge the national YMCA general secretaryship upon him again, but without success. In 1907 Mott brought out an abridgment of John Foster's essay *On Decision of Character*, as was noted in Chapter 2, above.

Although Mott derived a great deal from Henry Drummond and even Benjamin Franklin, his advice to young men on how to make their lives more efficient, rewarding, and exemplary grew out of his own experience. Counseling college students privately was possibly the most effective device included in his particular kind of evangelism: he gave every individual his absolute attention and prescribed much as J. E. K. Studd had advised at Cornell in 1887. The growing staff of youthful secretaries looked to him above all for spiritual guidance. He renewed his own resources through the Quiet Day and prayer circles, reading and devotions, and the morning watch, though the last became so difficult to maintain against a crowded schedule that he had to remind himself of its primacy in his annual "personal program"; Stewart revealed that sometimes the only outward evidences of it were a few hasty glances at Scripture and the humming of a hymn tune while shaving.

Stewart was aware that his chief was constantly "referring his work to his Heavenly Father," to the extent of occasionally asking his secretary to join in prayer that God might bless a letter just dictated. Mott never dropped the self-discipline that he had begun as a youth, setting himself physical, intellectual, "social and domestic," and spiritual goals for virtually every year. Each of these programs reflected his sense of particular loss of certain values due to the specific stresses of a given time. Stewart, who was in a position to know, testified that during his five-year tenure, Mott did not once lose his temper or speak a cross word to him or other associate, nor did he ever become angry under "provoking circumstances."[28]

Fundamental to Mott's survival and peace of heart and mind were Leila's constant support and the satisfaction and fulfillment provided by his growing family. Although tortured by loneliness when far from home, the joys of domesticity compensated when he returned. On her side, Leila said more than once that she would rather have John for one week than anyone else she had ever known for the rest of the year. She thus set an example and was a great encouragement to the wives of the staff around the world, as Ethan Colton described it to the author, of sacrificial service known colloquially as "YMCA widowhood." Long after his stint as Mott's secretary, Stewart, who married Leila Mott's sister Anna May, recalled that Mrs. Mott was her husband's "most sympathetic and yet most courageous" critic, and that no "masterpiece" went out without her "careful scrutiny." Mott "had to defend or even amend many of his statements of fact or opinion or his verbal phraseology under her gracious, but firm criticism."

The prime reason for installing a telephone at 75 Midland Avenue, Montclair, in the spring of 1904, was for John to be able to talk with Leila from his office, at that instance to keep constantly in touch with John L.'s bout with scarlet fever.

When Frederick Dodge Mott was born on August 3, 1904, almost the first person to know was Nettie F. McCormick, to whom the proud father wrote in his own hand, as he often did, that very morning; here was another personal bond and source of strength, flowing from one who had trusted and underwritten his vision since 1897. The birth of a second daughter, Eleanor, in 1907 brought great joy to her father, then in the Orient; his eccentric friend and supporter James Stokes insisted upon paying the costs of her expensive illness the next year. The burdens of both the Mott and White families continued: surgical operations, the financial and medical problems of his sisters and of Alice's children, of whom Bessie was a great favorite, and, in 1905, the not unexpected death of his father when John was in Paris, following which he became executor of the estate, thus entailing added responsibility for the welfare of his mother. To all of which might be added, although John did not undertake serious financial responsibility for it, brother-in-law Will's Biblical Seminary in New York.

Other than increasingly frequent sea voyages in the years 1904 to 1910, the retreat at Lac des Iles, Quebec, was Mott's greatest release from his self-imposed but nonetheless superhuman round. There, where there was yet no telephone, he was surrounded by his family and could learn to know and live and play with them. He shared in the Sunday worship services at the Ross home across the lake, best reached by rowboat or canoe. He loved to handle wood and, as the house grew and other structures were added, would himself select the materials and help with construction. Gradually, as guest accommodations were built, intimate friends and colleagues came to "the Canadian woods," in the seclusion of which Mott spent as much time as possible every summer. Yet Stewart observed this as "only a vacation in a relative sense." Mott usually awoke the family to an early morning plunge into the cold waters of the lake. Then, Stewart went on, "the morning was given to catching up on back reading of reports and the less urgent mail." Afternoon and evening were for exercise, the family, or reading aloud.

Mott's continuing single-minded devotion to his "first love" during the five years covered in this chapter was dramatically illustrated by his refusal of the executive secretaryship of the Federal Council of the Churches of Christ in 1909. He had entered enthusiastically into the genesis of the Council, having chaired a session of the planning conference in Carnegie Hall at which Robert E. Speer and Woodrow Wilson spoke in 1905; Mott introduced Wilson. After that conference he had written to his friend and fellow-Methodist Frank Mason North—who, according to his biographer, "shaped the social policies" of the American churches "more than any other" person at that time—that the decision to move toward federation was "the greatest and most significant" outcome of "any religious gathering ever held in North America, not only for its potential of economies and the elimination of overlapping, undercutting, "misunderstanding, friction and ill feeling" but also because "far heavier blows will be dealt against various forms of iniquity and injustice."[29]

Doubtless the tone of this letter heartened the Council's executive committee to approach Mott, which they did unanimously and with full recognition of his "reputation as a Christian leader" separate "in the public mind from any denominational connection." Publicity was given the selection, which received universal praise, and Mott was urged by Protestant leaders of every persuasion to accept. The filial relationship between Mott and Richard Morse was shown at its best in Morse's analysis of the call, written with confidence that his associate would not embark upon this "floating raft": the offer was less "in dimension and intrinsically" than the several responsibilities Mott was then carrying "in that combination of official positions of the first magnitude" that he had gradually assumed since graduating from college:

> Each new official position was intimately related as offspring to what you began with. Each is a link in a chain—a strong chain of responsibilities. You have become a leader and an expert within the Kingdom but in organizations non-ecclesiastical. Your life and leadership seem to belong to this sphere or realm which though non-ecclesiastical is of first importance in relation to the answer to our Lord's prayer "that these all may be one."
>
> I believe in the importance of the new office. It calls for a man of the first rank, but one younger perhaps than you and not yet committed as you are to organizations more mature and with such vital relation to all that concerns the development, influence and mission of the new Council which is as yet very young. I wish we could recommend them to the right young man—a young Brockman, or Colton or Fisher, Carter, or Phelps—who would grow with the growth of the Council.[30]

PART 4: Students of Europe and the World, 1904–1905

Of the fifty-six months between January, 1905, and August, 1909, Mott was away from North America during twenty-six—to Great Britain, France, Italy, South Africa, South America, Japan, Korea, the Philippines, China, Scandinavia, Russia, and eastern Europe. From the British SVM Quadrennial at Edinburgh in January, 1904, Mott had gone to Paris, where it was apparent that the French Student Movement had progressed significantly since its beginnings in 1895. He advised with the national student committee and its secretary, Pierre Bovet, who would accompany him to Italy. Marc Boegner, a theological student at the

Faculty of Protestant Theology, later recalled Mott's talk before a small group of students:

> I have never forgotten that evening when I saw John Mott for the first time, and I never shall. He was just forty years of age; his height, the beauty of his face, his straight, intelligent look, the energy which radiated from his whole personality, the unusual authority which emanated from his words and gestures, all combined to impress the students with a sense of moral nobility, absolute conviction and spiritual power.
>
> What did he say to us that evening? He took us with him to the universities in Asia, in South America and in Europe which he had just visited, stimulating the formation of student Christian movements wherever he went. But above all he confronted us with our own responsibilities, and made us realize that Christian students have a special vocation to serve Jesus Christ which they must accept and carry out in their own university. His words and his appeal were so direct, so urgent, so convincing, that the vigour of his faith and the firmness of his hope could not but touch our hearts. I went away deeply moved, overwhelmed by what I had just heard, and still more by the certainty that I had just met *a man* in the fullest sense, and a Christian man. [31]

Moving on to Italy where he touched six student centers—Turin, Torre Pellice, Milan, Venice, Florence, and Rome—Mott conducted "the first Christian students' congress ever held" in that country. It set up a national organization. A hundred students and professors came from twenty-eight institutions and there were fraternal delegates from France, Switzerland, Spain, and Portugal. The speakers included some of the "most influential Protestant pastors and professors in Italy." Mott spoke several times on Association methods, a session was photographed in the Colosseum, and a prayer service in five languages was held in the Catacomb of Domitilla where the Luther Hymn was sung and passages read from Hebrews 11 and 12. The closing session, featuring "un brilliantissimo discorso" by "signor Giovanni R. Mott," was presided over by the American ambassador. [32]

The voyage home from Naples to Boston was rough enough to keep Mott reading, mostly Italian history; for the first time in his travels his ship was two days late. It carried more than 700 steerage passengers whom he thought "not a very prepossessing looking lot of prospective citizens of America," but their desire to migrate was understandable "when you see their destitution in their home lands and their lack of opportunity to better their condition."

Mott returned to Great Britain the following January primarily to conduct evangelistic campaigns at Cambridge and Oxford. These were preceded by conferences on the recruitment of candidates for the ministry—the theme of his next book—at Edinburgh and Glasgow. At Cambridge he gave three addresses a day for ten days, and five hours daily to interviews. Although the students were at first reticent about this American evangelist, Mott's "uncommon personality" broke their reserve; he wrote to Postville that his meetings became the largest ever held there.

At Oxford, where the results were similar, an *Isis* columnist remarked that this "distinguished stranger" knew "what to say and what to leave unsaid." Though still a young man, Mott's wide experience and the force of his personality were "impressive."[33] The *Oxford Magazine* observed that Mott was a man of "great intensity of conviction and power of speaking who has studied the religious problems of University students throughout the world as probably no one else alive." Neither in his person nor in his methods was he to be regarded as a typical evangelist; there was no criticism.[34]

William R. Stewart explained how his chief could repeat the same addresses on similar themes, with each producing "an electric effect" on his hearers. Stewart said that Mott often quoted Moody's aphorism that "a sermon that is worthy to be given once, is worth repeating fifty times," and so took infinite pains to perfect every speech but always adapted it to "the viewpoint of a fresh audience." Even when his talks that had been printed were given before new audiences they never lacked "new power" because they were as fresh as great passages of Scripture. Stewart himself heard some of Mott's messages a dozen times, often in almost the identical words, but because of "fresh mental and spiritual preparation" the speaker became "the embodiment of a great living principle which had gripped him with moving power." Stewart likewise cited examples of the transformation of personality that resulted from Mott's private consultations with students. The only times he observed his chief to be "particularly fagged" were "during the days of evangelistic campaigns in the great educational institutions of the world" after hours of personal interviews, "where he was dealing with the sins of students. It was not the late hours but the carrying of the load of the sins of others" that tired him.[35]

Mott wrote to Mrs. McCormick that although Oxford had proved to be "a much more difficult and conservative field" than Cambridge, the results had been "even greater," numbers of "High Churchmen and men of other classes not ordinarily interested" having responded. His last presentation at Oxford was a farewell meeting with the student workers to perfect plans for the "conservation" of the results of the meetings.

Between the two university campaigns Mott had made a short trip to Wales "to be in touch with the revival there"; he saw and heard Evan Roberts, "a humble, simple man." In London R. A. Torrey and Charles M. Alexander were conducting an immense "mission"; Mott joined the crowd of 11,000 in the Royal Albert Hall, describing the choral music to his mother in glowing terms. He had earlier conferred with Fries on the details of the upcoming WSCF conference to be held at Zeist, the Moravian center in Holland, and the two had gone there to make final arrangements with their Dutch hosts. One evening he heard the debate on the dissolution of Parliament in the House of Commons, but his most significant appointment was on February 16 when SCM secretary Tissington Tatlow took him to Lambeth Palace to meet the Archbishop of Canterbury, Randall Davidson, whose assistance Mott craved in his project on recruiting university men for the ministry. Tatlow narrated the encounter, which was a first for both men, the appointment having been arranged by a third party.

> While our hansom careened down the Embankment towards the Palace, Mott laid his plans.
>
>> You don't know this man?
>> No.
>> Will he be sympathetic?
>> I don't really know; he's a very busy man and probably knows very little about the Student Movement. He'll very probably not want to become involved in a new interest, so is most likely, unless you really interest him, to attempt to be polite and yet get rid of us as quickly as possible.
>> Well, I'll introduce the subject of securing young men for the Ministry at once, and if his attention is not immediately caught, then I'll break off and begin to interest him about the Federation, and we'll start again on the Ministry when we have caught him.
>> Yes.
>> Now, we have got to interest him. I'll tell him about the students in the Far East and carry him round the world, and the minute I stop speaking you cut right in and pick up any points that you think I have missed. Don't give him a chance, don't let him say anything, we must interest him.
>> All right, I'll do what I can.
>> By the way, what do I call this man—my Lord?
>> No, you call him your Grace, but don't say it too often.
>
> On arrival at Lambeth we were greeted by a chaplain and within a few minutes were in the Archbishop's presence. I recall the scene vividly. The

Archbishop shook hands, motioned us to a couch where we sat side by side, and seated himself at his writing-table, across which he looked at us. He wasted no time, but immediately asked that we should state our business. Mott explained that he was making an inquiry on the subject of recruiting the ablest young men for the Ministry and was anxious to have the opinion of the Archbishop on the subject. The Archbishop interrupted him to explain that he had just appointed a committee on this very subject, and that until the committee had reported he felt it was impossible for him to say anything official on the subject. The interview showed every sign of an early end, but Mott's prearranged strategy was put relentlessly into operation.

Excuse me, your Grace, but I should like to tell you something about the work of the Student Christian Movement among young men.

Then without a pause Mott started with Japan and began describing his meetings in the University of Tokyo. I looked anxiously at the Archbishop to see how we would take it. As soon as Mott began to speak he bent back in his chair with a resigned look upon his face, as much as to say, "Alas! I am evidently in for it with this troublesome American." But as Mott spoke on, addressing the Archbishop exactly as if he was at a public meeting, his Grace's interest began to be aroused and within about five minutes he had his face in his hands with both his elbows on the table, and his gaze fixed on Mott in a concentrated frown of interest. Mott, having found an attentive auditor and a very important man rolled into one, was in his element, and with emphasis, eagerness and gesticulation, he proceeded with his address to the fascinated Archbishop. He must have spoken for at least half an hour, when suddenly without any warning he swung round to me, remarking, "Now my friend, Mr. Tatlow, has many more interesting things to say to your Grace." By this time the Archbishop was as putty in our hands and looked responsively at me to see what I had to say. Knowing Mott's ways and how carefully he stuck to his programme, I was ready, and cleared up one or two points in Mott's speech which by watching the Archbishop's face I had noticed had raised questions in his mind. After a few minutes the conversation became general between the three of us, and at the end of about two hours the Archbishop suddenly said, "I don't often meet two men who know their own minds as thoroughly as you two do; what do you want me to do about this subject of the Ministry?"

The upshot of the interview was that it was arranged that when Mott returned a week later from Holland, which he was just about to visit, there should be a specially called meeting of the Archbishop's committee to meet us and discuss the whole question. This was a committee presided over by the Bishop of Hereford (Dr. Percival) with the Rev. S. A. Donaldson as secretary. We had an extremely interesting meeting with the committee, the Archbishop himself attending. Mott made a speech on the subject of recruiting for the Ministry and then cross-questioned the committee, eliciting an amount of very interesting information from those present.

I took careful notes for Mott of what was said, which was put in the form of a memorandum for him. But Mott was not satisfied, he had not got what he wanted. What he wanted was a letter on the subject from the Archbishop which he could use as propaganda, to draw attention to the importance in different countries of the question of recruiting for the Ministry, and he mourned that he had nothing in writing from the Archbishop. I felt that his Grace had been so kind and interested that there was no reason why Mott should not write and ask him for a letter. Mott, however, was very timid about doing this, but egged on by me he wrote, and as I expected, received in response just the kind of letter he wanted. "Oh my, isn't this just fine," he said, as he displayed the letter; "I tell you, this will weigh a ton in some of the countries in which I shall use it."[36]

Such was the beginning of a dynamic friendship between a Methodist layman from Postville and a prince of the Church.

A few days later Mott gave a great speech to a metropolitan student meeting in London at the Mansion House; the Bishop of London presided. Mott's theme was "The Power of Jesus Christ in the Life of the Student." He was at his best. S. Wirt Wiley, observing Mott in London, marvelled at his influence with the British and his ready adaptation to their customs—silk hat, frock coat, afternoon tea—but nonetheless with the same "terrible earnestness" that characterized his activities at home.[37] Not long after this, the staff of the British Student Movement got out a special edition of their magazine in which they lampooned one another, especially Tatlow, and extended the coverage to Mott:

Awake! for Mott, that man of daring schemes,
Has marked strategic points, and cleared our dreams.

Mott's reactions were never known, but Leila disapproved:

THE GREAT ADVENTURER;

Or, "Mott will find out the way."

(From a 17th Century MS. recently unearthed in the Archives of the W.S.C.F.)

Over the New World,
And over the Old,
Where'er there's a student
To bring to the fold;
Through academies ancient,
Which tradition obey,
A pioneer patient,
Mott will find out the way.

Past all objections
That Croesus may urge,
Spite all the questions
Which in time must emerge,
Through problems the deepest
That students dismay,
Over rocks of the steepest
Mott will find out the way.

Where Bishops' palaces
The Movement ignore,
Where they politely
Show Trav. Secs. the door,
Where a Don dare not venture,
Lest he give himself away,
Federation can enter,
Mott will find out a way.

You may esteem him
Not made for the sea,
Or you may deem him
A coward to be,
But if a deck-cabin
In the centre be free
To capture a rich man
Mott will risk e'en the sea.

Though the field it be world-wide,
He will gallop it o'er,
Tho' the seas rise against him,
He won't stick to the shore,
Should a movement grow hollow,
Into heresy stray,
Mott will find wings to follow,
Bring it back to the way.

No manner of striving
Can cross his intent;
No amount of contriving
His tours will prevent.
For if points strategic
A nation display,
Of fatigue quite regardless
Mott will start on his way.[38]

It had been Mott's intention to remain abroad through the early part
of May, 1905, for two important conferences, but due to the terminal

illness of his father, he returned home the first week of March, going on to Postville at the end of the month. On the advice of the attending physicians he returned to New York, and finally took passage again on the last ship that would get him to Paris for the Golden Jubilee of the World's Alliance. On the eve of that event, word came "about Father's home-going." Unable to express how deeply he felt not to be with his mother and sisters, Mott wrote that very day of his own sorrow "about the end—or let me say the beginning, for I like to think of the truth that Father has really just entered into the largest life and is now free from all the weakness, and limitations of life on earth." Although they had all been prepared for this for months, John had hoped against hope that he could be at home when the end came, as the doctors had encouraged them to believe. "It must be a great satisfaction to you and Hattie," he wrote to his mother, "that you were able to minister unto him during these last months. We whose duties kept us away . . . cannot but regret it." The occasion brought him to "a more sympathetic understanding" of soldiers, sailors, missionaries, and others "whose duties call them to distant lands. I too am over here on duty; I surely would not have come for any selfish purpose."

A few weeks later, Richard Morse wrote John's mother a gracious letter assuring her of her son's keen and painful regret on account of his enforced absence. "But the errand and the work that he has accomplished at this time have been of the most critical importance. None of his associates could have substituted for him"; he was "one of the leaders indispensable to the accomplishment of the great work of peace, unity and progress" both at the Alliance conference in Paris and the WSCF at Zeist. "I am one of many who feel deeply grateful for the divine guidance which brought him to us in the critical sessions of these two world conferences, against his own preference. I am sure he was led to come in direct answer to prayer, yours and his and ours." Morse went on:

> When I think of the many years I have known John ever since his college days and of the intimate filial relation in our life work which he has so faithfully and helpfully sustained to me—the relation of an adult son on whom the father leans with an increasing gratitude, it seems strange that I am writing now for the first time to his mother to thank her for the very large part she has had in conferring this great inestimable blessing. Few can realize as I do the wisdom and strength he has brought to the administration and leadership of our work for students and for all classes of young men first on our own continent and then on all continents.
>
> But I know this has cost self-denial and self-sacrifice—many a heartache—not only to himself but to those who love him best and most of

all to his mother. But there is One who knows better than we the full meaning of such suffering in His name, knows also how to bring to His own something of the consolation He has Himself experienced. May these consolations be yours also, for human gratitude is indeed too often a broken reed to lean upon. But His love and grace can always supply all our need.[39]

The deliberations to which Morse referred were in committee and behind the scenes, but they concerned major issues in the life of the World's Alliance of YMCA's and marked the Paris Jubilee as a milestone. They resulted in a "healing of differences," reaffirmation of the Paris Basis, and comprised a first step toward providing "an internationally representative Executive." Mott gave what could be called a keynote address in which he reviewed the history of the Alliance and challenged it to "tremendous advance in the years right before us." He kept busy, securing delegate John Wanamaker's pledge of $100,000 toward "Y" buildings in Seoul, Peking, and Kyoto.[40]

The Zeist conference of the WSCF, held in "the glorious beauty of spring in Holland at the headquarters of the Moravian community" while the Russo-Japanese War raged on the other side of the globe, was "the most representative yet," with thirty nations, eighteen movements, five continents, and Australasia present. Among the delegates were friends from near and distant places where Mott had planted in his ceaseless journeys—Johannes Sandegren from Sweden, Paul Nicolay from Russia, J. Merle Davis there for Mott to call him to Japan—examples of how the Mott network operated. This meeting had been planned for Japan; Fries commented on how difficult it had been for Mott to relinquish a plan "which he had once accepted as given by God." The Federation would go to Tokyo two years hence.[41]

Yet Zeist was a significant gathering. Mott reviewed the decade of the Federation's history: its greatest achievement had been "what it has accomplished in the direction of realizing Christian unity"; he regarded the growing social consciousness of students in various movements, citing Holland, Great Britain, and the Harvard Association as "signs of encouragement," and urged the constituent movements to "take up the study of social questions, seriously, earnestly and thoroughly":

Students must be influenced to stand for bringing the Christian religion into every department and relationship of life ... the world of thought, family and social life, commercial and industrial life, municipal affairs, national problems and international relations. ... The men who are to have a leading part in helping to solve the social questions of our generation must have come from the universities; it is urgent that we prepare them for discharging their responsibilities.[42]

And, as he had recommended at home, Mott pressed students everywhere to "undertake some form of social work." Forward steps were taken at Zeist to relate "the world of woman students to the Federation"; like the Paris Jubilee of the Alliance, the Federation reaffirmed its Vadstena basis of membership; it voted to meet in Japan in 1907; and upon the insistence of the delegates from South Africa strongly urged the General Secretary to visit that subcontinent. Mott's closing address was one of his most powerful. Utilizing the military analogy and anticipating the next conference, he told how Joseph Neesima had, on his deathbed, marked on a map of Japan "the strategic positions which should be taken for Christianity," and how the missionary Guido Verbeck, who was born there in Zeist, "became a leader of modern Japan" by humbly hiding himself behind the Japanese during his long life among them.[43]

PART 5: South Africa and South America, 1906

In 1896, while the Motts were bringing Australasia into the Federation, Luther Wishard, with the chance assistance of Donald Fraser en route to his first missionary assignment in Livingstonia or Kondowi, Nyasaland, had organized the Student Christian Association of South Africa. In 1898 the South Africans began to request Mott to visit them. At Zeist they convinced him that he must go: their movement was in serious straits in the aftermath of the Boer War, and he had by then been back to all of the other national movements at least twice. He therefore prepared for a tour to South Africa and South America, the last major regions of the world that he had not visited, obtained some $10,000 from fifteen wealthy friends to pay for the trip, and soon after the Nashville Quadrennial, which Fraser had attended on furlough, sailed for Europe on March 15, 1906, with Leila, and William R. Stewart as secretary.

On shipboard rest and relaxation were the order of the day: Leila wrote Mother Mott that "these journeys" were "saving his life." After arrival in Paris, John touched base in Geneva, Barmen, and Utrecht in one whirlwind week before reaching London where he rejoined Leila and conferred at length with British leaders on strategy for promoting unity in the troubled South African Movement, obtained assurances of financial support, and received greetings from Oxford and Cambridge for the students of South Africa. He attended a meeting of the World's Committee of the Young Women's Christian Associations with Leila, and addressed 1800 people at Exeter Hall for the second annual meeting of the SCM.

Ruth Rouse joined them for the 17-day voyage to Capetown; all participated in the ship's games, Stewart excelling in the athletic events and Leila awarding the prizes. John spoke on the resurrection at an Easter service. The steamship company gave them an extra cabin for John's books; he started devouring them almost at once. Miss Rouse described the effect on the other passengers:

> He fills a heavy trunk with books (it needs iron bands). For the voyage to South Africa in 1906, it was filled with piles of Blue Books, biographies of Livingstone, Cecil Rhodes, Sir Bartle Frere, Kruger and Chako, the Zulu king of Slaughter, and histories of the Boer War, then so recent. Speculation was rife among the men on board about this man who sat on deck reading book after book and often, after tearing out a page or two, flinging them into the sea. One day, as he sat with his back to a lounge window, a young man stole inside, crept to the window determined to know in what deep subject this enigma was buried. He peeped, threw up his hands and whispered to the expectant crowd "King Solomon's Mines"! [a popular novel laid in Africa].[44]

On the morning of April 17, all arose early to see the sunrise over Table Mountain and the city of Capetown spread along its base, the bright crisp air reminding Leila of Colorado or California. By mid-afternoon the Motts and Miss Rouse were being welcomed at the YMCA Hall by a select group presided over by J. Hofmeyr, "the most influential politician of the country"; one of the welcoming addresses was by the Anglican archbishop. As the visitors were well aware, they would find the Boers still full of bitterness toward the British, insisting upon speaking Afrikaans to anyone who understood it, thus requiring Mott to use interpreters. Nevertheless, the Student Christian Movement, although predominantly Dutch but in a weakened condition, looked to Mott "to give them a missionary vision and to help them to win the students of British origin; it was a valiant effort to escape from one-sidedness," wrote Miss Rouse in retrospect. In a report letter, Mott compared the divisions and rivalries "between the different colonies and ports" to America before the Revolution or Australia before the Commonwealth.[45]

Furthermore, the strictly Calvinistic Dutch Reformed Church, to which most students belonged, was anti-mission, largely because it was anti-native and missionaries were champions of the Africans. Mott and Rouse found at once that there was no possibility of including black Africans, who outnumbered the white population ten to one, in the Movement, though they did temporize by entrusting them to the Student

Volunteer Movement. The racial situation was infinitely complex because of the presence of Oriental minorities such as the Indians championed by Mohandas K. Gandhi. The very youth of the Movement, only ten years old, and the lack of leadership among the few colleges and secondary schools confronted Mott with a situation not unlike that which he had faced in Australia and New Zealand a decade earlier.

The visitors found a very hearty welcome almost everywhere. Fortunately, this was matched with genuine goodwill and the fullest support by veteran leaders of the Dutch community such as Andrew Murray. Introductions brought ready entrée to the Anglican, Methodist, and Presbyterian churches and schools. Mott reverted to his earlier tactic of visiting every school and college, beginning with those in and surrounding Capetown; sometimes he was forced to speak four times a day. He used the themes developed for his world tour of 1901–1902 which had been published as *Christians of Reality*. He frequently met with groups of clergymen, presenting his ideas and questions on recruiting superior men for the ministry. He obtained information on conditions in South Africa from every person whose experience could be helpful, notably Clinton T. Wood, a Princeton Theological Seminary graduate of 1897, who was teaching at Wellington and who oriented him to the South African SVM. There were mass evangelistic rallies attracting as many as 3500 persons as well as student meetings, at which Mott used the themes of sin, temptation, and purity.

At Wellington both Motts satisfied a longing of years in meeting in his home "Clairvaux" the aging Andrew Murray, who could rightly have been called the patron saint of the South African student movement because of the aid he had given Wishard in 1896. John had discovered Murray's devotional tract *With Christ in the School of Prayer* while an undergraduate at Cornell, and his *Key to the Missionary Problem*, which laid the burden of responsibility for missions on the local pastor, was a stimulus to Mott as he planned *The Pastor and Modern Missions* and now discussed the issue with Murray. Murray was a man of action, leader of the Dutch Church, founder of several schools, and a protagonist of the Keswick way. Moody had brought him to the adult conference at Northfield where he had conducted the morning devotions for two weeks in 1895. Mott now sought his advice on the strategy of his tour.[46] Murray called on Leila briefly one evening, affording her the opportunity to tell him "how much he was loved in America." He in turn spoke of the "precious fellowship in Christ." She recorded in her diary that he made "an impression of saintliness such as few if any men ever have upon me."

Mott's larger campaigns were at Capetown, Stellenbosch, Paarl, Wellington, Grahamstown, King Williamstown, Lovedale, Bloemfontein, Johannesburg, Pretoria, Pietermaritzburg, and Durban. He touched all of the "important college towns" of the four colonies and he could report that he had opened the doors to "all the principal British colleges and schools." At small places Leila noted that he took his audiences "around the world in an hour and eighteen minutes" or gave "a compote of several addresses and a view of the world." Train travel, as yet primitive for the most part, through the strange desert country where ostriches roamed, inspired long letters home to the children. There were evangelistic rallies in desert towns and cordial hospitality in remote Dutch parsonages. One "best" hotel Leila thought "no great shakes."

Girls and young women listened respectfully to Leila and Miss Rouse, but Leila noted that they really wanted to hear John, whose most unforgettable experience was at the Scots Presbyterian boys' school at Lovedale, near Alice, Cape Colony, which "in methods, spirit and reputation" seemed similar to Tuskegee. The "intensity, power, and fruitfulness of the meetings" reminded him of his visits "at Yale in 1898, at Okayama, over four years ago, and at Oxford a year ago last winter." Audiences of 800 which included every tribe south of the Zambesi and groups of up to fifty who had walked "over the mountain from Healdtown" and from other places made an indelible impression upon the speaker:

> My addresses were translated into Kaffir by a most able native interpreter. Certain critical parts of my messages were translated into Sesuto also, in order to make doubly sure that my meaning be understood. There was an eagerness and earnestness about the attention of these young men which was both pitiful and inspiring. Just as the sea of faces of some of my Chinese, Japanese and Indian audiences lingers in memory, so will the vision of these hundreds of dusky faces of Zulus, Kaffirs, Basutos, Fingoes, Baralongs and other African tribes, never be forgotten.[47]

Next fall, his meetings at Howard University would remind him of Lovedale.

The "principal event," as of all Mott tours of this kind, was the "Student Missionary Conference" at Capetown May 17–20, "the largest student gathering ever held in South Africa." Official attendance was 526, with several hundred more crowding the facilities of Huguenot Hall. More than seventy white schools and colleges were represented, but neither Mott nor the conference records tell what transpired when "a most interesting delegation came from the native college at Zonnebloem," composed of three distinguished African princes: "Christopher Lobengula, son and heir of the late King of the Matabele; Isany Pilane, son of the King of the Bakhatla; and Joseph Moshesh, grandson of the first king and founder of the powerful Basuto race."[48] Opened by the Anglican Archbishop of Capetown, the program included speakers of all the major churches; Mott spoke five times and Leila once. Andrew Murray, nearing eighty and partly paralyzed, touched the hearts of his hearers with a "burning and prophetic message," "He Must Reign," and subsequently wrote the introduction to the Conference proceedings. The students subscribed £350 a year for two years toward the support of the Movement.

Mott compared the Capetown Conference to an SVM Quadrennial. Volunteers were held back from signing the pledge during the Convention to discourage emotional responses, but many had done so before he had left the country. As he looked back on his tour and the Conference he felt that his principal objective had been realized: for the first time since the terrible Boer War most of the differing Christian forces of the country had been brought together, a feat that could possibly be accomplished only by the Christian student movement "with its world-wide program" that afforded "a platform sufficiently broad and attractive to make even the beginning of this difficult work of unification at all possible."

Funds were raised to obtain a special secretary to work among the British and native schools; Oswin Bull, a Cambridge man, was later enlisted and found his life work in South Africa. Everywhere he could, Mott tried to enlist "leading men" in the Association cause. His visit stimulated international intercourse between the parent YMCA's in the United States and South Africa; beginning in 1910 an American International secretary, J. S. Tichener, served two years as secretary of the South African national committee. Everywhere Mott had been concerned to "lay upon the native young men . . . a burden of responsibility for the Christianization of their peoples," for Africa "can never be evangelized by white men alone or chiefly."[49]

Following the conference, a fund-raising luncheon, and a full day with the Movement executive committee, the Motts entrained for a vacation trip to Victoria Falls. Miss Rouse remembered "a thrilling day" at Kimberley, "when he read, thought and talked of nothing but diamonds, their origin, production and value." When the train stopped at remote places, the cries of wild animals could be heard. There were two days and nights, Leila wrote, comprising "one of the greatest experiences of our lives" seeing the Falls from all vantage points. The reader of their letters gains the impression that a large part of their enjoyment was the knowledge that David Livingstone was the discoverer of this wonder. They had "an exciting journey" upstream in a Canadian-style canoe paddled by four black men to the station of the *Mission de Paris* at Livingstone, where they met the Coissons, missionaries from Torre Pellice. Miss Rouse told how on the return trip to Johannesburg and work,

> we collaborated on notes for a monumental address (never delivered!) on "Seventeen Reasons why Victoria Falls is greater than Niagara." (He actually sent John L. a cable suggesting as much!) But it nearly broke his heart that he could not work in a visit to the World's View, the Rhodes' Tomb on the Matoppo Hills.

He had, she pointed out, a rare power of switching off the current of world affairs and living another life completely absorbed in something other than his work: without this power, he could never return to work with the freshness that he did.

The Motts returned through the Transvaal and Natal to take ship for South America at Durban, visiting a gold mine at Johannesburg, speaking at several meetings called on short notice, and organizing the first Association in Natal. They wondered how Ladysmith could have been defended as it had been during the Boer War. Learning that their sailing date had been postponed, Leila, while John itinerated from the same base, spent several days in intimate contact with the students and the dozen missionary teachers—"I had known most of them when they were students at home," John wrote his mother—of the Zulu mission of the American Board at Amanzimtoti, seven miles from the railway by ox-cart. This was one of the longest and most leisurely times either John or Leila Mott ever spent at an actual mission station.

Mott devoted one of these days of delay to extended conversations at Howick Falls with one of the forgotten men of the WSCF, G. B. A. Gerdener, who had planned the tour. That past January, Gerdener had begun what would be a significant ecumenical career as traveling secretary of the South Africa Student Movement. Dedicated to the ideal of unity, Gerdener was popular with students and would become a strong force in eventually reconciling all elements save a few die-hards to unity in the South African Movement. That Mott was deeply impressed by this young man is clear from his arranging for him to attend the WSCF in Tokyo the next year, then to visit Northfield and student centers in Britain and Europe. Gerdener eminently justified Mott and Rouse's estimate of him through the next fifteen years, devoting himself tirelessly to overcoming the isolation and provincialism that they saw as the greatest weakness of the South African organization.[50]

During the weeks Mott was in this part of Africa, Mohandas K. Gandhi, whose little farm was only a short distance from Durban, was organizing a group of Indians into an ambulance corps to offer their services to the government of Natal, in an effort to improve their image, during a Zulu uprising. In the course of what proved to be an abortive assignment, Gandhi, with time for uninterrupted contemplation, resolved that although married he would henceforth lead a life of chastity. Thirty years later, Mott would be a visitor to his ashram with whom Gandhi would discuss his frustration when this long-suppressed urge rose to confound him.[51]

Finally, on June 14, the Motts and Stewart sailed for Buenos Aires from Durban on the *Highland Mary,* a 3,000-ton tramp steamer of the Nelson Line—a "dreadful looking boat—too dirty and greasy" to endure, said Leila, helplessly—engaged in the cold storage meat trade out of Argentina. This would be the most dangerous and uncomfortable trip Mott ever made. It put to the severest test his travel motto from the first world tour: "With God anywhere, without Him, not over the threshold." The alternative had been to return to the Azores and await a ship to Buenos Aires. The decision to take the *Highland Mary* was "to save time and money." As it turned out, Stewart commented later, "we saved little of either, but we got our time and money's worth in experience."

Mott had made the captain "a generous cash payment" for the use of his cabin, high amidships, which had three ports that could be kept open most of the time; it was "well fitted up with wardrobe, table, six large drawers, two bunks, a washstand, and a desk." When Leila asked the chief steward what she might bring aboard to make the voyage more comfortable, he suggested "a billiard table and a piano," but she bought "beds with springs" that proved "quite comfortable," steamer chairs, extra pillows, and a stock of food. Calling at Capetown on the eighteenth, during which John spent the day with the SCM executive committee which had been called by telegram, Leila shopped frantically to supplement already large stores that would make them almost independent of the ship's mess with its "unspeakable" dirty tablecloths, and which three days had not commended. The hoard comprised more than fifty cans, boxes, and packets of biscuits, crackers, evaporated milk, fruits, preserves, raisins, coffee, tea, chocolate, and nuts, plus 120 bottles

of mineral water, 118 bananas, 108 oranges, ten pineapples, and a dozen
lemons.

Leila's diary was suspended when the ship nosed out of the
Capetown harbor into rain and fog to begin the 3800-mile passage across
the South Atlantic. John's lengthy log, addressed to son John L. at home
the day before the voyage ended, revealed "Papa" in a mood rarely if ever
exposed. Because of the danger, which is not mentioned, this document
adds significantly to a portrait of Mott under stress. The first week things
went reasonably well. Then, 1500 knots from Capetown, the moderate
westerly wind changed into an Antarctic gale:

> June 26th Run, 157. Very discouraging. Had wide board made to hold Leila
> in bed. A day for oranges and kind words.
> June 27th Run, 176. Wind, west, south-west and north-west. Great gale.
> Heavy sea. Mutiny among stokers; suppressed at 3 A.M. Awful night.
> No sleep. Captain stayed away from two meals. German-Polish
> woman driven to prayer.
> June 28th Run, 172. Strong north-west wind. Sea choppy. Heavy head
> swell. Captain sober today. Fog. First and only use of fog whistle.
> Much thinking among passengers and few words. Deep problems
> being solved.

One theorizes that the fog horn would echo from icebergs if there were
such; the route lay within the northern summer limits of floating ice.

> June 29th Run, 135. North-west wind. Awful gale. Heavy head sea.
> Squally. Overcast. Boat pitching and swinging through arc of 40 feet.
> Passengers ignorant and uncertain as to which end standing on.

The next day brought fine, clear weather, but the wind continued. "Rays
of hope pierce passengers' breasts." A sailing ship, the first since
Capetown, was sighted. Three more days of "confused sea," but moderate
runs.

> July 3rd Run, 230. West, northwest gale. Following sea. Sky overcast.
> Majestic billows, some running from forty to fifty feet high. One
> crashed over boat and poured into our cabin through ventilator open-
> ing which is 37 feet above water line. Spray dashed over top of
> steamer funnel. Final beans in cabin.

Stewart was soaked while taking dictation, holding the typewriter with
one hand. Yet, he reminisced, in spite of storm and peril, "the work went
on." "Hundreds of letters were written."

> July 4th Run, 89. Lowest ever made in all travels at home or abroad. Wind,
> north-west, west, south-west; also from other quarters. Fierce breezes,

gales and gusts. Seas confused; also passengers. German-Polish woman spent second night in prayer. Captain depressed. Threatened mutiny of second-class passengers against harmless stewards. Solemn protest from first-class passengers on principle, "Don't shoot the organist; he is doing the best he can." Sincere efforts to be patriotic. Stars and Stripes raised in cabin. Driven to ginger ale and Sherlock Holmes. Deep meditation.

The next day they ran 173 knots; there was a fresh west wind, rough choppy sea, but fine clear weather. On July 6 the run climbed to 206, with a light wind and so-called smooth sea, "restful hopeful feeling. Third-class passengers gave concert in open air, in seven languages."

July 7 Run, 237. Wind west to north-west. Great activity in letter-writing and packing in anticipation of landing tomorrow or next day. Only 241 knots from Buenos Aires. Clinching nail of resolution never to do it again; that is, never to travel "cold storage" again.[52]

The following morning Leila resumed her diary, the ship being in the roads of the La Plata, which reminded her of the Yangtze.

They were met by two able men, both of whom John had recruited: Bertram A. Shuman, who had come to Buenos Aires in 1901, and Charles J. Ewald in 1903. An Association, primarily for British and other Protestant men, had been established in 1902; as time passed, membership would rise to eighty percent Argentinian and work for students would be initiated. Their hosts took the Motts to the Grand Hotel, which seemed luxurious after the *Highland Mary.* Joined for dinner by the two men's wives, the brief week they were to have in the Argentine capital began with callers and planning. Mott plunged at once into a round of meetings, luncheons, dinners, and receptions. His principal intent, planned with Shuman over the previous months, was to stimulate the Buenos Aires Association to build on a challenging scale. Changing his emphasis from the WSCF to the foreign work, he offered a contingent gift of $100,000 toward that goal at a reception given by businessmen on the third day in a speech in which he told his hosts that theirs was "the most important city in the world without such facilities, and certainly the last city in the world of which this should be said." The offer was accepted, though the building was not completed and dedicated until 1912. Newspapers commented enthusiastically.

There were more receptions and opportunities to explain the building program to various civic and religious groups and to coach the fundraisers. Leila visited both Catholic and Protestant girls' schools, spoke a few times, and was tendered an elegant reception at the "new and beautiful" Palace Hotel. John became very much aware of the unique problems faced by an evangelical Protestant organization in a Catholic country; next year this membership issue would be aired at the International Convention.[53]

Taking ship July 13 for Rio de Janeiro, the Motts stopped briefly at Montevideo, where there was soon to be a building campaign, going on at once to São Paulo to meet the senior South American YMCA secretary, Myron T. Clark, who had been in Brazil since 1891 and was then in the midst of his second national conference. Mott immediately became engulfed in affairs related to this enthusiastic body:

> I gave five public addresses, conducted two conferences with pastors and missionaries on the problem of getting able young men for the ministry, presided over one conference with representatives of the American and British and Foreign Bible Societies to agree on a plan of federation of their activities throughout South America, held one meeting with the National Committee of the Young Men's Christian Associations about plans for the future, and held interviews with each of the principal delegates.[54]

He also called on the Minister of Education and the President of the Republic, while Leila visited and spoke at various schools and was entertained by numerous mission groups. John spoke at a meeting of "government students"; trouble was anticipated but did not develop.

In Rio the Motts found the Pan-American Congress in session and made the most of the presence of the United States Secretary of State Elihu Root, an old "Y" man. Both Motts went to a gala affair given by Root, John using all these events to meet "many of the leading statesmen of Brazil, as well as other prominent public men." He laid out the plans for Association expansion in Latin America in a "special interview" with Root, "who manifested the deepest interest and promised to receive a deputation in Buenos Aires, and at that time to make a speech endorsing Association work in Latin countries." During this conversation, Mott remarked that it was Association policy to minimize denominational differences and magnify unity in service. Root broke in with, "That is what McBurney used to say."[55] Myron Clark wrote in his diary that Mott's visit was "by all odds the largest event of the year." *Christians of Reality* was being issued in Portuguese; Clark had interpreted for Mott and been complimented on his skill.

The voyage home, August 2–20, was routine, there being short stops at Bahia and Pernambuco (Recife) where a new "Y" secretary was expected momentarily, and at Barbados and Martinique; John won at deck golf. In recapitulating his experience in South America he noted the "truly remarkable success" of the YMCA in the three major cities he had visited, the hearty support by virtually all Protestant bodies and "a growing number of the most enlightened Catholics" who did not disguise their sympathy, and the plight of students, who were "without a religion." Thus the conviction came to him with "overwhelming force" that "a special burden of responsibility rests upon the Christians of the United States for the establishment of Christ's Kingdom among the people of Latin America." Yet Ruth Rouse was to comment much later that not China, Japan, or Russia, but the Latin lands would prove to be "the Gibraltar of the student world."[56]

An anticlimax to the southern hemisphere tour was a quick train trip to Mexico City that October, with successful fund-raising in St. Louis en route and an evangelistic campaign at the University of Texas on the return trip. At Monterrey, Mott picked up Augustin E. Turner, newly assigned secretary there, to serve as guide and private secretary. As he had done in Buenos Aires, Mott offered the Mexico City Association $50,000 toward a building. Before he left, the Mexicans obtained a matching sum, which "lifted their faith so they now are going to enlarge the proposition and work for a total of from $300,000 to $400,000 Mex.," he wrote Leila. He had two interviews with Vice-President Corral, who was honorary president of the Association, and President Diaz gave him an "unhurried and profitable" interview: "He is a gentleman in every way. He spoke in the strongest terms in approval of our work and offered to interest the members of his cabinet and ask them to contribute to the enterprise." Turner recalled that in the course of one of Mott's addresses he surprised everyone by stopping his interpreter with "That is not what I said!"—although he did not know Spanish.[57]

Problems concerning Association membership of Catholics surfaced early in Latin America and in the Philippines. The Mexico City YMCA cut the gordian knot by making a list (this had never been done) of acceptable evangelical churches that included the Roman Catholic. At the International Convention in Washington in the fall of 1907 a realistic attempt was made to rephrase the traditional North American basis in the broader terms of the Paris statement, especially for student Associations, with some gain, but the Convention was stampeded by conservatives and the proposal failed. In the debate Mott found himself opposing William Jennings Bryan, who is reported to have said to the person seated next to him that he guessed he must be on the wrong side![58]

In recapitulating the year for Mrs. McCormick at the end of 1906—he had kept her informed throughout—Mott said that he had raised more than $400,000 toward buildings "for the great cities of Latin America" since returning. The next year he saw that Charles D. Hurrey was appointed continental secretary for South America, which made possible "comprehensive planning, the inauguration of Associations in new centers, the coordination of the Associations, and an increase of strength through fellowship." We should not forget that there is a Latin America, he charged the readers of his report letters, and if we include the Philippines, its population is almost equal to that of Anglo-Saxon America. It is related to us as Europe is not: "It is an America as much as the land we occupy." The Latin American countries are new countries like our own. They are experiencing growing pains similar to our own in "the building of great cities, extension of railways, and assimilation of foreign populations; and they are looking to us as to no other part of the world for guidance in all these matters. The solidarity of our interests rests also upon the identity of our fundamental political principles." The recent revival of interest in the Monroe Doctrine, "which has been tremendously quickened by the visit of Mr. Root, suggests religious as well as political responsibility. The Spanish and Philippine Wars have opened the eyes of the American people as never before to the urgent moral and spiritual claims of the Latin American peoples. We have come to realize the full force and aptness of the designation of South America as the 'neglected continent.' Is it not our solemn duty to atone for generations of neglect?"[59]

PART 6: Korea, the Philippines, and China, 1907

The Federation Conference in Japan, in early April, 1907, was not only, as Hans-Ruedi Weber insists, "the dawn of a new day" for Oriental students and the Asian ecumenical movement, it was one of the organization's most significant gatherings. Mott had prepared for it with foresight and imagination since it had been authorized at Söro in 1902, and had raised a special fund of well over $20,000 from a score of friends. On the eve of departure he confessed to Mrs. McCormick that it was "the most important mission on which I have embarked in these nineteen years of work among students of many lands."[60]

The trip began with a full day in Washington on December 31, 1906, where his chief appointments were with Secretary of State Elihu Root and Secretary of War William Howard Taft who was still the virtual Governor of the Philippine Islands, each of whom provided him with "valuable letters endorsing the main objects" he would be promoting. President Theodore Roosevelt being away, Mott "set things up so as to get him to write a letter" that would be forwarded.

It was more than usually difficult to leave home this time, with Leila expecting another child in May. Before settling into sleep on the fast *Pennsylvania Special* to Chicago late that New Year's Eve, he wrote her a letter that did not merely chronicle his activities:

> My Darling:
>   You have been in my thoughts and heart every waking moment since those holy moments together last night. Thank God for such a love— which grows and grows, and which, although partings are so hard, fills one with a sense of companionship and trust and soul rest. You were never so near and dear to me as now. Already I have begun to look forward to getting back to you and that joyful thought will stay with me to buoy me up during these busy weeks. And if we continue to call upon God out of pure hearts He will answer us and restore us to each other.
>   God bless you and ours my own dearest!
> Your husband,
> John

Met by Stewart in Chicago, Mott spent New Year's Day with his sister Clara and in clearing up correspondence. The next three days were at Postville. En route to the Coast he read Adolf von Harnack's *Expansion of Christianity*, writing Leila that it confirmed one's "belief in the SVM Watchword." He arrived in Portland via the *Overland Limited* Monday evening, January 7, and went into conference with the local YMCA staff; at midnight he took a sleeper to Seattle, spent Tuesday completing sailing arrangements, finished letter-writing, mailed the copy of his edition of Foster's *Decision of Character*, wrote Leila detailed comments on the reorganization of the National YWCA Board, and spoke at an Association banquet. The Richard Morses arrived and all sailed January 9 on the *Minnesota*, which, with its electric lights and fans, Mott thought the "finest boat on the Pacific." They arrived at Yokohama January 23 after a "most comfortable voyage" during which Mott read a score of books on Japan, Korea, and East-West relations. From Tokyo Bay he wrote Leila that in spite of the comforts of the ship he would rather have crossed on the *Highland Mary* if she might have been along, and that he was anticipating being back with her when the baby came: "Unless I am off on my reckoning I will be." He was adopting her suggestion that he keep "a brief journal." These diaries are the chief sources for his trips from this time on.

In five days "about as full as days can be packed" he went over with the staff and Japanese leaders every detail of the coming Conference, made protocol calls, attended luncheons, dinners, receptions, and outlined the purpose and plans of the gathering to various groups. Following adequate exploratory conversations he announced to the National YMCA Board the gift of $50,000 he had obtained for student Association hostels to be erected in Tokyo and other cities, and on January 29 left for his first visit to Korea, a shift in plans. He would return at the end of March.

Morse and Mott were joined at Shimoneseki by Brockman and Lewis from China. After the night ferry crossing to Fusan, they conferred on a wide range of Association matters throughout the long day's train ride on the newly built Japanese line to Seoul. From the car windows it was apparent that the Japanese were occupying the country in force, following the "protectorate" they had established in 1905.[61] Three days of "regal reception" began with an escort of hundreds of persons carrying Oriental lanterns from station to hotel, where addresses were given by "a member of the Privy Council" and a leading Korean pastor. The endless round of receptions, luncheons, and banquets that followed were, in Morse's words, a testimony to the "more strong and cordial receptivity" by the Koreans to Christianity than that shown by any other Oriental people.

That Korea was on the threshold of a religious revival at this tragic juncture in her history was evidenced by the growth of the Seoul YMCA to 900 members served by three International secretaries—Philip L. Gillett, who had been there since 1901, and Frank Brockman and George Gregg who had come in 1906. In addition to interviewing on his project on the ministry—the questionnaire now had thirty-two items—Mott spoke to groups of missionaries, businessmen, and educators as well as conferring with individuals. At two afternoon meetings, he talked on "The Power of Christ" to audiences of 2,500 young men; one of these meetings lasted three hours. Many came to the first one out of curiosity "and hoping that I had some political message which would bring them relief from the Japanese," he told Leila. Lewis, who described the scene, gained admission to the crowded hall by being pulled "by a strong arm reached down from above." No member of those audiences could have been more aware of the speaker's theme in his own heart and career than Mott's interpreter, the brilliant Baron Tchi Ho Yun, an intimate of Brockman at Vanderbilt and then head of the Southern Methodist Anglo-Korean School at Songdo, whose orations at Tokyo in both English and Japanese next April would bring distinction to Korea, and whose imprisonment by the Japanese in 1911 would become an international *cause célèbre.* [62] At the appropriate occasion Mott announced John Wanamaker's gift of $40,000 toward a building for the Seoul YMCA. He called on the Japanese Resident-General, the real ruler of the country, who "manifested hearty interest and approval" of Association policy.

Ransford Miller arranged for audiences with Emperor Kwang Mu on the last day of the visit. In full evening dress with white gloves, Mott and Morse were "met by official chair bearers and carried to the palace":

> On reaching the door of the audience room one bows to His Majesty, then when half way across the room one bows a second time, and when one has taken one's position immediately in front of him one bows a third time. In retiring one repeats this process, but goes out backwards, being careful not to show one's back to the Emperor. His Majesty was standing behind a little table. On either side of him were various court functionaries. Immediately by his side was the young Prince, about eleven years old. The Emperor shook hands with me both at the beginning of the audience and at its close. He asked me several questions through the interpreter. In answering I had good opportunity, which I improved, to tell him about our Association work and plans in Seoul, about the gift of Mr. Wanamaker, about the coming Federation Conference, and about my impressions of Korea. At the close he thanked me for the interest I had shown in the young men of his country. . . . When I withdrew from the audience room the little Prince followed. As he knows English we chatted with him a little while. He manifested special interest in what I told him of the Zoo in London. When asked whether he would like to visit America and England he replied that he would if his father would let him. [63]

In less than six months, the Emperor would be forced to abdicate in favor of "the little Prince." In 1910 the dynasty would be ended and the country annexed by Japan.

The audience had disrupted Mott's plans for travel to Manila, his next goal. Unable to "bribe the boat (to Japan) to wait for us" or to obtain a special train back to Fusan, the party was forced to travel on Sunday, a day spent "in Bible study and conversation regarding various important questions in our work," and in writing a long letter to Leila describing the picturesque welcome, the great evangelistic meetings, details of the audience, and the enthusiasm of the missionaries over their success in Korea. In his report letter, Mott concluded that Korea was a "dead-ripe" mission field; in 1908 he was quoted in the annual report of the Southern Methodist Church that if missions were adequately maintained and enlarged at once, "Korea will be the first nation in the non-Christian world to become a Christian nation."[64] Unfortunately, things were never predictable in the once "Hidden Kingdom."

In 1896 Mott had "steamed past the Philippines," which were still under the domination of "Roman ecclesiastics and were securely closed against Protestant influence." In 1904 he could say guardedly that the "cause of pure religion" had a "most hopeful opportunity" there. Any doubts about "the wisdom of the United States continuing to occupy" the Islands were dispelled by wide reading, his conferences with Taft, and by his whirlwind four-day visit to Manila of February 15–19, 1907— "about the most intense week of my life."[65]

Accompanied by Morse and Fletcher Brockman, he went into conference with W. A. Tener, International secretary who had been on the field only a few weeks, and Arthur Rudman who was leaving after a brief term. Their conversations were shortly expanded to include the local committees that had been working on the building project; Mott was astonished that the groundwork had been laid so well that by the end of the first day he could be fully in touch with the entire situation. The plan was to build a home for a "model Association for all these regions" primarily for European and American young men, to be expanded to the Filipinos as soon as possible. Here it was imperative that Catholics be included from the beginning; from 1907, said E. Stanton Turner, later general secretary and historian of the Philippine national movement, Mott pioneered in the use of the Paris Basis for this purpose.[66]

Mott's first public act was to present his credentials to General James F. Smith, the Governor-General, who was a Catholic; on the second day, he and Tener called on the Catholic Vicar-General and visited several Catholic schools and a church. Mott then conferred with Episcopal Bishop Charles H. Brent, whom he had met two years earlier en route to Europe; there is reason to believe that Brent encouraged him toward the inclusive membership policy.[67]

Meetings, conferences, individual consultations, beginning with breakfasts at 6:30 and running to 1:00 A.M., were the order of four days during which Mott gave seven public addresses, conducted two sessions of a secretaries' conference, held twelve board and committee meetings, visited several building sites, and interviewed a dozen prominent men including General John J. Pershing who conducted him around the grounds of Fort McKinley. At a banquet on the second day Mott announced the contingent gift of $75,000 gold toward the building project; most of the remainder was subscribed before the visitors left for the

U.S.A. two months later. Mott was deeply impressed by 800 "bright-minded" students at a mass rally where he spoke on "The Power of Sin." Bishop Brent dragooned him into substituting for a cathedral lecturer whose boat had been delayed; Mott went directly from there to follow Morse in speaking on the building project at a young men's banquet that was followed by a coaching session with workers. It must have been with the usual sense of relief that Morse and Mott took ship for China; although the voyage was disagreeable it gave them two days and three nights of rest. En route Mott summarized his reactions to the challenge of the Philippines. [68]

On this, Mott's third visit, he found "a new China" wherever he went. The Association movement, with which the WSCF was almost inextricably mixed, was well on its way to proving the forecasts of five years before; there were now twenty-eight Western secretaries, most of whom he had recruited and found support for. The increase in Chinese leadership was relatively greater. Robertson's program for the popularization of Western science was successful beyond imagination. Princeton-in-Peking now had a staff of three and there were Associations in eight cities. "Its growth," writes Shirley Garrett, "was explained by the fact that the Association stood for gradualist Western change. Its values paralleled those of traditional China, yet contained a dynamic that appealed to modernizers." The "Y" was playing a significant role in reform, bringing the concern for social action that was becoming vocal in the United States and several other national movements to focus upon Chinese needs as the modern merchants and the new student class accepted them. As the imperial government decayed and the revolution drew nearer, the YMCA, in Brockman's words, was finding itself "in touch with the highest aspirations of young China." Since Mott's previous visit alliances had been formed with each of China's urban elites, and Chinese officials were turning to the Associations for various programs. Robertson and Robert Gailey had introduced Western sports and by 1907 plans had been started for a Far Eastern Olympics; Robertson was finding youth more interested in athletics than in science. [69]

This visit, then, would be vastly different from Mott's previous ones. In twenty-five days he "concentrated on the eight great centers: Hongkong, Canton, Shanghai, Soochow, Nanking, Hankow, Peking, and Tientsin," and because of "the almost faultless preparations" the staff had made, accomplished more than had been possible before the Movement was so well established. In every place possible he threw himself "with the keenest interest into the work of evangelism." The meetings averaged more than 1,000 picked young men, every one crowding the largest hall obtainable and lasting three hours; in two cities temporary pavilions were constructed. "All the influential classes of young men" were accessible, open-minded, and responsive to his message, he believed.[70]

Wherever possible Mott paid protocol calls on, was entertained by, or himself honored the appropriate government officials. In Peking, secretary Gailey "brought it about" that "four of the leading members of the Wai Wu Pu of the Imperial Foreign Office" gave a dinner in honor of Mott, accompanied by Brockman, Gailey, and Walter Lowrie, the first such honor to foreigners. It provided Mott "a rare opportunity to meet in a personal way the most powerful group of men in the Empire," and he improved the occasion to set forth Association attitudes, especially in its non-controversial stance as regarded politics, and its methods. But Chinese youth would soon be looking for political commitment.

Gailey also arranged a tiffin in Tientsin, "the most progressive city of China," which was attended by "most of the leading officials" of the province of Chili. More important in Mott's estimation was an invitation to lecture on "The Aims of Education" to a distinguished audience of 300 officials and 1,700 "more mature students from the various government colleges." He devoted more than half of his speech to the ethical aspects of education and laid special emphasis on "the vital service which the Association renders to the cause of education by promoting the moral and religious development of the students." At the close of the address, the President of the Imperial University, who had presided, "not only endorsed the positions I had laid down, but urged upon the teachers and students the claims of what I had said." After the audience was dismissed the provincial commissioner and the President engaged Mott in a two-hour discussion of educational problems, during which he had further opportunity to testify concerning the goals of the Christian colleges.[71]

At Nanking, accompanied by Brockman, Lyon, and Pettus, Mott was received by the Viceroy Tuan Fang and forty of his officials; Mott spent an hour alone with him "in conversation on various topics related to education, the Association, and Christian missions." They were joined by the commissioner of education, and Mott invited Tuan to attend the forthcoming national conference in Shanghai. Earlier that day, Mott had addressed "a splendid company of young men" who crowded "to its uttermost limits" a "large meeting pavilion" on the campus of Nanking University; he was brilliantly interpreted by Wang Cheng-ting ("C. T. Wang"), himself a far greater orator than any foreign speaker and, because of his repute as a revolutionary, a student idol.[72]

Mott held a "private" conference with the two dozen International secretaries in China in Soochow for three days, regarding it as possibly of greater significance than the national conference itself. Between sessions and late in the evenings he talked individually with every man and with small groups having special concerns. Brockman and Lyon were usually included in the latter, Mott complimenting them later as men of states-manlike stature having already accomplished a work out of all proportion to their years, though he confided to Leila that Brockman's health was "much shattered," because of which his load must be reduced. Mott coached his men on the forthcoming China Centenary Missionary Con-ference, for which he would not stay. It would praise the YMCA and recommend its expansion, an endorsement he used to obtain vastly in-creased funds for both secretaries and buildings.[73] He and Brockman agreed upon a buildings budget of $346,000. By 1910 this had grown to $425,000; in 1912 there would be seventy-five International secretaries in China, the fruit of the SVM.[74]

The event of "capital importance" on this tour was the National Conference of the YMCA of China, Korea, and Hong Kong, held at Shanghai March 19–22. Mott spoke before three sessions but attended only a few, possibly because they were held in Chinese, but the gathering was notable in that he and Morse were the only Western platform speak-ers. Comprised of "the very flower of the Chinese Church," Mott charac-terized the Convention as "the most remarkable gathering of Oriental Christians ever held." More than 300 of the 350 delegates en route to Tokyo brought an international flavor. The Honorable Yun carried "two beautiful golden goblets" to Mott from the Emperor of Korea. Mott gave a tiffin at the Astor House for the representative of the Viceroy, who attended all sessions; he closed the Conference at a meeting of "great power" with an address on "Our Summons to a Great Advance," the theme he would recast at Tokyo, and later at Edinburgh.[75]

This visit was also packed with conversations with well-known missionaries—Roots, Taylor, Sheffield, Lockhart, Whitmore, Stuart, Meigs, Smith, Graves, Stephenson, Bryan, Parker, Anderson, Pott—and many more. When possible he quizzed them on recruitment for the ministry. There were numerous staff conferences to plan for five years ahead in China. Neither Mott's diary nor his letters mention recreation, the usual visits to places of interest, or relaxation. This was the "time of times" for China; not a moment was to be lost. If there was such, it was filled in "perennial conference" with Brockman and/or Lyon. As he reviewed his notes on the ship to Japan, Mott wrote his constituency:

The Association Movement has become indigenous in China. I am fully persuaded that were it to die out in America and Europe, it exists with such vitality and propagating power in China that it would ultimately spread from that country back to the West. [76]

In a packet of letters awaiting him at Shanghai there had been a disquieting note from Leila expressing fear that they had spent their last days together, to which he replied that he had never felt more certain "that our loving Father has many plans yet for us to work out together and it is my most joyous thought. Yes, I shall be with you for many a day and year."

> I only hope that I can get back to be with you at the time we welcome our new child. I find my mind and heart much stayed on this blessed event. Unless I am altogether off on the original reckoning [it] will come in May at the time corresponding to when we were in Bahia or Pernambuco. Still I recognize from an earlier experience when Irene came that we must take nothing for granted and that you should surely well in advance of such time surround yourself with every precaution and with those whom you most want and need. . . . I feel guilty not to be near you and yet we have seemed to be in the path of duty. Certainly God has been using me along the line on matters calling urgently for my help. . . . Everywhere secretarial problems must be dealt with in person. [77]

PART 7: The First International Conference in Asia: the WSCF at Tokyo, 1907

The most dramatic change in the student life of China and Japan that had taken place since Mott's visit five years earlier was the almost unimaginable migration of Chinese students to Tokyo following the abolition of the ancient examination system. Undoubtedly Mott and Brockman discussed this problem at length as their ship plowed the waters of the China Sea; they believed that "a disproportionate share of the leaders of the New China" would come from the ranks of those in Japan and abroad. Mott had expressed his concern for it when he outlined this trip to Mrs. McCormick months before. His mature plan was to build Christian hostels at strategic centers such as Waseda and Tokyo Imperial universities and to staff them with American and Chinese secretaries, of whom J. M. Clinton and C. T. Wang were the first. Mott made commitments of more than $50,000 at this time; ultimately this grew to $100,000. "Without doubt, the key to China is in Tokyo." Locations, staff, and administrative arrangements were major claims on his time in Japan. [78]

When Henry W. Luce, returning to China from a furlough, stopped in Japan for the Federation Conference, "the Island Empire was aglow with an expansive mood of friendliness—particularly for America, which had loudly applauded her sensational victory" over Russia. The Conference, meeting under the motto "Unum in Christo," made "an indelible impression" on Luce and his young son, the future publisher, though it was plain that much of the display expressed "political and nationalistic motives rather than religious convictions," as the Tokyo mayor's address of welcome would make abundantly clear. [79] Nevertheless, two Russians, Archbishop Nicolai of Tokyo and Baron Paul Nicolay of Finland and St. Petersburg, would address the Conference and fellowship together. Greetings rather than recriminations would be received from Buddhist and Shinto bodies. Because of heroic service to Japanese soldiers during the recent war—to which the Emperor had contributed 10,000 yen—the YMCA was enjoying great popularity; in 1907 there were fifty-eight student groups with 2,000 members and nine city Associations with as many members. The Tokyo "Y" was justly proud of its fine building in which the Conference met; surely no other delegate could have experienced a deeper satisfaction from the events that week than Jonathan T. Swift, the pioneer foreign secretary, who had given his patrimony toward it. There were now six International and fifteen Japanese secretaries. [80]

The Tokyo Conference of the World's Student Christian Federation was the first international gathering of any kind to be held in Japan or in Asia; its official languages were Japanese and English. It had been projected and approved at Söro in 1902 when Mott had taken seriously the invitation of the Japanese delegate. As early as July, 1903, he had outlined his ideas for it to Galen Fisher in detail, including a post-convention evangelistic campaign by teams of Japanese and foreign delegates which, he hoped, would "enable us to catch the ear of the whole country." This it did, receiving messages from President Roosevelt, King Edward VII, King Haakon of Norway, Prince Bernadotte, and Marquis Ito and the Japanese ministers of education and foreign affairs. Thus it "remained no small inner Christian affair" but became a national event where Christians and non-Christians spoke to one another. Morse wrote that it exceeded all expectations, being "the largest, the most representative, scholarly, and evangelistic" of the seven Federation meetings up to that time. Hans-Ruedi Weber, writing in 1964, regarded it as one of three major events in the early ecumenical history of Asia, a manifestation of things to come. Mott, even though he tried to avoid overstatement, assessed the Conference as "one of the most notable events in the history of Christianity in the extreme Orient." [81]

The first gathering of Federation representatives was the meeting of the General Committee, held April 1 and 2 in a private railway car en route between Tokyo and Nikko, and at the Nikko Hotel. These solid working sessions had been preceded by three days of concentration on mutual problems by the national secretaries of Japan, India, and China. Except for walks in the park at Nikko, "a marvel of wintry beauty . . . the mountains and trees and mausoleums covered with snow," wrote Morse of the "succession of temples in which Japanese art seems to have expended and exhausted itself in the expression of its highest, purest and most beautiful forms," this selected group of Mott's henchmen from around the world deliberated almost continuously, reaching all their decisions unanimously. Here were present not only the Japanese leaders Honda and Ibuka, but a roster of men Mott had recruited around the world: T. T. Wong and W. C. Chen from China, familiar names from Britain, Korea, the movements of Belgium, France, Holland, and Switzerland, Theophil Mann and Paul Humburg from Germany, Azariah and Carter from India, Fries and Eckhoff—founding fathers from Scandinavia, and Mott's most recent finds from South Africa, G. B. A. Gerdener and C. T. Wood. [82]

The Conference opened with a quiet session led by Honda and Fries. A symposium on student evangelization with Sherwood Eddy, J. S. Motoda, and E. T. Colton followed. That afternoon Viscount Tadasu Hayashi received the delegates at his official residence. The evening featured welcoming speeches by five Japanese officials: the Mayor of Tokyo, the Honorable Y. Ozaki, expressed his happiness in the knowledge that the Conference had been planned before the recent war, and compared Japanese ethics favorably with those of Christianity, confessing, perhaps a bit wistfully, that "we outsiders" did not know how to emulate the unity in heart and purpose of these delegates from twenty-five nations. Later, Count Okuma, in welcoming his guests at another garden party, remarked that if Christianity were to dominate the thought and life of the Orient, it would be indispensable "that it should be done by the might of the Japanese people." Fries countered that the members of the Federation knew only the power of the Divine Master and were united "to extend his gracious dominion over the hearts of students of all nations and races."

At still another garden party, this in the famous Kora-ku-en with cherry trees resplendent in artificial blossoms, Baron Shimpei Goto, president of the South Manchurian Railway, was so pleased with Mott's response to his address of welcome that he had it printed and distributed to a large circle. Mott referred to the Federation's uniting 2,000 universities in forty nations, binding together *in heart* as well as in understanding the future leaders of the nations—a fact comprehensible only in terms of Christ, the Great Magnet. He also referred to Japan's potential as mediator between the nations of East and West because she understood both "better than does any other land," a theme on which he would dwell for forty years. It was on occasions such as these that Mott was at his best. Impeccably dressed in the Japanese model of the European morning suit, he mingled among the groups from titled host and hostess to student delegate to turbaned Indian, with unfailing courtesy, ready to listen, fully respectful of the person of his auditor, and absorbed in that one's concerns. [83]

During the five and one-half days the 627 delegates, more than 500 of whom were Asians and 184 of them from outside Japan, from twenty-five countries, heard talks on the attitudes of scientists toward Christianity by Professor Alexander Macalister of Cambridge and Sir Alexander Simpson of Edinburgh, surveys of "the place of Christianity in the life of great nations and peoples" by speakers from Germany, Britain, Holland, the United States, India, Japan, and the American Negro W. A. Hunton on Africa, with others by M. Uemura, T. Miyagawa, Archbishop Nicolai, Baron Paul Nicolay, J. H. Adriani, Yun Tchi Ho, J. N. Farquhar, D. Ebina, Charles Fermaud, B. C. Sircar—a virtual roster of Asian ecumenical leaders, whose ranks would soon be joined by student delegates such as Soichi Saito and Michi Kawai. [84] The emotional high points of the Conference were reached in addresses by Professor E. I. Bosworth of Oberlin on "Jesus Christ, Our Lord," and Sherwood Eddy's "Appeal to the Heroic and Self-sacrificing." Mott gave the closing address as "The Call to a Great Advance": "The end of the exploration is the beginning of the enterprise. The end of the Conference is the beginning of the conquest. The end of the planning is the beginning of the doing."[85]

One of the hopes of the Chinese and Japanese planners of the Conference (most of the planning was done in the Orient) had been "to give the Occidental leaders definite knowledge of the status, needs, and successes of the Oriental movements," to afford them "immediate contact with some of the Associations," and to conduct evangelistic campaigns in Tokyo and other places in Japan. The Conference also stimulated the impetus toward work with women students. By the end of the sessions on Sunday evening, April 7—for Mott the "busiest week of my life"—the first two of these objects had been accomplished. The Conference subscribed 6,000 yen toward the Federation budget. As had numerous officers and delegates, Mott had evangelized during the week in

Tokyo, with some special services for Korean and Chinese students, climaxed by a mass meeting of more than 1200 Japanese students at the Central Tabernacle "crowded to its very limits." Fries and Mott spoke; their presiding officer was a student at the Imperial University who had been converted under Mott in Kumamoto five years before.

As Eddy appeared before these crowds of eager students, he became aware that the Chinese were far more responsive than the Japanese. Responding to Brockman's invitation to conduct an evangelistic tour in China, he found himself addressing as many as 4,000 students a day; in 1912–1913 he and Mott would meet with unprecedented response in their joint campaigns in China.

After a retreat and briefing by Mott fifteen to twenty deputation teams accompanied by interpreters fanned out from Tokyo to other student centers—Hurrey and Azariah to Yokohama, the British Garfield Williams with Davis and Tajima to Hirosaki, Karmarkar, Mann, Carter, and Honda to Okayama, Pourtales, Sautter, Farquhar, and Mott to Kyoto, Hunton and four others to Shidzuoka, Eddy to Kobe and Osaka, Frank Brockman to the Korean students in Tokyo, Colton to Moji and Kumamoto, Pierre de Benoit to Kanagawa, Paul Nicolay and Karl Fries to Fukushima. [86]

After Mott had boarded his train for Kyoto on Monday afternoon he was handed a cable message from Leila: "Undaunted." In the family code this meant the birth of a daughter and that all was well. He cabled back, "Rejoicing with you. God bless you and ours." A letter could not go sooner than his own ship in a week, but he at once wrote her four full pages of affection and apology for being "on this side of the world at this crisis with you." It had been the hardest experience of his life. He confessed that the cable had daunted him: "Coming so long before I expected it, it swept me off my feet with surprise and joy." Chiding Leila for not telling him the name she had "stored up for so long," he declared that he would cancel the Shanghai Centennial Conference and expect full details from her at Vancouver. He told Colton his news but thought it "just as well to let all these delegates get scattered and then to break it to our friends." Already he had been forced to subterfuge when asked how many children he had. After signing the letter to Leila he realized that in his excitement he had not thought to mention the Conference just concluded! On shipboard later he wrote to Mother that he could not stop at Postville: "The daughters in my family seem to have the knack of being ahead of me—for I was away also when Irene came." This baby was named Eleanor.

During the ten days before he could leave for home, Mott was almost as busy as during the Conference. In Kyoto, Osaka, Sendai, and Tokyo there were rounds of official calls, welcomes by municipal dignitaries, individual and group meetings with secretaries, recruiting talented Japanese for that profession, speaking on the theme of Japanese-American friendship, and almost every evening an evangelistic message to upwards of a thousand young men. In Kyoto he shared the platform with Pastor Eckhoff, who talked on the famous "Make Jesus King" cablegram that had been sent to Northfield from that very place in 1889, and that had later led to the formation of the Scandinavian Student Christian Movement. Mott assisted in the ground-breaking for a new building in Kyoto (John Wanamaker had thanked Mott for "the privilege of building the buildings for the YMCA in Korea, Pekin, and Kyoto") and somehow found time to slip away twice to see Japan's largest cherry tree in full bloom and illuminated far into the night. In Tokyo he had a rewarding conversation with Archbishop Nicolai, attended an Orthodox service, and gave a tiffin for the Japanese representatives about to sail to the States for the Jamestown Exposition.

The most dramatic of his evangelistic engagements was in Sendai. Part of the justification for that long trip was the opportunity for extended conversation with Fisher. They were met at the station by "a large and influential deputation including the Mayor, the Lieutenant Governor, a Member of the House of Peers, a Judge, the Chiefs or Heads of the different wards of the city, the principals of at least twenty schools, a number of Japanese pastors, several missionaries, prominent business men, two leading Buddhist priests and delegations of students." Although there were only two hours allocated for the meeting, welcoming speeches took up half the time:

> The Japanese anthem was sung. The Mayor addressed me with a flattering welcome to which I responded. Then the Lieutenant Governor welcomed me on behalf of the Governor and I made another response. The Mayor led the audience in three banzais for America and the other Treaty Powers. I then led them in three banzais for the Emperor and Japan. Following this I gave a Gospel address as it was my only opportunity. [87]

He and Fisher were back in Tokyo at 8:00 A.M. Two days later Mott sailed for Vancouver on the *Empress of China,* arriving there April 28 after a very comfortable voyage of 4,300 knots. Those eleven days not only provided rest and recreation but time for a couple of detective yarns, reflection on the meaning of the tour, and the writing of his summaries.

In looking back on the Conference, Mott emphasized its Eastern character: "Never has there been such an assembly of Oriental Christians. We had present in our sessions from day to day the very flower of the Asiatic church." The devotional and evangelistic notes had been clear and compelling, the emphasis on civic, social, and religious responsibilities of Christian students were timely and effective, the spirit of tolerance and brotherhood indicated by the reception accorded Nicolai's address. But,

> above all, the influence of this Conference will be enormous in uniting more closely than any other event the East and the West. Oriental and Occidental delegates have come forth from its sessions and its fellowship with a larger understanding of each other, with a truer appreciation of each other's points of view, with a more sincere intellectual respect and a deepening love for each other.[88]

The evangelism had been "genuinely spiritual and thorough," probably most effective as it prepared the way for "the regular Christian propaganda." In Japan, "the present is pre-eminently the time to reap." Japanese students are "the most open-minded in the world," and when the relation of Japan to Asia is considered, the words of a missionary may not be an exaggeration: The Conference and the evangelistic campaign "constitute the heaviest single blow ever struck by united Christianity in the non-Christian world." Altogether, this had been "the most significant and potential event" in his nearly twenty years' work among students. For once, wrote Weber long afterward, Mott had not overstated the case.

That winter, Yoitsu Honda, now the first bishop of a united Methodist Church of Japan, wrote in the first issue of the new Federation magazine, *The Student World,* that the effects of the Conference had been great in the provincial centers as well as in Tokyo itself. Many Japanese had been astonished by the concern for evangelism by the laymen as well as the professional Christian workers who had attended the Conference. It had "broken up the hard crust of prejudice," even in the Imperial normal colleges. City halls that had never been rented for Christian gatherings were now available. The Japanese Christian forces had been greatly encouraged and the example of cooperation was a "mighty Christian apologetic." The tendency toward "a narrow nationalism within the Japanese Church" had been redirected by this "welding of the ties of fellowship with the Christians of all lands." Christian workers and the Christian message were now finding "an unprecedented welcome everywhere." And, the Conference brought home to

Japanese Christians "a sense of their prestige in the Far East somewhat corresponding to the political prestige the nation enjoys"—not only a reason for elation but a cause for self-examination. [89]

Mott returned from this tour fully convinced that, in the words of John Morley, "in the waters of the Pacific there lies for America a risk and a possibility."

> Unquestionably the risk is great and grave if the best Christian sentiment of America does not actively, vigilantly, and generously carry forward the good work so well begun during these recent years. On the other hand, if we do press our advantage, the possibility of further advance is simply limitless.

In the Philippines the resident missionaries had insisted that the staff should be doubled and new programs added. Manila could become a model YMCA for the East:

> More than one-half the peoples of the earth live in countries which are within easy reach of the Philippine Islands. Their position with reference to the great Oriental world is such as to make Manila increasingly a great center for commercial activity and for influence on all lines. Here under the American flag with all that that means in the way of protection, freedom, and sympathetic backing, the conditions are favorable for developing agencies, methods, and spirit which will profoundly affect the character of work among all classes of young men throughout the Far East. [90]

When he addressed the SVM Conference at Liverpool in January, 1909, Mott focused all of his experiences in the Orient on "the urgency and crisis" there:

> There should be a masterly and united policy on the part of the missionary leaders of Europe and North America . . . [who] should come together, not simply to congratulate and criticize one another, or to exhort one another, or to educate one another, but to face these great crises, to study how they are to be met, and how to better coordinate our forces and to introduce practical means of cooperation and federation. . . . We should face the whole field, and not simply take it up in parts. We should face our whole generation, and not merely grapple with emergencies. We should face the whole range of missionary purpose. We should pay due regard to the principles of strategy with reference to places, to classes, to times, to methods. [91]

Not long afterward, Mott made perhaps his most lucid statement of the purposes of YMCA foreign work, in the course of an address to a conference of British secretaries:

> We have gone out to these foreign Associations to make ourselves, not indispensable, but dispensable. Our great idea in going out to these countries is to leave them as soon as possible; to plant the Association idea in the hearts and minds of the native young men, in order that they may propagate the Movement themselves, and let us go home as soon as may be. . . . This great work . . . is primarily a Chinese, a Japanese, an Indian, a native enterprise.[92]

Although the "Panic of 1907" seriously inhibited domestic fund-raising, Mott's solicitation for the large sums required to continue the expansion of the foreign work and equip its outposts with modern buildings barely hesitated, due not only to his skill but to the fact that his wealthy clientele was not seriously affected by such economic fluctuations. It was, in fact, exactly the opposite of that diminution of Protestant returns that scholars have recently found to have had their beginnings soon after the turn of the century. Ethan T. Colton, Mott's lieutenant at home base, with gargantuan labors requiring "rare faith, patience, and persistence," carried the foreign appeal to the conscience of individual Associations until it became an accepted part of the total program and budget. The historian of the foreign work referred to this period as the "halcyon years of the budget."[93]

Stimulated by the tours described in this chapter, Mott had put together by 1908 a list of building needs totaling more than a million dollars. He then asked John D. Rockefeller, Jr., to give half that sum. Rockefeller replied by sending Ernest D. Burton of the University of Chicago to survey the needs on the spot in "the Turkish Empire, India, China, and Japan." His findings were positive to the point of enthusiasm, and Rockefeller accepted Mott's challenge. Mott then planned a conference at a hotel in Washington, but when he asked President Taft to address it the President proposed that the gathering come to the White House. On October 20, 1910, Mott chaired a meeting of some 200 persons in the East Room. The President spoke, and Mott announced the Rockefeller gift. Surrounded by the elite of his foreign staff, which now numbered 132, assembled from Japan, the Philippines, Latin America, India, and China, together with several distinguished foreigners, and with guarantees in his pocket from John Wanamaker, George M. Perkins, James Stokes, Mrs. McCormick, and others, Mott audaciously increased the goal to a million and a half dollars for almost fifty buildings. More than half of it was subscribed that day; in the next few months he collected over two million dollars.[94]

PART 8: **The Students of Europe, 1908-1909**

Mott spent nine months in Europe between November, 1908, and July, 1909. There were two short trips before that, and on the eve of the 1908-1909 tour he published another book.

On the first of these crossings, the lively memory of his children on Christmas morning led him to his first use of ship-to-shore wireless to send them a greeting the next day. The goal of this trip was the British SVM Quadrennial at Liverpool in early January, 1909; on shipboard he polished four of the addresses to be given there. A feature of the conference, wrote a reporter, was Mott's speech on the Far East. The great Asiatic renaissance had begun:

> We saw out there in the Far East 'Japan leading the Orient, but whither?' We realized with him the awful danger of the Eastern awakening if it was not met with Christ, not gradually but immediately. The next ten or fifteen years is the most critical in the world's history.[95]

The meeting was to Europe "what Nashville was to America," Mott reported to Chairman Cleveland H. Dodge: there were 2,000 delegates from "all parts of the Continent" as well as from the British universities. The audience faced a banner carrying the watchword, while behind it was the WSCF motto, *Ut Omnes Unum Sint.* This was the last time the watchword was formally presented from the platform of the British SVMU, although Tatlow's oration on it was memorable. Mott was able not only to confer with delegates from numerous national movements but to lay plans for the next WSCF conference, to be held at Oxford in 1909.

In London, where his arrival was noted by the *Times* as it would be henceforth, he spoke to several missionary groups and the English National Council of the YMCA, attempting to raise their sights from five-and ten-pound solicitations to "gifts from men who would prefer to give £200 or £400 when they come to realize the tremendous importance of this foreign work." In Scotland he pressed the work in India and the Far East upon the National Council of the YMCA's, and while there "launched the Laymen's Missionary Movement at a large gathering of leading Christian laymen." In Glasgow he was the guest of Lord Overtoun who gave him £2,500, and in Edinburgh of Sir Alexander Simpson; these men he thought "the very salt of Scotland." On the return voyage he again made use of the ship-to-shore wireless for family greetings and to explain a twenty-four hour delay as "blizzard-bound."

Most of the time on the return trip and work at home "from eight

A.M. to ten P.M." for two weeks were devoted to the final preparation of the long-gestating series of lectures on recruitment of high-caliber candidates for the ministry. He gave them at Toronto in mid-February, 1908, under the auspices of five theological colleges. In March they were repeated at Berkeley for the seminaries of the Pacific Coast. Stewart, who transcribed them, described the process:

> With his facts marshalled under his outline, he started from New York on a transcontinental express for the Pacific Coast.... Dr. Fletcher S. Brockman went along as companion and critic. In a private compartment of the Pullman car the paragraphs were ground out from his orderly mind. Brockman performed ably the role of challenger of certain statements or adviser on various points, but there was little halting and no backward motion until, on the eve of our arrival at our destination, the first draft was complete in less than four days' time. On the homeward journey toward New York, the corrective of his audiences' response was applied, and the polishing process undertaken.[96]

The lectures were given again at Vanderbilt University, where "more ministers, editors and church officials were present than at either Toronto or Berkeley." Everywhere he was urged to publish them.

Trips such as that to San Francisco were never single-purpose sallies, which probably helps to explain how Mott could endure them. YMCA, college, evangelistic, and social visits were usually included. During a Midwestern trip he visited Clara and Mrs. McCormick in Chicago while a blizzard was raging; he was "seized with the front end of a cold," but in Postville, Mother's "heavy drafts of flaxseed tea," followed by "the beautiful Minnesota weather" at Northfield and recalling Henry Ward Beecher's jibe that "two long sermons [Mott gave four] would break up any cold—did the business." While in Postville he had arranged for a new coal-burning stove to replace a wood range and for central heat for the big house on West Williams Street. In San Francisco there was a luncheon and long discussion with Chinese students at the Fairmont, said to be "the finest hotel in the world." A day at Stanford, the Santa Clara Valley's fruit trees in full bloom, and the orange groves at Santa Barbara brought memories of the honeymoon tour of 1892 and yearnings for Leila. That spring there was a special evangelistic campaign at Princeton. June required Mott's presence at Lake Geneva, Montreat, Silver Bay, and Northfield.

This not unusual round was interrupted in July and August, 1908, by a brief trip to Europe for two summer conferences in Great Britain and Holland and several committee meetings to prepare for conferences in

1909 and 1910. Morse obtained funds for Mott and his colleague C. J. Hicks to enjoy an unusual vacation tour of Normandy and Brittany by private chauffeured motor car during a break. Mott was reminded of his French-Canadian neighbors at Lac des Iles and declared to his mother that he would always understand French history, literature, and life better. But it was a sin, he confessed to Leila, not to have our wives with us. Even so, he had to rest up at Interlaken before the next committee met.

The fall of 1908 was largely occupied with preparation for eight months in Europe and the publication of *The Future Leadership of the Church*. The book was based on the hundreds of interviews he had held around the world in the past six years, if not since 1888; in addition, a questionnaire had been sent to selected Southern ministers, YMCA and YWCA personnel, seventy-five WSCF leaders in all countries, the bishops of the Methodist Church, a select list of professors who had heard the lectures, a dozen friends in Australasia and in South Africa. As he had done with each previous book, Mott submitted the typescript to a large number of friends, clergymen, denominational executives, and others, but significantly this time to President Woodrow Wilson of Princeton, Mrs. McCormick, and President Theodore Roosevelt, with the desired results utilized to the fullest extent by an effective publicity agency.

Wilson gave it his "thorough approval," with some reservation on the minister's involvement in "all sorts of social activities" that might divert attention from "the effectual preaching of the Word."[97] Roosevelt wrote for a YMCA magazine in what the Boston *Evening Transcript* called the President's "most distinctively homiletical vein":

> Indeed this question of recruiting the ranks of the Christian ministry is one of world-wide interest and concern. But I do not speak only of ministers. I speak of all who take part in a broad and catholic spirit in work for the essentials of Christianity, of all who without regard to differences of sect will join with one another, and indeed with all good men in whatever way they worship their Creator, to bring nearer the reign of righteousness and of brotherly kindness on this earth. There must be union and co-operation among all good men who wish to see the spirit of true Christianity given practical expression in accordance with the biblical precept that 'by their fruits shall you know them.' There are opportunities of note in the world for all such men, be they clergymen or laymen. . . . The fight for righteousness, the effort to realize the kingdom of God in this world, is fraught with infinite hardship and risk, with the certainty of wearisome labor and discouragement, with danger to all who are feeble and faint-hearted. It is because of this very fact that the best, the most resolute, and the most daring spirits, should listen to the summons which calls them to the life of effort and conflict. We ask that men of heroic temper undertake the great

adventure. . . . So now the call of duty to undertake this great spiritual adventure, this work for the betterment of mankind, should ring in the ears of young men who are high of heart and gallant of soul, as a challenge to turn to the hard life of labor and risk, which is so infinitely well worth living.[98]

More than sixty magazines and papers, most of them secular, reviewed the book, all but one favorably. The Rochester *Democrat and Chronicle* commented on the President's "strong hold on the youth of the country" and declared that in endorsing Mott's book Roosevelt had "exercised his great influence for the furtherance of a cause than which there is none worthier or more important in all the range of human activities now commanding the interest of our people." The *Springfield Republican* thought that Mott's argument was presented so ably that it needed "no letters of recommendation." The only critical review appeared in *The Association Seminar*, the YMCA professional magazine, whose reviewer thought Mott had ignored the most fundamental questions young men would ask when confronted with the call to the ministry: if churches are to be consolidated and united, as he advocates, we would need fewer men, not more; ordained men are not "the only real leaders in promoting the work begun by Jesus"; many now active in "YMCA work, social settlement work, welfare work and many other forms of directly religious activity would in the last generation have studied theology and sought ordination"; Mott might have emphasized more than he did the "unnecessary obstacles which the churches keep in the way of able and earnest men who consider entering the ministry"—a point made by one or two other reviewers. [99] A few compared the book favorably to Bishop Brent's *Leadership*, published at almost the same time, but no reviewer suggested the possibility that a great many of the thousands of eager student volunteers who had been recruited for foreign missions might have entered the ministry.

Mott made very little direct use of the statistical material accumulated over twenty years, preferring to emphasize "the character or quality" of ministerial candidates rather than numerical or quantitative aspects of the problem. The need was not for numbers but for men of ability. After laying down requirements not unlike those he had often prescribed for the physical, mental, and spiritual qualifications for Association secretaries, he declared that ministers should "have a message and be conscious of a mission," able to give effective expression to their passion for Christ and for men. They should be men of intense moral enthusiasm, able to organize, lead, and inspire others to work, but above all "great in character." Citing Wilson's phrase, he described the ministry as "the only profession which consists in being something."[100]

Under a second heading, "The Urgency," Mott expanded at some length on the need of the Church for "men able to deal wisely with social questions" and cited James H. F. Peile's Bampton Lectures for 1907.[101] If the Church holds back in the present social crisis "it will not command the following of many keen minds and unselfish spirits." Quoting Walter Rauschenbusch and Reginald J. Campbell, he declared that the Church must have men of insight and sagacity capable of studying and understanding social conditions—competent to deal with the causes of misery and wrong as well as with the misery and wrong themselves: the call is to stop the battle, not merely to save the wounded. This is an unprecedented international opportunity and crisis, and the responsibility for it rests on the Christians of Great Britain, Canada, and the United States. "We must have great leadership for great movements." "Obstacles" to entering the ministry were secularism, outmoded theological seminary curricula, "inadequate financial provision," and the actual lack of recruitment—the last, in Mott's judgment, the "principal cause." It was the final chapter with its concluding phrase from J. R. Illingworth that caught the eye of President Roosevelt and naturally of many reviewers: "The pleasures of each generation evaporate in air; it is their pains that increase the spiritual momentum of the world."[102]

The book was issued by the North American YMCA's Student Department. A British edition came out early in 1909; the problem there was far greater and of longer standing. To supplement the book's appeal, a series of pamphlets was issued, each by a recognized denominational leader—George A. Gordon, Bishop William F. McDowell, W. W. Moore, Dean E. I. Bosworth, Phillips Brooks, Charles E. Jefferson, and Woodrow Wilson. These were later collected and published as *The Claims and Opportunities of the Christian Ministry*, to which Mott wrote a foreword.[103]

After his trip to the Liverpool Quadrennial in 1908, Mott had told Chairman Dodge that because the last several years had kept him "at the extremities of the world," he "ought to give several months to Europe" in 1909. The fulfillment of numerous pledges to do so began in November, 1908. Arrangements were complex: he would visit more than a dozen countries; Leila and the younger children would stay in Switzerland, while John L., now sixteen, was at the Hill School in Pennsylvania. Provision for his mother's and sisters' comfort and well-being was also necessary. "Helpful letters to all our diplomatic representatives in

Europe" were obtained from Secretary of State Root, and on October 9, together with Silas McBee, Mott lunched and visited for two hours with President and Mrs. Roosevelt on the balcony of the White House "looking toward the Washington Monument." The President provided him with a special letter to the students of Russia.[104]

Galen Fisher once wrote that Mott was happiest when in the midst of an evangelistic campaign. His first appointments abroad that fall were meetings at Oxford, London, Glasgow, and Cambridge that must have fulfilled his every prayer. Preparations at each place had gone on for months, Tatlow having first approached Mott as early as the spring of 1907. These campaigns may well have been his greatest in the Western world. They abundantly demonstrated J. H. Oldham's mature judgment that "in the range and long continuance of his influence no one in my lifetime could compare with Mott as a Christian evangelist among students."[105]

Well before Mott came to Oxford the *Isis* "Idolator" had made his "prostration before a real prophet." Mott, he wrote, "is in the true sense a great statesman. . . . he has a complete grasp of the great problems now confronting man." All religious elements cooperated: "Broad churchmen, low churchmen, high-churchmen even of Pusey House, as well as all classes of nonconformists, united, not only as individuals, but also through their student organizations," so that there was a real sense of anticipation. *Isis* continued:

> Vigour is the most prominent element in his composition. He is wholly without the winsome graces of the more poetic saints: and still more emphatically is he free from the sentimental excitement of the revivalist. His diction is the sternest prose; his view of life is sober and matter of fact; his handling of his subject is downright and direct. But as one listens, one begins to realise that, behind the statesmanship and vigour which are the first qualities to strike the hearer's mind, there is a life of quiet, simple, and unostentatious, but also quite absolute, devotion to the cause with which he has identified his whole being, and that this is the source of his power.[106]

The next week *Isis* reported that "many hundreds of us have heard that commanding speaker and statesman of the Church, Mr. Mott. There is something impressive about a thousand undergraduates in the Schools hearing what they were hearing, and being charged with the uplift of their generation. The striking daring of a life laid out so that the World Religion may become the Religion of the World, and the wonderful response that the world is making, were factors which lent their quota to the power of this remarkable series of meetings."[107] The *Oxford Magazine* commented on "the steady and earnest work" that had characterized the preparation for the meetings:

> The existence of this solid background of organized and disciplined purpose, as well as the severe restraint and practical common sense of Mr. Mott's addresses, should be a guarantee against the reaction which so often follows missions of the emotional type, and should also ensure that the enthusiasm he has evoked will not be allowed to run to waste, but result in a real extension and deepening of the religious life of Oxford. The afternoon lectures to graduates, especially the striking concluding lecture, left a vivid impression of great organizing genius, and that commanding grasp of "strategic points" which led him to see in the solidarity of the student world the possibility of putting a religious girdle round the earth, based on the principle of unity in diversity.
>
> Mr. Mott's unrivalled width of experience, his deep sincerity and earnestness, his vigorous terseness of speech and sound sense, cannot fail to make a great impression both on individuals and on the life of the University as a whole.[108]

Mott believed that some of the best work was accomplished in the smaller meetings:

> This was true of a notable intercession meeting of the keenest men, of a meeting of over sixty foreign missionary candidates together with over 100 other students seriously considering becoming missionaries; of a meeting with representatives of Oxford and Cambridge universities to discuss plans for a university which they are thinking of establishing jointly in China; of a meeting with some seventy American Rhodes Scholars; of a breakfast with Mohammedan students; of two conferences with leaders of the student religious societies; of a meeting with students of the women's colleges in Oxford; and last but not least of a luncheon with members of the Vincent Club, which includes the leading "Blues," or top-notch athletes and social men. . . . The meeting which time will show was by far the most productive was the closed gathering I held on the last night, limited to 230 men selected from the twenty-one colleges, with reference to their powers of leadership. Here I discussed in frankest manner the conservation of the results of my mission and the lines along which the religious life and work of the university should develop in the future.[109]

A correspondent of the *Daily Telegraph* credited the "remarkable success" of Mott's five days in Oxford to "his tact and judgment, no less than his moral earnestness" that had "made an impression alike upon seniors and juniors, which is not likely to be effaced." The *Evening Standard* adjudged that the remarkable results at Oxford presaged "a religious awakening only comparable with that which was originated by the late Henry

Drummond." Temple Gairdner declared that to live through a Mott mission was "a strenuous experience." No criticism has survived.[110]

The London campaign opened with a mass meeting in the Royal Albert Hall crowded with 10,000 persons—of whom a disappointing minority were students—to which Mott was introduced by the Bishop of London. His address, "Modern World Movements: God's challenge to the Church," dealt with nationalism, especially in Turkey and in China, "the impinging of the nations and races upon each other"—the shrinkage of the world which "accentuates the perils resulting from contact and mingling":

> It must be admitted that the beginning of the twentieth century seems to be marked by the recrudescence of international prejudices and hatred. Another peril is demoralization. . . . The less highly organized and the less civilized races are especially prone to fall under this fatal spell.

> Christianity must interpret the East to the West and the West to the East. This indispensable service cannot be accomplished by diplomacy, or by military prowess, or by commercial expansion, or as a result of the proclamation of social codes, or by the spread of higher education as such. No attitude of patronizing exclusiveness or superiority will avail. Only the spirit of Jesus Christ, illustrated in the character and practice and relationships of men, will suffice.

> The greatest single influence which can be exerted in the direction of counteracting the perils resulting from the closer mingling of the races, is the extension of the missionary propaganda. The missionary is the great mediator between the East and the West. . . . I cannot but think of them as Christian ambassadors, devoting all of their hours to errands which are tantamount in their significance to effective efforts to bind together the East and West with Christian bonds. . . . Without doubt they constitute the greatest force for the promotion of friendship, good-will, and brotherhood between races. Moreover, through their influence more than through any other cause, the East and West are coming to see that they are necessary to each other. They are demonstrating that the essential unity of the human race is discovered and realized only in and through Jesus Christ. . . . We are just beginning to learn that we have a Christ so large that He requires all the nations and all the races through which to reveal adequately His excellencies, communicate His power, and make possible the carrying out of His program.

Another great movement was the World's Student Christian Federation, which included "the future leadership of the Church":

> It is the great recruiting agency for the Christian ministry and for the foreign missionary forces. Moreover, it is to furnish the leading Christian laymen of our generation. It has, as one of its dominant ideals and objects,

the making of Jesus Christ known to the whole world in our day. To accomplish the realization of this ideal the native Christian students of Asia, Africa, and Latin America are uniting with the Christian students of Europe, North America, and Australasia. There has been nothing like this in the annals of Christianity.

"God is unmistakably summoning us to a larger unity." Mott startled his hearers as he worked into his peroration with:

After studying the world field, let me say that I firmly believe a carrying out of a comprehensive plan of cooperation in the missionary work of the various Christian communions would be the equivalent of doubling the missionary forces.[111]

We need no new organizations and movements, but we do need "a fresh and larger bestowal of superhuman power for the accomplishment of our stupendous task of enthroning Christ among all peoples and in all human relationships." This was one of Mott's most widely circulated addresses. The *Standard* found it "intensely interesting and inspiringly optimistic" in spite of his making "no pretensions to eloquence"—not being "an orator in the ordinary sense." It was printed in pamphlet form and circulated throughout the world student movement; it was not only a distillation of his reflections upon his world journeys but a challenge to the forthcoming Edinburgh World Missionary Conference.

The London campaign continued with four afternoon meetings in the lower auditorium of the new St. James Hall. Their effectiveness could be judged by the increasing stream of young men who came for personal interviews until Mott was unable to cope with the numbers. In addition, he spoke to students from eight theological colleges, and to some seventy Chinese students invited by Lord Kinnaird to his home. Possibly the largest result of this "splendid team play of the leaders" was to demonstrate "the feasibility of a successful work of evangelism in the midst of the baffling difficulties of metropolitan student fields."[112]

Mott reported briefly that his visit at Glasgow "was like that in London in point of difficulty," yet the methods and results were similar. "The hearty cooperation of men like Principal Macalister, Professor George Adam Smith, Dr. John Kelman, and Professor James Denney, as well as that of the student leaders, accounts for the success achieved." Sixty years later one of his hearers remembered the profound impression Mott's vivid description of conditions in India had made upon him.[113]

Cambridge had been unable to unite all church groups behind the mission and it was unfortunately scheduled during examinations, but due to "a few scores" who "worked like Trojans" they had "the most largely attended series of religious meetings ever held among undergraduates of Cambridge" and Mott was again unable to handle the numbers seeking interviews. Two members of Moody's famous "Cambridge Seven" were back from China and assisted in the follow-up. Mott, wrote a reporter, urged his hearers "to live as citizens of the world, and not merely as belonging to one country only." This was a call to "the strongest men of the University to go out and meet the need" in the Far East. As at Oxford, he spoke to a dozen smaller groups.[114]

After the Cambridge campaign, Leila took the children to Switzerland, where she set up headquarters at Chernix, near Montreux. John joined them for a happy Christmas, much needed rest, and preparation for the next round. Leila wrote to Clara:

> It's such a comfort to have John on the same side of the ocean. You would enjoy seeing him with the children. He's more and more a family man—I'm glad to say—for I do not think he ever would have had the gentler, softer side of him developed except by children of his own.

Beginning with what proved to be the largest Dutch midwinter conference, in Utrecht January 19 and 20, at which he left "an inspiration to a more holy and more consecrated life," Mott moved into a long-promised visit to Scandinavia. There was "a marked difference" from his reception in 1899; again accompanied by Karl Fries, who not only interpreted but was himself "a special source of strength," Mott received the warmest welcomes and farewells from singing groups at the railroad stations. His meetings were held in the aula of each university, in itself a sign of acceptance.[115]

At Christiania (Oslo) King Haakon VIII heard Mott's address on the crises in the Far and Near East and asked him to an audience. Upon the occasion of one of Mott's addresses in Christiania, his secretary, William R. Stewart, who had heard the self-same address a dozen times, was forced to rethink his own life plans afresh. Two years later he went to China as the first YMCA boys' work secretary to that country.[116]

In Stockholm Mott's general meetings attracted 3,000 persons; he visited the Bernadottes and found opportunity to call on Sven Hedin, "an interesting man and a genuine Christian," just back from Tibet. At Uppsala the Archbishop attended several times, and Mott was the guest of his old friend of Northfield 1890, now Professor Nathan Söderblom. The two found much of mutual concern, Mott urging Söderblom to write a life of Luther. A young man named Knut B. Westman, who became a professor at Uppsala, attributed the beginning of his interest in ecumenism to Mott's visit, noting that Mott had "in a splendid way added fuel to the flames" of a student revival that winter, when there were fresh outbursts of interest in Bible study, morning devotions, and personal evangelism, not only in Sweden but in Denmark.[117]

In Copenhagen Mott faced the largest student audience he had ever addressed in the Occident—1,400 men, which stimulated the reorganization of the Danish Student Christian Movement; gatherings of 2,000 and 3,000 heard him in churches and other halls. With Miss Rouse to interpret in Finland, students crowded the Helsingfors University aula and again Mott spoke to general audiences of 2,000; new Bible circles resulted everywhere. Fries attributed these great successes to "economic, moral, and social conditions in the different countries," but also to prayer.[118]

PART 9: **Russia, 1909**

Neither the Federation nor the parent YMCA had relaxed concern for Russia during the decade since Mott's visit of 1899. With the financial and personal backing of James Stokes the *Mayak* had grown steadily in acceptance and membership, and had served to a limited extent as a rallying point for such penetration of the student world as was possible under the repressive policies of the government. It was rather the continuous, careful, personal activity of Baron Paul Nicolay, beginning with German students in St. Petersburg, who gradually assembled tiny groups of Russian students. In 1903 Miss Rouse had met with ten of the women friends of the male members of a Student Christian Union. Under the strictest police surveillance a thousand students had come to a meeting with her in 1907, but only she and Nicolay were permitted to speak, so fearful were the police of student radicalism, a not unlikely apprehension because many students were revolutionaries, feared alike by government and populace. Robert Wilder had visited Russia in 1904. In addition, a potential Movement had to contend with distrust and suspicion on the part of the Church, the softening of which was one of Mott's principal objectives in 1909.[119]

Accompanied by Leila, Miss Rouse, Nicolay, and Stewart, and with the assistance of Franklin Gaylord and Erich L. Moraller of the *Mayak*, Mott's 1909 visit to Russia proved to be "one of the most wonderful experiences that have ever come to me in all these twenty and more years work among students in different nations." It even eclipsed the opportunity presented by the Chinese students in Tokyo. Not only were the Russian students without religion, but they despised Orthodox Christianity because they regarded the Russian Church as "the instrument of oppression and cause of the crying social crimes" with which they were familiar. Yet Mott found them possessed of "an essentially religious nature" and longing "for what only vital Christianity can give."

Contrary to his policy in 1899, Mott sought out Orthodox leaders to assure them that he had no intention of proselytizing. Gaylord took him to meet the Minister of Public Education, the Over-Procurator of the Holy Synod, S. M. Lukianov, and the Former Over-Procurator, Prince A. D. Obolensky. He also called upon Senator I. V. Meschaninov, president of the *Mayak* board, Father John Slobotskoi, and Professor S. F. Platonov, the historian. He spoke to a small private meeting of some members of the Duma. He was advised to concentrate on the student centers of St. Petersburg and Moscow, with a shorter time at Dorpat (Tartu); this worked out as eleven days in the capital, six in Moscow, and four in Dorpat.[120]

Mott was astonished that he attracted audiences upward of 500 each night. Conditions were apparently "providentially" just right, student disappointment over the failure of the 1905 revolution having dissipated sufficiently to drive many to religious introspection. People had said that students would never come "to hear the truth of God," he wrote later, but "over four hundred came to a meeting after two o'clock in the morning to show their interest and to find Jesus Christ as divine Lord and Savior." Stewart described what happened in Moscow:

> The set-up for the meetings in Moscow had to be left in the hands of an inexperienced girl student of twenty years, the only trusted person available. When she started her plans, her fellow students laughed at her, but she was so in earnest and so persistent that her enthusiasm caught on, and before the day of the meetings, she had every seat sold out in the large auditorium she had hired for the assembly. When I went to the first meeting, a few minutes late, I was not allowed in, for all the seats were occupied and the police, in order to keep matters under control, would not allow anyone to stand. Dr. Mott was a bit puzzled by the plan of selling tickets of admittance. He said, "The gospel message is free. I shall be responsible for the full expenses. Refund the money to the students." But the Russian workers who had come down with him from St. Petersburg persuaded him to let the matter stand. It is the only occasion, so far as I know, where there was an entrance fee charged to one of his evangelistic meetings.[121]

The young woman who performed this miracle five times, Alexandra Dobroliubov, subsequently worked for the Federation for a time among women students, aiding the heroic efforts of Rouse and Nicolay.[122]

In contrast to the laughter that greeted the name of Christ when Miss Rouse was in Russia only two years earlier, Mott found students uniformly quiet and entirely willing "literally to hang upon one's words." They thronged and pressed upon him, between speeches, on the streets, during his inspection of the *Mayak*, at his lodgings. Unable to grant individual interviews, he received groups; their questions revealed "soul struggles" and personal doubts rather than politics, temptations, or habits:

> With pathetic and tragic intensity, they are wrestling with the problem of trying to reconcile the presence of evil and suffering with the goodness of God, with the divorce they see between religion and morals, with the harmonizing of science and Christianity, and with the social crimes of the Church. . . . Most of them are living in the zone of pessimism and despair. I met, not one, but several students who were seriously contemplating suicide. . . . Strange as it may seem, I had to go to Russia in order to understand most fully and vividly the mission of Jesus Christ.[123]

Mott's files contain several touching letters from students at Dorpat, St. Petersburg, or his "attentive Moscow hearers" greeting him at Easter and expressing their "deep gratitude" for his days among them. Numerous individuals wrote testimonials and even some radicals expressed appreciation by admitting that Mott was a "long-headed fellow."[124]

When Mott stepped to the platform at the annual meeting of the *Mayak*, he was greeted with lengthy and enthusiastic applause as the "special delegate" of James Stokes, the American supporter of the *Mayak*. President Roosevelt's letter was received "with intense enthusiasm." There is no nation in the world, the President said,

> which, more than Russia, holds in its hands the fate of the coming years, and for this reason, not only should every young Russian feel a peculiar sense of responsibility, but all outsiders should likewise feel a special interest in the moral and ethical development of the mighty people which occupies so great and commanding a position alike in Europe and Asia.
>
> To the young men of Russia, as to the young men of America, I would especially urge the need of combining a high ideal with practical efficiency in carrying it out. Scorn the base and sordid materialists who would teach that power in any form, whether of money or political rule, justifies iniquity or is to be sought for at the expense of justice and fair dealing.
>
> The revolutionary and the reactionary play into one another's hands, for

each in turn, by his foolish and blind violence, by the fury of his excesses, makes good men turn in loathing from the side he champions.

I ask the young men of Russia to remember the duty that a great state owes in its international relations. Weakness is to be despised in the nation as in the individual. . . . Our aim in international affairs should be as our aim in private affairs. An upright man will not wrong his neighbor; and so all upright men should strive to see that the nation to which they belong refuses to wrong any neighbor, does justice to all within its gates as well as to the world outside, and makes the precepts of the golden rule its guide, exactly as it should be the guide of individuals in private life. The state must be practical and efficient; but the state should ever show its fealty to lofty ideals.[125]

The reading of the Roosevelt letter was followed by a "powerful" address on "The World Movement Among Young Men" by Mott, which was said to have "moved the audience with deep thought," bringing the realization that those present shared in that great "movement which works for righteousness in the life of the nation as well as of the world."

Although the halls where Mott spoke were consistently crowded to their "uttermost capacity," the time was not ripe for setting up a student organization in Russia. He favored the fostering of Bible circles under the continued tutelage of Nicolay, working through small groups in each student center; yet by 1913 there would be a Russian Movement worthy of inclusion in WSCF fellowship for a brief interlude before war and revolution destroyed it.

George M. Day, whom Mott recruited for service in Russia on his way home through Germany, later summarized this visit:

What was the secret of this wonderful response to Mr. Mott's message? Why was it that one of the original leaders of the Moscow circle, Miss [Dobroliubov], with apostolic faith engaged for five nights the largest hall in the city for the Mott meetings? Weary of the fruitless effort in politics, sick in mind and spirit, many even driven to suicide, these students with eagerness and gratitude welcomed Mr. Mott and his message. Of course those warmhearted, impulsive, long-suffering Russians responded to the fresh and virile interpretation of religion, to the manly summons to clean up the personal life, to the unveiling of the person of Christ as the friend and master of students. They could not help it. Never had they heard it in this wise before. Both the message and the man gripped them, found them. It was just what they needed and were hungering for.[126]

Yet the Holy Synod decreed that Mott should never be allowed to return to Russia.[127]

Following the visit to Russia, the Motts moved their base of operations from Chernix to Chexbres, nearer Lausanne, whence John went first to Italy to assist the small and struggling Movement he had fostered five years before. He held well-attended meetings in Naples and a small national conference in Rome. George Day, who accompanied him, reported in *The Student World* that "the main impressions of this conference were of hope and courage." It was the same in Portugal later that spring; in spite of heroic endeavors, the Movement did not take root in Catholic countries. Between these trips Mott attended a significant Student Mission Conference for all Germany at Halle, where his "world vision of student responsibility and opportunity was both an inspiration and a challenge, and his stirring Macedonian call to the university men of Germany fell on responsive ears."[128] We assume that he called on the aging Gustav Warneck, who had sent a message to the conference.

From Halle Mott went to Hungary, a Federation objective ever since Mott had appointed a corresponding member there in 1895. Fries and other WSCF representatives had paid short visits at various times, and had on occasion gathered large student audiences. Mott now visited the five principal student centers and met with enthusiastic responses. "In one place I delivered seven addresses in one day, and still the students followed me about to hear more." He attracted capacity audiences to the city hall in Budapest, but lack of leadership prevented organizing, so he assembled a small conference of leaders whom he coached in Association methods, chose "a strong man" to become permanent traveling secretary, and left hoping that an aggressive movement might be developed that would serve as an example to all of the Balkan states. Two years later the Federation would focus on this region with its conference at Constantinople.

As Mott was leaving Budapest he received a seven-page proposal from President Arthur Twining Hadley of Yale inviting him to become the head of a reconstituted Divinity School—the ultimate testimony to *The Future Leadership of the Church!* The offer was endorsed by a member of the Yale Corporation who had made a special trip to New Haven for the meeting at which it was unanimously voted, and who wrote on White House stationery—President William Howard Taft. En route to the Iberian Peninsula, Mott cabled Hadley that he would consider the call seriously; how seriously is indicated by the fact that he did not come to a final decision until December. At almost the same moment, word came of the death of his mother in Postville.

The climax of this long sojourn in Europe was the Federation Conference at Oxford in mid-July, 1909. In contrast to Tokyo 1907, which had been a large and evangelistic gathering, Oxford was a council of leaders dealing with the basic problems of the constituent movements, notably their attitudes toward social problems. The questionnaire on which Mott's report to Oxford was based had specifically asked what each national body had done "to promote the study of social problems" and to enlist members in "Christian social service." In his review of the quadrennium since Zeist (there was no summary at Tokyo) he spoke of the "unmistakable growth of interest" in and the "deepening sense of responsibility with reference to social questions." The British Movement had given these matters "the most earnest, continuous, and thorough attention," especially at the recent Matlock Conference, and he named five other movements that had emphasized this area, which "bids fair to be one of the truest and greatest services rendered by the Student movement to the world." He expanded the subject in a later section of his report which he called "The Possibilities of the Federation." The Conference program featured several addresses on the theme, with Charles W. Gilkey speaking for the American Movement. The preparatory number of The Student World that April had carried an article by William Temple, then a lecturer at Queen's College, who anticipated that this meeting would consecrate the "special sense of social responsibility and special efforts of social service" that were associated with Oxford. As Mott closed the Conference upon a high spiritual plane—"Losing Ourselves in the Cause"—the social and ethical notes were audible in each paragraph. [129]

PART 10: The SVM at Rochester, 1909–1910

The large public events in which Mott was involved during the few years described in this chapter concluded with the sixth SVM Quadrennial at Rochester, New York, December 29, 1909 through January 2, 1910. Keynoted by Eddy and Speer, its 3,728 delegates from 735 institutions heard Mott report that 4,377 Volunteers had sailed to mission posts since the beginning of the Movement in 1886. The past four years had been record-breaking for student giving, the launching of Yale-in-China, Princeton-in-Peking, the University of Pennsylvania's medical mission in Canton, Oberlin's project in Shansi, for an increase in mission study, and for the impact of the Movement as an "apologetic factor and force." Some, he said, consider that the greatest by-product of the Student

Movement is its "far-reaching influence in the direction of Christian cooperation, federation and union." Mott also spoke on the watchword, which was still viable in North America, and on "What is needed to meet the present world crisis." Leila wrote to Clara that John's head could easily be turned by the publicity if that were possible.[130]

Kenneth Scott Latourette and Samuel McCrea Cavert dated their commitment to the ecumenical enterprise to this conference, as did the China medical missionary R. J. Reitzel. Ross L. Finney, a Postville youth who would later teach at the University of Minnesota, was a delegate from Illinois Wesleyan; he attempted to assay the greatness of "Our John" as he saw him in action:

> It is the highness of the star he has hitched his wagon to. . . . This movement was the original conception of his inventive genius. But to my mind his ability to marshall and lead the hosts is attributable to another characteristic. I refer to his indescribable seriousness. In this, it strikes me, lies the real greatness of his personality. He believes in his enterprise with the tremendous faith of a prophet's vision.[131]

And, added Finney, "all who know his mother understand where he got the qualities that make him John R. Mott from Stockholm to Sydney, and from San Francisco and Oxford to Shanghai and Tokio."

Will Stewart disproved the adage that no man is a hero to his secretary. When he took the job in 1905 he was puzzled by Mott's stature which he expected to be stunted by Mott's lack of leisure for quiet study. "Link up your life to a great cause," one of Mott's appeals to students, was "manifest in his own life." The questionnaire, daily conference, and interview were a constant challenge. Stewart could find no "personal pride" in his chief; his "deep humility and teachableness were big factors in his growth." He often quoted St. John 9:4 ("I must work . . . while it is day"), and lived up to it on an average of fourteen hours a day, with emergencies requiring twenty-four. Interviews and conferences went on during meals. Dictation continued on the train morning and night. Mott must have rested "between heart-beats," Stewart concluded. Those who worked through a campaign with him could be exhausted but Mott would go on to another equally strenuous. During Stewart's five years, Mott did not take a single day off because of illness. When seasick, Mott would have Stewart read to him. An associate pointed out the difference between Mott and his colleagues: others' brains stopped functioning when they got tired; Mott's continued to turn out "high-grade work, even when . . . fagged." Mott, said Stewart, read Ephesians 5:16 as "buying up the opportunity" and practiced it.[132]

PART 11: **A Fork in the Road**

Mott gave his final word to President Hadley a few weeks before the Rochester Quadrennial. News of the offer was kept confidential, but the prominent members of the Divinity School faculty all urged him to accept. He conferred with Hadley. Charles S. Macfarland, who would soon accept the general secretaryship of the Federal Council of Churches, reminded him that the Yale Corporation had offered him "the opportunity of getting at the center" of the things he had projected in *The Future Leadership of the Church.* Newman Smyth, pastor of Center Church in New Haven, a noted liberal, whose ecumenical call *Passing Protestantism and Coming Catholicism* Mott had read, Charles Foster Kent, an admirer from early days at Northfield, Anson Phelps Stokes, Secretary of the University, Henry B. Wright, former Dwight Hall secretary but now a professor in the Divinity School, and Harland P. Beach, who had served the SVM for years, joined in urging his acceptance. The offer was part of President Hadley's effort to upgrade Yale from a college to a university, by obtaining as teachers "men who can *do* things." He also tried to lure George Adam Smith to the Divinity School, as he had attempted to get Ernest Rutherford, John Dewey, and G. Lowes Dickinson.[133]

Beach laid out in some detail the tensions between liberals and conservatives at Yale, revealing that Smyth had argued that a conservative element (which it was assumed Mott belonged to) was "always desirable in a great university."

> If you were to come to Yale . . . men would see that the ministry is a living, godlike service, worthy of the best that is in man. Your emphasis on the spiritual life would be felt and accepted by all the Faculty and students.[134]

He underscored Macfarland's point that the Yale post would be the "logical outcome" of his agitation in *Future Leadership.* Mott's analysis of his choice has not survived, but his own decision against the pastoral ministry must have been a pivotal factor. And was a professorship in a School that trained ministers "logical" for him?

Before they left Europe that August, Mott had confided in Morse, himself a Yale man. Morse's analysis was not unlike his dissection of the earlier Federal Council offer:

> Will the acceptance of the call help you . . . to perform more efficiently the work for students and on the foreign mission field to which you have consecrated your life and in which God has so signally blessed and is blessing you?

> For over twenty years you have happily carried on the work without iden-
> tifying yourself with any one university in any one nation. . . . Will iden-
> tification with the administration of one department in a leading university
> of your own country increase your standing, influence, and efficiency?

> Your position has been strengthened and your influence increased by the
> fact that you have held a mediating attitude between the various churches,
> and universities, and schools. A university of the so-called liberal type
> recognizes you as a conservative. To those of strong conservative views you
> seem to belong to the "Broad Church.". . . You could hardly identify
> yourself with any one institution and its school of thought without some
> damage to this neutral mediating position.

Since it had been assumed by Hadley that Mott would handle the Yale
assignment on a part-time basis, Morse wondered how Mott could add it
to his many portfolios and yet continue to administer and extend the
movements to which he was already committed; he felt that the Yale
situation itself "ought to have the undivided time and attention" of the
man who undertook it. Then he made a telling point:

> It seems to me that what is *incidental* in the many qualifications you possess
> for your present position is what they have discerned and coveted as your
> *chief* qualification for the office and work they desire from you. [135]

Mott also shared the problem with J. H. Oldham, who was by now
his intimate colleague in the planning of the World Missionary Conference to be held in Edinburgh the next summer. Oldham's response was
prophetic:

> I can hardly conceive of any opportunity—not even that of Yale—being
> equal to that which you have enjoyed in recent years, the opportunity of
> directing and powerfully influencing the lives of the strongest men in the
> years when they were most susceptible to far reaching influence. I should
> view with deep concern your being removed from an opportunity so su-
> preme.

Oldham then mentioned some reservations he held concerning the limitations of the YMCA foreign work and the possible restricting effect of
that limitation upon the WSCF.

> The burden of my thought is that your powers and influence are now too
> great—I dare not say what I think about those powers—for you any longer
> to serve any auxiliary or anything short of the Church of Christ itself.

"I think you would have to make" the kind of opportunity I crave for you,
he continued:

The sort of thing that hovers before my mind is that some international post might emerge as the result of the forthcoming conference in which you might serve *all* the [missionary] Societies rather than one particular society [the YMCA] pouring your influence and ideas into the work of each; and still leaving you free for the supreme work for which you are so preeminently gifted—the work of getting men. Only instead of picking men for posts of a special and limited kind you would pick the strongest men for the biggest posts under the various societies. You might thus wield a tremendous influence for the coordination and unification of the work throughout the world. . . . I shall pray with deep earnestness that you may be guided into a clear knowledge of the will of God. He has used you most wonderfully in past years. . . . I hesitate to think that the deep roots which you have struck in lands outside America are to be pulled up, and that your world-wide influence is to be exchanged even for such an opportunity as is presented at Yale. I wonder whether you know how profound has been your influence on some of us in Great Britain.[136]

Mott replied that this was "the most difficult situation" of his life. Oldham answered with the speculation that "perhaps the climax of your life work" might come in leading the movement they both expected to eventuate from Edinburgh.[137] Mott responded that he had considered that possibility.

When Mott finally sent his refusal to Yale, it was based upon the conviction that the new post ought to command "more rather than less time and vital force." After review of his "present work and field" and its probable foreseeable demands of the next few years, he felt that he must concentrate "any time and strength" he could gain upon them, rather than to undertake a new task.[138]

For many years Mott kept this correspondence in a file labelled "Forks in the Road." But the main highway had never forked. Since the summer of 1886 there had been side-roads with sometimes beckoning vistas, such as *Future Leadership* and Yale. Oldham was right. The Yale invitation helped clarify the perspective.

7

Edinburgh
1910, and After

*Mais c'est aussi cette conférence qui consacra
l'autorité de Mott dans le monde chrétien tout
entier et ouvrit un nouveau chapitre de sa vie*
—Marc Boegner[1]

THE WORLD MISSIONARY CONFERENCE held at Edinburgh, Scotland, in June, 1910, came at the climactic end of what Kenneth Scott Latourette aptly called "The Great Century" of the expansion of Christianity and of Western culture. It was more than a conference: it was "one of the great landmarks in the history of the Church," a "watershed in missionary discussion," Like a lens, it "summed up and focused much of the previous century's movement for uniting Christians in giving the Gospel to the world." Mott called it "the most notable gathering in the interest of the worldwide expansion of Christianity ever held, not only in missionary annals, but in all Christian annals."

He was intimately involved in preparation for it throughout three years. He headed the first of its eight preparatory commissions, presided at most of its sessions, and became chairman of its Continuation Committee. Latourette declared that in many ways he was "the master mind of the gathering." Gordon Hewitt points out that although the Conference was backward-looking in summing up a century's achievement of sharing the gospel with the peoples of Asia, it was saved from a "ruinous triumphalism" by its organization and methods of work that pointed forward; "this positive and creative aspect," he concluded, owed most to its chairman, John R. Mott, and its secretary, J. H. Oldham.[2] From the perspective of forty-five years of ecumenical history, Marc Boegner adjudged that Edinburgh established Mott's commanding position throughout the Christian world and opened a new chapter in his life.

342

PART 1: **The Preparation**

There had been a great missionary conference in London in 1888. Mott had taken part in one in New York in 1900.[3] But from the moment that a proposal for a third "ecumenical missionary conference" surfaced in the Foreign Missions Conference of North America in 1907, he expressed himself forcefully on the nature of such a meeting:

> To my mind the missionary enterprise at the present time would be much more helped by a thorough unhurried conference of the leaders of the Boards of North America and Europe than by a great popular convention. I feel strongly upon this point.[4]

That position became the point of departure as negotiations between American, German, Scottish, and English societies moved forward upon the mutual assumption that the conference should be held in 1910; Edinburgh 1910 was organized in accordance with Mott's dictum, but it was also "a great popular convention."

In January, 1907, the Foreign Missions Conference of North America accepted a Scottish invitation to a third missionary conference of world Protestantism to be held in their capital three and a half years hence. During that year, J. H. Oldham, whom Mott had known since 1891, had become a member of the host committee. During the Liverpool SVM Quadrennial of January, 1908, for which Mott made a special Atlantic crossing, he and Dr. George Robson, editor of *The Missionary Record* of the United Free Church of Scotland, sought an interview with Mott. The preparations for the conference were at that time for all practical purposes "in the hands of the Scottish committee," wrote Oldham,

> and we suggested to him that an international gathering should be internationally planned from the start. He seized the point immediately and took a swift decision. He promised that one of his first acts on returning to America would be to call a meeting of the Foreign Missions Boards and put the suggestion before them.[5]

That body was scheduled to meet the week of Mott's return. It appointed a special committee to further American preparation for the Edinburgh Conference, of which Arthur Judson Brown of the Presbyterian Mission Board was chairman, and Speer and Mott were members.[6] By the end of the week this group had produced a five-page document, signed by Brown and Mott, that it sent on its way to Edinburgh on January 31, 1908. One suspects that Mott had at least outlined it during his return voyage. "In less than a month," Oldham recalled,

> A letter arrived in Edinburgh, suggesting that an international committee should meet in the summer of that year, and undertaking to send a strong American delegation. . . . I learned that in the making of history chance meetings may have unexpectedly far-reaching consequences. By Mott's action the planning of the Edinburgh Conference was transformed from a national to an international committee. If this change had not taken place, the developments of the last fifty years would have been quite different from what they were. [7]

The letter set forth the American positions on the object, character, personnel, and program of the forthcoming Conference. It betrayed Mott's thinking and style, and the imprint of the Student Christian Movement was unmistakable, as W. R. Hogg rightly observed in *Ecumenical Foundations.* [8] The Conference, the two Americans began, should not be devoted primarily "to educational and inspirational purposes" as had London and New York, but ought to be given to "thorough study and consultation by the leaders of the foreign missionary forces of the world." It should be planned by an international committee and modeled upon the conferences at Madras in 1902 and Shanghai in 1907. Representation should be based on the seating capacity of the assembly hall, but in no case should there be more than 1,000 to 1,200 delegates; every Protestant foreign missionary agency ought to be represented, in proportion to the number of its missionaries or its budget; care should be taken to secure "men of large experience." Everything possible must be done to secure the presence of secretaries of societies and clergymen who are recognized leaders of the missionary enterprise "both on the mission fields and also at the home base."

The distinctive feature of this conference, the American spokesmen insisted, should be consideration of advance reports by study commissions dealing with seven or eight "matters of large importance and of timely interest at this stage of the missionary enterprise." Suggestions on the selection of and instructions to these commissions followed; "the forenoon and at least half of the afternoons" should be given daily to "the thorough discussion" of their reports. Evening sessions ought to feature inspirational addresses by "only the greatest missionary speakers in the English language." Each morning there should be one "deeply spiritual address." The recent Liverpool SVM Quadrennial practice of a daily twenty-minute prayer session should be followed. In conclusion, the

Brown-Mott document recommended deputation work throughout the British Isles on the model of Tokyo 1907.[9]

The Scottish committee also received remarkably similar proposals from the London group and from the German *Ausschuss*, the oldest cooperative missionary body, which became the continental agency for Edinburgh planning. All of the recommendations were accepted. An international planning committee was duly appointed and met at Wycliffe Hall, Oxford, in mid-July, 1908. Of nineteen members, Fries, Oldham, Mott, and Tatlow comprised a younger contingent that imprinted the Student Volunteer Movement outlook upon the proceedings. Oldham was made secretary of the meeting. Later, in view of the colossal work load contemplated, Mott moved that a full-time paid secretary be put in charge, something new. Oldham was selected for this strategic post—perhaps the most significant decision made at Wycliffe Hall that summer.

Thus began a professional collaboration between Mott and this diminutive Scot that would bind the two in common tasks that demanded the utmost from each until 1934; the bond thus created would tie the two men in an already realized spiritual unity as long as either lived. In 1891, when Mott had first visited Oxford, Oldham, an undergraduate in Trinity College, had been asked by a friend (one guesses A. G. Fraser or Temple Gairdner) to meet "at the station an American who was coming with an introduction to him, and to help show his visitor something of Oxford."[10] Nine years Mott's junior, Oldham was the product of a warmly evangelical Scottish home, a man with a single-track mind—as several, including Mott, would characterize him—a "thinker" and scholar, as different from Mott as could be imagined. A Bible student and author of a widely studied text on *The Teachings of Jesus* and much later a popular *Devotional Diary*, Oldham came to the preparatory committee with experience as a British SCM secretary, missionary and YMCA secretary in India, study in theology at New College, Edinburgh, and in missions under Warneck at Halle; he was then mission study secretary for the United Free Church of Scotland and for the British SCM.[11] If Mott master-minded Edinburgh 1910, Joseph Houldsworth Oldham was its chief engineer.[12] Their teamwork epitomized the fact of British and American missions being virtually a joint enterprise.

As the international planning committee worked its way through three long sessions a day at Oxford, Mott and Robson were delegated to redefine the subject areas of the commissions. These came out of the final committee process much as Brown and Mott had originally proposed them, with but one addition. Their officers were selected; Mott was made chairman of Commission I, "Carrying the Gospel to all the World," with Robson and Julius Richter of Germany as vice-chairmen.[13] The committee laid down the procedures for all commissions, set a deadline for their reports, and established a methodology for the selection of their personnel; it laid out the program, named various subcommittees including publicity, and of great significance for the success of the Conference, declared that no resolution could come before it that involved "questions of doctrine or Church polity with regard to which the Churches or Societies taking part . . . differ"—a prerequisite to Anglican participation.

It emphasized that comity and cooperation were to be stressed in every aspect of the planning and program. Each early release carried excerpts from or the full text of letters from President Theodore Roosevelt, William Howard Taft, and Lord Bryce, endorsing the Conference and its aims. And each release quoted both Oldham and Mott on the need for special prayers for the Conference itself, for each of the Commissions, and that "the Church, dominated by a fresh vision of an unevangelized world and of that coming ecumenical, Christ-redeemed, triumphant multitude whom no man can number, may consecrate herself, as never before, to the sublime task of making Christ known and loved and obeyed by all men."[14] In almost every aspect, the plan resembled that outlined in the Brown-Mott letter of January 31, 1908.

Due to his presence in Europe for almost half of the remaining time before the Conference met, Mott was able to attend several planning sessions and to confer with his colleagues. In the fall of 1908 he collaborated in the delicate negotiations aimed to bring the Anglican Church into the Conference, by writing a lengthy description of the plans for the prestigious The East and the West, the missions quarterly of the High-Church Society for the Propagation of the Gospel, and securing editorial approval. In this statement, which was reprinted and widely circulated, he emphasized that matters of polity or doctrine were forbidden by the constitution of the Conference. He managed to cite the recent Pan-Anglican Congress and to quote the current Lambeth encyclical that had declared that "waste of force in the Mission field calls aloud for unity." The Church, he declared, must be prepared to pay the price for results that will surely be "so extensive, so beneficent, and so valuable" as those anticipated. That price is that "all missionary societies and boards must heartily cooperate," and he believed that "every missionary agency of standing" would unreservedly do so.[15]

Mott played a very small part in the crucial negotiations (on which the success of the Conference really hung) that brought the Church of England into the enterprise. The chief credit goes to Oldham and Tatlow, but as Hogg puts it, the Student Movement was "directly responsible" and Mott's influence there hardly needs noting. William Temple wrote in 1915 that students ought to know that the Edinburgh Conference could never have been held "without their movement," and a historian of 1963 found that the "SVM emphasis helped mold the intangible atmosphere which permitted the Edinburgh Conference to advance beyond its predecessors."[16] However, the Archbishop of Canterbury, Randall Davidson, could hardly have forgotten his earlier introduction to Tatlow and Mott (which was related in Chapter 6). The two shared in the interview in July, 1909, at which Oldham and others asked him to address the Conference; ten months later he decided to do so.

Throughout the first half of 1909 Mott had kept in touch with Oldham and with the vice-chairmen of his Commission through voluminous correspndence involving scores of pages of single-spaced discussion of a whole gamut of issues, written from Chernix, Uppsala, or Moscow, and dealing with the printing of pamphlets or the Anglicans' reservations. Oldham came to America briefly to clarify some issues with the North American committee; Mott wrote pointed instructions from Moscow to his surrogate Hans Andersen in New York on how to handle the visit, ordering that special efforts be made to "convert" Oldham from what Mott considered his mistaken views on North American YMCA Foreign Work and that he should be prevented from talking privately with members of the Conference committee. Oldham, he avowed, was "by all odds the deepest thinker and most influential worker in the British Student Movement," and would not be "easily changed." Fortunately, the problems were adjusted and Oldham returned home satisfied that a serious crisis had been averted.[17] While in New Haven, Professor Harlan P. Beach "leaked" the forthcoming Yale offer to Mott so that Oldham was privy to the fact well before Mott received word; there followed months of statesmanlike exchange concerning the world organization that might emerge from Edinburgh and Mott's place in it.[18] At the end of June, Mott attended a planning session at York and conferred at length with Oldham.

That summer at Lac des Iles he spent "days in quiet thought, prayer and planning" that he later believed had led to significant results at Edinburgh: this was Item 6 of his life-list of "most creative" experiences. As 1910 drew nearer, the vast correspondence between Oldham and Mott increased. The potential for a continuing world organization grew steadily greater in both their minds. So important did Mott's future commitment to "some great and comprehensive work" loom in Oldham's vision that in September, 1909, when Mott was probably most agonized over the call to Yale, Oldham begged him to keep himself "free from other engagements until the Conference is over."[19]

For a time during the winter of 1909–1910 Mott hoped that Theodore Roosevelt and Admiral A. T. Mahan might be obtained as speakers for the Conference, but it proved impossible. From a letter that Roosevelt sent to the Conference, it is not difficult to speculate on what the ex-president might have said, but Mahan's possible message remains an enigma.[20] For months both Mott and Oldham were plagued, or so they regarded it, by letters and promotional materials from H. E. Wootton, a layman of Melbourne, Australia, asking for an opportunity to present the claims of a "'One' World Missionary Movement" which had been endorsed by several denominations in Australia and New Zealand. Wootton's plan and tactics seemed brash to Oldham, who referred him to Commissions I and VIII, the latter on cooperation and unity. However, it is apparent that this unorthodox scheme was but another straw in the ecumenical wind that became a gale before the end of the Conference. Wootton spoke powerfully and emotionally from the floor as a delegate when the continuation committee proposal was before the house.[21]

In the late winter Oldham received a letter from W. Nelson Bitton of the London Mission in Shanghai expressing disappointment that few Orientals were going to Edinburgh. Mott had earlier expressed himself as heartily in favor of such representation and complained to Oldham that he wished he might have "had better success" in getting the mission boards to include "at least one Oriental in each delegation" (the Conference being comprised of persons invited by them). As a result, there was considerable scurrying about and the group of distinguished Orientals increased somewhat. Oldham later recalled that it had been Mott "above all others who insisted in the face of a good deal of conservative opposition that the younger Churches should be represented."[22]

The preparatory period was appropriately climaxed for Mott when in mid-February, 1910, he received a letter from an excited Oldham conveying the unanimous invitation of the executive that he chair the sessions of the Conference. Although already a "master of assemblies," he replied that he was "quite overwhelmed" and would make the matter the subject of special prayer before deciding whether he ought to undertake such a responsibility. He must have received approval because he wrote Mrs. McCormick just before sailing that he was "trying to discover" his duty "in the face of such a great opportunity." Such were its unexpected demands that he advanced his departure by a week, leaving on April 20.

PART 2: Commission I

The study commissions proposed in the Brown-Mott recommendations of January, 1908, made the Edinburgh Conference unique. The concept and the achievement produced "something new" and set a precedent for later conferences. A by-product was the creation of an ecumenical atmosphere. Individual qualifications took precedence in the selection of the directors of these studies over denominational affiliation or any other claim.

The ink was hardly dry on the minutes of the international planning committee's Oxford, 1908, sessions when Mott started to work on his assignment, "Carrying the Gospel to All the World." One of his first acts was to solicit financial undergirding for the work of the eight commissions; he obtained $55,000, $7,000 of which was provided by Mrs. McCormick; the budget for Commission I was $9,900. The other preliminary task of importance was the selection of the members of Commission I. Four were chosen from his "household"—Hans P. Andersen, his able office secretary, Yale missions professor Harlan P. Beach, WSCF secretary Ruth Rouse, and SVM secretary Samuel M. Zwemer. The names of several others are familiar; the rest were missions executives based in Paris, London, New York, Boston, Herrnhut, Germany, Toronto, Philadelphia, and Husby, Denmark. In spite of Mott's own preferences, no "strong native leaders," as stipulated by the international planning committee, were included. This was true of all the Commissions, doubtless because of the postal lag that would have made the compilation of reports impossible within the time limits, and the fact that virtually everyone selected was accessible and had secretarial aid. There was voluminous correspondence with some, but all shared in the editorial process as the report took shape. Andersen served as Mott's assistant, and Charles H. Fahs, later to head the Missionary Research Library, was co-opted for half time.

At the Oxford meeting in the summer of 1908, Mott talked briefly with George Robson, one of his vice-presidents, but rushed ahead on his own with the preliminary development of the questionnaires to be sent to a worldwide list of missionaries. Several months later, Robson politely raised some questions, after which the most solicitous cooperation prevailed;[23] Mott corresponded constantly with Richter, his other vice-chairman, met him several times in Germany, and brought him to the Rochester SVM Quadrennial in January, 1910, when they conferred at length.

The Commission divided its task geographically and functionally, requiring several questionnaires. Mott, whose experience with such instruments began with his first world tour, edited them before they were sent to some 500 missionaries around the world. Here the scarcity of Orientals on the Commission might have been compensated, as Mott drew not only upon his own memory and files for qualified persons, but had the advantage over other chairmen of direct access to the worldwide YMCA network. Naturally he turned to Richter, Robson, and others for names. Even so, he included less than a score of non-Westerners; half of them were Japanese. This was, however, more than any other Commission consulted. Mott individualized the wording of his covering letters, which reached most correspondents after they had received a general statement concerning the Conference, such as a copy of his article in *The East and the West,* and advance instructions for the questionnaire. The correspondents who did not return their replies when expected were firmly reminded; the responses to all Commissions were extraordinary. For special problems, he called on his intimate friends: he asked Galen Fisher to write a section on Japan, D. Willard Lyon to read and criticize an almost-final draft on China, and James L. Barton of the American Board to advise on the Pacific Islands. Criticisms were frank, especially from those on intimate terms with the chairman.[24]

Inevitably problems of procedure and definition arose. Mott usually synthesized issues of content and in one case consolidated two subcommittees. He rarely took an arbitrary stand and always closed his letters, however firmly they may have set forth his own position, with thanks, commendation, and reminders of the necessity of prayer and, wherever possible, of conversation. As we know, while Mott was in Russia in the spring of 1909 Oldham came to America to resolve the problems created by Beach, Dennis, and Fahs' use in their *Atlas* of statistics that had implications distasteful to the Anglicans. The North American members of Commission I met at Mott's urgent command at least six times and got together in Edinburgh prior to the opening of the Conference.

The final process of editing the report was the prerogative of the chairman. His was the duty of digesting all the materials from the field and all the criticisms and suggestions. It goes without saying that Leila Mott shared largely in this. Toward the end of the editing, a Commission member implored Mott to write the final draft of a given section himself: the author's account "may not have the edge and vigor to it which these findings must possess. . . . I prefer to see the basis of criticism something that you yourself have written." William R. Stewart compared the intensity of this effort to that of 1906 when his chief had prepared simultaneously for the Nashville SVM Quadrennial and the trip to the southern hemisphere. Somehow the deadlines were met, and Mott sailed for Britain as planned—doubtless putting on the finishing touches during the voyage—although Oldham had despaired in the previous October, a betrayal of his ignorance of Mott's capacity for work. The report would be presented on the morning of the first working day of the Conference.

As if this were not enough, the moment that document was "put to bed" Mott turned to the writing, in Scotland, of a book based on the Conference reports that would capture the interest generated by the meeting. Stewart, who took much of the dictation, recalled the "most unideal circumstances for literary production" in which *The Decisive Hour of Christian Missions* was written. During the "extremely busy and hectic days" immediately prior to the opening, Mott had "dictated it to his two stenographers as rapidly as they could transcribe it on the typewriter." The only hope of getting such a job done, Mott explained to them, was "to commit oneself to accomplish it by a certain time," under the pressure of a publisher's deadline. He wrote Mrs. McCormick that he was devoting fourteen hours a day to it. When it appeared in late summer one reviewer hailed it as his greatest book.

A week before the Conference was to open, Mott and several congenial colleagues—Robson, the Oldhams, V. S. Azariah, Mrs. Alexander Whyte, wife of the Principal of New College, and a few others—withdrew to the Yorkshire village of Goathland for a three-day retreat. They spent much of their time "singly alone in the open moors" that surrounded them. For Mott, it was "weird" but a "very restful" time of "spiritual refreshing" that he had greatly needed. News of the unexpected death of King Edward VII, which "threw the whole nation into deep mourning," intensified for the Edinburgh planners their own as well as the nation's need "to rely more on God in this critical time." Mott remembered the Goathland retreat as the seventh event in his life-list of creative experiences.

PART 3: **High on "The Mound"**

In the midst of the Scottish acropolis of Edinburgh, not far from the Castle and near St. Giles' Cathedral, there stands the spacious Assembly Hall of the United Free Church of Scotland, the site of numerous historic events. Surrounded by the buildings of New College, which housed the ancillary enterprises of the Conference, the Hall itself, designed for such gatherings, seated each of the 1,200 delegates within sight and sound not only of the dais but so that a speaker anywhere in the room could easily "address the whole audience and directly face the larger half." The Chairman faced the entire congregation. For a working Conference it was ideal.

The Conference was preceded by a convocation of the University of Edinburgh at which honorary degrees were conferred upon fourteen Conference leaders including Mott (his first LL.D.), K. C. Chatterji, Robert E. Speer, General James E. Beaver (one of Mott's early sponsors), and President T. Harada of the Doshisha.[25] In a few carefully chosen words Mott acknowledged for the group "this most gracious act of adoption" by a university "founded in that spacious century in which the areas of discovery, invention, and knowledge were so widely extended and in which the bounds of liberty were so wonderfully enlarged" that it had been rendered hospitable to "the great purposes which have brought this World Missionary Conference within your gates."[26]

The pre-Conference business session resolved that the business committee, of which Mott was a member, should continue throughout the Conference; each Commission report must be presented within forty-five minutes and those wishing to speak to it must hand in their names the previous afternoon; the Chairman would have discretion to recognize speakers with due regard to "a fair representation of different countries and societies and to an adequate expression of differences of view"; the time allotted to each person in the discussion of the reports could not exceed seven minutes; "in all questions relating to order and procedure" the ruling of the Chairman would be final; standard rules of debate were laid down; Oldham's appointment as secretary and Mott's as "Chairman of the Conference in Committee" were confirmed. Lord Balfour of Burleigh was the President of the Conference.

The real opening of the Conference was on the evening of June 14, the delegates climbing the hill in the late rays of the northern sun, winding their way through a narrow court past the silent but dominating statue of John Knox to fill the Hall "from floor to ceiling." Because of denominational differences there could be no eucharist on this solemn occasion, but the prayer of the venerable Principal Alexander Whyte seemed to the chronicler of the Conference to bring the congregation "very near the Head and His universal Church." Lord Balfour then read to a standing audience a message from Britain's new and as yet un-crowned King George V, following which he spoke with strong personal conviction on the opportunity of the day, emphasizing and reemphasiz-ing unity.

The featured speaker was the Archbishop of Canterbury, Randall Davidson, whose presence forecast to many—especially those who had labored to get him there—the dawn of a new era of ecumenism. Not known as an orator, he nonetheless carried his hearers to new heights of expectation: "the place of missions in the life of the Church must be the central place." Secure for that thought its true place, "in our plans, our policy, our prayers; and then—why then, the issue is His, not ours. But it may well be that, if that come true, there may be some standing here tonight who shall not taste of death till they see the Kingdom of God come with power." Robert E. Speer spoke last: let only the barrier of unfaith be removed and "living faith will make it possible for Him to make use of us for the immediate conquest of the world."

When Mott rose to present the report of Commission I the morning of June 15, he had just turned forty-five years of age, but to a youthful usher and several others (ushers or pages were a unique feature at Edin-burgh) he still "looked young." He was "already an ecumenical figure of towering influence" who through half of those forty-five years had in reality worked tirelessly toward this moment. The dais at Edinburgh became for him a new ecumenical plateau, and as Oldham had forecast and Boegner perceived, opened a new phase of his career. During those June days, he personified the new generation of leadership that had come up through the Student Christian Movements of the world and would exert a strategic influence upon the Conference.[27]

Having asked Sir Andrew Fraser to take the Chair, Mott opened the first presentation of a Commission report—his own—with the comment that the assumption that the volume of over 300 pages had been read "may be a large one!" His preamble revealed not only the mind and hand of its chairman but the temper of Protestant missionary thought at the end of its "great century" as its leaders sensed it:

> It is a startling and solemnising fact that even as late as the twentieth century the Great Command of Jesus Christ to carry the Gospel to all mankind is still so largely unfulfilled. It is a ground for great hopefulness

that, notwithstanding the serious situation occasioned by such neglect, the Church is confronted to-day, as in no preceding generation, with a literally world-wide opportunity to make Christ known. There may have been times when in certain non-Christian lands the missionary forces of Christianity stood face to face with as pressing opportunities as those now presented in the same fields, but never before has there been such a conjunction of crises and of opening of doors in all parts of the world as that which characterises the present decade. It is likewise true that never on the home field have the conditions been more favourable for waging a campaign of evangelisation adequate in scope, in thoroughness, and in power. Therefore, the first duty of a World Missionary Conference meeting at such an auspicious time is to consider the present world situation from the point of view of making the Gospel known to all men, and to determine what should be done to accomplish this Christ-given purpose. . . . It is earnestly hoped that the way may have been pointed [by the labours of this Commission] to a more scientific study of the fields and problems, and, above all, that enough may have been done to impress the Church with the unprecedented urgency of the situation, and to create a sense of deep solicitude as to the grave consequences which must ensue if the present unique world opportunity be not improved. [28]

Thus, as James H. Nichols has put it, Edinburgh "spoke out of prewar optimism, Western complacency, and faith in progress."

Mott presented his summary in six "outstanding convictions and impressions" that had "laid strong hold upon us" during two years' work. The first was "the *vastness of the task* of evangelizing the world." The second was that "the time is really at hand—not coming—when the Christian Church should bestir itself as never before *in the countries of the non-Christian world in which it is already at work.*" The third conviction, not unexpected, was that "the time is also at hand when the Church should enter the so-called *unoccupied fields of the world,*" a long section that Gairdner, the popularizing reporter of the Conference, called "melancholy reading." The fourth conviction was that if this world-situation was to be met, there must be "*united planning and concerted effort*"; a well-considered plan of cooperation, entered into by the [180] Societies represented in this hall, carried out with "a sense of our oneness in Christ," would be more than the equivalent of doubling the missionary forces of the world! A loud burst of applause greeted this challenge; it was repeated not only when Mott expressed the hope that some kind of permanent international body would eventuate from the Conference but also upon any mention of such throughout the next week. The fifth impression gained by Commission 1 was that the evangelization of the world is not chiefly a European or American enterprise, "but an Asiatic or African enterprise," carried on by "still further developing the power of initiative, of aggressive evangelism, and of self-denying missionary outreach on the part of the Christians of Asia and Africa." Nowhere did the SVM watchword appear, though its spirit was often audible in a newer terminology. The Commission's last point was that "the vitality of the Church in the Christian countries" must be greatly enhanced. Mott closed with a paraphrase of the Archbishop's climax of the previous evening:

> The power is in this room, under God, to influence the hosts of Christendom to enter into the realisation of the sublime hope expressed by the speaker last evening, that before the eyes of some of us shall close in death, the opportunity at least may be given to all people throughout the non-Christian world to know and to accept, if they will, the living Christ![29]

When Mott resumed the Chair, thirty-four delegates commented, then and in the afternoon session. Four were Orientals; Eddy appealed for India and Brockman set forth the needs of Eastern students studying in the West.

If we recall Mott's meticulous plans for SVM Quadrennials since 1891, it should come as no surprise that he gave what was for him especially meticulous attention to his own preparation for the Edinburgh Chairmanship. Mathews, his biographer of 1934, interviewed numerous Conference participants and devoted six pages to this matter, concluding that Mott had not only read widely on European methods of parliamentary procedure but had talked with ecclesiastics and parliamentarians on both sides of the Atlantic.[30] Betty D. Gibson, who served the International Missionary Council for many years, recalled from her personal knowledge that "to the exhaustion and even exasperation" of his colleagues, Mott had insisted upon placing name-cards in the Hall: "Those whose mother-tongue was not English, and who were therefore apt to be a little slow off the mark in debate, had special attention and were placed so that they could easily catch his eye." Although he was criticized for it, he also gave prominence to certain Anglicans because of the importance of their presence.

The test of the chairman was the seven-minute rule, a standing order of the Conference. Mott, with the assistance of an electric bell that he rang inexorably after six minutes, enforced the rule upon "Bishop, Moderator, or Peer of the Realm," beginning with Bishop Gore, who was cut off in mid-sentence and resolutely refused to return to the podium despite popular clamor. At the end of seven minutes the bell—a novelty to most delegates—rang again; Mott stood, bowing slightly toward the speaker, or, as Miss Gibson noted, occasionally used a toe "to good effect."[31] It was also a rule that would-be speakers must hand their names to the Chair the day before. The "much-suffering Chairman," as Gairdner described Mott, had then to exercise the "unenviable responsibility of having to look purely to the interests of the debate, and of yet ensuring that neither race nor nation nor denomination nor 'school of thought' should feel neglected or aggrieved." Gairdner held that "every fair-minded person pronounced that their Chairman had in this case played his difficult part to perfection," adding that one morning Mott had confessed that if those who had been unable to speak the day before had been disappointed, "what must be the feelings of 'the Chair'!" Writing in the heat of excitement, Gairdner painted a rare yet vivid portrait of the Chairman:

> Not one man from either hemisphere could have filled that chair as it was filled by John R. Mott. Like every Speaker he never spoke—that is to say, he made no contribution to the debates themselves, except only on the day on which, as Chairman of a Commission, he had to bring forward its Report; yet his influence and personality was felt throughout the whole Conference. The whole physique of the man suggested strength, with its frame built on large lines, finely-moulded head, and rock-strong face. When a point of unusual interest was being hazarded, forward would come the big head, quick as light; the strong square jowl would be thrust forward, the broad brow knit and scowl (if the word may be used for a sight wholly gracious), the dark shaggy eyebrows almost meet, while from under their shadow shoots a gleam from suddenly-kindling eyes:—a very lion preparing to spring at an idea. . . . Thus, too, when he himself addresses an assembly, knits and kindles the craggy tender face; the voice vibrates with fierce emphases and stresses, while gestures of admirable justness accompany each point made. The single words seem literally to fall from his lips (the trite expression is for once justified), finished off with a deliberation that never slurs one final consonant, but on the contrary gives that consonant the duty of driving its word home. And so for the sentences also;—the conclusion of each, instead of dropping in tone, increases to a sort of defiant *sforzando*, which, when his earnestness is at its height, can be terrific. Every sentence is brought down like a blow; and, as when the heavy arm of some stone-breaker bangs blow on blow on the heart of a lump of stone, until it fairly smashes into fragments, not otherwise hammer the sentences of John R. Mott, with careful, scientific deliberateness, until, at the end, the audience finds itself, in a word—smashed. . . . And then the tenderness of the man comes out—as he deals with the fragments.
>
> Such consistent power is vested in no man save him in whom it daily accumulates by habitual communion with the one Source. And that, in fact, has been the secret in the case of this man, and the sole explanation

of his unique career as a Christian worker among the Colleges and the Churches, culminating in Edinburgh, 1910. . . .

Yet this heavy-weight fighter in the great Campaign had the lightest touch. That leonine gleam could be also a gleam of humour. Time and again, when the Conference was dragging from weariness, or when an awkward situation was developing and the tension was giving some anxiety, the light touch saved the situation;—one brief remark, dry-spiced with saving humour, would set things going rightly forward again. An audience which was probably radical and democratic in its general attitude, might not have cared to be told to limit, or even stop, its applause. But what audience can take it amiss when its Chairman requests it to "*applaud concisely*"? . . . Neither does an assembly, as a general rule, appreciate an intimation that it, like all assemblies, is apt to become long-winded. But it will even cheer that intimation from a Chairman who, when directing speakers "to look straight at the clock," adds that an acoustical peculiarity which makes this desirable "may possibly have other advantages."[32]

Another Scottish observer described the Chairman as "the mainspring of the Conference."

As Chairman, Mott recognized the few Orientals for whose presence he had labored, perhaps disproportionately. The Reverend Yugoro Chiba, Professor T. Y. Chang, the Honorable T. H. Yun, and the Reverend V. S. Azariah spoke to his presentation of the report of Commission I; in subsequent discussions he recognized old friends—Honda, Cheng, Ibuka, Harada, Chatterji—so that for the first time representatives of the "younger" churches (the adjective "native" began to disappear thereafter) were seriously heard from in a world gathering outside the student movement.[33]

President Takasu Harada of the Doshisha, Principal K. Ibuka of the Meiji Gakuin, and V. S. Azariah of India were chosen to address evening sessions on themes of East-West relations and cooperation. The young Azariah hesitated to unburden himself, "but great-hearted Dr. Mott had charged him to tell out freely and frankly what lay on his heart"; the address became "a tale of missionaries from overseas and their Indian colleagues that rather took our breath away," wrote his biographer, a delegate, describing what came to be known as "the first shot in the campaign against 'missionary imperialism.'" We can only comprehend "the love of Christ which passeth knowledge," through "spiritual friendships between the two races," cried this future Indian bishop who for ten years had been a YMCA secretary:

Through all the ages to come the Indian Church will rise up in gratitude to attest the heroism and self-denying labours of the missionary body. You have given your goods to feed the poor. You have given your bodies to be burned. We also ask for *love*. Give us FRIENDS![34]

(Both italics and capital letters are in the Conference *Minutes*.)

On the morning of "midsummer's day," June 21, which many delegates noted hopefully, the report of Commission VIII on "Cooperation and the promotion of unity" was moved forward for early consideration. Its essence was to create what became known as the Continuation Committee "to carry forward the work begun by the eight preparatory commissions, and, in general, to further the realization of the vision" that was being born there on The Mound. "International and representative" as well as interdenominational, it would avoid "the idea of organic and ecclesiastical union" while fostering comity and cooperation on the mission fields of the world.

Reading that report and the addresses of the day—there were no really negative voices—climaxing as they did the increasing sentiment in favor of some form of permanent body, one is reminded of the welling up of the "missionary gusher" that became the Student Volunteer Movement at Mount Hermon twenty-four years earlier. What thoughts may have coursed through the mind of delegate Robert P. Wilder! From the opening day, mention of cooperation, unity, or the creation of a body to continue the work of the Conference, had been greeted with applause. "The enormous section of Christendom represented at Edinburgh, 1910, *was ready for a Continuation Committee*," wrote Gairdner.

The most telling speech was a tour de force by the brilliant Cheng Ching-yi, who had interpreted for Mott on his 1907 tour in China. Now the pastor of an independent Chinese congregation in Peking and president of the YMCA of that city, his seven-minute oration, "solid and lean as an athlete in training," was a full argument for cooperation among the younger churches. After Azarish's outburst, it was Edinburgh's most remembered address.[35]

Following lengthy discussion, during which the widest expression of opinion, including that of Mott's and Oldham's former antagonist H. E. Wootton of Australia, was voiced, Mott put the question: "Shall the vote now be taken?" Sir Andrew Fraser, Chairman of Commission VIII, waived his right to close the discussion. Then came the dramatic moment, as Gairdner felt it:

"The Motion has been moved and seconded: those in favour of it say Aye!"

A roar: "*Aye!*" short as the monosyllable itself, but with a volume like a Handel chorus.

"Contrary, No!"

A silence, as voluminous as the former sound.

"The Motion is carried unanimously."

The Conference leapt to its feet and burst into the Doxology. The Continuation Committee was born.

Oldham wrote many years later that there had been sufficient "hesitations" on the part of numerous delegates that "without Mott's resolute leadership and skilled adocacy, the proposal would not have been carried." It was Mott also, he continued, "who was determined that the committee should not be a paper committee but an active one with a budget and a secretariat." But to Oldham in 1910 the all-important consideration "was that it enlisted the energies of John R. Mott in the service of the missionary movement. There was no suggestion or question in the mind of anyone that there could be any other possible chairman."

Oldham had at first shrunk from becoming the secretary of the continuing body, regarding the job as almost unmanageable. But his familiarity with and understanding of the German viewpoint, gained from his study with Warneck, brought the German delegation to him at a critical juncture. They had long favored the idea of a Continuation Committee but feared that they might be swamped by the "larger, wealthier Anglo-Saxon societies," an apprehension shared by other continental societies. They made it clear that "the only thing that would relieve them from their anxieties would be my consent to accept the secretaryship. . . ." Oldham continued;

> I also had a conversation with Dr. Frere, at that time the head of the Community of the Resurrection at Mirfield, and later Bishop of Truro, in which he told me that to take part in a permanent organization was, for the Anglo-Catholics, a bigger and more serious step than to participate in a particular conference. He went on to say that in the two years of preparatory work some of them had got to know me and realized that I understood and respected their point of view; if I agreed to become secretary, they would join in, but they would not give their trust to a man whom they did not know. I was thus put in a position which made refusal of the post very difficult. In particular, I was influenced by the fact that, if the Continuation Committee was formed, Mott would certainly be asked to be its chairman, and the advantages of enlisting his tremendous energies in the service of the missionary movement seemed to me so great a gain that I had no choice but to accept the office. [36]

On the final morning of the Conference, when Oldham rose to give announcements, he received an ovation. When the new Continuation

Committee first met, he was appointed secretary "to devote his whole time to the work." Mott was elected Chairman.[37] Of the thirty-five members of the new body, ten represented Great Britain, ten the Continent, ten North America, and one each South Africa, Australasia, Japan, China, and India; the last three were Honda, Cheng, and Chatterji.

For his short closing address on the last evening of the Conference, Mott took a familiar theme from David Livingstone that struck an answering chord in the hearts of most of his hearers, particularly those who had read or been present for his quite different application of it at the close of the 1907 WSCF Conference at Tokyo. "The end of the Conference is the beginning of the conquest. The end of the planning is the beginning of the doing."[38] Unlike Speer, Mott made no effort to be original; his purpose was to focus upon the task ahead the energies generated in those power-packed days on The Mound. Actually, this concept had been emphasized from the beginning of the preparations for Edinburgh; in 1908 the statement of aims and plans had declared that if the Conference were to fulfill the purpose of God, it "must be not an end but a beginning," because "what is to follow" must be of greater concern than "what we do before or during" it.

In the final moments of a gathering that seemed to realize that it had made history, Mott reminded the delegates that in their "oneness in Christ" they had discovered a fellowship that transcended all barriers, and challenged them to translate the facts and arguments they had heard into reality, for him almost a synonym for action: "I make bold to say that the Church has not yet seriously attempted to bring the living Christ to all living men." Reality will require that we not only revise our plans concerning the Kingdom, but the plans for our own lives, going with Christ into the garden. Further, "a sense of urgency should strike into the core of each one of us"—that urgency under which "Christ seemed to live":

> God grant that we all of us may in these next moments solemnly resolve henceforth so to plan and so to act, so to live and so to sacrifice, that our spirit of reality may become contagious among those to whom we go: and it may be that the words of the Archbishop of Canterbury on the threshold of this conference shall prove to be a splendid prophecy, and that before many of us taste death we shall see the Kingdom of God come with power.[39]

Almost threescore years later, Marc Boegner remembered that Mott's words "made his hearers look into their hearts." The Conference sang a hymn, was dismissed with the benediction, and passed into history, the judgment of which is that Mott had been "its most dynamic figure." "A single step," wrote Charles H. Brent, Episcopal Bishop of the Philippines, "has been taken toward a distant goal." Through the next twenty years Brent would guide further steps along one pathway toward the goals of unity, and Mott another, but for forty years. Missions historian R. Pierce Beaver called Edinburgh "the fountainhead of the modern Ecumenical Movement." How Mott helped to channel that stream is the principal theme of the remainder of this book.[40]

PART 4: Launching the Continuation Committee

Mott made "the end of the planning" the literal "beginning of the doing." When he spoke those words on Thursday evening, June 23, the Continuation Committee had already met for organization. Next day it worked almost nine hours under his gavel and on Saturday morning concluded twenty-four agenda items in another three-hour session. An Executive was set up, Eugene Stock and Julius Richter elected vice-presidents, ten committees appointed, the next meeting scheduled for 1911, and a provisional constitution adopted. Edinburgh thus proved its distinction from all such previous gatherings by setting in motion "a committee to perpetuate its ideas and continue its work." If, as a Scottish commentator suggested, the Conference presaged "a new day over all the world," Mott and Oldham were now authorized to usher it in. Yet neither they nor any of their contemporaries could have imagined that their first goal, the International Missionary Council, was still eleven years and a World War away. When Oldham looked back in his old age, he believed that their miniscule international body with its budget and secretariat could have been the first such in the modern world, anticipating proposals for the League of Nations by eight years.[41]

As the two men entered upon their new duties, they consciously or unconsciously began to build an organization that would increasingly resemble the international body that Gustav Warneck had depicted before the London Missionary Conference of 1888. Mott had been acquainted with Warneck since visiting the elder missionary authority in his home in Halle in 1899, and Oldham had subsequently studied under Warneck. It is highly improbable that they did not know of Warneck's plan; in any case the organization of the Continuation Committee, the emergency body that World War I evoked from it, and the International Missionary Council that grew out of these in 1921 were, in Latourette's words, "almost an exact embodiment" of Warneck's plans.[42] Warneck was one of four to whom Mott dedicated the volume of his *Addresses and Papers* on the Council and its forerunners.

Before leaving Great Britain, Mott conferred at great length with Oldham, on whose shoulders rested the immense task of editing and publishing the nine volumes reporting the Conference and of sending its messages to the Protestant churches of the world. Both men took extended vacations, Oldham to the Continent, Mott at Lac des Iles.

Mott dated the preface to *The Decisive Hour of Christian Missions* June 29, the day before sailing for Quebec and a summer with his family. That 250-page "first fruits of the World Missionary Conference" appeared in time to be reviewed in the October issue of *The Student World* by G. A. Johnston-Ross, who saw it as evidence of a new era in missions. A digest of the Commission reports, especially Commission I, it was "so startling, arresting, painstaking, and pain-giving" as to be "at once an education, an inspiration, a challenge, and a judgment." It reviewed the social ferment in Asia and the Near East and prescribed "the requirements for seizing the unique opportunity" of the moment for "a worldwide propagation of Christianity"—the Edinburgh proposals. Exposure of the Church's mismanagement of the missionary enterprise constituted "a rebuke, stern and authoritative." Behind the author stood the authority of the Commission: "'The issues are so great that there can be no trifling in the matter.' This is a new note," concluded Ross, "stern and peremptory; precisely the note that is needed in the Church's present apathy and unbelief and inveterate parochialism."[43]

The New York *Christian Advocate* rightly recognized the book as "the first concise and clarion utterance" of Edinburgh and Mott as its mouthpiece. After devoting half of a long review to Mott's qualifications, it spoke of the book's vivid descriptions (which were enhanced by dramatic photographs) of "the social ferment that is now working in so many of the hitherto unprogressive nations" and selected one sentence from the argument for a united front: the chief obstacle to advance is in the lives of Christians, who "*by their lack of vision, by their lack of wholehearted consecration, by their lack of efficient resolution, by their lack of heroic self-sacrifice, and by their lack of triumphant faith, prevent the complete realization of God's sublime purposes for the world.*"

The *Advocate* also recognized the wider implications of Mott's book and suggested that together with Gairdner's popularization of the Conference, *Echoes of Edinburgh*, it have a place beside Captain Peary's and

Colonel Roosevelt's recent best-sellers as "preeminent among the season's publications." Intended to be a missions study text for the SVM; it appeared under numerous imprints and was translated into German, French, Danish, and Swedish; it exercised a pervasive influence throughout those student movements and upon numerous individual members of that student generation whose dreams would be shattered by the Great War. The force of Mott's argument may be felt in his concluding sentences:

> Christ emphasized that the mightiest apologetic with which to convince the non-Christian world of His divine character and claims would be the oneness of His disciples. Experience has already shown that by far the most hopeful way of hastening the realization of true and triumphant Christian unity is through the enterprise of carrying the Gospel to the non-Christian world. Who can measure the federative and unifying influence of foreign missions? No problem less colossal and less bafflingly difficult will so reveal to the Christians of to-day the sinfulness of their divisions, and so convince them of the necessity of concerted effort, as actually to draw them together in answer to the intercession of their common and divine Lord.
>
> It is a decisive hour for the non-Christian nations. Far-reaching movements—national, racial, social, economic, religious—are shaking them to their foundations. These nations are still plastic. Shall they set in Christian or pagan molds? Their ancient faiths, ethical restraints, and social orders are being weakened or abandoned. Shall our sufficient faith fill the void?
>
> It is a decisive hour for the Christian Church. If it neglects to meet successfully the present world crisis by failing to discharge its responsibility to the whole world, it will lose its power both on the home and on the foreign fields and will be seriously hindered in its mission to the coming generation. Nothing less than the adequacy of Christianity as a world religion is on trial.
>
> It is indeed the decisive hour of Christian missions. It is the time of all times for Christians of every name to unite and with quickened loyalty and with reliance upon the living God, to undertake to make Christ known to all men, and to bring His power to bear upon all nations. It is high time to face this duty and with serious purpose to discharge it. Let leaders and members of the Church reflect on the awful seriousness of the fact that times and opportunities pass. The Church must use them or lose them. The sense of immediacy and the spirit of reality are the need of the hour. Doors open and doors shut again. Time presses. "The living, the living he shall praise Thee." Let each Christian so resolve and so act that if a sufficient number of others will do likewise, all men before this generation passes away may have an adequate opportunity to know of Christ.[44]

Such words, by "a modern apostle of authority and power," were widely pondered by the generation that would soon find itself engulfed in the Great War.[45]

Upon Oldham's return from holiday he wrote Mott a reminder of the more important issues and directions that had been raised in the exploratory meetings of the Committee, commenting that "there is not likely to be any lack of work" and suggesting that their primary task ought to be preparing the agenda for the 1911 meeting of the Committee, which, as it proved, was a major planning session. The relations of missions to governments seemed to be a priority; Oldham would spend some time that autumn establishing rapport with mission board executives, and was open to Mott's earlier suggestion that he visit America. He was thinking of the usefulness of something "in the nature of a news sheet" (which had been highly successful before and during the Conference) and occasional papers. As his thought progressed, he became certain that they ought to publish "a central missionary review, dealing with work all over the world."

In spite of, or perhaps because of, their differences of temperament and outlook, and their vastly different gifts, Mott and Oldham made an exceptional team. Oldham, sensitive to theological nuances and ecclesiastical subtleties, was quick to discern potential hazards in the complex relationships between the Committee and the two hundred or more boards it hoped to develop into its constituency. Mott, equally concerned with the central gospel message, perhaps tended to see individuals as members of groups and to measure their contributions in terms of finances or organizations. It is certain that his fund-raising made possible the Committee's program, but it is equally certain that his access to persons in high places and their enlistment in the enterprise were just as indispensable. Each made every effort to keep fully informed of the other's activities. Oldham proposed sending Mott copies of all his letters, making it clear that he would not "take any action whatever" without Mott's "sanction and approval." Mott suggested that Oldham instruct his secretary to make extra copies for him of "the most important" letters to "Christian leaders and others," erring on the side of sending "more, rather than less." As the fall advanced both men realized the importance of conversation; Oldham, with his wife, came to North America in December, visiting mission boards in Nashville and Toronto as well as New York City. He shared in the full evening report on Edinburgh to the annual meeting of the Foreign Missions Conference of North America.[46] In November Mott met informally with the North American members of the Committee on routine matters such as the date for the full meeting in Britain in 1911 and additional personnel on some of the sub-committees.

PART 5: "An Eirenic Itinerary"

When the Cunarder *Lusitania* sailed from New York for Southampton on her second eastward crossing, January 18, 1911, John and Leila Mott, the J. H. Oldhams, and the peripatetic editor of the American Episcopal journal *The Churchman,* Silas McBee, with his wife, were aboard.

McBee, an early and ardent worker for the Faith and Order Movement, was some dozen years Mott's senior; the two had met at least as early as that interview with President and Mrs. Theodore Roosevelt on the balcony of the White House in 1908 when the President promised Mott the letter to Russian students that Mott used with such telling effect during his trip to Russia in 1909. McBee was a member of both the American Executive and the International Committees of the Edinburgh Conference, but more significantly was Vice-Chairman of Commission VIII on Cooperation and Unity that had proposed the Continuation Committee. He had electrified the conference with a letter that he had obtained from the Roman Catholic Bishop of Cremona, Italy, who, with the tacit approval of the Vatican, had applauded the Conference with its quest for "a common ground of agreement" that could provide "a sound basis for further discussion, tending to promote the union of all believers in Christ." Now a member of the Continuation Committee, McBee was undertaking the trip at Mott's request "and in connection with the WSCF at Constantinople." His Anglican contacts opened Orthodox doors throughout this *Eirenic Itinerary,* as McBee entitled the compilation of articles he sent to his paper. [47]

Three days in London were filled with meetings of the executive bodies of the Continuation Committee and of the WSCF. McBee and Mott conferred with the Archbishop of Canterbury on the work of the Committee and on their tour. McBee described the conversation:

> Archbishop Davidson gave his full and hearty sympathy and approval in both directions. His discussion of the Edinburgh Conference and its Continuation Committee was vigorous and courageous and hopeful. I never felt the elements of essential greatness in the Archbishop so strongly. It was more than advice, more than abstract and general approval. It was a clear outline of constructive policy looking to the steady development of better understanding, better feeling, and better relations between Christian Churches everywhere. [48]

Mott remained at Lambeth to dine and spend the night; he canvassed a wide range of concerns with the Archbishop, including "Brent's plan" and his own growing dilemma of an overburden of work. It appears that Davidson advised him to hold on to the WSCF, the SVM, and the Continuation Committee. McBee and Mott were subsequently received at the Foreign Office by Sir Edward Grey, to whom letters of introduction had been sent by President Taft and Ambassador James Bryce; the Minister "entered into our plans and purposes" for forty minutes, promised introductions, and asked them to call upon him when they returned. McBee dined that evening with Baron von Hügel.

The McBees and Motts went next to Utrecht where the men met with the Dutch delegation to the forthcoming WSCF Conference: "A sturdier body of men in mind and character it would be difficult to find," commented McBee. During a week-end in Berlin, Prince Bernadotte of Sweden paid a call, the men visited Dr. Lepsius, Director of the Orient Mission, Leila Mott had a tooth filled and heard her first opera; McBee obtained a message to the Constantinople Conference from the Emperor, Mott being forced to leave for Switzerland, which rendered a joint audience impossible. Baron Paul Nicolay joined him, while the McBees went to Russia during Mott's three-week evangelistic tour of the universities at Lausanne, Geneva, Neuchâtel, Berne, Basle, and Zurich.

Since the first Swiss conference in 1895, Mott had been especially interested in the universities of that country because of their cosmopolitan nature, more than half of their students being from abroad. Due to "magnificent preparation" he reported that he was able to do as much in three weeks as he might normally accomplish in six; he "averaged four public addresses daily, and one day gave ten," many of them to Bulgarians, Greeks, and Russians—the last interpreted by Micolay. The Greek students sent home the texts of the addresses; when Mott arrived in Greece and in Constantinople there were pressing invitations to speak to the Greek colleges and to the Orthodox Theological Seminary at Halki.[49] The opening assemblies in the Swiss universities usually were in the university aula with the Rector presiding; they were always crowded. It was estimated that "considerably more than half of the student population of the country heard one or two of the messages," which dealt with "the best method of meeting successfully the moral, spiritual, and intellectual problems of students in the modern age." There was some violent opposition awakened where before there had been indifference "concerning religious and moral questions." Henri-Louis Henriod, a student leader, recalled much later that the campaign was illustrative of

Mott's techniques: "It had lasting results for the life of our Movement and its local units; it made a deep impression on a large number of students; it confirmed or inspired vocations to life service in the Christian cause."[50]

A young assistant pastor named Karl Barth wrote a long article about Mott for a student paper:

> Once I had come to realize that Mr. Mott was a spirited American and no professor of theology or philosophy, my interest in him then centred in the man himself. When I tried putting aside the glasses of a typical central European and those of the academic intellectual, I at once discovered that I was dealing with an unusual person, not, as they say in French, with a 'quelconque' but with a 'quelqu'un'. This much was clear to me, the man is unique, not one of the ever-present herd. He knows what he wants, and he wants what he knows. He is what we are always talking and writing books about: a personality. I let the impression of this personality have its effect upon me.
>
> First, Mott sees in the universities the focal point of mankind's spiritual life, which is to say, of life in general. Second, he thinks of every student as a future leader occupying some important post in the direction of men's affairs. Thirdly, he asks of the leader who holds such an important post that he be just, and by that he means inwardly and morally just. And fourthly he demands that the student be a disciple of Jesus, for it is through communion with Jesus that one becomes an inwardly and morally just person. Mankind—the universities—the student—the person—Jesus. That, I would say, is the way Mott thinks. For us this is all theory. We think about the separate links in this process, and we discuss the rightness and appropriateness of their relationship with one another. All well and good. But isn't it refreshing to meet for once a person for whom reflection and discussion have ceased before they ever got started, for whom the entire series is a whole, not just a theory but a process? For that is what it is. That is Mott's personality: something happens. And what happens is not just anything, but at once the ultimate and most important thing that can happen: man is judged by his aim and the aim is Mankind. I hope that among my readers there is no one who is not in some sense interested in or concerned about this fixed goal of Mott.
>
> But what does this mean in our case? It means that what we do is to study one particular part of this series and to work over it. In his essentially personal concern, one of us is *just* a student, another *just* a person, another *just* a Christian. Each of us recognizes to a certain extent that the other parts of the series of concerns are also justified, and some of us even dare, feeling rather dilettante about it, to concern ourselves with one of the other aspects. But basically we remain what we are, and as a punishment we are infected by acute or chronic cases of disease, we become either mere professionals or 'petit-bourgeois' or 'Holy Joes'.
>
> But in John R. Mott, we have for once had among us an essentially

healthy person. John Mott never stops at any one point as we do. His life is, on the contrary, a constant moving back and forth from the first to the last point in the series; he never stops at any one of them. He would bring mankind to Jesus, and by Jesus he is sent back to mankind. In Mott's view, the student is the most important instrument in this process, the chosen carrier and representative of this life process. For this reason Mott himself has become the apostle to and organizer of students. You may find his universalism quite American. I certainly do. I also shrug my shoulders, because I find it impossible to accept this attitude myself. But this process has appeared before us as a fact. When I think of the incurable splintering and sectarianism of our spiritual life, in which I also share, I cannot help saying that this Mott-process impresses me and that it would be a good thing if we had more such 'Americans'.[51]

In Basle and in Geneva, Mott introduced the American Laymen's Missionary Movement to mass meetings. Leila wrote the Postville family that it was her work "to take care of him so far as I can."

When the party was united in Cairo, McBee brought greetings for the WSCF at Constantinople from the Czar and from the King of Italy. At Luxor they visited J. P. Morgan "on his houseboat." Mott gave a series of four "Lectures on Social Subjects" to audiences of at least 2,000 young men in Cairo and studied the need for a city YMCA there. As in 1895, he visited missions at Assiut. He and McBee twice called upon the Patriarch of the Coptic Church, Cyril V, and the Coptic Archbishop of Alexandria, the latter declaring that they had given him "new ideas and new hopes." They spoke at the Coptic theological school, where both student body and faculty "gave the closest attention, questioning us keenly." They also attended Coptic and Arabic services, saw some ancient Coptic churches, visited United Presbyterian missions and an agricultural college, and were entertained in the home of W. H. T. Gairdner who had opened many doors for them.[52]

In Palestine, Mott spoke at Jaffa and at Jersualem where there were present in his audience Latins, Greeks, Protestants, Armenians, and even Moslems. On behalf of the Continuation Committee, he and McBee called on the Greek Orthodox Patriarch Damianos, presenting His Beatitude with a set of the nine Edinburgh volumes and receiving a handsome portfolio of the wildflowers of Palestine. The Patriarch returned their call and stayed more than an hour to discuss cooperation and unity. The Anglican Bishop Blyth gave them letters to the Orthodox Metropolitan of Beirut and the Patriarch of Antioch in Damascus.

Late one night, Mott went to the Mount of Olives to meditate, in spite of the cold. The next summer he shared his feelings of that and later moments informally with a student group at Northfield:

As I stood under those olive trees, there came to my mind thoughts of Another who had stood there. And then as I threaded my way across Samaria and the carpet decked fields of Galilee, and then as on a memorable Sunday afternoon I went with some friends to the little hill back of Nazareth, those words kept ringing in my ears: "Rising in the morning a great while before it was day, he went apart to pray." "Going into the mountain, he continued all night in prayer unto God." "He was alone praying." . . . And as I thought of these sayings I said to myself, "If these olive trees and hills and shores and deserts could tell all they know, they would tell of a prayer life characterized by constancy, by intensity, by reality, and by irresistible power."[53]

Unlike the Motts' experience of 1895, only part of the journey to Nazareth necessitated riding horseback; an all-day tain trip through Galilee in the full bloom of spring brought them to Damascus, thence to Beirut via Baalbek through walls of snow "much higher than the train."

Mott's week at the Syrian Protestant College, later the American University, at Beirut, was devoted chiefly to an evangelistic campaign directed toward the 650 students whose varied religious backgrounds were the most cosmopolitan he had ever encountered—Moslems, Jews, Druses, Bahais, Protestants, Orthodox Greeks, Greek Catholics, Gregorians, Armenian Protestants, Maronites, Roman Catholics, Copts, Syriac Christians, and Syrian Catholics. Philip Hitti, a student who was later to pioneer Near Eastern Studies at Princeton University, recalled that Mott came as a refreshing breeze in contrast to the stuffiness of most missionaries.

In a report letter, Mott described a day that was unusual, even for him:

> On the way from Beirut to Athens, we spent twenty-four hours in Alexandria. A great deal was crowded into that short time. The Alhambra Theater, largest in the city, was filled to overflowing with over 1,500 students, professors, and graduates of the Greek, Coptic, Catholic, Armenian, Protestant, and government schools, including hundreds of Moslems. Many could not gain entrance. In every particular it was like the meetings in Cairo.
>
> After giving one full address, the whole audience remained for me to deliver a second. I spoke also in the American Boys' School, in the leading Coptic college at the request of the Archbishop of Alexandria, and in the principal Greek college at the request of the Greek Patriarch. In addition to these various meetings, there were interviews with the missionaries as well as with the Patriarch of the Greek Church; and a wonderful hour was spent with Abbas Effendi, head of the interesting and growing Bahai Movement, which now claims over 2,000,000 adherents in Persia, the Turkish Empire, India, and Western lands.[54]

In Athens, Mott spent four days in visits and interviews concerning higher education, students and student organizations, and the student life of the University of Athens, talking with a variety of authorities from the minister of ecclesiastical affairs and of education to the "private priest of the royal family." En route to Constantinople his ship called at Smyrna, where he talked with both Archbishop Chrysostom, the Orthodox Metropolitan, and with the Armenian bishop; the former sent out runners and "brought together a meeting of 500 of the most influential Greeks in the district."[55]

PART 6: The WSCF at Constantinople, 1911

Mott's first journey around the world in 1895–97 had taken him far beyond the bounds of the YMCA's evangelical test of membership. This trip of 1911 was a prime ecumenical venture outside the limits of Anglo-American Protestantism. "Few indeed were the Patriarchs of any ancient Eastern church that he did not visit; with several of them he formed personal friendships," wrote Miss Rouse, who was at Constantinople. That this Federation Conference was a venture of faith was obvious from the fragile Christian base in Turkey, from the fact that there was only one facility in which it could be held, and that there was no continuing organization to follow it up. The plan seemed audacious: as recently as three years earlier it would have been impossible, yet when it was over Mott could write that "the convening of a world Christian congress within the gates of what some regard as the greatest citadel of the Mohammedan world bears witness to one of the most wonderful changes of modern times." As much as Tokyo 1907, Constantinople 1911 was an experiment.

Mott and his party arrived two weeks before the opening day. The times were not propitious: the Turkish revolution was only three years old, war was threatening with the Balkan States, there was a serious epidemic of cholera, the missionaries upon whom the burden of preparation and entertainment fell were hardly enthusiastic, and even the weather was gloomy—yet Mott insisted that it was "now or never" and the Oxford decision of 1909 held when the General Committee gathered. McBee noted that "with the aid of Robert College and friends in Constantinople" the Conference came off "as if Constantinople were designed for it," a result made possible largely by "the direct and indirect influence of the Orthodox Churches of the East and the Roman Church in Italy and the Levant." McBee had contributed significantly to this by visiting four Italian cardinals, the Exarch of Bulgaria, and the Patriarch of Constantinople while Mott was in Switzerland, and subsequently the Patriarch of Antioch, the Latin Archbishop of Beirut, and the Orthodox Metropolitan of that city.

Mott's audience with the Ecumenical Patriarch, Joachim III, was warm and friendly. "Your work is apostolic," His Beatitude said to Mott: "It will have the blessing of God, and I shall follow it always with prayer." Much credit for the local acceptance of the Conference must be given to Miss Rouse, who, a few months earlier, from a base at the American School for Girls, the sister institution to Robert College and co-sponsor of the Conference, had learned from the American professors and the students much concerning "the religious and racial groups represented" at the two schools—Greek, Armenian, Bulgarian, and Turk; Orthodox, Gregorian, and Moslem. She was received by the Ecumenical Patriarch and his "opposite number," the Armenian Patriarch; "to the profound astonishment of everyone" she received permission to address the latter's girls' schools. "Introductions from the Archbishop of Canterbury," she continued, "complete with official seals," worked wonders. Early in 1911, accompanied by Suzanne Bidgrain of France, she had visited Serbia and Roumania, "regions as unknown to us as Central Africa," where they found students, professors, and ecclesiastics "willing to come to Constantinople to see what this strange thing might be." Some of them learned of the Federation only "a week or so before it convened." Fries visited the Armenian theological seminary at Izmid, where he spoke to the students and was royally entertained.

The General Committee met on the island of Prinkipo several days before the Conference. "It was there," wrote Tissington Tatlow, secretary of the British SCM and subsequently its historian, "that we had an opportunity of supporting Mott and Baron Nicolay of Russia in an effort to make the Federation representative of Catholics, Orthodox, and Protestants." The question was the basis of membership; although Protestant in origin, the Federation had never shut its door to non-Protestants. Mott's trips to Russia, his Anglican contacts, the miniscule but persistent Catholic student groups in southern Europe and South America, and now his Orthodox explorations, "had stirred in him the desire for a wider fellowship than a Protestant student federation," thought Tatlow, but one must agree with Miss Rouse that this had always been his dream.[56] Edinburgh had now broadened his thrust.

At Prinkipo the Federation Committee agreed upon a new basis of membership and urged such of its constituent bodies "as may be affected by this resolution to consider the possibility of making their basis conform to this principle":

> The General Committee puts on record its opinion that no student, to whatever branch of the Christian Church he may belong, should be excluded from full membership in any National Movement within the Federation if he is prepared to accept the basis of the Federation, or whatever equivalent is approved by the Federation.

This resolution, the delayed fruit of Tokyo 1907 and Oxford 1909, and the "epochal" number of "long-haired and long bearded ecclesiastics" of the Eastern Churches who sat in the front row as the Conference met, made the gathering "a milestone in the history of the whole Church," declared Miss Rouse, who later edited an official *History of the Ecumenical Movement* together with Bishop Stephen C. Neill. A glance at the Constantinople Conference photo, she noted, "shows a picturesque variety of ecclesiastical costume, headgear and coiffure, such as was scarcely seen again until the Oxford and Edinburgh Conferences in 1937." Mott saw the Conference as "a splendid illustration of the real communion of Christian believers":

> There sat together in common counsel and fellowship day after day members of the Greek Orthodox, Syrian, Armenian, Coptic, Protestant, and Roman Catholic communions. A representative of the Armenian Patriarchate sat by the side of the representative of the Ecumenical (Greek) Patriarchate, and the President of the Greek Orthodox Theological Seminary, a leader of the Coptic Church and a Maronite Catholic from Syria were among the speakers.[57]

Robert College, the host to the Conference, had been established by American Protestants forty years earlier on a superb site a few miles north of the city.[58] Mott had been fascinated by it in 1895. Now, its proximity to the fifteenth-century battlements of Rumeli Hisar, its dramatic overview of the traffic on the Bosporus, and the presence of Asia immediately across the majestic strait, seemed to justify his selection of the site and to reinforce his opening words: "We meet," he declared, "to make attractive, compelling, visible, the fact of the World's Student Christian Federation. We cannot make this great ideal real in any way save by bringing delegates together from all the world." This Conference, even more than any of its predecessors, "will accentuate our oneness in Jesus Christ." It will summon the Christian students of the world to face an absolutely unique world situation. We meet at a plastic moment, in the danger zone of Europe, at a time of urgency. God will summon us here "to make His Kingdom co-extensive with the inhabited world."

Not only were the 200 delegates from thirty-three countries impressed by the messages McBee brought from the crowned heads of Europe, but also by Mott's letter from President Taft. Yet the most significant endorsement was that of the Ecumenical Patriarch, Joachim III, who had assured the delegation that waited upon him that he would help "in any way in my power" because he considered "such a conference to draw Christians into fellowship and cooperation as one of the most sacred causes."[59] There were ten Orthodox fraternal delegates and several times that many representatives of the eastern European countries and churches. A week before the Conference opened, Mott had spoken at the Orthodox Theological Seminary on the island of Halki; its President, the Reverend Archimandrite Germanos Strenopoulos, soon to be Ecumenical Patriarch and much later one of the first Presidents of the World Council of Churches, came.[60]

There were thirty delegates from "Asia Minor," a dozen from Turkey, eight from Bulgaria including a representative of the Exarch, seven from Syria, six from Hungary including Janos Victor, three from Egypt, one from Roumania, and eight from Russia in addition to Baron Nicolay, Alexandra Dobroliubov, and Alexander Nikitin; a dozen with non-Western names represented Robert College itself. There were three Chinese, three Finns, sixteen Germans, two Greeks, two Indians, two Japanese, a Mexican, nine from South Africa including G. B. A. Gerdener and Oswin Bull, and from New Zealand Constance Grant, Leila Mott's riding partner of 1896.

It had been planned that the Anglo-Americans would be distinctly in the minority. This produced the expected ecumenical impact upon the entire Protestant contingent, some of whom at first resisted broadening the basis of membership. As Mott commented in his report letter, the Conference "accentuated the essential oneness" of all true Christians "far more" than had Edinburgh. "Even more remarkable than its international aspect was its ecumenical character." The program was designed to stimulate theological and ethical discussion across denominational lines. It opened with a series of "apologetic lectures by distinguished European and American professors," notably Edward I. Bosworth, D. S. Cairns, M. E. Sadler, Erich Schaeder, J. N. Farquhar, and Nathan Söderblom. Presentations followed on "the application of Christ's teachings to modern life," by Burgoyne Chapman of Australia, President Howard S. Bliss of Beirut, the co-hostess President Mary M. Patrick of the American College for Girls, C. F. Andrews of India, and Silas McBee. The purposes of the Movement were discussed by a group of Western leaders: Rutgers of Holland, Wilder, Tatlow, Henry B. Wright, E. C. Carter, Raoul Allier of France, and Henry T. Hodgkin. The Orientals spoke on the "opportunities before the Student Movement" in Japan, China, and India; Nicolay, who had brought several delegates from the Balkans as well as his Russian contingent, described the situation in Russia.[61] Philip Hitti, a Maronite, depicted the characteristics of Syrian students,[62] and Charles J. Ewald summarized the needs of South America. Devotionals on the theme "The Realization of Jesus Christ" were led by the Orthodox K. C. Chacko of India, Gerdener of South Africa, the Anglican E. S. Woods, and the Chairman, Karl Fries, a Swedish Lutheran. The only platform addresses other than brief reports by Orthodox speakers were those by Chako and Nicolay, who also gave the devotional at the opening session. Through all these there ran the persistent Federation themes: the morning watch, prayer and Bible study, Christian fellowship and unity, the application of Christ's teachings to modern life, and missions.

The function of the WSCF as an ecumenical training ground was apparent in the effect of Constantinople on both mature and younger leaders who would play key roles in the movements leading to the World Council of Churches, notably Nathan Söderblom, for whom the Conference was "an earnest of things to come." He spent three weeks on the trip, visiting Orthodox patriarchs, bishops, and other leaders such as Germanos, as well as McBee, Woods, Hodgkin, Cheng-ting Wang, and Cairns. Söderblom concluded that "the history of Christianity is not at an end on earth; it has just begun."[63] Raoul Allier of the Sorbonne, President of the French SCM, was convinced "that no distinctively Protestant movement could or should be established in Orthodox lands"; he subsequently worked for the Federation in Greece and Roumania. Constantinople was a first WSCF for Pierre Maury, who later traveled in the Balkans also;[64] he would become its general secretary. Tatlow and Walter Seton were also granted an audience with the Ecumenical Patriarch, who approved fully of the request by the Western visitors that Eastern men join them "in working for the extension of Christ's kingdom."[65]

Constantinople was thus the opening of the WSCF in a more self-conscious manner than ever before as "an experimental laboratory of ecumenism." In retrospect Mott saw that feature as its unique characteristic: "not since the early Councils of the Christian Church—held in the part of the world where we met this year—has there been an assembly of Christians so representative of the entire Church." Others noted that the Federation's aims had been more productive of unity than the Councils of antiquity.

As at Tokyo in 1907, supplemental meetings, conducted in French, Greek, Turkish, and Armenian, were held in six parts of the city; some attracted as many as 10,000 persons. Mott gave several addresses: "never have I had more respectful or sympathetic attention." Two YMCA men, D. A. Davis and E. O. Jacob, had been sent to Constantinople not long before the Conference; they not only prepared for it, but later, joined by two YWCA workers, set up what proved to be a short-lived student Movement in the Turkish Empire. On the way home, ten deputations including Mott, Miss Rouse, and Baron Nicolay laid foundations for national movements in Greece, Serbia, Bulgaria, and Roumania. Those in the Balkans were most effectively developed by French-speaking workers such as Allier, Charles Grauss, and Henri Johannot of the Swiss Movement who, with Sherwood Eddy and Robert Wilder, "commanded great attention for their apologetic and evangelistic addresses." Some of these groups survived World War I.

McBee thought that Mott's closing speech, "a prophetic interpretation of the mission of the Federation," was easily "the most constructive and comprehensive statement" he had heard from the General Secretary; it could not have been made before Edinburgh or until the recent "rich experiences" of meeting Orthodox ecclesiastics. Mott reviewed "the processes by which a larger unity may be realized, and thus how we may hasten the answer of the prayer of our Lord that we all may be one":

> We shall hasten the realization of our Lord's desire and prayer that we may all be one by keeping before us our colossal task. Just as war fuses together a great and complex nation, even its different and conflicting political parties, so a true and vivid conception of the vastness and difficulty of the undertaking of world conquest for Christ will serve to draw His followers together. It is well that we recall that Christ has commanded us to give all men now living an adequate opportunity to know of Him. He has called us to Christianize the races and nations in every department of their life. He has summoned us to the reconstruction of the non-Christian world. It is His wish that the impact of the so-called Christian nations upon the non-Christian world be Christianized. He looks in a special sense to the universities which we represent to furnish the leadership for these truly great undertakings. This means that He looks to them for the guidance and directive energy to ensure concerted effort among His followers, for the rank and file of the Christians will continue to follow their leaders. Who can measure the unifying influence of the Watchword of the Student Volunteer Movement, "The Evangelization of the World in this Genera-

tion"? This Movement views the whole fact of Christianity in relation to the whole fact of the non-Christian world. The larger looms the task to be accomplished, the more imperative grows the demand that there must be unity in order to achieve the end. [66]

Mott's share in the post-Conference deputations was to visit the Universities of Belgrade and Sofia, accompanied by Miss Rouse and Baron Nicolay. The one Serbian delegate to Constantinople, Professor Lecco, secured the Belgrade University Hall for three apologetic lectures under the chairmanship of the Rector. Each meeting was "crowded to suffocation." The first two were disturbed by Social Democratic demonstrators, but there was no violence. The third night, wrote Miss Rouse, an eye-witness,

> when Dr. Mott was nearing the close of his witness to Christ, a battle royal broke out. Those who wished to hear and those who did not, hammered each other with chairs and anything else which came handy. The Rector and professors were helpless. Only after some bloodshed was Dr. Mott able to say a concluding word; he got safely out, with nothing worse than a little jostling. [67]

The results were "amazing and welcome." The event was proclaimed as the most exciting since the assassination of King Alexander eight years before! Students "flocked" to Mott for personal interviews and the press published all three lectures verbatim. This sole known instance of violence that threatened Mott's safety, exaggerated in the growing Mott mythology, provided a spectacular beginning for the Serbian SCM which would survive the Great War. Mott also spoke to the national Orthodox theological seminary in Belgrade.

In Sofia his meetings were less tempestuous but equally crowded and followed by many interviews. He conferred with the Orthodox Metropolitan Stefan, addressed the Bulgarian Orthodox seminary, and was asked to meet with its faculty. On the last day of his visit,

> Her Majesty, the Queen, sent for Baron Nicolay, Professor Panaretoff of Robert College, who had come to Sofia to serve as my interpreter, and myself. During the audience, which lasted some thirty minutes, she evinced most lively interest in the work which we had accomplished, and assured us of her desire to cooperate in every way in her power. She responded especially to my suggestions about the promotion of Bible study and the provision of student hostels. [68]

While their train lay over in Budapest the next day, Mott and Fries spoke at a banquet prepared by Janos Victor and a group of students.

The next stop was Vienna, to attend a meeting of the Executive of the World's Alliance of YMCA's and hopefully to fulfill a dream held since 1895, to organize an SCM in "that race whirlpool of Europe, the former Austro-Hungarian Empire." Miss Rouse, who participated, remembered that

> after endless negotiations, a curious federation of three movements within the Empire was formed, a German, a Czech, and a Polish Movement; while at the conference, Hungarian, Serbian and Bulgarian delegates watched suspiciously lest their interests should somehow be imperilled by what was proposed. So great was the racial and political difficulty that, incredible as it may seem, it was actually proposed that the official language of the loose combination should be English! A few months later that combination was blown sky-high by the first guns of the Great War.[69]

The Constantinople Conference not only changed and enlarged the Federation map, but created a new era of ecumenism. When Tatlow returned home to Britain, he found that well-informed ecclesiastics were "astonished with a great astonishment" at Mott's openings in "the Coptic, Armenian, Greek Orthodox and Bulgarian and Servian Churches."[70]

While Mott languished through a "drowsy session" of the World's Committee in Vienna on May 10, he wrote Leila that word had just come that King George of England would receive him and McBee on the fourteenth. They rushed to London.[71]

PART 7: Charting the Course of the Continuation Committee

The two presented themselves at Buckingham Palace shortly before noon. In a rare surviving letter to his wife, who was resting at Bad Nauheim, Mott described the audience, which lasted "a full half hour":

> Ambassador Reid accompanied us and introduced us. I was favorably impressed by His Majesty. He was direct, cordial, simple, democratic, earnest, vivacious. He drew us out first of all on our recent journeys. McBee gave an outline of the trip up to Constantinople, then I chimed in and described the Conference—its personnel, its character, its influence. I explained the large part that the British Empire has in the Federation. We talked a great deal on the unifying work and influence of the Federation among nations and churches. We dwelt on the problem of Xn unity. He deplored the number of denominations in England. He inquired about our attitude toward other religions. He spoke of his conversation with Dr. Jowett before his departure to America. Some of the conversation was political with Ambassador Reid. He endorsed strongly all that I said about

the importance of the student work. All in all it was a most satisfactory experience—one that I shall never regret.

I obtained some Buckingham Palace paper with monograms while there and wrote both Irene and John on it.

How happy I shall be to have you back in my arms again! May you have good restful, health-giving days this week!

With all my heart,
Your own
John[72]

Mott, McBee, and Oldham, who had come to London for lengthy discussion with Mott, now moved to the north of England, where the Continuation Committee convened at Auckland Castle May 16–19 as the guests of the Bishop of Durham, Handley C. G. Moule. The thirteenth-century castle and Durham Cathedral, thought McBee, were "at once a tower of strength and a virile admonition to the Committee. There was no room for small conceptions or petty work at this bulwark of the Northumbrian dioceses."

Throughout the more than three months Mott had been on the Continent and in the Levant, he and Oldham had threshed out an agenda and clarified most problems by telegram and a surprising correspondence, in view of Mott's constant movements. In four days Mott moved the Committee through eighty-eight items of business at sixteen sessions, punctuated by matins and evensong in the Castle Chapel and overseen by the "generous kindness and hospitality of the Bishop and Mrs. Moule."[73] Most of the members of the Committee were present, but Bishop Honda of Japan was ill, and Cheng Ching-yi of China, the Bishop of Gippsland, Australia, and Professor Marais of South Africa could not afford the time demanded by the trip, thereby reducing the Committee to a Western entity.

The Committee adopted a constitution, shuffled its subcommittees, accepted a budget, initiated the *International Review of Missions* under Oldham's editorship, and voted to meet in North America the next year. For this narrative, its most significant action was to ask Mott to consider whether he could "arrange to devote a considerable portion of his time" to it in visiting the missionary field, acquainting missionaries and native leaders with its work and plans, "studying how missionary bodies on the field and this Committee may be brought into the most mutually helpful relations, and assisting the work of the Special Committees in such other ways as may be determined by the Executive acting in consultation with them." The resolution was "carried with unanimity." Mott replied that the request "involved great and difficult readjustments in his work" and asked for earnest prayer for divine guidance; he "did not feel free to give any definite reply until he had the clear leading of God."[74] That leading was not long in coming; he had not been around the world for a decade: as requests began to come from the Orient during that quiet summer of rest, meditation, and prayer in the Canadian woods, it became clear that he should make the trip.

Before leaving England, Mott and McBee saw the Bishop of Winchester, Neville Talbot, who had been prevented from attending the meetings at Auckland Castle; Mott expected Talbot's advice to be helpful in his "final thinking" on the Committee's request. Mott had "over two hours alone" with the Archbishop of Canterbury, carefully reviewing the Committee's decisions. He and McBee reported to Sir Edward Grey on the Constantinople Conference and gave their impressions of the situations in Egypt, Turkey, and the Balkans. Four months after leaving New York, the Motts, McBees, Richard Morse, Dr. A. J. Brown of the Presbyterian Board, and Bishop Lambuth of the Southern Methodist Church, sailed for home on the *Caronia;* Mott wrote Oldham the first day out that it seemed "good indeed" to be on the ocean "with the prospect of a thorough rest." "Let us keep in closest touch with one another," he added, "through correspondence and intercession."

Two weeks after his return, Mott went to Princeton to receive an honorary degree that had been offered in 1910 by President Woodrow Wilson. Both men had been disappointed when it had to be postponed on account of Mott's being in Edinburgh. During the year, his friend Wilson had become Governor of New Jersey; Mott refused to be considered for the Princeton presidency.[75] When Wilson heard of it he declared, "Mr. Mott can't afford to take the presidency of a great university; Mr. Mott occupies a certain spiritual presidency in the spiritual university of the world." The citation accompanying the Princeton LL.D. has been cited by some as alleged evidence of the expansionist nature of the missionary movement:

> John R. Mott, honored by academic and religious bodies for his services in planning and extending the active Christian work of university students; devisor of national and international agencies for this work, particularly the World's Student Christian Federation; presiding leader in the World's Missionary Movement in Edinburgh in 1910; a traveler over four continents in search of room for work; a man of buoyant energy, deep consecration, astonishing success; a new Crusader bent on the Christian conquest of the world.[76]

Mott's response, couched in terms of "The Larger Princeton," would have pleased Wilson and possibly the expansionists, but it was less crass than such utterances are generally thought to have been.[77] Only a few days before, he said, Sir Edward Grey had spoken to him of the unique and grave opportunities for great religious and humanitarian enterprises that America might embrace without the opprobrium of ulterior political motive. "The larger Princeton lies far beyond this place" in education, diplomacy, medicine, leadership of the Church, in Christianizing national life as exemplified in "Princeton-in-Peking" and in the worldwide student movement—the last perhaps the University's greatest outreach.[78]

When news of the Continuation Committee's request to Mott began to penetrate SCM circles in Britain, Tatlow and other student leaders became concerned lest it be undertaken to the detriment of the WSCF. In a nine-page letter to Mott a few weeks after the Auckland Castle meeting, Tatlow described a conference at which the subject had come up; he had also talked with Oldham, who had "practically not thought of the matter at all from the point of view of the Federation." The assumption of the Committee appeared to have been that whatever Mott did for it would be at the expense of his efforts for the American YMCA. But, said Tatlow, Oldham is "a man of one idea," which at present is the Continuation Committee. He will "continue to manipulate things so as to get you to do a maximum of work for the Committee." Tatlow warned Mott that the Committee would inevitably become "an octopus"—in fact, it already had. Casual work won't be very helpful to it. He went on to remind Mott of the great needs of the Federation: Has not God called you to its work? You are needed in the next few years for a great deal of work on the continent of Europe, where you can accomplish much more than in non-Christian lands. I would like to enter a strong plea that you give some time before long to the strongest movements—Germany, Scandinavia, Ireland (which you have never visited), the provincial universities of England ("much harder nuts to crack than Oxford or Cambridge").[79] We do not have Mott's reply, but we do know that he was considering reducing his American load; his program of the next two years showed the effect of Tatlow's argument. And a year after that, all of his plans would be revised.

The first issue of the *International Review of Missions* appeared in January, 1912. It at once took its place as "the outstanding supraconfessional international journal in the field of missions." In it Mott set forth his concept of the Continuation Committee, reminding his readers that it had been established at Edinburgh by a unanimous vote that expressed a "thrilling sense of oneness of desire and purpose." Its aim was to "carry forward" the activities and "perpetuate the spirit" of Edinburgh, and to deal "more deliberately and systematically" with the great problems of missions, furthering the work of the several commissions "with a view to building up a science of missions on which statesmanlike policies may be based." It would serve as a clearing house, foster closer cooperation among agencies, and try to preserve the vision and to spread the spirit and atmosphere of the World Missionary Conference.

He described the functions of each of the new subcommittees, one of the most important of which was that on cooperation and unity; he announced that he would start "within a year on an extended and unhurried visit in an honorary capacity to the principal mission fields throughout Asia," while at the same time continuing "to discharge his duties" to the WSCF and the other movements to which he was related. He made it clear that the Continuation Committee was "not an end in itself," not a new missionary society, but "the servant of all." It had no ecclesiastical status or charter or authority to represent churches or missionary organizations, but would be "purely consultative and advisory." Citing several Edinburgh speakers, he emphasized that the Committee would strive toward unity in spirit and asked for the prayers of sincere Christians everywhere for "fresh stores of spiritual forces for the evangelization of the world."[80]

By the time of the second meeting of the Committee in September, 1912, its status and role were fairly well established. The fifteen-month interval since May, 1911, had tested the patience and resourcefulness of both chairman and secretary. Mott and Oldham had exchanged well over a hundred letters, many of them lengthy, and had conferred several times; they had learned that they could handle the most delicate issues, even their own personal disagreements, in utter frankness and trust. I have the growing conviction, wrote Mott from the Canadian woods, that "if we see eye to eye and heart to heart we shall be able by His good grace to render much larger and much needed service to His Kingdom." When Oldham sounded a similar note, Mott closed a long letter "Thanking God for a friendship which enables me to write as freely as I have done in this letter, without feeling that you will misunderstand." The smoothness with which eighty-six agenda items were dispatched during the Committee's five days at Lake Mohonk, New York, attested not only Mott's skill as a presiding officer but the unanimity made possible by careful planning and prior discussion.

At that fall meeting, the Committee faced frankly the diminution of enthusiasm for a permanent international body, partly because of the worsening international situation, and agreed to drop such plans, voting instead to increase its membership slightly. The vexing issue of the relations of missions and governments was referred to national organizations, but a strongly-worded letter was sent to the Ambassador of Japan in Washington protesting the imprisonment of Korean Christians—of whom the Honorable T. H. Yun who had represented his country at Edinburgh was perhaps the most prominent—for "alleged plotting against the Japanese Government." Letters were also sent to missionaries in Korea and the Committee engaged in a special prayer for the new Emperor of Japan, for the missionaries, and for the Korean Christians.

The major item of the Mohonk agenda was Mott's forthcoming tour for the Committee, the extensive plans for which were reviewed, suggestions made, and the Chairman assured not only of "the entire and hearty cooperation of the whole Committee in the arduous work which he is undertaking" but also its purpose "to support him in it by our intercession."[81] Before we trace that journey, which began in early October, 1912, we must notice certain of Mott's activities at home and in Europe after his return from Constantinople in the late spring of 1911.

PART 8: In Response to Tatlow's Challenge, 1912

It had been planned at Constantinople that Mott would visit the Dutch universities soon. In the fall of 1911, Tom Barker, secretary of the newly-formed Irish SCM, urged Tatlow to obtain Mott for a fortnight in Ireland "at the earliest possible date." Barker's reasons would appeal to Mott. These two assignments, interspersed with a dozen varied chores, took Mott to Britain and the Continent for almost three crowded but productive months from late January to early April, 1912.

On shipboard he prepared a five-page, single-spaced outline of his plans, messages, requirements, and schedule for the Irish staff and students to follow up while he was on the Continent. In London he met with Oldham, spoke in Queen's Hall to the annual meeting of the SCM, addressed a meeting of Wesleyan pastors, sat with the Continuation Committee's British members, and spent one evening with the Archbishop of Canterbury and another with the Bishop of Winchester at Farnham Castle where the Archbishop of York was also a guest.

In Holland he was teamed with Robert Wilder, spending a week each in Leiden and Delft. He spoke without an interpreter to audiences of 700 to 800 students, opening at Delft with a masterly use of Dutch illustrations beginning with reference to Hugo Grotius who had worked for peace through international law at that very place three centuries before. Other addresses dealt with "The Influence of Students in the Modern World," "Religion a Matter of the Will," and "Student Temptations." The numbers of inquirers reduced individual interviews to ten minutes. A student named Hendrik Kraemer, who became a missions authority, later recalled that Mott had widened his conception of that field:

> This stimulating influence he then had also on the plans of a small group of students to which I belonged, intending toward a more vigorous evangelistic approach in the student world. It struck me then that Dr. Mott always listened very intently, immediately seized the point of difficulty, and gave encouraging, illuminating advice on how to overcome the difficulties. Dr. Mott has meant to me personally a stimulating eye-opener.[82]

Mott also met with Chinese students from the Dutch Indies, gathered a group of South African students, and entertained fourteen Moslem princes from Java to urge on them "The importance of their studying Jesus Christ and His teachings."

"You can imagine my surprise," he wrote his sister Alice, "when one day there came to see me the Aide de Camp of the Queen," bidding him to an audience. He took full notes, including the protocol:

> I bowed to the Queen [Wilhelmina] and then to the Prince Consort as I entered. The Queen came forward and shook hands. Then the Prince Consort. They had me sit near and right opposite her, with the Prince the same distance to her right. After ½ hour the Prince had to go. Shook hands twice as he said good-bye and expressed his pleasure. The Queen bade me sit again and remain ¾ hour longer. At end she rose and thanked me and shook hands. JRM retired backwards. Queen bowed three different times as I went.

The wide-ranging conversation revealed the Queen's deep religious interests. She inquired about the current campaign, the Federation and his travel and whether he had visited the Dutch Indies, and his chairmanship of Edinburgh and of the Continuation Committee. She commented on the great need for missionaries and twice emphasized the need for unity. In response to her questions, Mott spoke of the interconfessional nature of the Federation, the Oriental students in Holland, England, and the United States, and "the great future" of the Dutch SCM, especially if it could have buildings for its activities. Three times the

Queen commented that his work must be "very interesting." Mott asked for the privilege of sending his latest book and inquired about Her Royal Highness, the Princess, which pleased the Queen. [83]

At The Hague he conferred at length with members of "two International Committees to grapple with the problems related to the [membership] basis of the student movements of the world and to plan the Congress of the WSCF, to be held in June, 1913." His schedule in Holland ended with meetings of missionary society leaders and laymen. These were followed by two days in Paris at Marc Boegner's request, seeing students and mission executives. The unexpected death of Alfred Boegner, Director of the Paris Société des Missions Évangéliques, a "Protestant saint" for whom Mott had held the greatest respect and affection, evoked a tribute that at once tightened the bond between Mott and the younger Boegner "more than ever," and which the latter recalled forty years afterward. [84]

En route to Ireland there was a full day with Oldham in London. Mott found not only an enthusiastic welcome in Belfast, but his host's reasons for inviting him were most congenial to his own ways of thinking. Met at the station by hundreds of cheering students, he was lifted on their shoulders and borne through a surging crowd to a carriage. Then the horses were taken off and the students pulled the vehicle to their Union where they welcomed him on the steps. Imagine Mott in top hat and morning suit:

> My heart is deeply touched and inspired. It is difficult if not impossible to express my emotions: I can best express my appreciation by saying that I feel at home. I come among you as a stranger but I assure you Ireland is not a stranger to me. At various times I have met many Irish students; my life of travel has acquainted me with the larger Ireland in the States, Canada, Australia, and South Africa. Then there is the still greater Ireland, the Ireland of ideas, ideals, tradition, scholarship, religion. No land in northern or western Europe has a more profoundly and helpfully influential spirit. I find myself in deepest sympathy and most heartily responsive to the spirit of the Irish nation. I am therefore deeply grateful for the privilege of coming among you. [85]

The American flag was then hoisted over the building and remained throughout Mott's stay. Barker, himself a Dublin man, was delighted. He had hoped that Mott would help students "to realize in a vivid way what is going on in the other parts of the Federation" and win them to face Irish questions—especially Home Rule—"with a definitely Christian outlook" that would supplant a narrow conception of the Kingdom of God limited to an attitude of "to hell with the Pope." There is a tremendous need of more "moral backbone" in the Irish colleges, Barker had written to Tatlow, adding that Irish Protestantism suffered tremendously from "provinciality of outlook."

After the mission, Barker wrote with great enthusiasm that 1,000 persons had heard Mott daily for three days; most had stayed each time for his second word "to those who are specially interested." The missionary meeting recruited at least ten men, and Mott's final coaching session for the workers summed up "a time of most direct and unmistakable answer to prayer" during which "the trend of public opinion in the university has been absolutely whirled into line with the ideals of Jesus of Nazareth." Catholics came in increasing numbers not only to the meetings but for private interviews. [86]

"In ways different but quite as genuine I was welcomed into the life of the university at Dublin," Mott wrote cryptically of his second week in Ireland, presumably from Trinity College, but said little more. Richard Pelly, another SCM secretary, told Tatlow in the midst of the campaign that audiences had averaged about 400. The second lecture dealt with the psychology of temptation; Mott led up to "a climax in his last suggestion—'associate with the Living Christ'—each word emphasized. With that sentence he ended and though it was the only religious thing he said all evening, the effect was electric." Later meetings were small and Pelly confessed to be a "little disappointed" because the place had not "really been gripped in any thorough way yet and 'the father of all Whales' (the staff enjoyed their digs at Mott) is I think a little tired. There is extraordinarily little fervor or reckless zeal dear to my . . . soul and the prayer meetings seem to be felt to be a burden and are very badly attended." Yet it was interesting to this Bible study secretary that Mott's appeal seemed to be "entirely to the moral nature and there is no theology in it. I must say I think the lack of something corresponding to Torrey's Bible Readings is a weakness."[87]

Mott's last Sunday in Ireland chanced to be St. Patrick's Day; he improved it with "a conference with selected leaders, students and professors from all the leading colleges" to plan an aggressive program for the Irish SCM, the potential of which Mott, sharing Barker's optimism, thought "difficult to exaggerate" in the "solution of the gravest problem of Ireland" by "promoting a closer unity between the radically divided and warring elements which make up the Irish nation."

Pausing briefly in London for another conference with Oldham on his way from Dublin to Berlin, Mott was the luncheon guest of a group of

members of the House of Commons, at which he spoke on the importance of religion and morality in education. In Germany he worked with
student leaders including Theophile Mann and Friederick Wilhelm
Siegmund-Schultze (half of whose salary he was raising) on the development of social centers and a secretary for the large population of foreign
students—centers destined to play a significant role during the Great
War when vast numbers would become refugees. [88] He then made a quick
trip to Copenhagen, where he "helped to found a most promising movement among the laymen," presumably the LMM.

In Geneva he met with several members of the Executive Committee of the World's YMCA who had been "called together to discuss with
me the future policy of the Committee." Convinced that the YMCA was
"much more backward in Europe than in the United States, Canada, and
Asia, largely because of the lack of a sufficient number of able leaders,"
he presented the group his program ideas for the expansion and clarification of the Committee's "work and policies," assuring them that the North
American International Committee had "no wish to be a competitor."[89]

In summarizing this tour, Mott declared that as chairman of the
Continuation Committee he had "undertaken and carried out a plan of
systematic visitation of nearly all the missionary societies of Europe,"
discussing "their problems, needs, and plans," always in terms of the
"absolutely fundamental" question of "better understanding and closer
cooperation between the societies of different churches and of different
nations."

An official of the White Star Line had shown special interest in the
SCM and had presumably offered Mott and Eddy, who returned home
together in April, 1912, passage on the *Titanic*. They did not accept,
taking the *Lapland* on April 8. As they docked in New York on the
fifteenth, word of the *Titanic* disaster was beginning to filter through. It
is said that the two men looked at each other and one voiced their
common thought: "The Good Lord must have more work for us to do."
Mott later confessed to Oldham that he "very nearly" took the *Titanic*:
"you may be sure I have been much solemnized." That was a crossing to
remember. [90]

PART 9: Taking Edinburgh to Asia: India

Mott's round-the-world journey of 1912–13 would more than make
up for the paucity of Orientals at Edinburgh and on the Continuation

Committee. It would dramatize the shift in mission ideology of which Edinburgh and the year 1914 were indicators. It would set the high-water mark of student evangelism both for Mott and for Eddy, now, through the largess of Mrs. McCormick, YMCA foreign work secretary for Asia, who would accompany him, and in many places this would become a triumphal procession. It would harvest the first ecumenical fruits from earlier WSCF plantings and provide Mott with the opportunity to inspect his far-flung YMCA enterprise.[91]

The tour had been in the planning stage since the Auckland Castle meeting of May, 1911. It was to be the most elaborately organized, the most fully staffed, the most widely publicized, and the most expensive—though at no cost to the Continuation Committee—world trip of his life. It cost $101,000, subscribed by some fifty friends including Nettie Fowler McCormick, John D. Rockefeller, Jr., Mrs. T. B. Blackstone, A. A. Hyde, Mrs. D. Willis James, Mrs. John S. Kennedy, C. D. Massey, Dr. Samuel Murtland, and L. H. Severance, whose $5,000 gifts were the largest. Mott took as aide and private secretary his son John L., who interrupted his junior year at Princeton for the experience. William G. Schram was financial secretary and photographer. Charles H. Fahs went as historian and archivist; his collections would provide the nucleus of the Missionary Research Library. Edward J. Webster was stenographer, making verbatim reports of all the conferences. Mott was armed with letters from several high officers of the Taft administration and with introductions and endorsements to the Anglican bishops of Asia from the Archbishop of Canterbury.[92] He took quantities of Edinburgh descriptive material, his usual complement of books on the countries to be visited, and an India-paper edition of the *Encylopedia Britannica*, which proved to be the most-used resource.

In June, 1912, when Mott's plans were rapidly consolidating, Oldham attended a conference of British missionary societies at which deep concern was expressed over the crisis in China and the problems it was creating for missions. To Oldham's embarrassment, the conference proposed that he accompany Mott on the China segment of the tour, so that the British societies could have an informed resource person at hand. Oldham could see both sides of the matter and left it to Mott to decide whether his responsibility to the fledgling *International Review of Missions* outweighed such a special request. The issue led to an extraordinarily frank yet affectionate exchange that intensified each man's respect for the other and brought Oldham to a firm decision that he should not go.

Mott was convinced that Oldham was indispensable to the *Review* and that it would be unwise for both men to be away from their offices when the new subcommittees were just beginning their work and the Japanese government was pursuing a policy of persecuting Korean Christians. Mott thought that the British need could be met otherwise and assured Oldham that the last thing he could want in the Committee was to give any member "the impression that you and I are not absolutely one." The two concluded after a time that the proposal may have been made for that purpose! Mott reminded Oldham that he had made every effort to be impartial in the selection of personnel to prepare for his work in each country. As Oldham knew, the tour was somewhat of an experiment on Mott's part to help him ascertain the will of God with regard to his own future commitments, for Richard Morse was again pressing the general secretaryship of the American YMCA on him, and it was inevitable that the Continuation Committee would ask for his full time.

Less possible of sublimation was John's desire for Leila to accompany him. Some of the funds he had raised could have been used for that purpose, including $100 toward her outfit, but for reasons unknown, doubtless family concerns, she did not go. Before he sailed on the *Lapland* October 5, he mailed her a note from the ship confessing that "it was harder to leave today than ever before" and asking her to meet him in the Far East. During the voyage he repeated his plea:

> Your love is the most precious possession I have and it is everything to me. Never was I more conscious than on that Saturday morning that you were absolutely and wholly mine. My only hope is that you have a like consciousness with reference to me. I think you surely do, for it is true. What a wonderful love and union. It enables us to endure this separation while it at the same time makes the one outstanding date the day when we can be together again.
>
> If you can make entirely satisfactory provisions for the Children I favor your coming to me after the Christmas Holidays. You can help me far more than you realize—in dealing with women missionaries at these Conferences, in counseling with me in my preparation for the Federation Conference and for reporting my tour, in reaching our united decision as to my future work (the problem has become more baffling rather than less so).[93]

Several more of his letters to her have survived; in every one he reiterated his request, made suggestions for her schedule, and finally sent a cable from Singapore. She came to Japan.

As had been his custom since their marriage, he reported to her much of the detail of the trip. John L. was "taking hold of his work splendidly" and was "a great help." The two had prayers together each morning. The shipboard routine included morning watch, exercise, prayer, and time for relaxation; the team was working well together. Two short days in London were given chiefly to Federation affairs; a breakfast address raised "over £600." He and Eddy went to the House of Commons where they had "a fine visit" with John Burns, the labor leader. A day in Paris was spent with Grauss, Allier, and DeBilly; Mott "joined the boys [John L. and Schram] for two hours in the Louvre," enjoying it more than ever. The journey continued to Marseilles on a "beautiful sunny day" with gorgeous autumn tints: "never did France look so attractive."

The voyage from Marseilles to Colombo on a Japanese ship was fully organized for rest, exercise, prayer, and work. Mott read a great deal on India and perused some "very light" literature Miss Rouse had given him, but he was engrossed in the "masterly and most interesting" report on "educational missions, the YMCA, and the YWCAs of Asia" lent him by its author, Professor Ernest D. Burton of the University of Chicago, with the approval of its sponsor, John D. Rockefeller, Jr. Mott spoke at worship. John L. complained that he did not have time enough for sleep because the party was "routed out at 7:00 A.M. for exercise and the Morning Watch but as [his] work hours are less than six" Father told him it was "all a matter of planning," since he and Eddy were working ten hours a day and still getting "more sleep than we did on land." Yet Mott was aware of and grateful for "spiritual growth" in his son. Mott protested to Leila that he ought to have had another year to get ready for this mission. At Port Said he posted two letters to her, leaving the second with a friend to mail a week later so she would not have so long a wait without a word from him.

This visit of the Mott-Eddy team was at a time of relative political calm in India. Eddy discerned signs of a new era. The possibility of a united Indian Church had been under discussion for thirty years and a few bodies had actually joined. Mott's primary purpose was, as he had explained to Archbishop Davidson, to bring about "a better understanding and closer cooperation" among the churches and missionary bodies. Invitational regional meetings comprising fifty to seventy "outstanding leaders" were held at Colombo, Madras, Bombay, Jubbulpore, Allahabad, Lahore, and Calcutta. Mott and Oldham had agreed months earlier on the principles for selecting the delegates and had sent these well ahead. Each regional meeting chose five representatives to a national conference that met in Calcutta. From one-sixth to one-fifth of the delegates to all of these were Indians. Unlike previous Mott conferences, the emphasis was upon a syllabus of forty-seven questions arranged under the subcommittee plan of the Continuation Committee and sent in advance to the participants. The regional conferences were not apprised of the findings of their predecessors, so presumably conducted their discussions without prejudice; nor did they all discuss the same questions. At the end of the tour Mott noted the clearly "united judgment and desire" not only of the India meetings but also of the entire twenty-one meetings of the tour.

Soon after his arrival in India, Mott wrote Leila that never in all their married life had he been caught in "such a net work of engagements and unforseen situations." There were audiences and receptions; lodging with Anglican bishops, part of his strategy, involved much protocol. In Madras the Governor invited the Roman Catholic archbishop to what proved "a wonderful interview" of more than an hour; in response to Mott's inquiry about how to foster unity, the prelate replied, "By prayer, by kindness and gentleness and courtesy, and by fellowship." Mott would cite that formula many times. In Bangalore on November 22 he laid the cornerstone for the new United Theological College, then under the principalship of his companion of 1899, L. P. Larsen. Mott took the concept on which the College was founded as his theme:

> This plan of a United Theological College is striking at the heart of the most fundamental problem of Christianity. . . . I see in this event. . . what epitomizes and promotes the cause of Christian unity . . . and greatly hastens its progress. . . . Being united in Christ, in our wish to be like him, we are one.
> I have studied this principle during the last three decades and I affirm that the present decade will surpass all the other three and will break all records in the number of things which Christian people of different denominations find it possible to do together.
> God calls us to be apostles of reconciliation, for the getting together of His children in love and efficiency. We need to raise up men of catholic minds, men of thorough knowledge of church history, men of vision and enthusiasm, of high ideals and passionate desire to accomplish the ideals of their Saviour. . . . The arranging of a formal union calls for the highest statesmanship. Christ implied that we should not drift into unity, but that we must take the initiative and be peace-makers.[94]

The India National Conference, December 18–21, 1912, fussed a bit because of external initiative and because no decennial gathering had been planned for that year, but "largely through Mott's superb chairmanship" accomplished a great deal, reviewing the findings of the regional meetings and itself covering the entire syllabus. It revived and strengthened "many old plans for cooperation," including the system of arbitration that had been in operation for a decade, set up a committee on survey (Mott promising the funds), and authorized regional bodies to be affiliated with it which it in turn was charged to assist. The prompt organization of this body and the resources it was able to command equipped it to step into the gap created in 1914 when the Great War orphaned German missions in India; it became "a solid foundation block in the world-wide network of missionary councils," and its policies "the standard missionary statement of the principles and practice of comity."[95] Prominent among the delegates or the committees it appointed were many whose names, with their connections to the Mott network, were or became related to the ecumenical movement in the subcontinent: Azariah, Carter, Farquhar, C. F. Andrews, S. K. Datta, K. T. Paul, S. C. Mukerji, Archie Harte. Mott wrote Leila that the national conference had exceeded his highest expectations and justified the tour.

The most spectacular aspect of the Mott-Eddy visit to India was their student evangelism. Other Western evangelists had been there but none addressed themselves solely to students or met the enthusiastic reception accorded these two. The Continuation Committee conferences were held in the college or university centers so that Mott was able to join Eddy in the after-meetings. Attendance averaged more than 1,000 a night and in the larger cities filled the biggest halls. There were some demonstrations and a little violence but the audiences were generally eager and attentive. Careful count was kept of attendance, the number of "enquirers," and of those being prepared for baptism. Mott recorded Eddy's "deepest conviction" that India was "ready for reaping if we are ready to reap" and Farquhar's judgment that there had never been "such a ripe time"; Datta had agreed. "Pamphlets for Enquirers" were issued: one of Mott's and Eddy's contributions to the series was *Constructive Suggestions for Character-Building*, which set forth briefly but pointedly the importance of public confession, baptism, and church membership. The pamphlet concluded:

> The great thing needed on the part of all who have read what is set forth in this pamphlet is conclusive thinking, or decision of character. By conclusive thinking is meant thinking thoroughly on the principles and facts and then arriving at a definite conclusion. By decision of character is meant the habit of settling questions as they present themselves. There is no greater danger or source of weakness in the life of a man than permitting himself to fall into the habit of procrastinating and compromising. . . . Let each one of us, with full purpose of heart, cost what it may, resolve that we will promptly and heroically, take each and all of the steps which have been indicated. *Now* is the accepted time. *Now* is the day of Salvation. *Now* is the time for action in matters that reach into eternity.[96]

The climax of the student enterprise was an All-India Student Conference at Serampore just prior to the winter holidays. Mott was "the lion." The previous summer he had written the YMCA staff the most detailed instructions for it, insisting that a decided majority of the delegates must be "advanced or mature Indian Christian students." The planners were to "break into much new territory." He was ready to supply $1,000 toward the costs. Students were brought into the planning process; they asked Datta, Paul, Azariah, and Apaswamy as well as Eddy and Mott to speak. One hundred ninety-four students came from seventy-two colleges. The majority of them traveled more than 2,000 miles. "Serampore," wrote Carter, "spelled their unification into a self-conscious national organization."

V. S. Azariah, a student secretary and delegate to Edinburgh whose speech there was one of the best-remembered, was consecrated Anglican Bishop of Dornakal during the Conference. Two days later, in the presence of the Conference, he performed his first episcopal act by baptizing two students, a Brahmin and a Kaisthya, who had been converted in Mott's meetings two weeks earlier. The sacrament was celebrated at dusk in the Hooghly River "at the very spot where Carey baptized his first convert over a century ago." The significance of a low-caste person's baptizing a Brahmin was not lost on the witnesses.

In Carter's restrained review of this "unusual time and season for the Indian Christian Church" he included among five chief events of the Mott-Eddy visit a "Syrian Church Unity Conference" that followed the student gathering. Disagreements had torn this ancient church of South India into factions—the Mar Thoma and the Malankara Churches. When Syrian students began attending Madras Christian College "a new window opened on the world for this ancient Church," especially when the brilliant K. C. Chacko attended the WSCF Conference at Constantinople in 1911. He and others now begged Mott to "use his influence to make peace." Mott agreed to try if the feuding ecclesiastics would come to Serampore. To everyone's surprise, they did. Although Orthodox historians have denigrated the significance of this event, it was highly regarded at the time and Mott's strategy deserves a paragraph. Housing and dining arrangements were planned to throw the antagonists together in the company of Mott, an Anglican bishop, and their Baptist hosts, whom Mott instructed to spare no expense for the food. The nineteen participants chose Mott to chair their discussions, which gave him several opportunities to pontificate on the desirability of cooperation and on one occasion to speak at some length on the sin of disunion. A continuation committee of which Chacko was a member met several times. After Mott and their hostess had seen the two Syrian archbishops off, he commented to her that they seemed very happy. Carter observed that the meeting had "publicly recorded the determination of leaders of the largest Christian community in India to unite with Christians of all communions in a forward movement for the evangelization of Southern Asia," which had been the context of Mott's appeal to his guests.[97]

Review of YMCA affairs in India was one of Mott's important objectives, though it was not publicized. There were now twenty-six North American secretaries, Carter had just begun his second highly successful term as national executive, "the tide of the Foreign Work of the International Committee was now coming to its flood," and, as Latourette says, "the 'Mott Era' was approaching its peak." Carter, Harte, and Farquhar had met Mott at Colombo with "problems mountain high all calling for prompt action." He held a conference with the entire staff and talked individually with each one but took Carter, Harte, Eddy, and son John L. to Darjeeling for a Christmas retreat and review of the seemingly perpetual tensions between American and British missionaries and YMCA leaders, Harte's quixotic temperament, Anglican relations, the best strategies for advance, the balancing of the claims of various cities for new buildings, and the strengths and weaknesses of each secretary. As on previous occasions the party rose at 3:00 A.M. for the six-mile climb to Tiger Hill to see Mount Everest at sunrise. Mott fell from his horse, bruising his leg; had not John L. been at hand, the incident could have been serious. At the staff conference, Mott was honored as usual; this time the Indian group presented him and his family with a splendid Bokhara rug that Harte, an expert, had selected.

"The words, 'Dr. Mott's visit,'" wrote Carter in retrospect, "summarize for hundreds of leaders many weeks of praying and doing—a period when he did not cause but certainly occasioned the passing away of an old order and the ushering in of a new." En route to China Mott conveyed his satisfaction to Oldham on the "magnificent" cooperation of the Anglicans: he was sending articles for a symposium on the continuation Committee conferences for the still new *International Review of Missions*. "In these Conferences God has carried us beyond our plans and expectations. I found myself again and again in the position of having to restrain. The missionaries and Indian leaders are ripe for cooperative effort and real spiritual leadership." In its next world survey of missions, the *Review* emphasized the large place the all-India Conference had given to making "the Indian Church in reality the most efficient factor in the Christian propaganda in the land," and to placing Indians on complete equality "in status and responsibility with Europeans." At this point, Mott concluded to Oldham, he was content "to let the others do the talking and writing." He would report first to the Committee.[98]

PART 10: Edinburgh in China

After a conference at Rangoon and another at Singapore that brought to Mott's attention the vast needs of the Netherlands Indies, which he would not visit until 1926, the party arrived in China late in January, 1913. This was not long after that brief moment in Chinese history when some historians have thought that there might have been "a swift and reasonably peaceful transition" to a new order. During 1912 the differences between President Yuan Shih-kai's party and that of Sun Yat-sen had hardened as Yuan tightened his grip on the central power. Missionaries were certain that the revolution was one of the great events of history and that it would expedite the opportunity for the expansion of Christianity. A few months after Mott left China, Sun's "second revolution" was suppressed and he was exiled temporarily.

Yet the revolutionary enthusiasm that probably produced the most favorable attitude toward Christianity in all of China's history was a major factor in the ostensible success of the Continuation Committee conferences and of Mott's and Eddy's student evangelism. Assurances of religious liberty had been obtained from Yuan. Sun, a professing Christian, and ranking officials attended special church services, supported the YMCA, and endorsed certain mission programs. There were public statements acknowledging the indebtedness of China to the Christian Church for the introduction of reforms. During Mott's audience with President Yuan he was asked to explain what he was telling the students:

> I was glad that that day I had an unusually good interpreter with me, and as the President seemed disposed to listen I took the better part of three-quarters of an hour to try to put as concisely as I could the message I was bringing to the students from one end of China to the other. After I had finished he made this very striking statement: he said, Mr. Mott, I have listened earnestly. Confucius teaches us the truth, but you have been telling about a personality who enables men to obey the truth.[99]

Eddy told of a special luncheon tendered him and Mott, at which the Vice-President, General Li Yuan-hung, "requested us to address his family and guests upon the subject of Christianity." There was another occasion when in a meeting Eddy recognized "one former governor, two generals, a legal adviser to the President, the director of China's national bank," and other prominent officials. At a formal banquet in Shanghai, Mott and Eddy found themselves among the business leaders of the country, one of whom, a Yale graduate, declared that China imperatively needed Christianity today "to furnish her with moral power," while another guest had come at the behest of a provincial governor to request a YMCA for his city.[100] This was the era during which friends of the Association were saying that "Confucius would have been a 'Y' man."

Eddy, who had already traveled extensively in China during these eventful years, saw in that country "the climax of the new era in Asia." Despite unsettled political and economic conditions, the YMCA was thriving. Nascent nationalism aided Mott's moves toward unity, for the Chinese were anxious to obtain control of the Christian Church in their country, as became apparent in the Committee conferences. W. E. Taylor, who managed the Mott-Eddy evangelistic campaign, reflected the views of the team when he wrote that "China is facing the greatest crisis of her history. She has undergone the greatest change of her 4,000 years. Her problems are enormous and almost overwhelming."

The new nationalism, which had been apparent in Cheng Ching-yi's speech at Edinburgh, surfaced in the first Continuation Committee Conference, at Canton, which resolved that "the Chinese Church, and not the foreign organization, is the permanent factor in the evangelization of China." It reappeared in the national conference's decision to speak of "The Christian Church in China." Although it had been but six years since the China decennial missionary conference had seated only a handful of nationals, one-third of the delegates to this China National Conference were Chinese Christians and this was the first time they and the missionaries had deliberated together. At this meeting, self-government, self-support, and self-propagation were stressed and denominational union encouraged. A China Continuation Committee was set up, calling to its secretaryship E. C. Lobenstine and a great favorite of Mott's, his brilliant interpreter, Cheng Ching-yi, whom Mott had pushed for the post. It proposed greater cooperation in both college and theological education as well as in the production of Christian literature and the reciprocal recognition of church discipline. A Chinese who helped write its report recalled Mott's "great acumen and statesmanship" as chairman. A. L. Warnshuis wrote that the conference had marked an epoch in the missions history of China: "The findings are the nearest approach to a science of China missions that has yet been made." Brockman wrote to

Gilbert Beaver that the meetings marked "a new era in the history of Christian work in China."[101]

Instead of evangelizing together as in India, Mott and Eddy separated in order to reach "twice as many students." Brockman, whom Mott had recently advised to refuse the presidency of Peking University, accompanied Mott everywhere. Attendance at meetings ranged from 1,000 to 3,000, with an average of 2,000. The largest halls were used; in some cities government officials provided public buildings; where none was available, pavilions were constructed of bamboo and mats, as at Nanking, where YMCA secretary L. Newton Hayes had no difficulty in building the facility but was thunderstruck when faced with filling it! He called in a Chinese wood-carver who produced a life-sized cartoon of Mott from a small photo. Prints were mounted on large red posters announcing the visit and these were distributed throughout the city; capacity audiences came. In 1969 Hayes recalled for the author his perception of Mott's personal development from visit to visit; having first seen him in 1896, Hayes had been struck by Mott's growth in ability to speak to the Chinese to a degree that few Americans achieved—in vocal inflection, grammatical usage, sense of conviction, and fitness of expression. And he was wonderful to interpret! Hayes added that Eddy also acquired such a facility.[102]

The 1913 campaign was in striking contrast to Mott's first visit to China, when the government schools had seemed like Gibraltar. By the time of his 1907 visit they had shaken down like Jericho, but this was now a ripe harvest. In Canton, Mott's first stop, a new theatre seating 3,000 had been reserved. Brockman suggested that they reach it early, but when they did it was already filled and the doors locked. Twenty leading officials of the province were seated on the stage. Mott spoke for an hour and a half, with "no appeal to the emotions, no recourse to stories or incidents to add interest. It was severely logical, straightforward, convincing, and made dynamic by the fire of Mott's own conviction," Brockman recalled. The speaker finished and sat down. Not a man stirred, from topmost gallery to stage. Mott asked the chairman what it meant. "They want another address." Mott gave it, but even then the audience left reluctantly. This evidence of interest grew as the campaign moved on. In three cities there were 2,400 "enquirers." Mott explained one instance by the fact of its being the Universal Day of Prayer for Students. Others pointed out that Mott and Eddy were Americans, not yet tainted by the suspicion with which the Chinese were increasingly regarding Britain and the European powers. Mott made much use of a letter from President Taft who declared:

It would be difficult to overstate the importance of the work which awaits these students in China who in these days prepare themselves thoroughly for leadership in the constructive work of the world. It is vital that in their preparation they give careful attention to all that ensures the development of strong character.[103]

The magnetism of a cluster of star converts also had its appeal to students: T. Z. Koo, C. T. Wang, Y. Y. Tsu, David Z. T. Yui. The climax of Mott's campaign was reached in Peking, where he spoke to "a mighty concourse" from the Altar of Heaven. Feng Yü-hsiang, later known as the "Christian General," dated his adoption of Christianity from this visit. W. E. Taylor, who organized and managed the evangelistic tour, calculated the total attendance at 137,000; 60,000 had attended Robertson's science lectures; there had been 35,000 different men.[104] Some observers were not happy with the Mott-Eddy methods, pointing out that the Chinese had flocked to hear the Americans out of curiosity rather than from a genuine desire to hear the gospel, and that baptisms did not increase. Such analyses seem to have been confined to German missions periodicals—earlier criticism of the SVM watchword will be recalled—and had little circulation in English-speaking circles.[105]

At this time there were some 100 foreign secretaries at work in China and the student enterprise was a department of the national Chinese YMCA. Mott had told Brockman a year before, as he laid out his plans, that he could give neither major nor particular attention to Federation or YMCA matters on this tour, and he did not. A secretarial conference was held at the conclusion of the China National Continuation Conference, but in actuality the "Y" staff did most of the spade work for those conferences and the evangelistic campaign was in reality a YMCA activity, arranged in each city by the local secretaries. In addition, Mott was responsible for the special programs that had helped to create interest in his meetings—C. H. Robertson's science lectures or Dr. W. W. Peters' medical evangelism being examples.[106] It could be said that in addition to his duties as national YMCA secretary for China, Brockman had carried the major burden of planning and administering not only Mott's evangelistic tour but the Continuation Committee Conferences, in all of whose deliberations and subcommittees YMCA men were prominent.

Much to Mott's and Oldham's gratification, the Anglicans had cooperated splendidly and the China Inland Mission and the American Presbyterians had been very much in evidence. From Dairen Mott could write to Oldham that "we went a great deal further in our relations to the Roman and Greek Catholic Churches in the Far East than we ever dreamed of elsewhere but I think none too far." He did not mention the problems that had concerned them during the planning stages of the tour, but Oldham thought the Shanghai resolution to cultivate friendly relations with Roman Catholics "likely to give trouble": sooner or later "we shall probably have a storm."

PART 11: Minister to China?

Just before Mott landed at Colombo in early November, 1912, his friend of many years, Woodrow Wilson, was elected President of the United States. The outgoing Taft administration had not recognized the new Republic of China, so that Wilson was faced not only with the issue of recognition but also with the appointment of a new diplomatic representative. The missionary community was pressuring him in favor of recognition. Sun Yat-sen congratulated Wilson upon his election and the president-elect responded warmly. [107]

While Mott was in Peking in late February, 1913, he sent Wilson, through their mutual friend Cleveland H. Dodge, a brief urging prompt recognition of the Chinese Republic. Mott cabled seven points:

China has won the right to recognition by progress achieved in a most difficult year. . . .

She presents evidences of stability: the country is quiet; no serious troubles; elections held without disturbances in 21 or 22 provinces; new provincial assemblies are electing senators this month; good feeling between sections; whole country united; principal possible rivals to Yuan are strongly supporting him; country prosperous; record year in crops and custom receipts; best men in power.

Recognition now would give America position of unique influence.

It would accord with our best traditions and with our greatest helpfulness to all other republics.

American ideals prevail in China more than those of any other land; China is speaking of us as the great sister republic and looking to us as to no other country.

Students returning from America are wielding predominant influence and therefore render it peculiarly appropriate that a nation which afforded them their inspiration and training should strengthen their hands.

If America is ultimately to recognize China, why not now?

Mott added that he found the "keenest disappointment and dismay" spreading among the best men, with "confidence in America's disinterestedness being greatly shaken." The inaugural message was being anticipated with "eager expectations." Prompt recognition would "enormously enhance our prestige in the East."[108]

Unknown to Mott, Wilson was at the very same time, conceivably with Dodge's approval [Dodge could have asked Mott for the above], considering Mott for the diplomatic post. In Wilson's mind, Mott possessed "as many of the qualities of a statesman" as any man of his acquaintance, with the added advantage of familiarity with conditions in China. Wilson also made it explicit to his secretary of state-elect, William Jennings Bryan, that he wanted "exceptional men" for diplomatic appointments; Mott was "one of a thousand." Wilson offered it to Mott in a cable on February 24 which he followed with a letter declaring that he had set his heart on Mott for "the Ambassadorship to China." With Bryan's concurrence, Wilson was willing to accept "any arrangements" that would allow Mott to fulfill his current obligations. Mott refused.

Immediately after his inauguration, Wilson marshalled Dodge and others to change Mott's mind, himself cabling to urge reconsideration because "the interests of China and of the Christian world are so intimately involved." Mott agreed. The President cabled that he was "eager to unite what you represent with what this government means to try to represent" and was therefore congenial to Mott's retaining his present posts. Missionaries on furlough in the States and a group of YMCA men in China reenforced Wilson's plea. Dodge cabled at length, although he could hardly have encouraged the President, knowing as he did Mott's attitude toward the Princeton presidency only a short time before.

Fortunately for Mott, Leila had joined him. The decision could be a mutual one. As they thought and prayed about the matter, "the long line of young men whom he had induced to enter professionally Christian occupations seemed to rise before him, and he felt that acceptance would be betrayal." He later told Colton that there were "too many men and women out over the world on lifetime missions, influenced by his representations, for him now to step out of the line." Leila wrote in her diary for March 31 that "it was a lovely day along the Inland Sea, with peach blossoms, orange trees laden with fruit, the famous Myajima Shrine with a torii out in the sea. We discussed and decided John's call to be U.S. Minister at Peking." A cable to Dodge was final: "Must decline truly great opportunity. This done with profound appreciation present situation and full sympathy with [Wilson's] policy. Could not fulfill serious obligations already assumed and do justice to new position."[109]

PART 12: Taking Edinburgh to Manchuria, Korea, and Japan

The fantastic experiences that characterized this Mott tour continued in Manchuria. There was no hall large enough to hold the students who wanted to hear him in Mukden, so at his own expense the governor built a pavilion to accommodate 5,000. Mott gave three addresses; the next day the 5,000 came back for three more talks; 600 signed cards pledging to study "the little books called the Gospels," to pray daily, and to take Jesus Christ as Lord and Saviour "as far as my conscience and reason will permit."

> The Commissioner of Education had been sent there by the governor and had heard the lectures. He said, "I want to say something. Young men, I have heard these lectures. I have been particularly interested in these three promises you have signed, and which Mr. Mott has explained seven times. (It took forty minutes to explain.) Now, I want to exhort you to keep these promises. . . ." That man was not a Christian![110]

The Continuation Committee Conference, attended by two Chinese to each Western Christian, set up a federal council for Manchuria "on the lines laid down by the China Centenary Conference" of 1907. It recommended that steps be taken to realize "a worthy autonomous Chinese Church," to study the successful methods of the Korean Church, to develop Chinese Christian leadership, and to push for a comprehensive program of Christian education at all levels.[111]

Mott found the situation in Korea politically "very tense" because of the repressive policies of the Japanese overlords, and the Church facing "delicate and grave problems," a serious deterioration since his previous visit in 1907. But through the good offices of the highly competent YMCA staff, chiefly Frank Brockman and Philip L. Gillett, he had "special meetings with the Japanese and with members of the government." The YMCA was thriving but found it almost impossible to remain aloof from the ever-present tension, which actually broke out in minor violence at least once in Mott's presence. It maintained an aggressive program among students; one of its promising young secretaries, Syngman Rhee, was in the United States hoping to raise funds at the time of Mott's visit, but Yun Tchi Ho was still in prison for alleged conspiracy against the regime.[112]

The Continuation Committee Conference was able to create an advisory committee somewhat like that formed in China, but was itself almost disrupted by a High churchman threatening to boycott it because it had not invited the Greek and Roman Catholic Churches, without which he contended that there could be "no true reunion of Christendom"; the issue was resolved by extending an informal invitation to those bodies. A large tent was erected for Mott's evangelistic meetings, which were attended by 3,000 "strong Korean men"—"a scene that I shall not forget through all the time that life lasts." With heroism because of the certainty of persecution, 300 of them "paid the price of open confession." Few pages of Leila Mott's diary for Korea lacked words such as sad, pitiful, tragic, and John would always see those "loving Korean faces" in his mind's eye.[113]

"In Japan as in the West it is an era of inward struggle, of restlessness, of testing the teachings and ideals of the past," wrote the elder statesman Count Shigenobu Okuma in the IRM a few months before Mott arrived for his fourth visit to the Sunrise Kingdom. It was also the end of an era, for on July 30, 1912, the Emperor Meiji had died. By this time, Christianity was recognized as a spiritual and moral force in Japanese society, as evidenced by the inclusion of Christians with Buddhists and Shinto representatives in what came to be known as the "Three Religions Conference" of 1911, an effort by the government to enlist the major religious bodies in the moral guidance of the country at a time of transition. This was paralleled by a new official emphasis on school attendance at the shrines, which created chronic problems for Christians.[114]

Due to the vastly different situation in Japan from either India or China, Mott followed a unique program that he had worked out with his national YMCA secretary Galen M. Fisher months before. There were already Japanese-led ecumenically-oriented bodies among youth and laymen which had fostered evangelistic campaigns and summer schools, as well as a Federation of Missions that greatly resembled the Federal Council of Churches in the United States, and of which it chanced that Fisher was chairman that year. Mott met first with the missionaries, then with the Japanese, the rosters of whom indicate that in this era of change a new generation of leaders, many of whom had come up through the YMCA, was taking over from the pioneers such as Bishop Honda who had died the year before. Finally there was a national conference of both, for which extensive preparation had been made by twenty commissions that produced a 175-page advance report; Fisher had been secretary of the planning group. Hogg evaluated the Continuation Committee Conferences as marking "a high point in Protestant missions in Japan," lifting the vision of the total task to a new level by placing major emphasis upon "Japan's complete occupation" and planning a three-year evangelistic campaign, a central Christian university, and a Continuation Committee for Japan.[115] In all three conferences the YMCA leadership was present but not conspicuous.

Mott had warned Fisher that he could give only minimal attention to YMCA affairs on this tour, but he did hold a meeting of secretaries and a student gathering. The latter brought some 400 professors and students from seventy Associations, causing Mott to compare it to the situation sixteen years earlier when there had been eight small student bands with a few score members. Now in 1913 he found that same Movement "waging a triumphant Christian propaganda." The unique feature of this student conference and of student life in Japan at the time was the social service or social gospel emphasis. Fred B. Smith, the American YMCA "evangelist to men," and Raymond Robins, a founder of the American Progressive Party, had been there earlier, as were Charles R. Henderson of the University of Chicago and Hamilton Mabie, editor of the *Outlook*, who was an exchange lecturer at Kyoto that year. The student conference was addressed by Francis G. Peabody of Harvard, author of *Jesus Christ and the Social Question*, and several Japanese spoke to social themes. The body split into small groups to visit factories, reformatories, and other institutions, led by "Christian officials of the Department of the Interior." With the increase of social and industrial problems, Fisher concluded, "we have begun none too early to educate Christian social engineers" in the current phraseology of American social gospel circles.[116]

Mott and Eddy evangelized among students in the largest centers. Whether in government or Christian colleges, each meeting, Mott reported with obvious enthusiasm, showed "great openness and responsiveness to the direct presentation of the claims of Christ," especially so at Kyoto, the center of Buddhism. Special lectures were given to Chinese and Korean students. In his informal platform style he described the climax of these gatherings a few weeks after returning home: the first night at Tokyo Imperial University it was like facing a stone wall. The next night he went there physically exhausted, yet "there came a hush on these men, and as we came to the holding up of the living Christ at the end of about two hours and a half—and, by the way, the meeting continued to nearly four hours—when it came to the last of the four tests there were over three hundred of these men acknowledging their purpose, first, to make a thoroughgoing study of the Gospels; secondly, to pray to

God daily for wisdom to find the truth and courage to follow it, and, thirdly, as far as their reason and conscience would permit them to do so, that they would take this Christ as their divine, personal Saviour and Lord." This was "an evidence of Christianity, an opportunity the like of which I have not heard in this twenty-five years of work among students."

Mott was in Japan at the height of the anti-Japanese agitation in California that produced the Anti-Alien Land Act of 1913. He cabled President Wilson that it was "seriously regarded here by all classes including Americans" and would embarrass American interests. The day before he sailed for home he had an extended conversation with Count Okuma concerning it. From his notes it is apparent that he was himself embarrassed, but tried to put the insulting action in the best light possible. He explained that it was necessary to distinguish between the several sources of information available in Japan, pointed out that California was not the whole of America, related this one unfortunate incident to a long history of friendly relations, and regarded it as an emergency rather than the deliberate intent of American statesmanship.

The Count, who was entirely familiar with the United States Constitution, found the act contrary to the American sense of justice and remarked that "we now have to teach the people of California that which you missionaries have taught us." There is such a thing as political psychology, he continued, but crowd psychology is surely dangerous. The way to solve this problem is to call in the aid of religion: laws are powerless to change public spirit or feeling. If I were to speak as a statesman, Okuma declared, I should say that we ought to claim our rights. If we go on demanding our rights it will end in a conflict, I fear, of might. This is why I will not resort to political measures to settle differences: we must turn to religion as a means of persuasion. Mott reported to President Wilson shortly after returning home.

Two months after Mott had left, Fisher wrote that in view of what Mott's conferences had accomplished he would "never regret the calories of effort expended in preparation"; they "marked a new era in the direction of nationwide planning and cooperation." The final one had been characterized by "the spirit of love and fraternity"; not a "harsh or footless word" had been uttered. A decade earlier such a meeting would have been impossible. In YMCA affairs, Mott's previous visits had been milestones, but this one "marked an epoch in the whole Christian movement of the country." Reviewing the part he and the Associations had played, he remarked wryly that "whether we wish to or not we secretaries in Japan have to get into scrimmage in every cooperative enterprise." And he had never witnessed "a saner presentation and a more careful sifting of results" than in the evangelistic effort.[117]

Eddy once remarked that Mott had done the work of two men on this world tour. Hans-Ruedi Weber, writing in 1964, compared the twenty-one Continuation Committee Conferences with much later gatherings: one is struck by the

> unanimity of the conclusions reached on many questions and one begins to wonder how far this was the work of the Holy Spirit, how far the work of Mott's chairmanship or perhaps the one through the other. Never up to the Laymen's Foreign Missionary Enquiry in 1930 and the Situation Conferences of the EACC in 1963 has such a thorough attempt been made to survey the missionary task in Asia and to enlist the best minds for this consultation. Actually one wonders whether the two latter attempts can really be compared with what happened in 1912–13. The participants lists of the twenty-one conferences show that John R. Mott achieved drawing the best minds, both foreign and national, into consultation. The findings sound now rather dry and conventional, but they must have been revolutionary in their time, for instance when the second sectional conference of Japan, which consisted exclusively of Japanese, said about missionaries: 'New missionaries must be graduates of colleges... Every new missionary, as far as practicable, should work for the first year or two under the direction of some experienced Japanese pastor, and so get acquainted with Japanese church members and become familiar with their manners, customs and habits of thinking.' Also older missionaries must constantly continue to study things Japanese, the findings say.[118]

About this time the editor of an American secular magazine wrote that missions had changed "from guerilla warfare to organized campaign." Even before Mott left Japan, Oldham had written:

> I think your heart must be full of thankfulness to God for all that He has wrought, which goes beyond our highest expectation. He has abundantly and marvellously answered our prayers. There will be a great task before us in the coming years to enter the doors of opportunity which have been so wonderfully opened.

Forty years later, Oldham wrote of this period, "what the younger Churches in Asia and in other fields owe to John Mott cannot be measured."[119]

PART 13: The Continuation Committee's Last Meeting

From before the Edinburgh Conference itself, Oldham had believed that Mott would find the opportunity of his life in serving the organization they were both certain would grow out of it. The 1912–13 trip was in part an experiment in alternatives to the American national YMCA secretaryship, which one feels Mott shrank from. Oldham had relayed to Mott the thought of Richter and others regarding Mott's "future work." "I do not think that I am likely to be mistaken with regard to the attitude of the Continuation Committee," he wrote, "and I feel certain that almost without exception every member of the Committee is counting on your continued leadership." He begged Mott to keep himself free "from all other conflicting claims until the Continuation Committee has had an opportunity in November [1913] of expressing its mind." To expedite this he suggested that Mott cultivate the mission societies of Great Britain and the Continent, taking special pains to plan "a certain amount of leisurely personal contact with a few of the leading men." Mott not only adopted this policy but accepted Oldham's personal invitation to stay with him in Edinburgh for two days of conversation prior to the Committee meeting.

This trip to Europe—October 15 to December 23, 1913—was primarily to attend the Continuation Committee meeting at The Hague in mid-November but was also to raise funds for WSCF expansion into Eastern Europe and the Levant. It was preceded by a luncheon with President Wilson, who provided Mott with a letter of introduction to the diplomatic and consular officers of the United States in Europe. From the *Lusitania* John wrote Leila that it had been "hard, very hard," to break away but he felt that she was with him "in a most real sense" so that he "went forth with courage." What a joy "to think of all our children!" He loafed, he said, during most of the voyage, but dictated a first draft of his all-important report to the Committee; he must "arrange in some way so that you can be with me on these journeys." From Oldham's home in Edinburgh he wrote that the first sessions of a tight schedule to meet with some thirty mission societies—one or two a day—was off to a good start; they were taking his visit "most seriously," as was indicated by good attendance. "Dealing with these Committees of mature, conservative administrators of missions is quite a different experience from that of working with undergraduates."

In London he dined with the Archbishop of Canterbury and his wife, "all alone—the three of us—for nearly three hours." Mrs. Davidson charged him to bring Leila the next time. "At these various luncheons, teas, dinners and suppers I am meeting all sorts of important people who will help our various causes in years to come." It was becoming increasingly clear that the Continuation Committee would take more rather than less of his time. Benjamin Barber, who had given up an assignment overseas to become Mott's personal aide, was proving to be "the greatest secretarial helper" he had ever had, "and that is saying very much."

In two action-packed days in Paris Mott renewed old friendships, reported to the Paris Missionary Society, spoke to an overflow congregation in the Oratoire, and advised the French SCM of which Charles Grauss was then the secretary. It was visits such as this that helped confirm Pastor Marc Boegner in ecumenism and to inspire Pierre Bovet to write the booklet Quelqu'un (not "quelconque"—just anyone, as Karl Barth had distinguished two years before) about him, which caused Mott to remark, "to publish such things, rather wait till I am dead!" This "powerful personality" was decisive for the ecumenical careers of Suzanne de Dietrich, Emmanuel Galland, Phillippe de Vargas, Robert Pont, Leo Viguier, Emmanuel Sautter, Paul Conord, and Charles Westphal, as several of them would testify.[120]

Mott presented his report on the morning of the first day of the Continuation Committee session at The Hague, together with the printed volume containing the findings of the twenty-one conferences. He summarized the results:

> (1) They enabled the leaders of the Christian forces in the different fields to face the wholeness of the missionary task. (2) They made a great and unique contribution in laying down principles of missionary policy and in improving missionary method. (3) Reports received from all parts of the field show that the conferences have resulted in a marked increase in the efficiency of missionary work. (4) The conferences furnished the occasion on which more truly than at any time in the past the native Church came into its own. (5) They exerted a large influence in drawing together the native Christian leaders and the missionaries. (6) They have established a link between the mission field and the World Missionary Conference in Edinburgh. (7) The conferences resulted in the formation of a representative committee in each important mission field to carry forward the investigations and other activities begun at the conferences, and to help to give effect to their findings. (8) In the course of the conferences many schemes of co-operation were discussed. (9) Indirectly the conferences did much to promote true Christian unity.[121]

Mott's impressions, wrote Hogg in 1952, revealed a conception and strategy of "world church" beyond anything he had written before:

> They disclosed the mind of a great statesman, acknowledging the limited authority of the Continuation Committee, yet planning in bold, sweeping terms with full expectation that his vision would commend itself to his constituency. As never before Mott wrote as though he were actually

engaged in knitting together a world church. The Committee, he declared, "should do everything in its power to strengthen the bonds of union between the new Churches in non-Christian lands and the Church Historic, the Church Universal."

There could be no greater danger than for native Christianity to become separate from historical, creedal, ecumenical, vital Christianity.[122]

On the fifth day, Dr. James L. Barton, chairman of the subcommittee on the secretariat, submitted a recommendation based on the assumption that "the Church is still far from making an adequate response to the call of God in our own time." The need is for "a larger use of the gifts of intercession, of corporate life, of personal service and of material wealth for the speedy occupation of the entire world in the name of our Lord Jesus Christ." This Committee should therefore offer its services to the missions societies in order to place at the disposal of the Church "that which has been entrusted to it of experience, knowledge, and influence." The resolution then proposed that the Chairman be asked "to devote a large part of his time and energy" to the Committee, "though without relinquishing his other work," because he was capable of rendering "a unique service of the most far-reaching significance at the present time." Among the duties "for which we believe him to have been specially fitted, and to which we now call him," were these:

1. The representation of the Committee's work and aims to Missionary Boards and Societies, and to such Bodies as they may represent.
2. The leadership in a deliberate, new and larger effort, so far as the Boards may call us to this task, to bring home to the whole Church the call to the service of the world, and to claim for this service, in the name of Christ, the highest and best gifts of mind, leadership and influence.
3. The maintenance of intimate relationships between this Committee and representative Bodies on the field.
4. The organization of further Conferences on the field, especially in Africa and the Near East.
5. The assistance of the various Special Committees in such ways as may, from time to time, seem to be desirable and possible.[123]

The recommendations were unanimously adopted. Mott thanked the Committee "and intimated his acceptance."

The Conference went on to lay down what became known as "The Hague principle"—that the only bodies authorized to determine missions policy were the boards, missions, and the churches themselves: thus the Continuation Committee was not to be another non-denominational body like the SCM or the YMCA but an interdenominational agency through which the missionary societies could function jointly. It also made it plain that it was not related organically to or responsible for its new counterparts in the Orient, though it anticipated a growing relationship of "mutual understanding and helpfulness." Mott gavelled the sessions through ninety-two items of business. When the Committee was received by the Queen, he made one of the addresses.

The day after the delegates separated Mott wrote to Oldham: "I look back with overflowing thankfulness to God for the many answers to prayer during the past few days, and the joy of fellowship with you." A week later during the enforced leisure of the train trip from Budapest to Scandinavia where he would report to mission societies, he brought Leila up to date in a thirteen-page letter in which he summarized his thoughts on "our life problem"—the opposing calls to the Continuation Committee (some members had assured him of "their desire to back me in any plans I might develop") versus the American YMCA secretaryship:

> I see more clearly that it will be harder to substitute for me in the C.C. activities than in those related to Mr. Morse's position. All my previous work seems to have prepared me for dealing with these larger international, interracial, and interdenominational questions.

The Committee would never meet again. The choice was taken out of Mott's hands.

PART 14: "The Frontier Stage Is Over": The WSCF at Princeton and Lake Mohonk, 1913

Ruth Rouse, the Federation's secretary for women through several decades and its chief historian, characterized the 1913 Conference as "at once more inclusive" and far-reaching than any one of its predecessors. It was the most widely representative, counted the largest proportion of undergraduate delegates, effected distinct interracial advances, and "marked the end of the pioneer stage of Federation history." By this time the WSCF had entered not only the Orient, Australasia, and South Africa, but the Balkans and the Near East. This advance was not solely geographical: it had "claimed for Christ" the worlds of women students, student migrations, foreign students, and "successive regions of thought and activity, social and ecumenical."

In addition to Miss Rouse's milestones it must be said that this was to be the last conference largely dominated by Mott as well as the last one held in the United States in his lifetime. And it was the last one cast in the exuberance of the waning nineteenth century: a German delegate who insisted that war was imminent met with sheer incredulity or was suspected of a perverse sense of humor. Mott's reasons for holding this Conference in the United States may be inferred in part from Miss Rouse's point that it was "a training conference in method." Delegates from other countries "found much to learn" from the methods and programs of the older American Movement, which was, one may add, at the very apex of its development under Mott's leadership and at the moment when he was considering resigning from it.[124]

Mott had made a sincere effort to obtain constructive criticism from the leaders and guests at Constantinople in 1911, and the program for the meeting at Lake Mohonk, New York, appears to have been democratically planned by the General Committee, to the extent that it could be when he made the budget and raised the funds. The British had been incensed at the idea of meeting in the States and had said so loudly, but they came. Charles J. Ewald, who had been assiduously cultivating the South American field, was bitter when he saw the program, with no place given to neglected Latin America and even the assigned topic on student work in Roman Catholic countries given to a Swiss. These were forgotten in the joy of fellowship and the foreign delegates' sheer wonder at America, the scenery, the sparkling spring weather, and the hospitality, behind the complex plans for which there is plainly discernible the master hand of the Federation's General Secretary who had raised $25,000 outside of the regular budget!

From the beginning, each Federation Conference had been preceded by a meeting of the General Committee, usually near and just prior to the Conference itself. In late May, 1913, the thirty-five members of the Committee met at Princeton, New Jersey, the birthplace of the modern American Student YMCA. It heard strong pleas for holding the next conference in China or India in 1915 but decided to storm Eastern Europe with a big convention at Prague in celebration of the five-hundredth anniversary of the martyrdom of John Huss. The basis of membership was modified in the direction of the British statement after a strong presentation by President Ibuka of Japan who pointed out that in some countries students had no conception of the nature of the Christian God or of historic Christian faith. Baron Nicolay held that there were many in Russia who claimed to be Christians but were ignorant of the Bible. The membership statement was revised to read: "To lead students to accept the Christian faith in God—Father, Son, and Holy Spirit—

according to the Scriptures and to live as true disciples of Jesus Christ."
The Russian Movement, the fruit of a decade of toil by Nicolay, was
admitted as the thirteenth member of the Federation, "and there was a
solemn prayer of thanksgiving for the blessing that had come to the work
in Russia"; this was Nicolay's last Federation conference, and one of the
greatest moments of his life. Delegates were also welcomed from Latin
America.

Near the end of the General Committee meeting, its members were
witnesses to a commemorative event that conveyed deep meaning to
many of the delegates and to those who participated in it. On the Princeton campus in 1876, Luther D. Wishard, who became the world's first
full-time Christian worker among students, had met the New York
philanthropist and YMCA leader, William E. Dodge, and his two sons,
Cleveland H. and William Earl; together they laid plans that eventuated
in the adoption of a student work program by the parent YMCA. Upon
his graduation in 1877, Wishard began the office he was to create and
develop for eleven years. Mott had succeeded him in 1888 when Wishard
went on an extended missionary journey.

On Memorial Day, May 30, a heroic bronze statue called "The
Christian Student" by the American sculptor Daniel Chester French,
well known for the "Minute-Man" on the Lexington Green and later for
the seated figure of the Lincoln Memorial in Washington, was unveiled
on the Princeton campus just north of Murray-Dodge Hall, itself a
memorial to two YMCA and Princeton leaders. One of French's best
pieces, the sculpture was modeled from photographs of William Earl
Dodge, who had died prematurely, and was the gift of Cleveland H.
Dodge. The reporter for The Student World, the Federation organ, described the figure as "a young collegian" in athletic uniform "partially
covered by an academic gown" whose face conveyed "a radiant harmony
of spiritual vision, steadfastness of purpose, and physical vigor." President John G. Hibben and Baron Nicolay preceded Mott in the brief
exercises.

Mott began by calling attention to the inscription, "To mark the
birthplace of the worldwide union of Christian students in work for
Christ." Noting that universities had from their beginnings been centers
of power and influence, he quickly moved to a theme he had voiced two
years before at the Princeton commencement, that in his travels he had
seen the university's influence at work in the service of the nation and
abroad. But here he ventured to suggest that its greatest service was in
stimulating and supporting the now worldwide union of Christian

students—of which many of his hearers were representatives. The statue suggested to Mott character, vision, and purpose—men who stood for open-mindedness, reality, and loyalty to Christ. Such were the casualties of the Great War and its aftermath of disillusion that the sculpture had later to be protected from student resentment by removing it to secret storage where it was forgotten for several decades.[125]

After the Princeton sessions the 275 delegates assembled in New York City were entertained by Miss Grace Dodge at her Riverdale mansion, and the large American contingent was coached by Mott, fresh from his world tour, on their duties as hosts:

> Remember that this is a great opportunity to learn. Never forget that you are the hosts. Study the names and backgrounds of each delegate in the Conference *Who's Who,* and interest yourself in their affairs. Do not speak disparagingly about any nation, race, or person, and do not boast of America or American things. Take the initiative in helping the lonely, neglected, or handicapped. Speak slowly and clearly. Above all, "let us make a spiritual impression," proving to our guests that we are far more concerned with evangelism, Bible study, and the dedication of our lives than with those popular misconceptions that Americans concentrate on organization, buildings, numbers, and finances.[126]

Most of the ninety-mile trip to Lake Mohonk was by river steamer up the scenic Hudson, the last segment, by horse-drawn coach, through verdant woods and meadows. Planned to nurture friendships among the delegates, the trip ended at the sprawling hotel that had been established four decades earlier in the mountains through which Mott's ancestors had once pressed their perilous way westward, and only about forty miles from his birthplace. Founded by the Quaker Smiley brothers and for years the host to conferences on international arbitration and on the American Indian, the resort, which Mott seems to have "discovered" not long before this, had become known as "a moral citadel" and indeed seemed to the delegates to be not merely a place but a symbol of "friendship for the Indian and the Negro, and the champion of international peace."

Mott and the planners had determined both to demonstrate the American Movement's growing concern with racial and social issues, and to provide it with an example of an integrated conference. "Duly coached by the American leaders," the Federation, wrote Miss Rouse, had made it known that it would not accept an invitation unless non-whites were admitted on equal terms. At Mohonk this had been practiced for years, but up to this time, in spite of much study, there had not been an American conference attended by both black and white students. The Americans acquiesced and invited thirteen Negroes, twenty Chinese, three "British Indians," five North American Indians (one of whom was Miss Ella Deloria from Oberlin), two Filipinos, nine Japanese, and one Korean.

The delegates drew lots for their seating at meals. All went well, although there is a possibly apocryphal story of at least one Southern white woman student sobbing to Mott that she could not face it, but coming to thank him for the experience at the end of the Conference. W. A. Hunton, a Negro YMCA secretary, sensed "most deeply the abiding spirit of brotherhood which ran like a golden thread through all the proceedings." The American Indians sent a message to their fellow Indian students across the country attesting to their conviction that "the one fundamental need of the Red Men is Jesus Christ" and that their race would "achieve a greater glory or vanish from the earth according as it receives or rejects" Him. They bade every Christian student "to stand up with us, and to take heart as never before," and called on all Christian agencies working in Indian student centers "to strengthen their hands in the endeavor to lead students to a personal adherence to Jesus Christ and to foster all influences working for a settlement of Indian problems along the lines of Christian statesmanship."[127]

In his report, Mott devoted more than a thousand words to a review of "the marked development of the social consciousness throughout the Federation," noting that the British Movement had set up such a department four years earlier and North America recently, of which "Mr. [Malcolm] Spencer, in England, Mr. [Richard H.] Edwards in America, Mr. Siegmund-Schultze in Germany, and the group of workers dealing with the Negro problems in the Southern states of America" were examples. Integration at American conferences would henceforth be easier, with marked advances the next year.

The Conference Who's Who recorded the names of a whole generation of young leaders who would make their contributions to ecumenism in every country represented.[128] In the absence of Fries, Ibuka of Japan was appointed acting chairman, and Baron Nicolay served as vice-chairman in C. T. Wang's place. The program was organized functionally. David S. Cairns of Aberdeen and Robert E. Speer spoke to "great religious themes." Mott's and Rouse's reports, which required sixty-four pages to print, literally covered "the religious forces in the universities of the world." Charles Grauss, secretary of the French Movement and author of Vers l'Unité Chrétienne, gave what Nicolay remembered as a brilliant address on the French influence in the Federation; Grauss' dedicated voice would be stilled on the battlefield before the WSCF met again. David Z. T. Yui brought a message from General Li Yuan-hung, Vice-President of the Republic of China, and spoke proudly of the crucial role Christian students were playing in his country. President Ibuka of the Meiji Gakuin in Tokyo opened the Conference; Mott closed it with "Our Best Days Lie in Front of Us." President Ellen F. Pendleton of Wellesley spoke on religion in the higher education of women, and Bishop Charles H. Brent gave a "deep" sermon on the ecumenical theme, showing the relation between the Federation and the Church and warning lest the former degenerate into a sect. Mott had prepared a special booklet of prayers for the Conference. Germanos, now Ecumenical Patriarch of Constantinople, who had attended the Conference at Robert College in 1911, sent an Orthodox priest to present his greetings. [129]

Instead of the evangelistic campaigns that had followed the last several WSCF conferences—notably begun at Tokyo in 1907—the foreign delegates visited among the eighteen North American summer conferences and a large number attended a secretarial training program in New York City. David S. Cairns, reflecting on the Conference, noted

> its international character and the prevailing youth of the delegates, the unflagging vitality of the whole proceedings. I do not remember one dull or depressing hour throughout the week, and there were not a few incidents of dramatic interest.

As he had looked over his audience, a vision of the great student world behind it, "over which the Spirit of God is brooding today, preparing the history of tomorrow," had crossed his mind:

> Paris, Vienna, Budapest, Berlin, Cracow, Moscow, Geneva, Sofia, Rome, Tokyo, Peking, Buenos Aires, Beirut, Cairo—has there been any field like it for Christian propaganda since the first age of the Church? Something here is maturing that, if it goes forward as it has begun, will reckon among the great forces of history, not a ripple or a current, but a tide.

Miss Rouse believed that the Federation "found itself" at Mohonk as "a world-embracing student Christian movement—international, interracial, ecumenical. We believed that we saw before us the path which God would have us take." [130]

After the Continuation Committee sessions in Holland that fall, Mott went to Vienna and Budapest to strengthen the hands of the Federation secretaries he was sending there and for whose support he had just raised funds in Great Britain: Robert Wilder—"our Mr. Wilder" to the Poles—and E. S. Woods of Great Britain, Miss Rouse, and Miss de la Faille. The quick trip was a steady stream of individual and group consultations climaxed by his giving seven addresses to the Hungarian leaders in one day and following them with a speech on "The Present World Situation" before "an immense company of the flower of the Christians of Buda Pest and the student delegates," thus breaking his own record for a single day, he wrote to Leila.

Again in the lakeside parlor at Mohonk just a year after the Federation meeting, he described the WSCF briefly to an arbitration conference and declared that his journeys during the intervening months had proved that the delegates had "not only received visions of a drawing together of the nations and races but are incarnating and realizing their visions." And he forecast that when the WSCF would next meet in "the danger zone of the world—in southeastern Europe and the Austro-Hungarian Empire," it would "seek to diffuse the atmosphere of Mohonk among those peoples." That opportunity never came.

PART 15: The Home Front, 1910–1914

The international activities described thus far in this chapter occupied somewhat more than one third of Mott's time between 1910 and August, 1914, in terms of days he could count, but much more than that in planning and promotion by correspondence and in committee. The rest went into his "first love," the SVM, and the YMCA foreign work, along with a dozen related responsibilities. Underlying all of these was the ever-increasing requirement of more and more funds as the optimism of the times inflated every enterprise.

By 1914 the American Student YMCA had seventeen national secretaries of whom half were specialists, in Bible study, preparatory school work, the theological schools, Indian schools, sex education, and "social study and service." Eight summer and winter conferences annually assembled almost 3,000 student leaders who in turn were guided by some 100 local campus secretaries; the latter had their own national get-together at Estes Park, Colorado, in 1913. New study courses including Fosdick's *Manhood of the Master* were introduced that year. David S. Cairns wrote in *The Student World* after a six-week visit to the States that the very magnitude of the American Movement suggested the risk of its evolving into "a church of a very peculiar kind," even possibly engaging in a sort of "chronic" rather than "acute" rivalry with the denominations. Mott was either too busy with world affairs, or subconsciously planned to leave the issue to his successor, for he did not meet the challenge of the denominational campus pastor movement which was beginning to make itself felt by 1914, and that partly because of the very success of the "Y's."[131]

After Edinburgh 1910 he no longer engaged in the frequent continent-wide campus evangelistic tours that had played such an important part in his earlier promotion of the Movement, concentrating instead on a few strategic campuses each year. In October, 1911, he visited the Canadian West from Winnipeg to Vancouver and later that winter toured in the American West and South. April, 1913, found him at the University of Iowa, the first week of March, 1914, at Columbia in a series of meetings sponsored by the dozen student Associations of the city of New York. The editor of the *Columbia Spectator* declared it to be "the most remarkable student religious campaign ever held at this University." Total attendance was estimated conservatively at 8,000; the lecture series ranked not only "among the best, but also among the best managed affairs held on this campus." The editor was intrigued by Mott's stress on the will: "Religion is a matter of the will. When our reason tells us what the truth is, then we must follow it." Mott had then pleaded with men not to allow "procrastination or cowardice" to prevent them from accepting Christianity "after the mind had been freed of all doubt as to its truth."[132]

A few weeks later he gave a similar series at Harvard and in May spent a week at Washington and Lee in Virginia, where the campaign was planned by a senior named Francis Pickens Miller. Miller had met Mott at a summer conference at the end of his freshman year. Impressed by the idea of religion as a matter of the will, Miller wrote in his autobiography that "here was a giant of a man":

> He talked about Moscow, Calcutta, Tokyo, and Rio de Janeiro as if they were nearby towns, and he spoke of people belonging to different nations and races as if they were members of the same society. This man extended my horizons to the whole habitable world and provided me with a universal frame of reference. For the next fourteen or fifteen years he was my hero.[133]

In the summer of 1912 Miller and his brother, who became a missionary to Iran, had attended Northfield, "a time for thinking deep thoughts and dreaming great dreams." The next summer the two young men had gone to the secretarial conference at Estes Park, Willis Weatherford hoping to obtain them for the YMCA secretaryship. A notable event of Francis' senior year was the "Mott campaign":

> Since I naturally liked administration, I set to work with a good heart to make our W & L campaign a model of its kind. . . . The committee structure worked well under competent chairmen, and I had an agent in each fraternity to distribute literature and get the boys out. Further, the administration and the faculty could not have been more cooperative. The result was that practically the entire student body as well as many townspeople attended the meetings. Mott was much impressed; he was even more impressed when mother gave him a photograph of Robert E. Lee which the General himself had autographed for her.

Mott wrote Mrs. McCormick that the week had been "splendid." For a great many years the picture of Lee on Traveler hung in his office. Miller served with David R. Porter in the preparatory schools for the next three years and in the parlance of the times became, in John L. Mott's phrase, one of his father's "fair-haired boys," succeeding Mott as Chairman of the WSCF in 1928.[134]

Although Mott continued to stress personal morality in his evangelistic addresses and in his Sunday services on the college and university chapel circuit, as well as at Northfield, Lake Geneva, or Blue Ridge, themes such as "Principles and Helps in Determining a Life Work" were popular with students, and the widening ethical concerns of the times became increasingly apparent. The zeal of Mott's younger colleagues must have caused Cairns to warn the American Movement against sinking "from a religious to a moral, philanthropic, and humanitarian level." At about the same time, William R. Moody, son of the evangelist, criticized Mott for moving too far in that direction. Mott replied that he held "as strong convictions as you do with reference to the cardinal points of our faith." This may have been a phase in the gradual separation of the moderate and conservative followers of D. L. Moody, as represented by the Northfield Schools in contrast to the Bible Institute in Chicago, whose directorship had once been offered to Mott by its founder, who recognized in him an irenic spirit similar to his own.[135]

Or it might have been a preview of the opening gulf between liberal and conservative Protestants that was widened by the publication of *The Fundamentals* at this time. Unlike Robert E. Speer, his lifelong friend and colleague, Mott did not contribute to those twelve booklets which were distributed to all English-speaking Protestant religious workers around the world by wealthy sponsors. At various times, Mott was related to at least four others of the authors—A. T. Pierson, Bishop H. G. C. Moule, Prebendary Webb-Peploe, and Charles R. Erdman. For Mott to have identified with this reactionary, divisive, and political movement would not only have been contrary to his spirit and attitudes but would have compromised his ecumenical leadership. Because of his constant contacts with the university and theological centers of the world, he could not possibly have adopted the dogmatic thought forms that came later to unite political power groups in the major denominations. This was a kind of controversy into which he would never enter, nor would he ever move as far to the left as the liberals whose theology became "secularized and innocuous." Franklin H. Littell's summary is to the point: "In Mott, simple piety and social concern, personal evangelism and organizational genius, were combined to a degree rare in the history of the church."[136]

Mott had no hesitation in endorsing the social gospel because of his position that "there are not two gospels, one social and one individual. There is but one Christ who lived, died, and rose again, and relates Himself to the lives of men." There can be no conflict "between the emphasis on the conversion of the individual and the regeneration of society," he or his associate Edward C. Jenkins editorialized in *The Student World* in 1912:

> The two are complementary, not contrasted. Evangelism without social work is deficient; social work without evangelism is impotent. [If we can] transform men within, they will soon change their surroundings. But how helpless we are to get at their real selves through the layers of prejudice and misconceptions, and to penetrate with the Gospel the wretchedness of bad housing, exhausting labor, and political chicanery. The social worker must have some message to carry that will inspire as well as arouse the fighting blood, give hope for clean hearts as well as clean streets.[137]

The social gospel emphasis in the SCM was not unrelated to the nation-wide propaganda of the "Men and Religion Forward Movement." This lay effort to reach men and boys with the gospel, which originated in the YMCA, found the social message so popular during the heyday of Progressivism that it became a virtual social gospel campaign, of which Walter Rauschenbusch could say that it had "made social Christianity orthodox."[138] Some of the prominent speakers of the Movement were attracted into the college field. Mott both spoke and wrote for it, and occasionally teamed with Sherwood Eddy or the Progressive Raymond Robins to stage social gospel campaigns on the larger campuses.

Robins, for whom a biography is awaited, was a striking personality, most attractive to younger men such as E. Stanton Turner or Conrad Hoffman who joined in these efforts. Robins had grown up in the West where he worked as a miner in the Rockies and had "struck it rich" in the

Alaska gold rush of 1899, during which he had a dramatic conversion experience the effects of which never left him. From a base in Chicago he sponsored liberal causes and in 1912 was one of the founders of the Progressive Party, running unsuccessfully for the Senate in Illinois in 1914. In the college year 1915–1916, he and John L. Childs, then on the staff of the Student YMCA's *Intercollegian,* visited forty-two campuses, one of which was the University of Kansas, where Mott also starred.[139]

In 1908 Mott had attracted E. C. Carter, student secretary at Harvard, to the national staff to promote and coordinate social service activities. A. M. Trawick came next. In 1912, when Carter moved to foreign service, Mott brought Richard H. Edwards from the University of Wisconsin where he had developed a unique program of wide-ranging discussions of current social problems including the Negro. The thoroughness of Edwards' approach, which represented the best contemporary social science, appealed to Mott. Under the tutelage of such men and through his own constant visitation of university centers, he was able to bring significant leadership to broaden the horizons of the SCM's.

The climax both in thought and in proposals for action by the Student Movement in the social realm came at a special conference called by Mott at Garden City, New York, in April, 1914. This "Conference on Social Needs" of the new Council of North American Student Movements, of which Mott was chairman, was almost the last significant meeting of its kind with virtually no students present. It brought together some sixty representatives of both the American and Canadian men's and women's student organizations—not only the secretaries charged with such concerns: Edwards, Weatherford—but also the outstanding social gospel leaders: Henry Sloane Coffin, Charles R. Henderson, Owen Lovejoy, Walter Rauschenbusch, and Harry Ward. Its report, *Social Needs of the Colleges of North America,* was hailed by *The Student World* as "a summons to penitence for our share in the corporate sins of society and to a new faith, a new order, a new devotion of service." Full of "explosive ideas," the booklet spoke of the denial of "Christ and His social teachings in our present civilization," and challenged students preparing for all professions to "solemn dedication of their lives to service under the leadership of Christ":

> The crisis of the hour calls for men and women consecrated enough to be willing to see our social order for what it really is, to acknowledge that, resting as it does on competition, it is unchristian and contrary to the will of Christ, and then to dedicate themselves to the thinking out of a solution that harmonizes with His teaching and to withstand the scorn, misrepre-

sentation and persecution of the men of this generation. More than all it calls for men and women of mighty faith in God, which nothing can shake, faith that will remove mountains of indifference, ignorance, and denial of the power of God to transform human society as well as individuals, according to the mind of Christ, faith which already sees the vision of a new order of human society, founded upon principles of cooperation and fellowship.[140]

The Conference proposed the broader social education of all college students and asked its parent body to enter into negotiations with the colleges and universities of the two countries to effect the necessary curricular changes.

Although Willis Weatherford was present, the Garden City Conference hardly touched upon the Negro problem in the United States, possibly because that issue did not seem to concern the Canadians. But the impetus from the WSCF at Mohonk was not to be lost and two weeks after Garden City Mott presided over a Negro Christian Student Conference of sixty whites and 600 blacks at Clark University in Atlanta, the first integrated gathering of its kind. Harlan P. Beach, who reported it for *The Student World*, rated Mott "the oustanding personality" but important parts were played by Booker T. Washington, Weatherford, William A. Hunton, and a group of southern white speakers. Mott opened the Convention with an address on "Fostering Right Race Relations" in which he struck a note of urgency in the "absolutely unprecedented world situation" of the moment—a theme with which he was much concerned as international relations in Europe deteriorated that spring. The address, however, dealt only indirectly with the immediate aspects of race in the American South, subtly placing them in the context of international relations and the unity being forced upon the human race by technology. The purpose of the Conference was not to raise issues but to get representatives of both races together in Christian fellowship.

Mott was followed by Washington, who spoke more directly to the immediate situation, counseling "faith in the future of our race," patience in cultivating the good will of the white man, modesty in advancing the Negro's claims "for justice and to be of service." Beach said that there had been a deliberate attempt to avoid "all divisive questions, such as those of color, politics, and social segregation, thus ensuring harmony and begetting a sincere friendliness." Common objectives for both races were the evangelization of Africa by joint effort, "the bond of common service in social betterment," and study of all the racial and social problems involved. From a perspective of sixty years this may seem an innocuous beginning but it was a start; it led to what became one of the most persistent and pervasive concerns of the American SCM's. At the time it was "one of the most significant conventions ever held in this country." Robert Moton, then head of Tuskegee Institute, who would become head of Hampton Institute following the death of Washington the next year, noting that the meeting had been initiated, planned, and presided over by Mott, added that it "did more than any other single thing to crystallize into real practical action and to draw into cooperative work the many groups of people interested in the development of better interracial understanding."[141]

Immediately after it, Mott wrote to Mrs. McCormick's daughter Mrs. Emmons Blaine, who was underwriting Weatherford's salary, that he felt humiliated that he had let so many years pass without becoming involved in this question and assured her that he would seek "to make up for lost time in any years of service" that might remain to him. And to Mrs. T. B. Blackstone, another Chicago supporter, who had helped with the expenses of the Conference, he wrote that it had done more than any previous event "to create right relations between the Christian leaders of both races" and expressed the belief that she would be pleased to know that the $2,500 she had given toward its cost had proved to be "one of the most profitable gifts" she had ever made.[142]

The interracial note had been characteristic of the SVM from its beginning, though it was usually heard in international terms. Wishard had invited foreign students including Orientals to Mount Hermon in 1886 and Mott had been deeply concerned about Chinese students in Japan and in the United States. He had brought into being a Chinese students' organization and had assigned a full-time secretary to it; when it met at Northfield in 1912 he spoke to it. The rationale for this was that the missionary assignment should be widened to include students in foreign environments. By softening the shock of adjustment through friendly assistance, organization, Christian fellowship, and in several cities Christian hostels, foreign students such as those Chinese studying abroad on Boxer funds would return home to positions of leadership imbued with Christian principles.

Basil Mathews, Mott's biographer of 1934, relates a bizarre and possibly partially apocryphal incident of this period which must have been told him by Mott. The story, which became part of the Mott legend, opened with a conversation between him and Cleveland H. Dodge concerning the needs of foreign students:

Mott chanced to mention that he had never met Andrew Carnegie. Dodge promptly took him to Carnegie's home. Carnegie soon stamped in, irritable from losing his golf game.

"I have brought you a man whom you ought to know," said Dodge, introducing Mott. "What has he got to say to us?" asked Carnegie. Mott plunged into the foreign student problem.

"You have got a charmer here," said Carnegie. "But why are you giving your life to such work? You are wasting your time. What is your plan?"

Mott outlined his scheme to assign able men to major university centers from Tokyo to New York in order to expose foreign students to the best instead of the worst side of Western civilization and to afford them "good comradeship and stimulating ideals." He concluded by asking Carnegie for $10,000 a year for several years.

Carnegie accepted if Dodge would match his pledge. Dodge met the challenge. On the way back down town they met the liberal philanthropist and former Morgan partner George Perkins and told him the story. "If you've got Carnegie in it there must be something to the proposition," Perkins replied and added his ten thousand.

The next evening Mott sat next to William Sloane, the New York furniture merchant and International Committee member, at a committee meeting and told him the story. "Let me add eight thousand dollars to that," said Sloane.[143]

The next day Mott launched the Committee on Friendly Relations among Foreign Students, which did yeoman service for several decades, much of it under the irrepressible Charles Hurrey. Not long after its founding Mr. and Mrs. Andrew Carnegie entertained seventy-five foreign students in their home: "There were Chinese, Japanese, Indians, Turks, Greeks, Syrians, Armenians and Persians present." By 1938 the Committee had six secretaries and an annual budget the size of the original outlay.

Just before Christmas, 1913, Mott returned from reporting on his world tour to the Continuation Committee and the missionary societies of Europe. On the last day of the year the seventh Quadrennial Convention of the Student Volunteer Movement opened in Kansas City. By this time 5,882 Volunteers recruited through the SVM had sailed to foreign fields and there were Volunteer groups in nine countries. Substantial excerpts from the Edinburgh 1910 findings were sent with the Kansas City advance materials, and the Convention itself manifested the influence of both Edinburgh and the British SVM Quadrennial of 1912 which had struck a resounding social note.

It is impossible to summarize in a few pages a convention attended by 5,000 representatives of 755 institutions, the reporting of which filled a volume of 800 pages with the addresses of more than 130 leaders, of whom twenty were Orientals. One of the five thousand recalled it half a century afterward:

> We were told that the whole world was rapidly turning toward the Christian faith and all that was needed was for a few more thousand American students to go abroad as ambassadors of the Kingdom of God. There was present an air of invincible confidence and optimism which swept many of the delegates out of their narrow and parochial lives and inspired them with a vision of a new heaven and a new earth. For those who were present, this conference in retrospect seemed like the glory of a golden sunset before black darkness descended upon the earth the following summer.[144]

The Reverend R. F. Horton of London wrote in *The Student World* that "the leaders were John Mott, Robert Speer, and Sherwood Eddy—men raised up for such work and such an occasion." This may have been the first time this triumvirate was so identified; it would not be the last. All three were laymen. Another delegate described the Convention for the *Christian World*, noting that although Mott had just returned from Europe he had appeared "vigorous and self-contained, showing no outward sign that the extensive journeys and prodigious labors of the past four years had worn upon him physically." Nor had the "exceptional honors" and "unprecedented reception in the Orient" inflated his ego:

> He is the same, simple, sincere, affable, approachable man that he was when D. L. Moody put his quickening touch upon him at Mount Hermon a quarter of a century ago. It would be a mistake to put even John R. Mott on a pedestal and affirm that the future of the student Christian movement depends solely on him. Already at Kansas City there was in evidence a group of men like-minded and with similar insight and power.

Francis Harmon, a freshman from the University of Virginia, heard Mott's challenge and said to himself, "this is he, Whom every man in arms should wish to be."[145]

In his opening address, Mott sounded themes that are not unfamiliar, but he gave them a new urgency and grandeur: For the first time, this International Convention meets in the Upper Mississippi Valley, where there is a spaciousness that has ever inspired men with vision to see things in the large, as has the pioneer spirit, the spirit of adventure, the spirit that not only sees visions but is not afraid of them, that makes effective what it sees.

> We have come here to face in its entirety the task that confronts the forces of Christianity as they look into the non-Christian world. . . . to remind ourselves that we who acknowledge Jesus Christ as our Lord . . . are all one . . . to realize the spiritual solidarity of the Christian students of North America, and to remind ourselves of a larger unity, the one that binds us to the Christian students of other lands and other races . . . to send out the call to the present generation of students of North America to face an absolutely unprecedented world-situation.[146]

Later in the week he devoted an entire address to the last theme, reviewing the impressions gained from his most recent travels, describing vividly specific incidents in Russia, Turkey, India, Ceylon, Korea, China, and Japan that added to the urgency of the situation. "The blush of shame has come to my cheeks," he exclaimed, as I have seen how the corrupt influences of so-called Western civilization are "eating like gangrene into the less highly organized peoples of the world." This speech would become a chapter in his next book.

In presenting the Executive Committee's report (it required thirty pages to print) he noted that almost 1,500 Volunteers had sailed since the Rochester Quadrennial of 1910. He closed the Convention with a meditation on the theme of "Daily Communion with God":

> At the beginning of this Convention, we gathered quickly around that central life-giving personality, Christ our Lord. He has loomed larger and larger in each succeeding hour. He is with us in this closing hour. We remember His practice of rising in the morning "a great while before day," and that He "departed into a solitary place, and there prayed." I leave this as the last question I will ask you in this Convention: If Christ found it necessary, or even desirable, to spend time unhurriedly alone with the Heavenly Father, can you and I afford to take the risk of doing without this life-expanding practice? God forbid that we should![147]

Speer, the second member of the lay triumvirate, spoke at the opening session and later gave one of the keynote addresses of the Convention, on the SVM watchword, reaffirming the historic slogan and attempting to "rearrange our emphasis" in the recognition of universality as the essence of Christianity and of the needs of the world. Mott, on behalf of the Executive Committee, refuted the British move to abandon the watchword, declaring that in view of its secondary effects as well as its direct benefits, it should be emphasized in the future even more than in the past. He could rightly claim, as he had in 1911 on the twenty-fifth anniversary of the founding of the SVM, that Edinburgh had brought Christians to look at the world as a whole, to confront "the world as a unit by the Christian Church as a unit." It had not been so in 1886. Later historians are agreed on the ecumenical importance of the pioneering role of the SVM.[148]

The social gospel emphasis was not as explicit at Kansas City in 1914 as it had been at Liverpool in 1914 where missions and social questions were combined. Yet it was a persistent theme, stated most dramatically by Sherwood Eddy and implemented as integral to mission by Charles R. Henderson, Shailer Mathews, A. M. Trawick, and speakers from abroad who described the need for Christianity in the social and political life of their countries. There were few, if any, conservatives and no identifiable fundamentalists on the program. It was clearly a new day in missions for all of the features of "The Modern Missionary," as James L. Barton, executive of the Congregational board delineated them some months later, were largely assumed. Mott, who was on intimate terms with Barton, would have concurred in his conclusion that the modern missionary "is a Christian worker of boundless vision, with the goal of his labor nothing less than nations transformed, new civilizations constructed on eternal foundations, and the ultimate consummation of the Kingdom of God on earth." In all this the missionary movement now reflected the goals of the social gospel and the Progressive era. Both Mott and Speer would have agreed with R. Pierce Beaver's much later judgment that in these years their own views remained "staunchly evangelical" yet "responsive to new insights and to a growing ecumenical consciousness," while at the same time "the aim and motive of the mission came to be grounded, not in proof-texts, but in the person, the work, and the lordship of Jesus Christ." So also would Sherwood Eddy, the third member of the triumvirate, who charged the departing delegates to action in the arenas of "human need and human service."[149]

During this period Mott was active in the Foreign Missions Conference of North America, serving on its executive Committee of Reference and Counsel and the Board of Missionary Preparation. He was twice delegated to ask the Rockefeller Foundation for financial aid to its projects. The larger of these was the request for a half-million dollars for a "common headquarters" building to house the Conference's growing activities. The Foundation preferred to provide furnishings and to make annual matching grants. This gift, "a good illustration of the wisdom of this helpful donor" (John D. Rockefeller, Jr.), proved "a veritable godsend." An entire floor was obtained at 25 Madison Avenue, with space not only for meetings but to house the archives and research materials that became the Missionary Research Library.[150]

As early as 1890 Mott had shown an interest in the acquisition and organization of archives and library materials when he contacted Orville Dewey, the originator of the Dewey decimal system of library classification. He early aspired to make the SVM collection of mission materials the best of its kind in the world and always took a personal interest in the exhibits at conferences. His first pamphlets included bibliographies and most of his own books listed titles for the working pastor's missions library or similar suggestions. By this time his personal library, kept at home, required the occasional skills of a professional. His personal archives and those of the WSCF that he accumulated likewise involved careful organization according to unique systems of classification that he may have developed himself.[151]

Shortly after the turn of the century, Mott met Charles H. Fahs, an experienced newspaper reporter, and obtained an increasing share of his time as research secretary, first on the two editions of the missions *Atlas* that was prepared under Harlan P. Beach (Fahs "did most of the work") for Edinburgh, which Fahs attended. In 1911 Mott sent Fahs to Germany to learn the language "and to become better acquainted with Continental methods and points of view." At Mott's suggestion Fahs served as secretary of the Lake Mohonk meeting of the Continuation Committee and was assigned to its commission on statistics; he was archivist and historian on Mott's 1912–13 world tour. It appears that Mott first asked for Rockefeller support for a missions research center in 1911, but the spring of 1914 brought the realization of a long-cherished plan. "The vision was yours, the basic funds for a firm and sound beginning were secured by you from Mr. Rockefeller," Fahs reminded Mott in 1947. For years the Missionary Research Library ranked as "the chief institution of its kind in the world," Mott reminisced in 1944. An example of its ongoing importance may be seen in its holdings of the vast correspondence between Oldham and Mott from before Edinburgh, utilized in this chapter, and extending another thirty years.

Throughout these years Mott's support of the Laymen's Missionary Movement, of which his brother-in-law J. Campbell White was general secretary from 1907 to 1915, evidenced his contention that "the layman must rise up and make Christianity what it was in the early days when every Christian was a missionary in the sense of spreading the faith," a position that Franklin Littell has described as "characteristic of the great American churches of his generation." After Edinburgh, Mott's many speeches before laymen's metropolitan, state, regional, or national conferences, or at luncheons and dinners, became more distinctly ecumenical in their thrust, and his appeal must have contributed substantially to the vastly increased financial support of missions that was realized in the two decades after 1906. Mott was one of the founders of the Movement (which grew out of the SVM Quadrennial of 1906) and inaugurated it in several European countries. It enlisted the support of Presidents Roosevelt, Taft, and Wilson, not to mention Admiral A. T. Mahan and many members of Congress.[152]

Under Mott's administration, with Colton and E. C. Jenkins as associates and Sherwood Eddy as secretary for Asia, the Foreign Work of the American YMCA flourished in the years immediately prior to the War. The building campaign launched at the White House in 1910 was successful beyond expectation and the number of secretaries on the field reached an all-time high with 240 men at work in 1913, thirty-six of them being recruits that year. About half devoted one or two terms to student work upon arrival at their assignments, thus building bases for the WSCF and inextricably mingling the two movements. In addition to Edward S. Harkness, the McCormicks, A. A. Hyde, G. W. Birks, John Wanamaker, the Rockefellers—father and son—and W. H. Hoover there were many whose contributions of capital funds and special gifts were in addition to their annual support of as much as $50,000 to the regular budget, which under Colton's tireless efforts reached $462,000 by 1915. The LMM had a notable positive effect. That these were the "halcyon years of the budget" was attested by the 1914 commendation of Mott by Starr Murphy of the Rockefeller Foundation that "your board never has a deficit."[153]

The secretaries sent out were instructed to make themselves dispensable as soon as possible. They were coached on how to develop local boards of directors, to spread influence by persuasion rather than largesse. Charles J. Ewald of Latin America believed this to be Mott's greatest contribution to the YMCA's international expansion and the chief factor in the rapidity of its growth. And there were few failures. Each man knew that Mott would never let him down; the resulting brotherhood was itself a major attraction into the profession. Mott possessed an uncanny ability to plumb the capacities of men to contribute to it, which provides a clue to the almost uniformly high caliber of the staffs not only of the YMCA foreign work but of the SVM and the WSCF. Wherever and whenever possible, and often unexpectedly, Mott added a personal and social bond; L. Newton Hayes recalled an occasion at a Silver Bay conference about 1914 when after an evening speech he and a few others shared in a midnight raid on the ice-box and Mott himself prepared a steak snack.[154]

Historians of the ecumenical movement trace three strands from Edinburgh. The first of these Mott wove through the Continuation Committee, which led to the International Missionary Council after the Great War. The second was Faith and Order, which grew largely out of the initiative of the Episcopal Bishop (of the Philippines) Charles H. Brent. Mott performed small parts in the early development of Faith and Order, having known Brent from at least as early as 1905. The two were agreed in their lifetime goals of uniting "all those churches which confess faith in Jesus Christ our Lord as God and Savior," the phrase used at the first World's YMCA conference at Paris in 1855 that moved on into history via the WSCF to the World Council of Churches.[155]

Fired by Edinburgh to "go away with some fresh duties to perform," Brent convinced the General Convention of his church that October to appoint a commission to promote a World Conference on Faith and Order. Unquestionably he discussed the proposal with Mott, who in turn canvassed it with Randall Davidson, the Archbishop of Canterbury, that winter; Davidson was to become an active supporter of the plan. It must have been a topic of frequent conversations between Mott and Silas McBee on their "Eirenic Journey" that next spring, 1911.

Early in 1913 Mott brought Tissington Tatlow of the British SCM to the States to travel among the Episcopal colleges in the hope of bringing more of them into the American Student Movement. When the WSCF met at Lake Mohonk that spring, Brent was a featured speaker and his intimate friend and collaborator in Faith and Order, Robert H. Gardiner, secretary of the F. & O. Commission, was an American delegate. Three weeks later Brent gave a similar address to the Northfield student conference, where during these years Mott was at the apex of his leadership.[156]

As the plans for the Faith and Order conference moved forward it was hoped that a preliminary gathering might be held in New York as early as 1917. Mott attended a planning committee meeting in March, 1914, where he suggested that a deputation be sent to the "Continent of Europe and the Levant" and offered to make contacts with knowledgeable persons who could provide interpreters and guides in the countries to be visited. As it turned out, most of these were from Student Christian Movement sources, such as Valdemar Ammudsen, a Danish member of the General Committee of the WSCF and later bishop, who supplied names and offered his own services. The War forced the abandonment of the project until the spring of 1919 when an American Episcopal commission did go to Europe and the Near East. Everywhere they were cordially received, particularly by the Eastern Orthodox; Mott's visits of 1911 and the WSCF's wartime programs helped pave the way.[157]

PART 16: The Guns of August, 1914

In perspective, Mott did not accomplish the Herculean tasks reviewed in this chapter out of a sense of duty or because he was a "workaholic." Rather, this was "the age of energy" and crisis was upon it. Edinburgh worked under a sense of urgency. Emil Brunner had not yet stated his "crisis theology" but Mott lived by the Biblical conviction that "now is the appointed time." He renewed the springs of his inner life and the sources of his physical energy daily at home or wherever he was, annually at Lac des Iles and with the friends of the Quiet Day. Like the human heart, he rested between beats, which is to say that he worked relaxed. He did it by planning his time, adhering to a schedule, refusing to be pushed by pressure. He was sustained by friends in prayer around the world, and his efficiency multiplied by the personal assistance of dedicated aides and private secretaries who had been tested in the crucible of the Association directorship and found willing to subordinate ambition or career to his personal service. Such were William R. Stewart from 1905 to 1910 and Edward C. Jenkins for the next three years; Hans P. Andersen, who filled this gap at various times, died prematurely in 1914. Benjamin R. Barber came into this relationship in 1913 and was at once "the greatest helper I have ever had"; he served happily, congenially, loyally, and with great skill as "man Friday" through the remainder of Mott's life.[158]

The years described in this chapter were the happiest ones at Lac des Iles, for all four children were there each summer. There were long hours for reading the books Mott had noted in his pocket diary and picked up around the world. Fishing in the lake was still rewarding. Each year there was a fresh pair of kittens, which John R. loved but never realized that Leila only tolerated. There came to be a guest house, one of the first occupants of which was Count Moltke of Denmark.

These periods of joy and renewal usually ended with August. In 1912 John wrote to Leila from Northfield on August 31, "What a happy Summer we have had. It will make the whole coming year richer and happier." On the same date in 1913 he repeated the theme: this had been a "wonderful" vacation. "I shall never cease to be thankful for it. You and each of the children mean more than ever to me and I enter the new year greatly strengthened thereby."

In 1914 the first weeks of the vacation at Lac des Iles lay under the darkening shadow of an assassination at Sarajevo. Although for months he had spoken of the Balkans as the danger zone of the world, like most Americans Mott expected the issue to sputter out. But instead, the lights of all Europe gradually went out, like the sinking *Titanic*, as the darkness of war settled over the Western world. In the evening of August 4, Mott took the sleeper from Montreal to New York. He awoke to the news that Germany had invaded Belgium. Perhaps there flashed across his mind a sentence from the Edinburgh message to the Church in Christian lands: "The providence of God has led us all into a new world of opportunity, of danger, and of duty." New duties demanded by the War would take him into danger and opportunity of which he had not dreamed.

8

Then Came the Test

It is impossible yet to take in the meaning of this terrible blow to all that we have been working for during the past few years. Our deepest need, I feel sure, is to continue to have faith in God, and to believe that not even human sin and madness can ultimately defeat His purpose of love for the world.
—J. H. Oldham[1]

I WOULD RATHER LIVE in the next ten years than in any time of which I have ever read or ever dreamed," John Mott told the Mohonk Conference of the WSCF in June, 1913. That decade would be the most fateful of his life and the apex of his career. It would drastically change and redirect his thrust, open vast areas of which he had hardly dreamed, and tax every ability beyond all previous demands. "It was the Great War which exacted the greatest toll," wrote Will Stewart, his former secretary, "not the super-human task to which he set himself" in 1914, but the shattering of the purposes "to which he had given a lifetime" that affected him, Stewart continued; even so, "he did not give up in despair" but set at once about saving the fragments.[2]

On stunt night at Northfield in 1913, Baron Nicolay had innocently but prophetically presented a cacophony of discord, with representatives of the nations each singing their national anthems in their native tongues. In hours the War reduced to chaos Mott's and millions of others' carefully laid plans. He was planning to live in Europe for two years in order to concentrate on the Near East, to cement ties with the Orthodox, to pursue the Christian approach to Islam; the Continuation Committee agenda for a September, 1914, meeting had been ready since June, and plans for the next World Missionary Conference were being considered. As the fabric of the Western world disintegrated, would the

430

WSCF network be disrupted? And what would happen to the YMCA foreign work and the worldwide missionary enterprise?

By cable and as fast as the steamships of that day could bring assurances of support and requests for aid to orphaned missions, such messages came to Mott from around the world. One of the first was a cable from leaders of the China Continuation Committee for financial aid to European missions in China. There were also shock waves from Orientals who were "very sorry to see such a war among European countries, which we are accustomed to think of as Christian countries." Could not Mott inspire some action to stop "this barbarous murdering" of Christians by Christians, asked a group of Japanese. Neither Mott nor Christendom itself could have done that. In fact, the concept of Western Christendom would also be a casualty. [3]

PART 1: The Present World Situation

The most pressing item on Mott's calendar for August, 1914, had been the scheduled meeting of the Continuation Committee at Oxford, September 17 to 24. He was booked to sail on the fifth of September. After a full day's work on the fifth of August, he returned to Lac des Iles for the long week-end. During that time the Germans began the destruction of the forts of Liège; on Friday, August 7, such of the luckless delegates to the Church Peace Union conference at Constance as had been able to reach London, organized what came to be known as the "World Alliance for International Friendship Through the Churches." Mott would later serve on its American executive. [4]

Also on that Friday, Mott learned two weeks later, Oldham and his associate Kenneth Maclennan assembled a group of British missionary leaders. They decided to postpone the Continuation Committee meeting "indefinitely" and to "look for action primarily" to the constituent national committees, through the Edinburgh office where possible. The two men offered their services to the British Conference of Missionary Societies and were made joint secretaries of that body. The group believed that the situation of Continental missionary societies would become "incomparably worse" than that of their own; the work of the Dutch and Paris societies would be "almost paralyzed through lack of funds" and the plight of the German bodies would be still more serious. By the end of the month Oldham wrote to Mott that missionary work on the Continent was in danger of "collapsing altogether." The August 7 meeting resolved to raise a fund to aid them and hoped that America could match twenty to twenty-five thousand pounds; as a "practical demonstration of the reality of Christian love and of its power to transcend national differences," such an expression would "give a demonstration of the solidarity created by the Edinburgh Conference that would have a valuable moral effect, and make a strong appeal to the friends of missions at home and to missionaries and the Church in the mission field."[5]

Thus in actuality the leadership of the Continuation Committee passed temporarily to its secretaries in Britain and to the British Conference, to the North American body through which Mott worked, and to bodies such as the China Continuation Committee or the National Missionary Council of India. As these shouldered their own burdens they were not only actualizing the spirit of Edinburgh but anticipating the International Missionary Council of the 1920's. The Continuation Committee, paralyzed by the War, became a shadow body to be utilized occasionally but having no real authority or existence.[6]

While Oldham was dictating a lengthy description of all this on Monday, August 10, he received a cable from Mott, now back at his desk for the next ten days, approving the cancellation of the Committee meeting and announcing his intention to make the crossing in September. Some of Oldham's letters did not come until the eve of his departure, but several cables, which we do not have, were exchanged and a British agenda set up for Mott, who also established appointments with Fries in neutral Sweden and with the officers of the World's YMCA in Geneva and Basle. He arranged for meetings with representatives of the FMCNA, a few foreign secretaries, mission board executives, the North American Student Council, and with President Wilson. Satisfied that he had made all possible preparations until the end of the American vacation period, he returned to the Lac for three more weeks of rest, meditation, and planning for what would be the most demanding autumn of his life. The Canadian YMCA's offer of service to the troops had already been accepted by the government; in actuality, the War was closer to Mott in the Canadian woods than in New York City.

That was only until the receipt of a cablegram from World Alliance officers in Geneva at the end of August. They set forth the needs of twenty million men under arms, of whom two hundred thousand were YMCA members:

World's Committee ready for co-operation army work with national committees. Dependent America for funding. No money in Europe. Can you
help with men and money?

Morse replied that they would do everything possible, and that Mott
would go to Europe to study the situation. When Mott returned to New
York in the third week of September, the first battle of the Marne had
been fought, the German Army was a mere twenty miles from Paris, and
was dug in north of the Aisne in the first of the infamous trenches that
would characterize the struggle to follow. And in the far corners of the
globe the Allies had begun seizure of German colonies, bringing chaos to
their missions. [7]

Oldham's first letter expressing his horror at the outbreak of the
War, which did not reach Mott until September 21, is a classic of the
ecumenical movement that must await his biography for full publication;
Mott marked these sentences:

> It is impossible yet to take in the meaning of this terrible blow to all that
> we have been working for during the past few years. Our deepest need, I
> feel sure, is to continue to have faith in God, and to believe that not even
> human sin and madness can ultimately defeat His purpose of love for the
> world. . . . I am sure that the first feeling in all our hearts must be one of
> penitence and contrition. We need not trouble about the distribution of
> responsibility. We need to get behind that to the fundamental fact that
> Christian Europe has departed so far from God and rejected so completely
> the rule of Christ that a catastrophe of this kind is possible. . . . We need to
> bow in deep humility before God. . . . We must strive . . . to maintain the
> international fellowship and love which we began to learn at Edinburgh. [8]

Oldham refused to sign a reply drafted by the Archbishop of Canterbury
to the German churchmen's "Appeal to Protestant Christians Abroad,"
but he believed strongly that he should prepare a statement for the
Review. Mott cautioned against anything conceivably open to misin-
terpretation, but Oldham persisted. The article, published in the October issue, was an ecumenical milepost. It affirmed the Edinburgh principles and asserted the need for "unity in the midst of strife." Not to
mention the War and its effects in the *Review*, he had written to Mott,
would indicate "an aloofness and a lack of human fellowship which
would be wholly inconsistent with the spirit of the Edinburgh Conference, and would be felt by most of our readers to be a repudiation of the
bonds that unite us with them." Mott later admitted "that God has used"
the article. During these weeks Oldham's Greek mind made him the

philosopher of the moment, while Mott's Roman mind drove him to plans for action.

Oldham experienced considerable difficulty in contacting German and other Continental missions leaders, but Mott had avenues open to him through the WSCF and the World's YMCA. He early turned to them to explore the possibilities of service to men in the armies and navies of the belligerents and of work among prisoners of war on both sides. He addressed himself to the actual ties that held together the constituent bodies of the Federation and utilized his numerous personal contacts with missions leaders, especially of the societies whose stations had been orphaned. The itinerary for his European trip in the fall of 1914 was set up through these agencies.

Before sailing on the *Nieuw Amsterdam* on September 29 he delivered to the printer the copy for his latest book, to be published by the SVM in December as *The Present World Situation*. Devoted to the missionary enterprise rather than the tragic current events, six chapters of its eight were revisions of lectures given the previous spring at Harvard and at Boston University, and at the Kansas City SVM Convention; one had been published in the IRM in April, and the final essay, on "Where to Place the Chief Emphasis in the Missionary Enterprise," was a fresh assessment in contrast to previous judgments based on his earlier world journeys.

> I am constrained to shift the emphasis entirely from numbers to quality, and especially to the spiritual aspect of the life and activity of the workers. . . . Beyond the shadow of a doubt the principal requisite is that of a far greater manifestation of spiritual vitality and power in all departments of the missionary movement. . . . The world-wide expansion of pure Christianity is essentially a spiritual and a superhuman movement. Therefore, the chief emphasis throughout the entire enterprise should be placed on the spiritual.

He did not revise the book upon the outbreak of the War, but said in its preface:

> That great catastrophe, however, lends a peculiar timeliness and meaning to the treatment of the subject. What a demonstration the War has furnished of the contention that the present is a time of danger. Who will say that the opportunity which is likely to confront the cause of Christ at the close of the struggle will not be more extensive than ever before? . . . What a colossal exhibition the War affords of the unchristian character of much of our so-called Christian civilization, and what a challenge it presents to the leaders of vital, Christlike Christianity to strive to bring in a new order wherein shall dwell righteousness, love and true peace![10]

In 1914 it could still be hoped that the War would end soon. By 1918 those goals were even more remote. With a presentation copy to Mrs. McCormick, Mott wrote that "The tremendous upheaval of the War lends added significance to the positions which I have taken." The main themes of the book would provide outlines for many lectures on "the religious meaning of the War" during the next four years.

Reviewers greeted the book as Mott's "greatest," "most valuable," or as a tract "for the times—a book of depth, of forcefulness, of exceptional interest." The Springfield *Republican* declared its author to be "one of the great constructive statesmen of the kingdom of God on earth" and that the "whole volume pulsates with the active, virile spirit of the writer, and its facts and conclusions ought to be absorbed by every churchman."[11] Tatlow saw it as presenting Mott's "ripening experience" and agreed with most reviewers that it had gained by having been written before the War. He quoted Mott as predicting that peace and unity would not come by drifting but by peace*making*. One of the longest and most perceptive reviews, by Charles L. Fry, appeared in a Lutheran magazine:

> This masterly book deals with the outcome of an Armageddon involving all races of mankind, in which every people of Protestant Christendom belongs to the Allies of the great King Emmanuel, including both Germans and Americans. In other words, it is the supreme problem of World-Evangelization which is here presented in a vivid new light. . . . If it was imperative for Protestant Christianity to federate its forces prior to the catastrophe, it will be ten-fold more imperative after the war closes. . . . When universal Protestantism in North America shall agree on its fundamental propositions, a long advance step will have been taken toward the brighter day which is about to dawn.[12]

Mott did what he could to hasten that day.

PART 2: **"One of the Most Nobly Useful Men in the World"**[13]

When President Wilson characterized Mott in those extravagant terms to a reporter for *Harper's Weekly* in March, 1914, he was speaking from long acquaintance. Mott must have first met Wilson when the latter lectured at Cornell during Mott's undergraduate days. While Wilson was an instructor at Wesleyan University the two met at college YMCA affairs, Wilson being active in the campus and regional Associations, an interest he maintained after moving to Princeton as professor and continuing throughout his University presidency. Mott was a frequent visitor to Princeton; Wilson contributed to his pamphlets on the Christian ministry and critiqued his manuscript for *The Future Leadership of the Church*. He shared with Mott both his educational ideals and plans and his problems with Dean Andrew F. West over the new graduate college. Wilson's slogan, "Princeton in the nation's service," epitomized Mott's concept of leadership; both of his sons went to Princeton. When Wilson wrote Mott early in 1910 that he was "genuinely disappointed" that the Edinburgh Conference would prevent Mott's being at commencement to receive an honorary degree that year, his regret was genuine. Wilson's offer to Mott of the post of minister to China in 1913 was reviewed in Chapter 7; immediately upon Mott's return from his world tour of 1912–1913 he reported to the President on affairs in the Orient and subsequently aided Wilson in the search for a qualified person for the China post.[14]

The congeniality of Wilson and Mott stemmed from their backgrounds yet was heightened by their mature assumptions. Wilson had had what he called the "unspeakable joy" of growing up in a southern Presbyterian manse; Mott learned Christian truth at a Methodist family altar; both were reared in families bound by strong ties of love and dominated by the urge for learning. Christian faith was the driving force in the lives of both men. Wilson used politics for ethical ends; Mott had sublimated his ambition for power by means of politics by channeling it through evangelism to the student movements and the ecumenical coordination of missions. As Arthur Link says, Wilson broke through the "iron shell" of Presbyterian legalism in mature life to a position approaching contextual or relativistic ethics, which one may adjudge comparable to Mott's reliance on the ethics of Holiness. Link also points out that by 1900 Wilson had reached the conclusion that men truly know God only through Jesus Christ.[15]

Both men rode the high tide of individualism in their youth, and both came to mature endorsement of the social gospel in the first decade of the twentieth century. By 1909 Wilson could say that "Christianity came into the world to save the world as well as to save individual men. . . . " That was the year of the WSCF Conference at Oxford that brought the social gospel to the attention of the student Christian movements of the world, under Mott's leadership. Wilson moved toward reform upon entering politics, and when Mott congratulated him in 1914 upon his progressive policies it was the major tenets of the "New Freedom" that he had in mind as well as Wilson's moral diplomacy in which he himself had been offered a strategic role; there would yet be two minor roles. "The significant fact" about the President's social vision, says Link, "was its origin, at least in part, in Wilson's Christian conscience," but its awakening was brought about by his widening political experience and the social gospel. Mott's conscience was early pricked by men such as Graham Taylor; his mature adoption of the social gospel was the product of his constant contacts with students and faculty members in the great universities of the world, the commitment of the young staff members he chose, and his world travels.

Mott's admiration for President Wilson was further augmented by Wilson's assertion of presidential leadership, for Mott both admired and advocated to youth the necessity for enlightened leaders. In May, 1914, the President joined a host of well-wishers who surprised Mott with congratulations on his forty-ninth birthday. In acknowledging Wilson's greeting Mott wrote in his own hand of his "profound appreciation of the remarkable way in which you are bringing to bear the principles of righteousness and unselfishness in all your relations to national and international affairs," his world travels having convinced him that Wilson was "lifting our nation into a high and large place in the thought of those whose opinions we most value." Three months later, he sent Wilson a telegram of sympathy on the death of Mrs. Wilson. The President replied that it was "very delightful to feel the warm touch of a friend's hand at such a time and your telegram has served to give me strength and courage."[16]

In addition to these bonds, Mott was on such intimate terms with the President's close friends and supporters the Dodges and McCormicks that he might almost have been accepted as a member of that inner circle. It was natural that as Mott's plans to assay conditions on both sides of the lines in Europe took shape in the fall of 1914, he should ask the President for an appointment and that one should be granted. In thirty-five minutes on September 16, which was not long after Wilson's proclamation of neutrality, Mott described to the President the effect of the War on Christian missions, on the worldwide work of the YMCA, and on the WSCF. To determine the opportunity and duty of American Christians "at this time and in these circumstances," it was being proposed that he go to Britain, France, and Scandinavia as well as to Holland, Switzerland, and Germany. He had come to the President for counsel, caution, and criticism, and hoped for assistance in obtaining access to those countries. Specifically, he requested a personal letter to the American ambassador in each of them and a safe conduct or foreign deputation to meet him if it were necessary to enter Germany. He then quickly summarized the plight of European missions, cited a recent letter from Dr. Herman Rutgers of Holland describing conditions, and mentioned several strong pleas for peace from Quaker and other sources to which he was close.[17]

The President promised the letters and a personal passport. He spoke of a message he had received from a Belgian delegation and about a cable from the Kaiser, using these as background for stating his strong desire "so to preserve our neutrality that at the right time we may be able to mediate." He quoted Napoleon's remark that no lasting peace was ever secured by force and commented on the settlement of the Franco-Prussian War and also on the Treaty of Berlin of 1878. The last entry in Mott's notes to the interview cited Secretary of State Bryan's remark to Viscount Chinda of Japan during the recent California anti-Japanese agitation: " 'Nothing is final between friends.' "[18]

In writing to Mrs. McCormick later that week, Mott told of Wilson's "most sympathetic interest" and explained that his previous program calling for nine months in Europe would need to be "deferred until another year." The short trip he was now planning would be "one of the most delicate and difficult and important missions" on which he had ever been sent; he hoped that during it they would mutually support one another in prayer. Just before sailing he mailed a short letter to a large circle of friends asking their "help in intercession" on account of the unusual nature of the undertaking:

> It is desired that I should (1) keep certain engagements in the British universities (the leaders ask this insisting that the students were never so solemnized and never so anxious to receive guidance); (2) study how the Christians of North America can best help safeguard the tremendously vital interests of the missionary societies of Europe in this time of unparalleled strain; (3) consider ways and means of promoting practical Christian helpfulness among the millions of men in arms; (4) encourage and counsel the sorely perplexed workers of the various European Christian Student Movements, so that they may be prepared to reorganize their forces and meet the peculiar opportunity at the close of the War; (5) do all in my power to help maintain among the Christian leaders of the different countries the international bonds of friendship which have been established with such wonderful promise in recent years.

> You will recognize instantly that on an errand of such delicacy, difficulty and possibilities, I shall stand in real need of your help in prayer every day of my absence. I am sure you will not fail me.[19]

They did not. The journey was not only safe but "wonderful" in a way no other trip had ever been.

PART 3: **"I Have Entered into Fellowship with the Sufferings of Great Peoples"** [20]

Mott sailed for Rotterdam on the neutral *Nieuw Amsterdam* on September 29, 1914. Learning by cable that he was on the high seas, Oldham wrote him in Holland that all of his training and experience had prepared him "for this most difficult task": "you may be enabled to render a greater service than any that you have yet done, and to be in God's hand an instrument of reconciliation and peace." Mott replied that it meant everything to him to have Oldham following him in prayer in what his colleague had well called his most difficult mission: "I am absolutely insufficient. But I begin to see His hand."

The British Navy suspected the *Nieuw Amsterdam* of carrying "conditional contraband" and detained her at Plymouth. Mott was delayed several days but managed to contact the SCM headquarters in London. "We got him off," wrote Miss Rouse, "and in a few hectic hours in London he managed to see the Federation officers and not a few British SCM and missionary society leaders, some of us accompanying him in the train to Folkestone for the steamer to Holland."[21] Those brief hours, which may have included a visit with the Archbishop of Canterbury, were enough to assure Mott, if the immense outpouring that had come to him at home had not, that the bonds of the Federation not only were holding but were daily being tightened; "almost everywhere," wrote Miss Rouse, "there was a new awakening to the need of God and of faith, a new readiness to listen to the Christian message."

Dr. Herman Rutgers, voluntary unpaid general secretary of the Dutch SCM, was the key to Mott's visit on the Continent. Rutgers, who made frequent trips to Germany and to Great Britain until the British government became suspicious, exemplified the Federation concept that communication was best carried on in conversation rather than in writing; Mott was later to subsidize Rutgers' travel and that of several other WSCF leaders who visited on both sides.[22] Holland served as the staging area for Mott's visit to Germany, but a trip that had been "eagerly anticipated" by the Belgians had of course been cancelled.

Mott and Rutgers were met in Berlin by Karl Fries, chairman of the WSCF, summoned by Mott from Stockholm, Christian Phildius, a German, the general secretary of the World's YMCA, and Pierre de Benoit of the Swiss SCM. "We had a wonderful time together" in Christian communion and fellowship, wrote Rutgers; there was "mutual trust and outspokenness" and the neutrals came to know their German friends far better "during these few days of conference in war time than during all the previous peaceful years." They also experienced "the misery and sorrow created by the war," visiting overcrowded hospitals and observing the endless lines of anxious inquirers at the Ministry of War seeking information on the dead and wounded; at the Student Movement head-quarters word came every day of "friends and members wounded or killed."[23]

The most impressive event of a crowded schedule was a visit to the camp at Döberitz where 3,000 British prisoners of war were being held. A religious service was arranged; Fries described it:

> The singing was so hearty that one expected to see the roof of the tent lifted by it, and the sermon was delivered by Mott. It was gripping. Tears might be seen in many eyes. I firmly believe that the impressions of that hour contributed in large measure to that deep sympathy on Mott's part with prisoners of war that impelled him to raise millions of dollars and send out scores of secretaries to alleviate their sad lot.[24]

Mott arranged with Phildius to provide £500 to start three or four men to work among soldiers and prisoners in Austria-Hungary and dis-patched him to Vienna with a letter to the American ambassador. A like sum was promised for similar work in France. This was the beginning of the vast prisoner of war (POW) enterprise that Mott would supervise for the World's Alliance of YMCA's and raise huge sums to support.[25]

He met with two other groups in Berlin. The leaders of the Student Movement (DCSV) included Dr. Georg Michaelis, its new president, who was to be for a short time imperial chancellor and Prussian minister-president in 1917; Dr. Niedermeyer, national secretary; his as-sociates, Pastors Le Seur and Kieser, "Mr. Spemann, and Mr. Siegmund-Schultze," and Paul Humburg. In private conversation with Michaelis, Mott heard a full, almost fanatical, defense of the German attitude toward England and Russia; after reaching home he wrote Michaelis that he had a much better understanding "of the heart and feelings of the German people." From these men he and the other neutrals learned of the devastation of the Movement by the War but turned at once to the planning of what became known as German Student Service, which Miss Rouse calls "the natural product of Christian concern for the needs of body, mind, and spirit, first of German students in the field, next of German soldiers, then of prisoners of war." With the cooperation of its President, who gave freely of his expertise as Prussian under-secretary of finance, and utilizing Siegmund-Schultze's experience with foreign student centers, this became an immense enterprise with a budget of 30,000,000 marks by 1918.[26]

Mott's other meetings were with leaders of German mission societies, notably Professor Richter whom he had known for some time as vice-chairman of the Continuation Committee, Adolph Harnack, Karl Axenfeld, G. Haussleiter, and Pastor Würz of Basle who was the chief channel of communication between the German and the Western members of the Continuation Committee. Oldham had oriented Mott to the Germans' state of mind, so that he was not surprised to find intense nationalism and fervent support of the War. Harnack, whose works Mott had studied at Cornell, gave him almost as impassioned a defense of the German course of action as had Michaelis, but attributed the stance of the English Christians to ignorance. Harnack described a weekly meeting of a group of leading Germans who were seeking an enduring foundation for peace.

Oldham, who had been in full communication with Würtz, had urged immediate aid to orphaned German missions, chiefly because communications between Germany and their mission fields had been cut off. Mott was also thanked heartily for proposing an American fund, a plan acceptable to the Germans only as a loan to be repaid, Axenfeld pointing out that the Paris Society was in much greater need than the German bodies.[27] The Germans welcomed Mott, comments Hogg, as the symbol "of all that is best in Christian, international missionary cooperation" and brotherhood. They were especially grateful that in spite of his inability to read or speak their language, Mott "had patience and sympathy enough to work through all our presentations and documents until he saw the whole situation in our light." Axenfeld, Director of the *Ausschuss,* acknowledged the need for Mott to remain neutral; "you came as a friend" and brought "the earnest desire to help us in our missionary work as well as is compatible with perfect neutrality." Later, he wrote Oldham a letter "full of the warmest affection," promising that nothing would ever break their "links of personal friendship." Oldham thought it displayed "good sense" and showed "no traces of excitement or unreason."

Back in Britain for two weeks, Mott found all agencies to which he was related and many others competing for his time until he was forced to cancel whole blocks of appointments that had been set up. Everywhere there was intense interest in his account of the attitudes of the Germans he had met, and he was likewise required to listen to the British defense of their course in entering the War. He came to see how, in Marc

Boegner's later judgment, the thunder-clap of August had "brutally suspended ecumenical work and in the belligerent countries threw the Churches back into an isolation that was often poisoned by Chauvinism." He conferred at length with Oldham, spoke with students in the universities at Glasgow, Aberdeen, Manchester, and Edinburgh, filling as many of Tatlow's requests as possible.

Mott went to Paris for most of the first week of November, being met at the St. Lazare Station by the young Swiss Frédérick de Rougement. "It was 10 P.M.," wrote de Rougement:

> Through the dark streets and the deserted public squares, we passed the Seine hardly being able to descry the shadowy lines of the bridges in the distance. From time to time a bright shaft of light searched the sky. We felt strange in that unknown Paris, so entirely in contrast to the usual Paris of life and light. It is war time.
>
> And still more, we could feel it, on the following morning when we met the members of the French Student Movement. The general secretary, Grauss, is somewhere on the battle front; almost all the members had been called to the colours; four came to the meeting and even these four are to be called before long. They said they felt very lonely and could hardly think of going on with the work in the midst of the practical difficulties; still they were trying their best to do so.... The universities are open and in them are students but as to the members of the local Associations, out of hundreds there were twenty to thirty left. And these thirty are very likely to be called also.... But they felt very lonely.
>
> And to them we went, Mr. Mott and myself representing the World's Federation, using the privilege of citizens of neutral countries.... In such a time as this the value of such a visit is increased tenfold. Surely it meant to our French brethren a new view of the situation.... All around them, they could see, now bodily represented in these members of the World's Federation, their fellow students in the whole world fighting with them and praying with them for the coming of the Kingdom of God, in spite of the seemingly insuperable present catastrophe. And surely they have gotten a new hope and a new faith. One of them writes to me: "Since Mr. Mott's coming we feel stronger. We had started working, but we had some doubts about the results... now we have an unshakable confidence."[28]

De Rougemont felt that the Swiss Movement had also derived "renewed courage and blessing" indirectly through himself from Mott's visit.

Miss Rouse long remembered that prayer meeting with Mott, fresh from Berlin, Suzanne de Dietrich, de Rougemont, Charles Westphal, Robert Pont, Paul Conord, and perhaps Raoul Allier. "In the first shock, to carry on had seemed almost impossible, but at the touch with the

Federation, faith and hope revived and bolder plans were made," as de Rougemont said. "Never shall I forget the passionate sincerity of the French students' prayers for their fellow members in the German Movement," Miss Rouse recalled. Mott reported that he had enjoyed a like fellowship with the Swedish, Dutch, and German-Swiss leaders.[29] The next spring President Allier of the French Movement wrote him:

> Many of our best members have been killed, but those who survive feel united by daily strengthening ties. The Federation is not an abstract term for our Christian students: it is a vital point. All their letters from the front show how greatly they feel the importance of our work. They are not discouraged.[30]

Allier's only son was one of those killed.

Mott returned to England and went immediately to Oxford, where on Sunday evening, November 8, he spoke in Balliol Hall to an audience "sobered in an extraordinary way" by the nation's struggle for its existence and hence "especially open to God's voice," as Oldham had earlier described the national mood. The *Oxford Magazine* editorialized that the service was "a remarkable one":

> To gather 400 undergraduates for a religious meeting is at any time a somewhat unusual thing, but it is especially so when that number means a third of those in residence. Dr. Mott held his audience completely. . . . His speech was mainly of a narrative kind, telling of the work of the Student's Christian Unions in all parts of the world, but it contained also telling appeals to his audience personally. Not the least interesting part of Dr. Mott's speech was his account of the work in France and Germany as it is affected by the War.[31]

This was one of the first of Mott's addresses on the spiritual impact of the War. He reviewed its adverse effects, showing how it had depleted the Movements in Britain, Germany, and France and had stopped the hopeful advances in southeastern Europe. War unsettles faith, confuses Christians in the Orient, and impairs the larger unity for which the world strives, he declared, but at the same time it reveals strength, calls forth helpfulness toward both allies and antagonists, reveals our shortcomings, tries faith by fire, presents great opportunities for evangelism to the wounded, to prisoners of war, to men in training and in service, and to those still in the universities where they are faced with the choice of military service or pacifist refusal.

And what of the situation after the War?, he asked. We cannot drift into peace: "blessed are the peace-*makers*," for they are needed in international cooperation. The War has deepened our acquaintance with God, His ways, His resources; men everywhere are turning as never before to the Bible and to prayer. Let us stand before Jesus Christ, submitting our unanswered questions to Him, professing Him, winning through to a Christianity worth professing, showing forth His spirit, placing our lives at His disposal at a time when whole nations are stretched to their limits, showing the spirit of justice, of kindness and compassion, of love, of sacrifice and service.

Upon these notes and during this visit to Britain, which did not yet have conscription, Mott began recruiting for the wartime services he had described; in four years that small cadre grew to an army of over 25,000 men and women.

During this final week in England, Mott talked at length, but never enough, with Oldham, spoke to a rally of laymen in London, conferred with missions leaders and met with SCM people on the tremendous student refugee problem. He interviewed former Prime Minister Arthur Balfour who would shortly take over the Admiralty from Winston Churchill, Viscount Bryce who had until recently been Ambassador to the United States, and A. Bonar Law, leader of the opposition in the House of Commons. He asked each of them a leading question concerning America's role in the War: Balfour believed that America should remain aloof but join in "the arrangements which will preserve peace," and that Germany should receive "a sound thrashing in order to humble pride and belief in the doctrine of might." Bryce held that the United States ought to join the peace and that now was the time to stabilize southeastern Europe and Turkey. Germany should not be humiliated but she must compensate Belgium: "it would be a mistake to talk of dictating peace in Berlin." Bonar Law was pessimistic as to the outcome of the War; England and the United States could agree on an international peace force but not Japan, France, or Russia; such a plan is not practical in this generation. Religion and ethics are swept away in the upheaval. [32]

As Mott reviewed his experiences on the voyage home, he must have taken profound satisfaction in the realization that the Federation was meeting a test for which it had not been designed. It was opening the channels for what would become "vast schemes of welfare for soldiers, prisoners of war, for refugee students," as Miss Rouse summarized the strenuous efforts that would be made by Mott, Fries, herself and every student worker "impartially to serve all" in every nation. The WSCF was the one worldwide organization that not only held together but was strengthened by its wartime activities. Its secretaries traveled almost as extensively as in peacetime. And when the conflict would finally end the Federation would take up the tasks of reconciliation with the same energy and determination that made it a force during the War.

This tour became item eight on Mott's life-list of "most creative experiences." As his ship neared New York, he wrote his sister Harriett that it had been not only a voyage of discovery but an attempt to help all countries in their hour of deep need and their groping for peace; lapsing into Midwestern idiom, he confessed: "I have been in the shadow during this entire trip. In a very true sense I have entered into fellowship with the sufferings of great peoples." Later he shared two incidents with an audience:

> The first home I visited in Europe was one in Germany. My host said thirty-one of his family have been called to the war, and that nine of the thirty-one had been killed or wounded. And the last home that I visited was that of Lord Balfour of Burleigh. He thought his older son was captured, but he learned that he had been killed five weeks before. He received a letter of condolence while I was there. As he read he choked up and said "Mott, finish it for me." So it was, going from one house of tears to another. [33]

Home in time for Thanksgiving and a twenty-third wedding anniversary at Wooster, Mott could not forget the prisoners at Döberitz and in every other camp. Ruth Rouse once recalled a much earlier day with the Motts and Principal David Cairns at Gettysburg when the two men had visited every corner of the battlefield and relived the conflict: "Mott's academic interest in battlefields seems to have waned since the Great War came and burnt its horror into his soul."[34] And it was said that this trip had aged him by ten years.

Because Leila was in Wooster, John spent the evening of the day of his arrival reporting at length to Cleveland H. Dodge, who suggested that he describe his tour to President Wilson. Charles R. Crane, Chicago philanthropist and Russophile, another member of that Progressive Democratic circle that included the Dodges and McCormicks, jotted on his Christmas card to the President that he hoped to be present when Mott would relate "the story of his wonderful journey."[35] Before leaving for Wooster, Mott wrote Wilson in his own hand that being in Britain, Germany, and France "at this possibly the most fateful moment in their life" had been "a never-to-be-forgotten experience"; he concluded his request for an interview with gratitude for the President's personal interest and cooperation on the journey, and with "sincere thankfulness to God for the wonderful and absolutely unique relation you sustain to the present world situation."[36]

In the interview, which took place on January 6, 1915, Mott expressed deep appreciation of the President's stand on neutrality, which was almost universally approved abroad. Citing his conversation with Harnack and others in Germany, as well as discussions in France and Britain, he believed that there was an "immense lot of thinking and study" going on in Europe about the outcome of the War and what should follow it. Men such as Sir Edward Grey thought it "most important not to limit America's rendering the greatest service by premature action or by injuring our neutrality"—we must "keep our moral powder dry." The British leaders believed that the War must be fought out, but with due regard for justice and a firm stand for rights, and that at its end America would have an "absolutely unique opportunity." Crane wrote next day that it had been "a wonderful evening."[37]

PART 4: "Remnant-Symbol" of the Continuation Committee

Prior to Mott's departure for Europe in the fall of 1914 he had brought the plight of orphaned Continental missions to the attention of the executive body of the FMCNA, the Committee on Reference and Counsel, and reported to it in detail upon his return. As a result the Committee recommended that each American mission board "should render all help in its power to any needy Continental missions which may adjoin their own missions," and that the Committee be authorized to secure if possible "an adequate central or general fund from which to help meet the most urgent needs of Continental missions which may not adjoin American missions, or which may be too large to be met by a contiguous American mission." The Committee also offered its services to the Continental societies "to assist them in any other practicable way."[38]

Implementation was another matter. Early in December Mott had described his trip at great length to John D. Rockefeller, Jr., delineating his "dominant impressions"—the internal unity, determination, confidence, self-justifying "holy war" attitudes of the belligerents, and the "indescribably awful" suffering that added up to "rivers of pain." He then proposed a centrally administered missions relief fund of from one-half to one million dollars, detailing the adverse effects of the War upon orphaned missions and numerous reasons why relief must come from America. He proposed to channel it through a central general fund because of the preoccupation of the denominational boards with their own problems, suggesting to Rockefeller that it be administered by the Committee on Reference and Counsel of the FMCNA on the recommendations of a joint advisory body, that payments be transmitted quarterly via the Standard Oil Company (which was already forwarding relief funds to Turkey), and that deficits be cleared up as a Christmas gift.

Rockefeller was cool to the proposal, which also did not appeal to the mission boards, but Mott had himself made chairman of the FMCNA sub-committee. It raised and disbursed $27,500 during 1915, the funds going chiefly to the Paris Society for its missions in Africa and to the China Continuation Committee for orphaned Continental missions in that country. In 1916, $16,000 was divided between the Paris Society and German missions in China and India; the next year $9,500 was budgeted for the Continuation Committees of China and Japan and the National Missionary Council of India. [39]

Mott increasingly found himself, as did Oldham, "the remnant-symbol" of the Continuation Committee, as Hogg was to put it. The functions of the Committee, moribund but not dead, continued to be the subject of careful consideration in the voluminous correspondence between Oldham and Mott throughout 1915, it becoming clear to Oldham early in the exchange that the Edinburgh body must be replaced after the War by an organization composed of national movements rather than individual denominations. In the exigencies of the moment both men found themselves daily called upon to advise on and dispose of requests, petitions, and appeals, which they both did in the spirit of the Committee, usually referring them to national bodies for action. Among their major preoccupations were a proposal to survey the Christian forces in India for which both obtained substantial contributions, a women's medical college in Madras, and the sub-committee on Christian literature. Each kept the other as fully informed as possible by mail but they found themselves increasingly using cablegrams. Affectionate and intimate as always, their letters ran to scores of pages, dealing in only one instance with a problem on which they disagreed, and that one was a matter of procedure. [40]

Both were concerned not only to secure reliable publicity in Britain and in the United States on the highly volatile issues of orphaned missions and the gamut of problems related to them but to maintain an ecumenical and ethical stance before the churches and the Christian public regardless of the emotions of the moment, a position rendered dangerously difficult upon the sinking of the *Lusitania* in May, 1915; Oldham bespoke himself somewhat more forcefully than usual upon hearing also the news of German use of poison gas. He considered resigning, but Mott declared that he would follow if Oldham left. Neither did. After all, there was no effective body to whom they could submit resignations! In a confidential letter to Mott, Oldham stated his personal belief that Germany was "rapidly setting herself in opposition to the sentiment of the world" and that when men [probably Americans] become convinced that the issue of the War is "between civilization and barbarism" rather than simply nationalism, they will unite "to bring Germany back to courses of sanity and reason and to restore her to a fellowship from which she has cut herself off." Mott replied:

> I cannot express adequately the depth and strength of feeling throughout this whole nation, even among many so-called German Americans. It is of first importance, of course, that even in the midst of such extreme provocations Christian leaders in the different countries should not forfeit their confidence in the Christian integrity of large numbers of Christians and Christian leaders in each of the countries concerned. . . . Some of us for the sake of all the coming years must preserve an unshaken faith in the fact that Christ has his own true witnesses in each nation, and, so far as is possible, we who are serving international Christian Movements must continue to remind others of this fact. This does not, as you clearly emphasize, mean that we might [not] in the strongest terms denounce that which we well know contravenes the example, principles and spirit of Christ.[41]

Both struggled to preserve a sane balance and to keep the long-range perspective of their life commitment in view. Oldham agreed when Pastor Marc Boegner expressed his belief that no attempt should be made until the War ended to bring together Germans, French, and English for the discussion of "anything relating to the Kingdom." He continued in intimate contact with Würtz, through whom he was kept in touch with German opinion, commenting to Mott on one occasion that "both the Germans and ourselves will need to suffer a great deal more before God can bring us into the purpose which He has for us. In neither country is the Church yet prepared to humble itself and to recognize its need of a complete conversion of heart."

Both Oldham and Mott were deeply concerned about post-war reconstruction, and as early as January, 1915, Oldham was giving the question "a good deal of thought," wondering how the churches could be brought to endorse "a positive constructive policy." In February Mott wrote Oldham that criticism of the United States in Britain must rest on misunderstanding and lack of information: already American opinion was one hundred to one in favor of the Allies, and he cited the discussion during a long evening "with President Wilson at the White House."[42] Between the lines in this correspondence Mott's own viewpoint may be seen shifting in that direction, if ever it had been otherwise, but he sedulously avoided any such commitment in public.

Throughout the war period Mott centered his mission activities in the FMCNA, working not only with its executive body but also on its Board of Missionary Preparation from 1915. He was a member of the Rockefeller China Medical Board from its inception in 1914. But the most significant event for missions with which he was identified in the years between 1914 and American entry into the War in 1917 was his participation in the Conference on Christian Work in Latin America that met in Panama in mid-February, 1916. Months before it he explained to Oldham that he was presiding over planning committees to give them the benefit of the Edinburgh experience. Latin America had been omitted from the Edinburgh agenda, but workers concerned for that area had met between sessions and agreed that a comparable conference was needed for Latin America. Three years later there came into being the Committee on Cooperation in Latin America, of which Robert E. Speer was chairman. This body sponsored a number of preparatory conferences, one of the most effective of which was held in Montevideo in June, 1914, under the auspices of the YMCA secretaries of Brazil, Uruguay, Argentina, and Chile, whose interdenominational stance and concern for students and the educated classes ideally qualified them for this responsibility.[43] Early in the preparation Mott visited Cuba and his lieutenant Ethan T. Colton went to Puerto Rico.

Mott took minor parts in the Panama Conference, served on several committees, exercised an advisory capacity, and lent men from his staff. Colton was a member of the committee on arrangements and because of his expertise in affairs south of the border chaired the commission on survey and occupation.[44] Harry Wade Hicks, who had had extensive YMCA experience under Mott, chaired the commission on the home base and served on the committee on arrangements. Fennell P. Turner, general secretary of the SVM, and Charles D. Hurrey, Secretary of the Committee on Friendly Relations among Foreign Students, both chaired working committees. Mott was chairman of an international advisory "committee of experts, interested in the public life of Latin America, Europe, and North America," and was selected at Panama to chair the business committee; he responded to the address of welcome and later spoke on "The Religious Significance of the World War."

On the first Sunday of the Conference the Roman Catholic Archbishop denounced it in a sermon that scandalized "the good people of Panama, Catholics as well as Protestants." A public reception was arranged and Mott was asked speak. William Adams Brown, who was later often critical of Mott, described the speech—"a unique opportunity to explain the spirit and purpose of our coming"—as having been presented "with his accustomed forcefulness and tact."[45] Charles H. Fahs, now of the Missionary Research Library, was secretary of the Conference. Charles J. Ewald, continental YMCA secretary for South America, was recording secretary in English. There were eight YMCA delegates in addition to Mott, Colton, Hurrey, and Turner; they were distributed throughout the organization of the Conference. Mott and Colton became members of the conference continuation committee's executive board. Miss Rouse accompanied the Motts to Panama; the Conference reminded her of a WSCF meeting, there being so many student leaders there. She went on to visit student centers in South America.[46] In speeches following the Conference, Mott urged the churches and their boards "to make a larger contribution to Latin America" during this "opportune moment" created by the War. The meeting had not been an achievement, he commented, but "a process of discovery."[47] It was also a partial compensation for Edinburgh's major omission.

PART 5: For the Millions of Men Now Under Arms

Before he left Europe in November, 1914, Mott acted vigorously to implement the programs that he initiated in Berlin and Paris. The first "Foyers du Soldats" (centers or "huts") were set up in the French army in the fall of 1914 under the direction of Emmanuel Sautter of the World's Alliance of the YMCA's. They were modeled on the American Army and Navy YMCA experience since 1898, which had included service to Japanese troops during the Russo-Japanese War of 1904-05. The Program spread from division to division until there were more than 1500 foyers by 1919 and the American YMCA had poured hundreds of men and women workers and some $9,000,000 into the effort. The plan spread to the British and Italian armies under other names, and after the entry of the United States into the War it accompanied American troops as the YMCA "Red Triangle." The prisoner of war work (POW) in the camps in Germany and Austria, launched by Mott while in Berlin, grew by the end of the War to a massive program serving five to six million men in almost every country involved in the struggle.

In January, 1915, he dispatched Archibald C. Harte, whose previous YMCA experience had been chiefly in India, to Berlin to work among British prisoners, even before approval had been obtained from the German government. By mid-March he had sent Harte $5,000 for additional secretaries and the construction of huts. C. V. Hibbard, who had accompanied the Japanese troops in 1904–05, was given comparable funds and sent to Geneva to instruct the staff. Mott insisted that "all this work among soldiers on the Continent should, so far as possible, be conducted under the supervision of the World's Committee," and though problems arose this policy was maintained throughout the enterprise. [48]

Simultaneously he began to enlist young men and women in the programs, first as summer service between college terms, challenging them wherever he went with this unique Christian opportunity. He spoke not only on college and university campuses but to civic groups, service clubs, the leaders of the churches, the state legislature of Iowa, and, in his own words, to "countless conferences and meetings." He gave several courses of lectures, wrote more than thirty pamphlets and scores of articles for newspapers, religious journals, and popular magazines. Beginning in March, 1915, he issued the first of a series of confidential newsletters entitled For the Millions of Men Now Under Arms, the purpose of which was to "throw interesting sidelights on the Christ-like service being rendered by the Young Men's Christian Association and the Student Movement in camps, in trenches, in hospitals, and in prisons"; it was sent to an enlarged prayer circle and to contributors. [49]

As the War dragged on, both home and foreign YMCA staffs were combed for top executives and for younger men to fill the ranks abroad. Ultimately, almost 26,000 men and women responded; for many it sublimated the Student Volunteer call during the War years when a Quadrennial could not be held and the missionary enterprise was universally hindered. Many of these youth possessed unusual qualities of leadership that placed them in positions of immense responsibility, but the process of recruitment was painfully slow. Harte agonized to Mott in December, 1915, that it was no longer possible "not to worry over the problem of men. Our opportunities grow. . . . I beg of you, if it be possible at all, get good men to us and get them to us soon. . . . We must fail if we continue to wait."

As the conflict spread, most of the American-inspired YMCA's around the world as well as others became involved with the troops of their own nations. As early as November, 1914, E. C. Carter had co-opted twelve men from half-a-dozen mission societies to accompany Indian troops to Europe, cabling Mott for $10,000 for support. Mott was commander-in-chief of the immense enterprise, which was, in his thought, dedicated to "the relief of physical suffering, mental strain, economic crisis" through fellowship with individuals everywhere by throwing out lines of "understanding, friendliness, and cooperation," and serving as an intermediary on countless occasions.[50]

He turned first to his wealthy friends for the funds to undergird these efforts. Although approved by the YMCA, they were his personal financial responsibility until April, 1917. An early contribution was $5,000 from Mrs. McCormick, who gladly redirected a pledge originally intended for Moslem conferences. Mott wrote her in March, 1915, that he had obtained eleven other $5,000 commitments but could easily use $150,000 because of the "almost unbelievable" expansion of the need: approval to work among British, Russian, French, and Belgian prisoners in Germany had just come and the French were asking for more secretaries. It was Mott's "daring faith," wrote Miss Rouse in retrospect, that obtained the funds for "these mighty undertakings" which made possible not only the work among prisoners and all men under arms but literally rescued student movements imperiled by war conditions, whether in neutral or belligerent lands, such as he had confronted in Paris.[51] The sums needed, and raised, would reach astronomical levels, especially after American entry into the War and the full development of the Red Triangle program.

PART 6: "A New Era in the Life and Work of the Whole Association Movement"

Upon the diminishing of Mott's duties as Chairman of the Edinburgh Continuation Committee and the lessening of what could actually be accomplished for missions and for the WSCF because of the War, the forces that had tried for twenty years to convince him that he should accept the general secretaryship of the American national YMCA renewed their efforts and in the summer of 1915 were successful.[52] Richard Morse, who had held that post since 1869, had proposed it to Mott in 1895 and 1897, and again in 1901, when Mott became the chief executive for the foreign but not the home work. Upon his acceptance of the chairmanship of the Continuation Committee in 1910 Mott had tried to reduce the work load involved in his other commitments, seeking the advice of members of the Committee's executive and of friends such as John D. Rockefeller, Jr., and the Archbishop of Canterbury.[53]

Colleagues in the WSCF worried lest the Committee replace the Federation in both his work load and his preferences, and counseled him to drop his commitments to the student and foreign departments of the YMCA, certain ones of them holding that organization somewhat in disdain and failing to understand what they called his "YMCA mentality," by which they meant his characteristically American lay rather than ecclesiastical orientation.[54] He seriously proposed dropping the student department in 1912 but was persuaded not to do so. At almost the same time, staff and organizational problems in the parent YMCA brought fresh overtures by Morse and by a new International Committee chairman, Alfred E. Marling. Mott asked to delay his response until after the world tour of 1912–13 at which time he again refused, although he received flattering endorsements from leading city Association men throughout the country and even more enthusiastic support from colleagues in the foreign work such as Eddy and Carter.

Here the matter lay, until two years, two study commissions, and six months of World War forced the organization to take a fresh look at itself. Mott was brought into lengthy consultation, to the enlightenment both of the International Committee and the hoped-for candidate. As these deliberations continued into the spring of 1915, Morse and his colleagues felt that they were making progress toward the goal for which they had "hoped, prayed, and worked for years." The shifts in Mott's world responsibilities seemed to suggest that he could be more favorably inclined. At this juncture he went to California for the month of May, during which he addressed an immense audience in Los Angeles on the religious significance of the War, visited colleges, and attended the national conference of Association secretaries, where, wrote Morse, "in personal fellowship and intercourse, considerations were presented to him that caused him during his long transcontinental journey home to give a thorough, patient, prayerful review to the entire problem." Leila Mott and the children accompanied John on this trip so that the review was mutual. On his 50th birthday cablegrams and congratulatory messages poured in from all over the world; it chanced that that was Association Day at the Panama-Pacific Exposition in San Francisco, where he also spoke. The events of the trip produced "a conditional consent" to the call and on June 8 he outlined his thinking to the Committee's senior secretaries.

Two weeks later, to Morse's "relief and joy," Mott, instead of outlining another refusal, named conditions—"some of them difficult to fulfill but none of them prohibitive"—upon which he might be able to accept. Morse later reminisced that "in the providential program of his life it was not until June, 1915, that the fulness of time had come for him to take this step, and my previous endeavors had been premature, but this only deepened the feeling of relief, release, gratitude, and satisfaction experienced by me on that memorable evening."[55] Those emotions were to be shared by the entire brotherhood.

As he had done at each major turning point in his career, Mott now brought the issue to Mrs. McCormick. On June 17 he presented her an eight-page brief in his own hand outlining his current and contemplated responsibilities, the main reasons for considering the general secretaryship, and his conditions of acceptance. His overall responsibility for the North American Student Movement would continue, but he had found an able successor to take over the Student YMCA in the person of David R. Porter; this was the only shift in the dozen agencies to which he was "responsibly related."[56] He listed thirteen "essential functions" of the head of the home department, the only division affected, since he was already head of the foreign work.

Since he could not "add days to the calendar, and as he is already living a full life," he explained to Mrs. McCormick that he must have several new associates: three for the home department comparable to the foreign work triumvirate of Colton, Eddy, and Jenkins; enlargement of his present personal staff to include an assistant private secretary, a research secretary and other necessary clerks and stenographers, and the services of his old and trusted colleague Gilbert A. Beaver, "to help in important and at times difficult personal negotiations."

In addition, Mott set as an absolute requirement of his acceptance the return of Fletcher Brockman from China to be his associate.[57] His reasoning becomes clear in the light of Latourette's later characterization of Brockman: "his capacity for organization and leadership, his comprehensive statesmanship, and his genius for friendship" had enabled him to fill the national secretaryship of China "with distinction." Mott assured Mrs. McCormick that Brockman would be "persona grata" everywhere as his personal substitute. She approved the package and subscribed $5,000 a year for five years to a $30,000 fund to undergird it;

the other guarantors were Cleveland H. Dodge, John D. Rockefeller, Jr., James Stokes, A. A. Hyde, and Cyrus McCormick.[58] From a train in Iowa the next week Mott thanked her:

> I have gone to you at every important crisis and at the time of every momentous decision in my life during the past twenty years and never without receiving invaluable help. Your intuition, your sympathy and your poise of judgment help me to see the path of duty and opportunity, just as your generous gifts have so many times made possible my entering the path. May God enable me to realize your own and His expectations![59]

Mott accepted on August 10 after a month at Lac des Iles during which there were long talks with his summer neighbors and extended prayerful sessions with the Brockmans. The decision was universally acclaimed by his colleagues, the secular and religious press, and the Association Movement.[60] The sentiment was well expressed in an editorial entitled "Religious Efficiency" in the *Los Angeles Times:*

> The Y.M.C.A. is to be congratulated on the selection of John R. Mott as its general secretary. Few organizations ever attain to the efficiency of the Young Men's Christian Association. This has not been alone because it was a society of laymen, but largely because the ranks of its workers have been filled with the trained flower of our colleges and universities. In the last twenty-five years very few men in the world have had a greater religious influence in the English-speaking universities of the world than John R. Mott. Japan and China have also felt this man's love and wisdom. He has served the remarkable apprenticeship that acquaints a man with every avenue of work in an organization. Mott is a peculiar combination of spiritual understanding and secular activity. He is in earnest about religion and has a fine capacity for doing things. With Mott in control the Y.M.C.A. should have a remarkable administration.[61]

In his letter of acceptance, which was severely edited by Leila, Mott reiterated the conditions that he had laid down (in the same words given to Mrs. McCormick), reported that Brockman had agreed, and set forth his attitude toward administration:

> In discharging this new responsibility I shall have as a guiding principle to discover how the Association may render throughout the world the maximum service to the Kingdom of God, especially as expressed in the Christian Church. It will be my constant effort to serve with impartiality all departments and phases of the work and to promote the solidarity of this complex and ever-expanding Movement. I shall be true to my strongest conviction concerning this and all other Christian enterprises, namely, that chief and constant emphasis must be placed on the spiritual, and, therefore, that the principal concern of all who are called to aid in any capacity, should be to bring into the lives of men the vitalizing and trans-

forming power of the Living Christ. At a time when the foundations of society are heaving and human supports are falling in confusion, how imperative it is that attention be riveted upon the One Sure Foundation— the same yesterday, today, and forever.

Notwithstanding the results which have been achieved by the Association Movement in the past and in spite of the present grave outlook throughout the world, the most fruitful service of the Young Men's Christian Association, as I firmly believe, lies in the days that are before us. While only a sense of Divine compulsion leads me to undertake these larger responsibilities, I should be untrue to my heart if I did not acknowledge that this opportunity to enter more fully than ever into the wonderful fellowship of this brotherhood is an inspiring privilege and honor.[62]

The underlying reasons for acceptance were less capable of public statement: the ecumenical stance of the YMCA, the shrinkage of the student and missionary worlds because of the War, the unprecedented opportunity the position offered to use the "Y" as the base for the War work programs and to undergird its own foreign thrust more adequately, his immense debt to Morse,[63] and the tremendous pressure that had built up through two decades and was now exerted by friends such as Cleveland Dodge and Cyrus McCormick, representative laymen whom Mott obviously preferred to ecclesiastics. In this position he reached the summit of lay leadership in American Protestantism, at its crest.

Mott's uprooting of Brockman from "the land of his heart adoption" came as "an absolute surprise" that "stunned and dazed and humbled" Brockman and his wife, as she described it to Leila Mott after they had reached a decision at the Lac. Three years before, when Brockman had been offered the presidency of Peking University, Mott had advised against acceptance because "when one has spent twenty years or more in specializing on one work he is not likely at the time in life where you and I find ourselves now to render as large or fruitful a service to his generation by changing as by continuing." Yet in long hours of intimate and prayerful discussion, in spite of their broken hearts at leaving China, the Brockmans came through a "blessed experience" to full acceptance of the new assignment. "If this is God's call we dare not hesitate to go," they had resolved when the first cablegram came. They took up their new work "with fear and trembling but with loyalty and devotion to our great Leader and to you two dear friends through whom the call of God came," Mary Brockman confided to Leila Mott. After days in conference in the Canadian woods the problems the two men faced initially appeared "bafflingly intricate and difficult." The Brockmans at first took rooms next door to the Motts in Montclair. Before Brockman could return to his beloved China there were to be nine "self-denying years, difficult years, exhausting," Mott later confessed, a tacit admission that the Mott-Brockman team had not been as effective as hoped. At a memorial service for Brockman in 1944, Mott declared he was "one of the dearest friends I have ever had."[64]

Some were critical of Mott for assuming that such a sacrificial dedication as Brockman's could readily be made or unmade, but that is to misjudge the depth of commitment and friendship between two men whose first-name relationship lasted almost sixty years.[65] Oldham, it will be recalled, had not felt drawn to the secretaryship of the Continuation Committee but accepted in order to assure Mott's commitment to it. In his letter of acceptance, Brockman told Mott that it was "absolutely necessary for the future of the Association work" that he(Mott) assume the post: "I concur with all my heart in the conditions upon which you have accepted." And to his lay chairman in China Brockman wrote that although the decision tore up "the very roots of our lives" he and his wife had been unable to follow their personal preferences because only Mott's leadership in America could meet the crisis here.[66]

PART 7: "A Peculiar Combination of Spiritual Understanding and Secular Activity"

Sherwood Eddy, who knew Mott far better than the editor of the *Los Angeles Times,* once remarked that for Mott organization "was not an end in itself. The essential thing was spiritual life." This was equally true of Brockman, which explains the compatibility of the two and why in spite of their ignorance of city Association work they could be welcomed as saviors of a Movement that was "staggered and embarrassed" by the burden of its new problems. It throws light upon Mott's concern in his acceptance that the YMCA render "maximum service to the Kingdom of God" especially as it is manifested "in the Christian Church."

Early in the joint planning of their work for the first year of partnership, Mott and Brockman proposed to "ascertain and where necessary put right the mind of leaders of the Church" concerning the "Y" and possibly to hold a series of conferences with them. They increased the religious work program of the entire Movement, laying down for the staff at a cabinet meeting in December, 1915, this policy:

> The International Committee stands for the prominence of the spiritual objective of this movement and the giving to the so-called religious work its true centrality. The religious work should be comprehensive, normal, pervasive, in accordance with the last word in reverent religious thought, evangelical, properly balanced between denominational and interdenominational interests, and aggressive.[67]

To this end also Mott restructured the national staff as a congenial group of intimates composing a cabinet bound in Christian fraternity and nourished on prayer. The fellowship of numerous retreats, a policy of frankness, and regular meetings in which he participated, completed the formula.

As the *Times* had said, the efficiency of the YMCA had not been achieved solely because it was a society of laymen, though that, it should be added, was of basic importance, but "largely because the ranks of its workers have been filled with the trained flower of our colleges and universities." Mott's national cabinet now became the "big team" that was the goal of many an ambitious and talented young man aspiring to a position of leadership in this unique organization. An example was Paul Super, city secretary at Honolulu, who was brought to headquarters in 1915: "The big games are played by the big teams," he told his wife. "I want to play on John R. Mott's big team, and as a member of his team, the signals he calls, I'll run."[68] Colton, who was quarterback for thirty years, wrote that "the give and take grew with the years into the fulness of the term 'fellowship' and beyond that."[69]

Mott picked able men and gave them wide latitude, a policy involving grave risks, but the marvel is that there were few failures. He read and retained the incredible details of their reports, proposals, and pet plans, so was constantly abreast of all developments across the Movement. He was also aware of their personal situations and problems. Whether he came to mean most to them as "a father, a brother, a friend, or a chieftain," as Colton once put it, he welded them into an extraordinarily effective squadron. It must have been that ability more than any other trait that had motivated a group of friends who had asked him a few years earlier to head a great central bank that had been projected (before the Federal Reserve system) to stabilize the financial structure of the country; it was his sense of single-minded dedication that could explain the possibly apocryphal aftermath of that offer—he was said to have burst into tears at the thought that his friends could have so misread his life purpose.[70]

The details of the new administration's program may be found in

Volume III of Mott's *Addresses and Papers* or in the author's *History of the YMCA*. In the spring of 1916 Mott called a small private conference of leading city Association secretaries to help chart the new city department that had been authorized at the time of his appointment. It soon became apparent there that program, ideology, and efficiency were all under question; in addition, the growth of organizations providing services that had been originated by the "Y" were becoming competitors. It was a genuine learning experience for the new general secretary and his associate.

The national YMCA Convention of that summer—Mott's "inaugural without a ceremony," meeting during a presidential campaign featured by Wilson's slogan "he kept us out of war"—heard and acted affirmatively on three dozen resolutions covering more than fifty proposals. It expanded program, staff, and budget, which necessitated moving the headquarters, this time to 347 Madison Avenue in the heart of mid-town Manhattan; that address became the locus of national and worldwide operations administered from the heart of the Western world and symbolizing YMCA identification with the larger currents of business and social life that swirled around it. [71]

Only four months after the resolutions of the 1916 Convention were implemented, America entered the War, which effectively shelved most of them and redirected the general secretary's duties for the duration. Richard Morse declared in 1918, in his last appraisal of Mott, that the first two years of the new administration had not only shown how "indispensable" Mott's leadership had proved to be but also "how essential he was to the improvement by the North American Associations of the vast opportunity this world war has presented to them of an unprecedented ministry to millions of young men under arms." [72]

Mott had described his new position to President Wilson in an interview November 8, 1915 when he characterized the work of the International Committee as touching "all states, all lands, all classes of young men"—in cities, rural areas, industry and the railroads, students, colored, Army and Navy. He had three great constituencies, he said: the young men of America, of the Orient and Latin America, and those under arms. After mentioning the Dodges, McCormicks, and Charles Crane, Mott spoke of the importance of conserving boyhood and young manhood, of the unifying power of great unselfish causes or purposes, and of young men as the stabilizing element of the country. On their behalf he appreciated the President's keeping the nation on an even keel and our moral powder dry, and thanked him and the state department and several ambassadors for cooperating in the work for soldiers, reporting on its growth and potential.[73]

One of the unusual reports to the International YMCA Convention of 1916 was that on the new National Council of the YMCA's of Canada, in the formation of which Mott had been active. It described an effective supervisory body forced "from the first month of the war" to concentrate on service to soldiers and faced with serious adjustments at home. A separation agreement of 1912 had proved entirely satisfactory. Mott had been involved in Canadian moves toward independence in the role of "master tactitian" along with Morse since 1901. Several of his close friends and summer neighbors at Lac des Iles were leaders of the Montreal Association and of the Canadian Movement.

When Morse and Marling, chairman of the International Committee, had convened an informal group to discuss Canadian problems at Toronto in 1911, Mott was unanimously chosen chairman. Nationalistic sentiment in Canada facilitated the proposal that the Canadian YMCA's organize a central supervisory body with one budget and one staff for the entire country. It was a clean break from the Movement in the United States, with the one outstanding exception of the foreign work, a feature that clearly reveals Mott's astute guidance; the agreements reached became the framework of the Canadian National Council.[74]

Mott and Morse further influenced the new organization by proposing the relatively youthful Charles W. Bishop to be its first national secretary. In the words of Murray G. Ross, historian of the Canadian Movement, "the decisive factor in the appointment was the influence of Morse and Mott":

> For these two men, Bishop was an excellent candidate. He was intimate with student work, a supporter of foreign work; he had a university education; he had not been a local general secretary; he was tactful and "diplomatic," yet had visions of greater days for the Y.M.C.A. This fitted the Morse-Mott pattern—one typical of their own successful careers.[75]

These developments, as Owen E. Pence remarked, provided an example (of which Mott was fully aware as he considered the call to the general secretaryship) "of modifying structure and institutional modes in favor of greater realism in service." The lesson was plain, for most of the problems facing the Movement in the United States were similar to those on which the Canadians had acted forthrightly. It would be a decade before the New York-based organization could take comparable steps.[76]

In the one area that the two Movements agreed to continue to support mutually, the foreign work, expansion had been so great and the criticism such that in 1915 a commission was named to review the entire enterprise. Its chairman, metropolitan secretary of Chicago, L. Wilbur Messer, who was considered the leading American city YMCA executive, had held aloof from support of the overseas venture and had appeared critical of Mott. But after a world inspection tour he endorsed what had been done in the past and recommended to the Convention of 1916 that steps be taken "to organize and carry through in the near future a comprehensive forward movement to augment greatly the resources of this part of our common work, and that the entire Brotherhood be called upon to support such an adequate policy of advance in all ways within their power." Mott's and Brockman's joy may be imagined, but both were realists enough to know that it would still take years of cultivation before foreign work support would become a budget item for the majority of local Associations. In 1915 Colton had complained that imposing a large share of the fund raising on Mott's shoulders was a misdirected use of administrative and spiritual resources for lesser needs. [77] However, the War years saw the program move "from strength to strength" with significant additions to staff and budget, while the calling of American foreign secretaries into War work opened large opportunities for nationals. Following America's entry into the War and in the 1920's the greatest advances on the foreign field would take place, although that budget had passed the half-million-dollar mark by 1916. [78]

Because the War had far less disruptive effect in the Orient and in Latin America than in Europe and the United States, these were ideal years to stimulate the foreign work there. There are no better examples than Mott's sending Augustin E. Turner to Chile in 1915 "to make a YMCA which had been organized for German and British young men into an Association for the Chileans." [79] In 1916 the vigorous and inventive E. Stanton Turner was sent to Manila. Such was his life investment in the Philippines that his autobiography could rightly be called *Nation Building;* he would remain in his adopted country when MacArthur evacuated the Islands in 1941. Mott's principle, Turner told the author, was "getting things started and letting us go our own way." Mott advised him to read liberal Catholic writers. Turner built a national and indigenous Movement and secretarial staff of Roman Catholic Filipinos; it became so firmly based that when the bishops issued an edict of excommunication, no one repudiated the "Y." As late as 1947 Turner was opposed by brother secretaries elsewhere for recruiting Catholics for the profession. Mott supported him to the hilt. [80]

When Stanton Turner went to Manila, it was as student secretary. At least half of the men sent to foreign fields by the North American YMCA's spent at least a term or two in student work. Thus from the beginning there was an intimate relationship between the foreign enterprise and the student department, both of which Mott headed until 1915. In actuality, his separation from the direct administration of his "first love," the college work, was divesting himself of detail, since he would continue to exert leadership as chairman of the North American Council of Student Movements and as Secretary of the WSCF. As general secretary of the YMCA all departments came under his purview.

There were still the great campus campaigns, enhanced by the expanding techniques of high-pressure organization and advertising and given added thrust by the social gospel and the War. Student departments, not only in the United States, were deluged with demands for special evangelistic meetings and round tables on religion. Mott chose a few at which he would appear at the psychological moment, speak to immense throngs, often on the religious significance of the War, and leave when the interest was at its height, being followed by teams of personal workers who effectively recruited volunteers for the growing War work enterprises. During the short period described in this chapter, he appeared at Oberlin, Cornell, and Yale; at the University of Kansas he was teamed with Raymond Robins, the noted Progressive. At Penn State among the many youths whose lives were changed was Arthur L. Carson, who was to serve in the Philippines. "I had never heard anything like it," he told the author, "Christ as a personal friend, a reality." He decided to try it; it worked.[81] Among the supporting members of these groups the name of David R. Porter appeared with increasing frequency.[82] In Porter, a Rhodes scholar from Bowdoin College, who had been traveling among the preparatory schools since 1907, Mott had at last found a successor. Under Porter the men's student movement continued to expand; one of its most notable features was the Negro field cultivated by Weatherford and Channing H. Tobias.[83] The Convention of 1916 directed Porter's department to work with cooperating denominations in providing a ministry in state universities.

Mott's "peculiar combination" may also be seen in his search for a new senior secretary of what had been known as the Religious Work Department, which was undergoing a transformation in the direction of what was really a new department of "Evangelism and Christian Education." The ideal candidate was Henry B. Wright, then of the Yale Divinity School, to whom he offered and urged the post: "You combine in

John Stitt Mott and Elmira Dodge Mott, John R. Mott's parents

John R. Mott, about age 12   *The Mott home on West Williams Street, Postville, Iowa*

Mount Hermon delegation, 1886: Mott at left in middle row; roommate George Ames upper right; F. H. Lee middle right

Barnes Hall, Cornell University

Mrs. John R. Mott (Leila Ada White)
and son John L. about 1893

Mott's Class of '88

White, Compton, Mott family reunion at the "White House," August, 1901: Mott,
upper right; Leila Mott with daughter Irene in front of her husband; Johnny Mott
front right

The home secretaries of the YMCA foreign department, about 1905: Ethan T. Colton, Mott, Hans P. Andersen

Robert E. Speer (left) and Mott at Northfield, about 1900

Mott with his first professional YMCA colleagues in the student work (l. to r.): Robert Weidensal, Luther D. Wishard, Charles H. Ober, Mott

The Founding Fathers of the WSCF: (l. to r.) Williamson, Siemsen, Mott, Eckhoff, Fries, Wishard

Vadstena Castle, Sweden

The Kumamoto Band, Japan, 1897

First meeting of the WSCF, Northfield, 1897

WSCF General Committee, Nikko,
Japan, 1907

Mott and Karl Fries, General Secretary and
Chairman of the WSCF, about 1905

Mott at YMCA convention, Melbourne,
1903

South Africa, 1906: Ruth Rouse, Leila
Mott, Will Stewart, Mott

Mott with J. H. Oldham

The World Missionary Conference at Edinburgh, 1910, Mott in the chair

World Tour, 1912–13 (l. to r.): S. H. Fowler, secretary to G. S. Eddy, John R. Mott, John L. Mott, C. H. Fahs, E. J. Webster

Lake Mohonk WSCF Conference, 1913: Robert Wilder, Baron Paul Nicolay, Mott, President Ibuka

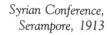

Syrian Conference, Serampore, 1913

The Root Mission aboard the Czar's royal train; Mott is eighth from left.

Mott with D. Willard Lyon at Harbin on the return from Russia 1917

"When I saw my boy in France": Mott with son John L., France, April, 1918

Pages from Mott's pocket ledger listing the contributors to the first War Work Fund ($3,000,000) of the YMCA in the spring of 1917

Meeting of department heads, YMCA War Work, Paris

Mott with Fletcher Brockman and David Yui, Hangchow, 1922

At the Haystack Monument, Williamstown, Massachusetts

John R., Leila, and Frederick D. Mott as guests of Viscount S. Goto and family, Tokyo, 1925

Arrival in Helsingfors, 1926

China Continuation Conference, 1922

Conference of missionaries to Moslems, Jerusalem, 1928

Mott with the Orthodox leaders, Jerusalem, 1928

Missionary Conference committee on findings, Melbourne, 1926

Mott and Margaret Holmes with D. K. Picken, National Chairman of Australia SCM, at Berwick, 1926

Family reunion, India, 1929: John L. Mott, Irene Mott, Celestine (Mrs. John L.) Mott, Eleanor Mott, J. R. M., Leila Mott.

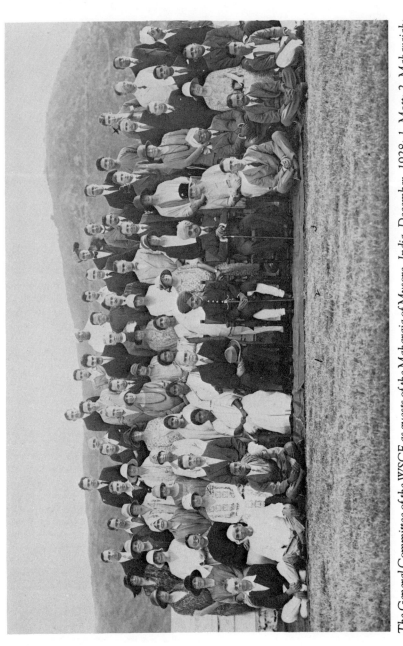

The General Committee of the WSCF as guests of the Maharaja of Mysore, India, December, 1928: 1. Mott; 2. Maharajah; 3. Yuvarajah of Mysore

Conference with Orthodox leaders, Athens, 1930

Committee of the International Missionary Council, Herrnhut, Germany, June, 1932

With Lord and Lady Allenby and the dedication of the Jerusalem YMCA, 1933

"In the heart of pagan Africa," 1934

With President Benes of Czechoslovakia, 1938

Five successive chairmen of the WSCF: W. A. Visser 't Hooft, Mott, Francis P. Miller, Robert C. Mackie, D. T. Niles

With his successors in the executive secretaryship of the National (U.S.A.) Student YMCA: A. Roland Elliott, David R. Porter, R. H. Edwin Espy

Consecrating the newly-formed World Council of Churches, Amsterdam, 1948: Mott is third from left.

The Honorary President with the six Presidents of the World Council of Churches, Amsterdam, 1948 (l. to r.): Bishop G. Bromley Oxnam, Archbishop S. Germanos, Mott, Geoffrey Fisher, Archbishop of Canterbury, Archbishop Erling Eidem of Sweden, Dr. Tsu-chen Chao

At the Nobel Peace Prize dinner, New York, December 19, 1946: Bishop G. Bromley Oxnam of the Methodist Church, Mott, Archbishop Athenagoras of the Greek Orthodox Church in the Western Hemisphere, Harry Emerson Fosdick, pastor emeritus of the Riverside Church, New York City

The headquarters of the World Alliance of YMCA's in Geneva, named for John R. Mott.

At Whitby World Council meeting, 1947

an unusual degree scholastic attainments with rich practical experience."
When Wright refused, Mott turned to his old and trusted colleague
Robert Wilder, who accepted an offer that specified that a third of his
time was to be spent in rest and study to keep him fresh to communicate
"the spiritual vision, spiritual life and spiritual impulses." Soon Wilder
was called on to administer the "Religious Work Bureau" of the National
War Work Council; there was little time for either rest or study. [84]

The spirit of the times may be read in the call to the Universal Day
of Prayer for Students, composed by Fries and Mott in late 1914, perhaps
while they were together on the Continent:

> Never in the history of universities and colleges has there been such need
> for united intercession on the part of students and of all other Christians
> who recognize the boundless spiritual possibilities of these centres of learn-
> ing, as in this fateful moment in the life of the world. . . . Nothing less than
> the overruling and irresistible working of the living God and the marked
> manifestation of His love and power in answer to prayer can bring true
> peace and harmony among people. . . . At a time when the foundations are
> heaving and everything seems to be slipping, it is supremely important to
> hold before men the central and abiding fact—"Jesus Christ, the same
> yesterday, today and forever." [85]

As the War dragged on and the likelihood of America's becoming a
belligerent increased, Mott's war-related enterprises grew as fast as men
could be recruited and funds obtained. By the time of his trip to the War
zones in the summer of 1916 Mrs. McCormick, John D. Rockefeller, Jr.,
and Cleveland H. Dodge were giving $50,000 each toward a fund of
$750,000. This added urgency to his basic message on the significance of
the War for religion, and the place of the all-embracing "Y" programs in
it. These utterances displayed Mott's "YMCA mind" at its fullest. Now
that he was its top executive and most fluent spokesman his speeches and
writings presented the Movement as a world force among students, a
ministry to young men in a score of foreign countries, the activities of the
World Alliance among prisoners of war, projects for railroad men, rural
work, a force to conserve the values of boyhood and young manhood
everywhere. It was a lay brotherhood, a fellowship, ecumenicity at work.
Its best days were to come.

PART 8: A "Most Dangerous" Journey, June–July, 1916

The records of this unique trip are scanty, due to the delicate nature
of Mott's errands, to censorship and his wish to avoid publicity, to the

conditions of travel, and to an extremely crowded schedule, although he took his son John L. as private secretary. Fortunately, during the return voyage from Christiania (Oslo) aboard the Scandinavian-American *Oskar II*, July 28–August 8, he reconstructed the itinerary, though the last page has not survived. But his small pocket account book has added some precious details and filled certain gaps. A few personal notes to conversations in Russia bear the stamp of the censor. If he wrote letters they have not survived.

Preparation for the journey was in part similar to that for the tour of 1914—explanations together with requests for prayer from friends such as Mrs. McCormick, who was supporting the student work in Russia. President Wilson gladly supplied not only the usual letters of introduction but commended Mott as his personal friend to several ambassadors. An unusual step was the presentation of Mott to Russian Archbishop Evdokim in New York by Charles R. Crane, who wrote his daughter that at his (Crane's) suggestion Mott was going on "another of his very important pilgrimages to Europe."

> His own work among the soldiers, both in the trenches and in the prison camps, takes him naturally there, so that he can go with a very important mission and yet not attract the attention that even quiet Colonel House now attracts, and supplement in a most valuable way, among the churches and universities of all the warring countries, the work the Colonel has done and the information he has gathered in the political world. I thought that I could enlarge Mr. Mott's usefulness by putting him in the right relationship with the Archbishop, who is a man widely known and greatly respected in Russia. The visit lasted perhaps an hour. Of course, I had previously laid the foundation for the interview by telling the Archbishop about Mr. Mott, his relations with the President, his own great work, and the estimate I myself placed on the value of the mission. The Archbishop was entirely sympathetic, fully recognized the gravity of the mission and cooperated in a wise and helpful way. . . . We all felt we were assisting at an historic meeting.[86]

Yet the trip was to be different. Oldham and others were instructed to make neither public commitments nor announcements. It would be a four-fold mission—for the army and navy work, POW's, the WSCF, and missions—but in addition there were delicate administrative matters to deal with and some were highly confidential. Service to the millions of men under arms was becoming a substantial enterprise, the many reports received from its executives indicated the need for face-to-face consultations, and in spite of the horror of it all, Mott felt a compulsion to visit the fronts.

He sailed again on the neutral *Nieuw Amsterdam,* which threaded her way safely through mine- and submarine-infested seas May 29–June 7, while the battle of Jutland took place in the North Sea. John L. Mott came to London from Aberdeen where he had been studying with Principal David S. Cairns; in six days father and son witnessed the effects of conscription and the incredible casualties of the first battle of Verdun. While John L. toured the city, his father conferred with Oldham, chiefly about orphaned missions, and with Tatlow, Wilder, Hodgkin, William Temple, Arthur Yapp of the YMCA, the Archbishop of Canterbury, Sir Edward Grey, and the American Ambassador, Walter Hines Page.

At Le Havre the Motts saw throngs of German prisoners on the docks, visited a POW camp, then inspected two *foyers* and a supply warehouse. In Paris Mott met Allier, talked with the general in charge of the prisoners' department of the Ministry of War, conferred with the Paris Missionary Society, and called upon the wife of SCM secretary Charles Grauss (whose husband had been in the trenches since the beginning of the war), leaving a gift of $150 with Sautter for her and a similar token for another. In Marseilles he met D. A. Davis and S. K. Datta of India, making staff assignments to the POW camps in the area. At Lyons there was a lunch with Protestant pastors and Red Cross workers; from his train window he conferred with Suzanne Bidgrain of the WSCF, and later inspected a *foyer* and held a student meeting.

Three days in Geneva were packed with student conferences, a reception, and discussions with the World's Committee of the YMCA, the Red Cross, and several consuls. Mott conferred with the American secretaries at work in the region and talked well into the night with de Rougemont and Rutgers. From Geneva the Motts traveled to Basle with Würtz, thence to Karlsrühe and Darmstadt where they visited a camp of French prisoners and a cemetery. Five days in Berlin revealed the awful casualties of Verdun again. There were visits to several POW camps; Mott spoke at Ruhleben, accompanied there by the American ambassador. [87] There were conferences with Harte, Rutgers, Hibbard, and with missions and student officers Mann, Niedermeyer, Siegmund-Schultze, Richter, and T. Hall, calls at the War Ministry, "lunch at Embassy with Chancellor &c." and a send-off to Vienna by Richter and Axenfeld at the train.

In Vienna Mott conferred with Phildius and all YMCA workers available, and called on the Red Cross committee and at the American embassy. [88] On July 1 he moved to Budapest the day the great battle of the Somme was launched on the western front, while the Brusilov offensive was at its height in the east. In the company of Janos Victor he visited prison camps, conferred with Red Cross people and others. Back in Vienna for another day he again met with his workers, with the American ambassador, and with numerous others before returning to Berlin, during which trip the Motts witnessed the excruciating tragedy of a trainload of prisoners.

Back at the Kaiserhof Hotel in the German capital, the chief conferred with Harte and Conrad Hoffman, lunched at the Embassy, entertained ten "war workers" at dinner, called at the Chinese and Danish embassies, and spoke with Von Jagow, the Foreign Minister. The long train trip to Copenhagen was made in the company of Karl Fries and others; during a day in the Danish capital he met with student leaders, saw Count Moltke and the American ambassador, and called on "Russian sisters." During a stop-over in Helsingborg he conversed with the Crown Princess of Sweden; at Malmo he visited the YMCA. In one day at Stockholm he called on two consuls, found time for shopping, and ran out to Uppsala to confer all too briefly with Nathan Söderblom, now Archbishop and engrossed in international peace plans and the exchange of prisoners between France and Germany.

The three-day trip by boat and train got the Motts to Petrograd late on the night of July 13; the next day there were conversations with Professor Samuel Harper of the University of Chicago, an expert on Russian affairs, with Frederick Corse of the New York Life Insurance Company, a long-time resident, with "Haggard and Anderson," and visits to Kazan Cathedral and the American Embassy. After a night trip to Moscow, Mott lunched with the mayor of the city, called at the Kremlin, visited several hospitals, attended two church services, and conferred with Gregory Alekseev, who oriented him to the current situation in Russia. The following day he conferred with the noted correspondent Harold Williams of the London *Times*, and on the 17th with the president of the "Union of Zemstvos" on the problems of transport confronting the POW program. On July 22, Mott conferred with Harte in Petrograd, the two drawing up an outline of the duties and responsibilities of the senior secretary in Russia and the division of labor between him and his associate.

The surviving record of Mott's itinerary ends in Moscow. In view of the interview with Archbishop Evdokim in New York it may be assumed that he saw some ecclesiastics. It is inconceivable that he did not confer with Baron Paul Nicolay on whose slender shoulders lay the burden of the Russian Student Movement, though Nicolay's biographer is silent on the matter. Very little concerning the tour appeared in print, doubtless to avoid any possible risk to the POW programs.[89] Yet the impact of this journey was in all probability the most profound of any trip in Mott's entire lifetime. Such optimism as he may have reflected earlier had been dissipated by the unmitigated horror of what he saw, smelled, and heard. He described one experience to a Methodist gathering that fall:

> The other day I was in Moscow and found in that one city twelve hundred military hospitals, all full and overflowing so that in many cases they had put beds out in the yards behind the hospitals and in the street. About this time I went down to the receiving hospital on the edge of Moscow and while I was there, there came in the twenty-ninth train of wounded that day. Those trains each average twenty cars and every car of the twenty-nine trains filled with men shot through with excruciating pain. I went the next day to one of the specialized hospitals filled solely with victims of facial wounds. What sights! I have prayed since that I might blot them out.[90]

In the spring of 1917 he described another incident to a great audience in Washington:

> I was visiting a hospital in Germany one day and I said to the Jewish surgeon who was taking me about: "Will you kindly explain to me the effect of modern instruments of destruction and modern warfare?" He hesitated. "Yes, yes," he said, "if you wish, I will." I did not realize what I was asking. Then we went about those never-ending wards. He explained the effect of shrapnel, of the high-explosive shells, of the three-cornered bayonet, of the sword-bayonet, of the lance, of concussion from shellfire. He showed me the victims of tetanus, of gas-gangrene and liquid fire, and I confess I almost sank at his feet.[91]

There was not only physical suffering. In the report letter that Mott composed during the voyage home for his friends and supporters such as Edward S. Harkness and Mrs. McCormick (who sent hers, underlined, to President Wilson) he spoke of the "vast range and depth of human suffering occasioned by the war," not only physical, but the "silent suffering of the anxious and the bereaved." He could not recall visiting a single home that "had not suffered affliction" nor a person across whose life "shadows had not fallen." No end of the awful struggle was in sight: "all these lands must suffer far more before there can be an enduring peace." In contrast to the climate of opinion in 1914, there was now an "alarming development of distrust, bitterness and hatred" everywhere.

Feeling toward America had changed completely:

> One of the best indications that we as a nation have been truly neutral is the fact that both sides in the present struggle regard our actions and policy with so much dissatisfaction and displeasure. Be that as it may, the present is not the time to argue with Europe, still less to criticize any of the nations now engaged in the war, or to make peace proposals to them.

He wrote of "the volume of unselfish activity and service" to be found in every part of Europe, but his "chief solicitude" was "lest the American people, because of our being at such long range and because of our lack of imagination and credence, fail to enter sufficiently into fellowship with the sufferings of the hundreds of millions of our brothers and sisters in Europe." This theme was emphasized over and over in his speaking during the next months. He continued to his friends:

> In the light of what I have seen, I fear that during the coming Autumn and Winter we shall witness immeasurably greater suffering than in either of the preceding years. It is essential that we not only continue to do all in our power to carry forward this practical and truly Christlike ministry to the bodies and souls of suffering men (of whom there are not less than five millions in the prison camps alone), but that we give ourselves more to prayer that God Himself may bring an end in His own way to a situation that has become impossible for men to control or for the world to bear.[92]

As he had done on some previous trips, Mott wrote out a dozen "Evidences of Answered Prayer." Life had been preserved and health shielded in spite of dangers on land and sea, of infections rampant in camps and hospitals; those at home were well. Doors had opened, thanks to President Wilson, the French Ambassador, and developments in Germany right after the visit there. Misunderstandings had been cleared up, confidence restored. Every appointment had been met, with no delays. He had borne a "message of hope and love to those who needed it." There had been opportunities to bear witness and to "promote better understanding and attitudes of feeling among leading men of the nations." Relationships had been renewed with leaders of the Christian movements with which he had been and continued to be connected. He had been kept from embarrassing his present or future influence and usefulness by "being drawn into newspaper or other declaration, or being misquoted or misinterpreted" by unsympathetic friends or others. New opportunities had been discovered and agreement reached on a policy for serving the soldiers and prisoners, and for forecasting plans for the period following the War, and he had realized more clearly than ever the uniqueness, and the indispensability of the suffering of Christ in promoting right relations between nations, races, and classes—"that His way of settling disputes is different from the way employed in this struggle."[93]

Between the time of Mott's return to New York and the opening of a new year's intensive round, there were only three weeks for rest and renewal at Lac des Iles. Even those precious days were broken by a summons to Washington.

PART 9: Peace, Pacifism, Mediation, and Relief

Few Americans had given serious thought to the ethical aspects of war and peace prior to the outbreak of the Great War in 1914. A notable exception was the Lake Mohonk Conferences on International Arbitration that met from 1895 to 1914, to which speakers came from many professions; Mott spoke there in 1905, 1908, and 1914.[94] The War brought an end to those meetings.

Mott was a charter trustee of the Church Peace Union from its establishment by Andrew Carnegie in February, 1914; one of the twenty-five at the dramatic meeting at which Carnegie set up and endowed the Union, he worked with it most of the rest of his life. It was one of the organizations in which he continued after becoming general secretary of the YMCA's. He was a member of the committee that planned the Union's first world conference, which had the misfortune to meet at Constance, Germany, on August 1, 1914. It regrouped in London to form the World Alliance for International Friendship Through the Churches; Mott served on the American continuing body and in several other capacities later. The next spring he was a signer, along with Robert E. Speer, A. J. Brown, Shailer Mathews, and others, of the Union's request to the American clergy to avoid pronouncements in support of either of the warring parties and to work for peace.[95]

Right after Thanksgiving, 1915, Mott received a telegram from Henry Ford inviting him to join a hundred representative Americans on a pilgrimage to the neutral Scandinavian capitals "to free the good will of Europe that it may assert itself for peace. . . . " Mott replied, "Other plans render it impossible to accept your most kind invitation."[96] That ill-starred effort at mediation was drowned in a wave of derision.

In the course of Mott's trip to Europe in 1914, he talked at length with Henry T. Hodgkin, a Quaker whom he had known at least since the latter volunteered for mission in China in 1905 and subsequently through Hodgkin's membership on the Edinburgh Continuation Committee. Hodgkin was a convinced pacifist and an organizer and chairman of the

British Fellowship of Reconciliation (FOR). Its members held that the Christian principle of love prohibited them from participation in war. They "considered pacifism a vocation, a duty, a religious imperative," as Carl Herman Voss has said. At just what point Mott became convinced of the FOR's position and joined is not clear, but he was instrumental in bringing Hodgkin to America in the summer of 1915. One result of Hodgkin's mission was the formation of an American FOR of which Mott's colleagues and intimates David Porter, Charles Hurrey, and Fletcher Brockman were members, with Gilbert A. Beaver the first chairman.

After Hodgkin's return to Britain in the fall of 1915, Oldham learned of Mott's action from him and hastened to advise against it. The news had "created an unfortunate impression in all quarters," said Oldham, because the FOR was regarded as being in effect a "stop the war" organization. It was strictly a British body, with no membership in Germany or Austria. To Oldham this meant that Mott was actually supporting "the very small minority of Christian people in England who desire peace at any price." The vast majority of earnest Christians in Great Britain were "conscientiously opposed to this view." The word "reconciliation" more nearly than any other term summed up what Oldham most desired and hoped for. But Hodgkin appeared to think primarily in terms of love for the Germans, whereas Oldham's—and the majority—view was that "love demands consideration for the countless generations yet unborn and for those great peoples of the East who are struggling into a new and unknown future." Oldham felt that Hodgkin's propaganda could only lead "to a defeat of the real interests of humanity."

Oldham was concerned that Mott's worldwide influence not be compromised by a viewpoint that if carried into action would mean that Germany could "reap the fruits of what appears to many as deliberate aggression." In his extraordinary book *The World and the Gospel*, published in July, 1916, Oldham gave further grounds for his position. He saw that Mott received a copy. There is no record of Mott's reply. Doubtless the two discussed the issue when they met in London on July 11, 1916. As was Mott's custom in such cases, he quietly withdrew from the FOR without damaging his friendships. In the fall of 1916 while the "preparedness" fervor was at its height in the United States, Beaver asked him to forward a statement of the Fellowship's position to President Wilson as one of several representations being made. Mott refused, explaining to "Dear Gilbert" that his understanding with the President and his knowledge of Wilson's purposes was such that he could not "consent to favor" the paper.[97]

In the fall of 1915, as the result of a cable from the American Ambassador to Turkey, Henry Morgenthau, Sr., Cleveland H. Dodge had invited some thirty leaders of religious and philanthropic groups to meet in his office. They organized to aid Armenians and Syrians victimized by the War and the genocidal disasters that were befalling those minorities. Mott was included; he was acquainted with at least half of those who were there—notably the chairman James L. Barton, the treasurer Charles R. Crane, and Arthur J. Brown, Dodge, Arthur Curtiss James, Frederick Lynch, Charles S. MacFarland, Frank Mason North, William Sloane, James M. Speers, and Rabbi Stephen S. Wise. Other bodies aiming at relief in Persia, Palestine, Turkey, and Syria subsequently joined this "Dodge Committee," which became "Near East Relief." Mott was a board member throughout the fifteen years of its life.[98] It proved to be another circle in which he worked with several of those Progressive admirers of the President, most of whom supported Wilson's campaign for re-election in 1916. Morgenthau came home from Turkey to assist in that effort; he and Mott shared in the jubilation of victory.[99]

Mott was a prime mover in a joint proposal with six others to Wilson that later led in part to the success of the United War Work campaigns after America entered the War. Mott phrased the idea in a telegram sent February 2, 1917:

> We the undersigned who have been in frequent informal conference looking toward better development of American relief measures in Europe desire to tender you our loyal sentiments and our support in any position which you may deem it wise for the country to assume; also to place our services at your disposal should you consider it advisable to create a national relief organization, which would provide an adequate patriotic fund for the support of the Red Cross and of other national measures of relief at home and abroad.

The signers were Mott, Cleveland H. Dodge, Herbert Hoover, Elliott Wadsworth of the American Red Cross, W. L. Honnold and Frederic C. Walcott for Belgian relief, and C. A. Coffin then chairman of the board of General Electric. The President, who apparently read only half of the message, replied next day that no telegram he had received had given him "such gratification"; it reflected "the spirit of America itself" and made him feel "stronger and more certain of the course to pursue."[100]

This was February 3, 1917, the day he severed diplomatic relations with Germany.

PART 10: The Joint High Commission with Mexico

Mott had hardly settled into his Canadian retreat for a desperately needed rest following the harrowing trip to Europe in the summer of 1916, when a telegram came from Secretary of State Robert Lansing relaying President Wilson's request that he serve on a Joint High Commission with Mexico to obtain "a settlement of our relations with our neighbor." Wilson begged Mott to accept because it was "imperative that I should have men whom I thoroughly know and absolutely trust." We want, he continued, a settlement "that will help the Mexicans."[101]

Relations with Mexico had plagued the Wilson administration from its inaugural; at the moment tension was high on both sides of the border and an American punitive force under General John J. Pershing had penetrated more than 300 miles into Mexico. Mott was fully aware of the YMCA services with those troops. It is impossible to sketch here the tangle of relationships that had brought the two countries to the brink of war in June, 1916, or to outline the problems discussed by the Commission. Mott accepted the assignment unaware that it would virtually immobilize him for more than four months. He informed his closest friends and in return received their assurances of prayerful approval.

The first orientation with the President was on August 22; it was attended by Mott and the other two American Commissioners, Franklin K. Lane, Secretary of the Interior, and Judge George Gray, a former Senator from Delaware, who had been a member of the International Permanent Court of Arbitration and of several peace commissions. The official meetings of the full Commission—the Mexican Commissioners were Luis Cabrera, Ignacio Bonillas, and Alberto J. Pani—began September 8 in New York and continued for *fifty* sessions held at first on the Connecticut shore near New London but principally at Atlantic City. Mott served as spokesman for the American team in a review with Wilson on October 5. His notes show a firm grasp of the issues and that he initiated numerous moves in the discussions; they could provide a wealth of information for a future historian concerned with the inner workings of the Commission. In addition to the seemingly endless regular sessions there were briefings, consultations with Chief of Staff General

Hugh L. Scott and with several political scientists, special interest hearings, and the necessary meetings of the three Americans.

An agreement was reached and signed on November 24, only to be rejected a month later by Mexican President Carranza because the protocol did not provide for immediate withdrawal of American troops from Mexican soil. The Commission could not handle that issue and broke up on January 15, 1917. Yet it had, as Arthur S. Link observes, "preserved the peace, and that fact alone justified its existence; and it had helped Wilson win the election by neutralizing the Mexican issue during the campaign."[102] A few days later the President, with involvement in the European war imminent, ordered Pershing to return to Texas.

Ethan Colton provides insights into "facets of the Mott character" brought to light through his activity on the Commission. Well down the stretch of tediously protracted and even deadlocked sessions, Mott described to Colton the Mexicans' "*dignidad,* Latin version of Oriental face." Not long before the presidential election, Mott learned that the Mexicans were interested in the campaign. He obtained Theodore Roosevelt's box at the Brooklyn Academy of Music where the Commissioners could hear and see the former president criticize Wilson's policies as "pussy-footing, unrealistic and dangerous." That night, aware of the Mexicans' presence, Roosevelt "pulled out all the stops on Washington's handling of the Mexican case," and called the rebels outlaw bandits whose country with two governments was locked in civil war, and that the party Wilson had recognized was bent on the confiscation of American private property. The proper recourse, Roosevelt went on, would be a Republican president who would put the house in order. Next morning Mott exclaimed to Colton: "Oh, it will do good. They will have to take into account that a successor may come to power, at the hands of a Party minded to shift from negotiations to military action."

Mott revealed to Colton some of the pressures exerted on the Commissioners by special interests. Not only the jingoes "joined in chorus," but the holders of mining, land, and industrial privileges. "The Hearst papers and the Chicago *Tribune* clamored for occupation of the country and an enforced settlement," Colton continued:

> Mott had one approach made to him. It came up on what might be calculated to be a soft side. Oil magnate Edward C. Doheny, so he represented, won $200,000 betting on Wilson's reelection. He offered to turn the sum over to YMCA objectives in Mexico. Acceptance could only be firmly if courteously declined.[103]

Colton administered the YMCA funds for the foreign work and therefore knew how Doheny's offer was handled, but the oilman later contributed to the first YMCA War Fund of $3,000,000, raised by Mott in the spring of 1917.

PART 11: America Joins the Allies

While Mott commuted between New York and Atlantic City, the battle of the Somme gradually ran out in rain and mud after more than a million men had been killed. Following his reelection on November 7, 1916 President Wilson opened negotiations in the hope of a "peace without victory," but when the Germans decided to gamble on winning before American aid could reach the western front and declared unrestricted submarine warfare (they were sinking 300,000 tons of shipping a month; this rose to 875,000 tons in April, 1917), he severed relations. On April 6, the United States declared war on Germany, after several more American ships had been sunk and the Zimmerman note to Mexico proposing an alliance was revealed.

Mott had planned another trip to Europe in the winter of 1916-17 but abandoned it. As the prospect of America's entering the conflict grew, some YMCA men foresaw the need to plan for services to the military, but few could grasp the magnitude of the task. The day war was declared, Mott, en route by train from Chicago to Bethlehem, Pennsylvania, telegraphed President Wilson on his own from "somewhere on the road" an offer of "the full service of the Association Movement." Four days later he assembled at Garden City, New York, again on his own initiative, a Movement-wide conference that proposed the creation of a National War Work Council (NWWC); this was ratified two days later by the International Committee. Mott was general secretary and William S. Sloane, New York furniture man and philanthropist, was chairman.[104]

On April 21 and 25 Mott conferred with President Wilson. On the first occasion he requested semi-official recognition of YMCA programs for the armed forces much as these had been approved in Canada, Great Britain, France, or Japan and for an endorsement similar to those the Associations in Britain had obtained from His Majesty, King George V; these were granted at once. A request for special military status for secretaries serving overseas met with some delay. Mott also conferred with the Secretary of War and the Secretary of the Navy. At the first meeting of the NWWC, April 28, he read a letter from the President commending earlier Association work for the military and expressing interest in the plans ahead; Wilson had also issued an executive order to the armed forces to "render the fullest practicable assistance and co-operation" to what would be called Red Triangle services at "posts and stations, and in camps and field." The Council adopted a budget of $3,000,000 to support its program for the American forces and took on Mott's POW and other wartime projects costing an additional $2,000,000 for the year. [105]

At the end of the interview of April 21, Wilson dropped a bomb in Mott's lap: "I want to ask you, will you go to Russia on a special diplomatic mission I am organizing?" Mott answered: "Mr. President, it seems like an impossible time for me to leave; but I believe in the principle of the selective draft, and you know both sides of the shield—if you think I can serve my country better in Russia than here, certainly I will go." Wilson replied: "I want you to go." [106]

When Mott returned to Washington the next week he gave the President his acceptance of membership in what became known as the Root Mission. Then in three hectic weeks he tried to put his several houses in order. Extraordinary powers were given to Brockman and associates. Mott spoke at a mass meeting of the Federal Council of Churches in Washington, obtained briefings on Russia, asked for the prayers of his friends, conferred with as many professional colleagues as possible, met with the Council of North American Student Movements, held the annual meeting of the YMCA International Committee, obtained more than $3,000,000 in pledges for the NWWC, and became a member of the Secretary of War's committee on training camp activities under Raymond B. Fosdick.

From the moment he barely caught the train from Washington to join the other members of the Mission on May 15, Mott was totally removed from his regular rounds until August eighth. His greatest adventure of travel had been the first world journey of 1895–97; the Root Mission would rank next.

9

Mission to Russia

I accepted this mission not as a political errand but because I saw in it a very important opportunity to promote the Kingdom of Christ.

W HEN MOTT gave President Wilson his acceptance of the assignment to Russia on April 25, 1917, the Provisional Government had been in office in Petrograd some six weeks and Lenin had been back in that city about ten days. The Russian Revolution was then generally regarded in the United States as the first step toward "a stable parliamentary system," and it was hoped that Russia could remain in the War as an ally. Wilson had recognized the new regime a few hours before Britain and France, and in his war message had referred to "the wonderful and heartening things that have been happening" in that nation which was "always in fact democratic at heart."

Credit advances had been authorized as early as April 3, but the first and possibly most important step toward inspiring and encouraging the Provisional Government was the sending of the Root Mission, a special delegation of nine distinguished Americans under the leadership of the elder statesman Elihu Root, former Secretary of State, Secretary of War, Senator from New York, and recipient of the Nobel Peace Prize in 1912.[1] The purpose of the Mission was to assure the new Russian government of America's whole-hearted welcome into the circle of great democracies and to confer on how the United States could best cooperate "in the prosecution of the war." History deflated both of these hopes.

PART 1: Envoys Extraordinary of the United States of America on Special Mission to Russia

Historians have been singularly united in their perplexity at Wilson's choice of Root, a conservative Republican, to head the Mission. He

476

appears to have accepted more out of a sense of duty than of concern; later he referred to the episode as a "grand-stand play" on Wilson's part—hardly a non-partisan comment. The other members were James Duncan, Vice-President of the American Federation of Labor; Charles Edward Russell, like Mott an Iowan—his father had been the abolitionist editor of a small-town newspaper—though the two found little in common, Russell being a muckraker and self-styled reformer who was expelled from the American Socialist Pary for accepting the assignment. [2] Samuel R. Bertron was a New York banker with some diplomatic experience; General Hugh L. Scott was still associated in the public mind with the Indian wars of the late nineteenth century; Admiral James H. Glennon went as naval representative.

For more than two decades Mott had been acquainted with Cyrus McCormick, Jr., through the YMCA and in other ways; McCormick was a Princeton classmate of Wilson. The Mission would cement Mott's friendship with Charles R. Crane, another wealthy Chicagoan, who supported numerous Slavic interests such as Orthodox Church choirs and Russian Studies at the University of Chicago; he was already supporting Mott's War projects, especially those in Russia. He had once had an audience with the Czar; although his was the first interview with Wilson as President, he refused the Russian ambassadorship but remained on intimate terms with the President, having advised on cabinet and ambassadorial posts and urged Wilson to include Mott in the Mission to meet the need for "at least one man of strong religious or spiritual power."[3] Crane had gone to Russia immediately after the March Revolution.

Scholars are also generally agreed that the Root Mission accomplished little, at least on the surface, though not all concur in George F. Kennan's verdict that "a mission so inauspiciously devised" left "a generally bad taste in everyone's mouth."[4] A more temperate and realistic view is Peter G. Filene's that the Mission's experience "symbolized the dilemma of policy and attitude through which Americans struggled in 1917,"[5] a time, it may be added, when they were resisting the end of what Henry F. May called "the age of innocence." All such judgments were unaware of Mott's emergence as the leading figure of the Mission and his influence upon President Wilson.

Having visited Russia less than a year before, and in 1899 and 1909, he was aware of the needs of the Russian Army for the services that he believed the YMCA could provide, and he grasped the opportunity to obtain the Provisional Government's approval and support for a new program comparable to those being rendered the British, French, and now the American forces in Europe. He had earlier established prisoner of war work in Russia and for Russian prisoners in Allied camps, and was therefore welcome in Russia.

Although he would be criticized for undertaking a non-neutral mission, Mott did so, in the words of Paul B. Anderson, his secretary in Petrograd who remained on through the YMCA experiment, as "an exercise in diplomacy to establish relations between the Christian people of America and the Christian people of Russia to their mutual benefit and for their common work in tackling the problems of war and peace throughout the world."[6] His acceptance of a place on the Mission was another evidence of the assumption, held with the President, of the parallelism between Protestant and American goals. His service on the Mexican Commission and his offer to Wilson of the services of the YMCA to the American armed forces were based on the same premises. It is not known whether he consulted with anyone other than Leila, though he confessed to Oldham that he had some anxiety about the effects upon his "future relationships." Oldham assured him that any service he might be able to render the Russian people "in this crisis in their history" would be of inestimable value; had the two been able to meet, Oldham would have urged Mott to go and was remembering him in prayer, as were other intimates such as Frank Mason North, Nettie McCormick, and his pacifist colleague Gilbert Beaver, all of whose prayers he had requested.[7]

Preparation for the Mission included extended briefings by Senator Root, whom Mott had known and admired since their contacts in South America in 1906. He conferred at length with Professor Samuel N. Harper of the University of Chicago, whom he had seen in Petrograd the previous July. Harper, whose chair was underwritten by Crane, was now confidential adviser to the State Department and generally regarded as the leading American authority on Russia. Mott renewed his Orthodox Church connections. The administration had not included a Jew in the Mission, although the largest Jewish population in the world then lived in Russia. At Harper's suggestion, Mott talked with Justice Louis Brandeis, who named several leading Jews whom Mott should meet.[8] Mott's most difficult problem, and it must be said the one he dealt with the least realistically, was provision for the administration of YMCA services to the American Army, which would arrive in France weeks ahead of schedule to the consternation of his lieutenants in Europe.[9]

Mott's appointment to the Mission was universally approved by both the secular and the religious press. The *Christian Science Monitor* declared that "probably no American" was better known abroad; it noted his acquaintance with several members of the new Russian government, who knew him as "a man who has done a remarkable work in the prison camps of belligerent countries, and who has brought comfort and relief to thousands of Russian prisoners." *The New York Times* alluded to the "profound admiration" of President Wilson for Mott. The New York *Christian Advocate* felt that Mott rounded out the Mission's personnel and in many respects would prove to be its *persona optima gratia.* The Boston *Evening Transcript* ranked him "next in importance to Root." The YMCA house organ, *Association Men,* felt that in drafting Mott the President had "laid a heavy strain" on the organization, but no one could be sent on a more important assignment. It also noted McCormick's appointment and concluded that Wilson had selected "the choicest type of American citizenship for the tremendous responsibilities" of the Mission. Of all these endorsements, Mott must have treasured most a personal note from John D. Rockefeller, Jr., assuring him of his prayers and "very great satisfaction" over the appointment, through which Mott would be in a position "to render a tremendous service to the New Russia. . . . "10

PART 2: **From Washington to Vladivostok**

German submarine warfare reached the height of effectiveness in April, 1917. It was therefore necessary for the Root Mission to travel west to Russia. Some thirty strong, it left Washington by regular train on the evening of May 15. Mott caught it at the last minute after a cordial conference alone with the British ambassador and Lord Balfour "chiefly about Russian matters." The delegation was briefed en route to Chicago by Professor Harper, who had prepared a forty-page memorandum covering developments in Russia down to May fourth and including biographical sketches of cabinet members they would likely meet. This was already obsolete, for as the Mission slept that night, Paul N. Miliukov, who had earlier lectured at the University of Chicago, was resigning as minister for foreign affairs and Alexander Guchkov as minister of war, the latter to be succeeded by Alexander Kerensky.11 Between trains in Chicago, Mott found time to see his sister Clara and to buy an armful of books to add to the trunkload he had already acquired.

He received a cable from Crane explaining some of the changes the Revolution had brought to the Russian Church. It had played no part in the Revolution, which was "entirely socialistic and material in aims," though there was an upheaval taking place in the Church, which Crane expected to be "separated from the state." In late June, laymen and clergy would hold conventions in Moscow dealing with Church affairs, and the "first general Church assembly or Sobor" in more than two hundred years had been called for September. Bishops and metropolitans had been dismissed; new ones would be appointed only after parish elections. Crane expected the new Church to be socialistic but democratic and free. "Glad you are coming as your work will now have entire freedom of expression and greater usefulness."[12] Actually the meeting to which Crane referred and before which Mott would speak was the All-Russian Congress of Clergy and Laymen, which met June 16–25. It was called by ecclesiastical liberals to develop support for reforms begun since the overthrow of the Czar and to stem the tide of conservatism rising in the Church. Mott later persisted in referring incorrectly to the body he addressed as the Sobor, which did not convene until after the Mission returned home.

While his train stopped next day in St. Paul, Mott managed a flying visit to his sister Alice. As the journey proceeded he wrote Leila that he was beginning to feel rested, was sleeping ten hours in his private compartment, had caught up on his correspondence, and felt relieved "to have the bridges burned for a while between me and my old work." Now he could concentrate on the new task—"and there is need of it." He spent most of the last day on the train talking with General Scott. McCormick joined the group at Seattle, where it arrived in the small hours of the morning of May 20 and sailed at once on the converted cruiser *Buffalo*.

The official log described the 4200-mile journey to Vladivostok with a touch of humor:

> For the first three days the weather was cold, disagreeable and becoming more and more foggy, with a fairly gentle sea, but enough to occasion a few casualties. Amongst the most serious of these was General Scott, who supported his suffering with a stoicism worthy of his old Indian friends.
> On the 23rd and 24th there was a considerable sea, with the wind abeam, which caused the *Buffalo* to stand up, or rather to roll over, to her well-merited reputation. During this period the convalescents had serious relapses, but about noon on the 25th the Unimak Pass was sighted, and upon entering it the sea became almost perfectly calm, the fog lifted, our struggles ceased and a wide and contagious cheerfulness prevailed.[13]

The course through Bering Strait was comparatively smooth, but fog rendered navigation extremely difficult. The log credited Mott with ingenuity in helping the passengers (the ship was given over entirely to the members and staff of the mission, except for its crew) to cope with the penetrating cold by playing deck golf; he wrote to his sister Harriett that he spent at least three hours a day in the open air playing this game "and in other forms of exercise"; Colonel T. Bentley Mott, Root's military aide, provided a sand-filled football that proved "an invigorating exercise." John Mott was frequently the winner or winning partner in the competition of strenuous daily exercise. Movies were shown several evenings, probably comprising the largest dose of this form of entertainment Mott had ever seen; the films ranged from social documentaries through current women's fashions. On May 30 the *Buffalo* reached Amphitrite Strait and safely entered the Sea of Okhotsk; there was a snowfall of several hours' duration; a small Asiatic land bird flew on board and was kept in the engine room.

Mott spent most of his time reading, and covered some twenty books during the voyage. At meals he sat at Senator Root's table, with General Scott, Bertron, McCormick, and Admiral Glennon.[14] John wrote to Leila that it was "a very rare privilege to be thrown in this most intimate way with Senator Root," with whom he had had unhurried conversations on all sorts of subjects, some of the most interesting of which had been about prominent men whom the Senator had known. His own estimate of Root as "our leading statesman—national or international" had not changed. He went on to characterize other members of the party:

> General Scott and Admiral Glennon are most democratic and likeable men and it is a constant pleasure to hear them tell of their experiences on land and sea. . . . Mr. Duncan, the Vice-President of the American Federation of Labor is a canny Scotchman and it is always interesting to hear his point of view. Mr. Russell is a so-called Socialist but there are so many types that this term conveys little idea of his position. He is a good sort and we all like him. Mr. Bertron is a New York broker who seems to have an unusually wide acquaintance. He is supposed to represent the capitalist interests and thought in our Commission. Mr. McCormick you know. His cabin and mine front on each other and we are together a great deal of the time. You may judge that we have become somewhat intimate when I tell you that we call each other by the first name.[15]

The first day out McCormick suggested to Root that he begin regular daily conferences "for mutual information and the consideration of all questions that were likely to come up." Root at first demurred. Mott and Bertron supported McCormick's proposal. Regular sessions began the next day.[16] At the first one Root reviewed President Wilson's directives; Mott recalled his earlier trip to South America with Root when the

Senator had become "sympatico" with the people and expressed hope for the success of this mission because of Root's ability to express "the true feeling of cordiality which the United States government and people" have for the Russians. As the daily conferences continued, conducted by Root in a stiffly formal manner, Mott raised his share of relevant issues that revealed both knowledge and awareness of the principal problems the mission would face. On some occasions, notably when Senator Root was in "a very excellent mood," a few would linger after a meal for intimate give-and-take, usually concerning politics and political figures with whom they were acquainted; once when they dissected William Jennings Bryan, Mott recalled that Bryan had told him he had not read a single book in a year, depending rather upon personal interviews for his information.[17] These conversations among men of pronouncedly differing opinions tended to divide them as progressives or conservatives rather than by party. Nonetheless a noticeable sense of unity began to emerge as the trip wore on.

One evening toward the end of the voyage, Mott and McCormick presented to Senator Root a matter they had discussed half-a-dozen times. Mott, who acted as spokesman, began by telling the Senator that he had been reading the latter's speeches and that the conviction had grown upon him of Root's "absolutely unique and exceptional qualifications for the presidency of the United States." But there was another mission for which he believed Root qualified "as no other living man in this or any other country," one "more significant and far-reaching" even than the presidency: the possibility of the Senator's taking "a leading part in the international Congress which will be held at the end of this War for the settlement of the many large and momentous international questions involved in the changed world situation." Root agreed that "that Congress and that . . . settlement will be the most important from the point of view of the interests of the whole human race that we have known in our day, or that we are likely to know in the coming days," and that in contrast to previous peace conferences which had been dominated by "the intrenched power of autocracy," this Congress would be "dominated by the forces of democracy." Mott added that he had also broached the matter to Cleveland H. Dodge. As the group broke up, McCormick said to Mott, "What you have been saying is so important that we must see what can be done about it."[18]

On the night of May 31 the ship confronted an ice pack, the "countless phosphorescent lights" of which, extending on all sides into the darkness as far as the eye could see, "presented a strange and uncanny

spectacle to those unacquainted with the ways of the northern seas." The
course was changed, and on June 1 passage through the Strait of La
Perouse brought the *Buffalo* into the Sea of Japan. After a final briefing
of the entire party on June 2, which Mott had requested, covering diet
and matters of security, the coast of Siberia was sighted. Early next
morning the ship sailed into the Golden Horn of Vladivostok but received no answer to her signals; it was the Russian feast of the Trinity, an
important religious holiday. The State Department had cabled the *Buffalo's* arrival date as June 4.[19]

PART 3: The Longest Rail Journey in the World

Among the dozen men to come aboard in mid-morning were Hugh A.
Moran, a YMCA worker in China who had been at Irkutsk for a year
and a half, who would serve as interpreter in both Russian and Chinese
and as Mott's private secretary, and Major Stanley Washburn, until a few
weeks earlier Russian correspondent for the London *Times,* who would
serve as assistant secretary to the Mission. In mid-afternoon the entire
entourage landed. There were a few moments of trepidation over the
greeting awaiting them by the local revolutionary "Executive Committee," but after some argument among their hosts and an exchange of
speeches they were finally received by it and a Soldiers' and Workmen's
Committee; in late afternoon they left for Harbin by special train.

At that junction, the next afternoon, General D. L. Horvat, Director of the Chinese Eastern Railway, entered the train—a "tall, erect,
soldierly looking man, of impressive personal appearance," whose "long,
flowing beard, worn in the distinctive Russian fashion, made him a
noticeable figure."[20] There were others, but quite unexpected were two
Chinese delegations representing warring factions, sent ostensibly to
greet the Mission and accompany it through Chinese territory, but with
the utmost seriousness to persuade Senator Root to return via China or
send a delegation there in order to relay a realistic picture of the desperate state of affairs to officials in Washington. No provision had been
made for a Chinese interpreter; fortunately Moran could fill the gap, but
he was so pressed that it was difficult to find time to eat.[21] While in
Harbin the Mission conferred with John F. Stevens and the other four
members of the American "railway commission" that had gone to Russia
to advise on the transportation problem.[22]

The next development was incredibly fantastic to Mott, the railway buff, who must have dreamed of the Trans-Siberian crossing ever since he saw it exhibited at the Paris Exposition in 1900: at Harbin the Mission was transferred to the ex-Czar's nine-car imperial blue train, the one, Mott wrote Hattie, "used by the deposed Emperor on his many journeys," though minus the Czar's personal coach. Pulled by two or three wood-burning locomotives, this luxurious conveyance would be the Mission's home for twenty-two days while traversing the more than 10,000 miles to Petrograd and back, much of it at fifteen miles per hour.[23] The principal car, a very long one containing dining room and parlor, was exactly as the royal family had left it, even to the Emperor's score-pad of a final card game; here he had signed his abdication only eleven weeks before. The conductor had traveled with the royal family for sixteen years and could recount many incidents concerning them. Each member of the mission had "a fine compartment—better than any I have ever seen in an American car"; Mott's was beautifully upholstered in green leather and had a sofa, a writing desk, cupboards, a bookcase, and a luggage compartment. At 6:35 P.M. the longest train trip in the world was begun, over a rail bed completed only a few years before despite incredible hazards compounded by permafrost, distance, revolution, disease, and bureaucracy.[24] The trip revealed the deterioration of the country's rail system; Mott's serenity was never ruffled, but there must have been some members of the Mission who wondered if they would ever reach Petrograd.

The group's daily routine centered around a two- to three-hour meeting after lunch, during which Russian newspapers were read, Senator Root submitted the addresses he planned to give, or various experts came aboard to provide briefings. Mott continued his reading program, devoting attention to books on Siberia such as the Norwegian explorer Fridtjof Nansen's *Through Siberia: The Land of the Future.* He also brought himself up to date as far as possible on the Russian Church, including the Service Book as compiled and translated by Isabel Hapgood, another project underwritten by Charles Crane.[25] Moran served as his secretary, much to Mott's pleasure. The weather was for the most part delightful, he wrote Hattie, like late May at home. "On every hand the country is ablaze with wild flowers." Never had he seen anything like as many; peasant children brought them to the train at every station. Stops were utilized for exercise, one occasion affording a tramp "for a mile or more into a magnificent pine forest." The people were uniformly "friendly and sympathetic," responding with cheers if Senator Root made a brief speech; "never has there been an action or word which we could interpret otherwise."[26]

In addition to the Commission meetings and his own reading, Mott daily interviewed men who possessed unique information or whose experiences qualified them as experts, beginning with Moran and Robert F. Leonard, both of whom had been in Siberia for some time; they described their prison camp work near Irkutsk. The possibilities of extending these services to Russian soldiers were canvassed; Donald A. Lowrie, who was already at work among both prisoners and soldiers with headquarters at Tomsk, reviewed his activities and encouraged his chief as to its significance; Mott authorized the purchase of a moving picture outfit and basic monthly expenses, with the admonition to "then ask local men to contribute."

After hearing these volunteers whom he had himself enlisted, Mott wrote home in a letter doubtless typed by Moran that he thought "we should send over scores of our best American workers to meet this need which I regard as one of the greatest opportunities which has ever come to us."

> If we enter the doors now it will lead to a great permanent work after the War. We can do no greater work to help America and the Allies than to press this effort which is calculated to do so much to improve the morale, discipline and character of the Russian troops. They number probably twelve millions.

By the time the Mission arrived in Petrograd, Mott's task was clear. In a fund-raising address for the YMCA War Work that October, he described the reasoning by which that conclusion had been reached:

> We did not go on a religious mission. But we had not gone far before we found this demoralization of the army, and regardless of our religious views, we came unanimously to this conclusion, that what the Russian army and navy needs is that which the YMCA is supplying in the American, English and Canadian armies. That was our unanimous conclusion. So, by the time we reached Petrograd, Senator Root said to me, "Mr. Mott, I want you to take this up with the authorities, military, naval, and civil, in Russia, and likewise with the ecclesiastical leaders."

The decision had been accelerated by the reports of the "Y" men he had met along the route:

> ... we found that some of our discerning secretaries, whom we had had over there for three years working among the enemy prisoners, not being able to stand it any longer, seeing this demoralization and knowing the Association principles, said, "We must see if we cannot do something in this army," and so in places as far removed as Turkestan in the south, Petrograd on the north, and Siberia, away out on the eastern front, they were trying out their plans. ... By this you could see what could be done in

the entire Russian army. The general in command in Turkestan was so much impressed with what had been done in our army that he sent our man to Petrograd to get permission to spread this work along the whole front. [27]

There were many other experts. August Heid, who had represented McCormick's International Harvester Company from Irkutsk to Vladivostok since 1908, described the deterioration of the economy and the armed forces. Stanley Washburn declared that the greatest need of the hour was effective publicity in Russia for Allied war aims. [28] A military attaché told Mott and McCormick that the Russian troops were about ready to lay down their arms. Mott talked at length with N. Eltekov, a member of the revolutionary governing body at Irkutsk, the capital of Siberia, who had come aboard at Harbin as host, and who was probably one of the more realistic sources with whom Mott conversed. On March 2, when word of the Revolution in Petrograd reached Irkutsk, Eltekov explained, the Governor and other high officials had been removed and a "local committee of Social Democrats" had taken charge. An election was anticipated; they had replaced the police because the people hated the sight of them. Eltekov anticipated a "democratic republic," but if anarchy should develop, a temporary dictatorship would be necessary, but there was no possibility of reaction returning to power. He favored Association work in the army and gave Mott numerous insights into the attitude of the Church to the Revolution. [29] Charles Stephenson Smith, A.P. correspondent who had come on at Vladivostok, reviewed recent events in China and Japan. There was an extensive briefing by Captain Karl Katterfield, a Russian army officer from the Baltics who had been assigned to expedite YMCA POW work; he covered the Russian military situation, the state of the Church, and the new Japanese "Monroe Doctrine." Vladimir Gorbatenko, First Secretary to General Horvat and his representative on the train and director of it, believed that the Revolution had come to stay; Lenin, still in Petrograd, "meddling in everything," should be arrested, but, he added, Kerensky did not dare do so even though Lenin's party was small; what was needed was a dictator. [30]

Aside from the spectacular scenery around Lake Baikal, the trip afforded few natural highlights. No untoward incidents occurred. Mott and McCormick made several small forays into the stations or towns where the train stopped long enough; at one place there were a hundred peasants, soldiers, and women sleeping anywhere. A six-hour layover allowed Mott ample time to buy a jasper box for Irene, together with some amethysts. After the train left Irkutsk its speed increased above the usual fifteen miles per hour; from the western descent of the Urals it sped across old Russia to reach Petrograd at 5:00 P.M. on Wednesday, June 13/ May 31 (Western, "new style" time, June 13, is used in this narrative; Russia was still on the "old style" calendar; there was a 13-day difference.)

The party was met at the "dingy and far from imposing" Nikolai station by an official delegation of more than twenty, including the new Minister of Foreign Affairs, M. I. Tereshchenko, the Minister of Finance, A. I. Shingarev, and the Chief of the General Staff, General Romanovskii. Ambassador D. R. Francis headed the Americans, who included Norman Armour, then third secretary of the Embassy. Mott's official escort was N. V. Nekrasov, then Minister of Transport; Franklin Gaylord, whom the reader met in Chapter 6, offered his services to Mott. Charles R. Crane joined the Mission on this occasion, having made part of his journey to Petrograd on the same ship with "Trotzsky and his crowd."[31]

PART 4: Guests in the Winter Palace

To its astonishment, the Mission was housed in the Winter Palace, left by its former royal tenants, now in protective custody at Tsarskoe Selo, as if they had gone for a weekend.[32] Here the Americans would be well insulated from the turbulence that frequently racked other parts of the capital city. To be "in this great palace associated as it has been through so many years with the Imperial Government and the autocratic regime" seemed to Mott "strange, almost unbelievable," as was the red flag floating over it. His third floor room, adjoining that of McCormick (who calculated that he was 440 steps from the front entrance) overlooked the palace gardens and the River Neva. Crane's room was beyond McCormick's; there was an elegant parlor for the guests of the three. Only Mott had a bathroom, which was utilized by the three. Gaylord piloted Mott and McCormick to a barber who gave them very good haircuts. The fare and appointments were sumptuous; most of the servants of the royal household were still there. "One feels almost guilty to sit down to these rich meals knowing of the great privation of multitudes who throng this city," then crowded with a million refugees. Grossly mismanaged for decades, Russian society could not long survive the chaos and defeatism, compounded by rising rents, lower wages, and shortages that daily grew by leaps and bounds.[33]

Edward T. Heald, in charge of the Petrograd office of YMCA prisoner of war work in Russia, once drove with Mott to the Palace. To

Heald's leading comment that the "socialist and Leninist agitation" on the front would prevent the Russians from ever fighting again, Mott replied that he thought the outlook "not favorable but not hopeless."[34] Neither he nor hardly any other person as yet realized the potential of the forces that had been unleashed by the Revolution. In the twenty-eight days since the Mission left Washington, the Provisional Government had been reorganized (as the "First Coalition"), Trotsky had returned to Russia, and Pitirim Sorokin, then a member of the Socialist Revolutionary Party and later a Harvard Professor, had confided to his diary the approach of "the tornado"; starvation was on the march, the word "anarchy" appeared increasingly in the speeches in the Duma, and Sorokin saw his country "rushing towards the abyss."[35] Yet none of the Americans or the Russians with whom they spoke had a clear understanding of the principles of Marxism or Leninism or of Lenin's program for establishing his party's rule over the Russian people. Perhaps Russell could have distinguished among the various forms of socialism espoused in Russia in 1917, but most Mission members, Mott included, certainly could not.

Next morning, June 14, there began twenty-six hectic, fantastic days. Mott would attend most of the multifarious group functions of the Mission, but his own assignment, many arrangements for which were set up by Crane, who usually accompanied him, was unique, as was that of each of his colleagues, some of whose activities were almost reduced to the perfunctory by lack of interpreters and secretaries. Mott would file a special report for Washington, covering in a modest way the highlights of his varied experiences, but his personal reactions were reserved for his letters home. He took voluminous notes and frequently described men and events to friends and audiences afterward. Only one contemporary Russian opinion of Mott has come to light: Dimitri Fedotoff White, the Russian naval officer attached to Admiral Glennon of the Mission, wrote in his diary the day the Mission arrived that Mott was "a very pleasant, mild-mannered man, very much like a clergyman of a well-to-do parish. He is genuinely anxious to help Russia and makes a good impression by his sincerity."[36] The general report of the Mission gave Mott little space, which led most historians to overlook the significance of what he did and some to ignore him, although his papers represent the largest coverage of conditions in Russia left by any of the group, with the possible exception of McCormick, who kept a detailed diary.[37]

The first days in Petrograd began with a service in the Royal Chapel inside the Palace, where "the finest Russian choir in the world" sang, although its ranks were somewhat reduced because of "vacations." Heald and Moran were invited to accompany the Mission on a tour of the Palace, including the hospital for wounded soldiers. "It was an unusual experience to be chatting around with such notables... while we discussed the revolution and Y.M.C.A. plans in this anti-revolutionary and anti-Y.M.C.A. outpost." Heald put his thoughts on paper:

> The life in the Winter Palace and on the train of the Czar will hardly give the American Commission glimpses of the real life of the people and of revolutionary Russia. I would like to have taken the Commission along with me on a visit I made in the tenement district of the factory end of town....
>
> ... If the American Commission could only see more of this seamy side of life in Peter's Capital they might understand more easily why it is so embarrassing for Minister of War Kerensky to entertain them, and why Kerensky is so difficult to make appointments with. The radical element hates bourgeois America which they consider this Commission represents and they bring pressure to bear on the Provisional Government to neglect the Commission. In spite of all this however the Commission has been shown great attention and cordiality from the liberal Russian elements who look to America for their salvation. The American Commission can certainly not complain about the imperial way they are being entertained in the grand suites of the Winter Palace where they have been assigned rooms. [38]

Then there were press conferences, official calls and receptions, but Mott shortly went about his own duties, calling first upon Ambassador Francis, later characterized by one of Root's biographers as "a charming old gentleman with no appreciation of what was going on in Russia,"[39] with whom he was already well acquainted. Crane then took him to the offices of the Holy Synod, where he met the associate of the Over-Procurator, A. V. Kartashev, who brought him up to date on ecclesiastical matters.[40] The Russian Church had undergone dramatic if not revolutionary changes. The Provisional Government had installed the "headstrong and erratic" Vladimir N. Lvov as Over-Procurator, whose authority continued as in pre-abdication times; Mott would spend many hours in conference with him.[41] The entire Church was pervaded by the spirit of revival and reform, stimulated by the new and unheard-of freedom of expression and discussion, and was seriously preparing for the new order to come.[42]

Friday, the 15th, was an eventful day, if only for the sheer volume of Mott's interviewing and note-taking. Frederick N. Corse, the New York Life Insurance official with whom he had talked in 1909 and again in

July, 1916, now foresaw the inevitable financial collapse of Russia. Alexander I. Guchkov, the well-to-do Moscow merchant, Octobrist, and Minister of War in the first Provisional cabinet, who had presented the Duma's demand for abdication to Czar Nicholas, and whom Mott had met in 1916, confided that Russia really had no government; Mott wished privately that Guchkov might be back in power. He felt similarly about Paul N. Miliukov, the Kadet leader (whom Crane had known for years) who had been Foreign Minister until a few weeks before, and who was on the whole more encouraging than Guchkov whose pessimism stemmed from his knowledge of the failure of the great offensive on the Austro-Hungarian front and the consequent increased demoralization of the army.[43]

Mott then dined with the Franklin Gaylords—Gaylord was Director of the *Mayak,* the Petrograd YMCA—where it was "very restful" to be in a home and to enjoy the opportunity to talk in a leisurely and free way about "many matters of common interest," which did not always mean professional concerns. Gaylord then took Mott to call on the Russian president of the *Mayak.* Later that evening Mott attended the official reception to the Mission by the Council of Ministers, meeting all of them but talking chiefly with the Prime Minister, Prince G. E. Lvov, the Minister of War, A. F. Kerensky, and the Minister of Education, A. A. Manuilov. Mott also took copious notes of the replies to his questions by Senator I. V. Meshchaninov, a member of the *Mayak* board, who hoped America would help Russia by providing capital and materiel.[44]

Saturday morning, the 16th, Mott was invited to attend a meeting of the Holy Synod's committee on revision of the curricula of the theological seminaries. To his surprise they asked him to speak to the subject of their inquiry after first outlining their traditional requirements to him. He was forced to gather his thoughts rapidly and then through an interpreter to try "to emphasize modern tendencies in theological education in the West" and to suggest possibly useful trends. He gave a quick survey of changing currents in many parts of the world and outlined four "chief new departures": missions, Christian social service or the social gospel together with field work, the spiritual classics, and the "new apologetics."

The first hour of that afternoon was devoted to an interview with the Prime Minister Prince G. E. Lvov, to whom Mott explained in detail "our work on behalf of the soldiers in France, England, America and other countries" and canvassed the possibilities of a similar work in the Russian army. "I met with a favorable response."[45] That night Crane and Mott went to Moscow.

PART 5: Two Days in Moscow

They spent a quiet Sunday visiting with the British Consul, R. H. Bruce Lockhart, and the American Consul, Maddin Summers, and his wife. Summers spoke Russian; his long experience in Russia provided realistic insights such as few others could give.[46] Mott also quizzed Crane at length, finding his attitude to be essentially pessimistic. In another conversation with Frederick M. Corse, Mott noted his opinion that "there may be counter-revolution and bloody hands before this work is done," that Russia was not a nation but "a conglomerate of nations," and that the country was on "a joy ride to bankruptcy." Crane introduced Mott to "a remarkable woman," Countess Bobrinskaya, who impressed him by her "unique gifts of leadership." Before dinner they wandered through the "wonderful cluster of churches and palaces" of the Kremlin; the view of the city was "overpowering" with its "hundreds of church domes and the thousands of crosses and steeples and bell towers... lighted up by the setting sun.... "

One of the most dramatic events of Mott's Russian trip took place the next evening, Monday, June 18, when he met with the Archbishop, six bishops, and the chief deacon of the "Old Believers" in the home of their Archbishop, "a little log house on the edge of the forest" on the outskirts of the city. As he recalled it later to Mathews, he faced "a circle of bearded ecclesiastics gathered round a table on which stood a white lighted candle." They described to him the life of this, the largest dissenting sect in the country, whose ten to fifteen million adherents had undergone fearful persecutions throughout the 250 years of their history. There was an exchange of ideas concerning the coming Great Sobor and the hope of reunion with the Orthodox Church. Mott emphasized that it was not size but vitality that constituted the power of a church. In his notes he indicated that the conference was from nine to ten-thirty. Then, Mathews recounts, "their choir, appearing like magic from the woods, sang their soul-shaking music to him under the stars."[47]

In mid-Siberia Mott had received a telegram from Crane relaying an invitation from Archbishop Platon to Mott to address the June Congress of churchmen in Moscow.[48] This trip was primarily for that purpose. Crane took Mott to meet the Archbishop, who was one of only two retained in the new Holy Synod appointed by Lvov. Mott insisted upon reviewing the remarks he planned to make, in spite of the Archbishop's demurrer. As Mott began to read, his host frequently exclaimed "Khorosho! Khorosho!" (good! good!). Crane recalled in his memoirs that as the Archbishop's enthusiasm rose he broke out with "Kak

Khorosho" (Oh, how good), and when Mott finished, "Oh, I would not dare touch it, I would not dare touch it!" But Mott insisted that he comment. Reluctantly the Archbishop said, "only one little thing—you might strike the war situation somewhat stronger." "Oh," said Mott, "Is the Church for the war?" "Don't have any doubt about it," responded the Archbishop, "the Church is for the war and is doing everything possible to sustain the army."[49]

Among the 1,072 delegates at the Congress Mott met the Reverend V. V. Aleksandrov, rector of the Russian Orthodox Cathedral of the Holy Trinity in San Francisco, whom he had previously seen at a YMCA convention, who now served as an ideal interpreter. After his conference with the Archbishop, Mott coached "the young priest" on his method of speaking, a tactic that Crane recognized as spelling success for the "carrying power" of his message, in contrast to Root's presentation of an entire speech with the interpreter merely summarizing his thought at the end.[50]

Since Mott included the verbatim text of most of his remarks in his *Addresses and Papers,* it may suffice to point out here that he began with a lengthy discourse on the natural friendship existing between the American and Russian peoples, then bringing in his personal experiences with Orthodox leaders around the world, beginning with the Ecumenical Patriarch and concluding with "the never-to-be-forgotten privilege of intimate association with the great Christian missionary and apostle, Archbishop Nicolai" of Japan. Next he expressed words of "solicitude and caution to the Russian Church in this critical hour," and lastly promised America's aid:[51]

> My third message is one of hope and reassurance. You are engaged in the greatest struggle which the world has ever known. I come to remind you that the United States is with you in this conflict to the very end. The American people love peace and hate war. We did all that we could do in justice to our conscience to keep out of this world war, but finally to be true to our souls and our highest guiding principles we found it necessary to join you and the other Allies.
>
> In doing so we have counted the cost and are ready to pay it. Since I left my home over ten millions of American young men have registered themselves as ready to serve their nation in this struggle in any way which the authorities may designate. This great host are being called up in lots of five hundred thousand each to be thoroughly trained. The week I left America fourteen great officers' camps were opened in which over forty thousand officers are being prepared for their responsibilities.
>
> Our Congress have already authorized the raising by loans and taxation for meeting the requirements of the war the equivalent of over thirty billions of roubles. Our various states and municipalities as well as the

national government have thrown themselves with earnestness into the work of preparation. All our great industries are being mobilized with reference to rendering the maximum of service in the war. The work of production and distribution has been put in the ablest hands for the same purpose, and our means of communication have been placed at the disposal of the Government. General Pershing and some of the first contingent of our troops have landed in France. We already have naval vessels at work in European waters. It may safely be said that ninety-nine percent, if not more, of the American people stand solidly behind our great President in the purposes which he has announced.

Let this message, therefore, remind you that you are not alone. Go back to all your parishes in the cities, towns and villages and tell the Russian people that America is with them. Say to them that just as Russia came to the help of America in the darkest hours of our history [by refusing to observe the British blockade of the thirteen colonies during the American Revolution], America now joins Russia in this moment of grave crisis. Tell them to stand firmly behind the Provisional Government. Tell them to be true to the Church that it may in this time of colossal strain preserve the solidarity of the nation.

Tell them that we believe that, in view of what Russia has already achieved in this war, in view of the wonderful sacrifices which the Russian people have already made, in view of the vast and vital issues at stake, and in view of the urgency of the situation and the gravity of the crisis, Russia and her Allies must continue steadfast to the end. Above all let the Church be unfailing in reminding the people that God only can enable us to accomplish His high and holy purpose. While everything else is changeable and changing Jesus Christ "is the same yesterday, today, yea, and forever."

Mott wrote Leila that he was interrupted at least twenty times by the Russian custom of rising and applauding. At the end of the address the audience arose instantly and joined in a hymn "calling upon the Holy Spirit to come upon us"; following this was the song *Many Years*. Then there were four spontaneous speeches of appreciation, the first by the president of the Congress, the last by the Over-Procurator of the Church. They spoke with "evident feeling," reflecting the sense "of the great company." When it was over, Mott added to Leila, "I had to go through the ordeal of being kissed by a number of the prominent men which I suppose was the climax evidence of their profound sympathy and approval."

Crane reported the event to President Wilson: Mott was accepted as your messenger, he wrote,

and made a most profound and moving discourse on the Church itself, its relationships to the Christian world, and the importance of its position,

not only in the empire but in America, and its relation to the winning of
the war. The assembly was greatly affected by the sympathy and wisdom of
the address. The foremost members of the body made most touching responses which were followed by the whole congregation rising and singing
the oldest and most beautiful hymn as an expression of their approval. One
of the members in responding said, 'The echo of this speech will not die
away here but within a short time will be heard in every parish in Russia. . . .'

"It was worth while having the Commission come here if that were the
one thing that it could accomplish—it certainly is the most important
thing," Crane continued to Wilson:

> It represented the heart of Russia and when Mr. Mott struck the war-note
> there was an immediate response and everyone instantly arose and
> applauded. It was a much more loyal, true and far-reaching note than one
> could possibly get from any political assembly.

He would send a fuller account to the *Christian Science Monitor,* and
concluded with "affectionate messages to the family and to the
Cabinet."[52]

That afternoon was almost as eventful, being spent in "unhurried
interviews" with Prince E. N. Trubetskoi, professor of the philosophy of
law at the University of Moscow, and with the Over-Procurator, Vladimir N. Lvov. Trubetskoi, who would be vice-president of the Sobor,
was a disciple of the philosopher Solovev who had labored for the unity
of Christendom and had pointed to the obligation of the Church in social
action; he told Mott that the address of the morning had reached a more
significant audience than the virtually moribund Duma would have given
him, because the Congress was larger, more representative, and would
have more influence with the people. Following an information session
at the American Consulate, Mott and Crane went to the Old Believers'
Cathedral where a special sacred concert was given for them. Mott told
Leila that this was "one of the most deeply moving hours" he had ever
spent. Peasants "gathered and stood quietly and reverently"; the
ecclesiastics explained the music. The two men returned to Petrograd
that night.[53]

PART 6: Baron Nicolay, the *Mayak,* and Emanuel Nobel

Back in the capital, the afternoon of the 20th was given to mission
meetings, a conference with Gaylord, and two hours with Baron Paul

Nicolay (Pavel Nikolai), sponsor of the Russian SCM, who had come from his home in Finland at Mott's request.[54] The evening was devoted to various Association matters. Thursday morning Mott and McCormick called on the Rumanian minister, M. Diamanti, who made a strong appeal to the Mission to go to Jassy, the temporary capital since the fall of Bucharest the previous December, "to see the king and queen, even if for only a day."[55] Archie Harte arrived and Mott conferred with him and Gaylord. There was an afternoon reception with fourteen speeches but for Mott the event of the day was a dinner for the Mission with the members of the *Mayak* board as guests at the home of Emanuel Nobel, nephew of the founder of the Nobel awards. Mott gave the address of the evening without an interpreter, since virtually the entire group of about twenty understood English. In talking with Nobel he heard again the oft-repeated phrase, "We are tired of the War." When Mott asked, "What will end the war?" Nobel replied, "The United States must give the answer, Russia cannot."[56] In his address, which McCormick thought short and very appropriate, Mott examined the "foundations of greatness in the life of a nation"—"the ideals, the character and the spirit of a people" cannot be made "free and triumphant apart from the help of true religion." Therefore, there should be agencies such as the *Mayak,* so successful in Petrograd, "securely planted, ably led and generously supported in all of the principal cities of Russia."

But there was another field in Russia for the work of the YMCA— among "the millions of Russian young men in the army and navy." Citing the desirable effects of such work at two thousand points in the British army, Mott revealed that since coming to Petrograd he had received a cablegram from France asking for 500 Americans "to enable them to extend *foyers du soldat* more widely and rapidly throughout the French army"; a similar request had recently been sent by the Italian government. As we know, on his way across Siberia, Mott had learned from Donald Lowrie of the work he had organized at Tomsk for Russian soldiers; Jerome Davis had set up a comparable program in Tashkent, and these were requests for more. Citing these, he asked: "Is this not a most opportune time to spread these agencies for the physical, mental and moral betterment of the soldiers among all parts of the great Russian army and into the navy as well?"

> I do not fear for soldiers when they are fighting or when they are drilling. The time concerning which I have anxiety is their leisure hours. Every soldier has a number of spare hours each day. Shall these hours be spent in

idleness, in dissipation and in unprofitable agitation; or shall they be spent in helpful recreation, in growth in knowledge and mental efficiency, in strengthening of character and in unselfish service among one's fellows? The Young Men's Christian Association has shown itself able to answer this vital question in the right way.

You Russians have "paid tremendous prices which we Americans can never adequately repay. Anything, therefore, which we can possibly do to strengthen your hands at this momentous hour, when with the other Allies you press on to achieve the full purpose of the war, we will gladly do."[57] From the dinner the Mission went directly to the train for Moscow.

PART 7: Two More Days in Moscow

On Friday, June 22, a "boiling hot day," Mott and Crane motored to the Troitskaya Lavra, a particularly venerated monastery and Church center fifty miles out in the country, where they joined the pilgrimage of the delegates to the Congress. Invited to return to Moscow in the private railway car of the Metropolitan of Moscow, the President of the Sobor, and the Over-Procurator, they "spent the two hours of the journey in intimate conversation with the last two going more deeply into certain matters" not covered in previous conversations. From the train Mott and Crane joined the Mission at the hall of the Moscow Duma just in time for a reception. "The strain of speaking and the long three hours' ride in a motor over a rough and dusty road had so used up John Mott," McCormick wrote in his diary, that after the reception he "felt in bad shape and took a room at the National Hotel." McCormick went to the Mission's train and brought in Dr. Curl, the Mission physician, who "treated Mr. Mott's throat with argyrol."

Next morning, well recovered, Mott rejoined the Mission as it made "a series of visits to the headquarters or halls of a number of organizations such as the Zemstvos, the cooperative societies, the munition workers, the Moscow Cooperative Bank, etc." In each place they listened to welcoming addresses and reports. Mott and Crane returned to the [Uspensky] cathedral and later called again on Countess Bobrinskaya, a conference that was continued the next day, a Sunday, during which the Countess took them to see "the most remarkable collection of icons in existence." They visited the School of Ecclesiastical Art and attended another special concert in honor of the Americans, this time by the

Choir of the Holy Synod. The Mission departed for the capital at an early hour that evening, "with a distinct sense of encouragement," according to the *New York Times*, [58] but twelve miles out of Moscow their special was sidetracked until midnight to allow the four regular trains to precede it. McCormick recounted how he and Mott spent a long "white night":

> After dinner John Mott and I took a walk up through the village. The air was warm and the locality was one very favorable to mosquitoes. The young women of the village as they walked around had their heads covered with veils, and it kept us busy warding off the attacks of these familiar little pests. The village was on a side hill, and like many of those at home, it consisted chiefly of one long street. We found that most of the young people had congregated down at the station, and were walking up and down the platform not far from our train so the village itself was comparatively quiet. The heavy log construction of the one-story Russian houses gives a village of this character a much more substantial look than is gained by seeing the lightly built and quickly constructed houses of an American town. Presumably the people of the village did not know who we were, but the fact that a special train was drawn up on a sidetrack was sufficient to arouse interest and curiosity on the part of the village people, so that men, women and even the children flocked to the train to have a look at it.
>
> Charles Crane greatly amused successive groups of children by performing a few simple slight [sic] of hand tricks by which he apparently swallowed a coin and then found it in the locks of a little girl, or under the arm of a boy in the audience. [59]

Monday was a very short day due to the delay of the train. Mott met with Professor Harper, who had arrived on Sunday, and would serve as his interpreter "in nearly all critical interviews." The two, together with Crane, spent the evening in the home of Baron Gintsburg, who was "without doubt one of the leading Jews of the world"; he gave his visitors "a very good idea about the hopes and fears of the Russian Jews," explaining that the religious equality brought by the Revolution had included the Jews, but to advocate Zionism, which had been popular before the war because of oppression, would now be a virtual crime because of the danger of diverting attention from vastly greater and more urgent issues before the Jewish community. If the liberal trends were to continue, he explained, the Jews would obtain their rights. He would like to see them play a representative part now, but it was not time for them to press for their specific rights, such as admission to the officers ranks in the military. [60]

Harte was also in Petrograd and briefed Mott on the pro-German attitude he had found in Sweden. On Tuesday, June 26, Mott, McCormick, and Harper conferred with S. I. Shidlovsky, chairman of the

Progressive Bloc of the Duma—whose political stance was "half-way between" Miliukov and Guchkov. Shidlovsky assured them that Harper was the only foreigner who had a clear understanding of the situation. Now in the second stage of revolution, Shidlovsky held, the Russians would reach the third stage when they eliminated the anarchists. The moment had come, he said, when Lenin should be detained: he is "sincere" but a fanatic "surrounded by pro-German agents." The Revolution is a pure revolution, not simply a change in government, and thus not like the French Revolution, having been a social revolution from the start. [61]

On Wednesday, June 27, the Rumanian minister again called to urge Mott and McCormick to go to Jassy "as an encouragement to the Rumanians" if the whole Mission could not go; this request came to Mott because of the "splendid work" of the YMCA as Harte had reported it. Because the Mission lacked instructions, they could not accept. General Scott met the King and Queen on his visit to the front. [62] Mott and McCormick also saw a British exhibit of movies of the War in France and were astonished to be told by their host that the pictures would probably have a deterrent rather than a favorable effect on Russian soldiers.

PART 8: Mott Addresses a Cossack Congress

That Wednesday, June 27, was both a red and a black letter day in Mott's life. At this time the All-Russian Constituent Cossack Congress of some 300 officers representing the several Cossack armies was meeting in Petrograd. It is not known just what the gathering was that Harper took Mott and Crane to, other than that it was composed of Cossack officers. "We just dropped in, without invitation or plan," Harper wrote his brother. "For an hour we talked to a group of a hundred, answering and putting questions back and forth." When the session opened they asked Mott to make a speech, with Harper translating:

> I speak not only for myself but also for all of my associates of the American Diplomatic Mission to Russia when I say that we appreciate profoundly your kindly courtesy and generous hospitality in admitting Mr. Crane and me to your important Congress and granting us the signal honor of bringing to you our message.
>
> We have been sent to Russia at this time by our President to assure the entire Russian nation of the good-will and sympathy of the American people, and likewise to discover the best ways in which our two great democracies can cooperate with one another, as well as with our Allies, in

achieving the supremely important ends which we have all set before us in the world war.

We esteem it an honor, indeed, to have this opportunity of meeting with these hundreds of chosen delegates of the ... Cossack armies, representing the seven million Cossack people. We are not unmindful of the indispensable part which you have had in building up and preserving the Russian nation. We well know that you constitute one of the strongest strains in the Russian nation. We respond with all our soul to the substance and spirit of the resolutions which you have prepared in this Congress—resolutions which so clearly, unequivocally and forcibly set forth the urgent duty of the Russian soldiers in order to meet the open and also the subtle dangers of the present most critical hour of the war.

It is always an inspiration to meet a company of men who give evidence that they know the way, that they are ready to go ahead, and that they have the contagious power to get others to follow them. Your insistence that the way to bring about the desired peace is by an immediate offensive has the true ring. Your reiteration of the determination of the great mass of the Russian people to tolerate no separate peace is precisely what we have expected from you. Your summons to the people to support the Liberty Loan and in other ways to strengthen the hands of the Provisional Government is also reassuring. Your clear-cut and fearless pointing-out of the deadly peril associated with the subtle propaganda and intrigues of the enemy within your gates is most timely. You clearly see that to wage a triumphant warfare at the front you must have no untaken forts in the rear.

We most heartily identify ourselves with all that his Excellency, the Italian Ambassador, has just said with reference to the splendid solidarity of the Allies, the righteousness of their cause, their determination to fight to the end, and their unshaken confidence in the successful outcome of their efforts and sacrifices.

We bring you good tidings from a far country—America; and that is, that the great American nation, after prolonged consideration, after counting the cost and with full determination to pay the cost, have decided to join with you and your Allies in the sublime cause of ensuring full opportunity and liberty for all nations large and small. We stand ready to throw into the struggle our full man-power ... our money power ... our powers of organization.

Above all we have entered the struggle with our moral forces, because the highest idealism, the finest conscience and the most self-effacing spirit of the American people have been with our President and our Congress in the great decision, and will be with them and our military leaders in giving to it full effect. Let the assurance of such cooperation on our part strengthen the members of this Congress as they go forth to perform their high duty.[63]

Mott had been led to believe that this group exerted a powerful influence, but if these were the Cossacks described by Sir Bernard Pares in his memoirs, the significance of the occasion was far less than Mott imagined.[64] Harper told Mott that the speech was hardly in "the role of the Secretary of the YMCA," but he wrote his brother that Mott had been "better able to seize the human side of this great revolution than the other men of the commission."[65]

Newspapers around the world picked up the speech, many merely commenting that Mott's appearance on the platform brought prolonged applause and that a strong resolution supporting the vigorous pursuit of the war had then been voted. The Chicago *Post* opined that of all the surprises produced by the War, few "could have been more unexpected than that presented in Russia this week when John R. Mott of the Y.M.C.A. stood up and told a lot of wild Cossacks that it was their duty to fight the war thru [sic] and that America would help them do it."[66] A German language daily in New York reported that Mott had congratulated the Cossacks on their unanimity and strength and had "declared that America will never leave Russia and the other Allies in the lurch." Stirred by the address, the paper went on, the Cossacks had unanimously passed a resolution in favor of an energetic continuance of the war.[67] The resolutions had actually been prepared prior to the Americans' visit.

But in far-off Shanghai the *Deutsche Zeitung für China* on July eleventh altered the speech to read that Mott had said that the Cossacks were the hope of Russia and the Germans enemies of civilization, especially of democracy.[68] When German missionaries in China reported this to the Fatherland, Mott's fitness to lead international Christian movements was at once fiercely and understandably challenged there and in the World's Alliance of the YMCA's, the World's Student Christian Federation, and the Edinburgh Continuation Committee, all of which had struggled to remain neutral. Although Mott subsequently labeled the Shanghai paper's perversion of his remarks an "absolute lie"—words normally out of character for him, and he would have been constitutionally incapable of making such a statement about the Germans for whom he had great affection and respect—he later defended his mission as having been strictly religious and ecclesiastical. In both fact and implication it was, however, hardly neutral.

The German government soon took steps to cancel all World's Alliance YMCA prisoner of war work in Germany and all such activity for German prisoners in England, France, and Switzerland, citing as its reasons Mott's membership in a political mission, the consequent increase of services to the Russian armies, and the widespread American propaganda in Russia attributed to the YMCA secretaries who were sent as soon as possible after Mott obtained the necessary permissions. Activation of this policy was avoided only by the most adroit diplomacy on the part of Alliance representatives sent to Berlin following an emergency session of the World's Committee executive at which Mott was present in Geneva in April, 1918.[69] The issue subsequently became compounded with that of German war guilt and exacerbated Mott's relations with the Germans for several years in spite of his heroic efforts on behalf of their "orphaned missions." It was ironed out in the WSCF in 1920 but hung on in the World's Alliance until 1931, on at least one occasion causing Mott to shed tears. It temporarily cooled the affection of some Swedes, including his intimate friend Nathan Söderblom, Archbishop of Sweden.

PART 9: A Speech to the Holy Synod

To return to that eventful June 27 in Petrograd, the early afternoon was given to a conference with Harte and Gaylord to draw up a constitution for Association work in Russia. Then Crane took Mott and Harper to meet Professor Thomas Garrique Masaryk of Prague, whom Crane thought "the greatest man in Europe"; Mott had met one of his daughters "years ago in connection with our growing Student Movement in Austria-Hungary." Masaryk, who was destined to be president of Czechoslovakia, was in Petrograd on behalf of Bohemian prisoners of war. He expressed grave doubts that the Russians could launch a strong offensive, yet voiced his hope that the War would strengthen democracy everywhere, even in Germany. Mott told Leila that Masaryk had thrown more light upon the causes of the War than anyone he had ever spoken with. He would later aid in introducing Masaryk to President Wilson.[70]

Under the date of June 27, Crane dictated a letter home describing the Mission as "a successful pilgrimage" that had reminded him of his Russian visit with Samuel Harper's father in 1900: "Indeed I am constantly amazed at the great similarity—of the positive identity—of the purposes, the sympathies, and the points of view of Dr. Mott and my older friend, President [William Rainey] Harper." Of Wilson's choice of Mott, Crane went on to comment: "The selection has been amply justified." In spite of all the military and other talents of the group, "the really great, inspiring and permanent achievements of the commission will be left by Dr. Mott," who reminded him "much of St. Paul."[71]

Crane took Mott that evening to share in "one of the charming things of the (pre-war) world"—the salon of Baroness Ikskul, to whose "principal literary salon" he had introduced the elder Harper in 1900. Crane greatly admired "the Russian lady presiding over the tea table and the samovar and directing the lively conversation, sometimes in several languages.[72] But on this occasion, the two men took advantage of the presence of V. I. Maklakov, a leader of the Kadet party, said to be "the most brilliant man in the Duma," to ask what Mott called "leading questions," from the answers to which they gained "valuable light on certain developments and tendencies of the Revolution."

Thursday morning Mott accompanied McCormick and Bertron to an interview with the acting minister of commerce and industry who displayed "ingenious charts" showing how the Government hoped to improve transport, but the Americans "were not surprised to learn that the new plans had not been as yet put into effect."[73] In addition to Mission meetings and interviews, Mott and Crane met that afternoon with a group of missionaries who were administering relief among the Armenians of the Caucasus. As members of the Near East Relief Committee in New York, which was sponsoring this work, they welcomed first-hand information. Mott also spoke that day with Sir George Buchanan, the British ambassador, whom Sir Bernard Pares once described as "England in Russia"; a leading Marxist, Pares went on, had said that Buchanan was a "great figure in Russian history."[74] Buchanan characterized the current leaders for Mott and referred obliquely to his own warning to the Czar of disaster to come.

Friday morning, June 29, Mott experienced "another wonderful opportunity"—one that seemed "almost unbelievable," he wrote Leila. He was invited to address the Holy Synod. "They gave me a free hand," he explained. McCormick, who, with Crane, accompanied Mott, recorded the event: Upon entering a long, upstairs room, to which they were conducted by the Over-Procurator, Lvov, they found nine archbishops or metropolitans in long black vestments:

> They wore high black hats, made of cloth with a silver cross at the top in the front, and from the back of the head hung long black veils extending backward and downward from the top of the hat. Each had a silver chain at the bottom of which hung a silver cross. Each of them had long hair and beards which evidently had not been cut. As we entered the room all those present arose, and Archbishop Platon welcomed us in broken English. His voice was low and rather thick, but his smile was genial.
>
> [There] were perhaps 100 delegates, some of them from the Orthodox Greek Church and others from the Old Believers—the conservative wing of the Greek Church which 200 years ago split off from the main body because they felt that the trend of the church was too much toward prog-

ress and modernism. The issue on which they split was a new translation of the Bible which the Old Believers felt contained some error. Archbishop Platon from the Caucasus presided. They gave us seats with the delegates, and we listened to the discussion. One of the most earnest and effective speakers was a big man with flowing white beard, thick gray hair, large red nose and white mustache cut very short. He was apparently about 54 years old and must have weighed not less than 250 pounds. Another speaker was a slender, pale man, with thin dark hair, and cavernous eyes. He was apparently about 45 and looked like a typical ascetic.

The question under discussion was the organization of the church and its relation to the state. One speaker held that their duty was to see that the church and its organization was perfected first and then they should consider its relation to the state. Another question under discussion was the fixing of the date for the church assembly [the Sobor] at which they are to vote upon the vital question of a re-union of the Orthodox Church and the Old Believers. August 15 was finally fixed upon as the date for this assembly to be held, in the Red Square in Moscow.

After a short time they asked Mr. Mott to address them. This was an honor rarely, if ever before, accorded to a Protestant. His address was a memorable one. It was translated sentence by sentence by Father Aleksandrov, of San Francisco, and it lost none of its impressiveness in the translation, for Father Aleksandrov, being accustomed to public speaking and the subject being one with which he was familiar, threw all of his fervor into the translation, as if he was making an address. [75]

This was one of the great speeches of Mott's life, although given to a small group. It was never published but he outlined it for Leila and, as usual, kept his notes:

I began by congratulating the leaders of this great Church on its achievements through all the centuries, giving these in outline. Then I congratulated them on their present opportunities and grave difficulties. After that I congratulated them on the future, showing them why the best days of the Russian Church lie in the years just before us.

The next heading of my address dealt with the eight great distinctive contributions which American Christianity has made to the common Christianity of the world [including the social gospel]. Of course I had in view in such a presentation bringing influence to bear indirectly on the Russian situation. I improved the opportunity to prepare the way for our own Movement in the work it desires to do in the cities, in the villages, in the universities, and above all in the army.

"They listened with the greatest intensity and with unmistakable sympathy to all that I said." There were statements of appreciation. On July 9 he could write Leila: "I have been assured by those who were present that the way is now wide open for us in Russia so far as the church is concerned." What an achievement it will be, he exulted, if these two bodies that have been separated for centuries should be drawn together. When he thought of the "reactionary, relentless and cruel way" in which the former resident of the very palace in which this event had transpired [K. P. Pobedonostsev, Over-Procurator 1880–1905, the most influential political figure of that time in Russia], had administered the affairs of the Church, Mott found it hard to believe that he could have had "such an opportunity" and that he had lived "to see the day of such stupendous changes."[76] The changes would be even more stupendous than he imagined.

PART 10: Conversations with the Over-Procurator

Altogether Mott had eight interviews with V. N. Lvov, the Over-Procurator, each of from two to five hours' duration. His copious notes reveal that they discussed not only "all of the pressing problems of the Church," as he wrote to Leila, but beginning with Lvov's personal practice of asceticism, also covered much Orthodox history and the current scandals Mott could not describe to his wife. Lvov gave him a confidential message for President Wilson that detailed the crimes of Rasputin (who had been assassinated December 29/30, 1916) and clarified the need and justification of democracy in the Church.[77]

John W. Long has edited and transcribed Mott's records of his several conversations with the Over-Procurator.[78] Lvov, who is not to be confused with Prince G. E. Lvov, explained the "terrible conditions" he inherited upon becoming Over-Procurator, and how he had tried to deal with the situation:

> I now see plainly that if the Revolution had not come the Church would have gone to pieces and a majority of its members would have gone elsewhere.
>
> Rasputin belonged to a sect called Clisty [Khlysty] or whips—a sect which was forbidden in Russia by criminal law. He was organizing a cult and teaching that salvation of [the] soul came through sexual relations with him. [The] most terrible thing is that [the] Czar and Czarina were in his favor. Otherwise, he had not so much favor. These high criminals who got into favor were put in through [the] influence of this arch-criminal.
>
> We investigated what he was doing in one lavra [monastery]. [The] Metropolitan [had] appropriated 75,000 rubles from [the] lavra and would have got 200,000 more but for [the advent of the] Revolution. [There were] all kinds of orgies. [They] brought girls there for the monks.

"I tried to correct the Synod peacefully," Lvov went on, so they might then start the purification of the Church themselves. This led to his demanding the removal of most of its members, which was done, thus explaining the small number present at Mott's address.

> Now in my work the best workers are not bishops but priests. Even now we have [in the Synod] two bishops who are good men but not good workers. Now you [can] understand why [our] clergy and laymen do not trust their bishops. This distrust is just.
>
> Our Church is an episcopal church so I am in a difficult position. It will be some time before [the] people will trust their bishops. [But] our Church cannot do without bishops. Now our electing system will in time make our Church healthy. When [the] people have elected[their] bishops they will be liked and loved.
>
> This Sobor [sic] has not invited any bishops. . . . [It was] only thanks to my suggestion [that] the Sobor [sic] allowed [the] High Procurator to invite . . . such bishops as can command [the] trust of the people. This is why we have only eight bishops here. Now to make [the] Church healthy we need to call the great Council [Sobor] to give the Church life, health and freedom. The difficulty . . . [is that] until we have enough bishops who will command [the] confidence of [the] people, the clergy and people will rise against them. [79]

On June 9/22, Lvov described how he had reformed the Church from top to bottom. Parish, district, and diocesan councils and committees had been organized.

> Every man and woman in the parish can vote for [their] parish council, parish committee and parish priest. Parish councils elect representatives for a district meeting and that district meeting elects [the] district council. [The] district meeting also elects representatives to elect a diocesan council. Bishops [are] elected by [the] diocesan council.
>
> We have no anarchy in the Church. Thus [the] Church has gone ahead of the State . . . which lacks the power and authority. [80]

Ten days later Lvov summarized what he believed he had accomplished, and commented on his predecessor:

> [The] most acute moment in [the] Church [situation] is passed. It [the Church] also had [a] revolution but I was able to guide its course. My task now is to gather round the Sobor all the best Russian Orthodox intelligentsia. This [the Sobor] will be a moral force, more so than the Constituent Assembly. The Provisional Government will not be able to oppose this great moral force of the Church.
>
> I am undoing everything which Pobedonostsev did. His book is hypocrisy, hypocrisy, hypocrisy. He got criminal papers about many bishops

and priests and instead of punishing them he placed his hand over the vast pile of [accusatory] papers and said: no, I have them under my hand. [81]

Doubtless Mott gave Wilson the gist of Lvov's comments. They contributed significantly to his own understanding of Russia and of Orthodoxy.

He and Lvov also discussed the reunification of the Old Believers with the Orthodox Church, which in Lvov's judgment would be "the greatest act in a thousand years." Mott supplied Lvov with information on the polities of the major Western churches. When Lvov spoke of his hopes for the Great Sobor, Mott advised him to take steps to secure delegates to the Constituent Assembly "who can look after the interests of the Church." [82]

After the meeting with the Holy Synod on the 29th, Lvov took Crane and Mott to lunch and to see several of the more interesting churches of Petrograd—that of Tsushima, erected to honor the men lost in the great naval battle of 1905 with Japan, and the monastery of Alexander Nevsky, where the Americans held "valuable conversations" with the Rector and with the head of the theological seminary. The "great improvements" under way in the Church were sources of gratification and encouragement to the visitors. Shortly after the Mission left Russia, the Church was placed under a new Ministry of Religion, headed by A. V. Kartashev, which took over the duties of the Over-Procurator. Mott would meet Lvov again in Paris after the war.

Somehow during that day Mott found time to talk with Shidlovski about the forthcoming Constituent Assembly, then planned for September. On the 30th he met with M. V. Rodzianko, [83] President of the Fourth Duma, lunched with Ambassador Francis, visited the American Hospital, and discussed the prospects of a Russian YWCA with Countess Sophia Panin, the "Jane Addams of Russia."

PART 11: A Special Service in Kazan Cathedral

Sunday, July 1, Mott believed would be remembered as "a notable day" in the history of relations between Russia and America "and in particular in the relations between the Russian Orthodox Church and American Protestant Christianity." Largely as the result of his contacts with the leaders of the Church, they proposed a special service in honor of the Mission. This was held in the Kazan Cathedral on Nevsky Prospect from ten until one, with "the saintly and noble Archbishop Platon, who

did such wonderful work for the cause of Christianity in America,"
officiating. The members of the Mission were given "a prominent and
important place to stand" within the royal gates and facing the choir.
Moran thought the Americans in their black morning coats presented a
drab contrast to the gorgeous, gold-embroidered robes of the clergy. Part
of the liturgy was read in English. Father Aleksandrov read the Gospel
and preached in English. As the service drew toward its climax "a most
unusual thing took place." Mott recounted it for Leila:

> One of the priests came to us Americans and invited the men members of
> the party to go behind the ikonostas which hides the altar save when the
> gates are open. There we observed the Archbishop administer the commu-
> nion in both kinds to the bishops and priests who were present. Then to
> the grateful amazement of all of us, five of our number were called forward,
> Mr. Crane, Mr. McCormick and myself from our Mission, Mr. Miller of
> the Railroad Commission and Mr. Gaylord, and the Archbishop adminis-
> tered the communion to each of us in both kinds. He also presented to
> each of us a little loaf of the blessed bread. For some reason which deeply
> touched me, the Archbishop singled me out of the party and kissed me. I
> am told that this is a very special mark of sympathy and confidence.

The Americans then returned to their previous places.

> The last part of the service was more overpowering than ever in its impres-
> siveness. One of the most wonderful moments was when the vast audience,
> men, women and children, broke out and sang together in perfect unison
> and with deep feeling the Lord's Prayer. There followed a period of inter-
> cession led by one of the priests, when they prayed for the army, for the
> President and people of the United States, the other Allies, all the Ameri-
> cans present at the service, the Russian prisoners of war, the Provisional
> Government, and other objects of special importance. [84]

Taking this service "all in all and what it represents," he continued, it
must constitute "one of the most significant events in all the history of
the relations between the great Christian communions."

In the formal exchange of written felicitations afterward, Mott invited the Russian Church, through the Over-Procurator, with whom he
had discussed the matter previously, to send "a delegation of able representatives" to a "Conference on Faith and Order" to be held in America
after the War. Mott was in close touch with the American leaders of the
Faith and Order movement; they had encouraged him to make such
contacts. Archbishop Platon and others of the Russian clergy were aware
of the F. and O. plans, since these had been discussed sympathetically by
the Holy Synod. Designed to bring together leaders and members of all

the great Christian communions that acknowledged "the Deity of Our Lord Jesus Christ," and to afford them the opportunity to set forth clearly their distinct "beliefs, principles, forms of government and methods of work," the gathering would tend "to hasten the answer to the prayer of Our Lord—'that they all may be one.'" Lvov responded that, to the extent of his responsibility, "suitable representatives of our Church" would be sent. [85]

That same Sunday afternoon, July 1, Mott, together with most members of the Mission, was an observer at a strategic point on the line of march of a great political demonstration (the "June Days," since June 18 in Russia was July 1 by the Western Calendar) indicative of the continuing struggle between the Provisional Government and the Soviets. He took great pleasure in jotting down the slogans from many banners and afterward felt that on the whole the demonstration was "decidedly in favor of the Government," a total misreading of the situation, doubtless produced by his enthusiasm and interests. If the Government could hold on through the forthcoming Constituent Assembly, Mott felt that "the permanent success of the Revolution will have been ensured." [86] That evening he spent long hours in conference with the eight "Y" men on the problems of "opening up and extending work in the great Russian army."

Early Monday Mott talked with Professor P. I. Astrov, a Moscow judge, concerning the "startling" extent of German, Austrian, and Bolshevik antiwar propaganda being circulated at the front. Astrov told Mott that *Pravda* was being distributed there in quantity, and read to him letters from soldiers begging for honest news. One declared his and his comrades' willingness to lay down their lives for Russia but feared for her—"show us the true road," one implored. In this "terrifying" situation Astrov confessed he had almost no help. The Root Mission would make strong recommendations on this.

Mott was then briefed on Polish affairs by the president of the official Russian committee on those matters, following which he had the first of two lengthy conversations with the noted Jewish lawyer, G. B. Sliozberg, who elucidated the favorable results of the Revolution from the standpoint of the Jews. Some time was given to discussion of Zionism, with which Sliozberg expressed little sympathy. That evening, news of the Russian offensive on the southwestern front brought "stupendous demonstrations" in the streets and parks. Later, Mott, together with Crane, Harper, Harte, and Father Aleksandrov, left for Moscow via private railway car as guests of the Over-Procurator. [87]

PART 12: **A Token of Oneness with the Orthodox**

This third and final trip to Moscow was primarily to enable Mott and Crane to witness the election of the new Orthodox Metropolitan on Wednesday, July 4. Tuesday afternoon was devoted to calls on N. I. Astrov, a member of the municipal government, the former mayor, M. V. Chelnokov, with whom Mott had lunched in 1916, Countess Bobrinskaya, and an official who had been instrumental in developing the Union of Zemstvos. Late that evening the two called on Dr. E. V. Chlenov, "one of the leading Jews of Russia," who had presided over the large Zionist Congress recently held in Petrograd, and to whom Justice Louis Brandeis had directed them. Mott again found sharp differences of opinion over Zionism. "Some of them regard it as the only hope of the Jews. Others regard it as the greatest danger."[88]

Wednesday, election day, proved to be another of "those great days which I have spent among Christians of other communions." At the Uspensky Cathedral in the Kremlin, Mott and Crane witnessed the impressive procession of ecclesiastics and delegates "bearing various sacred icons and other insignia of the Church" and the "surging crowds . . . lining the streets" and following it. The two Americans had been admitted to the delegates' area by special unanimous resolution of the assembly the night before, and were given places at the right between the altar rail and the ikonostasis, which afforded "one of the most picturesque and interesting sights which I have witnessed in any gathering." Mott also gloried in the singing, the "great solemnity and reverence," and the "evident depth of feeling" with which the congregation participated in the service. The actual balloting took place publicly in the cathedral and the votes were counted in the presence of the full assembly. The winner, Archbishop Tikhon, had been the first archbishop of the Russian Church in America, where he had served from 1898 to 1907.[89] The bishops of the Church endorsed the choice of the delegates, and the whole company sang the Te Deum and Many Years for the new Metropolitan.

Then, as was becoming almost commonplace, another unusual event transpired. Mott and Crane were summoned behind the altar and each was presented with a fourteenth-century icon from the Cathedral's collection, Mott's "representing our Lord" and given because of "the service which we had rendered Russia and in recognition of our Christian activity throughout the world." In presenting the icon, Archpriest Nikolai Liubimov "quite clearly" referred to the fact of Mott's being a Protestant but recognized his "oneness" with the Orthodox in "our belief in the one Divine Savior." The cleric, Mott wrote home,

> ... has a son who is in one of the prisoner-of-war camps in Germany. He told me that his son had written him repeatedly about the helpfulness of our Association and that in connection with it he had learned the English language. He is a graduate of Moscow University. I told him that I would arrange to have sent to his son from Copenhagen every two weeks a parcel of food. This moved the old man to tears.[90]

The Americans returned to Petrograd in their private car that night of July 4. While they were gone, the Bolsheviki had staged their first attempt to take over the Government but were defeated; machine guns had chattered and spit, and blood had been spilled in the streets.[91]

PART 13: Final Days in Petrograd

Upon arrival in the capital Mott and Crane lunched with Ambassador Francis. At four that afternoon, the British suffragette, Sylvia Pankhurst, took tea with the members of the Mission. Mott described the affair to Leila:

> ... She made a favorable impression upon me. Her visit here is timely. She is meeting with splendid response from the women of all classes. In some respects the women of Russia seem to be as well prepared for the Revolution as are the men. I think there is no doubt whatever about their receiving equal rights.

Later the same day he and Crane, Harte, who had been in Germany, Harper, Jerome Davis, and the Russian commissioner of prisoners of war, D. Navashin, met six Russian soldiers who had been prisoners in Germany and Austria. Some of them had escaped and others had been repatriated. They gave a detailed account of the "bad treatment" they had received and of "punishments" meted out to Russian prisoners. "It makes a startling story," Mott concluded.[92]

The next day Mott interviewed the several YMCA men and talked with Harold Williams, author of *Russia of the Russians*, then rated the best book on its subject.[93] He met three Russian officials: F. F. Kokoshkin, who would be murdered in his bed by the Bolsheviki the next January, briefed Mott on his hopes and plans for the future Constituent Assembly; L. Davydov, president of the Russian bank for foreign trade; and Prince D. I. Shakhovskoi, minister of welfare. Mott took copious notes on all of these conversations, prompting him to remark to Leila that he had the materials for a book if he chose to write one.[94]

Saturday, July 7, began with a conference of the Mission after breakfast to decide several delicate matters, one being McCormick's proposal of a cable to Washington recommending an additional credit to Russia. Mott sided with Root against the suggestion, while Russell supported McCormick; "the matter was left without decision."[95] Then there were protocol calls: Mott had an unusually profitable conference with British Labourite Arthur Henderson, a member of the War Cabinet who was in Petrograd as the head of a delegation not unlike the Root Mission. Oldham's reply to Mott's letter of May 16 arrived and was acknowledged with disappointment that Mott could not return home via Great Britain; nevertheless, "our coming has not been in vain. I have had evidence day by day that God sent me here for this particular time." His opportunities had come from directions not anticipated. Somehow that full Saturday he had been able to visit an Armenian shop where he purchased a dress, a waist, and a scarf together with ornaments and belts for Leila, and some books and a chess set. In the evening he took dinner alone with Foreign Minister M. I. Tereshchenko "in his beautiful apartments overlooking the Neva directly opposite the Fortress of St. Peter and St. Paul." This was a delightful two hours; Tereshchenko gave the impression of having "a clear perception of the problems of Russia." Mott described the evening as one of his "most stimulating and suggestive interviews."

Sunday, July 8, was "not exactly a day of rest," with the affairs of the Mission rushing toward conclusion. Mott filled it with protocol calls on the Over-Procurator, Archbishop, now Metropolitan Tikhon, later to be Patriarch; and the great Polish Roman Catholic bishop in Russia, Jan Cieplak. As it happened, the Over-Procurator Lvov was visiting the Catholic prelate when Mott arrived, the first time such a meeting had taken place in Russia. Mott took advantage of the ecumenical encounter to remark:

> . . . Here we are, representatives of the three great Christian communions—Russian Orthodox, Roman Catholic and Protestant. We have one Christ and we have common enemies. Surely we must come to understand each other better and learn to work together.

Receiving a sympathetic response from each of his hearers, Mott recounted the reply of the Roman Catholic Bishop of Madras to his question, "how shall we bring about the closer unity we so much desire to see?"

... First, we must pray more for unity; secondly, we must show one another true courtesy; thirdly, we must see more of each other. This also met with their hearty approval. We then discussed the proposed Conference on Faith and Order to be held in America within a few years after the war, and both of them have promised to cooperate.[96]

Mott dined late with the Gaylords and conferred with Gaylord, Harte, and Jerome Davis on the "Y" army work until midnight, agreeing that Gaylord and Davis would be associate national secretaries, with Gaylord to be "regarded as the senior" who would take the initiative in all matters of common concern. Several names were decided upon for a National Committee.[97]

The final day was crowded with "belated important interviews." The Mission left for Vladivostok in the imperial train at 11:00 P.M., Monday, July 9, both Russian and American officials giving them "a splendid send-off." Crane remained in Russia. After saying farewell to Mott, Edward Heald thought that the "chief" considered the opportunity here in Russia" to be "without parallel," noting in his diary that the Mission members who had visited the front had been "quite excited" over what they had seen. However,

> On the south western front the Czechs swept the Austrians off their feet, but the attacking regiments have not been supported by the Russian rear as they should have been, and the Leninist propaganda has spread a lot of disaffection in the ranks that may ruin the advance yet! On the western front instead of advancing the regiments have in some places opened up for the Germans to advance. We're not out of the woods yet by any means. It is a shame that all the outburst of enthusiasm and miraculous change of spirit of a week ago has nearly died out and there is more concern about the Bolshevik propaganda than there is hope for a successful advance.[98]

In actuality, Brusilov's great offensive on the Galician front, inspired in part by Kerensky's spectacular visit, had collapsed, and the badly disorganized Russian troops were completely defeated. The Bolsheviks now took the initiative and matters moved precipitately toward the October Revolution.

PART 14: "A Serious Mission Homebound"

If all members of the Mission were as exhausted as Mott they must have dropped into their luxurious berths with relief at the prospect of ten days of rest. Mott had often worked as long as twenty hours a day because they had been in Petrograd during the season of "white nights" when the sun set at eleven and rose at two-thirty; this, he remarked later, tempted a man "to do as we do in this country, to work all the time the sun is up." As the train rolled eastward, the countryside again "looked beautiful," a few days were warm and dusty but the nights cool, and everywhere the harvest was beginning. Whenever the occasion afforded, Mott and a colleague or two ventured into village shops, where he picked up more semi-precious stones, lace, and other gifts. There was a two-day delay at Viatka in European Russia where a wooden bridge had been burned; while the train waited in the station for tracks to be laid across a new bridge, several fires of suspicious origin broke out. Some newspapers later construed the episode as an anarchist plot to murder the Americans, but Mott merely remarked in a letter to Hattie that there was little doubt that the bridge had been burned "by the Germans and their tools," although he conceded that it "might have been a serious matter with us had it not been discovered in time." It was said that Senator Root "remained very cool during the incident."[99] The log described it in neutral terms.

While workmen readied the new bridge and the trainload of celebrities waited to move on east from the heartland of Mother Russia, the humorous weekly *Life* commented on the press releases concerning the Mission.

> We hear of Mr. Root, of Admiral Glennon, of James Duncan, the labor member of the deputation, and a little about General Scott. No doubt Mr. Crane and John R. Mott and the others are also active. The development of Mr. Mott as an international agent is very interesting. He, too, has a wise spirit, and is a man that even politicians may well keep an eye on.[100]

During the delay at Viatka, Mott, McCormick, and Moran hired a droshky for sightseeing and entered what they took to be a monastery in search of a cup of tea; they withdrew in embarrassment when it proved to be a nunnery. In further pursuit of refreshment they accosted a "young student" who was at first suspicious but when Moran mentioned Mott's name immediately became communicative and escorted them to the local inn; "he had heard of John Mott and his work for the young men of Russia."[101] Three months together produced a first-name relationship between Mott and McCormick; Cyrus presented albums of photographs to John and all the members of the Mission.

For years there circulated an apocryphal story that at some control point on the return trip (the incident occurred at the Manchurian border), Chinese inspectors discovered a cache of opium under the mattress in Mott's berth, the smuggler apparently having assumed that that compartment would not be searched. Actually, 20,000 rubles worth of the drug was found underneath some boxes of empty bottles elsewhere in the train.[102] The tale probably became associated with Mott by McCormick's telling it as a joke. Also at this check-point a cable came from Washington directing the Mission to return home directly from Vladivostok, which it had already planned to do.[103] Mott used the long train ride to rest, read, talk at length with members of the Mission and a few others who came aboard, edit his speeches and report letters, and review and clarify his many notes. Chinese representatives rejoined the party in Manchuria, but no member of the Mission was sent home via China, which had undergone further turmoil while the Mission was in Russia. At Harbin, Moran left to return to the States via Japan, and Willard Lyon, now senior YMCA secretary for China, joined Mott to confer during the twenty-four hour journey to Vladivostok; he brought word of "a chaotic condition of things in China during the last few weeks," referring to the revolt of Chan Chuang. For Mott, Lyon's presence was "the next best thing to visiting China." The two reviewed "the whole situation" there and discussed "all the important and pressing questions in our work."[104]

After twelve days the train arrived in Vladivostok around noon, July 21, the party now rested and ready for another bout with the icy, rolling Pacific. Bidding farewell to their Russian hosts in seemingly endless speeches and replies, the members of the Mission exchanged the royal luxury they had enjoyed for 10,000 miles of travel for the spartan accommodations of the *Buffalo* again. In mid-afternoon the ship disappeared into the fog. Mott again was a frequent victor in deck sports and found pleasure in watching the sea. On July 29 McCormick noted in his diary that "John Mott, who is understood to be a reliable authority with regard to things which he sees, reports having seen this morning one or more good sized whales." Crossing the international date line gave the party its sixth Sunday of the month. McCormick noted that there was some puzzlement as to how to spend it, but one wonders if Mott was reminded of his wish of thirty years ealier for 48-hour Sundays in which to accomplish his religious projects at Cornell! It chanced to be a calm, smooth day that made the occasion seem "more like a pleasure yachting party than a serious mission homebound," with myriads of birds on the water, spouting whales, seals in view, the magnificent mountains of Unimak Island in the background, and the Alaska Peninsula to the east.[105] Late Friday night, August 3, they docked in Seattle, having followed the same course as on the westward trip.

Mott was disappointed not to return via Japan, as he had been led to expect. "Had I known a little earlier," he chafed, "I would have had [Galen] Fisher come over to Manchuria to see me"[106] He was also lonely and disappointed that not a word had come from home or relatives since he left the States in May. The Mission was enthusiastically entertained in Seattle, where Root's speeches made headlines and a minor item reported General Brusilov's removal a few days earlier. Had he read older papers, Mott might have learned that on August 14 his SCM colleague Dr. Georg Michaelis had become Chancellor of Germany.[107] A special train over the Milwaukee Railroad (several members of the Mission took turns riding in the locomotive over the 440-mile electrified section) reached Chicago at 10:30 the third morning. At 12:30 they left by special train for Washington, arriving in the record time of three days, sixteen hours, and twenty-five minutes from Seattle. They were met at 10:25 A.M. in "seething heat" by Samuel Gompers and a minor State Department officer, and reported to the Secretary of State and the President in the afternoon.[108]

PART 15: **"The Best and Wisest of Christians"**

Whatever the final judgment of historians may be concerning the Root Mission and Mott's role in it, and that conclusion has not yet been reached, the experience was one of the more remarkable episodes of his career. His assignment was accomplished to the extent possible in Russia in the summer of 1917: to meet church officials, to convey the ecumenical regard and support of the Christians of America to them and through them to all Russians, to explore the possibilities of humanitarian YMCA work among Russian soldiers and sailors, and to lay the legal and administrative foundations for such a program. Neither Mott nor his peers and associates could forecast that this great effort, which ultimately elicited the unselfish service of several hundred men and women, begun as it was in hope but "ended in perplexity," would be frustrated by the Bolshevik Revolution.[109] Nor is a judgment final that overlooks the immediate humane values of selfless service to thousands of needy human beings, the victims of war and dislocation.[110]

Mott's relation to these services will be described in Chapter 10, but prisoner of war work, an independent entity, was to continue as a major YMCA activity in Russia. Authorities differ as to whether the first center for soldiers opened in Petrograd before Mott left with the Mission, or in Moscow on July 28; the ten American secretaries with whom he had conferred were augmented in the early fall by forty new men. Within a few weeks of the Mission's return Jerome Davis could write to Mott that in a personal interview Kerensky, now Premier, had granted the YMCA "blanket permission" to work "everywhere in Russia and at the front." In one sector they had been asked to open 200 clubs. Davis wondered if the American public realized what "unspeakable hardships" the Russian soldier had suffered "for his country and for us," paid as he was less than thirty cents a month and denied the YMCA privileges available to Allied armies the world over. There were now secretaries in Minsk, Kiev, Sarny, Odessa, and Kazan in addition to the cities previously mentioned. In Moscow the "Y" was already serving 25,000 men a week.[111]

Mott described his part in establishing all this in his special report to the Secretary of State. Convinced of the need by the experiments carried out by the secretaries already in the field, he had approached Premier Lvov, Tereshchenko, "and other members of the Cabinet" for the requisite approvals. He had "only a few words with Mr. Kerensky, who arranged to see me later but had not returned from the front when I left Petrograd."[112] He held a "long and favorable conference" with the Chief of the General Staff and with "other representatives of the War Ministry." Through Archie Harte's good offices, he also saw "a number of members of the Soldiers' Deputies, as well as many individual officers and soldiers." He also held inter-agency conferences on two occasions. On the basis of favorable conclusions so reached, Mott reported that he had

> diverted from the Prison Camp Work as many American secretaries as possible and . . . coached them with reference to beginning Association work on a large scale at the four principal garrison cities of Russia and Roumania: Petrograd, Moscow, Kiev and Jassy, and at two or three principal points at the front.

He had also cabled to America,

> for certain other men to come out immediately to join this force and . . . sent instructions to [his] office in New York to have a diligent search instituted at once to discover scores of the most likely candidates for such work so that, if we find ourselves in a position to extend this work on a large scale, we shall have men available to lead the enterprise.[113]

The requisite permissions were granted; almost 400 Americans served in Russia until the Bolshevik government terminated the program in 1923.[114]

In addition to setting up these far-flung services, Mott gained immensely from the Mission in knowledge of, and respect and affection for, the Russian people and their Church, its music, its saints and thinkers, the evangelical nature of its liturgy and service-book, and its constant and congenial emphasis upon the Resurrection. Throughout his career he would be concerned with the welfare of the Russian Church. During the dark days of Bolshevik persecution, he would instruct his secretarial friends to "find out what I can do to help them." He provided significant services to the emigrant communities of western Europe, always distinguishing between the Russian state and its people. Without doubt his experience with the Root Mission dispelled the last vestige of his heritage from the works of the German historian Harnack which he had studied at Cornell, that Orthodoxy was ossified. His extensive Orthodox overtures of the next twenty years were partly rooted in the Russian experience of 1917.

However, Mott's contacts in Russia were not exclusively with the state Church. He had spent a memorable evening with the leaders of the Old Believers and on other occasions talked with members of this, the largest dissenting sect. He also had "most profitable conferences with representatives of the Protestant forces in Russia, notably with Dr. Keen of the British and Foreign Bible Society and with Dr. Simons of the Methodist Episcopal Church," both of whom he thought were conducting their work "with great wisdom and evident acceptance." Save for Baron Nicolay there were no contacts with Lutherans, but

> memorable interviews were also had with the most distinguished and best trusted leaders of the seven millions of Russian and Polish Jews, which enabled me to penetrate more deeply into the heart of their problems. I am glad to believe that the Russian Revolution has at last ushered in a day of hope for these long-persecuted people. My conference with the Roman Catholic Bishop and with other representatives of that communion was likewise very satisfactory.[115]

The knowledge and experience thus accumulated greatly reenforced Mott's leadership of the organizations over which he presided and provided an inexhaustible resource for his many fund-raising speeches on behalf of both POW relief and services to men in arms. They also became building blocks for future ecumenical structures. If the Germans and Swedes, who expected him to be neutral, became disaffected for a while by what they regarded as a partisan and political stance, he was nonetheless able to forestall disruption of the several international bodies to which he was related and even retain his position as elected leader of them; in time he would convince them of the purity of his motives, if not of his neutrality. All in all, Mott returned home more than ever convinced of the truth of Theodore Roosevelt's message that he had carried to the students of Russia in 1909: "There is no nation in the world which, more than Russia, holds in its hands the fate of the coming years."[116]

The singular coldness displayed by the administration toward the Mission's recommendations and Wilson's perplexing lack of interest produced an appearance of failure,[117] but Mott immediately resumed his frequent contacts with the President. He was the spokesman for a subcommittee appointed by Root to prepare a succinct statement of the Mission's proposals for the President. After conferring over this document on August 30, his second or third meeting with Wilson since returning, Mott wrote to the President in his own hand on the train while returning to New York, offering certain clarifications of the proposed program, which was essentially directed toward staging educational [propaganda] campaigns for "strengthening the morale and cheering and raising the spirit" of the French and Italian armies as well as the Russian.[118] As time passed and their recommendations were not put into effect, in spite of a round of elegant luncheons, the members of the Mission began to feel that their services were not only no longer desired, but were resented at the State Department. The President had apparently dismissed them.[119]

Yet the significance of the Root Mission, which has invariably been treated as a failure, may need reevaluation. In contrast to the demise of the body itself, Mott, and apparently McCormick, Crane, and a few others, all trusted friends of the President, became Wilson's unofficial experts on Russia. During the next months they almost induced him to extend economic aid to Russia, possibly to be supervised by a commission that Mott was asked to head, but refused.[120] Such a step would have amounted to de facto recognition of the Bolshevik government, a policy with which Wilson was personally sympathetic. But the Allies pressured the President into military intervention, which certainly would have been opposed by Mott and the others named.[121] This is a problem for future investigation.[122]

Mott's relations with Wilson continued on an even more intimate level than before the Mission. In January, 1918, he began a conference with the President with an expression of gratitude for the chief executive's understanding of Russian problems. He quoted to Wilson the phrase from the poet Tiutchev that he had picked up from a prominent Russian in 1916: "You may not understand Russia, but you must believe in Russia."[123] It may have been in part as a result of Mott's counsel that Senator Root was somewhat surprised to find the President "very well informed on the Russian situation" when the delegation met with him after their return.[124] The conclusion is inescapable that Mott acquired the most thorough grasp of Russian affairs of any member of the Mission.[125] Crane believed that Mott's impact on "the minds and hearts of the Russian people" would be remembered for a century. Just prior to the departure of the Mission from Russia, he had written to a relative that Mott would be returning home "with a wider and deeper understanding of the present-day Russia and her problems than anyone else who has come here since President [William Rainey] Harper":

> He has seen a great variety of people and the wonderful sympathy and understanding he has, caused them to speak to him as I have known them to speak to no one else before. . . . I personally am very happy about his visit and entirely content with the message he takes home.[126]

Crane expected Mott "to get all of our family together—excepting me—soon after his arrival home and tell them of our really wonderful experiences."[127] In contrast, the Soviets would later regard Mott as the Mission's leading ideologist, a close personal friend and adviser to Wilson, and leader of the reactionary YMCA.[128]

As plans for another special commission to remain in Russia indefinitely took shape in the spring and early summer of 1918, Crane hoped that Mott could be induced to head it "for say three months, as a most important symbol."[129] Mott preferred to give the President some suggestions for the personnel of such a body, closing his letter with a commendation of the President's plan "to ensure a wise coordination of all that is being done and all that will be done on behalf of Russia by the various departments of the Government and by other agencies... here at home":

> Let me reiterate my conviction that you have been Providentially guided from the beginning in your attitude and policy with reference to Russia and the Russian people. In the midst of such confused counsels and conflicting national ambitions and in the face of much publicity propaganda, your own

course has been all the more remarkable. It is an impressive illustration of the value of having clear guiding principles and also sympathy with the aspirations of what have been aptly called "dark people" groping after larger light and liberty.[130]

It was such exchanges that brought Mott to know Wilson "more intimately" than any other president, and that led Wilson to characterize Mott as "certainly one of the most nobly useful men in the world."[131] The New York *Christian Advocate* had been clairvoyant in its forecast that Mott would be the *persona optima gratia* of the Root Mission. In August, 1918, Crane wrote to the President:

> You have near you the best and wisest of Slavs, Masaryk, and the best and wisest of Christians, Mott, to consult about moves that are more or less technical. You three are trusted by the whole world—and especially the Slavic world—and will do what is possible as opportunity offers.[132]

10

From War to Peace

*It is a shaken world. It is shaken to its very base. All
the foundations are heaving, yes, more, they are
slipping. . . . The world is under a strain the like of
which the human race has never known.*

MOTT FLED the heat of Washington as soon as the Root Mission's
immediate business was attended to on August 8 and 9, 1917.
That summer there was only one week's escape to the Canadian woods
from the imperious demands of six major organizations and nine active
committees and boards; he was planning to drop several as soon as possible.[1]

While the Root Mission was away, General Pershing had arrived in
France and his men had helped push the Germans back from Chateau
Thierry and Belleau Wood and had aided in clearing out the sector
between Rheims and Soissons. Although the British experiment with the
convoy, just begun, was to prove highly successful, the first shipload of
Red Triangle supplies had been torpedoed, a total loss. Nine million men
had been registered by the military draft, and the casualty lists from
France were beginning to convince Americans that this was the most
ghastly war in history.

Since mid-May the burgeoning War enterprises of the Associations
had been hampered by Mott's absence. In France, his lieutenant Edward
C. ("Ned") Carter had offered Pershing the YMCA's services in the same
spirit in which Mott himself had wired Wilson in April. Yet the lay
leaders of the YMCA found it as difficult as did the Congress to act upon
the urgencies of the moment. Without Mott's witness to the realities of
Europe they found it almost impossible to comprehend the magnitude of
the task to which he had committed them.[2] Not until September, six
months after America had entered the War, did the War Work Council
become fully involved in the overseas enterprise. It was the climax of

John Mott's life to inspire, direct, and raise the funds to support that vast ministry, the beginnings of which were described in Chapters 8 and 9. It was now being extended to all belligerents and their prisoners of war, and was to expand not only to the American Expeditionary Forces and the Allied armies and navies, but to a vast home front—war industries, training camps, ports of embarkation, ships at sea.

PART 1: "One of the Greatest Achievements of Peace in All the History of Human Warfare"

This praise by Chief Justice William Howard Taft after the War was hardly an exaggeration. The American YMCA's, he continued, served between four and five million American soldiers and sailors at home and abroad, "conducted nine-tenths of the welfare work among American forces in Europe," and "ministered to not less than nineteen millions of the soldiers of the Allied armies and extended its helpful activities to over five millions of prisoners of war." Almost five times the normal American YMCA staff were mobilized for this ministry with its strongly social overtones; of the 25,926 men and women who were recruited for it, 276 died or were wounded in service—approximately the same ratio of casualties as the armed services themselves: 355 were decorated, cited, or commended. [3]

Following the Root Mission, Mott sent his most trusted colleague, Ethan T. Colton, to Russia to administer the activities of a total of 400 secretaries, a program that continued until 1923, though a few individuals stayed on until 1926. Colton described Archie C. Harte and Carlisle V. Hibbard as "the two direct arms of Doctor Mott" in the outreach toward prisoners. Hibbard had been through the bitter experiences of the Japanese forces at war with Czarist Russia; Harte had been chaplain of a southern regiment in the Spanish-American War and had had extensive YMCA experience in India. He became ambassador-at-large, winning "the confidence of military chiefs, ministers of state, kings and empresses on both sides," using his irresistible personal charm to cross armed frontiers on behalf of enemy captives. John C. Traphagen, who afterward became president of the Bank of New York, Jerome Davis, to be a Yale professor, H. Dewey Anderson, subsequently author of studies and executive of the New Deal Temporary National Economic Committee, Francis P. Miller, to succeed Mott in the WSCF—each received his marching orders from Mott, as did many of those who remained on among Allied troops for the abortive projects at Archangel and Murmansk or with the international enterprise in Siberia and the Far East.[4]

Limitations of space restrict such citations, which could fill the remainder of this book. Russell M. Story saw service in Russia from 1917 to 1919 at Mott's behest. Myron T. Clark, YMCA pioneer in Brazil, was sent to organize the work among Portuguese troops. Y. C. James Yen developed a method of teaching a simplified Chinese alphabet to the coolies in Chinese labor camps in France; the idea was subsequently adopted in China. Anson Phelps Stokes, later secretary of Yale University and Canon of the Washington Cathedral, recorded that Mott had called him into his office early in the War to ask him to go to Europe as Educational Director of the YMCA army services, which he did, and at the end of the War organized the American Educational Commission.[5]

Conrad Hoffman, who had brought Mott and Raymond Robins to the University of Kansas for an evangelistic campaign in 1915, began POW work in England that year, then was allowed to remain in Germany after America entered the conflict, and from World YMCA headquarters in Berne administered the international POW program run by 65 secretaries from the neutral countries. It reached "across Europe and Siberia, south to Tashkent in Turkestan and Ahmednagar in India, and to German prisoners in Japan" until 1922.[6] Although there would be criticism of the YMCA administration of the Red Triangle canteens no serious flaws have ever been discovered in the POW program, which was the outgrowth of Mott's concept of an international service on a reciprocal basis in all countries, the only way prisoners of the Central Powers could be reached. After evaluating it in 1950 as "the greatest service rendered to the participants and victims of World War I by the YMCA," this author reaffirms that judgment and attributes the effectiveness of the POW effort to Mott's generalship, fund-raising, and selection of personnel.[7]

As was mentioned in Chapter 8, immediately after the United States entered the War Mott called an emergency conference to organize "possible service by the YMCA in connection with the proposed mobilization" of American troops. This was April 10, 1917, at Garden City, New York. As chairman, he proposed that the Associations direct their programs toward all men in all branches of the armed services, whether in camps or in transit or on leave, and where possible with huts and other facilities such as had proved effective in the Canadian experience and the Mexican border work. Means of recruiting and training secretaries were discussed, and it was emphasized that the best men should be sought rather than simply those who might be spared from the regular YMCA programs.

Mott then proposed a War Work Council, directly responsible to the International Committee of the YMCA, with William S. Sloane of New York as chairman. Mott became its general secretary. S. Wirt Wiley was director of publicity and obtained Bruce Barton, the editor of *Success* magazine, to serve as chairman of that committee. The Council was authorized on April 12 and a resolution issued calling for the mobilization of Association forces "to promote the physical, mental, social, and spiritual welfare" of the men of the current armed services. To undergird this a fund of at least $3,000,000 should be raised in the next thirty days, which Mott did almost single-handedly.

When the Council met for the first time on April 28, Mott explained his offer of the Associations' services to President Wilson, an action universally approved by the brotherhood; he had also talked with the Secretaries of War and of the Navy, pledging "our readiness to co-operate to the fullest extent." In the interim, YMCA leaders all over the country had "assumed the same patriotic attitude" and offered their services to headquarters. Mott also said that they would "continue to carry on abroad the unique service which the Association was rendering to the soldiers at the front, in the training camps, and in the prisoner-of-war camps"; the last would not presently come under the jurisdiction of the War Work Council, "though who could tell when the two would have to be united!" Mott climaxed the meeting with a short statement from President Wilson, who expressed his "sincere personal interest" in their "large plans." Raymond B. Fosdick's committee on training camps, of which Mott was a member, was also described, and it was reported that "many other organizations were trying to get into these camps, but the Secretary of War stated that he had decided to have only the Associations."[8] Robert Wilder reported on the plans for religious work to be carried on in the camps: "religious meetings, united prayer, Bible study, music, quiet rooms for personal devotion, Bible circulation, camp visitors from among clergymen, Christian workers, etc."

A week before the War Work Council got under way, its representatives met with those of the Federal Council of Churches—which had been concerned with the chaplaincy—to organize a joint cooperating committee on the training camps and the chaplaincy. They resolved to cooperate in the selection process for both chaplains and YMCA secretaries for the camps, asked chaplains and secretaries at the camps to confer regularly, and proposed a joint conference committee "to meet as occasion may require to insure the best understanding." That fall the Federal Council established a General Wartime Commission, though the YMCA representatives, apparently including Mott, at first vigorously opposed the move. Mott nevertheless became a member; William Adams Brown was its secretary, and Samuel McCrea Cavert became assistant secretary. Cavert, for whom this was the beginning of a lifetime of service with the Council, wrote in retrospect:

> In the main, the relation between Y.M.C.A. workers and chaplains was reasonably satisfactory. The "Y" huts were placed at the disposal of chaplains as needed; and the attitudes on both sides—with a few exceptions—were fraternal. But there was never any adequate definition of relationships between the churches and the Y.M.C.A. and the lack of it contributed to misunderstandings and rivalries. The vast program of the Y.M.C.A., although it leaned heavily on the churches for personnel and support, was launched without any clear agreement with them. Its War Work Council was set up without consultation with either denominational or interdenominational leaders. A little later, when a Cooperating Committee of the Churches was initiated by the Y.M.C.A., its members were chosen by the "Y" itself, not by the churches.
>
> The one established point of contact between the Y.M.C.A. and the churches was in the General Wartime Commission. Thanks to the representation of the "Y" in the Commission, and even more to relations of personal friendships and trust between the leaders on both sides, the overall picture showed more unity than might have been expected in the absence of common planning in advance.[9]

It should be noted that the "Y" was organized and ready to offer its services to the country on the day War was declared and that it had a leader capable of carrying it with him. The General Wartime Commission was not constituted until September 20, 1917.

In his memoirs William Adams Brown recalled that a small advisory committee representing Catholics, Protestants, and Jews had advised the Secretary of War "in all matters that had to do with religion," and had been extremely helpful and epitomized the ecumenical spirit at work. It included Father John Burke, editor of the *Catholic World* and secretary of the National Catholic War Council, whose idea it was; Speer, Brown, and Mott served on it.[10]

In the course of an interview with President Wilson on September 26, 1917, Mott raised several points concerning the chaplaincy and its relation to the YMCA. From his few notes it may be inferred that he explained that the "Y" regarded the secretaryship as sufficiently broad to include most of the functions of the chaplaincy. Seemingly unaware of the significance of the sacerdotal office to certain denominations, he appears to have assumed that the presence of some ordained men among Association personnel would be adequate; he inferred that ordained chaplains might constitute a sort of "fifth wheel" in some situations, and hoped that the churches would trust the Associations to perform these functions.[11]

But they did not, and "YMCA-church relations" were poor. In December, 1918, Mott assembled a representative blue-ribbon panel of twenty "Y" and church men and women to consider the matter. He outlined the situation as he saw it, and then listened to the comments. No holds were barred. The discussion appeared to clear the air, at least for the moment. Mott later gathered the points made in this meeting into a plea for mutual understanding and cooperation and published it as a twenty-page pamphlet called *The YMCA and the Evangelical Churches*. A few weeks later he spoke at the Fifth Avenue Presbyterian Church in New York on the task of the War Time Commission in demobilization, for which $10,000,000 in War Work Funds were set aside.

PART 2: **The Religious Signficance of the War**

Although most of the American clergy are alleged to have "presented arms" during World War I, it is instructive to examine the stance of the lay triumvirate "Mott, Speer, and Eddy," who were still at the summit of the leadership they had exerted for two decades. Early in the War, Eddy was brought back from China to speak to British soldiers in England and in France. He later mediated the misunderstandings between British and American troops at the front. He spent most of the War in Europe, and in 1918 wrote *The Right to Fight* but by 1924 repented with *The Abolition of War*.

On Tuesday and Wednesday, May 8 and 9, 1917, a month after the United States' declaration of war against Germany, and a week before Mott left for Russia with the Root Mission, the Federal Council held a mass meeting of representatives of its constituent bodies in Washington. The "call of the hour" was sounded by the Reverend Frank Mason North, prominent Methodist champion of the social gospel, currently president of the Council, and a close friend of Mott. North told his quasi-official audience that the churches were there to offer "sacrificial devotion" to the common welfare of humanity, that they should "resist with all their power" the "sordid influences of selfishness and materialism" of war, and "keep pure the springs of motive." They had come not to stimulate their patriotism or assert their loyalty but to accept responsibility, define their task, and determine their program.

Speer, assigned the topic, "The War and the Nation's Larger Call to World Evangelism," challenged the American churches to "witness to the possibilities that lie beyond the facts," to hold fast "on the world plane to an undertaking that will not let go the idea of a world brotherhood, that will work for it, and even in these days when mankind is rent asunder, will ignore the chasm and will send out its representatives across the whole world, speaking its message of a world love and holding fast to its dream of a world hope." This is the day for men to think not in terms of one nation's relationship to another nation only, but "in the wide terms of the interrelations of all men." In concluding, Speer laid down the guideline that he would attempt to follow in the Wartime Commission:

> We betray our mission and fail God if we shrink into a nationalistic sect that can conceive only of our own national functions, unless those national functions include for us the whole human brotherhood and the duty of speaking and thinking and living by the law of a world love. [12]

Agreeing with the official *Message* of the Council that had just been read, he endorsed the enlargement rather than the curtailment of the church's ministries. Yet, although Speer believed that the War was "righteous and necessary," when in 1918 he remarked that the United States was also guilty of some actions for which we had condemned Germany, he was criticized and vilified throughout the secular and religious press.

The extension of ministry through the YMCA to millions of men under arms was Mott's constant and inclusive theme throughout the War. In offering the services of the YMCA to the nation, and himself accepting diplomatic assignments, he endorsed the policies of President Wilson and thereby tacitly approved the War aims of the government. Like Speer, he never descended to the hate-mongering or emotional diatribes that characterized the utterances of those described by Ray H. Abrams in *Preachers Present Arms*—a sorry and one-sided account. Abrams mistakenly included Speer and Mott among scores of notables "who became converted in various degrees to the 'holy war' aims of the Allies." [13] Neither ever defended the struggle in such terms. Mott's experiences in Germany and in Great Britain in 1914 had shocked him into the realization that neither side could have a monopoly of righteousness. Whether or not the garbling of his speech to the Cossack officers in Russia served as a warning, Mott was careful in every public utterance

and in his writing to avoid any remark that could possibly be mis-
construed as critical of or derogatory to the Germans or their allies. One
is conscious of the tension between the American and the internationalist in him at this time.

Frank Mason North had called the attention of his audience in the
national capital to the separation of church and state under the American constitution as "the very condition of the sacrificial devotion of the
churches to the common welfare of community or nation." Perhaps as a
pragmatic layman Mott was less conscious of separation than were the
clergy, but his presence in Washington every two weeks during the
remainder of the War was evidence of the close wartime relations between government and the enterprises over which he presided. Had he
given the matter serious thought he would have agreed with the later
judgment of historian William W. Sweet that during the War "separation of church and state was suspended." Or was the YMCA program a
step toward the secularization of Christianity in the sense that that term
was to be used fifty years afterward?[14]

Although by 1916 Mott had retreated from the pacifist position to
which he had been temporarily converted by Henry Hodgkin, he did not
swing to the opposite extreme of joining the preparedness crusade of the
hour. There is no evidence that he in any way pressured the members of
his staff who held to pacifism: D. Willard Lyon, whose study guide *The
Christian Equivalent of War* (1914) was widely used throughout the
Movement; Gilbert Beaver, first chairman of the American FOR;
Fletcher Brockman, Mott's closest professional associate; Charles D.
Hurrey, who held a variety of student-related posts; and David Porter,
Mott's successor as senior secretary of the Student YMCA who would
influence it powerfully toward pacifism in the 1920's. The convinced
pacifist Kirby Page worked for Mott as a secretary during the summer of
1918; he too would influence the student pacifist movement of the next
two decades. Mott may well have felt himself vulnerable on this point
and perhaps secretly wished he could embrace their position, but as had
been the case more than once in his career, administrative necessity
outweighed personal preference.

C. Roland Marchand's analysis of this shift by many who withdrew
from the peace movement, in his *American Peace Movement and Social
Reform, 1898–1918,* throws light upon Mott's position. Men and women
who had seen the peace movement as part of "a wider campaign for
domestic and international order and stability" were consistent in aban-
doning it when it moved toward social upheaval and reform, and/or

"became critical of American foreign policy and seemingly overeager to mediate an end to a war in which Germany temporarily held the upper hand"—exactly what Oldham had pointed out to Mott. Further, suggests Marchand, such persons felt justified in withdrawing from the peace movement—but Mott did not leave the Church Peace Union—when association with it "might endanger the prospects of their primary reform cause. . . . "[15] Although his early neutrality had come under slight suspicion in Canada and Great Britain, perhaps because of his brief embrace of pacifism, at the time America entered the conflict Mott was in full agreement with President Wilson's view that a smashing Allied victory could only result in "a dictated peace, a victorious peace . . . an attempt to reconstruct a peace-time civilization with war standards."[16]

Mott was accused by Norman Thomas of side-stepping the issue of the mistreatment of conscientious objectors during the intolerance of 1918. Thomas had been shocked by the treatment received by his brother at the hands of intolerant "Y" men at training camp, and on the basis of several years' acquaintance with Mott, wrote personally to ask that the General Secretary investigate this "spiritual malpractice." Certain of Thomas' sentences must have cut Mott to the quick:

> My point is not that the Conscientious Objectors are right—you know my opinion on that matter—but that for a Christian organization to assume toward them the attitude of the YMCA is to come close to stultifying Christianity. . . . Surely I do not need to argue this point with you, for though you do not now agree with these Conscientious Objectors, in the case of some of them it was your own addresses at Northfield and elsewhere that gave them part of their spiritual background for their present stand; and as one of the founders of The Fellowship of Reconciliation in America, you are aware of some of the spiritual values involved in conscientious objection. I know the system is too big for you or any other one man to revolutionize, but is there nothing you and others of the wiser leaders can do to modify that attitude which tends, even in this hour of its popularity, to bring the YMCA into reproach among thoughtful men? . . . When under its auspices so often one hears preached a message of hate. . . .
>
> I think you ought to know what is being said, not only by men but by many men who have owed much to your leadership in the past, and who cannot feel that you view the present situation within the great organization you have done so much to create without some perturbation of spirit. Is it not possible for you to speak out on spiritual principles?[17]

Mott appears to have handed the letter to Beaver, what for he did not indicate. What else he did is not known, but it should not be assumed that he did nothing. Beaver was a member of the FOR, to which Thomas also belonged, and may have carried a message of reassurance to Thomas who was also critical of the treatment of objectors by the Army and of the Federal Council's seeming failure to protest.[18] Mott could well have spoken privately to appropriate officials in Washington on the larger issue, which would have been more in keeping with his approach to controversial matters. He may have disciplined individual "Y" workers, many of whom had been recruited hastily.

As may be imagined, the Church Peace Union was rent by internal disputes over its proper stance as War sentiment moved from neutrality to preparedness to jingoism. As a trustee, Mott was inevitably involved. He was hardly home from his first trip to the War zones in the late autumn of 1914 when he was asked to be president of an offshoot from the Union to be known as the "American League to Limit Armaments"—an early expression of anti-preparedness. He refused. By early 1916 some Union trustees, among them Mott, felt that the organization's leadership was going too far in embracing "politics" in the form of a stance regarding preparedness during a presidential campaign in which that was an issue.

The issuance of a potentially controversial statement by the Federal Council of Churches, in which Mott was also active, that might cause irritation or offense and in some way handicap relationships in the post-war period likewise seemed unwise—an attitude reminiscent of his earlier caution to Oldham against a statement on behalf of the Continuation Committee. By the summer of 1916 Macfarland of the FCC came to agree with Mott that this was no time to argue with Europe or to attempt peace-making. It was rather a time of unlimited opportunity for Americans to experience the compensatory benefits of "bravery, self-sacrifice, patriotic devotion, and Christian resignation" as well as to pursue the commercial profits from the War.[19]

After the United States became a belligerent, Mott supported the cause vigorously, championed the President, and called for victory. Although Mott was sympathetic with Wilson's aims, no evidence has appeared that he went on record in favor of the League of Nations during the period in 1919 and 1920 when the Federal Council, the Church Peace Union, and other Protestant bodies fought for it; he later supported it.[20] The vast YMCA programs were intended to boost morale and help keep America's fighting men in trim. Although some have interpreted this as jingoism or a "sellout," it was a straightforward attempt to serve "people caught in novel circumstances," as John F. Piper, Jr., put it.[21] It was, in fact, less self-interest on the part of the churches (and the YMCA, which Piper failed to note) than the discovery and implementa-

tion of new ministries to millions of persons facing new life-
situations—most of the YMCA's clientele being soldiers, sailors, or prisoners of war. Mott was one of few who realized that the War would be a
turning point not only for Western civilization but especially for the
American churches as they confronted the twentieth century which
would arrive belatedly in the 1920's. Under his leadership the YMCA, at
that time probably a more potent force than any single Protestant denomination and certainly much more so than the Federal Council of
Churches, set an unparalleled example in addressing itself to unprecedented needs.

Mott's constructive thought on the War was summarized in his
lectures, "The Religious Significance of the War," delivered at DePauw
University in 1917 but not printed. He compiled well over a hundred
pages of notes, culled by several assistants from hundreds of books, articles, and speeches. As Barton had remarked about Mott's manner of
speaking, these lectures contained "few flashes that strike the reader as
new," his strength consisting rather "in taking old truths and animating
them with the power of a big, vibrant personality." The ideas of many
writers appeared in what was apparently the final lecture of the series:

> At the close of the War there will be an unparalleled opportunity for
> reconstruction, for that will be a time of incalculable plasticity. The world
> that existed before the War has disappeared forever: we are living essen-
> tially in another era compared with two years ago. For the world it is a new
> birth, a great day of God such as comes only once in 100 or 1000 years.
> The means hitherto employed to prevent war have been proved in-
> adequate: treaties, alliances, the balance of power, secret diplomacy, force,
> preparation for war, and war itself: not even a fearful conflict like the
> present one will alter human nature or the nations to the depths of motiva-
> tion. Neither socialism nor organized Christianity has spoken clearly and
> compellingly. Nor have the arbitration movement, international law, the
> Hague conferences, the World Court, the League to Enforce Peace, or the
> peace societies.
>
> None of these has gone to the real roots of war: they have not brought to
> bear the only supreme power that can deal with the conscience, heart, and
> will of men—superhuman power. It is not primarily a matter of external
> arrangements or adjustments, valuable as these may be, but of internal
> changes in transformed human natures and lasting good-will as a result of
> conversion. Thus, all these things have been school-masters to bring us to
> Christ, whose religion is the one thing the nations of the world have not
> tried.
>
> We must, therefore, take Christ as Teacher and Lord. It is our belief that
> the principles of Christ are meant to be applied here and now and in every
> relationship, including the international. It rests with the Christian leaders

of Europe and America to establish a system of international life founded on justice and love as revealed to mankind by the teaching and life of Jesus Christ. Some of His principles and plans that are to be applied and followed are His conception of God, the Kingdom of God, the divine fatherhood and human brotherhood, the unity of believers, justice, the Golden Rule, service, and love.

We must wage a vast propaganda to create a new and right climate of opinion by laying siege to the whole constitution of man—reaching schools, colleges, the press, churches, literature, beginning with all Christians and applying the same comprehensiveness, strategy, and persistence that the world applies—in politics, commerce, or pressure groups. The danger is that we will try to get peace on too easy terms: it will not be a work of magic, nor can it be superficial or negative; it involves the reconciliation of contending forces, readjustment of disturbed conditions, and the changing of attitudes, motives, and ambitions.

Special responsibilities for these goals rest upon the clergy, upon laymen, upon students, and upon all to push the cause of missions because that is the one task vast enough and difficult enough and unselfish enough to pull the divided Christian forces into a real unity.

But let us not forget that this is a superhuman undertaking. It is the sovereign work of the spirit of God to flood men's hearts with love of God and therefore of men. He only can enable us to love the unlovely, or to love our enemies. It is possible for Him to end this war as suddenly as it began; it is also possible for Him to direct and govern the minds of those responsible for the treaty-making and the great readjustments that should follow the war so as to elimininate the seeds of future wars.

The unprecedented opportunities for real brotherhood rising from deep dissatisfaction with things as they are should drive us all to prayer as never before; although the occasion has no parallel in history, God's power is not exhausted: something far beyond our experience or imagination is possible. The crucial question for us in this time of times is whether we are going to believe in God a great deal less than we have believed, or a great deal more. There is no doubt which is the path of Jesus of Nazareth.[22]

PART 3: **When I Saw My Boy in France**

This was a sentimental age, or near the end of one. Almost every human emotion was played upon to sell Liberty Bonds and promote Red Cross or YMCA donations. When Mott spoke or wrote on "The Tradition of the American Mother" or "When I Saw My Boy in France," he evoked a response across the nation. He set forth without flourishes the concept on which these were based at a small luncheon tendered him in Chicago by Cyrus McCormick not long after the return of the Root Mission:

> Shall these men whom we love and honor and to whom we are related by these enduring bonds, shall they come back to us, whether they go overseas or not, shall they come back to us better men or worse men?[23]

Mott told his audience of millionaires that "a work on this broad base presents an irresistible appeal to the American people . . . and I understand that people." Proof came with the oversubscription of all War Work funds.

The idea for the piece on the American mother was given him by a general he met in France. The tradition was one of "the priceless treasures" being risked in "this battle for democracy." Mott used it in a promotional pamphlet for the United War Work campaign of 1918. Addressed "To the fathers and mothers who live in the homes with service flags," it described the YMCA and other agencies' ministries to men in uniform from travel with them on troop trains, through training camp, port of debarkation, and transport, to the huts sometimes under fire in France, resorts for men on leave, and services to prisoners of war. "Some day" these millions will come home—that is, most of them will, and the YMCA will have accompanied them "from the time they leave home until they return home, representing home to them during all the intervening months and preserving in truth the tradition of the American mother."[24] This propaganda bears the hallmarks of the advertising expert of the day, who was in fact Bruce Barton.

"When I Saw My Boy in France" was the cover story in the *American Magazine* for October, 1918. Addressed to the fathers of America in a sentimental style, it told how Mott, in uniform, and son John L., now in the 165th New York Regiment, met "in the muddy street of that little French town—my boy and I." They were able to talk "far into the night," and slept on the floor to avoid "cooties" (lice). I had wondered, Mott wrote, "whether, hating war as he always had, he could put his whole heart into the fight":

> I wanted to make sure that there was no lingering doubt in his mind that this war, and the winning of it, is for our generation the one thing that is supremely worth while. . . . In his mind was only one thought: pride that he could play a part in the great common struggle; eagerness to stay with it, to see it through. I heard no talk among the boys who are with my boy in France about the end of the war, only a fixed determination that it must *not* end until it is ended *right*.

For themselves, these boys had no fear; their only concern was lest the home folks worry: "Tell them that we're going to make them proud of us." Mott brought personal messages to the parents of John L.'s buddies; one, a rugged Irishman who came at night because of his work, asked, "How did he look?" As they talked, Mott thought, "Here is American fatherhood personified": in two million homes tonight hearts reach out to boys beyond the seas.

Mott (or perhaps it was Bruce Barton) then told the fathers of America that General Pershing's ideals were their ideals; that their boys were living clean lives in France; that the YMCA was doing for their boys what they would want to do if they could be there. "The Red Triangle huts are but branches of your home. The Y is being father and mother to your boy." He went on to describe the comforts provided, the program features, Sunday church services, the "wholesome, cheerful, kindly, good to look upon" women "like your wives and daughters" who serve as "sisters and mothers to your boys":

> War is a thing of bitterness and brutality and scars. But it is just as truly a thing of love, and of courage, and of triumphant faith. . . . War has sounded new depths in the hearts of us fathers of America. It has drawn us close to our sons. It has given us a knowledge of them and a reverence for them which years of peace never could have brought. We shall come out of this war worthier fathers of nobler and manlier sons. And we shall understand why it was that, when Jesus Christ sought to convey to the world the quality of God's love, He could express it only with the single word— Father. [25]

A box on the first page of this article featured the phrases in which three presidents, Theodore Roosevelt, Taft, and Wilson, had characterized Mott. [26]

The next article in that October American, picked up in a hut by a surprised John L. soon afterward, by Bruce Barton, was entitled "The Greatest 'Y' Man." It presented Mott as a man of the hour, a family man—with an informal photo of all six Motts at the Lac—a man of hard work, one who had set a goal for his life: "the complete abandonment of self-interest to the service of a vision—this is the secret of real greatness. It is the secret of John R. Mott." [27]

Widely reprinted in the secular and religious press, these articles played their part in putting the great War fund of 1918 over the top. Neither they nor any of Mott's utterances ever mouthed a word of hatred, a tirade against the Germans, or a call for vengeance. The most careful reading not only of his published addresses and those he selected to reprint thirty years later, but also of those taken down by a stenographer, and his own notes to a score more, reveals a complete absence of the popular atrocity tales and diatribes against the Kaiser or "the Hun."

The peroration of his report to the NWWC following his inspection tour in Britain, France, and Italy in 1918 represented the extent to which Mott let himself go in support of the War, save for his speeches in Russia the year before:

> There is all the difference in the world, there is the difference between victory and defeat, the difference between liberty and slavery, the difference in making this world livable for our children and our children's children, or something for which we shall hang our heads in shame. But we have got to pay colossal prices. It must be a military victory, and it must be a political victory. While we shall have to pay prices that may well cause our hearts to pause in this moment, God grant, my friends, that when the end comes and these boys of ours come back on the troop trains and the troopships, and you go down to the train to meet them—to meet your boy, or maybe go all the way up to New York or to Newport News to meet him, and as they come down those gangplanks, as they leap out of those car windows as well as doors, then as some of them are brought out on stretchers, then as some are led out, who will not be able to see with their eyes that did once see us, we will see them, God grant that none of us then may be afraid or ashamed because we left anything undone that we might have done in that year 1918, the climax year of the war. (Great applause.)[28]

PART 4: The Largest Voluntary Offering in History

Shortly after Mott returned from his first trip to the War zones in the late fall of 1914, he had challenged his staff with the idea of raising $250,000 to initiate a wartime YMCA ministry. A timid member wondered whether local "Y's" would respond to such an appeal. Mott is said to have snapped back, "I will be ashamed of them if they don't." They did. In the spring of 1917 when the War Work Council was organized on a budget of $3,000,000, he raised it from a group of friends in a few weeks.[29]

That summer, after he got back from the Root Mission, he proposed a drive for $35,000,000; it produced $54,000,000 for the YMCA. A year later the Associations joined six other service organizations in a United War Work Campaign that collected $188,664,230, which was 93 percent of $202,924,889 pledged;[30] Mott called it "the largest sum ever provided through voluntary offerings for an altruistic cause" in the history of mankind. He was the central figure in each drive. Altogether, Mott was instrumental in raising more than a quarter of a billion dollars during the period covered in this chapter.

In his conference with President Wilson on September 26, 1917, Mott explained the plans for the YMCA drive for $35,000,000 to underwrite an expanded War Work program inspired by "the opportunity of the hour in Russia and other countries." His recent experiences were unquestionably uppermost in his mind, having received by then not only full permission from the Kerensky government but a cable from Bishop Anatoly of Tomsk, "one of the three most influential religious workers in Russia," asking for more men. The President edited with his own indelible pencil a letter of endorsement provided by Mott, which George Creel, head of the government propaganda bureau, had drawn up.[31] The campaign was commended to "American individuals, families, and corporations" in a letter signed by George F. Baker, Cleveland H. Dodge, E. H. Gary, Arthur Curtiss James, J. P. Morgan, and John D. Rockefeller, Jr. Franklin K. Lane, Secretary of the Interior, also endorsed the canvass, and William G. McAdoo, Secretary of the Treasury, wrote to thank Mott for scheduling it after the Liberty Loan campaign of that fall.

Ex-President Theodore Roosevelt had been publicly critical of "Y" personnel, who he alleged were sheltered behind the lines when they should have been in the trenches. Mott bearded the "Bull Moose" at Sagamore Hill and emerged with a letter of endorsement:

> It was a very real pleasure to see you. I most heartily wish you all success in your desire to get the amount of money indispensable if the YMCA is to do the work which it alone can do for the soldiers.

From personal knowledge obtained from his daughter-in-law who was then with the "Y" in Paris, from his experiences of its programs in the Spanish-American War and among railway men, and especially because of its "large share" of the credit for the "successful construction" of the Panama Canal, Roosevelt now heartily approved the overseas programs of the Red Triangle:

> At this moment the work you are doing for our armies in France is of the utmost value to them; nothing could take its place. Any failure to back it up would be a veritable calamity to the army. I trust that the American people, whose sons, brothers, kinsfolk, and fellow countrymen are at the front, will think of their needs and will aid them by responding to your appeal with the heartiest generosity.[32]

Gilbert Beaver, Mott's intimate of twenty-five years and presumably an active pacifist, was working on the YMCA house organ, *Association Men*, in 1917. As the time for the drive approached, he asked Mott for "a brief message," not an official call to prayer, "which people do not read," but "a personal message and appeal from yourself":

> You have got the ear of the country now and they realize the titanic task before us and fully respond to the call to prayer. I wish I could be of help in selecting the topics that must be sympathetic with the present needs, the awful temptations to be faced, the rigors of the camp, the fierceness of the fight, the awfulness of the suffering, the significance of the victory which we reach for, pray for and as a nation are fighting for. What a joy it is to feel that the country is back of you in a great thing. [33]

And to the country Mott went, taking his appeal to the Associations to relay to the public.

The new demands for multiplied millions exceeded the potential of personal effort and the resources of his wealthiest supporters. As the chief executive of the national YMCA, he turned to it not only to shoulder the financial burden but also to provide the administrative expertise required by the drive. The YMCA had invented the intensive short-term campaign for raising funds for Association buildings and perfected it during the decade prior to World War I, largely under the leadership of Charles S. Ward, now with the Red Cross, whose advice Mott sought. [34] Drives for buildings at home were suspended during the War.

Mott now appeared in a new role. He had not previously been identified with this type of fund raising. Supported by a publicity bureau that was enlisting the volunteer services of some of the nation's top experts and backed by an experienced Movement, he set out on October first to kick off a drive set for November 11–19. Beginning in Pittsburgh he spoke to YMCA audiences in Chicago, Boston, Harrisburg, Philadelphia, New York, Buffalo, Utica, Newark, Detroit, Cleveland, Columbus, Baltimore, Hartford, and Rochester prior to November 15. There were usually two appearances in each city: the first a luncheon for a select group of Association sponsors augmented by community leaders and men of wealth, or parlor conferences such as those in the homes of George Eastman at Rochester or of Mrs. Arthur Curtiss James in New York; in Boston there was a select group of 200. In the evening there were mass meetings in large auditoriums such as Symphony Hall in Boston.

Mott's message was essentially that described in Parts 2 and 3, above, augmented by vivid illustrations from his recent experiences in Russia. He instructed Carter, Davis, and others to keep him informed by cable of unusual examples of heroism, sacrifice, workers carrying on under gas or shellfire attacks; he often read these to his audiences. His manner of speaking was far more relaxed and popular than usual, but still deadly serious. He lightened his messages with frequent accounts of conversations, name-dropping, and a skillful intermingling of statistics with anecdotes. Much use of the pronoun "I" gave a sense of reality; he was frequently interrupted by applause. An address given several times, "The Greatness of Our Undertaking," contrasted the needs of the War programs with the benefactions with which his hearers were familiar: missions, the regular YMCA programs, church support; he then compared these to the greater needs of the moment in terms of the strain and suffering imposed upon men and nations by the War, concluding that a great program and a great cause must be matched by great resources of men and money. In almost all of these speeches he appealed for volunteers for European service, such as William A. Sloane, Chairman of the War Work Council, "one of the busiest and wealthiest men of New York, who comes down to my office every morning and gives five-sixths of each day . . . and other businessmen who are placing their finest ability at our service in France, service that we could not hire with millions," or a Pittsburgh judge who gives his three months recess, or a rising young lawyer "whom I have just sent to Russia."[35]

Mott told the Boston City Club on October 11 that he expected New England to provide "at least $5,000,000 toward this $35,000,000," even if it called for sacrifice. Some individuals, firms, or families may have to give as much as $250,000 each, but "I fancy this much was done for the Red Cross. Nobody in this room will speak more highly than I will of the Red Cross"; the YMCA work deals, like the Red Cross, "not only with the bodies of men, but with the spirits of men and that is dealing with the morale of men." Because of what was at stake, Mott believed that many who had planned on contributions of $20,000 or $25,000 would need to raise them to $100,000, even if they had bought Liberty Loan Bonds. He then endorsed the current bond drive, declaring that one who has invested in it—the safest possible investment—should give some of the money so gained to the "Y" drive. And if that one claims that taxation prevents his having the funds, "let him not be afraid to cut into his principal, the way those men who have gone out there to put their lives at stake have cut into their principal, and their all. I am looking for men this year who are willing to cut into principal, and I am finding them in every city, and they are here in New England."[36]

The 1917 drive brought in $54,000,000. The Rockefeller Foundation gave one-tenth of the budget of $35,000,000. Nettie F. McCormick gave $100,000. Postville, Iowa, Mott's home town, contributed $2,800.[37] In exultation Mott wired President Wilson on November 20 his "great joy" not only over the results but for the "real generosity and sacrificial spirit" shown by every state and county, and his appreciation of Wilson's endorsement. He reiterated "the desire of our Movement" to strengthen the President's hands "in every way in our power." He then phoned the White House on behalf of himself and Cleveland Dodge to ask for a reply that day, for use in the closing hours of the campaign. Wilson answered that the results were "a national blessing."[38]

As early as Mott's March 6, 1918, conference with the President, the idea of a joint campaign the next fall had surfaced. Mott resisted, holding that the voluntary character of the organizations should be preserved. Naturally, the "Y" would reap a greater harvest from this kind of drive because of its proven expertise, but Wilson must have insisted, for when the two met in June after Mott's return from Europe, a joint campaign by seven agencies was agreed upon.[39] Plans went forward during the summer, not without some controversy, and on September 3 the President wrote belatedly to Raymond Fosdick, chairman of the Commission on Training Camps, asking him to request the seven "to combine their approaching appeals for funds in a single campaign."[40] The next day the group drew up an agreement to hold a "United War Work Campaign" for $170,500,000 during the week beginning November 11, and to distribute the funds on a pro rata basis of which the YMCA's share would be $100,000,000 or 58.65 percent. Cleveland H. Dodge was treasurer and Mott director-general.

Roman Catholic Bishop P. J. Muldoon described Mott's stance in a talk to a New York archdiocesan conference:

> When Mr. Mott was selected Director General, he said: "From this hour I am no longer a YMCA man. I have taken off the habit. I have become Campaign Manager for the United Drive." He took down every sign in his office which might indicate that it was the headquarters of the YMCA. Everything there now indicates that he is a representative of the United War Work Campaign.[41]

Muldoon also said that there had not been "one single criticism from any Bishop or priest in the United States," nor had any sign of friction with the other campaign managers been reported. There followed hectic "merger discussions and negotiations, involving, as they did for certain of the organizations, a threefold scrapping of the machinery, reorganization of the forces, and changing of the publicity program." The scant two-month period of preparation was vitiated by the Fourth Liberty Loan and a congressional election.

Mott's tactics were similar to those of the year before, but first he called upon his staff to take over his YMCA responsibilities so he could devote himself full time to the Campaign. He took a hotel room in New York and worked seventeen hours a day, going home only infrequently, to avoid crowds. Leila, who had a serious attack of the flu, worried about his meals and sleep.

Mott concentrated on the big givers: the Rockefellers and United States Steel stood at the top of the list with $5,000,000 contributions; no person of wealth in America was overlooked. Several dozen gave millions; scores were in six figures. Americans living abroad were approached through YMCA's and other agencies and contributed over $2,000,000, of which more than half came from China, $100,000 from the government of Cuba, $360,000 from Japan, and $100,000 from Mexico. [42]

Mott traveled in thirty-one states between September 20 and mid-November. Cyrus McCormick and John V. Farwell called together a small group of Chicago business leaders to hear him at a luncheon on September 23. Mott never missed trains, but when he arrived at the station the last train by which he could meet this engagement had left. He hired a special for $700 and, according to such authorities as may be relied on to verify a possibly apocryphal tale, arrived in time. [43] Rather than trying to cover all bases himself he coached groups of selected speakers, secured widespread publicity for his addresses—Barton was now head of this bureau—wrote for magazines and newspapers, and kept a careful eye on the timing of all releases.

Although the background for the drive was laid by "The Tradition of the American Mother" and "When I Saw My Boy in France," Mott struck a fresh keynote with a powerful oration on "Why We Need More Than $170,000,000." He began with homage to President Wilson for proposing the "splendid principle" of the united campaign, for the ecumenical aspects of which he thanked God. More than the stated goal was needed because of inflation, the rapid expansion of the American Army, the "most incredible growth" of the Navy, the great increases in civilian casualties, the widespread deployment of the armies in France, the shifting fronts with consequent losses of huts, and the increasing suffering of the British and French peoples. [44]

To the National Press Club of Washington he explained the advantages of agency cooperation in terms of economy, efficiency, mutual understanding, and the promotion of religious unity "without sacrificing anything that is distinctive." In these addresses he mentioned the Jews and Roman Catholics far more than in all of his career up to that time. He told the Press Club that he had said to the Jews that the YMCA could not do as well as they themselves in the safeguarding of their "religious positions and spirit," but that it would provide facilities for their workers; the same applied to Catholics "and all sincere followers of other sects." He believed that the President had in mind that the campaign and the united effort it represented would "promote unity among all of us."[45]

In the final weeks before the drive opened, a deadly influenza epidemic took twice as many American lives as were lost in the War itself. Mott's nephew, Ralph McAdam, died of it on a troop transport. It caused the speaking program virtually to be abandoned because of the bans against public gatherings of all kinds; Mott later cited one state in which forty percent of the fund workers were confined to their beds during the week of the Campaign. Colton described the UWWC executive meeting when the full implications of this were faced:

> Mott stood almost alone for proceeding. His own best laymen opposed him vigorously . . . on almost the eve of the appointed launching date. Against their judgment the majority did let him as Chairman of the campaign organization take the lonely responsibility for going ahead. Finance Chairman George W. Perkins came out of the room into the foyer beaten and baffled, exclaiming "What can you do with such a man?"[46]

A memo bearing the marks of Mott's authorship went shortly to all local workers, reminding them that both Liberty Loan and Red Cross campaigns had been successful under comparable handicaps, that the printed word had great power, that personal solicitation had not been outlawed, that small groups could meet, that the prohibition of public meetings (some could be held outdoors!) freed time for individual solicitation. They were urged to concentrate on large donors who were giving ninety percent of the funds; and, last but not least, "larger use than ever should be made of automobiles," especially in rural states such as Iowa: "No matter how much the epidemic may spread in that state, the Ford will carry its people over their goal for a large over-subscription." The author recalls agents wearing gauze masks ringing doorbells.

Not only was the Campaign hindered by the "flu," but the false armistice report of November 8 came on the very day that thousands of communities had planned their final coaching and organizational dinners and meetings; in many places the following day was declared a holiday. Then, "the greatest world news of modern times," the true Armistice, followed on November 11, the Monday the drive was to open. Mott stepped into the breach with this telegram to all state directors:

ON BEHALF OF UNITED WAR WORK CAMPAIGN COMMITTEE REQUEST YOU PROMPTLY RELAY TONIGHT TO EACH DISTRICT COUNTY AND IMPORTANT LOCAL CHAIRMAN OR DIRECTOR OUR UNITED CONCLUSION THAT NO MATTER HOW NEAR OR HOW DISTANT PERMANENT PEACE MAY BE THE LONG PERIOD OF DEMOBILIZATION AND THE PERIOD WHICH WILL PRECEDE DEMOBILIZATION WILL PRESENT GREATER NEED THAN EVER FOR THE SERVICE OF THE SEVEN COOPERATING ORGANIZATIONS AND THEREFORE THAT THE REQUESTED OVERSUBSCRIPTION OF FIFTY PER CENT IS MOST NECESSARY. OUR ADVISERS OF THE AMERICAN ARMY AND NAVY CONCUR IN THIS JUDGMENT. I HAVE CONFERRED ON THE SUBJECT WITH WAR DEPARTMENT AND PRESIDENT WILSON AND THEY STRONGLY EMPHASIZE NEED AND IMPORTANCE OF THIS WORK FOR THE PERIOD TO FOLLOW CESSATION OF HOSTILITIES. LETTER FROM PRESIDENT WILSON WILL APPEAR WITHIN TWO DAYS EXPRESSING HIS SATISFACTION THAT OUR PLANS HAVE BEEN ENLARGED TO RENDER THIS GREAT PATRIOTIC SERVICE. THE MONTHS FOLLOWING VICTORIOUS ENDING OF WAR WILL BE ACCOMPANIED WITH SPECIAL DANGERS. WE NEED NOT BE SOLICITOUS FOR OUR SOLDIERS AND SAILORS WHEN THEY ARE DRILLING AND FIGHTING AND CONFRONTING THE GREAT ADVENTURE OF LIFE AND DEATH BUT RATHER WHEN THIS GREAT INCITEMENT IS WITHDRAWN AND DISCIPLINE RELAXED AND HOURS OF LEISURE MULTIPLIED AND TEMPTATIONS ARE INCREASED. THE SEVEN ORGANIZATIONS WILL THEN BE MORE NEEDED THAN EVER TO PREVENT PERIOD OF DEMOBILIZATION BECOMING PERIOD OF DEMORALIZATION. IT TOOK OVER TWO YEARS TO COMPLETE DEMOBILIZATION AFTER THE FRANCO PRUSSIAN WAR EIGHTEEN MONTHS AFTER TURCO RUSSIAN WAR TEN MONTHS AFTER SOUTH AFRICAN WAR THIRTEEN MONTHS AFTER RUSSO JAPANESE WAR. ALL WITH WHOM WE HAVE CONSULTED AGREE THAT IT WILL REQUIRE MORE THAN ONE YEAR TO DEMOBILIZE AMERICAN FORCES. FOR THIS PERIOD OF GRAVEST DANGER OUR ORGANIZATIONS ARE PLANNING TO ENLARGE GREATLY OUR PHYSICAL AND SOCIAL PROGRAM BY PRESENTING SUCH HELPFUL COUNTER-ATTRACTIONS AS TO KEEP MEN FROM WRONG ASSOCIATIONS AND PRACTICES. WE ARE ALSO EXTENDING GREAT EDUCATIONAL PROGRAM INVOLVING USING OF THOUSANDS OF TEACHERS AND SPENDING MILLIONS OF DOLLARS ON TEXT BOOKS AND REFERENCE BOOKS. REMARKABLE RELIGIOUS PROGRAM WILL BE CONDUCTED INCLUDING USING OF LEADING RELIGIOUS PREACHERS AND TEACHERS OF AMERICA. TO OCCUPY ALL OF THE TIME OF OUR MEN IN THESE USEFUL WAYS WILL COST MUCH MORE THAN TO HELP THEM DURING FRAGMENTS OF THEIR TIME. WE THEREFORE CALL UPON ENTIRE AMERICAN PEOPLE TO SUBSCRIBE GENEROUSLY IN GRATEFUL RECOGNITION OF THE MARVELOUS SERVICE RENDERED BY OUR MEN AND WITH THE FIRM PURPOSE TO MAKE THE PERIOD OF DEMOBILIZATION NOT A PERIOD OF PHYSICAL MENTAL AND MORAL DETERIORATION OR WEAKENING BUT RATHER A PERIOD OF CHARACTER BUILDING OF GROWTH IN USEFUL KNOWLEDGE AND WORKING EFFICIENCY AND OF PREPARATION FOR ASSUMING LARGER RESPONSIBILITIES AS CITIZENS ON THEIR RETURN HOME. PLEASE GIVE THIS MESSAGE IMMEDIATELY TO PRESS.

John R. Mott[47]

On Sunday morning, the tenth, President Wilson's letter expressing his "earnest hope" for "abundant success" appeared in newspapers throughout the country. At Mott's telephoned request it had been added to at the last moment; the original document bears the familiar markings of the professor-president's indelible pencil. In addition there were endorsements by half of Wilson's cabinet, General Pershing, Marshall Foch, Chief Justice Taft, that "great sister organization the American Red Cross," the Roman Catholic hierarchy, Protestant pastors, and Jewish rabbis. As the first week of the Campaign neared its end, the directors in all forty-eight states received another telegram from Mott:

> PRESIDENT WILSON HAS JUST SENT IMPORTANT TELEGRAM ADDRESSED CONJOINTLY TO ME AS DIRECTOR GENERAL AND CLEVELAND DODGE AS TREASURER UNITED WAR WORK CAMPAIGN READING AS FOLLOWS:
>
>> QUOTE. WHITE HOUSE, WASHINGTON, NOVEMBER 15. 1918, I AM SURE THAT THE ENTIRE AMERICAN PEOPLE ARE FOLLOWING WITH EAGER AND RESPONSIVE INTEREST THE PROGRESS OF THE UNITED WAR WORK CAMPAIGN. NOW THAT THE CESSATION OF HOSTILITIES HAS COME WE HAVE ENTERED UPON A PERIOD IN WHICH THE WORK OF OUR SEVEN WELFARE AGENCIES ASSUMES IF POSSIBLE AN ADDED IMPORTANCE. THE INCITEMENT UNDER WHICH OUR SOLDIERS AND SAILORS HAVE BEEN WORKING IS WITHDRAWN, THEIR HOURS OF LEISURE ARE MUCH MORE NUMEROUS, THEIR TEMPTATIONS ARE GREATLY MULTIPLED AND INTENSIFIED. IT IS CLEAR THAT TO MINISTER TO THEM FOR ALL OF THEIR TIME IS GOING TO REQUIRE A LARGER FINANCIAL OUTLAY THAN WHEN THEY WERE BEING SERVED FOR BUT A SMALL FRACTION OF THEIR TIME. ONLY TWO DAYS REMAIN BEFORE THE CAMPAIGN CLOSES AND VERY MUCH MORE MONEY WILL BE NEEDED BEFORE THE DESIRED LARGE OVERSUBSCRIPTION IS SECURED. I CANNOT BUT BELIEVE THAT OUR PEOPLE FROM ONE END OF THE COUNTRY TO THE OTHER WILL RALLY IN GENEROUS AND SACRIFICIAL GIVING TO COMPLETE THIS FUND AND TO GIVE OUR MEN THIS FRESH AND UNMISTAKABLE EVIDENCE THAT WE ARE ALL STILL BEHIND THEM AND WITH THEM DURING THEIR PATIENT AND LONG VIGIL IN OUR BEHALF AND IN THE SOLE INTEREST OF COMPLETING THE HIGH PATRIOTIC DUTY ON WHICH WE SENT THEM FORTH. UNQUOTE.
>
> JOHN R. MOTT[48]

The deadline was extended to November 20. Mott's plea for "more than $170,000,000" was answered by a $33,000,000 oversubscription.

John D. Rockefeller, Jr., who knew the inside story of the drive, wrote to congratulate Mott on its "complete and overwhelming success." I do hope, he added, that very shortly "you can plan for at least some days of complete rest and change. . . . It is wonderful how well you have stood the prolonged and severe strain."[49] Nettie Fowler McCormick, confessing the difficulty of calling him "Dr." Mott—"Mr. Mott seems more like the much loved youth of long ago, so welcome at our house"—wrote that his praise was on a million lips for what he had done "in the *great crisis* in world-history of these four years past."[50] Mott was so tired that he dated several memos "1818" instead of 1918; he took one long week-end off and then ten days at Christmas at White Sulphur Springs, West Virginia. A Catholic colleague in the UWWC wrote in retrospect:

> John Mott in the present day has the conviction, and perhaps the aim, of John Wesley or John Calvin in their day, with a zeal and force that compel favorable consideration, and without the prejudice and animosity of the 16th century. He is like our own John Tetzel ... but is a better collector, and his selling argument—of man being his brother's keeper, of money being a stewardship, of bread cast upon the waters returning a hundred-fold—seems to get better results, or at least starts no schisms, as compared to the old-fashioned but still sound plea for prayers for the dead and faith without good works being of no avail.[51]

Galen M. Fisher described the UWWC as "the master-stroke" of Mott's money-raising career. The next June he was honored with the Distinguished Service Medal.[52] When the author spent a day with him in 1950, he referred again and again to the War Fund drive as the climax for which all previous solicitation had been but preparation.[53]

PART 5: From "Foreign Work" to "World Service"

Although the foreign venture of the North American YMCA's (Canada remained a partner after her administrative separation in 1912) suffered a slight hesitation at the outbreak of the War in 1914, each following year was successively reported as the best in its history. By 1919 the annual budget passed a million dollars, twice what it had been in 1915. The largest factor in this phenomenal increase, paralleling as it did the vast expansion of YMCA enterprises which have just been reviewed, was the impact of the statesmanlike and comprehensive report of the "Messer Commission" to the convention of 1916. L. Wilbur Messer had been somewhat typical of metropolitan general secretaries, in that he had not shown much enthusiasm for the foreign program and was somewhat cool toward Mott. In 1913–14 Messer devoted a sabbatical to a world tour of YMCA's, returning full of enthusiasm for what he saw, a result behind which Mott's subtle touch is discernible. Messer's report resulted in a reorganization of the Foreign Department but more importantly it laid the responsibility for funding the program on the local Associations.

By this time the building program adopted at the White House Conference of 1910, which had been largely Mott's enterprise, had been essentially completed. A less spectacular campaign, but one resulting in even larger contributions, was quietly, almost privately, launched by Mott in the late months of the War, having been planned as early as 1916: it was a major preoccupation during the long hours of relative leisure on the trip to and from Petrograd. Mott revealed his thinking to a meeting of the department in September, 1917, and developed his argument on several other occasions: "If we are truly to win this World War," he began, "we must concern ourselves more with winning the world." Unless we have a plan for enlargement, we may shrink, and in some places, collapse in inevitable defeat. The countries that we have not occupied ought not to be penalized because of the sins of Europe and America. "If you dislike the word sins," he interpolated, "let me use another word that you will accept": why should we penalize Asia, Latin America, and Africa because of the preoccupation of Europe and America [with war]? We must extend the plans of the YMCA to reach out to great areas of need because now is a time of "unparalleled opportunity, danger, and urgency in those parts of the world." We must send wise guides and leaders to non-Christian peoples. We must not settle back into a holding operation. "This is the time to deal in large dimensions. A Christ who is not able to deal simultaneously with the non-Christian world and the European War is not a Christ who is able to deal with the European War." Every moment of great suffering since Calvary has been a moment of creativity:

> I think of those unending crosses. I think of those multitudes of little crosses that I have seen over the fields of Eastern and Western Europe. I think with great vividness and distinctness of those countless homes that I have visited across which the dark shadow has been cast by this war. I think of those countless hospitals that I have visited. I think of the piercing cries of young wives and little children for the fathers and husbands who have gone forth to the war, and I say, there must be leadership somewhere among us to take advantage of this hour—this time of suffering—for great creative works.[54]

Mott may well have been emboldened to make this appeal in part because Colton had reported "vigorous sentiment" among the secretaries attending their professional conference a few weeks before in favor of maintaining the foreign enterprise at all costs during the War. Mott had spoken in this vein at a recent Canadian National Council meeting in Ottawa, and the viewpoint was widely circulated throughout the Movement.[55]

He projected a $5,000,000 foreign building program for 1917–22, to be obtained in large gifts by individual solicitation, in which he had the able assistance of Eddy and others including Colton after his return from Russia. The list of donors is a roster of Mott's friends and supporters of the era. According to his notes, John D. Rockefeller, Jr., in response to a "formidable appeal" drafted largely by Colton, "paid in full" $1,250,000. One pledge of $250,000 was "repudiated," several were "released" and a few proved "uncollectible." Cyrus McCormick gave $100,000, his mother $150,000. New names of large donors appeared: Kresge, Nichols, Jordan, Dollar, Lockhart, Crosby, Harkness, Severance, Ayer, Gamble, Scovill. Many designated their gifts for specific sites: Wuchang, Tainan, Calcutta Boys', Foochow, Dairen, Hankow, Kiangnan Conference site, Montevideo, Osaka, Madras, Seoul. Ultimately some $6,000,000 was raised.[56]

How the wartime operations of the American Associations led them into vast post-War expansion in eastern Europe will be a major theme in Chapter 11, but the essential fact was that what had begun thirty years before as a sending operation to peoples that sat in darkness was transformed by the War into a world service among equals. In 1923 the "overseas" work in Europe would be merged into the foreign division. It is impossible to deal with individual countries here, though it must be remembered that throughout this hectic period Mott was in constant touch with staff and developments in every city to which the American YMCA had expanded. At the risk of repetition it must be said with Latourette that the "expansion, the developments, and the diversification" of "Y" programs around the world were "by no means due entirely to funds and leadership from North America": these were "contributions to brother Movements," and Western secretaries were charged to make themselves unnecessary. Increasingly, local staffs were composed of nationals, a process greatly expedited by the calls to more than a score of American and Canadian foreign secretaries to serve on the War fronts.[57] Mott's convictions regarding world YMCA outreach and his ability to produce much of its funding were undoubtedly among the primary though underemphasized reasons why he had been called to the General Secretaryship in 1915.

PART 6: **Keeping the Home Fires Burning**

The enormous burden of the administration of the enterprises for which Mott was responsible was shared by a hand-picked team only a few of whose members could keep up with his limitless energy. Brockman proved to be a less able administrator than Mott had hoped, and there were moments when the patience of some colleagues was strained, chiefly because of failures of communication, but on the whole the headquarters staff performed to the satisfaction of their head, who rarely failed to tell them of his pleasure in their achievements. During the War years they traveled in North America more than he did, serving "as scouts to the chief," as one of them put it. Tied to commitments in New York City, he began to make increasing use of the long-distance telephone, which saved many a mile.

The exceptions to lessened domestic travel were Mott's speaking tours in behalf of the several War Funds and thirty trips to Washington where he spent thirty-three days between January, 1917, and April, 1920. This usually meant boarding a sleeper at Pennsylvania Station before midnight, so as not to lose precious daytime hours; a good night's sleep was assured and Mott would arrive in the capital fresh for a full day of appointments. Late afternoon or early evening return made it possible to sleep in his own bed in Montclair, though during the periods of greatest stress he could stay at one of the hotels in the Grand Central complex that was accessible from his office without going outdoors.

Although he once remarked that he had seen President Wilson on an average of every two weeks during the year and a half of American participation in the War, he went to Washington on a wide range of business matters that brought him in touch with cabinet members and high military and civilian members of the government, for he believed in going to the top. Only once did he apparently go over the heads of subordinates in an appeal directly to the President. After discussing the matter with Wilson on August 23, 1918, Mott wrote the next day setting forth the dilemma of the YMCA in France caused by delay in the issuance of passports for desperately needed personnel: There were, he pointed out, 2,834 men and 531 women "ready to sail in from one hour to two weeks"—700 of them waiting in New York City—if passports and steamer accommodations could be obtained. The "Y" had a ship available and could transport 1,200 if "the Military Intelligence Bureau of the War Department and the Passport Bureau of the State Department [will] cooperate with us to an exceptional degree to meet this emergency." A week later Wilson reported to Mott that he had taken up the matter with the Secretary of War, who had promised to press it "in order to expedite the departure of those who are straining at the leash."[58]

A high point of such visits was a June day in 1919 when Secretary of War Newton D. Baker, in a white linen suit, without fanfare other than the presence of news photographers, pinned the Distinguished Service Medal on Mott's black morning coat.[59]

Most of the meetings of the Commission on Training Camp Activities, chaired by Raymond B. Fosdick, of which Mott was a member, took place in Washington. Here he could bring to bear the experience of the YMCA upon certain unique problems created by the War. As Allen F. Davis put it in *Spearheads for Reform,* this was a medium through which "many of the diverse progressive movements that the settlements [to which must be added the YMCA's] had been promoting for years seemed to win acceptance"; some of "the most impressive victories" were won by the Fosdick Commission:

> With the aid of other private agencies the commission set out to apply the techniques of social work, recreation and community organization to the problems of mobilizing, entertaining, and protecting the American serviceman at home and abroad. They organized community singing and baseball, post exchanges and theatres, and even provided university extension courses for the troops. Moving out into the communities near the military bases, they in effect tried to create a massive settlement house around each camp. No army had ever seen anything like it before, but it was an outgrowth of the recreation and community organization movement, and a victory for those who had been arguing for the creative use of leisure time.[60]

Davis goes on to point out that the Fosdick Commission "continued the Progressive crusades against alcohol and prostitution," both of which goals, it may be added, were congenial to Mott, by obtaining legislation establishing zones around each military camp where prostitutes were prohibited, and outlawing the sale of liquor to men in uniform. The motto was "Fit to Fight," and by the end of 1917 every major red light district in the country had been closed and the army could be said to be "the cleanest since Cromwell's day." One is reminded of Mott's White Cross endeavors as a Cornell undergraduate, and his talks around the world on personal purity.

He continued as a member of the board of Near East Relief. Although he was on intimate terms with Wilson and the men whom Joseph L. Grabill describes in *Protestant Diplomacy and the Near East* as the president's "unofficial cabinet"—chiefly Cleveland H. Dodge and James L. Barton—there is no evidence that he participated in the intrigues Grabill describes on the part of that group to influence the President's policies toward Turkey and the Near East. Nor did he ever discuss such matters with Wilson, though his own experiences in Turkey in 1895 and in 1911 would naturally have made him sympathetic to their aims, especially those related to the Armenians.[61]

As General Secretary of the American YMCA, Mott was inevitably brought closer to several of its programs with which he had not previously been too familiar. Of these, boys' work appears to have intrigued him the most. Or perhaps the creative leaders of this program, such as David R. Porter but especially Edgar M. Robinson, were most effective in touching his interest in the training of future leadership and strengthening his long-held conviction that youth should be enlisted during the plastic years—a prime example of the influence of a department head upon his chief. Mott spoke autobiographically on "The Strategic Importance of Work with Boys": "The greatest visions I have ever known came to me as a boy out on the prairies of Iowa . . . boys have visions, the likes of which I do not find among the college men." The talk was published as a pamphlet.[62] In "The Reasons there should be a Special Work for Boys," he attacked the problem of delinquency. He reached the heights of wartime oratory with a speech in 1918 called "The Most Remarkable Generation of Boys the World has ever Known," an analysis of the need and a challenge to expand Association boys' work programs in the post-War era to meet the new social situation that would prevail.[63] Boys' work would become an international concern with him in the 1920's.

An area that was virtually second nature to Mott was the religious work department, directed by Robert Wilder until Colton returned from Russia in 1919. Their correspondence reveals the increasingly intractable problems resulting from the Associations' attempt to provide religious social services to the general population, as well as the stresses and strains that developed between the "Y" and the denominations. Among the department's tasks was the preparation and distribution of Christian literature that would serve the needs of men in the armed forces. Fosdick's *Meaning of Prayer*, with Mott's introduction, was reissued, as was the same author's *Manhood of the Master* and Richard H. Edwards' *Christianity and Amusements*. Endorsed by *The Student World* and other reviewers, thousands of these pocket-sized study or devotional booklets were distributed through the Red Triangle outlets at home and abroad, but the most popular was *The Social Principles of Jesus* by Walter Rauschenbusch, then the leading spokesman for the social gospel. The "Y" distributed 20,000 copies in the year of its publication, 1916; it had the largest circulation of all of Rauschenbusch's books.

The Atlanta Negro Christian Student Conference of 1914 had been a pivotal experience for Mott. The next year, as General Secretary, he acted to prevent D. W. Griffith's *Birth of a Nation* from being shown in YMCA's.[64] Soon after the United States entered the War, Willis D. Weatherford, student secretary for the South, called Mott's attention to the fact that although a disproportionate number of army camps would be located in the South, there were too few competent "Y" men to serve them. Mott authorized Weatherford to send 100 telegrams to talented leaders over his signature, which produced results. A War Workers' Training School was set up at the Blue Ridge conference center; Weatherford put eight contingents of 150 prospective "Y" workers through a three-week leadership course on which he reported frequently to Mott in New York.[65]

The eighth of these sessions was drawing to a close on Armistice Day, November 11, 1918. Weatherford, Will W. Alexander—who had received one of the Mott-Weatherford telegrams—and L. Wilbur Messer of Chicago, faculty members at Blue Ridge, gathered a small group of southern leaders to discuss the threat of racial violence that hung over the South as Negro veterans confronted poverty, racism, and lynching. A few weeks later the three talked with a group in Atlanta, deciding to try to set up an interracial council in every southern community. But this would be expensive. They went to New York seeking funds but found that "of all the leaders of war organizations in America," only Mott sensed the realities of the situation in the South. Alexander later recalled for biographer Mathews how with Mott's encouragement they had made their case to the NWWC:

> The Council was composed of business men, many of them of the type who headed the Red Cross and the Playground Association. Among the most prominent of them some violently opposed undertaking or participating in the sort of thing we were proposing. I remember very vividly that one business man, a prominent official in the War Work Council, was so opposed to the proposal that he left the room in a hot temper, and another man, equally powerful, opposed it. It looked as though the appeal was lost. Dr. Mott proved that he had not only vision, but courage. He stood firm and, as has usually been the case with organizations which he has built up, he was able to carry the organization with him. As I look back on it now, my impression is that most of the men who approved of the first gift of $75,000, did so because they believed in Dr. Mott, and not because they understood or sympathized with what we were trying to do. It was this first $75,000 that enabled us to start.[66]

The Commission on Interracial Cooperation thus came into being early in 1919. Weatherford ran "schools" again at Blue Ridge to "educate" some 1,200 white leaders while Alexander held a similar "school" in Atlanta for 500 Negroes. Subsequently supported by $400,000 more from the NWWC, this movement, which became the Southern Regional Council in the 1940's, "brought the best of both races face to face, and made them conscious of the friction points that existed." When the NWWC could no longer carry the project, Mott "assisted in making the plans which won the support of philanthropy generally throughout the country. Again and again he helped with counsel and advice and inspiration in times of discouragement." Alexander summarized Mott's long-range contributions to the Commission as having given it prestige and public acceptance: his insight led him "to support the movement in the face of the adverse opinion of men with whom he had the closest personal and official relations." His administrative experience not only in organizations but "with racial situations in other parts of the world" was of direct assistance, Alexander concluded.[67] Weatherford remembered many years afterward that the Commission had "brought about a new day in common understanding" and contributed powerfully to ridding the South of the menace of lynching. It was also influential in causing the YMCA to rethink its program for Negroes in the 1920's.

PART 7: Inspecting the Western Front

Mott made his most hazardous journey to Britain and the battle zones of France and Italy in April and May, 1918. Although German submarines were plentiful and ships were forced to pick their way carefully into mine-infested harbors, he was "conducted in safety through the perils of the sea." By the time of his arrival in London, April 1, the great German offensive from St. Quentin had broken through the British lines as far as Montdidier, and as he moved to France ten days later a second great German blow on the Lys again opened a wide breach in the British front—the lowest ebb of Allied strength. The authorities with whom he conferred believed that Germany had reached her maximum capacity to push westward, barring transfer of troops from the East. When American forces joined the French at Chateau Thierry in June (where John L. Mott would be in heavy fighting) and then in the second battle of the Marne, the Allies gained the initiative. As that summer dragged into fall, there was increasing but cautious optimism that victory was ahead.

Due to the great offensives on the western front, the interruption of
Channel traffic, and the closing of the French and Italian frontiers, Mott
could not plan an itinerary, but he did travel the entire length of the
battle zones from the Channel "along that vast bridge of steel and human
blood, across France and Italy, and on to Venetia, in the heart of the
Trentino."[68] This was the first trip during which he "did not give much
time to speaking," but conferred at length with the War Work staff in an
effort to ascertain "the immediate and prospective requirements of the
work" in order to promote its "unity and solidarity" both overseas and at
home. Such were his prestige and the demands for further expansion of
Red Triangle services that he was welcomed by royalty, by the highest
military command, and by top officials in each country. He and Charles
R. Watson were sent by the Foreign Missions Council to consult with the
British on the problems facing the Continuation Committee. Some time
was also given to the WSCF and to Russian affairs, for which last he
maintained a constant concern and perhaps considered himself still a
scout for President Wilson, whose letters of introduction Mott edited this
time.

Throughout the trip Mott enjoyed the closest fellowship not only
with Watson but with YMCA colleagues such as Carter and S. K. Datta,
and with D. S. Cairns of Aberdeen, J. H. Oldham, Marc Boegner in
Paris, and his own son John Livingstone. His expenses were paid by "a
friend." Among his grounds for gratitude to God at the end of the trip
were that every moment was "most fruitful," no time had been lost, all
objects were achieved, and he was kept in perfect health.

Beginning in Liverpool Mott's first act was to buy an overcoat. His
procedure was to visit national War Work headquarters, typical huts
(foyers in France, casas in Italy), and installations at ports, on transport,
in combat areas, and at hotels or resorts for men on leave. He held
"unhurried interviews with national executives" in each country; they
accompanied him almost all the time. He also conferred with divisional
and regional secretaries, who traveled with him, and met with local
workers "in every field." He required and received reports everywhere;
some of these were "exhaustive and remarkable," containing maps and
photographs, certain of which with General Pershing's permission he
would take home to show to the War Work Council.[69]

Personal conferences with prominent people "regarding important
aspects of the work" began in London with two conversations with the
Archbishop of Canterbury on April 2, when vice control was discussed
and the Archbishop declared that he would open the question of morality

in the House of Lords. One of these meetings may have been that quasi-apocryphal occasion on which Mott is said to have arrived at Lambeth Palace in the small hours of the morning in a state of perturbation and to have spent the rest of the night in deep discussion with the Archbishop.[70] At some point during this trip he talked with Ambassador Walter Hines Page, who advised him on the appropriate approach to the Italians.

During the interim since the collapse of the Continuation Committee, both its British and its American members and supporters had come to the conclusion that it must be replaced. Mott and Watson attended in London on April 4 a meeting Oldham had called at their convenience so they might confer with the "Standing Committee" of the British Conference of Missionary Societies. This group could not abolish or replace the Continuation Committee, but it recommended to its sponsors on both sides of the Atlantic that there should be a new agency "to deal with questions demanding immediate attention." Until a permanent body could be set up it would be called the "Emergency Committee"; Mott was elected chairman and Oldham and Maclennan secretaries.

Its directives, as Hogg has summarized them, were to handle all questions of governmental relations in which the societies were jointly interested (thus greatly strengthening Oldham's efforts in behalf of missions freedom), to "consider means to provide for war-impaired missions," and to act as "a clearing house and to harmonise the approach to major problems faced in common by all societies in the transition from war to peace." Within a few months this action had been ratified by both sponsors, the Continuation Committee moved to London and soon to "Edinburgh House" there, and a budget ratified. Thus was a major step taken from Edinburgh 1910 to the International Missionary Council of 1921: the new Emergency Committee, admittedly temporary, was an international body based on national missionary agencies, a proposal that had been dismissed as impossible at Edinburgh. During this week Mott also talked with Foreign Secretary Arthur Balfour concerning mission interests in Palestine and Syria.[71]

On April 5 Mott was accorded an audience with Queen Mary at Buckingham Palace between 2:30 and 3:15 P.M. The exact purpose is not clear, but news accounts of his remarks would have provided the British public with a succinct review of the current state of the War Work. The first matter discussed was the POW program, after which Mott reviewed Association services to British, French, Italian, and American troops. He told the Queen something of his plans for the next financial campaign at home and described the need to replace the 100 Red Triangle huts that had been lost in the recent German advance in Picardy. He expressed appreciation for the share taken by women in the work, and of the Queen's leadership and that of Princess Victoria who was also present. From Mott's notes the conversation appears to have touched upon Russia, and the names of Sir Arthur Yapp, chief executive of the British YMCA, and Archie Harte were mentioned. To enliven his reporting the event to Leila and daughter Irene (then cramming for entrance to Vassar that fall) he noted the room in which the audience was held, the seating, and that the Queen and the Princess were both dressed in blue.

On April 9 Mott went to Paris with Carter. Three to four weeks there, filled with routines similar to those followed in Britain, were punctuated by trips to the fronts, to Switzerland, and to Italy. On April 14 he spoke to the headquarters staff in Paris, emphasizing his pride in them and his personal appreciation. Bringing a message of assurance, he reviewed several of the more significant recent developments on the home front and in the structure of the work, the quality of volunteer activity and financial support, the improvement of the organization, and the expansion of services in the States. But, he declared, he had not come to make speeches or to witness the War, but "to see and learn" how to increase the efficiency of administration, to prepare for the next financial campaign, to "insure solidarity." The only limitations in the program were to be found in ourselves, he concluded, for there are none in our purpose, in the field itself, in the occasion, or in God.

On April 18 Mott talked with V. I. Maklakov, the Russian ambassador to France, whom he had met in Petrograd with the Root Mission, on developments since the return of the Mission. Pastor Marc Boegner later recalled, perhaps not entirely accurately, that on occasions such as this Mott had been "deeply concerned about our churches, our missions, and the Franco-American canteens for soldiers." There was, Boegner wrote in 1965, "a meeting of the [Paris Society] Mission Committee at which Mott, in the uniform of the YMCA, described his itinerary from continent to continent announcing 'the decisive hour for missions.'" Boegner noted that Mott had always seemed "well able to deal with any situation in which he was called to speak or act."[72]

Mott's trip to the battlefields probably took place between April 19 and 23, there being no entries in his pocket ledger for those days. On the 18th he had "shopped for John L." He met "his boy" in a village in Alsace. Young Mott had walked back from the front line, which chanced to be quiet. He came around a corner and there was his father. They talked at length and slept the night in their trench clothes. Mott's only description of the encounter was in the *American Magazine* article that October, mentioned in Part 3, above, and which John L. was surprised to pick up later in a canteen. Before leaving for home Mott gave Carter £20 for Johnny "if needed."

Mott told the War Work Council later that summer that he had been within "the sound and reach of shells all but two days" and described the "front lines," the trenches, and no man's land with the aid of maps brought out by permission:

> We then passed up into the advance section, or as the French would say, the zone of combat. There men's hearts begin to stand still. That is the great focus, as this map will show you. This map was corrected up to the hour that I left Paris. Up to the night I left Paris there were 606 dots representing Y.M.C.A. huts for soldiers—huts, dugouts, cafés, canteens, run in the interests of the American army and navy. We now have over 700 places where this particular industry is going forward.
>
> We go right up into the front-line trenches. I can just see one of those dugouts, out where I was the other night, between 11 and 2, in a wine cellar. I had to stoop to go down into the cellar; there was no ventilation except the door. I found over 100 American soldiers packed in there. The Y.M.C.A. canteen secretary told me he had been working sixteen hours, that he had made over 100 cups of chocolate, sending them out to the men in the front-line trenches. I came to another wine cellar under a front-line trench, in a village which had received 4,000 German shells that day— largely gas shells. The Secretary said one of the shells had fallen into the front end, and another at the other end, the Germans had evidently located it. The officer said, "You must not ever let more than twelve soldiers in at once, thus reducing the risk." I could tell you of scores of Y.M.C.A. men who are in the front lines. [73]

Near this time Mott lunched with General Pershing. Both men recalled their first meeting in Manila ten years before; Pershing commended the "Y" program in the Philippines and during the Mexican border affair. Mott explained that there would be another fund drive and inquired how many men the YMCA should plan to serve. He then spoke of his son. Pershing testified to the military value of the work and Mott mentioned President Wilson's interest in it. They discussed a declaration on the "venereal question," the increasingly difficult problem of adequate tonnage for Red Triangle supplies, and gave some attention to the problems of demobilization.

En route to Italy, Mott next went to Berne, where he conferred with Christian Phildius, and probably Harte and others, on the POW program being carried on in all countries by the World's Alliance of YMCA's, largely with American funds. In Geneva he attended a meeting of the executive committee of the Alliance. Italy had collapsed in the fall of 1917 and had been saved from total defeat by British and French troops rushed in to help hold a defensive line at the Piave; this stood until the end of the War, but the Italian troops were badly demoralized.

On April 30, 1918, Mott was granted an audience with King Victor Emmanuel III, at a small villa ten minutes from Padua. As he had done at Buckingham Palace, he made careful notes of the surroundings and of his impressions of the monarch, a small greying man with pleasing blue eyes and a good English vocabulary. Mott later spelled out some details for the War Work Council:

> The other day, the King of Italy, when I was down there on the southern front, sent for me and received me in audience in his little villa, right up there under shellfire, in a little room, I should say twelve feet square, with one simple iron bed and a little dresser and two hard chairs, and a few war maps on the wall. He had been cross-examining me, and saw the Red Triangle on my arm, and said, "What does that mean?" Well, gentlemen, I then had my opportunity literally to "preach Christ in Caesar's house." (Great applause.) When I had finished and explained what we are after— now notice this—he said, "Mr. Mott, I wish you would tell the American people to spread this work to the maximum in the entire Italian army." (Applause.)[74]

Mott had described the extent of the work in the Italian armies and elsewhere, mentioned President Wilson's interest in it, and gave a resumé of the POW program. The King pledged that Italy would hold on; Mott noted his dictum that "no such thing as injustice ever triumphed. No one who has tried to dominate the world has succeeded—Napoleon, Alexander, Charlemagne, Louis XIV." Both men had visited Russia and were perplexed by the revolution and lack of unity there; the King agreed with what was by now almost a cliché with Mott—"you may not understand Russia, but you must believe in her." Mott then told the King something of his own thirty years of travel, describing YMCA world service in terms of model programs for countries and for cities. They spoke of the effect of the War on religion. Mott noted the phrase "I've had it out with death": presumably they talked of how men became used to death at the front. Because of the King's request for YMCA services Mott remembered the occasion three decades later as a day of opportunity.

The next day he lunched with the King's cousin, the Grand Duke of Aosta; there were several colonels and generals present. The talk turned to the battle in progress on the western front; the generals were "entirely hopeful," believing that the Germans had spent their maximum effort and that the War would end by the spring of 1919. Mott found the company appreciative of the "Y" work as he described it in other countries. The Grand Duke "appealed for all that we can possibly do and that as soon as possible," after Mott had suggested 200 secretaries [only 150 could be obtained and because of transport the enterprise lagged].

Back in Paris, Mott devoted himself to administrative matters, convening both the headquarters and divisional executives and such visiting NWWC representatives as were available. A regional field organizational plan was worked out and put into effect late in June. Myron T. Clark of South America described all-day sessions under the joint leadership of Mott and Sir Arthur Yapp, chief British YMCA secretary. There arose a tremendous demand that Mott address all the workers in Paris. Time was somehow found and he did so at 5:30 on May 7 in the Wesleyan Church, which was "jammed full"; Clark thought it "magnificent."[75] Mott described the occasion to the War Work Council a few weeks afterward:

> As my last tour drew to a close, I said to our chief secretary, "Oh, that we might gain twenty-four hours, that I might conduct an Allied conference in Paris"; and by pushing up the night, as we have a habit of doing, we gained twenty-four hours, called an Allied conference in one of the hotels in Paris. Notice who were present: leaders of the Y.M.C.A. work in the English army—I don't like to use that word "English," I mean English, Scottish, Welsh, and Irish (Applause); of the Canadian army—by the way, they are a mighty close second to us;* of the Australian and New Zealand army; the South African army; the American, the French, the Italian— because I found three divisions of Italians blending their blood with the rest of us; the Portuguese army; the Indian cavalry; the Russian—by the way, the division that has suffered most in this recent offensive, relatively, has been that Russian division—that has fought a good fight. (Applause.) We are not through with Russia yet. (Great applause.)

After an aside on Russia, Mott returned to the Allied conference in Paris: there were

> leaders in the work among the Chinese laborers and the Chinese, who had come all the way from China, who came to work under constant shellfire; there we had the labor battalions of America, of Madagascar, of New Caledonia, of the West Indies, of Indo-China—gentlemen, I venture to say that never since Christ came among men have there been gathered

*Only rarely did Mott display this bumptiousness, which was so annoying to the Allies he was discussing.

within four walls leaders of so many great bodies of men, who had come together in one battlefield to unite under one great object, to make secure for time and eternity the liberties of the human race. (Great applause.) Therefore, the Y.M.C.A. has not only seen opportunity, but seized opportunity. [76]

The United States Navy brought Mott home to an unnamed port—possibly Newport News or Norfolk—as its guest between May 8 and 18; he paid the cost of his meals—$7.70. He found grounds for thanksgiving to God for the safety and health of the members of his family and for the carrying of his burdens by his colleagues; he had been preserved "in the midst of dangers in front line trenches and elsewhere under shell fire"; doors had opened across the closed frontiers of France and Italy, and there had been opportunity "to witness for Christ and His principles in high places, e.g., rulers, generals, etc., Caesar's household." He was also grateful that he could proclaim a message of hope in the darkest hours of the War, for his visit with John L., and that his own soul had been refreshed and enriched through fellowhsip with his colleagues. He reported to President Wilson the day of his arrival. [77]

During this tour of the YMCA fronts, Mott became increasingly aware of the growing criticism of the Red Triangle canteen operation. (Troops at the front expected to buy the same articles available at Army exchanges at home for the same prices.) In the perspective of sixty years this jarring note in an otherwise righteous enterprise is of minimal significance, but it offers a view of an almost hidden facet of Mott's character. As General Secretary of the American YMCA and of its War Work Council he took much of the blame personally. In essence the problem was that not until May, 1919, six months after the War was over, did the number of secretaries available to man these "grocery stores" rise to the original estimate of need, due to the bottlenecks in Washington and to submarine warfare and hence lack of tonnage. Canteens were operated at home by the Army; the YMCA added the cost of transport to its retail prices, but the War had ended before it was told that the Army was not charging for transport; as a refund it gave half a million dollars to the American Legion for welfare. Of the seven agencies providing services, the "Y" performed 90.55 percent of the total. Others gave away free the articles it was forced to charge for. The YMCA was the first on the field; it tackled the entire problem, which no other agency did. It repeatedly lost huts to enemy advance; they were costly to replace. By the end of 1918 Mott had requested the first of several government investigations that ultimately relieved the Associations of much opprobrium, but the conservatism of the War Work Council and the fact of a largely Protestant organization attempting both to run a business and to help men in need parlayed problems that brought Mott more than once to prayer "for patience and control."[78]

He addressed himself to the issues forthrightly. He preserved the outline of a talk on "Shortcomings and Weaknesses in Our Work for the A.E.F.," dated "May, 1818" (sic), that was either a presentation to the Paris staff or to the War Work Council. First and foremost, he began, there is the fearfully understaffed condition of the Movement; in addition, a number of key positions are either unfilled or held by inexperienced men without leadership capacity; some are not placed or replaced to the best advantage. We have poor business management in several areas. Failure to master the tonnage and other shipping problems is resulting in the work suffering almost everywhere for lack of supplies: we are, in fact, trying to make bricks without straw. Our weakest or least developed departments are personnel, post exchanges, the religious and educational work, and the program of movies. (Here he added later that he had taken up the matter of the exchanges with Washington on his return.) Relatively, we have neglected the Navy. There is a lack of coordination between New York and Paris and London. Not enough attention is being paid "to cultivating right relations with the French and British people and their leaders—both civil and military." We have not taken sufficiently long views: we seem to be dealing with emergencies rather than with a prolonged situation; we must make up our minds that we are in for a long war.

He worked out a strategy of seventeen points for himself, to begin with a series of pamphlets, their wide distribution, and the reorganization of the publicity department. There should be confidential letters written to Association departments and all secretaries and leaders asking for responsible help in dealing with the issues. A speakers' bureau should be set up. The work on the troop transports and at European ports should be improved and the best men should be placed in the hospital areas. "Study how to influence those who most influence public opinion." Try to get the cooperating organizations to see that it is in their interest to silence criticism. Facilitate a government investigation. Hold a series of coaching conferences, deal with returning secretaries, make constructive speeches, and personalize the issues as far as possible.

In actuality, he went further. On February 8, 1919, he spoke before a mass meeting of the League for Political Education in Carnegie Hall. There his strategy was to call attention to the approval accorded an overwhelming share of the total YMCA enterprise, while minimizing the criticism of "a comparatively small part." There were highly publicized dinners honoring General Pershing and Marshall Foch, whose fulsome praise of the "Y" constituted powerful counter-propaganda.[79] As the work of the NWWC was gradually phased out, a substantial part of its concluding effort was the preparation of a detailed two-volume history of the War enterprises, edited by Frederick Harris and introduced by William Howard Taft. This presentation was in itself a refutation of the criticisms, which were not mentioned. Taft paid a well-deserved tribute to Mott, "to whose initiative, genius for organization, and inspiring executive leadership" the work was chiefly due:

> He would seem to have been trained by Providence to do this work. There is no one of the present day who has a greater world vision of promoting the better side of all men and more experience fitting him to do so than Dr. Mott. His knowledge of the moral and religious spirit of peoples of all countries and of the effective method of reaching and stimulating that part of their natures is extraordinary. Leaders in centers of influence the world over have a familiarity with his genius and capacity. This has made him a great agent in the progress of civilization. No man knew so well as he did, when we were brought into the war, the problem we would have to meet, because he had made himself intimate with the conditions in all the war area by extended visits to the countries of the combatants and to their prison camps. Behind Dr. Mott was a thoroughly well-organized association of men in the YMCA who understood what welfare work meant, and who were eager and capable in solving the enormous problems of the war.[80]

The government had placed burdens that were "too heavy" on the YMCA. Nonetheless, Taft concluded, the story was a marvelous one of "American energy, executive genius, enduring patience, self-sacrificing Christian spirit and saving common sense."

PART 8: On Behalf of Missions

Although Mott was preoccupied with YMCA service programs during the War, his concern for missions never slackened. He held a mini-Quadrennial of the SVM at Northfield in the winter of 1917–18; it was attended by 700, the government having requested that there be no large meetings. His addresses on subjects such as "Shall a Program of Missions be Launched while the World is at War?" were heard with interest and published in a variety of magazines.

Oldham and Mott were in constant communication in spite of the slow service and occasional losses of the mails; important items were sent in duplicate by different ships. Oldham provided Mott with copies of all transactions of the British missionary bodies and of his memoranda to government, together with the replies. This included his intimate exchanges with Sir Arthur Hirtzell, permanent under-secretary at the India Office whom Oldham regarded as "a keen Christian" in whom the missionary enterprise had "a warm friend." Hirtzell, to Oldham's joy and his own relief, received Oldham as the sole representative of Britain's missionary societies, a quite unanticipated dividend from the unity movement initiated at Edinburgh in 1910. More than once Oldham urged Mott to come to Europe.

If such were possible, their comradeship deepened as the War intensified and their goals appeared to be increasingly threatened. In the spring of 1918, when the draft age for Britons was raised to fifty, Mott provided Oldham with a statement to the authorities on the indispensable nature of his service to the missionary movements of America and Europe. On November 14, 1918, while Oldham was ill, Mott wrote Miss Gollock, one of Oldham's colleagues, to "give him my love" and expressed his gratitude that the time had finally come to take up the old threads of cooperative international effort again.

On December 5, 1918, slightly over three weeks after the Armistice, Mott convened the American section of the Emergency Committee. The group outlined a strategy for presenting the issues related to missions to the American delegates to the forthcoming peace conference; a week later they met again, clarifying their aims and approaches. These were presented to the Foreign Missions Conference of North America at its annual session in New Haven, January 14–17, 1919. It handed the responsibility for pressing the case at the peace conference to James L. Barton, Charles R. Watson, and Mott, with authorization to go to Paris if necessary. Barton sailed in January. After President Wilson had gone to France, Mott cabled him on behalf of "all foreign missions boards of North America" their "deepest desire" that liberty of conscience, freedom of worship, "freedom for Christian workers to prosecute their educational, philanthropic, and other missionary work," and the right to hold property, be safeguarded "in the settlements of the peace conference." Mott and Watson sailed March 16, 1919.[81]

It was a great relief to travel again in the security of a great ship such as the *Mauretania* without threat of mines or submarines. The two men reached London from Southampton on March 21; John L. Mott had obtained a furlough to accompany his father as an aide. Mott's first appointment was an SCM conference in Surrey, reached by a long drive in an open motor, which resulted in a bad chill. He and Watson spent March 24 at the first meeting of the Emergency Committee, held at Bible House. Mott chaired the small group, to which no continentals had come although invited, while it forged a statement representing the "common agreement" of the British and American societies, to be presented to the British and American delegations at the peace conference in Paris and to the Prime Minister and the Foreign Secretary of Great Britain. The issues were the safeguards concerning which Mott had cabled President Wilson; a fresh issue was their application in the new mandates—the former German colonies. The Committee agreed to meet again when Mott and Watson returned from Paris.

That night Mott was a guest of the Archbishop of Canterbury at Lambeth Palace, together with the Bishop of Winchester and the Primate of Ireland. The conversation ranged over the peace conference, the mandates, the need for solicitude and tact in meeting the Germans again, and the prospects for a conference on Faith and Order. But Mott was extremely uncomfortable, for, as he wrote Leila, "that place is as chilly in cold weather as a house can be":

> I was in evening dress and attended prayers in the chapel where there never has been heat during all the centuries save what a few candles emit. The great drawing room with its lofty ceiling had one little fireplace. It is as though you had a fireplace on the outside of the church and sat around it in evening dress on a winter night. [82]

"So a real cold was fastened" upon him. He went to bed with it the next day but risked "pressing on to Paris" the following day, where George M. Perkins, a member of the United War Work Campaign executive, who was there inspecting YMCA enterprises, advised him to enter the American Hospital at Neuilly. One imagines that in spite of his illness Mott felt a new warmth toward France: since January 3 he had been a Chevalier of the Legion of Honor.

Confined for more than a week with what was diagnosed as "a light attack of the flu taken in hand just in time to break it," Mott held court from his bed: "By bringing people to me I did as much as though I had been about town and therefore spent very busy and profitable days," he explained to Leila, half-apologetically. The officers of the WSCF—Fries, Walter Seton, vice-chairman Cheng-ting Wang, head of the Chinese delegation to the peace conference, and Rouse—had their "first meeting in eight years as officers" around his bed, reviewing "the whole situation and projecting our post-war plans" and a conference to be held in August, 1920, to mark the Federation's twenty-fifth anniversary. The leaders of the French Student Movement came, as did the directors of the *foyers*; "many an hour" was spent with Carter, Perkins, and Brockman concerning the work for the AEF. Archie Harte and other YMCA heads came— those handling the projects for the Chinese, for the Russians, the Czechs, and the Poles in France, and for the POWS. [83]

After his release from the hospital, Mott, with Watson, lobbied among the members of the Peace Conference "about missionary interests," he wrote to Leila on April 13, describing the pervasive dissatisfaction with the "slow progress" of the negotiations; the air was "charged with criticism, uncertainty and pessimism." He had had a "splendid talk" with Col. House, President Wilson's personal advisor, but the President was "so fearfully pushed" that he had not tried to see him. In fact, Mott went on to Leila, "the President's popularity has greatly waned. It was inevitable in the presence of so many rival and conflicting ambitions and claims. I believe that he is doing his best to hold a straight course for what he believes to be right. He needs supplementing however in the practical application of his principles." [84]

Barton, Mott, and Watson learned from the Paris grapevine that their case would be greatly strengthened by including the French Protestants in their representations. It was their goal to have the proposed safeguards to religious freedom inserted in the covenants, the treaties, the mandates, and the covenant of the League of Nations. Opportunity for the first had passed before they arrived in France. They found that Oldham had foreseen the need in regard to the treaties and that there was already a clause in them that saved the German missionary properties, a great achievement to which the entire missionary movement was permanently indebted to the diplomacy and tireless efforts of the secretary of the Continuation Committee. In fact, Oldham had also laid the foundation for their representations concerning the mandates.

Watson later reported to the FMCNA that they had, with apparent success, gotten the ears of "certain committees and individuals" who had these matters in hand and they had taken them as far as possible with the British and American authorities. Oldham came to the United States and spoke at the FMCNA meeting of 1920. In introducing him Mott paid full tribute to the diminutive Scot's "constant vigilance," poise, rare penetration, and "general soundness of judgment," adding, "I know some people who have an international mind, but they lack an international heart that is responsive to the aspirations and the claims and the needs of other nations and races."[85] Although this varied legislation provided for the ultimate restoration of German missions, the German state of mind would be so exacerbated by the added opprobrium of war guilt that it would require much time and patience to achieve reconciliation.[86]

Mott's next move was a five-day trip to Italy, accompanied by Watson, Brockman, and John L., via "train deluxe in great comfort";

> We had a fruitful time with our workers studying postwar plans and the lines along which a permanent work had best be developed. We brought the men to Rome and so spent all the time there. Italy is most beautiful and sunny at this time of the year.[87]

On the return Mott touched Berne, Lausanne, and Geneva, and spent eight hours in critical sessions with the World's Committee of the YMCA. So great had the activities and influence of the American and British YMCA's become, that the central body felt threatened and a proposal had surfaced to divide it into European and Anglo-American entities. With Fries, Davis, and Harte present in addition to the regular members of the Committee, Mott raised major objections to the new idea:

> First we have been fighting this war in order that smaller nations and backward peoples might all have equal opportunity. The theory that certain large nations must dominate does not take into consideration such associations as Sweden and Norway. Secondly we have fought this war to protest against the idea that a treaty is a scrap of paper. The Constitution of the World's Committee has been built up after years of labour, with World's Conferences revising and improving it. Are we prepared to put it aside without consulting the alliances throughout the world?[88]

Christian Phildius thanked him afterward for his helpful visit, "which was a great encouragement to us all," and for the eminent services "rendered to us at the Versailles Conference and at your meetings with the English National Council in London. We know that the World's Committee possesses in you a strong advocate and we thank God for it." Mott likewise had eight or ten hours more with the Federation officers, three hours with missions leaders, and talks "with many individuals on all sorts of questions." Back in Paris there were full days of "conferences and committees and countless interviews."[89] When he wrote to Leila late on the night of April 23 he had been with Secretary Lansing, Colonel House, and General Bliss that day. As of that date, full documentation of the issues of missions freedom and related problems as the Emergency

Committee saw them were left with the peace negotiators.[90] For the first time in his long friendship with Wilson, he was unable to see the President, a final attempt having been frustrated by the Italian crisis.[91]

Early in the morning of April 24 the Mott party, including Cyrus McCormick, inspecting for the War Work Council, John L., and Carter drove to Coblenz to look over "our work in the Army of Occupation." From there they went to the British sections of the Rhine and thence through Belgium and "the devastated regions of Northern France," Mott crossing to Britain from Boulogne. Before starting on this final lap, he had written Leila that the peace conference was at its most critical stage. Paris was "charged full of criticism and more or less of pessimism." Mott told his wife that John L. had been a great help in every way, and added that "your YWCA are in front of big things over here but the difficulties are very great"; he had conferred with two of their representatives the day before.

On the evening of May 1, Mott entertained the Emergency Committee at dinner in London. The next day he presided over the second meeting of that temporary entity, on this occasion far more inclusive than a month earlier: Karl Fries represented the Swedish missionary bodies and Merle d'Aubigne the Paris Society; by invitation there were two from Denmark, one each from Holland, India, and Australia, and several staff members. The positions held by the group were clarified and most of the steps that had been taken at Paris were reviewed and approved. On Oldham's recommendation the Committee unanimously adopted a resolution urging common policies and simultaneous action by mission bodies in dealing with governments: this was likely "to become increasingly important in relation to the League of Nations." The objectives of the Emergency Committee ought therefore to be to consider in common those "questions affecting missionary freedom throughout the world, to facilitate common action by the national missionary organizations, and to authorize its officers to act on behalf of such national missionary organizations when requested by them to do so." The Committee then reviewed the current situation of each German mission around the world, to make certain that they would receive emergency support until restored. The temporary nature of the Committee was recognized but the need for such a body seemed inescapable; it was resolved to ask the British societies to release Oldham to devote full time to it, which was soon done.[92] Dr. J. W. Gunning of Holland and Dr. Henry T. Hodgkin, a guest, reported on a first delicate approach to the German missions leaders; they were found to be dejected and bitter.

Hodgkin told Mott in private that Würtz, in a 1917 letter never received, had reported Axenfeld as having said, "Don't blame Mott for the past but put on his conscience the responsibility for German missions for the future." Hodgkin described the "utter desolation" of "our German friends," who felt that they were regarded as moral outcasts. The splendid past of German missions had been the very life of their churches; without it he felt that they would languish. They considered themselves surrounded by enemies, cut off politically and economically. Although we have prayed with them, they feel that "we too regard them as moral lepers." If they could stretch out one hand toward us! They fear the Peace Conference. Hodgkin said that Axenfeld wondered how there could be a future for German missions when he was uncertain as to the Church's own future. Mott met only one German on this trip, Reinhold Schairer, a representative of the German SCM, with whom he talked in Geneva.

Informal approaches to the German missions officers were opened after the peace treaty was signed in June, 1919. The World Alliance for Promoting Friendship Through the Churches, meeting in Holland in October, 1919, asked the Continuation Committee to convene as soon as possible and to expedite the return of German missionaries to their stations. Five Germans attended the Alliance gathering, but they rejected any overtures until "the most fundamental and outstanding differences" between them and men like Mott, Oldham, and Ogilvie (of Scotland) could be ironed out in personal conference. After visiting the Continent that fall, Oldham became convinced that a small international gathering should be held the next spring. In preparation he and a few others met with five Germans in April for frank but difficult conversation; they were able to build a fragile bridge, convincing their former enemies that he, Mott, and other members of the Continuation Committee had in actuality been working on behalf of German missions.[93]

Mott returned home by slow ship in May, 1919. In June the American section of the Emergency Committee approved his and Watson's actions in Paris, accepted the recommendations of the British section, and among several other matters appointed Mott chairman of a subcommittee to handle any issues that might arise with the League of Nations. In August he wrote Oldham, who was ill again, from Lac des Iles that he was enjoying the best vacation in ten years and wished that Oldham and his wife might have shared it. Missions concerns continued to occupy the two men's exchanges through that fall; Oldham set up a visit to the United States, and Mott asked him to speak several times at the Student

Volunteer Quadrennial being planned for December 31, 1919–January 4, 1920 at Des Moines, Iowa. In addition there would be an assembly "of the greatest importance" of the burgeoning new Interchurch World Movement early in January; it would be "very desirable" that Oldham attend.

PART 9: **Student Volunteers in Revolt: Des Moines, 1920**

There had not been a full-sized, old-time SVM convention since 1914. Six thousand of the seven thousand persons who made this one the largest on record were students and faculty members. Mott, at home in the capital of his home state, was in his element, though quite aware of rumblings of discontent. He sounded the keynote with a short address on "The World Opportunity" in which he contrasted the optimism of 1914 with the bitterness, confusion, organized class hostility, and exhaustion of 1920, challenging his hearers to become active participants in building a new world by a thrust of fresh leadership that would apply the principles of Jesus Christ to industry, commerce, finance, and national and international politics. The watchword was not mentioned. [94]

As he had always done, Mott reported to the Quadrennial on the state of the Volunteer Movement. He chose to describe for this generation of students the highlights of its thirty-three ecumenical years since 1886. He spoke of the dynamics of prayer and of Jesus Christ as its attractive and impelling force, claiming that the 8,140 Volunteers on the mission fields of the world comprised one-third of all missionaries in service. In addition to missionaries from all major fields, world outreach was demonstrated by the presence of Fries, Oldham, Rutgers, R. G. Macdonald of Scotland, Henri-Louis Henriod, several Orientals, and Captain Pierre Maury of France, whom Mott asked specifically to work with Fries and Rutgers to devise ways and means of post-War reconciliation with former enemies in Europe. The older leadership was conspicuous: Speer, Eddy, Wilder, Zwemer, Watson, J. Campbell White, Bishop Logan Roots, Galen Fisher, Howard Bliss. There were also new and younger voices: David R. Porter, Samuel Guy Inman, Y. C. James Yen, Sam Higginbottom, Jesse R. Wilson, James I. Vance, "father" of the Interchurch World Movement, Tasaku Harada, Paul Kanamori, T. T. Lew, A. L. Warnshuis, Kenneth J. Saunders. The social gospel was pervasive; economic and social conditions in many countries were described and students were challenged with the opportunities in educational, medical, and agricultural missions as well as social reform at home.

But the students were in no mood to accept what they called "this piffle, these old shibboleths, these old outworn phrases."[95] They said they wanted the social gospel, though that was what Mott had challenged them with in his opening address. They wanted solutions to the problems of war and reconstruction, which again, Mott and Eddy told them, were the issues with which their generation must wrestle. Most of them were ignorant of the change in the concept of mission from the older attitude of Western superiority to concern for society and nation that had been quite clearly evinced at the Kansas City Quadrennial of 1914 and which the War had accelerated. If the planners had erred, they had failed to realize that thousands who would attend made no distinction between the Student YM–YWCA's and the SVM; in actuality, the Quadrennials had always been unifying centers of the entire coeducational intercollegiate organizations of the United States and Canada. Further, some veterans would remember the social gospel thrust of the 1914 Garden City conference and would expect a significant emphasis in that direction.

The revolt of the students at Des Moines, if it may be called that, may be understood if they are seen as the first contingent of post-War youth, a new generation described by Paula S. Fass as *The Damned and the Beautiful.* They were not there to listen. They did not want to be told. They could not sit still through unending hours of speeches as had their predecessors before the War. They wanted and needed to be heard, to deal with the immediate, and perhaps (unknowingly) to take a big step toward correcting that fateful fascination with the wonder and mystery of the Orient that had hypnotized their forbears and sent them off to China or the Antipodes out of sight, sound, and smell of the slums of Chicago or the injustices of sweated labor. They wanted to concentrate on the visible pressing social maladjustments at hand rather than "traditional questions of missionary work."[96]

They also wanted a greater share in planning such conferences and in the governance of the Movement. John L. Mott was among the dissidents. Henry P. Van Dusen, a 1919 Princeton graduate later to be President of Union Theological Seminary in New York City, became so obstreperous in a business session that, according to legend, Chairman Mott ordered him to sit down. Most of the resentment was directed toward Mott, though Eddy and Wilder were also recipients.[97]

Later that spring, so as not to appear to act in pique, Mott resigned his thirty-two year position as Chairman, assuming the honorary post of president.[98] He had been planning such a move for several years. The directions being pointed by the Emergency Committee were suggesting strongly that before long there would be an international missionary organization that would demand as much time and energy as he could give. The students had their way at the next Quadrennial, but Des Moines 1920 marked the beginning of basic changes in the SVM.[99] Mott neither forgot nor neglected this, the Movement that had evoked his first love at Mount Hermon in 1886.

PART 10: **Fiasco: The Interchurch World Movement**

The Foreign Missions Conference (FMCNA) at New Haven in January, 1919, that commissioned Mott, Barton, and Watson to press for religious freedom at Versailles, was exhilarated to hear the Reverend S. Earl Taylor, a Methodist missions executive who had once traveled for the SVM and would later earn the sobriquet "ecclesiastical buccaneer" from a Rockefeller aide, describe a grandiose scheme for the united support of missions to be called the "Interchurch World Movement" (ICWM).[100] Although it quickly spread across the Protestant landscape from foreign missions to home missions to social gospel to sociological research before an ignominious collapse in the spring of 1920, the primary appeal of the ICWM to Mott, at a time when he was shedding domestic responsibilities in favor of world commitments, was its original concern with foreign missions. He soon became seriously involved in it, but he was neither a founder nor an early supporter of this, the most ambitious plan ever fielded by Protestant boosters to amalgamate their forces.

The scheme had originated only a few weeks earlier; shortly after the signing of the Armistice in November, 1918, spontaneous stirrings had arisen in several American denominations toward what Taylor called "a new thought and a new place of leadership in this whole missionary enterprise," but it remained for the Reverend James I. Vance of the Southern Presbyterian missions board and a layman, C. H. Pratt, to invite representatives to an open meeting in New York on December 17, 1918, to discover "whether or not the churches were ready to unite in a joint foreign missionary campaign." Sentiment for a move "broader in its scope than foreign missions alone" quickly appeared, so home missions people were included in the call.

The tone was set by Vance's declaration that "the Church has come to the greatest hour in its history": the War has not saved the world; can the Church? If not, the world is bankrupt. Mott's brother-in-law, J. Campbell White, another promoter, and several others spoke; the idea of a great united campaign swept the meeting. The Laymen's Missionary Movement and the Men and Religion Forward Movement were recalled, but uppermost in the minds of many was the resounding success of Mott's $170,000,000 drive that had just secured pledges of more than $200,000,000.

That December 17, 1918, gathering in New York had appointed a committee of twenty, most of them dedicated promoters. Taylor was chairman; Vance, Cam White, Fred B. Smith—"America's greatest evangelist to men,"[101] Charles R. Watson, Robert E. Speer, and Mott were among the members. It recommended that a body to be known as the ICWM be organized. Ignoring the existence of the Federal Council of Churches, it proposed a "unified program of Christian service" in which the Protestant churches of North America would unite, "thus making available the values of spiritual power which come from unity and coordinated Christian effort, and meeting the unique opportunities of the new era." While it would be "primarily a Home and Foreign Missionary Movement," the ICWM was to be "broad enough to cover all those interests" outside of local church budgets "which are naturally related to the missionary enterprise through national agencies."

Taylor brought the proposal to the FMCNA in New Haven in January. There was extended discussion. Mott, who returned to New York for one day of the three-day session, did not participate. The FMC unanimously approved the creation of the ICWM and recommended that its own constituent boards join; it was constituted February 5-6, 1919.[102] Taylor became general secretary, the General Committee was chaired by Robert Lansing, and Mott was chairman of the executive committee. He addressed this meeting, which spent an entire day in prayer. His remarks have been preserved in part; they conveyed a message not unlike the conclusion of his DePauw lecture that was outlined in Part 2, above, but he went on to declare that it was now possible for Protestant Christianity to have "a plan that will be literally world-wide," which meant that "we shall shake the United States of America to a degree that has never before been done in any piece of planning."[103] Yet Mott's name appears infrequently in the official history of the Movement, in spite of his position. He spoke and wrote in its behalf, but one gains the impression in reading the archives that his enthusiasm gradually waned. The Movement had the advantage of his name and reputation for successful fund raising; much of his activity was in behind-the-scenes committee work. The ICWM was barely organized when he left the country on the errand to the Paris Peace Conference which has just been described.

A year was devoted to planning, organization, and selection of personnel for the ICWM. As it grew into a nationwide machine it was early realized that much of the leadership would need to be briefed if not trained, but certainly to be exposed to the oratory of the leaders. A World Survey Conference in Atlantic City in January, 1920, served as the climax of leadership training institutes held around the two countries. In preparation for it, Mott addressed a group of denominational forward movement leaders (there were several very successful parallel drives within some churches) in November, 1919, as they gathered to agree on goals, budgets, and relationships. He urged them "to create atmosphere" and to facilitate the solid support of the ICWM by its numerous constituencies and cooperating bodies, comparing the upcoming January, 1920, meeting to Edinburgh 1910.[104] He recommended to Fries and Oldham, both of whom were his guests, that they be at Atlantic City.

That gathering outdid most everyone's expectations: 1,700 leaders, "the controlling forces of American Protestantism," assembled in the upper room of the Steel Pier to hear three full days of presentations summarizing the surveys that had been months in preparation. In his introductory address Mott "showed how plainly the hand of God" had been in the Movement from its beginning, and he set the tone of the assembly:

> Without sacrificing our distinctiveness, we want to realize our unity and solidarity as we gather around the figure of our Lord with open minds, responsive hearts, and, I would say, hair-trigger wills—by that I mean wills that are eager to leap into action when we see a clear path.[105]

As chairman he was "always there with a firm guiding hand yet without obtruding himself; keeping things moving yet with no sense of driving; ready with the apt word yet without loquacity; knowing exactly how to steer clear of rocks and shoals yet not making the steering wheel too obvious," wrote Howard B. Grose, a friend and admirer, in *Missions*, adding that Mott could throw in "a touch of dry humor at the right time yet never at the expense of the dignity and propriety of a great occasion." What a contrast he was, Grose continued, to Earl Taylor, that "explosive dynamo," the executive secretary of the Movement, a seer who could make his hearers "see with him." Grose thought Mott's "calm steadiness" a "fine foil for Taylor's nervous impetuosity." In all, Atlantic City generated an atmosphere of "contagious faith and enthusiasm."

The conference reviewed the state of the organization, heard the reports of several committees, and discussed various criticisms and the defenses against them. But its main business was to hear summaries of numerous surveys, some of which had been made at great expense, of such diverse problems as migratory labor, missionary problems in China or Latin America, "the education of Christian leadership for the colored race," the problems of the church school, and rural conditions. Oldham seems not to have been impressed. In a carefully worked out memorandum prepared a month afterward, perhaps at Mott's request, he pointed out that "there is no such thing as survey in general" and that there were several types of surveys, much data for which already existed.[106]

One of the "most active" delegates at Atlantic City was John D. Rockefeller, Jr., who told the conference in what one reporter thought an "inspiring" address, that there could be no such word as "fail" in the future of the ICWM. There was instead, he said, the possibility of its almost infinite enlargement and extension: "I believe it will become the greatest force for righteousness in this whole world."[107] Although Rockefeller had been aware of the ICWM from its inception and had been urged to support it, only the previous November had he accepted an invitation from Mott to join an important committee.[108] From then on, quite possibly as a result of the acceptance he gained at Atlantic City, he "threw himself" into it, joining the Executive Committee and going on a continent-wide promotional tour with Taylor and a dozen other enthusiasts. More importantly, as Charles E. Harvey has shown, he provided a critically needed guarantee of funds to carry the ICWM through its financial campaign in the spring of 1920.[109]

The weeks immediately following the Atlantic City conference were critical. The fund drive was scheduled for early May, but the budget required drastic treatment in these final hectic days of preparation. Mott chaired committee session after committee session, for a time daily, until $336,000,000 was decided upon as the first year's goal.[110] He too faced a deadline—in mid-April for a long-planned trip to Europe. He became exhausted and with Leila went to White Sulphur Springs in West Virginia for a rest. They had hardly arrived when word came that his sister Harriett lay at death's door. Trains were not fast enough to get them to Postville before she died on March 10.

As the ICWM campaign neared, Rockefeller, contemplating it with tremendous excitement, begged Mott to remain in the country for it.[111] He did not, could not, because of longstanding commitments, resigning as planned but not until he had prepared a 20-point memorandum indicating where the organization needed to be tightened up and its weaknesses strengthened; this was an efficiency expert's analysis.[112] His position, as Galen Fisher put it, was responsible though not dominant. He felt some responsibility for the failure of the financial drive, which was the scandal of that spring, although it secured $176,000,000, 52 percent of the goal; it was the largest sum ever raised interdenominationally. Mott subsequently helped to raise funds to pay off the deficit, but Basil Mathews did not mention the ICWM in the Mott biography of 1934.

Mott sailed April 17 for England, to be gone for months. His friendly partnership with Rockefeller was undamaged and survived the collapse of the ICWM while he was away; Rockefeller was paying a third of the cost of the trip.[113] When asked by a reporter how his leaving at this critical juncture might affect the ICWM, Mott replied, "Not unfavorably, I am sure. The campaign is practically over, and I have done all I could to secure the result hoped for." He went on to explain that it had been "clearly understood" when he accepted the chairmanship of the Executive Committee that he would go on his "regular European tour this spring."[114]

Twenty years later Mott summarized the Movement's shortcomings: its goals had been "far too vast to be dealt with adequately within the set time limits," too little care had been given "to the selection of men qualified to master unprecedented and baffling conditions," for the leadership "was assigned largely to the promoter type" with lack of prophets, statesmen, and "wise master-builders." Mott did not mention them in 1939, but a few staff members regarded as radicals by ultra-conservatives gave the Movement a pink aura during the earliest of the post-War Red scares. He went on to note that the ICWM publicity had at times been "governed by the wrong motives and was too self-laudatory," and the management "had the reputation of extravagance," which it inherited from the War drives. The scheme to run the first drive on borrowed funds had been unwise, as was even the name Interchurch World Movement, for the plan was in reality a concurrent effort of the leading Protestant denominations with "all too little actual unity and fellowship." Denominational fears and rivalries, lack of collaboration, dissent, and jealousies also entered into the failure. But there were ecumenical gains, the surveys were useful, and certain of them were conserved under a Committee on Social and Religious Survey that Mott chaired; it later became the

Institute of Social and Religious Research. He headed it for a dozen years. [115]

PART 11: **Healing Wounds in Post-War Europe**

Mott's European tour of April 17 to August 21, 1920, was devoted to reconciliation, relief, and reconstruction. Among the last-minute items to be checked off a list of forty things to be done before April 17 were several college visitations, ten days of vacation, his resignation from the SVM, and meetings with two committees of the ICWM. His friendly supporters provided a $50,000 fund not only to meet his own expenses but those of secretaries, interpreters, and guides in each country, the costs of "many conferences and special gatherings" which some would be unable to attend without help because of inflation, and for "life and death relief cases here and there." The chain of command at national YMCA headquarters was established and the staff briefed on the journey. And there were letters of introduction from President Wilson.

Time was found for an interview by the religious journalist, Howard B. Grose, who described "five special objects of the present mission" in Mott's words. Doubtless because it was uppermost in his mind and affections, the first was to effect "a resumption of international action" by the WSCF. The next goal would be "to help bring about a similar renewal of international planning and co-operation" by the World's YMCA. A third would be to restudy the vast military and POW programs with a view to the continuing needs related to "twenty-three wars being waged in Europe, the Near East and Siberia." The fourth objective was "to help in bringing together again the Foreign Missionary forces of Europe and North America" in relation to the changing map of the world, especially in the former German and Turkish territories. His fifth objective, Mott told Grose, was "to sound out in the midst of the chaotic strife, pessimism and lingering death in parts of Europe, the Christian message of brotherhood, hope and vitality." Grose commented that Mott made the last statement "with a depth of feeling that cannot be conveyed in print." This tour would be "the most difficult and taxing, as well as the most needed, most timely, and probably most important mission" on which he had ever been sent—words that had been used before but which would be more true this time than ever.

No itinerary for this trip has survived, but Mott reported it in some detail to son John L., providing a few more intimate glimpses than usual.

A slow crossing on the White Star's *Baltic* provided time for rest and preparation. In London the most important conversations were with Fries, Rouse, and Walter Seton, treasurer of the WSCF, to plan for the Federation Conference that would come near the end of Mott's tour and climax it. There were extended talks with Oldham, who had been urging him to come as soon as possible, concerning the international missionary gathering that would be held at Crans, near Geneva, in mid-July. Daughter Irene had visited London and made some fast friends there; from this time on, Mott always looked them up when in the city.

In a week-end at Oxford, "over-crowded with undergraduates," Mott received "a great hearing" at Balliol Hall in pre-War style. He challenged his hearers to new leadership to replace men lost in the War, to apply Christian principles to society, to help "rising nations and peoples," and to confront the "vast secular and anti-Christian trends" of the time. "There was so much interest that I held an aftermeeting in the Hall of Queens across the street. It was filled and I was kept answering questions until toward midnight," he reported to son John L., now in India involved in work with villagers near Nagpur, in a warm letter reflecting a fine rapprochement between father and son. Mott added to John that he had run into Francis P. Miller and others, who sent their greetings; he had asked Miller to undertake a special mission that summer.[116]

Mott spent the most time in Paris where, during three different intervals, he conferred at length on the *foyers*; the American YMCA work was "pretty well completed." He was received by President Deschanel whom he thought "by no means such a forceful personality as Clemenceau." D. A. Davis, being groomed for a post with the World's YMCA, accompanied Mott on most of this tour. From Paris they went first to Italy, meeting with the American secretaries to plan the future YMCA program; it was later said that this visit gave "unity and direction as well as inspiration to the work" there. As of April 15, Mott had been awarded the Order of the Crown of Italy, which explains an odd entry for "scarfs and sashes" in his pocket ledger; presumably the honor was conferred on him and others at this time. He did not mention the decoration to John but described "one of the great spectacles of the Roman Catholic Church," a canonization ceremony:

> The whole made an impression of great ecclesiastical dignity and splendor but in honesty I must say it did not convey any spiritual impression. Rather one was reminded of a great human machine. How contradictory and out of harmony it all seemed in contrast with the humility and spirituality of Christ and His representatives of every age and of every land![117]

Traveling from Paris to The Hague, Mott saw much of "the terrible marks of the war and its desolation" in the devastated regions, but was amazed to observe that sixty percent of the area had been brought back under cultivation. His two days in Holland "were as always most enjoyable," partly due to meeting "scores of old friends." Half a day was spent with nine Dutch missions leaders including the J. W. Gunnings, father and son. They grilled him on his attitudes during the War and asked whether his intentions had been as an American or an internationalist. He countered with a recital of the positions set forth in many of his addresses, and explained his work on behalf of German missions both in fund raising and for religious liberty in the former colonies, his help to refugees, and the POW programs. Rutgers arranged a meeting with Dutch student leaders, at which Mott challenged them with the opportunities presented by the newly constituted countries, student migrations, "the Christianization of international relations," the new social, intellectual, and spiritual needs, and the reorganization of the WSCF at the forthcoming conference that should "enlarge its directive energies." Because of Holland's location, its neutrality and Oriental relationships, his hearers' linguistic access to foreign students, and because of Dutch history and traditions, they were peculiarly fitted to contribute to the Federation and to provide leadership. At Utrecht he spoke to a student audience on "Notes which Should Sound out from our Lives as Students in These Days"; the notes were hope, reality, loyalty, service, vitality.

Mott's first major effort at reconciliation with the Germans followed his visit in Holland when Miss Rouse and Rutgers accompanied him to Berlin, where, throughout most of the week of May 21 to 27, they were involved in "the most searching intercourse" with both student and missionary leaders. Both sides had wanted to open such discussions, the Germans having sent Mott a cable signed by Siegmund-Schultze, Theophil Mann, and others early in 1919 urging him to meet with them soon. When he was in Geneva later that spring he and Miss Rouse had met for several hours with Reinhold Schairer but little "visible reconciliation" had resulted.[118]

In preparation for the talks in Berlin, Mott had written out his reasons for going with the Root Mission, the chief of which was that it appeared to offer an unparalleled opportunity for service to the Kingdom of God, largely through expansion of YMCA services to men in uniform. In the course of the conversations, interpreted mostly by Conrad Hoffman, he branded the garbled version of his speech to the Cossack officers that had so shocked his German friends as an "absolute lie," claiming that it had been "a purely religious address." For them there were other problems: his "political" activities on the Mexican Commission, German war guilt, the Versailles treaties, the persistence of German misunderstanding of his efforts on behalf of their missions; even his friendship with President Wilson was suspect to these Lutherans. Pastor Paul Humburg, the new German national student secretary, was unconvinced of Mott's innocence and regarded the speech as improper for one in Mott's position as General Secretary of the WSCF, holding that Mott should resign or explain his actions. Mott chose the latter, in two stages; first in two days of eight to ten hours with Humburg and Johannes Weise, then with a select committee for two more exhausting days.

Yet Humburg still questioned the propriety of Mott's continuing to hold an international office in the ecumenical movement. The Germans remained convinced that Mott's idea of the Kingdom of God was too closely related to his belief in American democracy. As a matter of fact, some of Mott's intimate friends, among them Karl Fries, at one time shared the Germans' perplexity.[119] These grievances must be seen in the light of long-standing German distrust of Anglo-Saxon activism; the gulf between them and British-American viewpoints had opened as early as Mott's differences with Graf Pückler at Gross Almerode in 1895. Humburg was in fact a disciple and the biographer of Pückler, as well as the natural heir of nineteenth-century German pietism; it is understandable that he found Mott's "Kingdom of God" incomprehensible, especially in the context of the imponderables of American democracy. Nevertheless, he and several others would go to the WSCF meeting at St. Beatenberg, Switzerland, a month later.

On June 10 Mott described his experiences in Berlin in a lengthy letter to John L.:

> It made a greater draft on my physical energy, my patience and self control and the springs of spiritual feeling than any one experience I have ever had. It is impossible even for us who have passed through these days to describe it all. I must admit also that it is impossible for those of us who belong to the victorious nations to imagine the feelings of these defeated and suffering people. My errands were such as to enable me to get glimpses into their very souls.

He had been reminded every hour of their physical depletion and exhaustion, their isolation, loneliness, longsuffering, and extreme pessimism and despair.

There is also an infinite amount of pent-up and at times expressed bitterness. They unmistakably feel and believe that they have suffered great injustice. They suffer most under the impression that the rest of the world regards them as moral pariahs.

"All these intense feelings and convictions were concentrated on me," he went on, "as the representative of the Christian forces of the Allied nations."

Moreover, they had their severe personal grievances against me because of my trip to Russia (to organize the forces against Germany as they said) and because of my failure to do more to safeguard German missions. I spent seven very full days in Berlin. Never have I passed through such an ordeal but by God's grace I believe I showed myself a Christian. I was able to hold my temper and to say nothing of which I am ashamed, nor did I leave unsaid plain things which needed to be said in the right spirit. There had been countless misunderstandings and not all on one side. It took literally days—fifteen and eighteen hour days—to talk all these out.[120]

Mott also devoted "a great deal" of time to discussions with the German missions leaders. He talked at length with Adolph Deissmann and with Ernst Troeltsch, each of whom explained the bitter state of mind that was engulfing the country. Deissmann oriented him to the situation in Poland, where he would soon visit; Troeltsch analyzed the political situation in Germany. All misunderstandings were not cleared up, for that would "take many a year," but Germans came both to the missions conference at Crans and to the Federation Conference a few weeks later, at both of which further progress was made.

Mott next moved with Davis to "the most brilliant nation in Europe," newly independent Czechoslovakia. YMCA services to Czech legionnaires during the War and after had led to government requests for such programs in their army, and subsequently for civilians.[121] It was being said that "the Y stood as a moral bulwark against an ever-imminent anarchism" and that President Masaryk and his ministers gave it high praise as "a factor in keeping unrest out of the Army." Mott conferred for a day and a half with the seventy-five American YMCA men in the country; Davis described their work as giving the men under arms "a new conception of vital Christianity." New Testaments in Czech could not be printed fast enough and already Czech personnel were being trained in Bible study and Association methods; Mott spoke twice to this school. Numerous groups met with him to pledge their support as soon as a permanent civilian YMCA program could be started, and to urge the Americans not to withdraw until Czech leadership could be developed.[122]

Olga Masaryk, daughter of the President, whom Mott had met in Austria before the War, was laying foundations for a coeducational student movement. Mott addressed enthusiastic student audiences at Prague, Brno, and Bratislava, using a familiar theme, "The Battle Ground of Students of All Lands"; such was the response that a national convention was called. It was attended by students from the three universities and was endorsed by the government, and a national SCM came into being that summer.

Mott was received twice by President Masaryk, with whom he had last been in touch in June, 1918, when he aided in obtaining for Masaryk a meeting with President Wilson in Washington.[123] Masaryk explained the significance of Czechoslovakia's situation in central Europe and chided Mott for the lack of understanding of this by America and Britain, who overlooked the Roman Catholic influence there.[124] At a luncheon for Mott, a high government official expressed his compatriots' disillusion with organized religion and their fear that they could lose their liberty "through mixing with religious affairs." But the YMCA had epitomized "an humble ideal which bears out Masaryk's career, which is the greatest Christianity."

Mott's visit to Poland, July 8–17, was restricted but also enhanced by the Russian-Polish War, a Polish attempt to regain their eastern border of 1772; they were driven out of Vilna while he was there and the Russians temporarily advanced to the gates of Warsaw soon after he left. The American YMCA's were heavily involved in services to the Polish armies. As in Czechoslovakia, "Y" men and services had accompanied Polish troops home; these had been expanded until at the time of Mott's visit in 1920 there were forty installations under the direction of A. S. Taylor.

Mott's first contacts in Poland were with students of the university at Krakow, the "second oldest university on the Continent," he wrote John L. The Rector presided in a hall "packed with students and professors." It was "the first time a Protestant worker has addressed on religious lines this great Roman Catholic seat of learning." There was a demand for a national student conference; representatives from all six Polish universities came to it and a preliminary national organization was set up. In spite of their desperate needs, these students had not yet joined the ranks of The Damned and the Beautiful. So surprising had their response been in these Roman Catholic nations that Mott wished, in conclusion to John, that he might have "a whole life to give to student work in such countries as Poland, Czecho-Slovakia, the Balkan States and Russia, where countless doors have been opened as a result of our work for the prisoners-of-war and the soldiers."[125] The lifting of censorship and police controls were also important factors.

YMCA work at the front lines, which Mott and Davis visited by special railway car or train which took them "far into old Russia," maintained the usual program plus features provided by the government department of education. Mott gathered the forty American secretaries for a day and a half conference. In Krakow an audience of 4,000 soldiers "in one of our huts" listened intently to Mott. As he left the building "the soldiers caught me up and tossed me up and down and carried me out on their shoulders—one of their ways of showing special approval," he wrote his son. He reminded 1,500 soldiers in the Eagle Hut at Warsaw of Poland's great past and present, comparing their struggle for identity to the American Civil War. "You are going out to fight," he declared, but your most strategic battleground is in "the moral and spiritual arenas of temptation" and national and spiritual ideals. Davis described an even more impressive meeting "under the sound of the Bolshevik guns in that vast evergreen forest at the front when at sunset each company of soldiers formed and sang their evening prayer."[126]

Everywhere they went the Americans received public welcomes. "Not content with sending a delegation," Davis recalled, "the generals and mayors of the towns came in person to greet us and we were even met at stations by military music." They were received by General Pilsudski, the Chief of State, whom Mott described as "simple, direct, democratic, sympathetic," with "no signs of rank." The Minister of War gave an official luncheon in Mott's honor. The numerous toasts on these effusive occasions—which may have been of some embarrassment to the teetotaling Americans, since they never mentioned them—were to "the noble American nation," to its first citizen President Wilson, and to the health and long life of Mott, whose "warm and mighty words dropped like a refreshing rain from Heaven upon our hearts," encouraging us in "the hard struggle with the barbarians surrounding us." Mott expressed to son John his respect for the Polish women's battalions, which certainly included "many women of very strong personality and of flaming patriotism." This brief tour in Poland was "one of the most remarkable of my life," he summarized to John L., largely because of the favorable climate created by YMCA services to soldiers and POWs; it had been a great experience to travel in reunited Poland and to feel "the real thrill of its new national life."[127]

Nevertheless the two highest points of the tour were yet to come.

PART 12: **Wonderful Days at Crans**

The small missionary meeting the last week of June, 1920, which came to be known as the Crans Conference, for the Swiss town near Geneva where it was held, was pivotal in Mott's career. It has been described by Hogg, Latourette, and others chiefly as the planning session for the organization of the International Missionary Council, which it was, but Mott's role at the center of the controversies that were largely resolved there and his restoration as world missions leader by its principal recommendations, have not been fully recognized.[128]

Although the points raised by the German missions leaders against Oldham, Mott, and the Continuation and Emergency Committees were numerous and deeply-felt, it had been the garbled version of Mott's speech to the Cossacks in Petrograd in 1917 that had touched off a storm of protest against his remaining the head of the Continuation Committee. The German leaders and some Swedes believed that "this great world-figure, who personified supranational missionary cooperation, had entered the lists against them," as Hogg put it.[129] Senator Root's statements of the aim of the Mission to Russia further baffled them; an immense literature of protest and bewilderment appeared in the German missions press in 1917, culminating in a statement signed by a dozen German leaders repudiating Mott as Chairman of the Continuation Committee.

Neither an English translation of the statement nor Mott's reaction to it has come to light. Mott heard rumors but until Oldham sent him a translation in September, 1917, had not seen the document. It represented the most serious breach in the ecumenical movement up to that time. Oldham sympathized with Mott in what he knew must cause Mott "real grief." Because he had approved Mott's going with the Root Mission, Oldham could declare further that he had no doubt that "you have not the slightest cause to regret your course of action." But he hastened to add, "you will not, I am sure, on account of this action offer your resignation to the [Continuation] Committee." He was certain that the British members would not consent, "and the mere suggestion would aggravate the situation." If Mott resigned, Oldham would also. Neither did.[130]

He was speaking for Mott as well as himself when he reiterated his faith in the Committee: It was "not only an international fellowship but also an instrument for the more efficient prosecution of the missionary enterprise." This brought him to remark that, as Mott knew, he had "long been of the opinion that it must with the least possible delay give way to an international organization based on the existing national (missionary) organizations." Such a plan would be uppermost in the minds of both men throughout the next four years; a blueprint for it would be adopted at Crans. However, during the months following the German declaration, the terms of the Versailles Treaty had brought the issues to the fore again, and French insistence upon German war guilt did not help the efforts of Mott, Oldham, Hodgkin, and others toward reconciliation.[131] Mott's efforts in Berlin, just described, did not heal the breach but did bring four Germans to Crans in their personal capacities but not as official representatives of the *Ausschuss.*

Some forty persons from a dozen countries—former neutrals and belligerents—came as guests of Colonel and Madame van Berchem to the Chateau of Crans overlooking Lac Léman in the spirit of their hosts' prayers of months past that the conference might result in "increased international missionary understanding and effectiveness." Under the chairmanship of the irenic Bishop Logan H. Roots of China, there was frank speaking, sincere prayer, and realistic facing of issues; one of the great values was the opportunity for the Germans, whose spokesman was usually Julius Richter, to speak their minds. Mott chaired the business committee.

Oldham's preparatory booklet, *The Missionary Situation After the War,* which he "expounded" in an early session, provided documentary background on the relations of missions to governments and up-to-the-minute summaries of the status of most missions. It answered many of the Germans' questions. The meeting gave large attention to the new issue of governmental concern for education on mission fields, and to the status of each German mission. A lengthy resolution urged the return of German missionaries to their stations.

In *The Missionary Situation After the War,* Oldham outlined briefly the functions of a new international missionary organization; Mott laid down its spiritual foundations. Both the Continuation and Emergency Committees, temporary agencies called into being for limited purposes, had performed their tasks. All present felt the imperative need for a new body. Oldham and Mott had conferred and corresponded on the theme for a decade. There is no evidence that they agreed that Oldham should present the plan—Mott "took a back seat" at Crans—but its chances of adoption were doubtless better if he rather than Mott did so (Oldham had been outspoken on some War issues but had suffered no such opprobrium as did Mott). Following lengthy discussion the Crans group, which was neither the Continuation nor the Emergency Committee, yet in some sense both, unanimously proposed that there be brought into being an "International Missionary Committee," based on the principle adopted by the Continuation Committee at The Hague in 1913, with national agencies as constituent bodies. Its chief function would be as an international coordinating agency.

Crans recommended that Mott be chairman of the new entity, and Oldham its secretary, with a China missionary named A. Livingston Warnshuis as his associate. During the conversations leading to this far-reaching decision, Oldham, foreseeing the expansion of the new body's usefulness in the years ahead, suggested that it could even be "something that may represent the beginnings of a world league of churches."[132]

Mott gave two prepared talks at Crans. Early in the week he outlined the "essentials of an International Missionary Organization," for which he prepared with unusual care. This was not a blueprint but as forthright a statement of his ecumenical ideal as he ever uttered. There must be clear and strong conviction among the leaders of the various lands that we are members of one another, he declared; we are necessary to each other, and it is the mind of Christ that we should serve one another. A few, both officers and others, must give the work their best continuous thought. There must be a fixed policy and a determined effort to call out and enlist the distinctive and also the common contributions and full cooperation of each nation—large and small, weak and strong; there must be a fixed attitude of mind, a longing of heart, a settled purpose of will. Plans and practices must be such as to elicit the interest, confidence, and support of *at least* all the principal sections of the constituency. The men at the head must command the confidence of all; groups must meet frequently and lines of communication be kept open. There must be well thought out and accepted financial policies. The leaders must be appostles who will exert initiative—"blessed are the peace*makers!*"— men like Zinzendorf or Söderblom. Friendships must be kept in repair, and the whole must constantly be engaged in prayer.[133]

During a frankly confessional session on the final Sunday, Julius Richter, seeming to speak for his German colleagues, told the Conference that on the eve of his coming an "anarchistic revolt" had been feared and he had considered staying home to protect his wife and children, but he had come even though "full of apprehension." Such had been the atmosphere at Crans that the Germans could not describe all that the meeting had meant to them, he said, and it had renewed their deepest convictions concerning missions.

Mott was asked to give a closing address. It was an intimate talk. He spoke of the week's accomplishments as a "wonder work" in the renewal of contacts, the facing up to "some of the most difficult, pressing, and significant problems of Christian missions." We have reached the fresh conviction that we must have a united policy or understanding: *we must work toward a common mind.* We have agreed on a simple yet effective plan for international missionary organization and have come to a new realization of the importance of reasserting and maintaining at all costs the supremacy of spiritual facts and forces. God has done a humbling, healing, and recreative work here; we have seen His face as we have looked into the eyes of suffering souls, as we have reminded ourselves of the results of being without a shepherd, as we have experienced countless kindly, unselfish services, as we have walked day and night under the trees. An atmosphere of reality, loyalty, unselfishness, and hope has been created. And so, an enormous responsibility rests upon each of us, to communicate what we have received, to interpret it to others, to fill with living content the proposed organization which ought to afford a clear, strong lead to better international life. We are obligated as apostles of reconciliation to preserve and extend the atmosphere of hope, joy, and love that we have shared here.[134]

The Conference urged Mott to visit China in 1922 and to hold as soon as possible the Moslem conferences that had been planned before the War. Thus Crans was his vindication and a summons to a new era of missionary cooperation. Fries later insisted that no one knew "how much Mott did quietly throughout the entire war to help the hard-pressed German missionaries in fields under control of the entente powers." En route to his next assignment Mott wrote Oldham of his "sense of deep thankfulness to God for our wonderful days together at Crans." Years later he looked back on the meeting as a "widely representative" gathering of "leaders of both older and younger churches which, under the marked influence of the spirit of God, accomplished a wonderful ministry of reconciliation." And toward the end of his life he put it in that little list of the most sacred events of his career.[135]

The historian of the International Missionary Council placed Oldham and Mott in perspective at this juncture:

During the war years Mott had become a giant among the world's international figures, and Oldham had become probably the best informed missionary strategist in the world. Yet their work, their accomplishments for international missionary cooperation were little known beyond a relatively small circle of well-informed missionaries, ministers, and executive-leaders of Protestant churches. Their endeavors to knit together Protestantism's world Christian community were unequalled. Mott the grand statesman and Oldham the keen strategist—together they made a perfect team. To them, for their labours during World War I, the Christian community owes a great debt. [136]

PART 13: A Visit to Austria and Hungary

Only a few months before the War erupted in the Balkans, Mott had made a strenuous effort to establish a cooperating student movement in Austria-Hungary. From Crans he now went to Vienna and Budapest to evaluate the post-War situation and to further student relief in cooperation with the Friends' programs. Our only knowledge of this trip is his own account, written from Geneva to John L. on July 17, 1920:

> Austria has suffered greater hardship than any other country in the war . . . it is the most depressing of all the fields today. Everyone you meet is pessimistic. . . . Their industries are absolutely shattered. It was a rare thing to see any factory chimney smoking. . . . In no land have I found so many people starving or so much disease due to poor and insufficient food.

He found the work of "Hoover's Committee for feeding the children over six years of age" to be "simply wonderful," but university students and professors together with the middle class seemed "to be suffering the most of all."

> My trip to Hungary was almost prevented by the boycott which the Social Democrats of Europe had established with reference to Hungary. I could not make the trip by rail. The day before I planned to start for Budapest the Danube steamers were tied up. Private motor cars were not permitted. Finally the Friends' Mission loaned me a motor truck. We were unable to get a passport for any regular chauffeur. The head of the Transportation department of the Friends' Mission, who had had some experience in driving a car, consented to take Mr. Davis and myself to Budapest.

The visit to Hungary was "very much needed and very much blessed from every point of view." The Hungarians kept Mott talking "almost twenty-four hours in a long series of meetings, committees and interviews."

> We had a number of ordinary breakdowns going and coming. On our way back when we were almost at the Austrian frontier . . . the car struck a

> stone pile which set it to swaying as we were running at high speed. It almost turned over. In preventing this the driver started it toward a high precipice and we came within three feet of dashing over. He turned it so suddenly that one of the back wheels was crushed but this brought us to a stop within two or three feet of the precipice on the other side of the causeway.

They left the vehicle "in the hands of a villager" and with the aid of horses got across the Austrian frontier, spending the night at a village inn. "As fortune would have it," Mott continued to John, they found an electric tramway that took them into Vienna in time for him to make his return connections for Geneva. He left $1,000 with a professor in Budapest, presumably for immediate student relief, and paid the Friends $2,000 for the truck—an expense not anticipated in the budget![137]

Mott returned to Geneva for two days, then joined the eighteen senior American YMCA secretaries at work in eleven European countries whom he had summoned to a two-day session at Caux, near Montreux.[138] There followed several World's YMCA affairs, chief of which was the 1920 Geneva Plenary attended by men from twenty countries. This meeting marked the post-War beginning of Mott's aggressive leadership and the expansion of the world body. He summarized to John L. that he was "obliged" to serve at the Plenary in a position that gave him "the responsible task of helping to shape the policy of the World's Committee for the coming period with its large possibilities." The most significant of these were the decisions to designate D. A. Davis of the American YMCA, who had accompanied Mott on most of this tour, as a secretary of the world organization and Karl Fries to be similarly supported as General Secretary by the Scandinavian Movement.

That such a meeting was possible at all was due to delicate negotiations to bring French and Germans together that began months earlier, as had been the case in the Federation and the missionary movement. Galen M. Fisher provides an anonymous eyewitness description of an earlier meeting in Cologne:

> Three big Germans with short-clipped hair stalked into the conference room exuding wrath at every pore. They looked tough and angry. The French representatives were not too happy either. Dr. Mott and an Englishman took the brunt of the warm debate. The French softened up a bit and we all parted as Christian brethren. Mott was not the only peacemaker, but his self-control and tact were determining factors.[139]

One of the historians of the World's Alliance, Tracy Strong, its general secretary from 1937 to 1953, said that these conversations had been carried on "with great frankness and a common desire" to restore unity in Christ, but with "no immediate results."[140]

Without entering into the complex argument at the Geneva Plenary, it may be said that some progress was made there on this issue, but the problem persisted for a decade and arose again later. To a proposal that the World's Committee lay down the conditions on which fraternal relations be reestablished, Mott replied:

> The World's Committee could not determine the conditions. That is a matter between one alliance and another. It is the responsibility of each alliance to present the conditions on which it can resume relationships.

When Mott went on to say that "it is in the spirit of Christ that an international fraternity can be restored at all costs," a French delegate replied that it could not be "at all costs; not at the cost of morality." A compromise was adopted defining the aim of the World's Committee " to promote such conditions as shall make possible international thinking, planning, action, and fellowship." This was to be one of Fries' special objectives as he took office the next year.[141]

PART 14: "Do any of you know John Mott?" The WSCF in Wartime

Unlike many, if not most, international organizations, the WSCF did not break under the pressures, hatreds, and dislocations of the War. In fact, the War "had a remarkable effect in drawing out the loyalty to the Movement of all its parts," as Tissington Tatlow, chief British SCM secretary, put it.[142] Well could Mott declare in 1920 that its record had been "absolutely unique." It could not hold world conferences—the next one after Lake Mohonk 1913 was not until 1920—but the *Directory and Exchange List* appeared each year. The Day of Prayer for Students was "probably never more widely observed or more characterized by reality," services being held in Orthodox churches as well as Protestant. *The Student World* did not miss a single issue; it kept the constituent movements informed, and demonstrated to the most isolated the genuineness of the Federation's fellowship of love and prayer. Mott believed that it had proved as had no other body "the need for a world-wide student movement."[143]

Its people traveled almost as widely as in peacetime, rivaling Mott himself; Miss Rouse visited 29 countries in Europe and the Americas.

Canadians, Americans, and Europeans went to the Orient and to South America. Rutgers of Holland continued his trips across lines. Sherwood Eddy at first toured India and China, continuing the social evangelism he had shared with Mott in 1912–13 and stimulating Oriental thinking about the War in the West. Out of this ferment there came new Eastern student leadership for the post-War era.

The American student workers in Russia remained until the Bolshevik government forced them out and reduced the Russian Student Movement to martyrdom: Alexander Nikitin, whom Mott had recruited earlier, was found at the end of the War selling crusts of bread on the Galata Bridge in Constantinople. The YMCA men who rescued him put him back to work among Russian student refugees in Bulgaria, where, as in Roumania, a Movement survived.[144] Nevertheless, Miss Rouse could declare that "many Movements, both East and West, emerged greatly expanded or stronger for the strain of war." In Turkey itself, where all religious work in schools and colleges was forbidden, a Movement grew, producing a Christian testimony again to the point of martyrdom. That in Austria carried on a heroic work after being officially suppressed.[145] But there was a lost generation of leadership in all Western countries.

The War not only decimated the Federation's membership of some 200,000 students around the world, but made tens of thousands of them into refugees overnight, producing a problem of such magnitude that starvation and suicide became almost commonplace; waves of refugees from Belgium, Serbia, and Russia poured into France, Britain, Switzerland, the Near East, and North Africa, and some Europeans were caught in the Orient. National movements with Federation assistance set up *foyers* and heroic efforts were made to feed, relocate, advise, and meet religious needs. The Armenians were beyond reach, but every national Movement rendered yeoman service to the refugees within its borders. These ministrations were extended to students in POW camps, and the Federation contributed significantly to that specialized form of relief. A project to which students responded enthusiastically was the sending of libraries to prison camps.

The Student World provided news, in itself a component of hope. "Universities without walls" were opened. Students were urged to join the senior YMCA and YWCA War-related services. In the fall of 1916 the American student secretaries resolved at their setting-up conference to raise $150,000 from American students for these purposes; $170,500 came in, much of it at great sacrifice from students working their way through school. A year later a comparable drive set a goal of $1,000,000 only to exceed it by almost $300,000. The third year the total was $2,300,000.

Behind all this the General Secretary raised funds, kept in touch with the Movements in every nation possible, inspired individuals and local groups through his editorials in *The Student World,* called the Movement to prayer and sacrifice, encouraged Bible study and the morning watch, fostered the writing and mass publication in inexpensive format of popular religious classics such as Fosdick's *The Meaning of Prayer* or Rauschenbusch's *Social Principles of Jesus,* and held before his world constituency the goals of brotherhood, unity, and peace.

Mott's greatest service was the force of his own image. Miss Rouse tells how during the British advance in Serbia in 1918, a soldier who had been a founder of the Serbian SCM, called to the men in British uniform, "Are any of you students? Do any of you know John Mott?" "Yes," replied an Oxford SCM member. Friendship followed. The Oxford man later worked among Serbian students, some of whom had "first caught a glimpse of Jesus Christ as a living force in the world" at those meetings at Belgrade in 1911 when Mott's witness was challenged by rioters.[146]

PART 15: The "Great Event"—The Federation Meets Again

As that eventful summer of 1920 unfolded, Mott went on from Geneva to Berne for two days, perhaps for talks with Würtz, and then to Wengen in the Bernese Oberland, where, under the silent majesty of the Jungfrau, he could devote four days to preparation for the "great event," the first WSCF Conference since 1913. Expecting to lay down the primary responsibility for the Federation at this meeting, Mott prepared a lengthy report as a historical survey of the quarter century since its formation in 1895.

By popular demand this was expanded into a small illustrated book and published that fall as *The World's Student Christian Federation: Origin, Achievements, Forecast.*[147] Barely mentioning his own strategic part in the founding and growth of the Federation, he gave large place to the instrumentality of D. L. Moody, Henry Drummond, Luther Wishard, and James B. Reynolds in the preparatory stages, but emphasized the great work of men like Baron Nicolay and Orientals from Azariah to David Yui. This was the first time Mott cast himself in the role of elder statesman by placing his own works in historical perspective. When William Paton reviewed the book he was reminded of the "spiritual hopefulness" inherent in the Federation: "It has already considerably affected the movement for the reunion of Christendom."[148] Frank Sanders perceived the sane, unselfish, far-ranging thinking of the man who had led the "development of federated student activities for a generation."[149] But at the St. Beatenberg Conference, according to Miss Rouse, the report

> illuminated and steadied every discussion; provided a chart for the stormy days to come; made clear the principles which had brought the Federation so far on its way; induced a conviction that the idea of the Federation was God-given, and that it was an instrument for the carrying out of His purpose for the world.

Translated into five languages, it stood throughout the life of the Federation as its "most valued handbook," a monument both to it "and undesignedly to its author."[150]

As late as Mott's departure on this trip he had looked toward a twenty-fifth anniversary observance of the founding of the Federation at Vadstena, Sweden, its birthplace. But in London the other officers convinced him and Fries that this would be self-congratulatory and would appear to suffering, war-torn Europe to be backward rather than forward-looking. The times, some said, required penance and re-evaluation rather than celebration.

So the Conference met the first week of August, 1920, at St. Beatenberg, a resort overlooking Lake Thun, with the Jungfrau and the Bernese Alps in the background. Something less than a hundred delegates from twelve of the thirteen national constituent bodies came; almost a third represented non-Western, non-Protestant cultures. No Movement had disappeared since 1913. Several revered older leaders such as Baron Nicolay of Russia had died, were casualties of the War as was Charles Grauss of France, or would retire at this assembly. A new generation was coming to grips with the post-War student world and St. Beatenberg would be their orientation. Mott had anticipated this conference as the culmination of his tour of 1920 and was not disappointed. In the eyes of one delegate, he and Miss Rouse had "prepared magnificently." Sufficient time had elapsed since the War that national movements had gotten back on their feet, and former enemies could meet again.[151]

Mott's primary contribution to this meeting was the quarter-century review and forecast that has been described. He gave a second report on his personal activities since the Federation had last met at Lake Mohonk in 1913. In addition to the functions we have sketched, he spoke of funds raised for the Federation and for ten of the thirteen national movements and for the friendship and relief funds, and student secretaries recruited for fifteen countries. He had provided "men, dollars, coaching, and counsel" for student migrations. He explained briefly his resignation from the Student Volunteer Movement but not from missionary activity, spoke of evangelistic work on twenty campuses in seven countries and "many single appeals."

This provided a context for the most complete statement he would ever make in public concerning his War-related activities and their relation to his position as General Secretary of the Federation. His primary goal had been to serve and to keep alive the contacts of the various movements, to serve also the "vast numbers of present and former" Federation members who were involved in the War (which alone justified all the time spent) and especially those who were prisoners of war—whom he met everywhere.

Why did he not resign as General Secretary when America entered the War? As in the case of the Continuation Committee there was no functioning body to which a resignation could be presented. He had believed that his duty was to the large majority of the Federation constituency who had raised no question. He also felt a strong obligation to the large number of former members from the Central Powers who were prisoners of war. In the interest of *all* national movements, it was his further responsibility to hold on at the end of the War: "*no one could suddenly substitute for me.*" What then were the conditions under which he should continue? Only that he discharge all Federation functions with impartiality. This was most difficult: it was impossible! He knew that he would be misunderstood. But with trust in Christ and depending upon His resources he had concluded it to be his duty to continue.

Why had he not resigned upon joining the Root Mission to Russia? Because his assignment had been to the Russian churches and for the religious aspects of the Mission. His purpose was to broaden the relationships between American and Russian Christians. He had been forced to decide in a very few days: it was his own decision, but he had asked a special group of friends to pray that the decision might be the right one. The Mission turned into a "boundless opportunity."

Almost as if this were his swan song, Mott then named some thirty colleagues from the entire globe who had cooperated with him during the seven years since the Federation had last met. They best illustrated the spirit and policy of the WSCF: "Let those who think that War has stopped the activities and influence of the Federation ponder them and their works."

In conclusion, Mott presented his resignation. "For several months some who are here have known that my mind was made up that at the end of twenty-five years I should step down." It is needless, he suggested, to go into the reasons. It is best for the Federation. But he hoped there might yet be opportunities to serve. Karl Fries also resigned at St. Beatenberg, to become General Secretary of the World's Alliance of YMCA's. Mott paid strong if somewhat impersonal tribute to him.[152] The Federation made Mott Chairman in Fries' place, a post held until December, 1928. There would soon be six secretaries in Mott's place. Thus, although, as Miss Rouse once declared, the War brought Mott "perhaps nearest to martyrdom," he was again vindicated, this time by the organization that was his most creative achievement.

St. Beatenberg was epochal as a further forum in which the Anglo-American-German differences were aired. In a discussion of how to present the gospel to students, Pastor Humburg asked whether everyone there was "preaching the same Christ"; to go through business routines, he insisted at length, would be useless until that fundamental question was resolved. This confrontation with Humburg's traditional pietism outraged some Americans who privately considered Humburg a stupid and obstinate "humbug" whose criticism of Mott for "softpeddling [sic!] on references to the Cross in his masterly report" was absurd.

An intimate friend wrote to Leila Mott that "a man whose whole life has been via crucis needs no defense" and that Mott had answered Humburg "with marvellous gentleness and Christian grace." But young William Paton perceived Humburg's question as "the determination of one man not to gloss over, but to probe and understand what seemed to him real differences"; the resulting give-and-take had issued in "a wonderful sharing of outlook and conviction on the central facts of our faith"—a necessity in the Federation, and a forecast of its future theological concerns. For Paton, reconciliation had been faced and culminated at Beatenberg. Fries thought that session "the most important and valuable experience" of the week. Such a thing cannot be made, he continued to Mott in an analytical review of the Conference, "it was a gift of God. It brought us nearer each other and nearer the Cross than anything else could have done." The sight of four German youths in worn uniforms, the only clothes they had, may have contributed to the fraternal atmosphere. When the issue of Mott's mission to Russia came up, he insisted that he should not be blamed for it and that he did not regret it. Humburg agreed to drop the matter, to "close the files" on it. Yet he wrote in his own report that the War had revealed Mott as "not so much the 'great' Dr. Mott. We have learned better than before, where his limits as an American are." Nevertheless, Humburg admired Mott and his service to the Movement, writing him a few weeks after the Conference that he looked back to it "with a very thankful heart" and hoped that "these splendid days will be the beginning of a new understanding amongst the student movements." He also expressed this sentiment in a note to Mrs. Mott in which he spoke of the children's loss of their father's attention because of his journeys. Thus the social gospel-eschatological issue came into the open in the Federation years before it would surface in the ecclesiastically-oriented ecumenical movement at Stockholm in 1925. At Peking in 1922 and again at High Leigh in 1924 the WSCF would debate whether it had or could have a definite theology.[153]

At Beatenberg, Mott gave a talk, probably prepared at Wengen, but in any case inspired by the magnificence of the surroundings, on "the strength of the hills is yours also," that was remembered with gratitude by some as long as they lived. In the moments between sessions and committees, and late at night, he was tirelessly advising representatives of national movements, recruiting for the various Movements, or counseling those troubled by the times: "live on the utmost limits of your faith, not on your doubts," he told S. Ralph Harlow, who would invest his life in the chaplaincy of Smith College.[154]

The Conference took important actions in the areas of race and internationalism, established European Student Relief, sanctioned changes by nine members in their statements of purpose, authorized a hymnbook, and accepted an invitation to China for 1922. At no meeting, concluded Miss Rouse in her History, "did the Federation make so many bold and far-reaching decisions as it did at Beatenberg" in the midst of the uncertainties of a post-War world.[155]

On the westward voyage home, Charles D. Hurrey, who had been with Mott on most of this tour, wrote to Leila Mott:

In Vienna, Budapest, Berlin, Prague and a hundred other camps of darkness, agony, and death, the generous deeds of John R. are bringing joy and health and resurrection. Here's to him! May God bless him!

Hurrey, who was much of a wit, continued:

We all know he is in desperate need of a good rest—but no broken bones this time, please. Just the soul-refreshing intimacy of his family fireside, seasoned a little, perhaps, with a day [fishing] with Joe Posey—or a try at the motor boat.[156]

When the *Aquitania* docked in New York August 21, Mott hurried to Grand Central Station and a sleeper for Montreal—and Lac des Iles.

PART 16: The Strength of the Lakes and the Woods

Rarely had the peace of "the Canadian woods" been so needed or so satisfying as in the summer of 1920. Vacations there had been short and interrupted during the War, and in 1919 a broken ankle had hampered Mott's enjoyment. Both John and Leila Mott needed release from the iron discipline of commuting, the responsibilities that were at times too great, the perpetual pressure on a celebrity.

In addition to being "the great factor" in their family life, as Colton once commented, Leila was a member of the National Board of the Young Women's Christian Association from 1906 until 1922. Between September 1917 and December 1919 she was vice-chairman of its War Work Council, and until 1920 she was Chairman of its Overseas Committee, a very taxing assignment, since the YWCA sent out 433 workers; her Committee arranged transportation, Army clearances, authorization papers, temporary lodging, and met the thousand details and frustrations attendant upon its purpose.[157]

The Motts' own family circle of six had not been full at the Lac since 1915, John L. having been driving an ambulance or serving in the American Army beginning in 1916; by 1920 he was in India—to escape his father's shadow—at work among villagers. From the western front in May, 1918, he had written to his younger sister Eleanor, then eleven, thanking her for "letters and pictures and presents and Valentines" and wishing he might be going up to Canada for the summer, swimming in the lake and paddling down for the mail. If he could be there, she and Frederick, their younger brother, now a teen-ager, might well put him under the bed with their combined strength! Irene was a preparatory school student preparing for entrance to Vassar during the War years.

At times the Canadian summer cottage—called for a while *Huis ten Bosch*—after the royal Dutch summer residence—with extended guest facilities on an island from 1914, became the scene of Mott-White clan gatherings where aunts, uncles, cousins, and friends found the same relaxed atmosphere as did its host and hostess. Mother Mott came on occasion until her death in 1909, as did sisters Harriett, Clara—who presented an unforgettable sight rowing under a big hat—and Alice, whose daughter Bess was an especial favorite of her Uncle John; Leila's brothers and sisters brought broods of cousins for unforgettable vacations. Mott presided over this with joviality and was adored by all.[158]

War and death reached into all of these families. Lac des Iles was in a country that had been at war since 1914, and there were many losses not only among the Motts' friends who summered there but in the homes of their permanent French-Canadian neighbors, who had built the log house and its additions, guided on fishing trips, cut the firewood, filled the icehouse, and provided their every need each summer. John Mott's nephew Ralph McAdam, a Marine, succumbed to influenza en route to France. Wilbert White, Leila's nephew, a member of Rickenbacker's squadron, died in the bravest act Rickenbacker witnessed in the War, diving his plane into a German craft as it closed in on another American flyer.[159] Mott's sister Harriett died in 1920; the Postville home had been sold several years before.

The day after the Armistice was signed Leila Mott had written to Harriett, from a convalescent home where she was recovering from the flu, "Oh thank God it's *over*—this horrible nightmare. Now let's all spend the rest of our lives binding up the broken hearts and healing the wounds." From the thick of the War Work Campaign Mott had written to her "Thank God the end has come in Europe—not of the suffering and sorrow but of the cause of it all."

Mott never returned from a trip, even to the warring nations, without a suitcase of toys, gifts for all, and a large bottle of expensive perfume for Leila—if he had been to Paris. When he arrived at the Lac he shed his official personality, donned old clothes, adopted a nonsense vocabulary, played games with the children, roared at the antics of the customary pair of kittens, read aloud detective stories and other books picked up around the world, fished—sometimes lecturing the fish as though he were on a podium—swapped stories with cronies, tried desperately to learn swimming strokes that would more than keep him afloat, rowed and paddled, dragged brush and burned bonfires, and relaxed to Eleanor's piano playing. He led brief morning prayers in the living room; the days often ended with a fireside hymn-sing, a discussion, and his favorite refreshment, fresh fruit.

At least once each summer he tried out an address to be widely used the following year, by presenting it at one of the Sunday morning worship services in the Rosses' big house across the lake, which the whole family was expected to attend regularly. Leila insisted that there be no swimming on Sunday other than the usual morning dip (though Mott himself was less strict), but paddling home from the service was not infrequently so hazardous that the more venturesome teen-agers managed to fall into the water!

Yet the pressures of Mott's ongoing projects were so great that even here he could not set them entirely aside. Ethan Colton and his family were guests in the island cottage at the Lac in 1919; Colton noted that Mott "read prodigiously there, as at sea." Business that associates in New York could not dispatch accumulated and was brought to him once or twice during the summer. Colton observed that in the vacation interim it took "courage and resolution to crash the barrier."

The "Quiet Days" begun at the turn of the century meant much to Mott during the War years. That same small group of intimate friends met every year the day after Christmas to pray, meditate, contemplate the meaning of the War, share their deepest thoughts and most serious questions, and rededicate themselves to the service of their Lord. Mott usually attended a larger group with similar purposes that met in Princeton in September each year to center its thought around a specific theme.[160]

Although he stayed on at Lac des Iles as late as possible in 1920, Mott did not regain his old energy and enthusiasm. The problems to be faced in New York palled: both the War Work Council and the Interchurch World Movement had reached the mopping-up stage, criticism of them was persistent, and there were groundless charges that he and Rockefeller had wanted to eliminate local churches through the ICWM. Post-War witch hunts were in full cry, and some colleagues Mott trusted were under fire. Yet as 1920 drew to a close Mott was reassured by Rockefeller and five or six equally intimate friends and supporters that they would each provide $10,000 a year for five years for his personal staff, as needed "for service in connection with the various enterprises throughout the world to which you are giving yourself." Rockefeller, for one, added that he counted it "a privilege to help" in any way he could "to make possible the leadership you are giving to these several great world movements."[161]

A late report to President Wilson on the European trip of the spring and summer elicited some caustic comments. When Mott spoke to the President's query about France, Wilson replied, "France is now the head representative of imperialism." When Mott said that he could not understand Lloyd George's stance on Russia, Wilson answered, "Don't imperil your mind by trying to understand Lloyd George." In contrast Wilson expressed "an affectionate regard" for the Greek statesman Venizelos. [162]

During the fall of 1920 Mott traveled a little, but by mid-December was being forced to cancel appointments for health reasons. Colton recalled, though, that he "never saw him moody or giving way to depression." Even under the circumstances of that period Mott displayed what a modern editor called "grace under pressure." Soon after Christmas he went to the Grove Park Inn at Asheville, North Carolina, for an extended rest. Golf lessons and outdoor exercise helped, but Leila was too ill to follow until January. During their stay the Motts met Vice President-elect and Mrs. Coolidge. By the third week in February the Motts were well enough to travel. Six weeks in the Southwest through Indian country and at the Grand Canyon restored both to health for their return to New York in early April. [163]

Years later, when Mott outlined his activities during World War I in a rare autobiographical memo, he called it "Work for Peace." Howard Grose had commented before Mott went to Europe in the Spring of 1920 that the War had left lines upon his face. Long afterward, J. H. Oldham remarked that Mott was "never quite the same" after the War. Paul B. Anderson, who worked intimately with him for forty years, characterized the War period as "the peak but not the close" of Mott's career. [164]

11

Ecumenical Statesman

When the War is over, we shall be living in a new world.

—J. H. Oldham, 1915[1]

What we called foundations... have been found to be shifting sand. What we pointed to with such pride as pillars... have in recent years one by one fallen and crumbled at our feet—only one stands!

—J. R. Mott, 1919[2]

FEW IF ANY Americans were in better position to grasp the awesome realities of the "absolutely new world" of the 1920's than Mott. Thirty years of global travel and an intimate knowledge of the world derived from "inspecting the great battlefields of Christianity on every continent," he told the International YMCA Convention of 1919, had given him a perspective on the impoverishment, exhaustion, embitterment, sorrow, suffering and hunger that were following in the wake of the War. Although he did not then put the case in such terms, Mott went on to describe the global forces, including Bolshevism, that would mark the War as the turning point of Western civilization.

Already the unselfish, cooperative spirit of the War years was eroding: "We are by no means as unselfish as we were two years ago this week" when no demands had been too great, he reminded the Convention.[3] As normalcy pervaded America, and the "religious depression"[4] of the late '20's, and the economic collapse of 1929 slowed the expansion of his enterprises, his optimism would be put to the test. With the end of the age of American innocence, or of what some scholars described as the end of the Protestant era, Mott would come to retirement. He would not quit, but move out of the organizations of his youth and middle age into new international enterprises that had either come into being or reached

598

maturity largely because of the network of ecumenical connections that he had spent his life putting together.

Back in the full swing of activity in April, 1921, Mott looked back on his and Leila's recent rest and vacation in the Southwest as "the most profitable period" of his life. He "had time to think." He had seen "large dimensions": at the Grand Canyon "one realized the patient achievements of time and one was reminded vividly of the great reality that before these mountains were brought forth 'from everlasting to everlasting Thou art God.'" He also had seen the dimension of space; on a clear day there were views of 100 miles in all directions, of distant heavenly bodies at night. "One realized the littleness of things that fever our brows and occupy so much of our talking and writing, and we began to see things in the great divine perspective." And there was a third dimension in "the reaches of imagination": solitude is "as necessary for imagination as society is wholesome for character." But, he told an assembly of YMCA secretaries in Atlanta in April, 1921, it is not necessary to go to the desert for this experience. He had proved to himself since returning that it could be cultivated "in the subway, hanging to the strap, or in the surging crowd waiting to catch the ferryboat," or here in this busy conference—"to seek His face, to isolate myself, to have solitude." "It is a reality for which I contend, not a form."[5]

Thus restored to bodily and spiritual strength, Mott returned in the spring of 1921 to the unfinished business of his several positions. He spoke at Vassar the first weekend he was home, and met appointments in Washington, Buffalo, Chicago, Atlanta, and Toledo throughout April and early May of 1921. Both the War Work Council and the Interchurch World Movement were being liquidated, and plans for the organizational meeting of the International Missionary Council (IMC) were in process. As its General Secretary he must report at the annual dinner of the International Committee of the YMCA, and there were important matters to consider in the Student Movement.

The activities of Mott's mature years were also exemplified in a five-week trip he made to Europe between May 14 and June 22, 1921. In London he conferred with Oldham and others on the forthcoming organizational meeting of the International Missionary Council; at Geneva he met with the senior American YMCA secretaries for Europe on POW work and relief. In Holland the WSCF executive committee dealt decisively with the continuing need for student relief; the Utrecht Plenary of the World's Alliance of YMCA's elected him chairman of its business committee and welcomed his life-long friend Karl Fries as its General

Secretary, thus creating another aggressive partnership comparable to the Oldham-Mott team. This chapter is largely concerned with these expanding responsibilities.

PART 1: Establishing the International Missionary Council

The plans for international cooperation known as the Faith and Order Movement were so completely disrupted by the War that they virtually had to be started over again. But the far more developed missionary cooperative movement that had also been launched at Edinburgh in 1910 and which had been held together however tenuously by Oldham and Mott by means of the Continuation and Emergency Committees had never ceased to function throughout the conflict.[6] As was seen in Chapter 10, sufficient steps toward a restoration of unity were taken at Crans in 1920 that a permanent body could realistically be anticipated the next year. The historian of the International Missionary Council points out that although this was now eleven years after Edinburgh, the real marvel was that organization could be achieved in such a comparatively short time in view of the catastrophic events that filled most of those fateful years. The major factor in that achievement was the Oldham-Mott partnership: they allowed neither distance nor submarine warfare to interrupt their exchange of information, ideas, and mutual decisions. They rarely disagreed seriously and never feared to explore each other's questions or reservations. When the War ended and they could again meet without apprehension, every such occasion was an event of spiritual joy to each man.

As they worked to fulfill the mandates of Crans, the first and most important of which was to organize an international missions body, no detail was overlooked in planning for the all-important constituting session at Lake Mohonk the first week of October, 1921.[7] Mott himself went to the resort to make the arrangements. As the sixty members of the conference drove through the flaming fall colors up the long haul to the Mohonk Mountain House and from there viewed the wide panorama of mountain and valley, the choice of this incomparable site for their meeting must have suggested not only the careful preparation but also, as Mott might have said, the far-reaching outlook that was to characterize the conference.

In actuality, this event had been in the minds of Mott and Oldham since well before Edinburgh; its outcome would bear striking resemblance to a plan put forth by Gustav Warneck in 1888, with which both were familiar. Those who knew either Oldham or Mott at all well—there were at least seven who had held significant YMCA- and/or WSCF-related posts under Mott, and the others must have surmised as much—knew that the chairman and the secretary had worked over every aspect not only of the sessions but of the constitution, the budget, and the plans that would be proposed. Since Crans the two had exchanged dozens of long letters, memos, and documents, conferred in London, New York, and Asheville, and Oldham had spent the early part of 1921 in the United States and Canada, laying the groundwork during Mott's protracted absence on account of his and Leila's illnesses.

In his history of the International Missionary Council, *Ecumenical Foundations,* William Richey Hogg points out that Mohonk was primarily "a meeting of the home base of missions." Representatives came from the world, except Germany, whose sending agencies held that they could not cooperate as long as their missionaries were barred from Allied-held areas. Oldham had gone to Berlin in the spring of 1921 but had been unable to persuade the missions leaders to come. They were, he found, after an experience almost as traumatic as Mott's the previous year, more bitter than students and other professionals he met. A few, notably Richter, whom Mott also urged to come, were unhappy with the decision of their constituencies, but did not dare to attend even as individuals. [8] The Mohonk assembly nevertheless constituted the *Ausschuss* a charter member of the IMC, which gesture helped greatly to ease tensions and to bring about German cooperation.

The Council, which was a discussion body seated around a large square table, adopted the principle laid down at The Hague in 1913 that the new organization could be made up only of those churches, missionary societies, or boards that were "entitled to determine missionary policy." Like Edinburgh, it declared itself neutral on ecclesiastical or doctrinal questions, thus refusing to enter the territory of Faith and Order; nevertheless, it was united in belief that "it is the duty of Christians to witness to the gospel of Jesus Christ among all men," thus recognizing the unity of devotion to a common task. A third basic assumption was that the Council must be "entirely dependent on the gift from God of the spirit of fellowship, mutual understanding, and desire to cooperate."

Someone commented years later that Mott personified the IMC. The various functions set forth in its constitution, written by Oldham, comprised a resumé of the activities to which both men were devoting themselves. The Council, wrote Hogg, was created "to stimulate thinking and investigation on missionary questions," enlisting in the endeavour the best knowledge and experience and making the results available to all missions; "to help coordinate" the efforts of the different national missionary organizations and their member societies and "to bring about united action where necessary"; to "help to unite Christian public opinion" in support of freedom of conscience, religion, and missionary endeavour; to bring together the world's Christian forces to achieve "justice in international and inter-racial relations"; to publish *The International Review of Missions* and any other publication contributing to the study of missionary questions; and "to call a world missionary conference" if and when desirable.[9]

The Mohonk conference handed over to the new Council what functions remained with the Continuation and Emergency Committees. Under Mott's chairmanship and the seven-minute rule of Edinburgh it explored contemporary issues, most of which had been surveyed in papers circulated in advance in order to avoid lengthy presentations. Both Mott and Oldham had been determined to keep "the most firm control" over every moment lest the sessions degenerate into "aimless and unpractical" discussion "of large subjects." About midway in the conference Mott's 51-page paper on international missionary cooperation was presented. It was both an encyclopedic description of the possibilities and needs for cooperation at all levels, and a plea for and an inspirational defense of a body that would be "a spiritual organism—spiritual because grafted into the Living Christ."[10] Twenty-one delegates took part in the discussion that followed.

The Council authorized a questionnaire to missionary societies to probe their policies on indigenous churches and their leadership. It dealt at great length with freedom of religion, especially in Portuguese Africa and in French colonies, and urged the return of German workers to their missions. It discussed labor conditions in British East Africa and Portuguese Africa, but devoted the most attention to missionary freedom in the mandated territories about which Oldham had been concerned since the mandate system was first proposed. The Crans recommendation that Mott hold the series of conferences with missionaries to Moslems—which had been proposed before the War—was endorsed; he was also asked to attend the conference of the China Continuation Committee in 1922, and Oldham was encouraged to visit India.

The staff, soon to be enlarged by the addition of A. Livingston Warnshuis who would open an office in New York, was charged to give attention to key ethical questions—labor conditions, opium control, the growth of industrialization in Asia and its effects on human welfare. They were asked to study race relations "as these bear on missionary work," and to report at the next meeting on "the relation of the Negro community in America and the West Indies to missionary work in the African Continent." This recognition of the responsibility of the missionary enterprise for human problems was something new. Hogg concludes that when the delegates left the serene beauty of Mohonk, "they felt secure in the knowledge that at long last an International Missionary Council existed and stood ready to serve a world-wide missionary enterprise."

Its chairman had come to its leadership as the climax and fulfillment of his career, as had J. H. Oldham. The continuing collaboration of these two vastly different personalities became a phenomenon of the next decades—Oldham the intellectual and theological explorer, Mott the strategist. Toward the end of his career, Mott reminisced that the IMC officers had learned that they could not administer their great trust "from an office chair." Henceforth Oldham would also take to the road, as would younger staff members. Mott might have added that this had been a lifelong habit with him. In 1944 Mott could speak of the "enormous gains" to world missions resulting from the work of the IMC.

Two weeks after Mohonk, a new body, spiritually but not physically related to the IMC, was incorporated in New York State. Ostensibly the successor to the Interchurch World Movement (which was described in Chapter 10), it was known for two years as the Committee on Social and Religious Surveys and in 1923 named the Institute of Social and Religious Research. John D. Rockefeller, Jr., paid its bills and Mott, a great believer in research, was chairman until its dissolution in 1934. As Charles E. Harvey has reassessed the ISRR, it was a device worked out secretly by Rockefeller, through his surrogate Raymond B. Fosdick and staff, to continue ICWM programs in part, while serving as a front to fund some of the Interchurch debts by salvaging that defunct body's research program without revealing Rockefeller's behind-the-scenes involvement in the financing of the ICWM.[11]

Mott's intimate, Charles R. Watson, President of the American University in Cairo, gave part of his 1921 leave to setting up the Institute; upon his return to Egypt, Galen M. Fisher, who had served the YMCA in Japan since 1898, became director for the rest of the ISRR's life. Mott's and Fisher's ambitious early budgets were substantially trimmed by Fosdick, who held Rockefeller's veto power, yet during most of the decade they were allowed to spend $250,000 a year. Some fifty studies resulted.[12] The Institute was a regular agenda item at Mott's semi-annual consultations with Rockefeller.

Fosdick's fear that conservative criticism might touch Rockefeller, and Fisher's desire to study "any phase of the life of society" with which organized religion might be concerned, produced some tension. That Fisher often won out was demonstrated by Robert and Helen Lynds' *Middletown*, which scandalized Fosdick but after it became the Institute's best-known product earned his admiration. Mott's irenic hand and oft-expressed faith in research may be seen here; when the Institute's career came to an end he declared that its effort "to apply to religious phenomena the methods of social research without the distorting influence of ecclesiastical or theological bias" had been one of the significant, if less publicized, events of the decade. [13]

The cleavage between liberal and conservative religious viewpoints that developed during the 1920's was further illustrated in Robert E. Speer's opposition to Rockefeller's plans to substitute the Institute, another centralized agency outside of the controls of the denominations, for the Interchurch World Movement. Later, fortified by continental theology, Speer challenged the increasing secularization of religious enterprises and opposed Mott openly on the Laymen's Foreign Missions Inquiry, an Institute study, though it must be said at once that no such difference ever affected the depth and sincerity of the mutual affection and respect of Mott and Speer for one another. As controversy grew, Rockefeller began to lose interest in the Institute and phased it out in 1934. In the meantime the Jerusalem conference of 1928 authorized a Department of Social and Industrial Research for the International Missionary Council. It would be financed from many sources including the Carnegie Corporation.

PART 2: The World's Student Christian Federation Meets in Peking

At Lake Mohonk the International Missionary Council had endorsed the Crans recommendation that Mott represent it at a national missions meeting in Shanghai in late April, 1922. In the meantime, at Mott's behest, T. Z. Koo had traveled from China to Holland in 1921 to urge again China's invitation of 1913 to the Federation; his mission was successful and a major WSCF conference, prepared largely by the Chinese, was set for early April in Peking. Mott decided to spend eleven weeks in Japan, Korea, and China, his first trip to the Far East in nine years. [14]

Preparation for this tour included a first interview with President Warren G. Harding, which Mott opened by congratulating the President for convening the Washington disarmament conference, calling it "regulated sanity." Mott briefed the President on his coming trip. They discussed the international situation, Mott commenting that "the world knows that we are unselfish." He also spoke of Wilson's unselfishness at Paris. The same day Mott also talked with Secretary of State Charles Evans Hughes, expressing his appreciation of Hughes' "great work" toward the disarmament conference and of his aid in the struggle for religious liberty in the peace settlements. Mott also briefed Hughes on his trip; they discussed YMCA services to American troops still on the Rhine.

The first week in January Mott met with a record number of foreign diplomats who were in Washington for the disarmament conference. Nowhere did he explain the content of these talks, but that they most probably dealt largely with missionary matters is suggested by his naming the officials in a letter to Oldham, then in India. He had crowded into one long day, in appointments never less than one-half hour,

> important personal interviews with Sir John Jordan, a member of the British delegation to the Washington Conference; with Admiral Kato, the head of the Japanese delegation; with Minister Sze, Minister Koo, and Mr. Wang, of the Chinese delegation; with Secretary of State Hughes, of the American delegation; and with M. Sarraut, the acting head of the French delegation.

Hughes promised a message to the WSCF Conference, if Mott would write it. Mott had also spent a very profitable hour with ex-President Taft, and

> likewise with the Czechoslovak Minister Stepanek and with the Acting Russian Ambassador Bakhmetieff. I had an interesting visit with ex-Secretary of State Lansing. My guests at dinner were four or five of the leading Russians who were associated with the Kerensky Government, especially Prince Lvoff and Miliukov. [15]

"This does not exhaust the list by any means," he concluded to Oldham, regretting that it was not possible to share "all the important matters" with which the conversations had dealt. As a matter of fact, Mott almost never conveyed the details of an interview in writing; these must await his meeting Oldham in China and the relative leisure of the long voyage back to North America, on which Oldham would be a fellow-passenger. The next week Mott had an extended conference with John D. Rockefeller, Jr., briefing him on the trip and discussing the program for YMCA buildings in major cities in the Far East, in which Rockefeller was seriously interested.

John and Leila Mott's 1922 visit in Japan consisted of a week in mid-March devoted largely to the YMCA, students, and the preparation for a national missionary conference to be held in May, for which they would return en route home from China. Having been decorated with the Imperial Order of the Sacred Treasure, Third Class, in 1920, in recognition not only of his contributions to Association work in Japan but to his leadership in Red Triangle services during the War, Mott was now a person of even more consequence in Japan than at the time of his last visit in 1913. He paid courtesy calls upon the Premier, the Foreign Minister, the Mayor of Tokyo Baron Goto, and the American ambassador, all arranged by G. S. Phelps, who had succeeded Galen Fisher as national YMCA secretary. Mott met businessmen and YMCA leaders in Yokohama, Tokyo, Kyoto, and Osaka, addressed student rallies in Tokyo, spoke on the forthcoming missionary conference, met with YMCA professionals and the Japan National YMCA Committee. From the "Y" men the Motts learned of the critical illness of the three-year-old daughter of Tokyo Secretary J. Merle Davis. As Davis remembered it many years later, Mott

> recognized that we were facing the possibility of permanent separation from the Japan field, and great-heartedly urged us to take [the child] to Johns Hopkins Hospital. He further urged us to spare no expense, and promised that if the International Committee should feel unable to supply the costs, he himself would provide the money. [He] could not have been more tender and concerned had our Helen been his own child.[16]

En route to Seoul the Motts were interviewed and photographed by reporters for four newspapers; the South Manchurian Railway provided a first-class private car for their trip from Fusan; they were welcomed at way stations by missionaries and church school boys and girls. Several hours out of Seoul they were joined by the Honorable T. H. Yun, Frank Brockman, and S. Niwa of the Japan national YMCA. The welcome at Seoul by "a large company of leading Koreans, Japanese and foreigners" was virtually a public ceremony. During two crowded days at the Korean capital Leila Mott was entertained by Princess Pack and consulted on YWCA affairs. John was entertained by Prince Pack, missionaries and YMCA men, and was consulted on the problems created by the Japanese occupation of the country; he spoke to groups of interested Korean men. In a full day at Pyeng Yang Mott consulted with leaders of the YMCA, conducted a short conference with missionaries, and spoke to a mass meeting for men in the largest church in Korea while Leila and Miss Bidgrain of the WSCF staff spoke to a large audience of women in another church.

All personal Mott archives for the 1922 trip to China end with their departure from Pyeng Yang for Mukden. The usual diary was kept but it is missing and was not included in Mott's own table of contents of the papers he gave to Yale, nor is there mention of the Peking 1922 WSCF Conference in the Federation volume of his *Addresses and Papers.* Some especially distasteful incident or combination of such events may have caused him to put the journey out of his mind. Conversely, it might be hypothesized that in his new position as Chairman of the WSCF he did not feel the same compulsion to preserve its archives as had been the case during his general secretaryship, but that would not apply to the many other events of the tour. However this may be, Mott had invested immense energy and much time in obtaining young leaders possessing what he called "kindling power," such as S. Ralph Harlow of International College at Smyrna, in raising funds for the delegates' travel, and in preparation for the meetings of the General Committee which were held before and after the great popular Conference that was planned and very largely carried out by the Chinese. The entire enterprise was to be "preeminently Asiatic."

China had changed markedly since Mott's last visit a decade earlier. The Great War had not devastated Christian student work as had been the case in Europe. China had lived with war for a long time and was engrossed in building its new age, epitomized in the Chinese Republic, while the West was destroying itself. The Chinese renaissance, which urged examination not only of China's past but of all current knowledge and practice, symbolized by the promotion of respectable writing in a standard vernacular, was by 1922 several years along and had acquired great momentum among students. An Anti-Christian Student Federation had recently sprung up, in part a reaction against the coming of the WSCF but also inspired by a missions atlas entitled *The Christian Conquest of China,* the maps in which assigned the entire country to foreign missions boards. The Anti-Christians charged the WSCF with being opposed to science and open-mindedness and breathed out the most dire threats against it. This resulted in increased public notice for the Conference but it virtually nullified the effect of the post-Conference deputations, some of which had to cross fronts between opposing armies. The Conference motto, "Below Heaven One Family," an adaptation of a

Confucian saying to the Federation motto, "That they all may be one," needed to be understood "in the context of a war-ridden humanity full of political and race tensions," wrote a later historian. Save for one address on the centrality of Christ, and his chairmanship of both the General Committee and the larger Conference, Mott kept out of the limelight, though there was one unfortunate occasion when, at the reception by the President of the Republic, he made a speech while hundreds waited in line.[17]

The several forums of the popular Conference and the discussions on the Federation's purpose in the General Committee reflected the vast changes in the Orient and Africa since it had met in Tokyo fifteen years and a World War earlier. Delegates—virtually all native citizens of thirty nations—brought to the Chinese a sense of world fellowship that strengthened the Chinese Christian students' own identity, and here the fresh leadership of a new generation became apparent in C. T. Wang, David Yui, T. Z. Koo, Y. Y. Tsu, and Dr. Y. F. Wu.

In the minds of these young Chinese who organized the popular conference, the international and interracial issue was uppermost. At St. Beatenberg the Federation had added internationalism to its objectives. Early in the Peking General Committee meeting the issue of pacifism arose, pushed by Henry Hodgkin and supported by the delegations from India and Australasia and some Chinese, Koreans, and Filipinos. Most of the Western delegations were divided or certainly not persuaded that force is essentially evil. The Federation could not be true to its inclusive nature while adopting a dogmatic position. It resolved, therefore, to recommend to its member Movements that they face "the whole question of war and of those social and economic forces which tend to issue in war" in "the light of Jesus' teachings." This was, as Hans-Ruedi Weber points out, a realization of the cost of ecumenical commitment. This was the high-water mark of efforts to commit the Federation to pacifism, yet the Peking assembly was treated to "fresh surprises" of God's grace, as David R. Porter put it, when Alexander Nikitin of Russia was seen to embrace T. Z. Koo, and a Korean woman delegate became convinced of the imminence of the Kingdom of God by a Negro, Willis J. King of the U.S.A., who, she felt, drew his audience "nearer to God" than any other speaker. The Life and Work Conference that would meet at Stockholm in 1925 would draw up resolutions strikingly similar to those finally agreed upon by the WSCF at Peking.[18]

Dr. Georg Michaelis, chairman of the German Student Movement since before the War, who had served briefly as *Reichkanzler* in 1917, raised the issue of German war guilt. En route, he had been delayed and waited out the sailing of his ship at Hardenbroek, the Dutch SCM headquarters, where his host was the young Willem A. Visser t' Hooft. "His great concern in going to the world conference in China was to convince the outside world that the clause in the Versailles Treaty which made Germany alone responsible for the war was a lie and an example of shameful hypocrisy," Visser t' Hooft recalled in his Memoirs, adding that Michaelis "had little or nothing to say about Germany's share in war guilt and about the fundamental changes which were required in German politics for the sake of a new start in international relations." And Visser t' Hooft wondered whether this conservative old man really represented the mind of post-War Christian students in Germany.[19]

Michaelis received "a grateful hearing" from the General Committee at Peking, wrote Miss Rouse, but a young professor of missions from Yale, Kenneth Scott Latourette, opposed with some heat what he regarded as Michaelis' apocalyptic stance, regarding it as an impossible position. The Committee appears to have accepted Michaelis' contention that Germany had not been solely responsible. Mott, the chairman, kept a discreet silence. This disturbed Michaelis after the conference and he reopened the old German criticisms of Mott, charging that Mott constantly substituted "discussion, organization, and attempts at fraternization" for "clarification of the truth."[20] These issues did not die out, but in the next few years the Federation came to see that opposing viewpoints were integral to the universal inclusiveness that was its genius. Mott participated in the unsuccessful post-Federation deputation activities and left Peking on one of the last trains before the rail line was cut by the civil war. This was perhaps symbolic of the failure of the Conference to deal realistically with the issues raised by the powerful Marxist revolt that had been gathering strength in China since 1917. Yet not only in China but wherever the student Christian movements would substitute spirituality for intellectual grappling with contemporary historical issues, decline would set in.[21]

PART 3: A Pattern for National Councils of Churches

The China Continuation Committee Conference was held in Shanghai May 2-11, 1922. Attended by a thousand elected delegates, more than half of them Chinese, it evidenced the vigorous growth of the Church in China since the 1913 Mott conference whose delegates had been selected. Although he neither chaired nor prepared this meeting, and, as several have said, it was no "Mott conference" (some accounts did not mention his presence), he nonetheless exerted a pervasive influence on it through the new generation of Chinese leaders whom he had helped to enlist and train, notably the brilliant chairman Cheng Ching-yi, and T. T. Lew who uttered the phrase, "The Chinese Church shall teach her members to agree to differ and to resolve to love." The Conference produced a national body on the same basis as the International Missionary Council itself and became affiliated with it.[22] It was the first of some thirty such bodies in as many countries in the formation of which Mott would be instrumental. He was happy to observe that the indigenous leadership that had already taken over in the Chinese student and YM/YWCA movements was now "beginning to arise in the churches" in spite of continuing missionary paternalism.

Mott addressed the Conference at least twice. In a long speech published as "The present advantageous position of the world-wide Christian movement" he reviewed the plastic nature of the forces shaping the post-War world and related the reforming passion of the rising generation to the social gospel; in lands such as China "new and truly indigenous churches" were developing large measures of self-consciousness: the missionaries' prayer for "a self-directing, self-supporting and self-propagating Chinese Christian Church" was being answered before their very eyes. Yet even in this great hour of fruition, he cautioned, it may be an idle dream to think of accomplishing the Church's great aims "without true unity and cooperation." On another occasion Mott outlined "Some of the factors underlying [the] success of the National Christian Council of China," which were similar to those he had laid down at Crans for an international missionary body. He was influential in the selection of three secretaries for the new organization.[23] Mott also spoke in a coaching session with the central committee of the new Council on the functions of a national secretary, an outline he would use many times in the future, and which reminds one of his and Charles Ober's coaching sessions with college YMCA presidents thirty years earlier.

Hogg and Weber agree that the China National Christian Council emerged out of a welter of difficulties, not the least of which was a Fundamentalist controversy—if civil war were not enough. Oldham, who reached China well before Mott, sensed the situation and informed Mott. The critical issue appears to have been whether the China Inland Mission would require a creedal statement as the price of supporting the new Council. Mott spent two hours with D. E. Hoste, head of the Mission and leader of the conservatives. Apparently Mott succeeded in removing enough of Hoste's apprehensions that although the CIM did not join it did not oppose the Council.[24]

While in Shanghai, Mott also spoke before an association of universities and colleges on the "Burton Commission" report, a study of higher education in China that would be formative for years to come.[25] He laid the cornerstone of a new Navy YMCA and reviewed other Association building needs. Although the Shanghai Conference had passed strong resolutions of a social nature, especially on child labor and a living wage, the YMCA's "preferred to engage in constructive work [such as teaching literacy] rather than agitate for the immediate realization of such unrealistic visions." Marxism would gradually move Chinese students, labor, and some Chinese and American Association leaders, leftward, leaving the YMCA's with building centered programs of uplift that became identified with conservatism, although they occasionally passed resolutions calling for Christianizing industry. Nevertheless, such were the strength and prestige of the YMCA in 1922 that Sun Fo, the son of Sun Yat-sen, proposed that it join with the Kuomintang to "save China." When the Associations decided that this could not be done, Russia was invited. How much of this came to Mott's attention is unknown, but it adds a provocative paragraph to the story of how the West "lost" China to communism. Well before Mott's next visit, in the winter of 1925–26, the Chinese YMCA was being severely criticized and had undertaken a drastic reevaluation of its policies and objectives.[26] It was different in Japan.

In 1922 the Christian population of Japan numbered about one million; of this, however, only about one-third were church members, and of those perhaps one-third were active. The churches were small, only a handful having more than a few hundred members. Yet the decade had opened with great promise and activity on the part of the Christian community, the World Sunday School Convention having met in Tokyo in 1920. A prominent missionary could assure the mission enterprise that the ark of the Lord was safe in the care of the Japanese Church.[27]

The Japan Continuation Committee had been active since Mott helped to organize it in 1913, but by 1922 it had served its time and had called a conference to set up a permanent successor. This meeting was Mott's primary but not sole reason for another week in the Sunrise Kingdom in mid-May, 1922.[28]

As if to demonstrate the intimate relations between the YMCA and the Japanese churches, this National Christian Conference was held in the large hall of the Tokyo Association, which also was a denominationally neutral site. J. S. Motoda, who had been at Edinburgh 1910, was in the chair. To allay apprehension that the churches would be steamrollered into an alien imposed body, the Christian community had been told prior to Mott's arrival that he was not coming "to preside or attempt to foist the Mohonk program on them." He gave the keynote address on "The price to be paid to ensure the most effective and fruitful cooperation," the main lines of which he had developed at Crans and most recently in Shanghai; it was reported on the front page of the *Japan Advertiser*. Although he spoke again, on "Spiritual realization and spiritual renewal," this, like Shanghai, was no "Mott conference." Only one-fourth of the speakers were non-Japanese. The important outcome of the Conference was a Japan National Christian Council, organized some months later with Bishop K. Uzaki as chairman and William Axling and K. Miyazaki as secretaries; the older Federation of Churches merged with the new body. The Japan Council drew up a constitution with a strong "social creed" for the churches; it bore remarkable resemblance to the American Federal Council social creed but was adapted to Japanese conditions.[29]

Mott was of course involved in the affairs of the Japanese YMCA, whose work had not been seriously disrupted by the War. Entertained at dinner by its War Work Council, he gave a detailed review of Red Triangle services since the Russo-Japanese War. The forty "Y" secretaries of the whole country, with their wives, gathered for two days at Nikko (there were a few more Japanese than westerners) for a professional conference to which Mott gave five of his coaching talks. May 25, his birthday, was observed as "Dr. Mott Day"; when the session adjourned for tea, a photograph, and a "grand birthday cake," there was "jollification," including songs composed for the occasion and the presentation of an album of signatures. Leila shared happily in all of this.[30]

During the hectic days in Tokyo Mott spoke at funeral services for Soroku Ebara, the "Empire's leading Christian worker." He conferred at great length with the banker Viscount Shibusawa on Japanese-American relations, and had a long and friendly talk with Baron Shimpei Goto, the mayor of Tokyo, on "modern science and the religion of Jesus Christ." Socially, the climax of the Motts' week in Tokyo was their presentation to the Empress and the Prince Regent, who received them at the Shinjuku Imperial Gardens and entertained them at luncheon there "in recognition and appreciation," as the *Japan Advertiser* put it, of the work which

Dr. Mott has done "for the young men of Japan." This was the first of five audiences Mott would have with the young ruler who would become the Emperor Hirohito. The royal family contributed two thousand yen to the Japanese YMCA at this time. [31]

A few weeks later, when Mott reported on this trip to the Committee of Reference and Counsel of the Conference of Foreign Mission Boards of North America, he said that in Japan there had been inadequate preparation, much dissatisfaction, and many misconceptions. Nevertheless, a national council was greatly needed and with proper leadership, financial and organizational cooperation, it should (and did) eventuate. Conversely, the Chinese Church had "turned the theological corner" and was coming into her own as attested by the documents from the Shanghai conference. These differences were striking evidence of the tremendous changes taking place across a broad spectrum in both countries. The nine years since his previous visit seemed like an age: the Far East needed reinterpretation.

Mott had little summer for himself and family that year, 1922. July 24 found him in London, having brought Archie Harte with him, and his son Frederick as secretary. He saw Oldham that day, then met with the Federation secretaries; four days were given to the IMC executive at Canterbury, followed by five days in Copenhagen where the plenary of the World's YMCA and the World's Alliance for Friendship Through the Churches were both meeting. Mott spoke to the latter group in "his most optimistic vein that a world war had been a necessity in order to create, as a reaction, a renaissance movement all over the world." To this statement, one of his best friends, Archbishop Nathan Söderblom of Sweden, took strong exception and was led to reply in what his biographer calls "his possibly most challenging political address."[32] Mott went on to Prague via Berlin, held a third conference with the senior American YMCA secretaries for Europe at Teplice, Czechoslovakia, and attended the Passion Play at Oberammergau before returning home from Cherbourg.

PART 4: **Reorganizing the American YMCA**

"Significant readjustments have characterized the Young Men's Christian Association Movement in the United States since the World War," wrote Owen E. Pence in *The YMCA and Social Need*. The principal institutional modification that took place in the 1920's was the creation of a National Council to replace the International Committee that had governed the Movement for more than forty years.[33] The War Work Council had demonstrated what a unified national organization could accomplish in contrast to the loose relationship of two types of bodies having no organic ties to each other. As powerful city Associations and vigorous state bodies grew, their executives became fearful of the sheer size of the national organization while at the same time their relations with it became confused and often antagonistic. The infrequent national conventions—the source of authority—were at best unevenly representative and were increasingly dominated by the professionals. Mott's control of them amazed even his closest associates and henchmen.[34]

The convention of 1919 began a series of studies of these problems. By 1921 Mott and John D. Rockefeller, Jr., who is portrayed by his biographer as a perfectionist, had decided that the situation needed a thorough examination. Rockefeller offered to finance a comprehensive study that should result in modernization and economies, prevent overlapping, "bring about better co-ordination and co-operation" internally, and on the whole make the Movement "more logical, more effective, and more desirable."[35] The convention of 1922 accepted the offer and called a constitutional convention that met the next year at Cleveland.

As the research progressed, Mott and Rockefeller kept abreast of the findings. By the fall of 1923 Mott was having some misgivings. Certain proposals seemed drastic, he confided to Karl Fries. Fries' reply was revealing:

> Some of their effects must touch you very closely. It is a good thing not to be too tightly bound up with outward conditions and traditional connections, but to be all the more deeply rooted in the will of God and dependent only on Him. What we want is after all not this form or that but the coming of the Kingdom of Christ. May He ever keep us flexible and ready to do His errands.[36]

The recommendations, presented at Cleveland in the fall of 1923, and called the "Mark Jones" report for their author, would have set up a centralized body, which Mott probably preferred. But the "states rights" party rejected it. After five days of jockeying the Convention appointed a special committee to bring in a compromise proposal, which was for a federal system; it was adopted with enthusiasm and ratified nationwide. Mott had written his own preamble to the new constitution (in the small hours of the final day of the Convention) "as an ascription of praise, as a confession of faith, and as an act of dedication." It pledged the Movement to bring the boys and youth of North America "and the other lands served by our Associations" under the sway of the Kingdom of God. He could now reply to Fries that the Convention had been "nothing short of a wonder work of God," a unity having been achieved in the closing hours that had seemed impossible the day before: "It was indeed God's own doing."[37]

This heartfelt expression of relief and resolution may well have been in part because the reorganization had been a tacit criticism of Mott himself. For some time a few metropolitan secretaries, who were convinced that because he had no city Association experience he did not understand their problems, had been a sort of loyal opposition. Some felt that he used their organizations and in fact the entire Movement to further his foreign interests. The criticism sometimes became overt. Mott once showed Colton a vituperative letter from Wilbur Messer, metropolitan Chicago director. Colton remembered that "too moved to comment or be spoken to," Mott had gotten up, and "walked to the window for a long look away." From years of intimate contact Colton knew that Mott "could be hurt," but he never reacted in kind. The research for this biography turned up nothing to disprove Colton's statement. Mott's usual reply ito such a letter would begin "Dear Wilbur," although he normally reserved the first person for a very few close associates. S. Wirt Wiley, secretary at Rochester, New York, and Minneapolis before joining the national staff in 1925, observed to the author that Mott seemed to be entirely free of petty hostility or resentment during the entire period of reorganization, giving kindly attention to his harshest critics and opponents.[38] And there was an occasion when a long hassle over differences was broken off by taking the group to a popular play.

During the year between the constitutional convention of 1923 and the first convention of the new National Council at Buffalo in December, 1924, at which it was expected that he would be offered the general secretaryship, Mott wrestled with the problem of acceptance. He would be sixty in 1925, and all YMCA rules required retirement at that age. In April, 1924, the YMCA house organ *Association Men* reminded the Movement of this. Should he be an exception even though the new Council did not require the old limit? Friends such as Oldham had been urging him for years to leave the "Y" in order to give full time to the missionary enterprise.

Mott set down for himself the pros and cons and discussed the matter with his cabinet, but especially with Fletcher Brockman who as his associate was the most deeply concerned. Cabinet members "leaked" Mott's indecision to key secretaries and YMCA backers across the country, a score of whom implored him to continue. One pointed out that "the carping critic" had virtually disappeared and that another's "almost freakish flare-ups" were no longer taken seriously. "It is at an hour such as this that the Movement looks to you, its chosen and beloved leader," he declared. In the October issue of *Association Forum*, Buffalo secretary A. H. Whitford argued for Mott's re-election. Two weeks before the convention of 1924, Harry W. Stone, secretary at Portland, Oregon, issued an open letter to the National Council calling for Mott:

> There is no doubt that the great mass of association opinion is in favor of Dr. Mott as our leader for the new era, just as the overwhelming national sentiment made George Washington our first president, so that in spite of absurd gossip, criticisms, and weird suggestions he received the unanimous vote of the first electoral college. We have a unique leader in our brotherhood. It would surely seem that he had "come to the kingdom for such a time as this."

Nevertheless, Mott was still undecided when he boarded the train for Buffalo. But the outpouring of affection and esteem there overruled his doubts and he accepted, for a term that would be four years.[39]

Why did he? It was a vindication. The American YMCA was the power base for his worldwide enterprises and he relished the contacts it gave him with the leaders of his generation. He was a layman among laymen in the "Y" fellowship. His cabinet was composed of the ablest and closest friends of his life, and it functioned as a "varsity team" for which he called the signals. For the moment the recent deficits had been met. And Mott could not face retirement.

PART 5: A Fresh Mandate

In his closing remarks to the Constitutional Convention, Mott endorsed the new Council and pledged his heart and will to perpetuate the progressive atmosphere, spirit, and convictions that had won out over "our recent divisions." He anticipated ratification and assembled his new cabinet, just authorized, immediately upon adjournment.

There were to be new appointments at that level, and a fact noted by several was the number of men who had come up through the Student Movement. S. Wirt Wiley, who came in as head of a new home division early in 1925, recalled forty years afterward Mott's strong points as an administrator: his fine judgment of the strengths of men selected for differing functions, the careful delineation of responsibilities among them, and his encouragement of wide latitude and freedom of initiative. Wiley was often surprised by Mott's knowledge of the work of his people, the key to which was his phenomenal memory of their reports. Because of Mott's constant travel, most staff members saw little of him after his annual message, but cabinet members were kept in close personal touch by individual conference and week-end retreat. Mott did not limit his acquaintance with his associates to business matters, Wiley continued, but was concerned about their personal affairs and problems. When H. Dewey Anderson, the last "Y" man out of Russia, in 1926, returned, Mott invited him to his home in Montclair for a full week-end of talk. Anderson was surprised at Mott's concern for several plain people in Russia, but he found Mott "a very good interrogator, well informed, sharp"; he "looked right at you" and did not want to be trifled with. [40]

Colton, who had come to New York a quarter-century earlier than Wiley, noted that the team-work habit made Mott reluctant to decide on major policies when away; at home these were reached "after the issues had been canvassed thoroughly" in the presence of those best informed. Colton also remembered Mott's habit of telling his associates when they were making good. He was deeply grateful for the Chief's remarkable ability to comfort those in grief or anxiety. When Colton's only daughter died inexplicably in the bloom of young womanhood, Mott helped cushion the shock; both he and Leila made editorial comments on Colton's published tribute to her. Soichi Saito, the national YMCA secretary of Japan, was in New York when the catastrophic earthquake of 1923 struck Tokyo; he remembered all his life how Mott dropped everything to read scripture and pray with him. When Mott retired from the YMCA, Colton's comment that the staff had wondered whether he had meant the most to each of them "as a father, brother, friend or chieftain" summarized the matter. [41] Mott's personal staff continued to be supported by special gifts from his generous friends as long as he remained in the secretaryship, though the loss through death in 1923 of the sympathy and generosity of Mrs. McCormick, who had initiated this policy in 1897, was a deep sorrow. [42]

One of Mott's finest contributions to the YMCA was his share in obtaining the funds to establish the retirement system for its professional employees, agitation for which had surfaced in the secretarial organization as early as 1909. Mott negotiated a conditional Rockefeller gift of one million dollars that stimulated the raising of a four-million-dollar accrued liability fund with which the operation began in 1922. Other wealthy friends contributed and local Associations raised $300,000. Earl

Brandenberg, executive of the fund from 1922 to 1940, once admitted that this happened to be a money-raising project that Mott tended to put off, so he required Brandenberg to keep the pressure on him! Consummated "in the teeth of impossible financial conditions," the retirement plan was a notable step in upgrading the secretarial profession. Mott found a way to include the secretaries of the World's Alliance in its coverage. Although he often emphasized the importance of leadership and of adequate preparation for the secretaryship, Mott virtually ignored the financial needs of the two YMCA training schools, Springfield College at Springfield, Massachusetts, and George Williams College at Chicago, probably because of his own experience but also lest endorsement of their liberal teachings result in controversy and embarrass him with some conservative supporters. He considered Willis Weatherford's YMCA Graduate School in Nashville prophetic, but did little for it. His essentially autobiographical talks on the physical, intellectual, and spiritual life of the secretary, developed earlier, were in steady demand and were given frequently at professional gatherings; some of them achieved perennial usefulness, even into the 1970's.[43]

At one time or another during his secretaryship, Mott gave addresses emphasizing the spiritual aspects and potentials of the major Association programs for which he carried supervisory responsibility—religious work, the railroad YMCA, the physical program, activities for boys and young men, students—almost entirely elitist interests. Neither Mott nor the YMCA's nor the churches whose ideology they reflected were seriously concerned for the workers, whose plight more than any other factor save urban problems had precipitated the social gospel. By 1930 the National Council had no industrial staff. Yet such was Mott's concern for boys' work, and the Associations did try to reach boys of all social classes, that he supported Edgar M. Robinson's vision of promoting it on a global scale through the world's Alliance of YMCA's, underwriting and participating in the great boys' work conference at Pörtschach, Austria, in 1923.

But Mott's largest project in the first half of the 1920's was a special religious work emphasis campaign addressed to the increasing secularization of the "Y." It took him to eighty-five cities for consultations, staff conferences, and inspirational addresses. From Asheville to Albuquerque, Portland, Maine to Portland, Oregon, he counseled local staff to "give priority to religious work" because it was the heart of the YMCA. According to his own outline, the aim was to increase the spiritual vitality of the Movement. Early in the drive he told the professional staff of the Boston YMCA that confronting young men and boys with the living Christ was "in a sentence the objective of this continent-wide campaign": from it comes the great fruitage of the YMCA; it is the secret of world-conquering power and inescapably our greatest need; it is what the Church expects from us, the area of truest leadership; it is "what imparted a sense of divine mission to the call of each of us," and because the "Y" is at a fork in the road, between plans and vitality, contraction or expansion—our faith is involved. There were leaders' retreats in each region and in each city meetings with influential laymen, with clergymen and other professional religious leaders, with the entire working forces of the Associations, and where possible mass meetings of Christian men and of boys, "to confront them with the living Christ."[44]

Midway in the campaign it was reported that Mott had spoken 170 times with "great power and persuasiveness," and aggregate attendance had exceeded 30,000. Colton, who organized the campaign, or a member of his staff, preceded Mott and another followed up. In Butte, Montana, Colton was confronted by a local chairman—"an elderly seasoned Westerner given to profanity backed up with alcoholic breath"—who insisted that men would walk out of the meeting if Mott spoke about Christ and religion. The top male leadership of the city assembled in the hotel advertising the longest bar in America. Mott gave his address on "Why thinking men throughout the world believe in Jesus Christ as Savior and Lord," stopping "barely short of calling on them, one and all riveted to their seats, for decisions to begin the Christian life." Later the doubting chairman, "almost limp in a lounge chair," burst out to Colton: "My God, if we had preachers like that, the churches wouldn't hold the men."[45]

The campaign was planned to utilize the best of both of two approaches that were contending for attention throughout the Movement: the specialized religious work department, which was on the way out, and the newer view that each department should develop the Christian character of its own clientele. In spite of these Herculean efforts, traditional Bible studies and religious work departments diminished throughout the decade as Association leaders turned to "a broadly social interpretation of religion" to be instilled by the methods of progressive education. Mott was at home with the social gospel, acknowledging in the foreword of the collection of his messages in his campaign—*Confronting Young Men with the Living Christ*—that "the great social task of Christianity" had been "ever present" to his mind throughout it but the chief concern in these visitations had been "the vital relationship to the Lord of Life—the Source alike of all social achievement and of the highest individual attainment." The book was dedicated to the memory of George Williams, D. L. Moody, Henry Drummond, and Archbishop Nicolai of Japan. Although Mott and other old timers might lament "the absorption of a second generation of secretaries in administrative responsibilities in contrast to the first generation who conceived themselves to be primarily personal religious leaders of men," they could not counteract the influence of the followers of John Dewey. [46]

Some of the popular criticism of YMCA War Work and of Mott's share in the Interchurch World Movement lingered in parts of the country. He wrote a long, hard-hitting speech that met these head-on, giving it in places where needed but prominently in Atlanta at the first regional YMCA Conference in the South, in April, 1921. The YMCA is not a church, but it is a child of the Church, he began. It is controlled, recognized, and largely supported by the churches through their members. The Portland basis and the Paris basis of YMCA membership were framed by clergymen as well as laymen. It was at the invitation of missionaries that the YMCA expanded to "the less favored lands." Ignorance, lack of team work, of consultation, of fellowship, and poor thinking have contributed to poor relations between the "Y" and the churches.

The constructive portion of this speech covered some ten points, adroitly addressed to Association men, with nuances for the general public. Mott's basic assertions were that "every leader of the YMCA should regard himself as a recruiting officer for the Church of Jesus Christ," and "we must maintain the YMCA as an essentially religious, pronouncedly Christian and aggressively evangelistic and missionary movement." In Atlanta a long discussion period followed in which Mott answered, and parried, queries ranging from "how true is it . . . that you want to destroy denominations?" to the removal of pastors in favor of YMCA workers at Army camps in the South during the War. The reply ran to a thousand words and included the reading of lengthy telegraphic exchanges with the War Department.

A questioner from Arkansas said that some people in his state believed that Mott had launched the Interchurch World Movement to develop "a colossal system" of which he would be "the first great Pope." Mott replied with a thumbnail history of the Interchurch, introducing it with Mark Twain's word that "Truth is the choicest possession we have; therefore, let us economize it." He then pointed out that he had not been present at the organization of the ICWM and that its real founder had been James I. Vance of Nashville. A committee was formed and Mott's name included in it while he had been on vacation in the South. He had resisted being drafted for the position he finally took on its Executive Committee, he said, and then analyzed the weaknesses of the ICWM, in terms similar to those given in Chapter 10 above. He concluded a long statement by saying that he had not led the ICWM and that having raised $150,000,000 it could not be considered a real failure. He thanked God that he had been permitted to have a part in it and wished that there could have been "more hours and more strength and more influence to pour into it"—all this "in the interest of the Church of Christ which I love."[47]

As the fear of Bolshevism and hence of almost anything Russian spread after the War, Mott was called upon to defend the YMCA against criticism from conservatives. An early case was the lodging of charges against the Interchurch Movement, the Federal Council of Churches, and the YMCA for employing Harry F. Ward, F. M. Crouch, Jerome Davis, and Julius F. Hecker, whom a self-appointed investigator alleged were guilty of advocating radical ideas. John D. Rockefeller, Jr., brought the matter to Mott's attention on the eve of Mott's departure for Europe in April, 1920. Mott received a delegation that made similar allegations, and it fell to him to reply to Judge E. H. Gary of United States Steel. Mott defended Hecker and described the steps that had been taken to clear him prior to his being hired by the YMCA, but promised that if certain charges were to be proved he would be dismissed. Hecker was the only one of the four then employed by the "Y," and since Mott had just resigned from the Executive Committee of the Interchurch, he could but promise that its officers would "go into these cases with special care." Hecker and Davis would embarrass him again.[48]

A situation that came much closer to home revolved around Sherwood Eddy, whose conversion to the social gospel impelled him to join the Socialist Party. His bold advocacy of the United States' recognition of Soviet Russia brought repercussions. Eddy had taken the precaution of presenting his resignation from the staff of the National Council of YMCA's. Colton was present at the General Board meeting at which the matter came up:

> Dignified but deadly earnest debate took place on the motion to accept the proffered retirement. When all the laymen who wished to speak had done so, Mott quietly expressed his position. He believed there remained room in the YMCA for one of Eddy's character, talent and Christian devotion for continuing great usefulness, though some of his views diverged from

those of others. If not, there would seem not to be room for himself. When it came to voting two members raised their hands for what in the case would have amounted to dismissal [of Eddy]. [49]

As this incident became a part of YMCA folklore, other accounts appeared. According to one of them Mott had retorted:

It is strange if we must resign when we have a vision! If you must go out to get freedom to prophesy, why, I must go out, too. No movement is the right place for either of us if we can't speak out all that is in us from God to say. [50]

The most popular version was that Mott had simply said, "If Sherwood goes, I go." Eddy himself wrote that Mott had fought his battle "on principle against Judge Gary and the conservatives who conscientiously demanded my expulsion from the YMCA. He always defended the right of free speech for relatively radical doctrines. But he never spoke the radical word himself. That was not his job."[51] When Eddy wrote those words in 1934, in his first autobiography, A Pilgrimage of Ideas, or the Re-Education of Sherwood Eddy, Leila Mott thought the book too liberal for her sister and husband in China to show to their China Inland Mission or Southern Baptist friends.

PART 6: The Social Gospel and Mott's Theology

Mott believed it his duty to spur the organizations for which he was responsible into Christian social action. Although Eddy had gone on to say, in the context with which Part 5 concluded, that Mott "combined the rational processes of the philosopher and the statesman with the swift intuition of a woman as no other man I have known," he was a statesman, not a prophet. "He could not combine these contradictory qualities in one; it is almost impossible for a statesman who is a politician, a bishop or an organizer to be a prophet. The statesman must hold things and men together."[52]

Eddy expected a prophet to take a doctrinaire position such as absolute pacifism or socialism. Mott never assumed a dogmatic stance, but as editor, manager, or executive, he was a purveyor of ideas, a strategist, a promoter of programs—in this case one who encouraged the social application of Christian ethics. His utterances and actions during the turbulent twenties came from unequivocal commitment to social Christianity, especially in the areas of race and internationalism if not in economics.

The quest for Holiness that had fired Mott's youth turned him toward those perfectionist practices of interdenominational fellowship, lay leadership, and the primacy of ethics over dogma that, as Timothy L. Smith has shown, had "geared ancient creeds to the drive shaft of social reform." In the mid-nineteenth century it attacked slavery, poverty, and greed; in the last quarter of that century and the early twentieth, it provided powerful motivation for the social gospel. The main line of Methodism, in which Mott stood, discovered the social gospel late, but with fervor.[53] Social Christianity was a logical outgrowth from Mott's perfectionist theology; he was early aware of it, and brought it into the Student Movement soon after the turn of the century. It became more explicit upon the intensification of social issues and his greater awareness of them in the 1920's, when the American Student YMCA and the WSCF were both even more fully involved in it than before the War.

He urged the national YMCA, assembled at Atlantic City in 1921, to move "more nearly into the middle of the stream of the great Christian movement—that is, the effort to bring all social relations of young men under the rule of Jesus Christ." He told a group of secretaries in Japan in 1922 that one of the universal principles of the YMCA was to *"proclaim and illustrate the complete Gospel,"* by which he meant salvation not only of the individual but "salvation of society." The "Y" should insist in season and out of season that Christ should rule *all* life, and life in all its relationships. "We stand for a *great* Gospel," the two aspects of which are not in antagonism. "It is an idle dream to talk of society becoming Christian if the individual is not. They are inseparably associated."

In presenting a message to the new National Council of the YMCA's two years later, he called upon it to heed the heroic challenge of the "unprecedented industrial, international, and interracial situation throughout the world." In a review of the state of the Movement for its employed officers that same year, Mott included a long section on "the social conscience of the brotherhood" in which he recognized an increased momentum toward bringing the principles and spirit of Jesus Christ to bear upon social and racial issues. Three years earlier he had taken them to task for lack of "prophetic and heroic notes." In a program projection of 1925 he drew attention to the YMCA's potential "for helping to solve the most serious, most emergent problems of our generation"—social unrest, racial antagonisms, crime and lawlessness, international misunderstandings, the readjustment of relations between men and women. "The existence, strength, and gravity of these perils the world over, might well cause consternation were it not for the absolute sufficiency of the Lord Jesus Christ to meet this appalling array."[54]

Although Mott's popularity as a college preacher was much diminished in the 1920's, he spoke annually at Cornell and at Yale, with occasional stands elsewhere. In 1923 he told an audience at the University of Wisconsin that students everywhere were expanding their faith by applying it to the current world situation. Later that year at Cornell he gave an inspired adaptation of his great address at St. Beatenberg in 1920 on "The Strength of the Hills," in which he declared that the vital energies poured into our lives from the heights are not ends in themselves, they are not our own, they are His also, they are to be placed at the disposal of the Lord of Life and His program for mankind.

The SVM Quadrennial at Indianapolis in the winter of 1923–24 was the first that Mott neither planned nor chaired. One of his critics wrote of it as "the swan song of the founders," but Francis P. Miller, who would succeed Mott as chairman of the WSCF, observed that Mott had certainly not lost touch with students. In a long address, much of which must have fallen on deaf ears, Mott met his hearers' sceptical attitude sympathetically:

> The generation represented here is dissatisfied with the past and it certainly has a right to be. It is very much dissatisfied also with the present, and again I say it has a right to be. It is keenly critical. What has it not criticized? How much better this is, however, than the apathy, indifference, and inertia which have characterized far too many in the past. The present generation is the most alert and inquiring generation that the world has ever known . . . surging in its mind and heart are tides of new thought and social passion; where may not these tides bear it if but controlled by the living Christ and His unselfish representatives?[55]

Among the attractive traits he acknowledged in his youthful audience were hopefulness, idealism, adventure—"never quite so much needed as in these coming days of warfare, if the principles of Jesus are to have right of way in all human relationships." In the same address he confessed that among the many meanings of the SVM watchword for him had been the vivid appreciation of "both the social and individual aspects of the Christian Gospel and likewise their essential unity."[56]

When he addressed the 1928 SVM Quadrennial at Detroit, he developed the theme of a synthesis between the "old and never-to-be-neglected individual gospel and the equally true and indispensable social gospel of Christ," which "concerns every human being of every nation, of every race, of every condition, in the whole range of his being, in all his relationships—social, international, inter-racial—in all time and eternity." At Buffalo four years later he delineated the moving frontier of missions as less geographic than "social, economic, rural, racial, international," and set it in the context of a "larger evangelism." The primary purpose of the Church, he told these Volunteers, is "to make Jesus Christ known, trusted, loved, obeyed, and exemplified in the whole range of individual life and in all human relationships."[57]

Under Mott's general supervision as executive of the American YMCA, specialized work for blacks received a new impetus through the leadership of Channing H. Tobias beginning in 1924 and with the stimulating example of Max Yergan's mission to Bantu students in South Africa.[58] Black conventions were resumed, and at the one in 1921 Mott reminded the delegates that he and W. H. Hunton, the first black secretary, had entered the service of the brotherhood in the same year, 1888. Race, he went on, was a grave and urgent worldwide problem to the solution of which the YMCA's could contribute powerfully because of their interracial presence in fifty nations: they recognized the providential mission of each race in its individuality, its native leadership, its full development, and its self-expression. The YMCA assumes the Lordship of Christ and its corollary that all men are brothers in him, a principle that transcends "the accidents of race."

A constructive program for the black Associations, Mott went on, must apply these principles in individual, social, industrial, and national situations. Our work as well as our lives must express goodwill and brotherhood by seizing every opportunity to translate our ideals into practice. Nevertheless, there must be prayer to undergird all external arrangements, for we are called to be apostles of reconciliation, to be peace*makers*, for brotherhood is the hope of the world.

At a meeting of blacks held in connection with the Southern Regional YMCA Conference of 1921, Mott identified with the "hopes and aspirations of your race" and said that he felt "as one with you," both here and in Africa. "Let us press out into this great warfare against the forces of ignorance, prejudice and superstition," not doubting God and his leadership. And Mott pledged that his decisions would match his interest in the black program. To hopes expressed by a delegate from Virginia that the "Y" would "stand squarely for the principles of justice and Christianity with regard to relations of employer and employee" and in "relations between the races," Mott replied that its response would be "the supreme test of whether we are worthy of these times": do we have "the requisite heroism?" At this meeting, Will Alexander, who with W. D. Weatherford had organized the Inter-Racial Commission, was introduced by Mott, who must have taken quiet satisfaction in the knowledge, which was not mentioned, that he had opened doors of financial support for that major effort to improve race relations in the South. Mott again spoke at an interracial conference at Asheville in 1924, emphasizing "Processes of Ensuring Unity." The next year, when the black conference met in Washington, he outlined ways and means to occupy the field. Nevertheless, the American YMCA remained essentially segregated until well after World War II, though by then it was far ahead of the churches in moving toward integration.[59]

Mott's concern with race was also international. As editor of the WSCF magazine, *The Student World,* he devoted the entire July issue of 1921 to it. His introductory editorial was entitled "Inter-racial Problems and Christian Duty." After citing ancient sayings such as the Chinese aphorism that "All within the four seas are brothers," he declared that Christ had made this truth "one of the pillars of His teaching" and had based racial equality "for the first time upon a purely ethical and individual relationship to the Father of all" and bade His followers make disciples of all peoples and races on an equal footing. Then followed words not quite characteristic of Mott:

> It is against such background that the apostasy of many of Christ's professed followers to-day stands in such black relief. The hatred and abuse of coloured races by the whites, or of white races by the coloured is reminiscent of the jungle and of the primitive blood feud. That it persists even under the shadow of cross-tipped church spires proves not the impotence of Christ but the infidelity of his disciples.[60]

Articles followed by Inazo Nitobe, Y. Y. Tsu, R. R. Moton, M. N. Chatterjee, and Katsuji Kato. The editor commented that "the frankness, hopefulness, and kindliness with which all these writers discuss topics that ordinarily arouse cynical bitterness and intolerant denunciation are fresh evidence of the power of the Spirit of Christ to subdue even the demons of racial passion."[61]

At a great missionary conference in Washington in 1925 Mott set forth his basic convictions in this matter:

> Christ has not revealed himself solely or fully through any one nation, race, or communion. No part of mankind has a monopoly of His gifts. Every national and denominational tradition has a contribution to make which can enrich the Body of Christ.... For as in Christ, Who is the Head, there is neither Jew nor Greek, neither male nor female, barbarian, Scythian, bond nor free—not because He is none of these, but because He is all of them—so the Church which is His body cannot be perfected until they shall bring the glory and the honor of the nations into it—that is to

say, until the spiritual characteristics of every race and Christian name have been, not submerged, but brought to their individual perfection, in a perfect whole.

Thus Mott brought the Holiness ideal of his youth to full ethical impact.

Every race, every land—small as well as great, every denomination not only has the right but should have the opportunity, thus to express itself, thus to make its contribution. [62]

Such convictions not only motivated Mott's devotion to the ecumenical missionary movement and interracial understanding at home, but were the springs of his concern for peace.

He gave what proved to be his definitive address on "The Race Problem" in Australia in 1926. The infinite value of each race is a Christian conception; apparent racial inequalities are not the proper basis for judgment: all are equal in the sight of God, all are members one of another and hence are essential to each other, having one blood, sharing one Gospel, one discipleship, one Kingdom and Lord, one final judgment, and one heaven. He recommended the writers to whom he was indebted: Oldham, Speer, Weatherford, Basil Mathews, and Gandhi. On the practical side he urged the use of every device that could break down feelings of racial superiority or isolation—educational means, fellowship, personal contacts with persons of other races such as his own with Baron Goto, the cultivation of friendly relations among foreign students, fostering groups such as the Institute of Pacific Relations, efforts to cultivate right public opinion, the waging of a constant warfare against the roots of racial misunderstanding and strife, prayer, and striving for reconciliation. [63]

Limitations of space allow no more than mention here of Mott's other ethical concerns in the twenties. He endorsed some peace statements and kept active in the Church Peace Union but did not return to the Fellowship of Reconciliation. He recommended to his staff the first book by Kirby Page, an absolute pacifist who had been his secretary in the summer of 1918—*War: Its Causes, Consequences, and Cure.* [64] He supported the pacifistic programs of the North American Student Christian Movement, most of whose secretaries were pacifists. He talked with numerous delegates to the Washington Disarmament Conference and visited them on his world journeys, especially the Japanese. He was a consistent if not vocal supporter of the League of Nations. After a brief period of perplexity regarding the Bolshevik government of Russia, he branded communism as a malignancy, yet kept YMCA workers in the

Soviet Union as long as possible. He maintained a serious interest in the Russian emigré communities in Berlin and then in Paris, as will be shown. Financing of some of his more liberal projects came from Mrs. Emmons (Anita McCormick) Blaine, supporter of numerous progressive causes.[65]

The Kingdom of God, Mott told many audiences on his religious emphasis tours, ought to include the kingdoms of finance, commerce, industry, labor, the movies, the press, learning, and of society, because Christ is to be Lord of all or He is not Lord at all. The last phrase declared not only the wellspring of his social ethics but the source of his faith and the motivation of his career. From the moment of his youthful commitment to the Lordship of Christ that winter morning in his room at Cornell, the certainty of the Resurrection had been the guiding light of his life. Unlike the "bracing Christian individualism" of George Williams, the patron saint of every nineteenth-century "Y" man, whose message never altered, Mott's overview and vocabulary broadened with his worldwide experience and as the social gospel came into closer focus. To convey his meaning he would use such phrases as "the larger Christ," the "great gospel," the "larger evangelism," the "whole gospel," a "synthesis between the old and never-to-be-neglected individual gospel and the equally true and indispensable social Gospel of Christ."[66]

To the slander that Methodists had no theology and Mott was one of them—carelessly uttered by some of his younger colleagues who by the 1920's were making a point of being amused by his not infrequently extravagant verbiage—it should be replied that Mott simply assumed the eternal validity of what were for him the Christian truths; he was really not interested in theological systems as such. It is specious to assume that one for whom Christ was a real presence and God as near as breathing had no theology. Sherwood Eddy once put this in a few words:

> As truly as John Wesley, Mott can repeat the words of the great Augustine: "I take a whole Christ for my Saviour; I take the whole Bible for my staff; I take the whole Church for my fellowship."[67]

As had been the case with the Holiness of his youth, Mott's mature emphasis continued to be on the universality of Christian experience and fellowship rather than in an exclusive patch of dogma. His casual remark that his best claim to being a Methodist was because the world was his parish should be seen as much more than a reference to geography, whether or not he so intended it. It was not only an acknowledgment of his great debt to Wesley but an affirmation of his congeniality with all

Christians from those Roman Catholics who were open to ecumenical fellowship (he would have been delighted with Vatican II developments) through Orthodoxy and most Protestants to the Friends. Not that Mott held no basic Christian doctrines: he once rebuked William R. Moody, son of the evangelist, for accusing him of softness on the fundamentals. When a correspondent in England raised questions he replied that he had once held "the Unitarian position" but had long been an evangelical.

The clearest public confession of faith we have is Mott's statement before the distinguished audience honoring his retirement from the YMCA in 1928: "My lifework has not been built around a dead Christ but one alive forevermore," whose "supremacy and sufficiency" meet "the deepest longings and the highest aspirations of the human heart and of the human race."

> At His name ultimately every knee shall bow and every tongue confess that He is Lord of all. He not only was but is the living Christ. He communicates Himself to us as truly, as manifestly as any other fact of human experience. Our great work, as I have been trying to emphasize in my addresses, papers, and public conferences, is to make Jesus Christ known, trusted, loved, and obeyed, in the whole range of one's individual life and in all relationships. [68]

His favorite hymn was said to be "The Church's One Foundation." When, as President of the World's Alliance of YMCA's, he issued his last call to the week of prayer and world fellowship, the theme was "One Lord for One World."

If Mott must be inserted into one of the pigeonholes constructed by historians of American theology, the one that comes nearest to fitting is liberal evangelical, in the sense that, as H. Richard Niebuhr pointed out with regard to Charles G. Finney and earlier evangelicals, "now" is the time of times, of crisis, and of promise. [69] By the 1920's there was a good bit of Orthodoxy in Mott; as we shall see shortly, this was the period of his greatest involvement with the Eastern churches. He felt bound to them by mutual commitment to the victorious risen Christ who is worshipped through Orthodox liturgy and music. In the twenties he expedited the republication of an English version of the Service Book of the Orthodox Church. He attended Russian Orthodox Christmas services when he could. [70] He once named a dozen denominations and their leaders by whom his Christian experience had been enriched. He listed not only Methodism and most mainline churches but included the Moravians (who had profoundly influenced Wesley), at whose center in Saxony an IMC meeting was held in 1932, and the Friends, whose worship he had once characterized as truly "Holy Ghost religion." In his later years Mott formed a friendship with Rufus Jones, the Quaker leader, who greatly enhanced his long-standing appreciation of that tradition. Mott was, in fact, a kind of Quaker himself.

Prayer was the tie that bound this worldwide fellowship. In special situations Mott asked friends to pray for him not only for personal guidance but that God's will might be realized in the project at hand. The several prayer circles to which he belonged were sources of strength. It was as a man of prayer that some colleagues remembered him most vividly. [71]

The evangelical position commended Mott to Continentals from the early days at Gross-Almerode and Vadstena to the critical talks at Crans and St. Beatenberg. His own pietism gradually won most German and Scandinavian Lutherans, though it must be admitted that he did not respond to Lutheran worship with its emphasis on the death and suffering of Christ as he did to the triumphalist motif of Orthodoxy. D. Eric Stange, German national YMCA secretary, remembered that in the 1920's many of his constituents were attracted to Mott as a friend who shared their unique YMCA pietistic tradition that had stemmed from the nineteenth-century Association worker Friederick von Schluembach. Bishop Hans Lilje recalled that "some of our most valuable people" had likewise accepted Mott's own "rather simple evangelical faith" as "the kind of pietism the Germans understood"; as a consequence, he had "great influence" with them. A British colleague thought of this as a sort of "mysticism." [72]

On the other hand some German academic theologians were as late as 1925 still ringing changes on the wartime issues and picturing Mott as the archetypal American missionary who was "first of all an American and then a Christian," at the same time admitting that he was one of the most important Americans of his generation, surpassing even his friend President Wilson. One writer gave the traditional pietistic criticism of activism a somewhat different twist by claiming that American missions were an evidence of American cultural pluralism and accusing Americans of exporting a religion they no longer needed. Mott, he claimed, epitomized the American missionary enterprise, which he had shaped with a nationalistic character "inconsistent with the essence of Christianity." [73] Mott did not reply to such insinuations, though his friends occasionally did; some who knew him best believed that his Americanism occasionally did outweigh his commitment to internationalism.

Mott's assumptions concerning the perpetual crisis in human affairs were Biblical in origin:

> The sense of the immediacy of Christ and His work has been and is central with me. He is not static, but the fountain head of spiritual vitality and the generating source of all of the profound spiritual changes which have taken place and of the great creative work yet to be. [74]

In China in 1926 Mott talked to an intimate secretarial group on "My personal experience of Jesus Christ." This attitude enabled him to appreciate Continental theology as that developed, though he took little interest in it. This was in spite of its eschatological nature, an aspect that had been convincing in the early days of the SVM whose watchword was still a life commitment, a characteristic expression of his evangelical intensity. The evangelical approach, with its emphasis upon the will, explains his popularity with British students in the 1890's; their parents had responded similarly to Moody. [75] Mott's evangelicalism appealed to missionaries around the world because of their own motivation. John and Leila Mott were welcomed to Australia and New Zealand in 1896 because they stood in the evangelical tradition of those transplanted Victorian cultures. The universal appeal of evangelicalism will be seen in Mott's leadership of the Jerusalem missionary conference of 1928 in its symbolic setting on the Mount of Olives.

Mott avoided the Fundamentalist-Modernist controversies of the 1920's, as he did all argument, taking no part in them. The intimate Quiet Day fellowship of which he had been a member since the 1890's was saddened and driven to its knees in 1923 when two members of long standing wrote to say that they could no longer commune because the majority did not adhere to certain fundamentals. [76] Mott had early encouraged Harry Emerson Fosdick, who became immensely popular in student circles, but when Fosdick attacked the fundamentalists, Mott neither supported nor criticized him, although Fosdick's interpretive phrase "abiding experiences and changing categories" was doubtless congenial. The founder and longtime general secretary of the WSCF held, as the Federation itself came to believe (this was a two-way process of education), that theological differences should be mutually enriching rather than mutually exclusive. Mott had brought Harry Ward and Walter Rauschenbusch to the national student conference on social problems in 1914, and the Student YMCA was now in the 1920's led by liberals and some who were thought of as radicals, but John and Leila Mott maintained their personal friendship with the descendants of J. Hudson

Taylor, founder of the conservative China Inland Mission. A YMCA colleague described Mott as an "essentialist" rather than either a modernist or fundamentalist because he dealt "with intellectual, moral and spiritual essentials." It pained Mott that Robert Wilder moved to the conservative side in his last years.[77]

Mott's ecumenical stance was evident in broadening the YMCA basis of membership to include Roman Catholics in Catholic countries. His intimates came to feel that he had little personal interest in extending the strictly Protestant "Portland basis" on which the North American Associations had grown to maturity and power, preferring the broader "Paris basis" with its ecumenical inclusiveness. One of his colleagues commented that unlike Robert E. Speer, who was conservative and unyielding in such matters, Mott was sometimes too much the mediator.[78]

Mott had "a very natural sense of keeping abreast with movements," commented Bishop Hans Lilje. He was interested in the new theological trends of the late twenties, and, as Samuel McCrea Cavert said, in theologians as well as technical theology. In 1930, on Mott's invitation, Henry P. Van Dusen and Cavert assembled a small group of young theologians for a week-end. Mott "listened with both ears," said Henry Nelson Wieman, who chaired the discussions. During those two days Mott "did something magnificent, yet so subtle that those of us present never saw it until weeks and months had passed and we had opportunity to reflect upon it. When I think of it now a little shiver goes up my spine!" Wieman went on. Mott sat quietly as his young guests, who had never been through the night and the flood, "criticized and questioned the deepest convictions of his life," thought rather lightly of them, and "wanted to know whether they meant anything anyway." The bright young men said smart, keen things. They occasionally showed him where he was wrong—they who "had never caught the whole world in their arms and struggled to carry it like a wounded brother 'to the foot of the cross.'" At the end, Wieman related, just before we parted, Mott spoke briefly:

> Thanked us for coming and for our participation and then stated those simple convictions which had carried him through the great labor of his life, up the long mountain, through the dark sea. But he was not trying to persuade us. He was not arguing with us. He was scarcely talking to us. He was simply stating what he had so often stated, the simple faith by which he lived. Then he went away with that calm, unhasting step, with that manner that seems never ruffled, never excited, never anxious.

There is something like the mountains and the sea in John R. Mott. He will always be the same, very simple and a bit sublime.[79]

PART 7: Five Trips for Four Organizations

The major developments of the mid-1920's in four of the organizations to which Mott was related—the WSCF, the World's Alliance of YMCA's, the foreign outreach of the American Associations, the International Missionary Council—involved him in five tours between the spring of 1923 and the summer of 1926. During that time he visited most of the countries of Europe except Russia, and parts of North Africa and the Near East, several of them five times.

By far the largest program of the WSCF in the first half of the 1920's was European Student Relief. Mott not only obtained funds for it from Rockefeller and other sources, but contributed to the individual needs of national student and other staff members, even Pastor Humburg, when economic collapse or earthquake reduced to ruin the student worlds of Germany, Greece, Russia, Bulgaria, or Tokyo. He continued to administer the affairs of the Federation largely by correspondence with the secretaries, for which they were grateful. He held the major responsibility for the agenda of each General or Executive Committee meeting, conferring with the staff prior to each one. An important contribution was the presentation of the keynote address on a theme such as "The supremacy of the Lord Jesus Christ," or "Have I not seen Jesus Christ our Lord?" He edited *The Student World* until after the General Committee meeting at Nyborg-Strand, Denmark, in 1926, and remained on as Chairman until 1928.

The Executive Committee met in 1923, during the interim between the epochal Peking Conference of 1922 and the General Committee of 1924. The twenty members were the guests of Colonel and Mrs. van Berchem who had entertained that pre-IMC missionary group at their chateau overlooking Lac Léman at Crans near Geneva in 1920. By now the Federation secretaries were in such turmoil that they submitted their resignations to the Committee, a situation precipitated by the magnitude of their task, post-War crises, clashes of strong personalities, disagreement on policies, and Mott's withdrawal from the general secretaryship without specific definition of responsibilities among them. One version of the resignations was that they were in protest against the arbitrariness of the Chairman; they were not accepted. Mott prepared a memo for himself on the duties of the Chairman, and Henri-Louis Henriod, who would become Acting General Secretary, did likewise. [80] Mott was not happy with Henriod's proposals, yet this in no way marred their friendly collaboration, Mott frequently praising Henriod for the effective manner in which he administered the Geneva office. The division of responsibilities engaged the General Committee again in 1924, and there was a later attempt to define the duties of the Committee itself. [81]

Crans left a bad taste in many Federation mouths, Mott later writing Henriod that "we should not be proud of much of the time we spent there, but I believe that God has forgiven us and will overrule; but we certainly must avoid allowing ourselves to get into a similar state again." Yet there was one joyous occasion when the problems of trying to be a world body were forgotten in order to celebrate Mott's fifty-eighth birthday on May 25. Colonel van Berchem presented an immense birthday cake decorated with five large candles each for ten years and eight small ones, commenting that there should have been ten times as many because Mott had done the work of ten men throughout his lifetime. Soichi Saito, national "Y" secretary of Japan, translated a poem he had composed in Japanese:

> O lover of nature! O friend of young men and young women!
> O big brother of us all! O humble servant of God!
> Your heart beats with the world. Your vision is one Kingdom on earth. [82]

Charles Hurrey then gave one of his humorous monologues mimicking Mott's manner of delivery, "to the great merriment of all," including Mott, whose voice later gave audible proof that he had been deeply touched.

Miss Rouse declared in her history of the Federation that at High Leigh, an hour north of London, the next year, the General Committee's meeting marked a second "end of the frontier" era similar to that at Mohonk in 1913. The distribution of responsibilities was helped by making Henriod Acting General Secretary. The session was remarkable for the presence of Orthodox delegates from seven countries and for the election of Max Yergan, the black American secretary at work in South Africa, to the Executive Committee. A variety of theological viewpoints produced some tensions, which led J. H. Oldham to advise holding fast to opposing principles instead of trying to thresh out meaningless compromises. The new ecumenical hymnal prepared largely by Suzanne Bidgrain was used for the first time and a companion book of devotional resources was authorized after Mott illustrated out of his experience "the enrichment that would come to the spiritual life" of the Federation's members "from making use of the devotional resources of other Movements and of all the great Christian communions." Also at High Leigh, Roswell Barnes of the United States and Willem A. Visser 't Hooft of Holland (the latter having been a lay apprentice in European Student Relief under Conrad Hoffman for two years) argued strongly in favor of continuing that work. Both Mott and Henriod felt some disappointment with the session.

Although it is getting ahead of our story, mention must be made here of the General Committee meeting at Nyborg-Strand, Denmark, in 1926, which Mott opened with a searching talk called "The place whereon thou standest is holy ground." The most notable decision made there was to recognize the Russian Orthodox confessional position and thus to bring the fullness of Orthodoxy into the Federation. It was reported that European Student Relief had distributed more than $2,500,000 given by students of forty-two countries to their fellows in nineteen lands, thanks to the "marvelous resourcefulness" of its director, Conrad Hoffman, whom Mott had appointed in 1921. It was decided, however, to make the ESR into an autonomous body, International Student Service, which under wider sponsorship would perform a broader range of functions. Mott announced his intention to resign soon, which raised a unanimous protest from the secretaries and almost fifty delegates who signed a letter to Mrs. Mott asking her support and understanding of their need for his continued "help, his vast understanding, strength and loving care . . . his faith to strengthen ours" for "another period of leadership."[83]

In 1923, following a brief rest, Mott had gone from Crans to Pörtschach in southern Austria for the YMCA World Alliance conference on boys' work that had been in preparation for years by Edgar M. Robinson, now boys' work secretary for the Alliance. More than 800 delegates came from fifty-four countries, but disappointingly few from the Orient. Mott spoke several times, once introducing a distinguished visitor, Gennadios, the Greek Orthodox Metropolitan of Saloniki, head of a delegation requesting funds for a YMCA building in their city.[84]

It was at Pörtschach that young Visser 't Hooft first saw Mott in action:

> Now I could watch the great missionary statesman and evangelist operate in an international assembly. Speaking on "Boyhood—the Greatest Asset of Any Nation" he described the "new spirit moving on the troubled waters of the youth of the world" and defined the common element in all the

many new youth movements as "a protest against the past" and as "a burning desire for independence and self-determination." And he burst out: "Thank God, we have a Gospel which can influence and guide these overflowing tides of living interest and passion. To whom else shall they go?" That was a message which our tired European Christians could not afford to ignore. [85]

Within a few months Visser 't Hooft was called to Geneva by Robinson to discuss a boys' work position on the World staff and was appointed in the summer of 1924. During this time he came to know Mott "more intimately" through interpreting for him but especially on a trip to the States during which Mott took him to Yankee Stadium to see an Army-Notre Dame football game. Once when Mott was in Holland, Visser 't Hooft introduced his parents to him, on which occasion 't Hooft's mother told Mott that he was "like a spider and that no one who had been caught in his web could get out of it again." To which Mott is said to have made the courtly reply, "but, madam, you underestimate the great gift that God has made to us in your son." In his *Memoirs*, 't Hooft wrote that there was truth in his mother's remark: "I had indeed been caught in the web which he had spun—and I never did get out of it."[86]

As the Pörtschach conference receded into memory it took on added meaning for Mott, and he included it in that life-list of great events of his career compiled in old age. The World's Alliance Plenary that followed it approved Robinson's program and confirmed him in office. It wrestled with the Franco-German problem that, unlike the situation in the WSCF where it was solved comparatively easily, eluded Mott's and everyone's mediation until 1931, although an address he gave at the 1923 Plenary "deeply and favorably impressed" those Germans who were present. Plans were laid for the next World YMCA conference to be held in Helsingfors (Helsinki), Finland, in 1926, the first since 1913. Constitutional changes in the Alliance, toward which Mott had pressed since before the War, were initiated and became the subject of much correspondence between him and Fries, the new general secretary; the two worked with singleness of purpose to expand the program of the world body, which hitherto had been something of a Geneva club. Visser 't Hooft recalled that it was as if Mott had placed a bomb under the Alliance. Mott had always cultivated awareness of the Alliance fellowship among the American Associations and continued that emphasis. Its finances were chronically precarious during the twenties due to the impoverished conditions of much of Europe, especially Germany, and Mott helped as he could. Soon after its publication in 1923, Fries proposed that they find a way to distribute copies of *Confronting Young Men with the Living Christ* to German "Y" members who could not afford it, because it would "go a long way to conquer a certain distrust."

Several situations gave Mott and Fries some amusement in these months: Fries thought it rather "funny," after being Chairman of the WSCF for twenty-five years and on the most intimate terms with Mott, to need to ask him formally to appoint a Federation representative to Pörtschach. When Fries asked Mott to contribute an article to *The Sphere*, the Alliance magazine, his schedule made it impossible. It soon became necessary for Mott to ask Fries for one for *The Student World*. When Fries complied, Mott remarked that Fries was a better Christian than himself. On another occasion Mott sent a substitute paper for *The Sphere*, telling Fries the old joke about the prep school student who, when asked in an examination to name the major and minor Old Testament prophets, wrote, "far be it from me to discriminate between the prophets, but the kings of Israel were . . . ." Fries replied that he would have preferred the prophets! About this time he proposed a French translation of Mott's *Confronting Young Men*.

The XIX World Conference of the YMCA's, which met at Helsingfors during the "white nights" of 1926, was the great event of the twenties in the life of the World's Alliance. Ray V. Sowers, a delegate from the States, later to teach at Stetson University in Florida, remembered the magic of a night on the afterdeck of a ship in the Baltic when a group of choice spirits sat under the white sky munching fruit and swapping stories with Mott until sunrise. [87]

Fries retired at this meeting and Mott was elected Life Chairman, in which post he would be active until 1947. Some thought that he pushed out his elderly predecessor, Paul Des Gouttes, rather clumsily, without due recognition for years of dedicated service. Fresh from a tour of the Pacific basin (and here we are again slightly ahead of our story) Mott gave one of his great orations, "Opened doors in Front of the YMCA," based on Revelation 3:7-8. It was at this conference that Asian YMCA's began to play "a decisive role" in Alliance affairs when K. T. Paul of India took a prominent part in the deliberations and became one of the "big five" advisors to Mott. A deep impression was made by Paul's use of prayers adapted from Tagore. [88] At Helsingfors Visser 't Hooft observed that there was something intangible about Mott's leadership: often he would open a meeting with world-sweeping statements but leave the details to others. The still-feuding French and German delegates refused his mediation. He seemed to assume that leadership consisted mostly in stimulating people to think in larger dimensions. [89] In actuality this had always been Mott's method; in his younger days he had also done an immense amount of the spade work.

But the young boys' work secretary learned even more about Mott at Helsingfors. Asked to serve as his personal assistant, he became "a general dogsbody":

> It meant also that I was to be instructed in the art of running a complicated world conference by a man who had rightly been called "a master of assemblies." Mott took me to the big church where the main meetings would be held and went into every possible detailed question concerning seating, procedure, timing, etc. "Now you will sit behind that pillar," he said, "and you must look at me. When I give you a sign, this means that I need you. It may be that I have a message for somebody or that there is a crisis" (he loved that word). The result was that I spent most of my time looking all over the place for people who were required for meetings of one sort or another, bringing reports or resolutions to the printers and acting as Mott's interpreter. I saw little of the normal life of the conference, but I saw with what sense of strategy, of priorities, of human relations and of attention to detail Mott operated. [90]

Young William Temple had done this at Edinburgh in 1910 until Mott sent him off to Australia. It proved to be excellent training for a future Archbishop of Canterbury and for a future general secretary of a World Council of Churches!

In the mid-1920's the young International Missionary Council was feeling its way, moving "fearlessly but with caution." This was a time of perplexity for J. H. Oldham, who was depressed lest missions drift into a backwater "outside the main currents" that were shaping the world. He begged Mott to concentrate his entire attention on "the whole Church," for under Mott's leadership "a forward movement of the Christian forces" might be possible: "there is no one to take your place." Oldham could not imagine "any greater or more fitting crown" to Mott's life than something "far bigger and wider" than even the IMC chairmanship. There must be a "transformation in existing ideas of missionary work." As Oldham unburdened himself the friendship between the two men deepened; what Oldham hoped for was Mott's resignation from everything but the IMC. In 1928 Mott would relinquish the American YMCA secretaryship and the WSCF, but he would hold on to the World's Alliance of YMCA's.

As IMC chairman Mott guided its executive committee or its Council through the fundamentalist maze, through clarifications of its purpose and program, and in its selection of additional personnel. It met at

Canterbury (1922), Oxford (1923), and Atlantic City (1925) where the Jerusalem Conference of 1928 was projected as a "strong forward movement" of the Christian forces of the world, as Oldham had urged, and at Rättvik, Sweden (1926). Here Mott would finally agree to accept responsibilities "in addition to the duties of the chairmanship," thus becoming functionally the general secretary of the IMC.[91]

Mott's most spectacular, yet in the light of history most futile service for the IMC in the first half of the 1920's was a chain of conferences with missionaries to Muslims, held during 1924 in Algeria, Egypt, and Lebanon, and climaxed by a meeting at Jerusalem. This effort was first planned shortly after Edinburgh 1910 but was delayed by the War.[92] It was based on the naïve assumption, held for years, that Islam was on the verge of disintegration and that the time was ripe for a strong Christian thrust into the vacuum.

Since Napoleon's invasion of Egypt Islam had felt the secularizing influence of the West. The break-up of the Ottoman Empire had appeared to confirm the missionaries' hopes. A few of them exercised undue influence on their backers, and Mott listened, chiefly to James L. Barton of the Congregational Board (the ABCFM) whose involvement included Near East Relief and what one writer called "Protestant diplomacy." Even more convincing was Samuel M. Zwemer, for years a member of the "Quiet Day" prayer circle to which Mott belonged, whose narrow, almost fanatical advocacy was immensely persuasive.[93] Mott's own impressions of the Muslim world, gained first on his visit to Constantinople and subsequent horseback journey through Palestine in 1895 and another visit in 1911, supported by frequent interviews with authorities and much reading, brought him to agreement.

The Jerusalem conference of 1924 assembled eighty missionaries and converts out of Islam from all parts of the Muhammedan world including Indonesia, India, and China, as ostensible guests of the Greek Patriarch of Jerusalem in his church on the Mount of Olives, with Mott paying the bills. It concluded that Christian literature offered the most effective avenue to evangelization and took steps to organize a Christian council for the region; this was constituted in 1927, with Robert Wilder as its first secretary. From 1929 it was called the Near East Christian Council, with headquarters in Cairo.

Wide publicity was given to these "Moslem" conferences. The findings, together with a very respectable analysis of the problems, were put together in a 400-page survey of The Moslem World of Today, edited by Mott in 1925. He wrote the foreword and the concluding essay. Barton,

Gairdner, Zwemer, Speer, and a score more contributed. Mott spoke of the "thrill of a new life" in almost every Muslim land, and likened the "weakening of the sense of solidarity and moral unity" of such peoples to the break-up of the Holy Roman Empire.

> The threatened and impending disintegration of Islam calls for an adequate substitute. Only Christ and His programme can meet the need . . . . Only as the programme of Christianity is based upon a sympathetic understanding of the Moslems . . . is there any hope of winning them, but along that pathway there is infinite hope.

> We must either modify or abandon our faith or be logical, consistent, and apostolic and expand our plans and practice so as to give all Moslems opportunity to know Christ . . . . The essential victory or ultimate triumph of our Christian faith is involved as well as its validity and vitality. A Gospel which cannot, after being adequately brought to bear upon Moslems, win their minds and hearts and command the allegiance of their wills, must fail to satisfy the deepest longings and the highest expectations of the followers of other religions and of those without any religious faith. . . . The triumph of the Christian cause in other foreign fields and at the home base is involved in what takes place in the heart of the Mohammedan world. [94]

On shipboard a few days after the Jerusalem meeting, Mott wrote Henriod that the chain of conferences had constituted "one of the three or four greatest opportunities of my life. I shall never cease to be grateful to God for His sending me to these fields at this critical moment, a moment which I may say reverently has been a Day of the Lord."

No Mott tour was ever for a single purpose. On the journey of 1924 the next priority after the Muslim issue was the outreach of the American and World YMCA's into the countries of eastern and southeastern Europe. This required strenuous efforts toward rapprochement with the Orthodox Churches. The Motts' first commitment upon arrival in Jerusalem had been a dinner at Archie Harte's where they met the Greek Patriarch Damianos, whose house guests they would be at his residence on the Mount of Olives. Although the conference was served tea alfresco there, Orthodox participation consisted of an official visit and later an informal call by the Patriarch, described by the conference reporter as "a benignant, gracious soul, filling in every detail all the requirements romance has whispered of oriental ecclesiastical potentates." He brought with him on the first occasion bishops of the Syrian and Abyssinian Churches and blessed the conference "in the fashion of the East." Two days later he came again to give a special message of brotherly love and "to commission us anew, as it were, with the words of our Lord, 'Go ye into all the world.'" To confirm this sentiment, John and Leila Mott were each awarded the "Golden Cross of the Holy Sepulchre" by the Jerusalem patriarchate.[95]

The Jerusalem YMCA, founded in 1878, to which Mott had spoken in 1895, was now staging an extraordinary program aimed at both Jewish and Arab youth, under the dynamic direction of Archie C. Harte, whose grandiose dream of a great building that would be an example to the YMCA world did not fall upon deaf ears when outlined to Mott. Likewise in Cairo, Mott had been tremendously impressed by the Association program developed by Wilbert Smith, and he was making an effort at this time to introduce the YMCA to the Turkish men of Smyrna.[96]

In Beirut the Motts were guests of the young President and Mrs. Bayard Dodge of the American University. Mott had known Dodge since the latter's childhood when he used to dine at the Dodge home to discuss YMCA affairs with his father, Cleveland H. Dodge. There was a happy occasion in Beirut when the Dodges' young son, aged sixteen months, delighted everyone by taking his first unaided steps across a parlor full of people to Mott's arms. Bayard Dodge years later remembered Mott for his balanced judgment and initiative, a unique combination that he possessed in an unusual quantity, and that he never expressed himself on a controversial theological subject.[97] Mrs. Pierre Maury, who accompanied her husband with the Motts on part of this tour, admired not only Mott's qualities as chief and his mastery of public debate, but his human characteristics in domestic relations—his delicate regard for others and his charming courtesy that were in contrast to his authoritarian stance in a conference setting.[98] This visit to Beirut had been coordinated with a regional student conference of which Philip K. Hitti was chairman. Mott addressed six meetings, several of which reached 1,000 in attendance; Leila, who spoke to a YMCA group, thought this gratifying since fully half of the students were Muslims. Hitti remembered Mott as fresh and his influence intangible rather than stuffy like the missionaries.

The best-documented visit of this tour was to Greece, which had only recently been involved in war with Turkey before she could recover from the Great War.[99] In spite of unsettled conditions, perhaps because of them, he was welcomed enthusiastically. Throughout the centuries Greek life had been almost coterminous with Orthodox Christianity which had its chief center at Constantinople. The planting of YMCA's in Greece was, like similar movements across post-War eastern Europe, the result of a demand for civilian programs comparable to those provided to the Greek troops during the War; it depended upon rapprochement with the Orthodox Churches. Not only political authorities in Athens and Saloniki asked for Associations, but Mott received comparable requests from Church leaders.[100]

The visit took on aspects of a public celebration in view of the popularity of America, the wartime YMCA services to soldiers and refugees, the successful Association programs recently introduced, the highly effective work of Ulios L. Amoss, secretary at Saloniki, and D. A. Davis, European field secretary, who had cemented a warm relationship with the Orthodox hierarchy. The brilliant young professor Hamilcar Alivisatos of the University of Athens, who had met Mott in America shortly after the War, obtained the approval of Patriarch Meletios to start a YMCA in Athens. Such overtures were mutually helpful due in part to the lack of a youth program in the Orthodox Churches of Greece and the Balkans: the "Y" seemed ideally suited to meet this need and some of the highest ecclesiastical authorities served on YMCA boards. On Corfu, Metropolitan Athenagoras, later to become Archbishop of North America and subsequently Ecumenical Patriarch of Constantinople, himself organized and presided over an Association.[101]

Another factor that Alivisatos long remembered was Mott's obvious knowledge of and insight into Orthodoxy. Due to thirteen years of war and dislocation, many of the ecclesiastics Mott had met on his trip to Constantinople in 1911 were no longer active, but at the start of this journey he had conferred in London with Bishop Gore, one of the best informed Anglicans, who gave him the names of Orthodox persons to see in almost every city to be visited, from Cairo to Budapest. In Alexandria he had conferred with Greek Patriarch Photius and accompanied by Zwemer talked with the Patriarch of the Coptic Church. In addition to lengthy conversations with the Greek and possibly the Armenian Patriarchs resident in Jerusalem, he was now oriented in Athens to the nature of the several Christian men's societies in the city; the "Y" men on the field advised him at every point.

The Motts were received on the highest political and ecclesiastical levels by the Metropolitan of Athens and all Greece, the prime minister and his opponent who shortly took over that office, and the president of the University of Athens. In Saloniki Mott laid the cornerstone of the new YMCA building to be constructed in part with surplus American War Work funds on a site given by the government. With Henry Morgenthau, who was also being honored, he was entertained in the Governor's palace, had a street named for him, and was made an honorary citizen. Mott was decorated by the King with the "Higher Commandership of the Saviour"; in presenting the award at a state dinner, the Governor-General declared it to be for "the great services which he offered and is still offering to humanity at large and the Greek nation in particular." Mott spoke in an evangelistic vein at a special service in the Saloniki cathedral after being introduced by the Metropolitan (who had come to Pörtschach the year before) to an immense, packed congregation, as "one of the greatest Christians of the present day." This, wrote D. A. Davis, regional YMCA secretary who was accompanying the Motts, was the first time in the history of this ancient Church that Eastern and Western Christianity had "joined hands in presenting the challenge of Christ to youth." These events received wide publicity. [102]

Leaving Leila with friends, Mott, accompanied by Davis and A. K. Jennings, popular "Y" secretary who had done yeoman service among Greek refugees from Smyrna, left on the United States destroyer Edsall for a visit to the former Ecumenical Patriarch Meletios IV at the all-male monastic community Mount Athos, in the Aegean. After a three-hour ride on donkeys they were met by the ringing of monastery bells and were accorded the highest ecclesiastical honors by the Synod, to which Alivisatos had commended them. Mott addressed the assembled monks and talked with Meletios for eight hours. The Ex-Patriarch wrote in his own hand an introduction for Mott to take to his successor in Constantinople. Davis said that they left Mount Athos with a sense of having had "a rare opportunity for fellowship and invaluable counsel not only with a great soul but with one of the greatest statesmen of the Christian Church." To have won the confidence of the Eastern Churches for the YMCA at such a time made it "difficult to conceive of any greater opportunity for service." [103]

Peace had been restored to Turkey in 1923, yet as the train that brought Mott, Davis, and Jennings to Constantinople entered the station another was leaving carrying the royal family to exile. The Turkish Republic had been proclaimed only three months earlier; the Caliphate had just been abolished. Confusion prevented Mott from presenting his introduction from Melitios; Mustapha Kemal had just called for the suppression of the Patriarchate as a corollary to the abolition of the Caliphate. Mott conferred with Meletios' "dear friend" the Metropolitan of Albania, with Archbishop Kevork Arslanian (Professor Hagopian of Robert College interpreting), with Archbishop Anastazii of the Russian Church, and participated in a round-table discussion based on his questions on the current status of Islam. He may well have gained some appreciation of the Byzantine tradition in Orthodoxy. Davis commented that no post-War state had been "more thoroughly made over" than this new Turkey which in spite of much unrest was encouraging the YMCA to "render a service which no other organization is ready to render." On the whole these hopes were not realized but Mott continued to gain ground in the Orthodox world.[104]

Although Mott had made four stops in Athens and had given himself adequate time there and in Jerusalem, he finished the 1924 tour of the Balkans and eastern Europe by touching Belgrade, Sofia, Bucharest, Budapest, Vienna, Bratislava, Prague, Krakow, Warsaw, and Lodz in two weeks. In Belgrade he held what was a first meeting of YMCA secretaries working in the Balkans with their counterparts from England and the States. As they pooled their expertise it became clear that practically every Association program in use elsewhere in the world "for developing character and winning boys and men to Christ" was being utilized in these Orthodox countries "in full understanding and cooperation with lay and clerical leaders" of the Orthodox Churches.[105]

Welcomes, interviews with top political and ecclesiastical personages, meetings with lay leaders, crowded halls, and enthusiastic send-offs were less impressive than in Greece, but Mott's student audiences compared well with those of earlier times in the Orient; attention and response were gratifying. In Sofia a memorable impression was left with a group of university professors and students. King Boris of Bulgaria held him for an hour in discussion of spiritual matters. The Patriarch of the Serbian Church and the Metropolitans of Sofia and of Roumania gathered ecclesiastical and lay leaders to talk. The year before, Mott had been decorated with the Star of the Hungarian Red Cross. In all, he and Davis "visited and interviewed nearly every one of the official heads of Eastern Churches outside Russia"; everywhere they were received with "interest, sympathy and good will."

Because of secretary Paul Super's extraordinary success in building leadership for an indigenous YMCA in Roman Catholic Poland, Mott could describe it to the Archbishop of Canterbury on his way home as "our absolutely unique experiment." Mott was greeted in Krakow, Warsaw, and Lodz with state receptions and banquets, together with speeches of thanks for succor in the dark days of the War. General Sikorski, Minister of War, decorated him with the Cross of Commander of the Order of Polonia Restituta, said to be the highest honor bestowed upon a foreigner except a king or president. Several Polish speakers bracketed Mott with Wilson and Hoover as the Americans who would always be remembered in their country. Super believed that Mott's responses and addresses, "full of testimony to the place and power of Christ, profoundly moved the leaders of Poland, where such words from the lips of a layman are rare. Thus, our movement is not only pushed forward but lifted and given added spiritual tone."

All this was the more extraordinary because the YMCA was now incorporated as a Polish organization, all American interests having been turned over to the national body in 1923, though American funds continued to help provide buildings in key cities. In spite of his wish to withdraw in favor of a Pole as national secretary, Super was asked to stay on until retirement. In 1921, when he went to Poland, he had declared that the Association he would build must be Catholic, and so it was, in spite of some ecclesiastical resistance. At that time Mott, Super remembered, "rose to the idea, and agreed." Mott had, of course, inaugurated such a policy in Mexico, the Philippines, and South America years before. Although financial restrictions had reduced overseas personnel to a fourth of what they had been in 1921, Mott could tell the National Council of 1924 after this trip that "the work already reads like a romance," abounding in evidences "of the reality and conquering power of our faith" in Greek Catholic, Roman Catholic, and Moslem lands. Poland was an example of how American secretaries were "yielding executive responsibility to their native colleagues" as soon as "self-governing, self-supporting, and self-propagating" Associations were established.[106]

Hans Lilje, who would begin his general secretaryship of the German SCM in 1927, was already learning the elements of ecumenism from Mott. If we may paraphrase an interview, Lilje recalled that

> Mott overlooked divisions and boundaries. When he talked about blacks they were not just blacks, they were part of the ecumenical movement, or when in the days after World War I he talked to us Germans about the Poles or the Czechs or whomever, he had a magnificent way of making it clear that we were all on the same level, that there was no room for prejudice; it was amazing that the Germans said "he understands us." The Czechs adored him and said "he understands us," and the same with the Poles and others. These new nations that were fighting for their lives said, "this man knows us and is friendly and helps us." And the same was true of individuals: he had a way of letting one know that he cared for and respected him. I have beautiful memories of that. When he spoke to one in this way, that person felt honored for the rest of his life.[107]

Lilje also remembered that at its best Mott's give and take with an interpreter was like a game of ping-pong.

As the hold of the Soviet government tightened upon Mother Russia, streams of refugees found their way to the West. By 1924 there were three to four million in Germany, France, and elsewhere in Europe and America. They brought Orthodoxy to lands where the word had scarcely been known; among them were writers, philosophers, theologians, and prelates. As Paul B. Anderson points out, they took the initiative but Mott, the YMCA and YWCA and other agencies of which Anderson and G. G. Kullman were representatives, shared their quest for meaning in alien surroundings. In 1922 a union of Russian emigré students in Czechoslovakia had thanked Mott for aid. The next year a Russian SCM outside Russia was organized at a conference in Czechoslovakia that surprised everyone by its spirituality and loyalty to Orthodoxy, in contrast to the interdenominational character of previous student commitment.[108] While in the Balkans in 1924, Mott received from Ethan Colton, his most trusted advisor on Russian affairs, a confidential report that he digested en route and was thus well informed when he reached the emigré centers.

It was prophetic that his last important engagement on the Orthodox segment of this tour was a dinner and long evening of discussion at the Kaiserhof with a group of displaced Russian professors in Berlin the day after his triumphs in Poland—Berdyaev, Franke, Vyacheslavtsev, Karsavin, the Shidlovskys, and others. Mott reviewed his visits to half-a-dozen branches of the Orthodox family of churches plus the Coptic and Roman Catholic, and drew ecumenical conclusions, one of which was a trial balloon raising the possibility of a council of Eastern Churches. He took copious notes to the presentations and discussion by his hosts concerning the needs of the emigré community, which would soon move to Paris, where the Metropolitan Eulogios would become its leader. Berdyaev expressed his appreciation of Mott's understanding of Orthodoxy and described the crises through which it was passing. The conversation moved to the need for a theological school to provide continuity of leadership and to prevent the Orthodox Church from becoming passive, a matter that had been brought to Mott's attention twice before. Mott obtained a modest sum ($5,000) that assured the establishment of the Orthodox Theological Institute of St. Sergius in Paris; it opened in 1925 and was for some years the only Russian theological academy in the world; in 1931 it was recognized by the University of Paris. It provided a home and teaching post for Professors Bulgakov, Kartaschev, Zenkovskii, Fedotov, Florovskii, and other creative Russian thinkers. The contribution it has made to Orthodoxy is as extraordinary as its origins and original faculty. In 1940 it would confer an honorary doctorate of divinity on Mott as "one of its founders and constant friends."[109]

At that dinner in Berlin Mott had asked whether the emigré movement might profit from a theological periodical. Subsequently, Berdyaev's request for what became the magazine *Put'* ("The Way") seemed valid and Mott obtained funds to launch it in 1925. It became the outlet for the writing of Berdyaev and the other members of the group.[110] The most far-reaching proposal that evening at the Kaiserhof was for a publishing house. This led to the inauguration of a positive Orthodox editorial policy for the YMCA Press, which Mott had helped to establish in Prague in 1921. Berdyaev was its editor-in-chief for the remainder of his life; based in Paris, it has for more than fifty years published not only religious works but scores of other titles in Russian. It has been an outlet for writers who, like Berdyaev himself, were thus enabled to become a "world conscience"—Nabokov, Solzhenitsyn, Pasternak.[111] Few dinner parties have had such an impact.

PART 8: The Pacific Basin Tour of 1925–1926

En route to Japan, Mott told an audience of Cyrus McCormick's guests in Chicago that he was starting on a journey of 45,000 miles around the Pacific basin, into which you could put all the continents and islands of the world "and still have them surrounded by great stretches of water." Comparing the Orient of his first visit thirty years before to what he expected to find this time, he reminded his audience of the growing importance of the Far East and of its multiplying problems, and declared that it would not reject Christianity "because there you will find open doors." The primary purpose of this journey was to take soundings for the International Missionary Council on a world missions conference. He would also survey YMCA foreign work, meet with national student groups, and evangelize.[112]

Accompanied by their younger son Frederick and Ernest C. Brelsford as secretaries, with Fletcher Brockman as guide and interpreter, John and Leila Mott arrived in Yokohama December 17, 1925. In Japan and everywhere all arrangements were made by resident YMCA or missionary staffs, an ecumenical feat of no mean importance. Two unusual circumstances turned the Japanese spotlight on Mott: he was welcomed as a public benefactor because of the sums he had raised for relief and reconstruction following the earthquake of 1923;[113] and he was recognized as a friend of Japan and a mediator with an ambivalent America that had just insulted Japan with the exclusionary features of the Immigration Act of 1924, which he and many others had opposed vigorously. Breakfasts, luncheons, teas, banquets, speeches, and receptions were climaxed by an audience with the Prince Regent.[114]

The main theme of Mott's confidential talks with some of the country's highest officers was Japanese-American relations. His notes to these have not survived, but he had conversations with Prince Tokugawa, Viscount Shibusawa, Baron Shidehara, and Viscount Goto, whose house guests the Motts were in a new Western style villa. Later, in Melbourne, Mott said that the Immigration Act must be amended, not because of the risk of war but because it had produced a "festering sore, ever open to be aggravated."[115] Several speakers, including Tokugawa who invited present and former cabinet officers and members of the Diet to a luncheon honoring Mott, referred to his "constant endeavors for the betterment of the relations between his country and ours." The Prince Regent had expressed his appreciation to Mott for "promoting peace and right relations among the nations."

When Mott called upon Archbishop Sergius, successor to the great Nicolai, at the Russian Orthodox cathedral, Sergius accompanied him to the National Council of Churches conference at Kamakura, which had been called to meet with Mott; Sergius spoke several times. The conference heard Toyohiko Kagawa on Christmas Sunday and Mott addressed it more than once, being introduced as a missionary to a "much larger world" than Wesley's. Although there was some dissent, the group endorsed the proposal for an IMC world gathering. Brockman described the emotional impact of Mott's visit as having so affected one of his interpreters that the man broke down in tears and could not continue when Mott said that he wished he could remain longer than planned in Japan: "Such things do not occur easily in the Orient," Brockman added.[116]

Mott had obtained contributions toward the repair of Sergius' cathedral and its program. In gratitude the archbishop arranged a special choir concert on Christmas Eve, to which Mott invited fifty guests; he was given the archbishop's blessing and "Many Years" was sung for him and his family. En route to Korea Mott stopped in Osaka to inspect a new YMCA that he found "without a doubt our model building in all Asia."

Instead of rushing to Seoul, Mott spent the first day in Korea in consultation with Baron Yun Tchi Ho and others at Pusan where he was briefed on "the present situation and trends in Korea" under Japanese occupation, and the YMCA program was rethought in terms of current realities. The Mott party then went to Seoul for three incredibly full days, the chief business of which was a conference of "representative Christian leaders" called to discuss with Mott the unique problems of that country on which the IMC could be helpful, and to decide whether Korea favored a world IMC conference. As in Japan, the new discussion group method was used to obtain consensus; the sixty-odd delegates were divided into four sections, each of which brought findings to the entire body, which was chaired by Dr. Yun. The groups voted to reappraise the Christian enterprise in Korea ("methods which were adequate and effective in former times... in other countries... are not adapted to the present time"), and endorsed the proposal for an enlarged session of the IMC in Jerusalem. In striking contrast to his conference of 1913, Mott recorded, in this one practically all the speeches were made by Koreans. From the cold print of diary and reports there emerges fifty years later that poignancy that had ever touched Mott's heart about Korea, now invaded by a foreign power (they visited a Shinto shrine newly built on a hill overlooking the city) and its youth beginning to feel the corrupting influence of communism. Their last evening in Seoul the Motts dined with the Ransford Millers, his Cornell colleague, now American consul, "in their most interesting Korean house."[117]

Two weeks in China were "one of the most crowded periods of our lives," wrote Mott in his diary. Due to unsettled conditions in the North, they decided to stay in Shanghai, where the National Council of Churches conference, called at Mott's request, was held. Chaired by Dr. David Z. T. Yui, its roster included virtually all of the Chinese luminaries who were leading the Christian community, and an equal number of Westerners. There were seven groups whose findings were accepted by general consent, one of the more popular being that on Christianity and China's treaties with foreign nations. As in Japan and Korea the Jerusalem proposal was endorsed. The China conference *Report* referred to that city as "the birthplace of our common religion . . . than which no other spot on earth holds a greater religious interest for Eastern Christians," although some had thought that an Oriental site would be more attractive.

The crisis facing the YMCA in China had intensified since Mott's visit of 1922. It was under attack from many quarters; student interest was ebbing and receipts from businessmen were dropping sharply. Caught between the anti-Christian movement and communist criticism on the one hand and its traditional policy of political neutrality on the other, its principles bade it support the radical cause but it could not bring itself to do so. Its golden age in China was over, even though it would be saved temporarily by Chiang K'ai shek.[118]

Mott had asked David Yui to assemble a representative group of both Chinese and Western YMCA secretaries from all parts of the country to appraise the situation and develop a strategy. A series of papers on the issues were read, most of them by Chinese; Eugene E. Barnett, then executive secretary of the city division of the Chinese YMCA's, who had gone to meet Mott en route from Korea, and would become General Secretary of the American YMCA a decade later, gave one on the Association and the industrialization of China; D. Willard Lyon and F. S. Brockman also spoke, as of course did Mott, who found time for several student meetings, but these lacked the old enthusiasm. He held a small conference of the student secretaries of the country. One of the many personal interviews mentioned in his diary was a discussion of "extraterritoriality and fundamentalism" with D. E. Hoste, head of the China Inland Mission.

After a few hours in Hong Kong while their steamer lay over, the Motts arrived in Manila for a two-day visit, the first since 1907. Their host was E. Stanton Turner, then well into his remarkable leadership of the Philippine YMCA's. Sixty representatives of mission and church bodies heard Mott explain the Jerusalem proposal and endorsed it. Another group met at 7:00 A.M. to discuss relations with the Roman Catholic Church; the Motts then breakfasted with Governor-General and Mrs. Leonard Wood at Malacanang Palace. After a luncheon at the Chinese YMCA they boarded the *President Polk*. Mott spoke to a well-attended ship's worship service on a Sunday. From this perspective he wrote to Oldham, now in Africa, that he was being "led irresistibly toward some kind of world gathering, and this not too far in the future." His personal relation to it was not yet clear, but the trip was providing ideal conditions in which to discover, as could never have been possible at home, "the mind of God" with regard to it.[119] In three days at Singapore, he held a morning's discussion with "the leading missionaries of the various societies working in Malaysia and centering in Singapore," was dined by the Governor, and conferred about YMCA expansion in that region; Leila was horrified when the party witnessed a "pin-sticking" festival of self-torture at a Hindu temple.

A Dutch ship took them to Belawan, Sumatra, the port for Medan.[120] They were met by Herman Rutgers, the multilingual Dutch SCM secretary, who would explain and interpret throughout the five-week tour of Sumatra and Java, which Mott had anticipated ever since Queen

Wilhelmina had suggested it to him before the War. Everywhere there would be meetings with missionaries, interviews, calls upon government officials, and as much of the panoply that had come to feature a Mott tour as could be staged in a primitive country.

The first section of the trip across Sumatra was in two automobiles up to the central highland. Starting on a Sunday morning, the party attended a crowded church service at Siantar in the heart of the Batak region. The singing, by several choirs as well as the congregation, was impressive. Mott spent the afternoon with Johannes Warneck, the day's preacher, who was the head of the Rhenish mission. Warneck had some reservations about Mott's visit, but briefed him on the Bataks and accompanied the party on that portion of their tour. Some of the German missionaries were still resentful toward Mott over the wartime allegations, but this appears to have been resolved.

The next several days, en route to Sibolga on the south side of the island, held numerous surprises for a traveler as seasoned as Mott—Lake Toba with its immense island of Samosir, the unique architecture of the Batak buildings (which Mott noted were not only picturesque but showed splendid craftsmanship), the fine roads built by the Dutch, the spectacular remains of volcanic action, a self-governing leper colony, a fine church being paid for by its own members, a training school for Batak teachers, speaking to an immense congregation where there were great numbers of noisy babies on the backs of their mothers or sisters, visiting the memorial to the Congregational missionaries Munson and Lyman who were said to have been killed and eaten by cannibals in 1834, the 1800 curves in the road descending from the highlands to Sibolga—all through country where there was risk of malaria and typhoid.

The party took a ship from Sibolga to Padang, and another to Jakarta (Batavia), Java, for the longest stop in Indonesia. Mott's first public engagement was at a Chinese club which he urged to expand into a full multipurpose Association. At Buitenzorg he had a realistic interview with the Governor-General, who evinced a strong interest in the visit. Mott commended the cooperative policy toward German missions that had been pursued by the Dutch. Both men were concerned about the infiltration of communism. Mott brought greetings from Governor-General Wood of the Philippines, to which the reply was that the American government ought to make a firm decision on independence for those Islands: the Governor blamed President Wilson's ideals of self-determination for greatly increasing "the troubles of [colonial] administrators the world over," the only hint of coming agitation for independence that Mott heard. He asked about Methodist missionary work on the island. The Governor approved of it but was very critical of the Seventh-Day Adventists; the Pentecostals, he said, "stirred up the spirit of fanaticism." The Governor attended Mott's speech that evening.

While in this area the Motts were shown the famous Botanical Gardens at Buitenzorg, tea and quinine plantations, the great Buddhist monument at Borobedoer, the sultan's palace, a Javanese village morality play ("It was as interesting to watch the faces . . . as it was to watch the play"), rubber, copra, sugar, rice, teakwood, and tobacco plantations, several well-run hospitals, "The Nail" pinning Java to the globe. They were presented to Prince Mangkoenagara VII and his Princess, and observed the contrasts between a Javanese Christian village and a Muslim town. Mott was carried through the forest in moonlight up to Papandajan in a sedan chair while others rode horseback, Frederick going to the lip of the volcano Bromo itself in the company of Canadian friends en route around the world.

Although Mott spoke more than forty times to a variety of audiences, his most important engagements were a conference of youth leaders at Bandoeing and another of the Missionary Union of the Dutch East Indies at Jakarta. At Bandoeing he met and was immediately impressed by the Dutch SCM alumnus H. H. Kraemer, now "one of the ablest of the younger missionaries," who would soon become a leading theologian of missions. Mott spent much time with Kraemer during the remainder of the tour. At the Jakarta meeting Mott spoke on the "lessons to be learned from rising indigenous churches" and asked for consensus on four questions, for which he expressed gratitude even though the group itself was not satisfied with the manner in which they were answered. Comparable criticism was latent at other points. Rutgers sensed this and commented in his report that the time had been too short for Mott to absorb as much as he had hoped. Yet in spite of the heavy burden of speaking, the rigors of the tropics, and the fact of his being over sixty, Rutgers went on, Mott had obtained a good impression of missions there and of the importance of Indonesia itself. The Jakarta conference endorsed the Jerusalem proposal, though recommending that the site selection committee also consider British India, Singapore, and Manila. Applause greeted the proposal that Indonesia be represented "and the matter not be left to the Boards in Holland." Mott and Rutgers agreed that there was a great need for city YMCA's in Jakarta and Surabaja and tried to interest European and American sending agencies in establishing them.[121]

In reporting the tour of Sumatra and Java, Mott revealed his habit of observing the surroundings in which he worked: Java, he thought, deserved to be called "the pearl of the Orient"; in all his travels he had never seen "such richness of soil, abundance and variety of flora and fauna, of such beauty of landscape, and of such tides of fascinating human life." A chain of 140 volcanoes, "some dead, some sleeping, and some dangerously active," stretched the length of the island: "One is ever conscious . . . of the presence and working of great upheaving and creative forces in nature just as in the life and relationships of the tens of millions of people of these non-Christian races and religions." In writing to Oldham he enclosed a paragraph from a letter his recent guide Warneck had sent to a friend, saying that he had come to love Mott and was ashamed to have held some reservations about the visit: the two men had found a "beautiful and sympathetic understanding" which had widened Warneck's horizon and given him fresh incentives.[122]

It was not until a year later that Mott reported to the Queen of Holland. In doing so he described the affirmative factors about the islands and their government, the missionary situation, the Dutch program of education, and the helpful activities of the former members of the Dutch SCM. The weaknesses in the situation were the lack of agencies for character training, of organizations such as the YMCA to safeguard youth, of "voice, initiative, leadership, and influence on the part of the nationals in the indigenous Christian movement," the need for greater cooperation and unity, the lack of channels of communication between the Christian forces of Indonesia and those of the rest of the world. In view of the impact of the modern world on the most remote islands—nationalism, Pan-Islamism, communism—Christians needed to unite their forces and revise their strategy. Hence the importance of the Jerusalem meeting.

An important and quite unanticipated dividend from Indonesia for the Mott family was the decision of young Frederick, who, after observing the mission hospitals there, decided to enter the medical profession.[123] A very different result was Leila's illness with dengue fever soon after arrival in Australia; John came down with it in Sydney and was forced to reduce his activities for several days.

The Motts' four weeks in Australia had been planned with as much care by Margaret Holmes of the Student Movement as Mott himself devoted to his own preparation which had begun before he left home. Save for a minor hassle with reporters upon arrival at Brisbane the schedule moved like clockwork to Sydney, Melbourne, and Adelaide.[124] This was a time of relative prosperity if of smouldering political unrest in

Australia. There was considerable interest in prohibition and Mott's known stance on the exclusion of Japanese from the United States made him the target of newspapermen, assuring coverage everywhere. As in 1896 and 1903, he was welcomed into this still vaguely Edwardian society with equivalent pomp and circumstance, not only by mayors, governors, bishops and archbishops, but by university students, the clergy, the missionary community, and large audiences of church and YMCA orientation.

The climax of five days in Sydney was an evening affair in the Great Hall of the university, where thirty years before he had held the meeting that resulted in the formation of the University Christian Union. Under the auspices of that body, he now spoke for "over an hour and a quarter" on "Present-Day Trends in the Life of the World." The room was "packed to the limit" with students and alumni of the Movement; the presiding officer and many of the faculty were in academic dress, a "most impressive sight."[125] Mott had been speaking two to four times a day until the fever reduced it to one; nevertheless he went on to Melbourne on schedule but was forced to adopt a reduced regime for several days. Leila followed after recovery.

He gave his "Present Day Trends" address to an audience of 4,000. The large number of students present was occasioned in part by a front-page spread in the University of Melbourne student newspaper *Farrago* which had heralded his coming with a long laudatory sketch juxtaposed with verbatim excerpts from a sermon by the evangelist Gipsy Smith who had just been there. Mott was "a man of action, rather than a thinker. He has all the characteristics of a great general. He is able to enthuse and lead as few men can." The diatribe against Smith was vitriolic; it was headed *Il s'accuse*.[126] The next morning Mott addressed 600 ministers; he talked to the Rotary Club at noon; in the evening he spoke to a student audience at Ormond College.

The first of two major engagements in Australia was a student conference held at Berwick, some thirty miles from Melbourne, over the Easter week-end. Meticulously planned, it was a delegated body of some eighty leaders of the Christian Unions from the entire country. Mott gave an inspirational address once each day, but it was his chairmanship that made the most lasting impression; after briefing the conference on the subjects to be discussed, he broke it into small groups to report back. Forty-five years later, Edward Gault recalled that

> We then had a masterly demonstration of chairmanship I shall never forget. Dr. Mott asked the spokesman of each group to present their find-

ings. These he summarized on the blackboard in columns, in a clear hand, and often restated the report for the sake of brevity or clarity. By lunchtime we had before us a complete statement of the thinking of the whole group. My impression of Mott was that of a big man, in stature and mind, a bit aloof, even though light touches and humor were rare. [127]

Some of those touches were supplied by Leila and Fred Mott, who both contributed substantially to the spirit of the meeting.

Before Mott's second major event at Melbourne, he and Fred went to Adelaide for three days where John spoke to YMCA groups at a national athletic tournament, gave "Present Trends" in the largest hall of the university, spoke to various groups of students and faculty members, and addressed the Commonwealth Club on relations between Australia and the United States.

The prime object of visiting Australia in 1926 was to plumb opinion on missions and present the Jerusalem proposal. This was done at a specially called missionary gathering, advertised as a "Mott Conference" in spite of his strong protest, in Melbourne April 9 to 14. Held in the Collins Street Independent (Congregational) Church, it involved the missions bodies of virtually all of the Protestant churches of the Commonwealth. Its six surveys had been underway for months. Mott, at the height of his oratorical powers, gave ten of the addresses prepared for this tour to packed audiences; they were widely quoted in the daily press and in denominational papers for months afterward, as well as comprising sixty-five pages of the conference report. Among them were "Forces Released Through Cooperation," which had been written for the Washington Missionary Conference of 1925, and "The Race Problem," which surveyed dispassionately the worldwide aspects of that issue which was troubling Australians. He pointed out that segregation had so far been unsuccessful wherever tried—his answer to the "White Australia" policy:

> While some nations, like America, Australia, and Canada may have policies and legislation which prevent certain races from coming to us, we cannot, in this day of constantly improving communications, of industrial and commercial expansion, and of multiplying contacts in other departments of life, keep the aggressive elements of our own race from going forth to other parts of the world and mingling with their people. Thus inevitably the ideas, ideals, habits, and tendencies of one race will be brought to bear upon those of other races. . . . Generally speaking, the Christian conscience of the world, as far as I know, does not rest upon segregation as the ultimate ideal in the way of a solution of the race problem. The Christian spirit is necessarily missionary and inclusive, and cannot be content to let any barriers permanently remain between man and man. [128]

He then dealt with amalgamation and federation as proposed by some, but gave most attention to laying out "certain of the principles and teachings of Jesus Christ which, if applied to inter-racial relations, would, I honestly believe, dissolve the race problem through flooding the world increasingly with good will and unselfish action"—points set forth earlier in this chapter. The race issue down here, he wrote Oldham, is totally different from elsewhere.

The Conference heartily endorsed the proposal for a world missionary gathering in whatever form the IMC should decide upon. Leila wrote home that

> poor John almost wore out his throat making speeches. He's such an oracle out here that if it were needed part of my job would be to keep him humble. At every public meeting there must be a vote of thanks to the speaker and to the one who presides! You hardly recognize yourself [she had given some talks herself] or your relations by marriage in these eulogistic speeches.[129]

There were friends from 1896 and 1903 to see, and a trip into the bush to hear the Australian bell bird again (at Mott's request), before sailing from Sydney to Auckland. Pausing briefly in Wellington, Mott was asked to make a statement on prohibition, which he promised to do, but his main objective in coming to New Zealand was to attend a missionary conference in Dunedin. En route he was "very fully" interviewed by George F. Inglis of the *Otago Daily Times*—the most adequate and satisfying reporting Mott had enjoyed anywhere in the world, he indicated in his diary.

Met at Dunedin by a group including Principal William Hewitson of Knox College, with whom a remarkable fellowship developed during the short time the Motts were there, he was plunged at once into a maelstrom of events that included an oration to the assembled multitude celebrating Anzac Day during a Commonwealth Exposition and laying a wreath on behalf of the American nation! One afternoon he gave his address on religion as a matter of the will to a student group, and most of the audience insisted that he follow it with another talk.[130]

The national missionary conference, April 27–29, brought together some 150 delegates from the mission societies, student unions, and YM-YWCA's of the Commonwealth. Principal Hewitson presided. Mott gave five of the addresses, including "New Forces" and "The Race Problem." He worked with the findings committee, which heartily endorsed the plans for an IMC meeting at Jerusalem, expressed great concern toward the Maoris, and recommended the formation of a National Mis-

sionary Council, which would be a new move.[131] Between the sessions
Mott had several meetings with student groups, during which he urged
the reestablishment of the Student Volunteer Movement, which had
lapsed in New Zealand as well as in Australia.

The Motts worked their way back to Auckland slowly. Welcomes
and large audiences made the trip almost a triumphal procession. There
was a two-day student conference at Waikanae, at which Mott used the
blackboard technique again and gave several shortened addresses. During
five days in Auckland he produced the promised statement on prohibition, handing it to a delegation but also posting it to his reporter friend
Inglis in Dunedin and to others in Australia; it was published widely
throughout both countries.[132] He spoke in the largest church in Auckland, which was packed, and spent a good deal of time with students at
the university.

The long voyage to Vancouver was taken in a deluxe cabin in order
that five trunks could be kept open "to work over and classify all of our
materials." Leila commented that the two young secretaries had "worked
like Trojans"—John had never had a more willing or more efficient
team. There were two stops en route, the first at Suva, Fiji. Eight days
later the party enjoyed a day in Honolulu as their ship lay over. Mott
touched base with most of his interests, was the guest of honor at the
Commercial Club for lunch, and afterward conferred with the Hawaiian
members of the Institute of Pacific Relations, in which he was deeply
interested. The Institute at this time was the end result of a proposal at
Pörtschach, Austria, in 1923, for a Pan-Pacific conference as a useful
step to reduce tensions in the area. Mott had subsequently called leaders
of YMCA's in the Pacific area to Atlantic City where Frank Atherton
and Charles F. Loomis invited the conference to meet at Honolulu in
1925. John Merle Davis left his YMCA post at Nagasaki to become
executive of the Institute that grew out of this conference. At the moment of the Motts' Hawaiian stopover Davis was on a fund-raising tour
that took him along much of their route and to many of the same people.
Davis remained with the Institute until 1930, when he again connected
with the Mott network.[133]

Mott reported on this unique tour many times to a wide range of
organizations, but its real significance was that the Rättvik meeting of the
International Missionary Council in July, 1926 heard his report and
decided to hold a world meeting at Jerusalem in 1928. Also at Rättvik he
accepted the call of the IMC to devote an increasing share of his time to
it, a decision in which the Pacific Basin experience must have played a

large part. Oldham wrote after Rättvik that the more he thought about it the more did "the fresh dedication of ourselves to prayer seem to me the most significant thing that took place there."[134]

PART 9: Four Milestones of 1928

At both the Rättvik IMC executive in mid-July, 1926, and two weeks later at the Helsingfors World's YMCA Conference, Mott took on new responsibilities. He was charged by the former body with the huge task, together with Oldham and the staff, of organizing the Jerusalem meeting planned for 1928, and the oversight and chairmanship of two conferences "looking toward more effective missionary endeavor among Jews." The latter were held in April, 1927, at Budapest and Warsaw. The first world meetings of their kind, they led to IMC action that eventuated in the International Committee on the Christian Approach to the Jews; the WSCF was likewise concerned with Jewish students, but these projects do not appear to have been among Mott's larger enthusiasms.[135]

Mott had accepted the presidency of the World's Alliance with some limitations, yet he was to lead it into expansion of both program and staff—covering the secretaryships of Walter W. Gethman and Tracy Strong—that proved to be also a time of "disintegration and redintegration," as Strong characterized the years from 1926 to 1939. Mott anticipated certain problems of the pre-World War II era in his keynote address on "Open Doors" at Helsingfors; that conference also heard Max Yergan, Joseph Hromadka, and Bishop (later Patriarch) Athenagoras.[136]

While Mott was in Poland for the Jewish conferences of 1927, Paul Super co-opted him for the YMCA—"the most Polish thing in Poland," Mott called it. After a round of receptions and dinners, Super declared that though he had known Mott for twenty-five years he had never seen him "so colossal and commanding" or "so sympathetic, friendly, and lovably human." In connection with this tour Mott attended meetings of the World's Alliance, the WSCF, and of various missions bodies' executive committees.[137]

He went to Europe a second time in 1927 as an American Methodist delegate to the Lausanne Conference on Faith and Order, where he planned to meet with several Orthodox ecclesiastics and others informally. On reaching Lausanne he was stricken by an extreme attack of sinusitis and after one hour rushed back to Geneva for treatment, leaving

Friederick Siegmund-Schultze to relay his regrets. He hurried home, had an operation, and took another extended trip to the American Southwest to recover.[138]

Of the four milestones in Mott's career that were passed in 1928, the "enlarged" meeting of the IMC at Easter on the Mount of Olives at Jerusalem was the most significant.[139] Ever since he had camped in the Galilea region of the Mount in 1895, whence he watched the dawn creep over the Holy City each morning, Mott must have dreamed of bringing Christians from all corners of the globe to share the inspiration of this spot where Jesus went apart to pray. His was the major part in shaping the Jerusalem meeting, for he played the principal role in inviting and obtaining the delegates who came from fifty nations to what Hogg called "the first truly representative global assembly of Christians in the long history of the church."

All members of the Council were "on a level of full equality" and in proportionate representation. Because of a recent earthquake they were housed in barracks and a tent city, the women enjoying the hospitality of the nuns of the Russian Orthodox convent. Mott, now "a towering figure held in high esteem by Continentals," was largely responsible for a representative delegation of them, chiefly from Germany, who came in spite of reservations related to the "Message."[140] He also brought such marked leaders as President R. R. Moton of Tuskegee Institute and Cheng Ching-yi of China, while seeing to it that faith missions were represented. He found travel funds for some who could not afford the trip. At least fifty of those present had at one time been caught in Mott's web or were members of what we have called his network; more than a fourth came from what were by then being called the younger churches. Each of the leading national student movements was represented. Oldham, who had played a significant part in the planning but was growing sceptical of the value of meetings, was in Africa.

This multi-racial throng, many in colorful national garb, followed the footsteps of Jesus from Bethany to Jerusalem on Palm Sunday, prayed in the garden of Gethsemane on Maundy Thursday, trod the Via Dolorosa on Good Friday, and sang hymns at the Garden Tomb and heard the Greek Patriarch's choir on Easter. Patriarch Damianos, whom the Motts had met in 1924, and other Russian, Armenian, Coptic, and Abyssinian ecclesiastics (some of whom had felt overlooked in the preparations for the meetings) were entertained by the Council, but, strangely enough, did not participate in its deliberations.

Thus Mott's prayer for ecumenical spirituality and fellowship was fulfilled; years later he included this "conference on the Mount of Olives" in his life-list of creative meetings.

The small discussion groups were held in the German sanatorium and the Patriarch's summer palace. For fifteen days Mott chaired the plenary sessions in the Galilea Church, the seating plan before him but without the Edinburgh seven-minute bell which had been refurbished and offered by its maker! Hogg thought that Mott surpassed his superb performance at Edinburgh "if that be possible." He gave both the opening and closing addresses.[141]

Jerusalem 1928 was significant for recognizing secularism as the greatest competitor to Christianity. In contrast to Edinburgh, its concerns were not "with geographical areas, or with the numerical aspect of the missionary enterprise... but with the wide range of human relations—social, industrial, economic, racial, international," Mott pointed out. When Mott, Oldham, and Warnshuis had met in Mott's home in 1927 to consider the message of Jerusalem, they became convinced that the most serious contemporary threat was materialism or rationalism. They asked the Quaker leader Rufus Jones to write a preparatory paper. It declared that "the greatest rival of Christianity in the world today is not Mohammedanism or Buddhism or Hinduism or Confucianism but a world-wide secular way of life and interpretation of the nature of things." The idea was new to most delegates but it produced seminal results at Jerusalem (the discussion method was used effectively) and afterward around the world, especially in the Orient. It changed the context in which industrialization, the rural revolution, and the role of education were evaluated. Bishop Stephen Neill called the resulting division of opinion "the moment of the most acute tension between the more conservative and the more liberal wings of the missionary enterprise." Jones' statement had bordered on syncretism, which the biblicists and Barthians were quick to pick up; on the other hand the Anglo-American social gospel framework that was assumed was in itself somewhat superficial. Jerusalem also produced a fresh definition of a living and indigenous church that marked a real shift from mission-centered to church-centered thinking. This was the end of one era and the beginning of another. Mott summarized it in his foreword to Basil Mathews' journalistic account:

A thoroughly representative body of men and women... found it possible to arrive at a common understanding and to reach unanimous conclusions with reference to a policy for the worldwide Christian mission . . . to [so] re-think and re-state the message and the program as to make possible a clear direction for the Christian missionary enterprise in the momentous period that lies just ahead.[142]

Hans-Ruedi Weber found that "a new unity and unexpected fellowship" developed, in spite of "deep theological differences." Outgrowths from Jerusalem were a research organization, a revival of continental criticism of British and American thought, a fresh emphasis on evangelism, a new approach to the rural church, and another trip around the world by Mott. For as C. Y. Cheng said in a devotional address, "We must tarry in Jerusalem long enough to make sure that we get the vision, but, if we would keep it, we must hasten back to the uttermost parts of the earth to carry it out." For another decade Mott would be carrying his own Jerusalem vision of 1895 and now of 1928 to the ends of the earth.

Whether or not Jerusalem had neglected the Orthodox, Mott made up for it afterward. Shifting roles from his IMC chairmanship to the presidency of the World's Alliance of YMCA's, he plunged again into negotiations with the Eastern churches as he had in 1924. In Sofia, under his chairmanship, a group of distinguished Orthodox churchmen including metropolitan Stephan, laymen, and YMCA secretaries drew up a sort of concordat setting forth agreements that proved to be "of the highest importance for the ecumenical policy of the World's Alliance" and which were effective for years. This defined areas of mutual agreement and limitations: YMCA work was to be conducted in harmony with Orthodox principles and in consultation with its leaders, there was to be no proselytizing, and where the Bible was studied, interpretation should be "in full harmony with Orthodox doctrine." The last phrase was in fact a modification of the Paris basis of the YMCA but was readily ratified.[143] Mott thus set another important milepost in 1928. It was both a notable ecumenical move toward the West by the Orthodox and a step in Mott's accumulation of skills in ecclesiastical ecumenism.

Two years later a similar meeting was held at Kephissia, near Athens. The findings of the Sofia consultation were confirmed and elaborated by a somewhat larger and even more distinguished body. Some Orthodox suspicions had arisen since Sofia, but these were dealt with. The mission of the Orthodox to Islam was raised. It was probably at this meeting that someone intimated that there had been a lack of Orthodox zeal in this direction and one of the metropolitans is said to have replied somewhat warmly, "but, Dr. Mott, it must be remembered that the Orthodox Church has been preventing forty million perscns from becoming Moslems for five hundred years!" Mott promptly adjourned for tea.

A young staff member of the Alliance remembered long afterward that

> ... you saw Dr. Mott sitting there in the middle with the prelates around him, and there was no doubt who was the most truly prelatical of the prelates! I mean that not in an outward sense but in a substantial sense: and he brought into those meetings a readiness to listen to what the Orthodox churches had to say to those of the West at a time when hardly anybody was having that kind of discussion; there are still a good many people in the Eastern churches who had their first contact with any kind of ecumenical work through that early activity of Dr. Mott. [144]

Fred Field Goodsell of the American Board wondered what Mott was trying to do. His queries stirred "the deepest questions of Christian cooperation." He encouraged "the freest discussion, frankest unburdening of hearts and minds regarding Christian life and work." He watched his chances to "get in a telling statement now and then." Yet Mott appeared not to hold any hope for Christian unity in the near future; he saw the YMCA essentially as a channel for lay activity and that the Orthodox churches really wanted its help. He was strongly against any form of proselytizing. He truly believed that the Orthodox churches had rich treasures to bring to our common Christianity—mysticism, martyr history, piety. Another observer pin-pointed the pioneering nature of these ecumenical meetings as introducing the Orthodox participants to one another: many of them had never met before! [145]

Mott held a whole series of such consultations in the spring of 1933. He had gone to Palestine (then gorgeous in spring bloom) at Easter to share with Lord Allenby in the dedication of the Jerusalem YMCA building. [146] Meetings were held in Athens, Belgrade, Sofia, Bucharest, and Chantilly, near Paris. In the course of this journey Mott consulted with seven patriarchs and a host of lesser ecclesiastics and was received by the kings of Bulgaria and of Roumania. The largely Russian Chantilly meeting devoted a session to the relation of the Russian Church to the ecumenical movement. It honored Mott, who acknowledged that his introduction to Orthodoxy had been through the Russian Church. He spoke of how it had brought him to fresh study of the fathers and great councils, the creeds, the music, and "the mystical and contemplative notes which are largely explanatory of deeper depths." [147]

Mott set his third milestone of 1928 by resigning the General Secretaryship of the National Council of the American YMCA, effective with its October meeting, forty years after he had begun as a student worker. In an eloquent letter to the Council members he paid the deepest tribute to "that Christ-like Secretary . . . Charles K. Ober, and that model layman, Cleveland H. Dodge, . . . who drew me by unselfish guile into Association work." It had opened opportunities "such as come to few men." With what an unnumbered host of friendships the Brotherhood had enriched his life! And to the "little band of unnamed friends who for thirty-three of the forty years . . . have provided funds so that my salary and expenses and likewise those of my personal staff have not been a charge on the budget . . . is due a tribute of deepest gratitude. Above all would I humbly acknowledge the guiding, protecting, strengthening hand of the loving and ever-creative God vouchsafed on land and sea."[148]

Ever since the meeting on the Mount of Olives the call of the IMC had become more insistent. Another world journey would require Mott to be out of the country from November, 1928, to June, 1929, and the National YMCA needed full-time leadership. He was now sixty-three and had accepted the secretaryship for a limited time. One has the feeling that the administrative side of the job was beginning to pall. The arrangement with Fletcher Brockman as his associate had not worked out.[149] The Movement was caught in serious problems, such as the new community chest innovations, that were foreign to him. Mott once declared that his competence was in men and movements, not institutions and organizations. Some felt that his weaknesses as an administrator were becoming apparent in the National Council deficits and the shrinkage of the foreign enterprise, while others never ceased to admire him as the best administrator they had known. As the 1920's wore on, to protect diminishing energies he sought "more time for rest" in the schedules he prepared for himself, and there were some health problems.[150] The cumulative effect of all these was seen in a private interview the next year when both John and Leila Mott told a friend who had come to seek advice on taking an administrative post, that not since 1915 (when Mott accepted the general secretaryship) had he been able to make his best contribution to the YMCA because he was enmeshed in administrative detail that had to be mastered in order to function at all. His tenure had been "unwise use of manpower" and was a waste of his maximum potential.[151]

The retirement dinner for Mott produced tributes few men could have deserved. There were hundreds of messages from around the world, testifying to Mott's influence upon lives and careers. His successor, Fred W. Ramsey, another layman, put it well when he said that Mott "belongs to the nations, belongs to the world." John D. Rockefeller, Jr. said that he had been proud to call Mott his dear friend and that Mott's chief characteristics had been "utter unselfishness" and total devotion to the cause. Of all the words used to describe Mott, that evening and since, "statesman" is the most apt. Ethan Colton, an insider, spoke for the intimate colleagues of Mott's life, most of whom were present:

> For those of us who have had windows looking in upon the inner life it is given to witness to the miracles of grace there and to report their sources: Year on year, more prodigious labors. Greater prices paid. Before our eyes the expenditure from spiritual stores manifestly inexhaustible. The silent bearing of loneliness known only to great leaders. Good will that could not be embittered. Undiscourageable determination to understand differences. Love for the slow of heart, the confused and the obstinate. Patience with the mistakes of associates. (One who must have given many disappointments has yet to receive a first reproof.) Vision to encompass the largest projects colleagues conceived and habitually to expand them. Loyalty, accepting blame due others; and on endlessly until intimacies are reached sacredly kept in the archives of the heart.[152]

Colton recalled how a talk to students on prayer by Mott more than thirty years before had reached "the remoter farm belt" of South Dakota and had brought him into this fellowship: that message had revealed Mott's "first hand experience . . . that we have all seen increase in power and beauty with time. Here is the certain clue to the mystical reality of the life honored tonight and the reason for the honoring."

Mott's lengthy acknowledgment of the homage paid him became the fullest autobiographical sketch that he ever gave, save perhaps for the Mathews biography of 1934. Spoken in the relaxed, informal style usual at YMCA fetes, the address, which might be read by some as a pompous exercise in name-dropping, was in reality an extended acknowledgment of the sources of his inspiration and of his gratitude to all those from whom he had learned. He included not only the kings and presidents who had received him but the stenographers and private secretaries who had made possible "the spacing out" of his life span "and likewise much of its fruitage." Colleagues—from Barber and Beaver to Weidensall and Wilder—to whom his indebtedness could hardly be overstated, were legion. The climax of his speech was Mott's confession of "the supremacy and sufficiency of Jesus Christ to meet the deepest longings and highest aspirations of the human heart and of the human race."[153]

To provide him with an income and comparatively modest resources with which to carry out the varied projects that appealed to him as well as to meet the constant requests for aid from around the world, a corporation called "The Committee on the Work of John R. Mott" was set up. It paid Mott an annual stipend of $10,000 for the remainder of his life. In one of the first years it collected almost $170,000 but averaged around $50,000. The Great Depression and drastic changes in the tax laws meant that his days of vast financial operations were over. Nevertheless he lent his support to the drives to remove YMCA deficits and continued to obtain relatively modest grants for a fairly wide range of projects. Retirement did not mean that he left the YMCA: for years he advised, raised funds, and was regarded as its most valued senior consultant. Thus came to an end what Francis Harmon, general secretary from 1932, called the era of the great expansion of the YMCA.[154]

Mott passed his fourth milestone of 1928 in India when he resigned from the WSCF during the Federation's General Committee meeting at Mysore in December. We shall describe that exotic scene in Part 11.

PART 10: A Political Interlude

Mott's lifetime loyalty to the Republican Party had suffered but a temporary aberration during the presidency of Woodrow Wilson. After Wilson's retirement Mott asked to use his name as an honorary sponsor of European student relief; in 1921 Wilson's health was such that he declined Mott's invitation to attend the International Committee's annual dinner in Washington. The next year Wilson wrote a felicitous letter about Mott for the Student YMCA's observance of Mott's thirtieth year of service. Mott sent the former president a copy of *Service with Fighting Men* in 1923, which Wilson acknowledged with genuine interest.

On December 19, 1923, Mott exerted the *tour de force* of his lifetime of interviewing famous persons by talking with three presidents of the United States in one day. He began with William Howard Taft at 9:30 A.M., lunched with President Coolidge, and visited with his old friend Woodrow Wilson at 3:30. At his retirement dinner Mott described this final interview:

> There he was propped up in a chair, evidently in pain. I had just returned from an extensive journey throughout Europe and the Near East. I was able to bring him words of encouragement about the influence of his ideas and

policies. When I remarked that the new generation still believed in his "fourteen points" he broke in and exclaimed: "Mott, I must get well and help them." In a few days he passed away.[155]

Of the eight presidents he had known, Mott said, Wilson was "the most internationally minded and statesmanlike." He had had scores of consultations with him, beginning during Wilson's teaching days at Bryn Mawr and Wesleyan. He had been a formative influence in Mott's life and plans and "the most helpful critic" of two of his books. On that December day in 1923 the two had discoursed over European affairs, Wilson commenting that he would like to get the scalps of those who arranged the disgraceful treaty with Turkey, how sorry he felt for Germany, hoped the Germans would wipe France off the map ("that skunk Poincaré—he was a liar too!") but how amazing it was that we trusted them![156]

Mott had at least one appointment with President Harding, but became quite friendly with President Coolidge, endorsing his candidacy in 1924. The next year he took Eugene Barnett's report on the situation in China to the White House to discuss with the President. Mott secured Coolidge to speak to the national YMCA meeting of 1925, himself writing most of the speech. On February 20, 1927, Mott spent most of a day with the President; their talk was frankly political, chiefly concerning Coolidge's possible third term. From Mott's not entirely legible notes they appear to have agreed that if Al Smith were to be the Democratic candidate it would be highly desirable that the Republican Party be led by "one who will command the maximum confidence . . . of the Protestant and dry forces." After Jerusalem 1928 Mott reported to Coolidge and the two again discussed affairs in the Orient.[157]

Mott's acquaintance with Herbert Hoover began with Mott's visit to Stanford University in 1892, when Hoover was a freshman student. The two met on numerous occasions during the War and the acquaintance was picked up early in the 1920's through Mott's asking for Hoover's endorsement of European Student Relief. From 1922 Colton reported regularly to Hoover as secretary of commerce on the state of affairs in Russia and brought him to speak before the national YMCA in 1925, ghost-writing the address.

There is modest documentation of Mott's support of Hoover in 1928, but with his approval Colton directed a mini-campaign:

> I took a hand in both the nominating and election stages. In the former one, active pitch was made in Ohio. The professionals regarded the carrying of that state's national Convention delegates to be of strategic impor-

tance. And his success in the statewide primary did accelerate the winning of supporters across the country. We tied in with Charles P. Taft, II. At his request I secured from Mott, then overseas, a strongly worded cable endorsement of the candidacy that the promoters used widely in Ohio and elsewhere.[158]

Mott assembled a committee of editors of the religious press; Colton coordinated the distribution service that resulted. It emphasized prohibition, which was the paramount issue. As Colton put it four decades later, "the attack on the Democratic candidate centered on his over-riding advocacy of return to a legalized alcoholic liquor trade and his identification with Tammany Hall in New York City and State politics linked with the bossed machines of the Party in the big cities of the North." This group of editors tried to avoid the Catholic aspect by declaring in favor of "dryness" against "wetness." Colton barnstormed in his native state of South Dakota but the farmers there voted for Smith because of what they regarded as Hoover's ruinous farm policies. Just prior to election day Mott gave a press interview in which he declared his all-out support for Hoover. It was Hoover's "constructive statesmanship," his "sensitive and strong social conscience," which included Prohibition, his internationalism and humanitarianism, his concern for youth that evoked Mott's commitment.[159]

Mott's support of prohibition, which gave him publicity in Australia and New Zealand in 1926, was well known. He adopted the usual arguments for it—industrial efficiency, reduction of drunken driving, the majority votes in its favor—and added that it was "a boon of incalculable value not only for youth, but through them for every constructive cause which we have most at heart in the building of the nation." It was not a denial of personal liberty but an affirmation of "social conscience" which should take precedence over individual choice. He was often interviewed on the subject during his travels in Europe and frequently received front-page coverage on "That Failure and Farce in America." Hoover's endorsement of prohibition was an added reason for Mott's supporting him in 1928 and again four years later.[160]

In 1932 there was a movement to submit the dry issue to a popular referendum. Mott endorsed it and was featured on the front page of the *New York Times*. He favored it not only as an opportunity for the younger generation to express itself but also because many, such as John D. Rockefeller, Jr., were changing their minds. Mott was widely misquoted and some controversy ensued; the *Christian Century* disagreed with his position but made it clear that he had not followed Rockefeller into the wet camp. [161] After the election of 1932, Mott convened a group of persons interested in rethinking the whole problem. Fred B. Smith gave an eye-witness account of the meeting:

> It became apparent, within one hour after the session opened, that along with other persons the wildest, most impractical zealots were present and proposed to be very articulate in the discussion. For the most part they had not come to make a serious effort for a united constructive program . . . [but] to defend the past and to brand the "traitors" who had dared to think a new thought in this field.

> Sitting at the top table presiding was this man I had seen handle great assemblies of world leaders with such skill as I had never known in any other man. . . . I could not point to one single incident in these very complicated gatherings where he had seriously erred in judgment.

> But this Atlantic City gathering of prohibitionists, by the end of the first session, was clear out of his hands. As a matter of fact, I knew for a considerable part of the time that he did not know himself what some of these men and women were talking about.

> Near the end, when any kind or sort of agreement was shown to be impossible, Dr. Mott resorted to his favorite method in a crisis of that kind by suggesting that a "continuing committee" be appointed.

Mott was made chairman, but, Smith noted, no one ever heard of the committee. "No innocent boy, who in his curiosity explored a bumble-bee's nest, ever kept away from them more faithfully afterward than did Dr. Mott from this issue." Mott issued a statement of findings. He later expressed his belief that the failure of prohibition was largely due to the abandonment of the effective educational programs that had been an integral part of the temperance movement. [162]

In November, 1929, John and Leila Mott were President and Mrs. Hoover's overnight guests at the White House, and Mott saw Hoover with some frequency throughout the latter's term of office, discussing Eugene Barnett's report on Japanese aggression in China in 1931 and on another occasion talking alone with Hoover. Mott gave his wholehearted support to the President's campaign for reelection, but an effort to again enlist the agencies he had coordinated in 1928 fell on deaf ears; he sent his own "Reasons for the Re-election of President Hoover" to his constituency. In old age, Mott and Hoover refreshed their long friendship, and Hoover was among those who nominated Mott for the Nobel Peace Prize. [163]

PART 11: Taking Jerusalem 1928 Around the World

The first important event of Mott's eight-month globe-circling tour of 1928–1929 was the meeting of the 100-member WSCF General Committee at Mysore, India, during the first two weeks of December, 1928.[164] As the guests of the Maharajah of Mysore, the Committee members were welcomed with regal ceremony. The Maharajah arrived at the opening session "in a gorgeous state carriage accompanied by outriders on beautiful horses," was escorted to a throne, flanked by Mott, Henriod, K. T. Paul and others, and gave "in beautiful English" an address of welcome that Mott believed he had prepared "with the greatest care" (actually Stephen C. Neill had ghost-written it). K. T. Paul responded, as did Mott, whose bearing young Hans Lilje thought quite as majestic as that of the Maharajah.

The Committee's major business was the selection of both a new general secretary and a chairman, for Mott had determined to resign. Visser 't Hooft, who had not only been caught in Mott's web but had been tested by several years work with the World's YMCA and most recently as office secretary of the Federation, was delighted to move up to the general secretaryship, for the Federation had been for him as it was for Mott, a "first love." Mott had discussed the chairmanship earlier with Francis P. Miller, then treasurer, who had been a staff member of the American Student Movement, but he had refused. Miller was surprised to receive a cable from India announcing his election. He accepted and spent several months reorganizing the Federation. The chairmanship was a non-salaried position; at the earliest moment he sought out Mott for help in financing the organization, since he had no such clientele as had Mott. But Mott refused, a shattering experience for Miller:

> Mott had been my hero in a very special sense—endowed with the qualities of a great Christian leader and a world statesman. Suddenly the illusion faded: he was no hero at all, but a mere mortal man. During the next twenty-five years I did not see him or talk to him more than two or three times.

When Ethan Colton heard this story, he snorted, "Mott did that to all of us. Francis shouldn't have been so thin-skinned!"[165]

Some folklore accumulated around Mott's part in this epochal Federation gathering at Mysore. He, Henriod, Hromadka and others cabled a Christmas greeting to Archbishop Söderblom in Sweden, whose health had prevented his attending. There was a light moment when Mott, "feeling merry," tossed oranges from a basket to members of his audience.[166] When the General Committee demurred at a financial report showing a deficit for the previous year and was confronted with a larger one for the new year, Mott exploded: "From the beginning of time men have been making money. No one has ever taken any of it with him. Go out and get it!" Word of this comment apparently did not reach Miller! When Mott was delayed in handing the text of his closing address to Basil Mathews for the report, Mathews wrote what he believed Mott would say. "How did you know?" asked Mott. "I remembered," replied Mathews.

One senses that Mott had realized since the meeting at St. Beatenberg that the Federation was moving into waters beyond his depth and that his withdrawal was overdue, for Mysore marked a sharp turning point for the WSCF. Now under new leadership, theologically oriented toward the Continent of Europe, and confronted with problems almost unknown to its founders, it pursued quite different courses of action. But this only increased its ecumenical impact, the accumulated force of which would be discernible in moves toward a world council of churches, as writers such as Henry P. Van Dusen and Tissington Tatlow have shown. W. A. Visser 't Hooft called the chapter of his *Memoirs* on the WSCF, "Nursery and Brains of the Ecumenical Movement."[167]

The National Christian Council of India met with Mott at Madras over New Year's. He interpreted Jerusalem and spoke to several other themes. It was decided to make an intensive study of mass movements toward Christianity in India; Mott and William Paton assisted in framing the resolution authorizing it; Mott obtained funds for it from Rockefeller sources through the ISRR. He noted in his diary that the Indian National Council seemed to have found itself but thought the leadership relatively weaker than that in China or Japan. He attended a conference on rural problems (he would later become much involved in what came to be called "Agricultural Missions") and another on industrialization, and of course spoke at many small meetings.[168]

The remainder of thirteen weeks in India was devoted to relatively leisurely travel and visitation with son John L. and his wife Celestine, now engaged in industrial welfare and student work at Nagpur, and with daughter Irene, working among villagers in the same region. Eleanor Mott had come with her parents as secretary; William G. Schram was private secretary and fortunately for the record was photographer as well. There was a pleasure trip to the Khyber Pass; John and Leila chose the private railway car of a railroad executive but the young people went by automobile. When all went to Darjeeling, Celestine and Eleanor took the horseback climb for the dawn view of Everest while John and Leila enjoyed the mountains from their hotel. The party was entertained and garlanded by notables from the Viceroy down. An Indian who accompanied the Motts on one of their journeys was astonished at the respect and even deference Mott showed toward some beggars who came on the train at one stop.

Mott called upon Mahatma Gandhi at his ashram at Ahmedabad. Accompanied by Leila and a missionary named Wilson, Mott described his goals and programs and then asked Gandhi thirteen questions, writing down the replies next day. Gandhi answered promptly "and without time for meditation. He impressed me as perfectly frank, candid and sincere on all points except in dealing with my questions that bore on Jesus Christ and Christianity," Mott noted, adding that he was disappointed with Gandhi's "superficiality or evasion" of his questions dealing with the Mass Movement and with conversion. After circling the subcontinent from Madras to Bombay to Lahore to Calcutta and performing numerous YMCA and missions chores the Motts sailed for Rangoon in mid-February, Leila writing back to Irene their deep satisfaction in having gained a "deeper understanding of the life and surroundings and work of our children."[169]

Forty-eight busy hours in Rangoon saw Mott involved in specially called meetings of the Christian Council of Burma, to which he gave three addresses; he also made a speech to the anniversary celebration of the Rangoon YMCA. Taking ship to Penang and train to Bangkok, the party visited that city from February 27 to March 5. Upon arrival they were taken to a dazzling state ball where they witnessed "oriental splendor on every hand"—seeing the king and queen and the court in fancy dress. Mott might have worn the medal of the Order of the Crown of Siam that he had been awarded in 1919. He later interviewed five princes and questioned a leading abbot on "the lack of the propagandist spirit in Buddhism." Mott's principal business in Bangkok was a national conference of Christian workers, most of whom were Siamese (Thais), the first of its kind to be held there. The Jerusalem findings were the basis of the group discussions. Mott gave at least six addresses. The conference decided to form a national Christian council, another example of Mott's instrumentality in the creation of almost all such bodies around the world. The Boon Itt Institute, a sort of YMCA, and the presence of a descendant of Boon Itt who had been a member of the Mount Hermon Hundred of 1886, provided a nostalgic moment for Mott.[170]

The party went next to Manila for a five-day visit—Mott's longest there. Most of his time was given to "enlarged" meetings of the national Evangelical Union. He presided for three days, spoke on the significance of Jerusalem, and gave several other addresses. The discussion method was used; the most important development was the revision and adoption of a new constitution by which the Evangelical Union, dating from 1901, was reorganized into a National Christian Council. Mott coached its leaders on procedural matters and the selection of an executive secretary. The E. Stanton Turners took the Motts to Pagsanjan for a break, all enjoying "a most interesting and exciting trip in canoes up and down a series of swift rapids, through narrow and most beautiful gorges." Mott's last day was devoted to YMCA plans for extension and its unique inter-confessional program. [171]

The Motts reached Kobe on Easter Sunday, March 31, 1929. A launch met the ship to get Mott to a mass meeting of young men and women on time; his theme was "The Power of His Resurrection." From Kobe Mott went at once to Gotemba where he was featured at a four-day retreat for secretaries and lay leaders at the YMCA's Tozanso conference center; only ten of the forty-four present were non-Japanese. The round of affairs that followed, in Tokyo, was as crowded as any Mott tour; he met several who had welcomed him in 1896–1897. The climax of his calls upon government officials was an audience with the young Emperor Hirohito, whom he had earlier met as Crown Prince and Prince Regent. As in 1925, Mott used every opportunity to cultivate amicable relations between the United States and Japan. On April fifth he laid the cornerstone of the new Central (Kanda) YMCA. [172]

He was much in the company of Soichi Saito, G. Sidney Phelps, and Arthur Jorgensen, all of whom had been caught in his web. Saito, the national YMCA secretary, could be called a Mott disciple. Phelps, now senior American officer, was the statesmanlike "masterbuilder" type that Mott admired. Jorgensen was engaged in the unusual task of editing a continuing series of books in Japanese on biblical and Christian themes—encouraging Japanese to write, translate current Western authors such as Canon Streeter or Reinhold Niebuhr, and fostering some one-yen titles by Japanese. To launch the last-named project a life of Jesus by Bishop Y. Honda had been awarded a 500-yen prize. This project resembled that to which Mott had set J. N. Farquhar in India almost two decades earlier. Although Mott and Jorgensen did not always agree on details, Mott kept Jorgensen at it for two years past his normal retirement.

A National Council of Churches conference to implement Jerusalem had been held the past summer; now three regional meetings were called, at Kamakura, Nara, and Fukuoka, for Mott. He reemphasized the Jerusalem message and spoke to other themes. At Nara he had opportunity for fellowship with Toyohiko Kagawa whose "Kingdom of God Movement" to win a million souls for Christ was in part an emergent from Jerusalem. Though two more opposites could hardly be imagined—Kagawa returned to the slums of Osaka while Mott went to address the businessmen of that city at an elegant club—Mott subsequently obtained generous financing for certain of Kagawa's projects and for years would cite the diminutive evangelist as the kind of innovator needed to provide fresh thrust for the Christian enterprise.[173]

From Fukuoka the Motts rushed back to Shimonoseki and the ferry to Korea, reaching Seoul for what was for Mott a long visit, five days, the prime purpose of which was to attend a conference of the Korean National Council of Churches. He spoke at least six times before a highly appreciative body that was predominantly Korean. He lunched with his Cornell colleague R. S. Miller, with the Japanese governor, and on several occasions had opportunity to cultivate his acquaintance with Methodist Bishop James C. Baker. There were occasions in which Mott was the central figure in small gatherings of Koreans, Japanese, and Americans to foster "international goodwill among these leading Christians." He gave special attention to YMCA affairs, reviewing the rural program, the foreign staff, and the facilities.

Mott chose to enter China from the north, going from Seoul to Mukden over the South Manchurian Railway, which he noted had a smooth roadbed and high quality equipment and gave efficient service. After a day of rest with Leila's sister Anna May and her husband Will Stewart, Mott's former secretary, Mott described Jerusalem to a crowded conference of Christian workers from the entire region, interpreted by David Yui who had come to escort the Motts to Peking. The third day in Mukden, Mott took time off from the conference for luncheon with Marshall Chang [Hsueh-liang]:

> I spent nearly an hour with him and David Yui discussing in an intimate way some of his principal problems. In the course of the conversation I had opportunity to deal with his personal problem, and also to hold up Christ in a very special way.[174]

Later that afternoon Mott spoke at an evangelistic service for students on personal experience of Christ and the secret of victory over temptation;

128 gave in their names as inquirers, and Mott autographed copies of the New Testament for them. The Stewarts accompanied the party to Peking.

Several retreat conferences had been arranged in China to take advantage of Mott's presence, the first being in the Western Hills near Peking. Questionnaires had been prepared for the guidance of the discussion groups but Mott thought the results superficial. He gave several addresses, interpreted by Cheng Ching-yi. In no real sense were these "Mott" conferences, though he must have been the major attraction. Famine conditions in Honan Province caused him to send a lengthy cable to President Hoover, and Leila wrote home that the country was an armed camp. The Motts were, in fact, provided a bodyguard for travel between Peking and Hankow and were offered a special train which Mott did not accept. All through Honan, Leila noted, there were "troops or rather soldiers of our friend at the stations, guarding the bridges," and the like. The regional conference for central China was held at Wuchang, across the Yangtze from Hankow. It was there that Cheng Ching-yi made his famous appeal for an evangelistic campaign to double the church membership of China in the next five years. Mott followed with "The Summons to a Larger Evangelism" and spoke on several other occasions.[175]

It was probably during the four days the Motts were guests of Episcopal Bishop Logan H. Roots in Hankow that Leila Mott suffered what was later diagnosed as a heart attack. Realizing that something serious had happened, she wrote back to Anna May that the future seemed perplexing if she could not "stand traveling with John." Nevertheless, she held to most of the schedule for the remainder of the trip, such as this a few days later in Nanking:

> Leila, Eleanor and I, together with David Yui, and Mr. Mills, had dinner with General Chiang Kai-shek, Chairman of the Five Councils (popularly called the President of the Republic). Dr. H. H. Kung, Minister of Industry, Commerce and Labor, and Mrs. Kung were also present. The wife of the President and Mrs. Kung are sisters. Their brother is T. V. Soong, Minister of Finance. We spent a most enjoyable evening together. After dinner I spent over an hour with the President, David Yui serving as interpreter. Minister Kung was present most of the time, also Mills. In this conversation I raised in a most direct way a number of leading questions, which were answered with frankness by the President.[176]

Mott spoke several times at another regional meeting in Shanghai and held simultaneously a conference of the YMCA secretaries of China;

there was also a Christian literature conference. Willard Lyon accompanied him on May 18 to Hangchow where they attended the first four days of the seventh National Christian Council of China meeting, which took up Cheng's challenge.[177]

The Motts sailed for home from Shanghai on the *President McKinley* on May 24. The next day, John's sixty-fourth birthday, he received a wireless message announcing that the Emperor of Japan had bestowed upon him the First Order of the Sacred Treasure, having skipped the three steps from the honor he had received in 1920. Leila remained on shipboard when they docked in Kobe on a Saturday and John was whisked off for a whirlwind of activities. While the ship went on to Yokohama he rushed by train to Tokyo where he received the honor, was photographed wearing medal and sash (the retouch artist giving him a surprisingly Japanese mien), made a series of courtesy calls, was entertained at luncheon at the Peers' Club by Prince Tokugawa (Mott spoke at length on the situation in China and "with the greatest directness gave constructive suggestions bearing on the relations which Japan should sustain to China"), joined NCC discussions on a headquarters building, addressed a supper meeting on the million souls campaign, spent an evening on the student situation in Japan with Jorgensen and Bishop Baker, called on the aged Viscount Shibusawa to discuss the problem of promoting goodwill among the nations "and in particular between Japan and America," spoke at noon to the Union Club of Yokohama, and rejoined Leila on the *President McKinley* for Tuesday 3:00 P.M. sailing— seen off by a throng that included Russian Orthodox Archbishop Sergius, leaders of all the organizations he had worked with, and "a representative of the Goto family." Years later Mott named the series of conferences he had held in Japan and China on this tour of 1928–29 among the most creative of his life.

PART 12: **Africa, 1934**

Importuned for years to visit South Africa again, Mott finally did so in 1934. He was moved in part by Oldham's convictions concerning the "staggering" missionary potential of central Africa. "Since the unveiling of the Western Hemisphere there has been no greater event than the emergence of Africa," he wrote upon his return. How he reached that conclusion will emerge from an all-too-brief account of what was Mott's last long tour involving him in issues of great importance, and requiring a

great deal of courage on his part. Forty-five years later it seems amazing
that he was greeted with enthusiasm and could express himself freely in
South Africa, and that he achieved what was little short of a *tour de force*
in central Africa.[178]

Mott prepared for this trip with unusual care, taking special pains to
protect himself against the hazards of the tropics, which some felt he
should not risk at his age. Accompanied by Oliver McCowen of the
World Alliance staff to look after the many YMCA matters that would
arise, and R. S. Wort, a British YMCA man as secretary, Mott arrived in
Capetown April 9. Among the scores who honored him and attended his
meetings were some who had been at Northfield before the turn of the
century, many who recalled his missions at Oxford or Cambridge, and
more who had met him in 1906. Oswin Bull, whom Mott had recruited
for the South African Student Movement in 1908, and R. H. W. Shepperd, secretary of the General Missionary Conference of South Africa,
planned Mott's itinerary and accompanied him through most of it.
Everywhere he was greeted with open arms and much protocol, and was
heard eagerly. He devoted a good deal of time to the YMCA and to
students, but his chief concern was missions.[179]

The first conference was held in Wellington, near Capetown. It was
conducted much like those on Mott's Oriental tour. Before leaving
Capetown Mott had "a memorable visit" with General Jan Christian
Smuts. This was one of the "most inspiring and stimulating conversations" he had ever had with a public man. "He shared with me with the
greatest freedom and sympathy some of the deep experiences in his public
life, dwelling more particularly on his religious convictions and his guiding Christian principles."[180] As he moved from city to city, Mott used
about a dozen themes for his addresses, ranging from the power of the
Bible through the rising spiritual tide to the world outlook, always
adapted to the immediate situation.

The long train ride to Grahamstown tired Mott, but he was able to
rest at Lovedale during the next conference. He took great interest in
every detail of the important mission schools, hospitals, and printing
presses of the area. He presided over a regional conference at Bloemfontain and another at Durban. He spent several hours with John Dube, a
Zulu, "one of the leading native Christians of Natal," and spoke to at
least 3,000 attentive "natives" in a hall packed to suffocation. Moving
on to Pretoria, he presided over another conference but used his rest
period to see "the slums, the compounds and locations of the Natives,
African Indians, and Chinese," which revealed vividly "many of the

great needs of these populations as well as brought into view some of the more valuable constructive projects on their behalf." On Sunday, May 6, Mott addressed a vast united meeting of all the Dutch Reformed Churches of Johannesburg and vicinity in the City Hall, the service and his address being broadcast; he was told that people "apparently all over South Africa" had listened in. The next evening he gave his address on the race problem to an audience of five or six hundred in the Bantu Men's Social Centre, a "meeting of great intensity." The following Sunday he addressed three to five thousand natives on sowing and reaping, interpreted sentence-by-sentence into two dialects.

The general conference, for which the earlier ones had been preparatory, met at Bloemfontain May 15–16. Mott gave the keynote address under the title "A Fork in the Road," confronting his hearers with the choice between "a policy of expansion or contraction, between one of guiding on the past or the future . . . of united or separate action." Seven committees brought in reports that by common consent constituted "a clear and authentic lead for the Christian missionary forces of South Africa," one of these being the creation of a Christian Council that would eventuate two years later; Mott spent his final hours in Bloemfontain coaching the new secretary of that body, which would hold Dutch, Anglo-Saxon, and Africans together until after World War II.[181]

Mott now left for Southern Rhodesia. The next conference was at Bulawayo; during a break in the schedule he accomplished an urge of many years standing, seeing the grave of Cecil Rhodes and the "World's View" from the site, both of which exceeded his highest expectations; a serious gap in his enjoyment was Leila's absence. During the long train rides through uninteresting country Mott dictated as much as six hours a day; one of the books he relaxed with was Agatha Christie's *Murder on the Orient Express*. Two days were spent at Victoria Falls (Mosi-Ao-Funya), again missing Leila. He moved on into Northern Rhodesia (Zambia), finding on May 25 that there was no escaping his birthday when he was greeted with a cake in a missionary's home at Ndola, where the first regional conference for this section was held. McCowen returned to South Africa at this point and Mott went on to Elizabethville (Lubumbashi) in the Belgian Congo (Katanga) where he was met by Emory Ross, who had probably had the most to do with his making the trip, and H. Wakelin Coxill; a conference was held May 30–June 1. Mott spent a morning "inspecting" the copper mines and the mining company's facilities for its black workers.[182]

A leisurely train trip through the Kasai to Luluabourg allowed Mott and his guides to observe the native way of life and to see the upper reaches of the Congo. A regional conference took place at Mutoto, for which the preparation had been so adequate that the meeting marked "real advance" and "a splendid lead" for the region. Between sessions Mott was conducted to numerous missions stations and shown all phases of the work—as thorough a first-hand "inspection" as he had ever made. On a few occasions he spoke to gatherings of "natives." Someone snapped a picture of him with a group of dancing girls which, Coxill noted, "may have interested him, but did not seem to amuse Mott very much."

On June 12 Mott had his first long aeroplane ride on the seven-hour flight from Luluabourg to Léopoldville (Kinshasa). He noted that the plane was "splendidly managed" and the trip made "in great comfort." He took great interest in the scenery, since the flight was made between 3,000 and 4,500 feet. Writing to the Stewarts he was reminded not only of the trip with Leila and Will in 1906 but his mind naturally dwelt on the contrast between flight and the hardships endured by Stanley and Livingstone. The final conference took place at Léopoldville.

Mott kept these conferences on the highest level, wrote Coxill, adding that it was not surprising that they were immediately followed by "a great outpouring of the Spirit, when hundreds of Africans were led to seek Christ." Mott's own words were: "We are summoned to expose men and women more fully to the living Christ. He will make His own impressions—a transforming, enduring impression. Let us get people exposed to Christ." Although there was some criticism, a few thinking that Mott was not well enough informed for the task he attempted—and one who admired him greatly admitted that he was "somewhat of a steamroller and while he left a smooth track there were some rocks smashed down"—he succeeded in welding a very diverse group of missions people into a remarkable unity. Coxill wrote further:

> It was a rich privilege to watch the masterful dignity with which he steered the thoughts of missionaries of forty or more societies, of different nationalities and of varied traditions, towards one unanimous decision after another. He seemed to draw out the best that was in each of us. There was a delightful humility in the air . . . . Those who had been on the field for thirty or forty years offered their wise counsels with as much unassuming diffidence as the youngest members present.[183]

Coxill also recalled Mott's disappointment that the missionaries could not introduce him to more Congolese leaders, telling them of the remarkable initiatives nationals were taking in other lands he had visited, especially China. The missionaries explained that the Belgians did not favor the teaching of English, that these people had been wholly illiterate only two generations back, that few native pastors could have gained from his conferences. But Mott was not pleased: "Today (1965)," concluded Coxill, "we see how right he was, and his visit to Congo did much to encourage more African responsibility in and for the Church."

Mott did not leave the matter there. He spent much of his time on the long voyage back to Antwerp composing a report to Leopold III, King of the Belgians. The audience was granted on July 18. The young king greeted Mott cordially, putting him immediately at ease. "He evidently wanted me to speak freely and fully. A number of times I apologized for talking so much, but in every case he insisted that he wanted me to go on." Fully informed by Oldham concerning the problem, Mott adroitly praised the Belgian administration of the colony, then dwelt at length on the basic issue, "the securing of an equitable status and arrangement for the Protestant educational system." Mott read the statement he had written on the boat. The King asked questions which Mott "answered fully." All of Mott's notes to the audience have not survived but from correspondence with Oldham it is clear that the main point, which had concerned the IMC for some time, and about which Oldham had been needling the Belgian government, was that of religious liberty.[184]

As Mott reported to various missions bodies he pointed out that at long last the colonial powers were beginning to address themselves significantly "to the great human problem resulting from the invasion of the life of backward peoples by twentieth-century civilization"—inflamed race relations, lack of medical resources, the "white stumbling block," neglect of youth, inadequate educational facilities—but that in contrast there was "the remarkable work achieved by the Christian missionaries":

> When critics of missions point out that missionaries are concerning themselves exclusively with the individual as contrasted with the social aspect of the all-embracing integral gospel, and that their sole concern is with the life hereafter and not with the demands of the life of today, they expose their basic ignorance and superficiality. One of the glories of modern missions is the wonderful way in which throughout the African continent they have pioneered virtually all the more significant advances in the social and economic uplift of the various peoples.... The present moment, therefore, constitutes the time of times for Africa.[185]

PART 13: The Private Man Emerges

The African trip had been more leisurely than most before it, but the difficulties in trying to reduce the pace as Mott approached the age of seventy were demonstrated by the demands of 300 pieces of mail that

awaited him on his arrival in Belgium! Leila's heart attack also had such
an effect, for he seemed "to want me just to be around," she confided to
sister Anna May. "He couldn't have got on without her," commented a
friend. On the 1929 world tour they had slipped away from business and
socializing to hear the soprano Galli-Curci in concert at Hong Kong; as
time went on there were more such breaks and they were longer. They
even included occasional movies. He began to see more of his friends of
earlier years, found time to fraternize with contemporaries, and followed
World Series baseball and Ivy League football with enthusiasm. Somehow, the burden of bringing in the Kingdom began to weigh less heavily
than it had when Mott launched himself into the Age of Energy with
such vigor a half-century before. In the interim he had learned that "the
government is on His shoulders," not on John Mott's. The private man
could begin to separate himself from the image of the public servant. [186]

Not long after their last child, Eleanor, left home, the Motts disposed of the house in Montclair, New Jersey, and moved to a large airy
apartment overlooking the Hudson River in Yonkers, New York, making
it easier to commute to his office in mid-town Manhattan, which he kept
for many years. [187] Summers in Canada were lengthened; in the early
twenties there were unforgettable canoe trips into the Laurentians with
Fred, Eleanor, and Irene, the parents gaily enduring the hardships. In the
evenings Mott liked to read P. G. Wodehouse aloud. "It was a happiness
to be with him," wrote Eleanor of her father, "he made life richer in
every way for those around him." [188] Father was not a gadgeteer; though
he had worked in a lumber yard as a youth he had no practical skills as an
adult. In trying to learn to drive he almost wrecked the elegant Packard
automobile he was given at YMCA retirement. In the early thirties he
and Leila began wintering in Florida, at first on account of her health. A
deep sorrow for John was the death of his sister Clara, the musician, in
1925.

The Great Depression created havoc in the reduction of the foreign
YMCA staff, but there is no record of Mott's complaining, although he
was compelled to witness the apparent undoing of a precious part of his
life's work. He tended to rationalize such set-backs as "Advantages of
Testing-Times," the title of an oft-repeated lecture. A chronic burden
was brother-in-law Will White's Biblical Seminary, which Mott could
not bring himself to sustain financially, but with some grumbling did on
occasion help to bail out. Bank closings caused the Motts some temporary inconveniences, as they did everyone.

These years opened a few new interests for Mott, one of which was his appointment to an honorary board of the Washington Cathedral in 1932; he later became an honorary canon. In 1931 Brown University awarded him the LL.D. degree. He visited Oxford and Cambridge with "successful" results and carried tremendous weight as a speaker and evangelist in Europe, especially with young pastors and in missions circles. The tours of 1930 and 1931 in Great Britain, Scandinavia, and Czechoslovakia (where he was decorated with the Order of the White Lion by President Masaryk in 1930 and received the Masaryk medal in 1935) were virtual triumphs. Such popularity was based on the fact that Mott personified the world mission of the Church, as several of his contemporaries noted. [189]

The duties of the chairman of the International Missionary Council could not be reduced but they could be delegated and the pace could be slackened. When Mott went to the Orient again in 1935 he gave almost twice as much time to each country as in 1929. Speaking on the radio—and he was excellent in that medium—was far less demanding than barnstorming the country. There was no diminution in the quality of his spiritual and parliamentary leadership of the IMC executive meetings such as at the Moravian center Herrnhut in 1932 or Northfield in 1935.

He was in the vanguard of the "social gospel shift" in missions. His report of the 1928-29 world tour aroused the interest of John D. Rockefeller, Jr. and others. This led to the Laymen's Foreign Missions Inquiry and its report, *Rethinking Missions*, which was a scandal to Robert E. Speer and the majority of missions boards and their supporters because it seemed to destroy the prime motive for missions by its appreciative attitude toward other faiths. Since Mott was chairman of the Institute of Social and Religious Research, which did the study, carrying it out on a high level of excellence, he was criticized unduly. He doubtless held most of the forward-looking positions taken by the report, but publicly considered it desirable as "a fresh lead," citing Mark Twain's remark that "he was not so much troubled about the parts of the Bible that he did not understand and could not accept, as he was about those that he did understand and knew that he ought to accept." Speer refuted the study in *Rethinking Missions Reexamined,* but the friendship of the two men was not breached. When they next met at the Quiet Day both showed concern, but Mott observed to Samuel McCrea Cavert that he feared Robert was not quite sensitive enough to change. [190]

In the first half of the 1930's, Mott put into book/study guide form, as he had since *Strategic Points* in 1897, the distillation not only of his recent travel but of a lifetime of ecumenical observation that reflected both the contemporary missionary outlook and his own continuing sense of mission. Upon the invitation of Archbishop Söderblom, he lectured on the Olaus Petri Foundation in Sweden. With Leila's help (she wrote some parts of it and he dedicated it to her) he published *The Present Day Summons to the World Mission of Christianity* in 1931, an expansion of his recent Cole Lectures at Vanderbilt University, bringing together the main lines of his thinking during and since the tour of 1928–29.[191] The next year he gave the Ayer Lectures at Rochester Theological Seminary. These were published as *Liberating the Lay Forces of Christianity;* oddly enough, he hardly mentioned women, which some thought a blind spot with Mott in spite of his marriage partnership and the tremendous aid he had received from women from the day in 1895 when Mrs. George A. Coburn had made possible the first world tour and at its end Nettie Fowler McCormick had underwritten the World's Student Christian Federation.[192] In 1935 Mott provided the foreword to the *Conspectus of Cooperative Missionary Enterprises,* an IMC directory put together by the indefatigible and overburdened Charles H. Fahs and Helen E. Davis. Also in 1935 Mott produced a booklet called *Cooperation and the World Mission* for study in the student movements.[193]

There had also been an international survey, again funded by John D. Rockefeller, Jr., of the foreign expansion of the YMCA and YWCA. Carried out after Mott's resignation from the general secretaryship, it provided guidance for the transition forced by the Great Depression, but it paid homage to the structure Mott had built. Mott tried to keep out of these affairs but expressed himself freely in the committee meetings he did attend.

That Mott was becoming retrospective was evidenced by his authorization of a biography by Basil Mathews of the IMC staff. There had been plans to produce a biography in the mid-1920's but they were abandoned. Mathews' work appeared early in 1934 as *John R. Mott, World Citizen,* in time to send copies to a large number of friends as a 1933 Christmas gift. Both Mathews and Mott regarded it as descriptive of "the experiences and principles" of Mott's life that would serve as examples to youth rather than the strict purposes of biography. Hugh Vernon White, reviewing it for *The Missionary Herald,* asked, "Who is John R. Mott?" The book was a sharp reminder, he said, of the end of the era in which Mott had been the most representative figure. Mott would later claim that he did not want a biography, but in his later years he entered hundreds of identifying notes in his files.

A British reviewer pointed out that Mathews had described a man who had adapted the techniques of big business to the furtherance of the Kingdom of God. Mott was pictured in that role by Sir William Orpen, the well-known portraitist of the period, in a canvas for which a considerable sum was raised. Mott did not like it. It hangs in the offices of the WSCF in Geneva, perhaps the least appropriate headquarters of all of his enterprises in which to portray him in that role.[194]

Mott's seventieth birthday was celebrated by the World's Alliance at a memorable dinner in Geneva. He was given a superb bound volume of congratulatory letters and messages from Associations around the world, most of them on parchment, set in frames of indigenous art, calligraphy, or embossing. Instead of giving an autobiographical review Mott answered questions on how he would live his life again. Messages by the score came from everywhere. The most fitting was from the Archbishop of Canterbury, Geoffrey Fisher:

> He led us then;
> He leads us still.[195]

12

Retrospect
and Reward

"While life lasts I am an evangelist."
—Mott, in 1933 and 1954[1]

F EW MEN live to see the fruition of their life work as Mott witnessed the answer to his prayers for Christian unity in the International Missionary Council and the World Council of Churches. As he had earlier concentrated on the World's Student Christian Federation, the influence of which was pervasive and universal, in his last active years he gave himself fully to the IMC. Through its chairmanship he exerted both a symbolic and a direct influence upon the World Council "in process of formation."

In the winter and spring of 1936–37 he went to India to preside over the XXI World Conference of the World's Alliance of YMCA's at Mysore, which enjoyed the regal hospitality of the Maharajah like that shown the IMC in 1928.[2] Following it Mott had extended personal conferences and informal meetings with a host of missionaries, met Rabindranath Tagore, and again talked with Gandhi.[3] En route home he held missions conferences in Cairo and Khartoum, and cultivated the Orthodox in Palestine, Syria, and Turkey, presumably in the interest of the ecumenical conferences to be held at Oxford and Edinburgh in the summer of 1937.[4]

The next winter he presided for seventeen days over what he regarded as the greatest of the three world missions conferences—Edinburgh 1910, Jerusalem 1928, and now Madras, held on the new campus of Madras Christian College in the village of Tambaram at Christmastide 1938.[5] No longer confronted merely by humanistic secularism, the churches of sixty-nine countries, the younger ones being slightly in the majority, were now facing the demonic forces of communism, fascism, and revolution in a pre-war atmosphere. Prepared for by Mott, Oldham, and the staff almost from the close of the Jerusalem conference a decade earlier, Tambaram was significant, and hence ecumenically influential, as Hogg rightly says, for what it *was*—"a unifying event in the life of the whole church"—more than for what it *did.* "It is the Church," Mott declared in his opening address, "which is to be at the centre of our thinking and resolving these creative days." Africans who had never been together, for example, realized what it meant to be African Christians. Never, said Mott, "have Christians come together when men were bearing such impossible burdens, or undergoing such persecution and suffering." It was a great gift, wrote Visser 't Hooft, that Tambaram was held "just at the time when the World Council of Churches started its process of formation." Not only would the younger churches make the ecumenical movement truly worldwide, but the sense of fellowship that was the genius of Tambaram would undergird the process of formation through the war.[6] It was symbolic that shortly after Tambaram Mott should assist in the consecration of the Dornakal Cathedral with its blend of architectures witnessing to ecumenical Christianity; its bishop, Azariah, had been an ecumenical figure since Edinburgh 1910 and was a participant at Lausanne, Oxford, Edinburgh, and Tambaram.[7]

PART 1: The World Council of Churches "in Process of Formation"

What was Mott's part in the founding of the World Council? As the founder and builder of the World's Student Christian Federation his was a direct influence upon ten generations of college and university students from which its first leadership was largely drawn. The often heard comment that the ecumenical gatherings of the 1930's resembled WSCF alumni meetings was true; in a sense the World Conference of Christian Youth at Amsterdam in 1939 was a climactic example. Its chief organizer was R. H. Edwin Espy, who later was a successor of Mott as general secretary of the Student Volunteer Movement and executive of the National Student Work of the YMCA and became the general secretary of the National Council of Churches in the United States. Hundreds of delegates at this unprecedented world gathering of youth, representing more than seventy countries, were to become preeminent leaders in the churches, youth movements, and ecumenical organizations nationally and internationally. The delegates were recruited by nine world Christian organizations, to seven of which Mott had been closely related. The conference was in a true sense a bringing together of his lifetime of work with youth and was another evidence of what Saito meant when he called Mott "father of the young people of the world." A comparably pervasive influence also came from the ecumenical missionary movement of which Mott was the acknowledged leader as symbolized in his chairmanship of the IMC. [8]

Some have said that Mott entered the ecclesiastical ecumenical movement "late," that is, after the Life and Work and Faith and Order movements were well along and were considering next steps. Actually, the movements over which he presided were much further advanced than these two until the mid-1930's. He had known the leaders of both and had worked with them, unquestionably to their advantage, from their beginnings. His friendship with Nathan Söderblom, which began in 1890, was intimate. Although invited to give one of four keynote addresses, why Mott did not attend Söderblom's 1925 Stockholm conference is one of the unanswered puzzles of this biography. A possible clue is that all four of his children were to be at Lac des Iles that summer, perhaps for the last time. However, Mott had Söderblom fly to Helsingfors the next summer to address the World's Alliance of YMCA's. Mott was not at the Universal Christian Council for Life and Work in 1929, yet as Oldham moved into that orbit the two shared thoughts and plans, supplementing one another as always. Some observers believed that while Mott did not approve of Oldham's shift from the IMC to planning for Oxford 1937 he was sufficiently involved privately with Oldham that he deserved joint credit for the program and success of that conference. [9] Mott did attend the Chamby sessions of the Universal Christian Council in preparation for Oxford. Likewise, he had known Bishop Charles H. Brent of Faith and Order since well before Edinburgh 1910, shortly after which that movement had come into being. Mott had been a Methodist delegate to its preparatory conference in 1916, and went to Lausanne in 1927 in the same capacity but was forced by illness to leave; he kept in touch with Brent and knew Silas McBee intimately.

Mott participated in the moves that began to draw Faith and Order and Life and Work together in 1933, being kept fully informed by and advising constantly with Oldham. His participation began with the Princeton consultation of 1935. Fresh from world travel and immediate missionary contacts he contributed significantly to the meeting of the enlarged planning committee for Oxford 1937 that met at Westfield College, London, just before Oxford. A small group including Marc Boegner, William Temple, William Adams Brown, H.-L. Henriod and

Visser 't Hooft met in Mott's room each morning for prayer. Boegner remembered that Mott's influence was "tremendous." He immediately took the lead, the French pastor went on, "as the man who was to guide the deliberations of the Oxford Conference with the help of a number of chairmen including Dr. Lang, the Archbishop of Canterbury, Archbishop Germanos, Archbishop Eidem of Uppsala, Bishop Azariah, and Professor William Adams Brown." Henry P. Van Dusen later remembered that those who were "really carrying the heat and the burden of the day in the development of the ecumenical movement through the World Council" had found it necessary to "guard and restrain" Mott in his tendency to exert "a somewhat dominating influence" as his interest and enthusiasm for the cause increased, and of which some were quite willing to take advantage. [10]

Samuel McCrea Cavert proposed the name "World Council of Churches" for the body expected to eventuate from that summer's gatherings; such was the progress since the talks began four years earlier that Westfield voted in favor of putting the proposed plan into effect as soon as possible. "We have witnessed a miracle," exclaimed Oldham, who was largely responsible for it. Mott put down the Westfield meeting as the last item in his life-list of the most meaningful moments in his career. [11]

He was an important symbolic figure among the leaders on the platform of the 1937 Oxford Conference on Church, Community, and State, of whom the large majority were former SCM workers. As chairman of the business committee he was a weighty managerial person also; for his own reasons he asked W. A. Visser 't Hooft to sit with this body. Boegner recalled Mott's chairing of the full meetings:

> What a master he was of the art of controlling a debate! Always an erect figure, his glance, his energetic features and his dynamic vigour imposing respect, he combined humour with a firmly based authority. He knew how to cut short the over-talkative who exceeded the time limit. He made discreet selections from the names of those put down to speak, which allowed him to give a hearing, in what he considered the best order, to divergent or contradictory views. Mott was in large measure responsible for the success of the Conference. [12]

Oxford met at a time of very deep concern for the state of the German churches. Martin Niemöller had just been arrested, a powerful reason for uniting the branches of the ecumenical movement. "It was the influence of Mott, Temple and a few others which turned the balance," concluded Boegner. [13] John McKay thought that Mott had not been the ideal presiding officer at Oxford because of its subject matter, with which he was not really at home, the subtler real "meaning of the Church and the real differences between the churches" escaping him and actually being "gloriously irrelevant" to one whose single allegiance was to the Risen Lord.[14] Toward the end of the session the WSCF alumni present engaged in a fun session with a raucous bell to time their short speeches; when Mott was half through his remarks a very loud gong went off. Making a grand exit he exclaimed, "I will now confer with one of the Eastern Patriarchs." That was not entirely a laughing matter. The Orthodox had found the conference rough going; in addition there had been a real or fancied snub to Metropolitan Stephan, which Paul Anderson brought to Mott's attention. Mott grabbed his hat and rushed to the prelate's room: Stephan did not leave as threatened, but two others did.[15] A couple of hours after the Conference ended, Mott summarized it on the BBC: A visible and audible demonstration of an existing world fellowship, he said, its purpose was not only unity, but "that the world may believe." At Lac des Iles his voice came through so clearly that Leila could hear him breathe.[16]

At Faith and Order, which followed shortly at Edinburgh, Mott chaired the commission on next steps and shared the general chairmanship with Temple, Garvie, and Boegner. The plan for a World Council that had been agreed upon at Oxford came under attack by some who thought Life and Work was too political. Temple, Boegner, and Mott, wrote W. A. Visser 't Hooft, succeeded in convincing the vast majority of the delegates that the plan would strengthen rather than weaken the work for unity. Visser 't Hooft described how Mott operated: "I am deeply moved by the words of the Bishop of Gloucester," he began gently, "I have such complete trust in him, but I must be true to my heart," then coming down with a crashing blow: *"This plan* [for the WCC] *is the keystone in the arch we are building here."*[17]

A committee of fourteen, of which Mott was a member, met to resolve certain issues left over from both Oxford and Edinburgh; it found itself unable to act and called a larger meeting for May, 1938, at Utrecht, Holland. Hoping to hold a world assembly in 1941, this group established a provisional organization and chose officers. Mott was asked to be a vice-chairman; he is said to have replied, "I shrink from it, but I will take it." W. A. Visser 't Hooft became general secretary, well schooled by Mott.

The scene shifts back to Tambaram, where, seven months later, Mott emphasized the need for a solidly based World Council of

Churches. Anticipating the problems of relationships between Church and Mission, the conference proposed the establishment of a joint committee between the new Council and the IMC. This was adopted shortly afterward by the provisional committee of the World Council but the relationship was not stabilized until after Mott had moved off the scene. He had grave reservations about a world body not motivated by missions, and fears that the World Council might swallow the IMC.[18]

In the tragic summer of 1939 Mott and most of the members of the WCC administrative committee met at Zeist, Holland, in an attempt to move toward the first assembly of the new Council, but the disturbed international situation made concrete action impossible. Yet firm bases had been laid by this time for an interim American committee on the World Council, chaired by Mott, that had already met several times and would continue to do so for a much longer time than anyone then dreamed.

Very soon after Zeist the World Conference of Christian Youth assembled at Amsterdam, in August, 1939. Mott had been asked to speak on the deeper resources of his life, "and how it all began." He prepared with great care, calling the talk "The Christian as Ambassador." He began with a call to dedication and went on to remind his youthful audience of Schweitzer, Henry Hodgkin, Baron Nicolay, Kagawa, and Aggrey, and quoted Madame Chang Kai-shek's word that God had given her a work to do. In conclusion he told simply "the story of the mandate of Christ" to himself, beginning with Studd's visit to Cornell. His first love had been serving students "the world over" but it had broadened to embrace, in time of peace and of war, "all classes and conditions of men and boys," and then world missions had led to "helping to weave together in closer cooperation and unity the Christians of all nations, races, and communions." He told the story of the Kumamoto Band and its influence upon Japan. "God has some great design for this Conference": it is that we go forth from Amsterdam "with a vivid sense of what it means to be an ambassador of Christ at this great moment, and with an undiscourageable purpose to carry out His mandates cost what it may." The conference theme was *Christus Victor.*[19]

A few days later Hitler signed a non-aggression pact with Stalin. The following day Britain and Poland sealed a pact for mutual assistance; Germany invaded Poland, which brought a declaration of war upon her by France and Britain. Mott did not return to Europe until after hostilities ceased.

PART 2: The Private Man

Toward the end of the 1930's the Motts bought a pleasant bungalow across the street from Lake Eola in Orlando, Florida, and made it their permanent home, except for summers in Canada. Decorated by John's niece Bess McAdam, they thought it the prettiest place they had had. The housewarming was a party for all the workmen and their wives. Mott was "like a boy over a new toy," delightedly arranging his books and magazines. Here it was easier to reduce the ceaseless round of travel, but the Atlantic Coast Line's *West Coast Champion* took one to New York overnight. John did his daily constitutional by walking the mile around the lake, which reminded him of Lac des Iles. Leila surprised even herself by prevailing on him to occasionally go calling with her. He joined the First Methodist Church and attended. He supported the Orlando YMCA. The University Club and the "Animated Magazine" of Rollins College in nearby Winter Park afforded congenial audiences for some of his most anecdotal speeches, such as "My Experiences with Kings and Presidents." He gave his address on leadership to the students of Stetson University in nearby DeLand. He made an effort to sharpen the humor in his talks, which some thought a bit heavy-handed, by compiling jokes, but his true sense of humor was best displayed when he chaired a stimulating meeting. [20]

The guest book at 528 East Washington came to hold the names of scores of friends like Archie Harte who once came and took both Motts to see Shirley Temple in a movie; the Motts were shocked to learn that blacks could not attend the same theaters as whites in Florida. The Motts loved to celebrate birthdays and when a first grandchild came to Frederick and his wife Marjorie, he was christened in the grandparents' living room (they were still at Yonkers) and the silver loving cup that was used as a font, a gift from Korea, was given to the baby's parents. When abroad, especially in Germany, Mott would buy a cheap suitcase and bring it home full of toys, delighting in playing Santa Claus. There grew, especially after the elder Motts were at least semi-retired, an even closer family solidarity, frequently expressed in Leila's letters, such as at the time of Irene's fortieth birthday when her mother wrote how Irene had come "to gladden and enrich all our lives since" and John had responded to a reminder of the day with "wonderful, wonderful, wonderful," Leila adding "and he meant it too." Twice Irene Mott Bose's name appeared in lists of royal honors, once for the Kaiser-i-Hind medal. [21]

By carefully guarding her health, Leila was able to travel with John by 1936, accompanying him to Mysore; the diary for that trip was kept by her niece, Leila Compton, who was the Motts' girl Friday for several years. But there were numerous occasions when Mrs. Mott had to send her husband off "cheerfully rather than tearfully"—"I know he's helping somebody who needs him"—in spite of their growing need for one another and the desire "to talk everything over." But, she added, "distance does not separate." During the years just before America entered the War, he again traveled extensively across and up and down the country with the National Preaching Mission, for various YMCA affairs, to Mexico and to Central America and both coasts of South America, dedicated the 50-year Student Volunteer Movement monument at Mount Hermon School, spoke at the Methodist uniting conference and wrote a booklet on the merger, gave the Sprunt Lectures at Union Theological Seminary in Richmond, another series at Southern Methodist University, and a third to the College of Preachers at the Washington Cathedral. He shared the platform at a packed Carnegie Hall in New York with Sherwood Eddy and Henry Sloane Coffin to observe the centennial of the birth of D. L. Moody. He was honored by the Boy Scouts of America and was decorated by the governments of China and of Esthonia, and made honorary president of the YMCA of Czechoslovakia just before the Hitler invasion. "Your father," Leila wrote to Irene in 1938, "amazes us all as he is carrying, as J. D. R. said, the work of several men half his age.... He can get a big worthwhile [audience] anywhere. I think to stop completely would kill him off much sooner than to carry on and he loves to be doing, you know. It's unusual that the young leaders are still most glad to get him." Ten years later she wrote Irene again that Rockefeller, Cleveland Dodge, and others were urging him "to stop while he's still going strong and not peter out." All of this was in spite of increasing deafness in one ear, and some impairment of eyesight. [22]

The Sprunt Lectures were published in 1939 under the characteristic title *Five Decades and a Forward View;* they were essentially autobiographical. In 1938 he had published the results of his worldwide inquiry for the IMC as *Evangelism for the World Today.* When Reinhold Niebuhr, John C. Bennett, and others launched *Christianity and Crisis* in 1941, Mott was a member of the board of sponsors, but shortly withdrew without explanation. Somehow during the thirties his name appeared in a publication similar to Elizabeth Dilling's *Red Network,* but extended search has not recovered the details. [23] When the new Revised Version of the Bible appeared after World War II, he and Leila greeted it with enthusiasm.

PART 3: World War II

Mott is said to have burst into tears at the news of Pearl Harbor. That his Japanese friends could perpetrate such an act gave him the saddest day of his life. [24] But as head of the World's Alliance of YMCA's, he was already involved in prisoner of war work, which had begun in Europe two years earlier. This did not become the immense enterprise of the First World War, and Mott was in no such position to raise large sums for it, but it was a respectable effort. He obtained permission from the War Department for the YMCA to administer prisoner of war aid to German soldiers held in the United States, for which he was decorated by the West German government after the War. This time he was actively identified with the churches by serving on a joint commission for the chaplaincy that represented both the YMCA and the World Council. He lent his name to several relief and emergency organizations. At the end of the War he had an interview with President Truman. [25]

Mott traveled extensively in the Western Hemisphere during the War, increasingly by air. In 1943 he had a narrow escape from death when the *Champion* was derailed in South Carolina. His sleeper remained intact but Mott left it at once. Moments later the second section of the train crashed into the wreck; sixty-nine persons were killed. As when he missed the *Titanic*, Mott took his preservation as evidence that there was still work for him to do. [26]

This period brought a small revival of interest in him as a college speaker, and he visited a number of campuses. In 1943 his alma mater Upper Iowa conferred an honorary doctorate of letters on him, to which he responded before an admiring throng with a grand oration on the place of the university in the modern world. 1944 was a busy year for honors and speaking: in January he gave a series of lectures at Emory University, which were published as *The Larger Evangelism;* they were followed soon by the Shaffer Lectures at Yale Divinity School on "Christ and Our Latent Powers." [27] In the fall he was given an LL.D. by the University of Toronto. He assisted Sherwood Eddy in the preparation of the small centennial YMCA history, *A Century with Youth.*

Mott's most important functions during the war were ecumenical.

He played a significant part in the North American Ecumenical Conference held in Toronto in 1941. As president of the World's Alliance of YMCA's he issued its annual calls to the Week of Prayer which were unifying messages of hope sent around the world. From 1937 until late in 1946 he chaired the meetings (at least twenty-two of them) of the North American members of the provisional committee for the World Council, corresponded and advised extensively with the general secretary Visser 't Hooft, raised funds, and very much kept alive and active the ecumenical spirit on this side of the Atlantic. In 't Hooft's judgment, this was the greatest specific service Mott rendered to the embryonic World Council of Churches.[28]

In 1941, realizing that there was pressure from the younger leadership, he resigned the chairmanship of the International Missionary Council. Bishop James C. Baker became his successor. The dedication of the volume of his *Addresses and Papers* on the IMC revealed a great deal:

> To David Livingstone whose heroic, Christlike achievements furnished the governing missionary motive of my life; also to J. H. Oldham and Ch'eng Ching-yi, kindred spirits in the evolution of the International Missionary Council among the older and younger churches; and to Gustav Warneck, missionary historian, advocate, and critic.[29]

In 1944 the nascent World Council suffered an irreparable loss in the sudden death of William Temple, Archbishop of Canterbury. As soon after as possible, Marc Boegner, Bishop Bell, and Visser 't Hooft made their way to New York via Dakar, Port-Natal, and Trinidad to consult with Mott. "It was urgently necessary," Boegner wrote, "to restore normal ecumenical relations between the churches of Europe and the churches of North America, which had been somewhat weakened by six years of war."

> In this situation Mott gave us the most valuable help, thanks to his experience, his wisdom and his admirable vision of the *una sancta*. The memory I retain of the conversations we had at that time and the friendship that he showed me remain very precious to me. I can still see him standing in the pulpit of St. John the Divine [in New York] wearing the red robe of a Doctor of Divinity of Edinburgh University. He was 80 years old, but his power to communicate his convictions was as strong as ever.[30]

Shortly after the War, Japanese Christians made it known that they would like to reestablish fellowship with the American churches. The Federal Council sent a delegation of four, one of whom was Bishop Baker. Upon arrival in Tokyo they were told that the Emperor wished to meet them. Gone from the audience were the old trappings of ceremony. When the group sat down to talk it chanced that Baker was next to the Emperor. Almost at once he turned to Baker and asked, "And how is Dr. John R. Mott?" Later, Saito brought the Emperor's personal greetings to Mott on his first trip to the States after the War; Mott returned them in 1949, his last trip to the Orient, when he talked with Hirohito for an hour.[31]

In 1953, when R. H. Edwin Espy visited the ill and aging President Syngman Rhee of Korea in the badly bombed presidential palace at Seoul, the President's conversation, heard against the distant roar of bombers pursuing the enemy to the north, "was equally focussed on two subjects: the communists, for whom he had an implacable hatred, and John R. Mott, for whom he had unbounded admiration."[32]

At the earliest possible moment Mott went to Europe, where, as Norman Goodall described it, he became "a natural rallying-point" around whom were held the first post-War discussions between former "enemies." Goodall continued that this had been "the most stirring experience" he had had in the ecumenical movement:

> Not that he was quiescent; far from it. As chairman emeritus of the International Missionary Council he was sharing actively in our affairs . . . and in [the WCC's] critical operations between the end of the war and the Amsterdam Assembly Mott, as co-president, was vigilant and energetic. There was also a small *ad hoc* joint committee of the IMC and the emerging World Council; Mott was keeping a tight hand on this as its chairman . . . . Old and young, East and West, turned to him in confidence and gratitude; no senior statesman has ever exercised a more beneficent influence than did Mott in those early post-war days. His memory was still clear on the great events of a half century in which he had played such a forceful part—his unique contacts with Russia and the Orthodox Churches, his familiarity with Far Eastern affairs . . . his unrivalled knowledge of the student life of the world, and his kindling leadership in the world mission of the Church. Physically he was as imposing as ever—dignity in all his bearing, searching eyes, firm mouth, determined jaw and—not very frequently—the play of a smile touched with restraint which suggested that he could not allow himself too long a period of levity.[33]

In Germany Mott was greeted as a symbol of hope amid destruction and misery. Immense crowds of Christian youth heard him eagerly. He gave the national council of the German YMCA program suggestions that they were still using successfully twenty years afterward. Some of his addresses became the first Christian publications in Germany after the War.[34]

When Mott was in Switzerland early in 1946 for the first World's

Alliance committee session after the War, he took a brief holiday with Eugene Barnett to a ski resort near Lausanne:

> When we got onto the mountain train on Sunday afternoon en route to Geneva, a middle-aged Swiss dressed in mountain climbing garb, and his family entered our coach and took seats across the aisle from us. As they sat the man of the party spied Mott and crossed the aisle precipitately to greet him. "Dr. Mott!" he exclaimed. "Magnifique! You came to our school in Zurich when I was a small boy, 11 years old. I heard you speak only that once, but what you said that day—and the way you said it—changed my life."

When the two men reached Geneva, Mott introduced Barnett to the Archbishop of Canterbury. Later Mott told Barnett, "On this journey I have visited England, Norway, Denmark, Sweden and Finland. In all of those countries I have visited the primates of those churches, all of whom had worked with me in the Student Movement during their student days."[35] It was at this World's Alliance of YMCA's executive meeting that plans for worldwide study and visitations of the Associations, first proposed by Mott during the darkest days of the war, were initiated and implemented. The ensuing enterprise became "the largest and most important action ever launched by the World's Committee in the interest of the expanding world mission of the YMCA."[36]

PART 4: The Nobel Peace Prize

In 1946, John R. Mott, together with the pacifist Emily Green Balch,[37] was awarded the Nobel Peace Prize. The idea of nominating him for the 1934 Prize had come independently to Ethan Colton and to the Baroness Elizabeth van Boetzelaer van Dubbeldam of Holland, early in 1933. Colton coordinated the effort in North America and for the World YMCA, and Oldham and Paton obtained support in Europe. Together some 150 notables, beginning with President Truman, endorsed it. H. Dewey Anderson, for example, secured Herbert Hoover's support. Inevitably the project reached the newspapers. Aside from the anti-clerical stance of some in Norway, the only person of consequence to object was Norman Thomas, the American Socialist leader.[38] The sponsors were disappointed. The 1934 Prize went that year to Arthur Henderson, the British statesman, whom it chanced that Mott had met in Russia in 1917.

The 1946 announcement was a bolt from the blue. Mott's trip to

Oslo to receive the Prize was his first transatlantic flight. He was accompanied to Oslo by Hugo Cedergren of the World's Alliance. The Prize was awarded December 10, 1946. [39] In a brief response to the presentation address, Mott expressed his appreciation of "the high privilege" of being bracketed with Miss Balch, and summarized his life as "an earnest and undiscourageable effort to weave together all nations, all races and all religious communions in friendliness, in fellowship and in cooperation." In this worldwide effort he had concentrated on successive generations of youth; if he had a word to add, it would be "a word of abounding hope." Later he gave a short address on "The Leadership Demanded in this Momentous Time," a revised version of his speech to the University of St. Andrews in 1931. On this quite secular occasion he drew his illustrations from non-religious sources but concluded with "the all-important point" that Jesus Christ had summed up "the outstanding, unfailing and abiding secret of all truly great and enduring leadership" in the phrase " 'He who would be greatest among you shall be the servant of all.' He Himself embodied this truth and became 'the Prince Leader of the Faith,' that is, the leader of the leaders." The finest oratory of the events in Oslo was Bishop Berggrav's warm and sprightly talk at a mass meeting of the churches the next day: "To our generation you were the incarnation of a new scope for Christianity," he told Mott. [40]

Sweden added to the honors with the Prince Carl Medal and Finland gave Mott the Order of the White Rose. This was world news; the *New York Times* worked Mott's name into a crossword puzzle. In New York there were dinners sponsored by Cornell and a joint celebration by six national and world ecumenical bodies to which Mott had been related, and a happy welcome to Orlando. The next year the Serbian Eastern Orthodox diocese of the United States and Canada gave Mott its diploma and Cross of St. Joanikie. Several American church buildings and chapels created stained glass windows that included Mott's likeness. In 1949 his rank in the French Legion of Honor was raised to that of officer. [41]

PART 5: Amsterdam, 1948

"Amsterdam," wrote Marc Boegner, was "a great date in Mott's life." The two men, more intimate than ever, walked together in the procession to the great service in the *Concertgebouw* at which the World Council of Churches was constituted on August 23, 1948. Mott was the only person who had participated in or attended all five of the great ecumenical gatherings since Mysore. From the first meeting of the provisional committee in 1946 he had been one of the five provisional presidents with the archbishops of Canterbury and of Uppsala, Germanos of Thyateira, and Marc Boegner. Yet at Whitby in 1947 it had been apparent that new leadership was coming to the fore; people began to speak of the "post-Mott era."[42] At Amsterdam, for which he prepared meticulously, he chaired the business committee, which met daily over lunch. Bishop Y. Y. Tsu remembered not only his "genius in directing and planning" but his being "the life of the group with his wit and humor"; the Nobel Prize gave him "a sort of halo" in their eyes.

He was made Honorary President of the new Council. When word came that this special post was being created for him, plain evidence that he was being replaced by younger leadership, he told a story that he had heard from Rufus Jones about an elderly farmer who failed to deliver the usual vegetables one summer; when asked what was wrong he replied, "They say I've lost my mind, but I don't miss it."[43] Oldham's interpretation of the honorary presidency was on a different plane:

> In his life-long association with the ecumenical movement his judgment and decision were crucial at such a countless number of points, noticed and unnoticed, his influence on the lives of those who helped to shape the movement was so deep and extended, that one can say of him in a much more far-reaching sense than of any of his contemporaries that, had he not lived, the ecumenical movement would not have taken the form that it has done, and many fruitful growths in many different countries would not have taken place.[44]

Awareness of his "unrivalled contribution to the growth of the ecumenical outlook and of ecumenical activity" lay behind Mott's being given the unique position of honorary president, Oldham concluded.

It was fitting that Mott should be the first speaker at Amsterdam. Some thought his address "not a great success," but nevertheless "very moving." It was a brief review of the thirty-eight years since Edinburgh 1910, phrased in scriptural simplicity. Mott began:

> With hearts abounding in praise to God we come together today from all parts of the world to initiate formally the World Council of Churches. Hitherto He has led us; our expectation is from Him.

As though calling down a cloud of witnesses he named a score of "colleagues and master builders of different lands, races, and communions" who had passed on from their ecumenical pioneering. Most of them had

been his intimate colleagues. Then he spoke of the Student Volunteer
Movement that had sent out nearly 20,000 missionaries, and of the
World's Student Christian Federation that had united the students of
3,000 colleges and universities, "weaving together the future leaders of
the nations." The Young Men's and Young Women's Christian Associations were also uniting the leaders of tomorrow, and the International
Missionary Council, joining as it does the older and younger churches,
constitutes "one of the chief contributions of our gathering at Amsterdam." The new Council faces great problems and an uncertain future, yet
man's extremity is God's opportunity, and the fact that "we have a larger
Christ" is cause for hope. In what sense is He larger?

> He is One other than all the rest—other than those ancient holy men
> among the Hindus, One other than Buddha and Mohammed; One other
> than Moses and St. Paul; yes, other than all the rest. . . . He is indeed the
> Central Figure and Abounding Hope of our World Council of Churches. [45]

The widow of Archbishop Söderblom, aware of "the smile in his eyes,"
turned to her companion and said, "Only Mott is able to look forward."
Someone else commented that "this was the old Mott." No, was the
rejoinder, "this is the young Mott." [46]

The next day W. A. Visser 't Hooft took Mott to visit the youth
delegates, who were meeting in an old windmill. "Eventually he came—a
pink-faced grey-headed old man with bushy eyebrows—leaning on a stick.
The youth delegates stood up and cheered him spontaneously for three
full minutes. The old man stood there looking at us and the tears coursed
down his cheeks. . . . We who cheered him knew what the youth of the
world owed to him." [47]

PART 6: **Retrospection**

"I am anxious to keep in touch with you," Mott wrote to a WCC
official after Amsterdam. For several years that would be possible, but he
was already giving his attention to the past in a far greater measure than
ever before, by compiling six large volumes of his *Addresses and Papers.*
These comprise an authentic record, almost a history, of most of Mott's
affiliations with the SVM, the WSCF, the North American and World
YMCA's, and the IMC. The spade work for this consuming task was
done by Benjamin R. Barber and Nettie Tice, Mott's private secretary.
The dedications of these volumes are Mott autobiographical statements

par excellence. That on the SVM was dedicated to Robert Wilder, Fennell P. Turner, and Robert E. Speer; the second, on the WSCF, to its "brilliant chairman" Karl Fries, to Kajinosuka Ibuka, and Ruth Rouse. The others have been mentioned previously; each represented a major aspect of Mott's career, and the dedications named the partners of his endeavors and the human sources of his inspiration.[48]

Because of his longevity, about which he often joked in his last years, Mott was called upon to give or write memorials to a host of friends, colleagues, and spiritual companions. He had as numerous a network of international friendships as any man who ever lived, due in part to his phenomenal memory but chiefly to shared concerns and the fellowship of Christian brotherhood. Of the contemporaries with whom he worked intimately virtually throughout his life, only Colton and Oldham survived him. Before the World Council was organized at Amsterdam in 1948, the old leadership of the IMC had all died or retired, but Mott felt especially the deaths of William Paton, William Temple, Cheng Ching-yi, and Bishop Azariah, as he did the passing of D. Willard Lyon, pioneer YMCA missionary to China, whose "sacred dust" he and Sidney Phelps committed "to the deep at the mouth of the Yangtze" during Mott's last trip to the Orient in 1949. His talks on the occasions of memorials to these and others who had filled intimate places in his life—Brockman, Baron Nicolay, Robert E. Speer, Nathan Söderblom— were expressions of deep emotion and loyalty; they may be found in context in the six volumes and in the large correspondence kept up almost to the end of his life, such as a touching letter to the widow of Karl Fries, or a late renewal of his friendship with Raymond Robins, with Gilbert Beaver, and with Oldham. In the late 1940's he was a frequent visitor to Herbert Hoover's Waldorf Towers apartment, and it is not far-fetched to surmise that he was helpful in the writing of Hoover's *Memoirs*; certainly the two held identical views on much of the world's history since they had first met in 1892.[49]

When Mott resigned the presidency of the World's Alliance of YMCA's in 1947 he officially severed his active ties to the organization through which he had registered his life-long testimony to the place and the importance of the laity in the Christian enterprise. He had privately advised brilliant young men not to be ordained. During his later years he frequently challenged the laity to greater dedication and action. "Lay recognition and assumption of responsibility for the propagation of Christ's gospel throughout the world has ever been the secret of the triumphant spread of the Christian faith," he wrote in *Five Decades and a*

Forward View—a position from which he never varied. Oldham's and others' criticisms of his "YMCA streak" were evidences of their failure to understand his position and motivation. The Edinburgh conference at which he resigned from the Alliance unanimously elected him honorary president for life, for "the inspiring leadership" he had exerted since attending a World's Conference for the first time in 1891.[50]

PART 7: "Final"

In January, 1951, Mott sat silently through the annual Quiet Day with his friends, then went home and wrote "Final" on the notes he had taken. He did not go again. That June, the morning after he and Leila arrived at Lac des Iles, the main house was discovered to be on fire: there was no electricity to pump water. Neighbors formed a bucket brigade but despite heroic efforts the building burned to the ground. Gone were the souvenirs, scrapbooks, and mementoes of a lifetime of world travel.[51]

1951 was a year of last things. Mott attended his final Student Volunteer Movement Quadrennial, at Lawrence, Kansas. Carefully coached lest he become long-winded, he held his speech to two minutes less than the allotted time. "What a glorious thing it would be to be your age again and to have the great joy of demonstrating my faith in Jesus Christ in the terrible revolutions in which your world is now engaged," he exclaimed. The citation presented to him spoke of the gratitude of students around the world for "the countless ways" he had helped them "to take their place in the world Mission." The National Student Council of YMCA's and its senior body the National Council both recognized him at the convention marking the Association centennial that year; one of the most widely used photographs ever taken of Mott was snapped on that occasion.[52] Also in 1951, Mott attended the World Council of Churches' central committee at Rolle, near Lausanne. "His presence was a joy to everyone," Boegner recalled; he still radiated but his strength had begun to fail.

The next summer the Motts were preoccupied with the construction of a new house at the Lac. Leila, now 86, became ill by the end of the summer, remaining on at Queen Elizabeth Hospital in Montreal. She died there September 28, 1952, ending that remarkable marriage partnership begun at the "White House" in Wooster, Ohio, almost 62 years before. Her last breath was spent trying to convince her nurse that a picture of John hung on the bare wall before her. Her body was interred in Mount Hebron cemetery in Montclair, New Jersey. The National Board of the YWCA prepared a fitting resolution, written by Mrs. Robert E. Speer. Galen Fisher had just completed his biography, *John R. Mott: Architect of Cooperation and Unity;* he dedicated it to her. Hundreds of copies were sent to friends around the world. On an earlier occasion when her life had hung in the balance, John had composed an epitaph: "Counselor, comrade, traveling companion and inspiration."[53]

As soon as Mott could pull himself together, arrange for the closing of the Florida home, and find a traveling companion, he went to India, ostensibly to attend a World Council meeting at Lucknow but also to be near daughter Irene, the closest of his children to him. While at her home in Nagpur he became desperately ill with double pneumonia and was not expected to live. Yet Irene could write that "his courtesy, his sense of humor, his feeling of responsibility to his work, his love for my mother—all remained though [he was] quite out of his head." Even in his delirium he insisted that his dispatch case and his cane be kept near him. He repeated his favorite verse: "They shall mount up on wings as eagles. They shall run and not be weary. They shall walk and not faint." He recovered, to pray with Muslims on Fridays and to visit a Hindu temple with a friend. En route home he viewed a missionary exhibit in Geneva and gave a refreshing description of it on the radio.

Shortly after his return he married Miss Agnes Peter, a family friend of long standing.[54] She accompanied him on several trips, the last of which was to the World Council of Churches Assembly at Evanston, Illinois, in 1954. Sitting in the middle among the several presidents, he reminded many of Winston Churchill, who in old age was at times somnolent but on occasion "the old lion roused himself and roared." To Marc Boegner, occupying another president's chair, Mott incarnated "a half-century of struggles, of prayers, of faith, and of hope," yet everyone felt "sad and anxious because he had aged so much." Mott visited John Baillie's committee; when he was about to leave, D. T. Niles, the secretary, asked Baillie to suggest that Mott say a word. It was, "Gentlemen, when John Mott is dead, remember him as an evangelist." On another occasion he whispered to Henry Smith Leiper, "you must watch the IMC and not let it get swamped too soon." There were old friends to greet for the last time. Mott said to Francis P. Miller, "I have believed in you all along." Miller wished that he might have heard those words twenty-five years earlier. Mott never said farewell, only *au revoir*. When on another occasion he and Colton met for the last time "he gave me a blessing that follows down the rest of my life. With warm hand grasp and steady matching eyes" Mott said, "I love you." Boegner recalled the great acclamation the Assembly gave to Mott; when it stood to sing *The Church's One Foundation*, in the final service of worship, Mott sang every line of every verse with certainty and vigor, though with no printed words before him.[55]

Death is a place where I change trains, Mott had told a reporter at Amsterdam in 1948. A final schedule not of his making took him through that terminal on January 31, 1955, after a brief hospitalization. At Evanston, authorities of the Washington Cathedral—the Cathedral Church of Saint Peter and Saint Paul—had suggested that he be buried there; he asked to think it over. He and Agnes went to Postville en route home; she thought the rural cemetery there, swept by Hamlin Garland's "magic west wind of the prairie," too remote and hence inappropriate. In November, Dean Angus Dun made the invitation formal. Mott replied that he was honored and would come by to discuss it when he came to Washington. The next journey to the capital was from the other side of that final terminal. There was a state funeral in the Cathedral, attended by representatives of the world, followed by burial in the crypt of Saint Joseph of Arimathea. A stranger walking behind the casket asked what Mott's denomination had been. Almost anyone who was not a Methodist, answering that question, had to take a moment to recall.[56]

Memorial services were held in Orlando, New York, London, Geneva, and around the world. Messages came from everywhere. In 1965 the centennial of Mott's birth was observed widely; the decade had produced several hundred sketches about him, notably Robert Mackie's *Layman Extraordinary*, and the establishment of permanent memorials, including the impetus that led to this biography. One hazards that Mott would have thoroughly approved certain of these: naming the new Post-ville high school for him; the universal symbolism of calling the new Geneva headquarters of the World's Alliance of YMCA's "The John R. Mott House"; the "John R. Mott Memorial Lectures" established by the East Asia Christian Conference at its first meeting in 1959—the kind of tribute, as Norman Goodall wrote, "that Mott would have appreciated most—the honor of being associated with a new day"; and, he would have been delighted to meet the recipients of the "John R. Mott Fellow-ships" of the National Council of YMCA's of the United States, set up to recognize "truly outstanding professional leadership in the YMCA and to encourage further development of that kind of leadership."[57]

In *Five Decades and a Forward View* Mott had revealed the dynamic of his life:

One should school himself to take long views. Long views backward—back to the Old Testament prophets, back to the early Christians—to the arena and the catacombs, back to the Dark Ages where against the black background stand out some of the most hopeful and vital characters of all time, back to the reformers, the heretics, to those who have charted the new and better courses for mankind, back to the pioneers of modern missions on some of the great battlefields of Christianity. Surrounded with such a cloud of witnesses we cannot but run with patience, high hope and triumph the race that is set before us. Also we should even more concern ourselves with the forward view—the life-giving and unfading vision of the kingdoms of this world becoming the kingdoms of our Lord and His Christ that He may reign forever and ever. Those who live under the spell of this commanding vision, as well as of the memory of God's great goodness and faithfulness across the centuries, cannot be discouraged, dismayed, or defeated.

Above and through all we should keep our gaze riveted on Christ. He has spoken the adequate word for this confused and most severely testing decade and the fateful period that lies ahead—"In the world ye have tribulation; but be of good cheer; I have overcome the world."[58]

A few days before his death, Mott sent a message to the World's Alliance of YMCA's for its centennial observance later in 1955, which he was planning to attend:

Old things are passing away. All things may become new. Not by magic, nor by wishful thinking, but by self-sacrifice and the will to bring them about in the name of Jesus Christ.

Notes

These abbreviations are used in the notes:

CHH: The author.
CHH-Y: C. Howard Hopkins, *History of the Y.M.C.A. in North America* (New York: Association Press, 1951).
CtYD: Yale Divinity School Library.
JHO: J. H. Oldham.
JRM: Mott as author.
JRM-I, -II, -III, -IV, -V, -VI: *Addresses and Papers of John R. Mott* (New York: Association Press, 1946–1947), 6 vols.
JRM-Mn: Personal notes in Mott's handwriting; most are in the Yale Collection.
JRM-Y: The John R. Mott Collection, Yale University Divinity School Library, New Haven, Connecticut.
LWM: Leila White Mott (Mrs. John R. Mott).

Chapter 1: Young Man from Iowa

1. This is virtually all that is known of Thomas Mott (c. 1743–1813). The Mott homestead (John R. Mott's birthplace) and burial ground are on the south or west bank of the Willowemoc, directly below the western approach to the Interstate 17 bridge on the western side of Livingston Manor. They are reached via Riverside Street; a historical marker at the Town Library registers the fact of John R. Mott's birth nearby.

2. Elmira Dodge was the daughter of Israel and Mary Ann Green Dodge of Rockland; her ancestry is traceable to Tristram Dodge who settled in Taunton, Mass., in 1660; he came from Northumberland, England. Robert Dodge, *Tristram Dodge and Descendants* (New York, 1886).

3. Allan G. Bogue, *From Prairie to Corn Belt* (Chicago: University of Chicago Press, 1969), ch. 11; N. Howe Parker, *Iowa As It Is* (Chicago, 1855); Burleigh T. Wilkins, *Carl Becker* (Cambridge: Harvard University Press, 1961), pp. 8–10; A. M. Schlesinger, *In Retrospect* (New York: Harcourt, 1963), ch. 1; Bruce Catton, *Waiting for the Morning Train* (Garden City: Doubleday, 1972); R. A. Billington, "How the Frontier Shaped the American Character: Turner's Frontier Hypothesis," in A. S. Eisenstadt, ed., *The Craft of American History* (New York: Harper Torchbooks, 1966), vol. 1, ch. 9; Schlesinger, *The Rise of the City* (New York: Macmillan, 1933), ch. 3.

4. The subject of this biography was named John Mott by his parents. He added the "R." which he never spelled out, a custom of the time. The Library of Congress was incorrectly informed in 1904 that Mott's middle name was "Raleigh." He never used it, and there is no proof of it. Basil Mathews, who collaborated closely with Mott on the 1934 biography, neither used nor mentioned it. It appears on no formal documents. F. D. Mott to CHH (the author), Apr. 26, 1974: "His name is clearly John R. Mott. Mother was emphatic on the point that 'Raleigh' was someone's fabrication."

5. Herbert Quick, *Vandemark's Folly* (Indianapolis: Bobbs-Merrill, 1921), pp. 111-13.

6. John R. Mott (hereafter JRM), *Addresses and Papers*, vol. IV (New York: Association Press, 1947), p. 986 (hereafter JRM-IV, etc.).

7. JRM-IV, p. 990. H. E. Warner, *The Psychology of the Christian Life* (New York: Revell, 1910), pp. 13-15.

8. JRM home letter, Sept. 20, 1885. Detailed references to JRM's correspondence may be found in the "original" draft of this biography, at the Libraries of the Yale University Divinity School and of the National Council of the YMCA's at 291 Broadway, New York, NY 10007. The "home letters" are in the former Collection. Few personal letters to JRM survived a fire that destroyed the Motts' summer home in Canada in 1951.

9. Basil Mathews, *John R. Mott, World Citizen* (New York/London: Harper, 1934), p. 17.

10. CHH interview with President E. E. Garbee, Aug. 21, 1967.

11. Although Mott had said that he did not want another biography, notations such as this, of which there are a great many, were clearly for a biographer's use.

12. *Fayette Collegian* 3 (June, 1885), pp. 151-53.

13. *Fayette Collegian* 4 (Sept., 1885).

14. Mott, in a confused moment in 1946, said that he had gone to Michigan to study under Moses Coit Tyler, but Tyler was never a faculty member at Michigan; it was Adams he was interested in.

15. C. Howard Hopkins, *History of the YMCA in North America* (New York: Association Press, 1951), p. 184 (hereafter CHH-Y); see also JRM-IV, pp. 4-5.

16. JRM to "Dear Father," Nov. 29, 1885; Mott once reminded his parents that he had gotten on well while in Chicago, but there is no clue as to when or why he was there.

17. C. P. Shedd, *Two Centuries of Student Christian Movements* (New York: Association Press, 1934), pp. 236, 293-94; Mathews, *John R. Mott*, pp. 33-34; JRM-III, p. 5; JRM-IV, pp. 991-92; R. D. Clark, *The Life of Mathew Simpson* (New York: Macmillan, 1956), pp. 300-02.

18. JRM-III, p. 5; Mathews, *John R. Mott*, p. 35, from *Christian Students and World Problems, Report* of the Ninth International Convention of the Student Volunteer Movement, Indianapolis, 1923-25 (New York: SVM, 1924), pp. 63-64. I am grateful to Timothy L. Smith for reading and suggestions; see his *Revivalism and Social Reform* (New York/Nashville: Abingdon, 1957) and *Called Unto Holiness* (Kansas City: Nazarene Publishing House, 1962); see also C. E. Jones, *Perfectionist Persuasion* (Metuchen, NJ: Scarecrow Press, 1974), and F. D. Bruner, *A Theology of the Holy Spirit* (Grand Rapids: Eerdmans, 1970), pp. 40-44.

19. Wishard (1854-1925) was the first intercollegiate YMCA secretary: CHH-Y, pp. 276-79; Wishard, "The Beginning of the Students' Era in Christian History" (typescript, YMCA Historical Library). Ober (1856-1948), *Exploring a Continent* (New York: Association Press, 1929), and CHH-Y, index.

20. *The Christian's Secret* was by Hannah Whitall Smith, a Friend; first published in 1875, it has sold more than two million copies, with the latest reprint in 1978. For the White Cross Army, see CHH-Y, p. 385.

21. This account is based on JRM's letters home, the student-edited *Souvenir*, Mott's article in the CUCA *Bulletin*, and other primary materials in JRM-Y; see also CHH-Y, pp. 294–99; Shedd, *Two Centuries*, chs. 15–16; Ober, *Exploring*; Wishard, "Beginning." For Wilder (1863–1938), see his *The Great Commission* (London/Edinburgh: Oliphants [1936]), and Ruth Wilder Braisted, *In This Generation* (New York: Friendship Press, 1941).

22. JRM at the Northfield Conference of 1892; cited by Shedd, *Two Centuries*, p. 260; the original source was the *Springfield Union*, July 12, 1892, special Northfield edition.

23. Wilder's list was part of his and Forman's arsenal of materials distributed in the colleges during the next academic year; the copy in JRM-Y is probably the only one extant. In later compilations Mott was alleged to have put "world" in the space for the field anticipated; this is improbable, for he was concerned with India in 1886 and certainly had no foretaste of his worldwide parish.

24. JRM-I, p. 6, written in 1892.

25. JRM-III, p. 10.

26. James F. Findlay, Jr., *Dwight L. Moody, American Evangelist, 1837–1899* (Chicago/London: University of Chicago Press, 1969), p. 355, to whom I am indebted for criticism and suggestions. In 1914 Wilder defended the SVM watchword against the allegation that it had been associated with "a special view concerning the second coming of our Lord."

27. Robert T. Handy, ed., *The Social Gospel in America, 1870–1920* (New York: Oxford University Press, 1966), pp. 20–21; Arthur H. Link, ed., *The Papers of Woodrow Wilson*, vol. 6, *1888–90* (Princeton: Princeton University Press, 1969), p. 625.

28. *Divine Life and International Expositor* 10, no. 10 (Apr., 1887), p. 273; *Guide to Holiness* 44, no. 11 (Nov., 1886), p. 161. Clyde Binfield, *George Williams and the YMCA* (London: Heinemann, 1973), p. 222.

29. Paraphrased from John Foster, *Decision of Character*, abridged and with an introductory note by JRM (New York [1907]); J. E. Ryland, ed., *The Life and Correspondence of John Foster*, vol. 1 (London, 1848), p. 11; Foster's essays went through many editions; see also Mathews, *John R. Mott*, pp. 55–58, and Hugh A. Moran, *David Starr Jordan: His Spirit and Decision of Character* (Palo Alto: Daily Press, 1969), pp. 61–67.

30. Paraphrased, as note 29.

31. Mathews, *John R. Mott*, p. 55.

32. Ober, *Exploring*, pp. 74–76; see also CHH-Y, pp. 283f.

33. Morris Bishop, *A History of Cornell* (Ithaca: Cornell University Press, 1962), p. 269.

34. *The Association Bulletin* 3, no. 3 (Dec., 1887), p. 43.

35. R. H. Bainton, *George Lincoln Burr: His Life* (Ithaca: Cornell University Press, 1943), pp. 44–45, 129.

36. Ober, *Exploring*, p. 78 and his "Daily Statement [work record]," Mar. 19, 1888; Wishard, "Beginning," pp. 203–04.

37. JRM to Burr, Aug. 16, 1888. For the appeal of the YMCA to Mott, see CHH-Y, pp. 7, 106–09.

38. JRM-III, p. 7.

Chapter 2: "My First Love"

1. JRM-IV, p. 989.

2. P. E. Howard, *The Life Story of Henry Clay Trumbull* (Philadelphia: Sunday

School Times Co., 1905); R. E. Speer, *Men Who Were Found Faithful* (New York: Revell, 1912), pp. 156-70.

3. Richard C. Morse, *My Life with Young Men* (New York: Association Press, 1918), pp. 356-57; CHH-Y, pp. 122-24; Ruth Rouse, *The World's Student Christian Federation: A History of the First Thirty Years* (London: SCM Press, 1948), p. 37.

4. Howard Mumford Jones, *The Age of Energy: Varieties of American Experience, 1865-1915* (New York: Viking, 1970).

5. A. M. Schlesinger, *The Rise of the City, 1878-1898* (New York: Macmillan, 1933).

6. Blake McKelvey, *The Urbanization of America* (New Brunswick: Rutgers University Press, 1963).

7. CHH-Y, pp. 101-02, ch. 5.

8. S. E. Mead, *The Lively Experiment* (New York: Harper & Row, 1963). Clyde Binfield, *George Williams and the Y.M.C.A.* (London: Heinemann, 1973), pp. 220-22.

9. C. K. Ober, *Exploring a Continent* (New York: Association Press, 1929), pp. 44-45.

10. Ruth Wilder Braisted, *In This Generation: The Story of Robert P. Wilder* (New York: Friendship Press, 1941), p. 44.

11. CHH-Y, pp. 120-22.

12. For an obituary of C. H. Dodge (1860-1926) see the *New York Herald-Tribune*, June 25, 1926; a biographical sketch by E. T. Colton is in the YMCA Historical Library.

13. Fred L. Norton, *A College of Colleges* (New York/Chicago: Revell, 1889), p. 14; Murray D. Ross, *The Y.M.C.A. in Canada* (Toronto: Ryerson Press, 1951), p. 117.

14. William B. Whiteside, *The Boston Y.M.C.A. and Community Need* (New York: Association Press, 1951), pp. 96-97.

15. L. D. Wishard, "The Beginning of the Students' Era in Christian History" (typescript, YMCA Historical Library); Ober, *Exploring*, ch. 7; CHH-Y, pp. 276-79.

16. Ober, *Exploring*, pp. 79-83.

17. JRM-I, pp. 8-10; W. M. Beahm, "Factors in the Development of the SVM ...," University of Chicago Ph.D. dissertation, 1941, in *Schwartzenau* 3, no. 1, pp. 23-36; R. P. Wilder, *The Great Commission* (London/Edinburgh: Oliphants [1936]), p. 41; C. P. Shedd, *Two Centuries of Student Christian Movements* (New York: Association Press, 1934), ch. 17; CHH-Y, pp. 302-04; Braisted, *In This Generation*, pp. 43-44.

18 Ober, *Exploring*, pp. 65-66, 87-88.

19. William Richey Hogg, *Ecumenical Foundations: A History of the International Missionary Council* (New York: Harper, 1952), p. 87.

20. CHH-Y, pp. 292-93.

21. CHH-Y, p. 295; William H. Morgan, *Student Religion During Fifty Years* (New York: Association Press, 1935), pp. 12-18, 41-58; Ober, *Exploring*, pp. 62-63, 65.

22. CHH-Y, pp. 276-94.

23. William Seymour Tyler, *Prayer for Colleges* (Boston, 1878).

24. JRM-IV, p. 996.

25. Mott's coaching session with Brown had been on the same trip as that with Wishard; he noted that "the Southern fellows take hold with enthusiasm but don't have staying qualities." For Brown, see CHH-Y, pp. 215-20.

26. Ober, *Exploring*, pp. 79-80, from the YMCA *Yearbook* of 1889, pp. 35ff.

27. F. S. Brockman (1867-1944), *I Discover the Orient* (New York/London: Harper, 1935), p. 9; JRM-III, pp. 726-31.

28. Karl Fries, "John R. Mott as I Have Seen Him," in *God Jul: Läsning for Ung och Gammal* (Stockholm: Triangelförlaget A.B., 1932), translated by Hugo and Elsa Cedergren; JRM-III, pp. 169-76.

29. For Fries (1861–1943), see C. P. Shedd and others, *History of the World's Alliance of YMCAs* (London: SPCK, 1955), pp. 285–86.

30. CHH-Y, pp. 335–43; K. S. Latourette, *World Service* (New York: Association Press, 1957), pp. 109–10.

31. Interview, CHH with Mrs. H. E. Roberts, Postville, Iowa, Aug. 21, 1967.

32. *Exercises at the Dedication of Barnes Hall, June 16, 1889* (Ithaca: Cornell Christian Association [1889]), p. 36; CHH-Y, pp. 288–89.

33. Wilder, *Great Commission*, p. 44.

34. *Young Men's Era* 20, no. 10 (Mar. 8, 1894), p. 4.

35. Norton, *College*, pp. 51–52; CHH-Y, p. 330; Latourette, *World Service*, pp. 166–69.

36. George Sherwood Eddy (1871–1963), *Eighty Adventurous Years* (New York: Harper, 1955), pp. 26–30.

37. For Speer (1867–1947), see W. R. Wheeler, *A Man Sent from God* (Westwood, NJ: Revell, 1956).

38. JRM-I, pp. 3–19, is a revised edition; the original (1889), in JRM-Y, is inscribed by JRM: "The first pamphlet written by J. R. M."

39. JRM-IV, p. 996; JRM to "Dear Mother," Oct. 10, 1889.

40. CHH-Y, p. 282, from Wishard, "Beginning," p. 100; JRM used a photograph of the Haystack Monument as the frontispiece of the volume on the SVM in his *Addresses and Papers*.

41. JRM-III, p. 34. JRM notes, "Experiences dealing with Presidents," an address at the University Club, Winter Park, Florida, 1945 (in JRM-Mn XII. A.4).

42. Mrs. Taylor, who was also a benefactor of the College of Wooster and much later of the Westminster Choir College, accompanied the Motts on their first trip around the world in 1895–97 and gave generously to the SVM.

43. JRM-III, pp. 185–89; JRM preserved his notebooks and the rosters of the men who attended.

44. CHH-Y, pp. 350–54; CHH, "The Kansas-Sudan Missionary Movement in the Y.M.C.A., 1889–1891," *Church History* 21 (Dec., 1952), pp. 314–22.

45. Bengt Sundkler, *Nathan Söderblom, His Life and Work* (Lund: Gleerup, 1968), pp. 36–39; CHH-Y, pp. 306–08, 763, note 95; Marc Boegner, *The Long Road to Unity* (London: Collins, 1970), p. 60; CHH interview with Mrs. Brita Brilioth (daughter of Söderblom), Uppsala, July 10, 1968.

46. JRM-III, p. 727.

47. The pressed flower was intact when the author read the letter eighty years later, a testimonial to Mott's thoughtfulness.

48. Ober, *Exploring*, pp. 106–07 and ch. 8; Ober interview (probably with B. R. Barber), Apr. 6, 1926 (in JRM-Y, VI.3). One senses that Ober deliberately moved out of the student work to give Mott his opportunity.

49. CHH-Y, ch. 16.

50. Brainerd was chairman 1867–92; CHH-Y, pp. 142–43; JRM, "Cephas Brainerd and the YMCA" (typescript [1945]), p. 4. The vast majority of YMCA secretaries were unordained: CHH-Y, pp. 81, 106–09, 119–22, 161ff.

51. JRM to Wishard, June 28, 1890.

52. CHH-Y, pp. 276–77; D. Stuart Dodge, ed., *Memorials of William E. Dodge* (New York: Randolph, 1887); Carlos Martyn, *William E. Dodge, the Christian Merchant* (New York/London: Funk and Wagnalls, 1890).

53. CHH-Y, pp. 143–47 and index, "Brainerd."

54. JRM-III, pp. 711–12; CHH-Y, pp. 107–09.

55. CHH-Y, pp. 139, 751, note 146.

56. James Hastings Nichols, *History of Christianity, 1650-1950: Secularization of the West* (New York: Ronald, 1956), p. 436.

57. For J. C. White (1870-1962), see L. L. Notestein, *Wooster of the Middle West*, vol. 2 (Kent, OH: Kent State University Press [1969]), p. 108 and chs. 8-9; also *Who's Who in America*, 1942-43.

58. For W. W. White (1863-1944), see C. R. Eberhardt, *The Bible in the Making of Ministers* (New York: Association Press, 1949), part I. In 1978 the school was called the New York Theological Seminary.

59. The author's grandparents' home was similarly nicknamed because they were the Martin Van Buren Clevelands; their "White House" had an "East Wing."

60. Latourette, *World Service*, pp. 169-71; Miller later joined the United States Foreign Service in Japan, was Chief of Far Eastern Affairs, and Consul General at Seoul.

61. JRM probably read Robert Sinker, *Memorials of the Hon. Ion Keith-Falconer, M.A.* (Cambridge: Deighton, Bell & Co., 1890).

62. *Report* of the First International Convention of the SVM, Cleveland, February, 1891 (Boston [1891]), p. 7; Taylor also spoke at the farewell session, pp. 182-83.

63. JRM-I, p. 34; Wilder, *Great Commission*, ch. 8. T. L. Smith, *Revivalism and Social Reform* (New York/Nashville: Abingdon, 1957), p. 226; W. W. Sweet, *The Congregationalists: Religion on the American Frontier* (Chicago: University of Chicago Press [1939]), p. 50.

64. JRM-III, pp. 211-21; in CHH-Y, p. 353, the author mistakenly credited this tour de force to R. C. Morse. It was probably given first before the Association of General Secretaries at St. Joseph, Missouri, May 2, 1891.

65. Wilder, *Great Commission*, pp. 68, 72, 75-77; Tissington Tatlow, *The Story of the Student Christian Movement of Great Britain and Ireland* (London: SCM, 1933), ch. 2. Reynolds later entered social settlement work and was head of University Settlement House in New York City: Allen F. Davis, *Spearheads for Reform* (New York: Oxford, 1967), index; Shedd, *Two Centuries*, pp. 340f.

66. Shedd, *History*, p. 317 from Allier, "Beginnings of Federation Work in France," *Student World* (hereafter *StW*) (July, 1923), pp. 91f.; see also G. Richard, *La Vie et L'Oeuvre de Raoul Allier* (Paris: Éditions Berger-Levrault, 1948), ch. 6.

67. For Wishard's tour, which laid much of the groundwork for Mott's first world journey, see CHH-Y, pp. 302, 328-30, 344-47.

68. I am deeply indebted to Miss Leila Compton of Wooster, a niece of Mrs. John R. Mott, for an interview and much information and criticism, for family folklore (it was said that during Mott's first visit to the "White House" Leila asked her "impish brother" Cam if he had brought JRM there to meet her sister Anna May, to which he replied, "such was farthest from my thought"). I have also received materials from the alumni office of the College and from Professor Lowell W. Coolidge as Library Consultant. See notes 57-58, above.

69. *Young Men's Era*, Dec. 10, 1891, anonymous article, probably by S. M. Sayford; it is the only known account of the wedding. If the "R." in Mott's name stood for a name, he might well have used it on his marriage license, but did not, another proof that he did not have the middle name "Raleigh."

70. The story of the Compton boys is delightfully told in James R. Blackwood, *The House on College Avenue: The Comptons at Wooster, 1891-1913* (Cambridge/London: M.I.T. Press, 1968); they were related to the Whites by marriage.

71. Leila White Mott (hereafter LWM) Diary, Dec. 12, 1891.

72. Hugh A. Moran, *David Starr Jordan: His Spirit and Decision of Character* (Palo Alto: Daily Press, 1969).

73. JRM-III, p. 124.

74. JRM-III, p. 125; for McCoy and the San Francisco YMCA see Clifford M. Drury, *San Francisco YMCA: One Hundred Years by the Golden Gate* (Glendale, CA: Arthur H. Clark Co., 1963), chs. 5–7; CHH-Y, pp. 135, 197, 350. Of fourteen church colleges started in central California only one, the University of the Pacific at Stockton, has survived; one visited by Mott at Napa later joined Pacific, which had been at San Jose; the gold-rush mentality lacked concern for such private philanthropy.

75. JRM-III, pp. 126–131; JRM-IV, p. 1026.

76. JRM to "My dear Parents," July, 1891.

77. *Young Men's Era*, July 28, 1892, pp. 947–49; Northfield Special Edition, *The Springfield* (Mass.) *Union*, July 12, 1892.

78. *Directory of Oak Park including River Forest and Harlem . . .* (Oak Park, IL: Delos Hull, Publisher, 1893), p. 67.

79. Graham Taylor, *Pioneering on Social Frontiers* (Chicago: University of Chicago Press, 1930), p. 3; a list of ten best books on "Christian Sociology" had appeared in the *Intercollegian* 13 (Mar., 1891), p. 91; probably Mott had asked Taylor for it; he did supply such a bibliography for Mott's 1894 pamphlet *The Missionary Department of the College Association*.

80. Gilbert Beaver (1869–1951) was related to Mott enterprises for many years; they remained close friends as long as Beaver lived.

81. JRM to "My dear Hattie," Oct. 7, 1892. During the winter vacation of 1893–94 the Motts spent about three weeks in Louisville, sitting in on the classes of Professor John A. Broadus at Southern Baptist Theological Seminary; JRM home letters, Dec. 23, 1893, Jan. 16, 1894; Mott kept notes that indicate that Broadus dealt with Bible pedagogy as well as content.

82. JRM-III, p. 40.

83. JRM-V, pp. 676–91.

84. James F. Findlay, Jr., *Dwight L. Moody, American Evangelist, 1837–1899* (Chicago/London: University of Chicago Press, 1969), pp. 230–32, 245–46, 342; compare JRM-VI, pp. 93–102.

85. CHH-Y, pp. 188, 370; Findlay, *Dwight L. Moody,* pp. 116f.

86. Roger D. Woods, *The World of Thought of John R. Mott* (University of Iowa Ph.D. dissertation, 1965), p. 27; see also the excellent sketch of Moody by L. A. Weigle in the *Dictionary of American Biography*. When the centennial of Moody's birth was celebrated in 1937, the Northfield Schools invited the Bible Institute to participate but the move was not reciprocated.

87. Findlay, *Dwight L. Moody,* p. 220; Sundkler, *Nathan Söderblom,* pp. 38–39.

88. Findlay, *Dwight L. Moody,* p. 95, quoted from Daniels, *Moody and His Works,* p. 37.

89. JRM-III, pp. 155–159; although Mott later said that he had "attended and participated in" the Parliament (JRM-IV, p. 995), his address is not to be found in any of the several compilations of the speeches given there. For the Parliament, see Donald H. Bishop, "Americans and the 1893 Parliament of Religions," *Encounter* 31 (Autumn, 1970), pp. 348–71, and Egal Feldman, "American Ecumenism: Chicago's World's Parliament of Religions of 1893," *Journal of Church and State* 9 (Spring, 1967), pp. 180–99.

90. Agnes R. Fraser, *Donald Fraser of Livingstonia* (London: Hodder and Stoughton, 1934), pp. 26–27; JRM-II, p. 162; Rouse, *WSCF,* p. 52 and ch. 8.

91. *The Student Volunteer* 2, no. 3 (Apr., 1894), p. 45; JRM-I, pp. 34–35.

92. J. L. Nevius, "The Student Volunteer Movement," *Missionary Review of the World,* n.s. 6 (May, 1893), pp. 336–43; for A. T. Pierson's (the editor's) comments, see p. 379; JRM-I, pp. 39–40; Morgan, *Student Religion,* pp. 60–62. The original pledge was "I am willing and desirous, God permitting, to become a foreign missionary." It was

changed to "It is my purpose, if God permit, to become a foreign missionary." It was also decided to call it a volunteer declaration rather than a volunteer pledge.

93. Ernest R. Sandeen, *The Roots of Fundamentalism* (Chicago/London: University of Chicago Press, 1970), after declaring that the founding "conferences" of the SVM were "completely dominated" by millenarian speakers, which I have shown was not the case, admits that in later years these were less influential. However, there was only one founding conference—Hermon '86—and no others until 1891; the Quadrennials beginning in the latter year were far more significant even than 1886. He is correct in saying that Mott was "no millenarian" (p. 185).

94. JRM-II, p. 162.

95. Fries, "John R. Mott," pp. 2-3.

96. JRM-III, p. 222; for Williams, see Binfield, *George Williams.*

97. JRM to R. C. Morse, Aug. 31, 1894.

98. George Adam Smith, *The Life of Henry Drummond* (New York: Doubleday and McClure, 1898); Ruth Rouse, "Voluntary Movements and the Changing Ecumenical Climate," in Ruth Rouse and Stephen Charles Neill, eds., *A History of the Ecumenical Movement, 1517-1948* (London/Philadelphia: SPCK/Westminster, 1954), pp. 330-32; John C. Pollock, *The Cambridge Seven: A Call to Christian Service* (Chicago: Inter-Varsity Press, 1955).

99. The bibliography on Keswick is large. For earlier works see A. T. Pierson and Charles S. Harford; twentieth-century interpreters are Stephen Barabas and J. C. Pollock; for the relevance of Keswick to the YMCA see Binfield, *George Williams,* pp. 217-25, and George Marsden, "Fundamentalism as an American Phenomenon, A Comparison with English Evangelicalism," *Church History* 46 (June, 1977), p. 220.

100. Rouse, *WSCF*, pp. 96-97; Constance Padwick, *Temple Gairdner of Cairo* (London: SPCK, 1929), pp. 47-48; Fraser, *Donald Fraser*, p. 27; Tatlow, SCM, pp. 58-62. For Keswick 1894 see H. R. Coston, Jr., *The World's Student Christian Federation as an Ecumenical Training Ground* (Northwestern University Ph.D. dissertation, 1963; Xerox-University Microfilm #64-2469), pp. 70-71.

101. JRM-I, pp. 290-92; JRM to Morse, Aug. 31, 1894; Shedd, *History,* p. 354; Fraser, *Donald Fraser,* pp. 26-27.

102. JRM to "Dear Mother," Jan. 27, 1895.

103. JRM-III, p. 95.

104. CHH-Y, pp. 313-60; Latourette, *World Service,* ch. 3.

105. JRM-III, pp. 211-21; see note 64 above.

106. JRM-III, p. 93.

107. Morse, *My Life,* pp. 302-04.

Chapter 3: Students of the World United: Europe, the Near East, Ceylon, and India

1. JRM-VI, p. 527.

2. JRM-II, pp. 162-63.

3. JRM pocket ledger, 1895-97; other donors were John Englis, W. W. Wicks, James McCormick, R. S. Crawford, George Hague, Mrs. Helen Swift, and the International Committee which paid $1,000 per year as part-time salary; W. O. Grover, a Singer Sewing Machine executive of Boston became ill and his pledge was cancelled. David Gregg, *The Testimony of the Land to the Book* (New York: Revell [1895]). For Wishard's tour see CHH-Y, pp. 344-47.

4. Agnes R. Fraser, *Donald Fraser of Livingstonia* (London: Hodder and Stoughton, 1934), ch. 3; Tissington Tatlow, *The Story of the Student Christian Movement of Great Britain and Ireland* (London: SCM, 1933), p. 63.

5. Ruth Rouse, *The World's Student Christian Federation: A History of the First Thirty Years* (London: SCM Press, 1948), p. 57.

6. CHH-Y, pp. 362–69; Tatlow, SCM, pp. 65–66. Mott would modify this stance.

7. This was a joint conference of the SVMU and the Inter-University Christian Union; the latter changed its name to the British College Christian Union (BCCU) at this meeting: Tatlow, SCM, pp. 65–66.

8. Leila White Mott, Diary (unpaged), Aug. 4, 1895; hereafter LWM Diary.

9. L. K. Hall, *Doggett of Springfield* (New York: Association Press, 1964), ch. 4.

10. Rouse, *WSCF*, p. 58.

11. JRM-II, pp. 329–31.

12. Rouse, *WSCF*, pp. 59–60; the permission was obtained through Prince Bernadotte, second son of the King, whom Mott had met in 1894.

13. Rouse, *WSCF*, pp. 60–61.

14. JRM-II, pp. 464–66.

15. Rouse, *WSCF*, p. 61, from a memo prepared by H. W. Steinthal.

16. Mott's memory of some of the details was faulty: this account is based on Williamson's record. "Students of the World United" was Mott's alternate name had "Federation" not been adopted.

17. Karl Fries, "John R. Mott" (see ch. 2, note 28, above), p. 3; there were no serious disagreements or divergent viewpoints; the sessions appear to have dealt chiefly with administrative and editorial matters.

18. Rouse, *WSCF*, p. 62, sketches the founders. JRM, *The World's Student Christian Federation: Origin, Achievements, Forecast* (WSCF, 1920), has photos of the castle at Vadstena, of Moody and Drummond who in Mott's mind were prophets of the WSCF, of the six founders, the early officers, and facsimiles of Fries' notes to the organizing sessions.

19. Rouse, *WSCF*, p. 62; JRM-II, p. 164.

20. Ruth Rouse and Stephen C. Neill, eds., *A History of the Ecumenical Movement, 1517–1948* (London/Philadelphia: SPCK/Westminster, 1954), pp. 599–604, esp. 600.

21. "We were bound together as no other persons in the founding of the World's Student Christian Federation at Wadstena Castle in 1895 and its expansion on all continents until we handed it over to younger spirits. . . ." JRM to Mrs. Karl Fries, June 29, 1943, on the occasion of Fries' death. C. P. Shedd and others, *History of the World's Alliance of YMCAs* (London: SPCK, 1955), pp. 285–86, has a sketch of Fries.

22. L. D. Wishard, *A New Programme of Missions* (New York: Revell, 1895) is essentially autobiographical; see note 15, ch. 2, above.

23. World's Alliance of YMCA's, C.C.I. Minutes, Oct. 12, 1895.

24. JRM, *Strategic Points in the World's Conquest: The universities and colleges as related to the progress of Christianity* (New York: Revell, 1897), p. 41; this, Mott's first book, is based on his report letters; "strategic points" are colleges and universities; JRM-II has extensive excerpts from many report letters. JRM-II, pp. 508–11.

25. For the background of this situation, see James Eldin Reed, "American Foreign Policy, The Politics of Missions and Josiah Strong, 1890–1900," *Church History* 41 (June, 1972), pp. 230–45, esp. pp. 236–37. LWM Diary for Sept. 30 and Oct. 7, 1895. The author and his wife visited Robert College July 7, 1971, just prior to the Turkish government taking it over. We also experienced the bright moon over the Bosporus and over Jerusalem and the Dead Sea on consecutive nights, whereas the Motts' experience had to be separated by weeks.

26. Mott's report letters were the equivalent of a diary on this trip, since Mrs. Mott kept a daily record. See note 8, above.

27. Rouse, WSCF, pp. 63–64.

28. JRM, Strategic Points, pp. 52–54.

29. Amos Elon, The Israelis: Founders and Sons (New York: Holt, Rinehart and Winston, 1971), pp. 82–83.

30. Bertha Spafford Vester, Our Jerusalem (Garden City: Doubleday, 1950), pp. 63, 141, 150–51.

31. Peter Amann, "Prophet in Zion: The Saga of George J. Adams," New England Quarterly 37 (Dec., 1964), pp. 477–500, and S. Eidelberg, "The Adams Colony in Jaffa," Midstream III (1952), pp. 52–61.

32. C. H. Malik, "The Orthodox Church," in A. J. Arberry, ed., Religion in the Middle East, vol. 1 (Cambridge: Cambridge University Press, 1969), p. 320.

33. In the author's copy of The Palestine Pictorial Bible (London: Oxford, n.d.), the illustrations are remarkably true to life. A typical travel book of the period just after this is Robert Hitchens, The Holy Land (New York: Century, 1910). See also Elon, Israelis, p. 85; Mott filed a full series of articles from the Free Church of Scotland Monthly for 1895 that described and depicted places of interest in the Holy Land.

34. The Motts used the first edition of George Adam Smith, The Historical Geography of the Holy Land (New York: Armstrong, 1895); Joseph Cook, Orient, with Preludes on Current Events (Boston/New York, 1886), Lecture 1.

35. JRM, Palestine home letter #1, Oct. 27, 1895.

36. Vester, Our Jerusalem, p. 150.

37. Abba Eban, My Country (New York: Random House, 1972), p. 28.

38. LWM Diary. The Motts' agent, Rolla Floyd, was a survivor of the expedition described in note 31, above.

39. JRM, Palestine home letter #2, Oct. 28, 1895.

40. W. R. Moody, The Life of Dwight L. Moody (New York: Revell, 1900), p. 384.

41. See Elon, Israelis, pp. 82–83. Floyd accompanied the Motts to Jaffa.

42. K. S. Latourette, World Service (New York: Association Press, 1957), pp. 155–56; CHH-Y, pp. 287, 343–44, 658.

43. JRM-II, pp. 381–84; JRM-VI, pp. 119–24 is a later version of JRM's first address on the morning watch.

44. Norman Goodall, A History of the London Missionary Society 1895–1945 (London: Oxford University Press, 1954), pp. 15ff. S. C. Neill, Colonialism and Christian Missions (New York: McGraw-Hill, 1966), pp. 110ff. Latourette, World Service, ch. 5 and The Nineteenth Century Outside Europe: The Americas, the Pacific, Asia, and Africa, vol. 3 of Christianity in a Revolutionary Age (New York: Harper, 1961), pp. 407–15.

45. S. C. Neill, The Story of the Christian Church in India and Pakistan (Grand Rapids: Eerdmans, 1970), p. 98; R. P. Beaver, Ecumenical Beginnings in Protestant World Mission: A History of Comity (New York: Nelson, 1962), p. 88; W. R. Hogg, Ecumenical Foundations: A History of the International Missionary Council (New York: Harper, 1952), p. 24.

46. JRM-VI, pp. 102–11 (Lahore), pp. 111–19 (Calcutta).

47. JRM-VI, p. 110. Mott probably absorbed the idea of the morning watch from his contacts with Cambridge men: Tatlow, SCM, p. 33.

48. A Spiritual Awakening among India's Students (Poona, 1896), pp. 109–10; J. Campbell White edited this series of pamphlets, which was published for the SVM of India and Ceylon.

49. The student YMCA later withdrew from the parent body.

50. See note 48, above.

51. JRM-II, pp. 385–97; Strategic Points, ch. 9.

52. Basil Mathews, John R. Mott, World Citizen (New York/London: Harper, 1934), p. 341.

Chapter 4: Students of the World United: Australasia, China, and Japan

1. Clyde Binfield, *George Williams and the Y.M.C.A.* (London: Heinemann, 1973), pp. 194–99.

2. C. H. Goode, Jr., was listed as an official delegate in the souvenir booklet of *The Thirteenth Triennial International Conference and Jubilee Celebration of the Young Men's Christian Association* (London, 1894), p. 32; J. T. Massey, *The Y.M.C.A. in Australia* (Melbourne/London: F. W. Cheshire, 1950), pp. 343–44; letter, J. C. Massey to CHH, Feb. 18, 1974; I am indebted to Mr. Massey for critique and suggestions. Goode was later knighted.

3. Russell Ward, "The Social Fabric," in A. L. McLeod, ed., *The Pattern of Australian Culture* (Ithaca: Cornell University Press, 1963), pp. 6, 12–41. I am indebted to Professor McLeod for a critical reading of this section and also to Professors Kenneth J. Cable of the University of Sydney and D. W. A. Baker of the Australian National University for suggestions and bibliography.

4. John J. Virgo, *Fifty Years Fishing for Men* (London: National Sunday School Union, 1939); see also R. C. Morse, *My Life with Young Men* (New York: Association Press, 1918), p. 427.

5. JRM-II, p. 264; JRM, *Strategic Points in the World's Conquest: The universities and colleges as related to the progress of Christianity* (New York: Revell, 1897), pp. 112–14; LWM Diary, Apr. 6, 1896 and home letters point to the University of Melbourne; it was never identified positively.

6. Keith Sinclair, *A History of New Zealand* (West Drayton: Harmondsworth, 1959, also Penguin), quoted by J. J. Mol in A. L. McLeod, ed., *The Pattern of New Zealand Culture* (Ithaca: Cornell University Press, 1968), p. 165; I am indebted to Professor Sinclair of the University of Auckland for suggestions and materials.

7. LWM Diary, Apr. 21, 1896.

8. Ian Breward, *Godless Schools? A Study in Protestant Reactions to the Education Act of 1877* (Christchurch: Presbyterian Bookroom, 1967), p. 22, for example; some of Mott's hosts were involved in the controversy.

9. Mott's classes under J. G. Schurman at Cornell were the most likely preparation for these discussions, which Mott did not record.

10. Mol, as in note 6, above.

11. Breward, *Godless Schools*, p. 133.

12. A. T. Thompson, "Dr. John R. Mott. . . ," *Australian Christian World* (Sydney) XLII (Mar. 26, 1926), p. 10.

13. LWM Diary, May 2, 1896; JRM, "Prayer as a Factor in the Student Movement," typescript, June 25, 1911; probably a Northfield summer conference address.

14. Editorial, *YOUNG MEN* (Sydney) XVI, no. 11 (July 13, 1896), p. 105.

15. Johannes Heyer, *The Australasian Student Christian Movement*, pam. (Sydney, 1896), p. 7.

16. *Minutes*, Australasian Student Christian Union, June 8, July 1, July 4, 1896; I am indebted to the staff of the National Library of Australia at Canberra for painstaking courtesy. Mott's care for details is indicated in letters as well as the *Minutes* in this collection.

17. JRM-II, pp. 271–73.

18. A. S. Devenish, in *The Australasian Intercollegian*, excerpted in *Australian Christian World* (Sydney) XLII (Mar. 26, 1896), p. 9; LWM letter "En Route to Nagasaki," Nov. 7, 1896, in *The Southern Cross* (Dec. 25, 1896), p. 1241 (clippings, JRM-Y).

19. I am indebted to my colleague Professor Frank Kierman for a critical reading of this section and invaluable suggestions, and equally to Professor Shirley Garrett whose *Social Reformers in Urban China: The Chinese Y.M.C.A., 1895–1926* (Cambridge: Harvard University Press, 1970) has been a major source; other works upon which this

treatment rests are of course the Mott diaries, reports, and home letters; Norman Goodall, *A History of the London Missionary Society, 1895-1945* (London: Oxford University Press, 1954), pp. 146-47; K. S. Latourette, *History of Christian Missions in China* (New York: Macmillan, 1929), pp. 470-72 and note 31, p. 471; R. P. Beaver, *Ecumenical Beginnings in Protestant World Mission: A History of Comity* (New York: Nelson, 1962), ch. 4; John K. Fairbank, "China Missions in History," *Journal of Presbyterian History* 49 (Winter, 1971), p. 284; Victor Purcell, *The Boxer Uprising. A Background Study* (Cambridge: Cambridge University Press, 1963), p. 172; *Chinese Recorder and Missionary Journal* (Shanghai) 19 (1888), pp. 282-83, 358-64, 397-402, 465-72 and 20 (1889), pp. 89-90, 487-98.

20. In addition to her Diary, Mrs. Mott kept a record of the places visited, persons met, and miscellaneous items of interest.

21. CHH-Y, pp. 664-66; K. S. Latourette, *World Service* (New York: Association Press, 1957), pp. 247-50; Garrett, *Social Reformers*, pp. 44, 53-56, etc.; Lyon edited *The Evangelisation of China* (Tientsin, 1897), a compilation of the six addresses given by Mott at five conferences during this tour.

22. Irwin T. Hyatt, Jr., "The Missionary as Entrepreneur: Calvin Mateer in Shantung," *Journal of Presbyterian History* 49, no. 4 (Winter, 1971), pp. 303-27.

23. Roberto Paterno, "Devello Sheffield and the Founding of the North China College," in Kwang-Ching Liu, *American Missionaries in China. Papers from Harvard Seminars* (Cambridge: East Asian Research Center, Harvard University, 1966), pp. 42-92; Sidney A. Forsythe, *An American Missionary Community in China, 1895-1905* (Cambridge: East Asian Research Center, Harvard University, 1971).

24. Garrett, *Social Reformers*, p. 70.

25. LWM Diary, Oct. 13, 1896.

26. JRM-II, pp. 288-301.

27. JRM-I, pp. 292-95.

28. R. P. Beaver, "Editorial Foreword," in R. H. Drummond, *A History of Christianity in Japan* (Grand Rapids: Eerdmans, 1971), p. 9; (hereafter *Christianity in Japan*); see also John F. Howes, "The New Values and the Old," in Marius B. Jansen, ed., *Changing Japanese Attitudes toward Modernization* (Princeton: Princeton University Press, 1965), pp. 337-68.

29. The author is greatly indebted to Hugh Borton, author of *Japan's Modern Century*, 2nd ed. (New York: Ronald Press, 1970), for a critical reading of this section and numerous suggestions; the visit referred to was by Princess Chichibu, wife of Emperor Hirohito's younger brother, to the Friends' School in 1928; the Motts subsequently had many contacts with the Chichibus.

30. E. O. Reischauer, *Japan: The Story of a Nation* (New York: Knopf, 1970), p. 123.

31. Borton, *Japan's Modern Century*, p. 206.

32. Evarts B. Greene, *New Englander in Japan: Daniel Crosby Greene* (Boston/New York: Houghton, 1927), pp. 107-13.

33. Drummond, *Christianity in Japan*, p. 200; Ernest E. Best, *Christian Faith and Cultural Crisis: The Japanese Case* (Leiden: E. J. Brill, 1966), ch. 8 and pp. 84-88, 172 (hereafter *Japanese Case*).

34. Drummond, *Christianity in Japan*, p. 11; Irwin Scheiner, *Christian Converts and Social Protest in Meiji Japan* (Berkeley: University of California Press, 1970), pp. 185-87; Best, *Japanese Case*, pp. 146-50.

35. Drummond, *Christianity in Japan*, pp. 166-72; Scheiner, *Christian Converts*, ch. 4.

36. CHH-Y, pp. 318-35; Latourette, *World Service*, pp. 165-69; Reischauer, *Japan*, p. 135.

37. C. W. Iglehart, *A Century of Protestant Christianity in Japan* (Rutland/Toyko:

Tuttle, 1959), pp. 31–32, 49–53 (hereafter *Protestant Christianity*); the Kumamoto Band of 35 students, under the influence of Captain L. L. Janes, a graduate of West Point, took "an oath of Christian fealty... couched in terms of national liberty" on Hanaoka in 1876; a dozen of these men became famous in Japanese Protestantism; when the school closed and Janes left, most of them went to the Doshisha. JRM-III, p. 609. There were similar bands at Yokohama and Hokkaido.

38. Greene, *New Englander in Japan*, pp. 165–68; Inglehart, *Protestant Christianity*, pp. 96–97; Howes, "New Values," pp. 355f.; K. S. Latourette, *The Great Century in Northern Africa and Asia, A.D. 1800–A.D. 1914*, vol. 6 of *A History of the Expansion of Christianity* (New York/London: Harper, 1944), pp. 386–87, 389–90.

39. Kumato Morita, "Mr. Mott's Work in the Doshisha," *The Japan Evangelist* 4, no. 5 (Feb., 1897), pp. 144–45.

40. Oliver Statler, *Japanese Inn* (New York: Random, 1961); the Motts stayed at comparable inns on several occasions.

41. When the author visited the Fujiya in 1972 he was shown Mott's signature in the hotel register and the room the Motts occupied in 1896.

42. CHH-Y, pp. 334, 357; Latourette, *World Service*, pp. 168–70.

43. Bradbury taught English for several years, holding Bible classes in his home; his letters were published intermittently in the *Richmond Christian Advocate* (copies in JRM-Y).

44. For DeForest, see Charlotte B. DeForest, *The Evolution of a Missionary. A Biography...* (New York/Chicago: Revell [1914]).

45. Drummond, *Christianity in Japan*, pp. 339–55; Scheiner, *Christian Converts*, p. 134; Serge Bolshakof, *The Foreign Missions of the Russian Orthodox Church* (London: SPCK, 1943), pp. 77–78. Mott's notes to his interviews with Nicolai, as well as with Verbeck and many others, were copious; DeForest jokingly asked a friend if he had passed Mott's "examination" based on a questionnaire of 20-odd items which took from three to seven hours to answer.

46. Drummond, *Christianity in Japan*, pp. 188–89; Mrs. Mott noted in her diary that the "Unitarian element" was "so strong."

47. J. H. DeForest, "The Intercollegiate Union of Japan," *The Japan Evangelist* 4, no. 5 (Feb., 1897), p. 155.

48. LWM Diary, Jan. 19, 1897; for the Doshisha affair, see Best, *Japanese Case*, pp. 149–50; Iglehart, *Protestant Christianity*, pp. 96–97; Howes, "New Values," p. 355.

49. J. T. Swift, "The Visit of Mr. John R. Mott... to Japan," *The Japan Evangelist* 4, no. 5, (Feb., 1897), p. 148, and letter to R. C. Morse, Feb. 5, 1897.

50. Swift, "The Visit"; Mott was quoted in the *New York Times*, May 31, 1897, p. 5; see also Tsunegoro Nara, *History of Japanese Y.M.C.A.* (Tokyo: YMCA, 1959), pp. 86–90, to whom I am indebted for numerous courtesies.

51. JRM-II, pp. 416–27; *Strategic Points*, pp. 206–07.

52. JRM, *Strategic Points*, pp. 206–07; JRM-II, pp. 364–65.

53. JRM, *Strategic Points*, p. 213.

54. W. A. Visser 't Hooft, "Speech on the occasion of the John Mott Centenary Celebrations, 25 May, 1965" (transcript), p. 3. See also Rouse, *WSCF*, ch. 6 and JRM-II.

55. LWM Diary, Mar. 24, 1897.

56. Charles O. Burgess, *Nettie Fowler McCormick, Profile of an American Philanthropist* (Madison: State Historical Society of Wisconsin, 1962); *Dictionary of American Biography, Supplement 2* (New York: Scribner, 1958), p. 403.

57. JRM to Cyrus McCormick, Apr. 16, 1897; McCormick Collection, State Historical Society of Wisconsin, Madison, to which the author is indebted for all McCormick items cited in this book.

58. Mott's outline was essentially a current job analysis; the fund was administered by his employer, the International Committee of the YMCA's.

59. B. A. Garside, *One Increasing Purpose. The Life of Henry Winters Luce* (New York: Revell, 1948), pp. 122-23.

60. The JRM letter of April 16, 1897 was to the McCormick family.

61. James A. Beaver to JRM, Apr. 3, 1897.

62. Extravagance was a characteristic of American language and literature: H. M. Jones, *The Age of Energy* (New York: Viking, 1970); Robert N. Bellah, "Civil Religion in America," *Daedalus* (Winter, 1967), p. 5 etc.

63. JRM-II, pp. 6-9; JRM-I, pp. 283-88; JRM home letter, May 4, 1895; JRM, "The Vision of the Haystack Realized," pam. [1906], from *The One Hundredth Anniversary of the Haystack Prayer Meeting*... (Boston: American Board of Commissioners for Foreign Missions, 1907), pp. 187-99—for the significance of the "Haystack Band."

Chapter 5: Apostle of Unity

1. *The Student Volunteer* 6 (Oct., 1897), p. 10.

2. Irene Mott Bose (Sept. 17, 1899–Dec. 22, 1974) devoted her life to villagers in India. In 1944 her mother wrote on her birthday that as a college student she had loved the Greek word *eirene,* meaning "peace": "All through four months of illness, February to May, the word was with me so you came into the world named. And the name suited you...."

3. CHH interview with Mrs. Walter Judd, daughter of B. R. Barber, for many years Mott's private secretary; Mar. 31, 1970. The Oak Park house was sold for $4400 in 1900.

4. CHH interviews with E. T. Colton, Feb. 2, 1970; with Miss Leila White, Mrs. Mott's niece, May 10, 1971; with Miss Leila Compton, Mrs. Mott's niece, Aug. 26, 1967.

5. This sketch is based on the interviews in notes 3 and 4, materials from the alumni office of Wooster College, family correspondence, and JRM to his parents, July 24, 1898. Also CHH interview with Miss Bess McAdam, JRM's niece, Nov. 7, 1967; with Donald Budge and Robert Calhoun, Aug. 24, 1969 at Lac des Iles where I attended the final Sunday service in the Ross home; many conversations with Dr. and Mrs. Frederick D. Mott and several with Irene Mott Bose and John Livingstone Mott; interview with J. Edward Sproul, May 14, 1968. Karl Fries, "John R. Mott as I Have Seen Him," pp. 76-99, mss p. 8.

6. S. M. Cavert, *Church Cooperation and Unity in America, A Historical Review, 1900-1970* (New York: Association Press, 1970), pp. 14-15.

7. Owen E. Pence, *The Y.M.C.A. and Social Need* (New York: Association Press, 1946), pp. 110-11.

8. S. Wirt Wiley, "Impressions of Mott," memo prepared for CHH interview Mar. 2, 1968; JRM-III, pp. 675-82.

9. CHH-Y, pp. 559-62.

10. R. C. Morse, *My Life with Young Men* (New York: Association Press, 1918), pp. 302-04.

11. David McConaughy, *Pioneering with Christ* (New York: Association Press, 1941); McConaughy, "Notes on John R. Mott," typescript. This sketch is also based on interviews with S. M. Cavert, K. S. Latourette, and others; Cavert to CHH, Oct. 29, 1968; C. R. Erdman to JRM, Oct. 6, 1952 (there was also a larger "Princeton" prayer group); W. R. Wheeler, *A Man Sent from God: A Biography of Robert E. Speer*

(Westwood, NJ: Revell, 1956), pp. 269–70; Latourette, "John R. Mott: A Centennial Appraisal," *Religion in Life* 34 (Summer, 1965), pp. 381–82.

12. JRM-III, p. 168; JRM to N. F. McCormick, Dec. 5, 1899.

13. CHH-Y, pp. 625–30, 635–39; C. P. Shedd, *Two Centuries of Student Christian Movements* (New York: Association Press, 1934), pp. 303ff.

14. JRM-III, p. 162.

15. E. T. Colton (1872–1970), "As I Knew Him," *Old Guard News* 36 (May, 1965), pp. 1–2.

16. Colton, *Memoirs* (New York: YMCA Library, 1969), pp. 130–32.

17. Wilma Dykeman, *Prophet of Plenty: The First Ninety Years of W. D. Weatherford* (Knoxville: University of Tennessee Press, 1966), pp. 39–41, 45–50; CHH-Y, pp. 541 etc.

18. Ruth Rouse, "John R. Mott, An Appreciation" (Geneva: WSCF [1928]), pp. 22–23.

19. Colton, *Memoirs*, p. 34; Colton to JRM, Oct. 21, 1903.

20. JRM-VI, pp. 491–505; CHH-Y, pp. 163–64.

21. W. H. Morgan, *Student Religion during Fifty Years* (New York: Association Press, 1935), pp. 41–58.

22. JRM-III, pp. 49, 55.

23. C. K. Ober, "The Lure of the Work," *Association Men* 32 (May, 1907); Galen M. Fisher, *John R. Mott, Architect of Co-operation and Unity* (New York: Association Press, 1952), p. 109.

24. JRM to N. F. McCormick, Jan. 19, Dec. 12, 1899.

25. JRM, "Richard Morse—His Contributions to the Young Men's Christian Association," *Association Men* (Feb., 1927), pp. 260–61, 286.

26. When the author visited Cornell in 1967, Barnes Hall was being used as a book store.

27. JRM home letter, Jan. 16, 1901; the *Daily Palo Alto*, Jan. 14, 1901.

28. Letters between JRM and John D. Rockefeller, Jr., Sept. 13, 14, 25, 29, Oct. 1, 1900.

29. CHH-Y, pp. 276–79.

30. Colton, "As I Knew Him."

31. *The Harvard Crimson*, Mar. 7, 1901; JRM-II, pp. 252–54.

32. JRM-II, pp. 250–52; JRM-VI, pp. 231–32; JRM, "Foreword" to George Stewart, Jr., *Life of Henry B. Wright* (New York: Association Press, 1925); Ralph H. Gabriel, *Religion and Learning at Yale* (New Haven: Yale University Press, 1958), pp. 203–04. K. S. Latourette, *Beyond the Ranges, An Autobiography* (Grand Rapids: Eerdmans, 1967), pp. 28–31.

33. Gabriel, *Religion and Learning*, pp. 198–99.

34. JRM-VI, Part 1 etc.; JRM, *Christians of Reality* (Shanghai: National Committee College YMCA of China, 1902). CHH interview with Luther A. Weigle, July 23, 1970.

35. G. S. Eddy, *Pathfinders of the World Missionary Crusade* (New York/Nashville: Abingdon-Cokesbury, 1945), pp. 304–05.

36. JRM-VI, p. 84.

37. Morse, *My Life*, p. 77.

38. J. W. Chapman, *Life and Work of Dwight L. Moody* (Philadelphia: Universal Publishing Co., 1900), pp. 463–66; JRM, "The Influence of D. L. Moody on the Student Movement," *Intercollegian* 22 (Jan., 1900), pp. 87–88; JRM-VI, pp. 83–90.

39. Pieter Hendrick Muller, *Dwight Lyman Moody, Schets van zijn leven en arbeid, 1837–1899* (Den Haag: J. M. Voorhoeve [1949]), p. 46; I am indebted to Mark A. vanderHeyden for a translation.

40. Robert T. Handy, A Christian America: Protestant Hopes and Historical Realities (New York: Oxford University Press, 1971), p. 121.

41. Ecumenical Missionary Conference, New York, 1900, vol. 1 (New York: American Tract Society, 1900), pp. 95-103, 112; JRM-I, pp. 308-18.

42. For Luce, see B. A. Garside, One Increasing Purpose. The Life of Henry Winters Luce (New York: Revell, 1948).

43. Ruth Rouse, The World's Student Christian Federation: A History of the First Thirty Years (London: SCM Press, 1948), ch. 10; H. R. Coston, Jr., The WSCF as an Ecumenical Training Ground (Northwestern University Ph.D. dissertation, 1963; Xerox-University Microfilm #64-2469), pp. 71-72, (hereafter Ecumenical Training Ground).

44. Morgan, Student Religion, pp. 60-61; The Student Volunteer 6 (Dec., 1897), pp. 38-39.

45. Homiletic Review 40 (Dec., 1900), pp. 569-70.

46. The Student Volunteer 6 (Dec., 1897), pp. 33-35.

47. Douglas M. Thornton, "The Significance of the Cleveland Convention," The Student Volunteer 6 (Apr., 1898), p. 104.

48. The Student Missionary Appeal. Addresses at the Third International Convention of the SVMFM held at Cleveland, Ohio, February 23-27, 1898 (New York: SVMFM, 1898), pp. 274-75. See Clifton J. Phillips, "The Student Volunteer Movement and its Role in China Missions, 1886-1920," in John L. Fairbank, ed., The Missionary Enterprise in China and America (Cambridge: Harvard University Press, 1974), p. 102; R. Pierce Beaver, "Missionary Motivation through Three Centuries," in Jerald C. Brauer, ed., Reinterpretation in American Church History (Chicago: University of Chicago Press, 1968), pp. 131-33, 146; James S. Dennis, Christian Missions and Social Progress (New York: Revell, 1897-1906); Paul A. Varg, Missionaries, Chinese, and Diplomats (Princeton: Princeton University Press, 1958), pp. 71-74.

49. World-Wide Evangelization the Urgent Business of the Church. Addresses Delivered Before the Fourth International Convention of the SVMFM, Toronto, February 26-March 2, 1902 (New York: SVMFM, 1902), pp. 294-97. Beaver, "Missionary Motivation," p. 144.

50. Fisher, John R. Mott, pp. 99-100, also has a testimonial by K. S. Latourette.

51. LWM to N. F. McCormick, Apr. 16, 1902.

52. Robert P. Wilder, The Great Commission (London/Edinburgh: Oliphants [1936]), p. 84; see pp. 87 and 90 for the influence of JRM's Evangelization.

53. W. M. Beahm, "Factors in the Development of the S.V.M.F.M." (University of Chicago Ph.D. dissertation, 1941), abstract in Schwartzenau 3, no. 1, pp. 31-32; Beaver, "Missionary Motivation," pp. 149-51; Phillips, "SVM in China Missions," p. 95, points out that although millennialism helped to launch the SVM, it "quickly took on a life of its own," a viewpoint preferable to that of E. R. Sandeen, The Roots of Fundamentalism (Chicago/London: University of Chicago Press, 1970), pp. 172-87.

54. JRM-I, pp. 70-71.

55. JRM-I, p. 82; for JRM's other talks at Toronto, see pp. 339-46, 361-68.

56. Warneck appears to have tied the watchword to A. T. Pierson's millennialism and its proclamation, fearing that this would displace the conversion of men and the upbuilding of the Church: Tissington Tatlow, The Story of the Student Christian Movement of Great Britain and Ireland (London: SCM Press, 1933), pp. 109-10, ch. 7.

57. Rouse, WSCF, ch. 8; Rouse and S. C. Neill, eds., A History of the Ecumenical Movement, 1517-1948 (London/Philadelphia: SPCK/Westminster, 1954), pp. 328-29, 376. A history of the SVM remains to be written: CHH-Y, p. 630.

58. CHH-Y, pp. 316-17; K. S. Latourette, World Service (New York: Association

Press, 1957), ch. 3; Morse, *My Life*, pp. 362-69; C. K. Ober, *Exploring a Continent* (New York: Association Press, 1929), pp. 140-41.

59. Latourette, *World Service*, p. 70; Morse, *My Life*, pp. 302-04, 380-82, 431-33.

60. Eddy, *Pathfinders*, p. 297.

61. Latourette, *World Service*, p. 97; CHH-Y, p. 657; McConaughy, *Pioneering*, pp. 5-6, 57-58.

62. JRM notes, "McConaughy's Experience," Feb. 14, 1895.

63. Latourette, *World Service*, pp. 59-64.

64. Shirley S. Garrett, *Social Reformers in Urban China: The Chinese Y.M.C.A., 1895-1926* (Cambridge: Harvard University Press, 1970), p. 57; the church at Mount Hermon School supported Wilder; the Warren, Pennsylvania, YMCA underwrote B. R. Barber in India, as examples. Ober, *Exploring*, pp. 142-43; JRM-III, pp. 222-36. It may be noted that the Salvation Army publishes *The War Cry* seventy-five years later.

65. Frank W. Ober, ed., *James Stokes: Pioneer of Y.M.C.A.'s* (New York: Association Press, 1921).

66. John D. Rockefeller, Jr., to JRM, Nov. 12, 1900. Although JRM-Y has abundant JRM-Rockefeller materials, both it and the Rockefeller archives have a virtual hiatus between 1897 and 1900; I am deeply indebted to Joseph W. Ernst, Director of the Rockefeller Archive Center, for the items cited in this note and in note 67.

67. JRM to John D. Rockefeller, Jr., May 15, June 25 (2 letters), July 1, 5, 1902; Rockefeller to JRM, Apr. 25, 1901, Apr. 14, June 19, 30, July 7, 1902, June 2, 1903, May 15, 1904; various summaries of payments and expenditures of the capital funds, from both JRM-Y and Rockefeller archives.

68. C. P. Shedd and others, *History of the World's Alliance of YMCAs* (London: SPCK, 1955), p. 342.

69. Shedd, *History*, p. 374.

70. Fries, "John R. Mott," p. 3; the American Fries mentioned was probably James Stokes.

71. Shedd, *History*, p. 379.

72. Shedd, *History*, p. 384; JRM-IV, pp. 1037-42.

73. JRM-IV, pp. 1043-45.

74. Shedd, *History*, pp. 400, 415-16. The Paris Basis, adopted at the first international YMCA gathering in 1855, served as a universal basis for Association membership. It was the first great modern ecumenical statement: "The YMCAs seek to unite those young men who, regarding Jesus Christ as their God and Saviour according to the Holy Scriptures, desire to be His disciples in their faith and in their life, and to associate their efforts for the extension of His kingdom amongst young men." Shedd, *History*, ch. 4; CHH-Y, pp. 72-81.

75. JRM-IV, pp. 1045-48.

76. Rouse, *WSCF*, ch. 6; JRM-II, pp. 21-57; Morse, *My Life*, pp. 382-83.

77. Rouse, *WSCF*, p. 88; this was the beginning of the John R. Mott Collection later given to the Yale University Divinity School Library.

78. JRM Report Letter III, p. 2; Tatlow, SCM, pp. 165-66.

79. JRM Report Letter III; Rouse, *WSCF*, p. 66.

80. Rouse, *WSCF*, pp. 87-88.

81. Rouse, *WSCF*, p. 93; Rouse and Neill, *Ecumenical Movement*, p. 342; W. R. Hogg, *Ecumenical Foundations: A History of the International Missionary Council* (New York: Harper, 1952), pp. 95-97; JRM-II, pp. 3-31; Coston, *Ecumenical Training Ground*, pp. 17, 107-10.

82. Rouse, *WSCF*, ch. 5.

83. JRM-II, pp. 339-41.

84. James F. Findlay, Jr., *Dwight L. Moody, American Evangelist, 1837-1899* (Chicago/London: University of Chicago Press, 1969), p. 359.

85. *Cambridge Review* 19, no. 481 (Apr. 28, 1898), and no. 483 (May 12, 1898).

86. JRM-II, pp. 341-43.

87. Eddy, *Pathfinders*, p. 295.

88. Mott's lieutenant was W. H. T. Gairdner, who was completing a year as traveling secretary of the British Movement before going to Egypt as a missionary; Constance E. Padwick, *Temple Gairdner of Cairo*, 2nd ed. (London: SPCK, 1930), p. 56.

89. JRM-II, p. 344; *Cambridge Review*, May 12; *Oxford Review*, May 16; *Oxford Magazine*, May 11, 1898, p. 332.

90. It is probable that this was the occasion of Mott's first significant contact with Herman Rutgers, who would become the leader of the Dutch SCM.

91. Coston, *Ecumenical Training Ground*, pp. 36–38, from Raoul Allier, "Les Origines de la Fédération Française," *StW* 16 (July, 1923), pp. 94–96.

92. JRM home letter, June 1, 1898; Mott did not enter the controversy in religious circles concerning the implications of the war; W. S. Hudson, "Protestant Clergy Debate the Nation's Vocation," *Church History* 42 (Mar., 1973), pp. 110–18.

93. Mott was a guest of Moltke at his "magnificent palace," he wrote home, June 24, July 2, 1898.

94. JRM-II, pp. 24–32, 331–34, 524–32.

95. JRM-II, pp. 334–37.

96. JRM to "My dear Gilbert," Dec. 26, 1899. The WSI was the Western Secretarial Institute, predecessor of George Williams College.

97. Tatlow, *SCM*, p. 180; Fisher, *John R. Mott*, p. 28; Tatlow and Fisher both thought this an important introduction to Orthodoxy for Mott, but he did not use it. Pobedonostsev, Over-Procurator 1880–1905, is said to have been the most powerful figure in Russia during that time.

98. Tatlow, *SCM*, pp. 179–80; JRM-II, pp. 344–48.

99. JRM-II, p. 347; JRM-IV, p. 996; *Association Men* 32, no. 8 (May, 1907), p. 351.

100. The Diary of Larsen for these weeks was obtained from the Rigsarkivet, Copenhagen, through the kind offices of Mr. Sven Larson of Örebro, Sweden, and translated for me by Mr. James Foley; Carl Bindslev, *L. P. Larsen, Evangelist and Theologian* (Bangalore and Calcutta: United Theological College/YMCA Publishing House, 1962); Eddy, *Pathfinders*, pp. 104–11; JRM-II, pp. 466–76, 479–81.

101. JRM-II, pp. 471–72.

102. Sigfrid Estborn, *Johannes Sandegren och hans insats i Indien kristenheit*, vol. 10 (Uppsala: Studia missionalia Upsaliensia, 1968), p. 32; Basil Mathews, *John R. Mott, World Citizen* (New York/London: Harper, 1934), p. 162. A critic asserted that the student group in Lund was characterized by a strong American-Anglican influence; everyone worked and the initiative came from that. Mott's personality "worked devastatingly on lesser independent men so that they became his more or less soulless echoes." Dyvind Sjöholm, *Samvetets politik. Natanel Beskòw och hand omvärld intill 1921* (Uppsala, 1972), p. 187.

103. JRM-II, pp. 476–79.

104. Rouse, *WSCF*, pp. 77–78.

105. Rouse, *WSCF*, p. 162; Greta Langenskjold, *Baron Paul Nicolay, Christian Statesman and Student Leader in Northern and Slavic Europe*, tr. by Ruth Evelyn Wilder (New York: Doran, 1924), pp. 92–101; there are also biographies of Nicolay by S. A. van Hoogstraten (in Dutch) and Folke Winquist (in Swedish). Mott had conferred earlier with Arthur Hjelt who became a leader of the Finnish YMCA: Shedd, pp. 294, 365.

106. Rouse, *WSCF*, pp. 78, 161-63; JRM-I, p. 38; JRM-II, pp. 443-48; JRM-VI, pp. 376-77.

107. Wilder, *Great Commission*, pp. 89-90; Tatlow, *SCM*, pp. 109-10; the interview took place Apr. 27, 1899.

108. P. Kranz (Shanghai) to JRM, Nov. 14, 1901 was a translation of a review by Warneck.

109. Fries, "John R. Mott," p. 6; JRM-II, pp. 537-43.

110. C. R. Eberhardt, *The Bible in the Making of Ministers* (New York: Association Press, 1962), p. 62.

111. JRM-McCormick correspondence, summer, 1901, esp. July 17, July 30; Mar. 22, 1902. The Rockefeller wedding was Oct. 9, 1901; John Mott was in Japan, Leila at Wooster, JRM to JDR, Jr., Jan. 4, 1902.

112. JRM to "Dear Mr. Murray," Sept. 9, 1901.

113. JRM notes, "Proposed World Tour . . . Sept., 1901-Feb., 1902."

114. LWM to JRM, Sept. 6, 1901.

115. The questionnaire is appended at the end of the Notes to this chapter, pp. 724-25, below. See also JRM-II, p. 427.

116. Sources for this tour are JRM-Y, III, Diaries (entitled "Journal" in the case of this one tour), and V, Conferences and Visits; Japan interviews, 4 folders. See also JRM-II, pp. 427-33; Coston, *Ecumenical Training Ground*, has sketches of many leaders.

117. JRM-VI, p. 34. The sexual emphasis was often stronger and more explicit than in the printed versions; some addresses were translated into Japanese.

118. E. T. Colton, *Memoirs*, p. 143.

119. For Niwa, see Latourette, *World Service*, p. 168.

120. JRM Diary, p. 16, for Oct. 18, 1901.

121. JRM Diary, p. 15, Oct. 17, 1901.

122. Latourette, *World Service*, p. 170.

123. Sources for Mott's visit to China continue in those named in note 116; also Garrett, *Social Reformers*; Victor Purcell, *The Boxer Uprising* (Cambridge: The University Press, 1963); Stephen Neill, *Colonialism and Christian Missions* (New York: McGraw-Hill, 1966), pp. 158-59; Hans-Ruedi Weber, *Asia and the Ecumenical Movement, 1895-1961* (London: SCM Press, 1966), pp. 72-73; F. S. Brockman, *I Discover the Orient* (New York/London: Harper, 1935), ch. 4. Lyon estimated his losses at $1,500 "in U.S. Gold" (D. W. Lyon to "My dear Mott and Ober," Oct. 19, 1900). The YMCA recompensed its people. There is no evidence that it asked for or collected an indemnity as did most mission boards.

124. Brockman, *I Discover*, ch. 7; Garrett, *Social Reformers*, pp. 68-69, 74, 88-89, and ch. 4; Latourette, *World Service*, pp. 157-58; JRM-III, pp. 727-28; JRM-VI, p. 228; see Coston, *Ecumenical Training Ground*, for sketches of leaders.

125. JRM-II, pp. 301-02.

126. Garrett, *Social Reformers*, pp. 91-93, 99, 101, 108.

127. JRM Diary, p. 24, for Nov. 7-10, 1901; JRM-II, p. 302.

128. The addresses were "Christians of Reality," "The Use of the Tongue," "Be Filled with the Spirit," "The Place of Prayer in Our Work," "The Need of More of the Evangelistic Spirit," "Individual Work for Individuals," and "Christ our Pattern in Religious Work." Most were later reprinted in JRM-I to VI: e.g., VI, pp. 71-83, 139-46, 189-94.

129. Latourette, *World Service*, p. 156; Louis Hieb, *A Spiritual Pilgrimage and Selected Sermons*, pam. (Ponca, NE [1953]).

130. JRM-Y, V, Conferences and Visits, 1900-1910.

131. Sources for the India segment of this tour include Weber, *Asia*; Neill, *Colonialism*, pp. 107-10; K. S. Latourette, *The Great Century in Northern Africa and Asia,*

A.D. 1800–A.D. 1914, vol. 6 of A History of the Expansion of Christianity (New York/ London: Harper, 1944), pp. 211–14; and World Service, pp. 110–13.

132. JRM-VI, pp. 493–505.

133. JRM Diary, p. 39; Coston, Ecumenical Training Ground, sketches several of these leaders; for Satthianadhan, Welinkar, Karmarkar, and Banurji see S. Modak, Directory of Prostestant Indian Christians, vol. 1 (Ahmednagar, 1900), pp. 153–54, 202, 410–12.

134. Fisher, John R. Mott, p. 50; Sam Higginbottom, Farmer: An Autobiography (New York: Scribners, 1949), pp. 63–64.

135. JRM Diary, p. 41, for Dec. 30, 1901–Jan. 1, 1902.

136. JRM Diary, pp. 41½–42, for Jan. 8, 1902; Modak, Directory, p. 202; Weber, Asia, p. 96.

137. JRM Diary, pp. 41½–42, for Jan. 10, 1902.

138. Norman Goodall, A History of the London Missionary Society, 1895–1945 (London: Oxford University Press, 1954), p. 36; Eric J. Sharpe, Not to Destroy but to Fulfill: The Contribution of J. N. Farquhar to Protestant Missionary Thought in India before 1914 (Uppsala: Gleerup for Swedish Institute of Missionary Research, 1965), ch. 6.

139. JRM Diary, pp. 43–44, for Jan. 17–18, 1902.

140. JRM-VI, pp. 517–18.

141. JRM-VI, pp. 266–73; for other summaries see JRM-I, pp. 346–54; JRM-II, pp. 497–98, 532–36; JRM-III, pp. 354–57.

142. W. A. Visser 't Hooft, "Speech on the occasion of the John Mott Centenary Celebrations, 25 May, 1965" (transcript), p. 9; James A. Beaver to JRM, Apr. 3, 1897.

143. JRM-II, pp. 543–48; Weber, Asia, p. 57.

144. Rouse, WSCF, pp. 102–03, ch. 10.

145. JRM-II, p. 55.

146. Fries, "John R. Mott," p. 6; no conference was held in 1904.

147. Australian Christian World, Mar. 20, 1903, p. 9.

148. Unidentified clipping in JRM-Y, V, Conferences and Visits, Australia-New Zealand, 1903.

149. Morse, My Life, pp. 424–27; J. T. Massey, The Y.M.C.A. in Australia (Melbourne/London: F. W. Cheshire, 1950), pp. 49 etc. I am indebted to Mr. Massey for critical reading and many useful suggestions.

150. Margaret Holmes, "Some Reflections on the Student Christian Movement and the Ecumenical Movement," typescript prepared for this Project, 1970; I am deeply indebted to Miss Holmes for a multitude of courtesies including the planning and hosting of my visit to Australia in 1972.

151. Minutes, ASCU, Apr. 4 (?), 1903.

152. JRM-II, p. 281.

153. JRM-II, p. 278.

154. JRM-II, p. 303; the entire proceedings of the Melbourne and New Zealand Conferences were published as JRM, Australasia and the World's Evangelization . . . (Sydney: ASCU, 1903), p. 196; Mott gave seven addresses.

155. JRM, "A Forward Missionary Movement in Australasia," The Japan Evangelist, June, 1903, pp. 211–12; JRM-I, pp. 295–304; JRM-II, pp. 276–84.

156. JRM to "My dear Mr. Mills," Mar. 21, 1898: "In the judgment of all my associates, as well as in my own judgment, I am so responsibly connected with the Christian student movement with its various ramifications that it would be exceedingly undesirable, if not disastrous, for me to sever my connections with it either now or within the next few years." About 1900, Morse hinted at three other calls of this nature but did not name them; there were doubtless more.

157. JRM to N. F. McCormick, Dec. 1, 1898.

Appendix: 1901–02 Questionnaire

Investigation of the Young Men of Oriental Countries to be Carried on by John R. Mott in Connection with his Tour in the Far East, 1901–1902.

1. Number of young men in the land. Give authorities.
2. Distribution of young men with reference to cities, villages, etc.
3. Importance and influence of the young men of the country:
   (a) In political life.
   (b) In the professions.
   (c) In industrial and commercial life.
   (d) In social life.
   (e) In reform movements.
   (f) In the religions.
4. The economic conditions of young men:
   (a) Occupations... Number of young men in each.
   (b) Their working hours.
   (c) Their wages.
   (d) Necessary living expenses.
   (e) Holidays.
   (f) Their habits of saving and spending.
5. The home life of young men:
   (a) The strength of its hold.
   (b) Proportion away from home.
   (c) Usual age of leaving home.
6. Social relationships of young men:
   (a) To parents. (b) To brothers and sisters.
   (c) To clan. (d) To caste.
7. Education of the young man.
   (a) Relative number educated in different grades.
   (b) Subjects studied. Courses.
   (c) Educational ideals and standards.
8. What the young men are reading.
9. The young man's use of his leisure. Sports.
10. Young men's societies, clubs, guilds:
    (a) Objects. (b) Size. (c) Requirements.
    (d) Nature of organization.
11. Temptations, perils, forces of evil assailing young men:
    (a) Forms of manifestation. (b) Strength.
    (c) Results on body, mind, faith, property, society, etc.
    (d) Conditions favorable to yielding to temptation.
    (e) Attitude of young men toward sin.
    (f) How best fought, counteracted, or overcome.
12. Criminology of young men:
    (a) Crimes against person. (b) Crimes against property.
13. Religious distribution of young men.
14. The hold that the religions have on young men.
15. At what time and under what circumstances does a young man come into relation to religion?
16. If a religion is losing its hold on young men, why?
17. Facts showing the progress of Christianity among young men:
    (a) Relative to its progress among other classes.

(b) Relative to the progress of other religions among young men.

(c) Relative progress among educated and uneducated young men.

18. Why young men are becoming Christians:

(a) Reasons influencing them.

(b) Most successful means employed to influence them.

(c) Prevailing conception of the Christian life among Christian young men.

19. Why do not more young men become Christians?

20. How far can the regular missionary agencies in the country meet the needs of the young men converts?

21. Other agencies and influences helping to upbuild, save, and shield young men:

(a) Wherein are the non-Christian religions helpful?

(b) The other forms of Christianity?

(c) The government? (d) Native societies?

22. Wherein is the Young Men's Christian Association specially adapted to help the young men of the land?

23. Wherein the Association is able to sustain a helpful relation to other forms of missionary effort.

24. Difficulties in the way of the Association work.

25. Weaknesses in the Association work.

26. Encouragements in the Association work.

27. Ambitions and ideals of the young men of the land.

28. Characteristics of the young men:

(a) Favorable.

(b) Unfavorable.

(From JRM-Y, III. Diary of Trip Around the World, 1901-02.)

Chapter 6: Ecumenical Architect

1. *The Ecumenical Review* 7 (Apr., 1955), p. 282; unsigned editorial, probably by W. A. Visser 't Hooft.

2. C. Howard Hopkins, *The Rise of the Social Gospel in American Protestantism, 1865-1915* (New Haven: Yale University Press, 1940), pp. 146-48, 298-300; CHH-Y, pp. 625-30, 635-39; Ronald C. White and CHH, *The Social Gospel: Religion and Reform in Changing America* (Philadelphia: Temple University Press, 1976), pp. 210-13.

3. G. S. Eddy, *Pathfinders of the World Missionary Crusade* (New York/Nashville: Abingdon-Cokesbury, 1945), p. 308.

4. Andrew Carnegie, "Wealth," *North American Review* 148 (1889), pp. 653-64; Richard Hofstadter, *Social Darwinism in American Thought* (Philadelphia: University of Pennsylvania Press, 1945), pp. 31-32.

5. JRM, "Imitable elements of power in Christ as a worker," given at Postville, Aug. 6, 1893.

6. Dennis was an index item in the SVM Quadrennial *Report* for 1902; R. T. Handy, *A Christian America: Protestant Hopes and Historical Realities* (New York: Oxford University Press, 1971), pp. 132-33; R. Pierce Beaver, "Missionary Motivation Through Three Centuries," in Jerald C. Brauer, ed., *Reinterpretation in American Church History* (Chicago: University of Chicago Press, 1968), pp. 131-32, 145-46.

7. CHH-Y, pp. 483, 635-37. CHH interview with S. Ralph Harlow, Mar. 24, 1971.

8. JRM, Notes to an address at Dwight Hall, Oct. 22, 1905; R. H. Gabriel, *Religion and Learning at Yale* (New Haven: Yale University Press, 1958), p. 202.

9. JRM-III, p. 532; see also James H. F. Peile, *The Reproach of the Gospel* (London: Longmans, 1907), pp. 107ff.

10. White and Hopkins, *Social Gospel,* pp. 107–13; CHH-Y, pp. 636–37; Wilma Dykeman, *Prophet of Plenty: The First Ninety Years of W. D. Weatherford* (Knoxville: University of Tennessee Press, 1966), pp. 66–71.

11. JRM-III, p. 63; JRM to Nettie Fowler McCormick, Oct. 20, 1908; the purpose of this conference is not clear.

12. CHH interview with James C. Baker, June 10, 1969; C. P. Shedd, *The Church Follows Its Students* (New Haven: Yale University Press, 1938), pp. 70–71; CHH interview with Arthur Jorgensen, Apr. 2, 1970.

13. JRM, "The vision of the Haystack Band realized by the students of this generation," notes to an address at North Adams (Mass.), Oct. 10, 1906, also pub. as a pam. [1906] and in *The One Hundredth Anniversary of the Haystack Prayer Meeting . . .* (Boston: American Board of Commissioners for Foreign Missions, 1907), pp. 187–99.

14. Clipping from the New York *Evening Post,* 1906, in JRM-Y; Beaver, "Missionary Motivation," pp. 129–30, 141–45.

15. JRM-I, pp. 318–25; Tissington Tatlow, *The Story of the Student Christian Movement of Great Britain and Ireland* (London: SCM Press, 1933), pp. 344–45.

16. Edward Rowlands, "The Missionary Genius of St. Paul; insights from China experience," typescript, CtYD; Beaver, "Missionary Motivation," pp. 147–51. B. A. Garside, biographer of Henry Luce, declared in *One Increasing Purpose* (New York: Revell, 1948), pp. 47–48, that when Eddy, Luce, and Pitkin began to travel for the SVM, they refused to present "the old message of myriads of 'heathen' going into 'Christless graves' because they had not heard the Christian message." Theirs was "a gospel of love, a whole gospel which could make a new man from within, and could build a new society, a new China, a new world without." Compare G. S. Eddy, A *Pilgrimage of Ideas* (New York: Farrar and Rinehart, 1934), pp. 53–54.

17. J. H. Oldham to JRM, Feb. 2, 1904; JRM-I, pp. 318–25 and JRM-II, p. 348. Hereafter J. H. Oldham is abbreviated JHO.

18. Rowlands (note 16, above) thought the book still "fresh and appealing" when he wrote his memoirs fifty years later.

19. At this time, Methodist friends were urging Mott to consider various posts in the Methodist missions organizations.

20. Clipping from *World-Wide Missions,* Apr., 1905, p. 5; JRM-Y.

21. *The Baptist Missionary Magazine,* Apr., 1905, p. 167; JRM-Y.

22. *The Guardian,* Feb. 2, 1906.

23. JRM-VI, p. 535.

24. CHH interview with J. Gustav White, June 9, 1969; Beaver, "Missionary Motivation," p. 144.

25. Wm. M. Beahm, "Factors in the Development of the Student Volunteer Movement for Foreign Missions" (University of Chicago Ph.D. dissertation, 1941), abstract in *Schwartzenau* 3, no. 1, pp. 24, 31–32.

26. JRM, *Five Decades and a Forward View* (New York/London: Harper, 1939), ch. 2; JRM-I, pp. 129, 189.

27. The FMCNA, as it will be noted henceforth, underwent one or more name changes; Mott was never its chairman, but did head numerous committees; JRM-V, pp. 676–79.

28. Stewart, in JRM-VI, pp. 531, 538; CHH interview with Miss Helen White, Mrs. Mott's niece, May 10, 1971; CHH interview with E. T. Colton, Feb. 26, 1970.

29. JRM to Frank Mason North, Nov. 27, 1905, courtesy of Drew University Library; E. B. Sanford, ed., *Church Federation . . .* (New York: Revell, 1906), pp. 431–34.

30. Morse to JRM, Apr. 24, 1909; CHH-Y, pp. 528–29.

31. Marc Boegner, *The Long Road to Unity* (London: Collins, 1970), pp. 33-34; "John R. Mott: Fifty Years of Recollections," *Ecumenical Review* 17, no. 3 (1965), pp. 251-52; *Reformé*, 12 Feb., 1955.

32. Clipping from *L'Evangelista*, Jan. 28, 1904, p. 6; JRM-II, p. 350.

33. "Heard in the High," *Isis*, Feb. 18, 1905, pp. 221-22; JRM-II, pp. 352-54.

34. *Oxford Magazine*, Feb. 22, 1905, p. 210.

35. Stewart, in JRM-VI, p. 535.

36. Tatlow, SCM, pp. 253-56.

37. Memo prepared by S. Wirt Wiley for interview with CHH, Mar. 2, 1968.

38. *Warwicklania, Xmas, 1906:* The Movement, 22 Warwick Lane (London), E. C.

39. Morse to Mrs. J. S. Mott, May 18, 1905.

40. C. P. Shedd and others, *History of the World's Alliance of YMCAs* (London: SPCK, 1955), pp. 418-28; JRM-IV, pp. 1045-48.

41. Sigfrid Estborn, *Johannes Sandegren*, vol. 10 (Uppsala: Studia Missionalia Upsaliensa, 1968), p. 37; J. M. Davis, *An Autobiography* (Kyo Bun Kwan [1960]), p. 47. K. Fries, "John R. Mott as I have seen Him," typescript, JRM-Y, pp. 6-7.

42. Rouse, WSCF, p. 133; JRM-II, pp. 78-79.

43. JRM-II, p. 565.

44. Rouse, "John R. Mott," *StW* 23, no. 2 (Apr., 1930), pp. 118-20; the novel was by H. Rider Haggard.

45. JRM-II, p. 484; Rouse, WSCF, pp. 108-10.

46. C. K. Ober, *Luther D. Wishard, Projector of World Movements* (New York: Association Press, 1927), pp. 164-70; Johannes DuPlessis, *The Life of Andrew Murray of South Africa* (London: Marshall Bros., 1920), p. 443; W. M. Douglas, *Andrew Murray and His Message* (London/Edinburgh: Oliphants [1927]).

47. JRM-II, pp. 486-88; WSCF Report Letter, June 7, 1906; K. S. Latourette, *The Great Century in the Americas, Australasia, and Africa, A.D. 1800-A.D. 1914* (New York: Harper, 1943), pp. 353-54; R. H. W. Shepherd, *Lovedale, South Africa: The Story of a Century, 1841-1941* (Lovedale, C.P.: Lovedale Press [1940]), ch. 6.

48. JRM-II, p. 489.

49. Rouse, WSCF, p. 110; R. C. Morse, *My Life with Young Men* (New York: Association Press, 1918), pp. 427-28; JRM-II, p. 488; Oswin Bull, "JRM: Servant of Christ and Leader of Men," *The South African Outlook*, Apr. 1, 1955.

50. Miss Rouse overlooked Gerdener in her WSCF; for a sketch see H. R. Coston, *The WSCF as an Ecumenical Training Ground* (Northwestern University Ph.D. dissertation, 1963; Xerox-University microfilm #64-2469), pp. 226-27 (hereafter *Ecumenical Training Ground*).

51. Robert Payne, *The Life and Death of Mahatma Gandhi* (New York: Dutton, 1969), pp. 158-59.

52. JRM to "My dear John," July 7, 1906; JRM-VI, p. 529.

53. K. S. Latourette, *World Service* (New York: Association Press, 1957), p. 205; CHH interview with C. J. Ewald, Mar. 28, 1968; JRM-II, pp. 490-92.

54. JRM-II, p. 492; Latourette, *World Service*, pp. 204-05.

55. JRM-II, pp. 493, 498; Myron T. Clark Diary, July, 1906.

56. Rouse, WSCF, p. 110.

57. Latourette, *World Service*, pp. 226-27; memo prepared by Augustin E. Turner for interview with CHH, June 9, 1969.

58. Roger Dale Woods, *The World of Thought of John R. Mott* (University of Iowa Ph.D. dissertation, 1965), pp. 130-33; CHH-Y, p. 513; Galen M. Fisher, *John R. Mott, Architect of Co-operation and Unity* (New York: Association Press, 1952), pp. 39-43.

59. JRM-II, pp. 490-98.

60. JRM to N. F. McCormick, Dec. 11, 1906; Hans-Ruedi Weber, *Asia and the Ecumenical Movement, 1895-1961* (London: SCM Press, 1966), pp. 69-77.

61. Latourette, *World Service*, pp. 188–92; L. George Paik, *The History of Protestant Missions in Korea, 1832–1910* (Pyeng Yang, Korea: Union Christian College Press, 1929), pp. 346–47; JRM-II, pp. 438–440; Morse, *My Life*, pp. 464–65.

62. After Yun's release in 1915 he became general secretary of the Korean YMCA until 1920; Paik, *Protestant Missions*, pp. 185–86, said that "there has not yet been among the Korean people a Christian leader the equal of Baron Yun." Latourette, *World Service*, p. 193; F. S. Brockman, *I Discover the Orient* (New York/London: Harper, 1935), p. 101. Yun was a delegate to Edinburgh 1910.

63. JRM Diary, Feb. 3, 1907; JRM-II, p. 440.

64. Quoted by Paik, *Protestant Missions*, p. 353.

65. YMCA work had come to the Philippines with American armed forces in 1898, to be followed by organized but separate Associations for military personnel and American/European residents of Manila: Latourette, *World Service*, pp. 317f.; JRM-III, pp. 243–47 and Diary for Feb. 15–19, 1907; Gerald H. Anderson, *Studies in Philippine Church History* (Ithaca: Cornell University Press, 1969). W. H. Taft to JRM, Dec. 31, 1906.

66. CHH interview with E. Stanton Turner, June 9, 1969.

67. JRM's later contacts with Brent, and a few letters of this period, indicate the compatibility of their ideas.

68. JRM-III, pp. 243–47.

69. Shirley Garrett, *Social Reformers in Urban China: The Chinese Y.M.C.A., 1895–1926* (Cambridge: Harvard University Press, 1970), ch. 4, esp. pp. 77–78, 87, 101–02; Latourette, *World Service*, pp. 251–58.

70. JRM-II, pp. 305–06; JRM Diary, Mar. 5, 8, 10, 14, 1907.

71. JRM-II, pp. 307–08; JRM Diary, Mar. 5, 1907.

72. JRM-II, p. 308; JRM Diary, Mar. 10, 1907.

73. The Conference was composed entirely of Western personnel, with only a handful of Chinese as virtual spectators; it may have been that JRM did not want to compromise his well-known position on indigenous leadership by being present; most of his men were on Conference committees.

74. This was for 12 buildings in nine cities; Garrett, *Social Reformers*, p. 109 and note 101, p. 205; JRM Diary, Mar. 23, 1907; JRM-III, p. 323.

75. JRM-II, pp. 304–05; JRM Diary, Mar. 19–22, 1907; JRM-III, pp. 247–52.

76. JRM-II, p. 304.

77. JRM to LWM, Mar. 15, 1907.

78. Garrett, *Social Reformers*, pp. 103–08; JRM-II, pp. 549–55; Rouse, *WSCF*, pp. 143–44; Latourette, *World Service*, pp. 169–70, 173.

79. Garside, *One Increasing Purpose*, pp. 125–26; Weber, *Asia*, pp. 71–72.

80. Galen Fisher, *Handbook of the World's Student Christian Federation Conference, Tokyo, April 3–7, 1907* (Tokyo: Japanese YMCA Union, 1907), p. 34; C. W. Iglehart, *A Century of Protestant Christianity in Japan* (Rutland/Tokyo: Tuttle, 1959), pp. 118–19; CHH-Y, pp. 321–35; Latourette, *World Service*, pp. 166–69.

81. Morse, *My Life*, p. 470; Weber, *Asia*, p. 69; JRM-II, p. 433.

82. *Report of the Conference of the WSCF held at Tokyo, Japan, April 3–7, 1907* (New York city: WSCF [1906]); JRM Diary, Apr. 1–2; John F. Howes, "Japanese Christians and American Missionaries," in Marius B. Jansen, ed., *Changing Japanese Attitudes Toward Modernization* (Princeton: Princeton University Press, 1965), pp. 346–61.

83. JHO, *Ecumenical Review* 7, no. 3 (Apr., 1955), pp. 258–59; *Report*, pp. 190–92; Brockman, *I Discover*, pp. 167f.

84. Weber, *Asia*, p. 252; Fisher, *John R. Mott*, pp. 93–94; H. R. Coston, *The WSCF as an Ecumenical Training Ground* (Northwestern University Ph.D. dissertation, 1963;

Xerox-University Microfilm #64-2469), pp. 44-46; Rouse, *WSCF*, pp. 124-28; *Report*, pp. 233-40; Soichi Saito, "Dr. John R. Mott," typescript, 1949.

85. JRM-II, pp. 567-73; JRM Diary, Apr. 3-8.

86. Weber, *Asia*, pp. 76-77; Eddy, *Pilgrimage*, pp. 113-19; Greta Langenskjold, *Baron Paul Nicolay, Christian Statesman and Student Leader in Northern and Slavic Europe*, tr. by Ruth Evelyn Wilder (New York: Doran, 1924), pp. 162-67; Nicolay's handwritten report.

87. JRM Diary, Apr. 15, 1907.

88. JRM-II, p. 435.

89. Yoitsu Honda, "Some Results of the Federation Conference in Japan," *StW* 1 (Jan., 1908), pp. 4-7; D. W. Lyon, "Conference of the WSCF at Tokyo," *The Chinese Recorder and Missionary Journal* 38, no. 6 (June, 1907), pp. 353-54.

90. JRM-III, pp. 243-47.

91. JRM-I, pp. 326-38.

92. JRM-III, p. 261.

93. JRM to John D. Rockefeller, Jr., June 10, 1907; Latourette, *World Service*, pp. 64-65.

94. JRM-III, pp. 261-313; Fisher, *John R. Mott*, pp. 129f. E. T. Colton, *Memoirs*, pp. 46-52.

95. Tatlow, SCM, pp. 309-13; JRM-I, pp. 326-38; *StW* 1 (Apr., 1908), p. 43.

96. JRM-VI, p. 530.

97. *Future Leadership* was published both by the YMCA and the SVM in New York in 1908 and 1911 and in London in 1909; Wilson to JRM, Apr. 1, May 1, 1908; JRM to Wilson, May 5, 1908. I am deeply indebted to Arthur S. Link, editor of the Wilson papers, for numerous items and suggestions.

98. Theodore Roosevelt, "A Militant Ministry and Laity Alike Needed," *Men of Washington*, Feb. 4, 1909; *Association Men* 34, no. 1 (Oct., 1908), pp. 102-03, 117.

99. "W.G.B.," *The Association Seminar*, Dec., 1908.

100. JRM, *Future Leadership*, p. 12; for a comparable Wilson phrase, see White, Jr., and Hopkins, *The Social Gospel*, p. 184, the probable source of Mott's usage.

101. *Future Leadership*, p. 42; Peile, *Reproach*, pp. 107ff.

102. *Future Leadership*, p. 193.

103. *The Claims and Opportunities of the Christian Ministry* (New York: YMCA Press, 1911, 1913).

104. JRM-VI, insert, pp. 294-95.

105. JHO, *Ecumenical Review* 7, no. 3 (Apr., 1955), p. 256.

106. *The Isis* (Oxford), Nov. 14, 1908, pp. 85-86; JRM-II, pp. 356-58.

107. *Isis*, Nov. 21, 1908, p. 108.

108. *Oxford Magazine*, Nov. 12, 17, 1908.

109. JRM-II, pp. 356-58; W. W. Seton, "Mr. Mott in Great Britain," *StW* 2, no. 1 (Jan., 1909), pp. 31-32.

110. Clippings in JRM-Y, V. Conferences and Visits, 1908-09.

111. JRM-VI, pp. 248-65; Tatlow, SCM, p. 550.

112. JRM-II, p. 360.

113. Alexander Kerr to CHH, May 13, 1969.

114. *Cambridge Chronicle and University Journal . . .*, Dec. 11, 1908, p. 2; JRM-II, p. 361; *Cambridge Review*, Jan. 21, 1909, p. 186.

115. H. C. Rutgers, "The Dutch Winter Conference," *StW* 2, no. 2 (Apr., 1909), pp. 66-67; JRM-II, pp. 479-83. The aula is a large hall with stage, usually with classical or Baroque decor.

116. JRM-VI, p. 533.

117. JRM to Nathan Söderblom, Feb. 11, 1909 (courtesy of the University of Uppsala Library); Fisher, *John R. Mott,* p. 84.

118. JRM-II, p. 481; Marius Hansen to CHH, Feb. 16, 1968; CHH interview with Halfdan R. Høgsbro, July 19, 1968.

119. JRM-II, pp. 449–58; Rouse, *WSCF,* pp. 101–04; JRM-VI, pp. 376–77; Franklin Gaylord, "Breaking into Russia," in Frank W. Ober, ed., *James Stokes: Pioneer of Y.M.C.A.'s* (New York: Association Press, 1921); Colton, *Memoirs,* p. 144 and *Forty Years with Russians* (New York: Association Press, 1940); Coston, *Ecumenical Training Ground,* pp. 146–49.

120. JRM-II, pp. 451–56; JRM, "Prayer as a Factor in the Student Movement," address at Northfield, 1911, typescript; Nicolay's biographer does not mention Mott's visit to Russia in 1909; Lukianov was Over-Procurator 1909–11, Obolensky 1905–06.

121. JRM-VI, pp. 536–37.

122. Rouse, *WSCF,* pp. 112–13, 116.

123. JRM-II, p. 455.

124. Nicolay, "Mr. Mott's Visit to Russia (1909)," in JRM-II, pp. 449–51, from *StW* 2 (1909), pp. 101–04.

125. Insert between pp. 294–95, JRM-VI; Roosevelt to JRM, Oct. 12, 1908; James Stokes to Gaylord, Oct. 26, 1908.

126. George M. Day, "The Russian Student Movement," JRM-II, pp. 456–63, from *StW,* July, 1917; Fisher, *John R. Mott,* pp. 107–08. For Day, see JRM to H. P. Andersen, Apr. 22, 1909.

127. JRM War Fund address, Boston, Nov. 5, 1917, pp. 11–12; Basil Mathews, *John R. Mott, World Citizen* (New York/London: Harper, 1934), pp. 170–74, 197–99.

128. JRM-II, pp. 412–15; at Coimbra University Mott spoke on "The Power of Sin," an adaptation of an address given at Northfield in 1903: JRM-VI, pp. 11–19; G. M. Day, "The Rome and Halle Conferences," *StW* 2 (1909), pp. 104–07.

129. JRM-II, pp. 91–123, 573–79; Coston, *Ecumenical Training Ground,* pp. 36–37, 199–203, 209–10; Rouse, *WSCF,* pp. 137–39; *StW* 2, no. 2 (Apr., 1909), pp. 41–55, 121, 160; William Temple, "Oxford and Social Service," *StW* 2, no. 2 (Apr., 1909), pp. 52–55.

130. JRM-I, pp. 121–41; *Students and the Present Missionary Crisis. . .* (New York: SVM, 1910); *StW* 3 (1910), pp. 27, 61, 64, 77; LWM to Clara Mott, Jan. 8, 1910.

131. *Postville Review,* Jan. 7, 1910; Ross Lee Finney, *Personal Religion and the Social Awakening* (Cincinnati: Jennings and Graham, 1913) and *A Sociological Philosophy of Education* (New York: Macmillan, 1928); K. S. Latourette, *Beyond the Ranges. An Autobiography* (Grand Rapids: Eerdmans, 1967), p. 37; Fisher, *John R. Mott,* p. 105; R. J. Reitzel, *All in a Lifetime* (typescript, YMCA Historical Library [1972]), p. 102 and Reitzel to CHH, July 14, 1970 and Apr. 14, 1972.

132. JRM-VI, p. 528.

133. A. T. Hadley to JRM, Apr. 16, 1909; JRM to Hadley, June 12, 1909; George W. Pierson, *Yale College: An Educational History, 1871–1921* (New Haven: Yale University Press, 1952), p. 288.

134. Harlan P. Beach to JRM, Apr. 16, 1909.

135. Morse to JRM, Aug. 14, 1909.

136. JHO to JRM, Aug. 10, 1909.

137. JHO to JRM, Oct. 13, 1909.

138. JRM to Hadley, Dec. 11, 1909. It appears that Mott gave some lectures on missions at Yale Divinity School for several years, but the only record of them is the listing of his name as "Lecturer on Missions" in the *Bulletins of Yale University, The Yale Divinity School* for 1910 to 1912–13.

Chapter 7: Edinburgh 1910, and After

1. "Moreover, it was this conference that established Mott's commanding position throughout the Christian world and opened a new chapter in his life." Marc Boegner, "John Mott," *Reformé*, Feb. 12, 1955.

2. The literature on Edinburgh 1910 is immense: see Missionary Research Library *Occasional Bulletin* 11 (June 14, 1960), no. 5. Mott collected most major documents in JRM-V, pp. 1-178. W. H. T. Gairdner, *Echoes from Edinburgh, 1910* (New York: Revell [1910]) condenses the nine official volumes, with comments. Major secondary sources are W. R. Hogg, *Ecumenical Foundations: A History of the International Missionary Council* (New York: Harper, 1952), ch. 3, and K. S. Latourette in Ruth Rouse and S. C. Neill, eds., *A History of the Ecumenical Movement, 1517-1948* (London/Philadelphia: SPCK/Westminster, 1954), pp. 355-62. This treatment is based on the above and the voluminous archives in JRM-Y.

3. Hogg, *Ecumenical Foundations*, pp. 102-15. A missionary congress held in connection with the World's Parliament of Religions in Chicago in 1893 voted for and appointed a committee on a "World's Congress of Missions"; J. H. Barrows, *The World's Parliament of Religions*, vol. 2 (Chicago, 1893), p. 1538.

4. FMCNA, *Fourteenth Conference*, 1907, p. 102.

5. J. H. Oldham, "John R. Mott," *Ecumenical Review* 7 (Apr., 1955), p. 257.

6. FMCNA, *Fifteenth Conference*, 1908, p. 8.

7. JHO, "Reflections on Edinburgh, 1910," *Religion in Life* 29 (Summer, 1960), p. 330.

8. Hogg, *Ecumenical Foundations*, p. 107.

9. A. J. Brown and JRM, "On behalf of the North American Committee," to "The Reverend James Buchanan," Jan. 31, 1908.

10. JHO, "JRM," p. 256.

11. There is as yet no biography of Oldham. This sketch is based on JRM-Y and S. C. Neill, *Brothers of the Faith* (New York/Nashville: Abingdon, 1960), pp. 100ff.; G. S. Eddy, *Pathfinders of the World Missionary Crusade* (New York/Nashville: Abingdon-Cokesbury, 1945), pp. 277ff.; Hogg, *Ecumenical Foundations*, pp. 109-10; H. R. Coston, Jr., *The World's Student Christian Federation as an Ecumenical Training Ground* (Northwestern University Ph.D. dissertation, 1963; Xerox-University Microfilm #64-2469), pp. 62-65; Ruth Rouse, *The World's Student Christian Federation: A History of the First Thirty Years* (London: SCM Press, 1948), pp. 130-31.

12. Hogg, *Ecumenical Foundations*, p. 109; Latourete, *World Service*, p. 356, Henry T. Hodgkin wrote Mott from China Dec. 13, 1908 suggesting JHO for such a post.

13. Richter, a leading historian of missions, was named in the Conference records as Herr Pastor Julius Richter, D.D., Schwanebeck, Belzig, Germany; Robson was a member of the committee appointed by the Ecumenical Conference of 1900 at New York to plan for the next conference; he wrote the official brief history of the Edinburgh Conference (vol. 9 of the *History and Records . . .*) which JRM reprinted in JRM-V, pp. 1-19. For the titles of the seven other commissions, see JRM-V, pp. 7-8. Oldham related many years later that during this meeting, the snoring of one of the delegates kept Mott awake, so he packed his bag and went to a hotel for the duration.

14. FMCNA, 1910, pp. 122-23.

15. JRM, "A World Missionary Conference," *The East and the West* 6 (Oct., 1908), pp. 368-85; see also Bishop H. H. Montgomery's comments about Mott and the SVM introducing the above, and pp. 459-60.

16. Cited by Hogg, *Ecumenical Foundations*, p. 115, from *The Student Movement* 17

(1915), p. 96; Coston, *Ecumenical Training Ground*, pp. 73–80, 108, 277–80; Tissington Tatlow, *The Story of the Student Christian Movement of Great Britain and Ireland* (London: SCM Press, 1933), pp. 405–11.

17. The issue was the bearing of the method of presenting statistics upon the Anglican stipulation that the Conference must not concern itself with missions in Orthodox or Roman Catholic lands. JRM to H. P. Andersen, Mar. 16, 18, 1909.

18. JHO to JRM, Apr. 13, 1908; the Yale offer is discussed in Chapter 6, above.

19. JHO to JRM, Sept. 23, 1909.

20. Gairdner, *Echoes*, pp. 45–46. Mahan was a prominent Episcopal layman who often spoke and wrote on Christian issues and themes, but was in failing health at this time. Robert Seager II to CHH, Feb. 3, 1977.

21. Wootton's idea, which, as well as his identity, remains obscure, appears to have been a grass-roots plan for comity; the scheme had the endorsement of Joseph King, a LMS officer and "one of the outstanding religious leaders in Australia": Norman Goodall, *A History of the London Missionary Society, 1895–1945* (London: Oxford University Press, 1954), pp. 541–42; Joseph King to "Mr. T. H. Oldham," July 27, 1909; *LMS Chronicle*, Australasian ed., Apr., 1909; JHO to Wootton, June 3, 1909.

22. W. N. Bitton to JHO, Jan. 12, 1910; JRM to JHO, Feb. 16, 1910; JHO, *Ecumenical Review*, p. 258.

23. George Robson to JRM, Dec. 31, 1908; JRM to Robson, Jan. 11, 1909, two letters.

24. Ruth Rouse to JRM, Mar. 2, 1910.

25. Beaver was the father of Gilbert Beaver; he was Governor of Pennsylvania 1887–91, judge of the superior court of Pennsylvania subsequently; at Edinburgh he chaired an evening session and spoke to one of the reports.

26. Mott's citation spoke of him as "a dauntless crusader who has found his mission in the advancement of the spiritual side of university life," exercising "an extraordinary ascendancy over the students of all countries."

27. Betty D. Gibson, "Man Before His Time," *Life and Work* 20, no. 6 (June, 1965), p. 6; A. T. Thomson, "Dr. John R. Mott," *Australian Christian World*, Mar. 26, 1926, p. 10. The author is deeply indebted to Miss Gibson, Dr. A. G. Macdonald, and Dr. Robert Mackie for a round-table conference, July 25, 1968 at Edinburgh, and especially to Dr. Macdonald for a conducted tour of the Assembly Hall. He had been an usher in 1910 and testified to the importance of that experience; other ushers or pages who became leaders in the ecumenical movement were William Temple, Neville Talbot, H. G. Wood, K. E. Kirk, John Baillie, J. M. Campbell, and Walter Moberly. Tatlow, *SCM*, p. 411; Robert C. Mackie and others, *Layman Extraordinary: John R. Mott, 1865–1955* (New York: Association Press, 1965), pp. 44–45; Coston, *Ecumenical Training Ground*, pp. 4, 21–22, 86–89, 308–10.

28. Gairdner, *Echoes*, p. 68; J. H. Nichols, *History of Christianity, 1650–1950* (New York: Ronald Press, 1956), pp. 438–39.

29. Gairdner, *Echoes*, p. 92.

30. Basil Mathews, *John R. Mott, World Citizen* (New York/London: Harper, 1934), pp. 318–24.

31. The bell was contained in a "neat and compact" wooden box (8x5x3 inches) equipped with a long cable and pushbutton; it must have been rung by Mott himself because he took into account certain delegates' handicaps; it was provided by Harry W. Smith, treasurer of the Conference, who later refurbished it and offered it for use at the Jerusalem Conference of 1928: Smith to B. D. Gibson, Feb. 2, 1928.

32. Gairdner, *Echoes*, pp. 63–65.

33. Coston, *Ecumenical Training Ground*, pp. 80–82 and elsewhere provides invaluable biographical sketches of Oriental leaders; their exposure and influence were far out of

proportion to their small number: Hans-Ruedi Weber, *Asia and the Ecumenical Movement, 1895-1961* (London: SCM Press, 1966), pp. 132-33.

34. JRM-V, p. 681; Gairdner, *Echoes,* ch. 12.

35. Gairdner, *Echoes,* pp. 183-86.

36. JHO, "Reflections on Edinburgh, 1910," *Religion in Life* 29 (Summer, 1960), pp. 335-36.

37. When in 1942 Mott and Oldham recalled these years, JHO acknowledged his debt to Mott for choosing him and persuading him to accept the secretaryship, which was "the turning point" of his life: JHO to JRM, Mar. 16, 1942; JRM to JHO, Apr. 13, 1942.

38. Livingstone's words were: "I view the end of the geographical feat as the beginning of the missionary enterprise." David Livingstone, *Missionary Travels and Researches in South Africa* (New York: Harper, 1858), p. 718; W. G. Blaikie, *The Personal Life of David Livingstone, LL.D., D.C.L.* (New York: Harper, 1881), p. 190. Mott dedicated Volume V of his *Addresses and Papers* (New York: Association Press, 1947) to Livingstone, Oldham, Cheng Ching-yi, and Gustav Warneck. For JRM's Tokyo, 1907, address, see JRM-II, pp. 567-73.

39. JRM-V, p. 22.

40. C. H. Brent, *The Inspiration of Responsibility and Other Papers* (London: Longmans, 1916), p. 67; R. Pierce Beaver, *Ecumenical Beginnings in Protestant World Mission: A History of Comity* (New York: Nelson, 1962), pp. 78-79.

41. JHO, "Reflections," p. 336; he added that insofar as human agency was concerned, the Continuation Committee and its sequel were due "to the imagination and driving power" of Mott.

42. In Rouse and Neill, *Ecumenical Movement,* pp. 329, 363.

43. *StW* 3 (Oct., 1910), pp. 157-58.

44. JRM, *The Decisive Hour of Christian Missions* (New York: SVM, 1910), pp. 236-39.

45. *Decisive Hour* was widely used in the mission study movement in the churches of Scotland; that generation of youth regarded Mott as "in the direct line of the apostles": R. G. Macdonald to CHH, 9/7/69.

46. FMCNA, 1911, pp. 158-70.

47. Silas McBee, *An Eirenic Itinerary* (New York: Longmans, 1911), pp. 176-81; JRM-VI, p. 418. This narrative has also utilized Leila Mott's Diary but especially JRM's notes to his many conversations with Orthodox and other authorities.

48. McBee, *Eirenic Itinerary,* pp. 5-6.

49. Rouse, *WSCF,* pp. 142, 147-48.

50. H.-L. Henriod, "John R. Mott, Man of God," *StW* 48 (3rd quar., 1955), pp. 223-24.

51. "Karl Barth on JRM," unsigned article (probably translated by W. A. Visser 't Hooft), *Ecumenical Review* 7 (Apr., 1955), pp. 260-61; CHH interview with 't Hooft, June 18, 1968; Karl Kupisch, *Karl Barth in Selbstzeugnissen und Bilddokumenten* (Reinbeck bei Hamburg: Rowohlt, 1971), pp. 28-31. Eberhard Busch, *Karl Barth: His Life from Letters and Autobiographical Texts* (Philadelphia: Fortress Press, 1976), p. 58: I am indebted to John C. Bennett for calling the Busch statement to my attention.

52. Two of Mott's addresses were published in English and Arabic as *Lectures on Social Subjects* (Cairo: Nile Mission Press, 1911); devoted largely to personal purity, they stressed temptation and overcoming; more explicit than usual, one of them relayed the current view that "loss of semen results in lessened virility." JRM-II, pp. 320-24; JRM-VI, pp. 34-46.

53. JRM, "Prayer as a Factor in the Student Movement," typescript [1911].

54. JRM-II, pp. 500-01.

55. Mott's notes to the interviews and audiences of this tour are an invaluable

source (in JRM-Y, XII-a.3); JRM-II, p. 498; Tatlow, *SCM*, p. 416; CHH interview with Philip K. Hitti, Feb. 8, 1969.

56. Tatlow, *SCM*, p. 419; Rouse, *WSCF*, pp. 150–51; Tatlow to JRM, Jan. 25, 1911; JRM to Tatlow, Jan. 28, 1911.

57. JRM-VI, p. 393; the conference picture is in JRM, *The WSCF* (New York: WSCF, 1920), opp. p. 64 and in JRM-II, opp. p. 124; Rouse, *WSCF*, p. 154; Weber, *Asia*, pp. 64–65.

58. The College was opened in 1863, the Rumeli Hisar campus in 1871; the Turkish government expropriated it in 1971; CHH interview with President J. S. Everton, July 7, 1971; George Washburn, "Robert College," *StW* 4 (Jan., 1911), pp. 8–10; JRM-II, p. 514.

59. Rouse, *WSCF*, p. 154; McBee, *Eirenic Itinerary*, pp. 106–111; JRM-II, p. 512.

60. Mott would speak at Halki again later; CHH audience with the Ecumenical Patriarch Athenagoras I, July 6, 1971.

61. One of them, Andrei Petkov, later became a violent opponent of the YMCA in Bulgaria, organizing an Orthodox youth movement that was quite successful; he was subsequently Metropolitan of the Bulgarian Orthodox Church in North and South America and Australia: CHH interview with Archbishop Andrei, Mar. 3, 1969.

62. Conference *Report*, pp. 11, 229–30, 326.

63. Bengt Sundkler, *Nathan Söderblom: His Life and Work* (Lund: Gleerup, 1968), p. 98; the author is indebted to Bishop Sundkler for numerous courtesies, and to Gösta Thimon of the Uppsala University Library for a successful search for Mott-Söderblom correspondence that enriched his knowledge of the relationships between the two.

64. Rouse, *WSCF*, p. 157; Coston, *Ecumenical Training Ground*, pp. 241–44, 267–70, 312–13, 333; Allier, "Impressions on a Journey in Roumania and Greece," *StW* 7 (Oct., 1914), pp. 138–41.

65. Tatlow, *SCM*, p. 421; Suzanne de Dietrich, *Cinquante Ans d'Histoire* (Paris: Éditions du Semeur [1950]), pp. 57–58.

66. Conference *Report*, p. 269; for Mott's description of the Conference, see JRM-II, pp. 512–14.

67. Rouse, *WSCF*, p. 159; D. A. Davis, *Old Guard News* (Apr., 1965); Coston, *Ecumenical Training Ground*, pp. 130–45.

68. JRM-II, p. 286; Coston, *Ecumenical Training Ground*, pp. 180ff.; *StW* 4 (July, 1911), pp. 127f. Panaretoff became Bulgaria's first ambassador to the United States.

69. Ruth Rouse, *John R. Mott, An Appreciation* (WSCF [1928]), p. 10.

70. Tatlow to JRM, 21 June, 1911; JRM-II, pp. 284–88.

71. JRM to LWM, May 10, 1911. Mott's habit of writing while seeming to take notes annoyed some of his colleagues; CHH interview with Sir Frank Willis, July 17, 1968.

72. JRM to LWM, May 15, 1911; McBee, *Eirenic Itinerary*, pp. 128–30.

73. J. B. Harford and F. C. Macdonald, *Handley Carr Glyn Moule, Bishop of Durham. A Biography* (London: Hodder and Stoughton, 1922), pp. 327–29; Mott once said that the formulation of the morning watch idea came to him while strolling in Moule's garden at Cambridge, presumably in 1894.

74. Continuation Committee *Minutes*, 1911, item 41, p. 17.

75. JRM to Fletcher Brockman, Feb. 5, 1912.

76. C. P. Shedd, *Two Centuries of Student Christian Movements* (New York: Association Press, 1934), p. 304.

77. In contrast, the Edinburgh citation (see note 26 above) had emphasized Mott's activities among students.

78. Mott went on to emphasize the importance of leadership and advised the University to attract foreign students.

79. Tatlow to JRM, June 21, 1911; Rouse, Rutgers, Seton, and others joined in urging him to stay with the WSCF.

80. JRM-V, pp. 61-75, from *International Review of Missions* (henceforth IRM) 1 (Jan., 1912), pp. 62-78.

81. Continuation Committee *Minutes*, 1912, items 41, 49, 74.

82. Galen M. Fisher, *John R. Mott, Architect of Co-operation and Unity* (New York: Association Press, 1952), p. 99.

83. JRM-II, pp. 373-81; JRM to "Dear Alice," Feb. 23, 1912.

84. Alfred Boegner had been present at the FMCNA meeting of 1911; Marc Boegner, "John R. Mott: Half a Century of Recollections," *Ecumenical Review* 17 (July, 1965), p. 252.

85. JRM, notes, in JRM-Y, V, 1910-20.

86. Tatlow to JRM, June 21, 1911; Barker to Tatlow, 17/XI/1911; Barker, "Visit to Belfast," *The Student Movement*, 1912, in JRM-II, pp. 362-64.

87. R. L. Pelly to Tatlow, Mar. 18, 1912; I am indebted to the Librarian at British SCM headquarters, Annandale, for this and the items cited in note 86. A year later Tatlow was upset with Mott: Tatlow to JHO, 12 Nov., 1913. Mott had been at Dublin in 1894; see Ch. 2 above.

88. Rouse, *WSCF*, pp. 142, 144; Coston, *Ecumenical Training Ground*, pp. 246-47; Rouse and Neill, *Ecumenical Movement*, p. 509; for Siegmund-Schultze, see Herman Delfs, *Aktiver Friede* (Soest: Westfälische Verlags, 1972); Delfs planned a chapter on Mott's relations with Siegmund-Schultze but could not find a writer (H. Delfs to CHH, Aug. 11, 1976); see also *Lebendige Ökumene*, von Freunden und Mitarbeiten (Witten: Luther-Verlag, 1965).

89. JRM-II, pp. 372-73.

90. CHH interview with C. J. Ewald, Mar. 28, 1968; Fries to E. C. Jenkins, Apr. 18, 1912; JRM to JHO, May 4, 1912.

91. For this section, see JRM-II, pp. 399-411; JRM-V, pp. 79-178; C. H. Fahs, compiler, *The Continuation Committee Conferences in Asia, 1912-1913* (New York: The Chairman of the Committee, 1913); H. P. Beach, *The Findings of the Continuation Committee Conferences held in Asia, 1912-1913* (New York: SVMFM, 1913); G. S. Eddy, *The New Era in Asia* (New York: Missionary Education Movement, 1913); Hogg, *Ecumenical Foundations*, pp. 151-56; CHH-Y, ch. 17; Latourette, *World Service*; Coston as cited below. The financing of the tour is well documented including a CPA audit.

92. JRM to "My dear Lord Archbishop," June 14, 1912; courtesy of the Lambeth Palace archives.

93. JRM to LWM, Oct. 31, 1912.

94. Typescript of JRM's address kindly sent to CHH by the Reverend J. R. Chandran, Principal of the College, May 14, 1968.

95. S. C. Neill, *The Story of the Christian Church in India and Pakistan* (Grand Rapids: Eerdmans, 1970), pp. 146-47; R. P. Beaver, *Ecumenical Beginnings*, pp. 96-97; Beach, *Findings*, pp. 7-11. The author is indebted to the Reverend D. V. Singh for pointing out that Mott had been favorably impressed by the progress of comity in India several years earlier, and for directing me to the pages of the *Christian Patriot* for evidences of that progress.

96. JRM and G. S. Eddy, *Constructive Suggestions for Character Building, Pamphlet for Enquirers*, No. 2 (Calcutta: Association Press, n.d.), p. 12.

97. *Minutes* of "a conference of delegates from the Syrian Churches of Travancore held in Calcutta on the 1st and 2nd of January under the Presidency of Dr. Mott," typescript, p. 17 (Madras, n.d.); JRM-II, p. 411; JRM-VI, pp. 408-09; Weber, *Asia*, pp. 65, 204; Rouse, *WSCF*, p. 158; Rouse and Neill, *Ecumenical Movement*, pp. 652-53.

98. JRM to JHO, Nov. 25, 1912, Jan. 10, 11, 1913; IRM 2 (1913), pp. 269-90;

3 (1914), pp. 35-43. "Each C C Conference," Mott wrote his wife Dec. 5, 1912, "has its own distinctive individuality and makes its own distinctive contribution."

99. JRM, "The Bible as a world power," address to the Upper Canada Bible Society, Jan. 31, 1927.

100. For the China that Mott and his contemporaries experienced at this time, see JRM-II, pp. 309-19; G. S. Eddy, I Have Seen God Work in China (New York: Association Press, 1944); Eddy, New Era, pp. 87-135; F. S. Brockman, I Discover the Orient (New York: Harper, 1935); Shirley Garrett, Social Reformers in Urban China: The Chinese Y.M.C.A., 1895-1926 (Cambridge: Harvard University Press, 1970), ch. 5; P. A. Varg, Missionaries, Chinese, and Diplomats (Princeton: Princeton University Press, 1958); Weber, Asia, pp. 135-38.

101. JRM-II, p. 319; Hogg, Ecumenical Foundations, pp. 153-54; Y. Y. Tsu to CHH, July 28, 1969; F. O. Leiser to CHH, Sept. 28, 1970.

102. CHH interview with L. N. Hayes, June 6, 1969.

103. JRM-II, p. 311; StW 6 (July, 1913), pp. 103-06.

104. JRM-II, p. 319; Weber, Asia, pp. 79-80, 258-62; Eddy, New Era, pp. 120-25.

105. J. Genähr, "The Problem of Evangelization in China," typescript, from Evangelisches Missions-Magazin, Nov.-Dec., 1916 (JRM-Y).

106. LWM Diary, Mar. 15-16, 18, 1913; Eleanor W. Peter, William W. Peter, typescript (New York: YMCA Historical Library, n.d.), pp. 25ff.; Latourette, World Service, pp. 257-62.

107. The subject of this section has been partially covered by Eugene P. Trani, "Woodrow Wilson, China, and the Missionaries, 1913-1921," Journal of Presbyterian History 49 (Winter, 1971), pp. 328-51, and Michael V. Metallo, "American Missionaries, Sun Yat-sen, and the Chinese Revolution," Pacific Historical Review 47 (May, 1978), pp. 261-82.

108. JRM to C. H. Dodge, n.d.; in JRM-Y, Wilson file, 1913.

109. LWM Diary, Mar. 31, 1913; Colton, Memoirs (New York: YMCA Library, 1969), p. 137; Latourette, "JRM: A Centennial Appraisal," Religion in Life 34 (Summer, 1965), p. 379.

110. JRM, "An Unprecedented World Situation," Christian Workers Magazine (Aug., 1914), p. 782.

111. Fahs, Continuation Committee, pp. 371-85.

112. JRM-Y Rhee file; JRM-II, p. 438; Latourette, World Service, pp. 191-94; Rhee may have found it wise to be out of the country at that time; he held "unbounded admiration" for Mott throughout his lifetime: R. H. Edwin Espy to CHH, May 2, 1978. Yun was pardoned by the Emperor of Japan in 1915.

113. JRM, "The World Situation," an address at Cincinnati, May 18, 1913; Fahs, Continuation Committee, pp. 389-405; Hogg, Ecumenical Foundations, p. 154; LWM Diary, Mar. 25-29, 1913.

114. For views of Japan at this time, see Eddy, New Era, ch. 2; Tasuku Harada, "The Present Position and Problems of Christianity in Japan," IRM 1 (Jan., 1912), pp. 79-97; Count Shigenobu Okama, "A Japanese Statesman's View of Christianity in Japan" (an interview with Galen M. Fisher), IRM 1 (1912), pp. 654-58; R. H. Drummond, A History of Christianity in Japan (Grand Rapids: Eerdmans, 1971), pp. 243-45; C. W. Iglehart, A Century of Protestant Christianity in Japan (Rutland/Tokyo: Tuttle, 1959), pp. 135-51.

115. Hogg, Ecumenical Foundations, pp. 150-55; Weber, Asia, pp. 252-58; Fahs, Continuation Committee, pp. 409-67.

116. G. M. Fisher, Report for second quarter ending June 31 (sic), 1913; Latourette, World Service, p. 173; JRM-II, pp. 436-37; Tsunegoro Nara, A History of the Japanese YMCA (Tokyo: YMCA, 1959), p. 152, translated for CHH by S. Fujita; StW 7 (Jan.,

1914), p. 39; in an address before the Osaka YMCA Sun Yat-sen declared that the YMCA was established on a foundation of justice, humanity, and love and was "making great efforts to enable the peoples of the world to progress in the direction of international morality"; typescript, YMCA Library, Mar. 11, 1913.

117. JRM to President Wilson, Apr. 4, 1913.

118. Weber, *Asia,* p. 137; Beaver, *Ecumenical Beginnings,* p. 38.

119. JHO, "John R. Mott," p. 258; JHO to JRM, Apr. 3, 1913; StW 7 (Oct., 1914), pp. 150f.

120. Boegner, *The Long Road to Unity* (London: Collins, 1970), p. 40; Paul Conord to CHH, 13 Août, 1969; Conord, *Brève Histoire de L'Oecuménisme* (Paris: Collection "Les Bergers et les Mages," 1958), p. 71; Suzanne de Dietrich to CHH, Apr. 20, 1969, Mar. 16, 1970. Introduced by Raoul Allier, Mott spoke at the Temple de l'Oratoire du Louvre Nov. 11, on "Les Responsabilities du Monde Chrétien." For Allier, see Gaston Richard, *La Vie et L'Oeuvre de Raoul Allier* (Paris: Éditions Berger-Levrault, 1948), pp. 65–79.

121. JRM-V, p. 168; IRM 3 (1914), pp. 209–24.

122. Hogg, *Ecumenical Foundations,* p. 160.

123. *Minutes,* The Hague meeting, 14–20 Nov., 1913, item 138; JRM-V, pp. 177–78.

124. The 1913 Conference was reported in a 500-page volume (New York: WSCF, 1913); Rouse, *WSCF,* ch. 15; StW 6 (1913), pp. 32, 81–89, 110–13, 119–20, 155–56, and vol. 7 (1914), p. 118.

125. There is a photo of the statue in place in JRM, *The WSCF: Origin, Achievements, Forecast* (WSCF, 1920), opp. p. 46; JRM notes, "Statue at Princeton," May 30, 1913; CHH interview with Mrs. Margaret French Cresson, daughter of D. C. French, Aug. 20, 1969; CHH interview with Henry P. Van Dusen, June 22, 1970; F. D. Mott to CHH, Feb. 19, 1977. About 1965 the statue was repaired and transported to the French studio, Chesterwood, where it stands on the original base; it is on a 99-year lease to this National Trust for Historic Preservation property, Stockbridge, Massachusetts.

126. JRM notes, XIX.11.

127. Mohonk *Report,* pp. 492–96; Rouse, *WSCF,* p. 174; StW 6 (July, 1913), pp. 155–56; the statement was signed by Henry Roe Cloud, Sara W. Venne, Ella Clara Deloria, Henry Redowl, and Isaac Greyearth.

128. *Report,* pp. 469–97; Coston, *Ecumenical Training Ground,* pp. 264–77.

129. *Report,* pp. 464–65; in addition to the prayers in the compilation, Mott used some by Walter Rauschenbusch; the text of "Our Best Days" is in JRM-II, pp. 579–90.

130. Rouse, *WSCF,* p. 175; de Dietrich, *Cinquante Ans,* pp. 59–62; D. S. Cairns, "Impressions of the Federation Conference," StW 6 (July, 1913), p. 83.

131. JRM-III, pp. 63–67, 204–08; StW 5 (Oct., 1912), pp. 121–32, 6 (Oct., 1913), pp. 156–57; James C. Baker, *The First Wesley Foundation* (Parthenon [1960]), pp. 14–20; CHH interview with Baker, June 10, 1969.

132. JRM-II, pp. 258–62; StW 5 (Jan., 1912), pp. 36–37; JRM-VI, pp. 26–34, 46–54 was first given at Columbia in 1914; *Columbia Spectator* 57 (Mar. 7, 1914), pp. 1, 4; JRM to LWM, Apr. 25, 1913.

133. F. P. Miller (1895–1978), *Man from the Valley: Memoirs of a 20th Century Virginian* (Chapel Hill: University of North Carolina Press, 1971), p. 20.

134. Miller, *Man from the Valley,* p. 25, and "Plans for the Mott Campaign" (typescript, 1913) kindly lent the author by Col. Miller; CHH interview with Col. Miller, Mar. 22, 1969; JRM to Mrs. McCormick, May 4, 1914.

135. JRM to W. R. Moody, July 30, 1912.

136. There is no evidence that Mott was solicited to contribute to *The Fundamentals,* but there is a suggestion in a letter from him to his wife, Dec. 31, 1906, possibly related to their origins in a series of articles to be written for his brother-in-law W. W.

738   NOTES TO CHAPTER 7, PAGES 417-427

White by James Orr and others, for which Miss Gould had contributed twice as much as White had requested. For an astute comment on Fundamentalism, see S. E. Mead, *The Lively Experiment* (New York: Harper and Row, 1963), pp. 183–87.

137. Unsigned editorial, *StW* 5 (Oct., 1912), pp. 150–51.

138. CHH, *The Rise of the Social Gospel* (New Haven: Yale University Press, 1940), pp. 296–98; JRM-III, pp. 536–48; JRM, "Men and Religion," in Fayette Thompson, *Men and Religion* (New York, 1911), pp. 16ff.; JRM, "The World Problem," vol. 4, *Men and Religion Messages* (New York: Association Press, 1912), pp. 302–13.

139. Robins listed himself in *Who's Who* as "Leader, National Christian Social Evangelistic Campaign, 1915"; a biography of Robins is needed, but see the DAB sketch; JRM-II, pp. 188, 195. A long period of estrangement between Mott and Robins followed, but late in life they were reconciled: JRM-Y, Robins file.

140. *StW* 7 (July, 1914), p. 128; JRM to H. F. Ward, Mar. 10, Apr. 21, 1914, Feb. 2, 1915; Ronald C. White, Jr., and CHH, *The Social Gospel* (Philadelphia: Temple University Press, 1976), pp. 210–12.

141. JRM-II, pp. 254–58; JRM-VI, pp. 329–34, 335–38; Rouse, *WSCF*, p. 175; and Mathews, *John R. Mott*, pp. 303–04, speak of two conferences but I find records of only one.

142. JRM to Mrs. Emmons Blaine, May 20, 1914 (Anita McCormick Blaine papers, State Historical Society of Wisconsin); Mathews, *John R. Mott*, p. 303, quotes JRM to Mrs. Blackstone.

143. Mathews, *John R. Mott*, pp. 414–15; Fisher, *John R. Mott*, pp. 73–74; Latourette, *World Service*, p. 75.

144. Miller, *Man from the Valley*, p. 24; the Conference proceedings were edited by F. P. Turner, *Students and the World-Wide Expansion of Christianity . . .* (New York: SVM, 1914).

145. Address of Francis S. Harmon on the occasion of his election as general secretary of the International Committee (of the YMCA), Jan. 19, 1932, and CHH interview, Nov. 14, 1973; H. A. Bridgman, "Dr. Mott at Kansas City," *Christian World*, Jan. 22, 1914.

146. Report (note 144), pp. 3–6; JRM-I, pp. 203–06.

147. Report, pp. 17–47, 625–28; JRM-I, pp. 141–72.

148. Speer, in Report, pp. 99–111; JRM's closing address is pp. 42–45 of the Report; see also R. P. Wilder, *The Great Commission* (London/Edinburgh: Oliphants [1936]), pp. 84–85.

149. J. L. Barton, "The Modern Missionary," *Harvard Theological Review* 8 (Jan., 1915), pp. 3–17; R. P. Beaver, "North American Thought on the Fundamental Principles of Missions during the Twentieth Century," *Church History* 21 (1952), pp. 345–64; for Liverpool 1912, see Tatlow, *SCM*, pp. 441–50.

150. JRM-V, p. 680; FMCNA, 1915, pp. 50, 52–53; Rockefeller Foundation, *Annual Report* for 1915, pp. 29–31.

151. JRM to J. T. Bowne, Dec. 13, 1890; JRM to LWM, Dec. 4, 1913; no catalog of JRM's personal library has survived.

152. JRM-V, pp. 746–48; JRM-VI, p. 349; F. H. Littell, *From State Church to Pluralism* (Garden City: Doubleday-Anchor, 1962), p. 132; JRM, *Five Decades and a Forward View* (New York/London: Harper, 1939), ch. 2.

153. For the foreign work at this time see Latourette, *World Service*, pp. 64–69; CHH-Y, pp. 679–83; Colton, *Memoirs*, pp. 54–58; JRM-III, pp. 324–30.

154. CHH interview with C. J. Ewald, Mar. 28, 1968; Ewald to CHH, May 9, 1967; CHH interview with L. N. Hayes, June 6, 1969; CHH interview with H. S. Leiper, Mar. 5, 1968.

155. In 1935 Mott declared that he had been "identified with the Conference on Faith and Order from the days of the fruitful initiative of Bishop C. H. Brent." JRM, *Cooperation and the World Mission* (New York: IMC, 1935), p. 4; Coston, *Ecumenical Training Ground*, p. 19; Neill, *Brothers*, p. 48.

156. Tatlow to Archbishop of Canterbury, Feb. 11, 1913; Brent's addresses are in the Mohonk *Report*, pp. 214–24 and *StW* 6 (July, 1913), pp. 90–98; Brent, *Inspiration*, pp. 94–110.

157. Barbara A. Griffis, Ecumenical Librarian, The William Adams Brown Ecumenical Library, to CHH, Oct. 31, 1974; Rouse, *WSCF*, p. 158; Coston, *Ecumenical Training Ground*, pp. 212–14, from *In Memoriam: Bishop Valdemar Ammudsen, 1875–1936* (1937), p. 212.

158. CHH interview with Mrs. Walter Judd, Barber's daughter, Mar. 31, 1970; Fisher, *John R. Mott*, pp. 82–83; *StW* (July, 1914), p. 126.

Chapter 8: "Then Came the Test"

1. JHO to JRM, 5 Aug., 1914.
2. JRM-VI, p. 535.
3. K. Ibuka to JRM, Feb. 1, 1915; K. Muramatsu, H. Nakamura, T. Niwa, Tame Nishikawa, J. Kawamoto, K. Morita to JRM, Aug. 28, 1914; JRM to JHO, Aug. 27, 1914.
4. C. S. Macfarland, *Pioneers for Peace Through Religion* (New York: Revell, 1949), pp. 43–46.
5. JHO to JRM, 10 Aug., 1914.
6. W. R. Hogg, *Ecumenical Foundations: A History of the International Missionary Council* (New York: Harper, 1952), pp. 162–66.
7. JHO to JRM, 10, 27 Aug., 1914; JRM to J. L. Barton, Aug. 14, 1914 (ABCFM Archives, Houghton Library, Harvard University, by permission). C. P. Shedd and others, *History of the World's Alliance of YMCAs* (London: SPCK, 1955), p. 547.
8. JHO to JRM, 5, 28 Aug., 1914.
9. JHO, "The War and Missions," IRM 3 (Oct., 1914), pp. 623–38.
10. JRM, *The Present World Situation* (New York: SVM, 1914), pp. 207–08.
11. Springfield *Republican*, Feb. 28, 1915.
12. C. L. Fry, *American Lutheran Survey* (Mar. 22, 1915), pp. 41–42.
13. Woodrow Wilson, quoted by Howard A. Bridgman, "Today and Tomorrow with John R. Mott," *Congregationalist and Christian World* 99 (Apr. 6, 1914), p. 519, cited in *Harper's Weekly*, Mar. 21, 1914.
14. JRM-IV, pp. 996–97; Wilson, *The Minister and the Community*, pam. (New York: Student YMCA, 1909). Wilson to JRM, May 1, 1908; JRM to Wilson, May 5, 1908.
15. A. S. Link, "Woodrow Wilson and his Presbyterian Inheritance," in his *The Higher Realism of Woodrow Wilson* (Nashville: Vanderbilt University Press, 1971), pp. 3–20.
16. Wilson to JRM, Apr. 28, 1914; JRM to Wilson, May 30, 1914; Wilson to JRM, Aug. 15, 1914.
17. JRM notes "President Wilson interview, 12–12:35 P.M., Sept. 16, 1914"; see J. L. Grabill, "Cleveland H. Dodge, Woodrow Wilson, and the Near East," *Journal of Presbyterian History* 49, no. 4 (Winter, 1971), pp. 249–64.
18. Wilson, "To Whom It May Concern," Sept. 17, 1914 and others such as to Ambassador Stovall at Berne, same date.

19. JRM to Mrs. McCormick, Sept. 19, 26, 1914; JRM to J. L. Barton, Sept. 28, 1914 (ABCFM Archives, Houghton Library, Harvard University, by permission).

20. JRM to his sister Harriett, Nov. 24, 1914.

21. Ruth Rouse, *The World's Student Christian Federation: A History of the First Thirty Years* (London: SCM Press, 1948), p. 191.

22. Rouse, *WSCF*, p. 190; Tissington Tatlow, *The Story of the Student Christian Movement of Great Britain and Ireland* (London: SCM Press, 1933), pp. 518–21 describes Rutgers coming to his home after his ship had been torpedoed; Coston, *The World's Student Christian Federation as an Ecumenical Training Ground* (Northwestern University Ph.D. dissertation, 1963: Xerox-University Microfilm #64-2469), pp. 232–34, 250–52,

23. H. C. Rutgers, "A Visit to Berlin," *StW* 8 (Jan., 1915), pp. 12–17.

24. Karl Fries, "John R. Mott as I have seen Him," typescript, JRM-Y, p. 7.

25. Paul Des Gouttes to R. C. Morse, Sept. 3, 1914; Christian Phildius to Morse and to "My Dear Friend" (Mott), Sept. 7, 1914; JRM to Phildius, Sept. 25, 1914; E. Sautter to JRM, 10 Oct., 1914; document "Dr. Mott guarantees to provide . . . ," Oct. 19, 1914 (at Berlin). JRM-IV, p. 889. Shedd, *History*, pp. 547ff.

26. Rouse, *WSCF*, p. 200; Coston, *Ecumenical Training Ground*, pp. 246–47; F. Siegmund-Schultze, "Foreign Students in Berlin," *StW* 6 (Oct., 1913), pp. 129–32; 7 (July, 1914), p. 79; 8 (July, 1915), pp. 116–18; Karl Kupisch, *Studenen entdecken die Bibel* (Hamburg: Furche-Verlag, 1964), pp. 72–98; Hermann Delfs, *Aktiver Friede: Gedenkenschrift für Friedrich Siegmund-Schultze (1885–1969)* (Soest: Westfälische Verlagsbuchhandlung Mocker & Jahn, 1972); JRM notes to a conversation with Michaelis, Oct. 15, 1914.

27. JHO-JRM correspondence cited by Hogg, *Ecumenical Foundations*, p. 170; Axenfeld to JRM, Hogg, p. 404, note 80; I found no evidence that Mott met with the Archbishop of Canterbury that unplanned Oct. 12 in London; Mott gave much more than "marginal time" to missionary affairs on this trip.

28. F. de Rougemont, Fils, "The Value of the Federation in War Time," *StW* 8 (Jan., 1915), pp. 9–11.

29. Rouse, *WSCF*, p. 187; Paul Conord, *Brève Histoire de L'Oecuménisme* (Paris: Collection "Les Bergers et les Mages," 1958), p. 71; Conord to CHH, 13 Août., 1969, says that Charles Westphal, Robert Pout, and he himself were present.

30. Rouse, *WSCF*, p. 189; Allier to JRM, May 7, 1915, quoted by Rouse.

31. *Oxford Magazine* 33 (Nov. 13, 1914); Rouse, *WSCF*, pp. 194–98.

32. JRM's careful notes are in JRM-Y, Mn XII.A.6.

33. JRM, "Address on the War," typescript, used on various occasions, such as before the Iowa legislature, *Des Moines Evening Tribune*, Mar. 9, 1915.

34. Rouse, "John R. Mott," *StW* 23, no. 2 (Apr., 1930), p. 110; JRM to his sister Harriett, Nov. 24, 1914.

35. C. R. Crane to Wilson, Dec., 1914; from the Archive of Russian and East European History and Culture, Columbia University; papers of Charles R. Crane, Mss box 1232; by permission of Mr. John O. Crane.

36. JRM to Wilson, Nov. 26, 1914.

37. JRM notes to conference with Wilson, Jan. 6, 1915; Crane to Wilson, Jan. 7, 1915, permission as in note 35.

38. FMCNA 1916, p. 161.

39. JRM notes to "conference with Mr. John D. Rockefeller, Jr.," Dec. 7, 1914; FMCNA, 1916, p. 173; 1917, p. 85; 1918, p. 49.

40. JRM to JHO, Nov. 25, 1915, Jan. 12, 1916; Hogg, *Ecumenical Foundations*, p. 171.

41. JRM to JHO, May 19 (see also May 31), 1915; JHO to JRM, 11 May, 30 July, 1915.

42. JRM to JHO, Feb. 10, Mar. 17, 1915.

43. JRM-V, pp. 179-217; Augustin Turner traveled widely to obtain delegates to the Montevideo conference; CHH interview with Turner, June 9, 1969.

44. Ethan T. Colton, *Memoirs* (New York: YMCA Library, 1969), pp. 186, 255-59.

45. W. A. Brown, *A Teacher and His Times* (New York/London: Scribner, 1940), p. 221.

46. Ruth Rouse, "Panama Through SCM Eyes," *StW* 9 (1916), pp. 61-64.

47. JRM-V, p. 201.

48. JRM to C. V. Hibbard, Mar. 23, 1915; JRM to Emmanuel Sautter, Apr. 14, May 12, 1915; I am indebted to Jean-Paul Réymond not only for these and other occasional items but for securing the copying of the entire corpus of Mott correspondence with the World's Alliance for JRM-Y. See also K. S. Latourette, *World Service* (New York: Association Press, 1957), pp. 170-72, and Frederick M. Harris, *Service with Fighting Men* (New York: Association Press, 1922).

49. JRM notes, "My Activities in World War I," undated memo; for examples of early recruitment for work among soldiers and prisoners, see JRM to Harold C. Stuart, Mar. 29, June 7, 8, 23, July 1, Sept. 14, 1915 and Stuart, "Personal Impressions Gained while with the YMCA in the Training Camps of England," undated mss describing the "Flying Squadron," courtesy of Mrs. H. C. Stuart; J. Gustav White, *Caged Men*, unpublished mss describing work among prisoners, Hoover Library, Stanford; CHH interview with White, June 10, 1969; Raymond Reitzel, *All in a Lifetime*, vol. 1 (typescript, YMCA Historical Library [1970]), pp. 132-33, 143; Reitzel to CHH, July 14, 1970, Apr. 14, 1972.

50. JRM, "My Activities...."

51. Rouse, *WSCF*, p. 210.

52. Sources for Part 6 are JRM-III, pp. 395-408; CHH-Y, pp. 428-37; R. C. Morse, *My Life with Young Men* (New York: Association Press, 1918), ch. 25.

53. JRM notes to "Conference with John D. Rockefeller, Jr.," Dec. 19, 1910, with the Archbishop of Canterbury, Jan. 24, 1911; Morse to JRM, Nov. 14, 1913.

54. Ruth Rouse to JRM, 9-6-1911; Walter Seton to JRM, June 10, 1911; T. Tatlow to JRM, 21st June, 1911; Herman Rutgers to JRM, 22/6, 1911.

55. Morse, *My Life*, pp. 517-19; Morse to JRM, Sept. 5, 1915.

56. JRM-III, pp. 401-02.

57. JRM-III, pp. 402-06.

58. Mott's salary of $10,000 per year from the International Committee was not included; JRM to "Dear Mr. Gorton" (Mrs. McCormick's financial secretary), Sept. 23, 1915; JRM to L. W. Messer, Apr. 21, 1916.

59. JRM to Mrs. McCormick, June 22, 1915.

60. JRM-III, pp. 400-01; letters came from dozens of "Y" men and others.

61. *Los Angeles Times*, Aug. 27, 1915.

62. JRM to "Dear Mr. Marling," Aug. 10, 1915; in JRM-Y, pp. 400-01.

63. JRM notes, "50th Anniversary of R. C. Morse as Int'l Secy," Dec. 1, 1919; "R. C. M. 80 Yrs Old," Sept. 19, 1921; *Association Men*, Feb. 1927, reprinted in JRM-III pp. 714-18; JRM, "Foreword" to Morse, *My Life*.

64. Leila Mott to "Dear Anna" (Stewart) and "Dear Billy and Anna," Aug. 6, Sept. 2, 15, 1915; Mary Brockman to "Dear Friends (John and Leila Mott)," July-Aug., 1915; JRM-III, pp. 726-31; JRM's eulogy of Brockman was perhaps the longest and most moving he ever gave.

65. CHH interviews with Sir Frank Willis, July 26, 1968 and June 12, 1971.

66. Brockman to JRM, Aug. 10, 1915, in JRM-III, p. 406; Brockman to Wong Kok Shan, Aug. 21, 1915.

67. G. S. Eddy, *Pathfinders of the World Missionary Crusade* (New York/Nashville: Abingdon-Cokesbury, 1945), pp. 291–92.

68. Galen M. Fisher, *John R. Mott, Architect of Co-operation and Unity* (New York: Association Press, 1952), p. 109.

69. Colton, *Memoirs*, pp. 159–61; JRM-IV, pp. 976–78.

70. K. S. Latourette, "John R. Mott: A Centennial Appraisal," *Religion in Life* 34 (Summer, 1965), p. 379.

71. JRM-III, pp. 409–24; CHH-Y, pp. 436–37.

72. Morse, *My Life*, p. 521.

73. JRM notes to conference with Wilson, Nov. 8, 1915.

74. JRM-III, pp. 412–13; *Minutes* of the Conference on the supervision of the YMCA in Canada, Toronto, Dec. 29, 1911.

75. Murray G. Ross, *The YMCA in Canada* (Toronto: Ryerson, 1951), p. 268.

76. Owen E. Pence, *The YMCA and Social Need* (New York: Association Press, 1946), p. 135.

77. Colton, *Memoirs*, pp. 46–52.

78. Pence, *Social Need*, p. 129; CHH-Y, pp. 679–83; Latourette, *World Service*, pp. 67–70.

79. Memo prepared by Augustin E. Turner for interview with CHH, June 9, 1969; Latourette, *World Service*, p. 223.

80. E. Stanton Turner, "Impressions of the Manila Association," *StW* 9 (Oct., 1916), pp. 136–38; *Nation Building* (Manila: E. S. Turner, 1965); CHH interview with E. S. Turner, June 9, 1969; Latourette, *World Service*, p. 319.

81. CHH interview with Arthur L. Carson, Aug. 10, 1969.

82. For Porter (1882–1973), see CHH-Y, p. 639.

83. Channing H. Tobias, "The Student Movement Among American Negroes," *StW* 8 (July, 1916), pp. 111–16; W. D. Weatherford, "Has the Student Movement Developed a New Vocation?" *StW* 8 (July. 1916), pp. 103–10; see also "North American Indian Students," by R. D. Hall, *StW* 9 (1916), pp. 72–74, and by Paul Baldeagle, pp. 74–76.

84. *StW* 9 (Oct., 1916), pp. 155–56; Ruth Wilder Braisted, *In This Generation: The Story of Robert P. Wilder* (New York: Friendship Press, 1941), ch. 9.

85. *StW* 8 (Jan., 1915), pp. 32–33.

86. C. R. Crane to "J. C. B.," May 31, 1916; by permission.

87. Hoffman's report of Mar. 24, 1916 described "Gospel Meetings at Ruhleben," and included a list of some 150 names of men and their reasons for their "decisions."

88. Mott met R. J. Reitzel (note 49, above) at Vienna.

89. George M. Day, "The Russian Student Movement," *StW* 10 (July, 1917), pp. 241–49, reprinted in JRM-II, pp. 456–63, did not mention Mott's 1916 visit.

90. JRM, "The (Methodist) Missionary Conference," address to the Methodist Board of Foreign Missions, typescript, Nov., 1916, p. 17.

91. JRM, "The Church in the New World Situation," in C. S. Macfarland, ed., *The Churches of Christ in Time of War* (New York: Federal Council of the Churches, 1917), pp. 74–75.

92. Report letter sent to Mrs. McCormick, Edward S. Harkness, and others, Aug. 3, 1916.

93. JRM notes, "Evidences of Answered Prayer in connection with Trip of JRM to War Zones in June–July, 1916."

94. *Index of the Proceedings of the Lake Mohonk Conferences on International Arbitration, 1895–1914* (Lake Mohonk: Lake Mohonk Conference on International Arbitration, 1916); I am indebted to Mr. A. Keith Smiley for courtesies and hospitality in searching Mott items in the Lake Mohonk archives.

95. JRM-III, p. 401; Macfarland, *Churches*, pp. 19, 39–40, 46, 94, 198; Roger Dale Woods, *The World of Thought of John R. Mott* (University of Iowa Ph.D. dissertation, 1965), pp. 144–45.

96. Henry Ford to JRM, Nov. 24, 1915; Mott's reply is on the telegram in his hand.

97. Charles Chatfield, *For Peace and Justice: Pacifism in America, 1914–1941* (Knoxville: University of Tennessee Press, 1971), pp. 16–19; C. H. Voss, *Rabbi and Minister* (Cleveland/New York: World, 1964), pp. 144–45; JHO to JRM, Dec. 13, 1915; G. A. Beaver to JRM, Nov. 11, 1916 with JRM's reply in his hand on Beaver's letter; YMCA Library.

98. James L. Barton, *The Story of Near East Relief* (New York: Macmillan, 1930), ch 1; Grabill, Dodge, Wilson, and the Near East, pp. 254–55; *Protestant Diplomacy and the Near East* (Minneapolis: University of Minnesota Press, 1971), pp. 68–79; Herbert Hoover, *An American Epic* (Chicago: Regnery, 1960), II, 203–04.

99. JRM to Wilson, Nov. 10, 1916; Henry Morgenthau to JRM, Nov. 11, 1916.

100. JRM to Wilson, Feb. 2, 1917; Wilson to JRM, Feb. 3, 1917.

101. Robert Lansing to JRM, Aug. 18, 1916; JRM's detailed notes are a mine of information on the inner workings of the Commission; for background see A. S. Link, *Woodrow Wilson and the Progressive Era, 1910–1917* (New York: Harper, 1954), ch. 5.

102. Link, *Woodrow Wilson*, p. 143.

103. Colton, *Memoirs*, pp. 141–42.

104. CHH-Y, pp. 485–88; JRM-IV, pp. 743ff.

105. Wilson to JRM, 25 Apr., 1917; JRM-IV, pp. 743–56.

106. JRM, "The Opportunity of the Hour," address at the Second National Convention of the YMCA's of Canada, Ottawa, Nov. 3, 1917, pam. (National Council YMCA's of Canada, n.d.), p. 5. JRM address to Boston City Club, Oct. 11, 1917. JRM to Mrs. McCormick, May 16, 1917.

Chapter 9: Mission to Russia

1. Philip C. Jessup, *Elihu Root*, vol. 2 (New York: Dodd, 1938), ch. 43; Richard W. Leopold, *Elihu Root and the Conservative Tradition* (Boston: Little, 1954), pp. 116–22; Robert Bacon and James Brown Scott, eds., *Elihu Root: The Mission to Russia: Political Addresses* (Cambridge: Harvard University Press, 1918), pp. 91–147.

2. Sally M. Miller, *Victor Berger and the Promise of Constructive Socialism, 1910–1920* (Westport, CT: Greenwood Press, 1973), p. 173; Charles Edward Russell, *Bare Hands and Stone Walls: Some Recollections of a Sideline Reformer* (New York: Scribners, 1933), p. 292.

3. Charles R. Crane to Mildred Nelson Crane, June 27, 1917. The author acknowledges the kind permission of Mr. John O. Crane to utilize this and the other Crane items to follow, which are in the Archive of Russian and East European History and Culture, Columbia University. See also Crane to JRM, Mar. 24, 1917.

4. G. F. Kennan, *Russia Leaves the War* (Princeton: Princeton University Press, 1956), p. 22. See also T. A. Bailey, *America Faces Russia* (Ithaca: Cornell University Press, 1950); F. R. Dulles, *The Road to Teheran: The Story of Russia and America, 1781–1943* (Princeton: Princeton University Press, 1944); Peter G. Filene, *Americans and the Soviet Experiment, 1917–1933* (Cambridge: Harvard University Press, 1967); Alton Earl Ingram, *The Root Mission to Russia, 1917* (Louisiana State University Ph.D. dissertation, 1970: Xerox-University Microfilms #71–3418); W. A. Williams, *American-Russian Relations, 1781–1971* (New York: Octagon, 1971).

5. Filene, *Soviet Experiment*, p. 18; Ingram concludes that it would have been preferable if the Mission "had never made the journey."

6. Paul B. Anderson, "An Interpretation of John R. Mott, an American Citizen with World Horizons" (typescript, YMCA Library [1965]). The author owes a very large debt to Dr. Anderson for unusual assistance not only with this chapter but at numerous other points; see also Anderson, "Reflections on Religion in Russia, 1917–1967," in Richard H. Marshall, Jr., ed., *Aspects of Religion in the Soviet Union, 1917–1967* (Chicago: University of Chicago Press, 1971), pp. 11–33.

7. J. H. Oldham to JRM, 11 June, 1917; Creighton Lacy, *Frank Mason North, His Social and Ecumenical Mission* (Nashville: Abingdon, 1967), p. 227; JRM to Gilbert Beaver, May 16, 1917; JRM to Nettie Fowler McCormick, May 16, 1917.

8. Harper and Bernard Pares had traveled and studied in Russia together; for their method of research and reporting, see Pares, *A Wandering Student* (Syracuse; Syracuse University Press, 1948), pp. 136–38; Samuel N. Harper in Paul V. Harper, ed., *The Russia I Believe In* (Chicago: University of Chicago Press, 1945). For Mott's contacts with Root, see ch. 6, above, and JRM to Root, May 17, 1916; Root to JRM, May 19, 1916. For the meeting with Brandeis, see JRM to LWM, July 9, 1917, p. 8, and J. W. Long and CHH, "American Jews and the Root Mission to Russia in 1917: Some New Evidence," pp. 1–4; to be published in *American Jewish History*, LXIX, No. 4 (June), 1980.

9. CHH-Y, pp. 485–89.

10. John D. Rockefeller, Jr., to JRM, May 23, 1917.

11. Mott would speak with at least eight of the thirteen sketched by Harper; Harper to Richard T. Crane, Department of State, Apr. 4, 1917.

12. C. R. Crane to JRM, cable via the State Department over the signature of Robert Lansing, May 16, 1917.

13. This account is based on the official Log of the Mission, Mott's personal letters home, McCormick's Diary (hereafter CHMcC) with acknowledgment to the State Historical Society of Wisconsin, a 176-page record; McCormick, who had his personal secretary, was critical of the State Department for failing to provide interpreters and secretaries to all members of the Mission, June 22, p. 95; Paul B. Anderson attributed the relative ineffectiveness of some of them to these inadequacies (CHH interview with Anderson, Aug. 13, 1974).

14. CHMcC, May 20, p. 1.

15. JRM to LWM, June 2, 1917.

16. CHMcC, May 20, p. 4.

17. CHMcC, May 25, p. 15.

18. CHMcC, May 30, pp. 34–35.

19. Log, pp. 6–7.

20. Log, p. 9; CHMcC, June 4, p. 45. In this narrative, Russian proper names are spelled according to the Index (in vol. 3) of R. P. Browder and A. F. Kerensky, eds., *The Russian Provisional Government, 1917: Documents* (Stanford: Stanford University Press, 1961), with a few exceptions. For Horvat, see Kennan, *Russia Leaves*, pp. 189, 303–07, and John A. White, *The Siberian Intervention* (New York: Greenwood Press, 1969), pp. 97–99, 185–87, etc.

21. CHH interview with Hugh A. Moran, June 14, 1969 and photo by Moran of the group headed by Wang Ting-va, presumably the one that accompanied the Mission; Ingram, *Root Mission*, p. 28; Log, p. 10; CHMcC, June 5.

22. Stevens told CHMcC that it would require fifteen trains a day for 220 days to move the accumulated materiel: CHMcC, June 4, p. 46.

23. Jessup described the train as "resplendent" with the Czar's coat of arms; this is doubtful, for the Czar's private car had been invaded and damaged by rebels earlier and had been detached from the train. None of CHMcC's photos shows the insignia.

24. Jessup also erred in saying that the Mission boarded the Imperial train at Vladivostok. For conditions along the route, see C. E. Russell, *Unchained Russia* (New

York/London: Appleton, 1918), pp. 160–92; Fridtjof Nansen, *Through Siberia, the Land of the Future* (London: Heinemann, 1914).

25. Isabel Florence Hapgood, *Service Book of the Holy Orthodox-Catholic Apostolic (Greco-Russian) Church* (Boston/New York: Houghton, 1906); a revised edition was published in 1922 by Association Press, with an "endorsement" by Patriarch Tikhon that recognized Mott's agency in producing it.

26. JRM home letter, June 12, 1917; Mott expressed his pleasure in Moran's assistance; he had hoped to bring son John L. as secretary but this had not worked out.

27. JRM address to the Boston City Club, Oct. 11, 1917; stenographic report, pp. 14–15.

28. CHMcC, June 6, p. 55.

29. Log, p. 11; JRM-Mn, June 5, 1917; Mott's notes to this interview, more legible than some, are representative of the more than 70 pages taken in his shorthand. It has not been possible to document all of his interviews, some of which are only mentioned in the Log or in his home letters.

30. CHMcC, June 10, pp. 67–69.

31. C. R. Crane, to the editor of *The Commonwealth*, 5/2/33.

32. CHH interview with P. B. Anderson, Aug. 13, 1974.

33. Bernard Pares, *The Fall of the Russian Monarchy* (New York: Knopf, 1939), pp. 330–35.

34. E. T. Heald, *Witness to Revolution* (Kent, OH: Kent State University Press, 1972), pp. 103–04; CHMcC, June 5, p. 54; at the time, this phrase represented the thinking of the Mission; it had been used in a progress report cabled to the State Department from Manchuria.

35. Pitirim Sorokin, *Leaves from a Russian Diary* (New York: Dutton, 1924), pp. 50, 52, etc. Sorokin had been secretary to Kerensky and was later a professor at Petrograd University; banished in 1922 he taught at the University of Minnesota before going to Harvard: Browder and Kerensky, index, note 20, above.

36. Dimitri Fedotoff White, *Survival Through War and Revolution* (Philadelphia: University of Pennsylvania Press, 1939), p. 140.

37. CHMcC, June 22, p. 95.

38. Heald, *Witness*, p. 106.

39. Jessup, *Elihu Root*, p. 354; Kennan, *Russia Leaves*, pp. 32–41, describes Francis' tastes and habits as "the robust and simple ones of the American Middle West at the turn of the century...the portable cuspidor, with its clanking, foot-operated lid, may have been apocryphal; but there is no doubt that the Governor's preference for an evening's entertainment ran to good cigars, good whisky, and a few good cronies around the card table rather than to large and elegant mixed gatherings"; he took relatively little part "in the social doings of high Petrograd society."

40. Kartashev would succeed Lvov shortly; see John W. Long and CHH, "The Church and the Russian Revolution: Conversations of John R. Mott with Orthodox Church Leaders, June–July, 1917," *St. Vladimir's Theological Quarterly* 20, no. 3 (1976), note 10, p. 164.

41. See Part 10, below.

42. Paul B. Anderson, *People, Church, and State in Modern Russia* (New York: Macmillan, 1944), p. 45.

43. For Miliukov, see A. G. Mazour, *Modern Russian Historiography* (Westport, CT: Greenwood Press, 1975), pp. 146–49; Miliukov was a convinced westernizer and had been the Kadet party leader in the 3rd and 4th Dumas; Kennan, *The Decision to Intervene* (Princeton: Princeton University Press, 1958), pp. 325–26, comments that Mott, Crane, and McCormick were "strong partisans of the Kadet orientation." A brief sketch of Guchkov is in V. D. Medlin and S. L. Parsons, eds., *V. D. Nabokov and the Russian*

Provisional Government, 1917 (New Haven/London: Yale University Press, 1976), p. 34, note 5.

44. M. L. Levenson, comp., *Pravitel 'stvuiushcii Senat'* (St. Petersburg, 1912), p. 145.

45. JRM to LWM, June 25, 1917, p. 3.

46. According to Jessup, Summers had recently sent the State Department "some illuminating despatches" which were not read for some weeks and therefore could have had little or no effect on Lansing or the President at the time of the formation of the Mission: Jessup, *Elihu Root*, p. 354. Neither Mott's nor Crane's notes to these conversations in Moscow have survived; for Summers, see Kennan, *Russia Leaves*, pp. 43-45.

47. Basil Mathews, *John R. Mott, World Citizen* (New York/London: Harper, 1934), pp. 250-51; Long and CHH, "The Church," pp. 167-68.

48. Platon was then Exarch of Georgia and Chairman of the Holy Synod; after the defeat of the White Russians he emigrated and became presiding bishop of the Church in North America; for the body that Mott addressed, see Long and CHH, "The Church," p. 166, notes 20-21, and John Shelton Curtiss, *The Russian Church and the Soviet State, 1917-1950* (Boston: Little, Brown, 1953), pp. 16-22.

49. C. R. Crane, *Memoirs* [unpublished], p. 186.

50. Crane, *Memoirs*, p. 186.

51. JRM-VI, pp. 397-400, ends with the second point; the third as given here is as transcribed at the time, paragraphing added. Throughout his life Mott persisted in the error of calling this the "Great Sobor."

52. Crane, *Memoirs*, p. 186 noted that the address had the same effect on the vast audience as on the Archbishop the previous day.

53. JRM to LWM, June 25, 1917, p. 4.

54. Mott had been intimately related to Nicolay since 1899: save for this meeting, Mott appears to have had no contacts with students or the SCM on this visit; for Nicolay see Ruth Rouse, *The World's Student Christian Federation: A History of the First Thirty Years* (London: SCM Press, 1948), pp. 161-64; JRM-II, pp. 449-56; JRM-VI, pp. 376-77; and Greta Langenskjold, *Baron Paul Nicolay, Christian Statesman and Student Leader in Northern and Slavic Europe*, tr. by Ruth Evelyn Wilder (New York: Doran, 1924).

55. CHMcC, June 21, p. 91.

56. JRM notes, "Nobel, June 21, '17."

57. JRM, "Address at a dinner given by Mr. Emmanuel Nobel at his home in Petrograd," June 8/21, 1917; in JRM report of his activities for the Mission; also in *Recent Experiences and Impressions in Russia*, pam. (New York: YMCA, 1917), pp. 9-12.

58. Ingram, *Root Mission*, p. 158, from the *Times*, June 27, 1917.

59. CHMcC, June 24, p. 104.

60. JRM notes, "Baron Ginsberg," June 26, 1917, and Long and CHH, "American Jews," pp. 5-6 and note 18.

61. CHMcC, June 26, p. 107; E. T. Colton, *Memoirs* (New York: YMCA Library, 1969), p. 149.

62. CHMcC, June 27, p. 107; *Report* of the Mission, p. 28.

63. Verbatim text except for paragraphing; from JRM's *Report* to the State Department.

64. Pares, *Wandering*, pp. 240-41.

65. Harper, *Russia*, pp. 101-02.

66. Chicago *Post*, June 30, 1917.

67. A translation, in JRM-Y, from "*The Journal* (German), New York City, June 29, 1917"; the name of the paper was not included.

68. Karl Kupisch, *Studenten entdecken die Bibel* (Hamburg: Furche-Verlag, 1964), p.

124. J. H. Oldham to JRM, Oct. 15, 1917; P. B. Anderson, "The Declaration of German Members of the Continuation Committee, August, 1917," memo prepared Mar. 26, 1965.

69. Tracy Strong, "Service with Prisoners of War," in C. P. Shedd and others, *History of the World Alliance of the YMCAs* (London: SPCK, 1955), p. 553.

70. JRM to LWM, July 9, 1917, p. 2; Crane to Mildred Nelson Page, June 27, 1917; John W. Long and CHH, "T. G. Masaryk and the Strategy of Czechoslovak Independence: An Interview in Russia on June 27, 1917," *The Slavonic and East European Review* (London) 56, no. 1 (Jan., 1978), pp. 88–96.

71. Crane to Page, June 27, 1917.

72. Crane to "JCB and BC," Nov., 1930; Crane to "CSC," May 16, 1900. Baron Ikskul (Uxkull) was well known to American missions executives: FMCNA, 1907, pp. 60–61, 66, etc.

73. CHMcC, June 28, p. 109.

74. Pares, *Wandering*, pp. 238–41; Pares, *Fall*, pp. 422–23.

75. CHMcC, June 29, p. 111.

76. JRM to LWM, July 9, 1917; Colton, *Memoirs*, p. 145, says that the "Sobor" conferred an honorary degree on Mott; there is no other evidence of this, which, if it occurred, was more likely to have been by the Holy Synod. For some of the reasons for the generosity of the Russian Orthodox welcome to Mott, see Rouse, *WSCF*, p. 163 and Galen M. Fisher, *John R. Mott, Architect of Co-operation and Unity* (New York: Association Press, 1952), pp. 27–35.

77. Anderson, *People, Church*, p. 45. Lvov was discursive and confusing at best, which did not help with Mott's understanding of Church affairs: Anderson to CHH, Aug. 21, 1977. For an extended evaluation of Lvov see Medlin and Parsons, *V. D. Nabakov*, pp. 90–93.

78. The author is deeply indebted to his colleague John W. Long for a multitude of courtesies in the preparation, revision, and documentation of this chapter, especially the identification of many persons named in it, the spelling of Russian names, and for bibliographical materials unavailable to the author.

79. Long and CHH, "The Church," p. 170.

80. "The Church," p. 173.

81. "The Church," p. 175 and note 54.

82. JRM, *Report*, p. 2; Mathews, *John R. Mott*, p. 249.

83. For Rodzianko, see William Henry Chamberlin, *The Russian Revolution*, vol. 1 (New York: Grosset & Dunlap, 1965), pp. 70, etc.

84. JRM to LWM, July 9, 1917, pp. 5–6.

85. It appears that Mott was informally authorized by the Faith and Order leaders Gardiner and Manning to issue this invitation; JRM to "His Excellency the High Procurator of the Holy Synod," July 5, 1917; V. Lvov to JRM, July 6, 1917, both in JRM, *Recent Experiences*; JRM-VI, p. 401; also Barbara Griffis, Ecumenical Librarian, Union Theological Seminary, to CHH, Oct. 31, 1974.

86. Chamberlin, *Russian Revolution*, p. 162; P. B. Anderson to CHH, Aug. 21, 1977. That he did not take the threat of Lenin seriously is indicated by the fact of Mott's having jotted down the "Program of Lenin's Party" from *Pravda* a day or so prior to this incident (JRM-Mn VIII.2).

87. JRM to LWM, July 9, 1917, pp. 6–7; CHMcC, July 1, p. 119, listed the men as Harte, A. T. Burrie, N. P. Davis, E. B. Anderson (probably P. B. Anderson), E. T. Heald, Jerome Davis, H. A. Moran. For the Sliozberg interview, see Long and CHH, "American Jews," pp. 6–11.

88. JRM to LWM, July 9, 1917, p. 8, and Long and CHH, "American Jews," pp. 11–14.

89. For Lvov's characterization of Tikhon, see Long and CHH, "The Church," p. 178.

90. JRM to LWM, July 9, 1917, pp. 9-10.

91. Sorokin, *Russian Diary*, pp. 61-71.

92. Mott's notes assume the credibility of the witnesses; no doubts appear to have been raised. Three of the Americans present spoke and understood Russian; several of the "Y" men were familiar with the problem.

93. Williams would later be foreign editor of the London *Times;* Pares once described him as "linguist, saint, and scholar": *Wandering,* pp. 100, 122-25, 132, 181-83, 217.

94. JRM to LWM, July 9, 1917, p. 11. Unfortunately he did not do so.

95. CHMcC, July 7, p. 126.

96. JRM to LWM, July 9, 1917. If the author may be permitted a personal reminiscence, Mott's remark was repeated almost verbatim by Patriarch Athenagoras I, when I shared an audience with a Roman Catholic, July 6, 1971.

97. JRM-Mn, July 9, 1917.

98. Heald, *Witness*, pp. 111-12.

99. CHMcC, July 11, p. 133; July 12, pp. 137-38; clippings (JRM-Y), all bylined Tokyo, July 31, 1917, from the New York *Commercial,* the New York *Evening Sun,* and the Washington *Post;* a Mrs. Gregory Mason of New York was named as the source of the story; CHMcC said there were four or five fires, unquestionably incendiary; JRM to "Dear Hattie," Aug. 3, 1917; the Mission's train was delayed 32 hours.

100. *Life* (New York), July 12, 1917.

101. CHMcC, July 11, p. 133.

102. CHH interview with H. A. Moran, June 14, 1969; CHMcC, July 19, p. 151.

103. CHMcC, July 19, p. 151.

104. JRM to "Dear Hattie," Aug. 3, 1917.

105. CHMcC, July 29, pp. 170-71.

106. JRM to "Dear Hattie," Aug. 3, 1917.

107. Kupisch, *Studenten,* pp. 88-89.

108. CHMcC, Aug. 8, p. 176.

109. Donald E. Davis and Eugene P. Trani, "The American YMCA and the Russian Revolution," *Slavic Review* 33, no. 3 (Sept., 1974), pp. 469-91.

110. E. T. Colton, *Forty Years with Russians* (New York: Association Press, 1940), pp. 38ff.

111. Jerome Davis to JRM, received in New York, Oct. 30, 1917.

112. In a fund-raising address to the Boston City Club, Oct. 11, 1917, Mott described Kerensky:

He is a genuine, and a very magnetic, man, a man of remarkable personality, a man who just draws you, even though you do not understand Russian and he does not understand English, a man who in his person has been able to combine the divergent and warring parties of the Left, and who has carried that country through an almost impossible stage. I don't suppose he is a man who is equipped to do the building work that is required with the constituent assembly a few months later; but he is a man who ought to have our prayers, and may God help us to stand by him.

Stenographic report of JRM Address, "YMCA National $35,000,000 War Fund Campaign" (Boston), Oct. 11, 1917, p. 17.

113. JRM's report was Section VIII of "Appendices to Report of Special Diplomatic Mission to Russia, June-July, 1917," p. 3.

114. E. T. Colton (*Forty Years*) became the chief executive of this program; although it was closed out by the Soviets in 1923, a few Americans stayed on: H. Dewey

Anderson, *Always to Start Anew* (New York: Vantage, 1970), was the "last man out" in 1926; see also Davis and Trani, note 109 above.

115. JRM, *Recent Experiences*, p. 26.

116. JRM-VI, photostat facing p. 294.

117. Kennan, *Russia Leaves*, pp. 23-24.

118. JRM to "Mr. President," Aug. 30, 1917.

119. Ingram, *Root Mission*, p. 299. Wilson's treatment of the Mission may well have been related to his personal dislike of Root.

120. Colonel E. M. House to the President, June 4, 1918, in R. S. Baker, *Woodrow Wilson: Life and Letters*, vol. 8 (London: Heinemann, 1928-39), p. 160.

121. Eugene P. Trani, "Wilson and the Decision to Intervene in Russia," *Journal of Modern History* 48 (Sept., 1976), pp. 440-61.

122. John W. Long and C. Howard Hopkins are initiating the research for an article dealing with "The Root Mission and the Origins of American Intervention in Russia, 1918."

123. JRM notes to a conference with President Wilson, Jan. 17, 1918.

124. Robert D. Warth, *The Allies and the Russian Revolution* (Durham: Duke University Press, 1954), pp. 105-06.

125. It has not been possible to utilize all of Mott's notes to his many interviews, and doubtless some are missing. The personal or private nature of many of the conversations may have inhibited taking notes and their public use. That he shared his experiences with Wilson is well supported by numerous notes in addition to those cited. I am indebted to Professor Arthur S. Link, editor of the Woodrow Wilson papers, for a critical reading of this chapter and for generously allowing me to copy Wilson-Mott items not previously in JRM-Y, thus completing the coverage of Wilson materials in the Mott Collection.

126. C. R. Crane to Richard Crane, July 6, 1917.

127. C. R. Crane to "J. C. B.," July 12, 1917.

128. Davis and Trani, "American YMCA," p. 473, note 6.

129. C. R. Crane to Wilson, July 23, 1918.

130. JRM to "My dear Mr. President," July 24, 1918.

131. *Harper's Weekly*, Mar. 21, 1914, from H. A. Bridgman, "Today and Tomorrow with John R. Mott," *Congregationalist and Christian World* 99 (Apr. 6, 1914).

132. Crane to Wilson, Aug. 1, 1918; by permission.

Chapter 10: From War to Peace

1. JRM, notes, "Present Official Positions (c. 1917)," suggests that he regarded the YMCA, the WSCF, the SVM, the Continuation-Emergency Committee, the Council of North American Student Movements, and the NWWC as his major responsibilities; he hoped to give up the WSCF "in 1920 but possibly remain on the General Committee," to drop the "C.C. within a year," and the American SCM and SVM by 1919. Other relationships named were the FMCNA, the World's Alliance of YMCA's, the LMM, the Peace Union, the Alliance to Promote Friendship through the Churches, an FCC committee, the training camps committee; he overlooked Near East Relief.

2. CHH-Y, pp. 485-97; Frederick M. Harris, *Service with Fighting Men* (New York: Association Press, 1922), 2 vols.; Owen E. Pence, *The YMCA and Social Need* (New York: Association Press, 1946), pp. 139-43.

3. William H. Taft, "Foreword" to Harris, *Service*, vol. 1, pp. vii-ix; Pence, *Social Need*, p. 141; for the social note, see Donald E. Davis and Eugene P. Trani, "An

American in Russia: Russell M. Story and the Bolshevik Revolution, 1917–1919," *The Historian* 36, no. 4 (Aug., 1974), pp. 704–21.

4. E. T. Colton, *Forty Years with Russians* (New York: Association Press, 1940), pp. 36–37 and *Memoirs* (New York: YMCA Library, 1969), pp. 80–85; H. Dewey Anderson considered himself the "last man out" of Russia in 1926: CHH interview with Anderson, Apr. 1, 1970 and Anderson, *Always to Start Anew* (New York: Vantage, 1970), pp. 151–52.

5. Jerome Davis, *A Life Adventure for Peace: An Autobiography* (New York: Citadel Press, 1967); F. P. Miller, *Man from the Valley: Memoirs of a 20th Century Virginian* (Chapel Hill: University of North Carolina Press, 1971), pp. 28–36, 42–47 and CHH interview with Miller, Mar. 22, 1969; Davis and Trani, "The American YMCA and the Russian Revolution," *Slavic Review* 33, no. 3 (Sept., 1974), pp. 469–91; Orrin S. Wightman, "Excerpts from the Diary of an American Physician in the Russian Revolution," typescript, YMCA Library; Colton, *Forty Years,* pp. 188–92 lists those who served in Russia.

6. C. P. Shedd and others, *History of the World's Alliance of YMCAs* (London: SPCK, 1955), pp. 547–56; Galen M. Fisher, *John R. Mott, Architect of Co-operation and Unity* (New York: Association Press, 1952), pp. 83–84; H. R. Coston, Jr., *The WSCF as an Ecumenical Training Ground* (Northwestern University Ph.D. dissertation, 1963; Xerox-University microfilm #64-2469), p. 261.

7. Roger Dale Woods, *The World of Thought of John R. Mott* (University of Iowa Ph.D. dissertation, 1965), p. 163; CHH-Y, pp. 493–97.

8. JRM-IV, pp. 743–58; S. Wirt Wiley, *Memoirs* (New York: YMCA Library, typescript, 1963), pp. 230–35 and CHH interview with Wiley, Mar. 28, 1968; Wilson to JRM, Apr. 25, 1917, in JRM-IV, p. 754.

9. S. M. Cavert, *The American Churches in the Ecumenical Movement, 1900–1968* (New York: Association Press, 1968), p. 96 and CHH interview with Cavert, July 18, 1973; C. S. Macfarland, *Christian Unity in the Making* (New York: Federal Council of the Churches, 1948), p. 130; JRM-IV, pp. 756–58; Harris, *Service,* I, pp. 296–97.

10. W. A. Brown, *A Teacher and His Times* (New York/London: Scribner, 1940), pp. 236–37; John F. Piper, Jr., "The American Churches in World War I," *Journal of the American Academy of Religion* 38 (June, 1970), p. 155.

11. JRM notes, "The President," Sept. 26, 1917.

12. Piper, Jr., "American Churches," p. 151, from Macfarland, ed., *The Churches of Christ in Time of War* (New York: Federal Council of the Churches, 1917), p. 106.

13. R. H. Abrams, *Preachers Present Arms* (Scottdale, PA: Herald Press, 1969), pp. 55, 110–11; Woods, *World of Thought,* p. 154.

14. Quoted by Sydney E. Ahlstrom, *A Religious History of the American People* (New Haven: Yale University Press, 1972), p. 892, from W. W. Sweet, *The Story of Religion in America* (New York, 1950), p. 402.

15. C. Roland Marchand, *The American Peace Movement and Social Reform, 1898–1918* (Princeton: Princeton University Press, 1972), pp. 386–89.

16. Cited by Ahlstrom, *Religious History,* p. 882; Woods, *World of Thought,* pp. 152–53.

17. Norman N. Thomas to JRM, July 16, 1918; W. A. Swanberg, *Norman Thomas, the Last Idealist* (New York: Scribners, 1976), pp. 71–72.

18. Cavert, *American Churches,* pp. 99–100.

19. Marchand, *American Peace,* pp. 356–63.

20. James L. Lancaster, "The Protestant Churches and the Fight for Ratification of the Versailles Treaty," *Public Opinion Quarterly* 31 (Winter, 1967–68), pp. 597–619.

21. Piper, Jr., "American Churches," p. 154.

22. A paraphrase of JRM's notes, "At its close the War will Present an Unparalleled Opportunity for Reconstruction," JRM-Y, XIX.13.

23. JRM address to "Chicago Club," Oct. 2, 1917, p. 11.

24. The service flag, usually a small banner hung indoors in a window, displayed one star for each person from that home, business, or institution who was serving in the armed forces; a gold star signified a death. JRM, *The Tradition of the American Mother*, pam. (UWWC, 1918).

25. JRM, "When I Saw My Boy in France," *American Magazine* (Oct., 1918), pp. 6-8; CHH interview with John L. Mott and Irene Mott Bose, Nov. 29, 1970; E. C. Carter recalled this meeting quite differently: the two men met and talked, then Mott went on, silent for several hours; D. S. Cairns to "Miss Macdonald," May 16, 1918.

26. Roosevelt: "JRM is one of the men who have rendered the most consistently useful and disinterested service, not only to this nation, but to many other nations"; Taft: "One of the great men of this generation"; Wilson: "Certainly one of the most nobly useful men in the world."

27. Bruce Barton, "The Greatest 'Y' Man," *American Magazine* (Oct., 1918), pp. 9-10, 100.

28. JRM-IV, p. 894.

29. JRM Pocket Ledger for 1916-17, pp. 88-89, has the names and sums given by each donor.

30. Harris, *Service*, II, p. 521.

31. JRM-IV, p. 769; Wilson to JRM, Nov. 9, 1917.

32. JRM-IV, pp. 777-78; Basil Mathews, *John R. Mott, World Citizen* (New York/London: Harper, 1934), pp. 274-75.

33. G. A. Beaver to JRM, Oct. 10, 1917.

34. CHH-Y, pp. 596f.; C. S. Ward (telegram) to JRM, Oct. 18, 1917; Paul B. Anderson, "An Interpretation of John R. Mott, An American Citizen with World Horizons" (typescript, YMCA Library [1965]), p. 15.

35. For examples of these addresses, see JRM-IV, pp. 758-77; from July to October, 1917, his name was used as editor of a page "The YMCA in the War," *Ladies Home Journal;* one address was published in *Association Men* each month.

36. JRM-IV, p. 776.

37. George E. Vincent, President, The Rockefeller Foundation, to JRM, Dec. 28, 1917; JRM to Mrs. McCormick, Nov. 19, 1917; *Des Moines Register*, Nov. 23, 1917.

38. Wilson, telegram to JRM, Nov. 20, 1917.

39. JRM notes, "Pres. Wilson," June 18, 1918; the other organizations were the YWCA, the National Catholic War Council, the Jewish Welfare Board, War Camp Community Board, the American Library Association, and the Salvation Army.

40. JRM-IV, pp. 781-82.

41. Michael Williams, *American Catholics in the War* (New York, 1921), p. 201, cited by Harris, *Service*, I, p. 242.

42. JRM-IV, p. 805.

43. Irene Mott Bose to CHH, rec'd Oct. 4, 1967; CHH interview with J. Edward Sproul, May 14, 1968.

44. JRM-IV, pp. 784-97.

45. JRM address to the National Press Club, Washington, Sept. 19, 1918.

46. Colton, *Memoirs*, p. 136.

47. JRM-IV, pp. 797-98.

48. JRM-IV, p. 798.

49. John D. Rockefeller, Jr., to JRM, Nov. 25, 1918.

50. Nettie Fowler McCormick to JRM, Dec. 5, 1918.

51. Fisher, *John R. Mott,* p. 131.

52. *The New York Times,* June 15, 1919.

53. CHH interview with JRM, May 12, 1950.

54. JRM notes, "Why should the Association work be maintained and advanced during the War?" address at a department meeting, Sept. 12, 1917 and JRM-III, pp. 321-27.

55. Colton to JRM, Dec. 7, 1917; Murray G. Ross, *The YMCA in Canada* (Toronto: Ryerson, 1951), pp. 248-49.

56. JRM notes, "5,000,000 Building Fund" (JRM-Y): Mott indicated the disposition of each pledge on the master list of donors.

57. K. S. Latourette, *World Service* (New York: Association Press, 1957), pp. 70-71, 76-77, 417-18.

58. JRM to Wilson, Aug. 24, 1918; Wilson to JRM, 30 Aug., 1917.

59. See note 52, above; the citation in JRM-VI, p. 543, refers to Mott's activities "throughout the War" as related to the NWWC of the YMCA rather than the UWWC; a further honor was added in 1926.

60. Allen F. Davis, *Spearheads for Reform* (New York: Oxford University Press, 1967), p. 225.

61. Joseph L. Grabill, *Protestant Diplomacy and the Near East* (Minneapolis: University of Minnesota Press, 1971), ch. 4.

62. JRM-III, pp. 576-79.

63. JRM-III, pp. 579-84.

64. Mathews, *John R. Mott,* p. 308.

65. Wilma Dykeman, *Prophet of Plenty* (Knoxville: University of Tennessee Press, 1966), ch. 12; CHH-Y, pp. 540-42.

66. Mathews, *John R. Mott,* p. 302.

67. Mathews, *John R. Mott,* p. 303.

68. Sources for this trip are scarce, consisting chiefly of items such as speeches, notes to interviews, and correspondence.

69. JRM-IV, pp. 878-94.

70. Mott talked with the Archbishop twice on Apr. 2, 1918.

71. W. R. Hogg, *Ecumenical Foundations: A History of the International Missionary Council* (New York: Harper, 1952), pp. 183-84 mistakenly dated the April 4 Continuation Committee as Apr. 14; Mott was in Paris on Apr. 14.

72. Marc Boegner, "John R. Mott—Half a Century of Recollections," *Ecumenical Review* 17, no. 3 (July, 1965), p. 252.

73. JRM-IV, pp. 884-85.

74. JRM-IV, p. 889; Harris, *Service,* II, p. 372.

75. Myron B. Clark, Diary, May 6, 7, 1918.

76. JRM-IV, pp. 888-89.

77. JRM notes, "Pres. Wilson," June 18, 1918.

78. CHH-Y, pp. 497-504; JRM-IV, pp. 808-29.

79. JRM-IV, pp. 808-29, 851-64; see also Katherine Mayo, *"That Damn Y,"* (Boston: Houghton, 1920).

80. Harris, *Service,* I, p. x.

81. FMCNA, 1919, pp. 63-65, 128-37; 1920, pp. 37-38, 43-44, 70-89, 140-44; JRM cable to Lansing for President Wilson, Feb. 10, 1919.

82. JRM notes to interviews, Mar. 24, 1919; to LWM, Apr. 13, 1919.

83. JRM to LWM, Apr. 13, 1919; Ruth Rouse, *The World's Student Christian Federation: a History of the First Thirty Years* (London: SCM Press, 1948), p. 213.

84. JRM to LWM, Apr. 13, 1919.

85. FMCNA, 1920, pp. 72-75; C. R. Watson to JRM, June 17, 1919.

86. Hogg, *Ecumenical Foundations*, pp. 185–86.

87. JRM to LWM, Apr. 13, 1919.

88. Shedd, p. 474, from World's Committee *Minutes*, Apr. 17, 1919.

89. JRM to LWM, Apr. 23, 1919; Ch. Phildius to JRM, May 24, 1919.

90. JRM and C. R. Watson, "To the American Commission to Negotiate Peace," Apr. 23, 1919; Watson to JRM, June 17, 1919.

91. JRM to G. F. Close (confidential secretary to the President), Apr. 13, 15, 1919; Close to JRM, Apr. 14, 1919.

92. Hogg, *Ecumenical Foundations*, pp. 190–92; Emergency Committee *Minutes*, May 2, 1919.

93. Hogg, *Ecumenical Foundations*, pp. 192–95.

94. Burton St. John, ed., *North American Students and World Advance* (New York: SVM, 1920), pp. 17–19; JRM-I, pp. 370–72.

95. Woods, *World of Thought*, pp. 174f.; CHH interview with Lyman Hoover, Dec. 2, 1970.

96. Paula S. Fass, *The Damned and the Beautiful* (New York: Oxford University Press, 1977), pp. 335, 338, 346; there is no evidence that these students had been influenced by the Russian Revolution.

97. CHH interviews: with K. S. Latourette, Apr. 12, 1968; with John L. Mott, Nov. 29, 1970; with H. P. Van Dusen, June 22, Dec. 20, 1970.

98. JRM-I, pp. 375–77; SVM *Bulletin* 1, no. 2 (May, 1920), pp. 3–5.

99. Fass, *Damned*, p. 334; Milton S. Stauffer, ed., *Christian Students and World Problems. Report of the Ninth International Convention of the SVMFM, Indianapolis, Indiana, Dec. 28, 1923 to Jan. 1, 1924* (New York: SVM, 1924); W. M. Beahm, "Factors in the Development of the S.V.M.F.M." (University of Chicago Ph.D. dissertation, 1941), in *Schwartzenau* 3, no. 1, pp. 34–35; Ruth Wilder Braisted, *In This Generation: The Story of Robert P. Wilder* (New York: Friendship Press, 1941), pp. 151–54, 162; CHH-Y, pp. 642ff. Advocates of pacifism were present at Des Moines but they had not yet developed sufficient muscle to sway the Movement; the followers of Frank Buchman made an effort to capture it for their viewpoint: CHH interviews with H. P. Van Dusen, June 22, Dec. 20, 1970.

100. S. Earl Taylor, "Proposed Plans for the Inter-Church World Movement of North America," FMCNA, 1919, pp. 171–87. The principal source for the ICWM is Eldon G. Ernst, *Moment of Truth for Protestant America: Interchurch Campaigns Following World War One* (Missoula: Scholar's Press for the American Academy of Religion, 1972), which unfortunately does not utilize Rockefeller sources. I am indebted to Professors Valentin Rabe and Charles E. Harvey for suggestions and sources, especially Harvey's unpublished paper "John D. Rockefeller, Jr., and the Inter-Church World Movement of 1919–20."

101. Smith, *I Remember* (New York: Revell, 1936); CHH, "Fred B. Smith," *Dictionary of American Biography*, Supplement 2.

102. FMCNA, 1919, pp. 184–87.

103. *History of the Interchurch World Movement* (typescript, New York Public Library, West 34th St. Branch, ZKVA), organizational chart; possibly compiled by Raymond B. Fosdick, this 2-volume document is also at the Rockefeller Family Archives and in the American Theological Library Association's Microtext Project #38:I, ch. 1, pp. 48–49; JRM notes to his committee work.

104. Ernst, *Moment of Truth*, p. 57; JRM, "The Hour of Christian Opportunity," opening address, National Leaders' Training Conference, Nov. 5, 1919 (typescript, JRM-Y).

105. H. B. Grose, "The Interchurch World Movement Conference," *Missions* (1920), pp. 141–46.

106. JHO, "Memorandum on Survey" (to JRM), 14.II.20.

107. Grose, "Interchurch," p. 146.

108. JRM to John D. Rockefeller, Jr., Nov. 13, 1919; Harvey, "John D. Rockefeller, Jr.," pp. 7–8.

109. Harvey, "John D. Rockefeller, Jr.," pp. 8–9.

110. JRM notes; R. B. Fosdick, *John D. Rockefeller, Jr., A Portrait* (New York: Harper, 1956), p. 209.

111. Harvey, "John D. Rockefeller, Jr.," p. 13, citing Rockefeller, Jr., to JRM, Mar. 26, 1920.

112. JRM sent a copy of this 4-page memo to JHO, May 12, 1920.

113. Rockefeller, Jr., to JRM, Apr. 12, 1920; Rockefeller's pledge was for $15,000 of a $50,000 budget, open to an increase to $20,000.

114. H. B. Grose, "Dr. Mott's Mission to Europe," *Congregationalist and Advance*, May 13, 1920, pp. 642–43; also *United Presbyterian*, June 24, 1920; as of June 11, 1920, Grose signed personal letters on the stationery of the NWWC of the YMCA that were sent to a circle of influential persons, defending Mott's going on his tour and his having accepted a post in the ICWM with this proviso; Grose stated that Mott did not know he was writing.

115. JRM, *Five Decades and a Forward View* (New York/London: Harper, 1939), pp. 63–67; reprinted in JRM-V, pp. 748–49; for contemporary evaluations of the ICWM collapse, see James I. Vance ("father of the ICWM"), "What I Think of the Interchurch Now," *Congregationalist and Advance*, Dec. 9, 1920, p. 745; Anon., "Wildcat Campaigning by Ecclesiastics," *Current Opinion*, 1920, pp. 221–22; *The Continent* 51, no. 22 (May 27, 1920), p. 745.

116. JRM to J. L. Mott, May 15, 1920; Miller, *Man from the Valley*, p. 42.

117. JRM to John L. Mott, May 15, 1920; JRM-VI, pp. 541–42; D. A. Davis, *Visit to France, Italy, Czechoslovakia, and Poland with Dr. John R. Mott* (May–June, 1920), pam. (New York: International Committee YMCA's, 1920), pp. 4–5.

118. Coston, *Ecumenical Training Ground*, pp. 236–37, 320; Rouse, *WSCF*, p. 213; P. B. Anderson, "The Declaration of German members of the Continuation Committee, August, 1917," typescript, Mar. 26, 1965; Karl Kupisch, *Studenten entdecken die Bibel* (Hamburg: Furche-Verlag, 1964), p. 122; I am indebted to Anderson and to Walter Sundberg for critique and suggestions on this problem.

119. Kupisch, *Studenten*, pp. 124–27.

120. JRM to John L. Mott, June 10, 1920.

121. Latourette, *World Service*, p. 393; StW 13 (Jan., 1920), p. 36.

122. Davis, *Visit*, pp. 5–7; Harris, *Service*, II, pp. 469f.

123. John W. Long and CHH, "T. G. Masaryk and the Strategy of Czechoslovak Independence: An Interview in Russia on 27 June 1917," *The Slavonic and East European Review* 56, no. 1 (Jan., 1978), p. 96.

124. JRM notes, Conference with President Masaryk, Prague, June 7, 1920.

125. JRM to John L. Mott, June 10, 1920; Harris, *Service*, II, pp. 460–67, 470–71; Latourette, *World Service*, pp. 398–99; Davis, *Visit*, p. 8.

126. Davis, *Visit*, pp. 7–8; JRM to John L. Mott, June 29, 1920.

127. JRM notes, Conference with Field Marshall Pilsudski, Chief of State, June 11, 1920; Davis, *Visit*, pp. 7–8.

128. Principal sources for Crans are JHO, "A New Beginning of International Missionary Cooperation," IRM 9 (1920), pp. 481–94; JRM-V, pp. 222–28; Hogg, *Ecumenical Foundations*, pp. 194–98; Latourette, "Ecumenical Bearings of the Missionary Movement and the International Missionary Council," in Ruth Rouse and C. S. Neill, eds., *A History of the Ecumenical Movement, 1517–1948* (London/Philadelphia: SPCK/Westminster, 1954), pp. 363–66; for a photograph of Crans, see JRM-V, opp. p. 222.

129. Hogg, *Ecumenical Foundations*, pp. 172–73 and notes 91, 96; Anderson, "The Declaration."

130. JHO to JRM, 5 Sept., 1917; JRM to JHO, Sept. 24, 1917: In response to Oldham's translation of the German declaration, Mott wrote that he had not actually seen the statement itself previously, but had been "helped by all you have written in this connection."

131. The discussion of the issue by the American members of the Emergency Committee opened with "the French are ready for a meeting, for business, but not for reconciliation . . . not for cooperation"; JRM notes, Jan. 12, 1920.

132. Hogg, *Ecumenical Foundations*, p. 197, from JHO, *International Missionary Organization*.

133. JRM notes, Crans, June 24, 1920.

134. JRM notes, June 28, 1920; Mott also took part in the discussions of the relations of governments and missions, and of missionary education.

135. JRM-V, p. 682; Fries, "John R. Mott as I have seen Him," typescript, JRM-Y, p. 7.

136. Hogg, *Ecumenical Foundations*, p. 201.

137. JRM to John L. Mott, July 17, 1920; JRM pocket ledger for 1919–20, p. 39; somehow, during that week Mott managed to buy gifts to take home.

138. The sole record I have found of the 1920 meeting at Caux is a photograph, the gift of William G. Schram, comptroller for the American war services, who accompanied Mott on this tour.

139. Fisher, *John R. Mott*, p. 168.

140. Tracy Strong, "The World's Alliance in a Changing World," in Shedd, *History*, p. 477.

141. Strong, "World's Alliance," pp. 477–78.

142. Tissington Tatlow, *The Story of the Student Christian Movement of Great Britain and Ireland* (London: SCM Press, 1933), p. 518.

143. JRM-II, pp. 197–204, from JRM, *The WSCF: Origin, Achievements, Forecast* (WSCF, 1920), pp. 47–56 (excerpts from his report for 1920) provide the most authoritative account of the Federation during the War; Rouse, *WSCF*, chs. 16–18 gives more detail.

144. Rouse, *WSCF*, pp. 191–96, 216–17; Coston, *Ecumenical Training Ground*, pp. 177–80; Hans-Ruedi Weber, *Asia and the Ecumenical Movement, 1895–1961* (London: SCM Press, 1966), p. 81.

145. Rouse, *WSCF*, p. 221, citing S. Ralph Harlow, *Student Witnesses for Christ* (New York: Association Press, 1919).

146. Rouse, *WSCF*, pp. 158–59, 197.

147. See note 143 above.

148. *Church Missionary Review* (June, 1921), pp. 171–72.

149. StW 13 (1920), pp. 171–72.

150. Rouse, *WSCF*, p. 230.

151. The chief sources for the St. Beatenberg meeting are its *Minutes* and related papers in JRM-Y, WSCF Collection; Rouse, *WSCF*, ch. 20; JRM-II, pp. 160–229; StW 13 (1920), pp. 74–77, 118–19, 133–57; Coston, *Ecumenical Training Ground*, pp. 237–40; JRM notes; *Who's Who, Meeting of the WSCF, St. Beatenberg, July 30–August 7, 1920*, pam., p. 8. The decision not to meet at Vadstena may have reflected some resentment toward Sweden.

152. Rouse, *WSCF*, p. 228, from the Beatenberg *Minutes*.

153. C. D. Hurrey to LWM, Aug. 18, 1920; William Paton, "Beatenberg, 1920," StW 13 (1920), p. 146; Fries to JRM, Sept. 9, 1920; Kupisch, *Studenten*, pp. 126f.; P. Humburg to JRM, 18 Aug., 1920. Bengt Sundkler, *Nathan Söderblom, His Life and Work*

(Lund: Gleerup, 1968), p. 375, says that the "social" and the "eschatological approach," came out into the open for the first time at Stockholm." See also Coston, *Ecumenical Training Ground*, pp. 282–86, and Rouse, *WSCF*, pp. 267, 295–96.

154. CHH interview with S. Ralph Harlow, Mar. 24, 1971.

155. Rouse, *WSCF*, pp. 230–32.

156. Hurrey to LWM, Aug. 18, 1920. Joe Posey was a fishing companion.

157. I am indebted to Mrs. Elizabeth Norris, Librarian of the National Board of the YWCA, for Mrs. Mott's service: E. Norris to CHH, Feb. 3, Mar. 24, 1977; CHH interview with E. T. Colton, Feb. 26, 1970.

158. F. D. Mott to CHH, Nov. 14, 1977: "I recall the Brockmans, Hurreys, Barbers, and Coltons, and there were many others [who came to the new guest cottage]. This led to quiet and relative peace in the main house."

159. F. D. Mott to CHH, Nov. 14, 1977.

160. JRM notes; CHH interview with K. S. Latourette, Nov. 25, 1966.

161. Rockefeller, Jr., to JRM, Dec. 7, 1920.

162. JRM notes, "President Wilson," Nov. 21, 1920.

163. JRM to JHO, Feb. 16, 1921, suggests the heavy load Oldham undertook while in the United States, because of Mott's illness.

164. Grose, note 114 above; JHO, *Ecumenical Review* 7 (Apr., 1955), p. 257; Anderson, note 118 above, pp. 16–17; Colton, *Memoirs*, p. 138; JRM to Nettie Fowler McCormick, Dec. 22, 1920, Jan. 7, 1921.

Chapter 11: Ecumenical Statesman

1. JHO to JRM, Oct. 26, 1915.

2. JRM-III, pp. 658–67.

3. JRM-III, pp. 661–62; Mott was still receiving résumés of POW work that provided him with scores of case histories of individuals caught in the pincers of history.

4. R. T. Handy, "American Religious Depression, 1925–1935," *Church History* 29 (1960), pp. 3–16.

5. JRM-III, p. 674.

6. W. A. Brown, *Toward a United Church* (New York: Scribners, 1946), p. 61; W. R. Hogg, *Ecumenical Foundations: A History of the International Missionary Council* (New York: Harper, 1952), pp. 200–01; JHO to JRM, Oct. 26, Nov. 4, 1915.

7. Resources for the IMC at Mohonk are Hogg, *Ecumenical Foundations*, ch. V; JRM-V, pp. 222–41; *Minutes* of the IMC, Lake Mohonk, New York, U.S.A., October 1-6, 1921; the JHO-JRM correspondence.

8. JRM to Richter, May 2, 1921; JHO to JRM, 8 July, 1921.

9. Hogg, *Ecumenical Foundations*, p. 205.

10. JRM, "International Missionary Cooperation," IRM 11 (1922), pp. 43–72; it was printed as a pamphlet for the use of the conference.

11. C. E. Harvey, "John D. Rockefeller, Jr., and the Institute of Social and Religious Research, 1921–1934: A Key to the Ecumenical Movement," unpublished; I am indebted to Dr. Harvey for a critique of this section. JRM-V, pp. 742–45 is an excerpt from Galen M. Fisher, *The Institute of Social and Religious Research, 1921–1934* (n.p. [1934]).

12. Studies dealt with rural and urban churches, home and foreign missions, Christian education, theological education, and racial aspects of organized religion. Researchers included Edmund deS. Brunner, C. Luther Fry, Benson Y. Landis, H. Paul

Douglas, Mark A. May, Hugh Hartshorne, J. Quinter Miller, Benjamin E. Mays, Arthur L. Carson, and Edwin D. Starbuck.

13. JRM, "Foreword" to Fisher, *The Institute,* p. 5.

14. Sources for this tour are spotty; Ruth Rouse, *The World's Student Christian Federation: A History of the First Thirty Years* (London: SCM Press, 1948), pp. 280–81; Hans-Ruedi Weber, *Asia and the Ecumenical Movement, 1895–1961* (London: SCM Press, 1966), pp. 83, 262; StW (Jan., 1922), entire issue.

15. JRM to JHO, Jan. 12, 1922; JRM notes to visit in Washington, Jan. 5, 1922.

16. *John Merle Davis, An Autobiography* (Kyo Bun Kwan [1962]), pp. 74–75. Cleveland H. Dodge provided Mott with funds for this purpose.

17. CHH interview with K. S. Latourette, Apr. 12, 1968; R. P. Beaver, *Ecumenical Beginnings in Protestant World Mission: A History of Comity* (New York: Nelson, 1962), pp. 124–33.

18. Weber, *Asia,* p. 85; StW (1922), p. 104; H. R. Coston, *The WSCF as an Ecumenical Training Ground* (Northwestern University Ph.D. dissertation, 1963: Xerox-University Microfilm #64-2469), pp. 220, 336; CHH interview with H. S. Leiper, Mar. 5, 1968; Rouse, *WSCF,* pp. 274–77.

19. W. A. Visser 't Hooft, *Memoirs* (London/Philadelphia: SCM/Westminster Press, 1973), p. 11.

20. Karl Kupisch, *Studenten entdecken die Bibel* (Hamburg: Furche-Verlag, 1964), p. 133; CHH interviews with Latourette, Leiper; E. E. Barnett, *As I Look Back: Memoirs* (YMCA Library, typescript, n.d.), pp. 179–84; Ruth Rouse to JRM, Oct. 6, 1922; JRM to Rouse, May 12, Oct. 18, 1922.

21. Rouse, *WSCF,* p. 275 and ch. 26; Paul B. Anderson to CHH, Apr. 11, 1978, suggests that the turning point in China was 1922 rather than 1926 as Garrett (note 26 below, pp. 173–74) holds. Latourette, *Beyond the Ranges. An Autobiography* (Grand Rapids: Eerdmans, 1967), pp. 65–67.

22. Hogg, *Ecumenical Foundations,* pp. 211–12; Weber, *Asia,* pp. 140–41.

23. JRM-V, pp. 600–08; Mott wanted E. E. Barnett to take on the general secretaryship but Barnett was "sure that I did not have the capacity he had to keep so many balls in the air" and refused; Hodgkin, K. T. Chung, and Miss Y. J. Fan were appointed: Barnett to CHH, Oct. 7, 1966.

24. JHO to JRM, Apr. 26, 1922; Rowland M. Cross to CHH, rec'd Apr. 28, 1970.

25. Mott discussed the report before an Association of Universities and Colleges at Shanghai, May 1, 1922; for the Burton report see D. L. Lindberg, "The Oriental Educational Commission's Recommendations for Mission Strategy in Higher Education," University of Chicago Ph.D. dissertation, 1972.

26. Shirley S. Garrett, *Social Reformers in Urban China: The Chinese Y.M.C.A., 1895–1926* (Cambridge: Harvard University Press, 1970), pp. 170–83; CHH interview with L. N. Hayes, June 6, 1969.

27. For religious affairs in Japan at this time, see C. W. Iglehart, *A Century of Protestant Christianity in Japan* (Rutland/Tokyo: Tuttle, 1959), pp. 164–89; R. H. Drummond, *A History of Christianity in Japan* (Grand Rapids: Eerdmans, 1971), pp. 241–48.

28. In claiming to have visited Japan ten times, Mott counted this return as a separate tour; Saito and Nara kept their total at ten by incorrectly adding one on the return from the Root Mission, which Mott did not do.

29. *Japan Advertiser,* May 19, 1922; *Japan Evangelist* 39, pp. 172–76, 186–92; Hogg, *Ecumenical Foundations,* pp. 212–13; Weber, *Asia,* p. 141 and note 2; for the American Federal Council "creed" see CHH, *Rise of the Social Gospel* (New Haven: Yale University Press, 1940), pp. 316–17.

30. For the YMCA in Japan at this time, see Latourette, *World Service* (New York: Association Press, 1957), pp. 172–78.

31. *Japan Advertiser*, May 20, 23, 1922.

32. Bengt Sundkler, *Nathan Söderblom, His Life and Work* (Lund: Gleerup, 1968), pp. 331-32.

33. Sources for this section: CHH-Y, ch. 10; JRM-IV, pp. 909-952; Owen E. Pence, *The Y.M.C.A. and Social Need* (New York: Association Press, 1946), pp. 144-50.

34. E. T. Colton, *Memoirs* (New York: YMCA Library, 1969), pp. 76-77; CHH interview with Colton, Feb. 26, 1970.

35. Pence, *Social Need*, pp. 145-47, from the *Survey of the International Committee of YMCAs* (New York: privately printed, 1923); JRM-John D. Rockefeller, Jr., correspondence. Raymond B. Fosdick, *John D. Rockefeller, Jr., A Portrait* (New York: Harper, 1956), pp. 107-10.

36. Fries to JRM, Oct. 25, 1923.

37. JRM to Fries, Nov. 9, 1923; JRM-IV, pp. 916, 942-43; CHH interview with J. Edward Sproul, May 14, 1968.

38. Colton, *Memoirs*, p. 138; Robert E. Lewis was another critic. Mott wrote to D. A. Davis, Jan. 16, 1928, that a letter from Lewis filled him with "a sense of sadness" over what he called Lewis' total misapprehension of certain facts; Mott likewise refused to be drawn into criticizing colleagues about whom controversy centered: JRM to Mae P. Kaplan, Dec. 28, 1933, refusing comment other than commendation of Frank Buchman's work at Penn State "over twenty years ago." For Mott's statement at Messer's death, see JRM-III, p. 474.

39. H. W. Stone, "An Open Letter to the Members of the National Council of the YMCAs of the United States of America," Nov. 12, 1924; JRM-IV, pp. 937-40; Mott's salary was increased to $12,000.

40. S. Wirt Wiley, *Memoirs* (New York: YMCA Library, typescript, 1963); CHH interview with Wiley, Mar. 28, 1968; Colton, *Memoirs*, pp. 77f. CHH interview with H. Dewey Anderson, Apr. 1, 1970: Anderson's generalizations about Mott began with calling him a religious statesman who had faith yet lived in the world, and was always interested in the broad relationships of peoples and countries; he did not "pigeonhole" spirituality; he knew the top group in any situation, was himself on the borderline of the truly great; his interviews with leaders were not one-sided; he leaned toward the social gospel, even endorsing Jerome Davis' views; he never let one down, recognizing that there are younger and less spiritually-minded men who are not lost souls. For Anderson's Russian experience, see Harry D. Anderson, "Y.M.C.A. Expelled from Russia," *Literary Digest* 91, no. 37 (Nov. 20, 1926).

41. Colton, *Memoirs*, pp. 158-59 and "As I Knew Him," *Old Guard News* 36 (May, 1965), pp. 1-3; Colton to CHH, Nov. 3, 1967.

42. The family continued these arrangements for some years.

43. JRM-John D. Rockefeller, Jr., correspondence, 1921-22; CHH interview with Earl Brandenberg, Dec. 16, 1969; JRM-III, p. 461; JRM to Karl Fries, Oct. 17, 29, 1924; V. Schlaeppi to JRM, Oct. 28, 1929; Brandenberg named Raymond Kaighn as the first to propose the fund. L. K. Hall to CHH, Feb. 2, 1968 and *Doggett of Springfield* (New York: Association Press, 1964), pp. 122, 185. For the YMCA Graduate School see CHH-Y, pp. 610-14 and Wilma Dykeman, *Prophet of Plenty: The First Ninety years of W. D. Weatherford* (Knoxville: University of Tennessee Press, 1966), ch. 13. For Mott's suggestions to secretaries, see JRM-VI, pp. 493-505, 513-14; and Paul L. Hershey, ed., *Things of the Spirit* (Indianapolis), Apr-June, 1975; and Hershey to CHH, May 19, 1975.

44. JRM-III, pp. 576-658; CHH-Y, ch. 13.

45. Colton, *Memoirs*, p. 136.

46. JRM, *Confronting Young Men With the Living Christ* (New York: Association Press, 1923), p. 8; CHH-Y, pp. 590-93; Handy, "American Religious Depression," note 4 above.

47. JRM, *Addresses... at the First Southern Regional Conference (of the) YMCA, Atlanta, Georgia, April 28, 29, 1921,* pam. (n.p., n.d.), pp. 8–24; Mott repeated this address several times before large audiences. Much of the Baptist criticism was by J. B. Gambrel and appeared in the *Baptist Standard* of Dallas of which the issue of June 5, 1919 was a good example; see also JRM-IV, pp. 851–64.

48. JRM to "My dear Judge Gary," Apr. 8, 1920; JRM to John D. Rockefeller, Jr., Apr. 8, 1920; Rockefeller to JRM, Apr. 6, 1920; Ralph M. Easley to C. L. Close, Mar. 29, 1920.

49. Colton, *Memoirs,* pp. 137–38.

50. Galen M. Fisher, *John R. Mott, Architect of Co-operation and Unity* (New York: Association Press, 1952), p. 172.

51. G. S. Eddy, *A Pilgrimage of Ideas* (New York: Farrar and Rinehart, 1934), p. 206; Eddy, *Eighty Adventurous Years* (New York: Harper, 1955), p. 113; CHH interview with C. J. Ewald, Mar. 3, 1968.

52. Eddy, *Pilgrimage,* p. 206.

53. Timothy L. Smith, *Revivalism and Social Reform* (New York/Nashville: Abingdon, 1957), p. 8; CHH, *Rise of the Social Gospel,* p. 318.

54. CHH-Y, pp. 642–45; JRM-III, pp. 439–40, 462, 481, 487, 515–16; JRM-IV, pp. 932, 955–56.

55. JRM-VI, pp. 220–21.

56. JRM-VI, p. 234; Latourette, *Beyond the Ranges,* pp. 69–70; R. E. Lewis, "The Swan Song of the Founders," *Men* (1923-24), pp. 260ff.; Paula S. Fass, *The Damned and the Beautiful* (New York: Oxford University Press, 1977), p. 346.

57. JRM-I, pp. 214, 228, 238–39. In 1935 he spoke of "the social aspect of the all-embracing integral gospel": JRM-VI, p. 275.

58. CHH-Y, pp. 580–82.

59. *Minutes,* First Southern Regional Conference of the YMCA, with addresses by John R. Mott, Atlanta, 1921, pp. 54–55, 62, 64–65, 70–72. Ronald C. White and CHH, *The Social Gospel: Religion and Reform in Changing America* (Philadelphia: Temple University Press, 1976), pp. 93–96; Dykeman, *Prophet,* pp. 137–43; CHH-Y, pp. 727–29.

60. *StW* 14 (July, 1921), pp. 112–13.

61. Moton was the successor of Booker T. Washington as principal of Tuskegee, and was a member of the International Committee of the YMCA; he and Mott are pictured together in JRM-III, opp. p. 505 where in the text Mott reported the recent formation of 800 local and county interracial committees "in the southern region alone."

62. JRM-V, pp. 608–20.

63. This address was first given at a missionary convention in Washington, D.C., Feb. 1, 1925; it was printed in the *Report* of the Australian Missionary Conference of April, 1926; the version in JRM-V, pp. 608–20 is from the Australian copy; he also gave it in South Africa in 1934.

64. Harold E. Fey, ed., *Kirby Page, Social Evangelist: The Autobiography of a 20th Century Prophet for Peace* (Nyack, NY: Fellowship Press, 1975), pp. 32–34, 104; Charles Chatfield, *For Peace and Justice: Pacifism in America, 1914-1941* (Knoxville: University of Tennessee Press, 1971), p. 123; Roger D. Woods, *The World of Thought of John R. Mott* (University of Iowa Ph.D. dissertation, 1965), pp. 193–95.

65. JRM notes to an interview with Prof. S. N. Harper on Russia, Oct. 24, 1920; JRM-III, pp. 340–41; JRM to Mrs. Emmons Blaine, Nov. 23, 1918, May 25, 1926.

66. JRM-I, pp. 214, 228; IV, p. 999; VI, p. 275; Clyde Binfield, *George Williams and the Y.M.C.A.* (London: Heinemann, 1973), p. 15. Others have referred to Mott's stance as "holistic," and "balanced Christianity."

67. G. S. Eddy, *Pathfinders of the World Missionary Crusade* (New York/Nashville:

Abingdon-Cokesbury, 1945), p. 303; Mott himself had occasionally used this quotation from St. Augustine, e.g., JRM-III, p. 227. CHH interview with D. T. Niles, July, 1968.

68. JRM-IV, p. 999.

69. Kenneth Cauthen, *The Impact of American Religious Liberalism* (New York/ Evanston: Harper & Row, 1962), pp. 27–29; William R. Hutchison, *The Modernist Impulse in American Protestantism* (Cambridge: Harvard University Press, 1976), pp. 3–4; H. Richard Niebuhr, *The Kingdom of God in America* (Chicago/New York: Willett, Clark, 1937), pp. 138, 148–49, 156.

70. Isabel Florence Hapgood, comp. and ed., *Orthodox Church Liturgy and Ritual. English. Service Book . . .* (New York: Association Press, 1922); in his "indorsement," Patriarch Tikhon acknowledged Mott's part in the revision and republication of the work.

71. JRM to Paul de Schweinitz, Jan. 10, 1934; CHH interview with Henri Johannot, June 13, 1968.

72. CHH-Y, pp. 222–24; CHH interviews with D. Eric Stange, July 1–2, 1968; with Bishop Hans Lilje, July 18, 1968; with Sir Frank Willis, July 27, 1968; Karl Fries to JRM, Jan. 23, 1923; JRM to Fries, Feb. 13, 1923.

73. Karl Bornhausen, "Der Christliche Aktivismus Nordamerikas in der Gegenwart," in *Hefte der Theologischen Amerika Bibliothek*, no. 2 (Giessen: Alfred Toepelmann, 1925), pp. 40f.; I am indebted to Walter Sundberg for translation and discussion of this material. See also H.-L. Henriod to JRM, Mar. 20, 1925.

74. JRM-IV, p. 999.

75. K. S. Latourette, "John R. Mott: A Centennial Appraisal," *Religion in Life* 34 (Summer, 1965), p. 374.

76. JRM notes for Quiet Day, Dec. 26, 1923: data on the group is too scanty to identify "Howard" and "Best," from whom letters had been received.

77. CHH interview with Robert Mackie and friends, July 15, 1968, pp. 10–11; Fisher, *John R. Mott*, p. 153; F. Howard Taylor to Leila Mott, Oct. 12, 1934; CHH interview with Hans Lilje, p. 15.

78. CHH interviews with C. J. Ewald, Mar. 28, 1968; with Sir Frank Willis; with E. S. Turner, June 9, 1969; Colton, *Memoirs*, p. 137; Latourette, *World Service*, p. 223; Fisher, *John R. Mott*, pp. 40–43.

79. Henry Nelson Wieman, "John R. Mott," *Christian Century* 47, no. 42 (Oct. 15, 1930), pp. 1246–47. The meetings of "younger theologians" thus stimulated became significant for the IMC: Hogg, *Ecumenical Foundations*, p. 280; Van Dusen in Mackie, pp. 125–26.

80. For Henriod, see Coston, *Ecumenical Training Ground*, pp. 216–21 and Fisher, *John R. Mott*, pp. 90–91.

81. The WSCF secretaries presented their resignations to the Executive Committee May 17, 1923; JRM to Henriod, Oct. 27, 1923; CHH interview with D. T. Niles, July 13, 1968.

82. Yoshimichi Ebisawa, *Soichi Saito and the YMCA* (Tokyo, 1965), in Japanese; translation from p. 322; YMCA Library.

83. JRM-VI, pp. 182–87; Rouse, *WSCF*, pp. 221, 311; Zoë Fairfield and 50 secretaries and delegates to Mrs. Mott, 23 Aug., 1926; V. Marzinkovsky to JRM, Oct. 31, 1924; JRM to Marzinkovsky, Nov. 25, 1924.

84. Henri Johannot, "The Field of Action," ch. 15 in C. P. Shedd and others, *History of the World's Alliance of YMCAs* (London: SPCK, 1955), pp. 617–18.

85. W. A. Visser 't Hooft, *Memoirs*, p. 15.

86. Visser 't Hooft, *Memoirs*, pp. 16–18; others caught in Mott's net at Pörtschach were Johannot, Tracy Strong, Basil Mathews, and Alphons Koechlin.

87. CHH interview with Ray V. Sowers, Mar. 29, 1968.

88. For Fries' career, see Sundkler, *Nathan Söderblom*, pp. 166-67; Weber, *Asia* p. 101; JRM-IV, pp. 1056-94; Colton, *Memoirs*, p. 155.

89. CHH interview with Visser 't Hooft, June 18, 1968, and with Willis; J. T. Massey to CHH, 18 Feb., 1974, pp. 15-16.

90. Visser 't Hooft, *Memoirs*, p. 21: a "dog's body" is an errand-boy.

91. Hogg, *Ecumenical Foundations*, pp. 215, 223.

92. Hogg, *Ecumenical Foundations*, p. 237; JRM-JHO correspondence, 1912-13 and 1920-22.

93. CHH interview with Philip K. Hitti, Feb. 8, 1969; J. C. Wilson, *Flaming Prophet, The Story of Samuel Zwemer* (New York: Friendship Press, 1970); J. L. Grabill, *Protestant Diplomacy and the Near East* (Minneapolis: University of Minnesota Press, 1971); JRM-V, pp. 315-57; W. Montgomery Watt, "Religion and Anti-Religion," in A. J. Arberry, ed., *Religion in the Middle East*, vol. 2 (Cambridge: Cambridge University Press, 1969), pp. 609-27; the story is told that during a visit to Hagia Sophia in Constantinople, Zwemer had almost to be forcefully restrained by his friends from entering the pulpit to proclaim the gospel!

94. JRM, ed., *The Moslem World of Today* (New York: Doran, 1925), pp. vii-x, 378-79; Hogg, *Ecumenical Foundations*, p. 237.

95. Leila Mott home letter, Apr. 2, 1924; JRM-V, pp. 315-57; Hogg, *Ecumenical Foundations*, pp. 236-37; I am indebted to His Grace Vassilios, Archbishop of Jordan, the Chief Secretary of the Greek Orthodox Patriarchate, Jerusalem, for reading the two citations during an interview July 16, 1971 at the Patriarchate; the diplomas are numbered 2,006 and 2,007.

96. James M. Jarvie, who underwrote Harte's plan, was in Jerusalem at the time; there had, of course, been a British YMCA in Cairo long before the Wilbert Smith era.

97. American University was originally called the Syrian Protestant College. CHH interview with Bayard Dodge, Aug. 7, 1967; Dodge pointed out further that Mott's temperament was the opposite of Frank Buchman who, Dodge said, led people to talk and be concerned about themselves. Mott also advised Dodge against ordination.

98. L. (Mrs. Pierre) Maury to CHH, Mar. 7, 1970.

99. The Mott visit to Greece took place Feb. 29-Mar. 4 and Apr. 11-13, 1924.

100. During the War, the Metropolitan of Greece had come to Mott's office in New York to request that the YMCA be extended to Athens and every large city in Greece.

101. CHH interview with Alivisatos, July 8, 1968; Latourette, *World Service*, p. 385; Amoss' Christmas card of 1923 bore a photo of Meletios IV and four Metropolitans; Saloniki was an alternate site proposed during the agitation over suppressing the Patriarchate in Constantinople.

102. D. A. Davis, "Private letter... regarding visit of Dr. John R. Mott in Greece and Turkey," to "Dear Friends" from the *S. S. Fezara*, Mar. 16, 1924; Davis' letter is incorrectly dated in JRM-VI, pp. 412-15.

103. Davis, "Private letter," p. 3; the Mott files contain both Alivisatos' letter to the authorities at Mount Athos and Meletios' letter to the Patriarch; H. Alivisatos to JRM, Mar. 1, 1924.

104. Davis, "Private letter," p. 3; Latourette, *World Service*, p. 343; Basil S. Giannakakis, *International Status of the Ecumenical Patriarchate* (Cambridge, 1959), pp. 10-11. Arslanian told Mott that Gregorios was acting Patriarch or *locum tenens* and that Meletios IV had found himself "enmeshed in the antagonism between the Great Powers and between Greece and Turkey" and was "involving himself in political activities"; he had abdicated Nov. 10, 1923.

105. D. A. Davis, "Private Letter."

106. Paul Super, "Dr. John R. Mott in Poland, April 28-29-30, 1924. A Letter to

Association Friends"; JRM-III, p. 518; Latourette, *World Service,* pp. 398–401; CHH-Y, pp. 513–14, 674–75, 687, 704; Fisher, *John R. Mott,* pp. 44–45; JRM-VI, p. 542.

107. CHH interview with Lilje, July 18, 1968, a free transcription.

108. Paul B. Anderson points out that the few SCM members who remained in the USSR under persecution did so to inspire others in the West, but actually they were arrested while meeting in a private home in Leningrad in 1927, and were sent to forced labor, with no record of any of them since: Anderson to CHH, Apr. 11, 1978.

109. P. B. Anderson, "YMCA Russian Work as a Pioneering Enterprise in the Movement for Christian Unity," typescript, 1964, YMCA Library; D. A. Lowrie, *St. Sergius in Paris* (London: SPCK, 1954), ch. 2 and pp. 111–15; Coston, *Ecumenical Training Ground,* pp. 145–76; Colton, *Memoirs,* pp. 133–34; JRM-VI, pp. 418–20; Eulogius to JRM, May 22, 1940.

110. Anderson relates that when the Russians were ready to establish *Put',* Mott was in Geneva but Berdyaev did not have a Swiss visa, so the two met at Annemasse where they talked across the border; Berdyaev was convincing and Mott promised the money. Lowrie says that Berdyaev had more than 60 articles in *Put': Rebellious Prophet* (New York: Harper, 1960). I am deeply indebted to Dr. Anderson for critique and suggestions for this chapter.

111. Harrison E. Salisbury, "The Russian Writer as World Conscience," *Saturday Review/World,* July 27, 1974, pp. 18ff.; Lowrie, *St. Sergius,* pp. 168, 184, 201, 274.

112. This is one of the best-documented of Mott's tours: JRM-III, pp. 327–39., VI, pp. 514–17; there is an 88-page diary.

113. The rehabilitation fund for the YMCA in Japan totalled $1,150,000, of which $500,000 came from surplus War Funds and $325,000 was a conditional Rockefeller gift. The program continued through several years.

114. JRM Diary, Pacific Basin Tour, pp. 2–18; R. M. Miller, *American Protestantism and Social Issues, 1919–1939* (Chapel Hill: University of North Carolina Press, 1958), pp. 291–93; E. C. Jenkins telegram to JRM, Apr. 22, 1924; JRM-V, p. 366.

115. *Melbourne Herald,* Mar. 29, 1926, clipping in JRM-Y.

116. Hogg, *Ecumenical Foundations,* pp. 237–38; JRM, "New Strategies Which Through Closer Cooperation Will be Released Among the Christian Forces in Japan," *Japan Christian Quarterly* 1, no. 1, pp. 61–69; Diary, pp. 12–18; JRM-V, p. 367; Latourette, *World Service,* pp. 176–80.

117. Diary, pp. 18–22; JRM-V, pp. 368–75.

118. Diary, pp. 23–33; JRM-V, pp. 376–87; National Christian Council of China, *Report* of Conference on The Church in China Today . . . with Dr. John R. Mott . . . , Jan. 5–7, 1926 (Shanghai, NCC), p. 166; Garrett, *Social Reformers,* ch. 6; Barnett, *Memoirs,* vol. 1, ch. 15; Leila Mott home letter, Jan. 6, 1926.

119. Diary, pp. 33–35; Latourette, *World Service,* pp. 320–21; CHH interview with E. S. Turner, June 9, 1969; JRM to JHO, Jan. 29, 1926.

120. The sources for this segment of the tour are substantial: Diary, pp. 38–60; several files, JRM-Y, with clippings and notes; Leila Mott home letters; JRM-V, pp. 388–405.

121. Numerous reports and memos from Kraemer and Rutgers are in JRM-Y, V. Conferences and Visits, Dutch Indies, 1926.

122. JRM-V, pp. 400–05; JRM to JHO, Feb. 17, 1926.

123. Frederick Dodge Mott (1904–   ), second son and third child of John R. and Leila Mott, who interrupted his course at Princeton to go on this tour (he had accompanied his father on two previous trips to Europe), was graduated from that university in 1927. He studied medicine at McGill University and interned at Presbyterian-Columbia Medical Center, New York City. Entering the field of public health, he pioneered in group and public medical care programs first with several New Deal agencies, then with

the provincial government of Saskatchewan, finally as deputy minister. He later set up a special program in Appalachia for the United Mine Workers, following that with the executive directorship of the Community Health Association of Detroit. To climax his career he taught medical care at the University of Toronto. In 1975 he received the Distinguished Service Award of the Group Health Association of America. Dr. Frederick D. Mott has been most helpful at many points in the production of this work. He has read and commented on the entire manuscript, contributed invaluable materials to the Mott Collection, and in numerous letters, conversations, and as host at Lac des Iles helped me to better understand his father.

124. Sources for the Australia visit: JRM-V, pp. 405–14; Diary, pp. 61–73; Mott notes in JRM-Mn-V. 1925–26; *The Australasian Intercollegian* 29 (May, 1926) was given entirely to the Mott visit; his major addresses were published in *Australia Facing the Non-Christian World*, the *Report* of the Melbourne Conference in April (Melbourne: Alpha Printing Co., 1926), pp. 72–137; Memo prepared by Margaret Holmes, who had planned the Mott tour of 1926, for my visit in 1972. I am deeply indebted to Miss Holmes for a multitude of courtesies, and to the late Dwayne Orton, who made my trip possible. I am also indebted to Sydney M. Stevens, former general secretary of the Australian National YMCA, for hospitality and insights concerning Mott, and to the present staff of the Australian National YMCA.

125. After this affair, the Motts were entertained in the home of Sir Henry Barraclough, the Cornell colleague who had been so helpful in 1896, who was now Dean of the Engineering Department of the University.

126. *Farrago*, Melbourne, Mar. 26, 1926; courtesy of Miss Holmes and the University Library.

127. Holmes memo; Diary, pp. 65–67.

128. *Australia Facing*, pp. 72–137, esp. p. 111; JRM-V, pp. 608–20.

129. Leila Mott home letter, Apr. 23, 1926; JRM to JHO, Apr. 19, 1926; a reporter for the *Brisbane Courier*, Mar. 19, 1926, said that Mott's statement on "white Australia" was "very guarded" and that Mott intended to study the matter.

130. Sources for New Zealand: Diary, pp. 73–86; JRM-V, pp. 415–22; several files of clippings, notes, etc., in JRM-Y, V. Conferences and Visits; it is interesting to note (JRM-V, pp. 415–16) that some of the arrangements for Mott's 1926 tour were made by A. T. Thompson, who had been the first student to meet him in New Zealand in 1896. I am indebted to the Very Reverend J. S. Somerville, Master of Knox College, and to the Hocken Library there, for materials. See JRM to William Hewitson, May 1, 1926, and Hewitson to Mrs. Mott, 10 May, 1926.

131. Hogg, *Ecumenical Foundations*, p. 215; partial records of this conference are in JRM-Y, but CtYD has a complete *Report*; there were no Maoris present, but the conference gave a great deal of attention to them.

132. The content of the statement may be gleaned in part from clippings in the sources cited in note 130; Mott's stand on Prohibition is summarized in Part 10, below.

133. Davis, *Autobiography*, ch. 9; Davis to JRM, Nov., 1925; JRM to F. P. Miller, Apr. 22, May 1, 1927.

134. Hogg, *Ecumenical Foundations*, pp. 223, 226; JHO to JRM, 21 June, 9 Nov., 1926.

135. IMC, *The Christian Message to the Jews: Budapest-Warsaw Conferences, 1927. Special Papers* (Edinburgh, 1927); Hogg, *Ecumenical Foundations*, pp. 238–39.

136. Tracy Strong, "The World's Alliance in a Changing World," in Shedd and others, *History*, pp. 493–501; JRM-IV, pp. 1056–95.

137. JRM-III, pp. 350–54. D. A. Lowrie related that Mott so relished a rum-flavored dessert on one of these occasions that he asked for the recipe to take to Leila!

138. JRM to JHO, Oct. 1, 1927; JRM to A. W. Hanson, Sept. 23, 1927.

139. The primary sources for Jerusalem 1928 are the eight volumes of papers, reports, and addresses, published by the Council in New York and London in 1928; Basil Mathews wrote the popular account, *Roads to the City of God* (Garden City: Doubleday, Doran, 1928). Matters related to Jerusalem occupy the JRM-JHO correspondence for years; William G. Schram took and collected a large number of photographs; JRM-Y has three folders of Mott's notes and miscellaneous materials; JRM-V, pp. 242-82 concerns Jerusalem; his addresses are in vol. 8 of the official materials. The author visited Jerusalem in 1972, walked over the site, and interviewed Horatio Vester, whose mother, Mrs. Frederick Vester of the American Colony, author of *Our Jerusalem* (Garden City: Doubleday, 1950), was a member of the local committee on arrangements; I also talked with many others in Jerusalem; CHH interviews with delegates to Jerusalem 1928: Luther A. Weigle, July 23, 1970; S. M. Cavert, July 18, 1973; F. F. Goodsell, Nov. 9, 1970; John McKay, Dec. 13, 1974. Secondary sources are Weber, *Asia;* Hogg, *Ecumenical Foundation;* and Rouse and Neill, ed., *A History of the Ecumenical Movement, 1517-1948* (London/Philadelphia: SPCK/Westminster, 1954), pp. 366-69.

140. Mott held a meeting for continental and other delegates who were concerned over the preliminary papers, in Cairo just before Jerusalem opened: Hogg, *Ecumenical Foundations,* pp. 242-43.

141. Hogg, *Ecumenical Foundations,* pp. 242, 244-47; JRM-V, pp. 662-63; the London *Times* noted, Apr. 10, 1928, that the Eastern churches were not represented in the meetings, which was essentially true in spite of Mott's disclaimer that "a few of the delegates" were from the Orthodox churches; they were not in the *Who's Who.*

142. JRM, "Foreword," in Mathews, *Roads,* p. ix; Weber, *Asia,* pp. 154-63; Hogg, *Ecumenical Foundations,* pp. 243-58; S. C. Neill, *Brothers of the Faith* (New York/ Nashville: Abingdon, 1960), p. 86; JRM-V, p. 665.

143. For an excellent survey of these conferences, see Z. F. Willis, "That They All May be One," in Shedd and others, *History,* pp. 700-03; Colton, *Memoirs,* p. 154 and App. 11; Coston, *Ecumenical Training Ground,* pp. 192-97; CHH interview with Archbishop Andrei, Mar. 3, 1969; F. P. Miller, "Special Correspondence from Central Europe," *Christian Century* 45 (June 14, 1928), p. 776; JRM-III, pp. 376-78; Meletios sent Mott a blessing in August, 1926.

144. W. A. Visser 't Hooft, "Speech on Occasion of the John Mott Centenary Celebrations, 25 May, 1965," transcript.

145. Hogg, *Ecumenical Foundations,* p. 266; CHH interview with Fred Field Goodsell and excerpts from his "Commonplace Book #43," p. 9.

146. JRM to LWM, Apr. 10, 13, 1933; Vester, *Our Jerusalem,* p. 311; in his address, Mott paid high tribute to Archie Harte, who absented himself from the dedication because of changes in the plans and differences with those who had completed the project; there were serious problems in financing the completion of the building: JRM to Fred Ramsey, Nov. 9, 1932. CHH visit to the Jerusalem YMCA building and interview with secretary Minard, July 21, 1971.

147. JRM-VI, pp. 391-408; JRM to LWM, May 18, 1933; D. A. Davis, "John R. Mott confers with leaders of Orthodoxy," undated typescript.

148. JRM-IV, pp. 968-71.

149. Mott came to realize that he had done Brockman a great injustice in virtually compelling him to leave China in 1915 to become his associate, which he inferred in the memorial address he gave for Brockman in 1944, describing that nine-year period as "self-denying years, difficult years, exhausting" (JRM-III, p. 727); contemporaries regarded the relationship as roughly comparable to the vice-presidency of the United States. When confronted with his ignoring of Brockman, Mott was shocked. C. A. Herschleb to CHH, Feb. 12, 1969. In perspective it appears that Mott misjudged

Brockman's talents, which were inspirational rather than administrative: P. B. Anderson to CHH, Apr. 11, 1978.

150. Leila Mott to Anna Mae Stewart, Oct. 25, 1928. Fred B. Smith suggests that the YMCA post was less congenial to Mott than agencies such as the IMC (*I Remember*, p. 154), but S. Wirt Wiley felt the opposite. Mott was forced to miss the 1927 National Council meeting but had more influence on it than if he had been there—"we feel the presence of a silent figure out in the desert praying," Fred Ramsey had said: J. S. Tichenor to Leila Mott, Oct. 29, 1927.

151. CHH interview with Fred Field Goodsell, Nov. 9, 1970 and excerpts from Goodsell's "Commonplace Book #43"; Goodsell's interviews with the Motts were Oct. 18 and 28, 1929.

152. L. N. Hayes to CHH and interview, June 6, 1969; D. A. Davis in *Old Guard News*, Apr., 1965; there is a bound volume of letters from retired YMCA men on this occasion; Mott was not consulted concerning his successor but made it clear later that his choice was Wiley: CHH interview with C. J. Ewald, Mar. 28, 1968; for his attitude to the YMCA note the dedication of JRM-III. For Colton's tribute, see JRM-IV, pp. 976–78, and Colton's *Memoirs*, p. 199.

153. From the original pencil script of JRM-IV, pp. 985–1001.

154. The Rockefellers contributed annually to "The Work of John R. Mott" as long as Mott lived; in some years there were as many as thirty contributors of sums from $100 to $25,000 but the average was ten to fifteen contributors; in 1953 W. G. Schram compiled a total of $1,283,162, an average of $50,326 per year; for a late incident, see H. P. Van Dusen's contribution to Robert Mackie's *Layman Extraordinary: John R. Mott, 1865–1955* (New York: Association Press, 1965), p. 125. Cyrus McCormick wrote Mott Feb. 17, 1933, that he could no longer contribute as previously. Francis S. Harmon, "Address on the Occasion of his Election as General Secretary of the International Committee, Jan. 19, 1932—New York City," typescript, and CHH interview with Harmon, Nov. 14, 1973.

155. JRM-IV, p. 997.

156. JRM notes, "Interviews with 3 Presidents in One Day—Dec. 19, 1923." Grabill, *Protestant Diplomacy*, p. 80, quotes the *New York Times* as saying in its obituary for Cleveland H. Dodge that Dodge had been "the only early friend of President Wilson who remained his close friend to the end"; Mott may not have been as close to Wilson as Dodge but he was certainly his friend as long as Wilson lived.

157. Barnett, *Memoirs*, pp. 228–29; JRM to JHO, Oct. 21, Nov. 6, 1924, Feb. 22, 1927; JRM to D. A. Davis, Feb. 22, 1927.

158. Colton, *Memoirs*, p. 181.

159. Colton, *Memoirs*, pp. 135, 181–84; after the International Convention of 1925, at which both Coolidge and Hoover spoke, Colton's friends twitted him for having provided Hoover with a better speech than Mott had prepared for President Coolidge! For the Prohibition issue in the 1928 presidential campaign, see R. M. Miller, *American Protestantism*, ch. 4; CHH interviews with Colton, Earl Brandenberg, Dec. 16, 1969, and J. Edward Sproul, May 14, 1968. Mott's activities did not go uncriticized.

160. JRM, "Reasons for the Re-election of President Hoover," typescript, Oct., 1932.

161. *Christian Century*, June 19, 1932, p. 821; JRM, "Statement," June, 1932.

162. Smith, *I Remember*, pp. 154–56.

163. Miscellaneous Hoover-JRM correspondence and notes, some from the Herbert Hoover Presidential Library, courtesy of Thomas T. Talken, Director; E. E. Barnett, *Memoirs*, p. 276. Mott is said to have remarked once that he had instructed Hoover in the elements of relief work, but no verification has been found. H. Dewey Anderson obtained

Hoover's endorsement of Mott for the Nobel Prize: CHH interview with Anderson, Apr. 1, 1970.

164. Sources for Mysore: JRM-II, pp. 230-46; a full Diary; several hundred photos by W. G. Schram; CHH interviews with S. C. Neill, Apr. 27, 1967, with Margaret Holmes, July, 1972, with Hans Lilje, p. 13, with Ernest A. Payne, July 18, 1968, with H. S. Leiper, Mar. 5, 1968; Coston, *Ecumenical Training Ground*, pp. 257-59, 297-99.

165. F. P. Miller, *Man From the Valley: Memoirs of a 20th Century Virginian* (Chapel Hill: University of North Carolina Press, 1971), p. 63; Colton, *Memoirs*, pp. 125f.; CHH interview with Miller, Mar. 22, 1969.

166. D. T. Niles recounted that Mott had instructed Visser 't Hooft to deliver a note, "and run!" with it: CHH interview with Niles, July, 1968; Margaret Holmes recalled the orange-tossing incident.

167. 't Hooft, *Memoirs*, pp. 35-42; JRM-II, pp. 167ff.; Weber, *Asia*, pp. 56f.; H. P. Van Dusen, *World Christianity* (Nashville: Abingdon-Cokesbury, 1947), pp. 89-91; Coston, *Ecumenical Training Ground*, pp. 323-26; JRM-VI, pp. 391-95; Tissington Tatlow, *The Story of the Student Christian Movement in Great Britain and Ireland* (London: SCM, 1933); Ruth Rouse, *John R. Mott, An Appreciation* (Geneva: WSCF [1928]).

168. IRM, Oct., 1975, pp. 356f.; I. W. Moomaw, *Crusade Against Hunger* (New York: Harper & Row, 1966), pp. 44-53, credits Mott with starting Agricultural Missions and serving as its chairman for sixteen years; Hogg, *Ecumenical Foundations*, pp. 256, 273-74; JRM, "Foreword," to K. L. Butterfield, *The Rural Mission of the Church in Eastern Asia* (IMC, 1931).

169. LWM to Irene Mott, Feb. 24, 1929; JRM, "Foreword," to J. R. Chitambar, *Mahatma Gandhi, His Life, Work, and Influence* (New York: Winston, 1933); Mott's guide may have been Jesse R. Wilson.

170. For the remainder of the tour, see Hogg, *Ecumenical Foundations*, pp. 254ff.; Diary; JRM-V, pp. 523-76.

171. CHH interviews with Arthur L. Carson, Aug. 6, 1969, with E. S. Turner. June 9, 1969.

172. Tsunegoro Nara, *History of the Japanese YMCA* (Tokyo, YMCA 1959), p. 244; Mott and Brockman participated in the ceremony of "Teiosiki"; translation courtesy of S. Fujita.

173. CHH interview with Arthur Jorgenson, Apr. 2, 1970, with Mrs. G. S. Phelps, Dec. 14, 1972. I am indebted to Robert F. Hemphill for numerous items on Kagawa, and to John M. Nakajima, general secretary of the National Christian Council of Japan, for information on Mott's visits of 1925 and 1929: Nakajima to CHH, July 6, 1972. Weber, *Asia*, pp. 191-97; Drummond, *Christianity in Japan*, pp. 227ff.; Iglehart, *Protestant Christianity*, pp. 197-99, (note 27).

174. Diary, Apr. 25, 1929.

175. Diary, May 4-8; Hogg, *Ecumenical Foundations*, p. 265.

176. LWM to Anna Mae Stewart, May 20, 1929, Apr. 17, 1931; to Irene Mott Bose, May 6, 1932; Diary, May 10, 1929.

177. Diary, May 13-16, 1929; Hogg, *Ecumenical Foundations*, pp. 254-55. There was some opposition to Mott's pushing ahead with church union: Rowland H. Cross to CHH, rec'd Apr. 28, 1970; Dryden L. Phelps to CHH, Feb. 10, 1970; these men were aware of the declining prestige of the West in China at the time.

178. The Africa tour was a subject for correspondence between Mott and Oldham as early as 1928; it was largely financed by Mrs. Benjamin Moore of Montclair, NJ. The chief sources are a Diary, several folders of memos, reports, and plans; JRM-V, pp. 454-81.

179. StW 1 (Jan., 1908), p. 36; McCowen handled most of the YMCA business: "Notes on the Visit of Dr. Mott and Mr. Oliver McCowen to South Africa in the

Interests of the YMCA," typescript, 1934; Alexander Kerr to CHH, May 13, 1969; R. H. W. Shepperd to CHH, c. May, 1969.

180. Oldham was so incensed by a series of lectures Smuts gave at about that time that he wrote a booklet refuting them; JRM Diary, Apr. 16, 1934, p. 5.

181. K. S. Latourette, "Ecumenical Bearings of the Missionary Movement and the IMC," in Rouse and Neill, Ecumenical Movement, pp. 395–96. Mott had recruited and long supported Max Yergan in work among South African blacks; he made an effort to obtain Benjamin E. Mays for the Bantus in 1940–41 but Mays' call to the presidency of Morehouse College frustrated the plan: Mays to CHH, Feb. 17, 1970; Fisher, John R. Mott, p. 91.

182. Diary, pp. 8–9, 22–23; the Congo portion of this tour is heavily documented in JRM-Y, V. Conferences and Visits, 1934, and in Mott's notes. I regret my inability to utilize more fully the materials and insights given me in interviews with Emory Ross and Mrs. Ross on several occasions, with H. Wakelin Coxill, Aug. 26, 1970, and with George W. Carpenter, Aug. 29, 1969; C. C. Chesterman to CHH, July 15, 1970. Coxill, "Reminiscences of Dr. Mott," in Mackie, Layman, pp. 109–115. JRM to JHO, May 20, 1934.

183. Coxill, "Reminiscences," pp. 110–11; Hogg, Ecumenical Foundations, p. 266; JRM to JHO, June 4, 13, 1934.

184. Diary, pp. 33–34; JRM notes to his audience (in Mn III.9). He and Oldham had planned this strategy long before. See JRM, The Decisive Hour of Christian Missions (New York: SVM, 1910), pp. 42–43.

185. JRM-VI, pp. 274–75.

186. The distinction between the private man and the public servant is suggested by H. P. Van Dusen in Dag Hammarskjöld: The Statesman and His Faith (New York: Harper & Row, 1964), p. 124. This section is based on a variety of letters in which Mott informed his friends about family matters. CHH interview with Theodore O. Wedel, Mar. 31, 1970.

187. Mott's office at 347 Madison Avenue was reached by underground passage from Grand Central Station as well as from the street; during the remaining years he had his office at several locations in that area, convenient to the Yale Club which he used increasingly, especially after moving out of the city; the Yonkers apartment was at 293 North Broadway.

188. Eleanor Mott Ross to CHH, June 3, 1967. CHH interview with Miss Helen White, niece of Mrs. Mott, May 10, 1971.

189. CHH interview with Robert Mackie and friends, Edinburgh, July 25, 1968; Karl Fries, "John R. Mott as I have seen Him," typescript; T. Tatlow, "John R. Mott," Student Movement 13 (May, 1929), p. 23; JRM, "Leadership of the Constructive Forces of the World," address on the Walker Trust at the University of St. Andrews, Feb., 1931, in JRM-VI, pp. 351–68; Ernest A. Payne to CHH Aug. 8, 1968, has transcript of an address to a conference of clergy; Jesse R. Wilson to CHH, Oct. 29, 1968; JRM-I, pp. 355ff.; Mott's medals are at The John R. Mott House in Geneva: JRM-VI, p. 543. Estonia bestowed the Order of the Red Cross, second category, in 1938.

190. Charles E. Harvey attributes the demise of the Institute for Social and Religious Research in part to the expense of the Laymen's Inquiry and to Rockefeller's disenchantment, due largely to the controversies stirred up: see note 11, above. See also Fosdick, Portrait, pp. 213–20; JRM-I, pp. 233–47 and VI, pp. 321–29.

191. JRM, Present Day Summons to the World Mission of Christianity (Nashville: Cokesbury, 1931); the Manchester Guardian was critical of the style.

192. JRM, Liberating the Lay Forces of Christianity (New York: Macmillan, 1932); it was translated into Japanese the next year and into German in 1951; John D. Rockefeller, Jr., to JRM, Feb. 29, 1932.

193. JRM, *Cooperation and the World Mission* (New York: IMC, 1935; also SCM Press, London); JRM-VI, pp. 449–89 is a 1945 revision.

194. D. R. Porter was treasurer of the fund. Z. F. Willis to Paul B. Anderson, 24 Apr., 1965: "... Dr. Mott let me know in very certain terms that he didn't like the portrait... he saw to it that it wasn't displayed in John Mott House or in the offices of the WCC. ..."

195. JRM-VI, pp. 521–24; CHH interview with Sir Frank Willis; JRM to Wilfred Fry, July 31, 1935.

Chapter 12: Retrospect and Reward

1. JRM-VI, p. 521; CHH interview with D. T. Niles, July 13, 1968.

2. C. P. Shedd, *History of the World's Alliance of YMCA's* (London: SPCK, 1955), pp. 515–18; Basil Mathews, *Flaming Milestone, Report* of the XXIst World's Conference of YMCA's, Mysore, 1937; JRM-IV, pp. 1125–41.

3. I have been unable to find a record of Mott's conversation with Tagore, which was between Dec. 19 and 26, 1936; there were two meetings with Gandhi: Mahadev Desai, "Dr. Mott's Visit, I," *Harijan*, Dec. 19, 1936, pp. 359–62, and "Dr. Mott's Visit, II," Dec. 26, 1936, pp. 366–67; "Dr. Mott's Second Visit," *Harijan*, Dec. 10, 1938, pp. 369–74. I am grateful to Mrs. Irene Mott Bose for obtaining the texts of all three discussions; she remembered (having heard some of them) that Gandhi and her father seemed to be talking at rather than with one another, to some extent. It is probable that Gandhi brought up the problem of chastity at the 1936 meetings, because Desai did not record the entire conversation, and that was the year in which Gandhi had been obsessed with the matter: Robert Payne, *The Life and Death of Mahatma Gandhi* (New York: Dutton, 1969), pp. 460–67.

4. Mott's notes to these conferences with missionaries are among the most detailed of his career; see JRM-Mn XIIA.1. India, 1927–37; JRM to LWM, Mar. 12, 1937; Bertha Spafford Vester, *Our Jerusalem* (Garden City: Doubleday, 1950), p. 311; Mott had an interview with Lloyd-George June 27, 1936.

5. JRM-V, pp. 283–314, 297–320; JRM, *Five Decades and a Forward View* (New York/London: Harper, 1939), pp. 97–118; Linda Elaine Goodwin, *JRM as a Chairman of Assemblies* (Abilene Christian College M.A. thesis, 1969), pp. 117f. S. C. Neill, *Brothers of the Faith* (New York/Nashville: Abingdon, 1960), p. 111.

6. IMC, Fourth Meeting Madras, *The World a Mission of the Church* (London/New York: IMC, 1939); W. R. Hogg, *Ecumenical Foundations: A History of the International Missionary Council* (New York: Harper, 1952), pp. 300–01, 343; Hans-Ruedi Weber, *Asia and the Ecumenical Movement, 1895–1961* (London: SCM Press, 1966), p. 185; W. A. Visser 't Hooft, *Memoirs* (London/Philadelphia: SCM/Westminster Press, 1973), p. 59. "Pre-Madras Study: What is Evangelism?" JRM Papers, Missionary Research Library; JRM to F. F. Goodsell, 2/3/38 (ABCFM exec. vice-pres., 1938–39; domestic letters, Houghton Library, by permission); JRM to "Dear Friends," Nov. 19, 1934, JLM Coll., Stewart file.

7. JRM-VI, pp. 430–31.

8. Neill, *Brothers*, p. 145; H. P. Van Dusen, *For the Healing of the Nations* (New York: Scribners, 1940), p. 139; Galen Fisher, *John R. Mott, Architect of Co-operation and Unity* (New York: Association Press, 1952), p. 24; Ruth Rouse, *The World's Student Christian Federation: A History of the First Thirty Years* (London: SCM Press, 1948), pp. 139–40.

9. JRM to JHO, Mar. 7, 1936; CHH interview with Bishop Hans Lilje, July 18,

1968, 4. Söderblom to JRM, 28 Jan., 1925: "You are the man to give us a view of the responsibility, ideal, and the possibilities of the Church of today."

10. John C. Bennett to CHH, May 2, 1977; Marc Boegner, "John R. Mott, Half a Century of Recollections," *Ecumenical Review* 17 (July, 1965), pp. 252-53; H. P. Van Dusen to Galen M. Fisher, Jan. 8, 1952.

11. W. A. Brown, *Toward a United Church* (New York: Scribners, 1946), p. 140; JRM-Mn, "Some of the Creative Experiences of my Life," in JRM-Mn 1-A.

12. Marc Boegner, *The Long Road to Unity* (London: Collins, 1970), p. 110. John C. Bennett to CHH, May 2, 1977.

13. Boegner, "JRM," p. 253.

14. John McKay, "John R. Mott: Apostle of the Oecuminical Era," IRM 44 (1955), 338.

15. Visser 't Hooft, *Memoirs*, p. 74; Paul B. Anderson, "An Interpretation of John R. Mott, an American Citizen with a World Horizon," typescript.

16. JRM-VI, pp. 422-25; LWM to IMB, July 26, 1937. For an interesting sidelight see Fisher, *John R. Mott*, p. 97.

17. Visser 't Hooft, *Memoirs*, p. 80.

18. CHH interview with H. S. Leiper, Mar. 5, 1968.

19. JRM-VI, pp. 373-88.

20. CHH interview with Bess McAdam, Nov. 7, 1967; LWM to IMB, Jan. 24, 1944, Nov. 9, 1940, Mar. 1, 1939; LWM to IMB, Jan. 28, 1934. I am grateful to the Archivist of Rollins College for providing data on Mott's addresses there.

21. LWM to IMB, Sept. 18, 1939; CHH interview with Leila Compton, Aug. 26, 1967.

22. LWM to IMB, June 21, 1937; JRM to IMB, Feb. 24, 1941; JRM-Y, V. Conferences and Visits, Canada, 1937. JRM-VI, p. 544.

23. JRM, *Five Decades*; JRM, *Methodists United for Action* (Nashville: Board of Missions, The Methodist Church, 1939); I have seen the listing of JRM's name in one of the publications described but have been unable to locate it again. It could have been caused by his continuing interest in the Russian emigré community and his speeches on "Russia holds the fate of the coming years," his endorsement of Jerome Davis' books, or his defense of Eddy's moderate socialism.

24. Mott probably never learned that the bronze bust presented to him on his visit to Japan in 1935 was requisitioned by the government and melted down during World War II: CHH interview with M. Kimoto, Tokyo, June 8, 1972.

25. JRM to J. E. Manley, Sept. 10, 1939; *Orlando Sentinel*, Dec. 15, 1953; the decoration by the Federated Republic of Germany was the Commander's Cross of the Order of Merit. Mott encouraged the organization in 1943 and served on the Advisory Council of the Lithuanian Protestant Association, for which information I am indebted to Mrs. Frank Tishkius.

26. *New York Times*, Dec. 17, 1943, pp. 1, 18; JRM to E. E. Barnett, Dec. 18, 1943.

27. The Shaffer Lectures were summarized in the *Yale Divinity News* 40, no. 4 (May, 1944), pp. 1-2.

28. JRM to "Present and Former Members of the World's Alliance of the YMCAs," Oct. 27, 1943; CHH interview with W. A. Visser 't Hooft, June 18, 1968; JRM-VI, pp. 435-42; JRM-IV, pp. 1159-67; during the War Mott held two meetings of French- and English-speaking groups in Montreal arranged by Claude de Mestral: de Mestral to CHH, June, 1968 and interview, Aug. 27, 1969; CHH interview with Ernest Long, July, 1968. JRM-Y has complete *Minutes* of the WCC American Provisional Committee, Oct. 28, 1937 to Oct. 1, 1946.

29. JRM-V, dedication; A. L. Warnshuis, publicity release, "The IMC's Chair-

man," Jan. 15, 1942; JRM-V, pp. 699–741; CHH interviews with Charles Ranson, Dec. 4, 1968, J. W. Decker, Nov. 13, 1968, H. S. Leiper, Mar. 5, 1968.

30. Boegner, "JRM," pp. 254–55.

31. CHH interview with James C. Baker, June 10, 1969. JRM to S. Saito, May 9, 1947.

32. R. H. Edwin Espy to CHH, May 2, 1978.

33. Norman Goodall, "John R. Mott," *Christian World*, Feb. 10, 1955.

34. D. A. Davis, memo on JRM's mission in Germany, June 1–4, 1947; CHH interview with Hans Lilje, July 18, 1968, with Pastor Walter Arnold, July, 1968; various items in Arnold Jenny Collection, YMCA Library; interviews with D. Eric Stange, Robert H. Miller, Rose-Marie Balfanz, July 1–2, 1968; JRM, *Welt ohne Zukunft?*, pam. (Stuttgart: Kreuz-Verlag, 1946), is an address delivered Feb. 8, 1946; as many as 24,000 persons came to hear Mott during this visit. Dr. F. Schlingensiepen to CHH, June 5, 1968.

35. E. E. Barnett, *As I Look Back: Memoirs*, vol. 1 (YMCA Library, typescript), p. 147.

36. P. B. Anderson to CHH, Apr. 11, 1978; C. P. Shedd and others, *History*, pp. 522–26, 679–82.

37. Mercedes M. Randall, *Improper Bostonian: Emily Greene Balch* (New York: Twayne, 1964); for incidental references see Charles Chatfield, *For Peace and Justice: Pacifism in America, 1914–1941* (Knoxville: University of Tennessee Press, 1971) and Allen F. Davis, *Spearheads for Reform* (New York: Oxford University Press, 1967).

38. W. A. Swanberg, *Norman Thomas, the Last Idealist* (New York: Scribners, 1976), p. 161; JHO to Right Honorable J. Ramsey MacDonald, June 28, 1935; E. T. Colton, *Memoirs* (New York: YMCA Library, 1969), pp. 140–41; CHH interview with H. Dewey Anderson, Apr. 1, 1970.

39. The call to Oslo caught Mott in New York without a morning coat; he remembered that L. K. Hall, then director of Association Press, wore his size. A phone call brought Mrs. Hall with a coat from Kent, Connecticut, in time for Mott to catch his plane. At Oslo, mused Hall afterward, the King may have handed over the medal, but "the investiture came from me!": L. K. Hall to CHH, Feb. 2, 1968. Mott's share of the Prize was $16,843 in dollars: M. Tice to JRM, Apr. 27, 1953 at which time it was about $18,000.

40. *Les Prix Nobel en 1946* (Stockholm, 1948), p. 278; JRM-VI, pp. 351–68; Nobelstiftelsen, *Nobel: The Man and His Prizes* (Amsterdam, 1962), pp. 589–92. Among the scores of messages received, John D. Rockefeller, Jr., wrote "as your lifelong friend and fellow-worker. . . ."

41. JRM-VI, p. 544; Brooks B. Little, Director, Library and Museum, *The Upper Room*, to CHH, Apr. 19, 1975; a memorial carving of Mott was placed in the reredos of Trinity Church, Methodist, Springfield, Mass., in 1950: H. Hughes Wagner to JRM, May 6, 1954.

42. Hogg, *Ecumenical Foundations*, pp. 336–42. In these later years, Mott and Boegner became quite intimate, Mott staying with the Boegners when in Paris: JRM-Boegner corespondence, JRM-Y.

43. Y. Y. Tsu to CHH, July 28, 1969; CHH interview with Claude de Mestral, Aug. 27, 1969.

44. J. H. Oldham, "John R. Mott," *Ecumenical Review* 7 (Apr., 1955), p. 259; Sherwood Eddy, *Pathfinders of the World Missionary Crusade* (New York/Nashville: Abingdon, 1945), p. 291, gave "the final place to John R. Mott because he, possibly more than any other, was used of God to draw together and organize the Christian forces of our generation."

45. There are various printings of Mott's speech; I believe it to be one of the great

contributions to ecumenical literature; for another viewpoint see W. A. Visser 't Hooft, "Speech on the occasion of the John Mott Centenary Celebrations, 25 May, 1965," typescript, p. 8.

46. CHH interviews with Mrs. Brita Brilioth, Uppsala, July 10, 1968 and with J. O. Söderblom, Uppsala, July 17, 1968.

47. Chandran D. S. Devanesen, "Whither the Indian SCM?" based on a sermon at Madras Christian College, Mar. 12, 1972, typescript courtesy the Asia office of the WSCF to CHH, June 15, 1972. Mott considered Amsterdam the climax of his career: notes to a talk on "Lessons Learned."

48. CHH interview with Dr. and Mrs. Walter Judd, Mar. 31, 1970; B. R. Barber to JRM, May 21, 1945. Mott once called Barber an "old scoundrel," which shocked a British visitor who was unaware of colloquial usage of the term!

49. JRM to JHO, Sept. 23, 1943; JRM to Mrs. Karl Fries, 1943; JHO, "John R. Mott," p. 256; JRM cable to Mrs. D. Willard Lyon [Mar.–May], 1949. In the late 1940's Mott cultivated a friendship and correspondence with Sholem Asch: correspondence in JRM-Y.

50. JRM, *Five Decades*, pp. 30ff; JHO, "Reflections on Edinburgh, 1910," *Religion in Life* 29 (Summer, 1960), p. 337; JRM-IV, pp. 976–78; Weber, *Asia*, p. 63.

51. The fire was June 7, 1951.

52. Mott's remarks at the Lawrence SVM are in Archie R. Crouch, *Christ's Kingdom is Man's Hope* (New York: Association Press, 1952), p. 84; LWM to Irene Mott Bose, Jan. 30, 1952; JRM to Irene Bose, Feb. 2 or 26, 1952. The well-known photo of Mott with a young man pointing forward, taken at Oberlin in 1951, was managed by Max W. Clowers: Clowers to CHH, Jan. 14, 1976. Boegner, "John R. Mott," p. 256.

53. "Martha" to JRM, Oct. 2, 1952. JRM-Y has biographical materials on Mrs. Mott; JRM-VI had been dedicated to her earlier.

54. Miss Peter had been a friend since her World War I service; she had been devoted to the Washington Cathedral for many years; her brother was a canon there.

55. Marc Boegner, "John Mott," *Reformé* (Paris), 12 Feb., 1955; CHH interview with D. T. Niles, with Henry Smith Leiper; F. P. Miller, *Man from the Valley: Memoirs of a 20th Century Virginian* (Chapel Hill: University of North Carolina Press, 1971), p. 63; Colton, *Memoirs*, p. 161; Norman Goodall, "John R. Mott," obituary article, unidentified, 1955. CHH interview with Sir Kenneth Grubb, July 15, 1968. Mott had been invited to and was planning to attend the World's Alliance of YMCA's Centennial in Paris in 1955.

56. Roy L. Smith, "What will heaven be like?" *Christian Advocate*, Apr. 7, 1949; CHH interview with Dr. and Mrs. Paul B. Anderson, Dec., 1972, with Dr. and Mrs. Frederick D. Mott, Aug. 22, 1969 and other occasions; archives of the Cathedral including Angus Dun to JRM, 17 Nov., 1954, and JRM to Dun shortly afterward.

Although many were unaware of Mott's denominational affiliation, he was thought of by American Methodists as their most prominent member; he was a member of the Board of Managers of the Foreign Missionary Society of the Methodist Episcopal Church 1904-11, 1916-19 and an honorary member 1912-15 and 1920-36.

June 12, 1956, Irene Mott Bose to Dean Sayre of the Cathedral: "My father was at heart a humble man . . . [and] should have been buried quietly in the country cemetery beside my mother who had done so much more than anyone realizes to help in whatever he accomplished."

57. See for example the East Asia Christian Conference, John R. Mott Lectures II, *Christ's Ministry—and Ours*, published for EACC by the *Southeast Asia Journal of Theology* (Singapore, 1962), pp. 2–5, 7, 46. The Goodall quotation is from *A Decisive Hour for the Christian Mission*, cited by Weber, *Asia*, p. 68. A memorial tablet, provided by the Student Volunteer Movement, the World's Alliance of YMCA's, the Interseminary

Movement, the National Council of Churches, the National Council of the YMCA's, the World Student Christian Federation, and the United Student Christian Council, marks the burial place in the crypt; it bears the seals or shields of seven organizations. The Mott family gave two carved hymn-boards in memory of Leila and John Mott.

58. JRM, *Five Decades*, pp. 95–96.

Acknowledgments

*T*HIS BOOK is the outcome of a conviction on the part of members
of the National Council of Young Men's Christian Associations and of
the National Council of the Churches of Christ in the United States of
America, that a biography of John R. Mott should be prepared "to provide a definitive record of the life and work of a notable servant of God
and an uniquely effective world citizen." An extraordinary debt of gratitude is due to every member of the Committee that sponsored and implemented the project, obtained funds to underwrite and publish it, and
through fiften years guided it and counseled the author. I am more grateful than can be stated in brief space to each of them, but I owe a special
debt to the Chairman, Raymond P. Morris, for proposing that I undertake the writing, for his continuing support, and for a lifetime of friendship. All members of the Committee read parts of the manuscript, but
I am especially indebted to Robert T. Handy for critical comments on
the entire work, and to Paul B. Anderson not only for detailed critique
of Chapters 9 through 12 but for wisdom and guidance all along the way.
Each Committee member contributed uniquely. They were: Paul B. An-
derson, Eugene E. Barnett, R. Pierce Beaver, Clifford M. Carey, Samuel
McCrea Cavert, Gerrit B. Douwsma, R. H. Edwin Espy, Thomas G.
Graham, Lawrence K. Hall, Robert T. Handy, James M. Hardy, Violet
Henry, Edward H. Johnson, Tracey K. Jones, Jr., and Raymond P. Mor-
ris, Chairman. In addition, numerous staff members of the National
YMCA have made significant contributions of various kinds: Earl W.
Brandenberg, James F. Bunting, Ethan T. Colton, Clement A. Duran,
Robert W. Harlan, Francis S. Harmon, Joel E. Nystrom, and Edward
Sproul.

I am also indebted to secretaries Fredrick Franklin, W. Harold Denison, and Jean-François Reymond of the World Alliance of YMCA's; to Willem A. Visser 't Hooft, Eugene Carson Blake, Robbins Strong, Jens J. Thomsen, Paul Abrecht, and Eleanor Kent Browne of the World Council of Churches; to Frank Willis of the YMCA in Great Britain; to Frank G. Engels of the Australian Council of Churches and the friends he gathered to advise me—Messrs. Egan, Rennie, Stuckey, Vickery, and Way; to Secretary Yasutaro Owaku of the National Committee of YMCA's of Japan together with staff and friends—Messrs. Nara, Kimoto, Ikeda, Abe, Hongyo, and Saito; John M. Nakajima of the National Christian Council of Japan; to Walter Arnold, Eric Stange, Rosemarie Balfanz, and Robert H. Miller of the Reichsverband der CVJM Deutschlands; to Marjorie Ellmer of the Conference of Missionary Societies in Great Britain and Ireland; to Harold V. Jenner of the National Council of YMCAs of Australia together with staff and friends—Messrs. Stevens, Massey, Daddow, Top, Edna and Edward Gault, Gwenyth Fox, David Garrett, and David Garnsey.

A special debt of gratitude is owed to His Eminence Archbishop Iakovos of the Greek Orthodox Archdiocese of North and South America for his good offices in opening for me the way to an audience with His Holiness, the Ecumenical Patriarch, Athenagoras I, and to the Patriarch for that privilege.

Earlier biographers of Mott—Basil Mathews, Robert Mackie, Galen M. Fisher, and Roger Woods made my task easier and I am grateful to them.

Mott might have said that he was indebted to friends around the world for a host of favors; in addition to those named above, I have received assistance from the following, many of whom are appropriately acknowledged in the notes: L. S. Albright, Gerald H. Anderson, H. Dewey Anderson, His Eminence Archbishop Andrey of the Bulgarian Orthodox Church, Gordon W. Avison, D. W. A. Baker of the Australian National University, James C. Baker, Roswell P. Barnes, Domingo C. Bascara, M. Searle Bates, John C. Bennett, Marc Boegner, William Bradbury, Hugh Borton, Mrs. Yngve Brilioth, Eleanor G. Brown, Paul W. Brown, Kenneth J. Cable of the University of Sydney, George W. Carpenter, Arthur L. Carson, Hugo Cedergren, Max W. Clowers, Paul Conord, H. Wakelin Coxill, Earl and Mildred Cranston, Margaret French Cresson, H. C. Cross, Rowland M. Cross, Rena Datta, Donald E. Davis, Kay Dickson, Suzanne de Dietrich, Bayard Dodge, J. W. C. Dougall, and Roderick B. Dugliss.

Frank N. Elliott of Rider College, Francis C. Ellis, Paul D. Evans,

John Scott Everton of The American Colleges in Istanbul; Charles J. Ewald, James F. Findlay, Jr., George Garnsey, Shirley Garrett, Betty D. Gibson, Norman Gilkison and Mrs. H. P. Anderson of Auckland, New Zealand; Norman Goodall, Fred Field Goodsell, Kenneth Grubb, Marius Hansen, Rowland Harker, S. Ralph Harlow, Charles E. Harvey, Egbert M. Hayes, L. Newton Hayes, Robert F. Hemphill, Charles A. Herschleb, Elston J. Hill, Seward Hiltner, Philip K. Hitti, Halfsdan Høgsbro, Margaret Holmes and colleagues in Melbourne—Mr. and Mrs. Kenneth Horn, S. Yule, the Reverends Bakewell, d'Argaville, Sutherland, and J. Davis McCaughey, Master of Ormond College; Lyman Hoover, Arthur Jorgensen, Mrs. Walter H. Judd, Alexander Kerr, Mr. and Mrs. Edward W. Kozelka, Sven Larson, Kenneth Scott Latourette, Henry Smith Leiper, Fred O. Leiser, Hanns Lilje, Arthur S. Link, Ernest E. Long, John W. Long, R. G. Macdonald, John A. Mackay, Mrs. Pierre Maury, Kenneth L. Maxwell, Claude de Mestral, Michael V. Metallo, Francis Pickens Miller, and Hugh A. Moran.

Stephen Neill, D. T. Niles, Dwayne Orton, Ernest A. Payne, Clifford W. Petitt, Dryden L. Phelps, Mrs. G. S. Phelps, Clifton J. Phillips, James M. Phillips, James K. Quay, Karl K. Quimby, Valentin H. Rabe, Charles W. Ranson, Mrs. Samuel Rapp, Raymond J. Reitzel, Hildegard Ross, Harold J. Rounds, Mrs. Soichi Saito, William G. Schram, Robert Seager II, Clarence P. Shedd, R. H. W. Shepherd, Keith Sinclair of the University of Auckland; Dharam Vir Singh of Leonard Theological College, Jabalpur, India; Kenneth Slack of London, A. Keith Smiley Jr., Timothy L. Smith, J. O Söderblom, J. Sommerville, Master of Knox College, Dunedin, New Zealand; Ray V. Sowers, Mrs. Tracy Strong, Tracy Strong, Jr., Mrs. Harold C. Stuart, Walter Sundberg, and Bengt G. M. Sundkler.

Mrs. W. E. Taylor, Oliver S. Tomkins, Bishop of Bristol; Eugene P. Trani, Y. Y. Tsu, Augustin E. Turner, E. Stanton Turner, Eugene E. Garbee of Upper Iowa College, H. P. Van Dusen, Horatio Vester, Theodore O. Wedel, Luther A. Weigle, J. Gustav White, Francis Wilson, Jessie R. Wilson, Margaret Wishard, David Y. K. Wong and guests Andrew T. Roy, Kenneth C. K. Chung, Teng-Kiat Chiu, and others; Bertram R. Wyllie, Glora M. Wysner, Donald Coggan, Archbishop of York; Albright G. Zimmerman.

Sources

*T*HE JOHN R. MOTT Collection, housed in the Library of the Yale University Divinity School at 409 Prospect Street, New Haven, Connecticut 06510, U.S.A. is a comprehensive archive covering the entire life and career of its subject. Given to Yale by Mott, it was added to substantially by the family following his death, in both instances through the instrumentality of Raymond P. Morris, the Librarian. It has been enriched during the research and writing of this biography by remaining personal and family materials, given by the Mott children. Notable among these additions are Mott's shorthand notes to interviews, speeches, schedules, accounts, and letters, together with his pocket ledgers. I am deeply indebted to Irene Mott Bose, John Livingstone Mott, and Dr. Frederick D. Mott not only for materials but for their wholehearted cooperation; Dr. Frederick D. Mott has read the entire manuscript, and I have received substantial help from Mrs. John R. Mott's nieces the Misses Leila Compton and Helen H. White, and John R. Mott's niece, Miss Bess McAdam.

I owe an unusual debt to three libraries and their librarians: to Yale University Divinity School Library—Raymond P. Morris, Stephen L. Peterson, John A. Bollier, Jane E. McFarland, Martha Lund Smalley, and Helen B. Uhrich; to Princeton Theological Seminary, whose Faculty named me a Fellow during several years, to President James I. McCord who read the manuscript and encouraged me at many points, to Librarian Louis Charles Willard who made possible my long term use of a study room in the Speer Library and together with James Irvin and Mrs. E. L. Little provided over the years every service and facility I could ask for; and to the Historical Library of the National Council of YMCA's at 291 Broadway, New York, New York 10007—whose late librarian Virginia Downes provided not only copies of the papers of Mott's intimate YMCA colleagues such as Ethan T. Colton and Gilbert Beaver, but compiled bibliographies, obituaries, and memorials (in spite of this substantial transfer, the YMCA Library remains to my knowledge not only the largest but the only sizeable repository of other Mott materials outside of the Collection at Yale); I acknowledge a further debt to Mary P. Thorpe, John Randle, Cheryl Gaines, and Ellen Sowchek of the YMCA Library.

I am also indebted to Robert Paton of the National Library of Australia at Canberra for access to the archives of the Australian Student Christian Movement; to James Claydon of the University Library, Cambridge, England, for the use of newspapers describing Mott's visits to that University; to Margaret L. Moser of the Cleveland Public Library for assistance in obtaining the papers of Mrs. J. Livingstone Taylor; to John O. Crane for permission to consult the Charles R. Crane papers in the Archive of Russian and East European History and Culture at Columbia University and to Curator Lev Magerovsky for making them available; to Lawrence O. Kline, Lawrence D. McIntosh, and Kenneth E. Rowe of the Rose Memorial Library of Drew University for various items; to the Houghton Library and Harvard University for access to certain papers in the ABCFM Archives; to the Herbert Hoover Archives at Stanford and at West Branch, Iowa; to Lida L. Greene of the Iowa State Department of History and Archives; to the Hocken Library of Knox College, Dunedin, New Zealand; to E. G. W. Bill, Librarian, Lambeth Palace Library, London, for Mott items there; to the Library of Oberlin College for copies of the *Guide to Holiness*; to I. G. Philip of the Bodleian Library of Oxford University for access to student periodicals of that University; to Joseph W. Ernst of the Rockefeller Archive Center for Mott-John D. Rockefeller, Jr., items; to Evelyn Draper of Rollins College for data on Mott's participation in the "Animated Magazine" of that College; to William G. Schram for photographs and financial records; to Étienne Kruger of the Société des Missions Évangeliques de Paris.

I am especially indebted to the several collections and the librarians of Union Theological Seminary of New York City—particularly for the hundreds of letters exchanged between Mott and J. H. Oldham and other IMC and IMC-related personnel, provided in copy from the Missionary Research Library, a Mott-inspired archive, and to Barbara A. Griffis of the William Adams Brown Ecumenical Library, also at Union. Gösta Thimon of the Library of the University of Uppsala, Sweden, found fresh letters between Mott and Karl Fries in the latter's papers in that Library; John H. Bayless of the Washington Cathedral arranged for me to consult Mott items there. Useful papers and information concerning Leila White Mott were provided by Edward Arn and Professor Lowell W. Coolidge of the College of Wooster.

Through the good offices of Jean-François Reymond of the World Alliance of YMCA's, the immense correspondence of Mott with that body through the years was added to the Yale Collection in copy from the World Alliance archive at John R. Mott House in Geneva, Switzerland. Likewise, a variety of materials were obtained also in copy from the Library of the World Council of Churches in Geneva, A. J. van der Bent, Librarian, to whom I am deeply indebted. The World Student Christian Federation at Geneva also gave me access to their repository and allowed me to have copied a large number of items from their later archives (Mott had collected and given to Yale the early archives of the WSCF); and, finally, I am indebted to Elizabeth Norris, Librarian of the National Board of the Young Women's Christian Association of the U.S.A. for materials on Leila White Mott's relations to that Board.

In addition to those who made these acquisitions possible, and to those who operated the copy machines that reproduced them, I am indebted to scores of persons around the world for interviews and responses to my letters; most are named above or in the narrative or notes. Likewise I express my thanks to all the researchers and secretaries who participated in the project, but particularly to Rita Reed and Emily Kletzien. My largest debt is to my wife, Winifred Hawes Hopkins, for painstaking research, reading and critique of the manuscript and proofs, and because, as John Mott said of Leila, "she gladly faced the dangers and exacting demands" of foreign travel.

Bibliography

*B*ECAUSE a definitive bibliography of Mott's writings would be virtually impossible to compile, it is suggested that the reader consult the text, notes, and index. The first draft of the manuscript for this book is in the Mott Collection at Yale and in the YMCA Library in New York City; it footnotes many more items than could be included here. Mott utilized most of his ideas and arguments upon so many differing occasions and for such a variety of purposes that they are to be found under many headings. He allowed his articles and edited speeches to be published over and over, and numerous pamphlets were printed and reprinted worldwide in English and in translation. He compiled what he regarded as the cream of these ephemeral materials in the six volumes of his *Addresses and Papers*. Descriptions of his major books will be found in the text on the pages here indicated in parenthesis after each title:

Address and Papers, 6 vols. 1946–47
Christians of Reality, 1902 (p. 259)
The Claims and Opportunities of the Christian Ministry (Ed. by J. R. M.), 1911 (p. 326)
Confronting Young Men with the Living Christ, 1923 (pp. 619–20)
Cooperation and the World Mission, 1935 (p. 682)
The Decisive Hour of Christian Missions, 1910 (pp. 351, 362–4)
Evangelism for the World Today, As interpreted by Christian Leaders throughout the World (Ed. by J.R.M.), 1938 (p. 691)
The Evangelization of the World in This Generation, 1900 (pp. 226–27)
Five Decades and a Forward View, 1939 (pp. 691, 699, 702)
The Future leadership of the Church, 1908 (pp. 324–26)
The Larger Evangelism, 1944 (p. 692)

Liberating the Lay Forces of Christianity, 1932 (p. 682)

Methodists United for Action, 1939 (p. 769, note 23)

The Moslem World of Today (Ed. by J. R. M.), 1925 (pp. 639–40)

The Pastor and Modern Missions, 1904 (pp. 279–80)

The Present-day Summons to the World Mission of Christianity, 1931 (p. 682)

The Present World Situation, 1914 (pp. 434–35)

Strategic Points in the World's Conquest, 1897 (p. 207)

The World's Student Christian Federation: Origin: Achievements: Forecast, 1920 (pp. 589–90)

Mott also wrote Forewords to numerous books, from a memorial volume for Alfred Bertrand to Stephan Zankov's *The Eastern Orthodox Church*. He was the editor of *The Student World* and in a comparable capacity in all other organizations produced reams of reports and pamphlet releases: as in the case of his pamphlets, these are to be identified in the text and notes.

Index

Most entries for individuals, places, and colleges/universities indicate contact with Mott. Casual or background items are generally not included. Name changes from Mott's time are indicated by the current name in parentheses. Dates in entries such as Paris or Sydney indicate years of Mott visits or other involvement. His home letters are usually noted by content rather than recipient. His books (779–80) and some other items are each indexed alphabetically by title. These abbreviations are used:

CUCA: Cornell University Christian Association
FCC: Federal Council of the Churches of Christ in the U.S.A.
FMCNA: Foreign Missions Conference (Council) of North America
FOR: Fellowship of Reconciliation
ICWM: Interchurch World Movement
IRM: *International Review of Missions*
ISRR: Institute of Social and Religious Research
JRM: John R. Mott
LWM: Leila White Mott (Mrs. John R.)
NWWC: National War Work Council of the YMCA
SCM: Student Christian Movement (YMCA, YWCA, or Union)
SVM: Student Volunteer Movement for Foreign Missions
UWWC: United War Work Campaign
WSCF: World's Student Christian Federation
WW I: World War I
YMCA: Young Men's Christian Association
YMCA, IC: YMCA International Committee (parent body, US.A., Canada)
YMCA, Intercollegiate: Student YMCA
YWCA: Young Women's Christian Association

781

DATE DUE